T0180292

Lecture Notes in Computer Science 12953

More information about this subseries at http://www.springer.com/series/7407

Osvaldo Gervasi · Beniamino Murgante ·
Sanjay Misra · Chiara Garau ·
Ivan Blečić · David Taniar ·
Bernady O. Apduhan · Ana Maria A. C. Rocha ·
Eufemia Tarantino · Carmelo Maria Torre (Eds.)

Computational Science and Its Applications – ICCSA 2021

21st International Conference
Cagliari, Italy, September 13–16, 2021
Proceedings, Part V

 Springer

Editors
Osvaldo Gervasi (iD)
University of Perugia
Perugia, Italy

Sanjay Misra (iD)
Covenant University
Ota, Nigeria

Ivan Blečić (iD)
University of Cagliari
Cagliari, Italy

Bernady O. Apduhan
Kyushu Sangyo University
Fukuoka, Japan

Eufemia Tarantino (iD)
Polytechnic University of Bari
Bari, Italy

Beniamino Murgante (iD)
University of Basilicata
Potenza, Potenza, Italy

Chiara Garau (iD)
University of Cagliari
Cagliari, Italy

David Taniar (iD)
Monash University
Clayton, VIC, Australia

Ana Maria A. C. Rocha (iD)
University of Minho
Braga, Portugal

Carmelo Maria Torre (iD)
Polytechnic University of Bari
Bari, Italy

ISSN 0302-9743   ISSN 1611-3349   (electronic)
Lecture Notes in Computer Science
ISBN 978-3-030-86975-5   ISBN 978-3-030-86976-2   (eBook)
https://doi.org/10.1007/978-3-030-86976-2

LNCS Sublibrary: SL1 – Theoretical Computer Science and General Issues

This Springer imprint is published by the registered company Springer Nature Switzerland AG
The registered company address is: Gewerbestrasse 11, 6330 Cham, Switzerland

Preface

These 10 volumes (LNCS volumes 12949–12958) consist of the peer-reviewed papers from the 21st International Conference on Computational Science and Its Applications (ICCSA 2021) which took place during September 13–16, 2021. By virtue of the vaccination campaign conducted in various countries around the world, we decided to try a hybrid conference, with some of the delegates attending in person at the University of Cagliari and others attending in virtual mode, reproducing the infrastructure established last year.

This year's edition was a successful continuation of the ICCSA conference series, which was also held as a virtual event in 2020, and previously held in Saint Petersburg, Russia (2019), Melbourne, Australia (2018), Trieste, Italy (2017), Beijing. China (2016), Banff, Canada (2015), Guimaraes, Portugal (2014), Ho Chi Minh City, Vietnam (2013), Salvador, Brazil (2012), Santander, Spain (2011), Fukuoka, Japan (2010), Suwon, South Korea (2009), Perugia, Italy (2008), Kuala Lumpur, Malaysia (2007), Glasgow, UK (2006), Singapore (2005), Assisi, Italy (2004), Montreal, Canada (2003), and (as ICCS) Amsterdam, The Netherlands (2002) and San Francisco, USA (2001).

Computational science is the main pillar of most of the present research on understanding and solving complex problems. It plays a unique role in exploiting innovative ICT technologies and in the development of industrial and commercial applications. The ICCSA conference series provides a venue for researchers and industry practitioners to discuss new ideas, to share complex problems and their solutions, and to shape new trends in computational science.

Apart from the six main conference tracks, ICCSA 2021 also included 52 workshops in various areas of computational sciences, ranging from computational science technologies to specific areas of computational sciences, such as software engineering, security, machine learning and artificial intelligence, blockchain technologies, and applications in many fields. In total, we accepted 494 papers, giving an acceptance rate of 30%, of which 18 papers were short papers and 6 were published open access. We would like to express our appreciation for the workshop chairs and co-chairs for their hard work and dedication.

The success of the ICCSA conference series in general, and of ICCSA 2021 in particular, vitally depends on the support of many people: authors, presenters, participants, keynote speakers, workshop chairs, session chairs, organizing committee members, student volunteers, Program Committee members, advisory committee members, international liaison chairs, reviewers, and others in various roles. We take this opportunity to wholehartedly thank them all.

We also wish to thank Springer for publishing the proceedings, for sponsoring some of the best paper awards, and for their kind assistance and cooperation during the editing process.

We cordially invite you to visit the ICCSA website https://iccsa.org where you can find all the relevant information about this interesting and exciting event.

September 2021

Osvaldo Gervasi
Beniamino Murgante
Sanjay Misra

Welcome Message from the Organizers

COVID-19 has continued to alter our plans for organizing the ICCSA 2021 conference, so although vaccination plans are progressing worldwide, the spread of virus variants still forces us into a period of profound uncertainty. Only a very limited number of participants were able to enjoy the beauty of Sardinia and Cagliari in particular, rediscovering the immense pleasure of meeting again, albeit safely spaced out. The social events, in which we rediscovered the ancient values that abound on this wonderful island and in this city, gave us even more strength and hope for the future. For the management of the virtual part of the conference, we consolidated the methods, organization, and infrastructure of ICCSA 2020.

The technological infrastructure was based on open source software, with the addition of the streaming channels on YouTube. In particular, we used Jitsi (jitsi.org) for videoconferencing, Riot (riot.im) together with Matrix (matrix.org) for chat and ansynchronous communication, and Jibri (github.com/jitsi/jibri) for streaming live sessions to YouTube.

Seven Jitsi servers were set up, one for each parallel session. The participants of the sessions were helped and assisted by eight student volunteers (from the universities of Cagliari, Florence, Perugia, and Bari), who provided technical support and ensured smooth running of the conference proceedings.

The implementation of the software infrastructure and the technical coordination of the volunteers were carried out by Damiano Perri and Marco Simonetti.

Our warmest thanks go to all the student volunteers, to the technical coordinators, and to the development communities of Jitsi, Jibri, Riot, and Matrix, who made their terrific platforms available as open source software.

A big thank you goes to all of the 450 speakers, many of whom showed an enormous collaborative spirit, sometimes participating and presenting at almost prohibitive times of the day, given that the participants of this year's conference came from 58 countries scattered over many time zones of the globe.

Finally, we would like to thank Google for letting us stream all the live events via YouTube. In addition to lightening the load of our Jitsi servers, this allowed us to record the event and to be able to review the most exciting moments of the conference.

Ivan Blečić
Chiara Garau

Organization

ICCSA 2021 was organized by the University of Cagliari (Italy), the University of Perugia (Italy), the University of Basilicata (Italy), Monash University (Australia), Kyushu Sangyo University (Japan), and the University of Minho (Portugal).

Honorary General Chairs

Norio Shiratori	Chuo University, Japan
Kenneth C. J. Tan	Sardina Systems, UK
Corrado Zoppi	University of Cagliari, Italy

General Chairs

Osvaldo Gervasi	University of Perugia, Italy
Ivan Blečić	University of Cagliari, Italy
David Taniar	Monash University, Australia

Program Committee Chairs

Beniamino Murgante	University of Basilicata, Italy
Bernady O. Apduhan	Kyushu Sangyo University, Japan
Chiara Garau	University of Cagliari, Italy
Ana Maria A. C. Rocha	University of Minho, Portugal

International Advisory Committee

Jemal Abawajy	Deakin University, Australia
Dharma P. Agarwal	University of Cincinnati, USA
Rajkumar Buyya	University of Melbourne, Australia
Claudia Bauzer Medeiros	University of Campinas, Brazil
Manfred M. Fisher	Vienna University of Economics and Business, Austria
Marina L. Gavrilova	University of Calgary, Canada
Yee Leung	Chinese University of Hong Kong, China

International Liaison Chairs

Giuseppe Borruso	University of Trieste, Italy
Elise De Donker	Western Michigan University, USA
Maria Irene Falcão	University of Minho, Portugal
Robert C. H. Hsu	Chung Hua University, Taiwan
Tai-Hoon Kim	Beijing Jaotong University, China

Vladimir Korkhov	St. Petersburg University, Russia
Sanjay Misra	Covenant University, Nigeria
Takashi Naka	Kyushu Sangyo University, Japan
Rafael D. C. Santos	National Institute for Space Research, Brazil
Maribel Yasmina Santos	University of Minho, Portugal
Elena Stankova	St. Petersburg University, Russia

Workshop and Session Chairs

Beniamino Murgante	University of Basilicata, Italy
Sanjay Misra	Covenant University, Nigeria
Jorge Gustavo Rocha	University of Minho, Portugal

Awards Chair

Wenny Rahayu	La Trobe University, Australia

Publicity Committee Chairs

Elmer Dadios	De La Salle University, Philippines
Nataliia Kulabukhova	St. Petersburg University, Russia
Daisuke Takahashi	Tsukuba University, Japan
Shangwang Wang	Beijing University of Posts and Telecommunications, China

Technology Chairs

Damiano Perri	University of Florence, Italy
Marco Simonetti	University of Florence, Italy

Local Arrangement Chairs

Ivan Blečić	University of Cagliari, Italy
Chiara Garau	University of Cagliari, Italy
Alfonso Annunziata	University of Cagliari, Italy
Ginevra Balletto	University of Cagliari, Italy
Giuseppe Borruso	University of Trieste, Italy
Alessandro Buccini	University of Cagliari, Italy
Michele Campagna	University of Cagliari, Italy
Mauro Coni	University of Cagliari, Italy
Anna Maria Colavitti	University of Cagliari, Italy
Giulia Desogus	University of Cagliari, Italy
Caterina Fenu	University of Cagliari, Italy
Sabrina Lai	University of Cagliari, Italy
Francesca Maltinti	University of Cagliari, Italy
Pasquale Mistretta	University of Cagliari, Italy

Augusto Montisci	University of Cagliari, Italy
Francesco Pinna	University of Cagliari, Italy
Davide Spano	University of Cagliari, Italy
Giuseppe A. Trunfio	University of Sassari, Italy
Corrado Zoppi	University of Cagliari, Italy

Program Committee

Vera Afreixo	University of Aveiro, Portugal
Filipe Alvelos	University of Minho, Portugal
Hartmut Asche	University of Potsdam, Germany
Ginevra Balletto	University of Cagliari, Italy
Michela Bertolotto	University College Dublin, Ireland
Sandro Bimonte	INRAE-TSCF, France
Rod Blais	University of Calgary, Canada
Ivan Blečić	University of Sassari, Italy
Giuseppe Borruso	University of Trieste, Italy
Ana Cristina Braga	University of Minho, Portugal
Massimo Cafaro	University of Salento, Italy
Yves Caniou	University of Lyon, France
José A. Cardoso e Cunha	Universidade Nova de Lisboa, Portugal
Rui Cardoso	University of Beira Interior, Portugal
Leocadio G. Casado	University of Almeria, Spain
Carlo Cattani	University of Salerno, Italy
Mete Celik	Erciyes University, Turkey
Maria Cerreta	University of Naples "Federico II", Italy
Hyunseung Choo	Sungkyunkwan University, South Korea
Chien-Sing Lee	Sunway University, Malaysia
Min Young Chung	Sungkyunkwan University, South Korea
Florbela Maria da Cruz Domingues Correia	Polytechnic Institute of Viana do Castelo, Portugal
Gilberto Corso Pereira	Federal University of Bahia, Brazil
Fernanda Costa	University of Minho, Portugal
Alessandro Costantini	INFN, Italy
Carla Dal Sasso Freitas	Universidade Federal do Rio Grande do Sul, Brazil
Pradesh Debba	The Council for Scientific and Industrial Research (CSIR), South Africa
Hendrik Decker	Instituto Tecnolčgico de Informática, Spain
Robertas Damaševičius	Kausan University of Technology, Lithuania
Frank Devai	London South Bank University, UK
Rodolphe Devillers	Memorial University of Newfoundland, Canada
Joana Matos Dias	University of Coimbra, Portugal
Paolino Di Felice	University of L'Aquila, Italy
Prabu Dorairaj	NetApp, India/USA
Noelia Faginas Lago	University of Perugia, Italy
M. Irene Falcao	University of Minho, Portugal

Ana Paula Teixeira	University of Trás-os-Montes and Alto Douro, Portugal
Senhorinha Teixeira	University of Minho, Portugal
M. Filomena Teodoro	Portuguese Naval Academy/University of Lisbon, Portugal
Parimala Thulasiraman	University of Manitoba, Canada
Carmelo Torre	Polytechnic University of Bari, Italy
Javier Martinez Torres	Centro Universitario de la Defensa Zaragoza, Spain
Giuseppe A. Trunfio	University of Sassari, Italy
Pablo Vanegas	University of Cuenca, Equador
Marco Vizzari	University of Perugia, Italy
Varun Vohra	Merck Inc., USA
Koichi Wada	University of Tsukuba, Japan
Krzysztof Walkowiak	Wroclaw University of Technology, Poland
Zequn Wang	Intelligent Automation Inc, USA
Robert Weibel	University of Zurich, Switzerland
Frank Westad	Norwegian University of Science and Technology, Norway
Roland Wismüller	Universität Siegen, Germany
Mudasser Wyne	National University, USA
Chung-Huang Yang	National Kaohsiung Normal University, Taiwan
Xin-She Yang	National Physical Laboratory, UK
Salim Zabir	National Institute of Technology, Tsuruoka, Japan
Haifeng Zhao	University of California, Davis, USA
Fabiana Zollo	University of Venice "Cà Foscari", Italy
Albert Y. Zomaya	University of Sydney, Australia

Workshop Organizers

Advanced Transport Tools and Methods (A2TM 2021)

Massimiliano Petri	University of Pisa, Italy
Antonio Pratelli	University of Pisa, Italy

Advances in Artificial Intelligence Learning Technologies: Blended Learning, STEM, Computational Thinking and Coding (AAILT 2021)

Alfredo Milani	University of Perugia, Italy
Giulio Biondi	University of Florence, Italy
Sergio Tasso	University of Perugia, Italy

Workshop on Advancements in Applied Machine Learning and Data Analytics (AAMDA 2021)

Alessandro Costantini	INFN, Italy
Davide Salomoni	INFN, Italy
Doina Cristina Duma	INFN, Italy
Daniele Cesini	INFN, Italy

Automatic Landform Classification: Spatial Methods and Applications (ALCSMA 2021)

Maria Danese	ISPC, National Research Council, Italy
Dario Gioia	ISPC, National Research Council, Italy

Application of Numerical Analysis to Imaging Science (ANAIS 2021)

Caterina Fenu	University of Cagliari, Italy
Alessandro Buccini	University of Cagliari, Italy

Advances in Information Systems and Technologies for Emergency Management, Risk Assessment and Mitigation Based on the Resilience Concepts (ASTER 2021)

Maurizio Pollino	ENEA, Italy
Marco Vona	University of Basilicata, Italy
Amedeo Flora	University of Basilicata, Italy
Chiara Iacovino	University of Basilicata, Italy
Beniamino Murgante	University of Basilicata, Italy

Advances in Web Based Learning (AWBL 2021)

Birol Ciloglugil	Ege University, Turkey
Mustafa Murat Inceoglu	Ege University, Turkey

Blockchain and Distributed Ledgers: Technologies and Applications (BDLTA 2021)

Vladimir Korkhov	St. Petersburg University, Russia
Elena Stankova	St. Petersburg University, Russia
Nataliia Kulabukhova	St. Petersburg University, Russia

Bio and Neuro Inspired Computing and Applications (BIONCA 2021)

Nadia Nedjah	State University of Rio de Janeiro, Brazil
Luiza De Macedo Mourelle	State University of Rio de Janeiro, Brazil

Computational and Applied Mathematics (CAM 2021)

Maria Irene Falcão	University of Minho, Portugal
Fernando Miranda	University of Minho, Portugal

Computational and Applied Statistics (CAS 2021)

Ana Cristina Braga	University of Minho, Portugal

Computerized Evaluation of Economic Activities: Urban Spaces (CEEA 2021)

Diego Altafini	Università di Pisa, Italy
Valerio Cutini	Università di Pisa, Italy

Computational Geometry and Applications (CGA 2021)

Marina Gavrilova   University of Calgary, Canada

Collaborative Intelligence in Multimodal Applications (CIMA 2021)

Robertas Damasevicius   Kaunas University of Technology, Lithuania
Rytis Maskeliunas   Kaunas University of Technology, Lithuania

Computational Optimization and Applications (COA 2021)

Ana Rocha   University of Minho, Portugal
Humberto Rocha   University of Coimbra, Portugal

Computational Astrochemistry (CompAstro 2021)

Marzio Rosi   University of Perugia, Italy
Cecilia Ceccarelli   University of Grenoble, France
Stefano Falcinelli   University of Perugia, Italy
Dimitrios Skouteris   Master-Up, Italy

Computational Science and HPC (CSHPC 2021)

Elise de Doncker   Western Michigan University, USA
Fukuko Yuasa   High Energy Accelerator Research Organization
                                 (KEK), Japan
Hideo Matsufuru   High Energy Accelerator Research Organization
                                 (KEK), Japan

Cities, Technologies and Planning (CTP 2021)

Malgorzata Hanzl   University of Łódź, Poland
Beniamino Murgante   University of Basilicata, Italy
Ljiljana Zivkovic   Ministry of Construction, Transport and
                                 Infrastructure/Institute of Architecture and Urban
                                 and Spatial Planning of Serbia, Serbia
Anastasia Stratigea   National Technical University of Athens, Greece
Giuseppe Borruso   University of Trieste, Italy
Ginevra Balletto   University of Cagliari, Italy

Advanced Modeling E-Mobility in Urban Spaces (DEMOS 2021)

Tiziana Campisi   Kore University of Enna, Italy
Socrates Basbas   Aristotle University of Thessaloniki, Greece
Ioannis Politis   Aristotle University of Thessaloniki, Greece
Florin Nemtanu   Polytechnic University of Bucharest, Romania
Giovanna Acampa   Kore University of Enna, Italy
Wolfgang Schulz   Zeppelin University, Germany

Digital Transformation and Smart City (DIGISMART 2021)

Mauro Mazzei   National Research Council, Italy

Econometric and Multidimensional Evaluation in Urban Environment (EMEUE 2021)

Carmelo Maria Torre   Polytechnic University of Bari, Italy
Maria Cerreta   University "Federico II" of Naples, Italy
Pierluigi Morano   Polytechnic University of Bari, Italy
Simona Panaro   University of Portsmouth, UK
Francesco Tajani   Sapienza University of Rome, Italy
Marco Locurcio   Polytechnic University of Bari, Italy

The 11th International Workshop on Future Computing System Technologies and Applications (FiSTA 2021)

Bernady Apduhan   Kyushu Sangyo University, Japan
Rafael Santos   Brazilian National Institute for Space Research, Brazil

Transformational Urban Mobility: Challenges and Opportunities During and Post COVID Era (FURTHER 2021)

Tiziana Campisi   Kore University of Enna, Italy
Socrates Basbas   Aristotle University of Thessaloniki, Greece
Dilum Dissanayake   Newcastle University, UK
Kh Md Nahiduzzaman   University of British Columbia, Canada
Nurten Akgün Tanbay   Bursa Technical University, Turkey
Khaled J. Assi   King Fahd University of Petroleum and Minerals,
                             Saudi Arabia
Giovanni Tesoriere   Kore University of Enna, Italy
Motasem Darwish   Middle East University, Jordan

Geodesign in Decision Making: Meta Planning and Collaborative Design for Sustainable and Inclusive Development (GDM 2021)

Francesco Scorza   University of Basilicata, Italy
Michele Campagna   University of Cagliari, Italy
Ana Clara Mourao Moura   Federal University of Minas Gerais, Brazil

Geomatics in Forestry and Agriculture: New Advances and Perspectives (GeoForAgr 2021)

Maurizio Pollino   ENEA, Italy
Giuseppe Modica   University of Reggio Calabria, Italy
Marco Vizzari   University of Perugia, Italy

Geographical Analysis, Urban Modeling, Spatial Statistics (GEOG-AND-MOD 2021)

Beniamino Murgante	University of Basilicata, Italy
Giuseppe Borruso	University of Trieste, Italy
Hartmut Asche	University of Potsdam, Germany

Geomatics for Resource Monitoring and Management (GRMM 2021)

Eufemia Tarantino	Polytechnic University of Bari, Italy
Enrico Borgogno Mondino	University of Turin, Italy
Alessandra Capolupo	Polytechnic University of Bari, Italy
Mirko Saponaro	Polytechnic University of Bari, Italy

12th International Symposium on Software Quality (ISSQ 2021)

Sanjay Misra	Covenant University, Nigeria

10th International Workshop on Collective, Massive and Evolutionary Systems (IWCES 2021)

Alfredo Milani	University of Perugia, Italy
Rajdeep Niyogi	Indian Institute of Technology, Roorkee, India

Land Use Monitoring for Sustainability (LUMS 2021)

Carmelo Maria Torre	Polytechnic University of Bari, Italy
Maria Cerreta	University "Federico II" of Naples, Italy
Massimiliano Bencardino	University of Salerno, Italy
Alessandro Bonifazi	Polytechnic University of Bari, Italy
Pasquale Balena	Polytechnic University of Bari, Italy
Giuliano Poli	University "Federico II" of Naples, Italy

Machine Learning for Space and Earth Observation Data (MALSEOD 2021)

Rafael Santos	Instituto Nacional de Pesquisas Espaciais, Brazil
Karine Ferreira	Instituto Nacional de Pesquisas Espaciais, Brazil

Building Multi-dimensional Models for Assessing Complex Environmental Systems (MES 2021)

Marta Dell'Ovo	Polytechnic University of Milan, Italy
Vanessa Assumma	Polytechnic University of Turin, Italy
Caterina Caprioli	Polytechnic University of Turin, Italy
Giulia Datola	Polytechnic University of Turin, Italy
Federico dell'Anna	Polytechnic University of Turin, Italy

Ecosystem Services: Nature's Contribution to People in Practice. Assessment Frameworks, Models, Mapping, and Implications (NC2P 2021)

Francesco Scorza   University of Basilicata, Italy
Sabrina Lai   University of Cagliari, Italy
Ana Clara Mourao Moura   Federal University of Minas Gerais, Brazil
Corrado Zoppi   University of Cagliari, Italy
Dani Broitman   Technion, Israel Institute of Technology, Israel

Privacy in the Cloud/Edge/IoT World (PCEIoT 2021)

Michele Mastroianni   University of Campania Luigi Vanvitelli, Italy
Lelio Campanile   University of Campania Luigi Vanvitelli, Italy
Mauro Iacono   University of Campania Luigi Vanvitelli, Italy

Processes, Methods and Tools Towards RESilient Cities and Cultural Heritage Prone to SOD and ROD Disasters (RES 2021)

Elena Cantatore   Polytechnic University of Bari, Italy
Alberico Sonnessa   Polytechnic University of Bari, Italy
Dario Esposito   Polytechnic University of Bari, Italy

Risk, Resilience and Sustainability in the Efficient Management of Water Resources: Approaches, Tools, Methodologies and Multidisciplinary Integrated Applications (RRS 2021)

Maria Macchiaroli   University of Salerno, Italy
Chiara D'Alpaos   Università degli Studi di Padova, Italy
Mirka Mobilia   Università degli Studi di Salerno, Italy
Antonia Longobardi   Università degli Studi di Salerno, Italy
Grazia Fattoruso   ENEA Research Center, Italy
Vincenzo Pellecchia   Ente Idrico Campano, Italy

Scientific Computing Infrastructure (SCI 2021)

Elena Stankova   St. Petersburg University, Russia
Vladimir Korkhov   St. Petersburg University, Russia
Natalia Kulabukhova   St. Petersburg University, Russia

Smart Cities and User Data Management (SCIDAM 2021)

Chiara Garau   University of Cagliari, Italy
Luigi Mundula   University of Cagliari, Italy
Gianni Fenu   University of Cagliari, Italy
Paolo Nesi   University of Florence, Italy
Paola Zamperlin   University of Pisa, Italy

13th International Symposium on Software Engineering Processes and Applications (SEPA 2021)

Sanjay Misra   Covenant University, Nigeria

Ports of the Future - Smartness and Sustainability (SmartPorts 2021)

Patrizia Serra   University of Cagliari, Italy
Gianfranco Fancello   University of Cagliari, Italy
Ginevra Balletto   University of Cagliari, Italy
Luigi Mundula   University of Cagliari, Italy
Marco Mazzarino   University of Venice, Italy
Giuseppe Borruso   University of Trieste, Italy
Maria del Mar Munoz   Universidad de Cádiz, Spain
    Leonisio

Smart Tourism (SmartTourism 2021)

Giuseppe Borruso   University of Trieste, Italy
Silvia Battino   University of Sassari, Italy
Ginevra Balletto   University of Cagliari, Italy
Maria del Mar Munoz   Universidad de Cádiz, Spain
    Leonisio
Ainhoa Amaro Garcia   Universidad de Alcalà/Universidad de Las Palmas,
                                Spain
Francesca Krasna   University of Trieste, Italy

Sustainability Performance Assessment: Models, Approaches and Applications toward Interdisciplinary and Integrated Solutions (SPA 2021)

Francesco Scorza   University of Basilicata, Italy
Sabrina Lai   University of Cagliari, Italy
Jolanta Dvarioniene   Kaunas University of Technology, Lithuania
Valentin Grecu   Lucian Blaga University, Romania
Corrado Zoppi   University of Cagliari, Italy
Iole Cerminara   University of Basilicata, Italy

Smart and Sustainable Island Communities (SSIC 2021)

Chiara Garau   University of Cagliari, Italy
Anastasia Stratigea   National Technical University of Athens, Greece
Paola Zamperlin   University of Pisa, Italy
Francesco Scorza   University of Basilicata, Italy

Science, Technologies and Policies to Innovate Spatial Planning (STP4P 2021)

Chiara Garau   University of Cagliari, Italy
Daniele La Rosa   University of Catania, Italy
Francesco Scorza   University of Basilicata, Italy

Anna Maria Colavitti   University of Cagliari, Italy
Beniamino Murgante   University of Basilicata, Italy
Paolo La Greca   University of Catania, Italy

Sustainable Urban Energy Systems (SURENSYS 2021)

Luigi Mundula   University of Cagliari, Italy
Emilio Ghiani   University of Cagliari, Italy

Space Syntax for Cities in Theory and Practice (Syntax_City 2021)

Claudia Yamu   University of Groningen, The Netherlands
Akkelies van Nes   Western Norway University of Applied Sciences,
                            Norway
Chiara Garau   University of Cagliari, Italy

Theoretical and Computational Chemistry and Its Applications (TCCMA 2021)

Noelia Faginas-Lago   University of Perugia, Italy

13th International Workshop on Tools and Techniques in Software Development Process (TTSDP 2021)

Sanjay Misra   Covenant University, Nigeria

Urban Form Studies (UForm 2021)

Malgorzata Hanzl   Łódź University of Technology, Poland
Beniamino Murgante   University of Basilicata, Italy
Eufemia Tarantino   Polytechnic University of Bari, Italy
Irena Itova   University of Westminster, UK

Urban Space Accessibility and Safety (USAS 2021)

Chiara Garau   University of Cagliari, Italy
Francesco Pinna   University of Cagliari, Italy
Claudia Yamu   University of Groningen, The Netherlands
Vincenza Torrisi   University of Catania, Italy
Matteo Ignaccolo   University of Catania, Italy
Michela Tiboni   University of Brescia, Italy
Silvia Rossetti   University of Parma, Italy

Virtual and Augmented Reality and Applications (VRA 2021)

Osvaldo Gervasi   University of Perugia, Italy
Damiano Perri   University of Perugia, Italy
Marco Simonetti   University of Perugia, Italy
Sergio Tasso   University of Perugia, Italy

Workshop on Advanced and Computational Methods for Earth Science Applications (WACM4ES 2021)

Luca Piroddi	University of Cagliari, Italy
Laura Foddis	University of Cagliari, Italy
Augusto Montisci	University of Cagliari, Italy
Sergio Vincenzo Calcina	University of Cagliari, Italy
Sebastiano D'Amico	University of Malta, Malta
Giovanni Martinelli	Istituto Nazionale di Geofisica e Vulcanologia, Italy/Chinese Academy of Sciences, China

Sponsoring Organizations

ICCSA 2021 would not have been possible without the tremendous support of many organizations and institutions, for which all organizers and participants of ICCSA 2021 express their sincere gratitude:

Springer International Publishing AG, Germany
(https://www.springer.com)

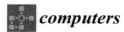

Computers Open Access Journal
(https://www.mdpi.com/journal/computers)

IEEE Italy Section, Italy
(https://italy.ieeer8.org/)

Centre-North Italy Chapter IEEE GRSS, Italy
(https://cispio.diet.uniroma1.it/marzano/ieee-grs/index.html)

Italy Section of the Computer Society, Italy
(https://site.ieee.org/italy-cs/)

University of Perugia, Italy
(https://www.unipg.it)

University of Cagliari, Italy
(https://unica.it/)

University of Basilicata, Italy
(http://www.unibas.it)

Monash University, Australia
(https://www.monash.edu/)

Kyushu Sangyo University, Japan
(https://www.kyusan-u.ac.jp/)

University of Minho, Portugal
(https://www.uminho.pt/)

Universidade do Minho
Escola de Engenharia

Scientific Association Transport Infrastructures,
Italy
(https://www.stradeeautostrade.it/associazioni-e-
organizzazioni/asit-associazione-scientifica-
infrastrutture-trasporto/)

Regione Sardegna, Italy
(https://regione.sardegna.it/)

Comune di Cagliari, Italy
(https://www.comune.cagliari.it/)

Città Metropolitana di Cagliari

Cagliari Accessibility Lab (CAL)
(https://www.unica.it/unica/it/cagliari_
accessibility_lab.page/)

Referees

Nicodemo Abate	IMAA, National Research Council, Italy
Andre Ricardo Abed Grégio	Federal University of Paraná State, Brazil
Nasser Abu Zeid	Università di Ferrara, Italy
Lidia Aceto	Università del Piemonte Orientale, Italy
Nurten Akgün Tanbay	Bursa Technical University, Turkey
Filipe Alvelos	Universidade do Minho, Portugal
Paula Amaral	Universidade Nova de Lisboa, Portugal
Federico Amato	University of Lausanne, Switzerland
Marina Alexandra Pedro Andrade	ISCTE-IUL, Portugal
Debora Anelli	Sapienza University of Rome, Italy
Alfonso Annunziata	University of Cagliari, Italy
Fahim Anzum	University of Calgary, Canada
Tatsumi Aoyama	High Energy Accelerator Research Organization, Japan
Bernady Apduhan	Kyushu Sangyo University, Japan
Jonathan Apeh	Covenant University, Nigeria
Vasilike Argyropoulos	University of West Attica, Greece
Giuseppe Aronica	Università di Messina, Italy
Daniela Ascenzi	Università degli Studi di Trento, Italy
Vanessa Assumma	Politecnico di Torino, Italy
Muhammad Attique Khan	HITEC University Taxila, Pakistan
Vecdi Aytaç	Ege University, Turkey
Alina Elena Baia	University of Perugia, Italy
Ginevra Balletto	University of Cagliari, Italy
Marialaura Bancheri	ISAFOM, National Research Council, Italy
Benedetto Barabino	University of Brescia, Italy
Simona Barbaro	Università degli Studi di Palermo, Italy
Enrico Barbierato	Università Cattolica del Sacro Cuore di Milano, Italy
Jeniffer Barreto	Istituto Superior Técnico, Lisboa, Portugal
Michele Bartalini	TAGES, Italy
Socrates Basbas	Aristotle University of Thessaloniki, Greece
Silvia Battino	University of Sassari, Italy
Marcelo Becerra Rozas	Pontificia Universidad Católica de Valparaíso, Chile
Ranjan Kumar Behera	National Institute of Technology, Rourkela, India
Emanuele Bellini	University of Campania Luigi Vanvitelli, Italy
Massimo Bilancia	University of Bari Aldo Moro, Italy
Giulio Biondi	University of Firenze, Italy
Adriano Bisello	Eurac Research, Italy
Ignacio Blanquer	Universitat Politècnica de València, Spain
Semen Bochkov	Ulyanovsk State Technical University, Russia
Alexander Bogdanov	St. Petersburg University, Russia
Silvia Bonettini	University of Modena and Reggio Emilia, Italy
Enrico Borgogno Mondino	Università di Torino, Italy
Giuseppe Borruso	University of Trieste, Italy

Michele Bottazzi	University of Trento, Italy
Rahma Bouaziz	Taibah University, Saudi Arabia
Ouafik Boulariah	University of Salerno, Italy
Tulin Boyar	Yildiz Technical University, Turkey
Ana Cristina Braga	University of Minho, Portugal
Paolo Bragolusi	University of Padova, Italy
Luca Braidotti	University of Trieste, Italy
Alessandro Buccini	University of Cagliari, Italy
Jorge Buele	Universidad Tecnológica Indoamérica, Ecuador
Andrea Buffoni	TAGES, Italy
Sergio Vincenzo Calcina	University of Cagliari, Italy
Michele Campagna	University of Cagliari, Italy
Lelio Campanile	Università degli Studi della Campania Luigi Vanvitelli, Italy
Tiziana Campisi	Kore University of Enna, Italy
Antonino Canale	Kore University of Enna, Italy
Elena Cantatore	DICATECh, Polytechnic University of Bari, Italy
Pasquale Cantiello	Istituto Nazionale di Geofisica e Vulcanologia, Italy
Alessandra Capolupo	Polytechnic University of Bari, Italy
David Michele Cappelletti	University of Perugia, Italy
Caterina Caprioli	Politecnico di Torino, Italy
Sara Carcangiu	University of Cagliari, Italy
Pedro Carrasqueira	INESC Coimbra, Portugal
Arcangelo Castiglione	University of Salerno, Italy
Giulio Cavana	Politecnico di Torino, Italy
Davide Cerati	Politecnico di Milano, Italy
Maria Cerreta	University of Naples Federico II, Italy
Daniele Cesini	INFN-CNAF, Italy
Jabed Chowdhury	La Trobe University, Australia
Gennaro Ciccarelli	Iuav University of Venice, Italy
Birol Ciloglugil	Ege University, Turkey
Elena Cocuzza	Univesity of Catania, Italy
Anna Maria Colavitt	University of Cagliari, Italy
Cecilia Coletti	Università "G. d'Annunzio" di Chieti-Pescara, Italy
Alberto Collu	Independent Researcher, Italy
Anna Concas	University of Basilicata, Italy
Mauro Coni	University of Cagliari, Italy
Melchiorre Contino	Università di Palermo, Italy
Antonella Cornelio	Università degli Studi di Brescia, Italy
Aldina Correia	Politécnico do Porto, Portugal
Elisete Correia	Universidade de Trás-os-Montes e Alto Douro, Portugal
Florbela Correia	Polytechnic Institute of Viana do Castelo, Italy
Stefano Corsi	Università degli Studi di Milano, Italy
Alberto Cortez	Polytechnic of University Coimbra, Portugal
Lino Costa	Universidade do Minho, Portugal

Alessandro Costantini	INFN, Italy
Marilena Cozzolino	Università del Molise, Italy
Giulia Crespi	Politecnico di Torino, Italy
Maurizio Crispino	Politecnico di Milano, Italy
Chiara D'Alpaos	University of Padova, Italy
Roberta D'Ambrosio	Università di Salerno, Italy
Sebastiano D'Amico	University of Malta, Malta
Hiroshi Daisaka	Hitotsubashi University, Japan
Gaia Daldanise	Italian National Research Council, Italy
Robertas Damasevicius	Silesian University of Technology, Poland
Maria Danese	ISPC, National Research Council, Italy
Bartoli Daniele	University of Perugia, Italy
Motasem Darwish	Middle East University, Jordan
Giulia Datola	Politecnico di Torino, Italy
Regina de Almeida	UTAD, Portugal
Elise de Doncker	Western Michigan University, USA
Mariella De Fino	Politecnico di Bari, Italy
Giandomenico De Luca	Mediterranean University of Reggio Calabria, Italy
Luiza de Macedo Mourelle	State University of Rio de Janeiro, Brazil
Gianluigi De Mare	University of Salerno, Italy
Itamir de Morais Barroca Filho	Federal University of Rio Grande do Norte, Brazil
Samuele De Petris	Università di Torino, Italy
Marcilio de Souto	LIFO, University of Orléans, France
Alexander Degtyarev	St. Petersburg University, Russia
Federico Dell'Anna	Politecnico di Torino, Italy
Marta Dell'Ovo	Politecnico di Milano, Italy
Fernanda Della Mura	University of Naples "Federico II", Italy
Ahu Dereli Dursun	Istanbul Commerce University, Turkey
Bashir Derradji	University of Sfax, Tunisia
Giulia Desogus	Università degli Studi di Cagliari, Italy
Marco Dettori	Università degli Studi di Sassari, Italy
Frank Devai	London South Bank University, UK
Felicia Di Liddo	Polytechnic University of Bari, Italy
Valerio Di Pinto	University of Naples "Federico II", Italy
Joana Dias	University of Coimbra, Portugal
Luis Dias	University of Minho, Portugal
Patricia Diaz de Alba	Gran Sasso Science Institute, Italy
Isabel Dimas	University of Coimbra, Portugal
Aleksandra Djordjevic	University of Belgrade, Serbia
Luigi Dolores	Università degli Studi di Salerno, Italy
Marco Donatelli	University of Insubria, Italy
Doina Cristina Duma	INFN-CNAF, Italy
Fabio Durastante	University of Pisa, Italy
Aziz Dursun	Virginia Tech University, USA
Juan Enrique-Romero	Université Grenoble Alpes, France

Annunziata Esposito Amideo	University College Dublin, Ireland
Dario Esposito	Polytechnic University of Bari, Italy
Claudio Estatico	University of Genova, Italy
Noelia Faginas-Lago	Università di Perugia, Italy
Maria Irene Falcão	University of Minho, Portugal
Stefano Falcinelli	University of Perugia, Italy
Alessandro Farina	University of Pisa, Italy
Grazia Fattoruso	ENEA, Italy
Caterina Fenu	University of Cagliari, Italy
Luisa Fermo	University of Cagliari, Italy
Florbela Fernandes	Instituto Politecnico de Braganca, Portugal
Rosário Fernandes	University of Minho, Portugal
Luis Fernandez-Sanz	University of Alcala, Spain
Alessia Ferrari	Università di Parma, Italy
Luís Ferrás	University of Minho, Portugal
Ângela Ferreira	Instituto Politécnico de Bragança, Portugal
Flora Ferreira	University of Minho, Portugal
Manuel Carlos Figueiredo	University of Minho, Portugal
Ugo Fiore	University of Naples "Parthenope", Italy
Amedeo Flora	University of Basilicata, Italy
Hector Florez	Universidad Distrital Francisco Jose de Caldas, Colombia
Maria Laura Foddis	University of Cagliari, Italy
Valentina Franzoni	Perugia University, Italy
Adelaide Freitas	University of Aveiro, Portugal
Samuel Frimpong	Durban University of Technology, South Africa
Ioannis Fyrogenis	Aristotle University of Thessaloniki, Greece
Marika Gaballo	Politecnico di Torino, Italy
Laura Gabrielli	Iuav University of Venice, Italy
Ivan Gankevich	St. Petersburg University, Russia
Chiara Garau	University of Cagliari, Italy
Ernesto Garcia Para	Universidad del País Vasco, Spain,
Fernando Garrido	Universidad Técnica del Norte, Ecuador
Marina Gavrilova	University of Calgary, Canada
Silvia Gazzola	University of Bath, UK
Georgios Georgiadis	Aristotle University of Thessaloniki, Greece
Osvaldo Gervasi	University of Perugia, Italy
Andrea Gioia	Polytechnic University of Bari, Italy
Dario Gioia	ISPC-CNT, Italy
Raffaele Giordano	IRSS, National Research Council, Italy
Giacomo Giorgi	University of Perugia, Italy
Eleonora Giovene di Girasole	IRISS, National Research Council, Italy
Salvatore Giuffrida	Università di Catania, Italy
Marco Gola	Politecnico di Milano, Italy

Pavan Kumar	University of Calgary, Canada
Anisha Kumari	National Institute of Technology, Rourkela, India
Ludovica La Rocca	University of Naples "Federico II", Italy
Daniele La Rosa	University of Catania, Italy
Sabrina Lai	University of Cagliari, Italy
Giuseppe Francesco Cesare Lama	University of Naples "Federico II", Italy
Mariusz Lamprecht	University of Lodz, Poland
Vincenzo Laporta	National Research Council, Italy
Chien-Sing Lee	Sunway University, Malaysia
José Isaac Lemus Romani	Pontifical Catholic University of Valparaíso, Chile
Federica Leone	University of Cagliari, Italy
Alexander H. Levis	George Mason University, USA
Carola Lingua	Polytechnic University of Turin, Italy
Marco Locurcio	Polytechnic University of Bari, Italy
Andrea Lombardi	University of Perugia, Italy
Savino Longo	University of Bari, Italy
Fernando Lopez Gayarre	University of Oviedo, Spain
Yan Lu	Western Michigan University, USA
Maria Macchiaroli	University of Salerno, Italy
Helmuth Malonek	University of Aveiro, Portugal
Francesca Maltinti	University of Cagliari, Italy
Luca Mancini	University of Perugia, Italy
Marcos Mandado	University of Vigo, Spain
Ernesto Marcheggiani	Università Politecnica delle Marche, Italy
Krassimir Markov	University of Telecommunications and Post, Bulgaria
Giovanni Martinelli	INGV, Italy
Alessandro Marucci	University of L'Aquila, Italy
Fiammetta Marulli	University of Campania Luigi Vanvitelli, Italy
Gabriella Maselli	University of Salerno, Italy
Rytis Maskeliunas	Kaunas University of Technology, Lithuania
Michele Mastroianni	University of Campania Luigi Vanvitelli, Italy
Cristian Mateos	Universidad Nacional del Centro de la Provincia de Buenos Aires, Argentina
Hideo Matsufuru	High Energy Accelerator Research Organization (KEK), Japan
D'Apuzzo Mauro	University of Cassino and Southern Lazio, Italy
Chiara Mazzarella	University Federico II, Italy
Marco Mazzarino	University of Venice, Italy
Giovanni Mei	University of Cagliari, Italy
Mário Melo	Federal Institute of Rio Grande do Norte, Brazil
Francesco Mercaldo	University of Molise, Italy
Alfredo Milani	University of Perugia, Italy
Alessandra Milesi	University of Cagliari, Italy
Antonio Minervino	ISPC, National Research Council, Italy
Fernando Miranda	Universidade do Minho, Portugal

B. Mishra	University of Szeged, Hungary
Sanjay Misra	Covenant University, Nigeria
Mirka Mobilia	University of Salerno, Italy
Giuseppe Modica	Università degli Studi di Reggio Calabria, Italy
Mohammadsadegh Mohagheghi	Vali-e-Asr University of Rafsanjan, Iran
Mohamad Molaei Qelichi	University of Tehran, Iran
Mario Molinara	University of Cassino and Southern Lazio, Italy
Augusto Montisci	Università degli Studi di Cagliari, Italy
Pierluigi Morano	Polytechnic University of Bari, Italy
Ricardo Moura	Universidade Nova de Lisboa, Portugal
Ana Clara Mourao Moura	Federal University of Minas Gerais, Brazil
Maria Mourao	Polytechnic Institute of Viana do Castelo, Portugal
Daichi Mukunoki	RIKEN Center for Computational Science, Japan
Beniamino Murgante	University of Basilicata, Italy
Naohito Nakasato	University of Aizu, Japan
Grazia Napoli	Università degli Studi di Palermo, Italy
Isabel Cristina Natário	Universidade Nova de Lisboa, Portugal
Nadia Nedjah	State University of Rio de Janeiro, Brazil
Antonio Nesticò	University of Salerno, Italy
Andreas Nikiforiadis	Aristotle University of Thessaloniki, Greece
Keigo Nitadori	RIKEN Center for Computational Science, Japan
Silvio Nocera	Iuav University of Venice, Italy
Giuseppina Oliva	University of Salerno, Italy
Arogundade Oluwasefunmi	Academy of Mathematics and System Science, China
Ken-ichi Oohara	University of Tokyo, Japan
Tommaso Orusa	University of Turin, Italy
M. Fernanda P. Costa	University of Minho, Portugal
Roberta Padulano	Centro Euro-Mediterraneo sui Cambiamenti Climatici, Italy
Maria Panagiotopoulou	National Technical University of Athens, Greece
Jay Pancham	Durban University of Technology, South Africa
Gianni Pantaleo	University of Florence, Italy
Dimos Pantazis	University of West Attica, Greece
Michela Paolucci	University of Florence, Italy
Eric Pardede	La Trobe University, Australia
Olivier Parisot	Luxembourg Institute of Science and Technology, Luxembourg
Vincenzo Pellecchia	Ente Idrico Campano, Italy
Anna Pelosi	University of Salerno, Italy
Edit Pengő	University of Szeged, Hungary
Marco Pepe	University of Salerno, Italy
Paola Perchinunno	University of Cagliari, Italy
Ana Pereira	Polytechnic Institute of Bragança, Portugal
Mariano Pernetti	University of Campania, Italy
Damiano Perri	University of Perugia, Italy

Federica Pes	University of Cagliari, Italy
Marco Petrelli	Roma Tre University, Italy
Massimiliano Petri	University of Pisa, Italy
Khiem Phan	Duy Tan University, Vietnam
Alberto Ferruccio Piccinni	Polytechnic of Bari, Italy
Angela Pilogallo	University of Basilicata, Italy
Francesco Pinna	University of Cagliari, Italy
Telmo Pinto	University of Coimbra, Portugal
Luca Piroddi	University of Cagliari, Italy
Darius Plonis	Vilnius Gediminas Technical University, Lithuania
Giuliano Poli	University of Naples "Federico II", Italy
Maria João Polidoro	Polytecnic Institute of Porto, Portugal
Ioannis Politis	Aristotle University of Thessaloniki, Greece
Maurizio Pollino	ENEA, Italy
Antonio Pratelli	University of Pisa, Italy
Salvatore Praticò	Mediterranean University of Reggio Calabria, Italy
Marco Prato	University of Modena and Reggio Emilia, Italy
Carlotta Quagliolo	Polytechnic University of Turin, Italy
Emanuela Quaquero	Univesity of Cagliari, Italy
Garrisi Raffaele	Polizia postale e delle Comunicazioni, Italy
Nicoletta Rassu	University of Cagliari, Italy
Hafiz Tayyab Rauf	University of Bradford, UK
Michela Ravanelli	Sapienza University of Rome, Italy
Roberta Ravanelli	Sapienza University of Rome, Italy
Alfredo Reder	Centro Euro-Mediterraneo sui Cambiamenti Climatici, Italy
Stefania Regalbuto	University of Naples "Federico II", Italy
Rommel Regis	Saint Joseph's University, USA
Lothar Reichel	Kent State University, USA
Marco Reis	University of Coimbra, Portugal
Maria Reitano	University of Naples "Federico II", Italy
Jerzy Respondek	Silesian University of Technology, Poland
Elisa Riccietti	École Normale Supérieure de Lyon, France
Albert Rimola	Universitat Autònoma de Barcelona, Spain
Angela Rizzo	University of Bari, Italy
Ana Maria A. C. Rocha	University of Minho, Portugal
Fabio Rocha	Institute of Technology and Research, Brazil
Humberto Rocha	University of Coimbra, Portugal
Maria Clara Rocha	Polytechnic Institute of Coimbra, Portugal
Miguel Rocha	University of Minho, Portugal
Giuseppe Rodriguez	University of Cagliari, Italy
Guillermo Rodriguez	UNICEN, Argentina
Elisabetta Ronchieri	INFN, Italy
Marzio Rosi	University of Perugia, Italy
Silvia Rossetti	University of Parma, Italy
Marco Rossitti	Polytechnic University of Milan, Italy

Francesco Rotondo	Marche Polytechnic University, Italy
Irene Rubino	Polytechnic University of Turin, Italy
Agustín Salas	Pontifical Catholic University of Valparaíso, Chile
Juan Pablo Sandoval Alcocer	Universidad Católica Boliviana "San Pablo", Bolivia
Luigi Santopietro	University of Basilicata, Italy
Rafael Santos	National Institute for Space Research, Brazil
Valentino Santucci	Università per Stranieri di Perugia, Italy
Mirko Saponaro	Polytechnic University of Bari, Italy
Filippo Sarvia	University of Turin, Italy
Marco Scaioni	Polytechnic University of Milan, Italy
Rafal Scherer	Częstochowa University of Technology, Poland
Francesco Scorza	University of Basilicata, Italy
Ester Scotto di Perta	University of Napoli "Federico II", Italy
Monica Sebillo	University of Salerno, Italy
Patrizia Serra	University of Cagliari, Italy
Ricardo Severino	University of Minho, Portugal
Jie Shen	University of Michigan, USA
Huahao Shou	Zhejiang University of Technology, China
Miltiadis Siavvas	Centre for Research and Technology Hellas, Greece
Brandon Sieu	University of Calgary, Canada
Ângela Silva	Instituto Politécnico de Viana do Castelo, Portugal
Carina Silva	Polytechic Institute of Lisbon, Portugal
Joao Carlos Silva	Polytechnic Institute of Cavado and Ave, Portugal
Fabio Silveira	Federal University of Sao Paulo, Brazil
Marco Simonetti	University of Florence, Italy
Ana Jacinta Soares	University of Minho, Portugal
Maria Joana Soares	University of Minho, Portugal
Michel Soares	Federal University of Sergipe, Brazil
George Somarakis	Foundation for Research and Technology Hellas, Greece
Maria Somma	University of Naples "Federico II", Italy
Alberico Sonnessa	Polytechnic University of Bari, Italy
Elena Stankova	St. Petersburg University, Russia
Flavio Stochino	University of Cagliari, Italy
Anastasia Stratigea	National Technical University of Athens, Greece
Yasuaki Sumida	Kyushu Sangyo University, Japan
Yue Sun	European X-Ray Free-Electron Laser Facility, Germany
Kirill Sviatov	Ulyanovsk State Technical University, Russia
Daisuke Takahashi	University of Tsukuba, Japan
Aladics Tamás	University of Szeged, Hungary
David Taniar	Monash University, Australia
Rodrigo Tapia McClung	Centro de Investigación en Ciencias de Información Geoespacial, Mexico
Eufemia Tarantino	Polytechnic University of Bari, Italy

Sergio Tasso	University of Perugia, Italy
Ana Paula Teixeira	Universidade de Trás-os-Montes e Alto Douro, Portugal
Senhorinha Teixeira	University of Minho, Portugal
Tengku Adil Tengku Izhar	Universiti Teknologi MARA, Malaysia
Maria Filomena Teodoro	University of Lisbon/Portuguese Naval Academy, Portugal
Giovanni Tesoriere	Kore University of Enna, Italy
Yiota Theodora	National Technical Univeristy of Athens, Greece
Graça Tomaz	Polytechnic Institute of Guarda, Portugal
Carmelo Maria Torre	Polytechnic University of Bari, Italy
Francesca Torrieri	University of Naples "Federico II", Italy
Vincenza Torrisi	University of Catania, Italy
Vincenzo Totaro	Polytechnic University of Bari, Italy
Pham Trung	Ho Chi Minh City University of Technology, Vietnam
Dimitrios Tsoukalas	Centre of Research and Technology Hellas (CERTH), Greece
Sanjida Tumpa	University of Calgary, Canada
Iñaki Tuñon	Universidad de Valencia, Spain
Takahiro Ueda	Seikei University, Japan
Piero Ugliengo	University of Turin, Italy
Abdi Usman	Haramaya University, Ethiopia
Ettore Valente	University of Naples "Federico II", Italy
Jordi Vallverdu	Universitat Autònoma de Barcelona, Spain
Cornelis Van Der Mee	University of Cagliari, Italy
José Varela-Aldás	Universidad Tecnológica Indoamérica, Ecuador
Fanny Vazart	University of Grenoble Alpes, France
Franco Vecchiocattivi	University of Perugia, Italy
Laura Verde	University of Campania Luigi Vanvitelli, Italy
Giulia Vergerio	Polytechnic University of Turin, Italy
Jos Vermaseren	Nikhef, The Netherlands
Giacomo Viccione	University of Salerno, Italy
Marco Vizzari	University of Perugia, Italy
Corrado Vizzarri	Polytechnic University of Bari, Italy
Alexander Vodyaho	St. Petersburg State Electrotechnical University "LETI", Russia
Nikolay N. Voit	Ulyanovsk State Technical University, Russia
Marco Vona	University of Basilicata, Italy
Agustinus Borgy Waluyo	Monash University, Australia
Fernando Wanderley	Catholic University of Pernambuco, Brazil
Chao Wang	University of Science and Technology of China, China
Marcin Wozniak	Silesian University of Technology, Poland
Tiang Xian	Nathong University, China
Rekha Yadav	KL University, India
Claudia Yamu	University of Groningen, The Netherlands
Fenghui Yao	Tennessee State University, USA

Contents – Part V

**International Workshop on Advanced Modeling E-Mobility
in Urban Spaces (DEMOS 2021)**

International Workshop
on Computational Geometry
and Applications (CGA 2021)

A Novel Line Convex Polygon Clipping Algorithm in E2 with Parallel Processing Modification

Vaclav Skala$^{(\boxtimes)}$ (iD)

Department of Computer Science and Engineering,
University of West Bohemia, 301 00 Pilsen, Czech Republic
skala@kiv.zcu.cz
http://www.VaclavSkala.eu

Abstract. This paper presents a new approach to line clipping by a convex polygon problem solution. The algorithm is based on a separation function, which separates the polygon vertices to the left or right hand side of the given line. It leads to numerically robust algorithms in comparison to the well-known Cyrus-Beck's algorithm and its modifications.

The proposed algorithm has $O(N)$ complexity, but supports parallel processing and simple implementation in hardware.

The presented approach has also impact to the algorithm design methodology and importance of a detailed analysis in algorithm development, if the algorithm robustness and efficiency is required.

Keywords: Line clipping · Line segment clipping · Cyrus-Beck algorithm · Convex polygon clipping · Homogeneous coordinates · Projective representation · Duality

1 Introduction

There are many algorithms for a line clipping or a line segment clipping by a convex polygon with many modifications. Probably the mostly published algorithms are devoted to a line or line segment clipping by a rectangular window in E^2, which was motivated by computer graphics output devices and Window-Viewport operations, the Cohen-Sutherand's (CS) [8] and Liang-Barsky (LB) [12] algorithms are the most known for line segment and line segment clipping in E^2 with several modification and improvements, e.g. Nicholl-Lee-Nicholl [13], Bui [2], Skala [16,33], Andreev [1], Day [5], Dörr [7], Duvalenko [6], Kaijian [10], Krammer [11], Liang [12], Sobkow [35] and Zhang [36]. Line clipping in E^2 using homogeneous coordinates was introduced by Nielsen [14] and optimized line segment clipping for the normalized window was published in Skala [26,31]. A new classification scheme for the line segment end-points is introduced in Skala [32].

Supported by the University of West Bohemia - Institutional research support No. 1311.

© Springer Nature Switzerland AG 2021
O. Gervasi et al. (Eds.): ICCSA 2021, LNCS 12953, pp. 3–15, 2021.
https://doi.org/10.1007/978-3-030-86976-2_1

However, clipping by a convex polygon is a little bit more complicated problem as it depends on number of vertices of the given convex polygon. Probably the Cyrus-Beck (CB) [4] algorithm is the most known for line segment and line segment clipping in the E^2 case having applicability also in the E^3 case for clipping by a convex polyhedron. The Cyrus-Beck algorithm has $O(N)$ computational complexity. The Cyrus-Beck algorithm was modified for non-convex polygons with self-intersecting edges and quadratic curves in Skala [17,18]. A line convex clipping algorithm based on space subdivision was introduced by Slater [34]. A line clipping algorithm based on shearing transformation was published by Huang [9], algorithm for a polygon clipping was published in Rappoport [15].

The algorithm for a line and line segment clipping by a convex polygon with $O(lgN)$ complexity was described in Skala [20]. Complexity decrease is possible due to "ordering" of vertex indexes of the convex polygon in the E^2 case. Unfortunately, this is not extensible for the E^3 case, i.e. line clipping by a convex polyhedron, as in the E^3 case no ordering of vertices is available. The algorithm with $O_{exp}(\sqrt{N})$ was introduced by Skala [23] for the case when the polyhedron is represented by a triangular mesh using information on the neighbours of triangles. A line intersection algorithm with a non-convex polyhedron in E^3 was introduced in Skala [21,25].

In the E^2 case, if the convex polygon is constant and many lines or line segments are to be clipped, it is possible to pre-compute the convex polygon using dual space representation and the point-in-convex polygon location strategy Skala [24]. Then, the line segment clipping algorithm is $O_{exp}(1)$ run-time complexity, Skala [22]. The algorithm was extended for the E^3 case in Skala [23].

In the following, a new approach to the line clipping by a convex polygon in E^2 is described in comparison to the Cyrus-Beck's algorithm.

2   Cyrus-Beck's Algorithm

The Cyrus-Beck's (CB) algorithm is well known and is used in many computer graphics courses due to its simplicity and applicability for the E^3 case.

The Cyrus-Beck's algorithm is based on direct intersection computation of the given line p in the parametric form and a line on which the polygon edge e_i lies, see Fig. 1, in the implicit form, i.e. on a solution of two linear equations (vector notation is used):

$$
\begin{aligned}
p: &\quad \mathbf{x}(t) = \mathbf{x}_A + \mathbf{s}\, t \\
e_i: &\quad \mathbf{n}_i^T \mathbf{x} + c_i = 0
\end{aligned}
\tag{1}
$$

Solving those equations, the parameter t for the intersection point is obtained as:

$$
e_i: \quad \mathbf{n}_i^T \mathbf{x}_A + \mathbf{n}_i^T \mathbf{s}\, t + c_i = 0
\tag{2}
$$

and therefore

$$
t = -\frac{\mathbf{n}_i^T \mathbf{x}_A + c_i}{\mathbf{n}_i^T \mathbf{s}}
\tag{3}
$$

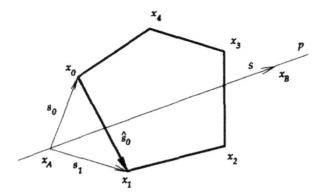

Fig. 1. Clipping against the convex polygon in E^2

It can be seen, that there is an instability of the algorithm as if the line p is parallel or nearly parallel to the edge e_i, the expression $\mathbf{n}_i^T \mathbf{s} \to 0$ and $t \to \pm\infty$. The fraction computation might cause an overflow or high imprecision of the computed parameter t value, see Fig. 2.

It is hard to detect and solve reliably such cases and programmers usually use a sequence like

$$\textbf{if } |\mathbf{n}_i^T \mathbf{s})| \ < \ eps \textbf{ then } a \ singular \ case$$

which is incorrect solution as the value *eps* is a programmer choice. Unfortunately, text books do not point this in spite of this dangerous construction as far as the robustness and computational stability is concerned.

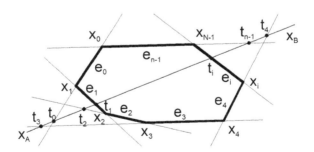

Fig. 2. Cyrus-Beck clipping algorithm against the convex polygon in E^2

The modification of the Cyrus-Beck's algorithm using the cross product for more reliable detection of the "close to singular" cases was described by Skala [19]. However, it is computationally more expensive and not solving the "close to singular" cases in total.

Algorithm 1. Cyrus-Beck's Line Clipping Algorithm

1: **for** $i := 0$ **to** N-1 **do**	
2: Compute $\mathbf{n}_i$ and c_i for all polygon edges	
3:	▷ pre-computation for the given convex polygon
4: **procedure** C-B-CLIP($\mathbf{x}_A, \mathbf{x}_B$);	▷ line is given by two points
5: $t_{min} := -\infty$; $t_{max} := \infty$;	▷ set initial conditions for the parameter t
6: $\mathbf{s} := \mathbf{x}_B - \mathbf{x}_A$;	▷ computation of the line coefficients
7: **for** $i := 0$ **to** $N - 1$ **do**	▷ for each edge
8: $q := \mathbf{n}_i^T \mathbf{s}$;	▷ pre-computation
9: **if** $abs(q) < eps$ **then** NOP;	▷ Singular case-usual solution
10: **else**	
11: $t = -(\mathbf{n}_i^T \mathbf{x}_A + c_i)/\mathbf{n}_i^T \mathbf{s}$;	
12: **if** $q < 0$ **then** $t_{min} := max(t, t_{min})$;	
13: **else** $t_{max} := min(t, t_{max})$;	
14: **end if**	
15: **end if**	
16: **end for**	▷ all convex polygon edges processed
17: **if** $t_{min} < tmax$ **then**	▷ intersection of a line and the polygon exists
18: { $\mathbf{x}_B := \mathbf{x}_A + \mathbf{s}\, t$; $\mathbf{x}_A := \mathbf{x}_A + \mathbf{s}\, t$; }	
19: **end if**	
20: **end procedure**	

The Cyrus-Beck's algorithm for a line clipping is described by the Algorithm 1. It can be easily modified for a line segment clipping just restricting the range of the parameter t to $<0,1>$, i.e.

$$<t_{min}, t_{max}> := <t_{min}, t_{max}> \cap <0,1>$$

It can be seen, that the algorithm complexity is of $O(N)$ and the division operation, which is the most consuming time operation in the floating point representation, is used N times. However, only 2 values of the parameter t are valid, i.e. $N-2$ computations of the parameter t are lost. Also reliable detection of the "close to singular" cases is difficult and time consuming.

In following, the S-Convex-Clip algorithms based on implicit formulation using projective representation will be presented. It is based on the classification of the window corners against the given line in the implicit form with high numerical stability.

3   Proposed Algorithm

The majority of line clipping algorithms in the E^2 and E^3 cases have been developed for the Euclidean space representation in spite of the fact, that geometric transformations, i.e. projection, translation, rotation, scaling and Window-Viewport etc., use homogeneous coordinates, e.g. projective representation.

This results into necessity to convert the results of the geometric transformations to the Euclidean space using division operation as follows:

$$\mathbf{X} = (X, Y) \quad \mathbf{x} = [x, y : w]^T \quad X = \frac{x}{w} \quad Y = \frac{y}{w} \quad w \neq 0 \tag{4}$$

where (X, Y) are the point coordinates in the Euclidean space E^2, while $[x, y : w]^T$ are in the homogeneous coordinates Skala [28–30]; similarly in the E^3 case. It should be noted, that ":" is used in the notation to point out, that the w is the homogeneous coordinate and has no physical unit in the contrary of the x, resp. y which has a physical unit, e.g. meters [m].

If a point is given in the Euclidean space, its homogeneous coordinates are given as $\mathbf{x} = [X, Y : 1]^T$, i.e. $w = 1$. The homogeneous coordinates also enable to represent a point close or in infinity, i.e. when $w \to 0$, and postpone the division operations. It leads to better numerical robustness and computational speed-up especially if GPU or SSE instructions are used.

4 S-Convex-Clip

Let us consider a typical example of a line clipping by the convex clipping window, see Fig. 1, and a line p given in the implicit form using the projective notation:

$$p : \quad ax + by + cw = 0 \quad, i.e. \quad \mathbf{a}^T \mathbf{x} = 0 \tag{5}$$

where $\mathbf{a} = [a, b : c]^T$ are coefficients of the given line p, $\mathbf{x} = [x, y : w]^T$ is a point on this line using projective notation (w is the homogeneous coordinate). It can be seen, that if the Eq. 5 is divided by $w \neq 0$, then:

$$a\frac{x}{w} + b\frac{y}{w} + c\frac{w}{w} = 0 \quad, i.e. \quad aX + bY + c = 0 \tag{6}$$

The advantage of the projective notation is, that a line p passing two points $\mathbf{x}_A$, $\mathbf{x}_B$ or an intersection point $\mathbf{x}$ of two lines p_1, p_2 can be computed due to the principle of duality as Coxeter [3] and Skala [30]:

$$\mathbf{p} = \mathbf{x}_A \wedge \mathbf{x}_B \quad, \quad \mathbf{x} = \mathbf{p_1} \wedge \mathbf{p_2} \tag{7}$$

where $\mathbf{a} \wedge \mathbf{b}$ is the outer product application on the vectors $\mathbf{a}$, $\mathbf{b}$ using homogeneous coordinates (application the cross-product $\mathbf{a} \times \mathbf{b}$ is used)

The line p is given by two points as:

$$\mathbf{p} = \mathbf{x}_A \times \mathbf{x}_B = [a, b : c]^T = \begin{bmatrix} \mathbf{i} & \mathbf{j} & \mathbf{k} \\ x_A & y_A & w_A \\ x_B & y_B & w_B \end{bmatrix} \tag{8}$$

where $\mathbf{i} = [1, 0 : 0]^T$, $\mathbf{j} = [0, 1 : 0]^T$, $\mathbf{k} = [0, 0 : 1]^T$. Now, an intersection point of two given lines is given as:

$$\mathbf{x} = \mathbf{p}_1 \times \mathbf{p}_2 = [x, y : w]^T = \begin{bmatrix} \mathbf{i} & \mathbf{j} & \mathbf{k} \\ a_1 & b_1 & c_1 \\ a_2 & b_2 & c_2 \end{bmatrix} \tag{9}$$

where $\mathbf{i} = [1, 0 : 0]^T$, $\mathbf{j} = [0, 1 : 0]^T$, $\mathbf{k} = [0, 0 : 1]^T$.

Let us consider an implicit function $F(\mathbf{x}) = \mathbf{a}^T\mathbf{x}$. The line p is then defined as $F(\mathbf{x}) = 0$. The clipping operation should determine intersection points $\mathbf{x}_i = [x_i, y_i : w_i]^T$, $i = A, B$, of the given line p with the convex polygon edges, if any. The line p splits the E^2 plane into two parts, see Fig. 1. The corners $\mathbf{x}_i$, $i = 0, ..., N-1$, of the convex polygon are split into two groups according to the sign value of the function $F(\mathbf{x}_i)$, $i = 0, \ldots, N-1$. It means that the ith corner is classified by a bit value c_i as:

$$c_i = \begin{cases} 1 & if\ F(\mathbf{x}_i) \geq 0 \\ 0 & otherwise \end{cases} \quad i = 0, \ldots, N-13 \tag{10}$$

and it is actually an application of the dot product as $\mathbf{a}^T\mathbf{x} \equiv \mathbf{a} \bullet \mathbf{x}$.

This leads to the $O(N)$ computational complexity of the S-Convex-Clip algorithm without the division operation use at all, see Algorithm 2.

Algorithm 2. S-Convex-Clip - Line clipping algorithm by the convex polygon

---

1: **procedure** S-Convex-Clip($\mathbf{x}_A, \mathbf{x}_B$);   ▷ line is given by two points
2:   ▷ $\mathbf{x}_k = [x_k, y_k : w_k]^T$; $i = A, B$
3:        $\mathbf{p} := \mathbf{x}_A \wedge \mathbf{x}_B$;   ▷ computation of the line coefficients - use the cross product
4:        **for** $i := 0$ **to** $N - 1$ **do**   ▷ to be done in parallel **par for**
5:            **if** $\mathbf{p}^T\mathbf{x}_i \geq 0$ **then** $c_i := 1$ **else** $c_i := 0$;   ▷ codes computation
6:        **end for**
7:                        ▷ the bit vector $\mathbf{c}$ contains code of all polygon vertices against the line p
8:        **if** $\mathbf{c} \neq [0...0]^T$ **and** $\mathbf{c} \neq [1...1]^T$ **then**   ▷ line intersects the window
9:            $i := TAB1[\mathbf{c}]$; $\mathbf{x}_A := \mathbf{p} \wedge \mathbf{e}_i$;   ▷ first intersection point
10:            $j := TAB2[\mathbf{c}]$; $\mathbf{x}_B := \mathbf{p} \wedge \mathbf{e}_j$;   ▷ second intersection point
11:            output($\mathbf{x}_A, \mathbf{x}_B$)   ▷ operator $\wedge$ means the cross-product application
12:        **else**
13:            NOP   ▷ line does not intersect the window
14:        **end if**
15: **end procedure**

As the indexes of the intersected are known at the lines 9 and 10 of the S-Convex-Clip algorithm, the relevant parameter t can be determined similarly as in the original Cyrus-Beck's algorithm or the coordinates of the intersection points computed directly using the outer product as shown in the algorithm.

It can be seen, that the S-Convex-Clip algorithm, see Algorithm 2, is quite simple. Computational complexity $O(N)$ is needed to determine the code vector **c** using *dot product* and only two intersection computations are needed, if an intersection exists. It means, that the algorithm requires:

- *dot product* operations: N (line 5)
- comparison operations in the floating point: N (line 5)
- *cross product* operations: 2 (lines 3 and 9,10)

The S-Convex-Clip algorithm is significantly computationally simpler than the Cyrus-Beck's algorithm and the causes of instability of the Cyrus-Beck's algorithm were removed.

It should be noted, that in the GPU and SSE instructions use, the algorithm gets much faster as the cross product and dot products takes one clock on GPU. Also the points of intersections remain in the projective notation, i.e. $\mathbf{x}_A = [x_A, y_A : w_A]^T$ and $\mathbf{x}_B = [x_B, y_B : w_B]^T$, which can be used for further processing without direct need to converting them to the Euclidean space. In this case, no division operations are needed at all.

Table 1. All cases for $N = 4$; N/A - Non-Applicable (impossible) cases

c	**c**	TAB1	TAB2	MASK		c	**c**	TAB1	TAB2	MASK
0	0000	None	None	None		15	1111	None	None	None
1	0001	0	3	0100		14	1110	3	0	0100
2	0010	0	1	0100		13	1101	1	0	0100
3	0011	1	3	0010		12	1100	3	1	0010
4	0100	1	2	0010		11	1011	2	1	0010
5	0101	N/A	N/A	N/A		10	1010	N/A	N/A	N/A
6	0110	0	2	0100		9	1001	2	0	0100
7	0111	2	3	1000		8	1000	3	2	1000

The values in TAB, illustrative table for $N = 4$ is presented by Table 1, can be generated synthetically for general N. As the table is symmetrical in some sense, only $1/2$ of the cases are needed to be generated; the other cases can be determined using the bit-wise negation, i.e. **not c**, and swapping columns TAB1 and TAB2.

It should be noticed, that there is no need to generate the whole Table 1 for the given N, especially if N is higher, as the intersected edges of the convex polygon can be easily detected from the bit vector **c**. It can be seen, that if there is a sequence "$\ldots 0, 1 \ldots$" or "$\ldots 1, 0 \ldots$" the relevant convex polygon edges are intersected. The Table 1 generation is to be used in the case of several lines and constant N of the convex polygon clipping, while the second possibility, i.e. finding "$\ldots 0, 1 \ldots$" and "$\ldots 1, 0 \ldots$", is to be used in cases, when N is changing.

As the clipping polygon is convex, the only two edges might be intersected. It means, that only one sequence ... 0, 1 ... and ... 1, 0 ... can occur, which simplifies detection of the edges intersected, if it is made "on the fly", not by using pre-generated table. Identification of those sequences is simple, just using binary shift and binary mask operations.

The proposed S-Convex-Clip algorithm can be easily modified also for the line segment clipping case similarly as in line segment against rectangular window Skala [27]. In this case, the MASK column of the Table 1 is used and this can be again generated for the given N or determined on the fly case by case.

It can be seen, that the proposed S-Convex-Clip algorithm is computationally robust, limiting unnecessary computations in the floating point representation. In addition, it does not use the division operation, if the resulting coordinates of the end-points of intersections are not needed to be converted to the Euclidean space.

5   Conclusion

This contribution describes shortly a new robust line clipping algorithm against a convex polygon with $O(N)$ computational complexity. It eliminates instability of "close to singular" cases, which causes instability in the Cyrus-Beck's algorithm. It also significantly reduces the floating point operations, especially division operations.

As the proposed algorithm uses projective notation, there is no need to convert points and polygon vertices from the homogeneous coordinates to the Euclidean space, which requires unnecessary division operations as well.

The algorithm is convenient for implementations using GPU or/and SSE instructions as it supports parallel processing and additional speed up as the cross product and dot product are implemented in hardware. Experiments proved over 10–15% speedup against the original Cyrus-Becks algorithm for small N and grows with the convex polygon vertices N substantially due to saving unnecessary intersection computation in the floating point representation.

Acknowledgment. The author would like to thank to colleagues at the University of West Bohemia for fruitful discussions and to anonymous reviewers for their comments and hints, which helped to improve the manuscript significantly. A special thanks belong to recent students of computer Science and the University of West Bohemia at Pilsen, who made many tests of line clipping algorithms developed and modified at the site.

Appendix A

The TABLE generation for a general N is a little bit tricky, but it is simple from the algorithm point of view. Let us consider $N = 6$ as an example. Then all the cases which can occur, except of lines that do no not intersect the convex polygon, are geometrically presented in the Table 5. It can be seen, that they are invariant to rotation, from the geometrical point of view. Analyzing all those cases, a simple pattern of similarity can be detected, see Table 2, Table 3 and Table 4. The cases S_0 and S_6 represent the cases, when a line does not intersect the convex polygon. The TABLE Tab. 1 for a general N-sided convex polygon is has $2^N - 1$ entries and many of those are the non applicable cases. However, the number of the "applicable" cases, which can occur in the line clipping, is $N*(N-1)+2$, only. In the case $N = 6$, we have 30 possible different intersections and 2 cases for the "not intersecting" cases, as we have to respect line segment orientation.

Table 2. Cases I & II; N means Non-Applicable N/A case

case	C_5	C_4	C_3	C_2	C_1	C_0	i_0	i_1	case	C_5	C_4	C_3	C_2	C_1	C_0	i_0	i_1
S_0	0	0	0	0	0	0	N	N	S_0	0	0	0	0	0	0	N	N
S_1	0	0	0	0	0	1	5	0	S_1	0	0	0	0	1	0	0	0
S_2	0	0	0	0	1	1	5	1	S_2	0	0	0	1	1	0	0	1
S_3	0	0	0	1	1	1	5	2	S_3	0	0	1	1	1	0	0	2
S_4	0	0	1	1	1	1	5	3	S_4	0	1	1	1	1	0	0	3
S_5	0	1	1	1	1	1	5	4	S_5	1	1	1	1	1	0	0	4
S_6	1	1	1	1	1	1	N	N	S_6	1	1	1	1	1	1	N	N

Table 3. Cases III & IV; N means Non-Applicable N/A case

case	C_5	C_4	C_3	C_2	C_1	C_0	i_0	i_1	case	C_5	C_4	C_3	C_2	C_1	C_0	i_0	i_1
S_0	0	0	0	0	0	0	N	N	S_0	0	0	0	0	0	0	N	N
S_1	0	0	0	1	0	0	1	0	S_1	0	0	1	0	0	0	2	0
S_2	0	0	1	1	0	0	1	1	S_2	0	1	1	0	0	0	2	1
S_3	0	1	1	1	0	0	1	2	S_3	1	1	1	0	0	0	2	2
S_4	1	1	1	1	0	0	1	3	S_4	1	1	1	0	0	1	2	3
S_5	1	1	1	1	0	1	1	4	S_5	1	1	1	0	1	1	2	4
S_6	1	1	1	1	1	1	N	N	S_6	1	1	1	1	1	1	N	N

Table 4. Cases V & VI; N means Non-Applicable N/A case

case	C_5	C_4	C_3	C_2	C_1	C_0	i_0	i_1	case	C_5	C_4	C_3	C_2	C_1	C_0	i_0	i_1
S_0	0	0	0	0	0	0	N	N	S_0	0	0	0	0	0	0	N	N
S_1	0	1	0	0	0	0	3	0	S_1	1	0	0	0	0	0	4	0
S_2	1	1	0	0	0	0	3	1	S_2	1	0	0	0	0	1	4	1
S_3	1	1	0	0	0	1	3	2	S_3	1	0	0	0	1	1	4	2
S_4	1	1	0	0	1	1	3	3	S_4	1	0	0	1	1	1	4	3
S_5	1	1	0	1	1	1	3	4	S_5	1	0	1	1	1	1	4	4
S_6	1	1	1	1	1	1	N	N	S_6	1	1	1	1	1	1	N	N

Algorithm 3. S-Convex-Clip-Table-Generator

```
 1: # This is a sequence for generating the TABLE #
 2: # This sequence can be further optimized #
 3: M := 2^N - 1;                          ▷ M is a bit vector of "1" of the length N
 4: for i := 0 to M do                              ▷ initialization of the TABLE
 5:     TAB1[i] := -1; TAB2[i] := -1;       ▷ "-1" means the "N' or "N/A" cases
 6: end for
 7: TAB1[0] := -1; TAB2[0] := -1;           ▷ settings for the "non-intersecting" cases
 8: TAB1[M] := -1; TAB1[M] := -1;
         ▷ bit-vectors are 2^N bit long independently of the unsigned integer length
 9: C_ones := M;           ▷ 2^N long bit mask           ▷ C_ones = [111...111]
10: C_zeros := 0;                                        ▷ C_zeros = [000...000]
11:
12: C_A := C_zeros + 1;                          ▷ setting the bit C_0 to "1"
13: k := N-1;  ▷ setting index if the index of the last edge - avoiding mod operation
14: for ii := 0 to N - 1 do                  ▷ for the each case I, II, ..., V, VI do
15:             ▷ C_A contains bit vector setting for the S_1 for all the cases I,..,VI
16:     Generate_Sequences(C_A, ii, k);
17:     C_A := (C_A shl 1);     ▷ shift left without carry - setting for all the S_1 cases
18:     k := ii;
19: end for
20:
21: procedure GENERATE_SEQUENCES(C_A, ii, k);          ▷ generation if the ii-table
22:     C_temp := C_A;
23:     for i := 1 to N - 1 do         ▷ setting the i-th row of the TABLE for the S_i case
24:         index := C_temp;           ▷ code C_temp converted to the unsigned integer
25:         TAB1[index] := k; TAB2[index] := i;
26:         carry := C_temp[N - 1];        ▷ set carry to the most left bit of the C_temp
27:                                        ▷ simulates the "circular shift" on N bits
28:         C_temp := (C_temp shl 1) + carry;
                                   ▷ shift left with carry transfer to the C_temp[0] bit
29:     end for
30: end procedure
```

It should be noted, that the generated codes respect the line, resp. line segment orientation as well Skala [27,31].

Table 5. All possible cases for $N = 6$ except of lines passing out the convex polygon

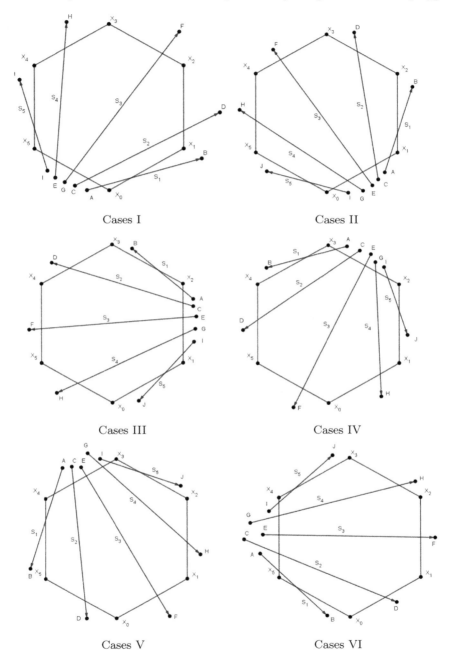

Cases I   Cases II

Cases III   Cases IV

Cases V   Cases VI

References

1. Andreev, R., Sofianska, E.: New algorithm for two-dimensional line clipping. Comput. Graph. **15**(4), 519–526 (1991)
2. Bui, D., Skala, V.: Fast algorithms for clipping lines and line segments in E2. Vis. Comput. **14**(1), 31–37 (1998)
3. Coxeter, H.: Introduction to geometry. Math. Gaz. **48**(365), 343 (1964)
4. Cyrus, M., Beck, J.: Generalized two- and three-dimensional clipping. Comput. Graph. **3**(1), 23–28 (1978)
5. Day, J.: A new two dimensional line clipping algorithm for small windows. Comput. Graph. Forum **11**(4), 241–245 (1992)
6. Duvanenko, V., Robbins, W., Gyurcsik, R.: Line-segment clipping revisited. Dr. Dobb's J. **21**(1), 107–110 (1996)
7. Dörr, M.: A new approach to parametric line clipping. Comput. Graph. **14**(3–4), 449–464 (1990)
8. Foley, D., van Dam, A., Feiner, S., Hughes, J.: Computer Graphics: Principles and Practice. Addison-Wesley, Reading (1990)
9. Huang, Y., Liu, Y.: An algorithm for line clipping against a polygon based on shearing transformation. Comput. Graph. Forum **21**(4), 683–688 (2002)
10. Kaijian, S., Edwards, J., Cooper, D.: An efficient line clipping algorithm. Comput. Graph. **14**(2), 297–301 (1990)
11. Krammer, G.: A line clipping algorithm and its analysis. Comput. Graph. Forum **11**(3), 253–266 (1992)
12. Liang, Y.-D., Barsky, B.: A new concept and method for line clipping. ACM Trans. Graph. (TOG) **3**(1), 1–22 (1984)
13. Nicholl, T.M., Lee, D., Nicholl, R.A.: Efficient new algorithm for 2D line clipping: its development and analysis. Comput. Graph. (ACM) **21**(4), 253–262 (1987)
14. Nielsen, H.: Line clipping using semi-homogeneous coordinates. Comput. Graph. Forum **14**(1), 3–16 (1995)
15. Rappoport, A.: An efficient algorithm for line and polygon clipping. Vis. Comput. **7**(1), 19–28 (1991)
16. Skala, V.: Algorithm for 2D line clipping, pp. 121–128. New Advances in Computer Graphics, NATO ASI (1989)
17. Skala, V.: Algorithms for 2D line clipping. In: EG 1989 proceedings (1989)
18. Skala, V.: Algorithms for clipping quadratic arcs. In: Chua, T.-S., Kunii, T.L. (eds.) CG International '90, pp. 255–268. Springer, Tokyo (1990). https://doi.org/10.1007/978-4-431-68123-6_16
19. Skala, V.: An efficient algorithm for line clipping by convex polygon. Comput. Graph. **17**(4), 417–421 (1993)
20. Skala, V.: O(lg N) line clipping algorithm in E2. Comput. Graph. **18**(4), 517–524 (1994)
21. Skala, V.: An efficient algorithm for line clipping by convex and non-convex polyhedra in E3. Comput. Graph. Forum **15**(1), 61–68 (1996)
22. Skala, V.: Line clipping in E2 with O(1) processing complexity. Comput. Graph. (Pergamon) **20**(4), 523–530 (1996)
23. Skala, V.: Line clipping in e3 with expected complexity O(1). Mach. Graph. Vis. **5**(4), 551–562 (1996)
24. Skala, V.: Trading time for space: an O(1) average time algorithm for point-in-polygon location problem. Theoretical fiction or practical usage? Mach. Graph. Vis. **5**(3), 483–494 (1996)

25. Skala, V.: A fast algorithm for line clipping by convex polyhedron in E3. Comput. Graph. (Pergamon) **21**(2), 209–214 (1997)
26. Skala, V.: A new line clipping algorithm with hardware acceleration. In: Proceedings of Computer Graphics International Conference - CGI, pp. 270–273 (2004)
27. Skala, V.: A new approach to line and line segment clipping in homogeneous coordinates. Vis. Comput. **21**(11), 905–914 (2005)
28. Skala, V.: Length, area and volume computation in homogeneous coordinates. Int. J. Image Graph. **6**(4), 625–639 (2006)
29. Skala, V.: Barycentric coordinates computation in homogeneous coordinates. Comput. Graph. (Pergamon) **32**(1), 120–127 (2008)
30. Skala, V.: Intersection computation in projective space using homogeneous coordinates. Int. J. Image Graph. **8**(4), 615–628 (2008)
31. Skala, V.: Optimized line and line segment clipping in E2 and geometric algebra. Ann. Math. Inform. **52**, 199–215 (2020)
32. Skala, V.: A new coding scheme for line segment clipping in E2. In: Gervasi, O., et al. (eds.) ICCSA 2021. LNCS, vol. 12953, pp. 16–29. Springer, Cham (2021). https://doi.org/10.1007/978-3-030-86976-2_2
33. Skala, V., Bui, D.: Extension of the Nicholls-Lee-Nichols algorithm to three dimensions. Vis. Comput. **17**(4), 236–242 (2001)
34. Slater, M., Barsky, B.: 2D line and polygon clipping based on space subdivision. Vis. Comput. **10**(7), 407–422 (1994)
35. Sobkow, M., Pospisil, P., Yang, Y.-H.: A fast two-dimensional line clipping algorithm via line encoding. Comput. Graph. **11**(4), 459–467 (1987)
36. Zhang, M., Sabharwal, C.: An efficient implementation of parametric line and polygon clipping algorithm. In: ACM Symposium on Applied Computing, pp. 796–800. ACM (2002)

A New Coding Scheme for Line Segment Clipping in E2

Vaclav Skala$^{(\boxtimes)}$ (iD)

Department of Computer Science and Engineering, University of West Bohemia,
301 00 Pilsen, Czech Republic
skala@kiv.zcu.cz
http://www.VaclavSkala.eu

Abstract. This contribution presents a new coding scheme based on Cohen-Sutherland line segment clipping algorithm, which enables to distinguish all possible cases easily. It leads to more efficient algorithm for a line segment clipping in E2. It also presents importance of a detailed analysis in algorithm development, if the algorithm robustness and efficiency is required.

1 Introduction

Many algorithms for a line clipping or a line segment clipping by a rectangular window have been published already. Probably the Cohen-Sutherand's (C-S) [7], Cyrus-Beck (CB) [3] and Liang-Barsky (LB) [11] algorithms are the most known for line segment and line segment clipping in E^2 and used in computer graphics courses. The CS algorithm uses end-point position coding to detect some cases, which leads to more efficient computation. However, in some cases 4 intersections of the line and the clipping window are computer; two of those are actually unnecessary. The CB algorithm was actually designed for a line clipping by a convex polygon. Several improvements of the C-B algorithm were published, e.g. Nicholl-Lee-Nicholl [12], Bui [2], Skala [28].

The line and line segment clipping are fundamental and critical operations in the computer graphics pipeline as all the processed primitives have to be clipped out of the drawing area to decrease computational requirements and also respect the physical restrictions of the hardware. The clipping operations are mostly connected with the Window-Viewport and projection operations. There are many algorithms developed recently with many modifications, see Andreev [1], Day [4], Dörr [6], Duvalenko [5], Kaijian [9], Krammer [10], Liang [11], Skala [27], Sobkow [29].

However, those algorithms have been developed for the Euclidean space representation in spite of the fact, that geometric transformations, i.e. projection, translation, rotation, scaling and Window-Viewport etc., use homogeneous coordinates, e.g. projective representation. This results into necessity to convert the

Supported by the University of West Bohemia - Institutional research support No. 1311.

O. Gervasi et al. (Eds.): ICCSA 2021, LNCS 12953, pp. 16–29, 2021.
https://doi.org/10.1007/978-3-030-86976-2_2

results of the geometric transformations to the Euclidean space using division operation as follows:

$$\mathbf{X} = (X, Y) \quad \mathbf{x} = [x, y : w]^T \qquad X = \frac{x}{w} \quad Y = \frac{y}{w} \quad w \neq 0 \qquad (1)$$

where X, Y are the point coordinates in the Euclidean space E^2, while $x, y : w$ are in the homogeneous coordinates [23,24]; similarly in the E^3 case.

If a point is given in the Euclidean space the homogeneous coordinates are given as $\mathbf{x} = [X, Y : 1]^T$. The homogeneous coordinates also enable to represent a point close or in infinity, i.e. when $w \to 0$, and postpone the division operations. It leads to better numerical robustness and computational speed-up, in general.

2   Line Segment Clipping

The line segment clipping operation in the E^2 and E^3 space is a fundamental problem in Computer Graphics and it has been already deeply analyzed. The line and line segment clipping algorithms against a rectangular window in E^2 are probably the most used algorithms and any improvements or speed up can have a significant influence on efficiency of the whole graphics pipeline. Many algorithms have been developed, e.g. the Cohen-Sutherland (CS) [7] for a line segment clipping against the rectangular window, the Liang-Barsky (LB) [11] and Cyrus-Beck (CB) [3] (extensible to the E^3 case) algorithms for clipping a line against a convex polygon and the Nichol-Lee-Nichol (LNL) [12] (modified by Skala [28]) are the most used algorithms.

However, some more sophisticated algorithms or modification of the recent ones have been developed recently, e.g. line clipping against a rectangular window, see Bui [2], Skala [15,17], line clipping by a convex polygon with $O(lgN)$ complexity, Skala [18] (based on Rappaport [14]) using ordering of the vertex indices, or algorithm with $O_{exp}(1)$ complexity using pre-processing Skala [20], line clipping by a window with quadratics arcs Skala [16], etc.

In the E^3 case, the algorithms have computational complexity $O(N)$ as there is no ordering of the vertices ordering in the E^3 case, however, the algorithm with $O_{expected}(\sqrt{N})$ have been developed by Skala [19–21].

In the following, the Cohen-Sutherland (CS) and the S-Clip algorithms based on implicit formulation using projective representation will be presented. The CS algorithm is based on end-points classification, while the S-Clip is primarily based on the classification of the window corner against the given line.

2.1   Cohen-Sutherland Algorithm

The Cohen-Sutherland (CS) algorithm for line segment clipping is a fundamental algorithm presented in computer graphics courses. It splits the 2D space into 9 areas defined by the rectangular clipping window, see Fig. 1. The line segment given by its end-points $\mathbf{x}_A$, $\mathbf{x}_B$ is classified and if not directly accepted or rejected, intersections with lines in which the window edges lie are computed and the intersection point found is then classified end the process is repeated, see Huges et al, see [8] for details. It is an analogy of the root bisection method in numerical mathematics.

2.2   End-Points Coding

A line segment is defined by its end-points x_A and x_B. The end-point position classification was used in the CS algorithms developed by Cohen-Sutherland [7]. Some additional coding for speedup were introduced in Bui [2], originally for the Euclidean space representation. The classification of the line segment end-points and the corners of the window mutual positions enables faster processing. It enables simple rejection of line segments not intersecting the window and direct acceptance of segments totally inside of the window, see Fig. 1.

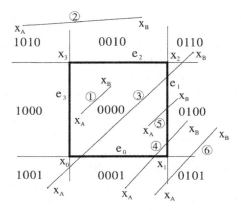

Fig. 1. The codes of line segment end-points

The end-points classification introduced in CS is represented by the Algorithm 1. If c_A and c_B are the codes of the end-points then the sequence catching those cases can be expressed as:

- **if** (c_A **lor** c_B) = [0000] **then** the line segment is totally inside
- **if** (c_A **land** c_B) $\neq$ [0000] **then** the line segment is totally outside

If the end-points of a line are given in the Euclidean space, i.e. $w = 1$, then the codes of the end-points are determined as in the Algorithm 1. However, in the general case, i.e. when $w \neq 1$ and $w > 1$, the conditions must be modified using multiplication, e.g. to $x \ w_{min} < x_{min} \ w$, etc., and then no division operations are needed.

Algorithm 1. End-point code computation

```
1: procedure CODE (c, x);                    ▷ code c for the position x = [x, y : 1]ᵀ
2:     c := [0000]ᵀ;                          ▷ initial setting
3:     if  x < xₘᵢₙ  then  c := [1000]ᵀ       ▷ according to x coordinate
4:         if  x > xₘₐₓ  then  c := [0100]ᵀ;
5:     if  y < yₘᵢₙ  then  c := c lor [0001]ᵀ   ▷ according to y coordinate
6:         if  y > yₘₐₓ  then  c := c lor [0010]ᵀ;
7:                          ▷ lor is all bits or - instead of algebraic + operation
8: end procedure
```

It can be seen, that other cases, see Fig. 1, cannot be directly distinguished by the CS algorithm coding, see the cases 4 and 6, and intersection points have to be computed, including the invalid ones, e.g. in the case 3 probably 4 intersections will be computed and 2 of those will be invalid. It is necessary to note, that the CS algorithm uses division operations in the floating point, which is the most time consuming operation.

2.3   S-Clip

Let us consider a typical example of a line clipping by the rectangular clipping window, see Fig. 2, and a line p given in the implicit form using projective notation:

$$p : ax + by + cw = 0, \quad i.e. \quad \mathbf{a}^T \mathbf{x} = 0 \tag{2}$$

where $\mathbf{a} = [a, b : c]^T$ are coefficients of the given line p, $\mathbf{x} = [x, y : w]^T$ is a point on this line using projective notation (w is the homogeneous coordinate). Advantage of the projective notation is, that a line p passing two points $\mathbf{x}_A$, $\mathbf{x}_B$ or an intersection point $\mathbf{x}$ of two lines p_1, p_2 can be computed as:

$$\mathbf{p} = \mathbf{x}_A \wedge \mathbf{x}_B, \quad \mathbf{x} = \mathbf{p_1} \wedge \mathbf{p_2} \tag{3}$$

where $\mathbf{a} \wedge \mathbf{b}$ is the outer product application on the vectors $\mathbf{a}$, $\mathbf{b}$ (actually the cross-product is used in this case, i.e. $\mathbf{a} \times \mathbf{b}$), see Skala [25].

The S-Clip algorithm [22] and its optimization for the normalized clipping window [26] use the window corners classification. This enables to determine which window edges are intersected by a line directly without additional intersection computation.

Let us consider an implicit function $F(\mathbf{x}) = \mathbf{a}^T \mathbf{x}$ representing a line, Eq. 2. The clipping operation should determine intersection points $\mathbf{x}_i = [x_i, y_i : w_i]^T$, $i = 1, 2$ of the given line p with the window edges, if any. The line splits the plane into two parts, see Fig. 2. The corners of the window are split into two groups according to the sign of the function $F(\mathbf{x})$ value. This results into Smart-Line-Clip (S-L-Clip) algorithm [22], see Algorithm 2.

The S-Clip line segment algorithm [22] is a slight modification of the S-L-Clip algorithm, which respect position of the line segment end-points and uses the end-point positions classification.

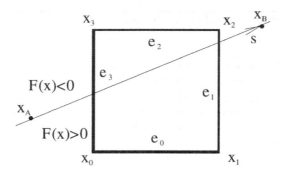

Fig. 2. Clipping against the rectangular window in E^2

Table 1. All cases; N/A - Non-Applicable (impossible) cases the MASK column is used for line segment clipping Skala [22]

c	c	TAB1	TAB2	MASK	c	c	TAB1	TAB2	MASK
0	0000	None	None	None	15	1111	None	None	None
1	0001	0	3	0100	14	1110	3	0	None
2	0010	0	1	0100	13	1101	1	01	0100
3	0011	1	3	0010	12	1100	3	1	0010
4	0100	1	2	0010	11	1011	2	1	0010
5	0101	N/A	N/A	N/A	10	1010	N/A	N/A	N/A
6	0110	0	2	0100	9	1001	2	0	0100
7	0111	2	3	1000	8	1000	3	2	1000

It means that the ith corner is classified by a bit value c_i as:

$$c_i = \begin{cases} 1 & if \ F(\mathbf{x}_i) \geq 0 \\ 0 & otherwise \end{cases} \quad i = 0, ..., 3 \quad (4)$$

The Table 1 presents the codes for all the situations (some of those are not possible). The columns **TAB1** and **TAB2** contain indices of edges of the window intersected by the given line (values in the **MASK** column are used in the S-Clip algorithm [22] for the line segment end-points).

It can be seen, that the S-L-Clip algorithm (see Algorithm 2) is quite simple and easily extensible for a line and line segment clipping by a convex polygon with $O(N)$ complexity as the Table 1 can be generated synthetically [22]. It is significantly simpler than the Liang-Barsky algorithm [11].

In the following, a new line segment clipping algorithm based on the Cohen-Sutherland and S-Clip algorithms.

3   Proposed Algorithm

The proposed algorithm is based on full classification of all possible cases based on the Cohen-Sutherland coding scheme. However, if the codes of the end-points

Algorithm 2. S-L-Clip - Line clipping algorithm by the rectangular window

```
 1: procedure S-L-Clip(x_A, x_B);                          ▷ line is given by two points
 2:    p := x_A ∧ x_B;                                     ▷ computation of the line coefficients
 3:    for i := 0 to 3 do                                  ▷ can be done in parallel
 4:        if p^T x_i ≥ 0 then c_i := 1 else c_i := 0;     ▷ codes computation
 5:    end for
 6:    if  c ≠ [0000]^T and c ≠ [1111]^T then              ▷ line intersects the window
 7:        i := TAB1[c];   x_A := p ∧ e_i;                 ▷ first intersection point
 8:        j := TAB2[c];   x_B := p ∧ e_j;                 ▷ second intersection point
 9:        output(x_A, x_B)            ▷ operator ∧ means the cross-product application
10:    else
11:        NOP                                             ▷ line does not intersect the window
12:    end if
13: end procedure
```

C_A and C_B are taken as integer numbers, see Table 2, and summed as $C_{AB} = C_A + C_B$, then the code C_{AB} gives us a composed code differentiating all the different cases Table 3 and the table is symmetrical. As the line segment $x_A\, x_B$ is actually oriented its orientation has to be respected in intersection computations.

Table 2. Numerical summation codes $C_{AB} = C_A + C_B$, IN - inside area, C - corner area, S - side area, n/a - non-applicable cases or outside case

			IN	C	S	C	S	C	S	C	S
	C_{AB}	C_B	0	5	4	6	2	10	8	9	1
	C_A		0000	0101	0100	0110	0010	1010	1000	1001	0001
IN	0	0000	IN	5	4	6	2	10	8	9	1
C	5	0101	5	n/a	n/a	n/a	7	15	13	n/a	n/a
S	4	0100	4	n/a	n/a	n/a	6	14	12	13	5
C	6	0110	6	n/a	n/a	n/a	n/a	n/a	14	15	7
S	2	0010	2	7	6	n/a	n/a	n/a	10	11	3
C	10	1010	10	15	14	n/a	n/a	n/a	n/a	n/a	11
S	8	1000	8	13	12	14	10	n/a	n/a	n/a	9
C	9	1001	9	n/a	13	15	11	n/a	n/a	n/a	n/a
S	1	0001	1	n/a	5	7	3	11	9	n/a	n/a

3.1 Classification of Possible Cases

The code C_{AB} gives us additional information on positions of the line segment end-points. If all the possible positions of a line segment are analyzed, then the following cases can be distinguished:

Table 3. Possible cases: n/a - non-applicable or solved by the C-S coding C - corner area, S - side area, IN - inside area End-points: IC - inside-corner, IS - inside-side; Cases: SS - side-side, SnCS - side-near corner - side, SdC - side-distant corner-side, CoC - corner-opposite corner, id: case re-indexing

		id	-1	0	1	2	3	4	5	6	7
	$Case$		IN	C	S	C	S	C	S	C	S
		C_B	0	5	4	6	2	10	8	9	1
	C_A		0000	0101	0100	0110	0010	1010	1000	1001	0001
IN	0	0000	IN	IC	IS	IC	IS	IC	IS	IC	IS
C	5	0101	IC	n/a	n/a	n/a	SdC	CoC	SdC	n/a	n/a
S	4	0100	IS	n/a	n/a	n/a	SnCS	SdC	SS	SdC	SnCS
C	6	0110	IC	n/a	n/a	n/a	n/a	n/a	SdC	CoC	SdC
S	2	0010	IS	SdC	SnCS	n/a	n/a	n/a	SnCS	SdC	SS
C	10	1010	IC	CoC	SdC	n/a	n/a	n/a	n/a	n/a	SdC
S	8	1000	IS	SdC	SS	SdC	SnCS	n/a	n/a	n/a	SnCS
C	9	1001	IC	n/a	SdC	CoC	SdC	n/a	n/a	n/a	n/a
S	1	0001	IS	n/a	SnCS	SdC	SS	SdC	SnCS	n/a	n/a

- INSIDE (IN) - the both end-points are inside
- OUTSIDE (n/a) - the line segment does not intersect the window
- Inside-Side (IS) - one end-point is inside, the second one is inside of a side area, see Fig. 3
- Inside-Corner (IC) - one end-point is inside, the second one is inside of a corner area, see Fig. 3
- Side - Side (SS) - the end-points are in the opposite side areas, see Fig. 4
- Side - near Corner - Side (SnCS) - both end-points are in the side areas sharing a common corner, see Fig. 4
- Side - distant Corner (SdC) - one end-point is inside of the side area, the second one is in the distant(opposite) corner area, see Fig. 5
- Corner - opposite Corner (CoC) - the both end-points are in the opposite corner areas, see Fig. 6

The most simple cases, i.e. the line segment is totally inside, resp. totally outside are easily detected by the bit-wise condition, i.e. by the original Cohen-Sutherland end-pointposition classification.

$$(C_A \text{ lor } C_B) = [0000], \quad \text{resp.} \quad (C_A \text{ land } C_B) \neq [0000]$$

After this, the simple cases as Inside-Side (IS) or Inside-Corner (IC) cases are detected by the logical condition

$$(C_A = [0000]) \textbf{ or } (C_B = [0000])$$

Now, the more complex cases are to be solved, i.e. Side-near Corner Side (SnCS), Side-distant Corner (SdC), Corner-opposite Corner (CoC) cases.

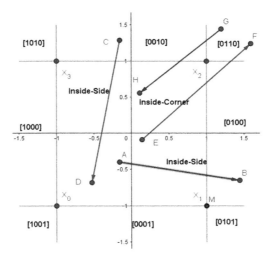

Fig. 3. Inside-Side (IS) and Inside-Corner (IC) cases

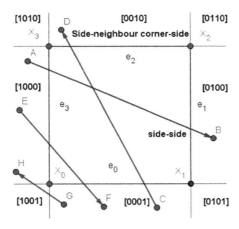

Fig. 4. Side-Side(SS) and Side-near Corner (SnC)

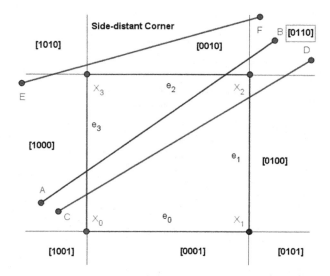

Fig. 5. Side-distant Corner (SdC) case

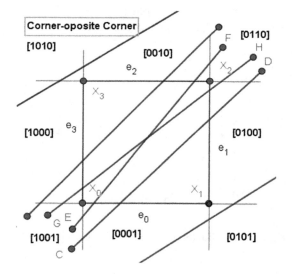

Fig. 6. The Corner-oposite Corner (CoC) case

The Table 3 presents all the cases for the summation code $C_{AB} = C_A + C_B$, while the Table 2 presents the C_{AB} values for each the case. It can be seen that non-trivial cases are actually formed by sub-tables 3×3 and the table itself is formally symmetrical. As a line segment is oriented actually, its orientation is to be respected in the algorithm. Unfortunately, the codes for C_A and C_B in the table Table 3 are not ordered according to the numerical values of the codes. As the simple cases, when at least one point is inside of the clipping window, are easily detectable, only more complex cases are to be distinguished and they are re-indexed.

The table Table 4 represents re-indexing of the code C_A, resp. C_B, so that the index of an area is ordered anti-clockwise starting at 0 from the right bottom side area; the id of the clipping window area is set to -1 for code efficiency only.

It can be seen, that the re-indexed value id gives also additional information, whether the end-point is inside of the side area or corner one, i.e. id is even or odd (except of the INSIDE case).

$$id \text{ and } [0001] = \begin{cases} [0000] \ corner \ area \\ [0001] \ side \ area \end{cases}$$

The one-dimensional array is used to end-points code re-indexing for cases of the codes C_A and C_B (non-applicable cases 11–15 removed).

$$id_A = TAB\_CODE\_INDEX[C_A] \quad id_B = TAB\_CODE\_INDEX[C_B]$$

Table 4. TAB_CODE_INDEX: Re-indexing table of edges and corners using [Left, Right, Top, Bottom] coding

C_A	C_A	$Type$	id	C_A	C_A	$Type$	id
0	0000	IN	-1	8	1000	S	5
1	0001	S	7	9	1001	C	6
2	0010	S	3	10	1010	C	4
3	0011	n/a	n/a	11	1011	n/a	n/a
4	0100	S	1	12	1100	n/a	n/a
5	0101	C	0	13	1101	n/a	n/a
6	0110	C	2	14	1110	n/a	n/a
7	0111	n/a	n/a	15	1111	n/a	n/a

It means, that the index id_A is giving a row in the Table 3 for the code C_A and the id_B is giving the column for the code C_B. As a consequence, if $id_A < id_B$ then the only upper triangle of the Table 3 is used, i.e. significant number of cases are reduced. The value of the code C_{AB} enables to distinguish different possible cases easily. However, as the line segment orientation is to be respected, the proposed algorithm, described in the next, has to respect it.

Algorithm 3. Q-CLIP

```
1: Global variables:
2:    real: x_min, y_min, x_max, y_max,                    ▷ x_min, x_max the window's corner
3:    array TAB_CODE_INDEX[0:10] = [ -1, 7, 3, -9, 1, 0, 2, -9, 5, 6, 4 ];
4:                    ▷ the value −1 means end-point is inside; −9 means the n/a case
5:    array TAB_CODE_CASE[0:15] =
6:       [ -1, -1, -1, 0, -1, 1, 1, 2, -1, 1, 1, 2, -1, 2, 2, 3 ];         ▷ C_AB re-indexing
7: procedure Q_CLIP(x_A, x_B);
8:                              ▷ All other procedures for clipping should be declared here
9:    C_A := CODE(x_A); C_B := CODE(x_B);                      ▷ set the C-S codes
10:                ▷ all logical operations land, lor, lxor are bit-wise operations
11:
12:                                             ▷ the whole line segment is inside
13:    if (C_A lor C_B) = [0000] then { DRAW(x_A, x_B); EXIT; }
                                             ▷ the whole line segment is outside
14:    if (C_A land C_B) ≠ [0000] then EXIT;
15:    C_AB := C_A + C_B;                          ▷ one end-point is inside cases
16:    # precompute directional vector s = x_B − x_A for better efficiency
17:    if (C_A = [0000]) or (C_B = [0000]) then {
18:       id_AB := TAB_CODE_INDEX[C_AB];                ▷ now, only the cases: IS or IC
19:       if (id_AB land [0001])= [0000] then
20:          { SOLVE_IS; EXIT }                  ▷ the IS case; C_AB ∈ {4,2,8,1}
21:       else
22:          { SOLVE_IC; EXIT }                  ▷ the IC case; C_AB ∈ {5,6,10,9}
23:       endif }
24:    endif
25:    # complex cases with two possible intersections
26:    id_case := TAB_CODE_CASE[C_AB];              ▷ re-indexing of non-trivial cases
27:    switch id_case do                           ▷ all complex cases classification
28:       case 0: { SOLVE_SS; EXIT; }                ▷ SS cases; C_AB ∈ {3,12}
29:       case 1: { SOLVE_SnCS; EXIT; }              ▷ SnCS cases; C_AB ∈ {6,5,10,9}
30:       case 2: { SOLVE_SdC; EXIT; }               ▷ SdC cases; C_AB ∈ {7,13,14,11}
31:       case 3: { SOLVE_CoC; EXIT; }               ▷ CoC cases; C_AB = 15
32:    end switch
33: end procedure
```

3.2 Q-CLIP Algorithm

The proposed clipping Q-CLIP algorithm is described by the Algorithm 3. The Q-CLIP algorithm solves the trivial cases first, i.e. the whole segment acceptance or rejection, then more complex cases are solved. It can be seen, that the Q-Clip algorithm is free of cycles, i.e. **while** and/or **for** cycle constructions, etc.

The implementation of the proposed algorithm is simple and straightforward, however, it should be noted, that:

– careful implementation is needed to solve each case, e.g. IC, IS . . . , as it influences efficiency of the algorithm significantly.

– use of **array of function** in-line construction might be more computationally efficient than the**switch** construction
– the bit-wise condition $(C_A \text{ lor } C_B) = [0000]$ differs from the condition $(C_A = [0000])$ **or** $(C_B = [0000])$ as it is the logical operation

It should be noted that the **Switch** instruction is to be implemented as an array of inline functions in order to avoid multiple **if** instructions in which the **Switch** instruction is actually translated.

The presented Q-CLIP algorithm can be easily modified for the case, when a line segment and vertices of the clipping window are given in homogeneous coordinates in general, i.e. when $w \neq 1$.

The proposed Q-CLIP algorithm was implemented in C and Pascal languages on 64bit MS Windows 10 operating system. Experiments made proved its superiority over the original Cohen-Sutherland algorithm, especially in the SdC and CoC cases. For each case, i.e. IC, IS, SnC, SdC, CoC the same number of line segments were generated randomly. The average speed up was over 15% nearly independent of the programming language used.

However, if vector operations with the homogeneous coordinate representation is used, similarly as in Nielsen [13], Skala [26], additional significant speed up can be expected if SSE instructions are used.

4   Conclusion

This contribution describes shortly a new coding scheme for the line segment clipping algorithm based on Cohen-Sutherland's algorithm using arithmetic operations to distinguish the fundamental cases eliminating unnecessary computations with clipping window edges. All the cases are easy to implement. However, computational efficiency is to be kept in mind in coding.

The experiments made proved the speedup over 10–15% against the original Cohen-Sutherland algorithm. Additional speed up can be expected if vector notation and vector operations are used for intersection computation.

The proposed algorithm presents a new coding scheme for distinguishing all the cases in line segment clipping in E^2. Similar approach can be taken for the line segment clipping in the E^3 case.

Acknowledgment. The author would like to thank to colleagues at the University of West Bohemia in Plzen for fruitful discussions and to anonymous reviewers for their comments and hints, which helped to improve the manuscript significantly.

References

1. Andreev, R., Sofianska, E.: New algorithm for two-dimensional line clipping. Comput. Graph. **15**(4), 519–526 (1991)
2. Bui, D., Skala, V.: Fast algorithms for clipping lines and line segments in E2. Vis. Comput. **14**(1), 31–37 (1998)

28   V. Skala

3. Cyrus, M., Beck, J.: Generalized two- and three-dimensional clipping. Comput. Graph. **3**(1), 23–28 (1978)
4. Day, J.: A new two dimensional line clipping algorithm for small windows. Comput. Graph. Forum **11**(4), 241–245 (1992)
5. Duvanenko, V., Robbins, W., Gyurcsik, R.: Line-segment clipping revisited. Dr. Dobb's J. **21**(1), 107–110 (1996)
6. Dörr, M.: A new approach to parametric line clipping. Comput. Graph. **14**(3–4), 449–464 (1990)
7. Foley, D., van Dam, A., Feiner, S., Hughes, J.: Computer Graphics: Principles and Practice. Addison-Wesley (1990)
8. Hughes, J.F., et al.: Computer Graphics: Principles and Practice, 3 edn. Addison-Wesley (2013)
9. Kaijian, S., Edwards, J., Cooper, D.: An efficient line clipping algorithm. Comput. Graph. **14**(2), 297–301 (1990)
10. Krammer, G.: A line clipping algorithm and its analysis. Comput. Graph. Forum **11**(3), 253–266 (1992)
11. Liang, Y.-D., Barsky, B.: A new concept and method for line clipping. ACM Trans. Graph. (TOG) **3**(1), 1–22 (1984)
12. Nicholl, T.M., Lee, D., Nicholl, R.A.: Efficient new algorithm for 2D line clipping: its development and analysis. Comput. Graph. (ACM) **21**(4), 253–262 (1987)
13. Nielsen, H.: Line clipping using semi-homogeneous coordinates. Comput. Graph. Forum **14**(1), 3–16 (1995)
14. Rappoport, A.: An efficient algorithm for line and polygon clipping. Vis. Comput. **7**(1), 19–28 (1991)
15. Skala, V.: Algorithm for 2D line clipping. In: Earnshaw, R.A., Wyvill, B. (eds.) New Advances in Computer Graphics, NATO ASI, pp. 121–128 (1989). https://doi.org/10.1007/978-4-431-68093-2_7
16. Skala, V.: Algorithms for clipping quadratic arcs. In: Chua, T.-S., Kunii, T.L. (eds.) CG International '90. pp, pp. 255–268. Springer, Tokyo (1990). https://doi.org/10.1007/978-4-431-68123-6_16
17. Skala, V.: An efficient algorithm for line clipping by convex polygon. Comput. Graph. **17**(4), 417–421 (1993)
18. Skala, V.: O(lg N) line clipping algorithm in E2. Comput. Graph. **18**(4), 517–524 (1994)
19. Skala, V.: An efficient algorithm for line clipping by convex and non-convex polyhedra in E3. Comput. Graph. Forum **15**(1), 61–68 (1996)
20. Skala, V.: Line clipping in E2 with O(1) processing complexity. Comput. Graph. (Pergamon) **20**(4), 523–530 (1996)
21. Skala, V.: A fast algorithm for line clipping by convex polyhedron in E3. Comput. Graph. (Pergamon) **21**(2), 209–214 (1997)
22. Skala, V.: A new approach to line and line segment clipping in homogeneous coordinates. Vis. Comput. **21**(11), 905–914 (2005)
23. Skala, V.: Length, area and volume computation in homogeneous coordinates. Int. J. Image Graph. **6**(4), 625–639 (2006)
24. Skala, V.: Barycentric coordinates computation in homogeneous coordinates. Comput. Graph. (Pergamon) **32**(1), 120–127 (2008)
25. Skala, V.: Intersection computation in projective space using homogeneous coordinates. Int. J. Image Graph. **8**(4), 615–628 (2008)
26. Skala, V.: Optimized line and line segment clipping in E2 and geometric algebra. Ann. Math. Inform. **52**, 199–215 (2020)

27. Skala, V.: A novel line convex polygon clipping algorithm in E2 with parallel processing modification. In: Gervasi, O., et al. (eds.) ICCSA 2021. LNCS, vol. 12953, pp. 3–15. Springer, Cham (2021). https://doi.org/10.1007/978-3-030-86976-2_1
28. Skala, V., Bui, D.: Extension of the Nicholls-Lee-Nichols algorithm to three dimensions. Vis. Comput. **17**(4), 236–242 (2001)
29. Sobkow, M., Pospisil, P., Yang, Y.-H.: A fast two-dimensional line clipping algorithm via line encoding. Comput. Graph. **11**(4), 459–467 (1987)

Solving the Coarseness Problem by ILP Using Column Generation

Allan Sapucaia$^{(\boxtimes)}$ [iD], Pedro J. de Rezende [iD], and Cid C. de Souza [iD]

Institute of Computing, University of Campinas, Campinas, Brazil
allansapucaia@students.ic.unicamp.br, {rezende,cid}@ic.unicamp.br

Abstract. A core problem in machine learning is the classification of points in high dimensions. In an attempt to minimize the resources required and facilitate data visualization, a recent effort has been made to project the points non-linearly onto the plane and apply classification methods. The quality of any such projection can be measured by evaluating how the resulting points of different classes are set apart. In this paper, we study integer linear programming (ILP) models to determine the coarseness of sets of bicolored points in the plane, which measures how well-separated these two classes are. The complexity of computing the coarseness of a point set is unknown, but conjectured to be NP-hard. We present a base ILP model for the problem with an exponential number of variables and constraints, followed by a series of improvements in the quality of its relaxation and close with an efficient column generation implementation. These modifications allow us to solve instances with three times as many points as the base model, within the same time and memory limits. By combining of our preprocessing techniques and a heuristic from the literature, we are even able to solve to proved optimality many instances of our benchmark in polynomial time. A comprehensive experimental study is presented to evaluate the impact of each improvement.

Keywords: Computational geometry · Combinatorial optimization · Coarseness

1 Introduction

In this paper, we study integer linear programming (ILP) models to determine the coarseness of sets of bicolored points in the plane. Given a bipartite planar point set $P = R \cup B$, with $R \cap B = \emptyset$, we call R (red points) and B (blue points) *classes of points* and say that P is a *bicolored set*. Intuitively, the *coarseness* of P is a measure of how blended the two classes of points of P are.

This work was supported in part by grants from: *Brazilian National Council for Scientific and Technological Development* (CNPq) #313329/2020-6, #309627/2017-6, #304727/2014-8; *São Paulo Research Foundation* (FAPESP) #2020/09691-0, #2018/26434-0, #2018/14883-5, #2014/12236-1.

O. Gervasi et al. (Eds.): ICCSA 2021, LNCS 12953, pp. 30–45, 2021.
https://doi.org/10.1007/978-3-030-86976-2_3

A core problem in machine learning is the classification of points in high dimensions, where two of the main issues are the necessary resources, time or memory, and the difficulty in visually representing the data. Non-linear projection techniques, such as t-SNE [12], are capable of projecting points from a high dimension onto the plane while attempting to preserve neighborhood relationships. These projections allow for the development of algorithms that first map the points to the plane and then work on classifying and presenting them. Successful applications of this approach can be found in [3,13] and [4].

In this context, non-linear projections can be evaluated by how well separated the classes of points are in the plane after projection. This evaluation is particularly useful for parameter tuning for the projection algorithms. The most popular metric for evaluating projections for classification problems is Normalized Cuts [17], which is based on graph theory. A geometric-based alternative metric is given by the *coarseness* of a point set that is discussed below.

As before, let $P = R \cup B$, with $R \cap B = \emptyset$, be a bicolored planar point set. From here on, unless stated otherwise, we assume that the points in P are in general position, i.e., no three points in P are colinear.

A subset $Q \subseteq P$ is an *island* if there is a convex region C such that $Q = C \cap P$. The set of all islands of P is denoted by $\mathcal{I}(P)$. We assume that the sequence of vertices of the convex hull of island Q, denoted $\mathrm{CH}(Q)$, is always given in counter-clockwise (CCW) order with respect to (w.r.t.) a point in its interior. Also, $\mathrm{INT}(Q)$ denotes the subset of points of Q that do not lie on the boundary of $\mathrm{CH}(Q)$. As island Q can be uniquely characterized by its convex hull, we may sometimes refer to Q simply by the CCW sequence of vertices of $\mathrm{CH}(Q)$. Two islands are called *disjoint* if their convex hulls are disjoint.

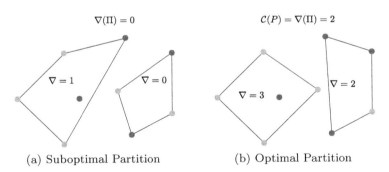

(a) Suboptimal Partition   (b) Optimal Partition

Fig. 1. Point set P and two partitions of its points into disjoint islands. (Color figure online)

We associate a *discrepancy* with each island $Q \in \mathcal{I}(P)$, given by $\nabla_Q = ||R \cap Q| - |B \cap Q||$. Moreover, the discrepancy of a partition $\Pi = \{Q_1, Q_2, \ldots Q_k\} \subseteq \mathcal{I}(P)$ of P into k pairwise disjoint islands, denoted ∇_Π, is given by $\nabla_\Pi = \min_{Q \in \Pi} \nabla_Q$. The *coarseness* of P, denoted $\mathcal{C}(P)$, is the maximum discrepancy among all possible partitions of P into pairwise disjoint islands. Figure 1 illustrates the concepts of discrepancy and coarseness.

Problem Statement. Given a bicolored planar point set, the *Coarseness Problem* consists in determining its coarseness.

This problem was first introduced in [5]. In that paper, the authors conjectured that the problem is NP-hard and studied theoretical bounds for the coarseness of point sets. They also proposed exact polynomial-time algorithms for two special cases: when the points are in convex position and when the partition is restricted to exactly two islands. The algorithm for the later case is reviewed in Sect. 4. Also, a work leading to polynomial algorithms for two other special cases is presented in [6], where the islands are restricted to lie within strips or within boxes. We are not aware of any studies in the literature that report experimental results regarding this problem.

Our Contributions. In this paper, we present an ILP model to compute the coarseness of bicolored planar point sets. We also investigate a number of improvements to the initial model, including a column generation approach, followed by a comprehensive experimental study that shows the impact of each refinement in terms of computational efficiency. The final model is able to solve instances with three times as many points when restricted to the same computational resources. Many of those instances are solved to proved optimality in polynomial time during preprocessing due to tight upper and lowerbound estimates. The benchmark used to assess the performance of the model is made publicly available to allow for future comparisons to our results.

This paper is organized as follows. In Sect. 2, we present a base ILP model for the Coarseness Problem. In Sect. 3, we improve the base model. Section 4 introduces a column generation algorithm. Lastly, Sect. 5 shows the empirical results comparing the improvements previously introduced.

2   ILP Model for the Coarseness Problem

In this section, we present the base ILP model for the Coarseness Problem.

Given a set P of n points, let $L(P)$ denote the set of $\Theta(n^2)$ line segments $\overline{jk}$ where j and k are distinct points in P. The *complete (geometric) graph* induced by P is $G(P) = (P, E(P))$, where $E(P) = \{\{j, k\} : \overline{jk} \in L(P)\}$. In this text, we refer to a segment $\overline{jk} \in L(P)$ and the corresponding edge in $\{j, k\} \in E(P)$ interchangeably. We denote by $S^C(P)$ the set of edge pairs whose corresponding line segments share an interior point, i.e., they cross each other.

Let LB and UB represent lower and upper bounds, respectively, for the coarseness of a given bicolored point set P. Associating a positive variable u_Q to each island $Q \in \mathcal{I}(P)$, a binary variable x_e for edge edge $e \in E(P)$ and a binary variable z_d for each possible discrepancy value d, we can express the Coarseness Problem as Model (1).

Constraint (1b) ensures that only one discrepancy value is selected, while Constraints (1c) ascertain that if an island is selected, its discrepancy is an upper bound on the discrepancy of the solution. Constraints (1d) guarantee that the points in P are partitioned into islands. Constraints (1e) enforce that if an island is being used, its edges are part of the solution. Constraints (1f), together with Constraints (1d), require the islands to be disjoint.

Notice that there is potentially an exponential number of islands.

From Constraints (1d) and (1e), it follows that having integer values for edge variables, (1h), implies that the island variables necessarily assume integer values. If edge variables are integral, their corresponding line segments define a planar subdivision. Now, assume that Q_1 and Q_2 are two different islands that share an edge and are fractional, i.e., $0 < u_{Q_1} \leq 1$ and $0 < u_{Q_2} < 1$, and $u_{Q_1} + u_{Q_1} < 1$. Since one of those islands must have and edge that is not shared with the other, at least one of the edge variables must assume a fractional value, which is a contradiction.

$$\max \sum_{LB \leq d \leq UB} dz_d \tag{1a}$$

$$\text{s.t.} \sum_{LB \leq d \leq UB} z_d = 1 \tag{1b}$$

$$u_Q \leq \sum_{LB \leq d \leq \nabla_Q} z_d \qquad \forall Q \in \mathcal{I}(P) \tag{1c}$$

$$\sum_{Q \in \mathcal{I}: p \in Q} u_Q = 1 \qquad \forall p \in P \tag{1d}$$

$$\sum_{Q \in \mathcal{I}: e \in \mathrm{CH}(Q)} u_Q = x_e \qquad \forall e \in E(P) \tag{1e}$$

$$x_e + x_f \leq 1 \qquad \forall \{e, f\} \in S^C(P) \tag{1f}$$

$$u_Q \in \mathbb{R}^+ \qquad \forall Q \in \mathcal{I}(P) \tag{1g}$$

$$x_e \in \{0, 1\} \qquad \forall e \in E(P) \tag{1h}$$

$$z_d \in \{0, 1\} \qquad \forall d \in \{LB, LB+1, \ldots, UB\} \tag{1i}$$

Prior to investigating the geometrical structure of P, we can set $LB = 1$ and $UB = \max_{Q \in \mathcal{I}(P)} \nabla_Q$ and solve the model by standard branch-and-bound (BnB) techniques, which rely on solving its linear relaxation obtained by dropping the integrality constraints on the variables. However, the relaxation is very weak, leading to a dual bound very close to UB. Moreover, another feature of this model that makes it hard to solve in practice is the exponential number of variables and constraints.

To overcome some of the deficiencies noted above, in the next section, we improve the quality of the relaxation by finding, in polynomial time, tighter values for LB and UB, and by adding a new class of constraints. Besides, in a subsequent section, a column generation approach to address the exponential size of the model is presented.

3 Improving the Base Model

In this section, we propose methods to find better values for the bounds, LB and UB, for the coarseness, as well as new constraints to strengthen Model (1).

As discussed in the previous section, the relaxation of our Model leads to a very weak dual bound. For many instances, this poor bound is attained by assigning to z_{UB} a value close to 1 and setting $z_{LB} + z_{UB} = 1$. Notice that the value of z_{LB} is an upper bound on all island variables due to Constraints (1c).

To illustrate this point, let us make reference to a benchmark of 30 randomly generated planar bicolored point sets of sizes $\{10, 15, \ldots, 60\}$ that we built for testing purposes. For each point, both x and y coordinates are randomly chosen in the interval $[0, 1]$ using uniform distribution and the colors are also assigned at random, with equal probability. This benchmark is available at [15]. Firstly, we observed that instances of size 20 are the largest that could be solved within one hour on a fairly standard computer (see Sect. 5) using the base model. Figure 2 shows the optimal value, the relaxation dual bound and the upper bound $UB = \max_{Q \in \mathcal{I}(P)} \nabla_Q$ for all thirty instances of size 20. For those instances, the difference between UB and the relaxation value, given as avg$\pm$stddev, is 0.017 ± 0.004.

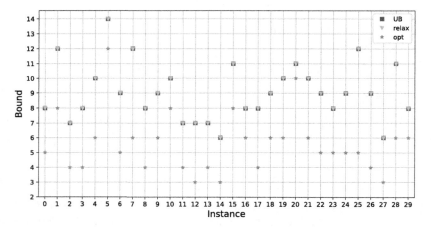

Fig. 2. Coarseness, UB and value of the relaxation given by the base model for instances with 20 points.

Based on these observations, we can infer that the quality of the relaxation could be improved by tightening the LB and UB bounds.

3.1 Lower Bound (LB)

By finding a tighter value for LB, we not only get a stronger bound, but can also eliminate from the model any island whose discrepancy is smaller than LB, effectively increasing solving speed and reducing memory requirements.

Clearly, the discrepancy of any partition of P into islands, i.e., a primal solution for Model (1), can be used to provide a lower bound. For example, a trivial solution would simply be to regard P as comprised of a single island.

Now, when the two classes of points that comprise P are linearly separable, there exists a partition that splits the points into two monochromatic islands, which obviously is an optimal solution to the coarseness problem for P.

As an educated guess, corroborated by the aforementioned extreme case, we suspect that partitions into at most two islands might lead to good quality solutions.

As discussed in the literature review (see the latter part of Sect. 1), there are results regarding bounds for the coarseness of a point set that may serve our purpose. In particular, we decided to use a polynomial time algorithm for the special case where the partitions are restricted to two islands, as it is efficient and straightforward to be implemented. That algorithm consists in finding a line that divides the plane into two islands with the largest minimum discrepancy. In spite of the $O(n^2)$-time algorithm from [5], for solving this special case, we opted for a trivial $O(n^3)$-time procedure since, for the instances at hand, $n = |P|$ is quite small. This algorithm inspects the partitions obtained by using the lines supported by the $\Theta(n^2)$ segments in $L(P)$, corresponding to edges in $E(P)$ and returns the best value found.

3.2 Upper Bound (UB)

Denote by z_{UB}^* the optimal solution to the relaxation of Model (1) for an instance P using LB as described previously and an upper bound UB. Note that since z_{UB}^* is an upper bound on the coarseness of P, we can take $UB = \lfloor z_{UB}^* \rfloor$ as a new upper bound, since coarseness is an integral number. This leads to an iterative procedure that successively finds decreasing upper bounds UB by solving the linear relaxation until this process converges, i.e., $UB = z_{UB}^*$. As the coarseness of P is bounded by $|P| = n$, there are a linear number of iterations which consist on solving the relaxation of Model (1).

In the next section, we show how to modify Model (1) so its relaxation can be solved in polynomial time through column generation. This will allow the iterative procedure we just discussed to be performed in polynomial time as well.

3.3 Least Discrepancy Constraints

We now improve Model (1) by observing that any optimal partition of discrepancy d must include at least one island of discrepancy d. This requirement can be expressed by the following linear constraints

$$\sum_{Q:\nabla_Q=d} u_Q \geq z_d \qquad \forall d \in \{LB, LB+1, \ldots, UB\}, \qquad (2)$$

which complements Constraints (1c).

Adding Constraints (2) prevents the solver from setting the value of z_{UB} close to 1 without actually including an island of discrepancy UB. Indeed, we observed that Constraints (2) improve the quality of the relaxation, as discussed in Sect. 5.

4   A Column Generation Algorithm

The number of variables and constraints in Model (1) makes it hard to solve instances in practice due not only to the high memory requirements, but also to the time spent enumerating them and building the model. In this section, we show how to use column generation to solve the linear relaxation of this model in polynomial time. For this, we need to improve a transient weakened version of the original model.

To create the set of all islands, we use an iterative procedure that generates islands by the size of their convex hull. Initially, we generate all single points, segments and islands whose convex hull is a triangle. Then, new islands are generated by adding a new point to the islands of the preceding convex hull size in such a way that the resulting island has all vertices from the previous island plus the new point as vertices. The algorithm stops when no new island can be expanded in this fashion.

Instead of enumerating all variables, we can solve the relaxation of Model (1) by starting with a small subset of variables and generating new ones when necessary. This approach, known as *Column Generation* [2], consists of iterating between two problems: the Restricted Master Problem (RMP) and the Pricing problem. The RMP solves the original model restricted to a subset of variables. On the other hand, given an optimal dual solution to the RMP, the Pricing problem seeks variables with positive (in the case of maximization problems) reduced cost that, when added to the RMP, will potentially increase the value of the objective function or, alternatively, certifies that no such variables exist, in which case the procedure stops. The solution of the last RMP is optimal for the relaxation of the complete model and, if the pricing algorithm runs in polynomial time, then the relaxation also is solved in polynomial time [10].

By associating dual variables $\alpha_Q \geq 0$ to Constraints (1c), β_p to Constraints (1d), γ_e to Constraints (1e) and $\delta_d \geq 0$ to Constraints (2), given a dual solution $(\overline{\alpha}, \overline{\beta}, \overline{\gamma}, \overline{\delta})$ we can write the pricing problem, obtained from the dual problem, as:

$$\overline{c} = \max_{Q \in \mathcal{I}} \left\{ -\overline{\alpha}_Q - \sum_{p \in Q} \overline{\beta}_p - \sum_{e \in \mathrm{CH}(Q)} \overline{\gamma}_e + \overline{\delta}_{\nabla_Q} \right\}. \tag{3}$$

If $\overline{c} > 0$, then Q has a positive reduced cost and must be added to the RMP.

Notice that before island $Q \in \mathcal{I}$ is included in the RMP, $\alpha_Q = 0$, and after it is included, its reduced cost is non-positive in any optimal solution of the RMP.

This being the case, to solve the pricing problem in polynomial time, we can use dynamic programming. A similar approach proved successful for solving the pricing problem in [14].

To express the pricing problem as a recurrence suitable for an efficient dynamic programming implementation, it suffices to weaken the model by combining discrepancy constraints (1c) in such a way that each dual variable is associated with a discrepancy value, similar to the dual variable associated with Constraints (2), instead of to individual islands. With this change, we can solve a recurrence that finds an island with the maximum reduced cost that has k as its leftmost and first point, ℓ and m as the second-to-last and last points and discrepancy d. Notice that, as is, we lack a necessary property to devise divide-and-conquer algorithms for the pricing problem (3), since knowing whether we have $\alpha_Q > 0$ is only possible after island Q is constructed by combining solutions to sub-problems, changing the reduced cost of Q.

This is done by adding together all Constraints (1c) with the same discrepancy d and noticing that, since we are partitioning n points of P into islands, we can have at most $\frac{n}{d}$ islands of discrepancy d in a solution. By doing this, we obtain the following constraints:

$$\sum_{Q:\nabla_Q=d} u_Q \leq \frac{n}{d} \sum_{LB\leq s\leq d} z_s \qquad \forall d \in \{LB, LB+1, \ldots, UB\}. \qquad (4)$$

We can lift the new constraints by including all islands with discrepancy lower than d, leading to these constraints:

$$\sum_{Q:\nabla_Q\leq d} \nabla_Q u_Q \leq n \sum_{LB\leq s\leq d} z_s \qquad \forall d \in \{LB, LB+1, \ldots, UB\}. \qquad (5)$$

By replacing Constraints (1c) with Constraints (5) and associating to them a dual variable η, we obtain the following final pricing problem:

$$\bar{c} = \max_{Q\in\mathcal{I}} \left\{ -\sum_{p\in Q} \bar{\beta}_p - \sum_{e\in\mathrm{CH}(Q)} \bar{\gamma}_e + \nabla_Q \sum_{s\geq\nabla_Q} \bar{\eta}_s - \bar{\delta}_{\nabla_Q} \right\}. \qquad (6)$$

We now solve this pricing problem using dynamic programming. We first provide an $O(n^5)$ algorithm and show how to improve the time complexity to $O(n^4)$.

To this end, we extend the concept of discrepancy so that we know the exact value of the resulting discrepancy when two islands are combined. For that, we introduce the notation $\nabla^\pm$ as the signed discrepancy. By assigning $\nabla^\pm(r) = +1$ for $r \in R$ and $\nabla^\pm(b) = -1$ for $b \in B$, the *signed discrepancy* of island $Q \in \mathcal{I}(P)$ is given by $\nabla^\pm(Q) = |R \cap Q| - |B \cap Q| = \sum_{p\in Q} \nabla^\pm(p)$.

Let $B(k, \ell, m, d)$ denote the maximum reduced cost from among all the islands with k as the leftmost point (and first in CCW order), ℓ as the second-to-last, m as the last point, and d as the signed discrepancy (w.r.t. the dual solution $(\bar{\beta}, \bar{\gamma}, \bar{\delta}, \bar{\eta})$). We say that (k, ℓ, m) is the *last triangle* of such islands. Figure 3 illustrates these concepts.

To simplify notation, let $D(d) = |d|(\sum_{|d|\leq s\leq UB} \bar{\eta}_s) - \bar{\delta}_{|d|}$ denote the sum of the dual variables associated with (signed) discrepancy d in (6) and $\Delta(k, \ell, m) = -\bar{\gamma}_{k,\ell} - \bar{\gamma}_{\ell,m} - \bar{\gamma}_{m,k} - \sum_{p\in(k,\ell,m)} \bar{\beta}_p + D(\nabla(k, \ell, m))$ denote the reduced cost of triangle (k, ℓ, m).

Given a triangle (k, ℓ, m) and a discrepancy d, we wish to determine whether there exists an island with maximum reduced cost that, once merged with triangle (k, ℓ, m), leads to discrepancy d. We can compute the discrepancy necessary for such an island to be mergeable with triangle (k, ℓ, m), and denote it by

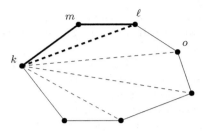

Fig. 3. An island whose last triangle is (k, ℓ, m). Dashed lines show how it is decomposed into triangles with k as the leftmost vertex. The edges of (k, ℓ, m) are emphasized.

$d'(k, \ell, m, d) = d - \nabla^{\pm}((k, \ell, m)) + \nabla^{\pm}(k) + \nabla^{\pm}(\ell)$. Note that since the points are in general position and k and ℓ are the only points shared by both the island and the triangle, the last two additive terms are necessary. To compute the resulting reduced cost of combining the triangle and an island, we need to consider that both share edge $\{k, \ell\}$, and also account for the reduced cost associated to their own discrepancy. Lastly, since a triangle can be regarded as an island, when its discrepancy is equal to the target discrepancy, island merging becomes optional.

Let P_k denote the list of points to the right of k, in increasing order of abscissae. Given a sequence of three points (k, ℓ, m) in the plane, we say that they are *colinear*, *positively oriented*, or *negatively oriented* depending on the value of the cross product $\vec{k\ell} \times \vec{\ell m}$ being 0, positive or negative. For simplicity, we say that $\text{CVX}(k, \ell, m) = \text{true}$ (or simply $\text{CVX}(k, \ell, m)$) if (k, ℓ, m) are positively oriented. We can combine an island whose last triangle is (k, o, ℓ) and triangle (k, ℓ, m) to form an island, as long as $\text{CVX}(k, o, \ell)$, so that (k, o, ℓ) is a triangle given in CCW order, and $\text{CVX}(o, \ell, m)$, to ensure convexity. Let $O_{k\ell m}$ denote the set $\{o \in P_k : \text{CVX}(k, o, \ell) \wedge \text{CVX}(o, \ell, m)\}$.

To simplify notation, we introduce an auxiliary recurrence $B_u(k, \ell, m)$, which computes a maximum reduced cost island that has (k, l, m) as its last triangle and discrepancy d by merging this triangle with another island. Using the aforementioned notation, these observations lead the following recurrence:

$$
B_u(k, \ell, m, d) = \begin{cases} -\infty, & \text{if } O_{k\ell m} = \emptyset \\ \left[\begin{array}{l} \displaystyle\max_{o \in O_{k\ell m}} \{B(k, o, \ell)\} + \Delta(k, \ell, m) + D(d) \\ \quad + 2\overline{\gamma}_{k,\ell} + \overline{\beta}(k) + \overline{\beta}(\ell) \\ \quad - D(\nabla^{\pm}(k, \ell, m)) - D(\nabla^{\pm}(d'(k, \ell, m, d)) \end{array} \right] & \text{otherwise} \end{cases} \quad (7)
$$

$$
B(k, \ell, m, d) = \begin{cases} \max\{B_u(k, \ell, m, d), \Delta(k, \ell, m)\} & \text{if } d = \nabla^{\pm}((k, \ell, m) \quad (8\text{a}) \\ B_u(k, \ell, m, d) & \text{otherwise} \quad\quad\quad (8\text{b}) \end{cases}
$$

A naive implementation of this algorithm would have a time complexity of $O(n^5)$. This is the result of having $O(n^4)$ states that require finding a maximum over $O(n)$ candidates plus the sum of costs associated with a triangle for each of them.

To calculate the costs associated with a triangle in constant time, we need to calculate $\sum_{p\in(k,\ell,m)} \overline{\beta}_p$ and $\nabla^{\pm}(k,\ell,m) = \sum_{p\in(k,\ell,m)} \nabla^{\pm}(p)$ in $O(1)$. Notice that the triangles are not necessarily empty. This can be realized using a technique presented in [8] for: given a set P of n weighted points, after an $O(n^2)$-time preprocessing, compute, in $O(1)$ time, the sum of the weights of all points within a query triangle with vertices in P. The basic idea is to precompute the sum above each segment in $L(P)$ and use an inclusion-exclusion principle to calculate the sum inside any triangle, based on its edges. To determine the signed discrepancy of a triangle, we assign weights $+1$ and -1 to points in R and B, respectively, and to compute the sum of the β variables of points within a triangle we associate to each point its β value.

To reach our proposed time complexity target, we adapt an angular sweeping technique first introduced to find the Maximum Cardinality Empty Convex Polygon [1], and recently employed in [14] to solve the pricing problem of an ILP model for the Minimum Convex Partition Problem. This technique allows us to compute the maximum within Eq. (7), which corresponds to finding a third-to-last point for the island being constructed, in amortized constant time.

While referring to Fig. 4, notice that, for fixed k and ℓ, if we visit the possible last points m in counter-clockwise order around ℓ, the list of candidates third-to-last points o can also be visited in counter-clockwise order in such a way that each candidate is only considered once. For further details, we refer the reader to [1] and [14].

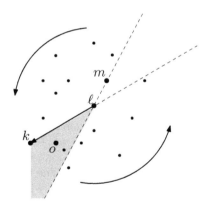

Fig. 4. Illustration of the angular sweep technique.

Finally, we use a technique of early stop to accelerate the convergence of the RMP. Instead of halting the column generation algorithm when the maximum reduced cost $\overline{c}$ is zero, we stop when it is small enough so that the floor of the current optimal of the RMP, z^*_{RMP}, cannot change. We can calculate a dual bound for the complete model based on the maximum reduced cost as $z^* \geq z^*_{\text{RMP}} + \bar{c}\kappa$, where κ is an upper bound on the number of islands in an optimal solution. Since we know that $z^* \geq LB$, we must have $\kappa \leq \lfloor \frac{n}{LB} \rfloor$. Finding a better LB reduces significantly the tailing-off effect, which is a frequent issue for column generation, when the value of z^*_{RMP} is very close to z^* and yet many iterations are needed to achieve a reduced cost of zero [11].

Now, we can solve to integrality the model that results from replacing Constraints (4) with (5) and adding Constraints (2), by using Branch-and-Price (BnP) [2]. We start the model with the islands corresponding to each individual point and use the pricing as described. When solving multiple relaxation, as in the case of the iterative procedure to find UB, we start the new relaxation with all islands generated to solve the previous one. Branching is done on edge and discrepancy variables.

5   Experimental Results

In this section, we show the positive impact of the modifications to the basic model described in the previous sections. All experiments were run on an Intel Xeon E5-2420 at 1.9 GHz and 32 GB of RAM, running Ubuntu 18.04. Models and algorithms were implemented in C++ v.11 and compiled with gcc 7.5. Geometric algorithms and data structures were implemented using CGAL 5.2 [18], using Gmpq for exact number representation. ILP models were implemented using SCIP 7.0.2 [9] with CPLEX 12.10 as the LP solver. In each experiment, we use the instances from the benchmark described in Sect. 3. A time limit of one hour was set for the ILP solver for each instance.

When running times are presented, we consider both the time to generate and to solve the model. Most of the data are presented in a standard boxplot, grouped by size. All data used to generate the figures is available at [15].

We begin by showing the impact of tightening the LB and UB bounds in the relaxation. In Figs. 5 and 6, the modifier +heuLB indicates that LB was found by a heuristic solution, +itUB means that the iterative procedure was used to find UB and the addition of the least discrepancy constraints is denoted by the +cut. The calculation LB and UB are considered the *preprocessing phase*.

Figure 5 shows the relative gap, computed as $\frac{\text{RELAX} - \text{OPT}}{\text{RELAX}}$, where OPT and RELAX are the values of an optimal integer solution and optimal relaxation solution, respectively, for instances of different sizes. The Base model could not solve instances with 25 or more points within one hour, while instances with at least 35 points did not fit in 32 GB of memory without column generation.

As expected, improving LB by finding the best partition into 1 or 2 islands has a positive impact in reducing the relative gap. The benefit of the least discrepancy constraints can also be noted. The iterative algorithm to find a better UB yields a tight bound for most instances.

Similarly, the total solving time for the same configurations is shown in Fig. 6. In order not to distort the scale and hinder details in the graph, two outlier instances with 30 points are not shown for the Base +heuLB +itUB +cut graph

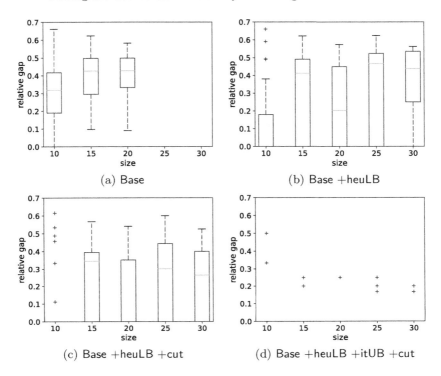

(a) Base

(b) Base +heuLB

(c) Base +heuLB +cut

(d) Base +heuLB +itUB +cut

Fig. 5. Relative gap for different configurations of the Base model.

as they took 2359 and 3980 s, respectively, to be solved. This experiment shows the impact in performance of the improved LB values, as that allows for the removal of a large number of variables, drastically reducing both solving time and memory consumption, which, in turn, raises the size of instances being solved from 20 to 30. Notably, the high quality bounds obtained by using the iterative algorithms to find UB come with a cost in overall time. This extra time is greatly reduced, along with the expected memory requirement, when solving the relaxations using column generation, as we will see.

Next, we show, in Fig. 7, the solving time to find exact solutions with and without the tighter UB, while still using the least discrepancy constraints and the LB found by the heuristic. As before, so as not to distort the scale, two outlier instances are omitted in Fig. 7b as they took 2594 and 4369 s, respectively, to be solved. Instances of more than 30 points could not fit in 32 GB of memory. Here, for most instances, we observe the advantage of using the iterative algorithm to find UB when it comes to solving the ILP. In such cases, the stronger bound compensates the extra time during preprocessing leading to an overall performance gain.

Lastly, as our paramount result, we focus now on the solving times using the same bounds as before, but employing column generation for both the iterative

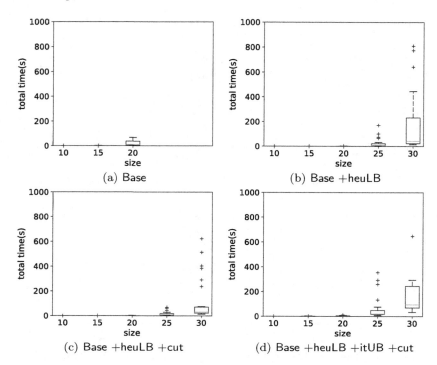

Fig. 6. Total solving time for the relaxation of different configurations of the model.

procedure to find *UB* and for the actual ILP, as depicted in Fig. 8a. Having thus lessened the memory limitation, larger instances could now be solved and we set aside a time limit of one extra hour just for the iterative procedure to find a tight *UB* value.

For the actual memory consumption, we refer the reader to Fig. 8b. Notice that the most remarkable development is the great reduction in memory usage, which allowed us to solve instances with three times the number of points as before, using one tenth of the total memory limit, on average. Moreover, the use of column generation sped up the procedure to find *UB*. For more details, see Table 1.

Notably, the combination of itUB and heuLB was able to solve to proved optimality a high number of randomly generated instances in polynomial time. This table also shows that even when limited to a total of one hour for preprocessing and solving, the usage of itUB increased the number of instances solved.

Table 1. Number of instances solved by different methods using column generation for different instance sizes. Solved in preprocessing indicates instances where $UB = LB$.

Method ↓ | **Size** →	10	15	20	25	30	35	40	45	50	55	60
# solved in preprocessing	27	25	28	26	26	25	23	21	27	19	18
# solved with itUB	30	30	30	30	30	29	28	23	28	21	20
# solved in 1h with itUB	30	30	30	30	30	29	28	23	27	19	18
# solved without itUB	30	30	30	30	30	28	27	20	26	13	17

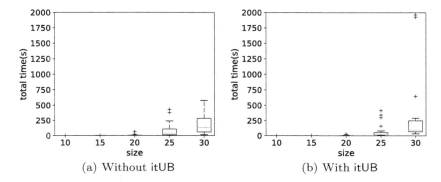

(a) Without itUB   (b) With itUB

Fig. 7. Total time for Base +heuLB +cut with and without itUB.

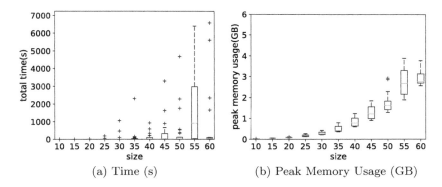

(a) Time (s)   (b) Peak Memory Usage (GB)

Fig. 8. Total solving time and peak memory usage for Base +heuLB +itUB +cut using Column Generation. Only instances that were solved to optimality are included.eps

Final Remarks

In conclusion, we showed that by using column generation, in conjunction with the improvements to the bounds on coarseness, we were able to solve to optimality instances of triple the size (up to 60 points) from our benchmark that the initial model could solve, with remarkably small memory requirement.

As to future work, we intend to investigate how to speed up the column generation procedure since its convergence is central for solving large instances quickly. Improving the heuristic is another venue of research, which might not only reduce the solving time for the relaxation but also lead to a larger number of instances that can be solved during preprocessing due to establishing a tighter lower bound.

Despite the fact that randomly generated point sets have a high probability of being in general position, it is important to consider how our model might be adapted for instances where this property may not be guaranteed. Besides the obviously intricate approach of considering all different cases of collinearity that may appear during island construction, it would be worth considering the alternative of applying symbolic perturbation schemes such as [7] or [16], notwithstanding their well known impact in time complexity, in practice.

References

1. Avis, D., Rappaport, D.: Computing the largest empty convex subset of a set of points. In: Proceedings of the First Annual Symposium on Computational Geometry, SCG 1985, pp. 161–167. ACM, New York (1985). https://doi.org/10.1145/323233.323255
2. Barnhart, C., Johnson, E.L., Nemhauser, G.L., Savelsbergh, M.W.P., Vance, P.H.: Branch-and-Price: column generation for solving huge integer programs. Oper. Res. **46**(3), 316–329 (1998). https://doi.org/10.1287/opre.46.3.316
3. Benato, B.C., Telea, A.C., Falcão, A.X.: Semi-supervised learning with interactive label propagation guided by feature space projections. In: Proceedings of the 31st SIBGRAPI Conference on Graphics, Patterns and Images (SIBGRAPI), pp. 392–399, October 2018. https://doi.org/10.1109/SIBGRAPI.2018.00057
4. Benato, B.C., Gomes, J.F., Telea, A.C., Falcão, A.X.: Semi-supervised deep learning based on label propagation in a 2D embedded space. CoRR abs/2008.00558 (2020). https://arxiv.org/abs/2008.00558
5. Bereg, S., Díaz-Báñez, J.M., Lara, D., Pérez-Lantero, P., Seara, C., Urrutia, J.: On the coarseness of bicolored point sets. Comput. Geom. **46**(1), 65–77 (2013). https://doi.org/10.1016/j.comgeo.2012.04.003
6. Díaz-Báñez, J.M., López, M.A., Ochoa, C., Pérez-Lantero, P.: Computing the coarseness with strips or boxes. Discret. Appl. Math. **224**, 80–90 (2017). https://doi.org/10.1016/j.dam.2017.02.022
7. Edelsbrunner, H., Mücke, E.P.: Simulation of simplicity: a technique to cope with degenerate cases in geometric algorithms. ACM Trans. Graph. **9**(1), 66–104 (1990). https://doi.org/10.1145/77635.77639
8. Eppstein, D., Overmars, M.H., Rote, G., Woeginger, G.J.: Finding minimum area k-gons. Discret. Comput. Geom. **7**, 45–58 (1992). https://doi.org/10.1007/BF02187823
9. Gamrath, G., et al.: The SCIP Optimization Suite 7.0. Technical report, Optimization Online, March 2020. http://www.optimization-online.org/DB_HTML/2020/03/7705.html
10. Grötschel, M., Lovász, L., Schrijver, A.: The ellipsoid method and its consequences in combinatorial optimization. Combinatorica **1**(2), 169–197 (1981). https://doi.org/10.1007/BF02579273

11. Lübbecke, M.E., Desrosiers, J.: Selected topics in column generation. Oper. Res. **53**(6), 1007–1023 (2005). https://doi.org/10.1287/opre.1050.0234
12. van der Maaten, L., Hinton, G.: Visualizing data using *t*-SNE. J. Mach. Learn. Res. **9**(86), 2579–2605 (2008). http://jmlr.org/papers/v9/vandermaaten08a.html
13. Peixinho, A.Z., Benato, B.C., Nonato, L.G., Falcão, A.X.: Delaunay triangulation data augmentation guided by visual analytics for deep learning. In: Proceedings of the 31st SIBGRAPI Conference on Graphics, Patterns and Images (SIBGRAPI), pp. 384–391, October 2018. https://doi.org/10.1109/SIBGRAPI.2018.00056
14. Sapucaia, A., de Rezende, P.J., de Souza, C.C.: Solving the minimum convex partition of point sets with integer programming. Comput. Geom. **99**, 101794 (2021). https://doi.org/10.1016/j.comgeo.2021.101794
15. Sapucaia, A., de Souza, C.C., de Rezende, P.J.: Coarseness of point sets - Benchmark instances and solutions (2021). http://www.ic.unicamp.br/~cid/Problem-instances/Coarseness
16. Seidel, R.: The nature and meaning of perturbations in geometric computing. Discret. Comput. Geom. **19**(1), 1–17 (1998). https://doi.org/10.1007/PL00009330
17. Shi, J., Malik, J.: Normalized cuts and image segmentation. In: 1997 Conference on Computer Vision and Pattern Recognition (CVPR 1997), Puerto Rico, 17–19 June 1997, pp. 731–737. IEEE Computer Society (1997). https://doi.org/10.1109/CVPR.1997.609407
18. The CGAL Project: CGAL User and Reference Manual. CGAL Editorial Board, 5.2 edn. (2020). https://doc.cgal.org/5.2/Manual/packages.html

Calculation of the Differential Geometry of the Intersection of Implicit Hypersurfaces in $\mathbb{R}^4$ with Mathematica

Judith Keren Jiménez-Vilcherrez[1]($\boxtimes$) , Ricardo Velezmoro-León[2]($\boxtimes$) ,
and Robert Ipanaqué-Chero[2]($\boxtimes$)

[1] Universidad Tecnológica del Perú, Av. Vice Cdra 1-Costado Real Plaza, Piura, Peru
C19863@utp.edu.pe
[2] Universidad Nacional de Piura, Urb. Miraflores s/n Castilla, Piura, Peru
{rvelezmorol,ripanaquec}@unp.edu.pe

Abstract. In geometry, knowing the differential properties of a curve at a point is very important, as it would help us understand its behavior around that point; even more so when said curve is generated by the intersection of hypersurfaces in $\mathbb{R}^4$. This paper describes a new Mathematica package, `Frenet4D`, that allows to visualize and calculate the Frenet frame of the curve given by the transversal intersection of three implicit hypersurfaces in $\mathbb{R}^4$ thus like the visualization of the respective hypersurfaces. The output obtained is consistent with Mathematica's notation and results. To show the performance of the package, several illustrative and interesting examples are described.

Keywords: Implicit hypersurface · Implicit–implicit–implicit intersection · Transversal intersection

1 Introduction

The implicit-implicit-implicit hypersurface intersection problem in $\mathbb{R}^4$, to calculate the differential properties of the intersection curve, has been fully developed in [6,7] based on [8] as well as in [11], although using different techniques. The results of both investigations provide explicit formulas to perform the above calculations, but all these calculations are done manually and this is a cumbersome process. Furthermore, none of these investigations shows geometric interpretations in their results.

The use of symbolic calculation systems to speed up calculations and perform geometric interpretations on research results related to various areas of mathematics is increasingly widespread [1,3–5,12]. However, we have not found any work that complements the results of the investigations mentioned in the previous paragraph. For this reason, we decided to carry out this investigation.

This paper describes a new Mathematica package `Frenet4D` that allows us to calculate the Frenet frame of the transverse intersection of three implicit hypersurfaces in $\mathbb{R}^4$, as well as the three curvatures, it also allows us to visualize the

© Springer Nature Switzerland AG 2021
O. Gervasi et al. (Eds.): ICCSA 2021, LNCS 12953, pp. 46–59, 2021.
https://doi.org/10.1007/978-3-030-86976-2_4

Frenet frame, at a given point on the curve and the hypersurfaces, demonstrate to the user a very useful tool for teaching and visualization. The results obtained are consistent with Mathematica's notation and results. The performance of the package is discussed throughout the paper using several illustrative and interesting examples.

The paper is organized as follows: Sect. 2 reviews the formulas necessary to calculate the properties of the differential geometry of a curve obtained by the intersection of three hypersurfaces implicit in $\mathbb{R}^4$. Then, Sect. 3 introduces the new Mathematica package, `Frenet4D`, and describes the commands implemented within. The performance of the package is also discussed in this section by using some illustrative examples. Finally, the conclusions are in Sect. 4.

2   Mathematical Preliminaries

Let us first introduce some notations and definitions (Many of the definitions and much of the terminology in this section may be found in [2,3,6,7,11,13]). The dot product of two vectors $u = (u_1, u_2, u_3, u_4)$ and $v = (v_1, v_2, v_3, v_4)$ in $\mathbb{R}^4$ is defined by

$$u \cdot v = u_1 v_1 + u_2 v_2 + u_3 v_3 + u_4 v_4$$

the norm of the vector u is

$$\|u\| = \sqrt{u \cdot u}$$

Let $\{e_1, e_2, e_3, e_4\}$ be the standard basis of $\mathbb{R}^4$, the cross product of three vectors u, v, w is defined as

$$u \times v \times w = - \begin{vmatrix} e_1 & e_2 & e_3 & e_4 \\ u_1 & u_2 & u_3 & u_4 \\ v_1 & v_2 & v_3 & v_4 \\ w_1 & w_2 & w_3 & w_4 \end{vmatrix}.$$

Some properties of cross product:

  i. $u \times v \times w = v \times w \times u = w \times u \times v = -w \times v \times u = -v \times u \times w = -u \times w \times v$
  ii. $u \cdot u \times v \times w = 0$
  iii. If $u \times v \times w = 0$ with $u \neq 0, v \neq 0$ y $w \neq 0$ then it may be the case that
     $u \parallel v, u \parallel w, v \parallel w$ or $u \parallel v \parallel w$
  iv. $\lambda (u \times v \times w) = (\lambda u) \times v \times w = u \times (\lambda v) \times w = u \times v \times (\lambda w)$

We will denote the differentiation of a curve with respect to the arc length s as $\alpha'(s) = \frac{d\alpha}{ds}$, $\alpha''(s) = \frac{d^2\alpha}{ds^2}$, $\alpha'''(s) = \frac{d^3\alpha}{ds^3}$ and $\alpha^{(iv)}(s) = \frac{d^4\alpha}{ds^4}$.

2.1   Regular Curve in $\mathbb{R}^4$

Let $\alpha : I \to \mathbb{R}^4$ be a regular curve parametrized by the arc length s, then from elementary differential geometry, we have

$$\begin{pmatrix} \alpha'(s) \\ \alpha''(s) \\ \alpha'''(s) \\ \alpha^{(iv)}(s) \end{pmatrix} = \begin{pmatrix} 1 & 0 & 0 & 0 \\ 0 & \kappa_1 & 0 & 0 \\ -\kappa_1^2 & \kappa'_1 & \kappa_1 \kappa_2 & 0 \\ -3\kappa_1 \kappa'_1 & -\kappa_1^3 + \kappa''_1 - \kappa_1 \kappa_2^2 & 2\kappa'_1 \kappa_2 + \kappa_1 \kappa'_2 & \kappa_1 \kappa_2 \kappa_3 \end{pmatrix} \begin{pmatrix} t(s) \\ n(s) \\ b_1(s) \\ b_2(s) \end{pmatrix}$$

where $t(s)$ is the unit tangent vector field, $n(s)$ is the unit principal normal vector field, $b_1(s)$ is the first unit binormal vector field, $b_2(s)$ is the second unit binormal vector field of α and k_i $(i = 1, 2, 3)$ are the ith curvature functions of the curve α. The Frenet frame along α is the orthonormal frame $\{t, n, b_1, b_2\}$ is given by

$$t(s) = \alpha'(s)$$
$$n(s) = \frac{\alpha''(s)}{\|\alpha''(s)\|}$$
$$b_2(s) = \frac{\alpha'(s) \times \alpha''(s) \times \alpha'''(s)}{\|\alpha'(s) \times \alpha''(s) \times \alpha'''(s)\|}$$
$$b_1(s) = b_2(s) \times t(s) \times n(s) \tag{1}$$

the Frenet-Serret formulas along α is given by

$$\begin{pmatrix} t'(s) \\ n'(s) \\ b'_1(s) \\ b'_2(s) \end{pmatrix} = \begin{pmatrix} 0 & \kappa_1 & 0 & 0 \\ -\kappa_1 & 0 & \kappa_2 & 0 \\ 0 & -\kappa_2 & 0 & \kappa_3 \\ 0 & 0 & -\kappa_3 & 0 \end{pmatrix} \begin{pmatrix} t(s) \\ n(s) \\ b_1(s) \\ b_2(s) \end{pmatrix} \tag{2}$$

Using 1 and 2 it is possible to see that the curvature functions of α are given by

$$\kappa_1 = \sqrt{\alpha'' \cdot \alpha''}, \kappa_2 = \frac{\alpha''' \cdot b_1}{\kappa_1} \text{ and } \kappa_3 = \frac{\alpha^{(iv)} b_2}{\kappa_1 \kappa_2}.$$

2.2   Regular Implicit Hypersurface

Let $f(x, y, z, w) = 0$ a regular implicit hypersurface i.e. $\nabla f \neq 0$, where $\nabla f = (f_1, f_2, f_3, f_4)$ is the gradient vector of f, $f_p = \frac{\partial f}{\partial x_p}$ $(p = 1, 2, 3, 4)$. Then the unit normal vector field of the hypersurface f is given by $N^f = \frac{\nabla f}{\|\nabla f\|}$.

Let $\alpha(s) = (x_1(s), x_2(s), x_3(s), x_4(s))$ be a curve on the hypersurface f, then we have

$$\alpha'(s) = (x'_1, x'_2, x'_3, x'_4), \alpha''(s) = (x''_1, x''_2, x''_3, x''_4), \ldots,$$
$$\alpha^{(v)}(s) = \left(x_1^{(v)}, x_2^{(v)}, x_3^{(v)}, x_4^{(v)} \right).$$

2.3   Curves in Hypersurface

Implicit Representation of Space Curve. The implicit representation for a curve in $\mathbb{R}^4$ can be expressed as an intersection curve between three implicit surfaces

$$f(x, y, z, w) = 0 \bigcap g(x, y, z, w) = 0 \bigcap h(x, y, z, w) = 0$$

Curves in Surface Parametrized by Arc-Length. Consider an implicit surface represented by $f : \mathbb{R}^4 \to \mathbb{R}$. A curve $\alpha(s) = (x(s), y(s), z(s), w(s))$ in which it is fulfilled $f(\alpha(s)) = 0$ defines a curve on an implicit hypersurface $f(x, y, z, w) = 0$.

3   The Package Frenet4D: Some Illustrative Examples

In this section, we show the `Frenet4D` package that will allow us to quickly and efficiently calculate the Frenet apparatus for the curve generated by the intersection of 3 implicit-implicit-implicit hypersurfaces at a point of the same; being very significant the fact that it can provide us with a graphical view in $\mathbb{R}^4$ of the hypersurfaces and the Frenet apparatus at the point given that it would be very difficult to obtain manually. In our opinion, the best way to show the power and functionalities of our package is through examples, these examples have already been discussed in [6,11] and whose answers are completely compatible with those provided by the package, so this is the approach that we will follow in this section. Firstly, we load the package:

```
<<Frenet4D.m
```

The commands incorporated in this package are:

```
Graphics4D, ImplicitPlot4D, Frenet4DForImplicit
```

The `Graphics4D` command allows you to obtain the graphics of primitives in 4D, i.e., points, lines, arrows, and polygons. The `ImplicitPlot4D` command plots the graphs of implicitly defined 4D solids. And, with the `Frenet4DForImplicit` command, the differential properties of curves given as the intersection of three implicit hypersurfaces are obtained.

Example 1. Consider the intersection of the three implicit hypersurfaces given by $f(x, y, z, w) = x^2 + y^2 + z^2 + w^2 - 2 = 0$, $h(x, y, z, w) = x^2 + y^2 + z^2 - w^2 = 0$ and $g(x, y, z, w) = x^2 + y^2 - x = 0$ and we calculate the Frenet frame $\{t, n, b_1, b_2\}$ along of the intersection curve α, as well as $\kappa_1(s)$, $\kappa_2(s)$ and $\kappa_3(s)$ are the first, second and third curvetures of $\alpha(s)$ at the point P0 $= \left\{\frac{1}{2}, \frac{1}{2}, \frac{\sqrt{2}}{2}, 1\right\}$.

First we define the hypersurfaces f, g and h

```
f[x_, y_, z_, w_] := x^2 + y^2 + z^2 + w^2 - 2
h[x_, y_, z_, w_] := x^2 + y^2 + z^2 - w^2
g[x_, y_, z_, w_] := x^2 + y^2 - x
P0 = {1/2, 1/2, Sqrt[2]/2, 1};
```

Frenet4DForImplicit returns the Frenet frame $\{t, n, b_1, b_2\}$ along α, as well as $\kappa_1(s)$, $\kappa_2(s)$ and $\kappa_3(s)$ are the first, second and third curvetures of $\alpha(s)$ at the point P0 $= \left\{\frac{1}{2}, \frac{1}{2}, \frac{\sqrt{2}}{2}, 1\right\}$.

```
{TT, NN, BB1, BB2, k1, k2, k3} = Frenet4DForImplicit[{
  f[x,y,z,w] == 0, g[x,y,z,w] == 0, h[x,y,z,w] == 0 }, {x,y,z,w},
  Point -> P0]
```

$$\left\{\left\{-\sqrt{\frac{2}{3}},0,\frac{1}{\sqrt{3}},0\right\},\left\{\frac{1}{\sqrt{39}},2\sqrt{\frac{3}{13}},\sqrt{\frac{2}{39}},0\right\},\left\{\frac{2}{\sqrt{13}},-\frac{1}{\sqrt{13}},2\sqrt{\frac{2}{13}},0\right\},\right.$$

$$\left.\{0,0,0,-1\},\frac{2\sqrt{\frac{13}{3}}}{3},-\frac{6\sqrt{2}}{13},0\right\}$$

The frenet4D variable is defined as follows:

```
frenet4D =
  Graphics4D[{ AbsolutePointSize[20], Point[P0],
  Red, Arrow[{P0, P0 + .5 TT}], Green, Arrow[{P0, P0 + .5 NN}],
  Cyan, Arrow[{P0, P0 + .5 BB2}], Blue, Arrow[{P0, P0 + .5 BB1}],
  ViewPoint -> {-0.8677623819257761, 3.0335880200886844,
  1.2224288007442063},
  ViewVertical -> {-0.12496031476425706, 0.2964760771820533,
  0.9468298978130967} }];
```

The following sentences allow us to obtain the graph of the hypersurface $f(x,y,z,w) = x^2 + y^2 + z^2 + w^2 - 2 = 0$.

```
S1 = ImplicitPlot4D[
  f[x, y, z, w] == 0, {x, 0.35, 0.75}, {y, 0.35, 0.75}, {z, 0.35,
  0.75}, {w, 0.75, 1.25}, Red];
Show[S1, frenet4D]
```

See Fig. 1 (top-left).

The following sentences allow us to obtain the graph of the hypersurface $g(x,y,z,w) = x^2 + y^2 - x = 0$.

```
S2 = ImplicitPlot4D[
  g[x, y, z, w] == 0, {x, 0.35, 0.75}, {y, 0.35, 0.75}, {z, 0.35,
  0.75}, {w, 0.75, 1.25}, Green]; Show[S2, frenet4D]
```

See Fig. 1 (top-right).

The following sentences allow us to obtain the graph of the hypersurface $h(x,y,z,w) = x^2 + y^2 + z^2 - w^2 = 0$.

```
S3 = ImplicitPlot4D[
  h[x, y, z, w] == 0, {x, 0.35, 0.75}, {y, 0.35, 0.75}, {z, 0.35,
  0.75}, {w, 0.75, 1.25}, Cyan]; Show[S3, frenet4D]
```

See Fig. 1 (bottom-left).

The following sentences allow us to obtain the graphs in the orthonormal frame $\{t, n, b_1, b_2\}$ at the point $\text{P0} = \left\{\frac{1}{2}, \frac{1}{2}, \frac{\sqrt{2}}{2}, 1\right\}$, the red vector represents the unit tangent vector, the green vector represents the unit normal vector, the blue vector represents the unit vector b_1 and the celestial vector represents the unit vector b_2 of the intersection curve of the hypersurfaces f, g and h.

```
Show[S1, S2, S3, frenet4D]
```

See Fig. 1 (bottom-right).

Example 2. Consider the intersection of the three implicit hypersurfaces given by $f(\mathrm{x},y,z,\mathrm{w}){=}(y-w)^3 + z = 0$, $h\,(x,y,z,w) = (y-w)^2 - x = 0$, $g\,(x,y,z,w) = y + w - 1 = 0$. and we calculate the Frenet frame $\{t,n,b_1,b_2\}$ along of the intersection curve α, as well as $\kappa_1\,(s)$, $\kappa_2\,(s)$ and $\kappa_3\,(s)$ are the first, second and third curvetures of $\alpha\,(s)$ at the point $\mathrm{P0} = \{1,0,1,1\}$.

First we define the hypersurfaces f, g and h

```
f[x_, y_, z_, w_] := (y - w)^3 + z
h[x_, y_, z_, w_] := (y - w)^2 - x
g[x_, y_, z_, w_] := y + w - 1
P0 = {1, 0, 1, 1};
```

Frenet4DForImplicit returns the Frenet frame $\{t,n,b_1,b_2\}$ along α, as well as $\kappa_1\,(s)$, $\kappa_2\,(s)$ and $\kappa_3\,(s)$ are the first, second and third curvetures of $\alpha\,(s)$ at the point $P0 = \{1,0,1,1\}$.

```
{TT, NN, BB1, BB2, k1, k2, k3} = Frenet4DForImplicit[{
  f[x,y,z,w] == 0, g[x,y,z,w] == 0, h[x,y,z,w] == 0 }, {x,y,z,w},
  Point -> P0]
```

$$\left\{\left\{\frac{2\sqrt{\frac{2}{3}}}{3}, -\frac{1}{3\sqrt{6}}, \sqrt{\frac{2}{3}}, \frac{1}{3\sqrt{6}}\right\}, \left\{-\frac{17}{6\sqrt{21}}, \frac{11}{6\sqrt{21}}, \frac{5}{2\sqrt{21}}, -\frac{11}{6\sqrt{21}}\right\},\right.$$

$$\left.\left\{\frac{3}{2\sqrt{7}}, \frac{3}{2\sqrt{7}}, -\frac{1}{2\sqrt{7}}, -\frac{3}{2\sqrt{7}}\right\}, \left\{0, -\frac{1}{\sqrt{2}}, 0, -\frac{1}{\sqrt{2}}\right\}, \frac{8\sqrt{\frac{7}{3}}}{81}, -\frac{6}{28\sqrt{2}}, 0\right\}$$

The frenet4D variable is defined as follows:

```
frenet4D =
  Graphics4D[{ AbsolutePointSize[20], Point[P0],
  Red, Arrow[{P0, P0 + .5 TT}], Green, Arrow[{P0, P0 + .5 NN}],
  Cyan, Arrow[{P0, P0 + .5 BB2}], Blue, Arrow[{P0, P0 + .5 BB1}],
  ViewPoint -> {-0.8677623819257761, 3.0335880200886844,
  1.2224288007442063},
  ViewVertical -> {-0.12496031476425706, 0.2964760771820533,
  0.9468298978130967} }];
```

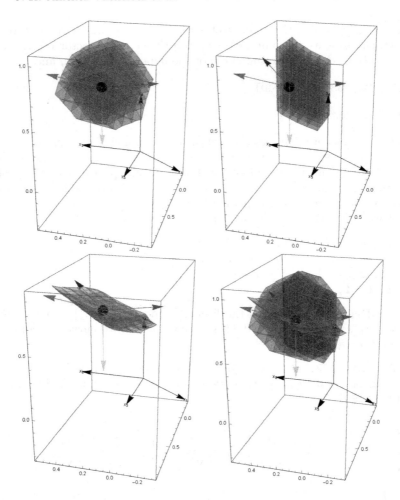

Fig. 1. Hypersurfaces $f(x,y,z,w) = 0$ (top-left), $g(x,y,z,w) = 0$ (top-right), $h(x,y,z,w) = 0$ (bottom-left) and graphical visualization of $f(x,y,z,w) = 0 \bigcap g(x,y,z,w) = 0 \bigcap h(x,y,z,w) = 0$ at the point $P0 = \left\{ \frac{1}{2}, \frac{1}{2}, \frac{\sqrt{2}}{2}, 1 \right\}$ (bottom-right)

The following sentences allow us to obtain the graph of the hypersurface $f(\mathrm{x}, \mathrm{y}, \mathrm{z}, \mathrm{w}) = (\mathrm{y} - \mathrm{w})^3 + z = 0$

```
S1 = ImplicitPlot4D[
    f[x, y, z, w] == 0, {x, 0.75, 1.25}, {y, -0.25, 0.35}, {z, 0.75,
    1.25}, {w, 0.75, 1.25}, Red];
Show[S1, frenet4D]
```

See Fig. 2 (top-left).

The following sentences allow us to obtain the graph of the hypersurface $g(x, y, z, w) = y + w - 1 = 0$

```
S2 = ImplicitPlot4D[
   g[x, y, z, w] == 0, {x, 0.75, 1.25}, {y, -0.25, 0.35}, {z, 0.75,
   1.25}, {w, 0.75, 1.25}, Green]; Show[S2, frenet4D]
```

See Fig. 2 (top-right).
The following sentences allow us to obtain the graph of the hypersurface $h(x, y, z, w) = (y - w)^2 - x = 0$

```
S3 = ImplicitPlot4D[
   h[x, y, z, w] == 0, {x, 0.75, 1.25}, {y, -0.25, 0.35}, {z, 0.75,
   1.25}, {w, 0.75, 1.25}, Cyan]; Show[S3, frenet4D]
```

See Fig. 2 (bottom-left).
The following sentences allow us to obtain the graphs in the orthonormal frame $\{t, n, b_1, b_2\}$ at the point PO $= \{1, 0, 1, 1\}$, the red vector represents the unit tangent vector, the green vector represents the unit normal vector, the blue vector represents the unit vector b_1 and the celestial vector represents the unit vector b_2 of the intersection curve of the hypersurfaces f, g and h.

```
Show[S1, S2, S3, frenet4D]
```

See Fig. 2 (bottom-right).

Example 3. Consider the intersection of the three implicit hypersurfaces given by $f(x, y, z, w) = x^2 + y^2 + z^2 + w^2 - 2 = 0$, $h(x, y, z, w) = (xw + yz)^2 + (xz - yw)^2 - 1 = 0$ and $g(x, y, z, w) = 2xyz - w(x^2 - y^2) = 0$ and we calculate the Frenet frame $\{t, n, b_1, b_2\}$ along of the intersection curve α, as well as $\kappa_1(s)$, $\kappa_2(s)$ and $\kappa_3(s)$ are the first, second and third curvetures of $\alpha(s)$ at the point PO $= \{1, 0, 1, 0\}$.
First we define the hypersurfaces f, g and h

```
f[x_, y_, z_, w_] := x^2 + y^2 + z^2 + w^2 - 2
h[x_, y_, z_, w_] := (x w + y z)^2+(x z - y w)^2 - 1
g[x_, y_, z_, w_] := 2 x y z - w (x^2 - y^2)
PO = {1, 0, 1, 0};
```

Frenet4DForImplicit returns the Frenet frame $\{t, n, b_1, b_2\}$ along α, as well as $\kappa_1(s)$, $\kappa_2(s)$ and $\kappa_3(s)$ are the first, second and third curvetures of $\alpha(s)$ at the point PO $= \{1, 0, 1, 0\}$.

```
{TT, NN, BB1, BB2, k1, k2, k3} = Frenet4DForImplicit[{
   f[x,y,z,w] == 0, g[x,y,z,w] == 0, h[x,y,z,w] == 0 }, {x,y,z,w},
   Point -> PO]
```

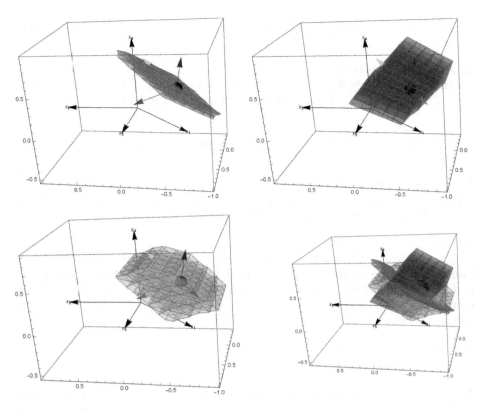

Fig. 2. Hypersurfaces $f(x, y, z, w) = 0$ (top-left), $g(x, y, z, w) = 0$ (top-right), $h(x, y, z, w) = 0$ (bottom-left) and graphical visualization of $f(x, y, z, w) = 0 \bigcap g(x, y, z, w) = 0 \bigcap h(x, y, z, w) = 0$ at the point $P0 = \{1, 0, 1, 1\}$ (bottom-right)

$$\left\{ \left\{0, \frac{1}{\sqrt{5}}, 0, \frac{2}{\sqrt{5}}\right\}, \left\{-\frac{1}{\sqrt{17}}, 0, -\frac{4}{\sqrt{17}}, 0\right\}, \left\{0, -\frac{2}{\sqrt{5}}, 0, \frac{1}{\sqrt{5}}\right\}, \right.$$

$$\left. \left\{\frac{4}{\sqrt{17}}, 0, -\frac{1}{\sqrt{17}}, 0\right\}, \frac{\sqrt{17}}{5}, -\frac{6}{5\sqrt{17}}, \frac{2}{\sqrt{17}}\right\}$$

The frenet4D variable is defined as follows:

```
frenet4D =
  Graphics4D[{ AbsolutePointSize[20], Point[P0],
  Red, Arrow[{P0, P0 + 2.5 TT}], Green, Arrow[{P0, P0 + 2.5 NN}],
  Cyan, Arrow[{P0, P0 + 2.5 BB2}], Blue, Arrow[{P0, P0 + 2.5 BB1}],
  ViewPoint -> {-0.8677623819257761, 3.0335880200886844,
  1.2224288007442063},
  ViewVertical -> {-0.12496031476425706, 0.2964760771820533,
  0.9468298978130967} }];
```

The following sentences allow us to obtain the graph of the hypersurface $f(x, y, z, w) = x^2 + y^2 + z^2 + w^2 - 2 = 0$.

```
S1 = ImplicitPlot4D[
  f[x, y, z, w] == 0, {x, 0.30, 1.2}, {y, -0.75, 0.75}, {z, 0.30,
  1.2}, {w, -0.75, 0.75}, Red];
Show[S1, frenet4D]
```

See Fig. 3 (top-left).

The following sentences allow us to obtain the graph of the hypersurface $g(x, y, z, w) = 2xyz - w(x^2 - y^2) = 0$.

```
S2 = ImplicitPlot4D[
  g[x, y, z, w] == 0, {x, 0.30, 1.2}, {y, -0.75, 0.75}, {z, 0.30,
  1.2}, {w, -0.75, 0.75}, Green]
```

See Fig. 3 (top-right).

The following sentences allow us to obtain the graph of the hypersurface $h(x, y, z, w) = (xw + yz)^2 + (xz - yw)^2 - 1 = 0$.

```
S3 = ImplicitPlot4D[
  h[x, y, z, w] == 0, {x, 0.30, 1.2}, {y, -0.75, 0.75}, {z, 0.30,
  1.2}, {w, -0.75, 0.75}, Cyan]
```

See Fig. 3 (bottom-left).

The following sentences allow us to obtain the graphs in the orthonormal frame $\{t, n, b_1, b_2\}$ at the point P0 $= \{1, 0, 1, 1\}$, the red vector represents the unit tangent vector, the green vector represents the unit normal vector, the blue vector represents the unit vector b_1 and the celestial vector represents the unit vector b_2 of the intersection curve of the hypersurfaces f, g and h.

```
Show[S1, S2, S3, frenet4D]
```

See Fig. 3 (bottom-right).

Example 4. Consider the intersection of the three implicit hypersurfaces given by $f(x, y, z, w) = x^2 + y^2 + z^2 + w^2 - 1 = 0, h(x, y, z, w) = x^2 + y^2 + z^2 - w^2 - 1 = 0$ and $g(x, y, z, w) = x^2 + y^2 - x = 0$ and we calculate the Frenet frame $\{t, n, b_1, b_2\}$ along of the intersection curve α, as well as $\kappa_1(s)$, $\kappa_2(s)$ and $\kappa_3(s)$ are the first, second and third curvetures of $\alpha(s)$ at the point P0 $= \{1, 0, 0, 0\}$.

First we define the hypersurfaces f, g and h

```
f[x_, y_, z_, w_] := x^2 + y^2 + z^2 + w^2 - 1
h[x_, y_, z_, w_] := x^2 + y^2 + z^2 - w^2 - 1
g[x_, y_, z_, w_] := x^2 + y^2 - x
P0 = {1, 0, 0, 0};
```

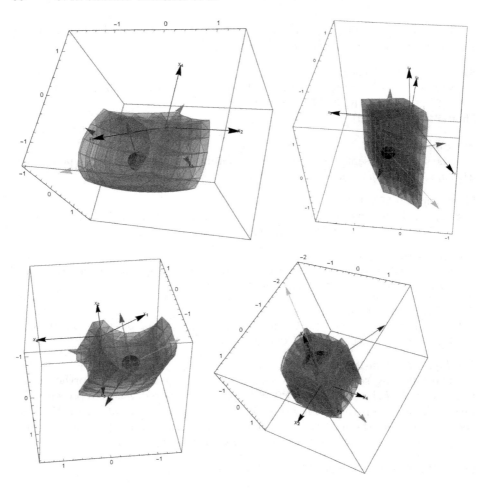

Fig. 3. Hypersurfaces $f(x, y, z, w) = 0$ (top-left), $g(x, y, z, w) = 0$ (top-right), $h(x, y, z, w) = 0$ (bottom-left) and graphical visualization of $f(x, y, z, w) = 0 \bigcap g(x, y, z, w) = 0 \bigcap h(x, y, z, w) = 0$ at the point P0 $= \{1, 0, 1, 1\}$ (bottom-right)

Frenet4DForImplicit returns the Frenet frame $\{t, n, b_1, b_2\}$ along α, as well as $\kappa_1(s)$, $\kappa_2(s)$ and $\kappa_3(s)$ are the first, second and third curvetures of $\alpha(s)$ at the point P0 $= \{1, 0, 0, 0\}$.

```
{TT, NN, BB1, BB2, k1, k2, k3} = Frenet4DForImplicit[{
    f[x,y,z,w] == 0, g[x,y,z,w] == 0, h[x,y,z,w] == 0 }, {x,y,z,w},
    Point -> P0]
```

$$\left\{ \left\{ 0, \frac{1}{\sqrt{2}}, \frac{1}{\sqrt{2}}, 0 \right\}, \{-1, 0, 0, 0\}, \left\{ 0, -\frac{1}{\sqrt{2}}, \frac{1}{\sqrt{2}}, 0 \right\}, \{0, 0, 0, 1\}, 1, \frac{3}{4}, 0 \right\}$$

The frenet4D variable is defined as follows:

```
frenet4D =
  Graphics4D[{ AbsolutePointSize[20], Point[P0],
  Red, Arrow[{P0, P0 + 1.5 TT}], Green, Arrow[{P0, P0 + 2.5 NN}],
  Cyan, Arrow[{P0, P0 + 1.5 BB2}], Blue, Arrow[{P0, P0 + 1.5 BB1}],
  ViewPoint -> {-0.8677623819257761, 3.0335880200886844,
  1.2224288007442063},
  ViewVertical -> {-0.12496031476425706, 0.2964760771820533,
  0.9468298978130967} }];
```

The following sentences allow us to obtain the graph of the hypersurface $f(x, y, z, w) = x^2 + y^2 + z^2 + w^2 - 1 = 0$.

```
S1 = ImplicitPlot4D[
  f[x, y, z, w] == 0, {x, 0.75, 1.5}, {y, -0.35, 0.75}, {z, -0.35,
  0.75}, {w, -0.35, 0.75}, Red];
Show[S1, frenet4D]
```

See Fig. 4 (top-left).
The following sentences allow us to obtain the graph of the hypersurface $g(x, y, z, w) = x^2 + y^2 + z^2 - w^2 - 1 = 0$.

```
S2 = ImplicitPlot4D[
  g[x, y, z, w] == 0, {x, 0.75, 1.5}, {y, -0.35, 0.75}, {z, -0.35,
  0.75}, {w, -0.35, 0.75}, Green]
```

See Fig. 4 (top-right).
The following sentences allow us to obtain the graph of the hypersurface $h(x, y, z, w) = x^2 + y^2 - x = 0$.

```
S3 = ImplicitPlot4D[
  h[x, y, z, w] == 0, {x, 0.75, 1.5}, {y, -0.35, 0.75}, {z, -0.35,
  0.75}, {w, -0.35, 0.75}, Cyan]
```

See Fig. 4 (bottom-left).
The following sentences allow us to obtain the graphs in the orthonormal frame $\{t, n, b_1, b_2\}$ at the point P0 $= \{1, 0, 0, 1\}$, the red vector represents the unit tangent vector, the green vector represents the unit normal vector, the blue vector represents the unit vector b_1 and the celestial vector represents the unit vector b_2 of the intersection curve of the hypersurfaces f, g and h.

```
Show[S1, S2, S3, frenet4D]
```

See Fig. 4 (bottom-right).

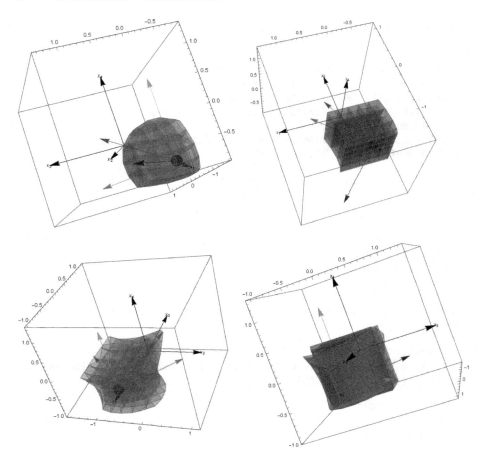

Fig. 4. Hypersurfaces $f(x, y, z, w) = 0$ (top-left), $g(x, y, z, w) = 0$ (top-right), $h(x, y, z, w) = 0$ (bottom-left) and graphical visualization of $f(x, y, z, w) = 0 \bigcap g(x, y, z, w) = 0 \bigcap h(x, y, z, w) = 0$ at the point P0 $= \{1, 0, 1, 1\}$ (bottom-right)

4   Conclusions

This paper proposes a new Mathematica package to calculate the properties of differential geometry of the curves given by the intersection between three implicit hypersurfaces in $\mathbb{R}^4$, according to the results obtained in [2, 6, 7, 9, 11, 13] and as a continuation of [3–5, 14] whose results coincide with those found in this work. The performance of the package is analyzed using two illustrative and interesting examples. All commands have been implemented in Mathematica and are consistent with the Mathematica notation and results [1, 10, 12]. The program is shorter and more efficient in my experience.

References

1. Anto, L.A., Fiestas, A.M., Ojeda, E.J., Velezmoro, R., Ipanaqué, R.: A mathematica package for plotting implicitly defined hypersurfaces in $\mathbb{R}^4$. In: Gervasi, O., et al. (eds.) ICCSA 2020. LNCS, vol. 12250, pp. 117–129. Springer, Cham (2020). https://doi.org/10.1007/978-3-030-58802-1_9
2. Badr, S.A.-N., Abdel-All, N.H., Aléssio, O., Düldül, M., Düldül, B.: Non-transversal intersection curves of hypersurfaces in Euclidean 4-space. J. Comput. Appl. Math. **288**, 81–98 (2015)
3. Burgos, G., Jiménez, J., Ascate, Y.: Frenet Serret apparatus calculation of curves given by the intersection of two implicit surfaces in $\mathbb{R}^3$ using Wolfram Mathematica v. 11.2. Sel. Matemáticas **6**(2), 338–347 (2019)
4. Jiménez, J.: Calculation of the differential geometry properties of implicit parametric surfaces intersection. Revista Científica Pakamuros **8**(1), 69–79 (2020)
5. Jiménez-Vilcherrez, J.K.: Calculation of the differential geometry properties of implicit parametric surfaces intersection. In: Gervasi, O., Murgante, B., Misra, S., Garau, C., Blečić, I., Taniar, D., Apduhan, B.O., Rocha, A.M.A.C., Tarantino, E., Torre, C.M., Karaca, Y. (eds.) ICCSA 2020. LNCS, vol. 12251, pp. 383–394. Springer, Cham (2020). https://doi.org/10.1007/978-3-030-58808-3_28
6. Aléssio, O., Düldül, M., Düldül, B.U., Badr, S.A.-N., Abdel-All, N.H.: Differential geometry of non-transversal intersection curves of three parametric hypersurfaces in Euclidean 4-space. Comput. Aided Geom. Des. **31**(9), 712–727 (2014)
7. Aléssio, O.: Differential geometry of intersection curves in R4 of three implicit surface. Comput. Aided Geom. Des. **26**(4), 455–471 (2009)
8. Patrikalakis, N.M., Maekawa, T.: Shape Interrogation for Computer Aided Design and Manufacturing, 1st edn. Springer, Heidelberg (2009). https://doi.org/10.1007/978-3-642-04074-0
9. Seok, H., Tae-wan, K., Cesare, B.: Comprehensive study of intersection curves in R4 based on the system of ODEs. J. Comput. Appl. Math. **256**, 121–130 (2014)
10. Torrence, B.F., Torrence, E.A.: The Student's Introduction to Mathematica and the Wolfram Language, 3rd edn. Cambridge University Press, Cambridge (2019)
11. Uyar Düldül, B., Düldül, M.: The extension of Willmore's method into 4-space. Math. Commun. **17**(2), 423–431 (2012)
12. Velezmoro, R., Ipanaqué, R., Mechato, J.A.: A mathematica package for visualizing objects Inmersed in $\mathbb{R}^4$. In: Misra, S., et al. (eds.) ICCSA 2019. LNCS, vol. 11624, pp. 479–493. Springer, Cham (2019). https://doi.org/10.1007/978-3-030-24311-1_35
13. Williams, M.Z., Stein, F.M.: A triple product of vectors in four-space. Math. Mag. **37**(4), 230–235 (1964)
14. Xiuzi, Y., Takashi, M.: Differential geometry of intersection curves of two surfaces. Comput. Aided Geom. Des. **16**(8), 767–788 (1999)

International Workshop on Collaborative Intelligence in Multimodal Applications (CIMA 2021)

Comparable Study of Pre-trained Model on Alzheimer Disease Classification

Modupe Odusami[1](✉), Rytis Maskeliunas[1], Robertas Damaševičius[2], and Sanjay Misra[3]

[1] Department of Multimedia Engineering, Kaunas University of Technology, Kaunas, Lithuania
modupe.odusami@ktu.edu, rytis.maskeliunas@ktu.lt
[2] Department of Applied Informatics, Vytautas Magnus University, Kaunas, Lithuania
robertas.damasevicius@vdu.lt
[3] Department of Electrical and Information Engineering, Covenant University, Ota, Nigeria
sanjay.misra@covenantuniversity.edu.ng

Abstract. The Alzheimer's disease (AD) is a type of dementia that affects millions of people worldwide every year and the occurrence will continue to be on the increase. The move to diagnose people suffering from AD at an earlier stage has been a daunting problem in mental health. In recent years, the advancement of deep learning in the likes of convolutional neural networks (CNN) has made a great effort towards an early detection of AD using magnetic resonance imaging (MRI) data. However, due to the need for highly discriminative features from MR images, it is still challenging to accurately use CNNs by training from scratch for early detection of AD. This paper aims to improve the early detection of Alzheimer's disease using deep learning for neuroimaging data. We have utilized the SqueezeNet, ResNet18, AlexNet, Vgg11, DenseNet, and InceptionV3 pre-trained models to automatically classify MR images. To validate our model, we experimented with the MR images obtained from the Open Access Series of Imaging Studies (OASIS) database. The average classification accuracy derived by SqueezeNet model for training and testing was 99.38% and 82.53% for binary class and multiclass, respectively.

Keywords: Alzheimer disease · CNN · Dementia · MR imaging · Transfer learning

1 Introduction

An irreversible progressive neurodegenerative disorder, called Alzheimer's Disease (AD), gradually destroys memory and induces complications in communication and carrying out daily activities such as speaking and walking [1]. Also, the progression of this disease slowly hips to an outspread loss of mental function such as memory defect, language impairment, disorientation, and personality change, eventually leading to death [2]. This disease is, currently, the paramount cause of neurodegenerative dementia in the world with an estimate of 131 million people projected to be living with dementia by 2050 [2]. The generic spread of AD represents a threat to healthcare and social systems

© Springer Nature Switzerland AG 2021
O. Gervasi et al. (Eds.): ICCSA 2021, LNCS 12953, pp. 63–74, 2021.
https://doi.org/10.1007/978-3-030-86976-2_5

[3], and even the drug to prevent or slow down cognitive decline in AD remains an unmet therapeutic need [4]. Thus, early, and accurate diagnosis of AD is of paramount need.

Therefore, accurate diagnosis of AD at the early stages based on the measurements of effective biomarkers can provide tangible information to assist researchers and clinicians develop a new treatment. A popular approach that is long-established in the diagnosis of AD is the neuroimaging techniques which are non-invasive and offer sufficient information for identifying abnormalities in the brain. Recently, several neuroimaging modalities, including structural Magnetic resonance imaging (sMRI) [5–7], functional magnetic resonance imaging (fMRI) [8–10], fluorodeoxyglucose positron emission tomography (FDG- PET) imaging [11, 12], amyloid positron emission tomography (PET), resting state- fMRI (rs-fMRI), and Diffusion tensor imaging (DTI) have been successfully utilized for AD diagnosis. However, some existing studies have successfully utilized a single modality to help to determine the onset of AD. For early diagnosis of AD, the most discriminating AD-related brain region based on MRI analysis includes the Cortical, Sub-cortical, and Hippocampus subfield [13–16]. For fMRI, some features such as Occipital_Mid_R, Precentral_L, Caudate_R, Postcentral_L, Temporal_Pole_Mid_L, Frontal_Inf_Oper_L, and Precuneus_L are highlighted in the discrimination of MCI and NCs [17–19]. As for FDG- PET, the average relative Cerebral glucose metabolic rate in the Precuneus, Superior Temporal gyrus in both hemispheres, Middle Frontal gyrus and superior frontal gyrus, middle cingulate cortex, and the angular gyrus in the left hemisphere [20, 21].

In recent years, several studies based on deep learning have focused on the analysis of MRI and showed that quantitative assessment of hippocampal atrophy via volumetric analysis can be utilized as a biomarker for AD [22–24]. In [25], a multi-task deep CNN model was proposed for hippocampus segmentation and hippocampus volumes based on the centroid of segmentation were computed for AD classification. An optimization technique was also proposed to measure hippocampus volume [26]. Hippocampal shape and intensity provide information that is independent of hippocampal volume [28]. In [29], the intensity and shape features on the decomposed image patches of the internal and external hippocampus are extracted for AD recognition.

Quite a few deep learning approaches have been successfully used to extract features from the hippocampus via different observations such as patched-based, voxel-based, and region-of-interest (ROI)-based. For instance, local patches, which are assembled into 2.5 dimensions, are extracted from MRI images [25]. Multi-task CNN learned features and extracted 3D patch covering the hippocampus based on the centroid of segmentation mask are passed as input to the 3D DenseNet model to learn more relevant features [26]. While most of the existing studies have focused on the use of CNN models by training from scratch [27–30]. However, training a model from scratch requires a large amount of dataset and consumes more time. The availability of pretrained models trained on large, labeled datasets such as ImageNet offer accurate learning models for deep feature representation. This approach that allows a pretrained network to be used as the starting point for a model on a second task is transfer learning. For example, authors in [31] utilized three pre-trained models to demonstrate the effectiveness of transfer learning to classify AD by updating all three model parameters. Here we present a comparative analysis of the effectiveness and sensitivity of different pre-trained models to classify

AD from MRI data. Open Access Series of Imaging Studies (OASIS) database of MRI scans of patients is used for the classification.

The contributions of this paper are summarized as follows:

- A new AD classification model based on deep transfer learning using whole-brain MR images for the classification of AD in the absence of preprocessing of the MR images with high accuracy is presented.
- The study focused on the detailed evaluation of binary (dementia or non-dementia) and multiclass (dementia or non-dementia or mild dementia) classification.
- The study compares the performance of different pretrained models such as AlexNet, Squuezenet, Inceptionv3, Resnet18, VGG16, DenseNet121 by applying a transfer learning method based on feature extraction.

The remaining paper is organized as follows: Sect. 2 includes a detailed literature survey of existing solutions. Section 3 describes the proposed method with an explicit explanation of transfer learning. The implementation details and the results obtained from our proposed method are presented in Sect. 4. Section 5 concludes the paper with future recommendations.

2   Related Works

The application of CNNs in classifying medical images has been a great success in the health care sector. However, training these models from scratch often needs a large amount of data. Therefore, the ImageNet dataset, consisting of millions of images has been used to train some CNN architectures, and this enables these models to utilize existing knowledge to know what to transfer, when to transfer, and how to transfer. The transfer learning performs some type of feature extraction scheme by training new layers after re-used layers to interpret their output. A good feature representation of the brain is identified at a reduced error rate and can allow a better prediction of AD patterns. The application of pre-trained CNN in different problems related to neuroimaging analysis has gained strength [32, 33]. For example, Authors in [34] utilized an end-to-end deep 3D CNN for the multiclass AD biomarker identification task, using the whole image volume from MRI. The study compared the performance of four pre-trained models and the best accuracy of 75.9% was obtained with the VGG network. The authors recommended the investigation of explainable techniques to understand brain regions involved in classification decisions. Authors in [35] presented a Siamese Vgg-16 model to classify dementia stages using a publicly available dataset open access series of imaging studies (OASIS) for evaluation. Authors in [36] presented a deep learning algorithm method using inception v3 CNN for detection of AD from ADNI data set. The proposed study considered the brain as a pixel-by-pixel volume in its classification. An efficient transfer learning architecture based on Pre-trained Alexnet was utilized to extract deep features in AD stage detection [38]. Authors in [39] proposed an efficient AD classification technique by fine-tuning a pre-trained AlexNet CNN model. The model was trained and tested for both binary and multiclass classification over the OASIS dataset. Authors in [38] investigated the use of transfer learning in the diagnosis of AD by exploring layer-wise transfer learning on CNN architecture. The required information for AD diagnosis was extracted from MRI slices. Comparative performance analysis of three pre-trained models which include (AlexNet, GoogleNet, and ResNet50 were further performed using MR images from the OASIS database [40].

3   Experiments and Results

In this study, we have compared the performance of AlexNet, Vgg-16, Inceptionv3, Resnet50, DenseNet121, and SqueezeNet networks in classifying MRI brain images into No Dementia, Mild Dementia, and Dementia as using Open Access Series of Imaging Studies (OASIS) database. The workflow for this study is depicted in Fig. 1.

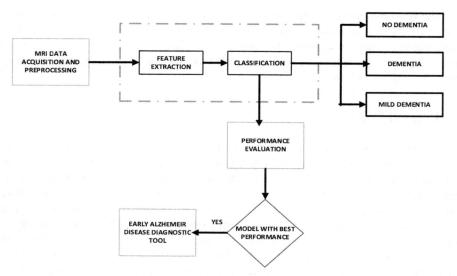

Fig. 1. Workflow used in this study

3.1   OASIS Dataset Description

The released data for the OASIS-3 dataset was utilized. The dataset consists of T1-weighted MRI of subjects with AD obtained from older adults between the age of 60 to 96 years. The subjects consist of 62 men and 88 women. Each image has a different number of slices, and a total of 1,566 slices for both non-dementia, mild dementia, and dementia were extracted. Figure 2 shows some examples of the slices that constitute the dataset used in this study. The first row corresponds to images with no dementia, the second row corresponds to images with dementia, and the third row corresponds to images with mild dementia.

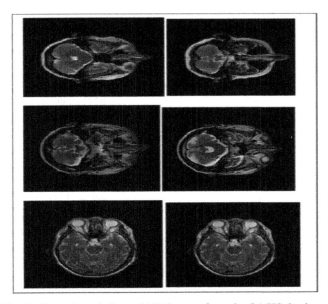

Fig. 2. Examples of slices of MR images from the OASIS database.

3.2 Experimental Setup

The base of CNN architectures are the convolutional and pooling layers, and the classifier consists of a couple of fully connected layers. We have reshaped the last fully connected layer of some of the pre-trained networks to have the same number of inputs as it was initialized and contains the same number of outputs as the number of classes in the dataset. For the training process, the stochastic gradient descent (SGD) optimization method was utilized to determine how to update the weights during training on the OASIS dataset for both binary and multiclass classification. Weight decay of 0.01 for L2 regularization was utilized through the optimizer. For each of the pretrained networks, various learning rates between 0.001 and 0.009 were tested, and a learning rate of 0.004 was utilized to train the pre-trained model. We have only trained the models for not more than 10 epochs and keeping the batch size at 8. This experiment was performed 5 times for each of the models to achieve the average classification accuracy of the model on different learning rates. The evaluation process for the OASIS dataset is conducted by using hold out. For the training (70%) and validation (20%) sets. The training dataset consists of 429 No Dementia, 390 Dementia, and 286 Mild Dementia. The validation data consist of 469. A data augmentation technique was implemented to increase the training samples. We have used PyTorch deep learning framework with anaconda for (Python 2.7; Python Software Foundation) to implement all pre-trained models because it easily offers transfer learning. All the models were trained on a single NVIDIA GPU. Table 1 shows the composition of the feature extraction layer of the pre-trained CNN models.

Table 1. Description of pretrained CNN models used in this study

Pretrained CNN model	Reshape layer for feature extraction	Composition of the reshape layer
Resnet18	Last layer (fully connected layer)	(fc): Linear (512 input layers, 1000 input layers, bias= **True**)
Alexnet	6th layer	**(6):** Linear (4096 input / 1000 output features, bias = True)
Vgg 16 with batch normalization	6th layer	(6): Linear (4096 input / 1000 output features, bias = True)
Squeeze net	1st layer (1x1 convolutional layer)	(1): Conv2d (512, 1000, kernel_ size = (1, 1), stride = (1, 1))
Densenet 121	Classifier layer	(classifier): Linear (1024 input / 1000 output features, bias = True
Inception v3	Two output Layers	(fc): Linear (768 input / 1000 output features, bias= **True**) (fc): Linear (2048 input / 1000 output features, bias= **True**)

3.3 Performance Evaluation

Three metric measurements which include accuracy, sensitivity (recall), specificity, and precision were used to evaluate the classification performance of pre-trained CNN models depicted in Table 1. The binary and multiclass classification will pro-duce four outcomes which include True positive (TP), True negative (TN), False Negative (TN), and False Negative (FN), all terms are from the confusion matrix.

4   Results and Discussion

In this study, we evaluated the performance of different pre-trained models such as AlexNet, Vgg-16, Inceptionv3, Resnet50, DenseNet121, and squeezeNet using MRI imaging dataset from the OASIS database to identify the best classifier using 70% training samples and 30% for validation. Tables 2 and 3 show the performance obtained for each of the pre-trained CNN models during training and validation for binary classification and multiclass classification, respectively. These results show that squeeze net gave the best performance with 99.38% accuracy for binary classification and 82.53% accuracy for multiclass classification on the validation dataset. This could be explained because the first convolution layer of the classifier extracts deep image features that the final classification layer uses to classify the input image. Additionally, we noted that Inception v3 gave the least performance of 90.99% accuracy for binary class classification while ResNet 18 gave the least performance of 67.51% for multiclass classification. All these results obtained from the binary classification corroborates the results reported by [30] where the results of the pre-trained deep learning models show the effectiveness of pre-trained models in AD classification. Figure 3. shows a graph that outlines

Table 2. Binary classification performance comparison of different pre-trained CNN models based on accuracy for training and validation

CNN pretrained model	Validation accuracy	Training accuracy
Resnet18	94.81%	96.86%
Alexnet	94.14%	95.98%
Vgg 16 with batch normalization	95.68%	99.36%
Squeeze net	99.38%	99.41%
Densenet 121	95.02%	98.28%
Inception v3	90.99%	92.32%

Table 3. Multiclass classification performance comparison of different pre-trained CNN Models based on accuracy for training and validation

CNN pretrained model	Validation accuracy	Training accuracy
Resnet18	67.51%	70.42%
Alexnet	72.15%	75.76%
Vgg 16 with batch normalization	67.68%	73.04%
Squeeze net	82.53%	86.40%
Densenet 121	67.72%	67.31%
Inception v3	76.30%	77.3%

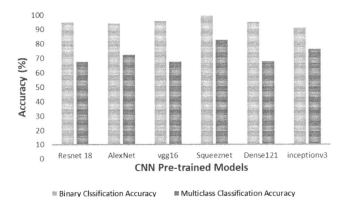

Fig. 3. Comparative results of various CNN models with binary and multiclass classification

the performance of the pre-trained networks against the number of classes utilized for classification.

The results from Tables 2 and 3 reveal that classification performance of the selected pre-trained models is affected by the number of predicted classes. The accuracy for multiclass classification is lower than the accuracy for the binary class. This could be an account of certain reasons. First, the data set may contain not enough variation. Second, the performance of each model might also be related to the mild changes in the structures between patients with no dementia and mild dementia. Hence, it is difficult for the models to extract informative features that distinctly separate three classes. Tables 4 and 5 show classification performance from each of the pre-trained CNN models during validation for binary and multiclass classification.

Table 4. Binary class classification performance of pretrained model during validation

CNN pretrained model	Specificity	Sensitivity	Precision
Resnet18	97.26%	90.50%	97.00%
Alexnet	97.48%	90.72%	97.36%
Vgg16 with batch normalization	97.92%	93.40%	97.80%
SqueezeNet	99.89%	98.88%	99.88%
Densenet121	91.80%	96.08%	91.97%
Inceptionv3	92.24%	89.72%	91.94%

Table 5. Multiclass class classification performance of pretrained model during validation

CNN pretrained model	Specificity	Sensitivity	Precision
Resnet18	87.81	74.75	77.50
Alexnet	89.59	77.86	79.03
Vgg16 with batch normalization	87.85	74.59	75.62
SqueezeNet	90.07	80.33	83.42
Densenet121	89.35	77.20	77.88
Inception 3	86.99	72.97	80.97

From Tables 4 and 5, SqueezeNet is showing the best classification performance with 99.89% specificity and 98.88% sensitivity for binary classification likewise a specificity of 90.07% and 80.33 sensitivity for multiclass classification. High specificity and sensitivity can guarantee high true positive and true negative rates, respectively. And as regards neurodegenerative diseases it is of a high preferential to have a high sensitivity for all patients with AD to be effectively and accurately identified early. The current experimental results have shown a good view in terms of classification accuracy, and sensitivity when compared the results with existing classification experiments for binary and multiclass classification, especially squeeze net with 99.38% and 82.53 accuracies for binary and multiclass, respectively. To further show the performance of the pre-trained models on the OASIS data set. Figure 4. shows the per-class classification performance for sensitivity.

From Fig. 4, the performance comparison of per-class classification results of the pre-trained models has demonstrated outstanding performance for accurately positively classifying dementia in the case of squeeze net and inception with 96.74% and 91.86% respectively. The poor performance of the pre-trained models for positively classifying mild dementia could be due to the close brain changes between dementia and mild dementia as the two classes are both associated with reduced cortical thickness and surface area in the brain regions [41].

We can conclude from Tables 5 and Table 6 that SqueezeNet is a strong pre-trained model for MR image classification. SqueezeNet produced the best training and validation accuracy among other models. The second highest accuracies were obtained by VGG16 and Inceptionv3 for binary classification and multiclass classification, respectively.

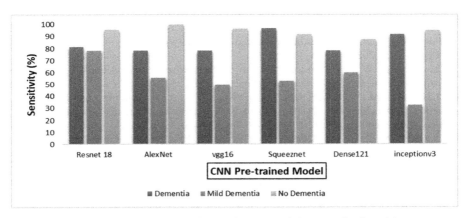

Fig. 4. Per class classification performance of the pre-trained models

5   Conclusion

Early detection of Alzheimer's disease remains a challenge, and deep learning classification has intrigued researchers due to its flexibility and ability to generate optimal findings. The availability of pre-trained models trained on big, labeled datasets like imageNet allows for reliable deep feature representation learning models.

Therefore, comparative analysis and evaluation of different pre-trained CNN architectures is presented in this study. We utilized transfer learning with a feature extraction approach using various CNN models which include DenseNet121, ResNet18, AlexNet, vgg16, SqueezeNet, and Inceptionv3 for accurate classification of MR images between three different classes, namely Dementia, No Dementia, and Mild Dementia. Analysis of the model was carried out by changing the learning rate and optimal performance was archived at 0.004 and 0.005 for binary and multiclass classification, respectively. The models had been well-trained for our OASIS dataset, and they were all effective at classification. SqueezeNet produced the highest validation accuracy of 99.38% and

82.53%. Hence, transfer learning as feature extraction using SqueezeNet is an effective technique to classify MR images into Dementia, Mild Dementia, and No Dementia.

In future, a visualization method could be added to the SqueezeNet to enhance the classification accuracy of multiclass classification.

References

1. Ebrahimighahnavieh, M.A., Luo, S., Chiong, R.: Deep learning to detect Alzheimer's disease from neuroimaging: a systematic literature review. Comput. Methods Programs Biomed. **187**, 105242 (2020)
2. Shao, W., Peng, Y., Zu, C., Wang, M., Zhang, D.: Alzheimer's disease neuroimaging initiative: hypergraph-based multi-task feature selection for multimodal classification of Alzheimer's disease. Comput. Med. Imaging Graphics **80**, 101663 (2020)
3. Battista, P., Salvatore, C., Berlingeri, M., Cerasa, A., Castiglioni, I.: Artificial intelligence and neuropsychological measures: the case of Alzheimer's disease. Neurosci. Biobehav. Rev. **114**, 211–228 (2020)
4. Zhou, K., He, W., Xu, Y., Xiong, G., Cai, J.: Feature selection and transfer learning for Alzheimer's disease clinical diagnosis. Appl. Sci. **8**(8), 1372 (2018)
5. Li, H., Habes, M., Wolk, D.A., Fan, Y., Initiative, A.D.N.: A deep learning model for early prediction of Alzheimer's disease dementia based on hippocampal magnetic resonance imaging data. Alzheimers Dement. **15**(8), 1059–1070 (2019)
6. Ke, Q., Zhang, J., Wei, W., Damaševičius, R., Woźniak, M.: Adaptive independent subspace analysis of brain magnetic resonance imaging data. IEEE Access **7**, 12252–12261 (2019). https://doi.org/10.1109/ACCESS.2019.2893496
7. Chandra, A., Dervenoulas, G., Politis, M., Initiative, A.D.N.: Magnetic resonance imaging in Alzheimer's disease and mild cognitive impairment. J. Neurol. **266**(6), 1293–1302 (2019)
8. Holiga, S., Abdulkadir, A., Klöppel, S., Dukart, J.: Functional magnetic resonance imaging in alzheimer' disease drug development. In: Perneczky, R. (ed.) Biomarkers for Alzheimer's Disease Drug Development, pp. 159–163. Springer New York, New York, NY (2018). https://doi.org/10.1007/978-1-4939-7704-8_10
9. Forouzannezhad, P., et al.: A survey on applications and analysis methods of functional magnetic resonance imaging for Alzheimer's disease. J. Neurosci. Methods **317**, 121–140 (2019)
10. Zhao, J., Du, Y.H., Ding, X.T., Wang, X.H., Men, G.Z.: Alteration of functional connectivity in patients with Alzheimer's disease revealed by resting-state functional magnetic resonance imaging. Neural Regen. Res. **15**(2), 285 (2020)
11. Ossenkoppele, R., et al.: Discriminative accuracy of [18F] flortaucipir positron emission tomography for Alzheimer disease vs other neurodegenerative disorders. JAMA **320**(11), 1151–1162 (2018)
12. Guo, J., Qiu, W., Li, X., Zhao, X., Guo, N., Li, Q.: Predicting Alzheimer's disease by hierarchical graph convolution from positron emission tomography imaging. In: 2019 IEEE International Conference on Big Data (Big Data), pp. 5359–5363. IEEE (2019)
13. Amoroso, N., et al.: Alzheimer's disease diagnosis based on the hippocampal unified multi-atlas network (HUMAN) algorithm. Biomed. Eng. Online **17**(1), 6 (2018)
14. Lian, C., Liu, M., Zhang, J., Shen, D.: Hierarchical fully convolutional network for joint atrophy localization and Alzheimer's Disease diagnosis using structural MRI. IEEE Trans. Pattern Anal. Mach. Intell. (2018)

15. Gupta, Y., Lee, K.H., Choi, K.Y., Lee, J.J., Kim, B.C., Kwon, G.R.: Early diagnosis of Alzheimer's disease using combined features from voxel-based morphometry and cortical, subcortical, and hippocampus regions of MRI T1 brain images. PloS one. **14**(10), e0222446 (2019)
16. Toshkhujaev, S., et al.: Classification of Alzheimer's disease and mild cognitive impairment based on cortical and subcortical features from MRI T1 brain images utilizing four different types of datasets. J. Healthcare Eng. (2020)
17. Bi, X.A., Jiang, Q., Sun, Q., Shu, Q., Liu, Y.: Analysis of Alzheimer's disease based on the random neural network cluster in fMRI. Front. Neuroinform. **12**, 60 (2018)
18. Hojjati, S.H., Ebrahimzadeh, A., Khazaee, A., Babajani-Feremi, A., Initiative, A.D.N.: Predicting conversion from MCI to AD by integrating RS-fMRI and structural MRI. Comput. Biol. Med. **102**, 30–39 (2018)
19. Wang, Y., Li, C.: Functional magnetic resonance imaging classification based on random forest algorithm in Alzheimer's disease. In: 2019 International Conference on Image and Video Processing, and Artificial Intelligence, Vol. 11321, p. 1132104. International Society for Optics and Photonics (2019)
20. Marchitelli, R., et al.: Simultaneous resting-state FDG-PET/fMRI in Alzheimer disease: relationship between glucose metabolism and intrinsic activity. Neuroimage **176**, 246–258 (2018)
21. Chen, D., et al.: Brain network and abnormal hemispheric asymmetry analyses to explore the marginal differences in glucose metabolic distributions among Alzheimer's disease, Parkinson's disease dementia, and Lewy body dementia. Front. Neurol. **10**, 369 (2019)
22. Uysal, G., Ozturk, M.: Hippocampal atrophy based Alzheimer's disease diagnosis via machine learning methods. J. Neurosci. Methods **337**, 108669 (2020)
23. Duan, Y., Lin, Y., Rosen, D., Du, J., He, L., Wang, Y.: Identifying morphological patterns of hippocampal atrophy in patients with mesial temporal lobe epilepsy and Alzheimer disease. Front. Neurol. **11**, 21 (2020)
24. Falgàs, N., et al.: Hippocampal atrophy has limited usefulness as a diagnostic biomarker on the early onset Alzheimer's disease patients: a comparison between visual and quantitative assessment. NeuroImage. Clin. **23**, 101927 (2019)
25. Li, F., Liu, M., Initiative, A.D.N.: A hybrid convolutional and recurrent neural network for hippocampus analysis in Alzheimer's disease. J. Neurosci. Methods **323**, 108–118 (2019)
26. Chitradevi, D., Prabha, S.: Analysis of brain sub regions using optimization techniques and deep learning method in Alzheimer disease. Appl. Soft Comput. **86**, 105857 (2020)
27. Islam, J., Zhang, Y.: Brain MRI analysis for Alzheimer's disease diagnosis using an ensemble system of deep convolutional neural networks. Brain Inf. **5**(2), 1–14 (2018). https://doi.org/10.1186/s40708-018-0080-3
28. Liu, M., Cheng, D., Wang, K., Wang, Y.: Multi-modality cascaded convolutional neural networks for Alzheimer's disease diagnosis. Neuroinformatics **16**(3–4), 295–308 (2018)
29. Feng, C., et al.: Deep learning framework for Alzheimer's disease diagnosis via 3D-CNN and FSBi-LSTM. IEEE Access **7**, 63605–63618 (2019)
30. Xia, Z., et al.: A novel end-to-end hybrid network for Alzheimer's disease detection using 3D CNN and 3D CLSTM. In: 2020 IEEE 17th International Symposium on Biomedical Imaging (ISBI), pp. 1–4. IEEE (2020)
31. Prakash, D., Madusanka, N., Bhattacharjee, S., Park, H.G., Kim, C.H., Choi, H.K.: A comparative study of alzheimer's disease classification using multiple transfer learning models. J. Multimed. Inf. Syst. **6**(4), 209–216 (2019)
32. Levakov, G., Rosenthal, G., Shelef, I., Raviv, T.R., Avidan, G.: From a deep learning model back to the brain—Identifying regional predictors and their relation to aging. Hum. Brain Mapp. **41**(12), 3235–3252 (2020)

33. Wee, C.-Y., Liu, C., Lee, A., Poh, J.S., Ji, H., Qiu, A.: Cortical graph neural network for AD and MCI diagnosis and transfer learning across populations. NeuroImage Clin. **23**, 101929 (2019). https://doi.org/10.1016/j.nicl.2019.101929
34. Folego, G., Weiler, M., Casseb, R.F., Pires, R., Rocha, A.: Alzheimer's disease detection through whole-brain 3D-CNN MRI. Front. Bioeng. Biotechnol. **8**, 1–14 (2020)
35. Mehmood, A., Maqsood, M., Bashir, M., Shuyuan, Y.: A deep Siamese convolution neural network for multi-class classification of Alzheimer disease. Brain Sci. **10**(2), 84 (2020)
36. Ding, Y., et al.: A deep learning model to predict a diagnosis of Alzheimer disease by using 18F-FDG PET of the brain. Radiology **290**(2), 456–464 (2019)
37. Nawaz, H., Maqsood, M., Afzal, S., Aadil, F., Mehmood, I., Rho, S.: A deep feature-based real-time system for Alzheimer disease stage detection. Multimed. Tools App. 1-19 (2020). https://doi.org/10.1007/s11042-020-09087-y
38. Maqsood, M., et al.: Transfer learning assisted classification and detection of Alzheimer's disease stages using 3D MRI scans. Sensors **19**(11), 2645 (2019)
39. Khan, N.M., Abraham, N., Hon, M.: Transfer learning with intelligent training data selection for prediction of Alzheimer's disease. IEEE Access **7**, 72726–72735 (2019)
40. Khagi, B., Lee, B., Pyun, J.Y., Kwon, G.R.: CNN Models Performance Analysis on MRI images of OASIS dataset for distinction between Healthy and Alzheimer's patient. In: 2019 International Conference on Electronics, Information, and Communication (ICEIC), pp. 1–4. IEEE (2019)
41. Yang, H., et al.: Study of brain morphology change in Alzheimer's disease and amnestic mild cognitive impairment compared with normal controls. General Psychiatry **32**(2), e100005 (2019)

Evaluation of Indoor Localisation and Heart Rate Evolution

Iuliana Marin$^{(\boxtimes)}$ and Arthur-Jozsef Molnar

SC Info World SRL, Bucharest, Romania
{iuliana.marin,arthur.molnar}@infoworld.ro

Abstract. The number of older adults and their proportion within the general population are expected to increase in the upcoming decades. Decision makers have turned to technology in order to provide cost-mitigating solutions. Assisstive systems have been developed for many of the challenges that can be addressed through technology. However, we find most of them to have singular focus, using proprietary equipment and communication protocols which makes them difficult to integrate into a comprehensive system. Our work was carried out in the development phase of a cyber-physical platform that enables seamless integration of third party vendor devices and applications into a configurable, extensible and cost-effective technological platform for elderly care. The present paper targets the integration of commercial off the shelf components into a real-time indoor localization system, which allows monitoring the older adult's level of activity and detecting potentially dangerous situations automatically. We present the initial results of our comparative evaluation on the accuracy of localisation and heart rate monitoring of persons within an indoor setting. We briefly present the integrated cyber-physical system developed as part of the project. We use intelligent luminaires that act as location beacons and detail the results of an experiment where we evaluated the performance of two different luminaire types. While our previous experiments have shown that room-level localisation of a moving subject was possible using custom-developed luminaires, we extended our evaluation to cover a cost-effective, commercially available alternative. Real-time location data was combined with heart rate information recorded using a commercially available smartwatch in order to obtain a more complete picture of the monitored person's level of activity. Our initial results showed that existing technologies can be configured and integrated into a more complex platform, which remains customizable according to each end user's needs.

Keywords: Ambient assisted living · Cyber-physical system · Indoor positioning · Trilateration · Heart rate evolution

1 Introduction

Population aging is expected to bring important long-term societal and economic changes to the developed world. The number of adults over 60 is expected to

© Springer Nature Switzerland AG 2021
O. Gervasi et al. (Eds.): ICCSA 2021, LNCS 12953, pp. 75–89, 2021.
https://doi.org/10.1007/978-3-030-86976-2_6

double by 2050 [24]. This is expected to increase healthcare, local and central government expenditures for assistance and care programs. Authors of [16] have found annual health expenditure to increase by 4% per year, with important funds allocated toward the care for the older adult population. This is compounded by recent medical advances not translating into an improved quality of life for older adults [24], where more targeted approaches are beneficial.

Existing technology-based solutions for assisted living allow intelligent automation at home through monitoring and controlling physiological parameters and the surrounding environment [17]. Assistance for autonomy at home allows remote control of the house and facilitates independent living for older adults or those suffering from chronic or short-term disability [5].

The current paper describes an integrative cyber-physical platform that aims to automate the process of developing customized, interconnected assistance solutions for home autonomy and assisted living. For instance, the solution allows tracing the movement path of the monitored person and lays the groundwork for value adding functionalities such as monitoring the level of activity and behavioural patterns. Our proposed system facilitates the design and implementation of various monitoring and assistance scenarios through an integrative system that allows for easy configuration of component modules such as additional hardware elements, software modules and the required communication protocols.

The proposed system is relevant to the current social and economic context that stimulates the creation of a new market for cost-effective home care solutions. The proposed platform allows easy integration of monitoring solutions for both physiological and ambient parameters. Thus, it is a generic solution for implementing a wide and varied range of monitoring scenarios targeting older adults or people with mild physical or mental impairments. Through the proposed functionality, the system will realize a substantial reduction in the production costs of customized home help solutions, with a significant impact on their commercial availability and market penetration.

The aim of the current paper is to report on our initial evaluation regarding the accuracy of indoor localisation when using commercially available smart bulbs as signal beacons, integrated with heart rate monitoring that is carried out using a commercially-available smartwatch. We used off-the-shelf smart bulbs to replace our previously developed custom hardware elements [15] of the i-Light Eurostars project in order to assess whether lower deployment and maintenance costs can be attained without sacrificing room-level detection of a moving person. We detail relevant related work in Sect. 2, and provide a brief description of our proposed system in Sect. 3. Our experimental evaluation in a home setting is detailed in Sect. 4, where we employ a common location and methodology to compare our custom developed hardware elements with a commercial alternative. The evolution of the heart rate is analyzed during the same period of time when indoor localization is performed. Finally, Sect. 5 provides our conclusions and future work.

2   Related Work

In recent years, the monitoring of physiological and ambiental parameters have become topics of real interest both within the scientific community and the industry. The European Union has recognized the long-term challenges heralded by the current wave of societal and demographic changes, and created the Active and Assisted Living Programme [1] to foster the co-creation of commercially-viable solutions based on technology.

Health-centric monitoring systems usually include several components, and have to address issues related to inter-device data exchange, recording and processing signals from ambient sensors and those reporting physiological parameters, as well as data storage and retrieval. In addition, as data includes health and location components, data security and confidentiality are of utmost importance, with special requirements related to its processing and storage, such as the European Union's GDPR regulations.

Such systems must also provide a way to represent the monitored environment. Some solutions are built around a two-dimensional map [11,18], while others use three-dimensional models [9,23]. They are used as data sources from which information such as door locations, furniture and gas sources can be extracted. They are also employed for storing the installation location for beacons and other physical equipment required for accurate indoor localisation.

In addition to processing sensor data, a monitoring system has to integrate ubiquitous communication technologies that provide real-time health services matching the context and the end-user requirements [19]. The Internet of Things (IoT) and the paradigm shift towards a system of interconnected smart devices [3] can bring additional value, with sensor-enriched nodes that can be used to monitor vital signs and other biometric parameters, collect data and transmit them over a network of nodes.

Numerous assisting devices are currently available commercially, and include those for drug administration, fall detection, alarm buttons, monitoring of vital signs, as well as complex solutions for recording and tracking more environmental parameters [21]. In the context of the COVID-19 pandemic, smart clothing has been designed for elderly users in order to non-intrusively monitor their daily habits, health and well-being [20]. Older adults are known to be in the highest risk bracket with regards to COVID-19, with the mostly likely chronic underlying conditions of heart disease (34%), diabetes (17%) and lung disease (15%) [26].

In the same context, quarantine code tracker wristbands made from waterproof paper and based on QR codes were used in China to monitor personal quarantine compliance [22]. The QR code was read by a dedicated mobile phone application which asked the user to walk around her/his home to determine the house boundaries. Monitoring was carried out over 14 d. If the person wearing the wristband wanted to leave their home before quarantine completion, a warning sound was played by their associated mobile phone. The person had to return back home after at most 15 s and confirm their presence.

Solutions that integrate multiple devices into systems for active living have yet to see wide scale commercial adoption. Most of the integrative solutions developed so far are found in the form of prototypes described in the scientific literature [4, 8, 27]. The main barrier to building such solutions is that most of these devices come with proprietary applications, use custom communication protocols and do not expose programming interfaces, making them impossible to integrate into third-party applications.

Currently, development costs represent the main reason for the slow adoption of IoT-driven solutions for assisted living. Thus, the final price is greatly influenced by the complexity of designing and developing these systems and by the need to engage highly specialized human resources. Another important factor regards the absence of tooling that enables automating the design, development, implementation and installation procedures for such solutions.

The system for which we carry out the present evaluation aims to automate the development of home autonomy support solutions, provide an easy-to-use design and development environment, as well as the ability to reduce the time and cost of developing customized solutions for a wide range of scenarios. Our system was designed and is currently under development around international standards for inter-device communication. This allows the integration of a multitude of third-party commercially available devices from the health and home automation sectors, facilitates the transfer of data from third party proprietary systems into ours, achieving plug-and-play interoperability. We believe this will provide access to the continuously developing market of active living and home autonomy solutions, as well as leverage the commercial results of previous research in the domain.

3   System Architecture

The current section briefly details the architecture of the *SMARTCARE* cyber-physical system. Its main objective is to facilitate active and safe living among older and at-risk adults using intelligent automation of their home environment, as well as by monitoring their vital signs and a suite of configurable ambient parameters. Our aim is for the system to enable people to live independently within their own homes, even in cases of chronic conditions or that of mild mental impairment. The system provides an event-based monitoring, automation and alerting platform. It consists of a number of heterogeneous smart connected devices, a data access services platform, offline analysis based on artificial intelligence, notifications, software utilities for system configuration and adaptation to the needs of the beneficiary, together with services aimed towards solution designers and system integrators.

The development of the ongoing project is carried out through end-user centric design that covers their needs and preferences, as well as catering towards requirements for deployment, configuration and maintenance from integrators and system administrators. Under these conditions, the *SMARTCARE* application offers two user interfaces, one for administration and one for users such as formal or informal care givers as well as for the end-users themselves.

The *DeveloperUI* component is dedicated to users with the role of integrator or system administrator. It offers multiple functionalities such as user management, role-based user right configuration, management of deployed devices and tools for configuring several aspects related to indoor location, monitoring and alert scenarios, project management, establishing business rules, as well as visualization of different available reports.

The end-user interface is designed for caregivers and the monitored persons themselves. In the case of monitored persons, the system provides a Virtual Assistant type application, which transmits data via the Gateway component, with a voice interface that facilitates predefined dialogues, voice notifications and voice commands. A graphical interface is available for manually entering vital sign values and other biophysical parameters and observations related to health. The system can also respond to a suite of commands and present notifications. A panic button can be actioned by the user in case of critical situations.

System users in a caregiver role can alter settings related to deployed equipment, can configure scenarios that will trigger real-time notifications and can view reports based on recorded data. Additionally, users registered as medical personnel can manage patient lists, medical observation sheets, establish and follow patient-level treatment as well as configure and receive real-time notifications.

The *SMARTCARE* system consists of the main components illustrated in Fig. 1:

- ***Devices layer*** - comprised of the connected devices deployed and registered within the platform. Together, they form the system's configurable and extensible physical layer
- ***Gateway*** - has the role of communicating and interfacing with deployed devices, environmental monitors and actuators as well as telemedicine solutions. The *DeveloperUI* component for device registration and configuration is part of this layer.
- ***Expert system*** - a cloud service layer that facilitates intelligent processing of the information received from the sensor network by defining and following rules for monitoring and alerting.

Connected equipments are deployed using the *DeveloperUI* component implemented using Python as a back-end and HACS (Home Assistant Community Store) for the graphical interface to facilitate the discovery, installation, renewal and deletion of monitoring devices associated with system users. This module is aimed to facilitate the design of solutions for specific home care applications. The *DeveloperUI* provides design templates for creating custom monitoring and support scenarios and enables their design and implementation through the automatic configuration of the Gateway and Expert system components. The *DeveloperUI* allows the interaction with smart connected devices and responds to events transmitted by them.

Components that interact with an Internet of Things domain track the devices in the beneficiary's home and consist of a central part and module-specific logic. These components make their information available through the

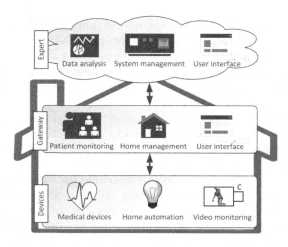

Fig. 1. *SMARTCARE* system architecture [2]

state machine and an event bus infrastructure which implements the publish / subscribe model. The event bus is used to disconnect components, such that components can react to each other's messages through the event bus. This enables integrating devices from different vendors and with different specifications using the event bus as an adaptation and translation layer.

Each user can subscribe to specific events. Users are notified when the event they subscribed to is posted on the event bus. Events can be published on the event bus when something happens. Components also record services in the service log to expose device controls. Components that respond to events that occur provide the logic for home automation, as well as involve services that perform common tasks. Each device is represented as an entity. An entity abstracts the internal operation of the *DeveloperUI* module. The device integrator extends an entity class and implements the properties and methods required for the specific device type.

Setting up a new device is done using a human-readable *yaml* configuration file. The provider is responsible for distributing the configuration on the *SMARTCARE* platform, redirects configuration entries and device discovery information, and collects entities for service calls. In addition, all platform entities are managed and updated when necessary. When adding entities, the feature register is queried to ensure that entities have correct identifiers. The entity register tracks entities and allows users to store additional settings for an entity. The *DeveloperUI* platform uses the configuration to query the external device and add entities.

The same module allows for the management of equipment and tools for configuring several aspects related to indoor localisation, monitoring and alerting. The configuration file is used to register new monitoring devices within the system. This is exemplified in Fig. 2a, which illustrates a number of smart connected devices: two bulbs, a spotlight, a motion sensor (placed under the red spotlight), three switches for manually operating the bulbs and spotlight, three sensors (round shape) for smoke detection, carbon monoxide, flooding, a panic button (placed between the switch and the socket), an intrusion detection sensor (with the vertical shape) and a smart power socket. Figure 2b illustrates the intelligent lighting elements used in our comparative evaluation. The left hand side shows a smart device that was custom developed as part of a previous research project, and which integrates sensors for measuring temperature, humidity and volatile compound levels. The right hand side illustrates a cost effective, commercially available smart bulb that can double as a signal beacon for indoor localisation.

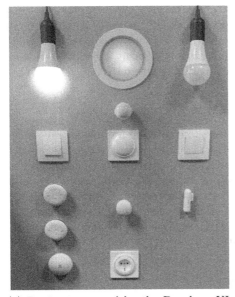

(a) Devices managed by the DeveloperUI module

(b) Custom developed smart lighting device (left) and Philips Hue bulb (right)

Fig. 2. Selection of intelligent luminaires

The system can help older adults who belong to the most fragile category during the COVID-19 pandemic, by monitoring their heart rate and the daily number of steps. For this situation, a Fitbit Versa 2 smartwatch was considered. It communicates with the associated smart phone of the older adult via Bluetooth. In order to retrieve data from the smartwatch, an account was created on the Fitbit platform[1]. The last part of the configuration *yaml* file contains the

---

[1] www.fitbit.com.

link to the smartwatch that monitors the heartbeat, calories consumed, and the number of steps taken during the current day.

The data from the Fitbit platform is imported into the DeveloperUI module every 30 min and includes the calories consumption, heart rate and the number of steps taken. The counter is reset at the end of each day.

4   Experimental Evaluation

The present section details our experimental evaluation and discusses its results. We dedicate the first subsection to describing the location and methodology of the experiment, as the presence and layout of walls and furniture can be the source of significant signal reflections that affect accuracy. We employ the same location and methodology as in our previous work [12], making results comparable. We present and discuss our findings within the second subsection, where we compare the accuracy obtained by replacing previously developed custom beacons with a cost-effective, commercially available alternative.

4.1   Experimental Setup and Conditions

The evaluation was carried out in an apartment situated in a multi-storey apartment building. The layout is illustrated in Fig. 3. Exterior walls are made of brick and cement and are 35 cm thick, while interior ones are made of brick and 17 cm thick. The expected effect of the building materials on the signal strength was described in our previous work [12]. Signal absorption appears because the corners of the rooms are made of iron-reinforced concrete pillars. During the movement of the monitored person, interference appears and the effects occur when computing the current indoor position.

4.2   Indoor Positioning Methodology

A Raspberry Pi 4 Model B was used to gather received signal strength indicator (RSSI) values from the three luminaires deployed where indicated by the yellow circles in Fig. 3. The device was connected to the system server via a stable WiFi connection. The monitored person carried a Bluetooth-enabled smart phone and was monitored by the deployed system. We repeated the scenarios from our previous research [12]. The person's movement is illustrated in Fig. 3. Starting next to the bed, the person moved near the hallway closet, from which they moved back next to the bed and then near the desk chair situated in the study room. At the start and finish, as well as between each movement phase, the person remained in the same place for a duration of about 60 s. The entire scenario was repeated a number of three times and in the same conditions. RSSI scans were carried out every five seconds.

The beacons employed in our previous research [12,15] were intelligent luminaires custom developed as part of a precursor research project and are shown on the left hand side in Fig. 2b. They consist of a Raspberry Pi unit and printed

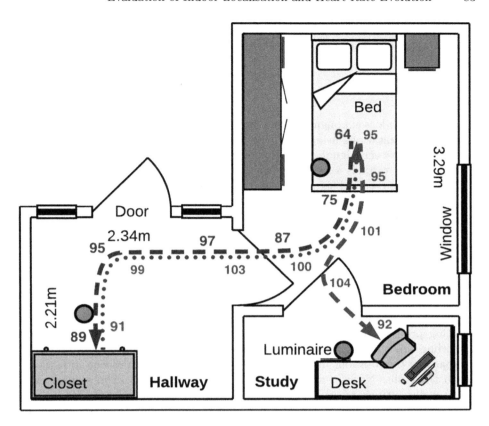

Fig. 3. Floor plan of the apartment used for the experiment. Arrows indicate user movement (a) from the bed to the closet (blue); (b) from the closet towards the bed (green) and (c) from the bed towards the desk (magenta) [12]; user heart rate is correlated with movement, with taken samples shown along the movement path. (Color figure online)

circuit board located inside a housing. The sensing elements, which include temperature, heat and volatile compound sensors are located in the center of the circular element in order to avoid heat emissions from the lighting module. Sensors were placed pointing downward to improve accuracy. For the present evaluation, we replaced these custom devices with a set of Philips Hue[2] intelligent bulbs, as shown in the right hand side in Fig. 2b. The Philips Hue bulb communicates with the Philips Hue bridge via the Zigbee protocol. While they lack additional sensing capabilities, adequate accuracy would allow them to be employed as cost-effective beacons that can replace custom hardware for localisation purposes.

Calculations for indoor localisation are carried out server-side, using the same approach regardless of deployed beacon type. First, trilateration is used in order

---

[2] https://www.philips-hue.com/.

to determine the distance between the monitored person and each deployed beacon using the [7] formula:

$$d = 10^{\frac{A-RSSI}{10 \cdot n}} \tag{1}$$

where:

- n is the path loss exponent and its value is determined empirically, with existing implementations using values between 2 and 6 for indoor environments.
- A represents the signal strength measured in dBm and computed at one meter. This value is a specific constant of each luminaire type.
- $RSSI$ is the received signal strength index, also measured in dBm.
- d is the calculated distance between the beacon and the user's device with activated Bluetooth.

The position of the monitored person is the intersection of the three circles constructed using the distances between each beacon and the user's device. However, multipath fading, differences in antenna orientation as well as the presence of objects and bodies (including the monitored person's own body) all lead to measurement errors. As such, the user's location must be approximated. We employ the Levenberg-Marquardt algorithm [6] illustrated in Fig. 4 to solve the resulting problem of nonlinear least squares by integrating the Gauss-Newton algorithm and the gradient descent method. The algorithm works iteratively, approaching the solutions in a way that is similar to gradient descent and switching to the Gauss-Newton method for fine tuning the result. The scenario was repeated three times to evaluate the consistency of the reported results.

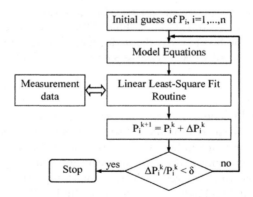

Fig. 4. Levenberg-Marquadt algorithm flow optimization [10]

The Levenberg-Marquardt algorithm determines an approximation of the (x, y) coordinates of the user's location from the following system of equations:

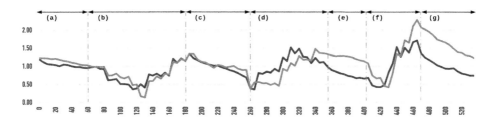

Fig. 5. Measurement of the mean localisation error (vertical axis, in meters, across three repetitions) when using custom developed (blue) and Philips Hue (gray) luminaires as beacons. Horizontal axis has the time expressed in seconds and is divided according to the evaluation stages: **(a)** standing near the bed; **(b)** walking towards the closet **(c)** standing near the closet; **(d)** walking back towards the bed; **(e)** standing near the bed; **(f)** walking towards the desk and **(g)** standing near the desk. (Color figure online)

$(x - x_i)^2 + (y - y_i)^2 = d_i^2$, where (x_i, y_i) are the coordinates of the ith smart bulb, $i \in \{1, 2, \cdots, n\}$, where $n \geq 3$. The algorithm sets an initial value for the parameter vector $P = [x, y]^T$, and in each iteration it replaces it with an updated estimation $P + \Delta$ [10]. The process stops once the step falls below a preset threshold. At least three luminaires are required, with previous research showing that additional devices can improve accuracy, especially in the case of large enclosures [13].

4.3   Results

Figure 5 and Table 1 show the mean errors obtained over the three repetitions of the experimental scenario. Both include our previous results [12] obtained using the same methodology, the same location, and using the custom hardware devices detailed in the previous sections.

Based on our previous research, [14], at least 60 s are required for RSSI values to stabilize. Each obtained position was calibrated by having every smart bulb to consider the previous three RSSI readings. Every position has associated the person's heart rate value which was triggered by using the Fitbit Versa 2 smartwatch in order to analyze its evolution based on the performed activity. Longer durations with the user standing lead to decreased error rates and heart rate values. Conversely, we record the largest errors for indoor localization during the shorter stages (f) and (g), when the person also moves between rooms. This activity also determines the increase of the heart rate.

The data in Fig. 5 shows comparable error rates between our custom devices and the Philips intelligent bulbs. In all cases, we observed that accuracy improved over time with a stationary user, which was confirmed by our previous research [15]. Scenarios (a) and (e), as well as (b) and (d) are worth a closer look, as they are related. In the first case, both represent a monitored user standing near the bed. In both cases the location was resolved with room-level accuracy, with the commercially-available devices being more accurate in scenario (e). With

Table 1. Mean error and standard deviation for the three repetitions carried out using the custom developed device (Old) and the Philips Hue smart bulb (New). Each repetition represented on a table row.

Repetition	Mean error (m)				Standard deviation (m)			
	Walking		Standing		Walking		Standing	
	Old	New	Old	New	Old	New	Old	New
#1	0.76	1.10	1.05	0.70	0.27	0.23	0.17	0.30
#2	0.86	0.75	1.25	0.82	0.36	0.32	0.12	0.29
#3	1.17	0.51	1.61	0.74	0.60	0.20	0.28	0.36

regards to the second scenario pair, they represent the same path, but traversed in opposite directions. Table 1 details mean error measurements and standard deviations individually for each repetition. We do observe important variance between them using both sets of devices. However, the accuracy remained suitable for room-level user detection across each run, with both sets of devices.

The average error and the standard deviation values are better for the experiments which involved the usage of the Philips Hue smart bulb. The initial experiment used a Raspberry Pi 3 Model B with Bluetooth 4.0 connectivity and a Bluetooth 4.1 mobile device. Our current experiment was based on the Philips Hue smart bulbs, complemented by a Raspberry Pi 4 Model B and a mobile device, both supporting the Bluetooth 5.0 standard, which doubles the bandwidth over Bluetooth 4.0 [25]. In addition, version 5.0 extends both indoor and outdoor signal ranges four times when compared to version 4.0. These are important considerations when using Bluetooth RSSI for accurate localisation and we believe them to be the source of the observed differences.

During the three repetitions of the scenario, the average heart rate of the monitored person while lying in bed was of 64 bpm. When the person moved from the bed towards the closet, the heart rate increased and reached a mean value of 82 bpm. After walking and reaching the closet, the heart rate was recorded at 92 bpm, due to the physical effort. When heading towards the bed, the heart rate increased again, reaching 97 bpm. Based on the gathered data, there is a clear connection between the recorded position and activity of the person on one hand, and their heart rate on the other. When at rest, the person's heart rate decreases and then stabilizes. As the person moves, the heart rate increases gradually, denoting that an activity is taking place. Heart rate measurements can play an important role as they can be used to determine the existence of critical situations. For example, a sudden change in heart rate, or heart rate variability can signal that medical intervention is required. Events like heart attacks, fibrillation or arrhythmia can be detected early, as well as kept under observation in case of preexisting conditions. Caregivers can be notified by the software system when such events are triggered and the movement of the monitored persons, together with their current location and updated measurements can be made available to help make an informed decision.

The fact that commercially available and cost-effective solutions were straightforward to integrate into the system, together with them matching the accuracy of previously developed devices is an encouraging result. These can be used in deployments where additional sensing capabilities such as smoke and volatile compound detection are not required, or in the case where the monitored person can make better use of functionalities specific to these devices. In addition, using commercially available solutions can lessen the psychological observer effect on targeted users, as these devices do not look out of place for the end-user, family members or visitors.

5   Conclusion

Western society is in the midst of important societal and demographic changes, with a continuously expected increase in the number of older adults and patients with chronic conditions. While life expectancy has generally risen in the last decades, we find that this was not accompanied by a corresponding increase in the quality of life for older adults [24].

Decision makers are invested in exploring technology as a potentially viable solution that can address current and expected issues, help older adults retain quality of life, all in a cost efficient manner. Technologies such as the Internet of Things accelerate the digitalisation of ambient monitoring, while transforming the lives of many persons. We believe that societal needs and technological progress are well aligned to create solutions with a profound and lasting impact on wide demographics.

In the present work we evaluated one alternative for providing a cost-efficient scheme for indoor localisation and heart rate monitoring using commercially available technology. We aim to further our work and use the platform under development as an integrative hub where innovative devices can be integrated so that it brings added benefit to older adults and their caregivers.

Acknowledgements. This work was supported by Romanian Ministry of Education and Research, CCCDI - UEFISCDI, project number 46E/2015, *i-Light - A pervasive home monitoring system based on intelligent luminaires* and project number PN-III-P2-2.1-PTE-2019-0756, *Integrative platform for home care assistance solutions*, within PNCDI III.

References

1. AAL - Active and Assisted Living Programme: ICT for ageing well (2016). http://www.aal-europe.eu/about/objectives/
2. Achirei, S.D., et al.: On the design of an iot based solution for assisted living. In: 2020 E-Health and Bioengineering Conference (EHB), pp. 1–4 (2020). https://doi.org/10.1109/EHB50910.2020.9280185

3. Bolívar Pulgarín, N.G., Cangrejo Aljure, L.D., Salcedo Parra, O.J.: eheart-bp, prototype of the internet of things to monitor blood pressure. In: 2019 IEEE/ACM International Conference on Connected Health: Applications, Systems and Engineering Technologies (CHASE), pp. 58–63 (2019). https://doi.org/10.1109/CHASE48038.2019.00025
4. Dias, M., et al.: A living labs approach for usability testing of ambient assisted living technologies. Lect. Notes Comput. Sci. **9186**, 167–178 (2015)
5. Dong, L.M., Piran, M.J., Han, D., Min, K., Moon, H.: A survey on internet of things and cloud computing for healthcare. Electronics **8**(7), 1–49 (2019)
6. Gavin, H.: The levenberg-marquardt method for nonlinear least squares curve-fitting problems. Department of Civil and Environmental Engineering, Duke University, pp. 1–15 (2011)
7. Goldoni, E., Prando, L., Vizziello, A., Savazzi, P., Gamba, P.: Experimental data set analysis of rssi-based indoor and outdoor localization in lora networks. Internet Technol. Lett. **2**(1), e75 (2019). https://doi.org/https://doi.org/10.1002/itl2.75, https://onlinelibrary.wiley.com/doi/abs/10.1002/itl2.75
8. Ham, S., Cho, H., Lee, H., Lee, G.: Prototype development of responsive kinetic façade control system for the elderly based on ambient assisted living. Architect. Sci. Rev. **62**(4), 273–285 (2019). https://doi.org/10.1080/00038628.2019.1614902
9. Jaworski, W., Wilk, P., Zborowski, P., Chmielowiec, W., Lee, A.Y., Kumar, A.: Real-time 3D indoor localization. In: 2017 International Conference on Indoor Positioning and Indoor Navigation (IPIN), pp. 1–8 (2017). https://doi.org/10.1109/IPIN.2017.8115874
10. Duc-Hung, L., Cong-Kha, P., Trang, N.T.T., Tu, B.T.: Parameter extraction and optimization using levenberg-marquardt algorithm. In: 2012 Fourth International Conference on Communications and Electronics (ICCE), pp. 434–437 (2012). https://doi.org/10.1109/CCE.2012.6315945
11. Lv, H., Feng, L., Yang, A., Lin, B., Huang, H., Chen, S.: Two-dimensional code-based indoor positioning system with feature graphics. IEEE Photonics J. **11**(1), 1–15 (2019). https://doi.org/10.1109/JPHOT.2018.2885985
12. Marin, I., Bocicor, M., Molnar, A.J.: Intelligent luminaire based real-time indoor positioning for assisted living. In: Proceedings of the 15th International Conference on Evaluation of Novel Approaches to Software Engineering (2020). https://doi.org/10.5220/0009578705480555
13. Marin, I., Bocicor, M.-I., Molnar, A.-J.: Indoor localization techniques within a home monitoring platform. In: Damiani, E., Spanoudakis, G., Maciaszek, L.A. (eds.) ENASE 2019. CCIS, vol. 1172, pp. 378–401. Springer, Cham (2020). https://doi.org/10.1007/978-3-030-40223-5_19
14. Marin, I., et al.: Indoor localisation with intelligent luminaires for home monitoring. In: Proceedings of the 14th International Conference on Evaluation of Novel Approaches to Software Engineering, pp. 464–471. SCITEPRESS-Science and Technology Publications, Lda (2019)
15. Marin, I., et al.: i-light—intelligent luminaire based platform for home monitoring and assisted living. Electronics **7**(10), 220 (2018). https://doi.org/10.3390/electronics7100220
16. de Meijer, C., Wouterse, B., Polder, J., Koopmanschap, M.: The effect of population aging on health expenditure growth: a critical review. Eur. J. Ageing **10**(4), 353–361 (2013). https://doi.org/10.1007/s10433-013-0280-x

17. Mshali, H., Lemlouma, T., Moloney, M., Magoni, D.: A survey on health monitoring systems for health smart homes. Int. J. Ind. Ergonomics **66**, 26–56 (2018). https://doi.org/10.1016/j.ergon.2018.02.002, https://www.sciencedirect.com/science/article/abs/pii/S0169814117300082
18. Puertolas-Montañez, J., Mendoza-Rodriguez, A., Sanz-Prieto, I.: Smart indoor positioning/location and navigation: a lightweight approach. Int. J. Interact. Multimedia Artif. Intell. **2**, 43–50 (2013). https://doi.org/10.9781/ijimai.2013.225
19. Pustokhina, I.V., Pustokhin, D.A., Gupta, D., Khanna, A., Shankar, K., Nguyen, G.N.: An effective training scheme for deep neural network in edge computing enabled internet of medical things (IOMT) systems. IEEE Access **8**, 107112–107123 (2020). https://doi.org/10.1109/ACCESS.2020.3000322
20. Scataglini, S., Imbesi, S.: Human-centered design smart clothing for ambient assisted living of elderly users: considerations in the COVID-19 pandemic perspective. In: Marques, G., Bhoi, A.K., Albuquerque, V.H.C., K.S., H. (eds.) IoT in Healthcare and Ambient Assisted Living. SCI, vol. 933, pp. 311–324. Springer, Singapore (2021). https://doi.org/10.1007/978-981-15-9897-5_15
21. Kishorebabu, V., Sravanthi, R.: Real time monitoring of environmental parameters using IOT. Wireless Personal Commun. **112**(2), 785–808 (2020). https://doi.org/10.1007/s11277-020-07074-y
22. Walline, J.: Quarantine wristbands, face masks, and personal freedom in hong kong. J. Emerg. Med. **59**(4), 604–605 (2020). https://doi.org/10.1016/j.jemermed.2020.06.048
23. Wang, W., Zhang, Y., Tian, L.: Toa-based nlos error mitigation algorithm for 3D indoor localization. Chin. Commun. **17**(1), 63–72 (2020). https://doi.org/10.23919/JCC.2020.01.005
24. World Health Organization: World report on ageing and health (2015). https://www.who.int/ageing/events/world-report-2015-launch/en/
25. Yaakop, M.B., Abd Malik, I.A., bin Suboh, Z., Ramli, A.F., Abu, M.A.: Bluetooth 5.0 throughput comparison for internet of thing usability a survey. In: 2017 International Conference on Engineering Technology and Technopreneurship (ICE2T), pp. 1–6 (2017). https://doi.org/10.1109/ICE2T.2017.8215995
26. Zimmerman, S., Sloane, P., Katz, P., Kunze, M., O'Neil, K., Resnick, B.: The need to include assisted living in responding to the covid-19 pandemic. J. Am. Med. Directors Assoc. **21**, 572–575 (2020). https://doi.org/10.1016/j.jamda.2020.03.024
27. Zubiete, E., Gomez Gonzalez, I.M., Medina, V., Gómez, J.: Design and implementation of a prototype with a standardized interface for transducers in ambient assisted living. Sensors **15**, 2999–3022 (2015). https://doi.org/10.3390/s150202999

Exercise Abnormality Detection Using *BlazePose* Skeleton Reconstruction

Audrius Kulikajevas[1]([✉]), Rytis Maskeliūnas[1][iD], Robertas Damaševičius[1][iD],
Julius Griškevičius[2], Kristina Daunoravičienė[2], Jurgita Žižienė[2],
Donatas Lukšys[2], and Aušra Adomavičienė[3]

[1] Department of Multimedia Engineering, Kaunas University of Technology,
51368 Kaunas, Lithuania
audrius.kulikajevas@ktu.edu
[2] Department of Biomechanical Engineering, Vilnius Tech, 03224 Vilnius, Lithuania
[3] Center of Rehabilitation, Physical and Sports Medicine, Vilnius University Hospital
Santaros Clinics, Santariškių g. 2, 08410 Vilnius, Lithuania

Abstract. There still exists a knowledge gap in the field of computer vision in respect of posture prediction and deviation evaluation is an important metric for various medical applications, that require posture abnormality quantization. Our paper proposes a deep heuristic neural network architecture, using *BlazePose* as a backbone, that is capable of reconstructing users skeleton from a real-time monocular video feed, using which we are able to evaluate the subjects performed exercise and measure the deviation from expected values. The proposed heuristics are able to identify and evaluate most of the abnormalities, with the highest indicator of postural issues being the spinal deviation accounting for 95%. Additional evaluation of real-time performance has shown that our method is capable of maintaining 23-ms response times, making it applicable to real-time applications.

Keywords: Exercise analysis · Posture estimation · Skeleton reconstruction · Abnormality detection

1 Introduction

Thanks to advancements of shallow artificial intelligence, mostly in the field of deep artificial neural networks (DANNs), we are able to solve more and more tasks that were previously hard to solve using classical approaches, allowing for fields like computer vision to expand into new frontiers. While the ANNs have been proposed more than half a century ago, only recently we are able to leverage them thanks in large part to parallelized computing systems, such as graphical processing units (GPUs) and tensor processing units (TPUs). Deep-learning based black-box models have shown state-of-the-art performance in a wide variety of real world applications, including medical applications. These can be ranging from driver fatigue detection [9], lung abnormality detection in X-ray imaging [18], detection of heart and blood vessel disease [15,38], diagnosing of

© Springer Nature Switzerland AG 2021
O. Gervasi et al. (Eds.): ICCSA 2021, LNCS 12953, pp. 90–104, 2021.
https://doi.org/10.1007/978-3-030-86976-2_7

cancer [40], hypoglycemia [35]. Early detection and evaluation of course of the disease for neurodegenerative disorders like Huntington's [21] and Parkinson's disease [1]. Predicting mortality rates [33] and wide variety of autism spectrum disorders [41]. In addition, machine learning has shown the ability to analyze electroencephalographic signals which can be used for brain-computer interfaces [8] or even developing new drugs and treatments [13] for various ailments.

Various ailments may cause various posture related impairments, these can range starting with Pompe disease [36,39], various neurological disorders [30] and general spinal injuries [20]. Additionally, bad posture onto itself can be a cause of health risks [11,27,31]. Patients abnormal posture analysis, while performing various exercises, may be useful for a physician in order to diagnose and/or evaluate posture-related illnesses, appropriate application of treatment and rehabilitation measures and evaluating their effectiveness. In this paper we propose deep neural network with heuristic analysis for the evaluation of 7 types common exercises as described by field experts: 1) shoulder flexion; 2) shoulder flexion and internal rotation; 3) shoulder flexion and internal rotation, elbow flexion; 4) shoulder extension and internal rotation; 5) shoulder flexion; 6) fool shoulder flexion; 7) shoulder adduction.

The majority of state-of-the-art human posture classification research focuses on the classification of posture without measuring the absolute deviation from the norm. Whereas, the methods that do provide deviation from correct results, generally depend on availability of special depth sensors in order to capture the human skeleton, making the accessibility of such approaches have a higher upfront cost. Instead, our approach uses state-of-the-art *BlazePose* [3] neural network as the backbone for skeleton reconstruction with which, in combination with our devised heuristics analysis, we are able to identify exercise abnormalities in addition to measuring the severity of abnormality ($\Delta\phi$) for the given exercise.

Our paper is organized as follows: firstly in Sect. 2 we present related works. Afterwards in Sect. 3 we present our methods and approach. Followed by results in Sect. 4, and finally Sect. 5 we present our conclusions.

2   Related Work

One of labor-related musculoskeletal ailment risk factors is the improper posture positions adopted by office workers. With one of direct consequences of inadequate posture being back pain, whereas indirectly linked improper posture ailments can range from cardiovascular disease, lumbar disease and even early mortality [5]. Some studies have suggested that body posture is an important predictor of stress [14,28] and mental fatigue [2].

There exist multiple solutions with regard to human posture detection. One of such solutions attempts to detect various course-grained posture operations such as *standing*, *bending*, *sitting* and *crawling* [32]. This solution was able to separate ergonomic from non-ergonomic values, however it does not provide the quantized error as feedback to determine if the posture is improving or deteriorating, in addition it requires a depth sensor in addition to closed-source software, which both increases underlying cost and reduces the solutions' reliability. Another attempt at predicting subject posture by using 3D motion analysis, allowing to identify such subject actions as *walking* and *falling* [16]. However, it does not provide the ability to differentiate between properly and improperly performed action in addition to being sensitive to lightning conditions. Other solutions attempt to detect the human position in an office environment [12], or to identify inadequate subjects posture using depth sensors such as Kinect [22,25,37]. Whereas structured light depth sensors are more robust against lightning conditions they are generally more noisy and have much higher initial costs, making them less-than ideal in certain applications. Other solutions depend on skeleton evaluation [23,29] which may fail due to occlusion in addition to the solutions becoming obsolete due to the discontinuation of the used depth sensing devices by the manufacturer. Some solutions however, avoid skeleton evaluation altogether, instead using semantically linked hierarchical tree, thus solving for occlusion problem [19] by predicting human posture with as little as 30% of the body visible in addition of having discrete posture prediction sub-states. Other approaches such as pulse-coupled neural networks were capable of recognizing moving human [42] skeleton in a crowded background, while others used 2D image mapped into 3D space to acquire depth information for full skeleton prediction [7]. 3D data obtained from both synthesis of depth from a monocular frame [17] and from depth sensors such as Kinect has other general applications such as gender recognition from body shape [6] or evaluation of physical performance from training exercises [34] (Table 1).

Table 1. Comparison of algorithms capable of human posture classification. Different methods are compared in terms of being applicable to monocular and non-monocular cameras, whether they are able to detect posture abnormalities, quantize the abnormality error and if they are occlusion resistant against other objects in the scene.

Method	Monocular	Detects abnormality	Quantize error	Occlusion resistant
Ray et al. [32]	✗	✓	✗	✗
Hsieh et al. [16]	✓	✓	✗	✗
Kulikajevas et al. [19]	✗	✓	✓	✓
Li et al. [22]	✗	✗	✗	✓
Liu et al. [25]	✗	✓	✗	✓
Wang et al. [37]	✗	✗	✗	✓
Ryselis et al. [34]	✗	✓	✓	✓
Proposed	✓	✓	✓	✓

While the mentioned approaches have shown the capability of classifying subject posture, they tend to lack the ability to quantify the error level that the posture has. In our paper, we propose heuristic approach as an extension to deep neural network posture estimation for the quantification of posture error.

3   Methods

3.1   Pose Estimation Pipeline

With the main focus of our approach is being real-time pose abnormality detection we need fast and robust way of detecting humanoid skeleton. While many approaches exist for humanoid skeletal analysis, we have opted to use *BlazePose* as our backbone, as it has shown to be one of the most-performant solutions using monocular cameras in terms of prediction speed, robustness and stability, this makes it more than suitable for our approach. In order to achieve real-time performance of the *BlazePose* each of its components have been designed to be suitable for real-time applications. This is done by making certain assertions and generalizations about the human body, i.e. that the best indicator for the human torso is the direction of the subjects face. Assertions like these allow for simplification of the pose estimation by using well established face detection networks that are capable of sub-millisecond performance—*BlazeFace* [4]. Additionally, based on the relationship between human torso and human head it is also possible to extrapolate other key body features such as the maximum radius of the human body, this allows for detecting such key features like the bodies center of mass, it's rotation and scale, which are required for the estimation of more complicated poses with very little computing cycle overhead. To estimate the pose a two-stage detector pipeline is used (see Fig. 1), where the detector located the Region-of-Interest (RoI) for the given image that is most likely to contain the subject, while the tracker predicts the joints within the given RoI.

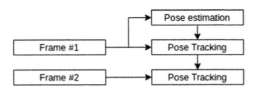

Fig. 1. Pose estimation pipeline. First frame is used to estimate the RoI of the subject that will be tracked, with the subsequent frames using previous frames' prediction to improve the pose tracking.

3.2   Network Architecture

While other methods for humanoid skeleton estimation tend to use computationally expensive heatmap predictions, instead *BlazePose* only uses heat and offset maps for supervised learning stage, the overview of the artificial neural network architecture can be seen in Fig. 2. Firstly, *BlazePose* downsamples a monocular image to 256×256, which is then used as the input for the ANN. A heatmap and an offset loss are used during the supervised training stage is used in order to improve the networks convergence by supervising the coordinate regression layers, however the supervision layers are then stripped from the final network.

This gives our backbone network the real-time performance that is critical for our applications. Unfortunately, the existing solution while fast proved to be too unstable to be used in medical applications. For this reason before applying our heuristics to the estimated skeleton we have added one-dimensional stabilization kernel which uses the last 5 frames in with Gaussian [10] which has greatly improved the estimation stability performance with very little abnormalities due to never frames having the highest weight impact into the final pose estimation.

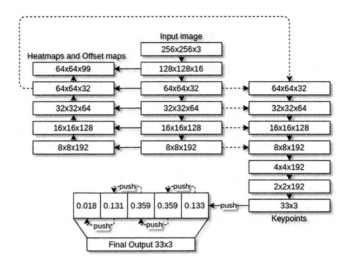

Fig. 2. *BlazePose* network architecture. Given a 256×256 RGB image neural network outputs 33 joint x, y coordinates in addition to probability if the given joint is visible in cases when it parts of the subject may be occluded. The output of *BlazePose* is then sent to stabilization kernel to stabilize the skeleton.

The output joint topology uses expands upon $COCO$ [24] skeleton topology, outputting 33 joints (see Fig. 3) for a given input image. Each of the joints containing their x and y coordinates in the image space in addition to the *visibility* probability, the latter is used to predict how likely the given joint is visible in the image, this is useful when the given joint may be occluded or out of frame.

Using transfer learning, we have trained our network using *Stochastic Gradient Descent* (SGD) [26], using learning rate of 5×10^{-3} and momentum of 0.9 for 1000 epochs with the batch size of 16, The network was implemented using Python and Tensorflow to allow for GPU accelerated training.

3.3   Exercise Abnormality Detection

In order to detect abnormalities in subject exercises we use multiple heuristic protocols based on the simplified skeleton posture predicted by the *BlazePose* backbone. We use these heuristics for 7 of our main exercises: 1) raise hand 90°

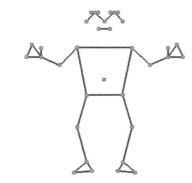

Fig. 3. 33 joints predicted by *BlazePose* skeleton joints

and move it to front (Hand 90° Side to Front); 2) raise the hand and place it on top of the head (Hand to top of Head); 3) raise hand and touch the nose (Hand to Nose); 4) raise the hand and touch lower back (Hand to Back); 5) raise the hand to front 90° (Hand 90° Up Front); 6) raise the hand 180° above the head (Hand 180° Up); 7) raise the hand 90° to the side (Hand 90° Side). Each of the exercises have special heuristics designed in order to evaluate the patients posture abnormality severity, see Fig. 4 for full UML activity diagram of the system. The heuristics we have chosen are based on contracted *BlazePose* skeleton (see Fig. 5). We reduce the 33 joints provided by the *BlazePose* into 17 joints and 2 reference axes. The joints are as follows: J1) right heel; J2) right knee; J3) right hip; J4) left heel; J5) left knee; J6) left hip; J7) spine bottom; J8) right wrist; J9) right elbow; J10) right shoulder; J11) left wrist; J12) left elbow; J13) left shoulder; J14) spine top; J15) right ear; 16); left ear; J17) nose. The 3 references axes: a) horizontal eye line axis; b) vertical spine axis.

Main Heuristics. The three main error heuristics that are shared between all the exercises is spine deviation error $\Delta\phi_{sp}$ (see Eq. 1), head deviation error $\Delta\phi_h$ (see Eq. 2) and shoulder deviation error $\Delta\phi_{sh}$ (see Eq. 3). These three main heuristics are used to classify healthy subject from one that suffers from an ailment which induces posture related abnormalities when performing exercises in addition to identification of abnormality severity.

$$\Delta\phi_{sp} = \arccos \frac{J14 - J7}{\|J14 - J7\|} \cdot b \tag{1}$$

$$\Delta\phi_{h} = \arccos \frac{J16 - J15}{\|J16 - J15\|} \cdot a \tag{2}$$

$$\Delta\phi_{sh} = \arccos \frac{J13 - J10}{\|J13 - J10\|} \cdot a \tag{3}$$

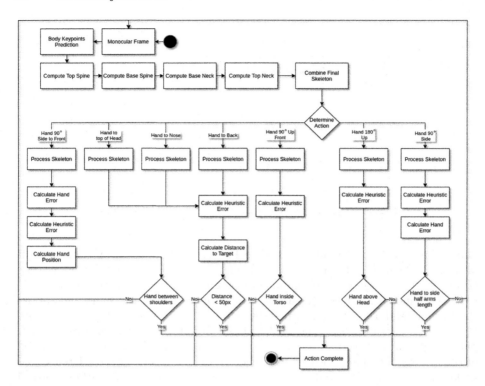

Fig. 4. UML activity diagram denoting our heuristic algorithm used for abnormality detection.

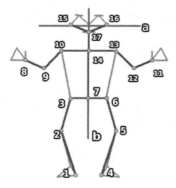

Fig. 5. Green—original *BlazePose* skeleton; blue—contracted skeleton. Additionally, we add world reference axes: a) horizontal eye line axis; b) vertical spine axis. Contracted skeleton along with references axes is used in our heuristic analysis. (Color online figure)

First heuristic $\Delta\phi_{sp} \in [-5°, 5°]$ is used as the main identifier to classify between a properly and improperly completed exercise, when the subjects' spine tilts more than $5°$ away from the vertical axis b the exercise is considered executed improperly, at this point physician is informed about exercise abnormalities and their severity. The $[-5°, 5°]$ grace range has been defined by experts. Additionally, $\Delta\phi_h$ shows how much the patients head has tilted from the a horizontal axis. As with $\Delta\phi_{sp}$, grace range for $\Delta\phi_h \in [-5°, 5°]$. This heuristic alone generally is unable to show if the person suffers from any ailment and is instead used in conjunction with others to better evaluate the deviation from norm. Finally, $\Delta\phi_{sh} \in [-5°, 5°]$ is used to evaluate the shoulder deviation from horizontal axis a, as with $\Delta\phi_h$] it is generally used for assessing the deviation from the benchmark exercise parameters instead of classification of healthy/unhealthy subjects.

4   Results

To evaluate the deep heuristic artificial neural network we validate it against our collected dataset consisting of 57 videos. To validate our heuristics we evaluate each of the heuristics ($\Delta\phi_{sp}$, $\Delta\phi_h$ and $\Delta\phi_{sh}$) capability to classify the subjects' performed exercise as either normal or abnormal. We have calculated deviation mean and Probability Density Function (PDF) for each of our heuristics. As we can see from Figs. 6 and 7, there is a clear separation of both probability density function indicating that $\Delta\phi_{sp}$ has very little overlap, indicating that patients' spine deviation from the vertical axis is a great indicator of any postural abnormalities that may be affecting the subject. When comparing $\Delta\phi_h$ spread in Figs. 8 and 9 we can see that while a person with a posture abnormality has a larger probability density function when compared to a healthy subject, this heuristic alone is not sufficient to evaluate if the person is healthy. In the same matter $\Delta\phi_{sh}$ has large overlap between sick and healthy subjects (see Figs. 10 and 11) meaning they alone cannot be used for classification. However, in conjunction they allow for finer evaluation of the severity of posture problems when performing the exercises. This assertion is further supported by Shoulder-Spine deviation chart seen in Fig. 12, where we can see that shoulder deviation alone is rarely an indicator of any posture abnormalities on its own accord. In similar matter Head-Spine deviation as seen in Fig. 13 head tilt alone is not good enough standalone indicator that the person is healthy or not. Additionally, we evaluate the deep heuristic neural networks ability to work in real time, the results can be seen in Fig. 14, as we can see that processing a single frame takes around 23 ms, this equates to around 43 frames per second, which is more than enough for real time video analysis. Finally, while our findings have been evaluated by the experts with clinical experience, further validation in a clinical environment is required and should be performed in future work.

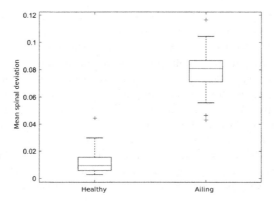

Fig. 6. Overall mean $\Delta\phi_{sp}$ deviation.

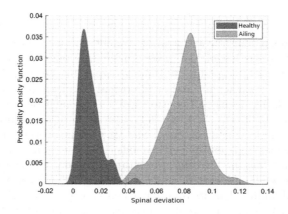

Fig. 7. Probability density function for $\Delta\phi_{sp}$ deviation.

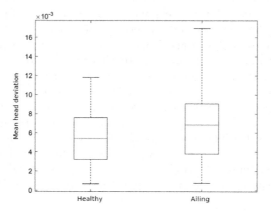

Fig. 8. Overall mean $\Delta\phi_h$ deviation.

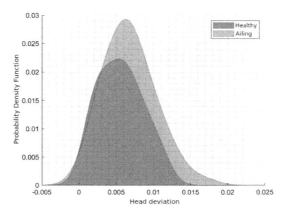

Fig. 9. Probability density function for $\Delta\phi_h$ deviation.

Fig. 10. Overall mean $\Delta\phi_{sh}$ deviation.

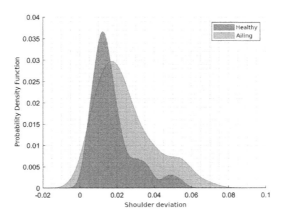

Fig. 11. Probability density function for $\Delta\phi_{sh}$ deviation.

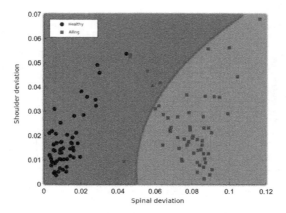

Fig. 12. $\Delta\phi_{sh}$ and $\Delta\phi_{sp}$ deviation correlation between normal and abnormal exercise.

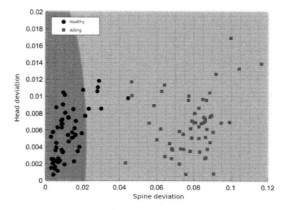

Fig. 13. $\Delta\phi_h$ and $\Delta\phi_{sp}$ deviation correlation between normal and abnormal exercise.

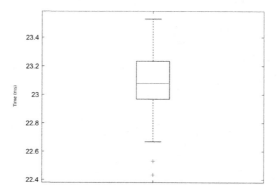

Fig. 14. Average time it took for processing of a single video frame.

5   Conclusions

We have proposed a deep heuristic neural network for, which is capable of estimating and classifying human pose in addition to providing angle of deviation from nominal exercise parameters. Experimental results have shown that the biggest indicator of the posture abnormalities were spinal heuristics accounting for 95% of all abnormalities. Furthermore, the given approach uses *BlazePose* model as its backbone neural network giving it 23-ms response times, which makes it suitable for the use in real-time systems. The results obtained confirm the fact that the proposed method is valuable and can be applied to determine the quality of patients' movement, to monitor the course of rehabilitation and to evaluate its effectiveness.

Author contributions. Conceptualization, R.M.; methodology, R.M.; software, A.K.; validation, A.K., R.M., R.D., J.G., K.D., J.Ž. and D.L.; formal analysis, R.M. and R.D.; investigation, A.K. and R.M.; resources, R.M.; data curation, A.K.; writing— original draft preparation, A.K. and R.M.; writing—review and editing, R.D. J.G., K.D., J.Ž. and D.L.; visualization, A.K. and R.M.; supervision, R.M.; funding acquisition, J.G., K.D., J.Ž. and D.L. All authors have read and agreed to the published version of the manuscript.

References

1. Almeida, J.S., et al.: Detecting Parkinson's disease with sustained phonation and speech signals using machine learning techniques. Pattern Recognit. Lett. **125**, 55–62 (2019)
2. Baker, R., Coenen, P., Howie, E., Williamson, A., Straker, L.: The short term musculoskeletal and cognitive effects of prolonged sitting during office computer work. Int. J. Environ. Res. Public Health **15**(8) (2018). https://doi.org/10.3390/ijerph15081678. https://www.mdpi.com/1660-4601/15/8/1678
3. Bazarevsky, V., Grishchenko, I., Raveendran, K., Zhu, T.L., Zhang, F., Grundmann, M.: Blazepose: on-device real-time body pose tracking. arXiv:abs/2006.10204 (2020)
4. Bazarevsky, V., Kartynnik, Y., Vakunov, A., Raveendran, K., Grundmann, M.: Blazeface: sub-millisecond neural face detection on mobile GPUs (2019). https://arxiv.org/abs/1907.05047
5. Cagnie, B., Danneels, L., Tiggelen, D.V., Loose, V.D., Cambier, D.: Individual and work related risk factors for neck pain among office workers: a cross sectional study. Eur. Spine J. **16**(5), 679–686 (2006)
6. Camalan, S., Sengul, G., Misra, S., Maskeliūnas, R., Damaševičius, R.: Gender detection using 3D anthropometric measurements by kinect. Metrol. Meas. Syst. **25**(2), 253–267 (2018)
7. Cao, B., Bi, S., Zheng, J., Yang, D.: Human posture recognition using skeleton and depth information. In: 2018 WRC Symposium on Advanced Robotics and Automation (WRC SARA), pp. 275–280, August 2018
8. Chai, R., Ling, S.H., Hunter, G.P., Tran, Y., Nguyen, H.T.: Brain-computer interface classifier for wheelchair commands using neural network with fuzzy particle swarm optimization. IEEE J. Biomed. Health Inform. **18**(5), 1614–1624 (2014)

9. Chai, R., et al.: Improving EEG-based driver fatigue classification using sparse-deep belief networks. Front. Neurosci. **11**, 103 (2017). https://doi.org/10.3389/fnins.2017.00103. https://www.frontiersin.org/article/10.3389/fnins.2017.00103

10. Dhulipala, S.L.N.: Gaussian kernel methods for seismic fragility and risk assessment of mid-rise buildings. Sustainability **13**(5) (2021). https://doi.org/10.3390/su13052973. https://www.mdpi.com/2071-1050/13/5/2973

11. Filho, N.M., Coutinho, E.S., Azevedo e Silva, G.: Association between home posture habits and low back pain in high school adolescents. Eur. Spine J. **24**(3), 425–433 (2014). https://doi.org/10.1007/s00586-014-3571-9

12. Fujimoto, Y., Fujita, K.: Depth-based human detection considering postural diversity and depth missing in office environment. IEEE Access **7**, 12206–12219 (2019)

13. Gawehn, E., Hiss, J.A., Schneider, G.: Deep learning in drug discovery. Mol. Inf. **35**(1), 3–14 (2015). https://doi.org/10.1002/minf.201501008

14. Hackford, J., Mackey, A., Broadbent, E.: The effects of walking posture on affective and physiological states during stress. J. Behav. Ther. Exp. Psychiatry **62**, 80–87 (2019). https://doi.org/10.1016/j.jbtep.2018.09.004. https://www.sciencedirect.com/science/article/pii/S0005791617302471

15. Han, T., Ivo, R.F., Rodrigues, D.D.A., Peixoto, S.A., de Albuquerque, V.H.C., Rebouças Filho, P.P.: Cascaded volumetric fully convolutional networks for whole-heart and great vessel 3D segmentation. Future Gener. Comput. Syst. **108**, 198–209 (2020)

16. Hsieh, J., Hsu, Y., Liao, H.M., Chen, C.: Video-based human movement analysis and its application to surveillance systems. IEEE Trans. Multimedia **10**(3), 372–384 (2008). https://doi.org/10.1109/TMM.2008.917403

17. Huang, K., et al.: Superb monocular depth estimation based on transfer learning and surface normal guidance. Sensors **20**(17) (2020). https://doi.org/10.3390/s20174856. https://www.mdpi.com/1424-8220/20/17/4856

18. Ke, Q., et al.: A neuro-heuristic approach for recognition of lung diseases from x-ray images. Expert Syst. Appl. **126**, 218–232 (2019)

19. Kulikajevas, A., Maskeliunas, R., Damaševičius, R.: Detection of sitting posture using hierarchical image composition and deep learning. PeerJ Comput. Sci. **7** (2021). https://doi.org/10.7717/peerj-cs.442

20. Langdon, E., Snodgrass, S.J., Young, J.L., Miller, A., Callister, R.: Posture of rugby league players and its relationship to non-contact lower limb injury: a prospective cohort study. Phys. Ther. Sport **40**, 27–32 (2019). https://doi.org/10.1016/j.ptsp.2019.08.006. https://www.sciencedirect.com/science/article/pii/S1466853X19300173

21. Lauraitis, A., Maskeliūnas, R., Damaševičius, R.: ANN and fuzzy logic based model to evaluate huntington disease symptoms. J. Healthcare Eng. **2018**, 1–10 (2018). https://doi.org/10.1155/2018/4581272

22. Li, B., Han, C., Bai, B.: Hybrid approach for human posture recognition using anthropometry and BP neural network based on Kinect V2. EURASIP J. Image Video Process. **2019**(1), 1–15 (2019)

23. Li, R., Si, W., Weinmann, M., Klein, R.: Constraint-based optimized human skeleton extraction from single-depth camera. Sensors **19**(11) (2019). https://doi.org/10.3390/s19112604. https://www.mdpi.com/1424-8220/19/11/2604

24. Lin, T.-Y., et al.: Microsoft COCO: common objects in context. In: Fleet, D., Pajdla, T., Schiele, B., Tuytelaars, T. (eds.) ECCV 2014. LNCS, vol. 8693, pp. 740–755. Springer, Cham (2014). https://doi.org/10.1007/978-3-319-10602-1_48

25. Liu, B., Li, Y., Zhang, S., Ye, X.: Healthy human sitting posture estimation in RGB-D scenes using object context. Multimedia Tools Appl. **76**(8), 10721–10739 (2017)
26. Liu, Y., Huangfu, W., Zhang, H., Long, K.: An efficient stochastic gradient descent algorithm to maximize the coverage of cellular networks. IEEE Trans. Wireless Commun. **18**(7), 3424–3436 (2019). https://doi.org/10.1109/TWC.2019.2914040
27. Lurati, A.R.: Health issues and injury risks associated with prolonged sitting and sedentary lifestyles. Workplace Health Saf. **66**(6), 285–290 (2018). https://doi.org/10.1177/2165079917737558. PMID 29251259
28. Nair, S., Sagar, M., Sollers, J., Consedine, N., Broadbent, E.: Do slumped and upright postures affect stress responses? A randomized trial. Health Psychol. **34**(6), 632–641 (2015). https://doi.org/10.1037/hea0000146
29. Niu, J., Wang, X., Wang, D., Ran, L.: A novel method of human joint prediction in an occlusion scene by using low-cost motion capture technique. Sensors **20**(4), 1119 (2020). https://doi.org/10.3390/s20041119
30. Nonnekes, J., Goselink, R.J.M., Růžička, E., Fasano, A., Nutt, J.G., Bloem, B.R.: Neurological disorders of gait, balance and posture: a sign-based approach. Nat. Rev. Neurol. **14**(3), 183–189 (2018). https://doi.org/10.1038/nrneurol.2017.178. http://www.nature.com/articles/nrneurol.2017.178
31. Nowotny, J., Nowotny-Czupryna, O., Brzęk, A., Kowalczyk, A., Czupryna, K.: Body posture and syndromes of back pain. Ortop. Traumatol. Rehabil. **13**(1), 59–71 (2011). https://doi.org/10.5604/15093492.933788
32. Ray, S.J., Teizer, J.: Real-time construction worker posture analysis for ergonomics training. Adv. Eng. Inform. **26**(2), 439–455 (2012)
33. Ripoll, V.J.R., Vellido, A., Romero, E., Ruiz-Rodríguez, J.C.: Sepsis mortality prediction with the quotient basis kernel. Artif. Intell. Med. **61**(1), 45–52 (2014). https://doi.org/10.1016/j.artmed.2014.03.004
34. Ryselis, K., Petkus, T., Blažauskas, T., Maskeliūnas, R., Damaševičius, R.: Multiple kinect based system to monitor and analyze key performance indicators of physical training. Hum.-Centric Comput. Inf. Sci. **10**, 1–22 (2020)
35. San, P.P., Ling, S.H., Nuryani, Nguyen, H.: Evolvable rough-block-based neural network and its biomedical application to hypoglycemia detection system. IEEE Trans. Cybern. **44**(8), 1338–1349 (2014)
36. Valle, M.S., Casabona, A., Fiumara, A., Castiglione, D., Sorge, G., Cioni, M.: Quantitative analysis of upright standing in adults with late-onset Pompe disease. Sci. Rep. **6**(1), 37040 (2016). https://doi.org/10.1038/srep37040. http://www.nature.com/articles/srep37040
37. Wang, W.J., Chang, J.W., Haung, S.F., Wang, R.J.: Human posture recognition based on images captured by the kinect sensor. Int. J. Adv. Rob. Syst. **13**(2), 54 (2016). https://doi.org/10.5772/62163
38. Wu, J., et al.: Risk assessment of hypertension in steel workers based on LVQ and fisher-SVM deep excavation. IEEE Access **7**, 23109–23119 (2019)
39. Zapata-Aldana, E., et al.: Muscle problems in juvenile-onset acid maltase deficiency (Pompe disease). Paediatrics Child Health **24**(4), 270–271 (2019). https://doi.org/10.1093/pch/pxy153. https://academic.oup.com/pch/article/24/4/270/5486550
40. Zhang, N., Cai, Y.X., Wang, Y.Y., Tian, Y.T., Wang, X.L., Badami, B.: Skin cancer diagnosis based on optimized convolutional neural network. Artif. Intell. Med. **102**, 101756 (2020). https://doi.org/10.1016/j.artmed.2019.101756. https://www.sciencedirect.com/science/article/pii/S0933365719301460

41. Zhou, J., et al.: Whole-genome deep-learning analysis identifies contribution of noncoding mutations to autism risk. Nat. Genet. **51**(6), 973–980 (2019). https://doi.org/10.1038/s41588-019-0420-0
42. Zhuang, H., Zhao, B., Ahmad, Z., Chen, S., Low, K.S.: 3D depth camera based human posture detection and recognition using PCNN circuits and learning-based hierarchical classifier. In: The 2012 International Joint Conference on Neural Networks (IJCNN), pp. 1–5 (2012)

An Efficient Approach for the Detection of Brain Tumor Using Fuzzy Logic and U-NET CNN Classification

Sarmad Maqsood[1], Robertas Damasevicius[1(✉)], and Faisal Mehmood Shah[2]

[1] Department of Software Engineering, Kaunas University of Technology, 51368 Kaunas, Lithuania
sarmad.maqsood@ktu.edu, robertas.damasevicius@ktu.lt
[2] Pakistan Space & Upper Atmosphere Research Commission, Karachi 75270, Pakistan

Abstract. Clinical diagnosis has increased marvelous significance in current day healthcare systems. This article proposes a brain tumor detection method using edge detection based fuzzy logic and U-NET Convolutional Neural Network (CNN) classification method. The proposed tumor segmentation system is based on image enhancement, fuzzy logic based edge detection, and classification. The input images are pre-processed using the contrast enhancement and fuzzy logic-based edge detection method is applied to identify the edge in the source images and dual tree-complex wavelet transform (DTCWT) is used at different scale levels. The features are calculated from the decayed sub-band images and these features are then categorized using U-NET CNN classification which recognizes the meningioma and non-meningioma brain images. The proposed method is evaluated using accuracy, sensitivity, specificity, and dice coefficient index. Simulation study demonstrates that the proposed technique achieves better performance, both visually and quantitatively in comparison with other approaches.

Keywords: Brain MRI · Medical image processing · Deep learning · Image classification · Segmentation · Fuzzy logic

1 Introduction

The enormous growth of cell areas in the brain can lead to tumors, which occur in people of all ages. Based on the area, size and location, these large tumor cells are divided into cancerous and non-cancerous cells [1]. The early stage of cancer cells is called benign and is referred to as the primary tumor area. The severe stages of cancer cells are called malignancies and secondary tumor area. Primary tumors are curable, and their growth controlled by taking the appropriate medications. The secondary tumor can be cured only if the affected patient receives adequate

© Springer Nature Switzerland AG 2021
O. Gervasi et al. (Eds.): ICCSA 2021, LNCS 12953, pp. 105–118, 2021.
https://doi.org/10.1007/978-3-030-86976-2_8

treatment with surgery or radiation [2]. Brain tumors are known to damage surrounding brain tissue, so tumor progression must be carefully assessed to extend patients survival time [3]. Magnetic resonance imaging (MRI) is determined to be one of the most common diagnostic approaches for brain tumors, and numerous MRI methods can be used to recognize the brain tumor. Each of the above MRI methods has a different relaxation time, so it can be used to recognize different brain tissues [4]. This deadly disease can be controlled early only by proper scanning the brain area at the initial stage to detect the tumor.

Due to the complexity and change in tumor structure and the similarity in intensity between tumor tissue and normal brain tissue, tumor segmentation is a difficult task. While certain tumors such as meningioma can be easily isolated, other tumors such as glioma and glioblastoma are problematic [5]. This makes manual segmentation of tumor a cumbersome task, and in some cases, due to the various appearance and vague shape of the tumor, changes in the oncologist's segmentation results may be observed. Therefore, an automatic segmentation method must be developed to facilitate this difficult task.

Meningioma is a tumor that procedures in the skull and protects the brain and the spinal cord. Specially, tumors form in a three-layered membrane called the meninges [6]. Meningiomas usually appear as extra axial lobar masses with distinct margins [11]. The existence rate of patients having meningioma is contingent on the size and location of the tumor area and the patient's age. Annexations, headaches, and limb weakness are signs of meningiomas. If caught early and treated with appropriate medical treatment, most malignant meningioma tumors can be cured. The diameter of benign meningioma tumors is approximately less than 2 mm and the diameter of malignant meningioma tumors ranges from 2 mm to 5 cm [3].

Manually identifying brain tumors and tracking their changes over time can be unvaried and error prone [6]. Since it requires an automated system to replace the traditional manual approaches. Previous methods have some limitations i.e., many traditional approaches use tagging methods to detect abnormal pixels in the brain region, existing methods cannot detect inner border pixels which are incompatible for various brain tumor detection systems. In this article, MRI is chosen as compared to computed tomography (CT) scanning because of the area enhanced by the contrast agent and its visibility, which can be well processed by various image processing methods [7]. MRI has been used to detect ischemic stroke lesions [8] and schizophrenia [9] in brain image slices. It also has been applied to detect tumour in other tissues such as breasts [10]. Therefore, numerous brain tumor detection approaches use MR imaging modalities.

The remaining paper is organized as follows. Section 2 study the notable related work on brain tumor detection. In Sect. 3 the detailed methodology of the proposed approach is discussed. Section 4 evaluates the performance of the proposed method in comparison with the other methods and, finally, Sect. 5 concludes this article with future research goals.

2   Related Work

Over the past few years, more and more work has been performed in the brain tumor segmentation field. This is determined by the significance of this topic in the medical society [3, 12, 13]. Different researchers have used different techniques to segment brain tumors. Currently, the deep learning based methods are considered as state-of-the-art in image-based recognition and segmentation of various cancers [14, 15] and other diseases [16, 17]. Khan et al. [18] uses two pre-trained CNN models (VGG19 and VGG16) for feature extraction. The best features were selected using the correntropy based joint approach and extreme learning machine (ELM) classifier is employed to classify the features. Seetha et al. [19] uses CNN for the brain tumors classification. They studied the structural variability of tumors around adjacent areas. The authors proposed a small kernel to keep the weight of each neuron small. Jasmine et al. [20] uses the adaptive neuro fuzzy inference classification technique to detect and locate tumors on MRI of the brain. The tumor areas are improved using histogram equalization technique without the detection of edges in brain images. Bansal et al. [21] used the swarm ant lion algorithm for the process of locating and detecting tumors in MRI. The method is likened with the probabilistic neural network to verify the effectiveness of the method. Devkota et al. [22] created a mathematical segmentation system of linear parameters to detect irregular tumor areas in brain images. The author derives statistical and texture characteristics of images from brain sources and divides the images into malignant or non-malignant images based on these calculated brain image characteristics. The tumor area was segmented using linear limited morphological processes. Ganeshkumar et al. [23] used the watershed segmentation technique to brain MR imaging to locate the tumor areas. The segmentation process uses a predetermined set of labeling methods, maximizing the precision of the tumor segmentation. Prasava et al. [24] presented a method to detect and recognize boundary pixels in brain images to segment tumor areas. This approach only detects the abnormal border of the tumor area but cannot detect the inner border of the tumor area. Lai et al. [25] presented a CNN method for semantic image segmentation. The authors suggest reducing the size of the convolution filter and reducing the input channels number to create the model more portable. Likewise, the author in [26] presented a lightweight CNN for real-time semantic segmentation. This method has omitted numerous connection areas to reduce the parameters of the network and rise the speed. Finally, Woźniak et al. [27] suggested a correlation learning mechanism (CLM) for deep learning models that fuses CNN with a classic neural network architecture. This support network helps the main CNN to find the most suitable filers for pooling and convolution layers, and the resulting architecture is used for brain tumor detection in CT scan images.

All the aforementioned methods achieved enhanced results, but still they exhibit several limitations such as many conventional approaches use tagging methods to detect abnormal pixels in the areas of the brain and existing approaches fail to detect the inside of the edge pixels, which is not appropriate for brain tumor detection systems.

3   The Proposed Method

The proposed approach for tumor segmentation and classification comprise of contrast enhancement, fuzzy logic-based feature extraction method, and classification. Firstly, the source brain image is pre-processed through contrast enhancement method for better visualization and then dual tree-complex wavelet transform (DTCWT) is employed to the improved image at different scale levels. Afterwards, the fuzzy-logic based feature extraction approach is used to find the edges. U-NET CNN is employed for the detection and classification of brain tumor imaging. The proposed framework contains two different modules: up sampling and the down sampling. The proposed U-NET CNN framework uses the perception of zero padding in both up sampling and down sampling to enhance the response of each layer. Figure 1 illustrates the workflow of brain tumor detection and classification.

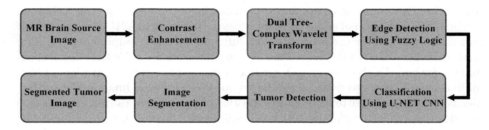

Fig. 1. Schematic diagram of the proposed system for brain tumor segmentation.

3.1   Pre-processing

To intensify the low contrast images the histogram equalization approach seems to be a more effective technique. Non-parametric modified histogram equalization (NPMHE) [30] is applied to increase the contrast and keep the average brightness of the source image.

Firstly, NMHE removes the spikes from the original histogram. After that the process clipped the histogram and computed the cumulative distribution function of the transitional rehabilitated histogram from the uniform one. After that it works as a weighting factor to create a final updated histogram. Equation (1) regulates a threshold and the pixels higher than the threshold contribute in the modified histogram as,

$$W_c(j) = r[j \mid H],\qquad(1)$$

where $r[j \mid H]$ is the occurrence probability of ith intensity-level given the horizontal contrast variation H. A measure of un-equalization (ζ_u) is calculated as in Eq. (2).

$$\zeta_u = sum(u - \varsigma_c v).\qquad(2)$$

The value of ζ_u is a pointer to those images which does not follow a uniform distribution. u is a uniform probability density function and $\varsigma_c v$ is a modified clipped histogram designed from the original histogram. The weighted factor of the modified PDF is given in Eq. (3).

$$\vartheta_F = (\varsigma_c v)W_c + (1 - \zeta_u)u. \tag{3}$$

The CDF of the image is attained from the reformed histogram ϑ_F in Eq. (4).

$$t_D(n) = \sum_{j=0}^{n} \vartheta_F(n). \tag{4}$$

The transformation operation $S(c)$ attained by using t_D given in Eq. (5).

$$S(c) = [(\alpha - 1)t_D(n) + \frac{1}{2}], \tag{5}$$

where $S(c)$ is used to obtain the contrast enhanced images. Contrast enhancement results improved the edges in the input images.

Figure 2 shows the enhancement from source brain images. From the image, it can be observed that after applying the enhancement method, the gradients of the image are enhanced keeping the information of the source image.

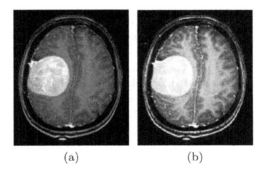

(a)   (b)

Fig. 2. Contrast enhancement result. (a) Source brain MRI, (b) Contrast enhanced image.

3.2   Dual-Tree Complex Wavelet Transform

This transform is employed to alter spatial resolution pixel to multi resolution pixel. The Discrete Wavelet Transform (DWT) is employed as a traditional decomposition technique for acquiring sub band images of numerous scales. DWT has a limit on offset variation, which affects the resolution factor at different zoom levels. This limitation can be overcome by using DTCWT to capture a broken sub band image. The DTCWT framework is intended with complex wavelet and complex scaling functions. The advantage of DTCWT is that it can extract edges from detail subbands, which are abundant in brain tissues. Those edges serve as discriminant features between diseased brain and healthy brain tissues [28].

The DTCWT operation is given in Eq. (6) as:

$$\psi(s) = \psi_r(s) + j\psi_{imj}(s) \tag{6}$$

The complex wavelet function having real and imaginary parts is expressed by Eqs. (7) and (8).

$$\psi_r(s) = \sqrt{2} \times \sum Q_r(s) \times \psi_r(2s - g) \tag{7}$$

$$\psi_{imj}(s) = \sqrt{2} \times \sum Q_{imj}(s) \times \psi_{imj}(2s - g) \tag{8}$$

The proposed method uses four levels of DTCWT to obtain the decomposed sub band images.

3.3   Feature Extraction

Fuzzy logic previously has been employed successfully for detection of edges in complex medical images such as retinal images [29]. Here, a fuzzy logic-based edge detection approach is presented to acquire the edges map of the contrast enhanced image. The workflow of the proposed fuzzy edge detection method is displayed in Fig. 3. A 3×3 convolution mask is created to obtain the grayscale neighborhood pixels values in the contrast enhanced image. The grayscale neighborhood pixels values acquired from the mask are preprocessed before the fuzzy inference system. The system is created to seize the processed values as the input. Then convert these values to a fuzzy plane. A library of fuzzy rules has been determined and displays the edge pixels of the output image. The output of the system is computed using the centroid technique and defuzzification according to the Mamdani's inference.

Firstly, a 3×3 convolution mask is created using the patterns shown in Fig. 4. These 16 fuzzy patterns represent a variety of possible boundary shapes. Select a pattern that mimics the type and orientation of edges that may appear. Patterns are examples of edges. The 'u', 'v', and 0 represent pixels in the edge model. The values $u = 0.5$ and $v = 1.2$ have been selected experimentally in this work. These values are fixed in all images. A recognizable addition is that increasing the number of models to 16 and above does not significantly improve the edge results. If the number of models is reduced, many edges are lost.

With 16 patterns all the edges are detected. After that, hesitation level or Intuitionistic Fuzzy Index (IFI) is found in Eq. (9).

$$IFI = \chi \times (1 - \psi(s)). \tag{9}$$

It calculates the Intuitionistic Fuzzy Divergence (IFD) between each element of the pattern, the size of the image window is the same as the pattern, and the

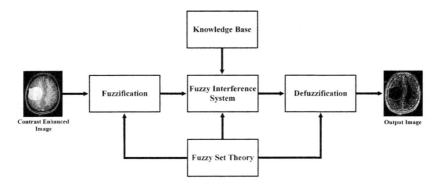

Fig. 3. Schematic diagram of the fuzzy logic-based edge detection method.

$$\begin{vmatrix} 0 & v & u \\ 0 & v & u \\ 0 & v & u \end{vmatrix} \begin{vmatrix} u & u & u \\ 0 & 0 & 0 \\ v & v & v \end{vmatrix} \begin{vmatrix} u & u & v \\ u & v & 0 \\ v & 0 & 0 \end{vmatrix} \begin{vmatrix} v & v & v \\ 0 & 0 & 0 \\ u & u & u \end{vmatrix}$$

$$\begin{vmatrix} u & u & u \\ v & v & v \\ 0 & 0 & 0 \end{vmatrix} \begin{vmatrix} u & v & 0 \\ u & v & 0 \\ u & v & 0 \end{vmatrix} \begin{vmatrix} 0 & 0 & 0 \\ u & u & u \\ v & v & v \end{vmatrix} \begin{vmatrix} v & u & u \\ 0 & v & u \\ 0 & 0 & v \end{vmatrix}$$

$$\begin{vmatrix} v & u & 0 \\ v & u & 0 \\ v & u & 0 \end{vmatrix} \begin{vmatrix} u & 0 & v \\ u & 0 & v \\ u & 0 & v \end{vmatrix} \begin{vmatrix} 0 & 0 & 0 \\ v & v & v \\ u & u & u \end{vmatrix} \begin{vmatrix} o & u & v \\ 0 & u & v \\ 0 & u & v \end{vmatrix}$$

$$\begin{vmatrix} v & v & v \\ u & u & u \\ 0 & 0 & 0 \end{vmatrix} \begin{vmatrix} v & 0 & u \\ v & 0 & u \\ v & 0 & u \end{vmatrix} \begin{vmatrix} v & 0 & 0 \\ u & v & 0 \\ u & u & v \end{vmatrix} \begin{vmatrix} 0 & 0 & v \\ 0 & v & u \\ v & u & u \end{vmatrix}$$

Fig. 4. Edge detection using 16 patterns.

maximum-minimum correlation of the equation is used to select the minimum IFD value in Eq. (10) as:

$$IFD(u,v) = Maxnumber[min(IFD(U,v))]. \tag{10}$$

The highest consequence is placed at the centered point in the image. Then, from the fuzzy domain matrix the edge images are transformed into the pixel images in the interval $(1-255) \times 255$ and after setting the threshold and applying the morphological operations the final image is obtained.

3.4   U-NET Based CNN Classification

The U-NET CNN is employed for brain tumor imaging detection and classification. The proposed framework contains two different elements: up sampling and down sampling. The down sampling component of the proposed U-NET

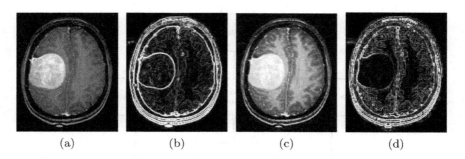

(a)   (b)   (c)   (d)

Fig. 5. Edge detection results. (a) Source brain MRI, (b) Gradient of (a) using fuzzy edge detection, (c) Contrast enhancement using NMHE [30], and (d) Gradient of (c) using fuzzy edge detection.

CNN framework contains six convolution sub-modules, and each convolution sub-module has three convolution layers. Every convolutional layer contains 32 filters with a 3×3 window size. The MRI of the brain of origin passes through each convolutional layer and generates posterior internal features. The size of the inner convolution function is important. To decrease the size of the internal features made by the convolution layer, a pooling layer is employed after the convolution submodule. The pooling layer is divided into averaging and maximum pooling. Average pooling locates a 3×3 mask on the inner feature set and then choose the mean of feature values as the final response from the pooling layer. Maximum pooling locates a 3×3 mask on the internal feature set and choose the maximum value of the feature values as the final response from the pooling layer. Therefore, by applying the proposed framework with maximum pooling, loss of functional value can be avoided. Unlike the inconsistent flow, the extended flow consists of sampling the feature map and immediately following it with a 2×2 size convolution. After concatenation, the convolution operation is applied on the two 3×3 kernels and ReLU is activated. Finally, by applying a 1×1 convolution to the last layer, a vector of each 56 component is assigned to the desired class (Fig. 5).

The proposed U-NET CNN operates the perception of zero padding for both up and down sampling to enhance the response of each layer that is not existing in the usual U-NET. Figure 6 shows the architecture of U-NET CNN. Figure 7 shows the benign and malignant meningioma brain images and Fig. 8 displayed the benign and malignant non-meningioma brain images. To segment out the tumor area the morphological gradient function is calculated using Eq. (11).

$$\phi(I(r,s)) = (I(r,s) \oplus D) - (I(r,s) \ominus D), \tag{11}$$

where $I(r,s) \oplus D$ denotes the elementary dilation function and $I(r,s) \ominus D$ denotes the elementary erosion function.

The gradients are computed using the Eq. (12).

$$\Delta(I(r,s)) = (I(r,s) \oplus D) - 2 \times I(r,s) + (I(r,s) \ominus D), \tag{12}$$

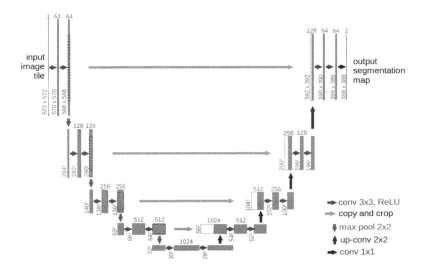

Fig. 6. U-NET CNN framework.

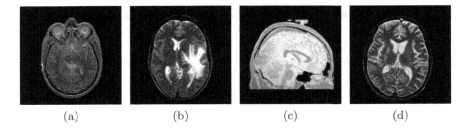

     (a)   (b)   (c)   (d)

Fig. 7. Non-meningioma benign and malignant brain images.

The tumor detection and segmentation of the brain image is shown in Fig. 9.

4 Simulation Setup

The implementation of the proposed technique is performed on a laptop having Intel(R) Core (TM) i7-9750H processor, 16 GB RAM, and one NVIDIA GTX 1650 GPU with 4 GB RAM in MATLAB environment. The experiments are evaluated on meningioma brain MR images. The dataset for the brain tumor detection is acquired from [31]. The dataset includes benign and malignant brain images containing a total of 708 brain MRI. The group of 571 meningioma brain MRI, 57 glioma brain MRI, and 80 pituitary brain MRI are available. This work contains a total of 571 meningioma brain MR images. To assess the performance of the proposed brain tumor detection and segmentation technique is employed on these images.

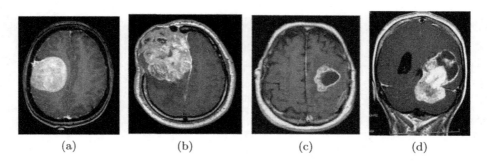

(a)   (b)   (c)   (d)

Fig. 8. Meningioma benign and malignant brain images.

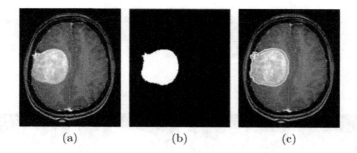

(a)   (b)   (c)

Fig. 9. Meningioma brain image. (a) Source image, (b) Tumor segmented image, and (c) Tumor extraction.

4.1   Results and Discussions

The Accuracy (Ac), Sensitivity (Sn), Specificity (Sp), and Dice coefficient index (DCI) metrics are used to estimate the performance of the proposed method. The highest value of these metrics presents better performance. These metrics are defined as follows.

$$Ac = \frac{K_{TP} + K_{TN}}{K_{TP} + K_{TN} + K_{FN} + K_{FP}} \times 100\% \tag{13}$$

$$Sn = \frac{K_{TP}}{K_{TP} + K_{FN}} \times 100\% \tag{14}$$

$$Sp = \frac{K_{TN}}{K_{TN} + K_{FP}} \times 100\% \tag{15}$$

$$DCI = \frac{2 \times K_{TP}}{2 \times K_{TP} + K_{FN} + K_{FP}} \times 100\% \tag{16}$$

where K_{TP} denotes the true positive, K_{TN} denotes the true negative, K_{FN} denotes the false negative, and K_{FP} denotes the false positive.

Table 1 demonstrates the simulation results of the proposed technique using the U-NET CNN classification method. The proposed system attains the Ac of

98.45%, Sn of 98.04%, Sp of 98.86%, and DCI of 96.95%. From Table 2, note that the proposed system for detecting the brain tumor using the U-NET CNN classifier attains better performance.

Table 1. Quantitative evaluation of the proposed approach using U-NET CNN.

Proposed method	
Parameters	U-NET CNN classification method (%)
Accuracy (Ac)	98.45
Sensitivity (Sn)	98.04
Specificity (Sp)	98.86
Dice coefficient index (DCI)	96.95
Classification accuracy (CAc)	98.59

Table 2 evaluates the proposed brain tumor detection system with other latest methods in terms of classification accuracy. Using the same dataset and the same number of meningioma brain MRIs, all methods were compared, and performance was evaluated quantitatively. The U-NET CNN classification method was used for brain tumor detection and segmentation, and 571 MRI of meningioma correctly classified 563 brain images of meningioma, and the classification accuracy rate reached 98.59%. From Table 2, it can be concluded that the proposed system has better accuracy of classification than other advanced methods. The performance of the proposed system is also determined using the receiver operating characteristic (ROC) curve and confusion matrix. The ROC curve and confusion matrix of the proposed U-NET CNN classification method are illustrated in Fig. 10.

Table 2. Performance comparison with other state-of-the-art approaches.

Authors	Methods	Classification accuracy (%)
Tripathi et al. [32]	Support Vector Machine (SVM)	94.63
Cheng et al. [33]	Linear discriminant analysis (LDA)	93.60
Badza et al. [34]	CNN classification	96.50
Proposed Method	U-NET CNN classification	**98.59**

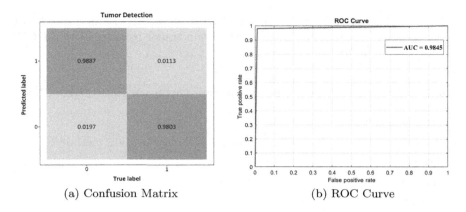

(a) Confusion Matrix   (b) ROC Curve

Fig. 10. Confusion matrix and ROC curve of U-NET CNN method.

5   Conclusion

Medical imaging has increased a solid status in modern day healthcare systems. This method proposes a brain tumor segmentation method using fuzzy edge detection and U-NET CNN classification method. This method uses a contrast stretching as a processing step to enhance the edge details in an image. A 4-level DTCWT is used to decompose the MR enhanced images into subband images. Edge detection methods based on fuzzy logic are used to find edge details on MR brain images. The proposed brain tumor detection method is evaluated by applying the proposed U-NET CNN framework. Simulation results prove that the proposed approach achieves better performance, in terms of both visually and enhanced information extraction when compared to other advanced techniques. The proposed classification method for brain tumor detection attains an accuracy of 98.59%. In future, the proposed method will further be analyzed for other application areas of biomedical image processing such as breast cancer recognition.

References

1. Bauer, S., May, C., Dionysiou, D., Stamatakos, G., Buchler, P., Reyes, M.: Multiscale modeling for image analysis of brain tumor studies. IEEE Trans. Biomed. Eng. **59**(1), 25–29 (2011)
2. Toğaçar, M., Ergen, B., Cömert, Z.: BrainMRNet: brain tumor detection using magnetic resonance images with a novel convolutional neural network model. Med. Hypotheses **134**, 109531 (2020)
3. Havaei, M., et al.: Brain tumor segmentation with deep neural networks. Med. Image Anal. **35**, 18–31 (2017)
4. Pereira, S., Pinto, A., Alves, V., Silva, C.A.: Brain tumor segmentation using convolutional neural networks in MRI images. IEEE Trans. Med. Imaging **35**(5), 1240–1251 (2016)

5. Ohgaki, H., Kleihues, P.: Population-based studies on incidence, survival rates, and genetic alterations in astrocytic and oligodendroglial gliomas. J. Neuropathol. Exp. Neurol. **64**(6), 479–489 (2005)
6. Jansson, D., et al.: Cardiac glycosides target barrier inflammation of the vasculature, meninges and choroid plexus. Commun. Biol. **4**(1), 1–17 (2021)
7. Ke, Q., Zhang, J., Wei, W., Damaševičius, R., Woźniak, M.: Adaptive independent subspace analysis of brain magnetic resonance imaging data. IEEE Access **7**, 12252–12261 (2019)
8. Kadry, S., Damasevicius, R., Taniar, D., Rajinikanth, V., Lawal, I.A.: U-Net supported segmentation of ischemic-stroke-lesion from brain MRI slices. In: 2021 Seventh International conference on Bio Signals, Images, and Instrumentation (ICBSII) (2021). https://doi.org/10.1109/icbsii51839.2021.9445126
9. Kadry, S., Taniar, D., Damasevicius, R., Rajinikanth, V.: Automated detection of schizophrenia from brain MRI slices using optimized deep-features. In: 2021 Seventh International conference on Bio Signals, Images, and Instrumentation (ICBSII) (2021). https://doi.org/10.1109/icbsii51839.2021.9445133
10. Kadry, S., Damasevicius, R., Taniar, D., Rajinikanth, V., Lawal, I.A.: Extraction of tumour in breast MRI using joint thresholding and segmentation - a study. In: 2021 Seventh International conference on Bio Signals, Images, and Instrumentation (ICBSII) (2021). https://doi.org/10.1109/icbsii51839.2021.9445152
11. Ostrom, T.Q., et al.: CBTRUS statistical report: primary brain and other central nervous system tumors diagnosed in the United States in 2010–2014. Neuro-oncology (2017)
12. Muzammil, S.R., Maqsood, S., Haider, S., Damaševičius, R.: CSID: a novel multimodal image fusion algorithm for enhanced clinical diagnosis. Diagnostics **10**(11), 904 (2020)
13. Maqsood, S., Javed, U., Riaz, M.M., Muzammil, M., Muhammad, F., Kim, S.: Multiscale image matting based multi-focus image fusion technique. Electronics **9**(2), 472 (2020)
14. Lahoura, V., et al.: Cloud computing-based framework for breast cancer diagnosis using extreme learning machine. Diagnostics **11**(2), 241 (2021)
15. Khan, M.A., Sharif, M., Akram, T., Damaševičius, R., Maskeliūnas, R.: Skin lesion segmentation and multiclass classification using deep learning features and improved moth flame optimization. Diagnostics **11**(5), 811 (2021)
16. Akram, T., et al.: A novel framework for rapid diagnosis of COVID-19 on computed tomography scans. Pattern Anal. Appl. (2021). https://doi.org/10.1007/s10044-020-00950-0
17. Sahlol, A.T., Elaziz, M.A., Jamal, A.T., Damaševičius, R., Hassan, O.F.: A novel method for detection of tuberculosis in chest radiographs using artificial ecosystem-based optimisation of deep neural network features. Symmetry **12**(7), 1146 (2020)
18. Khan, M.A., et al.: Multimodal brain tumor classification using deep learning and robust feature selection: a machine learning application for radiologists. Diagnostics **10**(8), 565 (2020)
19. Seetha, J., Raja, S.S.: Brain tumor classification using convolutional neural networks. Biochem. Pharmacol. J. **11**(3), 1487 (2018)
20. Johnpeter, J.H., Ponnuchamy, T.: Computer aided automated detection and classification of brain tumors using CANFIS classification method. Int. J. Imaging Syst. Technol. **29**(4), 431–438 (2019)
21. Bansal, S., Kaur, S., Kaur, N.: Enhancement in brain image segmentation using swarm ant lion algorithm. IJITEE **8**(10), 1623–1628 (2019)

22. Devkota, B., Alsadoon, A., Prasad, P.W.C., Singh, A.K., Elchouemi, A.: Image segmentation for early stage brain tumor detection using mathematical morphological reconstruction. Procedia Comput. Sci. **125**, 115–123 (2018)
23. Shanthakumar, P., Ganesh Kumar, P.: Computer aided brain tumor detection system using watershed segmentation techniques. J. Imaging Syst. Technol. **25**(4), 297–301 (2015)
24. Prastawa, M., Bullitt, E., Ho, S., Gerig, G.: A brain tumor segmentation framework based on outlier detection. Med. Image Anal. **8**(3), 275–283 (2004)
25. Lai, D., Deng, Y., Chen, L.: Deepsqueezenet-CRF: a lightweight deep model for semantic image segmentation. In: 2019 International Joint Conference on Neural Networks (IJCNN), pp. 1–8 (2019)
26. Liu, J., Zhou, Q., Qiang, Y., Kang, B., Wu, X., Zheng, B.: FDDWNet: a lightweight convolutional neural network for real-time semantic segmentation. In: IEEE International Conference on Acoustics, Speech and Signal Processing (ICASSP), pp. 2373–2377 (2020)
27. Woźniak, M., Siłka, J., Wieczorek, M.: Deep neural network correlation learning mechanism for CT brain tumor detection. Neural Comput. Appl. (2021). https://doi.org/10.1007/s00521-021-05841-x
28. Wang, S., Lu, S., Dong, Z., Yang, J., Yang, M., Zhang, Y.: Dual-tree complex wavelet transform and twin support vector machine for pathological brain detection. Appl. Sci. **6**(6), 169 (2016)
29. Orujov, F., Maskeliūnas, R., Damaševičius, R., Wei, W.: Fuzzy based image edge detection algorithm for blood vessel detection in retinal images. Appl. Soft Comput. **94**, 106452 (2020)
30. Poddar, S., Tewary, S., Sharma, D., Karar, V., Ghosh, A., Pal, S.K.: Nonparametric modified histogram equalisation for contrast enhancement. IET Image Proc. **7**, 641–652 (2013)
31. Cheng, J.: Brain tumor dataset. Nanfang Hospital and General Hospital, Tianjin Medical University, China (2017). https://doi.org/10.6084/m9.figshare.1512427.v5
32. Tripathi, P.C., Bag, S.: Non-invasively grading of brain tumor through noise robust textural and intensity based features. In: Das, A.K., Nayak, J., Naik, B., Pati, S.K., Pelusi, D. (eds.) Computational Intelligence in Pattern Recognition. AISC, vol. 999, pp. 531–539. Springer, Singapore (2020). https://doi.org/10.1007/978-981-13-9042-5_45
33. Cheng, J., et al.: Enhanced performance of brain tumor classification via tumor region augmentation and partition. PLoS ONE **10**(10), e0140381 (2015)
34. Badza, M.M., Barjaktarovic, M.C.: Classification of brain tumors from MRI images using a convolutional neural network. Appl. Sci. **10**(6), 1999 (2020)

Home Automation for People with Autism Spectrum Disorder

Jéssica Santo[1](✉) 🄳, Caique Z. Kirilo[1] 🄳, Marcelo Nogueira[1,2] 🄳, Nuno Santos[2,3] 🄳,
Ricardo J. Machado[2,3] 🄳, Luiz Carlos M. Lozano[1] 🄳, Álvaro Prado[1] 🄳,
and Juliana Carvalho[1] 🄳

[1] Software Engineering Research Group, Paulista University, UNIP,
Campus Tatuapé, São Paulo, Brazil
[2] School of Engineering, ALGORITMI Centre, University of Minho, Guimarães, Portugal
[3] CCG/ZGDV Institute, Guimarães, Portugal

Abstract. In an effort to reduce the crises of people with autism spectrum disorder
and increase their safety, a study was conducted on home automation so that,
through a medical protocol, it will be possible to configure situations and actions
that should be put into practice when the system identifies that the autistic stress
level is high. In addition, some studies were necessary to understand how the
autistic mind works, based on the literature and interviews with specialists in the
field. Through the developed system, it is possible to minimize the daily crises that
occur inside the home, working together with the treatments of chromotherapy
and music therapy.

Keywords: Autistic Spectrum Disorder · Stress level · Chromotherapy · Music
therapy

1 Introduction

Autism, from the Greek autós, means "of oneself". The term autism was coined in 1908
by Eugen Bleuler, a Swiss psychiatrist who used the term to describe the escape from
reality into an inner world (Cunha 2012).

The history of discoveries and achievements of autism is recent, it was classified as
a disorder of cognitive development in 1978, however, only in 1993 the syndrome was
added to the International Classification of Diseases of the World Health Organization.

Autism, according to Halpern (2019):

"Autism Spectrum Disorder (ASD) is a neurodevelopmental disorder characterized
by difficulties in communication and social interaction and by the presence of
repetitive or restricted behaviors and/or interests."

It is also considered a biological disorder that alters the brain's ability to understand
sensory stimuli, which are perceptions of smells, tastes, textures, sounds, lights, colors,
and everything that the human body is capable of feeling, making them sensitive to these
sensations (Garreau 1994).

© Springer Nature Switzerland AG 2021
O. Gervasi et al. (Eds.): ICCSA 2021, LNCS 12953, pp. 119–141, 2021.
https://doi.org/10.1007/978-3-030-86976-2_9

Considering that technology has been an ally in different areas and has been helping in several difficulties faced by mankind, an intelligent, safe and cozy environment was thought, aiming to help in nervous crises occurring in autistic people. The research in intelligent environments works to develop facilities and systems in order to help people in their daily activities and promote the saving of resources without reducing comfort (Rosa 2015).

Automating certain areas of the home can increase the effectiveness of a treatment, transforming previously uncomfortable rooms into quiet, cozy, and safe spaces.

In today's age, contact with technology is constant. Throughout each technological evolution, new methods and discoveries have been made with the intention of making human life easier. One example is the evolution of lighting, from candles to lamps. Thinking a little further ahead, lighting is something necessary for all human beings, but for some people it can be something more, it can be part of a treatment, a way to calm down and slow down the pulse through chromotherapy for example. According to Sui (1992): "Chromotherapy is a science that uses color to establish balance and harmony of body, mind, and emotions.

Based on researches conducted by the American Psychiatric Association in 2006, color therapy proved to be efficient in treating diseases. With this in mind, a project was developed to automate the lighting of a house based on the level of stress in which the autistic person finds himself.

The measurement of the stress level will be the sum of two factors: tension in the muscles, which according to Cielo et al. (2014) can be caused by stress, and the heartbeat, since, if tachycardia occurs frequently, even standing still, it may be related to situations of stress or anxiety (Loures 2002).

Thinking about the sound sense, which also becomes more sensitive for autistic people, it was designed a system of anti-noise windows and ambient sound, based on the study of music therapy.

"Music therapy is the professional use of music and its elements as an intervention in medical, educational, and everyday settings with individuals, groups, families, or communities that seeks to optimize their quality of life and improve their physical, social, communicational, emotional, intellectual, and spiritual health and well-being. Research, professional practice, teaching and clinical training in music therapy are based on professional standards according to cultural, social and political contexts." WFMT (2011).

The project also includes the automation of doors and windows with electric locks, ensuring the autistic's safety and helping the family's daily routine. It also has an emergency alert system for the family in case the stress level exceeds the average informed in the system.

According to the World Health Organization (WHO), there are approximately 70 million people in the world who have the Autistic Spectrum Disorder, and according to the study conducted by Goin-Kochel (2006), families with a higher family income usually receive the diagnosis of their child's ASD earlier than families with lower purchasing power, i.e., these people have better conditions to treat their children, because the sooner the diagnosis is made, the earlier the treatments begin, and the chance of control and the very understanding of how it works is better.

It is known that autism is a disease that can disable a person from having an ordinary and even independent life, so thinking about actions, devices, and possibilities for improvement is essential for families and people with this disorder.

The more help there is, the better they will live. There may not be or have not been a resolution to the disease, but minimizing and controlling it is a big step for them.

The existence of families who need help in their routines for having a dependent person is justified by Buscaglia (2006) as being a complex experience, full of difficulties and extreme responsibilities, since the autistic person may be partially or totally dependent on his/her parents. With the researches done, the possibility of integrating technology in treatments performed in patients with autism, such as chromotherapy and music therapy, was seen, and it is also possible to contribute to safety and stress reduction.

The Hospital Israelite Albert Einstein informed that about 150 thousand new cases of autism are diagnosed every year in Brazil, estimating today about 2 million autistic Brazilians and approximately 407 thousand only in the state of São Paulo. Based on this data, a study was carried out on the average socioeconomic status of families with autistic. The responsible for the research was Brazilian Association of Research Companies (2008), which carried out the analysis with the participation of 150 caregivers (Fig. 1), and from this total, 70.6% belonged to classes C1 (family income of R$1391), C2 (family income of R$933) and D (family income of R$618).

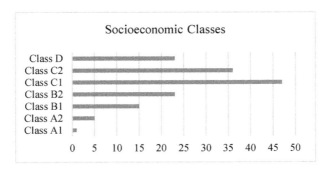

Fig. 1. Graphic of the socioeconomic survey. Source: Hospital Israelita Albert Einstein (2017)

Based on the data above, a project that would serve all families regardless of social class was elaborated, considering that there is the possibility of acquiring the equipment separately according to the individual needs of each autistic person.

2   Theoretical Reference

Autism
The Autistic Spectrum Disorder (ASD) is defined as a complex developmental disorder

that, from the behavioral point of view, has adverse implications on the development of communication and social environment (Gadia 2006).

According to the experts Sigman and Spence (2005), since it has not yet been possible to identify the causes, autism cannot be predicted or prevented, there is no cure or even particularly effective treatments.

Autism can manifest itself in varying degrees, however, certain signs can be considered "standard" and leading to diagnosis, such as repetitive and patterned behaviors with minimal interest in certain subjects and activities, absence of social interaction and communication. These symptoms can appear from early childhood, which corresponds to the period between birth and 6 years of age, and limit the individual's daily performance causing abnormal development (Gomes 2015).

In 1943, Kanner initially defined Autism as a condition with behavioral characteristics organized into three groups: social inability, language and communication problems, and the need for repetition, or sameness, then called Autistic Affective Contact Disorder.

Accordingly, Hans Asperger carried out a study called "Autistic psychopathy in childhood" in 1944, which confirmed the findings made until then, highlighting the preferential occurrence in early childhood boys who showed lack of empathy, low ability to make friends, motor mannerisms and unusual aspects in communication as tendencies to echo, they were also called little teachers, due to their ability to discuss a subject in detail.

In 1952, the American Psychiatric Association published the first edition of the Diagnostic and Statistical Manual of Mental Disorders DSM-1, which had nomenclatures, symptoms, and classifications used as a reference for researchers around the world.

During the 1950s, Kanner and Bettelheim supported the "refrigerator mother" belief, arguing that the disorder would be caused by emotionally distant family members, and the theory was called affective etiology or psychogenic theory. However, Bernard Rimland was the counterpoint to this theory, describing that there were four reasons to end the blaming of parents:

1. There were many parents who had other children who did not have autism;
2. If autism did indeed have a psychogenic origin, the disorder should disappear with psychotherapeutic treatment, which did not happen, according to studies based on this hypothesis;
3. The theory also defended the hypothesis that there had been a trauma in early childhood, but no patterns or reports were identified in which autism had started after a supposed trauma;
4. At least 23 parents in their database had been described as affectionate and cheerful, contradicting the idea of a "cold personality".

The year 1978 was marked with the understanding of the disorder. Michal Rutter classified autism as a disorder of cognitive development, proposing the definition based on four criteria:

1. Social delay and deviance not just as intellectual disability;
2. Communication difficulties such as absence of speech or even unusual use of it;
3. Unusual behaviors such as stereotyped movements and mannerisms;

4. Onset before 30 months of life.

The year was also marked by the elaboration of the DSM-3, where autism is recognized as a specific condition and is allocated to the new class called Invasive Developmental Disorders (IDD).

In 1981, psychiatrist Lorna Wing points out that autism is a spectrum of conditions and should be analyzed on different levels, since each individual could present specific difficulties. The term Asperger's Syndrome was coined.

According to studies conducted by Ivar Lovaas in 1988, the benefits of intensive therapeutic behavioral treatment were proven, with the result of his studies being an increase of 20 points on average in the IQ of children after two years of treatment.

In 2007, the UN established World Autism Awareness Day on April 2. In 2012, the Berenice Piana Law (12.764/12) was sanctioned in Brazil to guarantee the rights of people with Autism Spectrum Disorder.

In 2013, the DSM-5 started treating autism as a single diagnosis and aggregating different levels of severity. Asperger's syndrome, previously applied to milder cases, is no longer considered a separate condition.

Finally, within the current history, in 2015 the Brazilian Law of Inclusion of the Person with Disability (13.145/15) was created, increasing the protection of those with Autism Spectrum Disorder.

Spectrum disorder is a mental disorder that aggregates a diversity of conditions, but which have similarities and originate in some way from the same cause (Wing 1991).

Among the main symptoms of Autism Spectrum Disorder (ASD) are sensory difficulties. The brain of the person with ASD is unable to organize stimuli and give them meaning.

"Human beings are born with the basic capacity for sensory integration, however, it must be developed through interaction with the world and the adaptation of their body and brain to the many physical challenges during childhood. "(Caminha 2008).

According to Ayres (1972), there may be direct problems in the learning process in the autistic brain because of this social integrative difficulty, causing inappropriate behaviors, affecting his social life.

Sensitivity is divided into two categories: hypo sensitivity and hypersensitivity, and affects the five senses: hearing, sight, smell, touch, and taste. Because it is a spectrum, each autistic person may have a different sensitivity than the other; one autistic person may have sensitivity in all the senses while the other has sensitivity in only one (Table 1).

Hyposensitivity is observed when the autistic person relentlessly seeks to put his or her body in contact with the sensation that will be caused, i.e., does not run away from the sensation, such as looking directly at light.

According to Gallina (2019), researcher Judith Bluestone pointed to a possibility that hyposensitivity is actually a result of extreme hypersensitivity, in fact, high sensitivity would cause the person to totally block out a certain sensation.

This characteristic can be considered dangerous, since they may not perceive exhaustion, thirst or hunger.

Fig. 2. Parts of the brain affected by autism. Source: (The theory of mind, 2013)

Table 1. Descriptive Table of Hypersensitivity and Hyposensitivity. Source: Book More than Words (SUSSMAN 2004)

Hypersensitive	Hyposensitive
Movement (Fig. 2)	
Difficulties in activities that include movement	Need to swing and turn
Touch (Fig. 3)	
Touch is painful and uncomfortable	High pain and temperature threshold and like heavy objects on them
Vision (Fig. 4)	
Vision is distorted and bright objects and lights fragment images	High concentration on peripheral vision, because central vision is blurred, and also great depth perception
Hearing (Fig. 5)	
Magnified noise volume, distorted and confusing sounds, inability to limit certain sounds, and difficulty concentrating. This results in a high sensitivity to auditory stimuli	Sounds are only heard with one ear and there is no recognition of particular sounds. These individuals like crowded and noisy places, kitchens, doors, and objects
Smell (Fig. 6)	
Selects food, people, and objects by smell	Likes specific smells

Hypersensitivity is extreme sensitivity, generally causing autistic to flee from uncomfortable situations. This is a very recurring characteristic among autistics.

The individual with sensory hypersensitivity, whose perception of stimuli is intense, when present in environments of high stimulation, develops aggressive, impulsive, and frightened behavior.

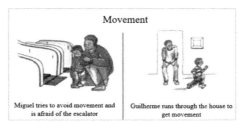

Fig. 3. Example of hypersensitive and hyposensitive – Movement. Source: Book More than Words (SUSSMAN 2004)

For autistic people who are hypersensitive to movement, there is a delay in motor development, problems with motor coordination, and a lack of dexterity.

The hyposensitive ones, on the other hand, have a need to be in constant movement, be it spinning, running, jumping, or swinging (Fig. 3).

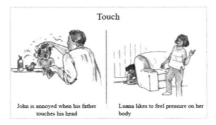

Fig. 4. Example of hypersensitive and hyposensitive – Touch. Source: Book More than Words (SUSSMAN 2004)

For autistic with hypersensitivity, characteristics such as fear of crowds, dislike playing games that can get them dirty, dislike being washed, combed or dried are common features for this type of sensitivity.

In the case of autistic with hyposensitivity, they have a high tolerance for pain, like to be upside down, and prefer tight-fitting clothing (Fig. 4).

Autistic with visual hypersensitivity avoid sunlight and glare because they cause headaches, dizziness and nausea when they use their vision, are afraid of moving objects, have difficulty determining distances, differentiate tones and colors, and do not like direct eye contact.

Autistic with hyposensitivity like to stare at lights or the sun, stare at moving objects, cannot perceive the presence of new people or objects in the environment, get lost when reading, and seek visual stimuli such as fans, pedestrians, fences, and textures (Fig. 5).

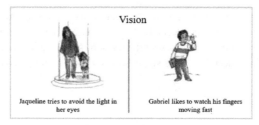

Fig. 5. Example of hypersensitive and hyposensitive – Vision. Source: Book More than Words (SUSSMAN 2004)

Fig. 6. Example of hypersensitive and hyposensitive – Hearing. Source: Book More than Words (SUSSMAN 2004)

Hypersensitive autistic, because they have very high sensitivity, usually cover their ears or hide in case of very loud sounds, avoiding noises such as high-pitched sounds, metallic sounds, and running water sounds.

Hyposensitive autistic like to talk loudly, prefer music and loud noises, making loud sounds in quiet environments (Fig. 6).

Fig. 7. Example of hypersensitive and hyposensitive – Smell. Source: Book More than Words (SUSSMAN 2004)

Hypersensitives avoid some smells because in some cases they become agitated. They choke on certain smells and foods are not attractive to them.

Hyposensitives like strong smells, preferring foods with strong smells, but have difficulty identifying certain smells, not identifying dangerous smells (Fig. 7).

It is known that autism is a developmental disorder and that it can present in varying degrees of severity. Despite these discoveries, the etiology of autism is still a matter of debate in the field of science, since its origin and treatment are not known for sure (Rotta 2007).

In the mild degree, autism is classified by difficulties in social interaction, but a little lighter, problems in changing the activity they are doing at that moment and problems with organization and planning.

In the moderate degree, the deficit in social skills is a little larger, even when the autistic person receives support, either in verbal or non-verbal communication, there is a certain limitation to start a social interaction. The moderate autistic person has difficulty in facing changes and presents repetitive behaviors more frequently.

The severe level has a diagnosis of much greater deficit in verbal and non-verbal communication than the moderate level, with even greater difficulty in social interaction, because besides not initiating an interaction as happens in the other two levels, severe autistic are not open to social interactions with other people. Moreover, in this grade, repetitive behaviors are even more pronounced.

Treatments

- **Chromotherapy**
  Several ancient civilizations used colors as a form of health treatment. The Chinese believed that color was related to Mythology and Astrology, associating each organ of the body with a specific color. Among the Greeks and Romans, many philosopher-medics went in search of knowledge of this medical science with the Egyptian priest-medics who built the colorful city Heliopolis (city of light), where colors were used in the treatment of the sick.
  According to Dr. Galioughi (1983), medical treatment using colors began in Egypt, where priest-medics treated the sick with colors using flowers and precious stones.

  "Chinese, Egyptian and Hindu manuscripts of that time show that these peoples possessed a complete system of chromology based on the law of correspondence between the septenary nature of man and the septenary division of the solar spectrum" (Marini 2007).

  On the other hand, there are beliefs that Chromotherapy originated in Ayurveda, a medicine practiced in India thousands of years ago, which associated color with the chakras, seven spiritual points of the body located along the spine, applying crystals, sounds, breathing exercises, massage, and medicinal plants that act on the energy centers of the human body (Brennan 2006).
  Chromotherapy was recognized as a complementary therapy to traditional medicine by the World Health Organization (WHO) in 1976.
  Chromotherapy is a science that uses colors to restore balance and harmony to the body, mind, and emotions, with the understanding that each color has a specific vibration and therapeutic capacity. This restoration is performed at the energetic level, taking advantage of natural resources (light energy, physical and mental) to help strengthen the individual (Sui 1992).
  The body is composed of colored energies (vibrations) and to adjust it, it is necessary to use identical colors and energies, projected with various functions according to the area of vibration, stabilizing the balance and providing healing, since the visible

light spectra release healing potentials in the physical body. The choice of colors can restore the body, mind, and spirit to their natural balance, focusing on health, not disease (Table 2).

Below is a list of colors and their indications for treatments:

Table 2. List of colors and their indications for treatments. Source: Silva R. C. (2006).

Color	Indication	Physiological effects	Emotional effects
Red	People with heart failure reject the color	Super stimulates the nervous system, stimulates emotions, and aids in recovery from fatigue and general weakening	It produces nervousness, stimulates bad temper, produces severe headaches, produces morbidity
Orange	Suitable for depressives or people with dysrhythmia	Increases the vitality of the nervous system, accelerates bone metabolism, aids in kidney disease	Restlessness
Yellow	Indicated for intellectual work	Increases blood pressure and aids in strengthening the health of tissues, organs, and bones	Stimulates concentration
Green	Suitable for hospital environments	It accelerates the liver metabolism, increases the speed of healing of post-operative tissues, lowers fever, and is a destroyer or decomposer of sick and dead cells	Tranquilizes the patient and improves balance
Blue	Indicated for children and for manic and violent patients	Lowers blood pressure, is soothing and mild anesthetic, refreshing	Reduces anxiety, stress, eliminates pain, and induces relaxation and sleep
Violet	Used in the treatment of serious infections. Do not use in the treatment of respiratory diseases, as it will stimulate the growth of lung virus	Antiseptic, regenerator of the exhausted and stressed nervous system with prolonged fatigue, and aids in tumor processes	In autism, blue stimulates a feeling of calmness and improved balance, representing lightness in the emotional aspect of the autistic person. The deepest of the colors, it transmits tranquility, harmony, and serenity

- **Music Therapy**

  In Ancient Greece, music was considered the Art of the Muses, being described as a divine revelation, and of extreme importance for harmonizing body and mind (Tyson 1981).

"While Hippocrates has been called the Father of Medicine, we can recognize Plato and Aristotle as the forerunners of music therapy. Plato recommended music for the health of the mind and body, and to overcome phobic anguish. Aristotle described its beneficial effects on uncontrollable emotions and to provoke the catharsis of emotions" (Leinig 1977).

According to Podolsky (1954), for the philosopher Plato, music is capable of providing mental and physical health, and there are several demonstrations of music as a healing element in Greek mythology, such as that of the Greeks Zenocrates, Sarpender, and Arion, who used the harp as an instrument to soften violent outbreaks of mania, preventing the method used from being physical force.

According to Tyson (1981), during the Renaissance, the interaction of music with medicine occurred through the rescue of the theory of the four humors, which unified the four elements and four humors of the body that would derive the four temperaments and associating with the theory of music, having as a result:

Element - Air, Mood - Blood, Temperament - Blood (joy, optimism, confidence and extroversion), Music Classification - High.

Element - Water, Mood - Phlegm, Temperament - Phlegmatic (shyness, apathy and tiredness), Music Rating - Tenor.

Element - Fire, Mood - Yellow Bile, Temperament - Choleric (irritability, intensity, impulsiveness and quickness), Musical Rating - Soprano.

Element - Earth, Mood - Black Bile, Temperament - Melancholic (artistic inclination, sadness, fear and introversion), Musical Rating - Bass.

The elements would influence temperaments, so an imbalance of the elements could alter human behavior, thus causing mental illness. Music then was used by means of an analysis corresponding elements to sounds (Tyson 1981).

For the physician Robert Burton (1621), music is the possibility to lower fears and rages and to cure "annoyances of the soul". In relation to melancholy, he pointed to music as a means to cheer and revive the soul, however, he warned about the harm and illness that "music could cause".

With the advent of Empiricism, a theory that claimed that knowledge came only from sensorial experience, studies on the physiological effects of music began, using musical elements such as rhythm, melody and harmony (Tyson 1981).

According to Costa (1989), the French psychiatrist Jean-Étienne Esquirol recommended music to his patients, expanding its use inside psychiatric hospitals, as he believed that the order and metrics of music could help in treating the mentally ill, recovering moral norms and socially adaptable behaviors, and awakening emotions in his patients.

Only in the mid-20th century was music therapy considered as a profession and discipline, and it was widely used for the physically and mentally handicapped, people with neurological disorders, language disorders, and blindness.

Music is an art form present in all cultures, and has been used as a form of entertainment or even as a form of treatment for disorders and diseases (Gfeller 2008).

Music therapy is a science with interdisciplinary and multidisciplinary basis, since its theoretical body has influences and foundations, besides music, in areas such as Psychology, Education, Medicine, and Philosophy. The technique aims to aid communication and encourage the relationship, motivation, and learning of patients by studying their reactions to sound-musical stimuli. (Smith 2000).

The literature on Autism reports that there is an intense relationship between sufferers of the disorder and music, being an excellent element for the study and understanding of emotions, since it can provoke positive and negative responses even in individuals from different cultures (Brattico 2011).

The therapeutic value is found in the capacity that music has to produce effects on the human being on biological, physiological, psychological, intellectual, social and spiritual levels (Blasco 1999). From the psychological point of view, music can favor emotional and affective development, reducing the anxiety of daily life, stress, and insomnia. Physically, it activates touch and hearing, stimulating blood circulation, breathing and reflexes.

In general, the objective of Music Therapy is to provide the expression of feelings, whether in the form of words, sounds, or even silences, and can help improve the quality of life.

Technical scope

- **Automation**

  In the technical scope, the concepts of automation, internet of things and human-computer interaction composed the study.

  Automation is a technique of making a process automatic, being information flow tasks, services performed or products manufactured. According to Black, (1998), the greater the number of human functions performed by a machine, the greater the degree of automation.

  Automation is a technology that guarantees the success of a process, since it was programmed with the objective of performing one or more functions always in the same way, thus ensuring equity in each process and reducing errors.

  In this process, it is possible to apply the understanding of "surplus value" by Karl Marx (1983): "[…] reduction in working time and the corresponding change in the proportion between the two components of the working day [...]". In other words, by increasing production through automation, manual work time is reduced.

  According to engineer Silveira, (2016), automation has seven main benefits, namely:

- Productivity;
- Cost reduction;
- Quality improvement in the process and its result;
- Safety;
- Competitive advantage;
- Precision;
- Remote Monitoring.

- **Human-Computer Interaction**

  Human-computer interaction is an area of computing that is, by definition, interdisciplinary, since it studies the behavior of human beings in relation to technology, whether with cell phones, refrigerators, etc.

  The IHC potential is a combination of robot characteristics (eg adaptability, accuracy, speed) with the properties of human cognitive abilities (eg problem solving). To facilitate this collaboration, humans need to work safely and interact with the robot. Furthermore, the robot must adapt to human behavior and anticipate human needs. Indeed, cognitive factors, including topics such as communication and perception, can greatly benefit HRI in general and production applications in particular (Prati 2020). HRI is also a science that studies the interaction of humans with robots, focusing on their behavior and attitudes towards robots in relation to the physical, technological and interactive characteristics of robots (Dautenhahn 2013).

- **Internet of Things**

  The popularity of the Internet of Things (IoT) has been growing steadily given its versatility and applicability in various fields (Maskeliunas et al. 2019).

  According to Ashton (1999), "The Internet of Things" is a technological revolution with the purpose of connecting equipment used daily to the world wide web.

  In order for the Internet of Things to exist, it is necessary to use smart objects, that is, objects that are equipped with a form of sensor, microprocessor, communication device, and energy source (Vasseur and Dunkels 2010).

  According to Santos (2016), the fundamental tools used in the Internet of Things for data transfer and processing are arrangements of various technologies that enable the integration of blocks:

  - Computation: Executes the local algorithm on smart objects;
  - Services: It has four areas, namely:
  - Identification, designed to map physical entities of interest to the user into virtual entities;
  - Data Aggregation, responsible for collecting and organizing data;
  - Intelligent collaboration, determines the reaction to a certain imposed scenario;
  - Ubiquity, deals with collaboration intelligently at different times and places where they are needed.
  - Semantics: Responsible for extracting knowledge from objects in the IoT.
  - Identification: Defines whether the object can be connected to the Internet or not.
  - Sensors/Actuators: Collect, store and forward data to storage centers.
  - Communication: Techniques used to connect smart objects.

After identifying the key items, it is then necessary to adapt the existing protocols, since there are paradigms that need to be overcome so that the intelligent object network can reach the standards determined by the global network (Loureiro 2003).

3   Methodological Procedures

The present work is characterized by exploratory, descriptive and explanatory research with the outlines of bibliographic research with a qualitative and quantitative approach, having as its nature the applied research, besides the experimental research.

According to Boccato (2006), the bibliographical research aims to solve a problem based on published theoretical references, evaluating and debating the various scientific contributions.

Applied research focuses on problems existing in the activities of institutions, organizations, groups or social actors. It is dedicated to detailed diagnosis, problem location, and solutions. It responds to the needs of "clients, social actors or institutions". Furthermore, it aims to generate knowledge for practical application (Thiollent 2009).

Exploratory research aims to provide greater familiarity with the subject, with a view to making it more understandable and explicit to the point where it is possible to build new hypotheses. It determines trends, environments, contexts and situations of study. (Gil 2007).

Descriptive research requires information about the subject to be researched in specific, describing its characteristics. This type of study aims to describe the facts and phenomena of a given reality (Trivinõs 1987).

Explanatory research presents the factors that determine or contribute to the occurrence of events, thus explaining the reason for each event through the results found. It can also be defined as the continuation of a descriptive research, since after the identification of the factors that determine a phenomenon, it is necessary for it to be described and detailed (Gil 2007).

For greater assertiveness in this study, a free interview was conducted as a method of communication, with a psychopedagogue with experience and direct contact with an autistic child, in order to understand more thoroughly the difficulties of the target audience of this study.

For the execution of this work, a bibliographic research was carried out, with the purpose of deepening the knowledge about the Autistic Spectrum Disorder, its levels and characteristics. An analysis was also made to define the sensory aspects that could be helped by technology in their treatment.

In sequence, a survey of requirements, prototyping and screen specification was done to determine exactly what would be developed in the practical prototype.

As methodology, we have:

– Free Interview as a communication method.
– Exploratory, descriptive and explanatory research.

And as fundamental methods for carrying out the research:

– Bibliographic research, with the purpose of deepening the knowledge about the Autistic Spectrum Disorder, its levels and characteristics.
– Requirements survey, prototyping and specification of the system screens.
– Development of the prototype.

4   Case Study

A field study was conducted with a psychopedagogue with experience and direct contact with an autistic child. In this study, it was discussed the benefits of having treatments like music therapy and color therapy in the home and how they could help in controlling and reducing the crises. It was also discussed the facility of having a record of the occurrences, heartbeat and muscle tension measurements for medical follow-up, helping in the direction of the treatments.

The question was raised to what extent the autistic can benefit from the automations presented, and the answer was the improvement of life in their routine, not only of the autistic, but of their legal guardians, by being confident that the house is properly equipped to better maintain the safety and comfort of those who need it.

5 The Prototype

The work consists of a set of automations and software that communicate with each other becoming a system that automates analog aspects of a residence according to the user's needs, manually or through analysis of the level of stress presented, aiming to assist in crisis control and in treatment of disabled people with Autistic Spectrum Disorder.

The objective of the software consists in controlling and monitoring the states of each automatic object installed in the user's residence, through its initial buttons, it is possible to change the state of an object and verify its current state, to make this control possible, the system has direct communication with the arduino (Fig. 8).

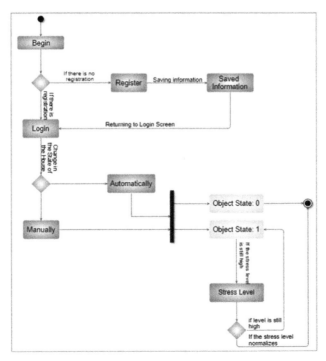

Fig. 8. State machine diagram. Source: Own Authors

The insertion of data and definition of situations and actions that should be put into practice when the system identifies that the autistic's stress level is high, will be done by the desktop system developed to configure this information. The system has as input the analysis of the user's stress level in the form of values identified via sensors and the manual input via the user's own request, that is, from an analysis of values and verification of requirements for each type of change, there will be a result as output of the change in the current state of the requested objects automatically, also allowing punctual changes without the need of an analysis of the stress level presented by the user (Fig. 9).

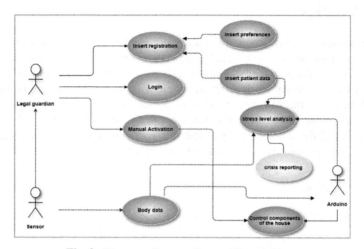

Fig. 9. Use case diagram. Source: Own Authors

The system will receive information about the level of stress and, according to the configured parameters, will analyze these settings regarding the necessary actions that should be put into practice in order to help in a possible crisis.

The communication is made between a Java object-oriented system, muscle and heart beat sensors and an Arduino board which controls the state of the house objects (Fig. 10).

The main objective of the arduino is to control the mechanisms that make objects that were previously analog or manual automatic, such as: the anti-noise system for doors and windows, the emergency door and window locks, and the lighting system.

In the project, for the anti-noise system to be possible, there are installed on the doors and windows of the house, fabric shutter curtains with acoustic insulation, which are activated via arduino, controlled by the software, with the purpose of inhibiting the internal noises that reach the residence.

The emergency lock system is composed of automatic locks, which in communication with the arduino and the main software, lock the doors and windows, so that in an emergency occurrence detected by the system, the locks are activated at the same moment, with the purpose of protection against a possible exit of the user or entrance of a third party whose risk of danger exists. The lighting system is composed of lamps that

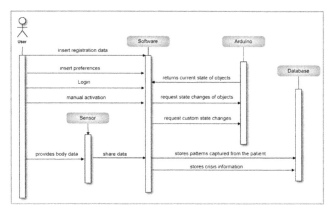

Fig. 10. Sequence diagram

have light level control and allow the change of the lighting color. The main objective of making their control automatic is so that there is total manipulation of the influence that the lighting states have on the user, once the software detects the need to change the current state of the light in a certain room, there is an instant change, making the environment as adapted as possible to the user's needs.

In general, the objective of the system is to provide interaction with all the components of the project, arduino, components of the residence and mainly the user, as well as an operating system provides communication between hardware and software, the system built in this project, has the purpose of being the main communication between user and machines, having as the only goal, to provide comfort and security for the main user and other residents of the residence (Fig. 11).

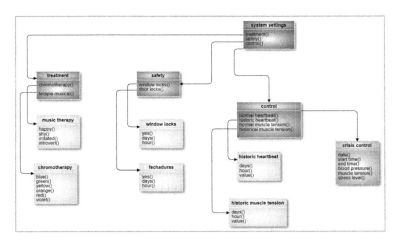

Fig. 11. Entity relationship diagram - system control. Source: Own Authors

The system can be activated in two ways: manually or automatically.

Manually, the user requests the change of state of the automatic component and from this request, the system sends an order to the Arduino, changing the state of the object, and keeps the information of the current state of the component, for example, the user requests the system to activate the anti-noise system of the doors and windows of the house, the system sends the order to the arduino, which activates the automatic blinds so that they cover the doors and windows, after the action of the Arduino, the software registers that the current state of the anti-noise system is active, leaving as the only input option, the request to deactivate the anti-noise system.

Done automatically, by reading the user's current stress level, for this input option, it is necessary for the system user to customize the way about which components of the house he would like to change and which state he would like depending on his stress level. Once the requirements to be changed are selected, the software will make the configured changes according to the user's stress level input.

As mentioned before, the measurement of the stress level will be given by the sum of two factors: muscle tension, which according to Cielo et al. (2014) can be caused by stress, and the heart rate, since, if tachycardia occurs frequently, even standing still, it can be related to stress or anxiety situations (Loures et al. (2002).

The human body presents a series of tension points, called trigger points. However, the most common point related to stress is tension in the trapezius, a muscle located in the neck (Fig. 12).

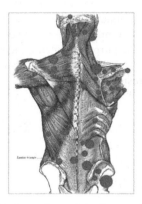

Fig. 12. Muscle tension points. Source: (Kelly 2017)

The sensor is responsible for picking up the electrical signal that the muscle generates when it contracts. It captures this small signal and amplifies it in the order of microvolts.

Regarding the alteration of the heartbeat, one of the most common causes, for people who do not have heart diseases, is due to stress situations.

Below is a table showing normal heart rate levels for women and men (Tables 3 and 4).

The sensors will work together, and if at any time only one of the two sensors identifies a level that is outside the configured standard, the system will check the second sensor to see if there is any change.

Table 3. Table of normal heart rate for women. Source: (Paschoal et al. 2009)

	Between 18 and 25 years	Between 26 and 35 years	Between 36 and 45 years
Excellent	54 to 60 bpm	54 to 59 bpm	54 a 59 bpm
Good	56 a 61 bpm	60 a 64 bpm	62 a 64 bpm
Below average	74 a 78 bpm	75 a 76 bpm	74 a 78 bpm

Table 4. Normal heart rate table for men. Source: (Paschoal et al. 2009)

	Between 18 and 25 years	Between 26 and 35 years	Between 36 and 45 years
Excellent	45 a 55 bpm	49 a 54 bpm	54 a 59 bpm
Good	57 a 61 bpm	67 a 61 bpm	60 a 62 bpm
Below average	71 a 73 bpm	72 a 74 bpm	73 a 76 bpm

The sum of these two factors, when above normal, will automatically trigger the system, which will have the function of identifying the best way to help the crisis to decrease or not to happen at all (Fig. 13).

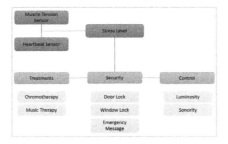

Fig. 13. Flowchart of the complete system. Source: Own Authors

The system will have three help options, and they can be activated together or separately.

In treatments, the system has the options Chromotherapy and Music Therapy, each of which can be configured according to the user's preference, or following the system's suggestion that will be based, in the case of music therapy, on the theory of the four elements, and, in the case of chromotherapy, on the theory of colors (Fig. 14).

Regarding security, the system will be connected to doors and windows that will have the locks activated when the system identifies a high level of stress, being also possible its configuration according to the user's preference. To unlock the locks, it will be necessary to manually deactivate the system.

The system will also trigger alert messages, warning the registered emergency contacts that the autistic person has a high stress level and is possibly in a crisis (Fig. 15).

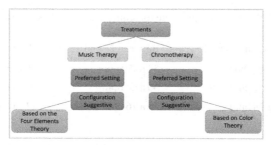

Fig. 14. Flowchart of the treatment system. Source: Own Authors

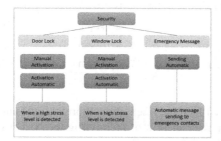

Fig. 15. Flowchart of the security system. Source: Own Author

In controls, the user can set the appropriate brightness level to make the autistic comfortable indoors, or he can leave the system Caiq automatic mode, adjusting the brightness as soon as it detects a brightness above the acceptable setting. The system will also activate the anti-noise windows when it detects a sound above the acceptable setting, also allowing the manual activation of this option (Fig. 16).

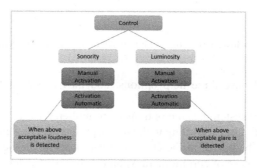

Fig. 16. Flowchart of the control system. Source: Own Author

6 Results e Discussions

From the case study, it was observed a sensitive improvement in moments of crisis, contributing to the control of anxiety and stress. Considering that this was a single case study, it was demonstrated that if this case study were extended to other people, it would become even broader and more effective.

In interviews realized with patients and their families, it was predicted that the system will be extremely beneficial in the daily control of the heartbeat, muscle tension and the stress level itself, providing a historic record that can be reported to the doctor with the date, time and the duration of the crisis.

7 Conclusion

With each passing day, the use of technology and artificial intelligence is growing and consolidating itself in the social sphere, actions that in the past were considered unimaginable are now part of everyday life, part of work, of family, of life. And it is with this thought of evolving people's knowledge and care, along with a desire that this subject does not stop here, with a mixture of satisfaction and social learning that this work was developed.

The system was thought of the autistic person and his/her family, being then a system of easy similarity and understanding, consisting of a cell phone or computer application, thus having an easy, fast and intuitive access, with an accessible price to all classes.

This was also an issue raised, currently, some existing equipment for the disabled in general, are marketed with high values for much of the population, which ends up making the cost and consequently the sale more expensive. The idea of ARSE is that it should be accessible to all classes, because this should go beyond commerce and profit, it should be a social project in search of improving the coexistence and experience with people who have this difficulty.

The study of the topic revealed to be ample and with potential for improvement even in the project that was presented in this article, providing future studies and analysis. For new studies, we will explore methods of detecting which of the human senses unleashed a crisis and which treatment was applied to reduce it.

The ARSE system has the intention of not only changing the way of life of autistic people, but that it is possible to change the technology called brain that exists inside each one, only then we will have a better society, able to respect everyone, always living in harmony.

Acknowledgements. "This work has been supported by FCT – Fundação para a Ciência e Tecnologia within the R&D Units Project Scope: UIDB/00319/2020".

References

Ayres, A.J.: Sensory Integration and The Child. Western, Los Angeles (1972)

Baptista, R.R., Cunha, G.D., Oliveira, A.R.: Aspectos fisiológicos e biomecânicos da produção de força podem ser usados no controle do treinamento de remadores de elite. Rev. Bras. Med. Esporte **14**, 427–430 (2008)

Black, J.: O Projeto da Fábrica com Futuro. Bookman, Porto Alegre (1998)

Blasco, S.P.: Compendio de Musicoterapia. Herder, Barcelona (1999)

Boccato, V.R.: Metodologia da pesquisa bibliográfica na área odontológica e o artigo. Rev. Odontol. Univ. Cidade São Paulo, São Paulo (2006)

Brattico, E., Alluri, V., Bogert, B.J., Vartiainen, N.: A functional MRI study of happy and sad emotions in Music with and without lyrics. Front. Psychol. **2**, 1–16 (2011)

Brennan, B.A.: Mãos de Luz: um guia para a Cura através do Campo de Energia Humana. Pensamento, São Paulo (2006)

Burton, R.: Anatomia da Melancolia (1621)

Buscaglia, L.: Os deficientes e seus pais: um desafio ao aconselhamento. Record, Rio de Janeiro (2006)

Caminha, C.R.: Autismo: Um Transtorno de Natureza Sensorial? PUC-Rio, Rio de Janeiro (2008)

Castells, M.: Sociedade em Rede: A Era da Informação: Economia Sociedade e Cultura. Paz e Terra, São Paulo (2002)

Cielo, C.A.: Síndrome de tensão musculoesquelética, musculatura laríngea extrínseca e postura corporal: considerações teóricas. Rev. CEFAC. **16**, 1639–1649 (2014)

Coriat, B.: A revolução dos robôs: o impacto sócio-econômico da automação. Busca Vida, São Paulo (1989)

Costa, C.M.: O despertar para o outro. Summus, São Paulo (1989)

Cunha, E.: Autismo e inclusão: psicopedagogia e práticas educativas na escola e na família. Wak, Rio de Janeiro (2012)

Dautenhahn: The Encyclopedia os Human-Computer Interaction. Berkshire Publishing school, Denmark (2013)

Espada, P., Martinez, O., Garcia-Bustelo, B., Lovelle, J.: Virtual objects on the Internet of things. Int. J. Artif. Intell. Interact. Multimed. **1**(4), 24–30 (2011)

Gadia, C.: Aprendizagem e autismo: transtornos da aprendizagem: abordagem. Artmed, Porto Alegre (2006)

Galioughi, D.P.: La Médicine des Pharaons (1983)

Gallina, L.P.: Toc Therapy: Design E Estimulação Multissensorial Para Crianças Com. Tea (Transtorno Do Espectro Autista), Bento Gonçalves (2019)

Garreau, B.: Effects of auditory stimulation on regional cerebral blood flow in autistic children. Dev. Brain Dysfun. **7**, 119–128 (1994)

Gfeller, K.: Music: a Human Phenomenon and Therapeutic Tool. American Music Therapy Association, Silver Spring (2008)

Gil, A.C.: Como elaborar projetos de pesquisa. Atlas, São Paulo (2007)

Goin-Kochel, R.P., Mackintosh, V.H., Myers, B.J.: How many doctors does it take to make an autism spectrum diagnosis? Autism **10**(5), 439–451 (2006). https://doi.org/10.1177/136236130 6066601

Gomes, P.T.: Autismo no Brasil: desafios familiares e estratégias de superação. In: Belo Horizonte, M.G., (ed.) Faculdade de Ciências Médicas, Universidade José do Rosário Vellano (Unifenas), Brasil (2015)

Halpern, A.A.: Manual de Orientação: Transtorno do Espectro do Autismo. Sociedade Brasileira de Pediatria (2019)

Henschel, A.H.: Cognição Socila na Era da Interação Humano-Robô. Cell Press, Cambridge (2020)

Kanner, L.: Autistic disturbances of affective contact. Nerv. Child. **2**, 217–250 (1943)

Kelly, K.: O que são pontos de gatilho? Quiropraxia, notícias e artigo (2017)

Leinig, C.E.: Tratado de Musicoterapia. Sobral Editora Técnica, São Paulo (1977)

Loureiro, A.A.: Redes de sensores sem fio. Simpósio Brasileiro de Redes de Computadores, Uberlândia (2003)

Loures, D.L.: Estresse Mental e Sistema Cardiovascular. Arquivos Brasileiros de Cardiologia (2002)

Marini, E.: Cromoterapia: dicas e orientações de como as cores podem mudar sua vida. Nova Era, Rio de Janeiro (2007)

Maskeliūnas, R., Damaševičius, R., Segal, S.: A review of internet of things technologies for ambient assisted living environments. Future Internet **11**(12), 259 (2019). https://doi.org/10.3390/fi11120259

Paschoal, M.A., Trevizan, P.F., Scodeler, N.F.: Variabilidade da frequência cardíaca, lípides e capacidade física de crianças obesas e não-obesas. Arquivos Brasileiros de Cardiologia **93**(3), 239–246 (2009). https://doi.org/10.1590/S0066-782X2009000900007

Podolsky, E.:. Music Therapy. Philosophical Library, Nova York (1954)

Prati, E.P.: Como incluir a experiência do usuário no projeto de interação homem-robô. Robótica e Manufatura Integrada por Computador. Department of Sciences and Methods for Engineering University of Modena and Reggio Emilia, Italy (2020)

Rosa, V.P.: Protocolo de comunicação para localização de objetos na casa inteligente. Revista Militar de Ciência e Tecnologia (2015)

Rotta, N.T.: Transtorno de aprendizagem: abordagem neurobiológica e multidisciplinar. Artmed, Porto alegre (2007)

Sigma, M.: Autismo e seu impacto no desenvolvimento. Centro para a Pesquisa e o Tratamento do Autismo, EUA (2005)

Silveira, C.B.: Sete benefícios conquistados através da Automação Industrial (2016)

Singer, T.: Tudo conectado: conceitos e representações da internet das coisas. Práticas Interacionais em Rede (2012)

Smith, M.P.: Melodia e harmonia ditam ritmo do corpo. Folha, São Paulo (2000)

Sui, M.C.: Cura prânica avançada: manual prático de cura prânica com cores. Ed. Ground (1992)

Therapy, W.F.: What is Music Therapy? (2011)

Thiollent, M.: Metodologia da pesquisa-ação. Cortez, São Paulo (2009)

Trivinõs, A.N.: Introdução à pesquisa em ciências sociais: a pesquisa qualitativa em educação. Atlas, São Paulo (1987)

Tyson, F.: Psychiatric Music Therapy: Origins and Development. Wiedner & Son, New York (1981)

Vasseur, J., Dunkels, A.: Interconnecting Smart Objects with IP. Morgan Kaufmann (2010)

Wing, L.: The relationship between Asperger's syndrome and Kanner's autism. In: Frith, U. (ed.) Autism and Asperger syndrome, pp. 93–121. Cambridge University Press (1991). https://doi.org/10.1017/CBO9780511526770.003

International Workshop
on Computational Science and HPC
(CSHPC 2021

Exploratory Analysis and Visualization of Brazilian Forest Data from the Forest Document System of the Brazilian Institute of the Environment

Matias Emir Luemba[1]([✉]) [iD], Nsiamfumu Kunzayila[2] [iD], and Wallace Casaca[1] [iD]

[1] Faculty of Science and Technology (FCT), São Paulo State University (UNESP), Presidente Prudente Campus, São Paulo, Brazil
matias.emir@unesp.br
[2] Bauru School of Sciences – São Paulo State University (UNESP), Bauru, São Paulo, Brazil

Abstract. This paper presents a study that makes use of several Exploratory Data Analysis and Information Visualization techniques to analyze forest data. Our goal was to carry out a data-driven investigation based on information from the so-called Forest Origin Document (DOF) system, which has been used by the Brazilian Institute for the Environment and Renewable Natural Resources (IBAMA) to control and supervise wood harvesting. The data utilized in this study have been obtained from the IBAMA's website. A comprehensive literature review covering the topics data analysis and visualization was conducted, allowing us to perform graphically oriented inspections and data-driven discussions when handling DOF-type data. Moreover, proposals have been presented in an effort to detect possible signs of fraud and illegality. Finally, by using data analysis tools, it was possible to originate different graphic models and data-based visualizations, thus obtaining summaries and preliminary results about the data of the Forestry Document system.

Keywords: Exploratory Data Analysis · Information Visualization · Forest Origin Document · Amazon Rainforest

1 Introduction

Exploratory Data Analysis (EDA) and Information Visualization (IV) are useful data-based tools successfully used to explore large amounts of records. They contribute to the understanding of several complex environmental and social challenges such as those related to wood harvesting and forest preservation. Thus, making data available as open repositories for research purposes has the potential to improve environmental governance, as well as to assist public policies for combatting illegal practices, hence supporting sustainable logging and agricultural production. These actions can corroborate the mitigation of gas emissions and the adaptation to climate changes [1].

© Springer Nature Switzerland AG 2021
O. Gervasi et al. (Eds.): ICCSA 2021, LNCS 12953, pp. 145–159, 2021.
https://doi.org/10.1007/978-3-030-86976-2_10

In Statistics, EDA helps data analysts to better understand the key characteristics of the data, mainly through methods based on visual inspection, which can lead to the formulation of new hypotheses and the design of novel validation experiments. Therefore, EDA is one of the main tasks in Data Science applications in the sense that the more data is pre-processed and visualized, the more information you can get and the better machine learning models you can train [2]. Concerning IV, it gathers a multiplicity of techniques and graphically oriented models for visual analysis and simulations. In fact, conventional visualization methods aim at simplifying data and highlighting relevant information based on domain experience [3].

Illegal logging makes it difficult to locate and quantify the wood being harvested from Brazilian forests, because harvesting often does not form large clearings that can be visualized from satellite images. The problem intensifies when one tries to track regions that do not leave clues which can be captured by satellites. These include logging in areas with difficult access, wherein the wood is transported by rivers. The falsification of documents is another critical issue [4]. Moreover, due to the high rate of illegal logging in protected areas and the lack of transparency in public data, the Amazon Forest turned out to arouse the interest of several Non-Governmental Organizations (NGOs). Since there is a large amount of data publicly available as part of the Forest Origin Document (DOF) system, such a collection is an interesting alternative to carry out data-based evaluations and visual inspection.

By conducting studies with open forest data, to ensure public transparency and a better overview of the logging in the Amazon Forest, in this paper we employ EDA and IV tools for exploring the DOF-IBAMA database. We focus on identifying discrepancies among millions of data records, including the detection of possible signs of fraud and illegality. By performing this exploratory analysis of DOF database, we seek:

- Improve social control over the logging, especially for Amazon Rainforest, to create robust instruments for transparency and systematic surveillance.
- Increase public knowledge about open data in the timber and forestry industry.
- Inspect the distances and transportation costs in the wood flow.
- Collect evidence of occurrence and volumes of different wood species.
- Tracking different types of forestry-derived products in the DOF database.
- Analyze the number of company indicators in different regions.
- Analyze the frontiers in the sense of "how data vary over the borders and migration to new frontiers and transportation routes".

We also intend to offer the visualization of the results concerning the following issues: (i) wood production and abundance, (ii) composition of wood species, (iii) technologies and generated products, (iv) wood prices and income, (v) number of companies in different regions.

The data used in this study consist of subsets (cutouts) taken from the original database of DOF system, because of the large volume of data in the full database. Thus, we select two particular subsets, which comprise the whole data of the Brazilian states of Acre and Rondônia from 2016 to 2018. By taking the DOF database of the IBAMA, we discuss the following points as motivation:

– Determine the sequence of wood flows and individual production chains. A difficult task to be evaluated in the datasets is the following: "how to map the log extraction path within the forest?".
– Determine the "mass balance" for the wood sector, towards answering the following question: "what is the total wood production in different parts of the chain, considering more raw materials from construction to final wood products?".
– Gathering evidence of illegal logging: "what is the variation, as measured from the database, to provide clues and basis for illegal logging?".

Therefore, the goal of this work is to analyze the DOF database of the IBAMA, seeking to identifying patterns and characterizing production chains and the behavior of timber companies. The exploration of species and volumes traded through visualization techniques and exploratory data analysis is another object of study, as well as the identification of possible signs of fraud and illegality concerning wood exploration and transportation.

This paper is organized as follows: Sect. 1 presents the introduction of the work and delineates the research scope, its motivation, and the intended objectives. Section 2 brings the theoretical foundation and literature review. Section 3 describes our study proposals and the methodological steps as conducted in this study. Section 4 gives the experimental results and their discussion, while Sect. 5 summarizes our findings and the conclusions of the work.

2   Basic Concepts and Related Work

As previously mentioned, EDA is a class of techniques that can be used to visually represent the knowledge deeply embedded in a given dataset [5]. In fact, EDA can be understood as the process by which a dataset is analyzed to interpolate useful information. This process usually describes the data in a visual way, allowing decision-making for business entities [6].

2.1   Data Visualization

Data visualization consists of a dynamic manner to quickly react to new developments using virtual environments, network technology, or new computer graphics algorithms. The user – the decision-maker – initially has a total idea about a scenario before focusing on the details, but observations from a graphical model can provide part of the relevant information [7].

2.2   Forest Origin Document System of the Brazilian Institute for the Environment and Renewable Natural Resources

DOF electronic records cover the transportation and the sale of forest-derived products and by-products of native origin, from the forest exploitation area to consumer companies. A single DOF record can contain different wood-derived products and their species, which are listed in the document from the entry of the record lines. However, the precarious filling of the document and the existence of incomplete data fields in DOF records make it difficult to be used for tracking purposes, as well as for social control of the wood chain, including more robust transparency mechanisms [1].

2.3   Brazilian Forests

Forest is any large area of land covered by trees or other woody vegetation areas where the crowns touch, forming a green "roof" [8]. The Brazilian Amazon Rainforest remained completely intact until the beginning of the modern era of deforestation, i.e., before the Transamazonica highway inauguration, in 1970. Deforestation rates in the Amazon have been increasing since 1991 with the deforestation process at a variable but accelerated pace. Although the Amazon Rainforest is deforested for a variety of reasons, livestock is still the predominant cause. In fact, medium and large livestock properties were responsible for around 70% of deforestation activities [9].

2.4   Transportation of Wood Products

The cost of transportation is an important issue when commercializing wood. As it is a bulky and dense product, transporting wood generally entails significant costs for the producer. The cost of domestic wood transportation represents, on average, 3.5% of revenue [10]. The portion of the cost referring to the transportation of native wood is around 12% of the definitive price of the product. According to [11], the cost of transportation represents 44.54% of the expenses related to logging in Brazil.

The vast majority of logs are conveyed from the forest to the processing zones through the 85% road network and, to a lesser extent, the 15% waterway. Road transport has also some peculiarities related to the quality of roads for wood transportation. On average, only 19% of transportation between the logging area and the processing industry is conducted by paved ways (good quality), 36% by poor roads (regular quality) and 30% by non-precarious roads (low quality) [12, 13]. There is a complexity in the transportation of wood due to the large number of variables involved in the process, such as climate variables, distances between the forest and the wood processing unit, maintenance costs, fuel, lubricants, tires, tariffs, among others, so that a decision must be made in order to minimize expenses and distances covered.

All costs involved in wood transportation are called total costs, and they are divided into fixed and variable costs. As variable costs, all expenses that vary as production changes are considered, i.e., fuel, lubricants, tires, and maintenance [14].

2.5 Wood Extraction

Legal logging is responsible for promoting sustainability through forest management plans. The forest-based sector extracted approximately 13 million m^3 of logs from Brazilian forests, feeding the wood processing sector to generate approximately R\$8 billion in annual revenues [15]. For sustainable exploitation, the authors in [16] considered the following aspects: 1st Costs of pre-exploratory activities in forest management (pre-exploratory activities, IBAMA fees, vine cutting and monitoring fees); 2nd Exploratory costs in the implementation of forest management (exploratory management costs, divided into the maintenance of main and secondary roads, opening of roads, trails, and displacements, in addition to hauling and felling trees.

2.6 Related Work

Several works have already been carried out concerning Exploratory Data Analysis and Visualization applied to forest data. Below, we present some of these reports, focused on environmental protection and wood sustainable management.

In [17], the authors evaluated the economic viability of the forestry activity in a sustainable forest management plan, in an area belonging to Fazenda São Pedro, in the municipality of Nova Monte Verde, Mato Grosso state. To determine the economic feasibility, the Revenue/Cost Ratio method was used. The exploration activity was economically viable, as it presented a Revenue/Cost Ratio of R\$ 1,70. Thus, considering administrative and exploratory expenses, the total net income was R\$560,405.51 (41.33%), generating, on average, R\$71,60 of net income per m^3. The authors reported in [18] that the production capacity of native forests varied according to environment and forest plannings so that it is possible to support the sustainability of the forestry. They also considered characterizing the potential of production and exploratory planning in a reserved area, located in Flona do Jamari - Rondônia (RO), to visualize the dynamics of timber production. They evaluated the aspects of the availability of forest resources and the practice of low-impact exploratory planning.

In [19], the authors analyzed the differences in the explored forest areas over the years 2007 to 2010, on a particular property in the Pará state using Lidar data. Their research estimated the area of canopy gaps per hectare, extracted from a canopy height model. Impacts on the forest understory were also assessed, by using a metric that calculates the proportion of returns below 0.5 m versus total returns. The obtained results indicated large significant differences in the number of canopy gaps between undisturbed and logged forests, but not between harvest years. Considering the work conducted in [12], the authors stratified a forest portion in the Amazon region, in structurally similar areas, by applying multivariate analysis-based techniques in order to improve the planning of forest production. They used methods that rely on clustering and discriminant analysis. A forest census was carried out, in which the following variables were analyzed: Number of trees, Average commercial height, Average diameter at breast height (DBH), Basal area and Commercial volume.

A data-driven study was carried out in [20], by performing exploratory research on the activity sector from secondary databases, as available at the Brazilian Institute of Geography and Statistics (IBGE) website. The computational models applied in the study proved to be effective in the task of highlighting the effects of increase/reduction of Gross Domestic Product (GDP), hence improving the rural development and green economy. In a similar work, the authors in [21] evaluated the fifteen main forest genera and species legally exploited in the Brazilian Amazon of Acre state. The number of authorizations issued for the exploitation of managed forests, the volume of wood, and the management area licensed by the Acre Environment Institute from January 2005 to August 2012 were also analyzed. Their findings showed that the area and volume of licensed timber had growth during the period, reaching the peak in 2010 and 2011.

Despite the vast number of studies, the majority of works focused on applications such as forest management, sustainable logging, vegetation index, among others. In recent years, only a few works have employed EDA and IV to explore forest data in Brazil from DOF system. Detecting possible signs of fraud and illegality from DOF-type data is another little-explored branch in literature.

3   Material and Methods

Our methodology consisted of taking the bibliographical survey of the literature, the construction of computing frameworks for exploratory analysis and visualization, the DOF system of the IBAMA, and Brazilian Forestry data. More specifically, to perform such analysis and data visualization, two subsets of the DOF system have been considered: the data sets of the states of Acre and Rondônia, under the interval ranging from 2016 and 2018.

The data were obtained from secondary and official resources, but they can also be downloaded from IBAMA website, as a set of spreadsheets grouped by states. Notice that IBAMA is the main agency responsible for the DOF database, which includes all the states of the federation, except Pará and Mato Grosso states, which use the Forest Products Commercialization and Transport System (Sisflora), and Minas Gerais, which takes the Integrated Environmental Information System (SIAM).

The data were analyzed using open-source software and tools, such as Python and Python-related libraries.

4   Results and Discussion

Since its implementation in 2006, the DOF system has been modernized and technically improved. Moreover, the total number of documents issued by the states of Acre (AC) and Rondônia (RO), to accompany the transportation of legalized wood and native products, grew substantially from 2011 to 2014. Concerning 2016 and 2017, Fig. 1 shows the year-on-year evolution of DOF emissions for the Brazilian states of Acre and Rondônia, where RO had a much higher number of DOFs issued.

Figure 2 shows the comparison of DOF emissions w.r.t the destination states of wood products in the Brazilian market, grouped by years. One can observe that the DOF emission destinations have been increasing year on year during the period.

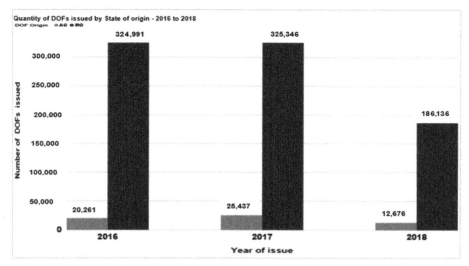

Fig. 1. Total number of Document of Forest Origin (DOF) issued between the years 2016 to 2018 by the Brazilian states of Acre (AC) and Rondônia (RO).

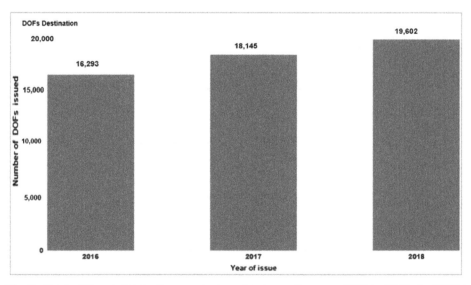

Fig. 2. Total of Forest Origin Documents, issued between the years 2016 to 2018, for DOFs' destination.

Table 1 shows the number of companies that send the timber sector in different regions between the years 2016 and 2018. Notice that the state of RO covers the highest number of companies in the North region of Brazil. In 2016 and 2018, 1,477 wood product shipping companies were registered in the North Region of the country.

Table 1. Total of wood product shipping companies in the North between 2016 to 2018.

Region/State	Companies
Brazil	**1,477**
North	**1,477**
Acre	149
Rondônia	1,328

Table 2. Total of companies receiving wood products in the different regions between the years 2016 to 2018.

Region/State	Companies
Brazil	**32,712**
North	**23,252**
AC – Acre	8,947
PA – Pará	7
AM – Amazons	70
RO – Rondônia	14,201
RR – Roraima	4
TO – Tocantins	23
Northeast	**929**
CE – Ceará	185
RN - Rio Grande do Norte	70
PB – Paraiba	82
AL – Alagoas	85
SE – Sergipe	75
BA – Bahia	299
PE – Pernambuco	68
PI – Piaui	35
MA – Maranhão	30
Southeast	**5,557**

(*continued*)

Table 2. (*continued*)

Region/State	Companies
SP - São Paulo	2,412
MG - Minas Gerais	2,038
RJ - Rio de Janeiro	690
ES - Espírito Santo	417
Midwest	**935**
DF - Federal District	100
GO – Goias	565
MT - Mato Grosso	125
MS - Mato Grosso do Sul	145
South	**2,039**
RS - Rio Grande do Sul	651
SC - Santa Catarina	526
PR – Paraná	862

Table 2 shows the number of companies directed to the timber sector in different regions between the years 2016 to 2018. The state of Rondônia has the largest number of companies represented in the activity of the national timber sector. Also, note that the North region holds most recipient companies - possibly as "intermediate" companies that receive products from several smaller companies in the region and ship them to large production centers such as São Paulo, Distrito Federal, and Rio de Janeiro.

Table 3. Summary of products presented by the DOF system.

Products	By-products	
Finished wood products	Soft	Floors and floors
	Portal or Jamb	Decks
	Lining (Lambril)	Tacos
	Solid Flat Door	Baseboard
	2-sided planed wood (S2S)	4-sided planed wood (S4S)
Round wood	Record	Roller
	Soft Platforms (TS)	Toretes
	Tortes (ts)	Chubby stands
Lumber	Wood (beam)	Wood (board)

(*continued*)

Table 3. (*continued*)

Products	By-products	
	Wood (plate)	Wood (beam)
	Batten	Block, square or fillet
	Wood (unfolded plank)	Wood (beam)
	Short beam	4-sided planed plate (S4S)
	Short kidney	Short board
	Wood (stem)	Little goats
	Short beam Slats	Short clapboard Short slat
Wood waste	Waste from the wood industry for industrial purposes	Wood industry waste for energy Purposes '
	Waste for energy purposes	Blade residue
Laminate	Unrolled Blade Knife blade	
Barbs	Chips (ts) Barbs	
Firewood	Firewood Firewood	
Chips	Chips	
Mourao	Posts	
Stacks	Stacks	
Bark	Cartridges	

Table 3 lists all products, and by-products registered in the DOF system. Notice that since there are many products derived from wood. As a result, these were categorized according to the summary of products presented in the DOF system. Lumber is the group that gathers the largest number of by-products, followed by Finished Wood Products and Wood Waste.

Considering the products reported in Table 4, Sawn wood is the one which holds the highest rates of commercialization and emission of DOF's documents in several regions between the years 2016 to 2018, representing 246,392,99 of the total of transported volume.

Table 5 tabulates the wood species transported between 2016 to 2018. From the listed species, one can observe that Caripé (*Licania longistyle*) was the one that presented the highest representation in the volume transported between the years 2016 to 2018, comprising more than 499 thousand cubic meters. Embirema (*Terminalia amazonica*) appears in the second place in this ranking, with a volume greater than 456 thousand cubic meters, and finally Jabota (*Calycophyllum spruceanum*), in the last position, with more than 151,000 m^3.

Table 4. Products and volumes transported and sold between 2016 to 2018 in Brazil.

Products	Year of marketing and transport			
	2016	2017	2018	Total volume
Finished wood products (cubic meters)	13,288,37	124,380,22	10,486,33	148,154,92
Round wood (cubic meters)	11,384,25	80,412,97	25,403,46	117,200,69
Wood (cubic meters)	180,798,67	48,345,86	17,248,46	246.392,99
Wood waste (cubic meters)	16,806,81	13,100,19	18,813,14	48,720,14
Laminate (cubic meters)	13,380,46	13,143,67	12,579,12	39,103,26
Chips (cubic meters)	9,255,59	15,298,30	13,565,37	38,119,25
Firewood	39,147,26	11869,80	17,750,64	68,767,71
Chip (cubic meters)	14,172,80	17,680,44	13,194,88	45,048,12
Bark	20,244,19	24,259,54	23,065,95	67,569,68
Coal	33,853,45	26,467,66	26,013,92	86,335,03

Table 5. Wood species transported in greater volume between 2016 to 2018.

Scientific name	Popular name	Volume (cubic meters)
Licania longstyle	Caripe	499,383
Terminalia amazonica	Embirema	456,611
Qualea paraensis	Jequitibá	423,034
Pithecellobium spp.	Jaguarana	413,641
Centrolobium paraense	Araribá	356,361
Inga spp.	Garlic	330,033
Qualea dinizii	Libra	312,103
Cedrelinga cateniformis	Cassava plant	269,113
Qualea dinizii	Cedar	254,275
Qualea spp.	Yellowish	241,411
Buchenavia macrophylla	Angelim	236,212
Calycophyllum spruceanum	Jatoba	151,967

Figure 3 shows the annual volume of wood transported, highlighting the years 2016 to 2018 in the state of Rondônia. Notice that there was a decrease in the volume of wood transportation in during three consecutive years in different states, except for the state of Rondônia.

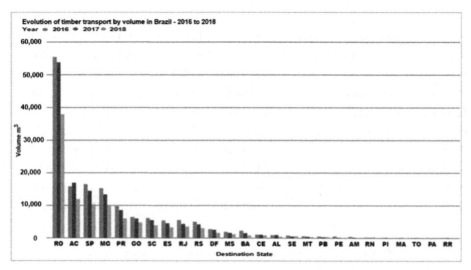

Fig. 3. Evolution of wood transport in Brazil - 2016 to 2018.

Figure 4 displays the transportation of wood products, organized by regions of Brazil between the years 2016 to 2018. From the plotted graphs, one can check that the main destinations of wood products are the North, Southwest, and South regions.

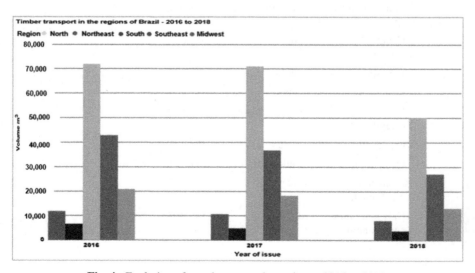

Fig. 4. Evolution of wood transport by regions - 2016 to 2018.

Figure 5 shows that most wood products come from the Amazon region. It was found that most of the cargoes of wood products in the Northern region are transported to the municipalities located in Rondônia and Acre, with Roraima and Tocantins having few records of transporting wood cargoes.

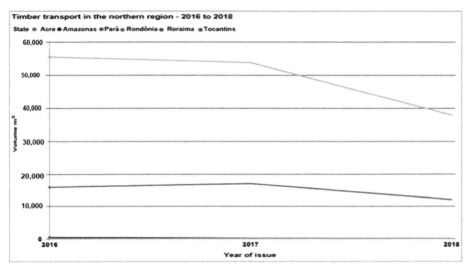

Fig. 5. Wood transport in the North - 2016 to 2018.

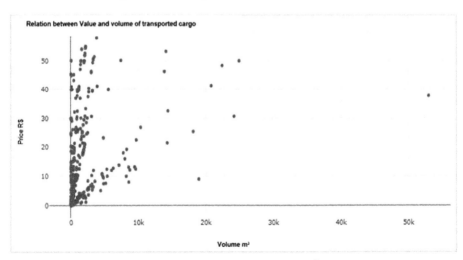

Fig. 6. Relation between the value (R$) and the volume (m^3) of the transported cargo

Finally, in Fig. 6, we discuss the relationship of the price against the volume of transported wood. From the plotted data, one can verify that some points holding a large volume of wood were registered at low prices, as well as small volumes of transported cargo with extremely high prices. This last case may be explained because some species of noble and protected trees have greater values when commercialized in the market. However, aiming at finding potential irregularities, we searched the spots where exceptionally low volumes and extremely high prices were declared in the DOF's documents. By inspecting these documents, we found out that the same shipping company declared all the records, which may be an indication of some kind of irregularity or documents filled out wrongly. Thus, this is a real case of data-driven analysis, wherein a ground check could be properly conducted in order to eliminate any doubts about the issue.

Still regarding Fig. 6, since the transportation cost varies as the distance changes, the location of the yard and consumption centers are strategic decisions and require detailed planning by the transportation companies. The longer the journey, the higher the unit cost per volume of wood transported. Several factors are related to the transportation of wood loads: the vehicle types, the distance of transportation, the unit value of the freight, the conditions in which the road mesh is found, the waiting time for loading and unloading, the load capacity in volume the vehicle carries, local and regional conditions. As a result, it is hard to perform a complete investigation only by taking DOF-type documents, requiring a more comprehensive investigation of different data resources.

5   Conclusion

This work applied Exploratory Data Analysis and Information Visualization tools on data from the Brazilian DOF system. We focused on exploring forest/wood data concerning two Brazilian states, i.e., Rondônia (RO) and Acre (AC), from 2016 to 2018. After carefully analyzing the forest data from DOF database, it was possible to better understand the relationship between different variables from the full database, as the total amount of extracted wood, transportation prices, destinations, etc.

The main wood shippers and recipients were also analyzed in this study, including the states with the highest / lowest number of transported wood loads and the relationship between price and volume of wood traded, as discussed in Fig. 6.

A future work, we intend to develop a new set of visually oriented tools to better explore DOF system data.

References

1. Bezerra, M.H., Morgado, R.P.: Research Report Open Data on Climate, Forest and Agriculture: An Analysis of the Opening of Federal Databases. Imaflora. Piracicaba, São Paulo (2017)
2. Samvelyan, A., Shaptala, R., Kyselov, G.: Exploratory analysis of Kiev city petition data. In: 2020 IEEE 2nd International Conference on Systems Analysis and Intelligent Computing (SAIC) (2020)
3. Zhang, M., Chen, L., Li, Q., Yuan, X., Yong, J.: Uncertainty-oriented ensemble data visualization and exploration using variable spatial spreading. IEEE Trans. Visual. Comput. Graphics. **27**, 1808–1818 (2020)

4. Scabin, A.: Illegal logging in the Anavilhanas archipelago (central Amazon): human variables that determine the spatial distribution of logging and structural effects on the most exploited taxa. National Amazon Research Institute. Manaus, Amazonas (2010)
5. Khan, S., Velan, S.: Application of exploratory data analysis to generate inferences on the occurrence of breast cancer using a sample dataset. In: IEEE. 2020 International Conference on Intelligent Engineering and Management (ICIEM) (2020)
6. Velleman, P., Hoaglin, D.: Applications, Basics, and Computing of Exploratory Data Analysis. Duxbury Press, Ithaca (1981)
7. Alves, C., Cota, M., Castro, M.: MLV-viewer: views with mining of data in decision support systems MLV-Viewer: data mining visualizations in decision support system. In: 2020 15th Iberian Conference on Information Systems and Technologies (CISTI) (2020)
8. OECO: what is a forest. https://www.oeco.org.br/dicionario-ambiental/29004-o-que-e-uma-floresta/. Accessed 15 Nov 2020
9. Fearnside, M.: Deforestation in the Brazilian Amazon: History, Indices and Consequences.
10. Fleury, P.: Strategic transport management. http://www.remade.com.br/br/revistadamad eira_materia.php?num=558&subject=Transporte. Accessed 21 Nov 2016
11. Machado, C., Pereira., R., Sant'Anna, G.: Forest roads: the determining in forest road transport (2003). http://www.remade.com.br/br/revistadamadeira_materia.php?num=367& subject=E%20mais&title=Estradas%20florestais:%20o%20fator%20determinante%20do% 20transporte%20rodovi%E1rio%20florestal. Accessed 15 Nov 2020
12. Pereira, D., Santos, D., Vedoveto, M., Guimarães, J., Veríssimo, A.: Amazon Forest Facts 2010. Amazon Institute of Man and Environment - Imazon. Belém – Brazil (2010), http://ift. org.br/wp-content/uploads/2014/11/FatosFlorestais_2010.pdf. Accessed 15 Apr 2021
13. Pereira, P., Ramos, J., Pereira, M., Schmidt, V.: Forest exploitation planning: a study in Brazilian Amazon. https://www.brazilianjournals.com/index.php/BRJD/article/view/3687/ 3494. Accessed 15 Mar 202021/03/15.
14. Berger, R.R., Carnieri, C., Lacowicz, P., Junior, P., Brasil, A.: Forestry transportation costs minimization using linear programming.https://revistas.ufpr.br/floresta/article/view/ 2277/1902. Accessed 10 Apr 2021
15. Juvenal, T., Mattos, R.: The forest sector in Brazil and the importance of reforestation, Rio de Janeiro (2002)
16. Passos, A., Dalfovo, W., Rosa, M.: Cost of legality in loggin in the state of Mato Grosso: implementation of forest management. https://journals.openedition.org/confins/29756. Accessed 15 Apr 2021
17. Bona, D., Silva, D., Pinheiro, L., Silva, E., Chichorro, J., Basso, M.: Income/cost of forestry exploration activity in a sustainable forest management plan in Amazonia – case study, https:// periodicoscientificos.ufmt.br/ojs/index.php/nativa/article/view/1807. Accessed 08 Apr 2021
18. Biazatti, S., Mora, R., Sccoti, M., Junior, J., Souza, L.A., Souza, L.: Planning and forest production in concession area in the western amazon. https://www.brazilianjournals.com/ index.php/BRJD/article/view/2317/2326. Accessed 09 Apr 2021
19. Pinagé, E., Keller, M., Dos-Santos, M., Spinelli-Araújo, L., Longo, M.: Temporal evaluation of logging effects using Lidar data. In: Proceedings XVII Brazilian Symposium on Remote Sensing - SBSR (2015). https://ainfo.cnptia.embrapa.br/digital/bitstream/item/123 636/1/3092.pdf. Accessed 09 Apr 2021
20. Pegorare, A.B., Mendes, D.R.F., Moraes, P.M.D., Costa, R.B.D., Constantino, M.: ANÁLISE DO IMPACTO DA PRODUÇÃO FLORESTAL NO DESENVOLVIMENTO ECONÔMICO E AMBIENTAL DE MATO GROSSO DO SUL. Revista Brasileira de Agropecuária Sustentável **8**(4), 9–18 (2018). https://doi.org/10.21206/rbas.v8i4.3032
21. Silva, F., Robert, R., Santos, A., Mendonça, S.: Quantification and assessment of the main forest species licensed for exploitation in the state of acre from 2005 to 2012. https://doi.org/ 10.1590/2179-8087.026212. Accessed 09 Apr 2021

Self-energy Feynman Diagrams with Four Loops and 11 Internal Lines

Elise de Doncker[1(✉)] and Fukuko Yuasa[2]

[1] Western Michigan University, Kalamazoo, MI 49008, USA
elise.dedoncker@wmich.edu
[2] High Energy Accelerator Research Organization (KEK),
1-1 OHO, Tsukuba, Ibaraki 305-0801, Japan
fukuko.yuasa@kek.jp
http://www.cs.wmich.edu/elise

Abstract. We consider 4-loop Feynman diagrams with 11 internal lines. The associated 10-dimensional loop integrals are calculated for four diagrams with massive internal lines, and we further handle the massless case of the diagram referenced in the literature as $M61$. The computations are performed with double exponential (DE), Quasi-Monte Carlo (lattice and embedded lattice rules) and adaptive integration algorithms, which do not require any user input regarding the integrand behavior. The lattice rule methods are combined with a transformation to help alleviate boundary singularities. The embedded lattice rules are implemented in CUDA C and their execution is accelerated using an NVIDIA Quadro GV100 GPU, whereas DE is parallelized over MPI and executed on an AMD cluster. Adaptive integration is performed with the ParInt multivariate integration package, which is also layered over MPI. For the massless $M61$ diagram we use a dimensional regularization approach and extrapolation. The results will be compared with respect to accuracy and efficiency, and verified with pySecDec.

Keywords: Feynman loop diagrams · Lattice rules · Adaptive integration · High performance computing · Dimensional regularization

1 Introduction

The Standard Model of particle physics developed in the last century is well established and has explained a wide range of physics phenomena. However, there remain several problems for which the model does not provide an explanation. For example, a theoretical prediction of the muon magnetic anomaly in the Standard Model provides an excellent result [2]. However, a recent highly precise measurement at Fermi National Accelerator Laboratory (FNAL) revealed that the discrepancy between experiment and theory has increased [1]. Not only by the anomaly but also by other unexplained problems, the limitation of the Standard Model has been recognized.

Therefore, precise tests of the Standard Model are inevitable and it is expected that further limitations will emerge from future experiments. In response, precise theoretical predictions are absolutely necessary. This means that a precise calculation of higher-order corrections in perturbative theory is required. Over the past two decades, significant advances have been made in analytical, semi-analytical and numerical methods

© Springer Nature Switzerland AG 2021
O. Gervasi et al. (Eds.): ICCSA 2021, LNCS 12953, pp. 160–175, 2021.
https://doi.org/10.1007/978-3-030-86976-2_11

in this research field. One of challenges is a precise evaluation of multi-loop Feynman integrals, which appear as a key ingredient in the calculations.

We have been developing fully numerical methods for the evaluation of multi-loop integrals with sufficient accuracy. Generally speaking, numerical approaches are computationally intensive. However, our methods succeed in performing the computation in a realistic time with the help of modern computer architectures. In this contribution, we will briefly describe our techniques and present recent developments taking 4-loop Feynman diagrams with 11 lines as an example.

Subsequently in this paper, we review background information on Feynman loop diagrams/integrals and on the numerical methods used, in Sects. 2 and 3, respectively. After an outline of automatic integration in Sect. 3.1, non-adaptive methods are covered in Sect. 3.2, including the double exponential (DE) method, and Quasi-Monte Carlo (QMC) approaches based on lattice rules, embedded lattice rules and stochastic rule families. The adaptive algorithm from the ParInt package is discussed briefly in Sect. 3.3. Sections 3.4 and 3.5 further specify the transformations used and the extrapolation, respectively. Results for the diagrams of Fig. 1 are reported in Sect. 4, including those for the massive diagrams in Sect. 4.1, and the massless diagram in Sect. 4.2. Appendix A.1–A.4 lists the main parts of the integrand functions.

2   Feynman Diagrams and Loop Integrals

A general form of the scalar Feynman integral in Feynman parameter (Euclidean) space is given by $\mathcal{F} = (4\pi)^{-\nu L/2}\mathcal{I}$ with

$$\mathcal{I} = \Gamma(N - \frac{\nu L}{2})\,(-1)^N \int_{\mathcal{C}_N} \prod_{r=1}^{N} dx_r\, \delta(1 - \sum x_r) \frac{C^{N-\nu(L+1)/2}}{(D - i\varrho C)^{N-\nu L/2}} \qquad (1)$$

$$= \Gamma(N - \frac{\nu L}{2})\,(-1)^N \int_{\mathcal{S}_{N-1}} \prod_{r=1}^{N-1} dx_r\, \frac{C^{N-\nu(L+1)/2}}{(D - i\varrho C)^{N-\nu L/2}} \qquad (2)$$

and where L is the number of loops, N is the number of internal lines, and ρ is an infinitesimal parameter preventing the denominator from vanishing. In the integrand function, C and D are polynomials depending on physical parameters and the topology of the diagram. For the instances covered here, D does not vanish in the interior of the domain, thus we have $\varrho = 0$. The space-time dimension ν is expressed in terms of a parameter ε, which approaches zero for regularization, $\nu = 4 - 2\varepsilon$. By eliminating the δ-function in (1), the N-dimensional unit cube integration domain $\mathcal{C}_N$ transforms into the $d = (N - 1)$-dimensional unit simplex $\mathcal{S}_d = \{\mathbf{x} \in \mathcal{C}_d \mid \sum_{j=1}^{d} x_j \leq 1\}$ in (2).

We further incorporate the normalization factor $n(\varepsilon)^4$ where

$$n(\varepsilon) = \frac{\Gamma(2 - 2\varepsilon)}{\Gamma(1 + \varepsilon)\,\Gamma(1 - \varepsilon)^2} \qquad (3)$$

The C and D functions are given in Appendix A.1–A.4.

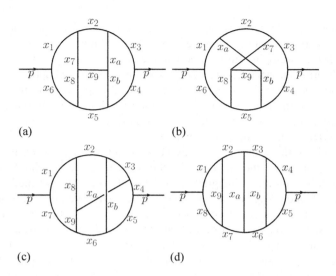

Fig. 1. 4-loop $N = 11$ diagrams (a) $M61$ [3,8,26,38]; (b) $M62$ [3,38]; (c) $M63$ [3,38]; (d) BH [5]

2.1   Loop Diagram Expansions

We will treat the $(L = 4)$-loop self-energy diagrams of Fig. 1 with $N = 11$ internal lines, thus the integrand behaves as $C^{1+5\varepsilon} / D^{3+4\varepsilon}$. For massive lines with all masses $= 1$, and $s = p^2 = 1$, we give results in this paper for all diagrams of Fig. 1, whereas for $M61$ in Fig. 1(a) we also handle the diagram with massless internal lines. The massless case of $M61$ (Fig. 1(a)) was considered in [8,26]. We covered the massless diagram of Fig. 1(d) in [20].

The integrals for the massless diagrams of $M61$, $M62$ and $M63$ satisfy an expansion in ε of the form

$$\mathcal{I} \sim \mathcal{I}(\varepsilon) = \gamma(\varepsilon) \sum_{k \geq \kappa} C_k \varepsilon^k \tag{4}$$

where γ is a factor that depends on ε, and $\kappa = -1$. Specifically, analytic results for these diagrams have been presented in the literature as an expansion in powers of ε with coefficients expressed in terms of Riemann zeta functions as follows.

$M61$, Fig. 1(a). We compute results for the massless case according to [3,34,38]

$$\mathcal{I} \sim n(\varepsilon)^4 \Gamma(3 + 4\varepsilon) \left(-\frac{10\,\zeta_5}{\varepsilon} + (50\,\zeta_5 - 10\,\zeta_3^2 - 25\zeta_6) \right.$$
$$\left. + (90\,\zeta_5 + 50\,\zeta_3^2 + 125\zeta_6 - 30\,\zeta_3\,\zeta_4 + 9.5\,\zeta_7)\,\varepsilon + \mathcal{O}(\varepsilon^2) \right) \tag{5}$$

$M62$, Fig. 1(b). Known results are from [3,38], corresponding to

$$\mathcal{I} \sim n(\varepsilon)^4 \Gamma(3 + 4\varepsilon) \left(-\frac{10\,\zeta_5}{\varepsilon} + (130\,\zeta_5 - 10\,\zeta_3^2 - 25\zeta_6 - 70\zeta_7) + \mathcal{O}(\varepsilon) \right) \tag{6}$$

M63, Fig. 1(c). The expansion for the massless case is [3,38]

$$\mathcal{I} \sim n(\varepsilon)^4 \Gamma(3+4\varepsilon) \left(-\frac{5\,\zeta_5}{\varepsilon} + (45\,\zeta_5 - 41\,\zeta_3^2 - 12.5\zeta_6 + 80.5\zeta_7) + \mathcal{O}(\varepsilon)\right) \quad (7)$$

BH, Fig. 1(d). The diagram (from [5]) is finite, with $\kappa = 0$ in (4). In [20] we gave numerical results for the constant C_0 in the expansion

$$\mathcal{I} \sim \Gamma(3+4\varepsilon)\,(C_0 + C_1\varepsilon + \mathcal{O}(\varepsilon^2)) \quad (8)$$

using lattice rules and adaptive methods for the massless case, where the analytic value is $C_0 = 35\,\zeta_7 \approx 35.2922$.

3   Numerical Methods

This section provides background information (as in [20]) on the termination criterion in automatic integration, non-adaptive and adaptive strategies, the transformations used, and extrapolation by the ϵ-algorithm [35,42].

3.1   Automatic Integration

Automatic integration methods act like a black-box, where the input includes the integrand specification $f(\mathbf{x})$, dimension (number of function variables) d and domain $\mathcal{D}$, with the objective to compute an approximation $\mathcal{Q}$ to an integral of the form

$$\mathcal{I} = \int_{\mathcal{D}} f(\mathbf{x})\,d\mathbf{x} \quad (9)$$

An (absolute) error estimate E_a is usually provided as well. To realize a termination criterion, requested absolute and relative accuracies (tolerances) t_a and t_r, respectively, and/or a maximum number of interactions or function evaluations may further be specified by the user. The algorithm then performs a prescribed number of iterations, or attempts to satisfy an accuracy requirement such as that of the integration packages Quadpack [32] and ParInt [15, 16, 19],

$$|\mathcal{Q} - \mathcal{I}| \leq E_a \leq t = \max\{t_a, t_r|\mathcal{I}|\}. \quad (10)$$

3.2   Non-adaptive Integration

Double-Exponential Method. The double-exponential method (DE) [39,40] transforms the one-dimensional integral

$$\int_0^1 f(x)\,dx = \int_{-\infty}^{\infty} f\,(\phi(t))\,\phi'(t)\,dt, \quad \text{using}$$

$$x = \phi\,(t) = \frac{1}{2}(\tanh\,(\frac{\pi}{2}\sinh\,(t)) + 1), \quad \phi'(t) = \frac{\pi\cosh\,(t)}{4\cosh^2(\frac{\pi}{2}\sinh\,(t))} \quad (11)$$

Due to the rapid decrease of the integrand (as $|t|$ increases) after the transformation, the infinite range can be truncated and a trapezoidal rule approximation may be suitable, provided the integrand is smooth inside the domain. This yields

$$I_h^{N_{eval}} = \sum_{k=-N_-}^{N_+} f(\phi(kh))\,\phi'(kh) \tag{12}$$

with mesh size h and $N_{eval} = N_- + N_+ + 1$ function evaluations. For multivariate integration, a product-wise application of formula (11) is used.

Lattice Rules. Rank-1 lattice rules provide an integral approximation over the unit cube of the form

$$\mathcal{Q}f = \mathcal{Q}(\mathbf{z},n)f = \frac{1}{n}\sum_{j=0}^{n-1} f(\{\frac{j}{n}\mathbf{z}\}) \tag{13}$$

Here $\mathbf{z}$ is a generator vector with components $z \in \mathcal{Z}_n = \{1 \le z < n \mid \gcd(z,n) = 1\}$, where gcd denotes the greatest common divisor, and $\{\mathbf{x}\}$ is a vector obtained by taking the fractional part of each component of $\mathbf{x}$ (see [37]). Classically n was taken prime [23,24] (so that $\mathcal{Z}_n = \{1,2,\ldots,n-1\}$); extensions to non-prime n are given in [29,31]. We precomputed the generators $\mathbf{z}$ for various n in [12,13,17,18], using the component by component (CBC) algorithm [30,31] either directly or via Lattice Builder [25], including the rules with 400,000,009 and 5^{13} points used for the results in Sect. 4 of this paper.

A sequence embedding of lattice rules is defined in [37], based on a rank-1 rule Q_0 and where each rule of the sequence applies a scaled copy of Q_0 to the subregions obtained by subdividing $\mathcal{C}_d$ into m equal parts in each of r coordinate directions. Denoting

$$\mathcal{Q}_r f = \mathcal{Q}_r^{(m)}(\mathbf{z},n)f = \frac{1}{m^r n}\sum_{k_r=0}^{m-1}\cdots\sum_{k_1=0}^{m-1}\sum_{j=0}^{n-1} f(\{\frac{j}{n}\mathbf{z} + \frac{1}{m}(k_1,\ldots,k_r,0,\ldots,0)\}) \tag{14}$$

for n and m relatively prime, the points of Q_r are embedded in Q_{r+1} for $0 \le r < d$. Q_r has $m^r n$ points and is of rank r for $1 \le r \le d$, and Q_d is composed of m^d scaled copies of Q_0. An error estimate for Q_d is calculated based on a sequence of rules $Q^{(i)}$, $1 \le i \le d$, of order $m^{d-1}n$ and embedded in Q_d [37]. The results for the 10-dimensional integrals ($d = 10$) in Sect. 4 of this paper are obtained with $m = 2$.

A stochastic family of rules can be considered as proposed by Cranley and Patterson [10], by adding a random vector $\mathbf{\Delta}$ to the integration points,

$$\mathcal{Q}(\mathbf{z},n,\mathbf{\Delta})f = \frac{1}{n}\sum_{j=0}^{n-1} f(\{\frac{j}{n}\mathbf{z} + \mathbf{\Delta}\}) \tag{15}$$

Averaging over a number of randomized (shifted) rule sums of the form (15) where $\mathbf{\Delta}$ has a multivariate uniform random distribution on $\mathcal{C}_d$ yields an integral approximation that has the integral $\mathcal{I}$ as its expected value [37]. An error estimate is given in terms of the standard deviation. This technique is applied by pySecDec [6].

3.3   Adaptive Multivariate Integration — ParInt

Adaptive automatic integration software includes HALF [11], Adapt [21], Dcuhre [4], Cuba [22], adaptive programs in Quadpack [14, 19, 32] and ParInt [15, 16, 19]. The basic global adaptive strategy follows the algorithm of Fig. 2, cf., [27, 33]. Our accuracy requirement for the global adaptive algorithm is given by (10), and the termination criterion tested in the course of the computations is of the form $E_a \leq t = \max\{t_a, t_r |\mathcal{Q}|\}$, where $\mathcal{Q}$ is the current overall integral approximation.

> Evaluate given region and initialize results
> Initialize priority queue to empty
> **while** (evaluation limit is not reached
>   and estimated error is too large)
> Retrieve region from priority queue
> Split region
> Evaluate subregions and update results
> Insert subregions into priority queue

Fig. 2. Adaptive region/task partitioning strategy

ParInt is a parallel automatic integration method implemented in C and layered over MPI (Message Passing Interface [28]). The user-specified domain is distributed over the participating MPI processes (workers), each of which successively selects and deletes the largest error subregion from its local priority queue (heap), subdivides this region, integrates over the parts, and inserts the children regions into the heap. The updates to the integral and error estimate are accumulated, and communicated with the controller process. A load balancing procedure further allows sending work from busy to idle or near-idle workers. Based on the distributed task partition strategy where each task processes one or more regions, the region subdivison algorithm tends to refine the domain around integration hotspots such as peaks, ridges and singularities.

3.4   Transformations

Since we rely on the loop integral representation (2) over a simplex domain, a transformation is needed from the simplex to the unit cube. Unless otherwise stated we transform the integral over $\mathcal{S}_d$ of (2) to $\mathcal{C}_d$ by the coordinate transformation

$$x_j = (1 - \sum_{k=1}^{j-1} x_k)\, y_j, \quad 1 \leq j \leq d \tag{16}$$

so that $\mathbf{y} \in \mathcal{C}_d$ and the Jacobian is $\prod_{j=1}^{d-1}(1 - \sum_{k=1}^{j-1} x_k)$.

Furthermore, while lattice rules are applied with a periodizing transformation of the integrand, we select a transformation that also suppresses singularities on the boundaries of the domain. We make use of Sidi's $\sin^m$-transformations [36] for $m = 6$,

$$\Psi_6(t) = t - (45\sin(2\pi t) - 9\sin(4\pi t) + \sin(6\pi t))/(60\pi), \quad \Psi_6'(t) = \frac{16}{5}\sin^6(\pi t)$$
$$\tag{17}$$

3.5   Extrapolation

With the goal of obtaining the limit numerically, we use the ϵ-algorithm [35,42] for a nonlinear extrapolation, and an implementation based on the code of *qext( )* from the QuadPack package [32]. The computation produces a triangular table, with a sequence of integral approximations as the entry sequence in the first column. The *qext( )* procedure computes a new lower diagonal of the table when a new entry is available, together with a measure of the distance of each element from preceding neighboring elements. In the construction of the triangular table, a table element *"new"* relative to preceding e_0, e_1, e_2, e_3 is obtained as

$$
\begin{array}{l}
e_0 \\
e_3 \; e_1 \; new \; = e_1 + 1/(1/(e_1 - e_3) + 1/(e_2 - e_1) - 1/(e_1 - e_0)) \qquad (18) \\
e_2
\end{array}
$$

and the distance for *new* is set to

$$
distance = |e_2 - e_1| + |e_1 - e_0| + |e_2 - new| \qquad (19)
$$

Then *qext( )* returns the new lower diagonal element with the smallest value of the distance estimate as the extrapolation result.

4   Numerical Results

4.1   Massive Diagrams

The GPU results were obtained on an x86_64 machine at KEK, with Intel(R) Xeon(R) Gold (dual) 6230 CPU@2.10 GHz, 20 cores (40 HT−hyper-threaded), under GNU/ Linux, with NVIDIA Quadro GV100 GPU and using CUDA C. The Quadro GV100 is a Volta architecture with compute capability 7.0, and with 5,120 cores and 640 tensor cores, 32 GB HBM2 (High Bandwidth Memory second generation) global memory, (boost) clock rate of 1,627 MHz, and memory clock rate 848 MHz. It performs at 33.32 TFLOPS for FP16 (half), 16.66 TFLOPS for FP32 (float), and 8.330 TFLOPS for FP64 (double) (from [41] and also using a device query program). The results in Tables 1, 2, 3, and 4 are computed in double precision.

The methods include *MPI + DE* and *OpenMP + Sidi 6*, which are run on AMD cluster nodes with a Ryzen Threadripper 3990X 64-Core (128 HT) CPU. According to [9], this CPU has a base clock speed of 2.9 GHz, observed boost clock speed of 3.4 GHz, and maximum boost clock speed of 4.3 GHz with lightly threaded workloads. *MPI + DE* employs 19 processes on one node, where DE evaluates 19 points in each coordinate direction. *OpenMP + Sidi 6* is multithreaded with 128 threads, for a lattice rule with $\approx 400M$ points and Sidi's $\sin^6$ (Ψ_6) transformation. Ψ_6 is also used for the *Sidi 6 Quadro GPU* results with $400M$- and 5^{13}-point lattice rules, and for the *Sidi 6 m = 2 Quadro GPU* embedded (2^{10}-copy) versions of the lattice rules with two copies in each coordinate direction. pySecDec 1.4.4 [6,7] comparison results are obtained on an AMD node (with 128 threads) for a Korobov-3 (shifted) rule, without use of a GPU.

Tables 1, 2, 3, and 4 display the resulting integral approximations, number of integrand evaluations, time in seconds, and an absolute error estimate (E_a) for the methods

Table 1. Results of DE, lattice and embedded lattice rules for $M61$ massive case (Fig. 1(a))

Method	Evaluations	Result	E_a	Time[s]
MPI + DE	$19^{10} = 6.131T$	-2.862726657918146 e-02		35,102
OpenMP + Sidi6	$400M$	-2.8596810730 e-02		2.70
Sidi6 Quadro GPU	$400M$	-2.859681073072325 e-02		0.23
Sidi 6 Quadro GPU	5^{13}	-2.863834054956898 e-02		0.66
Sidi 6 $m = 2$ Quadro	$400M \times 2^{10}$	-2.862717083713596 e-02	4.72 e-08	209.2
Sidi 6 $m = 2$ Quadro	$5^{13} \times 2^{10}$	-2.862717128087744 e-02	1.65 e-09	666.5
pySecDec Korobov-3	$337,940,896$	-2.862716229785056 e-02	5.59 e-09	117,046

Table 2. Results of DE, lattice and embedded lattice rules for $M62$ massive case (Fig. 1(b))

Method	Evaluations	Result	E_a	Time[s]
MPI + DE	$19^{10} = 6.131T$	-2.549545550207116 e-02		45,042
OpenMP + Sidi 6	$400M$	-2.5466771436 e-02		2.71
Sidi 6 Quadro GPU	$400M$	-2.546677143565166 e-02		0.23
Sidi 6 Quadro GPU	5^{13}	-2.551194982708940 e-02		0.68
Sidi 6 $m = 2$ Quadro	$400M \times 2^{10}$	-2.549545504404488 e-02	8.39 e-08	219.5
Sidi 6 $m = 2$ Quadro	$5^{13} \times 2^{10}$	-2.549545504820467 e-02	6.94 e-10	694.4
pySecDec Korobov-3	$337,940,896$	-2.549544878067482 e-02	4.57 e-09	142,359

Table 3. Results of DE, lattice and embedded lattice rules for $M63$ massive case (Fig. 1(c))

Method	Evaluations	Result	E_a	Time[s]
MPI + DE	$19^{10} = 6.131T$	-2.765508186953987 e-02		46,775
OpenMP + Sidi6	$400M$	-2.7643999940 e-02		2.81
Sidi6 Quadro GPU	$400M$	-2.764399993954736 e-02		0.24
Sidi 6 Quadro GPU	5^{13}	-2.766877323614956 e-02		0.69
Sidi 6 $m = 2$ Quadro	$400M \times 2^{10}$	-2.765491227212118 e-02	1.38 e-07	223.1
Sidi 6 $m = 2$ Quadro	$5^{13} \times 2^{10}$	-2.765491019803990 e-02	1.08 e-09	706.9
pySecDec Korobov-3	$337,940,896$	-2.765491546054626 e-02	5.61 e-09	119,274

Table 4. Results of DE, lattice and embedded lattice rules for BH massive case (Fig. 1(d))

Method	Evaluations	Result	E_a	Time[s]
MPI + DE	$19^{10} = 6.131T$	-9.341399988896524 e-02		29,845
OpenMP + Sidi 6	$400M$	-9.3338131744 e-02		2.67
Sidi 6 Quadro GPU	$400M$	-9.333813174440837 e-02		0.23
Sidi 6 Quadro GPU	5^{13}	-9.341291671067280 e-02		0.62
Sidi 6 $m = 2$ Quadro	$400M \times 2^{10}$	-9.340329476470503 e-02	4.34 e-07	201.1
Sidi 6 $m = 2$ Quadro	$5^{13} \times 2^{10}$	-9.340331509556005 e-02	5.20 e-08	638.9
pySecDec Korobov-3	$337,940,896$	-9.340331518736177 e-02	1.08 e-08	5,092

that supply a value for E_a. Based on this comparison and the estimated error, there is good agreement between the embedded lattice rules (*Sidi 6 m = 2 Quadro*), whereas the esimated error of the embedded 5^{13}-point rule is smaller. There is also good agreement between pySecDec and the embedded rules, in particular the embedded 5^{13}-point rule, but the latter is much more efficient with respect to execution times. *MPI + DE* is less accurate than pySecDec but faster, except for the *BH* diagram. We observe that its result for $M62$ agrees with the embedded lattice rules to 4.5×10^{-10}. As expected, the single lattice rule methods (*OpenMP + Sidi 6* and *Sidi 6 Quadro GPU*) are very fast but provide low accuracy in comparison.

4.2   Results for Massless $M61$

For the diagrams with massless internal lines, the space-time dimension is $\nu = 4 - 2\varepsilon$, which yields $\mathcal{I}(\varepsilon)$ with $C^{1+5\varepsilon}/D^{3+4\varepsilon}$ under the integral sign in (2). The massless case of $M61$ was covered in [8, 26], where [8] includes numerical results obtained via sector decomposition.

In this section we will compute the coefficient of $1/\varepsilon$ in the expansion (5) for $M61$ by approximating the limit of $\varepsilon \mathcal{Q}(\varepsilon)$ as $\varepsilon \to 0$. This gives a basis for dimensional regularization where $\nu \to 4$ as $\varepsilon \to 0$. The convergence of the sequence $\varepsilon \mathcal{Q}(\varepsilon)$ is accelerated by the ϵ-algorithm [35, 42] (cf., Sect. 3.5).

Tables 5 and 6 list the sequences $\varepsilon_\ell \mathcal{Q}^{(2)}(\varepsilon_\ell)$ for $\varepsilon_\ell = -1/b^\ell$ with $b = 1.2$ in Table 5 and $b = 1.15$ in Table 6. The integral approximation $\mathcal{Q}^{(2)}$ is an embedded $400M$-point lattice rule $\mathcal{Q}$ with $m = 2$, implemented using Sidi 6 on Quadro GPU. Also listed are the corresponding absolute error estimate E_a, execution time in seconds and the extrapolated sequence. The latter consists of elements selected from the lower diagonal of the triangular extrapolation table, computed according to (18).

As the estimated absolute error of the entry sequence increases to the order of 10^{-2}, this will limit the accuracy of the extrapolated result. The first extrapolation occurs at the third iteration (with three elements in the entry sequence), i.e., at $\ell = 7$ in Table 5 and at $\ell = 9$ in Table 6. The exact integral is $-10\,\zeta_5 \approx -10.369277551433699$. An accurate extrapolated result is reached at the 7th iteration (with five extrapolations), which is at $\ell = 11$ in Table 5 and at $\ell = 13$ in Table 6.

We further obtained results for this case with adaptive integration in ParInt, on the *thor* cluster in the Department of Computer Science at WMU. The MPI runs were performed on four Intel Xeon E5-2670, 2.6 GHz dual CPU nodes with 16 processes per node. The integral approximation, absolute error estimate, and time in seconds for the adaptive integration are given in Table 7, with their extrapolated values for a sequence $\varepsilon_\ell \mathcal{Q}(\varepsilon_\ell)$ with $\varepsilon_\ell = -1/b^\ell$, $b = 1.2$ and $\ell = 3, 4, \ldots$. The maximum number of integrand evaluations was set at $500B$.

The first sequence of extrapolation results (column 5) in Table 7 applies to the entry sequence starting at $\ell = 3$. Although the first three steps are erratic, convergence sets in after that. In fact, at $\ell = 7$, two results were available on the lower diagonal, including -17.85705981951788 besides the $169.7\ldots$ value listed. The latter was selected as it appeared with a slightly smaller *distance* estimate as given by (19).

The second sequence of extrapolation results (column 6) shows the behavior when the entry sequence is started at $\ell = 6$. Note that the second extrapolation, as it is started

Table 5. Results of embedded lattice rule and extrapolation for $M61$ massless case (Fig. 1(a)), $400M$-point rule, $m = 2$, sequence with $\varepsilon_\ell = -1/b^\ell, b = 1.2, \ell = 5, 6, \ldots$

ℓ	$\varepsilon_\ell \mathcal{Q}^{(2)}(\varepsilon_\ell)$	E_a	Time[s]	Extrapolated
5	-5.8670814834389446	4.045e-04	236.9	
6	-6.6010810209390192	9.334e-04	247.6	
7	-7.3290025451281524	1.736e-03	247.8	-94.50711787172600
8	-8.0025461298639637	2.795e-03	248.2	-16.34528520934288
9	-8.5955073617360025	4.044e-03	248.1	-12.95878306674803
10	-9.0962473167603335	5.377e-03	248.2	-11.81514810764655
11	-9.5035175173401605	6.665e-03	248.3	-10.33468561083054
12	-9.8237642007586796	7.636e-03	248.2	-10.30358698496245
13	-10.076829148927793	1.087e-02	248.3	-10.33470169032785

Table 6. Results of embedded lattice rule and extrapolation for $M61$ massless case (Fig. 1(a)), $400M$-point rule, $m = 2$, sequence with $\varepsilon_\ell = -1/b^\ell, b = 1.15, \ell = 7, 8, \ldots$

ℓ	$\varepsilon_\ell \mathcal{Q}^{(2)}(\varepsilon_\ell)$	E_a	Time[s]	Extrapolated
7	-6.1319925400428952	5.674e-04	236.2	
8	-6.6992591321666515	1.024e-03	247.6	
9	-7.2574395641246294	1.642e-03	248.2	-41.54754549845097
10	-7.7853886548937465	2.415e-03	248.4	-17.00529857230883
11	-8.2697056028975808	3.317e-03	248.7	-13.64562553847281
12	-8.7025765235833710	4.306e-03	249.2	-12.34478650059442
13	-9.0804943525783131	5.331e-03	249.5	-10.29791987579131
14	-9.4032831930914433	6.333e-03	249.4	-10.31245440302037
15	-9.6733449900103512	7.227e-03	249.2	-10.23243241946978
16	-9.8958550922968769	7.739e-03	249.3	-10.30299005253333
17	-10.084346379310391	1.145e-02	249.7	-10.35978087121498

at a later element of the entry sequence (column 1), generates a triangular ϵ-algorithm table that is a subtriangle of that started at an earlier entry element (as for the extrapolation sequence in column 5). However, the extrapolated value is selected at each iteration as the element with lowest distance estimate along the lower diagonal of the triangular table. This explains why some of the extrapolated values in columns 5 and 6 agree, while other ones are different.

While the extrapolation results are good, the adaptive integration is outperformed with respect to execution time by the lattice rules, which are indeed very efficient for this type of problem.

Table 7. Results of adaptive integration (ParInt) and extrapolation for $M61$ massless case (Fig. 1(a)), $500B$ integrand evaluations, sequence with $\varepsilon_\ell = -1/b^\ell, b = 1.2, \ell = 3, 4, \ldots$

ℓ	$\varepsilon_\ell \mathcal{Q}^{(2)}(\varepsilon_\ell)$	E_a	Time[s]	Extr. start $\ell = 3$	Extr. start $\ell = 6$
3	-4.91021341679181	0.00179	3292.7		
4	-5.20347093132543	0.00231	3310.5		
5	-5.84191584324681	0.00461	2818.2	-4.661073469965100	
6	-6.57615789432883	0.00275	2842.3	-0.948522306243995	
7	-7.31346988965485	0.00230	3371.6	169.7675893230898	
8	-7.98259667712166	0.00327	3385.2	-14.54898654030341	-14.54898654030341
9	-8.57201855470499	0.00501	3394.9	-12.93082342985936	-12.93082342985936
10	-9.06743566419856	0.00697	3398.1	-11.67834697610792	-11.67834697610792
11	-9.47072913855170	0.00826	3398.8	-11.26526383021044	-10.80236320496894
12	-9.78754291117960	0.01620	3398.0	-10.35212751126703	-9.900013844098643
13	-10.0284149761477	0.02240	3393.0	-10.22374747556268	-10.50801809515002
14	-10.2029760970888	0.03150	2876.7	-10.36314903844882	-10.36314903844882

5   Conclusions

We reported results incurred for diagrams with four loops and 11 internal lines, $M61$, $M62$, $M63$, and a diagram we call BH with reference to Binoth and Heinrich [5]. We employed automatic integration methods using QMC/lattice rules and adaptive integration, where the user is not required to specify characteristics of the integrand function − except for the function definition itself. It is clear from the function definitions in Appendix A.1–A.4 that it may be difficult to guage the actual integrand behavior.

The adaptive method is less efficient than the QMC embedded 2^d lattice copy rule in the dimensional regularization approach for the massless $M61$ problem. However, adaptive integration may be more versatile in general. The QMC embedded 2^d lattice copy rules compare favorably to pySecDec with respect to accuracy (which we used as a yardstick), but are much more efficient than the multithreaded pySecDec for these types of integrals.

To conclude, we observed that our fully numerical methods deliver good performance for computations of Feynman diagrams with four loops and 11 internal lines, with respect to accuracy and elapsed time. For further improvements, we will study suitable variable transformations in future work.

Acknowledgments. We acknowledge the support of the Grant-in-Aid for Scientific Research (JP17K05428 and JP20K03941) from JSPS KAKENHI, as well as the National Science Foundation Award Number 1126438 that funded the cluster used for the computations with ParInt in this paper. We also thank our colleagues, Dr. T. Ishikawa, Dr. H. Daisaka, Dr. N. Nakasato and Dr. J. Kapenga, for creating and maintaining computing environments supporting our Feynman integration work.

A C and D functions

The C and D functions for the diagrams of Fig. 1 are given in C code form below. We denote

$$x_{i_1...i_k} = \sum_{j=i_1}^{i_k} x_j \qquad (20)$$

We use $x_a = x_{10}$ and $x_b = x_{11}$. Obvious notations also include $xksq = x_k^2$.

A.1 M61, Fig. 1(a).

```
C = (x16*x5*x79 + x56*(x79*x8 + x7*x9) +
    x2*(x5*x678 + x67*x89 + x8*x9) +
    x1*(x2*x58 + x7*x89 + x23*x9 + x4*x9 + x8*x9) +
    x34*(x7*x89 + x6*x9 + x8*x9))*xab +
    (x16*x234578 + x2345*x78)*xa*xb +
    x34*(x1*x2*x5 + x5*(x6*x79a + x7*x89a) + x56*x8*x9a +
    x1*(x5*x79a + x8*x9a) + x16*x27*x89b +
    x2*(x7*x8 + x5*x678 + x78*x9b));

D1 = x34*(x1*x2sq*x589b + 2*x1*x2*(x589b*x7 + x8*x9) +
    x1sq*(x2*x589b + x5*x79a + x7*x89b + x8*x9a) +
    x2sq*(x5*x678 + x7*x8 + x6*x89b + x78*x9b)) +
    2*(x1*(x2*x3*x5 + x3*x5*x7) + x2*x3*(x5*x678 + x6*x8))*xa +
    x3sq*(x6*(x7*x89b + x8*x9a) +
    x1*(x2*x589b + x5*x79a + x7*x89b + x8*x9a) +
    x2*(x5*x678 + x7*x8 + x6*x89b + x78*x9b) +
    x5*(x6*x79 + x7*x89 + x8*x9 + x678*xa)) +
    (x1*x2sq*x589 + x1sq*(x27*x58 + x234578*x9) +
    2*x2*x3*(x7*x8 + x678*x9) + x3sq*(x7*x8 + x1*x9 + x678*x9) +
    2*x1*x2*(x589*x7 + x3*x89 + x8*x9) +
    x2sq*(x5*x678 + x67*x89 + x8*x9) +
    2*x1*x3*(x7*x8 + x7*x9 + x8*x9))*xab +
    (x1*x2sq + x1sq*x234578 + x1*x3sq + x23sq*x678 +
    2*x1*(x2*x378 + x3*x78))*xa*xb;

 D = D1 + C*x456789ab; // Massive diagram
//D = D1 - C*x123;      // Massless diagram
```

A.2 M62, Fig. 1(b).

```
C = x1*(x3*(x5*x79a + x7*x89b + x8*x9a) +
    x2*(x34*x589b + x58*x7 + x578*x9b) + x4*(x58*x79a + x7*x9b) +
    (x58*x7 + x34578*x9)*xab + x34578*xa*xb) +
    x2*(x58*x6*x7 + x5*x7*x89a + x578*x6*x9b + x5*x8*x9b +
    (x7*x8 + x578*x9)*xab + x34*(x5*x689a + x6*x89b + x89*xab) +
    x34578*xa*xb) + x34*(x5*(x6*x79a + x7*x89a + x8*x9a) +
    x6*(x7*x89b + x8*x9a) + (x7*x8 + x678*x9)*xab + x678*xa*xb) +
    x5*((x6*x7 + x7*x8 + x678*x9)*xab + x678*xa*xb) +
    x6*((x7*x8 + x78*x9)*xab + x78*xa*xb);
```

```
D1 = x3sq*(x56*x7*x8 + x5*(x6*x79+x2*x8) + (x1278*x5 + x16*x8)*x9 +
     x6*x7*x9b + x59b*x8*xa + x589b*(x16*x2 + x1*x7 + x1267*xa) +
     (x27*x8 + x12678*x9)*xb) +
     2*x1*x3*(x589b*x7*xa + x8*x9b*xa + (x79*x8 + x7*x9)*xb) +
     2*x2*x3*(x56*x79*x8 + x5*(x6*x79 + x7*x9) + x6*x7*x9b + x589b*x7*xa +
     x8*x9b*xa + (x79*x8+x7*x9)*xb)+
     x2sq*(x3479b*x5*x6 + x56*(x7*x8 + x34*x89) + (x5*x78 + x6*x8)*x9 +
     (x1*x58 + x6*x7)*x9b + x34*x58b*xa + x589b*(x1*x347 + x7*xa) +
     x3458*x9*xab + (x34*x6 + x34567*x8 + x7*x9)*xb + x58*xa*xb) +
     2*x1*x2*(x3a*x589b*x7 + (x34*x5 + x3*x8)*x9 + (x34*x58b + x8*x9)*xa +
     x345*x9*xab + (x379*x8 + x7*x9)*xb + x58*xa*xb) +
     x1sq*(x589b*(x2*x347 + x34a*x7) + x34*x58*x9a + x2*x58*x9b +
     x3458*x9*xab + x589*x7*xb + (x34 + x58)*xa*xb);

D = D1 + C*x456789ab; // Massive diagram
```

A.3 M 63, Fig. 1(c).

```
C = x8*(x6*x7 + x567*x9)*xb +
    (x1*x345689 + x2356*x789 + x4*x79 + x7*x89)*xa*xb +
    x2*((x3*x45 + x4*x6)*x789 + x35*(x6a*x789 + x78*x9) +
    x4*(x78*x9 + x789*xab) + (x56*x789 + x78*x9)*xb) +
    x4*(x6*(x7*x8a + x8*x9a) + x7*x8*x9ab + x67*x9*xa + x8*x9a*xb) +
    x1*(x345*(x69a*x8 + x69*xa) + x4569*x8*xb +
    x3*(x45*x689b + x69*xb) + x2*(x3*x4569a + x45*x69ab + x69a*xb)) +
    x5*(x67*(x8*x9a + x9*xa) + x7*(x6*x8a + x8*xb)) +
    x3*(x8*(x6*x7 + x67*x9) + (x6*x789 + x7*x89)*xa +
    (x6*x789 + x78*x9)*xb + x45*(x6*x789 + x7*x89b + x89*xb));

D1 = 2*x2*x4*(x8*x9a + x79*xa)*xb + 2*x1*x4*(x8*x9a + x9*xa)*xb +
     2*x1*x3*(x6b*(x5*x8 + x4*xa) + x4*(x69ab*x8 + x9*xa) +
     (x69a*x8 + x4a*x9)*xb) +
     x2sq*(x3*(x1*x4569a + x456a*x789 + x78*x9) +
     x45*(x1*x69ab + x6*x789 + x78*x9 + x789*xab) +
     (x1*x69a + x6a*x789 + x78*x9)*xb) +
     2*x1*x2*(x3*(x5*x689b + x4*x69ab + x4a*x89 + x69*x8b) +
     x45*(x69ab*x8 + x9*xa) + (x69a*x8 + x4a*x9)*xb + x34*xa*xb) +
     2*x3*x4*(x6*x7*x8a + x67*(x8*x9a + x9*xa) +
     (x8*x9 + x789*xa)*xb) +
     x1sq*(x2*(x3*x4569a + x45*x69ab) + x45*(x69ab*x8 + x69b*xa) +
     x3*(x45*x689b + x6*x8a + x8*x9 + x89*xa) +
     (x23*x69a + x6*x8a + x8*x9a + x9*xa)*xb) +
     2*x2*x3*((x5*x7 + x4b*x78)*x9 + x789*(x4*x6ab + x5*x6b + x6a*xb)) +
     x4sq*(x8*(x6*x79 + x7*x9) + (x6*x7 + x67*x89)*xa +
     x1*(x2689b*x3 + x28*x69ab + x69b*xa) +
     x2*(x36*x789 + x8*x9 + x7*x9ab + x89*xab) +
     (x79*x8 + x789*xa)*xb + x3*(x6*x789 + x7*x89b + x89*xb)) +
     x3sq*(x6*x7*x8ab + x1*(x45a*x689b + x69*x8b) +
     x2*(x1*x4569a + x456a*x789 + x78*x9) + x67*(x8*x9 + x89*xa) +
     (x69*x8 + x67*x9 + x789*xa)*xb + x45*(x6*x789 + x7*x89b + x89*xb));

D = D1 + C*x56789ab; // Massive diagram
```

A.4 *BH*, Fig. 1(d).

```
C = x189*xa*(x36*x45b + x45*xb)
    + (x189*x27 + x18*x9)*(x36*x45b + x45*xab + xa*xb);

D1 = x3sq*(x45b*(x189*x2 + x1*x79a) +
     x45*(x7a*x89 + x8*x9)) + 2*x1*x3*x4*x7a*xb +
     x34sq*(x7a*x89 + x8*x9)*xb +
     x1sq*(x45b*(x279a*x36 + x279*xa) + x279a*x45*xb) +
     x4sq*(x18*x36a*x9 + x189*(x27a*x36 + x7*xa + x2*xab) +
     x1*x79a*xb) + x189*x2sq*(x36*x45b + x45*xab + xa*xb) +
     2*x1*x9*(x45b*(x2*x36 + x3*xa) + x2*x45*xab +
     (x3*x4 + x24*xa)*xb) +
     2*x189*x2*(x4*xa*xb + x3*(x45b*xa + x4*xb));

D = D1 + C*x56789ab; // Massive diagram
```

References

1. Abi, B., et al.: Measurement of the positive muon anomalous magnetic moment to 0.46 ppm. Phys. Rev. Lett. **126**, 141801 (2021). (Muon g-2 Collaboration). https://doi.org/10.1103/PhysRevLett.126.141801
2. Aoyama, T., et al.: The anomalous magnetic moment of the muon in the standard model. Phys. Rep. **887**, 1–166 (2020). https://doi.org/10.1016/j.physrep.2020.07.006
3. Baikov, B.A., Chetyrkin, K.G.: Four loop massless propagators: an algebraic evaluation of all master integrals. Nucl. Phys. B **837**, 186–220 (2010)
4. Berntsen, J., Espelid, T.O., Genz, A.: Algorithm 698: DCUHRE-an adaptive multidimensional integration routine for a vector of integrals. ACM Trans. Math. Softw. **17**, 452–456 (1991)
5. Binoth, T., Heinrich, G.: Numerical evaluation of multi-loop integrals by sector decomposition. Nucl. Phys. B **680**, 375 (2004). hep-ph/0305234v1
6. Borowka, S., Heinrich, G., Jahn, S., Jones, S.P., Kerner, M., Schlenk, J.: A GPU compatible quasi-Monte Carlo integrator interfaced to pySecDec. Comput. Phys. Commun. **240**, 120–137 (2019). Preprint: arXiv:1811.11720v1 [hep-ph]. https://arxiv.org/abs/1811.11720. https://doi.org/10.1016/j.cpc.2019.02.015
7. Borowka, S., et al.: pySecDec: a toolbox for the numerical evaluation of multiscale integrals. Comput. Phys. Commun. **222**, 313–326 (2018). arXiv:1703.09692 [hep-ph]. https://www.sciencedirect.com/science/article/pii/S0010465517303028. https://doi.org/10.1016/j.cpc.2017.09.015
8. Carter, J., Heinrich, G.: SecDec: a general program for sector decomposition. Comput. Phys. Commun. **182**, 1566–1581 (2011)
9. cgchannel: 28 May 2020. http://www.cgchannel.com/2020/05/review-amd-ryzen-threadripper-3990x/
10. Cranley, R., Patterson, T.N.L.: Randomization of number theoretic methods for multiple integration. SIAM J. Numer. Anal. **13**, 904–914 (1976)
11. De Ridder, L., Van Dooren, P.: An adaptive algorithm for numerical integration over an N-dimensional cube. J. Comput. Appl. Math. **2**(3), 207–210 (1976)
12. de Doncker, E., Almulihi, A., Yuasa, F.: High speed evaluation of loop integrals using lattice rules. J. Phys. Conf. Ser. (JPCS), IOP Ser. **1085**(052005) (2018). http://iopscience.iop.org/article/10.1088/1742-6596/1085/5/052005

13. de Doncker, E., Almulihi, A., Yuasa, F.: Transformed lattice rules for Feynman loop integrals. J. Phys. Conf. Ser. (JPCS) IOP Ser. **1136**(012002) (2018). https://doi.org/10.1088/1742-6596/1136/1/012002

14. de Doncker, E., et al.: Quadpack computation of Feynman loop integrals. J. Comput. Sci. (JoCS) **3**(3), 102–112 (2011). https://doi.org/10.1016/j.jocs.2011.06.003

15. de Doncker, E., Genz, A., Gupta, A., Zanny, R.: Tools for distributed adaptive multivariate integration on now's: ParInt1.0 release. In: Supercomputing 1998 (1998)

16. de Doncker, E., Kaugars, K., Cucos, L., Zanny, R.: Current status of the ParInt package for parallel multivariate integration. In: Proceedings of Computational Particle Physics Symposium (CPP 2001), pp. 110–119 (2001)

17. Okada, H., Atluri, S.N. (eds.): ICCES 2019. MMS, vol. 75. Springer, Cham (2020). https://doi.org/10.1007/978-3-030-27053-7

18. de Doncker, E., Yuasa, F., Almulihi, A., Nakasato, N., Daisaka, H., Ishikawa, T.: Numerical multi-loop integration on heterogeneous many-core processors. J. Phys. Conf. Ser. (JPCS) **1525**(012002) (2019). https://doi.org/10.1088/1742-6596/1525/1/012002

19. de Doncker, E., Yuasa, F., Kato, K., Ishikawa, T., Kapenga, J., Olagbemi, O.: Regularization with numerical extrapolation for finite and UV-divergent multi-loop integrals. Comput. Phys. Commun. **224**, 164–185 (2018). https://doi.org/10.1016/j.cpc.2017.11.001

20. de Doncker, E., Yuasa, F., Olagbemi, O., Ishikawa, T.: Large scale automatic computations for Feynman diagrams with up to five loops. In: Gervasi, O., et al. (eds.) ICCSA 2020. LNCS, vol. 12253, pp. 145–162. Springer, Cham (2020). https://doi.org/10.1007/978-3-030-58814-4_11

21. Genz, A., Malik, A.: An adaptive algorithm for numerical integration over an n-dimensional rectangular region. J. Comput. Appl. Math. **6**, 295–302 (1980)

22. Hahn, T.: Cuba - a library for multidimensional numerical integration. Comput. Phys. Commun. **176**, 712–713 (2007). https://doi.org/10.1016/j.cpc.2007.03.006

23. Korobov, N.M.: The approximate computation of multiple integrals. Dokl. Akad. Nauk SSSR **124**, 1207–1210 (1959). (Russian)

24. Korobov, N.M.: Properties and calculation of optimal coefficients. Doklady Akademii Nauk SSSR **132**, 1009–1012 (1960). (Russ.). Eng. trans. Soviet Math. Doklady **1**, 696–700

25. L' Equyer, P., Munger, D.: Algorithm 958: lattice builder: a general software tool for constructing rank-1 lattice rules. ACM Trans. Math. Softw. **42**(2), 15:1–30 (2016)

26. Lee, R.N., Smirnov, A.V., Smirnov, V.A.: Master integrals for four-loop massless propagators up to weight twelve. Nucl. Phys. B **856**, 95–110 (2012)

27. Malcolm, M., Simpson, R.: Local versus global strategies for adaptive quadrature. ACM Trans. Math. Softw. **1**, 129–146 (1975)

28. MPI: http://www-unix.mcs.anl.gov/mpi/index.html

29. Niederreiter, H.: Existence of good lattice points in the sense of Hlawka. Monatshefte für Mathematik **86**, 203–219 (1978)

30. Nuyens, D., Cools, R.: Fast algorithms for component-by-component construction of rank-1 lattice rules in shift-invariant reproducing kernel Hilbert spaces. Math. Comp. **75**, 903–920 (2006)

31. Nuyens, D., Cools, R.: Fast component-by-component construction of rank-1 lattice rules with a non-prime number of points. J. Complex. **22**, 4–28 (2006)

32. Piessens, R., de Doncker, E., Überhuber, C.W., Kahaner, D.K.: QUADPACK, A Subroutine Package for Automatic Integration. Springer Series in Computational Mathematics, vol. 1. Springer, Heidelberg (1983). https://doi.org/10.1007/978-3-642-61786-7

33. Rice, J.R.: A metalgorithm for adaptive quadrature. J. Assoc. Comput. Mach. **22**, 61–82 (1975)

34. Ruijl, B., Ueda, T., Vermaseren, J.A.M.: Forcer, a FORM program for the parametric reduction of four-loop massless propagator diagrams. Comput. Phys. Commun. **253**(107198) (2020)
35. Shanks, D.: Non-linear transformations of divergent and slowly convergent sequences. J. Math. and Phys. **34**, 1–42 (1955)
36. Sidi, A.: Extension of a class of periodizing transformations for numerical integration. Math. Comp. **75**(253), 327–343 (2005)
37. Sloan, I., Joe, S.: Lattice Methods for Multiple Integration. Oxford University Press, Oxford (1994)
38. Smirnov, A.V., Tentyukov, M.: Four-loop massless propagators: an numerical evaluation of all master integrals. Nucl. Phys. B **837**, 40–49 (2010)
39. Sugihara, M.: Optimality of the double exponential formula - functional analysis approach. Numer. Math. **75**(3), 379–395 (1997)
40. Takahasi, H., Mori, M.: Double exponential formulas for numerical integration. Publ. Res. Inst. Math. Sci. **9**(3), 721–741 (1974)
41. Techpowerup. https://www.techpowerup.com/gpu-specs/quadro-gv100.c3066
42. Wynn, P.: On a device for computing the $e_m(s_n)$ transformation. Math. Tables Aids Comput. **10**, 91–96 (1956)

A Study of the Floating-Point Tuning Behaviour on the N-body Problem

Dorra Ben Khalifa[1(✉)] and Matthieu Martel[1,2(✉)]

[1] LAMPS Laboratory, University of Perpignan, 52 Avenue P. Alduy,
Perpignan, France
{dorra.ben-khalifa,matthieu.martel}@univ-perp.fr
[2] Numalis, Cap Omega, Rond-point Benjamin Franklin, Montpellier, France

Abstract. In this article, we apply a new methodology for precision tuning to the N-body problem. Our technique, implemented in a tool named POP, makes it possible to optimize the numerical data types of a program performing floating-point computations by taking into account the requested accuracy on the results. POP reduces the problem of finding the minimal number of bits needed for each variable of the program to an Integer Linear Problem (ILP) which can be optimally solved in one shot by a classical linear programming solver. The POP tool has been successfully tested on programs implementing several numerical algorithms coming from mathematical libraries and other applicative domains such as IoT. In this work, we demonstrate the efficiency of POP to tune the classical gravitational N-body problem by considering five bodies that interact under gravitational force from one another, subject to Newton's laws of motion. Results on the effect of POP in term of mixed-precision tuning of the N-body example are discussed.

Keywords: Computer arithmetic · Precision tuning · Integer linear problems · N-body problem · Numerical accuracy

1 Introduction

Reducing the precision of floating-point data, also called precision tuning, provides for many practitioners in High-Performance Computing (HPC) and related fields an opportunity for exploring trade-offs in accuracy and performance [16]. Compared to higher-precision data formats (e.g. `binary64` and `binary128`), lower-precision data formats result in higher performance for computational intensive applications such as lower resource cost, reduced memory bandwidth requirements and energy consumption: the performance of `binary32` operations on modern architectures is often at least twice as fast as the performance of `binary64` operations [1].

A number of tools has been developed to assist developers in exploring the trade-off between floating-point accuracy and performance [6,9,13–15,21]. A common purpose of these techniques is that they follow a try and fail strategy to reduce the precision with respect to an accuracy constraint: they create a program search

© Springer Nature Switzerland AG 2021
O. Gervasi et al. (Eds.): ICCSA 2021, LNCS 12953, pp. 176–190, 2021.
https://doi.org/10.1007/978-3-030-86976-2_12

space then tune either program variables or assembly instructions while the optimized data formats are dependent to the tuning inputs. If the accuracy of the results are not satisfying, some variables or instructions are removed from the search space and this process is applied repeatedly until a (locally) optimal solution is returned. In the best of cases of recent tools, the program is no longer treated as a black-box but an analysis of the source code and the runtime behaviour is performed in order to provide a customized search space classification and then to identify dependencies among floating-point variables.

Unlike existing approaches, POP [2–5] implements a static technique based on a semantical modelling of the propagation of the numerical errors throughout the code. This results in generating a system of constraints whose minimal solution gives the best tuning of the program, furthermore, in polynomial time. The key feature of our method is to find directly the minimal number of bits needed, known as bit-level precision tuning, at each control point to get a certain accuracy on the results. Hence, it is not dependant of a certain number of data types (e.g. the IEEE754 formats [1]) and its complexity does not increase as the number of data types increases. In practical terms, by reasoning on the number of significant bits of the program variables and knowing the weight of their most significant bit thanks to a range analysis performed before the tuning phase (details in Sect. 4), POP is able to reduce the problem to an Integer Linear Problem (ILP) which can be optimally solved in one shot by a classical linear programming solver (no iteration) − we use GLPK [17] in practice. The method scales up to the solver limitations and the solutions are naturally found at the bit level. Furthermore, POP implements an optimization to the previous ILP method. The purpose of this new method is to handle carry bits by being less pessimistic on their propagation throughout arithmetic expressions. By doing so, a second finer set of constraints is generated by POP and the problem does not remain any longer to a pure ILP problem (min and max operators are needed). Then we use policy iteration (PI) technique [7] to find optimal solutions.

Proposed Contributions. In this article, we validate the efficiency of our approach on one of the oldest problem of modern physics, the N-body problem [12]. An N-body simulation numerically approximates the evolution of a system of bodies that interact with one another through some type of physical forces, where N presents the number of bodies in the system ($N = 5$). The program implements a second order differential equation which needs to be solved to get a location of the bodies for a given timevalue. By varying the required accuracy by the user, we show experimentally that POP succeeds in tuning the N-body program (original program $\simeq$ 330 LOCs). As a result, the transformed program is guaranteed to use variables of lower precision with a minimal number of bits than the original one. Prior work on the precision of N-body simulations have been carried out for a long time [18]. Compared to other experiments carried out with POP [2,3], the N-body example presents new difficulties, mainly more complex computations and a wide range of values with different magnitudes.

The different experimental evaluations presented in this article are the following. First, we measure the distance between the exact position of the bodies,

`Jupiter`, `Saturn`, `Uranus` and `Neptune` (the `Sun` position is fixed), computed with 500 bits and the position computed with n bits where $n = 11, 18, 24, 34, 43$ and 53 bits. These distances are given for each body with different time of simulation (10 and 30 years). Second, we demonstrate on this example the ability of POP to generate an MPFR code [11] with the new data types returned by the solver. Furthermore, we measure the global analysis time taken by POP and the execution time of the MPFR generated code and we prove that POP returns solutions in a few of a seconds. The global analysis time includes the time of the program evaluation, the range analysis determination, the constraint generation and their resolution by the solver.

Roadmap. The rest of this article is structured as follows. Section 2 describes the existing approaches for precision tuning. In Sect. 3, we discuss the technique behind POP on the illustrative example of N-Body problem. In Sect. 4, we point out the key contributions made by POP to tune floating-point programs. Section 5 presents a comprehensive evaluation and the experimental results of POP on the N-body problem and concluding remarks are discussed in Sect. 6.

2   Related Work

As we have discussed, the general areas for floating-point precision tuning have been receiving a lot of attention. In order to attain optimally lowered precision, such approaches are divided into two categories: formulating precision tuning as an optimization problem using a static performance and accuracy model, and dynamically searching through different precisions to find a local optimum.

Static Performance and Accuracy Model. Prior work in static error analysis provides a foundation for rigorously determining what precisions are required to meet error constraints for particular closed form equations. In this context, the FP-TAYLOR tool [6] has proposed a method called Symbolic Taylor Expansions in order to estimate round-off errors of floating-point computations. Unlike dynamic tools, the precision allocation guarantees to meet the error target across all program inputs in an interval. Even so, FP-TAYLOR is not designed to be a tool for complete analysis of floating-point programs: conditionals and loops can not be handled directly. More recently, they have extended their work by performing a broad comparison of many error bounding analyses to ensure the mixed-precision tuning technique [24]. Darulova et al. [9] proposed a technique to rewrite programs by adjusting the evaluation order of arithmetic expressions prior to tuning. However, the technique is limited to rather small programs that can be verified statically. Basically, all the above methods suffer from scalability limitations and do not leverage community structure to guide the search. On the other hand, concerning scalability, POP generates a linear number of constraints and variables in the size of the analyzed program.

Dynamic Searching Applications. PRECIMONIOUS [21] is a dynamic automated search based tool that leverages the LLVM framework to tweak variable declarations to build and prototype mixed-precision configurations. It aims at finding the *1-minimal* configuration, i.e., a configuration where changing even a single variable from higher to lower precision would cause the configuration to cease to be valid. A valid configuration is defined as one in which the relative error in program output is within a given threshold and there is a performance improvement compared to the baseline version of the program. However, it does not use any knowledge on the structure of the program to identify potential variables of interest. Lately, a new solution called HiFPTUNER [13], which is an extension Of PRECIMNIOUS, uses dependence analysis and edge profiling to enable a more efficient hierarchical search algorithm for mixed-precision configurations. As with other dynamic tuners, HiFPTUNER's configurations are dependent on the tuning inputs, and no accuracy guarantee is provided for untested inputs. CRAFT [15] is a framework that uses binary instrumentation and modification to build mixed-precision configurations of existing binaries that were originally developed to use only double-precision. STOKE [23] is a general stochastic optimization and program synthesis tool to handle floating-point computation. Their algorithm applies a variety of program transformations, trading bit-wise precision for performance to enhance compiler optimization on floating-point binaries. Another dynamic tool is ADAPT [19]. It uses the reverse mode of algorithmic differentiation to determine how much precision is needed in a program inputs and intermediate results in order to achieve a desired accuracy in its output, converting this information into precision recommendations. Following the idea of program transformation, the AMPT-GA tool [14] selects application-level data precisions to maximize performance while satisfying accuracy constraints. AMPT-GA combines static analysis for casting-aware performance modeling with dynamic analysis for modeling and enforcing precision constraints. POP only focuses on the precision tuning problem. Hence, the input codes are taken as-is and we do not modify them. However, POP is compatible with other tools for program transformation for numerical accuracy [8, 22]. Typically, these tools reorder the computations to make them more accurate in the computer arithmetic. For example, for sums, numbers will be added in increasing order of magnitude.

3   Running Example

Our tool, POP, automates precision tuning of floating-point programs. We reduce the problem of precision tuning to determining which program variables, if any, can have their types changed to a lower precision while satisfying the user accuracy assertions. In this section, we introduce the gravitational planetary problem simulation code. For this example, we aim at modelling the simulation of a dynamical system describing

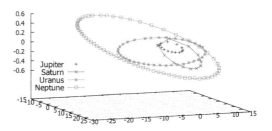

Fig. 1. Simulated movement of the bodies.

```
 1 days_per_year^{ℓ11} = 365.24^{ℓ10} ;
 2 dt^{ℓ13} = 0.01^{ℓ12};
 3 t^{ℓ15} = 0.0^{ℓ14};
 4 t_max^{ℓ17} = 1000.0^{ℓ16};
 5        [...]
 6 xJupiter^{ℓ39} = 4.8414316^{ℓ38};
 7 vxJupiter^{ℓ48} = 0.0016600767^{ℓ44}
 8 *^{ℓ47} days_per_year^{ℓ46};
 9 massJupiter^{ℓ63} = 9.5479196E-4^{ℓ59}
10 *^{ℓ62} solar_mass^{ℓ61};
11 xSaturn^{ℓ65} = 8.343367^{ℓ64};
12        [...]
13 vxSaturn^{ℓ74} = -0.002767425^{ℓ70}
14 *^{ℓ73} days_per_year^{ℓ72};
15 massSaturn^{ℓ89} = 2.8588597E-4^{ℓ85}
16 *^{ℓ88} solar_mass^{ℓ87};
17        [...]
18 while (t^{ℓ143} <^{ℓ146} t_max^{ℓ145}) {
19    dx^{ℓ757} = xJupiter^{ℓ753} -^{ℓ756} xSaturn^{ℓ755};
20    dy^{ℓ763} = yJupiter^{ℓ759} -^{ℓ762} ySaturn^{ℓ761};
21    dz^{ℓ769} = zJupiter^{ℓ765} -^{ℓ768} zSaturn^{ℓ767};
22    distance^{ℓ788} = sqrt(dx^{ℓ771} *^{ℓ774} dx^{ℓ773}
23    +^{ℓ780} dy^{ℓ776} *^{ℓ779} dy^{ℓ778} +^{ℓ786} dz^{ℓ782}
24    *^{ℓ785} dz^{ℓ784})^{ℓ787};
25    mag^{ℓ800} = dt^{ℓ790} /^{ℓ799} distance^{ℓ792} *^{ℓ795}
26    distance^{ℓ794} *^{ℓ798} distance^{ℓ797};
27    vxJupiter^{ℓ812} = vxJupiter^{ℓ802} -^{ℓ811}
28    dx^{ℓ804} *^{ℓ807} massSaturn^{ℓ806} *^{ℓ810} mag^{ℓ809};
29        [...]
30    vxSaturn^{ℓ848} = vxSaturn^{ℓ838} +^{ℓ847} dx^{ℓ840}
31    *^{ℓ843} massJupiter^{ℓ842} *^{ℓ846} mag^{ℓ845};
32        [...]
33    xJupiter^{ℓ2602} = xJupiter^{ℓ2595} +^{ℓ2601}
34    dt^{ℓ2597} *^{ℓ2600} vxJupiter^{ℓ2599};
35    xSaturn^{ℓ2683} = xSaturn^{ℓ2676} +^{ℓ2682} dt^{ℓ2678}
36    *^{ℓ2681} vxSaturn^{ℓ2680};
37        [...]
38    t^{ℓ2707} = t^{ℓ2703} +^{ℓ2706} dt^{ℓ2705};} ;
39 require_nsb(xJupiter, 11)^{ℓ2710};
40 require_nsb(xSaturn, 11)^{ℓ2716};
41        [...]
```

```
 1 days_per_year|56| = 365.24|56|;
 2 dt|56| = 0.01|56|;
 3 t|54| = 0.0|54|;
 4 t_max|53| = 1000.0|53|;
 5        [...]
 6 xJupiter|59| = 4.8414316|59|;
 7 vxJupiter|61| = 0.0016600767|61|
 8 *|61| days_per_year|61|;
 9 massJupiter|55| = 9.5479196E-4|55|
10 *|55| solar_mass|55|;
11 xSaturn|58| = 8.343367|58|;
12        [...]
13 vxSaturn|61| = -0.002767425|61|
14 *|61| days_per_year|61|;
15 massSaturn|53| = 2.8588597E-4|53|
16 *|53| solar_mass|53|;
17        [...]
18 while (t < t_max) {
19    dx|46| = xJupiter|46| -|46| xSaturn|47|;
20    dy|45| = yJupiter|45| -|45| ySaturn|46|;
21    dz|44| = zJupiter|44| -|44| zSaturn|45|;
22    distance|44| = sqrt(dx|46| *|46|
23    dx|46| +|45| dy|45| *|45|
24    dy|45| +|44| dz|35| *|35| dz|35|)|44|;
25    mag|44| = dt|44| /|44| distance|44| *|44|
26    distance|44| *|44| distance|44|;
27    vxJupiter|58| = vxJupiter|59| -|58|
28    dx|41| *|41| massSaturn|41| *|41| mag|41|;
29        [...]
30    vxSaturn|59| = vxSaturn|60| +|59|
31    dx|43| *|43| massJupiter|43| *|43| mag|43|;
32        [...]
33    xJupiter|53| = xJupiter|54| +|53|
34    dt|47| *|47| vxJupiter|47|;
35    xSaturn|53| = xSaturn|54| +|53|
36    dt|46| *|46| vxSaturn|46|;
37        [...]
38    t|53| = t|54| +|53| dt|38|;};
39 require_nsb(xJupiter, 11);
40 require_nsb(xSaturn, 11);
41        [...]
```

Fig. 2. Left: source program annotated with labels. Right: program with POP generated data types with ILP formulation.

the orbits of planets in the solar system interacting with each other gravitationally as shown in Fig. 1 (note that to for the sake of clarity of the graphic, Fig. 1 uses different simulation times for each body.)

We present, in Fig. 2, excerpts of code that measure the distance between the two planets Jupiter and Saturn. We assume that each body has its own mass (e.g. massJupiter, massSaturn), position (e.g. [xJupiter, yJupiter, zJupiter], [xSaturn, ySaturn, zSaturn]) and velocity (e.g. [vxJupiter, vyJupiter, zyJupiter], [vxSaturn, vySaturn, vzSaturn]). Moreover, we suppose that all variables, before POP analysis, are in double precision and that a range determination is performed by dynamic analysis on the program variables (we plan to use a static analyzer in the future). POP assigns to each node of the program's syntactic tree a unique control point in order to determine easily the number of significant bits of the result as mentioned in the left hand side corner of Fig. 2. Some notations can be stressed about the structure of POP code. We annotate each variable with its unique control point as we can observe in the left hand side program of Fig. 2, e.g. $\mathtt{xJupiter}^{\ell_{39}} = \mathtt{4.8414316}^{\ell_{38}}$ denotes that the variable $\mathtt{xJupiter}$ has the control point ℓ_{39} and assigned to the value 4.8414316 at control point ℓ_{38}. Considering that nsb denotes the number of significant bits of the variables, the statements $\mathtt{require\_nsb(xJupiter,11)}^{\ell_{2710}}$ and $\mathtt{require\_nsb(xSaturn,11)}^{\ell_{2716}}$ on the last two lines of the code inform the system that POP user wants to have 11 accurate binary digits on variables $\mathtt{xJupiter}$ and $\mathtt{xSaturn}$ at their control points ℓ_{2710} and ℓ_{2716}, respectively. Note that a result has n significants if the relative error between the exact and approximated results is less than 2^n.

The key feature of our approach is to generate a set of constraints for each statement of our program (more details in Sect. 4). In other words, the accuracy of the arithmetic expressions assigned to variables is determined by semantic equations, in function of the accuracy of the operands. Consider the program of the right hand side of Fig. 2. We display the POP output N-body program coupled with the generated data types. For a user requirements of 11 bits on variables $\mathtt{xJupiter}$ and $\mathtt{xSaturn}$, POP tunes successfully a large part of the variables of the program (number of constraints solved by GLPK $\simeq 3160$ with 2468 variables). For instance, the result of the measured distance between *Jupiter* and *Saturn*, on line 22 of the right hand side code of Fig. 2, is computed with 44 bits at bit level. Note that the full code contains other nsb requirements for the other bodies. The nsb given in the right hand side of Fig. 2 are greater than the nsb required on the final results since they have been skewed to ensure the precision of the whole code at any iteration. Let us also note that even if the computed nsb do not correspond to IEEE74 formats [1], one may either take the IEEE754 format immediately above the computed nsb or choose a multiple precision library such as MPFR [11] or POSIT [25] (we will discuss more about this point later in this article).

In the next section, we detail the ILP and the PI formulations of the precision tuning problem implemented in POP. Also, we present the nature of the constraints generated for the N-body problem and consequently the new data types already discussed.

4   Overview of POP

POP has been extended in several ways since its first introduction in [2–5]. It supports the four elementary operations, trigonometric functions, the square root function, loops, conditionals and arrays. Originally, the analysis in POP were expressed as a set of first order logical propositions among relations between linear integer expressions. Next, these constraints are checked by the Z3 SMT solver [20] in order to return a solution with a certain weight expressing the

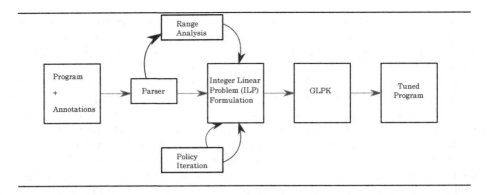

Fig. 3. POP overview.

number of significant bits of the variables. In the most recent version of POP, the intuition is to use no longer the non-optimizing Z3 SMT solver coupled to a binary search. By that means, we reduce the problem of determining the lowest precision on variables and intermediary values in programs to an Integer Linear Problem (ILP) which can be optimally solved in one breath by a classical linear programming solver as depicted in Fig. 3.

Our technique is independent of a particular computer arithmetic. In practice, we handle numbers for which we know their unit in the first place ufp and their number of significant bits nsb defined as follows. Recall that nsb stands for the number of significant bits of a number. The ufp of a number x is given in Eq. (1). This function is used further to describe the way roundoff errors are propagated across computations.

$$\mathsf{ufp}(x) = \min\{i \in \mathbb{Z} : 2^{i+1} > x\} = \lfloor \log_2(x) \rfloor \ . \tag{1}$$

Noting that the ufp of the variable values are pre-computed by a prior range analysis. More precisely, the current version of POP performs a dynamic analysis giving an under-approximation of the ranges. Our precision tuning is sensible to the ufp of the values. In other words, it is sensible to the order of magnitude of the ranges but not to the exact values. For example, we will obtain the same tuning with the ranges [3.4, 6.1] and [2.5, 7.8]. But, obviously we get a worst tuning if we use a much larger interval, e.g. [0.0, 1000.0]. In particular, the efficiency of our techniques for loops depends on the precision of the range analysis for loops.

Integer Linear Problem Formulation. In order to explain the obtained data types of our N-body program already illustrated in the right hand corner of Fig. 2, we present the system of constraints that corresponds to a pure ILP formulation as shown in Eq. (2). For the sake of conciseness, we will focus on lines 22 to 24 that measure the distance between the **Jupiter** and **Saturn** bodies (tuned program in the right hand corner of Fig. 2). To make it easier to follow our reasoning, we rewrite hereafter the statement under discussion annotated with the control points.

$$\texttt{distance}^{\ell_{788}} = \texttt{sqrt(}\ \texttt{dx}^{\ell_{771}} \times^{\ell_{774}} \texttt{dx}^{\ell_{773}} +^{\ell_{780}} \texttt{dy}^{\ell_{776}} \times^{\ell_{779}} \texttt{dy}^{\ell_{778}}$$
$$+^{\ell_{786}} \texttt{dz}^{\ell_{782}} \times^{\ell_{785}} \texttt{dz}^{\ell_{784}})^{\ell_{787}}$$

$$
C_1 = \begin{cases}
\mathsf{nsb}(\ell_{780}) \geq \mathsf{nsb}(\ell_{786}) + (-7) + \xi(\ell_{786})(\ell_{780}, \ell_{785}) - 7, \\
\mathsf{nsb}(\ell_{786}) \geq \mathsf{nsb}(\ell_{787}) + (-1) + 0, \\
\mathsf{nsb}(\ell_{774}) \geq \mathsf{nsb}(\ell_{780}) + 7 + \xi(\ell_{780})(\ell_{774}, \ell_{779}) - 7, \\
\mathsf{nsb}(\ell_{779}) \geq \mathsf{nsb}(\ell_{780}) + 6 + \xi(\ell_{780})(\ell_{774}, \ell_{779}) - 7, \\
\mathsf{nsb}(\ell_{785}) \geq \mathsf{nsb}(\ell_{786}) + (-3) + \xi(\ell_{786})(\ell_{780}, \ell_{785}) - 7, \\
\mathsf{nsb}(\ell_{787}) \geq \mathsf{nsb}(\ell_{788}), \mathsf{nsb}(\ell_{771}) \geq \mathsf{nsb}(\ell_{774}) + \xi(\ell_{774})(\ell_{771}, \ell_{773}) - 1, \\
... \\
\xi(\ell_{780})(\ell_{774}, \ell_{779}) \geq 1, \quad \xi(\ell_{786})(\ell_{780}, \ell_{785}) \geq 1 \\
\xi(\ell_{774})(\ell_{771}, \ell_{773}) \geq 1, \quad \xi(\ell_{779})(\ell_{776}, \ell_{778}) \geq 1 \\
\xi(\ell_{785})(\ell_{782}, \ell_{784}) \geq 1
\end{cases}
\tag{2}
$$

For this statement, POP generates 17 constraints as shown in system C_1 of Eq. (2). We assign to each control point (here 771 to 787) the integer variable nsb which are determined by solving the system C_1. The first two constraints of Eq. (2) are relative to the nsb of the additions stored at control points ℓ_{780} and ℓ_{786} respectively. The numbers computed corresponds to the ufp of the variable values e.g. $\mathsf{ufp}(\ell_{780}) = -1$. The following constraints that compute respectively $\mathsf{nsb}(\ell_{774})$, $\mathsf{nsb}(\ell_{779})$ and $\mathsf{nsb}(\ell_{785})$ are generated for the multiplication. The constraint $\mathsf{nsb}(\ell_{787}) \geq \mathsf{nsb}(\ell_{788})$ is for the square root function. Moreover, the constraint generated for $\mathsf{nsb}(\ell_{771})$ is relative to variable dx (same reasoning for variables dy and dz on their control points). Note that POP generates such constraints for all the statements of the N-body program.

Let us now focus on the last five constraints of system C_1. We introduce a constant function ξ. In the present ILP of Eq. (2), we assume that ξ is a constant function equal to 1. This function corresponds to the carry bit that can be propagated at each operation which is expressed by adding a supplementary bit on the elementary operation result. For instance, the constraint $\xi(\ell_{780})(\ell_{774}, \ell_{779}) \geq 1$ indicates that a carry bit is propagated on the result of the addition stored at control point ℓ_{780} which is correct but pessimistic (we highlight more the utility of ξ in the next paragraph). Finally, for a user accuracy requirement of 11 bits as displayed in Fig. 2. POP calls the GLPK [17] solver and consequently finds the least precision needed for all the N-body problem variables as we can observe hereafter (14636 is the total number of bits of the whole program after POP optimization).

$$\texttt{distance}|44| = \texttt{sqrt(}\ \texttt{dx}|46| * |46|\texttt{dx}|46| + |45|\texttt{dy}|45| * |45|\texttt{dy}|45|$$
$$+|44|\texttt{dz}|35| * |35|\texttt{dz}|35|)$$

Policy Iteration to Refine Carry Bit Propagation. In the ILP formulation in the above paragraph, we have over-approximated the carry bit function by $\xi = 1$. In contrast, this function becomes very costly in large codes if we perform a lot of computations and therefore the errors would be considerable. For example, if two operands and their errors do not overlap then adding a carry bit is useless. In what follows, we propose an optimization to use a more precise ξ function. Accordingly, when we model this optimization the problem will not remain an ILP any longer, with min and max operators that arise, as shown in the refined system of constraints C_2 of Eq. (3). Thus, we use the policy iteration method [7] to find an optimal solution.

$$
C_2 = \left\{
\begin{array}{l}
\mathsf{nsb_e}(\ell_{780}) \geq \mathsf{nsb_e}(\ell_{774}), \\
\mathsf{nsb_e}(\ell_{780}) \geq \mathsf{nsb_e}(\ell_{779}), \\
\mathsf{nsb}(\ell_{780}) \geq 7 - 6 + \mathsf{nsb}(\ell_{779}) - \mathsf{nsb}(\ell_{774}) + \mathsf{nsb_e}(\ell_{779}) + \xi(\ell_{780}, \ell_{774}, \ell_{779}), \\
\mathsf{nsb_e}(\ell_{780}) \geq 6 - 7 + \mathsf{nsb}(\ell_{774}) - \mathsf{nsb}(\ell_{779}) + \mathsf{nsb_e}(\ell_{774}) + \xi(\ell_{780}, \ell_{774}, \ell_{779}), \\
\mathsf{nsb_e}(\ell_{786}) \geq \mathsf{nsb_e}(\ell_{780}), \\
\mathsf{nsb_e}(\ell_{786}) \geq \mathsf{nsb_e}(\ell_{785}), \\
\mathsf{nsb}(\ell_{786}) \geq 7 - (-3) + \mathsf{nsb}(\ell_{785}) - \mathsf{nsb}(\ell_{780}) + \mathsf{nsb_e}(\ell_{785}) + \xi(\ell_{786}, \ell_{780}, \ell_{785}), \\
\mathsf{nsb_e}(\ell_{786}) \geq 3 - 7 + \mathsf{nsb}(\ell_{780}) - \mathsf{nsb}(\ell_{785}) + \mathsf{nsb_e}(\ell_{780}) + \xi(\ell_{786}, \ell_{780}, \ell_{785}), \\
\mathsf{nsb_e}(\ell_{774}) \geq \mathsf{nsb}(\ell_{771}) + \mathsf{nsb_e}(\ell_{771}) + \mathsf{nsb_e}(\ell_{773}) - 2, \\
\quad\ldots \\
\xi(\ell_{780})(\ell_{774}, \ell_{779}) = \min \left(\begin{array}{l} \max \left(6 - 7 + \mathsf{nsb}(\ell_{774}) + \mathsf{nsb_e}(\ell_{774}), 0 \right), \\ \max \left(7 - 6 + \mathsf{nsb}(\ell_{779}) + \mathsf{nsb_e}(\ell_{779}), 0 \right), 1 \end{array} \right) \\
\xi(\ell_{786})(\ell_{780}, \ell_{785}) = \min \left(\begin{array}{l} \max \left(-3 - 7 + \mathsf{nsb}(\ell_{780}) + \mathsf{nsb_e}(\ell_{780}), 0 \right), \\ \max \left(7 - (-3) + \mathsf{nsb}(\ell_{785}) + \mathsf{nsb_e}(\ell_{785}), 0 \right), 1 \end{array} \right)
\end{array}
\right\}
\tag{3}
$$

Equation (3) displays the new constraints that we add to the global system of constraints in the case where we optimize the carry bit of the elementary operations. Before introducing these constraints, we define in Eq. (4) the unit in the last place ulp of a number x.

$$
\mathsf{ulp}(x) = \mathsf{ufp}(x) - \mathsf{nsb}(x) + 1 \ .
\tag{4}
$$

The principle of the new ξ function is as follows: if the ulp of one of the two operands (or errors) is greater than the ufp (see Eq. (1)) of the other one (or conversely) then the two numbers are not aligned and no carry bit can be propagated through the operation (otherwise $\xi = 1$). Not surprisingly, our new system of constraint C_2 introduces a new integer quantity $\mathsf{nsb_e}$ which corresponds to the number of significant bits of the error which needs to be estimated. Formerly, let a number x, we define $\mathsf{ufp_e}(x)$ and $\mathsf{ulp_e}(x)$ as the unit in the first place and in the last place respectively of the error on x. From Eqs. (1) and (4), we have $\mathsf{ufp_e}(x) = \mathsf{ufp}(x) - \mathsf{nsb}(x)$ and $\mathsf{ulp_e}(x) = \mathsf{ufp_e}(x) - \mathsf{nsb_e}(x) + 1$ and consequently we can compute $\mathsf{nsb_e}(x)$.

In practice, policy iteration makes it possible to break the min in the $\xi(\ell_{780})$ (ℓ_{774}, ℓ_{779}) and $\xi(\ell_{786})(\ell_{780}, \ell_{785})$ functions of the two additions as shown in Eq. (3) by choosing the max between the terms. Next, it becomes possible to solve the corresponding ILP. If no fixed point is reached, POP iterates until a solution is found. By applying this optimization, the new data types of the statement of lines 22 to 24 in Fig. 2 are given as follows.

```
distance|41| = sqrt( dx|42| * |42|dx|42| + |42|dy|42| * |42|dy|42|
             +|41|dz|31| * |31|dz|31|)
```

By comparing with the formats already presented with the ILP method, it is obvious the gain of precision that we obtain on each variable and operation of

Table 1. Distances between the exact position (computed with 500 bits) and the position computed with n bits. Distances given for each body after 10 and 30 years of simulation. Followed by POP analysis time and the execution time of the MPFR generated code.

nsb	11	18	24	34	43	53
Simulation time: 10 years						
Jupiter	$5.542 \cdot 10^{-4}$	$1.650 \cdot 10^{-6}$	$1.577 \cdot 10^{-7}$	$4.998 \cdot 10^{-10}$	$5.077 \cdot 10^{-10}$	$5.076 \cdot 10^{-10}$
Saturn	$1.571 \cdot 10^{-3}$	$2.111 \cdot 10^{-5}$	$1.326 \cdot 10^{-7}$	$4.427 \cdot 10^{-10}$	$3.119 \cdot 10^{-10}$	$3.117 \cdot 10^{-10}$
Uranus	$2.952 \cdot 10^{-3}$	$2.364 \cdot 10^{-5}$	$1.140 \cdot 10^{-7}$	$3.072 \cdot 10^{-10}$	$7.212 \cdot 10^{-11}$	$7.236 \cdot 10^{-11}$
Neptune	$2.360 \cdot 10^{-3}$	$3.807 \cdot 10^{-5}$	$2.206 \cdot 10^{-7}$	$5.578 \cdot 10^{-10}$	$1.751 \cdot 10^{-10}$	$1.757 \cdot 10^{-10}$
Runtime	2'59	2'52	2'57	2'56	3'10	2'59
POP Time	25"	22"	22"	24"	23"	24"
Simulation time: 30 years						
Jupiter	$7.851 \cdot 10^{-4}$	$1.282 \cdot 10^{-5}$	$3.194 \cdot 10^{-8}$	$1.066 \cdot 10^{-8}$	$1.064 \cdot 10^{-8}$	$1.064 \cdot 10^{-8}$
Saturn	$3.009 \cdot 10^{-3}$	$1.934 \cdot 10^{-5}$	$2.694 \cdot 10^{-7}$	$1.7477 \cdot 10^{-8}$	$1.777 \cdot 10^{-8}$	$1.777 \cdot 10^{-8}$
Uranus	$6.839 \cdot 10^{-4}$	$6.132 \cdot 10^{-5}$	$8.901 \cdot 10^{-7}$	$5.105 \cdot 10^{-10}$	$1.464 \cdot 10^{-10}$	$1.457 \cdot 10^{-10}$
Neptune	$2.971 \cdot 10^{-3}$	$2.0227 \cdot 10^{-5}$	$2.469 \cdot 10^{-7}$	$3.869 \cdot 10^{-10}$	$4.775 \cdot 10^{-10}$	$4.779 \cdot 10^{-10}$
Runtime	2'39	2'45	2'43	2'56	2'48	2'40
POP Time	38"	39"	41"	37"	37"	37"

this statement. With the PI method, the total number of bits of the optimized N-body program is $\simeq$ 14335 (a gain of more than 300 bits compared to the ILP formulation). In term of complexity, for both ILP and PI methods, POP generates a linear number of constraints and variables in the size of the analyzed program and finds the best tuning of the variables in polynomial time.

5   Experimental Results

In this section, our goal is to evaluate the performances of POP in tuning the code simulating the behaviour of the different bodies of our example. We note that the N-body program has been excerpted (not fully) from [10] which relies on a second order differential equation solved by Euler's method. Now, we shed some light on the POP tool outline already depicted in Fig. 3. POP has been developed in JAVA. It uses the ANLTR v4.7.1[1] framework to parse the different input programs. As mentioned in Sect. 4, we reduce the precision tuning problem to an ILP by generating a set of semantical equations which can be solved by a linear solver. The integer solution to this problem, computed in polynomial time by a (real) linear programming solver, we use GLPK v4.65 [17], gives the optimal data types at the bit level.

---

[1] https://www.antlr.org/.

```
 1 xJupiter = mpfr(4.841431617736816,59)
 2 yJupiter = mpfr(-1.1603200435638428,60)
 3 zJupiter = mpfr(-0.10362204164266586,57)
 4 vxJupiter = mpfr(mpfr(0.001660076668485999,61)*mpfr(days_per_year,61)
           ,61)
 5 vyJupiter = mpfr(mpfr(0.007699011359363794,61)*mpfr(days_per_year,61)
           ,61)
 6 vzJupiter = mpfr(mpfr(-6.904600013513118E-5,61)*mpfr(days_per_year,61)
           ,61)
 7 massJupiter = mpfr(mpfr(9.547919617034495E-4,55)*mpfr(solar_mass,55),55)
 8[...]
 9 while( t<t_max):
10     dx = mpfr(mpfr(xSun,57)-mpfr(xJupiter,59),58)
11     dy = mpfr(mpfr(ySun,60)-mpfr(yJupiter,60),57)
12     dz = mpfr(mpfr(zSun,60)-mpfr(zJupiter,57),55)
13     distance = gmpy2.sqrt(mpfr(mpfr(mpfr(mpfr(dx,58)*mpfr(dx,58),58)
14 +mpfr(mpfr(dy,57)*mpfr(dy,57),57),57)+mpfr(mpfr(dz,46)
15                  *mpfr(dz,46),46),56))
16     mag = mpfr(mpfr(dt,56)/mpfr(mpfr(mpfr(distance,56)
17 *mpfr(distance,56),56)*mpfr(distance,56),56),56)
18     vxJupiter = mpfr(mpfr(vxJupiter,61)+mpfr(mpfr(mpfr(dx,56)
19 *mpfr(massSun,56),56)*mpfr(mag,56),56),60)
20     vyJupiter = mpfr(mpfr(vyJupiter,61)+mpfr(mpfr(mpfr(dy,54)
21 *mpfr(massSun,54),54)*mpfr(mag,54),54),60)
22     vzJupiter = mpfr(mpfr(vzJupiter,61)+mpfr(mpfr(mpfr(dz,55)
23 *mpfr(massSun,55),55)*mpfr(mag,55),55),60)
24     [...]
25     xJupiter = mpfr(mpfr(xJupiter,54)+mpfr(mpfr(dt,47)
26                  *mpfr(vxJupiter,47),47),53)
27     yJupiter = mpfr(mpfr(yJupiter,54)+mpfr(mpfr(dt,47)
28                  *mpfr(vyJupiter,47),47),53)
29     zJupiter = mpfr(mpfr(zJupiter,54)+mpfr(mpfr(dt,47)
30                  *mpfr(vzJupiter,47),47),53)
31     [...]
32}
```

Fig. 4. Python MPFR code automatically generated by POP for the N-body problem for a nsb requirement of 18 bits on the positions of the planets at the end of the simulation.

We ran our precision tuning analysis on the N-body problem with different nsb requirements on the program variables: 11, 18, 24, 34, 43 and 53 bits. This shows the ability of POP to tune programs in function of the IEEE754 formats (11, 24, 53) [1] as well as for arbitrary word length which can be encoded using libraries such as MPFR [11] or POSIT [25]. We test the efficiency of POP analysis in several ways. The experiments shown in Table 1 seek to measure the distances between the exact position of each of the bodies of our planetary system and the position computed with an nsb of 11, 18, 24, 34, 43 and 53 bits. The distances presented in Table 1 are given for a single position on the planets which follow the orbits previously presented in Fig. 1. The positions are taken after of 10 and 30 years of simulation time.

More precisely, for this experimentation, we generate the N-body program with all computations done on 500 bits (we assume that this gives the exact solution) and we also generate by the same manner an MPFR [11] code with the optimized data types returned by POP. For example, as we can observe in Table 1, for an nsb = 11, the distance measured for Jupiter is of the order

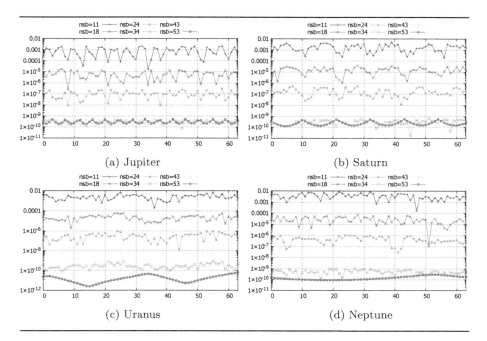

(a) Jupiter

(b) Saturn

(c) Uranus

(d) Neptune

Fig. 5. Distance between the exact and the computed position for the 5 bodies with 11, 18, 24, 34, 43 and 53 bits.

of 10^{-4} for 10 years of simulation which confirms the usefulness of our analysis: desirable results (also for the remaining planets) that respects the user nsb requirement where the worst error is of 2^{-11} for nsb = 11. For a simulation of 10 and 30 years, the runtime spent to measure these distances reaches maximally 2 minutes 59 seconds for an nsb = 53. Concerning the POP time, our analysis took as little as 25 seconds (nsb = 11) to find that we can lower the precision of the majority of variables of the N-body program for a simulation time of 10 years and does not exceed 41 seconds for a simulation time of 30 years (nsb = 24). With this speed, we believe that for large codes POP achieves its best tuning in a minimal time. Figure 4 depicts the capability of POP to generate automatically a Python MPFR version of the N-body program on the position of the planets at the end of the simulation. The MPFR code is annotated with the optimized formats returned by POP after analysis for nsb = 18. In the future, we plan to also generate code for libraries based on the POSIT number system[2].

We end this section by focusing on the curves of Fig. 5. For this experiment, we plot the distance between the exact and the computed position for each body at each instant of the simulation. This extends the results of Table 1 to all instants and not to specific ones. Consequently, we deduce from these observations that the measured error is controlled for the different planets at each iteration of the simulation.

---

[2] https://github.com/stillwater-sc/universal.

6   Concluding Remarks

The primary goal of our work was to provide a new approach for mixed-precision tuning, totally different from the existing ones. The novelty of our technique is to propose a semantical modelling of the propagation of the numerical errors throughout the code expressed as a set of constraints. We have defined two variants of methods. The first one corresponds to a pure ILP with an over-approximation of the carries in the elementary operations. The second one aims to use a more precise carry bit function and is solved by the policy iteration technique [7]. Both two methods have been implemented in our tool POP. We believe this static analysis performed by our automated tool is unique. The effectiveness of POP has already been demonstrated on a variety of programs coming from different fields.

In this article, we have shown that POP is able to tune the N-body program according to different number of significant bit required by the user. The results presented are promising in term of the analysis technique, speed and efficiency. The only limitation we can face is the size of the problem accepted by the solver. In addition, we have also shown that POP is able to generate code for multiple precision libraries, MPFR in practice, and we plan to integrate POSIT libraries in the near future.

Broadly speaking, our important future directions include handling Deep Neural Network's (DNNs) for which saving resources is essential. Also, code synthesis for the fixed-point arithmetic and assigning the same precision to pieces of code are perspectives we aim at explore at short term.

References

1. ANSI/IEEE: IEEE Standard for Binary Floating-point Arithmetic, STD 754-2008 edn. (2008)
2. Ben Khalifa, D., Martel, M.: Precision tuning and internet of things. In: International Conference on Internet of Things, Embedded Systems and Communications, IINTEC 2019, pp. 80–85. IEEE (2019)
3. Ben Khalifa, D., Martel, M.: Precision tuning of an accelerometer-based pedometer algorithm for IoT devices. In: IEEE International Conference on Internet of Things and Intelligence System, IoTaIS 2020, Bali, Indonesia, 27–28 January 2021, pp. 116–122. IEEE (2020)
4. Ben Khalifa, D., Martel, M.: An evaluation of pop performance for tuning numerical programs in floating-point arithmetic. In: International Conference on Information and Computer Technologies, ICICT 2021. IEEE (2021)
5. Ben Khalifa, D., Martel, M., Adjé, A.: POP: a tuning assistant for mixed-precision floating-point computations. In: Hasan, O., Mallet, F. (eds.) FTSCS 2019. CCIS, vol. 1165, pp. 77–94. Springer, Cham (2020). https://doi.org/10.1007/978-3-030-46902-3_5
6. Chiang, W., Baranowski, M., Briggs, I., Solovyev, A., Gopalakrishnan, G., Rakamaric, Z.: Rigorous floating-point mixed-precision tuning. In: Proceedings of the 44th ACM SIGPLAN Symposium on Principles of Programming Languages, POPL, pp. 300–315. ACM (2017)

7. Costan, A., Gaubert, S., Goubault, E., Martel, M., Putot, S.: A policy iteration algorithm for computing fixed points in static analysis of programs. In: Etessami, K., Rajamani, S.K. (eds.) CAV 2005. LNCS, vol. 3576, pp. 462–475. Springer, Heidelberg (2005). https://doi.org/10.1007/11513988_46

8. Damouche, N., Martel, M.: Mixed precision tuning with salsa. In: Proceedings of the 8th International Joint Conference on Pervasive and Embedded Computing and Communication Systems, PECCS 2018, Porto, Portugal, 29–30 July 2018, pp. 185–194. SciTePress (2018)

9. Darulova, E., Horn, E., Sharma, S.: Sound mixed-precision optimization with rewriting. In: Proceedings of the 9th ACM/IEEE International Conference on Cyber-Physical Systems, ICCPS, pp. 208–219. IEEE Computer Society/ACM (2018)

10. Demeure, N.: Compromis entre précision et performance dans le calcul haute performance. Ph.D. thesis, Université Paris-Saclay, January 2021

11. Fousse, L., Hanrot, G., Lefèvre, V., Pélissier, P., Zimmermann, P.: MPFR: a multiple-precision binary floating-point library with correct rounding. ACM Trans. Math. Softw. **33** (2007)

12. Gardarsson, M., Kjartan, K.: Some theoretical and numerical aspects of the n-body problem (2013, student Paper)

13. Guo, H., Rubio-González, C.: Exploiting community structure for floating-point precision tuning. In: Proceedings of the 27th ACM SIGSOFT International Symposium on Software Testing and Analysis, ISSTA 2018, pp. 333–343. ACM (2018)

14. Kotipalli, P.V., Singh, R., Wood, P., Laguna, I., Bagchi, S.: AMPT-GA: automatic mixed precision floating point tuning for GPU applications. In: Proceedings of the ACM International Conference on Supercomputing, ICS, pp. 160–170. ACM (2019)

15. Lam, M.O., Hollingsworth, J.K., de Supinski, B.R., LeGendre, M.P.: Automatically adapting programs for mixed-precision floating-point computation. In: International Conference on Supercomputing, ICS 2013, pp. 369–378. ACM (2013)

16. Lam, M.O., Vanderbruggen, T., Menon, H., Schordan, M.: Tool integration for source-level mixed precision. In: 2019 IEEE/ACM 3rd International Workshop on Software Correctness for HPC Applications (Correctness), pp. 27–35 (2019)

17. Makhorin, A.O.: GLPK (GNU linear programming kit). http://www.gnu.org/software/glpk/glpk.html

18. Makino, J., Kokubo, E., Fukushige, T.: Performance evaluation and tuning of GRAPE-6 - towards 40 "real" Tflops. In: Proceedings of the ACM/IEEE SC2003 Conference on High Performance Networking and Computing, Phoenix, AZ, USA, 15–21 November 2003, CD-Rom, p. 2. ACM (2003)

19. Menon, H., et al.: Adapt: algorithmic differentiation applied to floating-point precision tuning. In: Proceedings of the International Conference for High Performance Computing, Networking, Storage, and Analysis, SC 2018. IEEE Press (2018)

20. de Moura, L., Bjørner, N.: Z3: an efficient SMT solver. In: Ramakrishnan, C.R., Rehof, J. (eds.) TACAS 2008. LNCS, vol. 4963, pp. 337–340. Springer, Heidelberg (2008). https://doi.org/10.1007/978-3-540-78800-3_24

21. Rubio-González, C., et al.: Precimonious: tuning assistant for floating-point precision. In: International Conference for High Performance Computing, Networking, Storage and Analysis, SC 2013, pp. 27:1–27:12. ACM (2013)

22. Saiki, B., Flatt, O., Nandi, C., Panchekha, P., Tatlock, Z.: Combining precision tuning and rewriting. In: IEEE Symposium on Computer Arithmetic (ARITH) 2021. IEEE (2021)

23. Schkufza, E., Sharma, R., Aiken, A.: Stochastic optimization of floating-point programs with tunable precision. In: Proceedings of the 35th ACM SIGPLAN Conference on Programming Language Design and Implementation, PLDI 2014, pp. 53–64. Association for Computing Machinery (2014)
24. Solovyev, A., Baranowski, M.S., Briggs, I., Jacobsen, C., Rakamarić, Z., Gopalakrishnan, G.: Rigorous estimation of floating-point round-off errors with symbolic taylor expansions. ACM Trans. Program. Lang. Syst. **41**(1), 1–39 (2018)
25. Uguen, Y., Forget, L., de Dinechin, F.: Evaluating the hardware cost of the posit number system. In: Sourdis, I., Bouganis, C., Álvarez, C., Díaz, L.A.T., Valero-Lara, P., Martorell, X. (eds.) 29th International Conference on Field Programmable Logic and Applications, FPL 2019, Barcelona, Spain, 8–12 September 2019, pp. 106–113. IEEE (2019)

Multiple-Precision Arithmetic of Biot-Savart Integrals for Reconnections of Vortex Filaments

Yu-Hsun Lee$^{(\boxtimes)}$ and Hiroshi Fujiwara

Graduate School of Informatics, Kyoto University, Kyoto 606-8501, Japan
{andylee,fujiwara}@acs.i.kyoto-u.ac.jp

Abstract. In this paper, we show an efficient application of multiple-precision arithmetic to numerical computation of the Biot-Savart integral, which is a mathematical model of motion of vortex filaments. Since it is a non-linear integro-differential equation, numerical methods play a significant role in analysis. Hence reliable schemes are desired even though their computational costs are high. Multiple-precision arithmetic enables us to estimate rounding errors quantitatively, and comparing various precision arithmetic. Thus we conclude reliability of numerical results. In particular, reconnection of vortex filaments is investigated, and we meet oscillation of numerical solutions due to singularity. The proposed method clarifies that the divergence immediately after reconnection is still reliable in terms of rounding errors.

Keywords: Computational fluid dynamics · Vortex reconnection · Numerical instability and reliability · Multiple-precision arithmetic

1 Introduction

We consider dynamics of incompressible fluid occupying whole $\mathbb{R}^3$, whose velocity is denoted by $\vec{v} = \vec{v}(\vec{x})$ at $\vec{x} \in \mathbb{R}^3$. Its vorticity is defined by $\vec{\omega} = \mathrm{rot}\,\vec{v}$, and conversely, the Biot-Savart law gives $\vec{v}$ from $\vec{\omega}$ under the hypothesis of incompressibility. Let $C \subset \mathbb{R}^3$ be a non self-intersecting smooth curve, and suppose that vorticity concentrates on C with constant circulation. If $\vec{\omega}$ tangents to C at every point, then it is called a vortex filament. Let us denote the vortex filament at time t by $C = \{\vec{x}(t,s) ; t > 0, s \in I(t)\}$ with the arc length parameter s belonging to an interval $I(t) \subset \mathbb{R}$. It is then well known that C has self-induced velocity which is described by the Biot-Savart law

$$\frac{\partial \vec{x}}{\partial t}(t,s) = \frac{\Gamma}{4\pi} \int_{I(t)} \frac{(\partial \vec{x}/\partial s)(t,s') \times (\vec{x}(t,s) - \vec{x}(t,s'))}{\left|\vec{x}(t,s) - \vec{x}(t,s')\right|^3} ds', \quad t > 0, s \in I(t) \quad (1)$$

The second author was supported in part by JSPS KAKENHI Grant Numbers JP19H00641 and JP20H01821.

where Γ is circulation and $|\cdot|$ is the Euclidean norm in $\mathbb{R}^3$. Since the Biot-Savart law (1) is a non-linear integro-differential equation with a singular integral kernel, it is hard not only to prove well-posedness, i.e. unique existence of the solution and stability in a suitable normed space, but also to analyze the behavior of vortex filaments analytically. Therefore approximation methods have been developed so far (see [13,14,18] and references therein), and several computational approaches have been presented in recent years with the help of rapid growth of computational resources. The local induction approximation [5,9] and its correction [3,10,19], and regularization methods [15–17] are known as conventional methods, including treatments of singularities. Although numerical methods are indispensable in the analysis of the motion of vortex filaments, their reliability have not been investigated as the authors' best knowledge.

Recently Kimura and Moffatt have numerically observed the occurrence of singularities in C, where it is self-intersecting in their dynamics obeyed by (1) starting from non-self-intersecting smooth curves as initial conditions[11,12]. This is called *reconnection* of vortex filaments, which attracts a lot of interest in connection with smoothness of solutions of fluid dynamics.

In this paper, we discuss reliability of reconnection of vortex filaments from the standpoints of numerical computation. Particularly we concentrate ourselves on estimation of behavior of rounding errors, which give serious influences in unstable numerical processes. In time evolution problems, stability of numerical schemes indicates that the accumulation of computational errors is not crucial, hence it is one of fundamental concepts for reliability of numerical solutions. Since it is hard to prove stability of schemes theoretically in most cases, we develop a practical and efficient strategy to estimate accumulation of rounding errors.

The rest of this paper is arranged as follows. Section 2 briefly describes the numerical scheme proposed by Kimura and Moffatt. Our proposed methodology is presented in Sect. 3, and we show its efficiency and feasibility in Sect. 4 by case studies.

It should be noted that *stability* depends on a choice of topology where we discuss numerical schemes and corresponding solutions. Although terminology of *stability* with absence of function spaces is abuse, we use it for clarity.

2   Numerical Schemes for Motion of Vortex Filaments

In this section the numerical method for (1) is presented which is used in this paper. The method has been proposed by Kimura and Moffatt [11,12], and is efficient to avoid the singularities of the integral kernel in spite of its simplicity.

Firstly we assume that initial shape of the vortex filament is a closed curve, and has parameterization as $C_0 = \{\vec{x}(0, \theta) \, ; \, 0 \leq \theta < 2\pi\}$. Let Δt be a positive number, N be a power of two, and $\theta_j = 2\pi j/N$ for $0 \leq j < N$. Then we allocate N nodes $\vec{x}(0, \theta_j)$ on C_0, and for each time step $t_k = k\Delta t$, we calculate

$$\Delta s_j = \frac{|\vec{x}_{j+1} - \vec{x}_j| + |\vec{x}_j - \vec{x}_{j-1}|}{2}, \quad 0 \leq j < N, \qquad (2)$$

where $\vec{x}_j = \vec{x}(t_k, \theta_j)$ with identifying $\vec{x}_{-1} = \vec{x}_{N-1}$ and $\vec{x}_N = \vec{x}_0$ for periodicity. Then the Biot-Savart integral (1) is discretized as

$$\vec{v}(\vec{x}_i) = \frac{\Gamma}{4\pi} \sum_{\substack{0 \leq j < N \\ j \neq i}} \frac{\vec{t}_j \times (\vec{x}_i - \vec{x}_j)}{|\vec{x}_i - \vec{x}_j|^3} \Delta s_j, \quad 0 \leq i < N.$$

Particularly singularity in integration is approximated with ignoring the influence from neighborhood of $\vec{x}_i$. The unit tangent vector $\vec{t}_j$ is calculated by the fast Fourier transform (FFT), and the classical Runge-Kutta method is adopted for time-stepping. Then we can find $\{\vec{x}(t_k, s_j) ; 0 \leq j < N\}$ which approximates C at $t = t_k$.

Secondly, we consider the case when the initial condition $C_0 = \{\vec{x}(0, p) ; p \in \mathbb{R}\}$ is an unbounded curve. Let N be a positive integer, $h = \pi/(2N)$, and we introduce $p_j = \sinh\left(\frac{\pi}{2}\sinh(jh)\right)$ for $-N \leq j \leq N$. Then C is approximated by $2N + 1$ nodes $\vec{x}(p_j)$, and the double exponential rule [20] imply an approximation of (1) by

$$\vec{v}(\vec{x}_i) = \frac{\Gamma}{4\pi} \sum_{\substack{-N \leq j \leq N \\ j \neq i}} \frac{\vec{t}_j \times (\vec{x}_i - \vec{x}_j)}{|\vec{x}_i - \vec{x}_j|^3} \Delta p_j, \quad -N \leq i < N$$

where

$$\Delta p_j = \frac{\pi}{2} h \cosh(jh) \cosh\left(\frac{\pi}{2}\sinh(jh)\right)$$

and $\vec{t}_j$ is calculated from the five-point finite difference. Finally, the classical Runge-Kutta method is also employed for time-stepping.

3   Quantitative Estimate of Rounding Errors by Multiple-Precision Arithmetic

In scientific numerical computations, all real numbers and their arithmetic are approximated by floating-point arithmetic. In the standard numerical computation environments, it is hard to estimate the influence of them. We propose the use of multiple-precision arithmetic to estimate rounding errors introduced by this approximation.

On digital computations, a floating-point number consists of sign, exponent, and fractional parts. Since each part has finite information, rounding errors are inevitable in number representations and their arithmetic. Though rounding errors are thought to be sufficiently smaller than discretization errors so that they are negligible in scientific computation, they may accumulate rapidly in unstable numerical processes and give fatal influences. On the other hand, rounding errors depend on various issues, such as expressions in user programs and execution orders of arithmetic. Thus it is infeasible to estimate them theoretically in advance.

The double precision arithmetic defined in IEEE754 standard [2] is widely used in scientific computation. IEEE754 double precision has 53-bits in its fractional part which corresponds to approximately 16 decimal digits. However, in some advanced scientific and engineering computations, influence of rounding errors is serious. In such cases, particular algorithms must be designed so as to reduce rounding errors depending on problems or parameters in computations.

One of efficient strategy to reduce rounding errors is extending precision of the fractional part of floating-point numbers. Recently a quadruple precision arithmetic environment *quadmath* [7] has been implemented in the de facto standard compiler GNU Compilers Collection (GCC) on AMD64 and Intel64, which are popular processor architectures for PC. Furthermore, one of the authors has proposed a multiple-precision arithmetic environment *exflib* [6] which is suitable for scientific and engineering computation on AMD64 and Intel64 architectures. Exflib enables us to specify arbitrarily computational precision in advance, and provides user-friendly interfaces so as to use same expressions as the built-in types in the programming language C++. Table 1 shows bits length and precision of floating-point types used in the present research.

Table 1. Precision of floating-point types used in experiments. In exflib, 50 decimal digits is specified as desired computational precision.

Type	Total (bits)	Sign (bits)	Exponent (bits)	Fraction (bits)	(decimal digits)
IEEE754 double	64	1	11	53	(15.95)
quadmath	128	1	15	113	(34.02)
exflib, 50 digits	256	1	63	193	(58.10)

In order to estimate influences of rounding errors, we process computation with three different precisions and compare their results. Under the assumption that the results with exflib (50 digits) are most accurate among them, we are able to estimate rounding errors in results with IEEE754 double precision or quadruple precision arithmetic by using those with exflib (50 digits) as a reference.

4   Numerical Examples

This section is devoted to exhibiting efficiency and feasibility of the proposed method by case studies. In numerical experiments, the computational environment shown in Table 2 is used, and all computations are processed by the use of 32 threads parallel computation by OpenMP. Throughout the section, Γ is set to $4\pi/50$.

Table 2. Computational environment

CPU	Ryzen Threadripper 2990WX (3.0 GHz, 32 cores)
Memory	DDR4-1866 128GB
OS	CentOS Linux 7.9.2009
C++ Compiler	GCC Version 4.8.5
FFT	fftw Version 3.3.8
exflib	Version 20180620

4.1 Figure-of-Eight Vortex Filament

We consider as an initial condition

$$
\begin{aligned}
x(\theta) &= 0.5 \sin 2\theta, \\
y(\theta) &= 2.5 \sin \theta, \\
z(\theta) &= 0.05 \cos \theta,
\end{aligned}
\tag{3}
$$

with $0 \le \theta < 2\pi$. In discretization, we allocate N nodes $\vec{x}(\theta_j)$ with $\theta_j = 2\pi j/N$, $0 \le i < N$ with $N = 8192$. Using the Runge-Kutta method with $\Delta t = 4 \times 10^{-5}$, numerical results at $t = 0.0024 \ (= 60\Delta t)$ are depicted in Fig. 1 (a) and (b), which are respectively obtained by the standard double precision arithmetic and 50 decimal digits computation by multiple-precision arithmetic. Oscillations appear in both results, while numerical results with a smaller $\Delta t = 2 \times 10^{-5}$ are smooth shown in Fig. 1 (c).

Adopting $\Delta t = 2 \times 10^{-5}$ enables us to meet numerical reconnection of the vortex filament around estimated reconnection time which is approximately $t \approx 0.3385$. Figure 2 (a) and (b) are respectively numerical results immediately before and after the reconnection by the standard double precision, where purple and green parts mean that they are in $z > 0$ and $z < 0$ in the initial condition (3). Numerical results in Fig. 2 (b) has disturbance similarly to Fig. 1 (a) and (b).

In order to evaluate rounding errors quantitatively, we process the computation with quadruple precision arithmetic, and 50 decimal digits computations. Errors between double precision arithmetic and 50 decimal digits

$$
\max_j \frac{\left| \vec{x}^{(\text{double})}(k\Delta t, s_j) - \vec{x}^{(50 \text{ digits})}(k\Delta t, s_j) \right|}{\left| \vec{x}^{(50 \text{ digits})}(k\Delta t, s_j) \right|}
\tag{4}
$$

and those between quadruple precision arithmetic and 50 decimal digits

$$
\max_j \frac{\left| \vec{x}^{(\text{quadruple})}(k\Delta t, s_j) - \vec{x}^{(50 \text{ digits})}(k\Delta t, s_j) \right|}{\left| \vec{x}^{(50 \text{ digits})}(k\Delta t, s_j) \right|}
\tag{5}
$$

are shown in Table 3. In the results errors in $t \le 0.342$ are small as rounding errors, and oscillations in Fig. 2 (b) commonly appears in those with quadruple

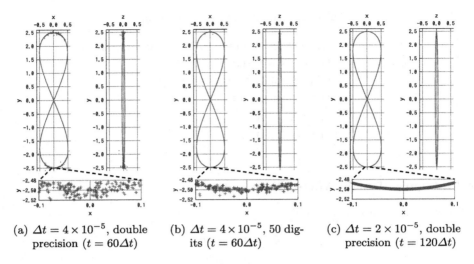

(a) $\Delta t = 4 \times 10^{-5}$, double precision ($t = 60\Delta t$)

(b) $\Delta t = 4 \times 10^{-5}$, 50 digits ($t = 60\Delta t$)

(c) $\Delta t = 2 \times 10^{-5}$, double precision ($t = 120\Delta t$)

Fig. 1. Numerical results for figure-of-eight vortex filament, $t = 0.0024$, $N = 8192$. The results (a) and (b) has oscillations, while the results (c) is smooth.

precision arithmetic and 50 digits computation. This implies that rounding errors do not give any influence to the oscillation in $t \leq 0.342$, including Fig. 2 (b). Therefore numerical results are reliable in terms of rounding errors.

Table 3. Maximum relative Euclidean distance in figure-of-eight vortex filament, the estimated reconnection time is $t \approx 0.3385$

t	Error in double (4)	Error in quadmath (5)
0.320	7.63×10^{-13}	4.28×10^{-31}
0.338	1.14×10^{-12}	3.65×10^{-31}
0.342	1.34×10^{-8}	9.41×10^{-27}
0.344	1.60×10^{2}	1.01×10^{-2}

In this case, most of computational time are consumed in finding tangent vectors by FFT and summation as discretization of the Biot-Savart integral. Table 4 shows them with $\Delta t = 2 \times 10^{-5}$ and $N = 8192$ for $0 \leq t \leq 0.4$ ($= 20000\Delta t$). We use FFTW3 with the FFTW_MEASURE flag for double and quadruple precision arithmetic [1], and the iterative algorithm [4,8] for 50 decimal digits implemented by the authors. Quadruple precision arithmetic and 50 decimal digits computation consume extraordinary longer time than those of double precision arithmetic, since their arithmetic are implemented as software libraries. However,

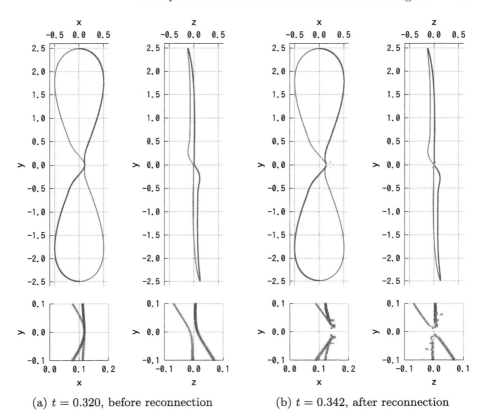

(a) $t = 0.320$, before reconnection   (b) $t = 0.342$, after reconnection

Fig. 2. Numerical results for before and after of the reconnection in figure-of-eight vortex filament with $\Delta t = 2 \times 10^{-5}$ and double precision arithmetic. After reconnection ($t \approx 0.3385$), disturbance appears illustrated in (b).

it is effective to verify the computational results, and it means that the proposed methods are effective and practical for evaluation of accumulation of rounding errors.

4.2   Tent-Shaped Vortex Filament

We consider another example started from an initial shape

$$x(p) = \pm c \cos \theta \cosh p,$$
$$y(p) = \frac{c}{m} \sinh p,$$
$$z(p) = -c \sin \theta \cosh p,$$
(6)

with $c = 0.1$, $m = 0.35$, $\theta = \pi/4$ with $p \in \mathbb{R}$. Note that this consists of two distinct unbounded curves illustrated in Fig. 3. We allocate nodes $\{\vec{x}(p_i) \, ; \, -N \leq i \leq N\}$ defined by

Table 4. Computational time for figure-of-eight vortex filament (unit : d = days, h = hours, m = minutes, s = seconds)

	Tangent	Summation	Total
double precision	47 s	24 m 11 s	25 m 09 s
quadruple precision	12 m 30 s	1 d 18 h 28 m	1 d 18 h 41 m
exflib, 50 digits	19 m 45 s	2 d 15 h 21 m	2 d 15 h 42 m

$$p_i = \sinh\left(\frac{\pi}{2}\sinh(ih)\right), \quad h = \frac{\pi}{2N}$$

with $N = 800$. Thus there are $2N + 1 = 1601$ nodes on one of two curves (totally 3202 points).

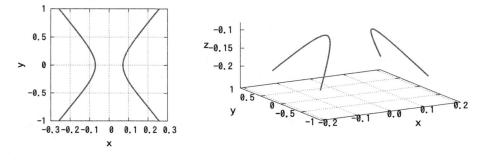

Fig. 3. Initial condition of tent-shaped vortex filament (6)

By starting from the initial nodes with $\Delta t = 4 \times 10^{-5}$, the numerical results at $t = 0.008$ ($= 200\Delta t$) have disturbance depicted in Fig. 4 (a) and (b), where double precision arithmetic and 50 decimal digits computations are employed respectively. The results indicate that oscillation is amplification of discretization errors. On the other hand, disturbance does not appear in Fig. 4 (c) if smaller $\Delta t = 2 \times 10^{-5}$ is adopted.

The choice of $\Delta t = 2 \times 10^{-5}$ and $N = 800$ enable us to reproduce reconnection. Figure 5 (a) and (b) depict numerical results around reconnection time, which is approximately $t = 0.5058$ in the tent-shaped model.

We process the same scheme with quadruple precision arithmetic and 50 decimal digits computations. The errors between double precision arithmetic and 50 decimal digits computation (4), and those between quadruple precision arithmetic and 50 decimal digits computation (5) are shown in Table 5. The results are almost same as the figure-of-eight vortex filament example, and major ingredients of differences for $t \leq 0.5074$ are not rounding errors.

Table 6 shows the computational time for $0 \leq t \leq 0.52$ ($= 26000\Delta t$). In this case quadruple precision arithmetic and 50 decimal digits computation spent substantially longer computational time than double precision arithmetic.

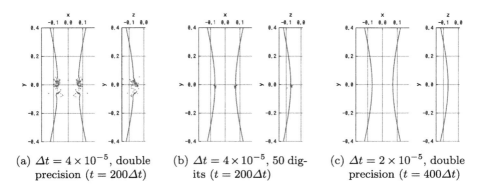

(a) $\Delta t = 4 \times 10^{-5}$, double precision $(t = 200\Delta t)$

(b) $\Delta t = 4 \times 10^{-5}$, 50 digits $(t = 200\Delta t)$

(c) $\Delta t = 2 \times 10^{-5}$, double precision $(t = 400\Delta t)$

Fig. 4. Numerical results for tent-shaped vortex filament, $t = 0.008$, $N = 800$

Table 5. Maximum relative Euclidean distance in tent-shaped vortex filament, the estimated reconnection time is $t \approx 0.5058$

t	Error in double (4)	Error in quadmath (5)
0.4500	2.20×10^{-12}	7.07×10^{-31}
0.5040	2.47×10^{-12}	7.47×10^{-31}
0.5074	9.48×10^{-8}	1.33×10^{-26}
0.5100	1.21×10^{20}	5.37×10^{3}

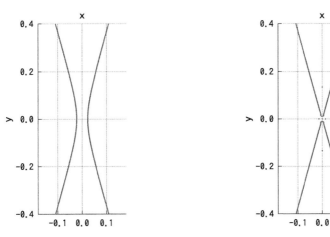

(a) $t = 0.4500$, before reconnection

(b) $t = 0.5074$, after reconnection

Fig. 5. Numerical results for reconnection in tent-shaped vortex filament, $\Delta t = 2 \times 10^{-5}$, double precision

Table 6. Computational time for tent-shaped vortex filament (unit : h = hours, m = minutes, s = seconds)

Environment	Time
double	2 m 36 s
quadruple precision	4 h 54 m 26 s
exflib, 50 digits	7 h 58 m 19 s

5   Concluding Remarks

This paper presents an estimate strategy of rounding errors by high-accurate arithmetic. Its feasibility is exhibited in numerical computations of vortex filaments, and reliability of numerical reconnection is concluded from numerical results although the reconnection of vortex filaments is involved with occurrence of singularity of smooth solutions and is sensitive to computational errors. The proposed method gives a quantitative and concrete estimate in spite of consuming substantial amount of computational time.

For high-accurate numerical computation, we have to pay attention to discretization errors in addition to rounding errors. Our numerical experiments in Fig. 1 and Fig. 4 suggest appearance of disturbance much earlier than the reconnection, and it is reduced by taking smaller time steps. As analogous to the numerical analysis of partial differential equations such as the wave equation and the heat equation, it indicates conditions for numerical stability of the scheme. In other words, the balance of temporal and spatial discretization parameter choice is crucial for reliable numerical computations, which will be discussed in a forthcoming paper.

Acknowledgments. The authors would like to express their gratitude for Professor Yoshifumi Kimura (Nagoya University) for his fruitful suggestions and discussions.

References

1. FFTW. http://www.fftw.org. Accessed 1 Mar 2021
2. ANSI/IEEE 754-1985 standard for binary floating-point arithmetic (1985)
3. Baggaley, A.W., Barenghi, C.F.: Spectrum of turbulent Kelvin-waves cascade in superfluid helium. Phys. Rev. B **83**, 134509 (2011)
4. Briggs, W.L., Henson, V.E.: The DFT: An Owner's Manual for the Discrete Fourier Transform. Society for Industrial and Applied Mathematics (1995)
5. Da Rios, L.S.: Sul moto d'un liquido indefinito con un filetto vorticoso di forma qualunque. Rend. Circ. Mat. Palermo **22**, 117–135 (1906)
6. Fujiwara, H.: exflib. http://www-an.acs.i.kyoto-u.ac.jp/~fujiwara/exflib. Accessed 1 Mar 2021
7. GCC libquadmath. https://gcc.gnu.org/onlinedocs/libquadmath/. Accessed 1 Mar 2021

8. Gentleman, W.M., Sande, G.: Fast fourier transforms: for fun and profit. In: Proceedings of the November 7–10, 1966, Fall Joint Computer Conference, AFIPS 1966, pp. 563–578 (Fall). Association for Computing Machinery, New York (1966)
9. Hama, F.R.: Progressive deformation of a curved vortex filament by its own induction. Phys. Fluid **5**, 1156–1162 (1962)
10. Hänninen, R., Baggaley, A.W.: Vortex filament method as a tool for computational visualization of quantum turbulence. Proc. Natl. Acad. Sci. U.S.A. **111**(Suppl. 1), 4667–4674 (2014)
11. Kimura, Y., Moffatt, H.K.: Scaling properties towards vortex reconnection under biot–savart evolution. Fluid Dyn. Res. **50**(1), 011409 (2017)
12. Kimura, Y., Moffatt, H.K.: A tent model of vortex reconnection under biot-savart evolution. J. Fluid Mech. **834**, R1 (2018)
13. Majda, A.J., Bertozzi, A.L.: Vorticity and Incompressible Flow. Cambridge University Press, Cambridge (2001)
14. Moore, D.W., Saffman, P.G.: The motion of a vortex filament with axial flow. Philos. Trans. R. Soc. London Ser. A **272**, 403–429 (1972)
15. Oshima, Y., Noguchi, T., Oshima, K.: Numerical study of interaction of two vortex rings. Fluid Dyn. Res. **1**(3), 215–227 (1987)
16. Pumir, A., Siggia, E.D.: Vortex dynamics and the existence of solutions to the Navier-Stokes equations. Phys. Fluid **30**(6), 1606–1626 (1987)
17. Rosenhead, L.: The spread of vorticity in the wake behind a cylinder. Proc. R. Soc. Lond. A **127**, 590–612 (1930)
18. Sarpkaya, T.: Vortex element methods for flow simulation. In: Advances in Applied Mechanics, vol. 31, pp. 113–247. Elsevier (1994)
19. Schwarz, K.W.: Three-dimensional vortex dynamics in superfluid ^{4}He: homogeneous superfluid turbulence. Phys. Rev. B **38**, 2398–2417 (1988)
20. Takahasi, H., Mori, M.: Double exponential formulas for numerical integration. Publ. Res. Inst. Math. Sci. **9**, 721–741 (1973/74)

Acceleration of Multiple Precision Matrix Multiplication Based on Multi-component Floating-Point Arithmetic Using AVX2

Tomonori Kouya[✉][iD]

Shizuoka Institute of Science and Technology,
2200-2 Toyosawa, Fukuroi 437-8555, Japan
kouya.tomonori@sist.ac.jp

Abstract. In this paper, we report the results obtained from the acceleration of multi-binary64-type multiple precision block and Strassen matrix multiplications with AVX2. We target double-double (DD), triple-double (TD), and quad-double (QD) precision arithmetic designed using certain types of error-free transformation (EFT) arithmetic. Furthermore, we implement SIMDized EFT functions, which simultaneously compute with four binary64 numbers on x86_64 computing environment, and by using help of them, we also develop SIMDized DD, TD, and QD additions and multiplications. In addition, AVX2 load/store functions were adopted to efficiently speed up reading and storing matrix elements from/to memory. Owing to these combined techniques, our implemented multiple precision matrix multiplications were accelerated more than three times compared with non-accelerated ones. Our accelerated matrix multiplication modifies parallelization performance with OpenMP.

Keywords: Multiple precision floating-point arithmetic · Matrix multiplication · AVX2 · Parallelization

1 Introduction

The scale of scientific computation is becoming increasingly large, and obtaining the user-required accuracy of approximation for ill-conditioned cases requires more fractional digits in floating-point numbers than for a IEEE754 binary standard, such as binary32 (24-bits fraction) or binary64 (53-bits). To obtain a precise approximation, it is critical to adopt multiple precision floating-point (MPF) arithmetic, which can handle more fractional digits than binary64.

The implementation of MPF arithmetic is currently categorized into two groups: multi-digit type, based on integer arithmetic, and multi-component-type (or multi-term), which is constructed by several binary32 or binary64 numbers. The QD library by Bailey et al. [1] represents the latter, whereas the former is represented by GNU MPFR (Multiple Precision Floating-point Reliable

Supported by JSPS KAKENHI (Grant Number JP20K11843) and Shizuoka Institute of Science and Technology.

library) [8], which is based on the multiple precision natural number arithmetic (MPN) kernel of GNU MP (GNU Multiple Precision arithmetic library) [12]. Both libraries are coded using C and C++ languages, and the MPN kernel is accelerated by assembler codes for various CPU architectures.

MPLAPACK based on MPBLAS [9] is an efficient MPF linear computation library that employs QD, MPFR, and bridge functions. ATLAS [11] and Open-BLAS [10] were created because the original reference BLAS, based on simple Fortran codes, has plenty of room for acceleration, and further accelerated MPF BLAS libraries are expected.

It is well known that multi-component MPF arithmetic can be accelerated using SIMD instructions, such as AVX2. Lis [6,13] is one of the most optimal AVX2-based linear and sparse linear computation libraries, and it has achieved over three times speedup using AVX2 [14].

In this paper, we report the performance of our implemented binary64-based multi-component MPF block and Strassen matrix multiplications using a technique similar to that of Lis. The targeted precisions are double-double (DD), triple-double (TD), and quadruple-double (QD) arithmetic. We adopted SIMDized error-free transformation functions on the x86_64 CPU architecture to extend the performance of these three precision MPF linear computations. QD-based addition is also utilized to obtain better performance in TD arithmetic. In our implementation, a new data structure for the MPF vector and matrix is introduced to accelerate the load and store its elements with AVX2. Owing to these efforts, we realized a higher performance for all types of MPF arithmetic than those of the Rgemm function of MPBLAS. Furthermore, we modified the speed of parallelization with OpenMP for block matrix multiplication in the AMD EPYC environment.

We determined that our Strassen matrix multiplication could not be accelerated on a CPU with more than eight cores, and that block matrix multiplication performed better than Strassen matrix multiplication on such CPUs.

2 Acceleration of DD, TD, and QD Matrix Multiplication with AVX2

Multi-component MPF arithmetic is constructed using several hard-wired binary32 or binary64 numbers and various functions of the so-called error-free transformation (EFT) [3]. The DD, TD, and QD precision MPF numbers are constructed with two binary64, three binary64, and four binary64 numbers, respectively. The most significant component (one leading binary64 number) of DD, TD, and QD precision numbers possesses the most significant digits of the entire MPF number.

Using DD precision arithmetic, it has been reported that basic linear computation can be accelerated with SIMD instructions, including AVX2, because DD arithmetic does not include complicated branches in its addition, subtraction, multiplication, and division. In contrast, TD and QD arithmetic require renormalization processes, including some conditional branches. Therefore, we are required to implement these renormalization as simple loops, where we consider each binary64 number in the _m256d data type of AVX2, including three or four binary64 numbers. Because we completed all DD, TD, and QD arithmetic using the _m256d data type as API interfaces, our MPF matrix multiplication library has been simply implemented and accelerated with AVX2.

2.1 Error-Free Transformation with AVX2

As we explained earlier, we only implemented the _m256d data type to express and accelerate linear computation with multi-component MPF arithmetic. Therefore, C APIs such as _mm256_[add, sub, mul, div]_pd, and _mm256_fmadd_pd as fused multiply add (FMA) [2], were embedded in the required EFT functions, such as QuickTwoSum, TwoSum, and TwoProd. Subsequently, these functions were implemented as AVX2QuickTwoSum (Algorithm 1), AVX2TwoSum (Algorithm 2), and AVX2TwoProd (Algorithm 3), respectively. In these SIMDized EFT functions, a, b, s and e are _m256d data type, and include four binary64 data such as $a = (a_0, a_1, a_2, a_3)$, $b = (b_0, b_1, b_2, b_3)$, $s = (s_0, s_1, s_2, s_3)$, and $e = (e_0, e_1, e_2, e_3)$.

Algorithm 1. $(s, e) := $ AVX2QuickTwoSum(a, b)

$s := $ _mm256_add_pd(a, b)
$e := $ _mm256_sub_pd$(b, $_mm256_sub_pd$(s, a))$
return (s, e)

Algorithm 2. $(s, e) := $ AVX2TwoSum(a, b)

$s := $ _mm256_add_pd(a, b)
$v := $ _mm256_sub_pd(s, a)
$e := $ _mm256_add_pd(_mm256_sub_pd$(a, $_mm256_sub_pd$(s, v))$, _mm256_sub_pd$(b, v))$
return(s, e)

Algorithm 3. $(p, e) := $ AVX2TwoProd(a, b)

$p := $_mm256_mul_pd$(a, b)$
$e := $_mm256_fmadd_pd$(a, b, -p)$
return(p, e)

2.2 SIMDized DD Addition and Multiplication

Because DD arithmetic is the simplest of the multi-component MPF arithmetic, its addition and multiplication needed for matrix multiplication, which directly adopt SIMDized EFT functions, can be easily implemented, as shown in Algorithm 4 and 5. One standard DD precision number is constructed with two binary64 as $x[2] = (x[0], x[1])$. Therefore, in SIMDized DD arithmetic, each array element of $x[2]$ is expressed as one _m256d variable, as $x[0] = (x[0]_0, x[0]_1, x[0]_2, x[0]_3)$ and $x[1] = (x[1]_0, x[1]_1, x[1]_2, x[1]_3)$. AVX2DDadd and AVX2DDmul simultaneously execute four calculations with $x[2]$ and $y[2]$, in which they have four DD numbers: $(x[0]_i, x[1]_i)$ and $(y[0]_i, y[1]_i)$ $(i = 0, 1, 2, 3)$. In these DD arithmetic, all temporary variables are expressed as the _m256d data type.

Algorithm 4. $r[2] := \text{AVX2DDadd}(x[2], y[2])$

$(s, e) := \text{AVX2TwoSum}(x[0], y[0])$
$w := \text{\_mm256\_add\_pd}(x[1], y[1])$
$e := \text{\_mm256\_add\_pd}(e, w)$
$(r[0], r[1]) := \text{AVX2QuickTwoSum}(s, e)$
return $(r[0], r[1])$

Algorithm 5. $r[2] := \text{AVX2DDmul}(x[2], y[2])$

$(p_1, p_2) := \text{AVX2TwoProd}(x[0], y[0])$
$w_1 := \text{\_mm256\_mul\_pd}(x[0], y[1])$
$w_2 := \text{\_mm256\_mul\_pd}(x[1], y[0])$
$w_3 := \text{\_mm256\_add\_pd}(w_1, w_2)$
$p_2 := \text{\_mm256\_add\_pd}(p_2, w_3)$
$(r[0], r[1]) := \text{AVX2QuickTwoSum}(p_1, p_2)$

As previously introduced, Lis [13] and MuPaT [14] realized a DD linear computation with AVX2 that is approximately three times faster. They utilized C macros to implement SIMDized DD arithmetic. In contrast to Lis and MuPat, we adopted the C static inline functions of the SIMDized EFT for DD, TD, and QD linear computations. In the remainder of this section, we describe these algorithms using AVX2 and their performance.

2.3 SIMDized TD Addition and Multiplication

Fabiano et al. proposed an optimized triple-word arithmetic [4]. In this arithmetic set, the renormalization of triple word numbers adopts VecSum and VSEB(k) (VecSum with Error Branch). Our SIMDized TD arithmetic can be implemented with AVX2 instruction, AVX2VecSum, and AVX2VSEB(n). AVX2VecSum can be fully implemented with AVX2 functions, whereas

AVX2VSEB(n) is not completely SIMDized owing to the conditional branch embedded in it.

TD addition (TDadd) calculates $r[3] = (r[0], r[1], r[2])$ as the sum of $x[3] = (x[0], x[1], x[2])$ and $y[3] = (y[0], y[1], y[2])$. The standard approach is to merge sorting all elements of $x[3]$ and $y[3]$, normalizing them by VecSum, and expressing $r[3]$ as the TD number by VSEB(3). The following AVX2TDadd (Algorithm 6) is implemented using AVX2. This algorithm is not sufficiently accelerated with AVX2 owing to the poor performance of the merge(-sort) function and incomplete AVXVSEB(n).

Algorithm 6. $r[3] := \text{AVX2TDadd}(x[3], y[3])$

$(z_0, ..., z_5) := \text{AVX2Merge}(x[0], x[1], x[2], y[0], y[1], y[2])$
$(e_0, ..., e_5) := \text{AVX2VecSum}(z_0, ..., z_5)$
$(r[0], r[1], r[2]) := \text{AVX2VSEB}(3)(e_0, ..., e_5)$
return $(r[0], r[1], r[2])$

As demonstrated in the results obtained by benchmark tests, AVX2TDadd cannot be accelerated completely with AVX2. Therefore, as an alternative, we applied QDadd (Algorithm 8) as TD addition (TDaddq) with a substitution such as $x[3] = y[3] = 0$. In our TD matrix multiplication, we adopted TDaddq and AVX2TDaddq as default TD additions.

For TD multiplication, Fabiano et al. proposed an accurate version and a fast version. We selected the latter as the default TD multiplication (TDmul) and implemented AVX2TDmul with AVX2.

Algorithm 7. $r[3] := \text{AVX2TDmul}(x[3], y[3])$

$(z_{00}^{\text{up}}, z_{00}^{\text{lo}}) := \text{AVX2TwoProd}(x[0], y[0])$
$(z_{01}^{\text{up}}, z_{01}^{\text{lo}}) := \text{AVX2TwoProd}(x[0], y[1])$
$(z_{10}^{\text{up}}, z_{10}^{\text{lo}}) := \text{AVX2TwoProd}(x[1], y[0])$
$(b_0, b_1, b_2) := \text{AVX2VecSum}(z_{00}^{\text{lo}}, z_{01}^{\text{up}}, z_{10}^{\text{up}})$
$c := \texttt{\_mm256\_fmadd\_pd}(x[1], y[1], b_2)$
$z_{31} := \texttt{\_mm256\_fmadd\_pd}(x[0], y[2], z_{10}^{\text{lo}})$
$z_{32} := \texttt{\_mm256\_fmadd\_pd}(x[2], y[0], z_{01}^{\text{lo}})$
$z_3 := \texttt{\_mm256\_add\_pd}(z_{31}, z_{32})$
$s_3 := \texttt{\_mm256\_add\_pd}(c, z_3)$
$(e_0, e_1, e_2, e_3) := \text{AVX2VecSum}(z_{00}^{\text{up}}, b_0, b_1, s_3)$
$r[0] := e_0$
$(r[1], r[2]) := \text{AVX2VSEB}(2)(e_1, e_2, e_3)$
return $(r[0], r[1], r[2])$

As a trial approach, we implemented TDmulq, which was converted to QDmul for the TD multiplication, although it could not realize a higher speed than TDmul. Therefore, to implement the TD matrix multiplication, we adopted the TDaddq and TDmul sets, as well as those of AVX2TDaddq and AVX2TDmul.

2.4 SIMDized QD Addition and Multiplication

For QD arithmetic, we selected a lighter addition and multiplication (sloppy addition and multiplication), and then we implemented AVX2QDadd (Algorithm 8) and AVX2QDmul (Algorithm 9) with AVX2Renorm as the renormalization of QD numbers with AVX2.

Algorithm 8. $r[4] := \text{AVX2QDadd}(x[4], y[4])$

$s_0 :=\_\text{mm256\_add\_pd}(x[0], y[0])$
$s_1 :=\_\text{mm256\_add\_pd}(x[1], y[1])$
$s_2 :=\_\text{mm256\_add\_pd}(x[2], y[2])$
$s_3 :=\_\text{mm256\_add\_pd}(x[3], y[3])$
$v_0 :=\_\text{mm256\_sub\_pd}(s_0, x[0])$
$v_1 :=\_\text{mm256\_sub\_pd}(s_1, x[1])$
$v_2 :=\_\text{mm256\_sub\_pd}(s_2, x[2])$
$v_3 :=\_\text{mm256\_sub\_pd}(s_3, x[3])$
$u_0 :=\_\text{mm256\_sub\_pd}(s_0, v_0)$
$u_1 :=\_\text{mm256\_sub\_pd}(s_1, v_1)$
$u_2 :=\_\text{mm256\_sub\_pd}(s_2, v_2)$
$u_3 :=\_\text{mm256\_sub\_pd}(s_3, v_3)$
$w_0 :=\_\text{mm256\_sub\_pd}(x[0], u_0)$
$w_1 :=\_\text{mm256\_sub\_pd}(x[1], u_1)$
$w_2 :=\_\text{mm256\_sub\_pd}(x[2], u_2)$
$w_3 :=\_\text{mm256\_sub\_pd}(x[3], u_3)$
$u_0 :=\_\text{mm256\_sub\_pd}(y[0], v_0)$
$u_1 :=\_\text{mm256\_sub\_pd}(y[1], v_1)$
$u_2 :=\_\text{mm256\_sub\_pd}(y[2], v_2)$
$u_3 :=\_\text{mm256\_sub\_pd}(y[3], v_3)$
$t_0 :=\_\text{mm256\_add\_pd}(w_0, u_0)$
$t_1 :=\_\text{mm256\_add\_pd}(w_1, u_1)$
$t_2 :=\_\text{mm256\_add\_pd}(w_2, u_2)$
$(s_1, t_0) := \text{AVX2TwoSum}(s_1, t_0)$
$(s_2, t_0, t_1) := \text{AVX2ThreeSum}(s_2, t_0, t_1)$
$(s_3, t_0) := \text{AVX2ThreeSum2}(s_3, t_0, t_2)$
$t_0 :=\_\text{mm256\_add\_pd}(\_\text{mm256\_add\_pd}(t_0, t_1), t_3)$
$(r[0], r[1], r[2], r[3]) := \text{AVX2Renorm}(s_0, s_1, s_2, s_3, t_0)$
return $(r[0], r[1], r[2], r[3])$

Algorithm 9. $r[4] := \text{AVX2QDmul}(x[4], y[4])$

$s_0 := \texttt{\_mm256\_add\_pd}(x[0], y[0])$

$(p_0, q_0) := \text{AVX2TwoProd}(x[0], y[0])$

$(p_1, q_1) := \text{AVX2TwoProd}(x[0], y[1])$

$(p_2, q_2) := \text{AVX2TwoProd}(x[1], y[0])$

$(p_3, q_3) := \text{AVX2TwoProd}(x[0], y[2])$

$(p_4, q_4) := \text{AVX2TwoProd}(x[1], y[1])$

$(p_5, q_5) := \text{AVX2TwoProd}(x[2], y[0])$

$(p_1, p_2, q_0) := \text{AVX2ThreeSum}(p_1, p_2, q_0)$

$(p_2, q_1, q_2) := \text{AVX2ThreeSum}(p_2, q_1, q_2)$

$(p_3, p_4, p_5) := \text{AVX2ThreeSum}(p_3, p_4, p_5)$

$(s_0, t_0) := \text{AVX2TwoSum}(p_2, p_3)$

$(s_1, t_1) := \text{AVX2TwoSum}(q_1, p_4)$

$s_2 := \texttt{\_mm256\_add\_pd}(q_2, p_5)$

$(s_1, t_0) := \text{AVX2TwoSum}(s_1, t_0)$

$s_2 := \texttt{\_mm256\_add\_pd}(s_2, \texttt{\_mm256\_add\_pd}(t_0, t_1))$

$s_1 := \texttt{\_mm256\_add\_pd}(s_1, \texttt{\_mm256\_mul\_pd}(x[0], y[3]))$

$s_1 := \texttt{\_mm256\_add\_pd}(s_1, \texttt{\_mm256\_mul\_pd}(x[1], y[2]))$

$s_1 := \texttt{\_mm256\_add\_pd}(s_1, \texttt{\_mm256\_mul\_pd}(x[2], y[1]))$

$s_1 := \texttt{\_mm256\_add\_pd}(s_1, \texttt{\_mm256\_mul\_pd}(x[3], y[0]))$

$s_1 := \texttt{\_mm256\_add\_pd}(s_1, q_0)$

$s_1 := \texttt{\_mm256\_add\_pd}(s_1, q_3)$

$s_1 := \texttt{\_mm256\_add\_pd}(s_1, q_4)$

$s_1 := \texttt{\_mm256\_add\_pd}(s_1, q_5)$

$(r[0], r[1], r[2], r[3]) := \text{AVX2Renorm}(p_0, p_1, s_0, s_1, s_2)$

return $(r[0], r[1], r[2], r[3])$

Excluding AVX2Renorm, all parts of AVX2QDadd and AVX2QDmul were sufficient for full implementation with AVX2; hence, a maximum increase of speed can be achieved with AVX2 rather than DD and TD. Additionally, they are completely faster than MPFR 212-bits matrix multiplication. Therefore, the results obtained from the SIMDized QD arithmetic verify that the over-quad-double MPF arithmetic with AVX2 is potentially more efficient than the MPFR arithmetic.

2.5   DD, TD, and QD MFLOPS with Element-Wise Addition and Multiplication of Vectors

The vector data structure that we implemented for multi-component MPF matrix multiplication is presented in this section. Although it is standard to use each MPF variable as one element of the array that expresses vector and matrix, we implemented one set of several arrays with each component of the vector or matrix element, as it is necessary for us to derive the maximum performance using the _m256d data-type of AVX2. Owing to these methods of expressing the MPF vector, highly performed continuous load and store instructions, such as _mm256_load_pd and _mm256_store_pd functions, can be utilized to read and store elements of a vector or matrix by four elements at once.

Therefore, our MPF vector and matrix data structure have two binary64, three binary64, and four binary64 arrays as DD, TD, and QD linear computations, respectively. By adopting these data structures, the TD linear computation case, as shown in Fig. 1, two sets of three calls of load functions can settle down two operands of AVX2TD[add, mul] (`bncavx2_rtd_[add, mul]`). Our adopted vector or matrix data structure for AVX2 can reduce the process time required to read and write, because it eliminates the need to read each binary64 number.

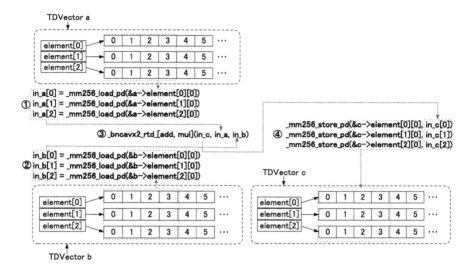

Fig. 1. TD vector data type that can be treated with load/store instructions

In the remainder of this paper, we adopted two types of computational environments to evaluate the implemented codes.

Corei9. Intel Core i9-10900X (3.6 GHz, 10 cores), 16 GB RAM Ubuntu 18.04.2, GCC 7.3.0

EPYC. AMD EPYC 7402P (1.5 GHz, 24 cores), 64 GB RAM, Ubuntu 18.04.5, GCC 7.5.0

AVX2 instruction has also a set of _m256 data-type that holds eight binary32 numbers. For confirmation, we also implemented binary32-based multi-component SIMDized MPF arithmetic and ran benchmark tests on both Corei9 and EPYC environments, but their performance did not improve over those of binary64-based SIMDized MPF arithmetic.

We demonstrated DD mega floating-point operations per second (MFLOPS), TD MFLOPS, and QD MFLOPS on a Corei9 environment to compare with three types of element-wise addition and multiplication of vectors in Fig. 2, Fig. 3, and Fig. 4. In these FLOPS tests, we adopted two n-dimensional real vectors

$\mathbf{a} = [a_1\ a_2\ ...\ a_n]^T$ and $\mathbf{b} = [b_1\ b_2\ ...\ b_n]^T$ as random numbers. Thereafter, we evaluated the number of additions or multiplications per second by computing each element, such as $a_i + b_i$ or $a_i \cdot b_i$. "AVX2 L/S" depicts MFLOPS with SIMDized calculation and AVX2 Load/Store instructions, "AVX2 Set" SIMDized calculation and AVX2 Set function (_mm256_set_pd) and normal substitution to arrays, and complete "Normal" standard calculation without using any AVX2 instructions. The DD, TD, and QD MFLOPS values are presented on the vertical axis, and n is the length of the vectors in the horizontal axis.

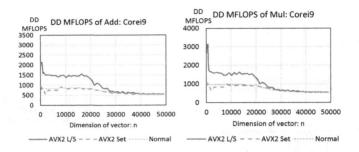

Fig. 2. DD MFLOPS of DD element-wise addition and multiplication of vectors

Figure 2 illustrates three types of DD MFLOPS. DD arithmetic requires less computation than TD or QD; therefore, the utilization of AVX2 load/store instructions is largely effective for the cache memory of a CPU. In fact, when all elements of the vectors are stored in cache memory, the DD MFLOPS is 1.5 times larger than the other two types of DD computations. For vector sizes beyond cache memory, both DD addition and multiplication for all types of calculations have the same performance.

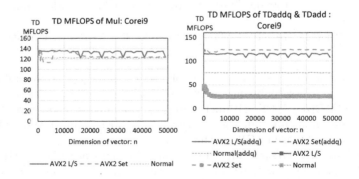

Fig. 3. TD MFLOPS of TD element-wise addition and multiplication of vectors

Figure 3 presents the TD MFLOPS for different processes. As can be observed in the MFLOPS of the original triple-double addition (TDadd and AVX2TDadd) presented in the left figure, they realized approximately 26 TD MFLOPS owing to the poor performance of the merge function in Algorithm 6; hence, SIMDization is ineffective for them. In contrast, TDaddq performed well at 75 TD MFLOPS, and AVX2TDaddq with load/store instructions also achieved approximately 115 TD MFLOPS, with AVX2 set at 123 TD MFLOPS. The TD addition to the Corei9 environment is an exceptional case in which the AVX2 load/store performance is less than that of the AVX2 set. Otherwise, TDmul cannot achieve sufficient efficiency with AVX2, as more than approximately 20 TD MFLOPS is achieved. Through these performance tests, we can infer that cache memory is not effective for TD arithmetic.

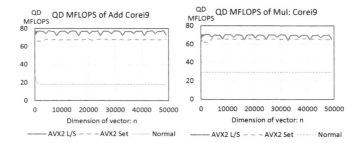

Fig. 4. QD MFLOPS of QD element-wise addition and multiplication of vectors

Figure 4 illustrates QD MFLOPS on the Corei9 environment. Similar to TD arithmetic, cache memory is never effective for QD arithmetic, and AVX2 can provide maximum performance for both QD addition and multiplication. AVX2QDadd is four times faster than normal QDadd, whereas AVX2QDmul is two times faster than normal QDmul. We can expect better performance for longer multi-component MPF arithmetic with AVX2.

As demonstrated above, MPF MFLOPS and SIMDized arithmetic with AVX2 load/store instructions can achieve the best performance for almost all cases. These results are similar to those of EPYC. Therefore, we can expect high-performance matrix multiplication with AVX2 for DD, TD, and QD arithmetic.

3 Benchmark Tests of DD, TD, and QD Matrix Multiplication

To evaluate the performance of the multi-component MPF matrix multiplication, we consider a dense real matrix multiplication to obtain $C := AB \in \mathbb{R}^{n \times n}$, where $A = [a_{ij}] \in \mathbb{R}^{n \times n}$, $B = [b_{ij}] \in \mathbb{R}^{n \times n}$ and c_{ij}, and the elements of C are obtained as

$$c_{ij} := \sum_{k=1}^{n} a_{ik} b_{kj}, \tag{1}$$

To draw the power of cache memories in the majority of current CPUs, "block" algorithms are adopted in dense matrix multiplications, which normally divide A and B into small block matrices with fewer rows and columns than the block size $n_{\min}$. We fixed $n_{\min} = 32$ for the benchmark tests in this study.

The "Strassen" algorithm is a divide-and-conquer method [5]. For even dimensional matrices A and B, four divided matrices are prepared and $C := AB$ is obtained, as shown in Fig. 5. We have already implemented BLAS level 1 MPF functions such as array substitution, vector addition, and scalar multiplication, as well as BLAS level 2 MPF functions such as matrix-vector multiplication, which are necessary for the Strassen algorithm.

Among all types of matrix multiplication, we adopted the row-major method to access the elements of matrices and parallelized them using OpenMP [7].

We fixed matrices A and B as follows:

$$A = \left[\sqrt{5}\,(i + j - 1) \right]_{i,j=1}^{n}, \quad B = \left[\sqrt{3}\,(n - i) \right]_{i,j=1}^{n}.$$

Because all elements were positive, there was no significant loss of significant digits in matrix multiplication. We determined one or two decimal digits of loss for all types of matrix multiplication.

All the codes for matrix multiplication were written in C or C++ languages, and the major programs adopted for the benchmark, including Rgemm of MPBLAS, were compiled with the following options:

```
g++ -O3 -std=c++11 -mavx2 -mfma -fopenmp
```

MPBLAS 0.8.0, which was downloaded in June 2019 from Github, was installed and used in our C++ benchmark programs.

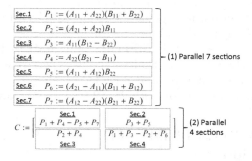

Fig. 5. Strassen matrix multiplication and its parallelization

3.1 Computational Time of Serial Matrix Multiplication and Comparison with Rgemm (MPBLAS)

First, we present the results obtained by serial matrix multiplication on both the Corei9 and EPYC environments in Table 1. In the tables, the "B" fields, "B + A," "S" fields, and "S + A" represent the computational time (s) of block matrix multiplication, block matrix multiplication with AVX2, Strassen matrix multiplication, and Strassen matrix multiplication with AVX2, respectively. The computational time ("M" fields) provided by the Rgemm of MPBLAS are presented in the rightmost columns of the tables. The underlined values in the tables below indicate the minimal computational time for the number of dimensions n in the environment.

We have previously reported that serial Strassen matrix multiplication and parallelized versions for large n are more efficient than the Rgemm of MPBLAS [7]. Our accelerated versions of block and Strassen matrix multiplication with AVX2 can be achieved more than twice as fast as the MPBLAS for any size of matrices. Although TD arithmetic is currently not supported by MPBLAS, we can confirm that the computational time of TD matrix multiplication is located between DD and QD arithmetic for any size and any type of algorithm.

3.2 Speedup Ratio of Parallelization and Computational Time

Next, we present the results of the parallelization using OpenMP. As a typical case of the speedup ratio of parallelization, we presented Fig. 6 on Corei9. As shown in this figure, we can infer that stable speedup has been achieved for block matrix multiplication by approximately 10 threads and that the speedup ratio of the Strassen matrix multiplication was limited by approximately six times using more than eight threads. This limitation occurs owing to Strassen's parallelization method, which produces new threads in recursive calls. We assume that the scheduling of many threads in calls is not executed smoothly.

In contrast to the Corei9 environment, although the EPYC environment always suspends the parallelization performance with over 16 threads for DD, TD, and QD matrix multiplications (the left figure of Fig. 7), AVX2 can eliminate the limitation of parallelization, as demonstrated on the right side of Fig. 7. The DD and QD matrix multiplication on the EPYC can be described as TD.

The limitation of the speedup ratio of the parallelized Strassen matrix multiplication is demonstrated to be similar to that in the Corei9 environment, and AVX2 cannot eliminate the failure of parallelization. We infer that to improve the performance of parallelized block matrix multiplication for over eight threads on CPUs with many cores, it is necessary to completely rewrite the Strassen routine.

Table 1. Serial computational time of matrix multiplication (unit: s): Corei9 (left) and EPYC (right)

DD : Corei9						DD : EPYC				
n	B	B+A	S	S+A	M	n	B	B+A	S	S+A	M
1023	7.84	2.46	4.35	<u>1.57</u>	5.98	1023	9.27	2.37	5.00	<u>1.43</u>	7.55
1024	7.86	2.46	4.34	<u>1.55</u>	6.00	1024	9.31	2.37	4.98	<u>1.41</u>	7.54
1025	8.61	2.68	4.40	<u>1.59</u>	6.01	1025	10.16	2.57	5.03	<u>1.44</u>	7.59
4095	507.8	162.7	212.3	<u>74.47</u>	390.7	4095	595.3	163.6	243.6	<u>68.04</u>	482.8
4096	509.1	161.8	212.5	<u>74.07</u>	390.7	4096	609.1	163.6	243.6	<u>67.75</u>	484.0
4097	518.0	161.7	213.3	<u>74.94</u>	391.0	4097	611.4	152.6	244.7	<u>71.03</u>	483.8
TD : Corei9						TD : EPYC				
1023	50.06	20.54	26.75	<u>12.64</u>	N/A	1023	61.12	21.19	32.18	<u>12.97</u>	N/A
1024	50.10	20.54	26.96	<u>12.48</u>	N/A	1024	61.15	21.16	31.98	<u>12.78</u>	N/A
1025	54.28	22.56	26.95	<u>12.61</u>	N/A	1025	66.46	23.17	32.20	<u>12.89</u>	N/A
4095	3202	1316	1276	<u>619.5</u>	N/A	4095	3918	1379	1555	<u>632.3</u>	N/A
4096	3205	1317	1276	<u>618.6</u>	N/A	4096	3934	1378	1554	<u>631.5</u>	N/A
4097	3272	1345	1287	<u>620.5</u>	N/A	4097	4002	1387	1561	<u>634.2</u>	N/A
QD : Corei9						QD : EPYC				
1023	102.8	31.41	54.90	<u>19.55</u>	73.76	1023	127.8	42.82	71.23	<u>25.17</u>	83.95
1024	102.9	31.40	54.71	<u>19.41</u>	76.04	1024	127.8	42.78	71.10	<u>25.07</u>	84.18
1025	111.8	34.41	55.23	<u>19.63</u>	74.12	1025	139.6	46.88	71.55	<u>25.32</u>	84.47
4095	6491	2013	2720	<u>970.5</u>	4729	4095	8177	2753	3440	<u>1245</u>	5384
4096	6493	2013	2721	<u>968.6</u>	4730	4096	8188	2754	3438	<u>1243</u>	5390
4097	6624	2059	2725	<u>972.6</u>	4727	4097	8371	2808	3449	<u>1247</u>	5394

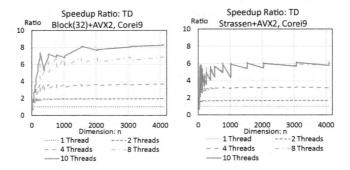

Fig. 6. Speedup ratio of parallelized TD block matrix multiplication on Corei9

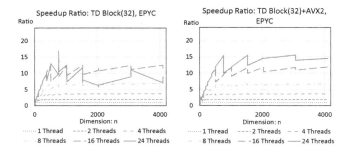

Fig. 7. Speedup ratio of parallelized TD block matrix multiplication on EPYC

Table 2. Seconds of parallelized matrix multiplication: 10 threads on Corei9 (left) and 24 threads on EPYC (right)

DD : Corei9 10 Threads				DD : EPYC 24 Threads				
n	B	B+A	S	S+A	n	B	B+A	S	S+A
1023	1.15	0.35	0.86	0.39	1023	0.78	0.20	0.80	0.59
1024	1.15	0.35	0.69	0.33	1024	0.73	0.20	0.77	0.54
1025	1.23	0.37	0.79	0.38	1025	0.79	0.22	0.84	0.57
4095	61.51	19.68	33.28	16.63	4095	160.68	10.74	35.67	25.43
4096	61.97	19.67	32.60	16.19	4096	191.24	10.72	35.24	24.90
4097	62.65	19.42	34.20	16.44	4097	169.09	10.28	36.26	25.23
TD : Corei9 10 Threads				TD : EPYC 24 Threads				
1023	7.65	3.03	4.57	2.91	1023	4.88	1.81	5.16	2.80
1024	7.67	3.02	4.11	2.07	1024	6.18	1.81	4.68	2.30
1025	8.12	3.22	4.30	2.13	1025	9.01	1.95	4.85	2.36
4095	409.94	159.68	202.34	107.08	4095	549.21	95.02	229.31	117.44
4096	410.48	159.66	196.19	100.55	4096	437.79	94.76	223.25	109.44
4097	416.29	162.04	198.99	101.92	4097	570.95	95.98	225.54	110.36
QD : Corei9 10 Threads				QD : EPYC 24 Threads				
1023	15.23	4.65	9.12	3.43	1023	26.95	3.35	8.91	4.07
1024	15.22	4.64	8.73	3.13	1024	28.98	3.37	8.40	3.50
1025	16.18	4.95	8.88	3.20	1025	27.35	3.60	8.53	3.56
4095	824.23	247.43	437.68	158.57	4095	863.46	171.27	415.35	179.00
4096	822.68	247.48	431.15	153.63	4096	865.12	171.13	407.80	170.27
4097	834.92	251.47	434.29	155.50	4097	882.51	172.95	410.26	171.72

Table 2 presents all computational time (s) with the same number of threads similar to those of the cores on Corei9 (10 cores) and EPYC (24 cores).

As shown in Table 2, block matrix multiplication tends to be increasingly faster than the Strassen on a CPU with many cores, owing to the limitations posed by parallelization of Strassen matrix multiplication. In fact, Strassen matrix multiplication is the fastest on Corei9, and more cases of shorter block matrix multiplication are observed on EPYC. We expect parallelized block matrix multiplication with DD, TD, and QD precision to be the fastest on a CPU with over 32 cores.

4   Conclusion and Future Work

Based on the accelerated DD, TD, and QD MPF matrix multiplication implementations in AVX2, we can confirm that block matrix and Strassen matrix multiplication show much higher speedup than the previous implementations. Furthermore, we can confirm that the speedup ratio is not limited by paralleling it with OpenMP, and it is stabilized in the EPYC environment.

Although the current implementation of parallelized Strassen matrix multiplication has exhibited a limitation of acceleration in CPUs with more than eight cores, BLAS level 1 and 2 MPF functions have been implemented owing to their required implementations in Strassen matrix multiplication. We will apply and develop linear and nonlinear algorithms with our accelerated MPF linear computation library in our future work.

References

1. Bailey, D.: QD. https://www.davidhbailey.com/dhbsoftware/
2. Intel Corp.: The intel intrinsics guide. https://software.intel.com/sites/landing page/IntrinsicsGuide/
3. Dekker, T.J.: A floating-point technique for extending the available precision. Numerische Mathematik **18**(3), 224–242 (1971) https://doi.org/10.1007/BF01397083
4. Fabiano, N., Muller, J.M., Picot, J.: Algorithms for triple words arithmetic. IEEE Trans. Comput. **68**, 1573–1583 (2019)
5. Golub, G.H., Loan, C.: Matrix Computations (4th ed.). Johns Hopkins University Press (2013)
6. Hishinuma, T., Fujii, A., Tanaka, T., Hasegawa, H.: AVX acceleration of DD. Arithmetic between a sparse matrix and vector. Parallel Process. Appl. Math., 622–631 (2014)
7. Kouya, T.: Performance evaluation of multiple precision matrix multiplications using parallelized Strassen and Winograd algorithms. JSIAM Lett. **8**, 21–24 (2015). https://doi.org/10.14495/jsiaml.8.21
8. Fousse, L., Hanrot, G., Lefèvre, V., Pélissier, P., Zimmermann, P.: MPFR: a multiple-precision binary floating-point library with correct rounding. ACM Trans. Math. Softw. **33**(2), 13 (2007). http://doi.acm.org/10.1145/1236463.1236468
9. MPLAPACK/MPBLAS: Multiple precision arithmetic LAPACK and BLAS. http://mplapack.sourceforge.net/
10. OpenBLAS. http://www.openblas.net/

11. ATLAS. http://math-atlas.sourceforge.net/
12. Granlaud, T., GMP development team: the GNU multiple precision arithmetic library. https://gmplib.org/
13. Kotakemori, T., Fujii, S., Hasegawa, H., Nishida, A.: Lis: Library of iterative solvers for linear systems. https://www.ssisc.org/lis/
14. Yagi, H., Ishiwata, E., Hasegawa, H.: Acceleration of interactive multiple precision arithmetic toolbox MuPAT using FMA, SIMD, and OpenMP. Adv. Parallel Comput. **36**, 431–440 (2020)

Object-Oriented Implementation of Algebraic Multi-grid Solver for Lattice QCD on SIMD Architectures and GPU Clusters

Issaku Kanamori[1]([✉]), Ken-Ichi Ishikawa[2], and Hideo Matsufuru[3]

[1] RIKEN Center for Computational Science (R-CCS), 7-1-26,
Minatojima Minamimachi, Kobe 650-0047, Japan
`kanamori-i@riken.jp`
[2] Core of Research for the Energetic Universe,
Graduate School of Advanced Science and Engineering, Hiroshima University,
1-3-1 Kagamiyama, Higashi-Hiroshima 739-8526, Japan
`ishikawa@theo.phys.sci.hiroshima-u.ac.jp`
[3] High Energy Accelerator Research Organization (KEK),
1-1 Oho, Tsukuba 305-0801, Japan
`hideo.matsufuru@kek.jp`

Abstract. A portable implementation of elaborated algorithm is important to use variety of architectures in HPC applications. In this work we implement and benchmark an algebraic multi-grid solver for Lattice QCD on three different architectures, Intel Xeon Phi, Fujitsu A64FX, and NVIDIA Tesla V100, in keeping high performance and portability of the code based on the object-oriented paradigm. Some parts of code are specific to an architecture employing appropriate data layout and tuned matrix-vector multiplication kernels, while the implementation of abstract solver algorithm is common to all architectures. Although the performance of the solver depends on tuning of the architecture-dependent part, we observe reasonable scaling behavior and better performance than the mixed precision BiCGSstab solvers.

Keywords: Multi-grid solver · Lattice QCD · Fugaku · SIMD · OpenACC

1 Introduction

Lattice QCD simulations have been one of the most challenging subjects in high performance computing in science. As increasing the precision of experimental data in elementary particle and nuclear physics, theoretical calculation is required to provide correspondingly precise predictions. Lattice QCD simulations are not only the first principle calculation of the strong interaction but also providing nonperturbative procedure to examine the candidates of new physics.

© Springer Nature Switzerland AG 2021
O. Gervasi et al. (Eds.): ICCSA 2021, LNCS 12953, pp. 218–233, 2021.
https://doi.org/10.1007/978-3-030-86976-2_15

A typical bottleneck in numerical simulations of lattice QCD is the linear equation for the Dirac fermion operator that is a large sparse matrix. As the simulated system becomes closer to the real system the linear equation becomes more difficult to solve because of larger lattice size and smaller quark mass parameter that increases the condition number. Therefore variety of improved algorithms have been developed for solving this linear equation. At the same time, numerous efforts have been devoted to exploit the new architecture of computers.

Multi-grid algorithms are widely used in solving large linear system. This type of algorithms applies coarsening of the lattice to define a matrix of smaller rank which reflects the long range effect of the original matrix while is easier to solve. The solution on the coarse lattice is used as a preconditioner of the original linear equation solver. A simple geometric coarsening, however, does not accelerate linear equation solvers in lattice QCD. It has been demonstrated that algebraic coarsening with adaptive setup is needed [1–5].

A direct trigger of this work is a need of porting the multi-grid algorithm to the supercomputer Fugaku [6] that has been installed at RIKEN Center for Computational Science (R-CCS) and provided for shared use recently. To make use of its potential arithmetic performance, one needs to implement a code that exploit the specific structure of the architecture. The A64FX architecture of Fugaku adopts the SIMD arithmetic operation in units of 512-bit length. While the same SIMD width is also adopted in the Intel AVX-512 instruction set architecture, their micro architectures are different, especially, in the instructions across the SIMD lanes needed for complex number arithmetics. Indeed different data layouts achieve better efficiency for the AVX-512 and A64FX architectures, as shown later.

Another important target of this work is GPU clusters, or systems with accelerator devices in general, which have been increasingly adopted as recent large-scale supercomputers. Such systems require heterogeneous parallelization code for the host processors and many-core devices. To implement the device kernel, several frameworks are available such as OpenACC, CUDA, and OpenCL. We adopt OpenACC in this work.

Under this situation, it is desirable to establish a code design that keeps machine specific implementation minimum while allows construction of algorithms in generic manner. The goal of this paper is to develop such a framework to implement the multi-grid algorithm applicable to various architectures exemplified for A64FX, Intel AVX-512, and an NVIDIA GPU cluster. To realize these contradicting issues, we adopt the object-oriented program design and specify the interface that the architecture specific code must provide. As a framework for implementation, we adopt a general purpose lattice QCD code set Bridge++ with extension to add a code that is tuned for specific architecture. We discuss how much the algorithm and optimization of code for specific architecture can be separated.

This paper is organized as follows. In the next section, we briefly introduce the linear equation in lattice QCD that is the target problem of this work. Section 3 summarizes the multi-grid algorithm implemented in this work. Section 4 describes our code implementation. Section 5 shows performance results measured on the following systems: Oakforest-PACS of JCAHPC (Intel Xeon Phi

KNL cluster), Fugaku, and the Cygnus system at Univ. of Tsukuba (NVIDIA V100 cluster). The last section is devoted to conclusion and outlook.

2 Linear Equation in Lattice QCD Simulations

In this section, we introduce the linear equation problem in lattice QCD simulations to least extent for understanding the following sections. For the formulation of lattice QCD and the principle of numerical simulation, there are many textbooks and reviews (e.g. [7]).

The lattice QCD is a field theory formulated on a four-dimensional Euclidean lattice. It consists of fermion (quark) fields and a gauge (gluon) field. The latter mediates interaction among quarks and are represented by 'link variable', $U_\mu(x) \in SU(3)$, where $x = (x_1, x_2, x_3, x_4)$ stands for a lattice site and $\mu = 1, 2, 3, 4$ is the spacetime direction. In numerical simulations the lattice size is finite: $x_\mu = 1, 2, \cdots, L_\mu$. The fermion field is represented as a complex vector on lattice sites, which carries 3 components of 'color' and 4 components of 'spinor', thus in total 12, degrees of freedom on each site. The dynamics of fermion is governed by a functional $S_F = \sum_{x,y} \psi^\dagger(y) D[U]^{-1}(x, y)\psi(y)$, where $D[U]$ is a fermion matrix acting on a fermion vector $\psi(x)$. A Monte Carlo algorithm is applied to generate an ensemble of the gauge field $\{U_\mu(x)\}$, that requires to solve a linear equation $x = D^{-1}\psi$ many times.

There is a variety of the fermion matrix $D[U]$ depending on the way to discretize the continuum theory. As a common feature, the matrix is sparse because of the locality of the interaction among quarks and gluons. In this paper, we examine the $O(a)$-improved Wilson fermion, also called clover fermion matrix,

$$D_{x,y} = [1 + F(x)]\delta_{x,y} - \kappa \sum_{\mu=1}^{4} \left[(1 - \gamma_\mu)U_\mu(x)\delta_{x+\hat{\mu},y} + (1 + \gamma_\mu)U_\mu^\dagger(x - \hat{\mu})\delta_{x-\hat{\mu},y} \right],$$
(1)

where x, y are lattice sites, $\hat{\mu}$ the unit vector along μ-th axis, and the hopping parameter $\kappa = 1/(8 + 2m_0)$ related to the quark mass m_0. $F(x)$ is a 12×12 Hermitian matrix made of link variables, which is introduced to reduce the finite lattice spacing artifact. As mentioned above, the link variable $U_\mu(x)$ is a 3×3 complex matrix acting on the color and γ_μ is a 4×4 matrix acting on the spinor degrees of freedom. Thus D is a complex matrix of the rank $4 \cdot 3 L_x L_y L_z L_t$. It is standard to impose the periodic or anti-periodic boundary conditions.

As a general feature, as decreasing the quark mass m_0, the linear equation becomes more and more difficult to solve since the condition number of the matrix increases. Another general feature common to fermion matrices is so-called γ_5-Hermiticity, which is a remnant of the Hermiticity of fermion operator in the continuum theory:

$$D^\dagger = \gamma_5 D \gamma_5, \quad \gamma_5 = -\gamma_1 \gamma_2 \gamma_3 \gamma_4.$$
(2)

The byte-per-flop of the clover fermion is 0.94 for single precision arithmetics.

3   Multi-grid Algorithm

This section describes the multi-grid algorithm applied in this paper. We first settle the convention to represent vectors. Adopting the style in the quantum mechanics, we denote a vector as $|x\rangle$ and its Hermitian conjugate $\langle x|$. They are vectors in the original fine lattice, and the vectors on coarse lattice is represented with suffix 'c', such as $|x\rangle_c$. For simplicity we describe a single level multi-grid algorithm, while a multi-level implementation is straightforward. The linear equation to be solved is

$$D|x\rangle = |b\rangle. \tag{3}$$

In the following, we first describe the general feature of the multi-grid algorithm and then technical details specific to the lattice QCD problem.

Solver Algorithm with Preconditioner. The multi-grid algorithm works as a preconditioner of iterative Krylov subspace solvers. While there is a variety of choice for this outer solver, in this work we employ the BiCGStab algorithm with flexible preconditioner summarized as follows [9].

BiCGStab algorithm with flexible preconditioning

$|x\rangle := |x_0\rangle, \ |r\rangle := |b\rangle - D|x_0\rangle, \ |\tilde{r}\rangle := |r\rangle, \ |p\rangle = |r\rangle$
M is the preconditioner and $|x_0\rangle$ is the given initial guess.
for $i = 0, \ldots, n$ do
$\quad \alpha_i = \langle\tilde{r}|r_i\rangle/\langle\tilde{r}|DM|p_i\rangle$
$\quad |x_i\rangle := |x_i\rangle + \alpha_i M|p_i\rangle, \quad |s_i\rangle := |r_i\rangle - \alpha_i DM|p_i\rangle$
$\quad$if($\big||s_i\rangle\big|^2$ is small enough) break
$\quad |t_i\rangle := DM|s_i\rangle, \quad \omega_i := \langle t_i|s_i\rangle/\langle t_i|t_i\rangle$
$\quad |x_{i+1}\rangle := |x_i\rangle + \omega_i M|r_i\rangle, \quad |r_{i+1}\rangle := |s_i\rangle - \omega_i DM|s_i\rangle$
$\quad$if($\big||r_{i+1}\rangle\big|^2$ is small enough) break
$\quad \beta_i = (\alpha_i/\omega_i)\langle\tilde{r}|r_{i+1}\rangle/\langle\tilde{r}|r_i\rangle, \quad |p_{i+1}\rangle := |r_{i+1}\rangle - \beta_i(|p_i\rangle - \omega_i D|p_i\rangle)$
end

If the preconditioner M provides an approximate solution, $Mx \sim D^{-1}x$, the algorithm works efficiently. As an example of such a preconditioner, multi-precision solver is known to work efficiently, in particular on a system whose performance is regulated by its memory bandwidth. The version of algorithm we use has two break points as described above.

Multi-grid Algorithm. Figure 1 schematically explains the idea of the multi-grid algorithm. In some way we define the vectors on a coarser lattice, $|b\rangle \rightarrow |b\rangle_c$. This process is called 'restriction'. Defining the matrix D_c multiplied to this coarse vector correspondingly, one solves the linear equation

$$D_c|x\rangle_c = |b\rangle_c. \tag{4}$$

From this solution on the coarsened lattice, one can construct an approximate solution on the original fine lattice: $|x\rangle_c \rightarrow |x\rangle$ (called 'prolongation'). This is

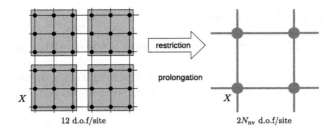

Fig. 1. Schematic description of the multi-grid algorithm. A domain X on the fine lattice is mapped to a site X on the coarse lattice.

a basic strategy of the multi-grid preconditioning. In addition, some operation called 'smoothing' is applied so as to improve the overlap of the approximate solution with the solution on the fine lattice, which contains the high frequency modes being not incorporated in the coarse solver. The smoother can be applied either before or after the coarse solver, or even both before and after.

Equation (4) is easier to solve than the original linear equation due to its smaller rank, and to be solved not necessarily with high accuracy. In lattice QCD simulation, as quark mass decreases, the Dirac matrix D becomes dominated by the low frequency modes that is well approximated by the coarse solution vector.

Construction of Coarse Grid Operator. To construct a coarse vector, we prepare N_{nv} so-called null space vectors that contain contribution from the low modes; $|i\rangle$, $i = 1, \ldots, N_{nv}$. Since the quality of $|i\rangle$ governs the efficiency of the multi-grid preconditioner, we describe a way to generate them later in this section. Having prepared $|i\rangle$, we divide the original lattice into N_D domains each composed of typically 4^4 sites. Each domain, labeled with a capital letter as X, is mapped to one site on the coarse lattice. Let us express the i-th null space vector whose nonzero components are restricted to a domain X as $|X, i\rangle$. At this stage we have totally $N_{nv}N_D$ independent vectors. We further double the number of vectors effectively by applying projections in the 4-component 'spin' space into two subspaces labeled by $s = +, -$[1]. The total number of independent vectors is thus $2N_{nv}N_D$ which is labeled by $I = \{s, i, X\}$. Since these projections into domain X and spin subspaces is local and almost trivial in the implementation, we need to keep only N_{nv} vectors $|i\rangle$.

Let us assume that vectors $2N_{nv}N_D$ vectors $\{|I\rangle\}$ are orthonormalized: $\langle I|J\rangle = \delta_{IJ}$. Denoting the component of a coarse vector $|x\rangle_c$ as $x(I)$,

$$x(I) = \langle I|x\rangle. \tag{5}$$

This operation reduces the degrees of freedom from $12L_x L_y L_z L_t$ to $2N_{nv}N_D$.

---

[1] We apply projection matrices $P_\pm = (1 \pm \gamma_5)/2$ in the spin space, where γ_5 is a 4×4 matrix defined in Eq. (2) and satisfies $(\gamma_5)^2 = 1$. Noting that the matrix D satisfies γ_5-Hermiticity $(\gamma_5 D)^\dagger = (\gamma_5 D)$ and that γ_5 approximately maps an eigenmode of $\gamma_5 D$ with eigenvalue λ to a one with $-\lambda$, one can show that use of the projected spin basis is equivalent to a low rank approximation of the Hermitian matrix $(\gamma_5 D)$.

Prolongation is performed by

$$|x'\rangle = \sum_I x(I)|I\rangle. \tag{6}$$

Note that $|x\rangle$ and $|x'\rangle$ are in general different. The coarse Dirac fermion matrix $D_c(I, J)$ is represented as

$$D_c = \langle I|D|J\rangle. \tag{7}$$

Numerical Steps. To summarize with a little more details, the multi-grid preconditioner is composed of the following steps.

(0) Building of null space vectors (setup stage)

(0-a) Initial setup: We start with N_{nv} independent random vectors. In general, multiplying an approximate D^{-1} amplifies low frequency modes. For this purpose, several iterations of arbitrary iterative solver algorithm may suffice. Instead of simply using D on fine lattice, we employ the Schwartz alternating procedure explained below. After the vectors are orthonormalized to $\langle I|J\rangle = \delta_{IJ}$, the coarse Dirac matrix D_c is determined accordingly to Eq. (7).

(0-b) Adaptive improvement: Once the initial null space vectors and coarse matrix are prepared, we use the multi-grid preconditioner itself (steps (1)–(2) bellow) as an approximate D^{-1} to further amplify the low frequency modes in the null space vectors. The coarse matrix is simultaneously updated accordingly. This improvement process may be repeated several times.

Provided the null space vectors and coarse matrix, we employ the following multi-grid preconditioner. Each step is a Richardson refinement, $|x\rangle + M_i(|b\rangle - D|x\rangle) \mapsto |x\rangle$ with $M_i \simeq D^{-1}$ $(i = 1, 2)$.

(1) Refinement on the coarse grid: The approximate solver M_1 is made of the following three steps.

(1a) Restriction: For a given source vector for the preconditioner, Eq. (5) is applied to make a vector on coarse lattice.

(1b) Coarse matrix solver: The linear equation on coarse lattice (4) is solved with a standard way. We employ the BiCGStab algorithm with an additional stabilization [8] in this work. This is not necessarily performed with high precision.

(1c) Prolongation: The solution vector of Eq. (4) is prolonged to make a fine vector with Eq. (6). The prolonged vector is used in the refinement of approximate solution on the original lattice.

(2) Smoother: We insert a smoother after the coarse grid refinement. As M_2 in the Richardson process, Schwartz Alternating Procedure (SAP) with fixed iterations is used in this work for which details are described below.

Note that once the null space vectors are obtained in the step (0a) and (0b), they are repeatedly used for different right hand side vectors $|b\rangle$.

Schwartz Alternating Procedure (SAP). Schwartz alternating procedure helps to reduce the communication in solving large linear system. It was introduced in [10,11] as a domain-decomposed preconditioner to the lattice QCD, and then used as an efficient smoother in the multi-grid algorithm [5].

One first divides the lattice into subdomains each containing *e.g.* 4^4 sites which should be practically determined by observing the numerical efficiency. One defines the Dirac matrix D_{SAP} by turning off the interaction across the domains. This implies that if each domain lies within a node, inter-node communication does not exist in D_{SAP}. We set the SAP domain to be the same as the domain of coarsening in the multi-grid algorithm. Splitting the domains into even and odd groups, $D_{\mathrm{SAP}}^{(e)}$ and $D_{\mathrm{SAP}}^{(o)}$, practical Schwartz alternating procedure is defined as follows.

Schwartz Alternating Procedure (SAP) with fixed iterations

$|x\rangle := 0, \quad |r\rangle := |b\rangle$
for $i = 1, \ldots, n$ do
$\quad |x\rangle := |x\rangle + M_{\mathrm{SAP}}^{(e)}|r\rangle$
$\quad |r\rangle := |b\rangle - D|x\rangle$
$\quad |x\rangle := |x\rangle + M_{\mathrm{SAP}}^{(o)}|r\rangle$
$\quad |r\rangle := |b\rangle - D|x\rangle$
end

In this algorithm $M_{\mathrm{SAP}}^{(e/o)}$ is an inner-domain solver, $M_{\mathrm{SAP}}^{(e/o)} \simeq (D_{\mathrm{SAP}}^{(e/o)})^{-1}$. For this approximate solver, we adopt the MINRES algorithm with fixed number of iterations, 6. While the number of SAP iterations n is one of the tuning parameters in the multi-grid algorithm, we set it to 4 in this work.

Related Works. Applications of the Multi-grid algorithms to lattice QCD have been developed in last 15 years [1–3]. Not only for the Wilson-type fermion matrix applied in this work, it is applied to the domain-wall fermion [4]. The SAP is introduced to the multi-grid algorithm in Ref. [5]. Their implementation was ported to K-computer [12]. As for the optimization for recent architecture, application to the Xeon Phi series is investigated [13]. Among widely used lattice QCD code sets, Grid [14,15] contains a branch with multi-grid solvers. QUDA [16,17], which is a lattice QCD library on GPUs, also contains multi-grid solvers. The data layout for Fugaku in the current work is a generalization of a solver library (not multi-grid) for Fugaku [18].

4   Implementation

4.1   Multi-grid Algorithm

To apply the multi-grid algorithm to variety of computer architecture, it is desirable to separate the algorithm and code implementation on specific architecture as much as possible. A guideline to accomplish it is the so-called object-oriented

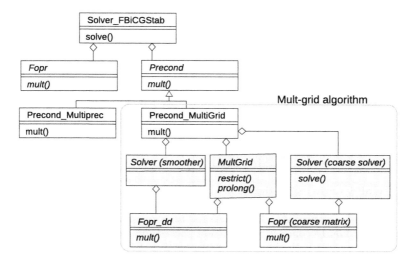

Fig. 2. Class diagram for the multi-grid algorithm. The objects of classes in blue color are implemented in single precision arithmetics. (Color figure online)

programming. As a code framework, we employ a general purpose lattice QCD code set Bridge++ [19, 20] which is written in C++ based on the object-oriented design. Bridge++ has been used to investigate a recipe of tuning on Intel AVX-512 architectures [21, 22].

Figure 2 displays a simplified class diagram of our implementation. All the classes are implemented as C++ template class for which a template parameter AField is omitted in the Figure. AField itself is a template class that holds field data with specific precision and architecture such as AField<float, SIMD>, where the second template parameter is an **enum** entry. The objects in the blue colored classes are constructed with single precision arithmetics. We show only the abstract classes except for the top level solver (BiCGStab algorithm with flexible preconditioning) and two subclasses of the preconditioner, Precond. One may choose a multi-precision solver as a preconditioner instead of the multi-grid algorithm.

Most of the ingredients of multi-grid algorithm is implemented independently of the fermion matrix and architecture. For a specific fermion matrix, e.g. the clover fermion in this work, one needs to implement subclasses of Fopr and Fopr_dd, where the latter represents a domain-decomposed version of the former. One can apply optimization for the specific architecture to this implementation. While the smoother is represented as an abstract Solver class and can be any solver, we use SAP solver in this work. In a subclass of MultiGrid class, functions for restriction and prolongation are implemented for the specific fermion matrix. A blocked version of linear algebra is used in these operations. Such blocked linear algebraic functions may effect the performance significantly and thus are implemented as a functional template code for each architecture.

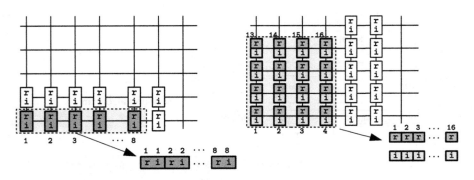

Fig. 3. The SIMD layouts for the AVX-512 (left panel) and A64FX (right) architectures. In the figure, r and i represent real and imaginary part of a complex number on each lattice site, respectively. On the AVX-512, 8 complex numbers are packed to a SIMD variable while 16 complex numbers are packed to 2 SIMD variables (one for the real part and the other is the imaginary part) on the A64FX.

In the case of the clover fermion, we therefore need to implement three objects in addition to the standard fermion matrix: the domain-decomposed version of the fermion matrix (AFopr_Clover_dd class), the matrix on the coarse lattice (AFopr_Clover_coarse class), and a set of blocked version of linear algebraic functions such as dotc and axpy. The last ingredients are provided as C++ template functions. These parts are possible to optimize independently from the construction of the algorithm. In the following, we summarize the features of our target architectures and procedures of tuning.

4.2   Implementation for Intel AVX-512 Architecture

We start with the implementation of our multi-grid code for the Intel AVX-512 architecture. Intel AVX-512 is the latest SIMD extension of x86 instruction set architecture. The 512-bit SIMD length corresponds to 8 double or 16 single precision floating point numbers. In the following we consider the single precision case with which the preconditioner is implemented. We pack 8 complex numbers that are consecutive in the x-direction[2] as displayed in the left panel of Fig. 3. This implies that the size of the domain in x-direction is a multiple of 8 and it is indeed fixed to 8 in this work. For the coarse operator, we instead pack the internal degree of freedom to the SIMD variables to avoid a strong constraint on the local coarse lattice size. Since each coarse grid vector has $2N_{\mathrm{nv}}$ complex components, N_{nv} is constrained to be a multiple of 4.

The implementation of the fine grid operators inherits the previous works [21,22] and uses the L2 prefetch in the full operator D. Although it has been tuned for D, the same prefetching pattern is used in the SAP operator.

---

[2] This corresponds to the case (a) in [21,22].

4.3 Implementation for A64FX Architecture

After the success of K computer, RIKEN decided to develop the post-K computer as a massively parallel computer with the Arm instruction set architecture with scalable vector extension (SVE). The development has successfully resulted in the Fugaku supercomputer manufactured by Fujitsu that has been installed at RIKEN R-CCS and provided for shared use since March 2021. In addition to Fugaku, there are several systems with the same architecture. The A64FX architecture adopted in Fugaku has 512-bit SIMD length that amounts to 16 single precision floating point numbers. The SIMD instructions are directly specified in a C/C++ code through ACLE (Arm C Language Extension).

The linear equation solver for the Dirac matrix in lattice QCD simulation has been one of the target applications in the development of the Post-K project that has lead to the Fugaku supercomputer. As a product of so-called co-design study, an optimized code named QWS (QCD Wide SIMD) library has been developed [18]. Through this investigation, it has been found that better performance is achieved by treating the real and imaginary parts in different SIMD vectors. Simplest implementation is achieved by packing 16 sites in x-direction into one SIMD vector for FP32, as adopted in the QWS library. For the implementation of the multi-grid algorithm, however, this implies that the domain size would be multiple of 16 at least in x-direction. This is rather strong restriction for examining the efficiency of the algorithm. Thus we decided to develop another code that packs the sites in x-y plane as depicted in the right panel of Fig. 3. This enables for example to pack 4×4 sites into a single SIMD vector for FP32 and increases the flexibility in choosing the parameters.

We develop a library of fermion matrices with the above 2D SIMD packing and with the same convention and data layout as QWS. Tuning of this library is still underway by employing ACLE by making use of the techniques established in the development of QWS.

4.4 Implementation for GPU Clusters

In implementation of a code for GPU, the first question is which offloading scheme is to be adopted. Two types of approaches are available: API-based libraries (CUDA, OpenCL, etc.) and directive-based ones (OpenACC and OpenMP). The former enables detailed manipulation of threads as well as the use of local store shared by a set of device cores. The latter is easy to start and suitable for incremental development. After preparatory study by comparing OpenCL and OpenACC, Bridge++ adopted to develop the offloading code mainly using OpenACC because of its simplicity and less effort in maintaining the code.

For the fermion matrix on original lattice, we assign the operations on each site to one device thread. The data layout is changed so that the so-called coalesced memory access is realized on the devices. For the matrix-vector multiplication on coarse lattice, computation of the vector component corresponding to one null space vector on each coarse site is assigned to one thread. In the case of GPU clusters, severe bottleneck is data transfer between the host processors and devices. Thus we implement a code that minimizes such data transfer and if necessary replace the general code with optimized code by exploiting the specialization of template in C++.

5   Performance Result

We measure the performance of the multi-grid algorithm on the following three lattice sizes of gauge configurations labeled as A–C[3].

- A: $32^3 \times 64$ lattice provided by PACS-CS collaboration [23].
- B: $64^3 \times 64$ lattice provided by Yamazaki *et al.* [24].
- C: $96^3 \times 96$ lattice provided by PACS collaboration [25].

These configurations are available through the Japan Lattice Data Grid [26,27].

The block size for the multi-grid setup is fixed to 8×4^3. The number of test vectors is set to 32 except for some benchmarks of matrix multiplications. Since these numbers should be tuned for each configurations, the throughput we investigate in this work may not be optimal. In addition to the solver, the performance of the matrix-vector multiplications is examined in the weak scaling setting, of which smaller local volume on Oakforest-PACS and Fugaku corresponds to running set A on 16 nodes.

For comparison, we also measure the elapsed time to solve the same system with a mixed precision BiCGStab solver. It uses the same flexible BiCGStab algorithm and the preconditioner is a single precision stabilized BiCGStab [8], the same algorithm used to solve the coarse system in the multi-grid solver.

5.1   Performance on Intel Xeon Phi Cluster

We use the Oakforest-PACS system of JCAHPC. The compiler is Intel compiler 2019.5 and the option used is `-O3 -no-prec-div -axMIC-AVX512`. We use cache mode of the MCDRAM and set the number of the thread to 2 per core.

In the left panel of Fig. 4, the weak scaling of the matrix-vector multiplication is plotted in two cases of local volume. For the smaller local volume case, the domain-decomposed operator is faster than the full operator as expected from the absence of communications. The tuning described in [22] for full operator works quite efficiently for a larger local volume so that its performance exceeds that of the domain-decomposed operator. Note that a naive roof line limit of the full operator is about 450 GFlops. The coarse operator is slower than the others. This is because the local volume is smaller than the fine lattice so that the cost of the neighboring communication becomes relatively larger, in addition to the lack of detailed tuning such as prefetching.

---

[3] Although the condition numbers are not provided, B has a significantly smaller value than the others. The lighter pion mass implies the larger condition number, which amounts 156, 512, and 145 MeV for the configuration A, B, and C, respectively.

Table 1. Elapsed time for the multi-grid solver. The 'solve' is for solving excluding the setup time. The ratios tabulated are time for solving the coarse solver, running the smoother, restriction and prolongation (R/P), and the other in the multi-grid preconditioner. For comparison, timing of mixed precision BiCGStab is also tabulated as 'MBiCGs'. The block size is fixed to $8 \times 4 \times 4 \times 4$. 'OFP' denotes Oakforest-PACS.

Sys.	Conf. label	# of nodes	N_{nv}	Elapsed time [s]		Fraction in the solve				MBiCGs [s]
				Setup	Solve	Coarse	Smoother	R/P	Prec. other	
OFP	A	16	16	5.6	35	29%	53%	5.2%	7.6%	54
	A	16	32	16	23	62%	26%	4.5%	4.0%	
	B	16	32	161	28	27%	50%	13%	5.9%	41
	B	32	32	65	13	28%	50%	11%	6.1%	22
	C	16	32	813	763	44%	35%	11%	4.8%	2801
	C	96	32	113	175	53%	29%	6.5%	5.5%	499
	C	192	32	60	80	51%	28%	5.6%	5.9%	297
Fugaku	A	16	32	107	31	33%	40%	19%	3.2%	121
	B	16	32	893	51	17%	48%	23%	6.6%	97
	C	96	32	688	213	34%	42%	18%	3.1%	1125
	C	216	32	314	111	41%	34%	18%	2.8%	512
Cygnus	A	1	32	500	198	50%	26%	20%	2.7%	–
	A	16	32	78	79	37%	13%	47%	1.7%	–
	B	16	32	263	21	23%	40%	27%	4.8%	–

The elapsed time and time budget are listed in Table 1. Once the null space vectors are prepared ('setup'), the multi-grid algorithm is faster than the mixed-precision solver. However, the overhead of setup becomes not negligible as the condition number decreases, as exhibited for configuration B. The fraction of the coarse solver and smoother depends on the configuration and the number of nodes, while the remaining part of the preconditioner including the restriction/prolongation is kept small. The performance of the multi-grid solver is 120–190 GFlops per node, which depends on the size of local volume and the fraction of the coarse grid solver.

5.2   Performance on Fugaku

On Fugaku, we use the Fujitsu compiler with the Clang mode. The version of the compiler is 1.2.31 and the option is `-Nclang -fopenmp -Ofast`. When we measured the performance, May 2021, jobs with a small number of nodes (<385) are not guaranteed to have physically close allocation in the 6-dimensional mesh-torus network. In this setting, frequent neighboring communication of the matrix multiplication kernel of QCD may interfere with communication of other jobs. We therefore secure a large enough number of nodes for which continuous torus geometry is guaranteed and then use a subset of them by specifying a rank map.

The performance of each matrix-vector multiplication is plotted in the right panel of Fig. 4. There is plenty of room for improvement, since the node of Fugaku has roughly the same peak performance as Oakforest-PACS and larger memory bandwidth. Note the difference of the scale between panels in the figure.

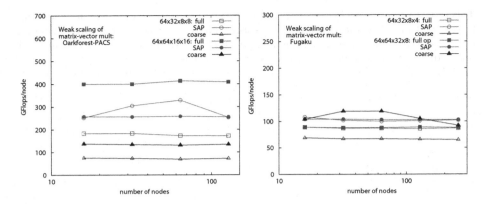

Fig. 4. Weak scaling of matrix-vector multiplication on Oakforest-PACS (left panel) and Fugaku (right panel) with two different local lattice volumes, 5.2×10^5 and 4.2×10^6 lattice points per node. The matrices are full matrix D, domain decomposed operator D_{SAP} used in SAP in the smoother, and the coarse operator used in the coarse solver. The block size is $8 \times 4 \times 4 \times 4$ and number of null space vector N_{nv} is 32.

The SAP operator is fastest than the full operator as expected. Although the code is still in the middle of tuning, the coarse operator with larger local volume sometimes outperforms the SAP operator. All kernels show a good weak scaling.

The elapsed time and time budget are listed in Table 1. Compared with Oakforest-PACS, restriction and prolongation take larger fractions. This is because we have applied ACLE tuning to only a part of matrix vector multiplication, and the linear algebraic functions have still not been tuned. The solving time is shorter than the mixed precision BiCGStab solver in all cases. Taking the setup time into account, the latter is faster for configurations A and B. Note that once the setup is finished, one can solve the linear equation with different right hand sides repeatedly, which is a typical situation in lattice QCD simulation. In such a case, the multi-grid solver may become an efficient solution. The total performance of the solver is 83–96 GFlops per node, which is in between the performance of coarse matrix and D_{SAP}.

5.3   Performance on GPU Cluster

As an example of GPU cluster, we use the Cygnus system at University of Tsukuba. Each node of Cygnus is composed of two Intel Xeon processors (Xeon Gold 6126, 12 cores/2.6 GHz) and four NVIDIA Tesla V100 GPUs. Although 32 nodes of Cygnus have FPGA devices connected with dedicated network, we do not use this type of nodes. Each V100 GPU has 5120 CUDA cores which amounts to 14 TFlops for FP32 arithmetics. The memory bandwidth of the GPU global memory is 900 GB/s. The bus interface is PCIe 3.0 with 16 lanes. The nodes are connected by Infiniband HDR100 x4 network. We use the NVIDIA HPC SDK 20.9 compiler with CUDA 11.0 and the MPI library MVAPICH2-GDR 2.3.5.

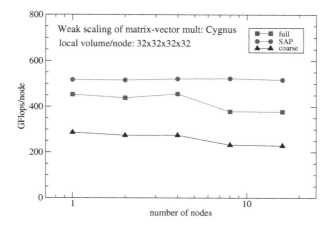

Fig. 5. Weak scaling plot of the performance of matrix-vector multiplications on Cygnus. The local volume per node is set to 32^4.

The code is compiled with options `-O2 -ta=tesla:ptxinfo,cc70`. We found that `-fast` option rather decreases the performance of the device kernel. Since most arithmetically heavy operations are performed on GPUs, multi-threading on the host processor contributes the performance little, and thus we switched it off in this measurement.

Figure 5 displays the weak scaling plot of the performance of matrix-vector multiplications for D (full), D_{SAP}, and coarse matrix D_c in single precision. To keep large enough local volume even after the coarsening, we measure the performance with lattice size per node 32^4. This lattice is divided to four GPU devices on each node. We observe that the performances of D and coarse matrix decrease about 15% between 4 and 8 nodes while that of D_{SAP} stays unchanged, as the effect of changing the MPI parallelization in (x, y) to (x, y, z) directions. Considering the device memory bandwidth above and the byte-per-flop of the matrix D, 0.94, further optimization may be possible. For this purpose, CUDA or OpenCL would be required to employ for more detailed tuning.

The elapsed time and time budget are listed in Table 1. The configuration C is not available due to insufficient memory size of the maximum number of nodes (16) in our budget. On Cygnus, we do not measure the mixed-precision solver due to the lack of time for preparation. General tendency of the time budget in the multi-grid algorithm is similar to the SIMD architectures. The fractions of restriction and prolongation, however, tend to be larger due to the data transfer between the hosts and devices required for these steps in the current implementation. The result implies that the current implementation is also efficient for the architecture with GPU accelerators.

6   Conclusion

In this paper, we implemented a multi-grid solver for lattice QCD on two SIMD architectures and GPU clusters. On all the architectures, the multi-grid solver accomplished sufficient acceleration of elapsed time in solving linear equation under typical parameter setup. Although setup of the null space vector requires non-negligible time, once they are prepared, solving the linear equation for each source vector is significantly accelerated. In the measurement of physical quantities in lattice QCD simulations, one frequently encounters the situation to repeat such processes, for which the multi-grid algorithm would be a powerful solution.

By separating the architecture-specific code from the construction of algorithm, it has become possible to tune for each architecture independently. While present implementation is not very optimized, one can concentrate on each architecture for individual requirement. In this paper, we focus on one type of fermion matrix. Application to other type of matrix, such as the domain-wall fermion, is underway. Application to other recent architectures, such as the NEC SX-Aurora TSUBASA with vector architecture, is also planned.

Acknowledgment. The authors would like to thank the members of lattice QCD working group in FS2020 project for post-K computer and the members of Bridge++ project for valuable discussion. Numerical simulations were performed on Oakforest-PACS and Cygnus systems through Multidisciplinary Cooperative Research Program in CCS, University of Tsukuba, and supercomputer Fugaku at RIKEN Center for computational Science. Some part of code development were performed on the supercomputer 'Flow' at Information Technology Center, Nagoya University, and Yukawa Institute Computer Facility. We thank the Japan Lattice Data Grid team for providing the public lattice QCD gauge ensemble through the grid file system. This work is supported by JSPS KAKENHI (Grant Numbers 20K03961 (I. K.), 19K03837 (H. M.)), the MEXT as "Program for Promoting Researches on the Supercomputer Fugaku" (Simulation for basic science: from fundamental laws of particles to creation of nuclei) and Joint Institute for Computational Fundamental Science (JICFuS).

References

1. Brannick, J., Brower, R.C., Clark, M.A., Osborn, J.C., Rebbi, C.: Adaptive multigrid algorithm for lattice QCD. Phys. Rev. Lett. **100**, 041601 (2008). https://doi.org/10.1103/PhysRevLett.100.041601
2. Babich, R., et al.: Adaptive multigrid algorithm for the lattice Wilson-Dirac operator. Phys. Rev. Lett. **105**, 201602 (2010). https://doi.org/10.1103/PhysRevLett.105.201602
3. Osborn, J. C., et al.: Multigrid solver for clover fermions. In: PoS LATTICE2010, p. 037 (2010). https://doi.org/10.22323/1.105.0037
4. Cohen, S.D., Brower, R.C., Clark, M.A., Osborn, J.C.: Multigrid algorithms for domain-wall fermions. In: PoS LATTICE2011, p. 030 (2011). https://doi.org/10.22323/1.139.0030
5. Frommer, A., Kahl, K., Krieg, S., Leder, B., Rottmann, M.: Adaptive aggregation based domain decomposition multigrid for the lattice Wilson Dirac operator. SIAM J. Sci. Comput. **36**, A1581–A1608 (2014). https://doi.org/10.1137/130919507
6. Sato, M., et al.: Co-design for A64FX manycore processor and "Fugaku". In: Proceedings of the International Conference for High Performance Computing, Networking, Storage and Analysis (SC 2020), Article 47, pp. 1–15. IEEE Press (2020)

7. Lattice Quantum Chromodynamics. Springer, Dordrecht (2017). https://doi.org/10.1007/978-94-024-0999-4
8. Sleijpen, G.L.G., van der Vorst, H.A.: Maintaining convergence properties of BiCGstab methods in finite precision arithmetic. Numer. Algorithm **10**, 203–223 (1995). https://doi.org/10.1007/BF02140769
9. Vogel, J.A.: Flexible BiCG and flexible Bi-CGSTAB for nonsymmetric linear systems. Appl. Math. Comput. **188**, 226–233 (2007). https://doi.org/10.1016/j.amc.2006.09.116
10. Luscher, M.: Lattice QCD and the Schwarz alternating procedure. JHEP **05**, 052 (2003). https://doi.org/10.1088/1126-6708/2003/05/052
11. Luscher, M.: Solution of the Dirac equation in lattice QCD using a domain decomposition method. Comput. Phys. Commun. **156**, 209–220 (2004). https://doi.org/10.1016/S0010-4655(03)00486-7
12. Ishikawa, K. I., Kanamori, I.: Porting DDalphaAMG solver to K computer. In: PoS LATTICE2018, p. 310 (2018). https://doi.org/10.22323/1.334.0310
13. Georg, P., Richtmann, D., Wettig, T.: DD-αAMG on QPACE 3. EPJ Web of Conferences, vol. 175, p. 02007 (2018). https://doi.org/10.1051/epjconf/201817502007
14. Grid: https://github.com/paboyle/Grid
15. Boyle, P.A., Cossu, G., Yamaguchi, A., Portelli, A.: Grid: a next generation data parallel C++ QCD library. PoS LATTICE 2015 (023) (2016). https://doi.org/10.22323/1.251.0023
16. QUDA: https://github.com/lattice/quda
17. Clack, M.A., Babich, R., Barros, K., Brower, R., Rebbi, C.: Solving lattice QCD systems of equations using mixed precision solvers on GPUs. Comput. Phys. Commun. **181**, 1517 (2010). https://doi.org/10.1016/j.cpc.2010.05.002
18. QCD Wide SIMD library. https://github.com/RIKEN-LQCD/qws
19. Lattice QCD code set Bridge++. https://bridge.kek.jp/Lattice-code/
20. Ueda, S., et al.: Development of an object oriented lattice QCD code 'Bridge++'. J. Phys. Conf. Ser. **523**, 012046 (2014). https://doi.org/10.1088/1742-6596/523/1/012046
21. Kanamori, I., Matsufuru, H.: Practical implementation of lattice QCD simulation on intel Xeon Phi knights landing. In: Proceedings of the Fifth International Symposium on Computing and Networking (CANDAR 2017), 19–22 November 2017, Aomori, Japan (2017). https://doi.org/10.1109/CANDAR.2017.66
22. Kanamori, I., Matsufuru, H.: Practical implementation of lattice QCD simulation on SIMD machines with Intel AVX-512. In: Gervasi, O., et al. (eds.) ICCSA 2018. LNCS, vol. 10962, pp. 456–471. Springer, Cham (2018). https://doi.org/10.1007/978-3-319-95168-3_31
23. Aoki, S., et al.: [PACS-CS]: 2+1 flavor lattice QCD toward the physical point. Phys. Rev. D **79**, 034503 (2009). https://doi.org/10.1103/PhysRevD.79.034503
24. Yamazaki, T., Ishikawa, K.I., Kuramashi, Y., Ukawa, A.: Helium nuclei, deuteron and dineutron in 2+1 flavor lattice QCD. Phys. Rev. D **86**, 074514 (2012). https://doi.org/10.1103/PhysRevD.86.074514
25. Ishikawa, K. I. et al. [PACS]: 2+1 flavor QCD simulation on a 96^4 lattice. In: PoS LATTICE2015, p. 075 (2016). https://doi.org/10.22323/1.251.0075
26. Japan Lattice Data Grid. https://www.jldg.org/
27. Amagasa, T., et al.: Sharing lattice QCD data over a widely distributed file system. J. Phys. Conf. Ser. **664**, 042058 (2015). https://doi.org/10.1088/1742-6596/664/4/042058

Development of Open-Source-Based Software Planetary Atmospheric Spectrum Calculator (PASCAL) Specified for Millimeter/Submillimeter Observation of Titan with ALMA

Takahiro Iino[(✉)] [ID]

Information Technology Center, The University of Tokyo, 2-11-16 Yayoi, Bunkyo-ku, Tokyo 113-8658, Japan
iino@nagoya-u.jp

Abstract. To illustrate planetary atmospheric environment, such as a three-dimensional structure of trace gases, combination of high precision millimeter and submillimeter-wave spectroscopic remote-sensing and an advanced information processing technology is crucial. By combining the open-source radiative transfer code Planetary Spectrum Generator (PSG) and the Python libraries SciPy and astropy, we have constructed the molecular profile derivation tool Planetary Atmospheric Spectrum CALculator (PASCAL), which focuses on analysis of data of Titan observed by the Atacama Large Millimeter/submillimeter Array (ALMA). PASCAL successfully retrieved the vertical profile of an isotopomer of a gaseous hydrogen cyanide ($H^{13}CN$) $J = 3$–2 rotational transition, where J is the rotational constant, from ALMA archival data. Further, it successfully determined that the northern high-latitude region has 27% higher column density than the south as seen in the intensity map. In addition, an installed parallelization method succeeded in decreasing the calculation time with its parallel speedup value $\sim$20 using 32 processors applying coordinate parallelization.

Keywords: ALMA · Planetary atmosphere · Radiative transfer · Parallel processing

1 Introduction

For the observational study of planetary atmospheres, high-dispersion spectroscopy gives us important information, such as the atmospheric structure, composition and dynamics. In particular, because the line-shape of the observed spectrum varies with respect to atmospheric pressure, complete fitting of a modeled spectrum to the observed spectrum reveals the vertical distribution of trace species. A numerical technique to derive the vertical structure of molecular abundance or temperature structure from the observed spectrum is called a retrieval method. The method consists of two different numerical techniques, a radiative

© Springer Nature Switzerland AG 2021
O. Gervasi et al. (Eds.): ICCSA 2021, LNCS 12953, pp. 234–244, 2021.
https://doi.org/10.1007/978-3-030-86976-2_16

transfer technique which produces modeled spectrum, and an optimizing method to derive the vertical physical properties convolved in the spectrum. Both techniques are very complicated because they include and consider many quantum physical processes, three-dimensional path of ray, and numerical difficulties. Each research group develops its own retrieval or at least the radiative transfer codes for their target, purpose and wavelength. For example, Non-Linear Optimal Estimator for Multivariate Spectral Analysis (NEMESIS) was developed to reduce the data observed by the *Cassini* spacecraft and is currently used mainly by NASA [6]. In addition, the Atmospheric Radiative Transfer Simulator (ARTS) is widely used in the remote sensing research [1] of both Earth and planetary atmospheres.

Recently, many astronomical observatories have made their observation data available as an archive to maximize its scientific output. To drive planetary atmospheric studies, reducing the burden of the retrieval methods is crucial for many researchers to analyze their own and archived observation data. Among such observation archive, we have focused on the archived data of the Atacama Large Millimeter-submillimeter Array (ALMA) for planetary atmospheric science. As we have reported already [4], ALMA has kept observed solar system objects as the standard absolute flux calibrator. Thus, ALMA stores a vast amount of planetary observation data. In particular, calibrated data of Titan, the largest moon of Saturn, have drawn attention. Since Titan has a thick atmosphere that contains many volatiles, understanding its atmospheric chemistry processes is one of the key science themes in our solar system planetary atmospheric science. For example, researchers have recently detected complicated molecular species, such as C_2H_5CN [3] and C_2H_3CN [8], isotopologues of nitriles (e.g. [2,5,11]), and time variation of minor species [13]. The comprehensive use of ALMA archival data is a key method for the further understanding of Titan's complicated atmospheric chemistry. For that purpose, we have developed a semi-automatic method for converting calibration data into scientific data and produced more than 2000 three-dimensional Flexible Image Transport System(FITS) datasets that store spectral data in each two-dimensional coordinate [4]. FITS is a standard data archive format widely used for astronomical data science developed in 1970s [9]. For the analysis of the data, development of a radiative transfer tool focusing on ALMA observation is needed. The recent improvement of open-source software has the potential to enhance astronomical research activity. The comprehensive use of such software reduces the burden of software development and enables us to evaluate the analyzed results using them. In this paper, we report the construction and evaluation results of our own retrieval code Planetary Atmospheric Spectrum CALculator (PASCAL) which utilizes open-source software for radiative transfer and optimization.

2   Scheme and Experiment

2.1   Overview

PASCAL mainly consists of the open-source radiative transfer code Planetary Spectrum Generator (PSG) [14], an astronomical Python code library astropy [10]

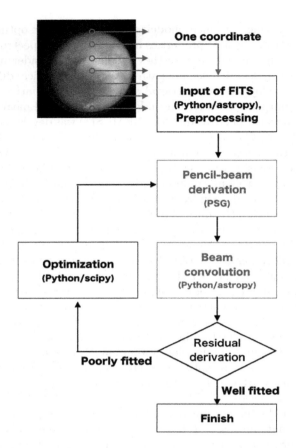

Fig. 1. A flow-chart of PASCAL to derive the vertical molecular abundance at one coordinate. Red symbols are parallelized processes (Color figure online).

and an optimizing method function included in SciPy. Figure 1 shows the flow chart of PASCAL to retrieve a molecular profile of one specific location on Titan. To reduce the calculation time, a parallelizing method is used for both radiative transfer and entire process. To obtain the spatial variation of the molecular profile, one needs to run the program to consider each coordinates.

PSG was developed by the NASA/Jet Propulsion Laboratory. PSG can consider a wide variety of planetary atmospheric observations, from in-situ satellite-based measurement to ground- and space-based observations. Frequency coverage is wide enough to consider wavelengths from UV to radio. Atmospheric structures of planets, major satellites, and minor bodies are implemented already.

PSG can be ran locally by installing it as the Docker container system. To run PSG, one has to prepare a config text file which describes the instrument setting and atmospheric structure such as pressure/altitude, temperature and composition. Besides, users can install packages developed for the specific use. In this study, a package which contains a molecular line database is installed. Once the PSG is installed, one can run the software via Application Program Interface (API) using curl command. After the calculation, PSG returns the result in the form of two column text that has channel and intensity field. An example of returned result is shown in Fig. 2. PSG can be run online by calling the address of NASA/JPL, which is easy to use but the calculation time is much longer than installed version.

For the beam convolution, the Python library, astropy, is used. Since the spatial resolution of ALMA is not infinite, observed area includes various optical paths. Thus, using PSG, PASCAL produces many spectra considering various emission angle as shown in Fig. 2, and convolves them into one spectrum by considering the shape of the beam. Because ALMA's beam typically has elliptical Gaussian shape, the contribution of each pencil beam has to be taken into account using astropy. The astropy is also used for FITS file handling.

To obtain the vertical distribution of the molecular gas, so called the retrieval analysis, we used SciPy package, a Python based package specified for the scientific research of mathematics, physics and engineering. SciPy consists of many libraries for scientific computing. Among them, we used a non-linear least-squares library for the retrieval analysis.[1] The library is a wrapper around MIN-PACK, a FORTRAN library for the least-squares method. Using the library, one can reproduce the vertical abundances of temperature and molecular abundance profiles by producing the molecular line spectrum and comparing it with the observed one.

The specifications of the computer used for the experiment are summarized in Table 1.

Table 1. Specifications of computer and storage used for test calculation

Item	Spec
CPU	Xeon Gold 6230 (20 cores, 40 threads, maximum frequency: 2.1 GHz) ×2
RAM	ECC Registered DDR4 2666 MHz 192 GB (16 GB × 12)
System disk	1.0 TB NVMe SSD
Data disk	214 TB RAID50 SAS
OS	Ubuntu Linux 16.04 LTS

---

[1] https://docs.scipy.org/doc/scipy/reference/generated/scipy.optimize.leastsq.html.

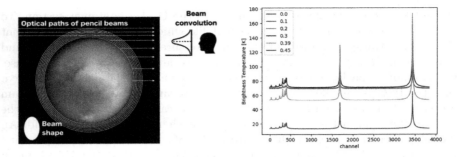

Fig. 2. Left: A model of pencil beam calculation. Pencil beams are convolved with respect to the coordinate of beam center and beam shape indicated in the bottom left. Right: Examples of pencil beam spectra calculated with respect to the distance from the disk center of Titan.

2.2 Radiative Transfer and Sample Data

PSG produces pencil beam with respect to the location on disk, frequency, temperature profile and molecular vertical abundances. A model and examples of pencil beam calculation is shown in Fig. 2. Along with the variation of optical path, the number of pencil beam produced in the code for nadir and limb viewing were 20 and 30, respectively, which correspond to ∼0.01 and ∼0.005 arcseconds spatial resolution, which is 10 times finer than the typical spatial resolution of ALMA, 0.2–0.4 arcseconds. For the test of Radiative transfer and retrieval, a strong rotational transition of the isotopologue of hydrogen cyanide ($H^{13}CN$) J = 3–2 was used. The right panel of Fig. 2 shows some examples of pencil beams for the range of distance from the apparent disk center expressed in arcseconds. The beams for 0.0 to 0.3 arcseconds are for nadir direction, 0.39 and 0.45 are for limb direction. The continuum is produced via Collision Induced Absorption processes, which has an extremely broad line-shape. Variation of the line-shape is due to the variation of optical path length with respect to the emission angles. Typically, line intensity gets increased when the path length gets longer because of increase of molecular column density.

The archived observation data of 2012.1.00453.S was used for the experiment. The observation date and an apparent diameter of Titan was July 7, 2014 and 0.78 arcseconds, respectively. An observed spectrum is shown in the left panel of Fig. 3 with a blue curve. A coordinate of the beam is the center of the disk. Lines seen in this spectrum are CH_3CN, $HC^{15}N$ and $H^{13}CN$ from left to right, respectively. The red curve over-plotted on observation is a retrieved spectrum. A red curve shown in the bottom of the panel is residual between model and observation. Vertical profile of both CH_3CN and $HC^{15}N$ were not retrieved, thus the large residual is seen under the two emission lines. A right panel of Fig. 3

is an integrated intensity map of the data shown in arbitrary unit. As clearly seen, $H^{13}CN$ emission is concentrated on the northern hemisphere due to the seasonal change. In this study, it is expected that the spatial variation of $H^{13}CN$ is obtained by the retrieval analysis. Three white cross marks are the coordinates used for the retrieval experiments described in next subsection.

The radiative transfer calculation was performed by PSG installed on a Windows 10 virtual machine set up with VMware workstation virtual machine software. The code transfers a dataset that describes atmospheric data, the molecular abundance profile, spectroscopic settings and so on to PSG. PSG returns the calculated spectrum as a standard text, which is saved to a RAM disk that has an extremely high disk I/O.

On Titan, atmospheric temperature profile is known to exhibit both spatial and time variation. Thus, the applied temperature profile is chosen from the previously obtained ones [12]. The modeled atmosphere is divided into 30 horizontal layers from the surface to the top of the atmosphere where the pressure level is 10^{-5} mbar.

2.3   Retrieval Analysis

The obtained residual between model and observation is transferred to SciPy for the retrieval. The vertical profile of the molecular abundance is controlled automatically to fit the modeled spectrum with the observed one. As an initial profile, a so-called "a priori", previously determined one is used. In this case, the profile obtained by [7] was applied. First, to coarsely determine the profile, the entire a priori profile is simply scaled to fit the spectrum. Then, the volume mixing ratio of some of the layers are modified for the fine profile determination. Values of the rest of the layers are interpolated. Fitting is performed to minimize the residual. The frequency range to measure the residual and the chi-square value is ±100 MHz for $H^{13}CN$. Typically, the number of retrieval iterations needed to converge was up to ~100 for each Titan's coordinate. A red curve in the left panel of Fig. 3 show the best-fit spectrum of disk center position. The fitting succeeded in decreasing the residual within the observed random noise level. A left panel of Fig. 4 shows a retrieved result of three coordinates. Northern hemisphere exhibits higher mixing ratio than other two coordinates other than at low altitude. The derived column densities of three coordinates converted to the main isotopologue are 4.2, 2.9 and 3.3×10^{17} molecules cm^{-2} for N, C and S coordinates, respectively.

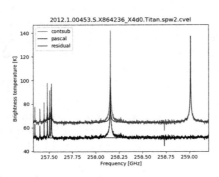
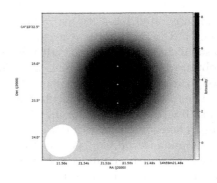

Fig. 3. Left: Observed (blue) and retrieved (red) model spectra of Titan. The residual is also plotted at the bottom of the panel. For the retrieval, the $H^{13}CN$ ($J = 3$–2) rotational transition locates at $259\,GHz$ which is present at right side of the panel was used. Emission lines at the left edge of the panel is $J = 14$–13 transitions of CH_3CN molecule. Right: An integrated intensity emission map of $H^{13}CN$. A white ellipse at bottom left and cross markers are the synthesized beam and Titan's coordinates used for the retrieval calculation. (Color figure online)

The right panel of Fig. 4 shows the variation of chi-square values with respect to each retrieval iteration. In this case, the first 15 iterations were for coarse scaling and remaining iterations were for fine retrieval, respectively. The derived vertical profiles of three coordinates are shown in Fig. 4.

2.4 Parallelization

Since the Titan's atmospheric trace gases are known to exhibit a time variation of its vertical profile, number of ALMA data should be used for retrieval to reveal the time variation of three-dimensional distribution of each gases. Without parallelization, each iteration takes $\sim30\,s$, thus, the total derivation time on the central meridian line with 8 points and 100 iterations is $24000\,s$. Thus, implementation of a parallelizing method to reduce the calculation time is crucial for its scientific application.

The entire code for one coordinate, including radiative transfer, was parallelized using the `multiprocessing` method of Python. Since the method does not use node-to-node communication, the number of used processes is limited to the maximum number of threads of the computer. In this study, the radiative transfer parallelization calculated pencil beams in parallel by running PSG simultaneously. In turn, coordinate parallelization ran the entire code in parallel to retrieve the vertical profile of different coordinates on Titan simultaneously. While the beam convolution process was parallelized also, it could not decrease

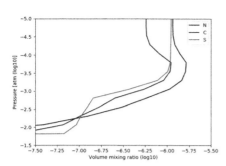
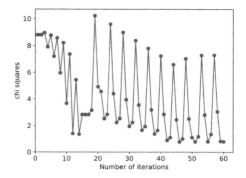

Fig. 4. Left: Retrieved vertical profile of $H^{13}CN$ at Titan's three different locations. N, C and S are for north, disk center and southern hemisphere, respectively. Right: Variation of chi-square values for the residual between modeled and observed spectra of Titan with respect to the number of iterations.

the calculation time. Effectiveness of the parallelization was estimated by calculating the parallel speedup $s(p)$, which can be obtained by the following equation:

$$s(p) = \frac{t(1)}{t(p)} \tag{1}$$

where $t(p)$ is time for one radiative transfer or vertical profile determination with p processors. Ideally, without any overhead time, the parallel speedup is equal to the number of processors. For the radiative transfer parallelization, note that the number of processors is limited to 16 because of the limitation of the virtual machine. In turn, for the coordinate parallelization, we measured the time needed for the entire process of vertical profile derivation. Figure 5 shows the parallel speedup of both parallelization tests. The tested numbers of processors were 1, 2, 4, 8 and 16 for radiative transfer and 1, 2, 4, 8, 16, 32 and 64 for coordinate parallelization. As the error bars, standard deviation of each iteration time or entire processing time is shown.

For the radiative transfer parallelization, $s(p)$ did not improve for p > 8. Because the number of pencil beams calculated in PASCAL is ∼30, improvement of parallel speedup for radiative transfer is still needed. Since each radiative transfer calculation does not need storage I/O and communication between processes, parallel speedup should be more efficient. In this study, we installed the PSG Docker container on the virtual machine. The indirect call of PSG may be the cause of the overhead of parallel speedup.

Coordinate parallelization exhibited a better speedup in the high-p region. Because the number of physical cores is 40, $s(p)$ does not improve above p = 40, although the number of threads is 80. For the coordinate parallelization, low speedup efficiency may be caused by the Hyper Threading function, or the storage I/O to read a large FITS file that has 1.5 GB in size. From a scientific point of view, calculations for the derivation of the latitudinal variation of a molecular profile should be performed only on central meridian line. Thus, the number of coordinates on Titan is no more than ~10, which is equivalent to 0.08 arcseconds spatial step, considering that the finest spatial resolution of ALMA at Band 6 or 7 as 0.1 arcseconds. Thus, the combination of both parallelization methods is useful considering the scientific purpose and benefit of parallelization.

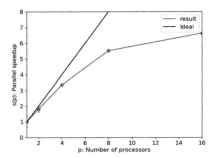 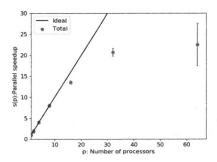

Fig. 5. Parallel speedup measured for the radiative transfer and vertical profile measured at multiple coordinates. Coordinate parallelization shows a higher speedup than the radiative transfer.

3   Summary and Future Prospects

In this study, we successfully retrieved the vertical structure of the isotopologue of hydrogen cyanide at different coordinates of Titan. The obtained result is consistent with the distribution of the integrated intensity, and it demonstrated that the PASCAL code is useful for the automated derivation of three-dimensional molecular abundances on Titan.

To use the results of PASCAL, solution of the following problems is needed:

- Application and testing for other molecules are insufficient. For example, for the HC_3N molecule, SciPy could not converge after many iterations to decrease the residual within the standard deviation of the spectrum.
- The error bar produced by SciPy retrieval is much smaller than that of retrieval results. For example, the error for $H^{13}CN$ derivation was as low as several percent for the entire altitude. However, previous submillimeter observations of HCN reported an error of ~50% at high altitude [13]. Evaluation and new implement of the errors are needed.

Acknowledgements. TI is grateful to Mitaro Namiki of Tokyo University of Agriculture and Technology for his advices on the entire study. Also, TI is also grateful to Hideo Sagawa for discussions about the improvement of retrieval program and usage of ALMA data. Authors are grateful to Geronimo Villanueva, a developer of PSG, for his kind support for the usage of PSG. This work was financially supported by a Telecommunications Advancement Foundation, JSPS Kakenhi grants (17K14420, 19K14782) and an

Astrobiology Center Program of National Institutes of Natural Sciences (NINS) grants. This paper makes use of the following ALMA data: ADS/JAO.ALMA#2012.1.00453.S. ALMA is a partnership of ESO (representing its member states), NSF (USA) and NINS (Japan), together with NRC (Canada), MOST and ASIAA (Taiwan), and KASI (Republic of Korea), in cooperation with the Republic of Chile. The Joint ALMA Observatory is operated by ESO, AUI/NRAO and NAOJ.

References

1. Buehler, S.A., Mendrok, J., Eriksson, P., Perrin, A., Larsson, R., Lemke, O.: ARTS, the atmospheric radiative transfer simulator - version 2.2, the planetary toolbox edition. Geosci. Model Dev. **11**(4), 1537–1556 (2018). https://doi.org/10.5194/gmd-11-1537-2018

2. Cordiner, M.A., et al.: Interferometric imaging of Titan's HC_3N, $H^{13}CCCN$, and $HCCC^{15}N$. Astrophys. J. **859**(1), L15 (2018). https://doi.org/10.3847/2041-8213/aac38d, http://stacks.iop.org/2041-8205/859/i=1/a=L15?key=crossref.3db3b0a1e328504fc7cc09382363bbb3

3. Cordiner, M.A., et al.: Ethyl Cyanide on Titan: spectroscopic detection and mapping using ALMA. Astrophys. J. **800**(1), L14 (2015). https://doi.org/10.1088/2041-8205/800/1/L14, http://stacks.iop.org/2041-8205/800/i=1/a=L14?key=crossref.d304cda239aa0a7fa1c22fbf25847529

4. Iino, T., Namiki, M., Yamada, T.: A feasibility study of exhaustive analysis of ALMA calibration data for the creation of big-data driven solar system astronomy. JAXA Res. Dev. Rep. J. Space Sci. Inform. Jpn. **7**(1), 19–32 (2018). https://doi.org/10.20637/JAXA-RR-17-009/0003

5. Iino, T., Sagawa, H., Tsukagoshi, T.: $^{14}N/^{15}N$ isotopic ratio in CH_3CN of Titan's atmosphere measured with ALMA. Astrophys. J. **890**(2), 95 (2020). https://doi.org/10.3847/1538-4357/ab66b0, https://iopscience.iop.org/article/10.3847/1538-4357/ab66b0

6. Irwin, P.G.J., et al.: The NEMESIS planetary atmosphere radiative transfer and retrieval tool. J. Quant. Spectrosc. Radiat. Transf. **109**(6), 1136–1150 (2008). https://doi.org/10.1016/j.jqsrt.2007.11.006

7. Marten, A., Hidayat, T., Biraud, Y., Moreno, R.: New millimeter heterodyne observations of Titan: vertical distributions of nitriles HCN, HC_3N, CH_3CN, and the isotopic ratio $^{15}N/^{14}N$ in its atmosphere. Icarus **158**(2), 532–544 (2002). https://doi.org/10.1006/icar.2002.6897, http://linkinghub.elsevier.com/retrieve/pii/S0019103502968971

8. Palmer, M.Y., et al.: ALMA detection and astrobiological potential of vinyl cyanide on Titan. Sci. Adv. **3**(7), 1–7 (2017). https://doi.org/10.1126/sciadv.1700022

9. Pence, W.D., Chiappetti, L., Page, C.G., Shaw, R.A., Stobie, E.: Definition of the Flexible Image Transport System (FITS), version 3.0. Astron. Astrophys. **524**(10), A42 (2010). https://doi.org/10.1051/0004-6361/201015362

10. Robitaille, T.P., et al.: Astropy: a community Python package for astronomy. Astron. Astrophys. **558**, A33 (2013). https://doi.org/10.1051/0004-6361/201322068

11. Serigano, J., et al.: Isotopic ratios of carbon and oxygen in Titan's co using ALMA. Astrophys. J. **821**(1), L8 (2016). https://doi.org/10.3847/2041-8205/821/1/L8, http://arxiv.org/abs/1602.07707, http://stacks.iop.org/2041-8205/821/i=1/a=L8?key=crossref.65db31dc4452e5223c4a0886fb6e5050

12. Thelen, A.E., et al.: Spatial variations in Titan's atmospheric temperature: ALMA and Cassini comparisons from 2012 to 2015. Icarus **307**, 380–390 (2018). https://doi.org/10.1016/j.icarus.2017.10.042

13. Thelen, A.E., et al.: Abundance measurements of Titan's stratospheric HCN, HC_3N, C_3H_4, and CH_3CN from ALMA observations. Icarus **319**(June 2018), 417–432 (2019). https://doi.org/10.1016/j.icarus.2018.09.023, https://linkinghub.elsevier.com/retrieve/pii/S0019103518304184

14. Villanueva, G.L., Smith, M.D., Protopapa, S., Faggi, S., Mandell, A.M.: Planetary spectrum generator: an accurate online radiative transfer suite for atmospheres, comets, small bodies and exoplanets. J. Quant. Spectrosc. Radiat. Transf. **217**, 86–104 (2018). https://doi.org/10.1016/j.jqsrt.2018.05.023

International Workshop
on Computational Optimization
and Applications (COA 2021)

Implementation of Robust Multi-objective Optimization in the Build Orientation Problem

Marina A. Matos[1], Ana Maria A. C. Rocha[1(✉)], Lino A. Costa[1], and Ana I. Pereira[2]

[1] ALGORITMI Center, University of Minho, 4710-057 Braga, Portugal
mmatos@algoritmi.uminho.pt, {arocha,lac}@dps.uminho.pt
[2] Research Centre in Digitalization and Intelligent Robotics (CeDRI), Instituto Politécnico de Bragança, 5300-253 Bragança, Portugal
apereira@ipb.pt

Abstract. Additive manufacturing (AM) is an emerging technology to create 3D objects layer-by-layer directly from a 3D CAD model. The build orientation is a critical issue in AM and its optimization will significantly reduce the building costs and improve object accuracy. This paper aims to optimize the build orientation problem of a 3D CAD model using a robust multi-objective approach, taking into account the staircase effect and the support area characteristics. Thus, the main objective is to obtain a robust Pareto optimal front, composed of solutions that are not quite sensitive to perturbations in the variables. In this manner, a set of robust solutions is presented as alternatives and the decision-maker can identify the compromise solutions and choose according to his/her preferences.

Keywords: Additive manufacturing · 3D Printing · Robust multi-objective optimization · Build orientation

1 Introduction

3D printing is an additive manufacturing (AM) technique used by several companies for manufacturing a wide range of 3D objects. A 3D object is built from 3D model data, by adding layer-by-layer of material, using a variety of materials, such as plastic, resin, rubber, ceramics, glass, concrete and metal [1]. Currently, AM processes are being used in different areas such as medical sciences (e.g. dental restorations and medical implants), jewellery, footwear industry, automotive industry, aircraft industry among others [2–4].

This work has been developed under the FIBR3D project - Hybrid processes based on additive manufacturing of composites with long or short fibers reinforced thermoplastic matrix (POCI-01-0145-FEDER-016414), supported by the Lisbon Regional Operational Programme 2020, under the PORTUGAL 2020 Partnership Agreement, through the European Regional Development Fund (ERDF). This work has been supported by FCT – Fundação para a Ciência e Tecnologia within the R&D Units Project Scope: UIDB/00319/2020.

© Springer Nature Switzerland AG 2021
O. Gervasi et al. (Eds.): ICCSA 2021, LNCS 12953, pp. 247–259, 2021.
https://doi.org/10.1007/978-3-030-86976-2_17

In the last years, AM has been used much more efficiently to improve part quality, process planning and post-processing, while reducing processing time and cost [4]. This technology also has the advantage of better resource efficiency, the parts produced have greater durability and it is possible to produce parts on a small scale sizes and complex geometry [3]. In addition, AM has the main advantage of being flexible and allowing the development of parts produced in different orientations. Furthermore, for a given build orientation it can generate less waste of material in the production of parts and requires less time and costs in its development [3]. The selection of the best build orientation is a critical issue because it affects several factors such as the number of generated supports, printing time, material cost, final part quality, shrinkage, distortion, support volume, and support area [4,5].

In the literature, a number of studies have been carried out in order to select the optimal build orientation for a 3D CAD model. Over the years, different approaches have been taken to determine the orientation of a 3D model based on single-objective optimization [6–9]. Matos et al. in [5] used a global optimization method, the Electromagnetism-like algorithm, to optimize six printing quality measures in order to find the optimal build orientations of six 3D CAD models. Moreover, different multi-objective approaches have been developed in order to determine a set of trade-off optimal build orientations, when optimizing more than one quality measure simultaneously [10–15]. For example, in [16] the authors applied the NSGA-II multi-objective method to determine the Pareto optimal set of build orientations based on four quality measures (the support area, the build time, the surface roughness, and the overall quality of the surface).

Recently, the main focus on some multi-objective optimization studies is finding the global best solutions that are less sensitive to the perturbation of the decision variables in its neighborhood [17,18]. In this case, researchers are interested in finding the so-called robust solutions. Robust optimization aims to find robust solutions, which are solutions that are not quite sensitive to small perturbations in the variables [17]. The robust optimization deals with uncertainties in variables making the objective functions have stochastic behaviors [18].

In robust optimization, the parameters of an optimization problem are not deterministic but uncertain, since their values depend on the scenarios which may occur [19]. Over the past few years, researchers have studied the single-objective uncertain optimization problems as well as the robustness concepts for multi-objective optimization problems, where in the first case, the problems are transformed into deterministic multi-objective problems by treating each scenario as an objective function [19,20].

In this paper an implementation of robust multi-objective optimization in the build orientation problem is presented. Firstly, the robust multi-objective problem is presented in the context of the build orientation optimization of a 3D CAD model. In this study, the Rear Panel Fixed model is used. The multi-objective genetic algorithm based on NSGA-II is applied to determine the robust Pareto optimal solutions that optimize the final quality of a 3D object, based on two specific criteria: the staircase effect and the area spent with external supports. Therefore, a step-by-step implementation of the robust multi-objective optimization for a given solution of the build orientation problem is described. Finally, the robust Pareto optimal solutions obtained are analyzed, in order to demonstrate their sensitivity towards two kinds of small perturbations in their decision variable values.

This article is organized as follows. Section 2 describes the model and the quality measures optimized in this study are presented in Sect. 3. The robust multi-objective approach is described in Sect. 4. The robustness analysis of the build orientation optimal solutions obtained in the numerical experiments is presented and discussed in Sect. 5. Finally, Sect. 6 contains the conclusions of this study.

2   Model

The 3D CAD model that will be used in this study is the Rear Panel Fixed (see Fig. 1(a)) which has vents on both sides. The size of the model is different from the side panels, but the side panels for left and right are equal [21].

Initially, the 3D model data is based on a 3D mesh model, created by structures built in CAD software and then converted into a surface tessellation language (STL) format, which is the standard file type used by the most common 3D print file formats. The STL file describes only the surface geometry of a 3D object, without color, texture, or other common attributes of the CAD model, representing the 3D solid object through triangular faces. The more complex the models are, the greater their number of triangular faces (see Fig. 1(b)).

(a) 3D CAD representation   (b) Triangular representation

Fig. 1. Rear panel fixed model.

The Rear Panel Fixed model is defined by 3008 triangles, a volume of 46.2 cm^3 and 676 slices for a layer thickness of 0.2 mm (layer thickness used in this work).

3   Quality Measures

The best build orientation for a given 3D object is determined using different measures that are studied in order to obtain an improvement in the surface quality. The surface quality of an object can be influenced by many different parameters, in particular the layer thickness as well as the amount of generated supports. In this study, the build orientation optimization of a 3D model is based on two measures: the staircase effect and the support area.

The staircase effect occurs when the layers stay inside or outside the contours of the original models, giving the perception of a layer. The error associated with the staircase effect is due to the layer thickness and the slope of the part surface [6,9].

Mathematically, the staircase effect, SE, is as follows

$$SE(\theta) = \sum_i L(\theta_i) \tag{1}$$

where θ_i is the angle between triangle facet i of model surface considering the build orientation θ [5,22]. The function $L(\theta_i)$ represents the length of the step for each triangle i and it is defined by

$$L(\theta_i) = \begin{cases} \dfrac{t}{\tan(\theta_i)}, & \text{if } \tan(\theta_i) \neq 0 \\ 0, & \text{if } \tan(\theta_i) = 0 \end{cases} \tag{2}$$

where t is the layer thickness.

The other measure of the quality used in this study is called the support area, that corresponds to the total contact area of the external supports with the object [5,8,13]. Mathematically, the support area, SA, is given by

$$SA(\theta) = \sum_i A_i \left| d^T n_i \right| \gamma \tag{3}$$

where A_i is the area of the triangular facet i, d is the unit vector of the direction of construction, n_i is the normal unit vector of the triangular face i and γ is a threshold function that takes the value of 1 if $d^T n_i < 0$ and 0 if $d^T n_i > 0$ (for more details see [22]). In this study, a 3D printer with a fixed platform (z-axis) is considered so that the direction vector is $d = (0, 0, 1)$.

Figure 2 shows the SE and SA landscapes for the Rear Panel Fixed model, respectively. Note that both objective functions are nonconvex and have multiple local optima.

4   Robust Multi-objective Approach

This section presents the robust multi-objective problem approach considering the two objective functions: staircase effect and the contact supports area. An illustrative example is also presented.

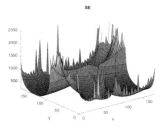
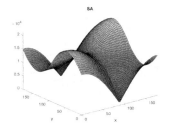

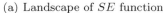

(a) Landscape of SE function   (b) Landscape of SA function

Fig. 2. Landscape of SE and SA functions for the Rear Panel fixed model.

4.1   Robust Multi-objective Problem

In this study, a robust multi-objective problem, with respect to δ-neighborhood, is defined by

$$
\begin{aligned}
\min\ & \{f_1^{\text{eff}}(\theta), f_2^{\text{eff}}(\theta)\} \\
\text{s.t.}\ & \theta \in S
\end{aligned}
\tag{4}
$$

where $\theta = (\theta_x, \theta_y)$ is the decision variables vector, $S = [0, 180]^2$ is the feasible search space and f_j^{eff}, for $j = 1, 2$, is a mean effective objective function given by

$$
f_j^{\text{eff}}(\theta) = \frac{1}{|B_\delta(\theta)|} \int_{\alpha \in B_\delta(\theta)} f_j(\alpha) d\alpha
\tag{5}
$$

where the set $B_\delta(\theta) = \{(\alpha_x, \alpha_y) \in \mathbb{R}^2 : \theta_x - \delta \le \alpha_x \le \theta_x + \delta,\ \theta_y - \delta \le \alpha_y \le \theta_y + \delta\}$ is the δ-neighborhood of the solution θ and $|B_\delta(\theta)|$ is the hypervolume of the chosen δ-neighborhood.

Given a point θ, to compute the mean effective objective function, $f_j^{\text{eff}}(\theta)$ defined in (5), for $j = 1, 2$, for a given perturbation of δ, the simple bounds θ^l and θ^u should be calculated as follows. The lower bound should be determined as $\theta^l = \max(0, \theta - \delta \mathbf{1})$ and the upper bound is defined as $\theta^u = \min(\theta + \delta \mathbf{1}, 180)$, considering the lower and upper bounds of the set S and $\mathbf{1}$ representing the vector with the same dimension as θ with ones in all coordinates.

Since the set $B_\delta(\theta)$ is a rectangular region, the hypervolume can be calculated as $|B_\delta(\theta))| = (\theta_x^u - \theta_x^l)(\theta_y^u - \theta_y^l)$.

The function $f_1^{\text{eff}}(\theta)$ represents the mean effective objective function associated with the staircase effect (SE) and can be calculated as

$$
f_1^{\text{eff}}(\theta) = SE^{\text{eff}}(\theta) = \frac{1}{|B_\delta(\theta)|} \int_{\theta_y^l}^{\theta_y^u} \int_{\theta_x^l}^{\theta_x^u} SE(\alpha_x, \alpha_y) d\alpha_x d\alpha_y
\tag{6}
$$

where $SE(\theta)$ was defined in (1).

Similarly, the function $f_2^{\text{eff}}(\theta)$ represents the mean effective objective function associated with the support area (SA) and can be calculated as

$$f_2^{\text{eff}}(\theta) = SA^{\text{eff}}(\theta) = \frac{1}{|B_\delta(\theta)|} \int_{\theta_y^l}^{\theta_y^u} \int_{\theta_x^l}^{\theta_x^u} SA(\alpha_x, \alpha_y) d\alpha_x d\alpha_y \qquad (7)$$

where $SA(\theta)$ was defined in (3).

To solve the double integrals Simpson or Trapezoidal rules can be applied.

4.2   Illustrative Example

To illustrate the calculation of the mean effective objective functions, the orientation point $\theta = (90, 0)$ and the perturbation $\delta = 2$ were considered.

In this case, the set $B_2(90, 0)$ is defined as

$$B_2(90, 0) = \{(\alpha_x, \alpha_y) \in \mathbb{R}^2 : 88 \le \alpha_x \le 92, \ 0 \le \alpha_y \le 2\}$$

and the hypervolume is $|B_2(90, 0)| = 4 \times 2 = 8$.

The next step is to calculate the double integral defined in (6) and (7). In this case, the trapezoidal rule with $n = 4$ subintervals was used, having stepsizes of $h_x = 1$ and $h_y = 0.5$ associated to the variables α_x and α_y, respectively. Then, the domain region $B_2(90, 0)$ will be discretized as shown in Table 1.

Table 1. Discretized values of α_x and α_y for $n = 4$ subintervals.

j	0	1	2	3	4
α_x^j	88.0	89.0	90.0	91.0	92.0
α_y^j	0.0	0.5	1.0	1.5	2.0

In order to compute the double integral, the values of $SE(\alpha_x^i, \alpha_y^j)$, $i, j = 0, \ldots, 4$ are presented on Table 2.

Table 2. $SE(\alpha_x^i, \alpha_y^j)$ values for $i, j = 1, \ldots, 4$.

$SE(\alpha_x^i, \alpha_y^j)$	α_x^0	α_x^1	α_x^2	α_x^3	α_x^4
α_y^0	1917.3	3346.3	31705.7	4517.6	2393.5
α_y^1	1870.2	3038.4	6243.0	3143.4	1982.8
α_y^2	1753.1	2497.0	3351.8	2536.8	1785.3
α_y^3	1609.5	2058.4	2390.0	2072.7	1615.5
α_y^4	1470.5	1753.6	1918.6	1756.1	1465.6

Considering the auxiliar function, $\overline{SE}(\alpha_y^j)$, $j = 0, \ldots, 4$,

$$\overline{SE}(\alpha_y^j) \approx \frac{h_x}{2} \left[SE(\alpha_x^0, \alpha_y^j) + 2 \sum_{i=1}^{n-1} SE(\alpha_x^i, \alpha_y^j) + SE(\alpha_x^n, \alpha_y^j) \right],$$

Table 3. $\bar{SE}(\alpha_y^j)$ values.

j	0	1	2	3	4
$\overline{SE}(\alpha_y^j)$	41725.0	14351.0	10155.0	8133.5	6896.3

where the calculated values of $\overline{SE}(\alpha_y^j)$, $j = 0, \ldots, 4$, are shown in Table 3.
Finally, the approximation of the double integral is given by

$$SE^{\text{eff}}(90, 0) \approx \frac{1}{8} \frac{h_y}{2} \left[\overline{SE}(\alpha_y^0) + 2 \sum_{j=1}^{n-1} \overline{SE}(\alpha_y^j) + \overline{SE}(\alpha_y^n) \right] = \frac{28475.0}{8} = 3559.4.$$

In a similar way, the value of $SA^{\text{eff}}(90, 0)$ is obtained as,

$$SA^{\text{eff}}(90, 0) = \frac{9935.2}{8} = 1241.9.$$

5 Experiments

The numerical results are presented in this section.

5.1 Details

In this paper, the elitist NSGA-II proposed by Deb et al. [23] implemented in
the `gamultiobj` function from MATLAB® [24] environment is used to solve the
bi-objective robust optimization problem defined in (4), where SE^{eff} is given by
(6) and SA^{eff} is given by (7). More information on the topics mentioned above
can be found in [21].

The population size and the maximum number of generations was set to
50 (default value) and 600, respectively. The default values for the remaining
parameters of the `gamultiobj` function were used. Due to the stochastic nature
of the optimization algorithm, 30 independent runs were performed. By default,
the Pareto fraction is 0.35 and therefore, in each run, 18 non-dominated solutions are found (0.35 × population size). The *Simplify 3D* software (a 3D model
printing simulator) allows to visualize the solutions found for the Rear Panel
fixed model [25].

5.2 Results

In this section, the results obtained for the Rear Panel Fixed for two different
values of δ-neighborhood are discussed. The approximations to the robust Pareto
optimal fronts for the robust bi-objective optimization problem for $\delta = 1$ and
$\delta = 2$ are presented.

In the following graphs, the set of robust non-dominated solutions obtained
among the 30 independent runs are plotted with a red circle. Representative

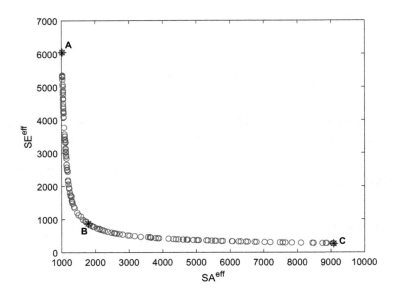

Fig. 3. Robust Pareto front obtained for SA vs. SE problem with $\delta = 1$. (Color figure online)

efficient solutions (marked with a black asterisk) are selected from the robust Pareto fronts and considered to analyze the trade-offs between the objectives and identify the characteristics associated to these solutions.

Figure 3 shows the robust Pareto front obtained for SA^{eff} vs. SE^{eff} problem with $\delta = 1$. It can be seen that solution A is the solution with the best value of SA^{eff} and solution C is the solution with best value of SE^{eff}. On the other hand, solution B is near the elbow curvature of the robust Pareto front. This solution seems to be a good trade-off since a small improvement in SA^{eff} will cause a large deterioration in SE^{eff}.

In Table 4, for the selected solutions from the robust Pareto front, the decision variable values, θ_x and θ_y, and the corresponding SA^{eff} and SE^{eff} values for $\delta = 1$ are presented.

Table 4. Robust solutions for $\delta = 1$ perturbation.

	θ_x	θ_y	SA^{eff}	SE^{eff}
A	90.45	0.00	1021.19	6047.18
B	93.66	4.66	1788.09	871.43
C	180.00	44.95	9081.89	260.74

It can be observed that solution A with the best SA^{eff} value corresponds to $\theta_x = 90.45$ and $\theta_y = 0.00$. It should be noted that, for instance, solution

$\theta_x = 90.00$ and $\theta_y = 0.00$ does not belong to the robust Pareto-optimal set for $\delta = 1$, i.e., it is not robust for a perturbation level of $\delta = 1$. This solution was found as a non-dominated solution without considering robustness in [21].

Solution C with $\theta_x = 180$ and $\theta_y = 44.95$ has the best value of SE^{eff}. Note that this solution is also obtained without considering robustness (see [21]) and, therefore, it is a robust solution.

Solution B with $\theta_x = 93.66$ and $\theta_y = 4.66$ may be interesting for the decision-maker since moving to neighbor solutions is not attractive in terms of the trade-offs between SA^{eff} and SE^{eff}.

In Fig. 4, the robust Pareto front obtained for SA^{eff} vs. SE^{eff} problem with $\delta = 2$ is presented.

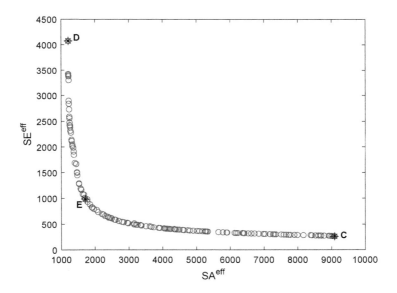

Fig. 4. Robust Pareto front obtained for SA vs. SE problem with $\delta = 2$

Solutions in this robust Pareto front are different in terms of SE^{eff} values when compared with those of Fig. 3. In this figure, solution D has the best SA^{eff}. Conversely, solution C has the best value of SE^{eff}. Solution E is a trade-off solution between the two objectives.

When the robust Pareto fronts from Fig. 3 and Fig. 4 with different values of δ are compared, it can be seen that the minimum SA^{eff} portion of the Pareto fronts becomes more and more non-robust. It can be observed a movement of the robust Pareto front along the complete range of optimal solutions due to the average function values computed by Eq. (5). In the minimum SE^{eff} portion of the Pareto fronts, the solutions are more robust since this effect is not observed. Actually, the extreme solution C is the same in both robust Pareto fronts. Thus, the minimum SA^{eff} region is more sensitive to decision variables perturbations than the minimum SE^{eff} region, for which the two robust Pareto fronts are almost identical. In terms of decision variables, it can be seen that fluctuations or perturbations in θ_x represents a great effect is SE^{eff} values.

Table 5. Robust solutions for $\delta = 2$ perturbation.

	θ_x	θ_y	SA^{eff}	SE^{eff}
D	90.95	0.00	1209.47	4074.10
E	93.47	3.75	1707.54	984.67
C	180.00	44.95	9081.89	260.74

Table 5 shows the decision variables and SA^{eff} and SE^{eff} for selected solutions from the robust Pareto front for $\delta = 2$. It can be observed that solution D with the best SA^{eff} value corresponds to $\theta_x = 90.95$ and $\theta_y = 0.00$. This extreme solution D is different from the solution A obtained with $\delta = 1$. This means that solution A is robust for $\delta = 1$, but becomes non-robust for $\delta = 2$. As for a perturbation of $\delta = 1$, solution C with $\delta_x = 180$ and $\delta_y = 44.95$ is robust and the best in terms of SE^{eff}. Solution E with $\theta_x = 93.87$ and $\theta_y = 3.75$ is an intermediate alternative for the decision-maker in terms of SA and SE.

In Table 6 the decision variable values, and the SA and SE values computed by (3) and (1), for the selected solutions from the robust Pareto fronts for $\delta = 1$ and $\delta = 2$ are presented.

Table 6. Computed values for the robust solutions for $\delta = 1$ and $\delta = 2$. perturbation

	Optimal solutions		Values from (3) and (1)		Robustness	
	θ_x	θ_y	SA	SE	$\delta = 1$	$\delta = 2$
A	90.45	0.00	961.56	6902.95	✓	✗
D	90.95	0.00	1087.50	5497.59	✓	✓
E	93.47	3.75	1628.65	957.02	✓	✓
B	93.66	4.66	1769.92	867.97	✓	✓
C	180.00	44.95	9078.06	260.39	✓	✓

In this table, it is also indicated the robustness of solutions for each value of δ. Taking into account the values of SA and SE computed by (3) and (1), it can be observed that all these solutions are non-dominated solutions. All solutions are robust to small perturbations of $\delta = 1$. However, solution A is not robust for $\delta = 2$. Moreover, it can be observed that $\theta_y = 0$ for solution D and A. The variation on the objective function values is due to the θ_x decision variable. A perturbation on θ_x produces a significant effect, specially, on SE values as can be seen in Table 6.

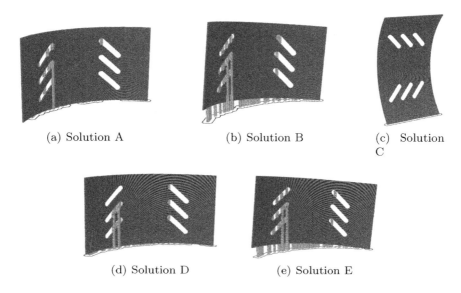

(a) Solution A   (b) Solution B   (c) Solution
                                                                C

(d) Solution D   (e) Solution E

Fig. 5. Visualization of the representative robust solutions.

In Fig. 5, the orientations of the representative robust solutions can be visualized. Solution A is not robust for $\delta = 2$ due the sensitivity of SA and SE to variations on θ_x. This can be observed in Fig. 5(a) and Fig. 5(d) where a small variation on θ_x changes the support area as well as the staircase effect. This can be seen in Fig. 2(a) in which in the vicinity of $\theta_x = 90$ and $\theta_y = 0$, there exist a large variability of the values of SE. For robust solutions D, E and B, as θ_x increases, the value θ_y also increases in a small amount. Their representations given in Fig. 5(d), Fig. 5(e) and Fig. 5(b) show the increase of support area and the reduction of the staircase effect due to the gradual change of orientation. In Fig. 2(a) and Fig. 2(b), it can be seen that from in the vicinity of $\theta_x = 90$ and $\theta_y = 0$ towards the region close to $\theta_x = 180$ and $\theta_y = 45$, there exist a plateau in both objectives and therefore, the solutions are robust. Solution C, represented in Fig. 5(c), has the largest support area due to its vertical position and the smallest staircase effect. This is a robust solution since the variability around this point is very small as can be observed in Fig. 2(a) and Fig. 2(b).

6   Conclusions

The build orientation optimization of 3D parts is one of the crucial factors to obtain the best final quality of the part surface.

In this work, an implementation of the robust multi-objective optimization in the build orientation problem was presented. Two quality measures were used in order to find robust optimal solutions for the Rear Panel Fixed model: the staircase effect and the support area.

The robust multi-objective optimization is briefly described. The experiments were conducted for two perturbation values $\delta = 1$ and $\delta = 2$.

The robust Pareto fronts obtained with the two different perturbation values, composed of solutions that were not quite sensitive to perturbations, were analyzed and compared. It was possible to conclude that small perturbations in the first component of θ represents a great effect in the SE^{eff} function.

In this way, the robust solutions will help the decision-maker to identify the compromise solutions and choose the best build orientation according to his/her preferences.

References

1. Ngo, T.D., Kashani, A., Imbalzano, G., Nguyen, K.T., Hui, D.: Additive manufacturing (3D printing): a review of materials, methods, applications and challenges. Compos. Part B Eng. **143**, 172–196 (2018)
2. Bikas, H., Stavropoulos, P., Chryssolouris, G.: Additive manufacturing methods and modelling approaches: a critical review. Int. J. Adv. Manuf. Technol. **83**(1–4), 389–405 (2016)
3. Ford, S., Despeisse, M.: Additive manufacturing and sustainability: an exploratory study of the advantages and challenges. J. Clean. Prod. **137**, 1573–1587 (2016)
4. Zhang, Y., De Backer, W., Harik, R., Bernard, A.: Build orientation determination for multi-material deposition additive manufacturing with continuous fibers. Procedia CIRP **50**(2016), 414–419 (2016)
5. Matos, M.A., Rocha, A.M.A.C., Pereira, A.I.: Improving additive manufacturing performance by build orientation optimization. Int. J. Adv. Manuf. Technol., 1–13 (2020)
6. Pereira, S., Vaz, A., Vicente, L.: On the optimal object orientation in additive manufacturing. Int. J. Adv. Manuf. Technol. **98**(5–8), 1685–1694 (2018)
7. Phatak, A.M., Pande, S.: Optimum part orientation in rapid prototyping using genetic algorithm. J. Manuf. Syst. **31**(4), 395–402 (2012)
8. Rocha, A.M.A.C., Pereira, A.I., Vaz, A.I.F.: Build orientation optimization problem in additive manufacturing. In: Gervasi, O., et al. (eds.) ICCSA 2018. LNCS, vol. 10961, pp. 669–682. Springer, Cham (2018). https://doi.org/10.1007/978-3-319-95165-2_47
9. Thrimurthulu, K., Pandey, P.M., Reddy, N.V.: Optimum part deposition orientation in fused deposition modeling. Int. J. Mach. Tools Manuf. **44**(6), 585–594 (2004)
10. Brika, S.E., Zhao, Y.F., Brochu, M., Mezzetta, J.: Multi-objective build orientation optimization for powder bed fusion by laser. J. Manuf. Sci. Eng. **139**(11), 111011 (2017)
11. Golmohammadi, A., Khodaygan, S.: A framework for multi-objective optimisation of 3D part-build orientation with a desired angular resolution in additive manufacturing processes. Virtual Phys. Prototyping **14**(1), 19–36 (2019)
12. Gurrala, P.K., Regalla, S.P.: Multi-objective optimisation of strength and volumetric shrinkage of FDM parts: a multi-objective optimization scheme is used to optimize the strength and volumetric shrinkage of FDM parts considering different process parameters. Virtual Phys. Prototyping **9**(2), 127–138 (2014)

13. Matos, M.A., Rocha, A.M.A.C., Costa, L.A., Pereira, A.I.: A multi-objective approach to solve the build orientation problem in additive manufacturing. In: Misra, S., et al. (eds.) ICCSA 2019. LNCS, vol. 11621, pp. 261–276. Springer, Cham (2019). https://doi.org/10.1007/978-3-030-24302-9_19
14. Mele, M., Campana, G.: Sustainability-driven multi-objective evolutionary orienting in additive manufacturing. Sustain. Prod. Consumption (2020)
15. Padhye, N., Deb, K.: Multi-objective optimisation and multi-criteria decision making in SLS using evolutionary approaches. Rapid Prototyping J. **17**(6), 458–478 (2011)
16. Matos, M.A., Rocha, A.M.A.C., Costa, L.A.: Many-objective optimization of build part orientation in additive manufacturing. Int. J. Adv. Manuf. Technol., 1–16 (2020)
17. Deb, K., Gupta, H.: Searching for robust pareto-optimal solutions in multi-objective optimization. In: Coello Coello, C.A., Hernández Aguirre, A., Zitzler, E. (eds.) EMO 2005. LNCS, vol. 3410, pp. 150–164. Springer, Heidelberg (2005). https://doi.org/10.1007/978-3-540-31880-4_11
18. Deb, K., Gupta, H.: Introducing robustness in multi-objective optimization. Evol. Comput. **14**(4), 463–494 (2006)
19. Botte, M., Schöbel, A.: Dominance for multi-objective robust optimization concepts. Eur. J. Oper. Res. **273**(2), 430–440 (2019)
20. Sülflow, A., Drechsler, N., Drechsler, R.: Robust multi-objective optimization in high dimensional spaces. In: Obayashi, S., Deb, K., Poloni, C., Hiroyasu, T., Murata, T. (eds.) EMO 2007. LNCS, vol. 4403, pp. 715–726. Springer, Heidelberg (2007). https://doi.org/10.1007/978-3-540-70928-2_54
21. Matos, M.A., Rocha, A.M.A.C., Costa, L.A., Pereira, A.I.: Multi-objective optimization in the build orientation of a 3D CAD model. In: Gaspar-Cunha, A., Periaux, J., Giannakoglou, K.C., Gauger, N.R., Quagliarella, D., Greiner, D. (eds.) Advances in Evolutionary and Deterministic Methods for Design, Optimization and Control in Engineering and Sciences. CMAS, vol. 55, pp. 99–114. Springer, Cham (2021). https://doi.org/10.1007/978-3-030-57422-2_7
22. Jibin, Z.: Determination of optimal build orientation based on satisfactory degree theory for RPT. In: Ninth International Conference on Computer Aided Design and Computer Graphics, p. 6. IEEE (2005)
23. Deb, K.: Multi-Objective Optimization Using Evolutionary Algorithms. Wiley, New York (2001)
24. MATLAB: version 9.6.0.1214997 (R2019a). The MathWorks Inc., Natick, Massachusetts (2019)
25. SIMPLIFY3D, I.S.S.: version 4.0.0 (2017). Simplify3D LLC., Legal Dept, Simplify3D (2017)

Resource Assignment Problem for Fleet Management Considering Outsourcing: Modelling and a Decomposition Approach

Filipe Monnerat[1,2] , Joana Dias[1,3] , and Maria João Alves[1,3(✉)]

[1] CeBER and Faculty of Economics, University of Coimbra, Av. Dias da Silva 165,
3004-512 Coimbra, Portugal
mjalves@fe.uc.pt
[2] Universidade Federal de Viçosa, Viçosa, Brasil
[3] University of Coimbra, INESC Coimbra, Rua Sílvio Lima, Pólo II,
3030-290 Coimbra, Portugal

Abstract. Many institutions have to manage internal and external resources to assure the realization of working trips. In this work we consider two different types of resources: vehicles and drivers. The assignment of these resources to trips is interlinked, since the number of drivers will depend on the number of assigned vehicles, and also on other characteristics of the trip itself. Furthermore, it is possible to improve the use of resources if they can be shared between compatible trips: trips that have compatible origin and destination pairs and are also compatible regarding the realization time periods. Instead of considering internal resources only, this work presents a new model where the possibility of outsourcing is also considered. This problem can be interpreted as an extension of the Generalized Assignment Problem, that is known to be NP-hard. An optimization approach is also proposed, based on the decomposition of the problem. Computational tests were performed to assess the solutions produced by the model and the behaviour of the decomposition approach. The computational results show that the developed model is capable of representing in a faithful way the problem, and the algorithmic approach presents a better performance when compared with a general solver applied to the whole problem.

Keywords: Combinatorial optimization · Generalized assignment problem · Fleet management · Outsourcing

1 Introduction

This work addresses a fleet management problem, where vehicles and drivers must be assigned to working trips that have to take place in predetermined time periods. These trips have also predetermined routes, so routing optimization does not need to be considered. The objective is to determine resource assignment minimizing total cost. One of the challenges of this problem is the fact that the assignment of drivers and vehicles cannot be done independently of each other. The number of vehicles needed

© Springer Nature Switzerland AG 2021
O. Gervasi et al. (Eds.): ICCSA 2021, LNCS 12953, pp. 260–273, 2021.
https://doi.org/10.1007/978-3-030-86976-2_18

depends on the vehicle availability and on the number of passengers that will travel. The number of drivers depends not only on the number of vehicles assigned but also on the trip's characteristics: a long trip may require more than one driver per vehicle in order to respect legal and safety obligations, for instance.

In a previous work, a similar fleet management resource assignment problem has already been tackled [1]. However, only internal resources were considered, which does not fully illustrate the situation in most institutions. In the present work, we consider the possibility of both internal and external resources being used, making explicit the possibility of resorting to outsourcing whenever that is needed (because no internal resources are available) or it is beneficial in terms of cost minimization. Furthermore, we also propose a decomposition method for the calculation of solutions that takes advantage of the characteristics of the problem at hand, but that can also be applied to other problems with similar structures. This decomposition method leads to an optimal solution of the problem provided that the subproblems are solved to optimality.

The motivation for this work came from the identification of this problem in a real institution (a public Brazilian university) and the need to properly address it from a resource management point of view. Several data sets were created, with different characteristics, aiming to assess the solutions calculated for the developed model and the behaviour of the decomposition optimization algorithm proposed. This approach is compared with the use of a general solver for the entire model (without decomposition).

Although there is an extensive published literature related to fleet management problems, a large part is focused on vehicle routing problems. Souza et al. [2] considered the vehicle routing problem for a patient transportation system, using a heterogeneous vehicle fleet. Lukman et al. [3] studied the fleet management optimization problem for winter services' resource assignment, having as starting point the Chinese postman problem. Hoff et al. [4] studied the industrial aspects of fleet composition combined with routing in maritime and rail transport, giving an overview of the combined problems of routing and composition of the fleet in transport. The authors show the importance of the subject and the difficulties associated with solving this type of problems, concluding that most studies discuss tactical decision-making and investigate the use of metaheuristics due to the difficulty of solving larger instances. An identification of the most relevant problems in fleet management for different means of transport was carried out in [5] referring to problems of routing and scheduling of vehicles, dynamic fleet management, private and public urban transport, dial-to-ride transport and specific problems related to air, sea, rail and intermodal transport. Loxton et al. [6] considered the problem of forming a new heterogeneous fleet of vehicles. The authors developed an algorithm based on dynamic programming to determine the fleet composition that minimized cost. A short literature review on the fleet sizing problem can be found in [7]. More recently, a heterogeneous fleet management system deployed to collect waste with each route being able to start and end in different warehouses has been developed and is described in [8]. The dynamic fleet management problem is also studied in [9], considering explicitly uncertain demand and service levels chosen by the customer. Billhardt et al. [10] address dynamic fleet management in real-time in an event-based architecture with simultaneous task allocation and vehicle allocation. Fleet management problems in the airline industry have also been studied [11, 12]. In a recent work, Zhang et al. [13] studied the fleet management problem considering not only the determination of vehicles' utilization schedules but also decisions regarding vehicles' purchasing and retirement schedules. Dauer and Prata [14] studied the vehicle allocation and trip scheduling problem assuming the existence of multiple depots, a heterogeneous fleet and the existence of time windows.

The work presented here differs from the works cited. The set of vehicles available is known, the fleet is heterogeneous and previously determined. All the defined trips must take place, with scheduling and routing decisions already made. Each trip is a route that starts and ends at the origin (the institution) and has predetermined stops. The goal is to optimize the assignment of vehicles and drivers to the planned trips, within a defined planning horizon, allowing for outsourcing (acquisition of full transport service for a trip), so that costs are kept as low as possible. This problem can thus be interpreted as an extension of the generalized assignment problem (GAP), which is NP-hard. However, it differs from the multi-resource GAP since a task (trip) needs two separate resources (vehicles and drivers), and the requirements of one of the resources (drivers) will depend on the number of assigned units of the other resource (vehicles). Moreover, tasks do not take place all at the same time, so the time limits in which they occur must be considered when considering resource capacity limitations and sharing possibilities.

The main contributions of this work are the description of a resource assignment problem for fleet management considering internal and external resources, and the development of a decomposition approach that is able to calculate optimal solutions for this problem and can also be applied to problems with a similar structure (an implicit timeline that affects the way resource assignment can be done).

This manuscript is organized as follows. The proposed model is presented in Sect. 2. Section 3 describes the decomposition approach. Section 4 presents the computational experiments and results. Section 5 presents some conclusions.

2   The Proposed Model

The model considers the simultaneous assignment of vehicles and drivers to travel requests, as well as the possibility of having trips with no internal resources assigned and resorting to outsourcing. For these requisitions, the number of passengers, the destination and the schedule are predefined. The number of drivers that must be considered for every vehicle used is also known.

This model follows closely the one described in [1], except for the outsourcing modelling that is new in the model presented herein.

Considering the existing information about the destination and schedule of the trips, two data matrices with binary elements must be created. One is the compatibility matrix, which indicates whether two requests are compatible in time and space (they have the same destination or one of them is on the route of the other trip), and therefore can share resources. The other one is a non-overlapping matrix that indicates whether two requests have no period of time in common (i.e., do not overlap). These matrices determine whether the same resource can be assigned to two different trips: if the trips are not compatible, the same vehicle/driver cannot be assigned to both trips, unless they occur in different periods of time. If these trips do not overlap regarding their realization time periods, then the same resource can be used for both. If the trips are compatible, they can share resources (vehicles and drivers).

As compatible trips correspond to situations that share the same route, or one trip is a sub-route of another one, to simplify the constraints of the model it is assumed that all the trips are ordered by increasing costs of drivers, vehicles and outsourcing. Since these costs are mainly related to distance and travel time, it is realistic to assume that the same order applies to the different costs (drivers, vehicles and outsourcing) and even to the number of drivers required for each vehicle. Therefore, this assumption does not limit the application of the model.

The notation used is defined as follows:

$i = 1, \ldots, V$ is the index used for vehicles, with V the total number of vehicles owned by the institution.

$j = 1, \ldots, J$ is the index used for trips, with J the total number of trips to consider in the defined planning horizon.

$m = 1, \ldots, M$ is the index for existing drivers, employed by the institution, with M the total number of existing drivers.

C_{ij} = cost of assigning vehicle i to trip j, $\forall i, j$

D_{mj} = cost of assigning driver m to trip j, $\forall m, j$

F_j = cost of using outsourcing for the realization of trip j, not using any other internal resources, $\forall j$

P_j = total number of passengers associated with trip j, $\forall j$

Q_i = number of seats in vehicle i, $\forall i$

n_j = number of drivers per vehicles needed for trip j, $\forall j$

Compatibility matrix: $A = [a_{jj'}], \forall j, j' : j < j'$

$$a_{jj'} = \begin{cases} 1, & \text{if trips } j \text{ and } j' \text{ are compatible, meaning they} \\ & \text{can share resources} \\ 0, & \text{otherwise} \end{cases} \quad , \forall j, j' : j < j'$$

Non-overlapping matrix: $B = [b_{jj'}], \forall j, j' : j < j'$

$$b_{jj'} = \begin{cases} 1, & \text{if trips } j \text{ and } j' \text{ do not have any intersection} \\ & \text{in their realization timings} \\ 0, & \text{otherwise} \end{cases} \quad , \forall j, j' : j < j'$$

We should note that, by definition, $a_{jj'} + b_{jj'} \leq 1, \forall j, j'$.

The decision variables represent the assignment of resources to trips.

$$x_{ij} = \begin{cases} 1, & \text{if vehicle } i \text{ is assigned to trip } j \\ 0, & \text{otherwise} \end{cases} \quad , \forall i, j$$

$$z_{ijj'} = \begin{cases} 1, & \text{if trips } j \text{ and } j' \text{ share vehicle } i \\ 0, & \text{otherwise} \end{cases} \quad \forall i, j, j' : j < j'$$

$$Z'_{jj'} = \begin{cases} 1, & \text{if trips } j \text{ and } j' \text{ share any vehicle} \\ 0, & \text{otherwise} \end{cases} \quad \forall j, j' : j < j'$$

$$X'_{ij} = \begin{cases} 1, & \text{if vehicle } i \text{ is assigned to trip } j \text{ and to other compatible trips} \\ & \text{sharing resources with } j \\ 0, & \text{otherwise} \end{cases} \quad , \forall i, j$$

$$Y'_{mj} = \begin{cases} 1, \text{ if driver } m \text{ is assigned to trip } j \text{ and to compatible} \\ \text{trips that use the same vehicle} \\ 0, \text{ otherwise} \end{cases}, \forall m, j$$

$$O_j = \begin{cases} 1, \text{ if trip } j \text{ does not use internal resources and its realization} \\ \text{is guaranteed by outsourcing} \\ 0, \text{ otherwise} \end{cases}, \forall j$$

The model can be formulated as follows:

Objective function (1) guarantees the minimization of total costs. Taking advantage of the ordering of the trips by increasing cost it is possible to assure an adequate accounting of the proper costs to consider whenever there are shared resources between different trips. The first three terms of (1) concern, respectively, vehicle, driver and outsourcing costs. The last term is a perturbation term (with ε a positive very small number), which aims to avoid unnecessary sharing in case of alternative optimal solutions.

$$Min \sum_{i=1}^{V} \sum_{j=1}^{J} C_{ij} X'_{ij} + \sum_{m=1}^{M} \sum_{j=1}^{J} D_{mj} Y'_{mj} + \sum_{j=1}^{J} F_j O_j$$
$$+ \varepsilon \sum_{i=1}^{V} \sum_{j=1}^{J} \sum_{j':j<j'} z_{ijj'} \tag{1}$$

Subject to:

Constraints (2) guarantee the coherence between decision variables X'_{ij} and x_{ij} : a vehicle i can be assigned to trip j and other compatible trips that share the same vehicle ($X'_{ij} = 1$) only if vehicle i is assigned to trip j ($x_{ij} = 1$). Constraints (3) and (4) assure the coherence between decision variables $Z'_{jj'}$ and $z_{ijj'}$: $Z'_{jj'}$ must be equal to 1 if trips j and j' share at least one vehicle, but it must be equal to 0 if j and j' do not share any vehicle.

$$X'_{ij} \le x_{ij}, \quad \forall i, j \tag{2}$$

$$Z'_{jj'} \ge \frac{1}{V} \sum_{i=1}^{V} z_{ijj'}, \quad \forall j, j' : j < j' \tag{3}$$

$$Z'_{jj'} \le \sum_{i=1}^{V} z_{ijj'}, \quad \forall j, j' : j < j' \tag{4}$$

Constraints (5) guarantee that every passenger in every trip has an available seat in one of the vehicles assigned to the respective trip. Passengers can be divided by different vehicles, and one vehicle can transport passengers from different trips. Guaranteeing that enough seats do exist is only necessary if outsourcing is not used. If outsourcing is used, it is implicitly guaranteed that all the necessary resources will be available. M represents a sufficiently large positive number.

$$\sum_{i=1}^{V} Q_i x_{ij} + M O_j \ge P_j + \sum_{j':j<j'} P_j Z'_{jj'}, \quad \forall j \tag{5}$$

Constraints (6) establish the coherence in the assignment of each vehicle to different trips: a vehicle i can only be assigned to two different trips j and j' if they are compatible

$(a_{jj'} = 1)$ or if they do not have any overlap in their realization time periods $(b_{jj'} = 1)$; otherwise, the vehicle i can only be assigned to one of the trips.

$$x_{ij} + x_{ij'} \leq \left(a_{jj'} + b_{jj'}\right) + 1, \forall i, j, j' : j < j' \tag{6}$$

Constraints (7) state that two trips j and j' cannot share a vehicle i (i.e., $z_{ijj'} = 0$) if they are not compatible ($a_{jj'} = 0$) or they do not have any time overlapping ($b_{jj'} = 1$); otherwise, these trips can share vehicle i provided that this vehicle is assigned to both trips.

$$z_{ijj'} \leq \left(1 - b_{jj'}\right)a_{jj'}\frac{x_{ij} + x_{ij'}}{2}, \forall i, j, j' : j < j' \tag{7}$$

Constraints (8) ensure that $z_{ijj'} = 1$ (the vehicle i is shared by j and j') for trips compatible and using the same vehicle.

$$z_{ijj'} \geq a_{jj'} + x_{ij} + x_{ij'} - 2, \forall i, j, j' : j < j' \tag{8}$$

Constraints (9) guarantee that the necessary number of drivers are assigned to each trip, whenever outsourcing is not used.

$$\sum_{m=1}^{M} Y'_{mj} \geq n_j \sum_{i=1}^{V} X'_{ij} - \mathbb{M}O_j, \forall j \tag{9}$$

Constraints (10) assure that a given driver m can only be assigned to two trips j and j' if they share some vehicle(s) or those trips do not have any temporal intersection $(b_{jj'} = 1)$.

$$Y'_{mj} + Y'_{mj'} \leq \sum_{i=1}^{V} z_{ijj'} + b_{jj'} + 1, \forall m, j, j' : j < j' \tag{10}$$

Constraints (11) and (12) guarantee the correct consideration of resource assignment costs. For all the trips that share the same vehicle i, variable X'_{ij} is equal to one only if j represents the most expensive trip (it corresponds to the larger index j). Constraints (12) together with (9) ensure the proper assignment of Y'_{mj} (drivers) whether the trips share the same vehicle or not. In the case of sharing, the driver is assigned to the trip with the longest journey. If outsourcing is used to realize a given trip, then no internal resources need to be assigned. This is ensured by constraints (13).

$$X'_{ij} \geq x_{ij} - \sum_{j' : j < j'}^{J} z_{ijj'}, \forall i, j \tag{11}$$

$$Y'_{mj} \leq 2 - z_{ijj'} - Y'_{mj'}, \forall i, m, j, j' : j < j' \tag{12}$$

$$x_{ij} + O_j \leq 1, \forall i, j \tag{13}$$

All variables are binary.

$$x_{ij}, X'_{ij} \in \{0, 1\}, \forall i, j$$

$$Y'_{mj} \in \{0, 1\}, \forall m, j$$

$$z_{ijj'} \in \{0, 1\}, \forall i, j, j'$$

$$Z'_{jj'} \in \{0, 1\}, \forall j, j'$$

$$O_j \in \{0, 1\}, \forall j$$

3 Problem Decomposition

The first attempt made to calculate the optimal solution for instances considering the described model used a general solver, Cplex. Whilst Cplex is capable of significantly reducing the number of variables in the pre-processing stage, by a priori fixing some of these variables, the optimality gaps obtained where large and the computational times were also significant, as it will be shown in Sect. 4. The difficulties experienced by the general solver motivated the development of a dedicated optimization procedure.

The main idea was to take advantage of the timeline that implicitly exists in the data, and that allows us to understand whether trips can be compatible and can share resources or they do not have any intersections considering their realization time periods. Actually, if it is possible to determine disjoint sets such that no trip in one set has any time intersection with any other trip in the other set, then it is possible to decompose the original instance into two smaller instances that can be easier to solve using a general solver.

This decomposition is made in an automatic and iterative way, trying to balance as much as possible the number of trips that are placed in each set. This can be done resorting to the resolution of an auxiliary linear integer programming problem that takes only seconds to solve. The procedure is repeated for every subset found, until it is not possible to subdivide these sets any more, or the number of trips in each set is already very small. It is possible to end up with a decomposition tree of the problem instance. Figure 1 depicts an example of a decomposition tree for one of the generated instances. The instance has a total of 122 trips. This initial set was divided in two smaller sets, both with 61 instances. The subset on the left was further divided in two smaller sets, one with 47 trips (that was not possible to subdivide any more) and another with 14. The procedure continues until the leaves in the decomposition tree represent sets that should not or cannot be further subdivided.

Let us consider R as representing the set of all the trips of the original instance. The objective is to decompose R into two subsets $R1$ and $R2$. According to the non-overlapping matrix B of the original instance, $b_{jj'} = 1$ means that there is no time overlapping between trips $j, j' \in R$, and $b_{jj'} = 0$ means that some time overlapping does exist between the two trips. If there is time overlapping, then the trips have to be placed in the same set (independently of having or not shared resources assigned to them later on). This is the only way to assure that the global solution that will come up from the resolution of all these subproblems can indeed be the optimal solution for the original

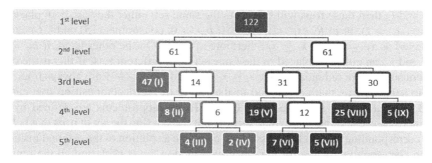

Fig. 1. Example of a decomposition tree

instance. Then, $b_{jj'}$ has to be equal to one for every trip pair (j, j') such that $j \in R1$ and $j' \in R2$. If $b_{jj'} = 0$, then trips j and j' will have to be placed together either in $R1$ or $R2$.

Let $|R1| = \alpha$ and $|R2| = \beta$, such that $\alpha + \beta$ is the total number of trips in R. Let x_j be a binary variable that is equal to 1 if $j \in R1$ and is equal to 0 if $j \in R2$.

The Decomposition Problem (DP) can be defined as follows:

$$Min(\alpha - \beta) \tag{14}$$

subject to:

$$x_j \le x_{j'} + b_{jj'} \quad \forall j < j' \tag{15}$$

$$x_j \ge x_{j'} - b_{jj'} \quad \forall j < j' \tag{16}$$

$$\sum_{j \in R} x_j = \alpha \tag{17}$$

$$\sum_{j \in R} (1 - x_j) = \beta \tag{18}$$

$$\alpha \ge \beta \tag{19}$$

$$x_j \in \{0, 1\} \quad \forall j \in R$$

$$\alpha, \beta \ge 0$$

The objective function (14) minimizes the difference $(\alpha - \beta)$ and constraint (19) defines $\alpha \ge \beta$, but the objective and the constraint could also be defined as the opposite: min $(\beta - \alpha)$ with $\alpha \le \beta$. The aim is to keep the subsets as balanced as possible, so the objective function is defined by the minimization of the non-negative difference of the sizes of the subsets, α and β, with α and β values defined in (17) and (18).

Constraints (15) and (16) guarantee the non-overlapping character of all the trips belonging to different sets. Thus, $b_{jj'} = 0 \Rightarrow x_j = x_{j'}$. If there is some overlap between trips j and j', then these trips will belong to the same set: either they are both placed in $R1$ ($x_i = x_j = 1$), or in $R2$ ($x_i = x_j = 0$). If $b_{jj'} = 0$, constraints (15) and (16) can be interpreted as $x_j \leq x_{j'}$ and $x_j \geq x_{j'}$; therefore $x_j = x_{j'}$. On the other hand, if $b_{jj'} = 1$, trips j and j' can either be placed in the same set or in different sets. If this is the case, these constraints are redundant since $x_j \leq x_{j'} + 1$ and $x_j \geq x_{j'} - 1$ are always true.

The subproblems that correspond to the leaves of the decomposition tree can be solved using a general solver, e.g. the Cplex. These subproblems are defined by the same model presented in the previous section, but considering the set of trips that belong to the corresponding subset. It is possible to calculate a solution to the original instance, and the corresponding value for the objective function, by considering all the optimal values for the decision variables (the union of all the decision variables in all the instances contains all the original decision variables). The global objective function value can be calculated by the sum of all the subproblems' objective function values. If some or all of the subproblems are not solved to optimality, it is possible to calculate the maximum optimality gap. Let K be the number of solved subproblems, and $Cost_k$ the objective function value obtained for subproblem $k = 1, \ldots, K$ to which corresponds a gap equal to gap_k. Knowing that the relative gap given by the solver is calculated as $\frac{|bestbound - bestinteger|}{bestinteger}$, then $gap_k = \frac{Cost_k - Bestbound_k}{Cost_k} \iff Bestbound_k = (1 - gap_k)Cost_k$. The total cost of the solution for the original instance is $Total\ Cost = \sum_{k=1}^{K} Cost_k$, with a maximum gap equal to $gap = \frac{TotalCost - \sum_{k=1}^{K} Bestbound_k}{TotalCost}$.

Summing up, the computational times associated with the resolution of each one of the subproblems leads to the total computational time of this approach (the computational times of the auxiliary decomposition problems DP are negligible).

4 Computational Experiments

4.1 Experimental Setting

The instances were generated having as starting point the case study described in [1]. Considering the real data of a public Brazilian university, a total of 122 trips was considered (corresponding to a normal working month), with the following available internal resources: 28 vehicles with 9 different passenger capacities; 24 drivers, each one belonging to one of two different sets, according to the corresponding working contracts and the impact of these contracts on the assignment cost of a driver to a trip. The trips are all taking place within a radius of 600 km from the origin (the institution itself). The average total distance travelled is equal to 440 kms (with trips ranging from 97 to 1067 kms). The trips have different number of passengers associated, between 1 and 52. The number of drivers per vehicle that has to be considered is either 1 or 2, depending on the travelled distance. From this original set, two groups with a total of 40 instances each were then created. The first group contains 20 instances (A-T) and considers a vehicle fleet equal to the set of the base instance. The second group also contains 20 instances (A-T) but considers a vehicle fleet composed of 16 vehicles of lower capacity only (up to 5 passengers). Within each group, some of the data were randomly generated (namely the time periods associated with the realization of each trip) to test the DP with different trips' compatibility and non-overlapping characteristics, but always guaranteeing the coherence of the data. Instances within each group (1A to 1T; 2A to 2T) were built with an increased number of trips' overlapping. This means that instances identified as A present less time overlapping than the other instances of the same group, and this overlapping increases from A to T. The compatibility between two trips depends both on the time compatibility and on the spatial compatibility (i.e., destinations). Increasing time overlapping from A to T increases the possibility of compatibility between trips but decreases de degree of decomposition by the DP approach. Table 1 summarizes this information.

Table 1. Percentage of compatible trips (CT) in the different generated instances

Instance	A	B	C	D	E	F	G	H	I	J
% CT	2.40	2.70	3.30	3.80	3.90	5.70	6.40	7.10	7.10	7.90
Instance	K	L	M	N	O	P	Q	R	S	T
% CT	9.60	9.80	10.90	10.90	11.30	14.30	14.70	16.70	19.90	22.10

Instances built in this way allow to assess the impact of trip compatibility in the sharing of resources and the use of outsourcing. Random data generation associated with each instance considered the following:

- Each vehicle has an associated cost per km travelled, randomly calculated considering the size of the vehicle and considering as base the data obtained from a specialized company [15] from the city of São Paulo.
- For group 1, the number of seats of each vehicle was randomly generated, considering a variation of $+1$ or -1 from the original data. For group 2, only the smallest vehicles were considered.
- The number of passengers associated with each trip is generated from the original dataset, considering random changes between $+1$ or -1.
- The outsourcing costs were calculated based on the mean cost of the vehicles with smaller capacity ($\overline{C}_{vs}$), plus the average cost of drivers ($\overline{D}_m$) multiplied by the needed number of drivers for each trip (n_j) and divided by the average number of available seats in the smaller vehicles (Q_{vs}). This reference value is then multiplied by a number randomly generated (σ) within the interval $[-0,10; +0,30]$. The obtained result is then multiplied by the number of passengers associated with each trip (P_j). This means that $F_j = \left(\frac{\overline{C}_{vs} + \overline{D}_m \times n_j}{Q_{vs}} \right) \times \sigma \times P_j, \forall j$.

Complete data of all the problems are available at:
https://www.uc.pt/en/feuc/mjalves/DataFleetManagement/data_40inst
The computational experiments were run in an Intel Xeon Silver 4116, 2.1 GHz, 12-core CPU, 128 GB RAM. The general solver used was Cplex, with a time limit of 18000 s for all the instances to be solved. To be able to compare the behaviour of the

general solver applied to the whole problem and the decomposition method, whenever the decomposition approach needed more than 18000 s in total, Cplex was run again for the whole problem considering exactly the same total computational time.

4.2 Computational Results

We will first compare the times and objective function values (costs and gaps) obtained with the decomposition method and with the general solver. Then, the characteristics of the solutions will also be analysed.

Considering the instances from group 1, both Cplex and the decomposition approach were able to find the optimal solution in only 3 instances out of 20. It is possible to conclude that both methods have increased difficulties in solving the problems as the time overlapping increases, presenting successively larger gaps (the gap is greater than 80% for 1T). It was not possible to find the optimal solution for instances belonging to group 2, within the computational time limits defined. The same pattern of having an increased gap with an increased time overlapping of the trips is also observed, but the gaps obtained are lower than the ones obtained for group 1. For both groups, the decomposition method was able to find better solutions than Cplex in most of the instances, and it was able to produce better bounds for solutions with gap different from 0. However, the decomposition approach still leads to solutions with a significant optimality gap in instances where trips have a large overlapping. Tables 2 and 3 summarize these results.

Analysing the obtained solutions, it is possible to classify the assignment of resources to trips into three different classes: trips that share resources, trips that do not share resources and the ones that are outsourced. In group 1, on average, 83.44% of the trips shared resources, with this value varying between 69.67% and 94.26%. Outsourcing was used on average in 5.7% of the trips, reaching a maximum of 28.69% in one of the instances. Outsourcing shows a trend of increasing with the increase of the compatibility and time overlapping between trips. Actually, this increase in the compatibility and time overlapping can have two distinct consequences: until a certain point it will promote resource sharing; however, beyond a certain level, there are too many trips taking place at the same time and there are not enough resources to be able to cope with all the trips.

Instances in group 2 are characterized by having a homogeneous fleet of small vehicles. In this setting, it is necessary to resort to outsourcing much more frequently: on average 28.20% of the trips are outsourced, being the largest percentage equal to 47.54% for instance 2T. As the number of available seats per vehicle is small, the use of shared resources is limited even when there are compatible trips. It is more often used when all of the compatible trips have a low number of passengers. If this number increases, then the use of more own vehicles to assure the needed capacity turns out to be more expensive than outsourcing the trip. Whilst it is not possible to compare these solutions with solutions manually defined by the people in charge of this assignment, since some of the data have been randomly generated, we have already concluded that the use of this type of models leads to better solutions than the ones that are manually created for cases in which outsourcing was not considered [1]. Adding an extra degree of freedom (outsourcing) makes this problem even harder to solve manually, so we believe this is a valuable tool for organizations that have to deal with similar situations.

Table 2. Computational results obtained for Group 1 instances.

	Resolution of the whole problem by CPLEX				Decomposition method			
	Total time	Gap	Best solution	Best bound	Total time	Gap	Best solution	Best bound
1A	18000	0.66%	**31976.48**	31764.85	141	0.00%	**31976.48**	-
1B	276	0.01%	**30391.12**	30388.09	63	0.00%	**30391.12**	-
1C	18000	2.29%	**27894.15**	27256.47	15083	0.00%	**27894.15**	-
1D	25522	8.20%	**27803.4**	25524	25519	4.35%	27898.92	26686.07
1E	20021	4.30%	**29064.64**	27813.72	20017	1.76%	31192.36	30643.5
1F	54233	14.53%	25893.51	22130.57	54225	10.32%	**25417.85**	22795.84
1G	72707	24.43%	27115.35	20491.62	72695	18.53%	**26186.32**	21335.22
1H	54011	22.98%	27291.7	21021.09	54005	16.52%	**25867.43**	21594.41
1I	55315	27.97%	25802.17	18585.39	55314	19.86%	**24632.85**	19740.05
1J	37909	41.87%	26409.92	15352.56	37907	36.94%	**25667.31**	16186.59
1K	48158	40.09%	25699.41	15396.74	48156	31.64%	**23786.58**	16259.87
1L	67915	46.71%	28061.11	14953.62	67913	41.13%	**27567.88**	16229.4
1M	54025	47.45%	**27329.03**	14361.62	54010	44.18%	27461.56	15329.47
1N	83545	51.03%	23328.49	11424.56	83534	42.76%	**22378.8**	12810.28
1O	36038	55.02%	31715.1	14265.6	36036	51.14%	**29391.53**	14361.17
1P	36048	66.94%	37803.61	12497.98	36048	62.37%	**35402.92**	13320.81
1Q	36038	55.29%	29231.47	13069.63	36035	54.10%	**28746.54**	13194.22
1R	36007	70.27%	36607.29	10884.84	36007	68.49%	**34716.5**	10939.08
1S	36007	80.72%	**38410.77**	7403.76	36002	83.82%	44618.06	7217.68
1T	36005	82.53%	**44704.04**	7811.1	36004	82.37%	45873.14	8089.7

Finally, we would like to emphasise that these problems are difficult to solve but the use of a general solver has revealed to be more efficient than dedicated metaheuristics. The development of a metaheuristic for this problem is a highly complex task, due to the difficulty of guaranteeing solution feasibility. We have extended to the proposed model a *matheuristic* previously developed for the model without outsourcing [1]. However, the solutions obtained were worse than those obtained by Cplex. This observation motivated the development of the deterministic decomposition approach proposed in this paper.

Table 3. Computational results obtained for Group 2 instances.

	Resolution of the whole problem by CPLEX				Decomposition method			
	Total time	Gap	Best solution	Best bound	Total time	Gap	Best solution	Best bound
2A	16482	4.43%	67568.92	64575	18766	0.35%	**67465**	67232.1
2B	15582	6.76%	66131.35	61663.83	37200	0.66%	**66085.9**	65646.57
2C	37474	7.77%	65707.65	60603.58	37443	4.06%	**65622.18**	62959.46
2D	30898	16.95%	70947.14	58924.48	73070	8.20%	**70162.15**	64408.76
2E	52159	13.97%	70250.19	60436.07	52140	8.73%	**70097.85**	63980.04
2F	108093	26.66%	71599.11	52508.05	108076	16.26%	**70797.88**	59283.14
2G	72484	31.29%	68156.21	46829.34	72468	20.18%	**67327.06**	53742.24
2H	54035	24.77%	69505.31	52291.42	54033	22.50%	**68654.86**	53205.79
2I	90530	28.29%	79655.33	57124.12	90505	20.03%	**76243.93**	60970.8
2J	72304	34.65%	80162.45	52384.68	72302	26.36%	**78503.18**	57809.16
2K	36772	38.70%	75930.69	46542.57	36767	30.06%	**74588.05**	52165.52
2L	72122	43.72%	74247.11	41783.63	72120	33.39%	**71520.26**	47641.03
2M	54056	45.73%	78290.2	42488.9	54055	39.52%	**74851.17**	45273.35
2N	72038	45.07%	79071.17	43436.64	72035	32.01%	**76591.46**	52074.12
2O	36168	41.87%	80247.75	46644.7	36166	34.39%	**76516.2**	50204.98
2P	36093	46.92%	80112.62	42521.84	36092	41.61%	**77427.41**	45207.15
2Q	37002	51.29%	69498.76	33854.7	37002	43.52%	**68482.77**	38681.25
2R	36030	50.89%	80475.72	39520.84	36005	46.58%	**78894.72**	42146.03
2S	36006	63.21%	79986.84	29423.82	36002	60.26%	**79859.43**	31738.97
2T	36043	53.86%	88228.4	40712.68	36001	47.49%	**87748.68**	46080.04

5   Conclusions

This work presents a model and algorithmic approach for an extension of the GAP: the problem of assigning two distinct resources (drivers and vehicles) to a set of tasks (trips), where the assignment of one resource is dependent on the assignment of the other. If the tasks are compatible, they can share resources. The model also includes the possibility of outsourcing. This work was motivated by the identification of an existing decision-making problem in a public Brazilian University.

This problem is NP-hard and it has proved to be very difficult to solve by using a general solver (Cplex). This motivated the development of a dedicated approach based on the decomposition of the problem. Trips in the original instance can be iteratively divided into smaller disjoint sets, guaranteeing that there is no time overlapping between trips that are in distinct sets. The decomposition approach was able to calculate, for most of the instances, better solutions with lower gaps. Although the gaps obtained for instances with high overlapping between trips is still considerable, it is possible to conclude that the use of this model and the algorithmic approach can efficiently automate the decision-making process. It enables to reach solutions that are better than the solutions calculated manually promoting greater sharing of resources.

Acknowledgements. This work has been funded by national funds through FCT – Fundação para a Ciência e a Tecnologia, I.P., Projects UIBD/00308/2020 and UIDB/05037/2020. The first author has been supported by CAPES Proc. 009345/2013–02 BEX.

References

1. Monnerat, F., Dias, J., Alves, M.J.: Fleet management: a vehicle and driver assignment model. Eur. J. Oper. Res. **278**(1), 64–75 (2019). https://doi.org/10.1016/j.ejor.2019.03.021
2. Souza, A.L.S., Bernardo, M., Penna, P.H.V., Pannek, J., Souza, M.J.F.: Bi-objective optimization model for the heterogeneous dynamic dial-a-ride problem with no rejects. Optim. Lett. **5**, 1–20 (2021). https://doi.org/10.1007/s11590-020-01698-6
3. Lukman, R.K., Cerinšek, M., Virtič, P., Horvat, B.: Improving efficient resource usage and reducing carbon dioxide emissions by optimizing fleet management for winter services. J. Clean. Prod. **177**, 1–11 (2018). https://doi.org/10.1016/j.jclepro.2017.12.142
4. Hoff, A., Andersson, H., Christiansen, M., Hasle, G., Løkketangen, A.: Industrial aspects and literature survey: fleet composition and routing. Comput. Oper. Res. **37**, 2041–2061 (2010). https://doi.org/10.1016/j.cor.2010.03.015
5. Bielli, M., Bielli, A., Rossi, R.: Trends in models and algorithms for fleet management. Procedia - Soc. Behav. Sci. **20**, 4–18 (2011). https://doi.org/10.1016/j.sbspro.2011.08.004
6. Loxton, R., Lin, Q., Teo, K.L.: A stochastic fleet composition problem. Comput. Oper. Res. **39**, 3177–3184 (2012). https://doi.org/10.1016/j.cor.2012.04.004
7. Ertogral, K., Akbalik, A., González, S.: Modelling and analysis of a strategic fleet sizing problem for a furniture distributor. Eur. J. Ind. Eng. **11**, 49–77 (2017). https://doi.org/10.1504/EJIE.2017.081428
8. Markov, I., Varone, S., Bierlaire, M.: Integrating a heterogeneous fixed fleet and a flexible assignment of destination depots in the waste collection VRP with intermediate facilities. Transp. Res. Part B Methodol. **84**, 256–273 (2016). https://doi.org/10.1016/j.trb.2015.12.004
9. Shi, N., Song, H., Powell, W.B.: The dynamic fleet management problem with uncertain demand and customer chosen service level. Int. J. Prod. Econ. **148**, 110–121 (2014). https://doi.org/10.1016/j.ijpe.2013.09.010
10. Billhardt, H., et al.: Dynamic coordination in fleet management systems: toward smart cyber fleets. IEEE Intell. Syst. **20**, 70–76 (2014). https://doi.org/10.1109/MIS.2014.41
11. Hane, C.A., Barnhart, C., Johnson, E.L., Marsten, R.E., Nemhauser, G.L., Sigismondi, G.: The fleet assignment problem: Solving a large-scale integer program. Math. Program. **70**, 211–232 (1995). https://doi.org/10.1007/BF01585938
12. Abara, J.: Applying integer linear programming to the fleet assignment problem. Interfaces (Providence) **19**, 20–28 (1989). https://doi.org/10.1287/inte.19.4.20
13. Zhang, L., Gu, W., Fu, L., Mei, Y., Hu, Y.: A two-stage heuristic approach for fleet management optimization under time-varying demand. Transp. Res. Part E Logist. Transp. Rev. **147**, 102268 (2021). https://doi.org/10.1016/j.tre.2021.102268
14. Dauer, A.T., Prata, B.: Variable fixing heuristics for solving multiple depot vehicle scheduling problem with heterogeneous fleet and time windows. Optim. Lett. **15**(1), 153–170 (2020). https://doi.org/10.1007/s11590-020-01577-0
15. Tabelas de Frete Company: Jardim Paulista, São Paulo-SP, Brasil (2019). https://www.tabelasdefrete.com.br. Accessed 08 Aug 2019

A Two-Stage Heuristic for a Real Multi-compartment and Multi-trip Vehicle Routing Problem with Time Windows

Catarina Pena[2], Telmo Pinto[1,2(✉)] ⓘD, and Maria Sameiro Carvalho[2] ⓘD

[1] Univ Coimbra, CEMMPRE, DEM, Coimbra, Portugal
`telmo.pinto@dem.uc.pt`
[2] Centro ALGORITMI, Universidade do Minho, Braga, Portugal
`sameiro@dps.uminho.pt`

Abstract. This paper addresses the multi-compartment and multi-trip vehicle routing problem in a fuel distribution company. A decision support system (DSS) to automatically produce daily routing plans was developed. The company delivers three fuel types using a heterogeneous fleet of multi-compartmented vehicles with a maximum capacity expressed in fuel liters. Additional and real constraints are imposed, such as time windows and compulsory breaks. A constructive heuristic based on the Clarke and Wright savings algorithm was adapted in order to embed all business constraints. This constructive heuristic was developed in three steps. In the first step, all the previously mentioned constraints were taken into account. In the second version of the algorithm, the multi-trip case was incorporated. In order to improve the quality of the solution, an exchange of compartments mechanism and two local search procedures were developed. One of the local procedures was based on local search movements within each route, while the other one was based on movements between distinct routes. Solutions are displayed using a georeferenced-based platform allowing for a spatial representation of data to be analyzed. The achieved results show that the total traveled distance can be reduced by approximately 14%. The main contribution of this work is to offer the company a DSS for route planning without any additional cost that may enable fast and efficient planning of the entire company's distribution sector.

Keywords: Vehicle routing problem · Multi-compartment · Multi-trip · Decision support system · Fuel distribution

1 Introduction

Nowadays, and in the scope of the Industry 4.0, companies are exploring the use of Information and Communication Technologies (ICT). This exploration will allow higher efficiency and better effectiveness of their operations while

© Springer Nature Switzerland AG 2021
O. Gervasi et al. (Eds.): ICCSA 2021, LNCS 12953, pp. 274–289, 2021.
https://doi.org/10.1007/978-3-030-86976-2_19

enhancing the organization's faster adjustment to the current dynamic environment. One of the areas where these technologies should be developed is the distribution [21].

In the distribution field, the Vehicle Routing Problem (VRP) plays an important role. Generally, the objective of VRP is to build a set of routes that minimize transport costs, associating a vehicle and a driver to each route, starting and ending in the same depot, so that all customers are served, taking into account that their demand is previously known. However, several constraints are inherent to the real problems that depend mainly on the nature of the products to be transported, the quality of service required, and the features of customers and vehicles. Such issues may significantly increase the complexity of these problems [2].

In this paper, we present a real-world problem context arising from the distribution sector. More precisely, we address the case of a Portuguese retail fuel distribution company. Usually, this type of company has restricted access to any decision support systems, using basic procedures to deliver a set of tours for each vehicle. Typically, the quality of routing solutions highly depends on the previous experience of the planner operator and/or vehicle drivers. Such approach lacks systematization and does not ensure the efficiency of produced solutions or acceptable levels of service. These facts strongly motivated our approach: the overall objective of this paper is to provide a decision support system to the distribution problem of a company in the fuel retail distribution sector. The motivation of this paper is to deepen the promising results of a previous work presented in [19]. In that contribution, the authors only addressed two constructive approaches: one of them considers the route planning without replenishments, and the other one considers the multi-trip case instead.

Additionally, we suggest another constructive approach and a local search method based on two neighborhood structures. Furthermore, a decision support system was developed using *Microsoft Excel* (under *Visual Basic Language platform*) combined with an interactive interface providing several functionalities to allow daily planning operations such as the record of new customers, new orders processing, and the design of a set of routes to be performed by the existing resources in a predefined slot of time. Additionally, the integration with a geographical information system and the inclusion of optimization procedures provides efficient solutions and, at the same time, allows the production of several reporting features to improve the overall performance of the distribution system.

This paper is organized as follows. Section 2 presents a brief state of art concerning VRP and, particularly, VRP with fuel distribution. Section 3 presents the definition of the real problem at the company. The solution methods are presented in Sect. 4. Section 5 describes the DSS developed at the company. Section 6 shows computational experiments, and the obtained results are discussed. Finally, Sect. 7 reports the main conclusions and final considerations regarding some possible future developments.

2   Literature Review

A huge number of variants and extensions can be found in the literature. We will give focus to the most common ones, and the most related one to the problem addressed in this paper, as follows:

- Capacitated Vehicle Routing Problem (CVRP): It is the basic version of the VRP. The name derives from the constraint of having vehicles with limited capacity Q. Customer demands are deterministic and known in advance. Deliveries cannot be split, and thus an order cannot be served using two or more vehicles. The vehicle fleet is homogeneous, and there is only one depot [22,24];
- Vehicle Routing Problem with Time Windows (VRPTW): In this VRP variant, the capacity constraint still holds and each customer i is associated with a time window $[a_i, b_i]$ and with a service time s_i. The nature of the time windows could be soft or hard. In the first case, the customer may be served after the upper bound of the time window, but a penalty is set for the service. In the second case, the same is not possible. If the vehicle arrives at a customer earlier than a_i, the vehicle must wait until the service is possible [16,22,24];
- Multi-Compartment Vehicle Routing Problem (MCVRP): In this variant, vehicles are compartmented in order to deliver products that are incompatible [15] or if their contact may be unstable or even dangerous. On the other hand, different types of products may need different conditions. The most common real-world examples are the trucks for selective waste collection or the petroleum distribution systems that deliver different types of fuel to retailers using multi-compartmented vehicles;
- Multi-Trip VRP (MTVRP): In this variant, the focus is given to the distribution of low quantities of products, and thus, several routes may be performed by each vehicle [5].

Note that the main goal is to minimize the overall cost or the traveled distance in all variants. According to [23], the data requirements and the complexity of urban planning and transportation problems have caused a growing interest in the use of decision support systems at the operational, tactical, and strategic planning levels. The significance and ability to use DSS to assist in fleet management on a daily or weekly basis has been widely recognized. Once adequate graphical interfaces are very important to represent solutions in routing problems given their strong spatial component. ICT can also play an important role in constructing user-friendly tools embedding algorithms, graphical interfaces, and access to remote data through the Internet [14,23].

The VRP was introduced in [12], exactly for the fuel transportation problem. Since then, this problem has awakened the interest of several researchers. Thus, in the last decades, several versions of the VRP for fuel transportation have been developed. In this section, a brief review of the literature contributions in this area is presented. Table 1 summarizes the main research works and dimensions addressed in the context of the fuel distribution problem.

The station replenishment problem is closely related to MCVRP, due to the different types of fuel that these companies transport. In [12], multi-compartment vehicles or the heterogeneous fleet variant are not considered. However, the authors recognized that it was important to include these variables.

Most of the contributions referred to in Table 1 tackled the multi-compartment VRP variant. However, only two approaches took into account time windows, and just three approaches considered the multi-trip case. The contribution presenting the highest number of variables is presented in [8]. However, the number of customers visited on each trip was limited to six since each compartment could only load one order. The last two contributions gave great importance to inventory management too. Additionally, due to the complexity of this type of problem, only three exact approaches were presented.

Table 1. Main characteristics of fuel distribution VRP problems, adapted from [8,19].

Ref.	Unlimited fleet	Homogeneous fleet	Multi-compartment	Time windows	Customers (each route)	Multi-trip	Exact approach
[12]	Yes	Yes	No	No	Several	No	No
[3]	No	No	Yes	No	Several	Yes	No
[1]	No	No	Yes	No	Several	No	Yes
[18]	No	No	Yes	No	Several	No	Yes
[9]	Yes	No	Yes	No	Up two	No	Yes
[10]	No	No	Yes	No	Up two	No	No
[11]	No	No	Yes	Yes	Up four	Yes	No
[8]	No	No	Yes	Yes	Up six	Yes	No
[20]	Yes	Yes	Yes	No	Up three	No	No
[25]	Yes	Yes	Yes	No	Up four	No	No
[26]	Yes	No	Yes	No	Several	Yes	Yes

3   Problem Description

This paper addresses the case of a Portuguese fuel retailer in the north of the country. Due to its chemical characteristics, fuel is included in the group of dangerous goods [4]. For this reason, it is guided by stricter legislation when compared to ordinary goods.

Three types of fuel are delivered (road, agricultural, and heating diesel) from a warehouse to several customers geographically dispersed in the north of Portugal (approximately 25 customers). The company has a heterogeneous fleet of four vehicles with multiple compartments of different capacities for fuel distribution: one vehicle has five compartments, the other two vehicles have two compartments and, the smallest vehicle has one compartment.

The company receives several orders to be performed on the following day. Each order is composed of the product type, product quantity, an interval of time in which the delivery may occur (time window), the address of the customer, and the road access constraints if any.

Before this work, the routes were planned in the early morning for each day. It is important to note that before the DSS implementation for route planning, this planning was empirically performed by a distribution manager, and the routes were defined by drivers. In the first phase, the employee responsible for the operational management of this area distributes orders by available drivers. In a second phase, the drivers create routes empirically based on their experience. If a new customer in an unknown area arises, the drivers use Google Maps to help to achieve the new location. Therefore, it was a disaggregated planning process involving several people and with a low level of control.

Frequently, the same driver returns to the depot to reload the vehicle, and it performs a new route. Therefore, the multi-trip variant must be considered.

The objective function is the sum of all traveled distances. However, there is a set of issues related to the level of service that will be analyzed.

4   Solution Method

Due to the complexity of the addressed problem, we suggest a two-stage heuristic that guarantees a global solution. The first stage consists of the application and adaptation of the well-known Clarke and Wright savings algorithm [6] as it was proposed in [19] for this problem. In the second stage, a local search approach is suggested. In order to make our paper self-contained, we present the two constructive heuristic approaches from [19], followed by the presentation of our newly developed procedures. Note that the authors considered first the relaxed algorithm version without considering the multi-trip variant. Therefore, and since the vehicle's compartments have different capacities, a mechanism was embedded to increase the efficiency of the solutions through the exchange of products among each compartment. We called it the exchange of compartments mechanism.

Constructive Heuristic without Multi-Trip – V1 [19]. The Clarke and Wright savings algorithm [6] has two versions: the parallel and the sequential version. In our constructive approach, the parallel version is used due to its performance. The algorithm was implemented in the following steps:

Step 1. For each pair of customers (i, j), a saving is computed by $S_{ij} = C_{i0} + C_{0j} - C_{ij}$ with $i, j = 1, \ldots, n$ and $i < j$, where C_{ij} represents the cost of traveling from i to j.

Step 2. Create n routes $(0, i, 0)$ for $i = 1, \ldots, n$ where n is the number of customers.

Step 3. Order the savings in decreasing order.

Step 4. Order the vehicles in decreasing order of capacity.

Step 5. Starting from the first saving, and for each saving S_{ij}, test if there are two routes, one starting with $(0, i, \ldots, 0)$ and other ending with $(0, \ldots, j, 0)$ that can be feasibly merged. Whenever two routes are combined, $(0, i, 0)$ and $(0, j, 0)$ are deleted and the arc (i, j) is introduced. This process is repeated while $S_{ij} \geq 0$.

When two single customers are merged, the first available vehicle (starting from the vehicle with the largest capacity) is assigned to the route. A feasible merge is performed when all capacity constraints and time windows are satisfied. The product load is distributed by the vehicle compartments. If the time windows are not feasible initially, the feasibility of the route is verified in reverse order. A solution with unvisited customers was considered as a feasible solution since the company makes the same assumption. If this happens, the customer is assigned to the next plan, providing that the time window constraint is always satisfied.

Constructive Heuristics with Multi-Trip Case – V2 [19]**.** In a second step, the replenishments were incorporated into the algorithm, i.e., the multi-trip case. Each vehicle performs a set of trips $T_b = \{1, \ldots, |T_b|\}$, in each planning period.

New Constructive Heuristics with Multi-Trip and an Exchange of Compartments Mechanism – V3. In this version of the algorithm, an exchange of compartments mechanism was incorporated. The aim of this mechanism is to improve the quality of solutions generated by the constructive heuristic through the load exchange between every two compartments, whenever it is possible. In Fig. 1, an order of 600 liters of heating diesel must be introduced into the vehicle. As it can be seen, in the initial phase, it is not possible to introduce 600 liters of heating diesel into the vehicle. So, the exchange of compartments mechanism starts by testing the load exchange between compartments 1 and 2. However, Fig. 2 shows that this exchange is not possible since the load in compartment 1 is larger than the capacity of compartment 2. Thus, the exchange is not performed. Thereafter, the load exchange between compartments 1 and 3 is tested. However, this movement does not enable the introduction of the order since the heating oil compartment remains the same, as shown in Fig. 3. Once again, the movement is not performed. The last movement tested is the load exchange between compartments 2 and 3. As it can be seen in Fig. 4, this movement allows the introduction of the order (600 liters of heating diesel) into the vehicle. Thus, this exchange is performed. The final solution is presented in Fig. 5. This mechanism finishes when a better feasible solution is found or when all movements are tested.

Subsequently, two local search procedures were implemented, aiming to improve the quality of solutions. The first one is based on movements within each route, while the second one is based on movements between two routes. Both mechanisms are presented below.

Intra-Route Local Search – V3,1. For each iteration, this local search mechanism tests the exchange of positions between two customers in the same route. If the objective function is minimized and the solution remains feasible, the movement (exchange of positions between the customers) is made. This process is repeated for all pairs of customers in all the routes generated by the constructive heuristic. For the sake of clarity, an example is provided in Fig. 6: it is possible to observe that movement $(C1, C2)$, starting from an initial route

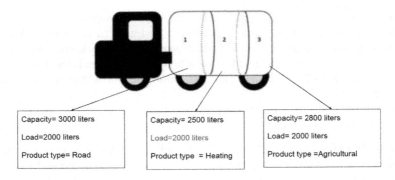

Fig. 1. Exchange of compartments: initial phase (adapted from [7]).

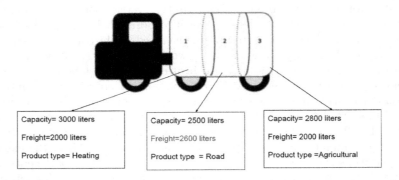

Fig. 2. Exchange of compartments: movement 1 (adapted from [7]).

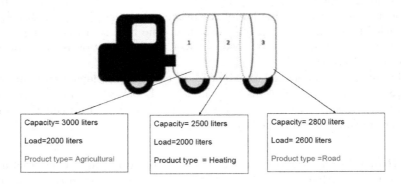

Fig. 3. Exchange of compartments: movement 2 (adapted from [7]).

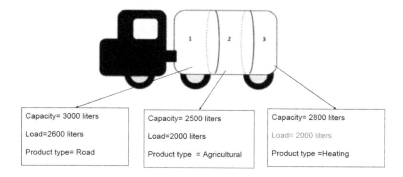

Fig. 4. Exchange of compartments: movement 3 (adapted from [7]).

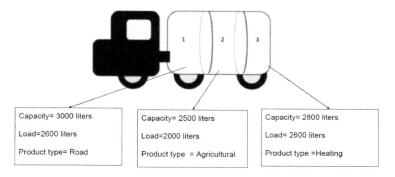

Fig. 5. Example of the exchange of compartments mechanism – final solution (adapted from [7]).

R_i. If the movement produces a decrease in the value of the objective function, the movement is performed, and the process is restarted with the new obtained route (new R_i). If the movement does not minimize the value of the objective function, no change is made to the original route, thus advancing to the next movement (C1, C3). This process must be repeated until all movements for all routes are tested.

Local Search Between Two Routes – V3,2. The second mechanism of local search introduced in the algorithm is based on relocate movements applied in [17]. Each movement requires the specification of two stops. For each customer, a neighbor list is built. The maximum size of the neighbor list is three. The neighbor list is composed of the three nearest customers in a different route. The movement (C3, S2) is presented in Fig. 7: two movements are tested: the first one is the insertion of customer S2 in the position immediately before C3, and the second movement tests the insertion of S2 in the position immediately after C3.

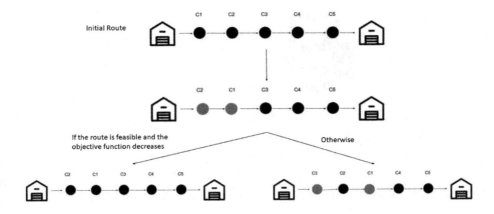

Fig. 6. Example of intra-route local search.

5   Decision Support System

A decision support system was developed using *Visual Basic Language* from *Microsoft*, using the VRP Spreadsheet Solver [13] as a starting platform. *Microsoft Excel* was considered by the company as the most convenient solution since the company is already familiar with this software. The architecture of the DSS is illustrated in Fig. 8.

Any process is made up of an input, output and a rule set, which limits the process. The DSS also works as a process. The inputs for this DSS are:

- Depot, opening hour and loading time;
- Data set of orders: customer ID number, name and address, delivery address, quantity, type of product, time windows, service time, and access restrictions;
- Set of available vehicles.

This DSS has a database with information about customers, with the ID number, name, address, geographical coordinates, and access constraints. The customer information is automatically inserted just by filling in the customer ID number. If the customer is not on the database, the user will be informed, and the customer data may be inserted into the database before introducing the order. The geographical coordinates of the customer address can be introduced by the user or be computed by the DSS. Additionally, the DSS also has a database with information about vehicles, with the license plate, fuel consumption per 100 km, number of compartments, and capacity. This database can also be edited. If all data is inserted, the user can generate planning through the selection of this option. The main output is a set of routes, each one assigned to a vehicle. Furthermore, the developed DSS also returns a set of complementary information associated with each route, such as the arrival and departure time for each customer and the depot; waiting time at each customer; route length (in Kilometers); fuel consumption (in Liters); route time (in hours); quantity and

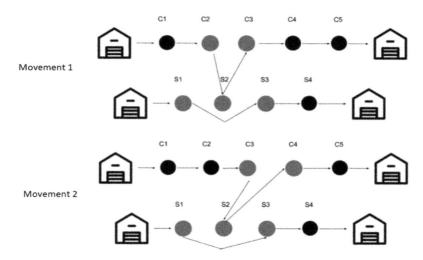

Fig. 7. Local search between two routes adapted from [17].

type of product assigned to each compartment and the vehicle usage. A table is generated for each route with the information referred to above. Additionally, the set of routes can be visualized on a map, as seen in Fig. 9. In this example, the starting point is the warehouse 20 and 7 customers are visited through three routes.

Finally, the user can analyze the generated routes. Then, he/she can validate all routes or eliminate one or more routes. In the end, the main data of each validated route are added to a database, with the generation date, vehicle's license place, starting and ending time, fuel consumption, the number of customers, and quantity of each type of fuel transported. So, the KPIs (Key Performance Indicators) are updated. The measured KPIs are the number of routes, the traveled distance, the fuel consumption, the visited customers, the quantity loaded of each type of product.

Additionally, this information is also presented in a set of charts, which are related to the different parameters analyzed by a period of time that can be defined by the user Fig. 10, such as: bar chart of traveled distance; bar chart of fuel consumption; bar chart of the number of visited clients; bar chart of the amount of each type of loaded fuel; bar chart of the number of visited clients per vehicle; Pie chart of the quantity loaded of each type of product. This feature allows the graphical visualization of performance indicators, referred to above, and it is constantly updated. So, the developed DSS takes into account the capacity of each compartment, time windows, and customers' access constraints. Additionally, the DSS also considers that different types of products cannot be mixed. The DSS needs internet access to operate since the real distances among customers, the distances between customers and the depot, and the geographical coordinates are calculated through *Bing Maps*.

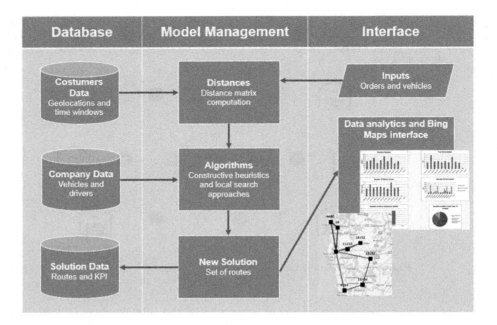

Fig. 8. Architecture of the DSS.

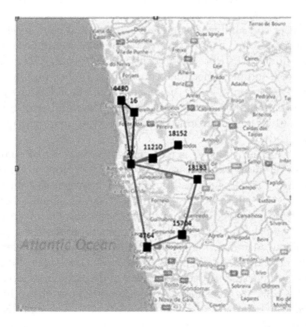

Fig. 9. Interface for visualization of routes on a map.

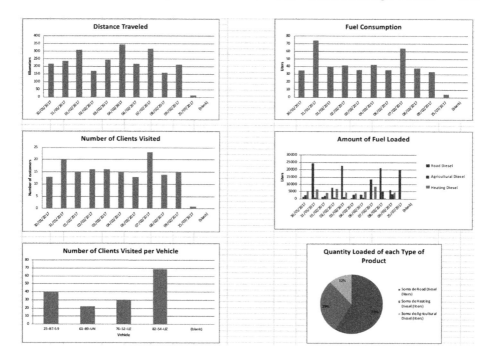

Fig. 10. Graphical representation of performance indicators accounted for by DSS.

6   Computational Results

In order to validate solutions produced by the DSS, data from the company was collected for 10 consecutive days (excluding Sunday). During these days, the drivers reported the traveled routes, the used vehicles, and the traveled distance. Combining this information with the list of deliveries for each planning period makes it possible to compute all parameters.

Five performance indicators have been used to assess the overall performance of the distribution system and to validate and compare obtained solutions: traveled distance (in kilometers); fuel consumption (in liters); time spent on distribution (in hours); average vehicle usage and the level of service. As for the level of service, the percentage of delivered orders was considered. In order to approach the real scenario, in each planning procedure it was considered: a set of vehicles used in the company; an average speed of 55Km/h; a loading time of 20 min; service time of 15 min and depot opening time from 8 a.m. until 7 p.m. Note that times and average speed are based on the collected data in the period referred to above. The five versions of the algorithm presented above were tested using real instances, and the results from computational experiments are shown in Table 2.

In the three first parameters (traveled distance, time spent on distribution, and fuel consumption), Table 2 shows that all versions of the algorithm present

Table 2. Results of real case and 5 versions of algorithm

Parameters	Real case	V1	V2	V3	V3,1	V3,2
Traveled distance (kilometers)	2828,5	2883	2621	2443	2428	2428
Time spent on distribution (Hours)	538,5	517,6	457,4	443,2	440,5	440,1
Fuel consumption	132,3	112,1	111,2	107,2	106,7	106,7
Level of service	93%	96%	97%	96%	96%	96%
Average vehicle usage	57%	66%	59%	56%	56%	57%

gradually better results with the increase of complexity of algorithms. Nevertheless, V1 presents a larger amount of traveled distance than the real case. However, this version also presents a higher average vehicle usage. The largest variations are found between V1 and V3. Both versions of V3 do not present a significant impact on the analyzed parameters. All versions present a higher level of service than the real case, but V2 has the best result for this parameter. The behavior of the traveled distance is shown in Fig. 11: V1 presents a traveled distance increase of 2% when compared to the real case. All other versions of the algorithm present a traveled distance in the overall solution that is lower than the one in the real case.

The results of the final algorithm show a 14% reduction in traveled distance, an 18% reduction in fuel consumption, a 19% reduction in time spent on distribution, and an increment of 3% in the level of service. The average vehicle usage remains the same. During the analyzed period, 166 orders were collected. The computational times increased slightly with the increase of the algorithm complexity. However, just a few seconds are needed to have a solution.

The first version of the algorithm does not take into account the multi-trip case. However, after testing several daily plans, the computational results presented had worse performances when compared to the results of the real case in terms of traveled distance. This fact is due to the shortest planning horizon. In many cases, since the possibility of performing multi-trips was not considered, the first saving values (merges) were wasted due to the lack of capacity of vehicles or to the time windows constraints.

As expected, in the first three parameters (traveled distance, time spent on distribution, and fuel consumption), the overall solution quality increases with the complexity of the algorithms. Although V3,1 and V3,2 have a better global solution, it has very similar values in all parameters and close values to the V3. Therefore, the local search contribution did not have a major impact. Version V2 has the highest level of service. Nevertheless, all versions of the algorithm have a global solution better than the real case regarding this parameter. Table 2 shows that the best usage of vehicle capacity is performed by V1.

The potential savings of the proposed DSS consists of a reduction of up to 5900 km, 1700 Fuel liters, and 640 work hours per year. These values were calculated through an arithmetic average of 258 working days per year. This is the number of days of distribution in the company during a given year.

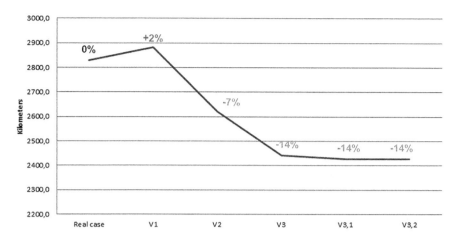

Fig. 11. Percentage changing in traveled distance parameter, compared to the real case.

7 Conclusions and Future Work

In this paper, a two-stage heuristic for a real-world multi-compartment VRP problem is proposed. Some real constraints are considered, such as the limited capacity, time windows, multi-compartments. Different approaches were developed: the first version without replenishments; the second one considers the multi-trip case; the third version also includes an exchange of compartments mechanism and finally, the last two versions of the algorithm with two local search procedures. The first one is an intra-route local search method, and the second one is a local search inter-route method. Generally, the last version of the algorithm (V3,2) is the most robust algorithm version. Therefore, this is the version to be incorporated into the DSS.

Despite positive results found in preliminary tests, the main contribution of this work is to offer to the company a DSS for route planning without any additional cost. This enables fast and efficient planning of the entire distribution sector. Currently, route planning is an automatic process that can be validated by the distribution manager. Real-world situations have a lot of unpredictable variables and, for this reason, any output of DSS may need human validation. Additionally, the DSS allows the company to monitor with detail the distribution activity.

Future work may include: the extension of the analyzed period to be used as an instance for computational experiments; the incorporation of multi-depot variant into the algorithm; the distinction between hard and soft time windows, and thus the user could choose if the time windows must be respected or if the time windows should be respected. The future work referred to above will increase the complexity of algorithms. Therefore, more efficient methods should be implemented to tackle that complexity.

Acknowledgements. This research is sponsored by national funds through FCT – Fundação para a Ciência e a Tecnologia, under the project UIDB/00285/ 2020. This work has been also supported by FCT – Fundação para a Ciência e Tecnologia within the R&D Units Project Scope: UIDB/00319/2020.

References

1. Avella, P., Boccia, M., Sforza, A.: Solving a fuel delivery problem by heuristic and exact approaches. Eur. J. Oper. Res. **152**(1), 170–179 (2004)
2. Baldacci, R., Bartolini, E., Mingozzi, A., Roberti, R.: An exact solution framework for a broad class of vehicle routing problems. CMS **7**(3), 229–268 (2010)
3. Brown, G.G., Graves, G.W.: Real-time dispatch of petroleum tank trucks. Manage. Sci. **27**(1), 19–32 (1981)
4. Cardoso, V.M.: The road transport of dangerous goods in Portugal (O transporte rodoviário de mercadorias perigosas em Portugal). Revista Segurança **224**, 22–27 (2015)
5. Cattaruzza, D., Absi, N., Feillet, D., Vidal, T.: A memetic algorithm for the multi trip vehicle routing problem. Eur. J. Oper. Res. **236**(3), 833–848 (2014)
6. Clarke, G., Wright, J.W.: Scheduling of vehicles from a central depot to a number of delivery points. Oper. Res. **12**(4), 568–581 (1964)
7. Coelho, L.C., Laporte, G.: Classification, models and exact algorithms for multi-compartment delivery problems. Eur. J. Oper. Res. **242**(3), 854–864 (2015)
8. Cornillier, F., Boctor, F., Renaud, J.: Heuristics for the multi-depot petrol station replenishment problem with time windows. Eur. J. Oper. Res. **220**(2), 361–369 (2012)
9. Cornillier, F., Boctor, F.F., Laporte, G., Renaud, J.: An exact algorithm for the petrol station replenishment problem. J. Oper. Res. Soc. **59**(5), 607–615 (2008)
10. Cornillier, F., Boctor, F.F., Laporte, G., Renaud, J.: A heuristic for the multi-period petrol station replenishment problem. Eur. J. Oper. Res. **191**(2), 295–305 (2008)
11. Cornillier, F., Laporte, G., Boctor, F.F., Renaud, J.: The petrol station replenishment problem with time windows. Comput. Oper. Res. **36**(3), 919–935 (2009)
12. Dantzig, G.B., Ramser, J.H.: The truck dispatching problem. Manage. Sci. **6**(1), 80–91 (1959)
13. Erdoğan, G.: An open source spreadsheet solver for vehicle routing problems. Comput. Oper. Res. **84**, 62–72 (2017)
14. Lin, C., Choy, K.L., Ho, G.T., Lam, H., Pang, G.K., Chin, K.S.: A decision support system for optimizing dynamic courier routing operations. Expert Syst. Appl. **41**(15), 6917–6933 (2014)
15. Mendoza, J.E., Castanier, B., Guéret, C., Medaglia, A.L., Velasco, N.: A memetic algorithm for the multi-compartment vehicle routing problem with stochastic demands. Comput. Oper. Res. **37**(11), 1886–1898 (2010)
16. Mester, D., Bräysy, O.: Active guided evolution strategies for large-scale vehicle routing problems with time windows. Comput. Oper. Res. **32**(6), 1593–1614 (2005)
17. Muyldermans, L., Pang, G.: On the benefits of co-collection: experiments with a multi-compartment vehicle routing algorithm. Eur. J. Oper. Res. **206**(1), 93–103 (2010)
18. Ng, W.L., Leung, S., Lam, J., Pan, S.: Petrol delivery tanker assignment and routing: a case study in Hong Kong. J. Oper. Res. Soc. **59**(9), 1191–1200 (2008)

19. Pena, C.M.D., Pinto, T., Carvalho, M.S.: A constructive heuristic for the multi-compartment vehicle routing problem: an approach for a fuel distribution company (2017)
20. Popović, D., Vidović, M., Radivojević, G.: Variable neighborhood search heuristic for the inventory routing problem in fuel delivery. Expert Syst. Appl. **39**(18), 13390–13398 (2012)
21. Ramos, T.R.P., de Morais, C.S., Barbosa-Póvoa, A.P.: The smart waste collection routing problem: alternative operational management approaches. Expert Syst. Appl. **103**, 146–158 (2018)
22. Rizzoli, A.E., Montemanni, R., Lucibello, E., Gambardella, L.M.: Ant colony optimization for real-world vehicle routing problems. Swarm Intell. **1**(2), 135–151 (2007)
23. Santos, L., Coutinho-Rodrigues, J., Antunes, C.H.: A web spatial decision support system for vehicle routing using google maps. Decis. Support Syst. **51**(1), 1–9 (2011)
24. Toth, P., Vigo, D.: Vehicle routing: problems, methods, and applications. Soc. Ind. Appl. Math. (2014)
25. Vidović, M., Popović, D., Ratković, B.: Mixed integer and heuristics model for the inventory routing problem in fuel delivery. Int. J. Prod. Econ. **147**, 593–604 (2014)
26. Wang, L., Kinable, J., Van Woensel, T.: The fuel replenishment problem: a split-delivery multi-compartment vehicle routing problem with multiple trips. Comput. Oper. Res. **118**, 104904 (2020)

On the Integration of Industrial Data and Analysis with Simulation in a Company of the Cork Sector

Catarina Mesquita[1], António A. C. Vieira[2,3] 🆔, Luís Dias[2(✉)] 🆔,
Guilherme B. Pereira[2] 🆔, and José A. Oliveira[2]

[1] Department of Production and Systems, University of Minho, Braga, Portugal
a77642@alunos.uminho.pt
[2] ALGORITMI Research Centre, University of Minho, Braga, Portugal
{antonio.vieira,lsd,gui,zan}@dps.uminho.pt
[3] CEFAGE Research Centre, University of Évora, Évora, Portugal
avieira@uevora.pt

Abstract. Nowadays, companies are constantly seeking to develop tools to increase productivity, production flexibility and the quality of their products, or to reduce costs, delays and their exposure to risks. In fact, such improvements can be achieved in the scope of product as well as of process improvement. In industrial contexts, often, such improvements can be achieved by implementing tools to access the intended information in due time, such as Decision Support Tools. Aligned with the aforementioned, this project was developed in the context of a cork industry, dedicated to the agglomeration of cork and other materials, such as rubber, foams and recycled plastics, and the transformation of these same agglomerates into products, such as joints, footwear, floors, consumer goods, acoustic coatings and sports surfaces. More specifically, tools for the automated access to information were developed, namely, a reference search tool that meets the specified requirements of managers from the company, as well as a tool to search the available dimensions or production steps for a given product. Moreover, and infield of process improvement, a set of simulation models were also developed using SIMIO. First, there was a survey and parameterization of the critical factors of the line, so that the simulation could be elaborated, and afterwards the balancing of the system was studied, considering different scenarios. Depending on the type of roll to be produced and according to the type of packaging, the balancing of the system varies. Other scenarios were studied for when the system is not balanced, in order to avoid this occurrence. All in all, the set of tools that were developed led to a considerable reduction of the time spent by human resources on accessing critical information, as well as an improvement of the analysis of their industrial processes.

Keywords: Information integration · Cork industry · Decision Support Tools · Simulation · Process improvement · Product improvement

O. Gervasi et al. (Eds.): ICCSA 2021, LNCS 12953, pp. 290–303, 2021.
https://doi.org/10.1007/978-3-030-86976-2_20

1   Introduction

Companies are constantly aiming for the overall improvement of their products and processes. In fact, such constant pursue allows them to attain benefits such as the increase of productivity, production flexibility and the quality of their products, or the reduction of several costs, amongst others. Nevertheless, a critical barrier to such goals is often the access to critical industrial information in due time. As such, the conception of solid Decision Support Tools (DST) is mandatory, which should allow the access to the intended industrial information, as well as assist sound decision-making concerning industrial processes [1].

The scope of this work consists of a project conducted in the area of industrial and engineering management in a real company of the cork industry. In this company, the need to develop a set of tools that could facilitate and automate the access to industrial information, as a more efficient overview and analysis of certain critical processes arose. To address this need, tools for automation of information search were developed using standard and widely adopted tools in industry, such as Microsoft Excel, Microsoft Access and VBA (Visual Basic for Applications). As such, the purpose of this paper is to document this work, emphasizing the main faced difficulties in working in a real industrial environment, as well as in establishing the main benefits that were achieved.

Microsoft Excel is a widely popular spreadsheet due to its versatility. It is useful to analyze data, create charts, automate tasks with macros, among other functions [2, 3]. VBA allows automating, customizing and extending the functionalities of Microsoft Excel, through programming code. In this way, it allows the development of applications, such as functions and procedures that respond to the needs of data analysis [4].

In its turn, Microsoft Access allows the development of database management systems, is easy to use, access and distribute. Access is often the first choice of relational database software, since it is possible to quickly create useful database solutions, and is widely available for industry community. It may not have all the performance features of other software used by the community specialized in database management solutions, such as SQL Server, but for many situations it has the most frequently used or necessary features. In fact, there are many challenges that can be solved by Access, without having to invest in expensive and complex software [5, 6].

The design of a DST should address business problems and questions with well-defined purposes. However, the risk of developing muscle artifacts without added value is high and it is therefore important to have a considerable background in the area of industrial management, which represents an important advantage in the development of these artifacts. For example, the application of Lean principles and tools might allow the acceleration of the creation and development of software.

Regarding process improvement, the requirement to simulate certain production lines of rewinding and automatic packaging of composite agglomerated rollers for the study of system balancing, according to the characteristics of the roller and packaging, also arose. Simulation involves the generation of an artificial history of the real system and its observation and analysis, in order to extract data or conclusions (inferences) about the operational characteristics of the represented real system [7]. In fact, simulation is a very convenient methodology for assessing a possible solution, and the interactions between these elements over time, under stochastic conditions, due to its ability to study complex systems that involve a set of resources with their own characteristics, machines, human collaborators, random factors, availability of secondary material, energy, location of each of these concepts, movement of raw materials, warehouses, queues, and others. Through the simulation of the system, it was possible to analyze and study the balancing of several scenarios, according to the characteristics of the rolls and the packaging. For unbalanced scenarios, alternatives were studied to avoid this occurrence.

This paper is structured as follows. Second section discusses the materials and methods used in this research, i.e., it starts by identifying the relevance of the problem at hand, so that the adopted methodology can be explained thereafter. Third section describes the interaction with the set of tools developed for the access to product data under several dimensions. Fourth section describes the set of simulation models that were developed for the purpose of allowing a better analysis of critical processes, and, finally, last section discusses the main findings and establishes future research topics aligned with this research.

2 Materials and Methods

This section describes the materials and methods used in this research. The section starts by identifying the description of the critical situations that were observed whilst conducting the initial field observations. Bearing the most relevant issues and other aspects in mind, a methodology was established for this research, which is described in the second subsection.

2.1 Problem Statement

The issues that originated this research can be summarized as related to process and product improvement. As such, the first group of issues concerns the access to critical product information, hence allowing more efficient analysis to the products of the company. The second group consists of being able to better analyze the processes to which said products go through.

Access to Critical Product Information
In the operations section of the cork company, there are several departments, one of them is Engineering, which encompasses, in turn, other sub-departments: the Product Engineering, Design Engineering, Continuous Improvement and Circular Economy. Each of these departments is responsible for fulfilling the established tasks.

The Product Engineering Department, among other activities, is responsible for responding to information requested by customers from the commercial department. For example, information on which references can meet certain requirements and on the possibility of designing a new product.

A reference consists of a four-digit code and for each reference the components and their proportions used to obtain a given mixture are determined. From this mixture one can agglomerate blocks, cylinders and/or sheets cured with the required thickness (FCE). However, for each of the references it is established which molds can be used.

The requirements that customers can choose are, for example, material density, product dimensions and type of finish. The product engineering team has this type of information gathered in Excel files, or is contained in the memory of some collaborators.

When a customer requests a new product, it is also the responsibility of the product engineering to study the possibility of designing that product and associate an internal production cost. To this end, it is necessary to define the agglomerate to be used, to analyze the technical limitations of the equipment and, if the production of this new product is feasible, to define the production processes through which the material has to pass.

In order to answer which references, limitations were found in the reference selection work, as there is a dispersion of information in several files, which leads to more time spent in searching, retention of information in supervisors or other employees, that hinders access to this information and increases the possibility of human errors, and the absence of research automation tools that facilitate the search of information.

In order to study the possibility of designing a new product, the Engineering Department not only needs to know the characteristics of each reference, but also needs to know the technical limitations of the equipment and the various production flows that exist. This information is also dispersed in several files or is retained in the memory of some supervisors or other collaborators. These conditions, again, cause more time to be spent searching for information and a greater likelihood of human error. Moreover, the absence of research automation tools also makes it difficult to search for information.

Thus, to decrease the time of human resources spent in the collection, management and selection of information and to decrease the probability of occurrence of errors, tools for automation of information research will be constructed: a reference search tool that meets the intended requirements and a tool to search for available dimensions or production steps.

Analysis of Critical Processes
The cylinders resulting from the agglomeration process can be rolled into rolls in the rolling mills. The automatic rollers rewinding and packaging lines contain an innovative technology that allows the rollers to be rewound and packaged automatically. However, they do not work completely alone, they need two collaborators. One employee is responsible for laminating the cylinders and the other employee is responsible for the entire packaging area.

In a first phase, the first collaborator places a cylinder in a mill, which laminates the cylinder to carry out the cleaning operation. After these setup operations, the already cleaned cylinder is rolled to the desired thickness and forms a continuous cork roller. This continuous roller advances to the rewinder, where it is rolled and cut, forming the final rolls to the desired length.

There are two lines of rewinding and automatic packaging of composite chipboard rolls in parallel. Each line contains a rolling mill, a rewinder and a conveyor belt. The same developer who performs the setup operations is also responsible for fine-tuning the thickness at which the cylinder is being rolled and for ensuring the correct functioning of the rolling mills and rewinders.

After the rewinding operation, the rollers follow the conveyors to the packing area, where the second collaborator is responsible for all the processes that take place here.

The rolls can be packed in plastic, cardboard and/or box. If the roller is packed in plastic there is a machine that automatically performs this operation. If the roller is packed in carton, the packing process is manual, carried out by the second collaborator. After the roller is packed, the collaborator transports it to the pallet. After the pallet is complete with rolls, the pallet is packed. Finally, the collaborator moves the set formed by rails, to then be collected and puts a new pallet in the respective location.

On the automatic rewinding and packaging lines of composite agglomerated rolls there are several factors that determine the system's production cadence, namely, the thickness and length of the intended roller and the type of packaging used. The smaller the thickness of the rollers, the longer the rolling time of the cylinder, as greater control and precision of the machine is required. The rewinder, in turn, adapts the speed at which it rolls and cuts the rollers so that there is no material accumulation between the two machines. Finally, depending on the type of packaging, the cycle time of the packing station varies, and plastic packaging is the one that has the lowest cycle time associated, since there is a machine that automates this process.

The characteristics of the roller and packaging influence the functioning of the system. For this reason, depending on the production, the system may be balanced or not. When the system is not balanced, the packaging zone cannot give flow to the rollers that arrive upstream and the employees stop one of the lines to prevent the rollers from being piled on the conveyors. This happens when the cycle time of the first stations is less than the cycle time of the packaging area. Thus, in order to predict the system balance according to production and to study solutions that prevent this accumulation of rollers, a simulation of the automatic rewinding and packaging lines of composite agglomerated rollers was constructed [8, 9].

2.2 Methodology

This subsection addressed the methodology adopted for this work. In this sense, Fig. 1 demonstrates the methodology used for the development of automation tools for information searching purposes.

As the figure suggests, it was necessary to initiate with the collection and organization of a series of data [10, 11]. The characteristics of each reference were collected and organized in a database, and processing equipment and production flows were studied. This information was organized in tables and flowcharts. Subsequently, the presentation of the available molds or the production steps to obtain a product was automated, using Microsoft Excel and VBA, and the selection of references that comply with the user's requirements was automated, through Microsoft Access and VBA. In addition, the task of updating the database was automated, for the removal of obsolete references and the addition of new references.

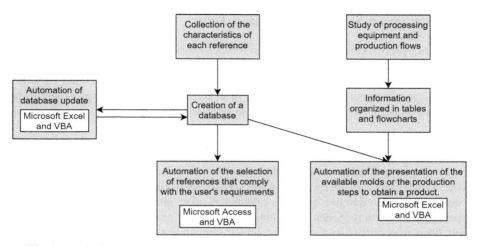

Fig. 1. Methodology used for the development of information research automation tools

In addition to the access to critical industrial information, it was also necessary to provide analytical tools to analyze complex systems, such as production environments. Figure 2 demonstrates the methodology used for the development of automation tools for information research.

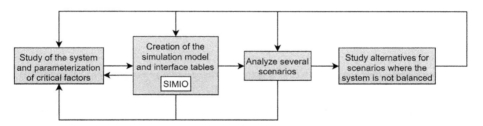

Fig. 2. Methodology used for the development of simulation tool

As such, for the construction of simulation models – and in a first step -, the system was studied and the critical factors of the lines were surveyed and parameterized. From this information the simulation of the system was constructed, using the SIMIO software, which is a general purpose discrete-event simulation software based on intelligent objects [12]. In this tool, users can blend animation and logic development in a single approach. Furthermore, the tool also allows users to specify the behavior of individual entities, hence allowing agent-oriented simulation [8, 11]. Then several scenarios were studied, and for the scenarios where the system was not balanced, alternatives were analyzed. Furthermore, as the figure suggests, it is possible to be in a stage of the work and have to go backwards in the process flow to any stage to reconsider some of the initial steps, due to the complexity of dealing with the behaviour of the system, as well as with the available data.

3 Information Search Automation Tools

This section presents the main requirement fulfilled by the developed tools. In this regard, first, the tools are displayed searching for information of certain references. Thereafter, the tool is displayed searching for the available dimensions and production steps for certain products. Finally, a brief discussion in terms of the impact of the proposed set of developed tools for the company of this case study is addressed.

3.1 Search Tool for References that Meet the Requirements

The tool developed in Access and VBA aims to streamline the information search process. After completing a form, the program selects and presents a list of references that meet the requirements entered in the form. The parameters taken into consideration are: product type, agglomeration type, density, rolling thickness and product dimensions. All tables have been imported from Excel files, which contain the entire database created. In addition, links have been established with these files, so that whenever an update is made to this database, the program is also updated. In the queries, all restrictions were established with logical expressions that allow the selection and presentation only of references that meet the requirements entered in the form. For example, Fig. 3 shows the search for references that obtains a rubber board, with density between 1000kg/m3 and 1300kg/m3, with 5mm thickness, 900mm length and 600mm width (the interface of the tool is shown in Portuguese).

Moreover, Fig. 4 presents a list of the references that meet the requirements entered and the indication of the molds that can be used, with the indication of yes or no. In addition, the yes* indicates which mold is most used for the agglomeration of the mixture in each reference.

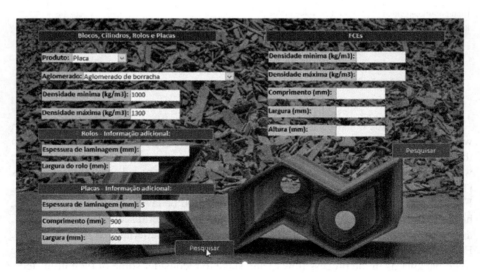

Fig. 3. Interface Menu of the tool for searching references

Referência ▾	Área ▾	Densidade ▾	CAE(915x915mm)x6in ▾	CAF(1000x1000mm)x6in ▾	CAB(1270x660mm)x6in ▾
1150	Aglomerado de borracha	1100,00	Sim	Não	Não
1177	Aglomerado de borracha	1025,00	Sim	Sim	Sim
1302	Aglomerado de borracha	1100,00	Sim*	Não	Não
1310	Aglomerado de borracha	1000,00	Sim	Sim*	Não
3510	Aglomerado de borracha	1000,00	Não	Sim	Sim
AMB9	Aglomerado de borracha	1250,00	Sim	Não	Sim
CM62	Aglomerado de borracha	1200,00	Sim	Não	Não
N733	Aglomerado de borracha	1050,00	Sim*	Não	Sim
NC80	Aglomerado de borracha	1015,00	Sim*	Não	Sim
RU04	Aglomerado de borracha	1030,00	Sim	Sim	Sim
S700	Aglomerado de borracha	1070,00	Sim*	Sim	Não
VC95	Aglomerado de borracha	1250,00	Sim	Sim	Não

Fig. 4. List of the references shown after the research

3.2 Search Tool for Available Dimensions or Production Steps

For the construction of the tool for available dimensions or production steps, interfaces have been developed that bridge the information entered by the user with the program, to present the requested data. These interfaces were created in the VBA User forms.

The user can search the available dimensions of molds for the agglomeration of cylinders and blocks for a given reference and can also ascertain whether a given product, plate, FCE roller, can be produced and, if it can, it indicates the production steps for obtaining that product.

In the main menu, the user can perform searches, delete or add references to the database and access the spreadsheets, where the database is located and where auxiliary calculations are performed. There are four buttons that perform these four tasks. Figure 5 shows the main menu.

If the user wishes to perform a search, enter the reference code and select one of the five products: block, cylinder, roller, plate or FCE. After clicking the Next button, the program checks if the entered reference is actually present in the database. Then, either a new form is opened, or the requested information is presented, according to the type of product selected.

If the user wants to make any changes to the tool or access the database tables, the Open Sheets button must be clicked. Otherwise, if the user wants to delete a reference from the database, enter the reference code, then the Delete Reference button should be clicked. Clicking this button sends a message to the user to confirm the execution of this action. If the user wishes to remove the database reference effectively, then in all tables in the database the reference records are removed. Finally, if the intention is to add a reference to the database, the Add Reference button should be clicked, and a new form appears, which must be filled with the data of the characteristics of the new reference.

Fig. 5. Interface Menu of the tool for available dimensions or production steps

3.3   Results: Impact of Information Search Automation Tools

The members of the product engineering team measured the time they spent researching references that met certain requirements and researching available dimensions or production steps for a given product. First without the use of search automation tools and then with the use of tools.

The average time per search without the use of the tools is 12 min and 40 s and the average time per search with the use of the tools is 1 min. Thus, it can be observed that there was a significant reduction of 92% of the average time performed by research. Thus, less time of human resources is spent on the collection, management and selection of information. Such time could, therefore, be used to perform other more added-value tasks, hence greatly improving the productivity of the company.

Moreover, the problems of information dispersion in the various files and the retention of information in supervisors or other collaborators ceased to exist, since the information is centralized. The tools also increase the reliability of the results, since the possibility of human errors is less.

4   Simulation

In this section, in a first phase, the objects and entities used to represent the system are presented. Thereafter, several examples of the simulation in operation are presented and discussed, for different types of rolls and packaging, in order to make an analysis of the system balance.

4.1 Simulation Model Development Approach

To prepare the simulation of the area under study, the system with objects and entities was first represented. Figure 6 shows the realization of this first stage, in which there was a representation of the layout of the rewinding lines and automatic packaging of composite chipboard rolls.

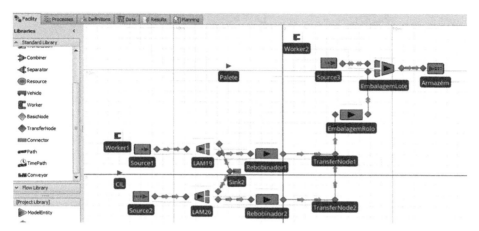

Fig. 6. Overview of the representation of the system through objects and entities in SIMIO.

Two entities were created, the CIL entity and the Palete entity, representing, respectively, cylinders and pallets. To create such entities, two Source objects were used. Thus, such entities are then directed to the LAM1 or LAM2 Separators, which represent the mills. At this point, a worker performs the setup operations on each of the rolling mills and as a product resulting from the rolling process, a continuous roll and waste is formed. The waste goes to the Sink objects, and the roll is directed to a Server object that models the rewinder processes, where the rolls are rolled to the desired length. Then the rollers pass through the conveyors, to the packing area. Here, first the rolls are individually packaged by Worker2 in the EmbalagemRolo Server and then the Worker2 transports one roll at a time to a Combiner object that is responsible for packing the entities. Finally, entities of the packing type are also created to enable this process. When the number of rolls required to form a batch is gathered, a worker packs the batch in the Combiner object and these lots are afterwards collected and placed in the warehouse. Figure 7 shows a 3D view of the system under analysis during its execution.

Since there are parameters that influence the operation of the entire system, it was necessary to establish such parameters, which bridge the data entered by the user, allowing the respective variance in the simulation to occur. As such, the user has to insert the following information in order to setup each simulation scenario:

- thickness and length of the intended roller;
- how many rolls each pallet takes;
- whether the packaging of the rollers is made in plastic, cardboard or box;

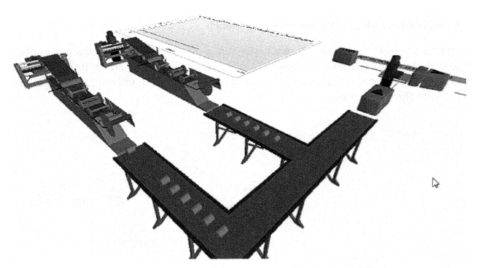

Fig. 7. Representation 3D of the system using SIMIO software

- whether or not the pallet packaging carries wrapping tape

From these variables the simulation automatically calculates additional relevant variables for the execution of the simulation, enabling the correct representation of the real system. Furthermore, while additional parameters could be easily created, these were the ones that were considered to be the main ones, as per agreed with the remaining involved stakeholders.

4.2   Results: Analysis of Various Scenarios

The system of roll rewinding and roll packing lines may be balanced or not in accordance with the characteristics of the roll, length and thickness, and the packaging. For the purposes considered in this work, the system is considered to be balanced when there is no stock build-up between rewinding and packaging. Nevertheless, it should be noted that the main purpose of the display of this tool is not to analyze the results per si, but rather to demonstrate the possibility of using this tool to analyze this systems performance, its potentialities, as well as the benefits that can be obtained by developing this tool, in an environment where there was no system to centralize relevant industrial data. In this regard, scenarios in which rolls of 6 mm of thickness and 27 m long were produced were considered. The following scenarios were considered for the sake of this work:

- Experiment A: Two rewind lines are considered;
- Experiment B: One of the two rewinding lines was blocked;
- Experiment C: The resources in the packaging area were doubled, two employees and two plastic packaging machines.

In its turn, Table 1 represents three examples of scenarios that can be executed in the simulation.

Table 1. List of scenarios that were considered in this work.

Experiment	Stockpiling	Laminator Rate of Occupation (%)	Packer 1 Rate of Occupation (%)	Packer 2 Rate of Occupation (%)	No. of rolls produced/ shift
A	Yes	82%	85%	–	280
B	No	41%	47%	–	155
C	No	82%	42%	26%	375

The system is balanced when there is no stock build-up between rewinding and packaging. It was found that the system is not balanced for experiment A, rolls 6 mm thick and 27 m long, where the packaging of the rolls is in plastic and each pallet takes five rolls. From experiment A, other scenarios were studied, always keeping the characteristics of the roller and the packaging, but changing some features of the system.

In experiment B one of the two rewinding lines was blocked. As expected, the system was balanced, but it was found that workers' occupancy rates were below 50%, which represented very low labor utilization.

For experiment C, the two lines were kept running and the resources of the packaging zone were doubled, two employees and two plastic packaging machines. The system is balanced and there is an increase of 58.67% of production per shift compared to experiment B, which represents a significant increase of more than twice the production.

Analyzing experiment A again, with the simulation, it was found that as time passed there was stock accumulation, but the packing area was eventually able to give flow to the accumulated rollers, since the number of accumulated rollers always returns to zero throughout the shift.

Comparing the production of example C and example A, there is a 9% increase in the production of rolls. Thus, example C is the option that ensures higher roll production per shift. However, example A is the option that brings less costs, there is a greater use of existing manpower and equipment, but it is necessary to incorporate an intermediate buffer.

5   Conclusions

In industrial contexts, the continuously improvement of processes and products is a crucial aspect in the improvement of competitiveness. To achieve such goal, companies require proper access to information, as well as solid artefacts that allow the analysis of complex systems, such as industrial environments. In light of this, this paper documents the work conducted to develop a set of tools that integrate industrial data, hence contributing for the efficient distribution of information, which can serve several purposes, as discussed throughout this paper.

To sum up, tools for the automation of the access to product information were developed, namely a reference search tool that meets the specified requirements, as well as a tool for searching available dimensions or production steps for a given product. Microsoft Excel, Access and Visual Basic for Applications were used to build these tools. Furthermore, several simulation models were also developed so that allow several types of analysis to be conducted over complex systems.

The average time per search was calculated without and with the use of the developed tools and it was verified that there was a significant reduction of the average time required to access the intended information. Thus, less time of human resources is spent on the collection, management and selection of information, which can be used to work on more added-value tasks. Moreover, problems such as the dispersion of information throughout several files (and even in the minds of certain individual collaborators) cease to exist, since the information is centralized. The tools also increase the reliability of the results, since the possibility of human errors is less.

On another hand, while information search tools allow a streamline access to information, system simulation allows additional levels of analysis, since it allows users to observe behaviours and dynamics and test various scenarios. For this paper, certain scenarios of production lines of rewinding and automatic packaging of composite chipboard rolls were simulated using the SIMIO software. For this purpose, firstly, a survey and parameterization of the critical factors of the production line were conducted so that the simulation could be elaborated and then the balancing of the system was studied in the face of different scenarios. Depending on the type of roll to be produced and according to the type of packaging, the balancing of the system varies. Other scenarios were studied for when the system is not balanced, in order to avoid this occurrence. As verified, the simulation allows an improvement of the analysis of the system's behaviour, as well as key performance indicators to be estimated under given conditions. The visual aspect of being able to observe the dynamics of the materials, machines, workers and other elements throughout time was also a valuable output of the simulation models.

In terms of future work, other areas could be studied and included, such as associating costing to the production tasks. On the other hand, including optimization models to synergize with the simulation models could also be pondered, as well as evaluating the possibility of incorporating the projections outlined by the simulation results in the designed information tools, hence providing additional insights for decision-makers.

Acknowledgments. This work has been supported by FCT – Fundação para a Ciência e Tecnologia within the R&D Units Project Scope: UIDB/00319/2020.

References

1. Tripathi, K.P.: Decision support system is a tool for making better decisions in the organization. Indian J. Comput. Sci. Eng. **2**(1), 112–117 (2011)
2. Aggarwal, A.K.: An excel-based decision-making tool (2004)
3. Pinto, M.: Microsoft Excel 2010 (2010)
4. Carvalho, A.: Automatização em Excel (2017)
5. Chung, L: Microsoft Access or Microsoft SQL Server : What's Right in Your Organization ? (2004)

6. Carvalho, J.V. , Azevedo, A. Abreu, A.: Microsoft Access 2010. 2010(May), 3–5 (2010)
7. Banks, J.: Handbook of simulation: principles, methodology, advances, applications, and practice (1998)
8. Vieira, A.A.C., Dias, L., Santos, M.Y., Pereira, G., Oliveira, J.A.: Supply chain hybrid simulation: from big data to distributions and approaches comparison. Simul. Model. Pract. Theory **97**, 101956 (2019)
9. Vieira, A.A.C.: Microssimulação para avaliar o impacto da introdução de pré-semáforos em cruzamentos, Master's Thesis, University of Minho (2013)
10. Singh, R.J., Sohani, N., Marmat, H.: Supply chain integration and performance: a literature review. J. Supply Chain Manag. Syst. **2**(1), 37–48 (2013)
11. Vieira, A.A.C., Dias, L., Santos, M.Y., Pereira, G., Oliveira, J.A.: Simulation of an automotive supply chain using big data," Comput. Ind. Eng. **137**, 106033 (2019)
12. Dias, L.M.S., Vieira, A.A.C., Pereira, G.A.B., Oliveira, J.A.: Discrete simulation software ranking – a top list of the worldwide most popular and used tools. Winter Simulation Conference. IEEE Press. Piscataway, NJ, USA, pp. 1060–1071 (2016). https://www.informs-sim.org/wsc16papers/095.pdf

A Maximal Margin Hypersphere SVM

Rui Malha[1] and Paula Amaral[1,2(✉)]

[1] Nova SST—FCT Nova, Campus de Caparica, 2829-516 Caparica, Portugal
paca@fct.unl.pt
[2] NovaMaths CMA Nova, Campus de Caparica, 2829-516 Caparica, Portugal

Abstract. In this work we propose a generalization of the Support Vector Machine (SVM) method in which the separator is a curve, but the concept of margin and maximization of the margin is still present. The idea of using different functions for the separation has been explored in particular in the scope of hyperspheres. However, most of these proposals use two spheres, using concepts different from maximal margin or one sphere but with a poor performance when data from the classes have a linear shape. In this paper we present a formulation of the linear SVM that generalizes it to a spherical separation shape, but still maximizing the margin. A linear relaxation of this quadratic formulation is also presented. The performance of these two formulations for classification purpose is tested and the results are encouraging.

Keywords: SVM · Automatic classification · Non-linear SVM

1 Introduction

Today we have sensors connected to houses, bodies, cars, machines, trees, animals. The act of monitoring reached a hyperbolic state in the era of Big Data, 4th industrial revolution, internet of things (IOT), smart cities, smart cars, smart appliances.

Interpreting and classifying these types of data requires good classification methods. Support Vector Machine (SVM) have been used with success in classification [2] and several generalizations of the boundary function have been proposed in the literature.

In this paper we propose a spherical separation, maintaining the concept of maximal margin. The key feature consists in letting the radius out of the minimization purpose so that, the sphere can approximate a linear separation by enlarging the radius and putting the center away from the centroid of the points. Most methods seek to minimize the ratio and so they have a poor performance for data with linear shape. We formulate and solve this nonlinear SVM for a set of generated data and for set of real data from a repository commonly used for this type of studies. This leads to a quadratic optimization problem and we

This work is funded by national funds through the FCT - Fundação para a Ciência e a Tecnologia, I.P., under the scope of the project UIDB/00297/2020 (Center for Mathematics and Applications).

also propose a linear formulation that can give an approximate solution to this quadratic problem.

The paper is organized in the following way: After this introduction we present the classical SVM method introducing the formulation from a pure optimization perspective without resorting to classical formulas of distance of a point to a line. This helps to understand the formulation of the classical SVM. In Sect. 3 we present a survey in spherical SVM to highlight the contribution of the methodology proposed in this paper. In Sect. 4 we develop our method including the linear formulation and, present in Sect. 5, before the conclusions, the numerical experience.

2   The Standard SVM

In this section we are going to review the SVM method and describe the fundamentals of the theory behind, using a pure optimization interpretation.

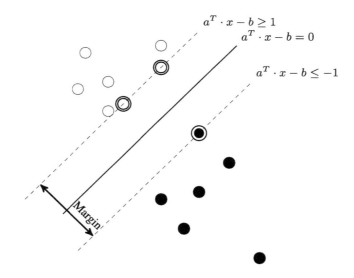

Fig. 1. SVM with two features ($\mathbb{R}^2$)

SVM is a supervised classification method. It uses two sets of labeled data, one to find a frontier that separates two or more classes of data (the training examples) and the other to test the accuracy of the classification (the testing examples). In the classical SVM the frontier is defined by a hyper-plane. The frontier is defined so that the examples of the separate categories are divided by a clear gap (the margin in Fig. (1)) that is as wide as possible. New points are automatically predicted to belong to a category based on the side of the gap on which they fall. In addition to performing linear classification, SVMs can efficiently perform a non-linear classification using what is called the kernel trick, implicitly mapping their inputs into high-dimensional feature spaces.

In the next section we are going to explain the classic SVM using a pure optimization perspective. We will ignore the formula of the euclidean distance of a point to a line in $\mathbb{R}^2$ and deduce it from an optimization point of view.

2.1   The Distance of a Point to a Plane as an Optimization Problem

The distance of a point (x_j^1, x_j^2) to a line $r \equiv w_1 x_1 + w_2 x_2 = b$ is a known algebraic formula that can be obtained by an optimization perspective. We want to find the closest point in r to (x_j^1, x_j^2) according to some measuring distance $D(\cdot)$.

$$\min_{x_1, x_2} D\left((x_j^1, x_j^2), (x_1, x_2)\right)$$
$$s.t. \ w_1 x_1 + w_2 x_2 = b$$
$$x_1, x_2 \in \mathbb{R}$$

Using for instance the half of the square of the euclidean distance we obtain:

$$P: \ z = \min \frac{1}{2}\left((x_j^1 - x_1)^2 + (x_j^2 - x_2)^2\right) \tag{1}$$
$$s.t. \ w_1 x_1 + w_2 x_2 = b \tag{2}$$
$$x_1, x_2 \in \mathbb{R} \tag{3}$$

For a general optimization problem

$$z = \min f(x) \tag{4}$$
$$s.t. \ Ax = b \tag{5}$$

the optimal solution can be found by solving the system

$$\begin{cases} \nabla f = A^T \lambda \\ Ax = \quad b \end{cases} \tag{6}$$

where λ are the Lagrangian multipliers. For problem P we obtain

$$\begin{cases} \nabla f = \begin{bmatrix} (x_j^1 - x_1) \\ (x_j^2 - x_2) \end{bmatrix} = \lambda \begin{bmatrix} w_1 \\ w_2 \end{bmatrix} \\ w_1 x_1 + w_2 x_2 = b \end{cases} \tag{7}$$

so using (7) in (1) we obtain

$$2z^* = \lambda^2 w_1^2 + \lambda^2 w_2^2 = \lambda^2 \|w\|^2 \tag{8}$$

solving (7) in order of x_1, x_2

$$x_1 = x_j^1 - \lambda w_1 \tag{9}$$
$$x_2 = x_j^2 - \lambda w_2 \tag{10}$$

and replacing it in $w_1x_1 + w_2x_2 = b$

$$w_1(x_j^1 - \lambda w_1) + w_2(x_j^2 - \lambda w_2) = b \tag{11}$$

we obtain

$$\lambda = \frac{w_1x_j^1 + w_2x_j^2 - b}{\|w\|^2} \tag{12}$$

Finally, from (8) and (12) we obtain the distance D_j of a point (x_j^1, x_j^2) to the line $w_1x_1 + w_2x_2 = b$

$$D_j = \sqrt{2z^*} = |\lambda|\|w\| = \frac{|w_1x_j^1 + w_2x_j^2 - b|}{\|w\|} \tag{13}$$

2.2 The SVM Problem

Given a set of training examples (x_j, y_j) for $j \in N = \{1, \ldots, n\}$, corresponding to two classes (one class with $y_j = 1$ for $j \in N_1$ and the other with $y_j = -1$ for $j \in N_2$), in order to find a hyperplane defined by a vector w that maximizes the margin, and such that the points from distinct classes lie on opposite sides of the hyperplane, we need to solve the following optimization problem:

$$SVM: v = \max_{j \in N} \min_{w_1, w_2} D_j \tag{14}$$
$$s.t.\ w_1x_j^1 + w_2x_j^2 - b \geq 1 \text{ for } j \in N_1 \tag{15}$$
$$w_1x_j^1 + w_2x_j^2 - b \leq -1 \text{ for } j \in N_2 \tag{16}$$
$$D_j = \frac{|w_1x_j^1 + w_2x_j^2 - b|}{\|w\|} \text{ for } j \in N \tag{17}$$

This maxmin problem can be reformulated as

$$SVM: v = \max \delta \tag{18}$$
$$s.t.\ w_1x_j^1 + w_2x_j^2 - b \geq 1 \text{ if } y_j = 1 \tag{19}$$
$$w_1x_j^1 + w_2x_j^2 - b \leq -1 \text{ if } y_j = -1 \tag{20}$$
$$\frac{|w_1x_j^1 + w_2x_j^2 - b|}{\|w\|} \geq \delta \text{ for } j \in N \tag{21}$$

which is equivalent to

$$SVM: v = \max \delta \tag{22}$$
$$s.t.\ y_j(w_1x_j^1 + w_2x_j^2 - b) \geq 1 \text{ for } j \in N \tag{23}$$
$$|w_1x_j^1 + w_2x_j^2 - b| \geq \delta\|w\| \text{ for } j \in N \tag{24}$$

Since together with constraints (23) $|w_1 x_j^1 + w_2 x_j^2 - b| = yi(w_1 x_j^1 + w_2 x_j^2 - b)$ we may combine (23) and (24) and obtain

$$SVM : \ v = \max \delta \tag{25}$$

$$s.t. \ y_j(w_1 x_j^1 + w_2 x_j^2 - b) \geq \delta \|w\| \ \text{for} \ j \in N \tag{26}$$

Finally since the problem is invariant to re-scaling of the parameters, we may constraint $\delta\|w\|$ to be equal to any constant in particular 1 and in that case $\delta = \frac{1}{\|w\|}$. Considering that to maximize $\frac{1}{\|w\|}$ is equivalent to minimize $\|w\|$ we obtain the well known SVM problem formulation

$$SVM : \ v = \min \|w\| \tag{27}$$

$$s.t. \ y_j(w_1 x_j^1 + w_2 x_j^2 - b) \geq 1 \ \text{for} \ j \in N \tag{28}$$

There will be some points, in each class for which the margin in Fig. (1) is attained. They are the support vector and are signaled by a double circle in Fig. (1).

3   SVM with Hyperspheres for Classification - A Small Survey

Inspired by SVM [7] proposed by Vapnik, some efforts have been made to improve SVM, in particular, using hyperspheres for classification.

Table 1 resumes some of the papers that constitute a milestone in the development of generalization of SVM based on spheres.

Spherical classifiers were first introduced into pattern classification by Cooper in 1962 [6] and subsequently developed and generalized by many other researchers. Support vector data description (SVDD), [21–23], is an one-class (the target class) classification method. The goal is to devise a closed decision boundary that may distinguish a member of this class from the rest of the feature space, characterized by center and radius $R > 0$ and described by the support vectors. The boundary can also be used to detect novel data or outliers. The model in [21–23] seeks to find a minimum radius hypersphere containing almost all the data from this class. To allow the possibility of outliers in the training set, the distance from data points to the center need not to be strictly smaller than the radius, but these larger distances should be penalized introducing slack variables measuring the distance to the boundary, if an object is outside the description. The sum of the slacks variables is included in the objective function parameterized by a constant as a trade-off between the volume of the hypersphere and the errors.

Different versions of classifiers have been extended from SVDD. These classifiers include maximal-margin spherical-structured multi-class SVM (MSM-SVM) [12], Twin support vector hypersphere (TSVH) [18] and Twin-hypersphere support vector machine (THSVM) [17]. These models find two hyperspheres, one for each class, and classifies points according to which hypersphere a given point

Table 1. Cronological list of papers.

Year	Title	Reference
1999	Support vector domain description	[23]
2002	Uniform object generation for optimizing one-class classifiers	[21]
2004	Support vector data description	[22]
2005	Pattern classification via single-spheres	[24]
2007	A new maximal margin spherical structured multi-class support vector machine	[12]
2009	A fixed-center spherical separation algorithm with kernel transformations	[5]
2009	A new maximal-margin spherical-structured multi-class support	[12]
2010	Least squares twin support vector hypersphere (LS-TSVH) for pattern recognition	[15]
2010	DC models for spherical separation	[3]
2012	Margin maximization in spherical separation	[4]
2013	Sphere Support Vector Machines for large classification tasks	[20]
2013	A twin-hypersphere support vector machine classifier and the fast learning algorithm	[17]
2014	Twin support vector hypersphere (TSVH) classifier for pattern recognition	[18]
2016	A maximum margin and minimum volume hyperspheres machine with pinball loss for imbalanced data classification	[25]
2016	Twin pinball loss support vector hypersphere classifier for pattern recognition	[11]
2017	Steel surface defect classification using multiple hyperspheres support vector machine with additional information	[10]
2017	Linear approach for twin-Hypersphere support vector machine	[13]
2018	Multi-class classification method based on support vector machine with hypersphere for steel surface defects	[9]
2019	Support vector machine with quantile hyperspheres for pattern classification	[14]
2019	A spheres-based support vector machine for pattern classification	[16]

is relatively closest to. The samples in one class are as many as possibly covered by the corresponding hypersphere, whereas the samples in the other class are as far as possible from this hypersphere.

Other approaches related to spherical separation [25] uses maximum margin and minimum volume hyperspheres machine with pinball loss (Pin-M3HM) and least squares twin support vector hyperspheres (LS-TSVH) [15].

A support vector machine with quantile hyperspheres (QHSVM) for binary classification [14] was proposed by Maoxiang et al. (2019). Here, the idea is similar to SVDD, however, it needs to build two hyperspheres with the same center. Considering two boundary hyperspheres (BHSVM) where target samples are inside hyperspheres with radius R+ and negative samples are outside hypersphere with radius R-. BHSVM maximizes the shortest distance between two classes by minimizing the volume of the first and maximizing the volume of the second, to keep margin as big as possible. QHSVM is generated by introducing the pinball losses in BHSVM.

In this paper, contrary to other approaches we don't minimize the radius. We propose to solve a SVM that is similar to the classic SVM in the sense that we attempt to maximize the margin. The only difference is that the separation boundary is a curve and so it can better adjust to the shape of points as depicted in Fig. 2. Locally, the larger the radius and the further away the center is from the centroid of the points, the closer the boundary is to a line. In this sense it is a generalization of the classic SVM, but that works well even if the data from one class lies in the interior of the second class.

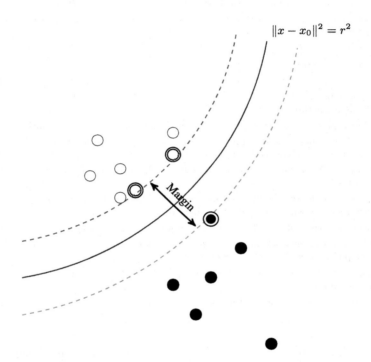

$$\|x - x_0\|^2 = r^2$$

Fig. 2. Non-linear SVM with two features ($\mathbb{R}^2$)

4   A Maximal Margin Hyphersphere SVM Method

Consider a set of $N = \{1, 2, \ldots, n\}$ points each one with $M = \{1, 2, \ldots, m\}$ features and distributed in two separable classes C_1 and C_2, such that $N_1 = \{1, 2, \ldots, |C_1|\}$ and $N_2 = \{1, 2, \ldots, |C_2|\}$.

The goal is to find a maximal separation function $f(x, \theta)$, where θ are the parameters of the function, and $\delta \geq 0$ measures the separation, such that:

$$f(x, \theta) \leq b - \delta \text{ if } x \in C_1$$

$$f(x, \theta) \geq b + \delta \text{ if } x \in C_2.$$

In general we may consider $b = 0$, so to find the optimal θ and δ an optimization problem of the following type must be solved:

$$G : v_G = \max h(\delta) \tag{29}$$
$$s.t. f(x_i, \theta) \leq -\delta, \quad \text{if } i \in N_1 \tag{30}$$
$$f(x_j, \theta) \geq +\delta, \quad \text{if } j \in N_2. \tag{31}$$
$$\delta \geq 0 \tag{32}$$

where $h(\delta)$ is a strictly increasing function on $\mathbb{R}^+$.

Spherical SVM have been proposed in the literature to define a non-linear separation between two sets of data with different labels $y = -1$ for $x \in C_1$ and $y = 1$ for $x \in C_2$. The common procedure is to find a sphere centered at some point inside the cloud of points defined by one set, such as the centroid. Sometimes two spheres are proposed each one with center in the centroid of each set. However, these methods will have a poor performance if the points are distributed along a line. In this paper we propose to define a sphere were the center is not necessarily rooted at the center of the points and may even be far outside the centroid if necessary. In this way, depending on the center and the radius, the separation curve may approximate, or not, a linear separator, a margin may be defined as in the linear SVM which we aim to maximize.

4.1 SVM with Spherical Boundary Maximizing the Separation Margin

Our proposal is to find a radius r and a center x_0 of a hypersphere such that the points of one class C_1 fall inside and the points in C_2 fall outside the hypersphere, as in Fig. (2).

$$\|x - x_0\|^2 \leq r^2 \rightarrow x \in C_1$$
$$\|x - x_0\|^2 > r^2 \rightarrow x \in C_2,$$

and there is a margin δ separating the points in each class

$$\|x - x_0\|^2 \leq (r - \delta)^2 \rightarrow x \in C_1$$
$$\|x - x_0\|^2 > (r + \delta)^2 \rightarrow x \in C_2$$

So the goal is to find x_0 and positive r that maximizes non-negative δ.

$$S_0 : v_0 = \max h(\delta) \tag{33}$$
$$s.t. \|x_i - x_0\|^2 \leq (r - \delta)^2, \quad \text{if } i \in N_1 \tag{34}$$
$$\|x_i - x_0\|^2 \geq (r + \delta)^2, \quad \text{if } i \in N_2 \tag{35}$$
$$\delta, r \geq 0$$

We are going to consider in (33) $h(\delta) = \delta$ and we assign a label $y = \pm 1$ to differentiate the classes. The definition of the label of each class is irrelevant, so we may assume that for $x \in C_1$ we have $y = 1$ and for $x \in C_2$ we have $y = -1$. So from

$$\|x - x_0\|^2 - r^2 - \delta^2 \leq -2r\delta \Rightarrow x \in C_1 \Leftrightarrow y\left(\|x - x_0\|^2 - r^2 - \delta^2\right) \leq -2r\delta \text{ for } y = 1$$

$$\|x - x_0\|^2 - r^2 - \delta^2 > 2r\delta \Rightarrow x \in C_2 \Leftrightarrow y\left(\|x - x_0\|^2 - r^2 - \delta^2\right) \leq -2r\delta \text{ for } y = -1$$

we obtain, the following equivalent problem:

$$S_1: \ v = \max \delta \tag{36}$$

$$\text{s.t. } y_i\left(\|x_i - x_0\|^2 - r^2 - \delta^2\right) \leq -2r\delta \text{ for } i \in N \tag{37}$$

Let us consider $z = \begin{bmatrix} x_0 \\ \delta \\ r \end{bmatrix}$, $\quad Q_i = \begin{bmatrix} y_i I(n) & 0 & 0 \\ 0 & -y_i & 1 \\ 0 & 1 & -y_i \end{bmatrix}$, $\quad v_i = \begin{bmatrix} -y_i x_i \\ 0 \\ 0 \end{bmatrix}$.

Let e be a vector of dimension $n + 2$ of zeros except in the $n + 1$ component which is equal to one. S_1 can be rewritten as:

$$S_1: \ v = \max e^T z \tag{38}$$

$$\text{s.t. } z^T Q_i z + 2v_i^T z \leq -y_i x_i^T x_i \text{ for } i \in N \tag{39}$$

The Lagrangian function is given by:

$$L(z, \lambda) = e^T z - \sum_{i \in N} \lambda_i \left(z^T Q_i z + 2v_i^T z + y_i x_i^T x_i\right) \tag{40}$$

and

$$\nabla_z L(z, \lambda) = e - \sum_{i \in N} \lambda_i \left(2Q_i z + 2v_i\right) \tag{41}$$

and from $\nabla_z L(z, \lambda) = 0$ we obtain considering $X^y = [y_i x_i]$

$$z = \left(\sum_{i \in N} \lambda_i Q_i\right)^{-1} \left(e - \sum_{i \in N} \lambda_i v_i\right) = \left(\sum_{i \in N} \lambda_i Q_i\right)^{-1} \left(e - V\lambda\right). \tag{42}$$

Considering $\lambda^+ = \sum_{i \in N} \lambda_i$ and $\lambda_y^+ = \sum_{i \in N} y_i \lambda_i$ then

$$\left(\sum_{i \in N} \lambda_i Q_i\right)^{-1} = \begin{bmatrix} \frac{1}{\lambda_y^+} I(n) & 0 & 0 \\ 0 & \frac{\lambda_y^+}{\lambda^{+2} - \lambda_y^{+2}} & \frac{\lambda^+}{\lambda^{+2} - \lambda_y^{+2}} \\ 0 & \frac{\lambda^+}{\lambda^{+2} - \lambda_y^{+2}} & \frac{\lambda_y^+}{\lambda^{+2} - \lambda_y^{+2}} \end{bmatrix}$$

and so

$$z = \begin{bmatrix} x_0 \\ \delta \\ r \end{bmatrix} = \begin{bmatrix} \frac{X^y \lambda}{\lambda_y^+} \\ \frac{\lambda_y^+}{\lambda^{+2} - \lambda_y^{+2}} \\ \frac{\lambda^+}{\lambda^{+2} - \lambda_y^{+2}} \end{bmatrix}$$

and

$$r - \delta = \frac{1}{\lambda^+ + \lambda_y^+} = \frac{1}{\lambda_1^+} \qquad (43)$$

$$r + \delta = \frac{1}{\lambda^+ - \lambda_y^+} = \frac{1}{\lambda_2^+} \qquad (44)$$

where $\lambda_1^+ = \sum_{i \in N_1} \lambda_i$ and $\lambda_2^+ = \sum_{i \in N_2} \lambda_i$.

Notice that the points x_i for $i \in N$ with $\lambda_i > 0$ are the support vectors. If $i \in N_1$ they fall on the curve $\|x - x_0\|^2 = (r - \delta)^2$ and if $i \in N_2$, they fall in the curve $\|x - x_0\|^2 = (r + \delta)^2$. Since there is at least one support vector by class then the denominators (43) and (44) do not vanish. Also, given that the number of support vectors is small we expect most of the dual variables to be zero. Since the problem is not symmetric, contrary to the linear case, the formulation must be solved twice, considering $y_i = 1$ for $i \in N_1$, $y_i = -1$ for $i \in N_2$ and also for $y_i = -1$ for $i \in N_1$, $y_i = 1$ for $i \in N_2$.

4.2   A Linear Relaxation of the Quadratic Formulation

From the constraints formulation (34) and (35) of S_0 we obtain

$$\|x_i - x_0\|^2 + 2r\delta \leq r^2 + \delta^2, \text{ if } i \in N_1 \qquad (45)$$

$$\|x_i - x_0\|^2 - 2r\delta \geq r^2 + \delta^2, \text{ if } i \in N_2 \qquad (46)$$

$$\delta, r \geq 0$$

and so from (45) and (46) we have

$$\|x_i - x_0\|^2 + 2r\delta \leq r^2 + \delta^2 \leq \|x_j - x_0\|^2 - 2r\delta \text{ for } i \in N_1, j \in N_2 \Leftrightarrow$$

$$\Leftrightarrow \|x_i\|^2 - 2x_i^T x_0 + \|x_0\|^2 + 2r\delta \leq r^2 + \delta^2 \leq \|x_j\|^2 - 2x_j^T x_0 + \|x_0\|^2 - 2r\delta \text{ for } i \in N_1, j \in N_2$$

$$\Leftrightarrow \|x_i\|^2 - 2x_i^T x_0 + 2r\delta \leq r^2 + \delta^2 - \|x_0\|^2 \leq \|x_j\|^2 - 2x_j^T x_0 - 2r\delta \text{ for } i \in N_1, j \in N_2$$

So, any feasible solution of S_0 verifies the constraints.

$$\|x_i\|^2 - 2x_i^T x_0 + 2r\delta \leq \|x_j\|^2 - 2x_j^T x_0 - 2r\delta \text{ for } i \in N_1, j \in N_2$$

there is

$$4r\delta + 2(x_j - x_i)^T x_0 \leq \|x_j\|^2 - \|x_i\|^2, \text{ for } i \in N_1, j \in N_2$$

Taking $\theta = r\delta$ we obtain the following relaxation problem for S_0.

$$SRL_0 : \max \theta \qquad (47)$$

$$\text{s.t. } 4\theta + 2(x_j - x_i)^T x_0 \leq \|x_j\|^2 - \|x_i\|^2, \text{ for } i \in N_1, j \in N_2 \qquad (48)$$

$$\theta \geq 0 \qquad (49)$$

But this problem may be unbounded, because from

$$4\theta \le \|x_j\|^2 - \|x_i\|^2 - 2(x_j - x_i)^T x_0,$$

if $2(x_j - x_i)^T x_0 < 0$ then x_0 can be chosen such that $-2(x_j - x_i)^T x_0$ is arbitrarily large. To solve this issue we propose introducing an indirect regularization technique. Instead of adding to the objective function $-k\|x_0\|$ where k is a parameter we introduce a new variable ρ and a new constraint, in the above formulation obtaining:

$$SRL_1(k): \quad \max \theta + k\rho \tag{50}$$

$$\text{s.t. } 4\theta + 2(x_j - x_i)^T x_0 \le \|x_j\|^2 - \|x_i\|^2 \text{ for } i \in N_1, j \in N_2 \tag{51}$$

$$4\theta + 2(x_j - x_i)^T x_0 \ge \rho \text{ for } i \in N_1, j \in N_2 \tag{52}$$

$$\theta \ge 0 \tag{53}$$

The next example illustrates the application of the quadratic and linear formulation.

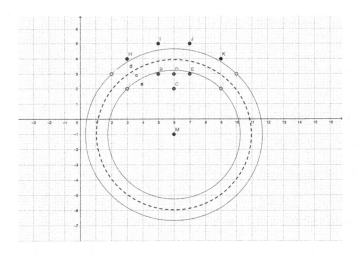

Fig. 3. Spherical separation using the quadratic formulation

Example 1. Consider the set of points in $\mathbb{R}^2$ from two classes, each with 6 elements.

Class1 | x_1 | 3 | 5 | 6 | 6 | 7 | 9 |
|---|---|---|---|---|---|---|
| | x_2 | 2 | 3 | 2 | 3 | 3 | 2 |

Class2 | x_1 | 2 | 3 | 5 | 7 | 9 | 10 |
|---|---|---|---|---|---|---|
| | x_2 | 3 | 4 | 5 | 5 | 4 | 3 |

For the quadratic formulation we obtained $x_0 = (6, -1)$, $r = 4.9497$ and the margin, $\delta = 0.7071$. The support vectors are $(3, 2)$ and $(9, 2)$ for Class 1 and $(2, 3)$ and $(10, 3)$ for Class 2. This solution is depicted in Fig. 3.

For the linear formulation we obtained $x_0 = (6, -1.5)$, $\theta = 3.75$, $r = 5.3153$ and the margin, $\delta = 0.7055$. The support vectors are $(1, 2)$, $(5, 3)$, $(7, 3)$ and $(9, 2)$ for Class 1 and $(2, 3)$ and $(10, 3)$ for Class 2 . This solution is depicted in Fig. 4.

5 Computational Experience

The goal of the numerical experience is to test the accuracy of the quadratic (38–39 in Sect. 4.1) and linear (50–53 in Sect. 4.2) models and compare against the classical SVM approach for real and generated data.

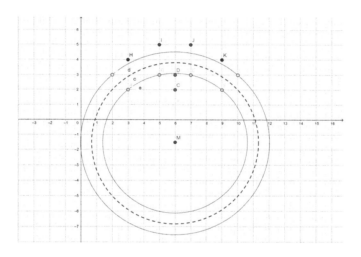

Fig. 4. Spherical separation using the linear formulation

Experiments were run on a computer with an Intel(R) Core(TM) i7-8550U processor, 1.80 GHz, 8.00 GB of RAM, 64-bit operating system, running on Windows 10, version 20H2. We code our method on Matlab R2019a, and we used BARON software [19] version 13.0.1, running on Matlab with MAT-LAB/BARON interface version v1.69. The BARON solver was used to solve the quadratic formulation. To run the classical SVM we used the Statistics and Machine Learning Toolbox from Matlab version 11.5.

The real data used was the *Seeds* data set, available from UCI Machine Learning Repository [1]. This data set considers three different varieties of wheat with 70 elements each, and the set is constructed with measures of seven geometric attributes. In our experiments we used only two spherically separated sets (140 objects). We performed 20 trials, choosing in each one, randomly, a set for training with 80 objects (40 of each class) and a set for testing with 60 objects (30 of each class).

We build also an artificial data set in order to have two sets, spherically separated, each one with three attributes. So, for set A we consider 50 points $a_i = (a_{i_1}, a_{i_2}, a_{i_3})$ so that: a_{i_1} satisfies a Gaussian distribution $N(2,2)$, a_{i_2} satisfies a Gaussian distribution $N(5,2)$ and $a_{i_3} = a_{i_1}^2 + a_{i_2}^2$. For set B we considered also 50 points $b_j = (b_{j_1}, b_{j_2}, b_{j_3})$ so that: b_{j_1} satisfies a Gaussian distribution $N(2,1)$, b_{j_2} satisfies a Gaussian distribution $N(3,1)$ and $b_{j_3} = 40 + b_{i_1}^2 + b_{i_12}^2$. From the 50 elements we randomly chose 25 points as the training set, the remaining 25 being the test set. As for the *Seeds* database we performed 20 trials.

Table 2. Accuracy results

Data set	SVM model		
	P_1 Quadratic	Linear	Classic (MATLAB)
Artificial	99,20	95,30	95,70
Seeds	97,17	96,25	95,42

Given a specific classification method, for every trial i, $i = 1, \ldots, 20$, considering that the test set has $n_i^1 = n_{1i}^1 + n_{0i}^1$ elements in class 1 and $n_i^2 = n_{1i}^2 + n_{0i}^2$ elements in class 2, the well classified element in class 1 and 2 are given by n_{1i}^1 and n_{1i}^2 respectively, and the number of misclassified objects is given by n_{0i}^1 and n_{0i}^2, for class 1 and 2 respectively. The accuracy of each method can be inferred by studying the proportion of well classified objects P_1 or of misclassified objects P_0, given by,

$$P_1 = \frac{1}{20} \sum_{i=1}^{20} \frac{n_{1i}^1 + n_{1i}^2}{n^1 + n^2}, \quad P_0 = \frac{1}{20} \sum_{i=1}^{20} \frac{n_{0i}^1 + n_{0i}^2}{n^1 + n^2}.$$

Table 2 presents the overall proportion of correctly classified objects P_1, for the testing sets in the 20 trials. Since P_0 can be obtained directly from P_1 there is no need to explicitly present it.

The results for both data sets show a better classification performance when using the quadratic model. For the linear model, the performance was slightly worse with the artificial data and better with the *Seeds* data set, when compared to the classic SVM. To test the statistical significance of the difference between the accuracy of two models, we used the Resampled Paired t Test [8]. The test statistic is given by,

$$t = \frac{\sqrt{20}\hat{p}}{\sqrt{\frac{\sum_{i=1}^2 (p(i) - \hat{p})^2}{n-1}}} \tag{54}$$

where $\bar{p} = \frac{\sum_{i=1}^n (p^{(i)})}{n}$ and $p^{(i)}$ is the difference, in trial i, between the proportion of well classified objects of the two methods. The null hypothesis states the equality of the accuracy of both methods against the alternative hypothesis of that one of them is more accurate than the other. Table 3 and 4 present the result of the statistical tests for the real and generated sets respectively. Globally there is only statistical evidence of the out performance of the Quadratic model in comparison with the Classic model.

Table 3. Statistical hypothesis test for the *Seeds* data

Alternative hypothesis	$\bar{p}$	Statistic t	p-value
Quadratic more accurate than Classic	0,018	3,367	0,002
Quadratic more accurate than Linear	0,009	1,764	0,047
Linear more accurate than Classic	0,008	1,365	0,094

Table 4. Statistical hypothesis test for the generated data

Alternative hypothesis	$\bar{p}$	Statistic t	p-value
Quadratic more accurate than Classic	0,035	5,872	0,000
Quadratic more accurate than Linear	0,039	5,224	0,000
Classic more accurate than Linear	0,004	0,395	0,348

6   Conclusions

In this paper we presented a formulation with a hypersphere separation, maximizing the margin. The formulation is a generalization of the classical SVM. We derived a linear relaxation for this problem and developed a regularization procedure for avoiding unboundedness. The preliminary results seem promising, and we obtained a good approximation for the quadratic solution computationally cheaper since it is based on a linear formulation. We intend to explore in the future the dual problem and to adjust the formulation to non-separable classes and multi-class classification.

Acknowledgments. We would like to thank the reviewers for their valuable comments and suggestions that helped to improve our manuscript.

References

1. Uc irvine machine learning repository. https://archive-beta.ics.uci.edu/
2. Abe, S.: Support Vector Machines for Pattern Classification. Springer, London (2005). https://doi.org/10.1007/1-84628-219-5
3. Astorino, A., Fuduli, A., Gaudioso, M.: A fixed-center spherical separation algorithm with kernel transformations for classification problems. J. Glob. Optim. **48**, 657–669 (2010). https://doi.org/10.1007/s10898-010-9558-0

4. Astorino, A., Fuduli, A., Gaudioso, M.: Margin maximization in spherical separation. Comput. Optim. Appl. **53**, 301–322 (2012). https://doi.org/10.1007/s10589-012-9486-7

5. Astorino, A., Gaudioso, M.: A fixed-center spherical separation algorithm with kernel transformations for classification problems. Comput. Manag. Sci. **6**, 357–372 (2009). https://doi.org/10.1007/s10287-007-0051-2

6. Cooper, P.W.: The hypersphere in pattern recognition. Inf. Control **5**(4), 324–346 (1962). https://doi.org/10.1016/S0019-9958(62)90641-1, https://www.sciencedirect.com/science/article/pii/S0019995862906411

7. Corinna, C., Vladimir, V.: Support-vector networks. Mach. Learn. **20**, 273–297 (1995). https://doi.org/10.1007/BF00994018

8. Dietterich, T.G.: Approximate statistical tests for comparing supervised classification learning algorithms. Neural Comput. **10**(7), 1895–1923 (1998). https://doi.org/10.1162/089976698300017197

9. Gong, R., Wu, C., Chu, M.: Multi-class classification method based on support vector machine with hyper-sphere for steel surface defects. In: 2018 37th Chinese Control Conference (CCC), pp. 9197–9202 (2018). https://doi.org/10.23919/ChiCC.2018.8483656

10. Gong, R., Wu, C., Chu, M.: Steel surface defect classification using multiple hyperspheres support vector machine with additional information. Chemom. Intell. Lab. Syst. **172**, 109–117 (2017). https://doi.org/10.1016/j.chemolab.2017.11.018

11. Gong, R., Wu, C., Chu, M., Wang, H.: Twin pinball loss support vector hypersphere classifier for pattern recognition. In: 2016 Chinese Control and Decision Conference (CCDC), pp. 6551–6556 (2016). https://doi.org/10.1109/CCDC.2016.7532177

12. Hao, P.Y., Chiang, J.H., Lin, Y.H.: A new maximal-margin spherical-structured multi-class support vector machine. Appl. Intell. **30**(2), 98–111 (2009). https://doi.org/10.1007/s10489-007-0101-z

13. Ketabchi, S., Moosaei, H., Razzaghi, M.: Linear approach for twin-hypersphere support vector machine. Adv. Model. Optim. **19**, 79–85 (2017)

14. Chu, M., Liu, X., Gong, R., Zhao, J.: Support vector machine with quantile hyperspheres for pattern classification. PLoS ONE **14**(2) (2019). https://doi.org/10.1371/journal.pone.0212361

15. Peng, X.: Least squares twin support vector hypersphere (LS-TSVH) for pattern recognition. Expert Syst. Appl. **37**(12), 8371–8378 (2010). https://doi.org/10.1016/j.eswa.2010.05.045, https://www.sciencedirect.com/science/article/pii/S0957417410004562

16. Peng, X.: A spheres-based support vector machine for pattern classification. Neural Comput. Appl. **31**(1), 379–396 (2017). https://doi.org/10.1007/s00521-017-3004-x

17. Peng, X., Xu, D.: A twin-hypersphere support vector machine classifier and the fast learning algorithm. Inf. Sci. **221**, 12–27 (2013). https://doi.org/10.1016/j.ins.2012.09.009, https://www.sciencedirect.com/science/article/pii/S0020025512005919

18. Peng, X., Xu, D.: Twin support vector hypersphere (TSVH) classifier for pattern recognition. Neural Comput. Appl. **24**(5), 1207–1220 (2013). https://doi.org/10.1007/s00521-012-1306-6

19. Sahinidis, N.V.: BARON 21.1.13: Global Optimization of Mixed-Integer Nonlinear Programs, User's Manual (2017)

20. Strack, R., Kecman, V., Strack, B., Li, Q.: Sphere support vector machines for large classification tasks. Neurocomputing **101**, 59–67 (2013). https://doi.org/10.1016/j.neucom.2012.07.025

21. Tax, D.M.J., Duin, R.P.W.: Uniform object generation for optimizing one-class classifiers. J. Mach. Learn. Res. **2**, 155–173 (2002)
22. Tax, D.M.J., Duin, R.P.W.: Support vector data description. Mach. Learn. **54**(1), 45–66 (2004)
23. Tax, D.M., Duin, R.P.: Support vector domain description. Pattern Recognit. Lett. **20**(11), 1191–1199 (1999). https://doi.org/10.1016/S0167-8655(99)00087-2, https://www.sciencedirect.com/science/article/pii/S0167865599000872
24. Wang, J., Neskovic, P., Cooper, L.N.: Pattern classification via single spheres. In: Hoffmann, A., Motoda, H., Scheffer, T. (eds.) DS 2005. LNCS (LNAI), vol. 3735, pp. 241–252. Springer, Heidelberg (2005). https://doi.org/10.1007/11563983_21
25. Xu, Y., Yang, Z., Zhang, Y., Pan, X., Wang, L.: A maximum margin and minimum volume hyper-spheres machine with pinball loss for imbalanced data classification. Knowl.-Based Syst. **95**, 75–85 (2016). https://doi.org/10.1016/j.knosys.2015.12.005, https://www.sciencedirect.com/science/article/pii/S0950705115004773

A Randomized Direct-Search Approach for Beam Angle Optimization in Intensity-Modulated Proton Therapy

Humberto Rocha[1,2]([✉]) [iD] and Joana Dias[1,2] [iD]

[1] FEUC, CeBER, University of Coimbra, 3004-512 Coimbra, Portugal
{hrocha,joana}@fe.uc.pt
[2] INESC-Coimbra, University of Coimbra, 3030-290 Coimbra, Portugal

Abstract. Intensity-modulated proton therapy (IMPT) is a very promising alternative for radiotherapy due to the unique depth-dose characteristics of protons that allow better trade-offs between tumor irradiation and organ sparing. Optimal selection of proton beam directions – beam angle optimization (BAO) – plays a decisive role in further improving these trade-offs having a profound impact on the quality of dose distributions, particularly because in IMPT the number of beams is typically lower than in intensity-modulated radiation therapy for photons (IMRT). Computational time efficiency becomes even more critical in the optimization of proton beam directions due to the increased degrees of freedom provided by different levels of energy and the existence of different scenarios for robust IMPT plans. In this study, we consider direct-search methods to address the IMPT BAO problem given their good performance in the resolution of the IMRT BAO problem. In order to test the effectiveness of reducing the number of polling directions at each iteration, both in terms of computational time and quality of the solution, a strategy for randomly selecting a reduced number of polling directions among a set of evenly distributed directions across quadrants is proposed. This strategy considers a set of probabilistic directions, where a descent direction exists with a given probability, instead of deterministic directions that guarantee at least one descent direction. For the prostate cancer case used in the computational tests, the randomized strategy proposed shows that considering as few as two polling directions improved significantly the computational time while the resulting treatment plan is at least as good as that obtained by the deterministic method. In future work, this type of randomized approximation has to be extended and tested in different cancer cases to validate the excellent performance found for a single prostate cancer case.

Keywords: Derivative-free optimization · Direct-search · Random directions · Beam angle optimization · Protons

O. Gervasi et al. (Eds.): ICCSA 2021, LNCS 12953, pp. 320–332, 2021.
https://doi.org/10.1007/978-3-030-86976-2_22

1   Introduction

The number of cancer cases will grow by 63.1% in 2040, according to the World Health Organization [1]. More than half of all the cancer patients will need some form of radiotherapy (RT), either with curative or palliative intent. Technological advances and emergence of new treatment modalities are two of the key factors that contribute to the continuous improvement of RT treatments and make RT treatment planning an area of research constantly evolving.

The goal of RT is to eliminate the cancer cells by irradiating the tumor with a prescribed dose while sparing, as much as possible, the surrounding organs. Irradiation with photon beams is clearly mainstream in RT treatments but the use of proton beams, in particular intensity-modulated proton therapy (IMPT), presents itself as a very promising alternative due to the unique depth-dose characteristics of protons: dose is slowly deposited along the beam path before reaching a sharp peak, known as the Bragg peak, rapidly falling to almost zero beyond the peak [2]. This characteristic allows for treatment plans where a better compromise can be reached between the irradiation of the tumor and the inevitable radiation of adjacent structures, not possible with other treatment modalities. Nevertheless, obtaining high-quality treatment plans taking the most possible advantage of the unique characteristics of this treatment modality requires the optimization of different parameters including the optimal selection of proton beam directions.

In IMPT, the number of beams is typically lower than in intensity-modulated radiation therapy for photons (IMRT), being the selection of the beam directions even more critical. In addition to the smaller number of directions, the differentiating characteristics between protons and photons makes the selection of the irradiation directions in IMPT more complex. There are more degrees of freedom due to the availability of different levels of energy, and it is necessary to consider robustness due to the existence of different sources of uncertainty. Thus, obtaining optimal beam irradiation directions in a clinically acceptable time becomes even more important considering the existence of different possible scenarios required for robust plans.

The beam angle optimization (BAO) problem, i.e., the optimal selection of irradiation directions, is a very difficult problem because it is a highly non-convex optimization problem [3]. Typically, the measure used to compare the quality of different beam ensembles, and thus to guide the BAO search, is the optimal value of the fluence map optimization (FMO) problem [4], the problem of finding the optimal fluence intensities for each beam. Obtaining the optimal FMO solution for a given beam angle ensemble is time costly mainly because it requires a complete dose computation. Thus, the beam angle optimization problem can be seen as the optimization of an expensive multi-modal black-box function which results in a computationally time consuming procedure.

In previous works, direct-search methods proved to be suited for BAO in IMRT [5–11]. Although direct-search approaches require few function evaluations to converge, several attempts were made to further improve its computational time performance, including considering FMO surrogates [5] or reducing the search space [9]. Recently, different studies proposed direct-search approaches that use few (random) directions in each iteration, with numerical benefits but at the cost of guaranteed convergence to a local minimum [12,13]. Nevertheless, the almost-sure probabilistic convergence proved for these approaches translates into quality results in practice with faster computational time [13].

In this study, we propose a randomized direct-search method for BAO. Considering a prostate cancer case treated with IMPT, the proposed probabilistic approach obtained quality solutions compared to the ones obtained by the deterministic counterpart, in a faster computational time. The paper is organized as follows. In the next section we briefly describe deterministic and probabilistic direct-search methods. IMPT for a prostate cancer case is presented in Sect. 3. In the following section, the randomized direct-search proposed for BAO is described. Computational tests are presented in Sect. 5 and conclusions are made in the last section.

2 Direct-Search

Direct-search methods are a class of widely used derivative-free optimization algorithms and, as such, only use function values never resorting to any type of derivative. One of the most popular direct-search method is the Nelder-Mead method [14]. That is the algorithm underlying *fminsearch* in MATLAB [15]. The Nelder-Mead method is a simplex method that moves and manipulates the vertices of a simplex in $\mathbb{R}^n$, i.e., $n + 1$ affinely independent points. In this work, we will focus on directional direct-search methods that use a set of directions, instead of simplices, to move to novel points when a decrease (considering minimization) in the objective function is obtained.

2.1 Deterministic Direct-Search

Deterministic direct-search methods consider a set of directions that correspond to a positive basis (or a positive spanning set). A positive basis for $\mathbb{R}^n$ is a set of directions (non-null vectors) that span $\mathbb{R}^n$ with nonnegative coefficients, but no proper subset does. A positive spanning set contains at least one positive basis [16]. A positive basis for $\mathbb{R}^n$ has at least $n + 1$ directions (in this case is called minimal positive basis) and at most $2n$ directions (in this case is called maximal positive basis). The main motivation for using positive bases in directional direct-search methods is that at least one of its directions forms an acute angle with the negative gradient vector (unused and/or unknown) which means that this direction is a descent direction unless the current iterate is already a stationary point [17].

Direct-search methods evaluate the function in the neighborhood of the current iterate, x_k, at points of the form $\mathbf{x}^k + \alpha_k d_i$, where α_k is the step along directions d_i of a positive basis (or a positive spanning set) D_k. This procedure, called polling, aims to decrease the function value at the current iterate and is the core step of direct-search methods displayed in Algorithm 1. An optional step, called search step, can also be performed. In this step, a finite number of trial points S_k can be evaluated, not necessarily in the neighborhood of the current iterate. When the search step fails to improve the function value, or $S_k = \emptyset$, the polling around the current iterate takes place. When both search and poll steps fail to decrease the function value, the step size, α_k, is decreased – the most common choice is to halve the step size as displayed in step 3 of Algorithm 1. If one of the steps manage to find a point that improves the function value at the current iterate then α_k is increased or kept – the most common choice is to keep the same step size as displayed in step 4 of Algorithm 1.

Algorithm 1. Direct-search algorithm

Initialization:

  - Choose initial point $\mathbf{x}^0 \in \mathbb{R}^n$.
  - Choose initial step size $\alpha_0 > 0$.

For k = 0, 1, 2, . . .

  1. Search step:
     Evaluate f at a finite number of points, S_k.
     If $\exists\, \mathbf{x}^{k+1} \in S_k$: $f(\mathbf{x}^{k+1}) < f(\mathbf{x}^k)$, select $\mathbf{x}^{k+1}$ and go to step 4.
     Otherwise, go to step 2.
  2. Poll step:
     Choose a set of poll directions, D_k.
     If $f(\mathbf{x}^k) \leq f(\mathbf{x}), \forall \mathbf{x} \in \{\mathbf{x}^k + \alpha_k d_i : d_i \in D_k\}$, $\mathbf{x}^{k+1} = \mathbf{x}^k$ and go to step 3.
     Otherwise, choose $\mathbf{x}^{k+1} = \mathbf{x}^k + \alpha_k d_i : f(\mathbf{x}^{k+1}) < f(\mathbf{x}^k)$ and go to step 4.
  3. $\alpha_{k+1} = \frac{1}{2} \times \alpha_k$.
  4. $\alpha_{k+1} = \alpha_k$.

Selection of the set of poll directions, D_k, is one of the distinguishing features of a direct-search method. Commonly used minimal and maximal positive bases are $[I\ -e]$, with I being the identity matrix of dimension n and $e = [1 \ldots 1]^T$, and $[I\ -\ I]$, respectively. When all directions of D_k are explored at each iteration, polling is called complete and leads to the convergence of the gradient to zero for the whole sequence of iterates [18]. Polling is called opportunistic when the first poll direction leading to descent is taken, obtaining a subsequence of iterates where the gradient is driven to zero [19]. In this case, the order of the poll directions may influence the computational performance of the method [20].

2.2 Probabilistic Direct-Search

The main motivation for exploring probabilistic approaches for direct-search is the need of evaluating the function on at least $n + 1$ (minimal positive base) polling points to ensure the convergence of deterministic methods. For a large dimensional space (large n) and particularly for expensive (in terms of computational time) functions to evaluate, convergence might be too slow. Recent numerical experiments suggested that polling directions randomly generated not necessarily fulfilling the positive spanning property compare favorable to the traditional use of positive bases (or positive spanning sets), particularly if the number of directions is considerably less than $n+1$ (which can go down to two) [12]. Direct-search methods (Algorithm 1) were extended by assuming that the set of polling directions D_k includes only a descent direction with a certain probability [13]. Nevertheless, that probabilistic approach enjoys almost-sure global convergence (convergent with probability one) provided the polling directions D_k are uniformly distributed on the unit ball [13]. Thus, Algorithm 1 remains the same for probabilistic direct-search methods except D_k, in poll step, where random directions uniformly distributed on the unit ball are considered without restrictions on the number of directions (can be as low as one).

3   IMPT for a Prostate Case

The prostate case considered in this study is included in the matRad package [21], an open source RT treatment planning system written in MATLAB. The rectum and the bladder are in the vicinity of the prostate and for that reason are the organs-at-risk (OARs) included in the treatment planning optimization. The tolerance doses considered for this two OARs are mean doses of 50 Gy. The remaining normal tissue, called Body, is also included in the optimization just to certify that dose is not accumulating elsewhere. The prescribed dose for the planning target volume (PTV) - tumor plus a margin - is 68 Gy. Considering the appropriate options in matRad, as displayed in Fig. 1, the fluence optimization for IMPT can be formulated as a quadratic nonlinear model that penalizes deviations from the prescribed/tolerated doses, implying that overdose or underdose may be clinically accepted at reduced levels, but are decreasingly acceptable for increased deviations from the prescribed/tolerated doses [22].

Two lateral parallel opposed beams are illustrated in Fig. 1 as they correspond to the most commonly used beam angle configuration for prostate proton therapy. For being widely used in clinical practice for prostate IMPT, this two-beam ensemble will be used as benchmark in our computational tests.

4   Randomized Direct-Search for BAO

IMPT BAO is a very challenging optimization problem that considers the determination of how many and which irradiation directions (angles) should be used in the treatment. For prostate cancer cases, appropriate beam selection is even more critical as proton therapy typically uses only a couple of beams. For that reason, optimal two-beam ensembles are aimed for the prostate case in study. The couch, where the patient lies during treatment, is also a degree of freedom. Figure 2 displays the benchmark two-beam ensemble (in red), possible coplanar beam directions (in black), when the couch is fixed at zero degrees, and possible noncoplanar beam directions (in blue), when couch is allowed to rotate.

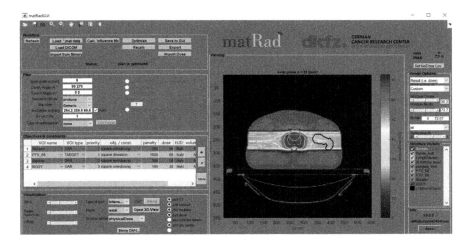

Fig. 1. IMPT for the prostate case from matRad package [21].

As highlighted before, BAO can be seen as the optimization of an expensive multi-modal black-box function, f, where the gantry angles, θ, and the couch angles, ϕ, for a two-beam ensemble are the input of f:

$$\min f(\theta_1, \theta_2, \phi_1, \phi_2)$$

s.t. $(\theta_1, \theta_2, \phi_1, \phi_2) \in \mathbb{R}^4.$

Note that this problem would be simpler if only coplanar beam directions were considered ($\phi_1 = \phi_2 = 0$) as the number of variables would be only two in a smaller search space ($\mathbb{R}^2$). The objective function $f(\theta_1, \theta_2, \phi_1, \phi_2)$ that measures the quality of the beam angle ensemble $(\theta_1, \theta_2, \phi_1, \phi_2)$ is the optimal value obtained by running the IMPT described in the previous section for each fixed set of two-beam ensembles.

We have developed deterministic direct-search approaches for BAO that were able to obtain high-quality treatment plans [5–11]. Although these approaches imply a computational time that is compatible with the clinical practice, these computational times are significant and can represent a drawback in some practical situations. The direct-search approaches for BAO we have developed consider the maximal and minimal positive bases highlighted in Sect. 2.1, which for this prostate case correspond to the directions (column-vetors) of the matrices

$$\begin{bmatrix} 1 & 0 & 0 & 0 & -1 & 0 & 0 & 0 \\ 0 & 1 & 0 & 0 & 0 & -1 & 0 & 0 \\ 0 & 0 & 1 & 0 & 0 & 0 & -1 & 0 \\ 0 & 0 & 0 & 1 & 0 & 0 & 0 & -1 \end{bmatrix} \text{ and } \begin{bmatrix} 1 & 0 & 0 & 0 & -1 \\ 0 & 1 & 0 & 0 & -1 \\ 0 & 0 & 1 & 0 & -1 \\ 0 & 0 & 0 & 1 & -1 \end{bmatrix},$$

respectively. One of the advantages of the directions of these positive bases is that for an appropriate choice of the initial step-size (power of two) all iterates

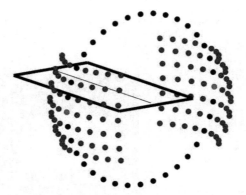

Fig. 2. Coplanar beam directions are displayed in black while some of the possible noncoplanar beam directions are displayed in blue. Benchmark 2-beam ensemble is displayed in red. (Color figure online)

will have integer values until the step-size becomes inferior to one, which is an interesting feature for the problem at hand.

The probabilistic direct-search approach tailored for BAO has the exact same algorithm (Algorithm 1) as the deterministic one except for the set of directions D_k that drops the need to be a positive spanning set. Gratton et al. suggested polling directions D_k that are uniformly distributed on the unit ball [13]. Instead of considering the l_2-norm, that would loose the feature described in the previous paragraph, we propose the use of the l_1-norm and randomly selecting directions uniformly distributed by quadrants. Figure 3 illustrates the proposed directions for two- and three-dimensional search spaces. Note that the number of possible directions is 2^n which is equal to $2n$ for a 2-dimensional search space but will be increasingly larger than $2n$ for higher dimensional spaces.

For the prostate case considered in this study, the IMPT BAO search space is four-dimensional with possible polling directions proposed corresponding to the column-vectors of the following matrix

$$\begin{bmatrix} 1 & 1 & 1 & 1 & 1 & 1 & 1 & 1 & -1 & -1 & -1 & -1 & -1 & -1 & -1 & -1 \\ 1 & 1 & 1 & 1 & -1 & -1 & -1 & -1 & 1 & 1 & 1 & 1 & -1 & -1 & -1 & -1 \\ 1 & 1 & -1 & -1 & 1 & 1 & -1 & -1 & 1 & 1 & -1 & -1 & 1 & 1 & -1 & -1 \\ 1 & -1 & 1 & -1 & 1 & -1 & 1 & -1 & 1 & -1 & 1 & -1 & 1 & -1 & 1 & -1 \end{bmatrix}.$$

Considering the benchmark two-beam ensemble as starting solution and an appropriate initial step-size, following any of these polling directions will always give an iterate with integer values as desired. The maximum number of random polling directions used at each iteration will, in theory, determine the pace of the algorithm. As important as verifying the computational time performance of the proposed randomized approach is to perceive the quality of the solutions obtained.

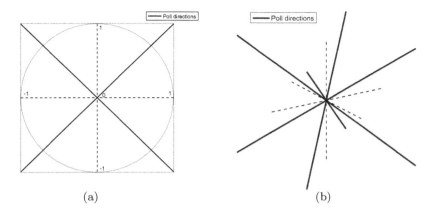

Fig. 3. Poll directions, one for each quadrant, considered for two-dimensional – (a) and three-dimensional – (b) problems.

5   Computational Results

A personal computer with MATLAB R2016a version running an Intel i7-6700 processor @ 2.60 GHz was used for the computational tests. The prostate case considered is included in the matRad package, that was used for IMPT fluence optimization by selecting the appropriate options. IMPT BAO optimization was performed considering both deterministic direct-search approaches (with maximal – $2n$ polling directions – and minimal – $n + 1$ polling directions) and randomized direct-search approaches (with a maximum of one, two, $n + 1$, $2n$, $3n$ and $4n = 2^n$, polling directions randomly chosen at each iteration). Opportunistic polling was considered without performing search step, i.e., $S_k = \emptyset$. Results obtained were compared with the two-beam benchmark ensemble. The goal of including deterministic direct-search approaches in the computational tests is to further benchmark the results obtained by randomized approaches as results obtained by deterministic methods have already proved to be of high-quality [10]. The purpose of allowing an increased maximum number of polling directions at each iteration in randomized approaches is twofold. First, to acknowledge if more polling directions will make a difference in the quality of the solutions obtained, regardless of the computational time. Second, when considering more than $2n$ of the possible poll directions defined in Sect. 2.2, we always end up with a positive spanning set. Thus, in this case, we have a set of polling directions that is deterministically descent, i.e., there is at least one direction that is guaranteed to form an acute angle with the negative gradient vector, instead of being probabilistically descent which is the case when we randomly consider at most $2n$ polling directions.

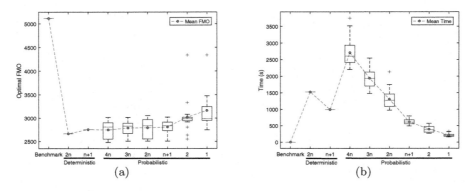

Fig. 4. Optimal FMO obtained by the different approaches – (a) and the corresponding computational times in seconds – (b).

As BAO is always performed resorting to the optimal FMO value, this is a natural measure to compare the quality of the solutions obtained by the different approaches. The optimal FMO value of the benchmark beam angle ensemble is 5114.82 while for the solutions of deterministic noncoplanar BAO solutions considering the maximal and the minimal positive basis are 2662.58 and 2753.35, respectively. These solutions manage to improve 48% and 46% the optimal FMO of the benchmark beam angle ensemble. The randomized approaches obtain a different solution each time the algorithm is run. For that reason, each randomized approach was run twenty times. The median (best) optimal FMO value of randomized noncoplanar BAO solutions, considering $4n$, $3n$, $2n$, $n+1$, 2 and 1 directions each iteration are 2808.52 (2480.31), 2826.79 (2503.8), 2834.77 (2503.8), 2832.83 (2505.52), 2985.26 (2547.94) and 2989.08 (2744.06), respectively. Figure 4 summarizes the performance of the different approaches both in terms of quality of solutions, as measured by the optimal FMO value, as in terms of computational times (in seconds). All BAO solutions clearly outperform the benchmark solution in terms of optimal FMO value, being deterministic BAO solutions slightly better than average randomized BAO solutions. It is interesting to see that randomized BAO solutions show no benefits from the possible inclusion of more poll directions while considering few random directions only present a small degradation of average results, that for 2 polling directions manage to obtain similar best results. In terms of computational times, the reduction of the maximum number of polling directions shows great benefits, with decreases to one third or half of the computational time when considering a maximum of 2 random directions compared to deterministic $2n$ or $n+1$ directions, respectively.

Although BAO solutions considerably improved the optimal FMO value of the benchmark solution, a set of other metrics is typically used in clinical practice to assess the quality of a treatment plan. A graphical instrument that gathers most of these metrics is the dose-volume histogram (DVH). The DVH displays the fraction of a structure's volume that receives at least a given dose. Ideally, the DVH line for the PTV should be at 100% volume until the prescribed dose

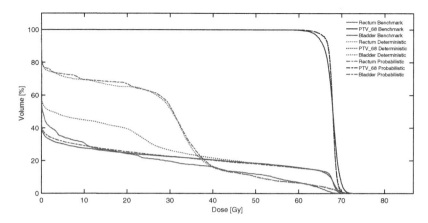

Fig. 5. Cumulative dose-volume histogram comparing the results obtained by considering the benchmark 2-beam ensemble and the 2-beam ensembles obtained by the BAO procedure with a deterministic maximal positive basis and a probabilistic selection of at most 2 poll directions at each iteration.

is reached and then immediately fall to 0%, while for OARs the DVH line would ideally fall immediately to zero at 0% of the OAR volume meaning that no dose was received. Figure 5 displays the DVH results for the benchmark 2-beam ensemble, for the BAO solution obtained by the deterministic approach with $2n$ directions (the best deterministic approach in terms of optimal FMO value) and by an average BAO solution of the probabilistic approach with 2 directions (the solution with best trade-off between optimal FMO value and computational times). By simple inspection of the DVH curves, we can verify that tumor coverage is similar for both BAO solutions that clearly outperform the benchmark solution in this important feature. In terms of organ sparing, benchmark solution obtained the best results. Interestingly, while rectum sparing is similar for both BAO solutions, the deterministic approach with $2n$ directions is outperformed by the probabilistic approach with 2 directions in terms of bladder sparing.

Figure 6 displays the different two-beam ensembles whose DVHs were compared in Fig. 5. Although the polling directions followed are different as well as the maximum number of directions allowed in each iteration, it is interesting to acknowledge that the solutions obtained by deterministic and randomized methods are spatially close, which may indicate these regions as appropriate to irradiate this patient.

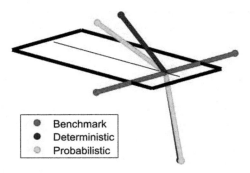

Fig. 6. Benchmark 2-beam ensemble is displayed in red while 2-beam ensembles obtained by the BAO procedure considering a deterministic maximal positive basis and a probabilistic selection of at most 2 poll directions in each iteration are displayed in blue and green, respectively.

6   Conclusions

In clinical practice, the number and directions of beams in an IMPT treatment plan are manually selected based on prior trial-and-error experience. However, the optimal selection of beam irradiation directions can deeply impact the quality of dose distributions. On one hand, the number of beams considered in IMPT is lower than in IMRT, typically 2–3 beams and rarely more than 4–5, which makes the optimal selection of beam irradiation directions more decisive. On the other hand, mainly because of high dose gradients in proton therapy, uncertainty due to anatomical variations but also other uncertainty factors specific of proton therapy, need to be addressed through robustness embedded in the optimization loop, including the optimal selection of beams. Thus, in proton therapy, decision on best beam ensembles cannot be based on dosimetric criteria alone, but must also take into consideration different sources of uncertainty. Nevertheless, assuming that robustness can be mostly handled by the FMO problem, strategies successfully developed for IMRT can be tested for IMPT.

In addition to the need for robustness, computational time becomes even more important in the optimization of irradiation directions by proton beams due to an increased number of degrees of freedom (e.g., different energy levels). In this study, we consider direct-search methods to address the IMPT BAO problem given their good performance in the resolution of the IMRT BAO problem. In order to test the effectiveness (both in terms of computational time and quality of solution) of reducing the number of polling directions at each iteration, moving from a set of deterministic directions (that guarantee at least one descent direction) to a set of probabilistic directions (where a descent direction exists with a given probability), we propose a strategy of random choice of polling directions evenly distributed across quadrants.

The proposed randomized strategy shows, for a prostate cancer case, that considering few polling directions (e.g., two) improved significantly the computational time at the cost of slightly decreasing the quality of the solution obtained. This is one of the differences from recent works on probabilistic descent that reported improved numerical behavior both in terms of computational times as well as the quality of the solution obtained when only two polling directions are considered. Nevertheless, although the optimal FMO value using only two polling directions was not the overall best, the resulting treatment plan is at least as good as that obtained by the deterministic method.

In future work, this type of randomized approximation has to be tested in more cases to validate the excellent performance found only for one prostate cancer case. Furthermore, different cancer sites where more beams are used, e.g. skull base cancer, have also to be tested to validate these approaches for optimization problems in higher dimensions. Inclusion of robustness must also be fully incorporated which was not the case in this preliminary study. Finally, different strategies for randomly selecting polling directions must be tested as well, as the success of this approach is closely linked to this choice.

Acknowledgments. This work has been supported by the Fundação para a Ciência e a Tecnologia (FCT) under project grants UTA-EXPL/FMT/0079/2019, PTDC/CCI-INF/28030/2017, UIDB/05037/2020 and UIDB/00308/2020.

References

1. Cancer tomorrow. http://gco.iarc.fr/tomorrow/home. Accessed 17 Mar 2021
2. Mohan, R., Grosshans, D.: Proton therapy-present and future. Adv. Drug Deliv. Rev. **109**, 26–44 (2017)
3. Craft, D.: Local beam angle optimization with linear programming and gradient search. Phys. Med. Biol. **52**, 127–135 (2007)
4. Rocha, H., Dias, J., Ventura, T., Ferreira, B.C., Lopes, M.C.: Beam angle optimization in IMRT: are we really optimizing what matters? Int. Trans. Oper. Res. **26**, 908–928 (2019)
5. Rocha, H., Dias, J., Ferreira, B.C., Lopes, M.C.: Selection of intensity modulated radiation therapy treatment beam directions using radial basis functions within a pattern search methods framework. J. Glob. Optim. **57**, 1065–1089 (2013)
6. Rocha, H., Dias, J., Ferreira, B.C., Lopes, M.C.: Beam angle optimization for intensity-modulated radiation therapy using a guided pattern search method. Phys. Med. Biol. **58**, 2939–2953 (2013)
7. Rocha, H., Dias, J., Ferreira, B.C., Lopes, M.C.: Pattern search methods framework for beam angle optimization in radiotherapy design. Appl. Math. Comput. **219**, 10853–10865 (2013)
8. Rocha, H., Dias, J., Ferreira, B.C., Lopes, M.C.: Noncoplanar beam angle optimization in IMRT treatment planning using pattern search methods. J. Phys.: Conf. Ser. **616**, 012014 (2015)
9. Rocha, H., Dias, J., Ventura, T., Ferreira, B.C., Lopes, M.C.: A derivative-free multistart framework for an automated noncoplanar beam angle optimization in IMRT. Med. Phys. **43**, 5514–5526 (2016)

10. Ventura, T., Rocha, H., Ferreira, B., Dias, J., Lopes, M.C.: Comparison of two beam angular optimization algorithms guided by automated multicriterial IMRT. Phys. Med. **64**, 210–221 (2019)

11. Rocha, H., Dias, J., Ventura, T., Ferreira, B., Lopes, M.C.: An automated treatment planning strategy for highly noncoplanar radiotherapy arc trajectories. Int. Trans. Oper. Res. (2021)

12. Gratton, S., Vicente, L.N.: A merit function approach for direct search. SIAM J. Optim. **24**, 1980–1998 (2014)

13. Gratton, S., Royer, C.W., Vicente, L.N., Zhang, Z.: Direct search based on probabilistic descent. SIAM J. Optim. **25**, 1515–1541 (2015)

14. Nelder, J.A., Mead, R.: A simplex method for function minimization. Comput. J. **7**, 308–313 (1965)

15. Lagarias, J.C., Poonen, B., Wright, M.H.: Convergence of the restricted Nelder-Mead algorithm in two dimensions. SIAM J. Optim. **22**, 501–532 (2012)

16. Alberto, P., Nogueira, F., Rocha, H., Vicente, L.N.: Pattern search methods for user-provided points: application to molecular geometry problems. SIAM J. Optim. **14**, 1216–1236 (2004)

17. Davis, C.: Theory of positive linear dependence. Am. J. Math. **76**, 733–746 (1954)

18. Kolda, T.G., Lewis, R.M., Torczon, V.: Optimization by direct search: new perspectives on some classical and modern methods. SIAM Rev. **45**, 385–482 (2003)

19. Torczon, V.: On the convergence of pattern search algorithms. SIAM J. Optim. **7**, 1–25 (1997)

20. Audet, C., Dennis, J.E., Jr.: Mesh adaptive direct search algorithms for constrained optimization. SIAM J. Optim. **17**, 188–217 (2006)

21. Wieser, H.-P., et al.: Development of the open-source dose calculation and optimization toolkit matRad. Med. Phys. **44**, 2556–2568 (2017)

22. Aleman, D.M., Kumar, A., Ahuja, R.K., Romeijn, H.E., Dempsey, J.F.: Neighborhood search approaches to beam orientation optimization in intensity modulated radiation therapy treatment planning. J. Glob. Optim. **42**, 587–607 (2008)

Optimal Control by Multiple Shooting and Weighted Tchebycheff Penalty-Based Scalarization

Gisela C. Vieira Ramadas[1]([⊠]) [iD], Edite M. G. P. Fernandes[2] [iD],
Ana Maria A. C. Rocha[2] [iD], and M. Fernanda P. Costa[3] [iD]

[1] Research Center of Mechanical Engineering (CIDEM), School of Engineering
of Porto (ISEP), Polytechnic of Porto, 4200-072 Porto, Portugal
gcv@isep.ipp.pt
[2] ALGORITMI Center, University of Minho, Campus de Gualtar,
4710-057 Braga, Portugal
{emgpf,arocha}@dps.uminho.pt
[3] Centre of Mathematics, University of Minho, Campus de Gualtar,
4710-057 Braga, Portugal
mfc@math.uminho.pt

Abstract. Numerical direct multiple shooting (MS) methods have shown to be important and efficient tools to solve optimal control problems (OCP). The use of an MS method to solve the OCP gives rise to a finite-dimensional optimization problem with a set of "continuity constraints" that should be satisfied together with the other algebraic states and control constraints of the OCP. Using non-negative functions to measure the violation of the "continuity constraints" and of the algebraic constraints separately, the finite-dimensional problem is reformulated as a multi-objective problem with three objectives to be optimized. This paper explores the use of a multi-objective approach, the weighted Tchebycheff scalarization method, to minimize the objective functional and satisfy all the constraint conditions of the OCP. During implementation, a penalty term is added to the Tchebycheff aggregated objective function aiming to force and accelerate the convergence of the constraint violations to zero. The effectiveness of the new methodology is illustrated with the experiments carried out with six OCP.

Keywords: Optimal control · Multiple shooting · Tchebycheff scalarization

---

This work has been supported by FCT – Fundação para a Ciência e Tecnologia within the R&D Units Project Scope: UIDB/00319/2020, UIDB/00013/2020 and UIDP/00013/2020 of CMAT-UM. We also acknowledge the financial support of CIDEM.

O. Gervasi et al. (Eds.): ICCSA 2021, LNCS 12953, pp. 333–349, 2021.
https://doi.org/10.1007/978-3-030-86976-2_23

1   Introduction

In this paper, we consider solving an optimal control problem (OCP) by a direct multiple shooting (MS) method, and explore the use of a weighted Tchebycheff scalarization method to take care of the simultaneous minimization of three objective functions. An OCP is a constrained optimization problem that has a set of dynamic equations as constraints. There are three types of OCP that differ in the formulation of the functional to be optimized: OCP in the *Bolza form*, in the *Lagrange form* and in the *Mayer form*. They are equivalent and it is possible to convert a problem in one of the forms into another one [1]. Here, we assume that the OCP is in the *Mayer form*:

$$\min_{\vec{u}(t) \in U} \ J(\vec{y}(t), \vec{u}(t)) \equiv M(T, \vec{y}(T))$$

$$\text{s.t.} \quad \vec{y}'(t) = \vec{f}(t, \vec{y}(t), \vec{u}(t)), t \in [0, T], \ \vec{y}(0) = \vec{y}_0, \ \vec{y}(T) = \vec{y}_T, \quad (1)$$
$$0 = h_e(t, \vec{y}(t), \vec{u}(t)), e \in E, \ t \in [0, T],$$
$$0 \geq g_j(t, \vec{y}(t), \vec{u}(t)), j \in F, \ t \in [0, T],$$

where $\vec{y} \in \mathbb{R}^s$ is the vector of state variables, $\vec{u} \in U \subset \mathbb{R}^c$ is the vector of control, U represents a class of functions (in particular functions of class C^1 and piecewise constant), $E = \{1, 2, \ldots, l_h\}$ and $F = \{1, 2, \ldots, l_g\}$ [1]. In the problem of Mayer, the functional is not an integral but a function M that depends in general on the dependent variables $\vec{y}$ and the final point of the t-domain T. For simplicity, we assume that the initial point of the t-domain is 0.

In the OCP we want to find $\vec{u}$ that minimizes the objective functional J subject to the dynamic system of ordinary differential equations (ODE) and the mixed states and control (equality and inequality) constraints.

Methods for solving OCP like (1) can be classified into two classes. In an indirect method, the first-order necessary conditions from Pontryagin's maximum principle are used to reformulate the original problem into a boundary value problem [2]. On the other hand, direct methods solve the OCP directly. They transform the infinite-dimensional OCP into a finite-dimensional optimization problem that can be solved by efficient nonlinear programming (NLP) algorithms. All direct methods discretize the control variables but differ in the way they treat the state variables.

In a direct MS method the t-domain is partitioned into smaller subintervals and the system of ODE is integrated in each subinterval independently. Besides the control variables, the new *state start values* (for the state variables) at each subinterval make the decision variables of the finite NLP problem [2,3]. When a direct MS method is used to solve the OCP, a set of "continuity constraints" must be defined and should be satisfied together with the other algebraic mixed states and control constraints. To solve the resultant finite NLP problem, well-known NLP methods can be used, namely a sequential quadratic programming procedure or an interior-point method [3,4]. To reduce the need for numerical (or analytical) derivatives, a first-order descent method based on the filter methodology has been proposed in [5].

To minimize the objective function and satisfy all the constraints - the "continuity constraints" and the algebraic constraints - the herein proposed methodology reformulates the NLP problem as a multi-objective optimization (MOO) problem with three objectives to be simultaneously optimized. Thereafter, the weighted Tchebycheff scalarization method is used to solve the reformulated finite MOO problem. We also take advantage of the weighted Tchebycheff method by solving problems with non-convex Pareto fronts and force the simultaneous minimization of the objectives by adding a penalty term to the weighted Tchebycheff scalar function.

The paper is organized as follows. Section 2 introduces the direct MS method for solving the OCP in the *Mayer form*, Sect. 3 shows the mathematical formulation of the finite NLP problem and the objective functions that are required to be simultaneously minimized. Section 4 briefly presents the basic multi-objective concepts, the objective function to be minimized in the weighted Tchebycheff scalarization context and the details concerning the new algorithm. Section 5 illustrates the implementation of the methodology with six OCP and we conclude the paper in Sect. 6.

2 Direct Multiple Shooting Method

In a direct MS method, the controls are discretized in the NLP. On a specific grid defined by $0 = t_1 < t_2 < \cdots < t_{N-1} < t_N = T$, where $N - 1$ is the total number of subintervals, the control $\vec{u}(t)$ is discretized, namely using a piecewise constant: $\vec{u}(t) = \vec{q}^{\,i}$, for $t \in [t_i, t_{i+1}]$ and $i = 1, \ldots, N - 1$, so that $\vec{u}(t)$ only depends on the control parameters $\vec{q} = (\vec{q}^{\,1}, \vec{q}^{\,2}, \ldots, \vec{q}^{\,N-1})$. Besides the discretized controls, the *state start values* at the nodes of the grid - herein represented by $\vec{x}^{\,i} \in \mathbb{R}^s$, $i = 1, 2, \ldots, N - 1$ - are also decision variables of the NLP problem [2]. The variables $\vec{x}^{\,i}$, $i = 1, 2, \ldots, N - 1$ are the initial values for the state variables for the $N - 1$ independent initial value problems on the subintervals $[t_i, t_{i+1}]$:

$$\vec{y}'(t) = \vec{f}(t, \vec{y}(t), \vec{q}^{\,i}), \text{ for } t \in [t_i, t_{i+1}] \text{ and } \vec{y}(t_i) = \vec{x}^{\,i}.$$

The continuity of the solution trajectories $\vec{y}^{\,i}(t; \vec{x}^{\,i}, \vec{q}^{\,i})$ is guaranteed by satisfying the "continuity conditions":

$$\vec{y}^{\,i}(t_{i+1}; \vec{x}^{\,i}, \vec{q}^{\,i}) = \vec{x}^{\,i+1}, \; i = 1, \ldots, N - 1, \tag{2}$$

as well as the initial state, $\vec{x}^{\,1} = \vec{y}_0$, and the final state, $\vec{x}^{\,N} = \vec{y}_T$, constraints. The dynamic system is then solved by an ODE solver on each shooting subinterval $[t_i, t_{i+1}]$ independently, and the state variables $\vec{y}(t)$ are considered as dependent variables $\vec{y}(t, \vec{q})$.

3 The NLP Problem

We assume that the NLP problem is a non-convex constrained optimization problem (COP). We also assume that the OCP is in the *Mayer form*, the ODE system has initial and boundary state values, and algebraic equality and inequality constraints, involving state and control variables, are present. The dynamic system is solved, in each subinterval $[t_i, t_{i+1}]$, by the explicit 4th order Runge-Kutta integration formula based on 5 points. The mathematical form of the COP is the following:

$$
\begin{aligned}
\min_{\vec{x}^i,\, i \in I_N; \vec{q}^i,\, i \in I} \quad & M(T, \vec{y}(T)) \\
\text{s.t.} \quad & g_j(\vec{y}^i(t; \vec{x}^i, \vec{q}^i), \vec{q}^i) \leq 0,\, t \in [t_i, t_{i+1}], i \in I, j \in F \\
& h_e(\vec{y}^i(t; \vec{x}^i, \vec{q}^i), \vec{q}^i) = 0,\, t \in [t_i, t_{i+1}], i \in I, e \in E \\
& \vec{y}^i(t_{i+1}; \vec{x}^i, \vec{q}^i) - \vec{x}^{i+1} = 0, i \in I,\ \vec{x}^1 - \vec{y}_0 = 0, \vec{x}^N - \vec{y}_T = 0\,,
\end{aligned}
\tag{3}
$$

where $I = \{1, \ldots, N-1\}$ and $I_N = I \cup \{N\}$. In order to solve the optimization problem (3), the objective function, the "continuity constraints" $\vec{y}^i(t_{i+1}; \vec{x}^i, \vec{q}^i) - \vec{x}^{i+1} = 0, i \in I$, the initial state and the final state constraints, and the algebraic equality and inequality constraints must be evaluated by solving the ODE system. An optimal solution to the problem (3) satisfies all the constraints and achieves the least objective function value.

To measure the violation of the "continuity constraints", initial state and final state constraints, the following non-negative function is used

$$
\theta(\vec{x}, \vec{q}) = \sum_{l \in L} \sum_{i \in I} (y_l^i(t_{i+1}; \vec{x}^i, \vec{q}^i) - x_l^{i+1})^2 + \sum_{l \in L} (x_l^1 - y_{l_0})^2 + \sum_{l \in L} (x_l^N - y_{l_T})^2\,,
\tag{4}
$$

where $L = \{1, 2, \ldots, s\}$. If the solution $(\vec{x}, \vec{q})$ satisfies these constraints, $\theta(\vec{x}, \vec{q})$ is zero; otherwise it is positive. Similarly, the non-negative function, p, used to measure the algebraic equality and inequality constraints violation, is defined as follows:

$$
p(\vec{x}, \vec{q}) = \sum_{j \in F} \sum_{i \in I} \max \left\{ 0, g_j(\vec{y}^i(t; \vec{x}^i, \vec{q}^i), \vec{q}^i) \right\}^2 + \sum_{e \in E} \sum_{i \in I} h_e(\vec{y}^i(t; \vec{x}^i, \vec{q}^i), \vec{q}^i)^2,
\tag{5}
$$

where $p(\vec{x}, \vec{q}) = 0$ when the corresponding constraints are satisfied, otherwise $p(\vec{x}, \vec{q}) > 0$.

In this paper, the constraint violation functions $\theta(\vec{x}, \vec{q})$ and $p(\vec{x}, \vec{q})$, and the optimality measure $M(T, \vec{x}, \vec{q})$, are used to reformulate the COP (3) into a tri-objective optimization (TOO) problem. In this TOO problem, both the feasibility measures – defined by the above defined constraint violation functions – and the optimality measure (defined by the objective function $M(T, \vec{x}, \vec{q})$) are minimized simultaneously.

To simplify the notation, the letter x will be used to denote the vector of the decision variables $x = (\vec{x}, \vec{q})$ (with $n = sN + c(N-1)$ components) and $f_1(x) = \theta(x)$, $f_2(x) = p(x)$ and $f_3(x) = M(T, x(T))$. Thus, the TOO problem is the following:

$$
\min_{x \in \Omega \subseteq \mathbb{R}^n} (f_1(x), f_2(x), f_3(x))\,,
\tag{6}
$$

where $x \in \mathbb{R}^n$ is the vector of the decision variables, n is the number of decision variables, Ω is the feasible search region (often called *feasible decision space*) and the components of the vector $\vec{f} : \mathbb{R}^n \to \mathbb{R}^3$ are the objective functions (also called criteria, payoff functions, or cost functions) to be optimized. The feasible criterion space $\mathcal{F}$ is defined as the set $\mathcal{F} = \{\vec{f}(x) \text{ such that } x \in \Omega\}$. This set is also called the *attainable set*. However, we note that there are points in the feasible objective space that do not correspond to a single point $x \in \Omega$. The space $\mathbb{R}^n$ is called the decision space and $\mathbb{R}^3$ is called the objective space.

When the objective functions are not conflicting, it is possible to find a solution where every objective function attains its minimum [6]. However, if the objectives are conflicting, i.e., the improvement of one objective leads to another objective deterioration, one single optimal solution does not exist, but a set of alternatives - the non-dominated solutions - further ahead called Pareto optimal set. The decision-maker then selects one (or more than one) compromise solution, among the alternatives, that better satisfies his/her preferences.

4   Multi-objective Optimization

The process of optimizing systematically and simultaneously a collection of objective functions is called MOO [7]. The simultaneous optimization of several objectives has been attracting the attention of scientific researchers, since it is possible to find a set of solutions that represent different compromises between the objectives. The decision-maker is then able to choose the solution that better suits his/her goals.

4.1   Basic Concepts

First, and assuming that the number of objectives, m, is greater than 1, the definition of dominance is presented.

Definition 1. *A vector $\vec{f} = (f_1, \ldots, f_m)$ is said to dominate $\bar{\vec{f}} = (\bar{f}_1, \ldots, \bar{f}_m)$ if and only if*

$$\forall i \in \{1, \ldots, m\} \ f_i \leq \bar{f}_i \ \text{ and } \ \exists i \in \{1, \ldots, m\} \ \text{ such that } f_i < \bar{f}_i. \tag{7}$$

When two solutions $\vec{f}^1 = \vec{f}(x^1)$ and $\vec{f}^2 = \vec{f}(x^2)$, $x^1, x^2 \in \Omega \subseteq \mathbb{R}^n$ are compared, one of these three cases is true: i) $\vec{f}^1$ dominates $\vec{f}^2$, ii) $\vec{f}^1$ is dominated by $\vec{f}^2$, iii) $\vec{f}^1$ and $\vec{f}^2$ are non-dominated. The next definition states the condition for a feasible solution to be a Pareto optimal solution.

Definition 2. *Let $\vec{f} \in \mathbb{R}^m$ be the objective functions vector. A solution $x^1 \in \Omega$ is said to be Pareto optimal if and only if there is no other solution $x^2 \in \Omega$ for which $\vec{f}(x^2)$ dominates $\vec{f}(x^1)$.*

This means that x^1 is a Pareto optimal solution if there is no other feasible solution, x^2, which would decrease some objective f_i without causing a simultaneous increase in at least one other objective. In MOO, there is no single optimal solution, but a set of optimal solutions called Pareto optimal set (in the space of the decision variables). The corresponding function vectors are said to be non-dominated (ND) (see [8] for details concerning MOO).

Definition 3. *Given a MOO problem with objective function vector $\vec{f} \in \mathbb{R}^m$ and the Pareto optimal set X^*, the Pareto optimal front (PF*) is defined as:*

$$PF^* = \{\vec{f} = (f_1(x), \ldots, f_m(x)) \quad such \ that \ x \in X^*\}.$$

4.2 Scalarization Approaches to MOO

The goal of a MOO algorithm is to find a good approximation to the Pareto front PF^* (and to the Pareto optimal set), i.e., to find a reasonable number of Pareto function vectors which are evenly distributed along the Pareto optimal front. The most popular methods to solve the MOO problem produce an approximation to the PF^* directly [9]. They are stochastic methods and although they are naturally prepared to produce many solutions, since they are in general population-based techniques, the computational effort to achieve the solutions is substantial.

Alternatively, a single solution can be found by aggregating the objective functions into a scalar objective function that is used in a single-objective optimization (SOO) context. When combining the objectives, a vector of weights should be provided by the decision-maker prior to the optimization. In order to be able to obtain an approximation to the PF^*, the SOO method must be run as many times as the desired number of points using different vectors of weights [10]. The most used aggregation method is the weighted sum approach that assigns to each objective function f_i, of the vector $\vec{f}$, a non-negative weight w_i, minimizing the function that is the weighted sum of the objectives. Although this function is differentiable and simple to implement, it suffers from a drawback since certain Pareto optimal solutions in non-convex regions of the Pareto optimal front cannot be found.

Alternatively, the weighted Tchebycheff approach also assigns a vector of weights to the objectives and relies on a nonlinear weighted aggregation of the functions f_i to form a single objective [11,12]. Thus, it is able to deal with a non-convex Pareto front [13]. In the minimization context, the resulting SOO problem has the form

$$\min_{x \in \Omega} \Psi(x; \vec{w}) \equiv \max \left\{ w_1 \left| f_1(x) - z_1^U \right|, \ldots, w_m \left| f_m - z_m^U \right| \right\} \qquad (8)$$

where $\vec{w} = (w_1, \ldots, w_m)$ is the vector of weights satisfying $w_i \geq 0, i = 1, \ldots, m$ and $w_1 + \cdots + w_m = 1$, the vector $\vec{z}^U = (z_1^U, \ldots, z_m^U)$ is the ideal (or Utopia) point in the objective space, i.e., $z_j^U = \min\{f_j(x) \text{ such that } x \in \Omega\}$, $j = 1, \ldots, m$. Each term can be view as a distance function that minimizes the distance between the solution point and the ideal point in the objective space. Minimizing $\Psi(x; \vec{w})$ can provide approximations to the complete Pareto optimal front by varying the vector of weights [8,10]. The function is not smooth at some points but the use of a derivative-free method to minimize $\Psi(x; \vec{w})$ overtakes this issue.

In our problem, z_1^U and z_2^U are known in advance, since f_1 and f_2 are constraint violations.

4.3   Weighted Tchebycheff Algorithm for OCP

In this section, the main ideas of the proposed methodology are presented in Algorithm 1. The algorithm has been designed to simultaneously minimize the three above defined objective functions $\theta(x)$, $p(x)$ and $M(T, x(T))$ using a weighted Tchebycheff scalarization approach that takes advantage of a penalty term to accelerate the convergence of the constraints violation to zero.

Algorithm 1. Weighted Tchebycheff algorithm with a penalty term for OCP

Require: n (number of decision variables), N_w, N_{runs}
 1: Generate a set of N_w weight vectors, $\vec{w}^i$, $i = 1, \ldots, N_w$ with positive components
 2: **for** $r = 1$ to N_{runs} **do**
 3:    Compute z_3^U and $Viol$ using Algorithm 2
 4:    Set $z_i^U = 0$, $i = 1, 2$
 5:    Given $x^0 \in \Omega$ based on the ODE initial conditions
 6:    **for** $j = 1$ to N_w **do**
 7:       Set $Viol_{old} = Viol$
 8:       Compute $x(\vec{w}^j)$, an approximation to the subproblem

$$\min_x \ \Psi(x; \vec{w}^j) + \mu_j \left(w_1^j f_1(x) + w_2^j f_2(x) \right),$$

        using x^0 as initial approximation, where $\mu_j = 2^\kappa$ and $\kappa = \lfloor \frac{j}{2} \rfloor$.
 9:       Set $Viol = f_1(x(\vec{w}^j)) + f_2(x(\vec{w}^j))$
10:       **if** $Viol < Viol_{old}$ **then**
11:          Update z_3^U with the current value $f_3(x(w^j))$
12:       **end if**
13:       Update $x^0 = x(\vec{w}^j)$
14:       Set $F_i^{r,j} = f_i(x(\vec{w}^j))$, $i = 1, 2, 3$
15:    **end for**
16: **end for**
17: Identify the ND solutions among $(F_1^{r,j}, F_2^{r,j}, F_3^{r,j})$, $j = 1, \ldots, N_w$, $r = 1, \ldots, N_{runs}$.

Relative to the ideal point $\vec{z}^U$, the tested strategy considers $z_1^U = z_2^U = 0$ all over the iterative process and z_3^U is initially estimated using a payoff table, as shown in Algorithm 2. A large set of points in the decision space are randomly generated in Ω, the corresponding function vectors are evaluated and the smallest f_3 value is identified to give the estimate of z_3^U. There is a different estimated value for each run. During the inner cycle that runs for all vectors of weights $\vec{w}^j$, $j = 1, \ldots, N_w$ (from line 6 to line 15 in Algorithm 1) the z_3^U is updated with the most recent value of $f_3(x(\vec{w}^j))$, if the sum of f_1 and f_2 (therein called $Viol$) for that $\vec{w}^j$ has decreased relative to that of the previous $\vec{w}^{j-1}$.

Another important issue addressed in Algorithm 1 is the initial approximation provided to the NLP solver. The x^0 for the first subproblem (in the inner cycle), corresponding to the weights vector $\vec{w}^1$, is generated taking into account the ODE initial conditions. For the remaining subproblems, x^0 is the solutions of the previous subproblem (see lines 5 and 13).

Finally, the penalty term that is added to the Tchebycheff objective function (8) for the minimization in each subproblem is justified by the need to force even further and accelerate the decrease of the objective functions f_1 and f_2 (constraint violations θ (4) and p (5) respectively). The penalty parameter μ is set initially to one and doubles every two subproblems. See line 8 in Algorithm 1.

Algorithm 2. Generate payoff table to compute z_3^U

Require: n (number of decision variables)
 1: **for** $j = 1$ to $50n$ **do**
 2:     Randomly generate $x^j \in \Omega$
 3:     Compute $f_i^j \equiv f_i(x^j)$, $i = 1, 2, 3$
 4: **end for**
 5: Set $z_3^U = \min_{j=1,\dots,50n} f_3^j$
 6: Set $Viol = \max_{j=1,\dots,50n}(f_1^j + f_2^j)$

---

5   Numerical Results

In this preliminary study, the `fminsearch` from MATLAB® is tested to compute $x(w^i)$, in line 8 of the Algorithm 1. For all experiments, the options for `fminsearch` are set as follows: 'MaxFunEvals' $= 1000n$, 'MaxIter' $= 500n$ and 'TolFun' $= 1e - 04$, where n is the total number of decision variables in the finite optimization problem. Parameter values for all the illustrated problems are: number of runs, $N_{runs} = 5$ and number of subintervals in $[0, T]$, $N = 10$. We note that the addition of more subintervals gives very little improvement in the optimal objective values, but greatly increases the overall computational effort.

To generate the weight vectors (see line 1 of Algorithm 1), the simplex-lattice design method for generating an evenly distributed set of weights in a simplex is used. The constructive method for the creation of a $\{m, q\}$-simplex lattice, presented in [14], is used to obtain the uniformly distributed vectors of weights. With $m = 3$ (number of objectives) and $q = 8$ ($q + 1$ is the number of points on each axis), a total of 45 design points are created. Since only design points that have positive components seem adequate for this TOO problem, a total of $N_w = 21$ vectors of weights are selected. Figure 1 shows the 55 design points of the $\{3, 8\}$-simplex lattice and the 21 selected points of the simplex.

The best solution obtained by the algorithm is selected from the final computed ND solutions, after running the algorithm 5 times. It corresponds to the final ND solution that has the least value of $Viol$. The results are shown for six problems: "trajectory", "VanderPol", "obstacle", "reactor","Fuller" and "Tankreactor". Table 1 contains the best solutions obtained for the selected problems and Fig. 2, 3, 4, 5, 6 and 7 display:

- (a) the 3-dimensional approximation to the Pareto front
- (b) the 2-dimensional projection $f_1 - f_3$ of the Pareto front (for Problem 1) and the trajectory in the state space (for Problems 2–6)

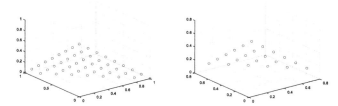

(a) Points of the {3, 8}-simplex (b) Selected 21 design points

Fig. 1. Design and selected points of the {3, 8}-simplex lattice

- (c) the state variables of the selected best solution
- (d) the optimal control of the best solution.

We note that the solutions computed after repeating the process 5 times ($N_{runs} = 5$, corresponding to the outer cycle) are displayed in the (a) (and (b) for Problem 1) plots with a 'blue' filled circle and the final ND solutions (after the 5 runs) are identified with a 'red' bigger open circle.

Problem 1. "trajectory" – Find $u(t)$ that minimizes J (with $T = 3$ fixed):

$$\min_{u(t)} J \equiv \int_0^T \left(y^2(t) + u^2(t) \right) dt$$
$$\text{s.t. } y'(t) = (1 + y(t))y(t) + u(t), \ t \in [0, T]$$
$$y(0) = 0.05, \ y(T) = 0, \ |y(t)| \le 1, \ |u(t)| \le 1, t \in [0, T].$$

For Problem 1, the initial provided x^0 is $y(t_i) = 1, \ i \in I_N$ and $u(t_i) = 0, \ i \in I$. The best computed solution in terms of constraints violation (identified among the final 44 ND solutions) is $(\theta, p, M) = (7.8962\mathrm{e}{-}10, \ 0, \ 0.023928)$, as depicted in Table 1. This table also shows the run (among the 5 runs) where the best solution was obtained, and j corresponds to the index of the weights vector $\bar{w}^j$ in that run. In Table 2, a comparison with other results in the literature is shown. This table displays t (time in seconds required to obtain the reported solution), fe (number of function evaluations required to produce the solution), as well as t_{avg} (average time for Algorithm 1 to produce a solution over the 5 runs and 21 weight vectors) and fe_{avg} (average value of function evaluations – over the 5 runs and 21 weight vectors). Figure 2 shows the plots above mentioned relative to this problem. The selected solution is very satisfactory and the profiles for the state and control are as expected.

Problem 2. "VanderPol" – Find $u(t)$ that minimizes J (with $T = 5$ fixed):

$$\min_{u(t)} J \equiv \frac{1}{2} \int_0^T \left(y_1^2(t) + y_2^2(t) + u^2(t) \right) dt$$
$$\text{s.t. } y_1'(t) = y_2(t),$$
$$y_2'(t) = -y_1(t) + (1 - y_1^2(t))y_2(t) + u(t), \ t \in [0, T]$$
$$y_1(0) = 1, \ y_2(0) = 0, \ y_1(T) - y_2(T) + 1 = 0 .$$

Table 1. Best selected solutions

Problem	ND solutions	(θ, p, M)	run (j^a)
"trajectory"	44	(7.8962e−10, 0, 0.023928)	2 (14–21)
"VanderPol"	42	(2.0699e−07, 0, 1.716531)^b	5 (21)
"obstacle"	8	(4.7033e−11, 0, 0.652339)^c	1 (21)
"reactor"	52	(8.3010e−12, 0, 0.552876)	3 (21)
"Fuller"	62	(2.1857e−07, 0, 3.133665)^d	1 (21)
"Tankreactor"	39	(6.4011e−08, 0, 0.026682)	1 (21)

^{a} j corresponds to the index of the vector of weights ($j = 1, \ldots, N_w$).
^{b} another interesting ND solution (4.14976e−05, 0, 1.692121) from run 5 ($j = 15$).
^{c} another interesting ND solution (4.3023e−10, 0, 0.185424) from run 4 ($j = 21$).
^{d} another interesting ND solution (3.2306e−05, 1.4921e−07, 3.105910) from run 3 ($j = 15$).

Table 2. Solutions comparison

Problem	Algorithm 1		Other methods	
	fe/fe_{avg}	t/t_{avg}	$(\theta, p, M)/M$	fe (t)
"trajectory"	413*/3094	0.62*/4.30	(8.848e−11, 0, 0.264)^a	21494 (22.5)
"VanderPol"	966/16943	0.54/9.77	$M = 1.6860^b$	$6^\ddagger + 6^\dagger$ (0.31)
"obstacle"	1293/6676	0.72/3.92	(1.31e−08, 4.88e−10, 2.46)^a	52702 (53.7)
			$M = 0.03180^c$	− (0.66)
"reactor"	1505/16504	1.07/9.36	$M = 0.572162^d$	− (0.29)
"Fuller"	1171/15959	0.74/9.26	$M = 3.0305914^e$	−
"Tankreactor"	2223/20669	1.36/12.56	(9.950e−05, 0, 0.036)^a	16320 (18.0)
			$M = 0.02680^f/0.028196^g$	−

* average of 8 runs with 8 weight values (equal function vectors). ‡ number of gradient evaluations;
† number of function evaluations. ^{a} [5]; ^{b} [3]; ^{c} [15]; ^{d} [16]; ^{e} [1]; ^{f} [17]; ^{g} [18].

For Problem 2, the best computed ND solution was found among 42 final ND solutions. The initial approximation $y_1(t_i) = 1$, $y_2(t_i) = 0, i \in I_N$ and $u(t_i) = 0.5, i \in I$ is used, see Tables 1 and 2. Figure 3 displays the ND solutions, the trajectory in the state space, the state variables and control relative to the best solution. The two selected solutions and the profiles for the states and control (of the identified best solution) are similar to those shown in [3].

Problem 3. - "obstacle" Find $u(t)$ that solves (with $T = 2.9$ fixed):

$$\min_{u(t)} J \equiv 5y_1(T)^2 + y_2(T)^2$$
$$\text{s.t. } y_1'(t) = y_2(t)$$
$$y_2'(t) = u(t) - 0.1(1 + 2y_1(t)^2)y_2(t), \ t \in [0, T]$$
$$y_1(0) = 1, \ y_2(0) = 1,$$
$$1 - 9(y_1(t) - 1)^2 - \left(\frac{y_2(t) - 0.4}{0.3}\right)^2 \le 0, \ -0.8 - y_2(t) \le 0, \ |u(t)| \le 1, \ t \in [0, T].$$

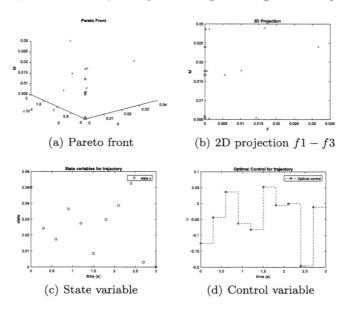

(a) Pareto front

(b) 2D projection $f1 - f3$

(c) State variable

(d) Control variable

Fig. 2. ND solutions and state and control variables for Problem 1 "trajectory" (Color figure online)

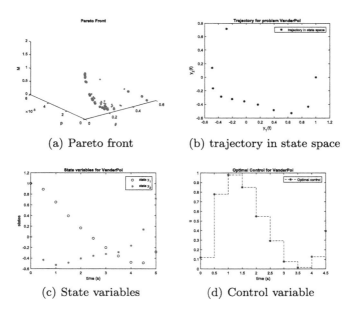

(a) Pareto front

(b) trajectory in state space

(c) State variables

(d) Control variable

Fig. 3. ND solutions, trajectory, and states and control for Problem 2 "VanderPol"

For Problem 3, the best solution was found among 8 final ND solutions. The initial approximation $y_1(t_i) = 1$, $y_2(t_i) = 1, i \in I_N$ and $u(t_i) = 1, i \in I$ is used and the results are shown in the Tables 1 and 2. Figure 4 displays the ND solutions, the trajectory in state space, the trajectory of the state variables and control relative to the best solution. The two solutions identified in Table 1 are satisfactory and the profiles of the state variables and control (relative to the defined best solution) follow the pattern shown in [15] (where larger numbers of subintervals in $[0, T]$ are used).

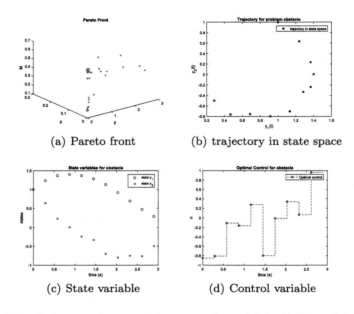

(a) Pareto front   (b) trajectory in state space

(c) State variable   (d) Control variable

Fig. 4. ND solutions, trajectory and states and control for Problem 3 "obstacle"

Problem 4. "reactor" – Maximize yield of $y_2(t)$ after one hour operation by manipulating a transformed temperature $u(t)$:

$$\max_{u(t)} J \equiv y_2(T)$$
$$\text{s.t. } y_1'(t) = -y_1(t)\left(u(t) + \frac{u^2(t)}{2}\right)$$
$$y_2'(t) = y_1(t)u(t), \ t \in [0, T]$$
$$y_1(0) = 1, \ y_2(0) = 0, \ 0 \le y_1(t), y_2(t) \le 1, \ 0 \le u(t) \le 5, \ t \in [0, T].$$

For Problem 4 the best computed solution was found among 52 final ND solutions. The initial approximation $y_1(t_i) = 1$, $y_2(t_i) = 1, i \in I_N$ and $u(t_i) = 0, i \in I$ is used and the results are shown in the Tables 1 and 2. The usual plots are shown in Fig. 5. The profiles of states and optimal control are identical to those shown in [16].

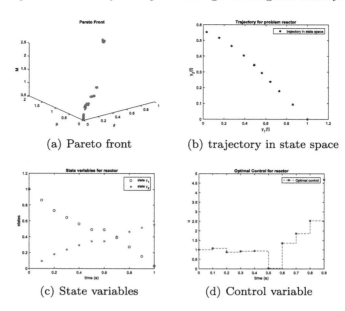

(a) Pareto front

(b) trajectory in state space

(c) State variables

(d) Control variable

Fig. 5. ND solutions, trajectory and states and control for Problem 4 "reactor"

Problem 5. "Fuller" – Minimize J (with $T = 8$ fixed) in this OCP linear in the control:

$$\min_{u(t)} J \equiv \int_0^T y_1^2(t)\, dt$$
$$\text{s.t. } y_1'(t) = y_2(t),$$
$$y_2'(t) = u(t), \ t \in [0, T]$$
$$y_1(0) = 2, \ y_2(0) = -2, \ y_1(T) = 2, \ y_2(T) = 2, \ |u(t)| \le 1, \ t \in [0, T].$$
$$|u(t)| \le 1, \ t \in [0, T]\ .$$

The initial approximation used is $y_1(t_i) = 2,\ y_2(t_i) = -2, i \in I_N$ and $u(t_i) = 1, i \in I$. From the results shown in Tables 1 and 2 and Fig. 6, relative to Problem 5, we can conclude that the proposed methodology is able to compute reasonably good solutions and the profiles of the trajectory in state space, the trajectory of the states y_1 and y_2, and the control u, are identical to those presented in [1].

Problem 6. "Tankreactor" – In a continuous stirred-tank chemical reactor, y_1 represents the deviation from the steady-state temperature, y_2 represents the deviation from the steady-state concentration and u is the effect of the coolant flow on the chemical reaction:

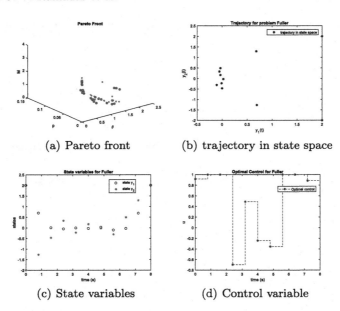

(a) Pareto front   (b) trajectory in state space

(c) State variables   (d) Control variable

Fig. 6. ND solutions, trajectory and state and control variables for Problem 5 "Fuller"

$$\min_{u(t)} J \equiv \int_0^T \left(y_1(t)^2 + y_2(t)^2 + Ru(t)^2 \right) dt$$

$$\text{s.t. } y_1'(t) = -2(y_1(t) + 0.25) + (y_2(t) + 0.5) \exp\left(\frac{25 y_1(t)}{y_1(t)+2} \right)$$

$$- (y_1(t) + 0.25)u(t)$$

$$y_2'(t) = 0.5 - y_2(t) - (y_2(t) + 0.5) \exp\left(\frac{25 y_1(t)}{y_1(t)+2} \right), \quad t \in [0, T]$$

$$y_1(0) = 0.05, \ y_2(0) = 0.$$

The optimal solution reported in [17], for $T = 0.78$ and $R = 0.1$, is $J^* = 0.02680$. Using the initial approximation $y_1(t_i) = 0.05$, $y_2(t_i) = 0$, $i \in I_N$ and $u(t_i) = 0$, $i \in I$, the results obtained by Algorithm 1 are shown in Tables 1 and 2. The identified best solution is very satisfactory and the resulting plots (c) and (d) in Fig. 7 are similar to those in [18].

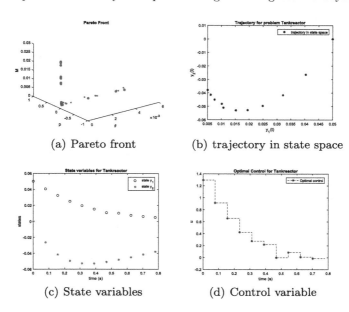

(a) Pareto front

(b) trajectory in state space

(c) State variables

(d) Control variable

Fig. 7. ND solutions, trajectory and states and control for Problem 6 "Tankreactor"

6   Conclusions

A weighted Tchebycheff scalarization methodology is proposed to solve a finite-dimensional nonlinear optimization problem that arises from the use of a direct multiple shooting method when applied to an OCP.

The proposed methodology aggregates three objective functions. Two of them measure constraint violations – from the "continuity constraints" and from the algebraic state and control constraints – that are required to be as close as possible to zero, and the other is the optimality measure – the objective functional from the OCP. Moreover, a penalty term is added to the Tchebycheff objective to force the constraint violations to decrease even faster. The preliminary numerical experiments show the effectiveness of the methodology when compared to similar strategies. A significant reduction in function evaluations (and time) and objective function improvements are achieved with the proposed methodology, when compared to the multiple shooting descent-based filter method presented in [5]. The comparison with other direct multiple shooting techniques (and even with indirect methods) shows similar computational effort and very good approximated solutions in general.

Acknowledgments. The authors wish to thank two anonymous referees for their comments and suggestions to improve the paper.

References

1. Frego, M.: Numerical methods for optimal control problems with applications to autonomous vehicles. Ph.D. thesis, University of Trento (2014)
2. Assassa, F., Marquardt, W.: Dynamic optimization using adaptive direct multiple shooting. Comput. Chem. Eng. **60**, 242–259 (2014)
3. Bock, H.G., Plitt, K.J.: A multiple shooting algorithm for direct solution of optimal control problems. IFAC Proc. Vol. **17**(2), 1603–1608 (1984)
4. Diehl, M., Bock, H., Diedam, H., Wieber, P.B.: Fast direct multiple shooting algorithms for optimal robot control. In: Diehl, M., Mombaur, K. (eds.) Fast Motions in Biomechanics and Robotics. Lecture Notes in Control and Information Sciences, vol. 340. Springer, Heidelberg (2006). https://doi.org/10.1007/978-3-540-36119-0_4
5. Ramadas, G.C.V., Fernandes, E.M.G.P., Rocha, A.M.A.C., Costa, M.F.P.: A multiple shooting descent-based filter method for optimal control problems. In: Gaspar-Cunha, A., Periaux, J., Giannakoglou, K.C., Gauger, N.R., Quagliarella, D., Greiner, D. (eds.) Advances in Evolutionary and Deterministic Methods for Design, Optimization and Control in Engineering and Sciences. CMAS, vol. 55, pp. 377–392. Springer, Cham (2021). https://doi.org/10.1007/978-3-030-57422-2_24
6. Angelo, J.S., Barbosa, H.J.C.: On ant colony optimization algorithms for multi-objective problems. In: Ostfeld, A. (ed.) Ant Colony Optimization - Methods and Application, InTech Europe, pp. 53–74 (2011)
7. Marler, R.T., Arora, J.S.: Survey of multi-objective optimization methods for engineering. Struct. Multidisc. Optim. **26**, 369–395 (2004)
8. Miettinen, K.: Nonlinear Multiobjective Optimization. Kluwer Academic Publishers, New York (1999)
9. Deb, K.: Multi-Objective Optimization using Evolutionary Algorithms. Wiley, Hoboken (2001)
10. Feng, Z., Zhang, Q., Zhang, Q., Tang, Q., Yang, T., Ma, Y.: A multiobjective optimization based framework to balance the global and local exploitation in expensive optimization. J. Glob. Optim. **61**, 677–694 (2015)
11. Zhang, Q., Liu, W., Tsang, E., Virginas, B.: Expensive multiobjective optimization by MOEA/D with Gaussian process model. IEEE T. Evol. Comput. **14**(3), 456–474 (2010)
12. Steuer, R.E., Choo, E.U.: An interactive weighted Tchebycheff procedure for multiple objective programming. Math. Program. **26**, 326–344 (1983)
13. Emmerich, M.T.M., Deutz, A.H.: A tutorial on multiobjective optimization: fundamentals and evolutionary methods. Nat. Comput. **17**, 585–609 (2018)
14. Das, I., Dennis, J.: Normal-boundary intersection: an alternative method for generating Pareto optimal points in multicriteria optimization problems, Institute for Computer Application in Science an Engineering, NASA Langley Research Center - Hampton, VA 23681-0001, Tech. rep. (1996)
15. Schlegel, M., Stockmann, K., Binder, T., Marquardt, W.: Dynamic optimization using adaptive control vector parameterization. Comput. Chem. Eng. **29**(8), 1731–1751 (2005)
16. Tamimi, J., Li, P.: Nonlinear model predictive control using multiple shooting combined with collocation on finite elements. IFAC Proc. Vol. **42**(11), 703–708 (2009)

17. Kirk, D.E.: Optimal Control Theory: An Introduction. Dover Publications Inc., New York (2004)
18. Wang, X.: Solving optimal control problems with Matlab - indirect methods. ISE. Dept., NCSU, Raleigh, NC 27695, Tech. rep. (21 pages). http://solmaz.eng.uci.edu/Teaching/MAE274/SolvingOptContProb_MATLAB.pdf

Assessing the Deployment of Electric Mobility: A Review

Sarah B. Gruetzmacher[1] (ID), Clara B. Vaz[1,2] (ID), and Ângela P. Ferreira[1(✉)] (ID)

[1] Research Centre in Digitalization and Intelligent Robotics (CeDRI),
Instituto Politécnico de Bragança (IPB), Campus Santa Apolónia,
5300-253 Bragança, Portugal
`a42827@alunos.ipb.pt`, {`clvaz,apf`}`@ipb.pt`
[2] Centre for Management and Industrial Engineering (CEGI/INESC TEC),
Bragança, Portugal

Abstract. The transport sector of the European Union is the only sector of the economy that has been increasing its emissions since 2014. To reduce the use of fossil fuels and achieve the greenhouse gas emissions mitigation target, many countries are focusing on the deployment of electric vehicles. This paper aims at analysing recent literature on the deployment of electric vehicles (EV) and typifying objectives, methods and indicators generally exploited, to better understand the state of the art on this topic. The Web of Science database was used and the results showed that the interest in the topic of electric vehicles has been increasing exponentially since 2010. The main significant indicators and the assessment methodologies were analysed. The indicators identified were aggregated in four main clusters: environmental, economic, social and technical indicators. Although the factors that contribute to EV deployment can vary depending on the regions specific characteristics, most of the research studies pointed out that the main contributors are the high density of recharging points, the existence of government monetary incentives and the lower operational cost of EV.

Keywords: Electric vehicles · Deployment · GHG emissions

1 Introduction

To meet the climate goal set in the Paris Agreement and achieve climate neutrality by 2050, the European Union (EU) set in 2014 a target of 40% reduction in the domestic greenhouse gas (GHG) emissions by 2030 when compared to 1990 levels [1,2]. All Member States should contribute to the overall reduction with the efforts allocated among them on a basis of relative Gross Domestic Product (GDP) per capita. Regulation (EU) 2018/842 [3] presents the targeted percentage reduction for each country to achieve by 2030 calculated using 2005 GHG emissions levels. Figure 1 shows these targets as red dots, in addition to the GHG emissions evaluated in 2018 in blue, both compared to 2005 levels (i.e., 100%).

© Springer Nature Switzerland AG 2021
O. Gervasi et al. (Eds.): ICCSA 2021, LNCS 12953, pp. 350–365, 2021.
https://doi.org/10.1007/978-3-030-86976-2_24

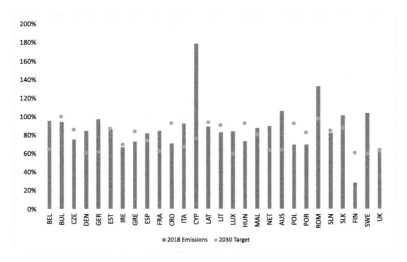

Fig. 1. 2018 GHG emissions and 2030 targets for EU countries, compared to 2005 levels. Adapted from [3,4]. (Color figure online)

Half the EU countries have already achieved their target, but some work still needs to be done, especially since the EU pursues a GHG emissions reduction of 55% and will come with a new proposal by June 2021 [5]. The contributions to reduce the emissions should be made by all sectors of the economy, i.e., industry, transport, electric energy production, residential and commercial and also agriculture [3]. However, despite technological improvements, the GHG emissions from Europe's transport sector have increased since 1990, as shown in Fig. 2 [2,6]. In 2018, this sector was responsible for 28% of the EU's total GHG emissions or 21% when excluding international aviation and shipping [8].

Passenger cars largely dominate the inland passenger transport, accounting for 83% of the total volume. Unfortunately, this mode of transport remains very oil dependent. In 2019, the sales of petrol passenger cars in the EU maintained their best sellers position with almost 60% of the total sales of the year and over 73% of the transport related GHG emissions in Europe came from road transportation, as shown in Fig. 3(a) [2]. Under this transportation mode, passenger cars are the main contributors, accounting for more than 60% of the total GHG emissions from road transport (Fig. 3(b)) [8–10].

To reduce the emissions from the transport sector some important changes were proposed in the White paper on transport strategy from 2011 [11]. One of these changes aims at a drastic reduction in the utilization of petrol vehicles, by halving their number by 2030 and phasing them out of the cities by 2050. Another paradigm shift is to use cleaner energies on road transport which is fundamental for a low carbon transition where the electrification of the transport sector has a fundamental role.

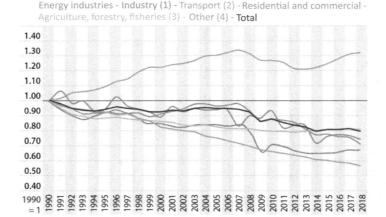

Fig. 2. Variation of GHG emissions by sector from EU-27 [7]. (1) Emissions from manufacturing and construction, industrial processes and product use. (2) Excluding international maritime, but including international aviation. (3) Emissions from fuel combustion and other emissions from agriculture. (4) Emissions from fuel combustion in other (not elsewhere specified), fugitive emissions from fuels, waste, indirect CO_2.

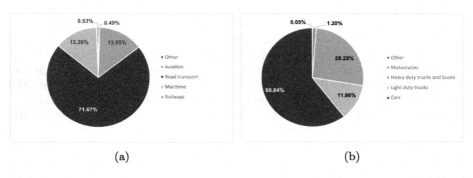

Fig. 3. Share of GHG emissions from transport in the EU (a) by transport mode and (b) by road transport mode. Adapted from [10].

From the above, it is clear why the electric mobility area has been receiving much attention and significance in recent years, and the electric vehicle fleet is expanding at a rapid pace. Worldwide, the number of passenger cars sold in 2020 has decreased by 15.3% when compared to 2019 values, and in the EU market this decline was of 23.7% [12]. The registrations of new passenger cars have fallen significantly across the globe due to the outbreak of the COVID-19 pandemic in the beginning of 2020. In the same period, the electric vehicles (EV) sales have increased due to a raised awareness on environmental issues and also tax/fiscal incentives: 3,24 million electric vehicles were sold worldwide, which is 43% more than the previous year. Europe registered 1,4 million new EV during 2020, a growth of more than 137% from 2019 [13].

The deployment of EV is a strategy used by many countries to reduce the use of fossil fuels and further mitigate GHG emissions [1]. The aim of this paper is to exploit and analyse recent literature on the deployment of electric vehicles regarding their environmental and energy sustainability, aiming at typifying objectives, methods and indicators to better understand the state of the art on this topic.

This paper is organized as follows: Sect. 2 gives some context into the electric propulsion-based vehicle, introducing the existing EV types and the EU policies related to their deployment; Sect. 3 presents the literature review on electric vehicles deployment, the indicators identified, the methodologies and main results from the source papers. Finally, Sect. 4 rounds off the paper, drawing the conclusions of this work.

2 Electric Propulsion-Based Vehicles Context

Electric vehicles were among the first vehicles introduced in the 1800s and by 1900 they represented a third of all road vehicles [14]. However, limitations on the battery technology and the scarce grid electrification, combined with cheap oil prices and technological development of the internal combustion engine (ICE) vehicles, drove the interest away from EV. Nowadays, climate change, concerns on the environment and the forthcoming end of the oil age due to depletion of world reserves, have brought the interest back to the EV in the last decades.

2.1 Existing Types of Electric Propulsion-Based Vehicles

Currently, there are a few different types of powertrain configurations for electric vehicles, as stated hereinafter.

The battery electric vehicles (BEV) are fully electric vehicles that rely on one or more electric motors for propulsion. The energy is obtained from electrical charging points and stored in the batteries [15]. The battery is also charged through regenerative braking. BEV have zero tailpipe emissions, however, as will be discussed later in this paper, their actual emissions depend on the carbon intensity of the primary energy source, from which is obtained the electricity.

Another type of EV are the plug-in hybrid electric vehicles (PHEV). PHEV are primarily powered by an electric motor with a plug-in battery and uses an ICE to extend the cruising range. The battery can be charged using the plug-in, by the ICE or through regenerative braking [14].

Hybrid electric vehicles (HEV) are powered by a combination of a conventional ICE and an electric motor, to improve its fuel efficiency. The battery cannot be plugged in for charging, it is replenished by energy generated by the ICE and regenerative braking [16].

Finally, electric vehicle can be powered through a fuel-cell, named fuel-cell electric vehicles (FCEV). Their typology is similar to BEV, by using an electric powertrain, but, it uses a full cell stack device to produce electric energy [17]. The fuel cell is an electrochemical device that converts the chemical energy of hydrogen into electrical energy and heat. The hydrogen is combined with an oxidizing element (often oxygen) inside the fuel cell stack and the reaction produces water, heat and electricity, the later powering the electric motor [18]. The electric energy generated by a fuel cell can directly power the traction motor of the vehicle or it can be stored in a battery or a ultra-capacitor. Most FCEV have a battery for recapturing braking energy, providing extra power during short acceleration moments and to smooth out the power delivered from the fuel cell [19].

Figure 4 summarizes the main differences between EV powertrains types. For petrol and diesel cars, the local and method for refuelling is well-established and straightforward. However, for plug-in electric vehicles (PEV), i.e. BEV and PHEV, the recharging process can be accomplished in different locations, at different charging rates, depending on the vehicle model and/or the electric power available. A learning curve will be necessary in the transition to PEV and should focus on enabling a behaviour shift to electric mobility by addressing issues such as lack of infrastructure related to EV, preconceptions and doubts from the general public and lack of awareness among public administrations and citizens concerning electric mobility [20,21].

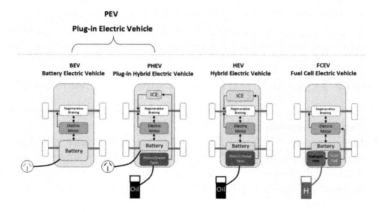

Fig. 4. Differences between the types of EV available [22].

2.2   Policies Related to Electric Vehicles

To foster the deployment of electric vehicles, governments worldwide have introduced an increasing number of incentives at the consumer-level, such as purchase subsidies and parking privileges [23]. By 2020, in the EU, 26 out of the 27 countries have applied some kind of fiscal measure to stimulate EV purchase.

Twenty countries offer incentives to buyers and 6 countries only offer tax reductions or exemptions for electric cars. The monetary value of these incentives varies greatly across the EU. Table 1 presents a summary of the countries that provide tax exemptions or reductions for the acquisition and/or ownership of EV. It also shows the countries that offer monetary purchase incentives and the values applied. A more detailed overview of these benefits can be seen in [24].

Concerning to car manufacturers, one of the policies set by the EU to push the electrification of road transportation forward is to limit CO_2 emissions of their fleet [25]. Regulation (EU) 2019/631 sets a mandatory target for the average emission of the manufacturer's overall fleet of new passenger cars of 95 g of CO_2 per kilometer by 2021 [26]. To reach this limit, a great market introduction of partially and full EV is required [25]. Mathieu et al. [8] mention that although the CO_2 emission standards were created as a climate regulation, they can also be seen as a great industrial policy since it propels the car industry to invest and supply the zero emissions technologies in Europe for the near future.

The growing sales of electric cars across Europe in the last years have resulted in a significant drop in new car CO2 emissions. In 2020, they reached 111 g/km, 9% bellow the 2019 levels of over 122 g/km, which is the largest drop since the standards came into effect in 2008 [8]. Figure 5 shows the market share of plug-in electric vehicles (BEV and PHEV) in the EU and the 5 countries with the highest market share by 2020. Ten of the 28 countries (EU-27 + UK) have surpassed 10% market share for PEV.

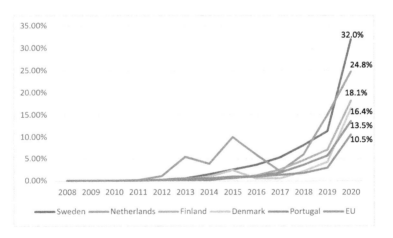

Fig. 5. PEV market share of the top 5 EU countries and the EU. Adapted from [27].

Furthermore, the GHG emissions reduction potential from EV is heavily dependent on its energy efficiency and the carbon intensity of the primary source for electricity generation. Nevertheless, an average EV using electricity characterised by the current global carbon intensity (518 g CO2-eq/kWh), over their life cycle, emits less GHG than the average ICE vehicle using gasoline [28]. The

Table 1. Summary of countries that have tax benefits and purchase incentive (values in Euro) for passenger EV. Adapted from [24].

Country	Tax benefits		Purchase incentive		
	Acquisition	Ownership	BEV	PHEV	FCEV
Austria	x	x	3000	1250	3000
Belgium	x	x	–	–	–
Bulgaria	–	x	–	–	–
Croatia	x	x	9200	4600	–
Cyprus	x	x	–	–	–
Czech Republic	x	x	–	–	–
Denmark	x	x	–	–	–
Estonia	–	–	5000	–	–
Finland	x	x	2000	–	–
France	x	–	3000–7000	3000–7000	3000–7000
Germany	x	x	7500–9000	5625–6750	7500–9000
Greece	x	x	15% cashback (up to 5500)	–	–
Hungary	x	x	1500–7350	1500–7350	1500–7350
Ireland	x	x	up to 5000	up to 5000	–
Italy		x	up to 6000	up to 6000	up to 6000
Latvia	x	x	–	–	–
Lithuania	–	–	–	–	–
Luxembourg	–	x	5000	2500	5000
Malta	x	x	–	–	–
Netherlands	x	x	–	–	–
Poland	x	–	8300*	–	20000*
Portugal	x	x	3000	–	–
Romania	–	x	10000	4250	–
Slovakia	x	x	8000	5000	–
Slovenia	x	–	7500	4500	–
Spain	x	x	4000–5000	1900–2600	–
Sweden	–	x	6000*	1000*	–
United Kingdom	x	x	up to 3000	–	–

(*) Values given in local currency and converted to Euro.

avoided emissions in road transport outbalance the higher emissions from the electricity generation and, according to the European Commission projection, by 2050, a 10% reduction of the total emissions from all sectors could be achieved [6]. From a technological point of view, the fleet electrification, combined with the penetration of renewable energy sources to generate electricity and the advances in energy storage, such as green hydrogen systems, are the best approaches for further reducing GHG emissions.

3   Review Methodology on Assessing the Electric Vehicles Deployment

3.1   Systematic Approach

A review on the literature was performed to analyse the methodologies used to assess the deployment of electric vehicles through a set of indicators. A search was made for articles between 2010 and 2021, evaluating the deployment of electric vehicles. Only articles published on journals were chosen from the Web of Science (WoS) database.

The first search for the term "electric vehicles" on the WoS database, in the 2010 to 2021 period, returns more than 16 thousand articles. Only in the first quarter of 2021, 742 articles on this theme have already been published. Figure 6 shows the growing interest in this subject in the past ten years.

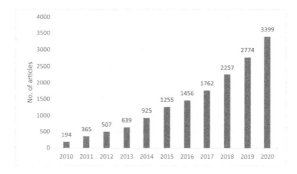

Fig. 6. Number of articles on electric vehicles published by year.

A keyword analysis using the VOSviewer software [29] divided these articles into four clusters, enabling to identify the main areas of study in this theme. The first cluster relates to batteries development, modeling and performance, as well as their degradation and recycling potential. Another cluster is defined with works related to the EV design, such as system, motor and energy management. The third cluster is composed by works analysing the EV impacts on the energy system and generation. These works deal with demand response, smart grids, renewable energy and power quality. Finally, the last cluster includes works in the area of interest of this paper, that are related to EV deployment and adoption, government policies and incentives and sustainable mobility.

To reduce the search for relevant papers in the subject under analysis, relevant keywords from the selected cluster were selected and applied in the search engine: "electric vehicles", "sustainab*" and "deployment" OR "adoption". From this search, it was possible to identify several indicators that have been used to assess the deployment of EV through quantitative methodologies. Table 2 summarizes the main significant indicators under use, the paper source and also the assessment methodology. The objectives, indicators and methodologies from the selected works, as well as their main conclusions are presented hereinafter.

3.2 Analysis and Discussion

Onat et al. [30] explore the suitability of BEV in the United States and identifies the policy strategies that are necessary to increase their competitiveness in each state. A novel multi-criteria decision-support framework is proposed based on Data Envelopment Analysis (DEA) and Agent-based modeling (ABM). DEA is used to assess the efficiency of using BEV in each state using the inputs operation cost and environmental impact (GHG emissions, energy consumption, water withdrawal and consumption) and the output data (the service provided per vehicle-miles travelled); ABM estimates the future market share using as inputs the government subsidies, social acceptability and the availability of charging infrastructure in each state. By coupling the relative performances from DEA and the possible market share from ABM the relative policy inefficiencies are revealed. DEA is a non-parametric technique that assesses the efficiency of a set of homogeneous decision making units (DMU) in using a multiple inputs to produce multiple outputs. It identifies the efficient DMU, which define the efficient frontier, enabling to quantify the inefficiency of the remaining DMU [31]. DEA uses mathematical linear programming to derive weights for inputs and outputs of each DMU, avoiding the subjectivity observed in others methods or expert-based weights assignment [30]. ABM is a discrete-event simulation approach in which the system under analysis is modeled as a collection of autonomous decision-making entities called agents [32]. ABM enables to simulate the interactions among different agents in a virtual environment. Each agent individually assesses its situation and makes decisions on the basis of a set of rules [30]. The work divides the states into four groups regarding their utilization score and efficiency score in order to suggest prioritization on investment in electric power generation or in policies for BEV adoption. Each state requires its own set of policy recommendations, however, this work helps to narrow down the main targets for future policies.

The authors Wang et al. [33] assess the city readiness for EV adoption through the analysis of 25 demonstration cities using a Partial Least Square (PLS) path model and a clustering analysis approach. A PLS path model with five factors (latent variables) was used in the analysis. These factors consist of government policies and investments, charging infrastructure construction and operation, business models and maintenance service system, consumer awareness education, operation scope and environmental benefits. Each latent variable is measured by a set of manifest variables collected from the summary report for each city. PLS Path Model is a method of structural equation which allows to estimate complex cause-effect relationship models with latent variables. Thus, the PLS path model consists of two parts, the measurement model, describing the relationships between latent variables and manifest variables, and the structural model, which describes the relationships among the latent variables [33].

Table 2. Reviewed literature summarized.

Reference Region	Objective	Methodology	Indicators
Onat et al. (2017) [30] US states	Analyse the suitability of BEV	Data Envelopment Analysis (DEA) and Agent Based Modeling (ABM)	– GHG emissions – Energy and water consumption – Operation cost – Government incentives – Social acceptability – Charging infrastructure
Wang et al. (2015) [33] Chinese cities	Assess the city readiness for EV adoption	Partial Least Square (PLS) path model	– Government incentives – Charging infrastructure – Maintenance services – Consumer awareness education – Environmental benefits
Thiel et al. (2019) [34] EU countries	Analyse the impacts of EV policies in different areas	DIONE and SHERPA models	– EV/recharging point ratio – EV market share – Charging infrastructure – Job creation – GHG emissions – Energy demand
Neves et al. (2019) [38] 24 EU countries	Analyse factors supporting the transition EV	Panel-Corrected Standard Errors (PCSE)	– No. of policies on EV – Employment rate – Education level – Industrial Production Index – GDP per capita – Fuel and electricity prices – GHG emissions – Charging infrastructure – Battery price, range and capacity – Renewable electricity generation – Patents in the transport sector
Wang et al. (2019) [40] 30 countries	Identify factors that promote EV adoption	Multiple linear regression method	– EV market share – Government incentive – Charging infrastructure – Environmental performance index – Fuel and electricity price – Income – Vehicles per capita
Javid et al. (2017) [41] California counties	Explore factors related to PEV purchasing and estimate their penetration	Multiple Logit Regression Analysis	– Car sharing – Income and education – Charging infrastructure – Fuel price
Neves et al. (2020) [31] 20 European countries	Calculate the efficiency scores for BEV adoption and EV policies and examine their determinants	DEA and fractional regression	– EV market share – No. of policies – Industrial production index – Brent crude oil prices – Electricity intensity – No. of BEV models in top 10 sellers – Renewable electricity generation – Charging infrastructure – Services added value – Imports/exports rate – Government incentives – Socioeconomic indicators
Yong et al. (2017) [44] 24 countries	Analyse the factors affecting the deployment of EV	Fuzzy-set qualitative comparative analysis	– EV penetration rate – Charging infrastructure – GDP per capita – Government incentives – Free charging points

The results in [33] show that the latent factors that most affect the city readiness of EV adoption are the charging infrastructure, government policies and investment. Based on the scores derived from the PLS path model, the clustering analysis is used to classify the 25 cities in terms of city assessment of EV adoption.

Thiel et al. [34] develop a holistic assessment of the impact of the EV deployment plans of the European Union. To assess the recharging point sufficiency, the ratio of EV per recharging point was calculated and maps with infrastructure density were produced for each member state. A new model is proposed to calculate job impact, using as input the infrastructure deployment, value added and productivity to estimate the gross job creation. The DIONE model is used to project pollutant emissions from the future EV shares. DIONE is a fleet impact model owned by the European Commission that is used to analyse fleet composition scenarios of European road transport up to 2050, including the projection of vehicle fleet composition, fuel consumption, pollutant emissions and energy consumption [35, 36]. The pollutant emissions results from the DIONE are then employed in the SHERPA model. The SHERPA (Screening for High Emission Reduction Potentials for Air quality) is an air quality model with open access owned by the European Commission which produces air pollutant concentrations for each region. By assuming a linear relationship between concentration and emission changes, SHERPA allows the identification of regions where the pollution originates, the ranking of the sources of air pollution and also the simulation of the impact of air quality plans scenarios [34, 37]. This work concludes that the EU needs to take further actions in the deployment of publicly accessible recharging points by, for example, implementing incentives for their build-up.

Neves et al. [38] analyse factors that promote the EV adoption, including BEV and PHEV using data from 2010 to 2016 for a panel of 24 EU countries. A Panel-Corrected Standard Errors (PCSE) model is used to analyse the factors driving the market share of BEV and PHEV individually, and all EV together. The factors analysed include several areas, such as government policies (number of policies on EV), social aspects (employment rate and education level), economic indicators (Industrial Production Index, GDP per capita, fuel price and electricity price), environmental indicators (GHG emissions) and technical aspects (number of charging stations per 100 thousand inhabitants, battery cost, battery range, battery capacity, renewable electricity per capita, patents in the transport sector). PCSE is a panel regression model used to deal with the presence of contemporaneous correlation in time-series data. This model accounts for the deviations from spherical errors, allowing for better inference from linear models [39]. The results show that policies should be focused on BEV or PHEV, instead of EV as a whole, since factors that support BEV are different from the ones for PHEV.

Wang et al. [40] also identify the key factors that promote EV adoption. The relationship between these factors and the EV market share for the year 2015 in 30 countries is explored using multiple linear regression method. This method assesses the linear relationship between one dependent variable and several independent variables using ordinary least squares. This study shows that chargers' density, fuel price and road priority are significantly positive factors correlated with a country's electric vehicle market share.

Javid et al. [41] explore the potential factors that can be attributed to the purchasing of PEV, in order to estimate their penetration in 58 California counties. Data from demographic and travel-related characteristics, socioeconomic variables, infrastructural and regional specifications were used to estimate the PEV penetration rate using Multiple Logistic Regression applied to a 2012 California Household Travel Survey dataset which includes both PEV and conventional car buyers' information. The logit regression model enables to predict a dichotomous dependent variable based on a set of independent variables, being the log odds of the dependent variable modeled as a linear combination of the independent variables. This study identifies that household income, maximum level of education in the household, car sharing status, charging stations density, and gas price in the region are the significant factors for PEV adoption.

In Neves et al. [31], DEA is used in a first stage to calculate the efficiency scores for 20 European countries of BEV adoption and policies supporting electric mobility. In a second stage, using the efficiency scores previously calculated, the Fractional Regression Model (FRM) enable to identify the significant determinants of electric mobility. FRM is a regression method used wherein the dependent variable is within the interval $[0, 1]$, being the estimation based on Quasi Maximum Likelihood method suggested by Papke and Wooldrige (1996) [42]. Since the DEA efficiency corresponds to the dependent variable, FRM is used in the second stage to identify their significant determinants [43]. This paper finds that few countries are performing on the efficiency frontier. Additionally, renewable electricity generation and the existence of peak periods of demand during the day decreases the efficiency scores.

Yong et al. (2017) [44] employ a fuzzy-set qualitative comparative analysis (fsQCA) to analyse the factors affecting the EV deployment and draw policy implications for EV promotion. The fsQCA is a form of succession of qualitative comparative analysis (QCA) since variables can get all the values within the range of 0 and 1. The fsQCA is a social science method that combines qualitative (case-oriented research) and quantitative (variable-oriented research) analysis. The study concludes that to promote electric vehicles countries should focus on tax exemptions, purchase subsidies and spreading charging infrastructure.

3.3   Main Results

From the performed survey, it is possible to grade the indicators into four main groups: environmental, economic, social and technical indicators. Thus, the environmental indicators include the GHG emissions, energy and water consumption, renewable electricity generation, environmental benefits and the Environmental Performance Index. The economic indicators encompass the government incentives, GDP per capita, fuel and electricity prices, operational costs, maintenance services, battery prices, import/export rate and the Industrial Production Index. The social indicators comprehend job creation, income, EV social acceptability, consumer awareness education, number of policies on EV, employment rate, vehicles per capita, car sharing and service added value. Finally, the technical indicators include the charging infrastructure, free charging points, EV typology market share and penetration rate, number of BEV models on the top 10 sellers maintenance services, battery range and capacity, patents in the transport sector, energy demand and electricity intensity.

A general analysis of these indicators showed that the ones related to the charging infrastructure were the most frequently used in the assessment approaches, followed by the EV market share and government incentives. The methodologies employed are diverse, depending on the type of data used and the various possible approaches to explore the EV deployment or adoption.

From this research analysis, it is possible to identify a trend on policy plans being region specific, since the characteristics and necessities can vary significantly. Nevertheless, most authors pointed out that the main contributors to the deployment of electric vehicles are a high density of recharging points, the existence of government monetary incentives, such as tax exemptions and purchase subsides, and the lower operational cost of EV (electricity vs. fuel prices).

4   Conclusions

Although most sectors of the EU economy have been reducing their GHG emissions, the transportation sector has been increasing their emissions since 2014. Since most of these emissions are related to the road transport and specifically passenger cars transport, the EU countries strategy is focused on the electrification of the sector. Even though EV are not yet commercially competitive with ICE vehicles, namely in terms of driving range, EV sales have been increasing, with some countries recently reaching a 10% market share. In 2020, registrations of electric vehicles in the EU have increased 137%, when compared to 2019, mainly caused by the promotion of different scheme of incentives, tax exemptions or reductions for the acquisition and/or ownership of EV in European countries.

The objective of this paper was to analyse existing literature on the deployment of electric vehicles and typifying objectives, methods and identify relevant indicators for assessing the deployment of electric vehicles. This issue is included in one of the main clusters of papers published in the literature related to EV deployment and adoption, government policies, incentives and sustainable mobility. Using the Web of Science database, a search was made for articles evaluating the deployment of EV that applied various methodologies to a set of indicators. The main significant indicators and the assessment methodologies were analysed, and the first ones were aggregated in four main clusters: environmental, economic, social and technical indicators.

Although the factors that contribute to EV deployment can vary depending on the regions specific characteristics, most of the research studies pointed out that the main contributors are a high density of recharging points, the existence of government monetary incentives and a lower operational cost of EV.

As the EV market deploys, research directions should be updated to include for instance driving range, fostered by improved storage systems, and green electricity availability. Also, new electricity market frameworks, on a two-way grid edge concept towards a decentralized and transactive electric grid, have the potential to affect the transition to electrified road transportation.

Acknowledgments. This work has been supported by FCT – Fundação para a Ciência e Tecnologia within the Project Scope: UIDB/05757/2020.

References

1. Hou, F., et al.: Comprehensive analysis method of determining global long-term GHG mitigation potential of passenger battery electric vehicles. J. Cleaner Prod. **289**, 125137 (2021)
2. European Environment Agency. Transport: increasing oil consumption and greenhouse gas emissions hamper EU progress towards environment and climate objectives. https://www.eea.europa.eu/themes/transport/term/increasing-oil-consumption-and-ghg. Accessed 22 Mar 2021
3. Regulation (EU) 2018/842 of the European Parliament and of the Council of 30 May 2018. https://eur-lex.europa.eu/legal-content/EN/TXT/?uri=uriserv:OJ.L_.2018.156.01.0026.01.ENG. Accessed 16 Apr 2021
4. Eurostat: Greenhouse gas emissions by source sector. https://appsso.eurostat.ec.europa.eu/nui/show.do?dataset=env_air_gge&lang=en. Accessed 16 Apr 2021
5. Climate & energy framework. https://ec.europa.eu/clima/policies/strategies/2030_en. Accessed 21 Apr 2021
6. European Environment Agency. Electric vehicles and the energy sector - impacts on Europe's future emissions. https://www.eea.europa.eu/themes/transport/electric-vehicles/electric-vehicles-and-energy. Accessed 21 Mar 2021
7. European Commission: EU Transport in figures. Statistical pocketbook 2020. Publications Office of the European Union, Luxembourg (2020). https://doi.org/10.2832/491038
8. Mathieu, L., Poliscanova, J.: Transport & Environment 2020: Mission (almost) accomplished (2020)
9. Feckova Skrabulakova, E., Ivanova, M., Rosova, A., Gresova, E., Sofranko, M., Ferencz, V.: On electromobility development and the calculation of the infrastructural country electromobility coefficient. Processes **9**(2), 222 (2021)
10. European Environment Agency. Share of transport greenhouse gas emissions. https://www.eea.europa.eu/data-and-maps/daviz/share-of-transport-ghg-emissions-2#tab-dashboard-01. Accessed 23 Mar 2021
11. European Commission: White Paper on Transport: Roadmap to a Single European Transport Area: Towards a Competitive and Resource-efficient Transport System. Publications Office of the European Union (2011)
12. European Automobile Manufacturers Association. Economic and Market Report - EU Automotive Industry: Full-year (2020). https://www.acea.be/uploads/statistic_documents/Economic_and_Market_Report_full-year_2020.pdf. Accessed 12 Apr 2021
13. EV-Volumes. The electric vehicles world sales database. https://www.ev-volumes.com/. Accessed 27 Mar 2021
14. Niestadt, M., Bjørnåvold, A.: Electric road vehicles in the European Union: Trends, impact and policies. European Parliamentary Research Service (2019)

15. Pielecha, J., Skobiej, K., Kurtyka, K.: Exhaust emissions and energy consumption analysis of conventional, hybrid, and electric vehicles in real driving cycles. Energies **13**(23), 6423 (2020)
16. Egbue, O., Long, S., Samaranayake, V.A.: Mass deployment of sustainable transportation: evaluation of factors that influence electric vehicle adoption. Clean Technol. Environ. Policy **19**(7), 1927–1939 (2017). https://doi.org/10.1007/s10098-017-1375-4
17. Tanç, B., Arat, H.T., Baltacıoğlu, E., Aydın, K.: Overview of the next quarter century vision of hydrogen fuel cell electric vehicles. Int. J. Hydrogen Energy **44**(20), 10120–10128 (2019)
18. Das, H.S., Tan, C.W., Yatim, A.H.M.: Fuel cell hybrid electric vehicles: a review on power conditioning units and topologies. Renew. Sustain. Energy Rev. **76**, 268–291 (2017)
19. Alternative Fuels Data Center. https://afdc.energy.gov/vehicles/how-do-fuel-cell-electric-cars-work. Accessed 1 Apr 2021
20. Pollák, F., et al.: Promotion of electric mobility in the European union-overview of project PROMETEUS from the perspective of cohesion through synergistic cooperation on the example of the catching-up region. Sustainability **13**(3), 1545 (2021)
21. Spöttle, M., et al.: Research for TRAN Committee – Charging infrastructure for electric road vehicles, European Parliament, Policy Department for Structural and Cohesion Policies, Brussels (2018)
22. The Driven. The ICE age is over: Why battery cars will beat hybrids and fuel cells. https://thedriven.io/2018/11/14/the-ice-age-is-over-why-battery-cars-will-beat-hybrids-and-fuel-cells/. Accessed 28 Mar 2021
23. Fluchs, S.: The diffusion of electric mobility in the European Union and beyond. Transp. Res. Part D Transp. Environ. **86**, 102462 (2020)
24. European Automobile Manufacturer Association. Overview - Electric vehicles: Tax benefits & purchase incentives in the European Union. https://www.acea.be/publications/article/overview-of-incentives-for-buying-electric-vehicles. Accessed 2 Apr 2021
25. ERTRAC, EPoSS and ETIP SNET: European Roadmap: Electrification of Road Transport. 3rd Edition, Version: 10 (2017)
26. European Commission. Regulation (EU) 2019/631 of the European parliament and of the council, https://eur-lex.europa.eu/legal-content/EN/TXT/PDF/?uri=CELEX:32018L2001&from=EN. Accessed 23 Mar 2021
27. European Alternative Fuels Observatory. https://www.eafo.eu/ Accessed 29 Mar 2021
28. International Energy Agency. Global EV Outlook 2019: Scaling up the transition to electric mobility, https://webstore.iea.org/download/direct/2807?fileName=Global_EV_Outlook_2019.pdf. Accessed 22 Mar 2021
29. VOSviewer. https://www.vosviewer.com/. Accessed 25 Apr 2021
30. Onat, N.C., Noori, M., Kucukvar, M., Zhao, Y., Tatari, O., Chester, M.: Exploring the suitability of electric vehicles in the United States. Energy **121**, 631–642 (2017)
31. Neves, S.A., Marques, A.C., Moutinho, V.: Two-stage DEA model to evaluate technical efficiency on deployment of battery electric vehicles in the EU countries. Transp. Res. Part D Transp. Environ. **86**, 102489 (2020)
32. Bonabeau, E.: Agent-based modeling: methods and techniques for simulating human systems. Proc. Nat. Acad. Sci. **99**(suppl 3), 7280–7287 (2002)
33. Wang, N., Liu, Y.: City readiness system assessment of electric vehicle adoption in China. SAE Int. J. Mater. Manufact. **8**(3), 678–684 (2015)

34. Thiel, C., et al.: Assessing the impacts of electric vehicle recharging infrastructure deployment efforts in the European Union. Energies **12**(12), 2409 (2019)
35. Harrison, G., Krause, J., Thiel, C.: Transitions and impacts of passenger car powertrain technologies in European member states. Transp. Res. Procedia **14**, 2620–2629 (2016)
36. Thiel, C., Drossinos, Y., Krause, J., Harrison, G., Gkatzoflias, D., Donati, A.V.: Modelling electro-mobility: an integrated modelling platform for assessing European policies. Transp. Res. Procedia **14**, 2544–2553 (2016)
37. Thunis, P., Degraeuwe, B., Pisoni, E., Ferrari, F., Clappier, A.: On the design and assessment of regional air quality plans: the SHERPA approach. J. Environ. Manag. **183**, 952–958 (2016)
38. Neves, S.A., Marques, A.C., Fuinhas, J.A.: Technological progress and other factors behind the adoption of electric vehicles: Empirical evidence for EU countries. Res. Transp. Econ. **74**, 28–39 (2019)
39. Bailey, D., Katz, J.N.: Implementing panel corrected standard errors in R: the PCSE package. J. Stat. Softw. **42**(CS1), 1–11 (2011)
40. Wang, N., Tang, L., Pan, H.: A global comparison and assessment of incentive policy on electric vehicle promotion. Sustain. Cities Soc. **44**, 597–603 (2019)
41. Javid, R.J., Nejat, A.: A comprehensive model of regional electric vehicle adoption and penetration. Transp. Policy **54**, 30–42 (2017)
42. Papke, L.E., Wooldridge, J.M.: Econometric methods for fractional response variables with an application to 401 (k) plan participation rates. J. Appl. Econometrics **11**(6), 619–632 (1996)
43. Ramalho, E.A., Ramalho, J.J., Henriques, P.D.: Fractional regression models for second stage DEA efficiency analyses. J. Prod. Anal. **34**(3), 239–255 (2010)
44. Yong, T., Park, C.: A qualitative comparative analysis on factors affecting the deployment of electric vehicles. Energy Procedia **128**, 497–503 (2017)

High-Dimensional Constrained Discrete Expensive Black-Box Optimization Using a Two-Phase Surrogate Approach

Rommel G. Regis[(⊠)] [iD]

Saint Joseph's University, Philadelphia, PA 19131, USA
rregis@sju.edu

Abstract. This paper develops an extension of a surrogate-based algorithm for high-dimensional discrete constrained black-box optimization called CONDOR that can be used when no feasible initial point is provided. The proposed extension uses a two-phase approach where the first phase searches for a feasible point whose objective value is then improved in the second phase. Each iteration of Phase I identifies the infeasible points that are nondominated according to three criteria: number of constraint violations, maximum constraint violation, and sum of squares of constraint violations. Then, multiple trial points are generated in some neighborhood of a randomly chosen nondominated point. The function evaluation point is then chosen from the trial points according to the predicted values of the above criteria. Moreover, each iteration of Phase II generates multiple trial points in some neighborhood of the current best feasible point. Then, among the trial points that are predicted to be feasible, the function evaluation point is chosen according to the predicted objective value and distance from previous sample points. In the numerical experiments, radial basis function (RBF) surrogates are used and the proposed algorithm is applied to test cases and to a benchmark based on a car structure design problem that has 222 discrete ordinal variables and 54 black-box constraints. The proposed method outperforms a genetic algorithm and a direct search method in terms of the number of function evaluations to obtain a feasible point and in the best feasible objective value obtained within a relatively limited computational budget.

Keywords: Constrained black-box optimization · Discrete ordinal variables · High-dimensional optimization · Surrogates · Radial basis functions

1 Introduction

Many surrogate-based approaches have been developed for constrained black-box optimization where surrogates are used to approximate expensive black-box objective and constraint functions that could take a few minutes or many hours to evaluate for a given input. These black-box functions might be expensive because their values are outcomes of computational fluid dynamics (CFD) or finite element (FE) simulations. Some of these methods use Kriging or Gaussian Process (GP) models (e.g., [3,7,21]) while others use Radial Basis Function

© Springer Nature Switzerland AG 2021
O. Gervasi et al. (Eds.): ICCSA 2021, LNCS 12953, pp. 366–381, 2021.
https://doi.org/10.1007/978-3-030-86976-2_25

(RBF) models (e.g., [1,18,25]). Most of these surrogate approaches for expensive black-box optimization have been developed for continuous optimization problems and relatively few of them can handle discrete variables [2]. Among the surrogate approaches for nonlinear integer or mixed-integer problems include the methods in [5,10,11,14,15,17,22,29]. However, most of these surrogate-based discrete black-box optimization methods have only been tested on problems with less than 25 variables and some do not handle black-box constraints (e.g., [15,29]). Moreover, surrogate methods that are suitable for high-dimensional problems with hundreds of discrete variables and many black-box constraints are still somewhat rare. One example is the CONDOR algorithm [26] and another is a constrained multi-objective evolutionary algorithm CMOEA/D assisted by an Extreme Learning Machine (ELM) surrogate [19]. The latter is designed for multi-objective constrained optimization, but it can be adapted for single-objective constrained optimization with discrete variables. CONDOR and ELM-assisted CMOEA/D have been tested on the 3-car Mazda benchmark problem [12,16] that involves 222 discrete variables and 54 black-box inequality constraints. CONDOR was applied to a single-objective version while ELM-assisted CMOEA/D was applied to the full multi-objective version of the Mazda benchmark. This paper proposes an extension of CONDOR that uses a two-phase surrogate approach to handle challenging high-dimensional constrained discrete expensive black-box optimization problems such as the Mazda benchmark.

Formally, this paper aims to find an approximate optimal solution to the following constrained optimization problem with ordinal discrete variables:

$$\min_{x \in \mathbb{R}^d} f(x)$$

s.t.
$$G(x) = (g_1(x), \ldots, g_m(x)) \leq 0 \tag{1}$$
$$x^{(i)} \in D_i \subset \mathbb{R}, \ i = 1, \ldots, d$$

where $x^{(i)}$ is the ith decision variable (the ith entry of $x \in \mathbb{R}^d$), and D_i is the finite set of the possible discrete ordinal settings of $x^{(i)}$. In practice, the elements in D_i do *not* have to be integers. They may be fractional values that the ith variable can take. For example, in the 3-car Mazda benchmark [12], $x^{(1)}$ takes on values from $D_1 = \{0.9, 0.95, 1.0, 1.2, 1.4, 1.5\}$. Moreover, the objective function $f(x)$ and the constraint functions $g_j(x)$, $j = 1, \ldots, m$ are black-box functions whose values are obtained from a computationally expensive simulation. In this paper, we assume that the simulations are deterministic and that there is no noise in the calculation of $f(x)$ and $G(x)$. The issue of noise in function evaluations will be addressed in future work.

In problem (1), the finite set $\prod_{i=1}^d D_i$ of (feasible and infeasible) points in $\mathbb{R}^d$ is the *search space* for the problem. The lower and upper bounds of the decision variables are given by $\ell_i := \min D_i$ and $u_i := \max D_i$ for $i = 1, \ldots, d$. For the proposed method, one *simulation* at a given point $x \in \prod_{i=1}^d D_i$ yields the values of the objective function $f(x)$ and all the components of the constraint function $G(x)$. However, some alternative optimization algorithms in the numerical comparisons require that separate calls are made to the objective function $f(x)$ and the constraint function $G(x)$ and that more calls are made to the latter than the former in one iteration. Hence, in the numerical experiments, the methods are sometimes compared after some fixed number of objective and constraint function evaluations instead of a fixed number of simulations.

The CONDOR (CONstrained Discrete Optimization using Response surfaces) algorithm [26] is a surrogate approach that can handle computationally expensive and high-dimensional constrained black-box problems involving discrete ordinal variables and many black-box inequality constraints. CONDOR that uses RBF surrogates for the objective and the constraints significantly outperformed a genetic algorithm and NOMAD [13] on a high-dimensional benchmark problem based on a car structure design problem from Mazda [16] given a relatively small computational budget and when the algorithms are given an initial feasible point. The 3-car Mazda benchmark has 222 discrete ordinal variables and 54 black-box constraints [16] and is much larger than most application and test problems in the literature. Unlike the ELM-assisted CMOEA/D in [19] where the constraints are aggregated and reduced to only three constraints, CONDOR uses a surrogate for each for the 54 inequality constraints in the Mazda benchmark. However, CONDOR [26] requires at least one feasible initial point, which can be difficult to obtain in some engineering applications.

This paper proposes the *Two-Phase CONDOR* algorithm, which extends the capabilities of CONDOR to solve high-dimensional constrained discrete black-box optimization problems when no feasible initial point is given. The method is designed to quickly obtain a feasible point and then find other feasible points with better objective function values using only a relatively small number of simulations. In Phase I of the proposed algorithm, all previously evaluated points are infeasible and the algorithm searches for a feasible point using surrogates for the constraint and objective functions. In Phase II, the algorithm improves on the objective function of the feasible point found in Phase I. Two-Phase CONDOR is implemented using RBF surrogates and is applied to discrete versions of three artificial test problems. It is also tested on the 3-car Mazda benchmark with 222 discrete variables and 54 black-box constraints using a computational budget of only $10d = 2220$ simulations. The proposed method outperforms a genetic algorithm and the direct search method NOMAD [13] in terms of the number of function evaluations to obtain a feasible point and in the best feasible objective function value obtained within the given computational budgets.

2 The Two-Phase CONDOR Algorithm

2.1 Algorithm Description

This paper proposes the *Two-Phase CONDOR (CONstrained Discrete Optimization using Response surfaces)* algorithm for finding an approximate optimal solution to the computationally expensive constrained discrete black-box optimization problem in (1). The proposed method uses a two-phase approach to extend the surrogate-based CONDOR algorithm in [26] so that it can be used when no feasible point is available among the initial sample points. The original

CONDOR algorithm assumes that at least one feasible initial point is provided, but this might not be the case in some applications and finding such a feasible point can be challenging for high-dimensional problems with many constraints. The first phase of Two-Phase CONDOR finds a feasible point while the second phase searches for a solution that improves on the feasible point found in the first phase. In both phases, surrogates for the objective and constraint functions are used to select the points where the expensive simulations are carried out. The use of a two-phase approach for surrogate-based constrained optimization with continuous variables has been employed in the COBRA algorithm [25] and its extension SACOBRA [1]. However, Two-Phase CONDOR not only deals with ordinal discrete variables, its strategies for selecting the simulation points in both phases differ from those in the COBRA and SACOBRA algorithms.

As with any surrogate-based approach, Two-Phase CONDOR begins by selecting an initial set of points in the search space where the simulations will take place. These points may be generated by using a space-filling design that is suitable for discrete search spaces or by simply randomly selecting points uniformly from the discrete search space. Then simulations are performed to get the values of the objective and constraint functions at the initial points. These function values are then used to fit the initial surrogates. For constrained optimization problems, there is typically no guarantee that a feasible point is available among the initial points. Hence, Phase I of the proposed algorithm uses surrogates for the constraints and the objective to find a feasible point for the problem. Then, Phase II searches for a solution that improves on the objective function value of the first feasible point found using again the surrogates for the constraints and the objective. If there is a feasible point among the initial sample points, then the algorithm simply proceeds to Phase II and behaves in the same way as the original CONDOR algorithm in [26].

Phase I of the proposed method employs a multi-criteria approach in determining its best previously evaluated sample points, which are all infeasible in this phase. In particular, in every iteration of Phase I, the algorithm identifies the sample points that are nondominated according to three criteria: number of constraint violations, maximum constraint violation, and sum of squares of the constraint violations. These criteria are pairwise conflicting in general. For example, for $x = [x^{(1)}, x^{(2)}, x^{(3)}] \in \mathbb{R}^3$, consider the constraint function $G(x) = \left(\frac{5}{6}x^{(1)} + \frac{1}{2}x^{(2)} - x^{(3)}, \frac{1}{3}x^{(1)} - \frac{1}{15}x^{(2)} + \frac{1}{15}x^{(3)}, -\frac{2}{3}x^{(1)} - \frac{1}{15}x^{(2)} + \frac{16}{15}x^{(3)}\right)$ and the points $[1, 0, 1]$, $[0, 1, 1]$ and $[1, 1, 1]$. Then $G([1, 0, 1]) = (-1/6, 2/5, 2/5)$, $G([0, 1, 1]) = (-1/2, 0, 1)$ and $G([1, 1, 1]) = (1/3, 1/3, 1/3)$. Note that $[0, 1, 1]$ has the smallest number of constraint violations, $[1, 1, 1]$ has the smallest maximum constraint violation, and $[1, 0, 1]$ has the smallest sum of squares of the constraint violations.

After obtaining the nondominated points based on the constraint violation criteria, the algorithm fits or updates the surrogates for the objective and constraint functions. Next, the algorithm chooses a nondominated point uniformly at random from the current set of nondominated points and then generates many trial points in some neighborhood of this nondominated point. The trial points are generated by perturbing some or all of the current variable settings of the chosen nondominated point as described below after the pseudocode. To select the simulation point, the algorithm uses the surrogates for the constraints to identify the *eligible* trial points, which are those that are predicted to be feasible. If none of the trial points are predicted to be feasible, the eligible trial points are those that have the smallest number of predicted constraint violations. The simulation point is then chosen from these trial points as the one with the best weighted combination of scaled values of the maximum predicted constraint violation (*MPCV criterion*) and scaled values of the sum of squares of the predicted constraint violations (*SPCV criterion*) as was done in the Two-Phase POSEIDON algorithm for constrained discrete multi-objective optimization [27]. On the other hand, if there are trial points that are predicted to be feasible, then the simulation point is chosen from these eligible trial points to be the one that minimizes a weighted combination of the scaled predicted objective value (*surrogate criterion*) and scaled distance from previous sample points (*distance criterion*) as was done in the ConstrLMSRBF algorithm [24]. Next, a simulation is performed to get the values of the objective and constraint functions at the chosen trial point. The algorithm goes through the iterations in Phase I until a feasible point is found, after which the algorithm proceeds to Phase II.

An alternative method for selecting the simulation point in Phase I is to use a multi-objective optimization algorithm to identify Pareto optimal points that provide a trade-off among the number of predicted constraint violations, the maximum predicted constraint violation, and the sum of squares of the predicted constraint violations subject to surrogates of the constraints. From these Pareto optimal points, the simulation point can be selected. This approach requires a multi-objective optimization algorithm that can handle discrete variables and constraints and will be explored in future work.

In every iteration of Phase II, the algorithm again fits the surrogates of the objective and the constraints and identifies the feasible sample point with the best objective function value. Next, the algorithm perturbs the variable settings of the current best feasible point multiple times to generate many trial points in some neighborhood of this best point. Then, as in Phase I, the surrogates for the constraints are used to determine the eligible trial points, which are those that are predicted to be feasible or at least those that have the smallest number of predicted constraint violations. Among these eligible trial points, the simulation point is selected to be the best trial point according to a weighted ranking of scaled values of two criteria as was done in [24]: predicted value of the objective function (*surrogate criterion*), and minimum distance between the trial point and the previously evaluated sample points (*distance criterion*). Once the best trial point is selected, a simulation is performed to get the values of the objective and constraint functions at that point, and then the algorithm iterates until the maximum number of simulations has been reached.

Below is a pseudo-code that outlines the main steps of the Two-Phase CONDOR algorithm for approximately solving the constrained discrete black-box optimization problem of the form (1).

Two-Phase CONDOR Algorithm

(1) *(Initial Simulations)* Run simulations to get the values of $f(x)$ and $G(x)$ at an initial set of points $\mathcal{I}_0 = \{x_1, \ldots, x_{n_0}\}$ in the search space $\prod_{i=1}^{d} D_i$. Set the simulation counter $n \leftarrow |\mathcal{I}_0| = n_0$ and the sample points $\mathcal{P}_{n_0} = \mathcal{I}_0$. If one of the points in $\mathcal{I}_0$ is feasible, go to Step 3 (Phase II).

(2) *(Phase I Iterations)* While a feasible sample point has not been found or while $n < n_{\max}$ do:

(a) *(Determine Nondominated Set)* Identify the sample points $\mathcal{N}_n^* \subseteq \mathcal{P}_n$ (all infeasible) that are nondominated according to three criteria: number of constraint violations, maximum constraint violation, and sum of squares of the constraint violations.

(b) *(Build Surrogates)* Build or update the surrogate for the objective $s_n^f(x)$ and the surrogates for the constraints $s_n^{g_i}(x)$, $i = 1, \ldots, m$ using info from all previous sample points $\mathcal{P}_n$.

(c) *(Generate Trial Points)* Select a point x_n^* uniformly at random from $\mathcal{N}_n^*$ and generate many trial points $\mathcal{T}_n$ in some neighborhood of x_n^*. (Described below.)

(d) *(Identify Eligible Trial Points)* Evaluate the surrogates for the constraints $s_n^{g_i}(x)$ at the trial points $\mathcal{T}_n$ and identify the trial points $\mathcal{T}_n^*$ that are predicted to be feasible or at least those with the smallest number of predicted constraint violations.

(e) *(Choose Simulation Point)* If the trial points in $\mathcal{T}_n^*$ are predicted to be feasible, then do (i) below, else do (ii).

  (i) Evaluate the surrogate for the objective $s_n^f(x)$ at the trial points in $\mathcal{T}_n^*$ and choose the simulation point x_{n+1} to be the trial point in $\mathcal{T}_n^*$ with the best weighted combination of scaled values of the surrogate and distance criteria.

  (ii) From the eligible trial points $\mathcal{T}_n^*$, choose the simulation point x_{n+1} to be the trial point with the best weighted combination of scaled values of the MPCV and SPCV criteria.

(f) *(Simulate)* Perform one simulation at x_{n+1} to get the values of $f(x_{n+1})$ and $G(x_{n+1}) = (g_1(x_{n+1}), \ldots, g_m(x_{n+1}))$. Set $\mathcal{P}_{n+1} = \mathcal{P}_n \cup \{x_{n+1}\}$ and reset $n \leftarrow n + 1$.

end.

(3) *(Phase II Iterations)* While $n < n_{\max}$ do:

(a) *(Identify Best Feasible Point)* Determine the feasible sample point with the best objective function value x_n^*.

(b) *(Build Surrogates)* Build or update the surrogate for the objective $s_n^f(x)$ and the surrogates for the constraints $s_n^{g_i}(x)$, $i = 1, \ldots, m$ using info from all previous sample points $\mathcal{P}_n$.

(c) *(Generate Trial Points)* Generate many trial points $\mathcal{T}_n$ in some neighborhood of x_n^*. (Described below.)

(d) *(Determine Eligible Trial Points)* Evaluate the surrogates for the constraints $s_n^{g_i}(x)$ at the trial points in $\mathcal{T}_n$ and determine the trial points $\mathcal{T}_n^*$ that are predicted to be feasible or at least those with the smallest number of predicted constraint violations.

(e) *(Choose Simulation Point)* Evaluate the surrogate for the objective $s_n^f(x)$ at the trial points in $\mathcal{T}_n^*$ and choose the simulation point x_{n+1} to be the trial point in $\mathcal{T}_n^*$ that with best weighted combination of scaled values of the surrogate and distance criteria.

(f) *(Simulate)* Perform one simulation at x_{n+1} to get the values of $f(x_{n+1})$ and $G(x_{n+1}) = (g_1(x_{n+1}), \ldots, g_m(x_{n+1}))$. Set $\mathcal{P}_{n+1} = \mathcal{P}_n \cup \{x_{n+1}\}$ and reset $n \leftarrow n+1$.

end.

(4) *(Return Best Feasible Point)* Return the best feasible solution x_n^* and the values $f(x_n^*)$ and $G(x_n^*) = (g_1(x_n^*), \ldots, g_m(x_n^*))$.

In every iteration of the proposed algorithm, many trial points are generated in some neighborhood of a center point, which is either the chosen non-dominated point in Phase I or the current best feasible point in Phase II. A trial point is generated by changing some of the variable settings of the center point. As with the original CONDOR algorithm [26], each component is modified with a certain probability, which we denote by p_{pert}. A perturbation consists of changing the current value of a discrete variable by either increasing or decreasing its value by a few discrete steps. The neighborhood depth parameter, which we denote by $depth_{\mathrm{nbhd}}$, is the percentage of the number of settings that the variable is allowed to increase or decrease. For example, in the 3-car Mazda benchmark [16], there are 9 possible settings of $x^{(17)}$ given by $D_{17} = \{0.9, 0.95, 1.0, 1.2, 1.4, 1.6, 1.8, 2.0, 2.1\}$ and suppose the current setting of variable $x^{(17)}$ at the current center point is 0.95. If $depth_{\mathrm{nbhd}} = 20\%$, then $x^{(17)}$ is allowed to take 20% of the possible discrete values for that variable above or below the current value. Hence, $x^{(17)}$ may be increased or decreased from 0.95 up to $\lceil 0.2(9) \rceil = 2$ discrete steps, and so, $x^{(17)}$ is allowed to take on the possible settings $\{0.9, 1.0, 1.2\}$. Note that the current setting of 0.95 is excluded from the possible values in order to force the value of $x^{(17)}$ to change.

2.2   Radial Basis Function Interpolation Model

The Two-Phase CONDOR algorithm can be implemented using any type of surrogate such as Kriging or Gaussian process modeling [3,8], radial basis functions (RBF) (e.g., [1,23,25]) and neural networks (e.g., [6]). The numerical experiments below use the RBF interpolation model in Powell [23], which is described below. Fitting this model involves solving a linear system that possesses desirable mathematical properties such as a guarantee that the interpolation matrix is nonsingular under mild technical conditions. This RBF model is suitable for the Two-Phase CONDOR on the Mazda benchmark because it has been successfully applied to high-dimensional problems with over a hundred decision variables and many black-box inequality constraints (e.g., see [1,24,25]). In contrast, Kriging models sometimes suffer from numerical issues and can be computationally expensive to build on high-dimensional problems with hundreds of variables.

Next, we describe how to build this RBF model. Let $u(x)$ be the objective or one of the constraint functions. Suppose the function values at the $x_1, x_2, \ldots,$

$x_n \in \mathbb{R}^d$ are known, so that we have the data points $(x_1, u(x_1))$, $(x_2, u(x_2))$, $\dots, (x_n, u(x_n))$. The RBF model from Powell [23] has the form:

$$s_n(x) = \sum_{i=1}^{n} \lambda_i \phi(\|x - x_i\|) + p(x), \quad x \in \mathbb{R}^d,$$

where $\| \cdot \|$ is the 2-norm, $\lambda_i \in \mathbb{R}$ for $i = 1, 2, \dots, n$, $p(x)$ is a linear function in d variables, and ϕ can take many forms such as the *cubic* form ($\phi(r) = r^3$), the thin plate spline ($\phi(r) = r^2 \log r$), or the Gaussian form ($\phi(r) = \exp(-\gamma r^2)$, where γ is a hyperparameter). A cubic RBF model is used in the numerical experiments because it does not require a hyperparameter that needs to be tuned and because of its success in previous RBF methods (e.g., [24,25]). More details about how to fit this model are found in Powell [23].

3   Numerical Experiments

3.1   Description of the Test Problems and the Mazda Benchmark

The proposed Two-Phase CONDOR method is tested on discrete modifications of the well-known benchmark problems G7 ($d = 10$ variables, $m = 8$ constraints), G9 ($d = 7$, $m = 4$) and G19 ($d = 15$, $m = 5$) (e.g., see [25]). The modified problems are referred to as G7-Discrete, G9-Discrete and G19-Discrete. The number of discrete settings for each variable in the modified problems ranged from 6 to 18 and the number of points in the search spaces are 1.99×10^{10} for G7-Discrete, 1.30×10^7 for G9-Discrete, and 1.12×10^{17} for G19-Discrete.

Two-Phase CONDOR is also tested on a single-objective version of the 3-car Mazda Benchmark [9,12,16,20] that is based on a car structure design problem. This benchmark has 222 discrete ordinal decision variables (thicknesses of structural parts) and 54 black-box inequality constraints (including collision safety performances), and it is among the largest application-based benchmark problems in expensive black-box optimization. The objective is to minimize the total weight of three types of Mazda cars (Mazda CX-5 (SUV), Mazda 6 (LV), and Mazda 3 (SV)) subject to the constraints. Each decision variable can only take values from a finite number of discrete settings ranging from 4 to 18. Moreover, the total number of possible combinations of values of the discrete variables is 4.4427×10^{198}, which is very large even by astronomical standards.

Evaluating the constraint functions in the design optimization of car structures requires running expensive simulations, but the evaluation of the Mazda benchmark is fast because the collision safety constraints are modeled by response surface approximations [12]. Moreover, calculating the objective function is relatively cheap since it is simply the total weight of three types of cars. However, in this paper, the objective function is also assumed to be black-box and expensive, which is the case in other applications. Future work will consider variants of the proposed method that take advantage of inexpensive objective functions. The Mazda benchmark is challenging for surrogate optimization because it has hundreds of decision variables and many black-box constraints, and it is larger than the vast majority of test problems used in surrogate-based optimization. In addition, it is not easy to obtain feasible points for the problem by uniform random sampling because the size of the discrete feasible region is very small relative to the astronomically large discrete search space. Non-surrogate methods such as evolutionary algorithms and direct search methods are not expected to produce feasible points quickly on the Mazda benchmark and this is confirmed in the numerical experiments. More details about the Mazda benchmark can be found at https://ladse.eng.isas.jaxa.jp/benchmark/index.html.

3.2   Experimental Setup

Two-Phase CONDOR is implemented using RBF surrogates with the cubic form $(\phi(r) = r^3)$ and three variants are considered: *CONDOR (RBF-local)*, *CONDOR (RBF-global)*, and *CONDOR (RBF-mixed)*. The first performs more local search for Phase I and Phase II, the second allows more global search for both phases, and the third is a mixture of more global search for Phase I combined with more local search for Phase II. The second phase of the first two variants coincide with the original CONDOR methods tested in [26], which only work when a feasible initial point is given. In each of the two phases, the three variants generate $20d$ trial points from the current center point (either a nondominated point in Phase I or the current best feasible point in Phase II) in each iteration. Moreover, the values of the perturbation probability p_{pert} and the neighborhood depth parameter $depth_{\text{nbhd}}$ vary in a cyclical manner in all variants. In particular, the algorithm parameters $(p_{\text{pert}}, depth_{\text{nbhd}})$ vary according to the following cycles: CONDOR (RBF-local) uses $\langle(0.5, 30\%), (0.1, 10\%), (0.05, 10\%),$ $(0.01, 10\%)\rangle$ as in [26], CONDOR (RBF-global) uses $\langle(0.5, 50\%), (0.3, 50\%),$ $(0.2, 10\%), (0.1, 10\%), (0.05, 10\%)\rangle$ as in [26], and CONDOR (RBF-mixed) uses the same cycle as CONDOR (RBF-global) for Phase I and the same cycle as CONDOR (RBF-local) in Phase II.

When the perturbation probability p_{pert} is fixed, the number of variables modified in the chosen center point is a binomial random variable whose mean is $d \cdot p_{\text{pert}}$. This means that when CONDOR uses $p_{\text{pert}} = 0.01$ in the Mazda benchmark, $d \cdot p_{\text{pert}} = 222(0.01) = 2.22$ variables are modified on average. Combining this with a depth parameter of 10%, CONDOR generates trial points that are highly local and close to the current center point. On the other hand, when CONDOR uses $p_{\text{pert}} = 0.5$, the number of variables modified on average is $222(0.5) = 111$, and combining this with a depth parameter of 50%, the algorithm yields trial points that are far from the center point and that have potential explore the search space globally.

The three variants of Two-Phase CONDOR are compared with NOMAD [13] and Matlab's Genetic Algorithm (GA) solver [28] with various crossover fractions. Before GA and NOMAD are applied, the possible discrete ordinal values of each variable are mapped to the integers 0, 1, 2, up to the maximum number of possible discrete values minus one. NOMAD is run on Matlab through the OPTI toolbox [4] and using its default settings. GA mostly used default settings, but with different crossover fractions set to 100%, 75%, 50% and 25%. Moreover,

GA is run with a population size of $5d$ for the artificial problems and 300 for the Mazda benchmark as in [12]. It would be best if CONDOR is compared with another surrogate-based method. Unfortunately, there does not seem to be any publicly available code for a surrogate-based algorithm for constrained discrete black-box optimization. As mentioned earlier, only a relatively small number of surrogate-based methods in the literature can be used for discrete black-box optimization [2], and even less can handle high-dimensional constrained black-box optimization problems.

Each algorithm is run for 30 trials on the artificial benchmark problems up to a maximum of $40d$ simulations (equivalent to $80d$ function evaluations when counting objective and constraint function calls separately). For the single-objective Mazda benchmark, each algorithm is run for 10 trials up to a maximum of $10d = 2220$ simulations (equivalent to $20d = 4440$ objective and constraint function evaluations). For a fair comparison, the CONDOR and GA algorithms used the same initial population in each trial. NOMAD also used the same initial points used by GA and CONDOR except that one of these initial points is chosen as the starting point of the algorithm. This starting point is chosen from among the initial points with the smallest number of constraint violations to be the best according to a weighted combination of scaled values of two criteria: maximum constraint violation and sum of squares of constraint violations. Moreover, the first trial on the Mazda benchmark used the same initial population as the one used in earlier experiments [16]. For the other trials on the Mazda benchmark and for all trials on the artificial problems, an initial population was obtained by randomly selecting points using a uniform distribution on the search space. In almost all trials, except for two trials on G9-Discrete, none of the points in the initial population are feasible, so the CONDOR algorithms started with Phase I.

All numerical experiments are carried out in Matlab 9.4 using an Intel(R) Core(TM) i7-7700T CPU @ 2.90 GHz, 2904 Mhz, 4 Core(s), 8 Logical Processor(s) Windows-based machine. The Mazda benchmark is run on Matlab through a system call that runs the executable provided in [16].

3.3 Results and Discussion

Table 1 shows the mean and standard error over 30 trials of the number of objective and constraint function evaluations (including those for the initial population) it took the different algorithms to obtain a feasible sample point on the artificial benchmark problems. The results for CONDOR (RBF-mixed) are not included since its Phase I is identical to that of CONDOR (RBF-global). Moreover, the results for GA with a crossover fraction of 25% are not included since they are comparable to the other GA results. Note that the CONDOR algorithms consistently required much less objective and constraint function evaluations to obtain a feasible point than NOMAD and GA on the artificial problems. Also, the results for the local and global variants are comparable with the global variant performing slightly better on the G9-Discrete and G19-Discrete problems.

Next, Table 2 shows the mean and standard error over 30 trials of the best feasible objective function value obtained by the CONDOR and NOMAD

Table 1. Mean (over 30 trials) of the number of objective and constraint function evaluations to obtain a feasible point on the test problems. The number inside the parenthesis is the standard error of the mean.

Test problem	CONDOR (RBF-local)	CONDOR (RBF-global)	NOMAD	GA (CR = 100%)	GA (CR = 75%)	GA (CR = 50%)
G7-Discrete	**168.87 (8.20)**	176.73 (12.71)	260.80 (11.38)	656.23 (32.69)	709.63 (34.98)	688.27 (42.05)
G9-Discrete	78.00 (3.24)	**75.93 (2.58)**	122.87 (8.41)	98.43 (8.04)	109.37 (8.94)	> 166.47
G19-Discrete	156.13 (0.88)	**154.93 (0.46)**	288.80 (11.43)	828.00 (74.26)	706.40 (50.26)	588.13 (45.19)

Table 2. Mean (over 30 trials) of the best feasible objective function value obtained by the algorithms in $80d$ objective and constraint function evaluations on the test problems. The number inside the parenthesis is the standard error of the mean.

Test problem	CONDOR (RBF-local)	CONDOR (RBF-global)	CONDOR (RBF-mixed)	NOMAD
G7-Discrete	**51.17 (5.66)**	65.97 (7.50)	60.57 (9.29)	69.00 (7.59)
G9-Discrete	728.00 (5.97)	**704.53 (3.15)**	725.07 (7.57)	746.23 (8.38)
G19-Discrete	341.52 (21.02)	**294.34 (16.70)**	343.70 (16.83)	1329.59 (389.62)

algorithms in $80d$ objective and constraint function evaluations on the artificial problems. The results for GA are not included since some of its trials did not even find a feasible sample point within the given computational budget. Note that the CONDOR algorithms consistently obtained better feasible objective function values than NOMAD (and also GA) especially on G19-Discrete.

The Two-Phase CONDOR algorithms are also compared with GA and NOMAD in how quickly they are able to obtain a feasible sample point on the Mazda benchmark. Figure 1 shows the mean of the minimum number of constraint violations (left plot) and the mean of the best sum of squares of constraint violations (right plot) over 10 trials obtained by the different algorithms at computational budgets up to about 2400 objective and constraint function evaluations on the Mazda benchmark. Both plots include error bars that correspond to 95% t confidence intervals for the mean. The t distribution is used in the calculation of confidence intervals since the number of trials for each algorithm is small. GA results are obtained for various crossover fractions of 25%, 50%, 75% and 100%. However, to simplify the presentation of the results, only the results for crossover fractions of 50% and 100% are shown since the other results are similar. Again, CONDOR (RBF-mixed) is not included in these comparisons since its Phase I is identical to that of CONDOR (RBF-global).

Figure 1 shows that the Two-Phase CONDOR algorithms are able to quickly reduce both the number of constraint violations and the sum of squares of the constraint violations of its sample points to zero and consistently yield feasible sample points within a relatively small number of objective and constraint function evaluations on the Mazda benchmark. Moreover, the results for Two-Phase CONDOR are much better than those for NOMAD and GA. In fact, none of

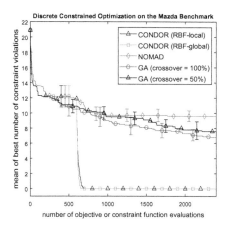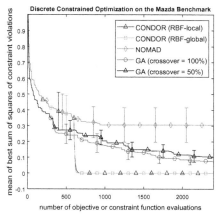

Fig. 1. Mean over 10 trials and 95% t confidence intervals for the minimum number of constraint violations (left) and the best sum of squares of the constraint violations (right) obtained by the Two-Phase CONDOR algorithms and alternative methods at different computational budgets on the Mazda benchmark.

Table 3. Number of simulations to feasibility and first feasible objective value obtained for 10 trials of Two-Phase CONDOR on the Mazda benchmark.

Algorithm	Trial 1	Trial 2	Trial 3	Trial 4	Trial 5	Trial 6	Trial 7	Trial 8	Trial 9	Trial 10	Mean
CONDOR	340	331	320	331	325	318	324	312	310	347	325.8
(RBF-local)	3.0779	3.0369	3.1085	3.0464	3.0992	3.0998	3.0895	3.0751	3.1020	3.1461	
CONDOR	319	319	313	318	313	328	323	324	315	313	318.5
(RBF-global)	3.1005	3.0967	3.1048	3.0868	3.0980	3.0645	3.1281	3.0067	3.0468	3.1160	

the trials of NOMAD and GA yielded a feasible sample point within the budget of $20d = 4440$ objective and constraint function evaluations (equivalent to $10d$ simulations). These results show the difficulty in obtaining a feasible sample point for the high-dimensional and highly constrained Mazda benchmark.

Next, Table 3 shows the number of simulations (including those for the initial population) it took the CONDOR algorithms to obtain a feasible sample point and the corresponding feasible objective function value for 10 trials on the Mazda benchmark. The last column of this table shows the mean of number of simulations needed to achieve feasibility for the algorithm. GA and NOMAD are not included since they did not produce any feasible sample point in any of the trials within the computational budget that is equivalent to $10d$ simulations.

Table 3 shows how quickly and consistently the CONDOR algorithms are able to obtain a feasible sample point within a small number of iterations on the Mazda benchmark while neither NOMAD nor GA found a feasible point within the equivalent of $10d = 2220$ simulations. In fact, removing the initial population size of 300 from the mean values in Table 3 shows that it only takes an average of 25.8 and 18.5 simulations for CONDOR (RBF-local) and CONDOR

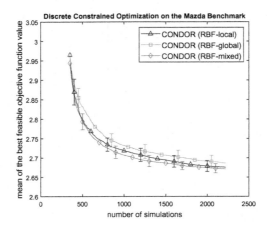

Fig. 2. Mean over 10 trials and 95% t confidence intervals for the best feasible objective value found by Two-Phase CONDOR algorithms at different computational budgets.

(RBF-global), respectively, to find a feasible point. Also, the global variant of Two-Phase CONDOR found a feasible point in less simulations than the local variant on the Mazda benchmark. Recall that the global variant found a feasible point in slightly less function evaluations than the local variant on G9-Discrete and G19-Discrete. This indicates that a more global search strategy for Phase I of the Two-Phase CONDOR might be more effective in achieving feasibility.

Next, Fig. 2 shows the mean of the best feasible objective function value over 10 trials obtained by the Two-Phase CONDOR algorithms at different computational budgets on the Mazda benchmark. As before, the error bars correspond to 95% t confidence intervals for the mean. The plots start at a budget of 350 simulations since all trials of the CONDOR algorithms have found a feasible sample point at this budget (see Table 3). Moreover, the mean of the best feasible objective function values (and standard error in parenthesis) obtained by the three variants after $10d = 2220$ simulations on the Mazda benchmark are 2.6757 (0.0060) for the Local variant, 2.6866 (0.0067) for the Global variant, and 2.6712 (0.0052) for the Mixed variant.

Figure 2 shows that the three variants of Two-Phase CONDOR have comparable performances with some slight advantage for CONDOR (RBF-mixed) in the best feasible objective function value obtained during Phase II. However, the earlier result in [26] comparing one trial each of the local and global variants of the original CONDOR when the feasible initial point from [16] is provided shows better performance for the local variant. These results, which are averaged over 10 trials, suggest that there is still some slight advantage for the local variant over the global variant on the Mazda benchmark. Recall that the global variant found a feasible point faster than the local variant. By using the search strategy of the global variant in Phase I and the search strategy of the local variant in Phase II, the mixed variant seems to perform slightly better than both the local and global variants on the Mazda benchmark. This might be because the more global search strategy in Phase I provides more diverse sample points for building the surrogates that are used to approximate the objective and constraints in both feasible and infeasible regions of the search space. More accurate surrogates are helpful in making progress in finding a feasible point in Phase I and in improving the best feasible objective function value in Phase II.

4   Summary and Conclusions

This paper introduced the surrogate-based Two-Phase CONDOR algorithm, which extends the CONDOR method [26] for high-dimensional and computationally expensive constrained black-box optimization problems with discrete ordinal decision variables and many black-box inequality constraints. The original CONDOR algorithm requires a feasible initial point while Two-Phase CONDOR can be used even when such a feasible point is not available. In Phase I, the algorithm searches for a feasible point by using the surrogates of the constraints and objectives. In Phase II, the algorithm finds a solution that improves on the objective function value of the feasible point found in Phase I.

Three variants of Two-Phase CONDOR that employ cubic RBF surrogates are tested on discrete versions of three well-known artificial benchmark problems and also on the Mazda benchmark, which is based on a car structure design problem that has 222 discrete ordinal variables and 54 black-box constraints. The CONDOR (RBF-local) variant uses a more local search strategy for Phase I and Phase II, CONDOR (RBF-global) uses a more global search strategy for both phases, and CONDOR (RBF-mixed) uses a mixture of more global search in Phase I with more local search for Phase II. Numerical results show that the Two-Phase CONDOR algorithms required much less objective and constraint function evaluations to find feasible sample points compared to NOMAD and GA on the artificial test problems. Moreover, they generally obtained better feasible objective function values than NOMAD and GA on the artificial problems. In fact, some of the trials of GA did not even yield a feasible point within $80d$ objective and constraint function evaluations on these problems. On the Mazda benchmark, the results also show that the Two-Phase CONDOR algorithms consistently found a feasible sample point within a relatively small number of Phase I iterations while the GA and NOMAD algorithms did not find any feasible sample points in all of the 10 trials within $20d = 4440$ objective and constraint function evaluations (equivalent to $10d = 2220$ simulations).

In addition, the global and mixed variants of Two-Phase CONDOR required slightly less function evaluations than the local variant to find a feasible point on two of the three artificial problems and on the Mazda benchmark. This indicates that a global search strategy might be more effective for Phase I of the algorithm. However, the performances of the three variants are comparable in terms of the best feasible objective value obtained in Phase II. Overall, these results suggest that the Two-Phase CONDOR algorithm is promising for discrete expensive black-box optimization involving hundreds of variables and many black-box constraints when an initial feasible point is not provided.

Acknowledgements. Many thanks to Dr. Takehisa Kohira for explaining some of the details of the Mazda Benchmark.

References

1. Bagheri, S., Konen, W., Emmerich, M., Bäck, T.: Self-adjusting parameter control for surrogate-assisted constrained optimization under limited budgets. Appl. Soft Comput. **61**, 377–393 (2017)
2. Bartz-Beielstein, T., Zaefferer, M.: Model-based methods for continuous and discrete global optimization. Appl. Soft Comput. **55**, 154–167 (2017)
3. Bouhlel, M.A., Bartoli, N., Regis, R.G., Otsmane, A., Morlier, J.: Efficient global optimization for high-dimensional constrained problems by using the kriging models combined with the partial least squares method. Eng. Optim. **50**(12), 2038–2053 (2018)
4. Currie, J., Wilson, D. I.: OPTI: lowering the barrier between open source optimizers and the industrial MATLAB user. In: Foundations of Computer-Aided Process Operations, Georgia, USA (2012)
5. Dong, H., Wang, P., Song, B., Zhang, Y., An, X.: Kriging-assisted Discrete Global Optimization (KDGO) for black-box problems with costly objective and constraints. Appl. Soft Comput. **94**, 106429 (2020)
6. Dushatskiy, A., Mendrik, A.M., Alderliesten, T., Bosman, P.A.N.: Convolutional neural network surrogate-assisted GOMEA. In: GECCO 2019: Proceedings of the Genetic and Evolutionary Computation Conference, pp. 753–761 (2019)
7. Feliot, P., Bect, J., Vazquez, E.: A Bayesian approach to constrained single- and multi-objective optimization. J. Global Optim. **67**, 97–133 (2017)
8. Forrester, A.I.J., Sobester, A., Keane, A.J.: Engineering Design via Surrogate Modelling: A practical guide. Wiley, New York (2008)
9. Fukumoto, H., Oyama, A.: Benchmarking multiobjective evolutionary algorithms and constraint handling techniques on a real-world car structure design optimization benchmark problem. In: GECCO 2018: Proceedings of the Genetic and Evolutionary Computation Conference Companion, pp. 177–178 (2018)
10. Garrido-Merchán, E.C., Hernández-Lobato, D.: Dealing with categorical and integer-valued variables in Bayesian Optimization with Gaussian processes. Neurocomputing **380**, 20–35 (2020)
11. Kim, S.H., Boukouvala, F.: Surrogate-based optimization for mixed-integer nonlinear problems. Comput. Chem. Eng. **140**, 106847 (2020)
12. Kohira, T., Kemmotsu, H., Oyama, A., Tatsukawa, T.: Proposal of benchmark problem based on real-world car structure design optimization. In: GECCO 2018: Proceedings of the Genetic and Evolutionary Computation Conference Companion, pp. 183–184 (2018)
13. Le Digabel, S.: Algorithm 909: NOMAD: nonlinear optimization with the MADS algorithm. ACM Trans. Math. Softw. **37**(4), 44:1–44:15 (2011)
14. Liu, B., Sun, N., Zhang, Q., Grout, V., Gielen, G.: A surrogate model assisted evolutionary algorithm for computationally expensive design optimization problems with discrete variables. In: 2016 IEEE Congress on Evolutionary Computation (CEC), Vancouver, BC, pp. 1650–1657 (2016)
15. Luong, P., Gupta, S., Nguyen, D., Rana, S., Venkatesh, S.: Bayesian optimization with discrete variables. In: Liu, J., Bailey, J. (eds.) AI 2019. LNCS (LNAI), vol. 11919, pp. 473–484. Springer, Cham (2019). https://doi.org/10.1007/978-3-030-35288-2_38

16. Mazda Benchmark Problem. https://ladse.eng.isas.jaxa.jp/benchmark/index. html. Accessed 30 Apr 2020
17. Mueller, J., Shoemaker, C.A., Piche, R.: SO-I: a surrogate model algorithm for expensive nonlinear integer programming problems including global optimization applications. J. Global Optim. **59**, 865–889 (2014)
18. Nuñez, L., Regis, R.G., Varela, K.: Accelerated random search for constrained global optimization assisted by radial basis function surrogates. J. Comput. Appl. Math. **340**, 276–295 (2018)
19. Ohtsuka, H., Kaidan, M., Harada, T., Thawonmas, R.: Evolutionary algorithm using surrogate assisted model for simultaneous design optimization benchmark problem of multiple car structures. In: GECCO 2018: Proceedings of the Genetic and Evolutionary Computation Conference Companion, pp. 55–56 (2018)
20. Oyama, A., Kohira, T., Kemmotsu, H., Tatsukawa, T., Watanabe, T.: Simultaneous structure design optimization of multiple car models using the K computer. In: 2017 IEEE Symposium Series on Computational Intelligence (SSCI), Honolulu, HI, pp. 1–4 (2017)
21. Parr, J.M., Keane, A.J., Forrester, A.I., Holden, C.M.: Infill sampling criteria for surrogate-based optimization with constraint handling. Eng. Optim. **44**(10), 1147–1166 (2012)
22. Pelamatti, J., Brevault, L., Balesdent, M., Talbi, E.G., Guerin, Y.: Efficient global optimization of constrained mixed variable problems. J. Global Optim. **73**, 583–613 (2019)
23. Powell, M.J.D.: The theory of radial basis function approximation in 1990. In: Light, W. (ed.) Advances in Numerical Analysis, Volume 2: Wavelets, Subdivision Algorithms and Radial Basis Functions, pp. 105–210. Oxford University Press, Oxford (1992)
24. Regis, R.G.: Stochastic radial basis function algorithms for large-scale optimization involving expensive black-box objective and constraint functions. Comput. Oper. Res. **38**(5), 837–853 (2011)
25. Regis, R.G.: Constrained optimization by radial basis function interpolation for high-dimensional expensive black-box problems with infeasible initial points. Eng. Optim. **46**(2), 218–243 (2014)
26. Regis, R.G.: Large-scale discrete constrained black-box optimization using radial basis functions. In: 2020 IEEE Symposium Series on Computational Intelligence (SSCI), pp. 2924–2931 (2020). https://doi.org/10.1109/SSCI47803.2020.9308581
27. Regis, R.G.: A two-phase surrogate approach for high-dimensional constrained discrete multi-objective optimization. In: GECCO 2021: Proceedings of the Genetic and Evolutionary Computation Conference Companion, pp. 1870–1878 (2021)
28. The Mathworks: Matlab Global Optimization Toolbox (2018)
29. Zaefferer, M.: Surrogate Models for Discrete Optimization Problems. Ph.D. thesis, Technische Universität Dortmund (2018)

A Clustering Algorithm Based on Fitness Probability Scores for Cluster Centers Optimization

M. Fernanda P. Costa[1]([✉]) [iD], Ana Maria A. C. Rocha[2] [iD],
and Edite M. G. P. Fernandes[2] [iD]

[1] Centre of Mathematics, University of Minho, Campus de Gualtar,
4710-057 Braga, Portugal
mfc@math.uminho.pt
[2] ALGORITMI Center, University of Minho, Campus de Gualtar,
4710-057 Braga, Portugal
{arocha,emgpf}@dps.uminho.pt

Abstract. In the present paper, we propose an iterative clustering approach that sequentially applies five processes, namely: the assign, delete,
split, delete and optimization. It is based on the fitness probability scores
of the cluster centers to identify the least fitted centers to undergo an
optimization process, aiming to improve the centers from one iteration to
another. Moreover, the parameters of the algorithm for the delete, split
and optimization processes are dynamically tuned as problem dependent functions. The presented clustering algorithm is evaluated using
four data sets, two randomly generated and two well-known sets. The
obtained clustering algorithm is compared with other clustering algorithms through the visualization of the clustering, the value of a validity measure and the value of the objective function of the optimization
process. The comparison of results shows that the proposed clustering
algorithm is effective and robust.

Keywords: Clustering analysis · Fitness probability score ·
Differential evolution

1 Introduction

Clustering is an unsupervised machine learning task and consists of grouping a
set of data points in a way that similarity of the elements in a group – also called
cluster – is maximized, whereas similarity of elements in two different groups, is
minimized. Clustering methods can be categorized as partitioning, hierarchical,
fuzzy, density-based or model-based methods. The most popular are the partitioning and hierarchical clustering. There are different types of partitioning

This work has been supported by FCT – Fundação para a Ciência e Tecnologia within
the R&D Units Project Scope: UIDB/00013/2020 and UIDP/00013/2020 of CMAT-
UM.

O. Gervasi et al. (Eds.): ICCSA 2021, LNCS 12953, pp. 382–396, 2021.
https://doi.org/10.1007/978-3-030-86976-2_26

clustering methods being the K-means clustering the most popular [1]. These methods subdivide the data set into K clusters, where K should be specified *a priori*. Each cluster is represented by the centroid (mean) of the data points belonging to that cluster. Hierarchical methods do not require the *a priori* specification of the number of clusters and the result of the clustering can be easily visualized in a tree-based representation of the data, known as a dendrogram. Partitioning and hierarchical clustering are suitable to find spherical-shaped clusters or convex clusters, i.e., they work rather well when clusters are compact and separated. On the other hand, when non-convex clusters and outliers (or noises) are present in the data set, they inaccurately identify clusters. Density-based clustering algorithms are the most appropriate for this type of data. DBSCAN is a popular density-based clustering technique that was introduced in [2]. It can find out clusters of different shapes and sizes from data containing noise and outliers. Alternatively, with clustering algorithms that cannot separate clusters that are non-linearly separable in the input space, the use of a kernel function tackles the problem. The idea is concerned with (before clustering) mapping the points to a higher-dimensional feature space (the kernel space) using a nonlinear function. Then, the kernel-based clustering method partitions the data points that are linearly separable in the new space [3].

Applications of clustering are varied and emerge in the field of data mining [4], in bioinformatics [5], pattern recognition [6], image processing, to name a few.

Since clustering can be seen as an optimization problem, well-known optimization algorithms, in particular metaheuristics, may be applied in clustering analysis. Varied contributions have been made in this area [7–13]. In general, metaheuristics have been combined with the K-means clustering, e.g., [9, 11, 14] However, contrary to the K-means, and other K-means combinations with metaheuristics, that require knowledge of the number of clusters in advance, it is possible to design an algorithm that dynamically adds, deletes and merges clusters based on a fitness function to evaluate the goodness of the clustering result.

The clustering algorithm presented in this paper resorts to this type of mechanisms to try to find the optimal (or near-optimal) clustering. Thus, the main contributions of this article include the definition of the algorithm parameters that are dynamically computed and depend on the characteristics of the data set. Furthermore, at each iteration of the algorithm, not all cluster centers but only a few of them are identified as the least fitted centers, and undergo an optimization process. The proposed clustering algorithm has mechanisms to merge two nearby clusters, delete the smallest cluster, split the largest cluster, and optimize specifically selected cluster centers iteratively. Although these mechanisms are similar to others in the literature, this article greatly contributes to this field of cluster analysis by proposing the definition of the parameter values - target values and thresholds - that are problem dependent and dynamically computed.

The paper is organized as follows. Section 2 describes the proposed clustering algorithm and shows details concerning the problem dependent parameters. In Sect. 3, the results relative to two sets of data points with two attributes and two sets with four and thirteen attributes respectively are shown. Finally, Sect. 4 contains the conclusions of this work.

2   Clustering Algorithm

Let a set of n patterns or data points, each with a attributes, be given. These patterns can also be represented by a data matrix $\mathbf{X}$ with n vectors of dimension a. Each element X_{ij} corresponds to the jth attribute of the ith pattern/point. Thus, given $\mathbf{X}$, a partitioning clustering algorithm tries to find a partition $\mathcal{C} = \{C_1, C_2, \ldots, C_K\}$ of K clusters (or groups), in a way that similarity of the patterns in the same cluster is maximum and patterns from different clusters differ as much as possible. The partition must satisfy three properties:

1. each cluster should have at least one point, i.e., $|C_k| \neq 0$, $k = 1, \ldots, K$;
2. a point should not belong to two different clusters, i.e., $C_i \bigcap C_j = \emptyset$, for $i, j = 1, \ldots, K$, $i \neq j$;
3. each point should belong to a cluster, i.e., $\sum_{k=1}^{K} |C_k| = n$;

where $|C_k|$ is the number of points in cluster C_k. Since there are a number of ways to partition the patterns and maintain these properties, a fitness function should be provided so that the adequacy of the partitioning is evaluated. Therefore, the clustering problem could be stated as finding an optimal solution, i.e., partition $\mathcal{C}^*$, that gives the optimal (or near-optimal) adequacy, when compared to all the other feasible solutions.

2.1   Clustering Algorithm with Centers Optimization

The partitioning clustering algorithm herein proposed does not require *a priori* specification of the number of clusters. Although for the initialization, a number of clusters must be specified, K, and the corresponding centers (that represent the clusters), $m_1, m_2, \ldots, m_K$ randomly selected (or generated), the algorithm iteratively adds, merges and deletes centers (removing the correspondent clusters) according to some problem dependent rules that vary dynamically as the iterative process progresses.

In Algorithm 1, the five main steps of the proposed clustering algorithm are shown - from line 6 to line 10. This is an iterative process that automatically finds the optimal clustering.

Briefly, after a set of cluster centers being randomly generated in the region of the data points, each point is assigned to a cluster based on the minimum distance of that point to all the centers. Then, clusters may be merged and deleted if the smallest distance between the cluster centers is below a threshold and the number of points in a cluster is considered very small relatively to the number of data points in the set. Furthermore, the cluster with maximum hypervolume may be split into two new clusters if its hypervolume exceeds a target value. The algorithm checks again if clusters may be merged or deleted. Finally, a set of the current cluster centers are identified as the least fitted centers, according to their fitness probability scores - further ahead described - and undergo an optimization process.

Algorithm 1. Clustering Algorithm

Require: a number of attributes, n number of data points, $\mathbf{X} = (X_{i,j})$, $i = 1, \ldots, n$, $j = 1, \ldots, a$ data set; $It_{\max}$
1: Set $K = \max\{2, \lceil 0.01n \rceil\}$; $N_{\min} = \max\{2, \lceil 0.05n \rceil\}$; $It = 1$
2: Compute $\underline{X}_j = \min_{i=1,\ldots,n} X_{i,j}$ and $\overline{X}_j = \max_{i=1,\ldots,n} X_{i,j}$ for $j = 1, \ldots, a$;
3: Compute $A_{\min} = \min_{j=1,\ldots,a}(\overline{X}_j - \underline{X}_j)$;
4: Randomly generate a set of cluster centers m_k, $k = 1, \ldots, K$ using

$$m_{k,j} = \underline{X}_j + rand(\overline{X}_j - \underline{X}_j) \text{ for } j = 1, \ldots, a$$

   where $rand$ is a uniformly distributed number in $[0, 1]$.
5: **repeat**
6:    Assign points to current cluster centers $m_k, k = 1, \ldots, K$ using Algorithm 2
7:    Merge clusters that have the two closest centers and remove the cluster with fewer points, using Algorithm 3, $\eta_D = \frac{1}{K} A_{\min}$ and $N_{\min}$
8:    Add one cluster by splitting the cluster with maximum hypervolume using Algorithm 4
9:    Merge clusters that have the two closest centers and remove the cluster with fewer points, using Algorithm 3, $\eta_D = \frac{2}{K} A_{\min}$ and $N_{\min}$
10:    Compute improved positions for the least fitted cluster centers (maintaining the fitter ones as constant) by optimizing the fitness function (WCD in (6)), using Algorithm 5
11:    Set $It = It + 1$
12: **until** $It > It_{\max}$ or cluster centers do not move
13: **return** K^*, $m_k, k = 1, \ldots, K^*$ and $\mathcal{C}^* = \{C_1^*, \ldots, C_K^*\}$.

To find which cluster to assign a point X_i ($i = 1, \ldots, n$), the simplest idea is to find the closest distance from that point to a center m_k ($k = 1, \ldots, K$), i.e., if the index of the closest center is k_i, then

$$d_{i,k_i} = \min_{k=1,\ldots,K} \|X_i - m_k\|_2. \tag{1}$$

Algorithm 2 presents the main steps of this idea. If no points have been assigned to a cluster, the center will be deleted.

During the iterative process, the two closest clusters to each other, measured by the distance between their centers, may be merged if the distance between their centers is below a threshold, herein denoted as η_D. This parameter value is dynamically defined as a function of the search region of the data points and also depends on the current number of clusters. Furthermore, if the cluster with the lowest number of points is considered very small relatively to the number of data points in the set, i.e., if $|C_{k_i}| < N_{\min}$ where $|C_{k_i}| = \min_k |C_k|$ and $N_{\min} = \max\{2, \lceil 0.05n \rceil\}$ is the threshold, the points are coined as 'noise', the cluster is removed and the center is deleted, see Algorithm 3.

Algorithm 2. Assigning Algorithm
***
Require: K, cluster centers m_k, $k = 1, \ldots, K$ and the data set $\mathbf{X}$
1: Set $C_k = \emptyset, k = 1, \ldots, K$
2: Compute $d_{i,k} = \|X_i - m_k\|_2$ from a data point X_i, $i = 1, \ldots, n$ to cluster center m_k, $k = 1, \ldots, K$
3: **for** $i = 1$ to n **do**
4:     Identify $\min_k d_{i,k}$ and the index $k_i \in \{1, 2, \ldots, K\}$ of closest center
5:     Assign point X_i to cluster C_{k_i}
6: **end for**
7: **for** $k = 1$ to K **do**
8:     **if** $|C_k| = 0$ **then**
9:         Delete m_k (and remove C_k)
10:     **end if**
11: **end for**
12: Update K
13: **return** m_k and C_k, $k = 1, \ldots, K$
***

Algorithm 3. Deleting Algorithm
***
Require: K, m_k, C_k for $k = 1, \ldots, K$, $\eta_D > 0$, $N_{\min}$
1: Compute $D_{i,j} = \|m_i - m_j\|_2, i = 1, \ldots, K - 1, j = i + 1, \ldots, K$
2: Identify $D_{i_m, j_m} = \min_{i,j} D_{i,j}$ (indices $i_m, j_m \in \{1, 2, \ldots, K\}$)
3: **if** $D_{i_m, j_m} \le \eta_D$ **then**
4:     Replace center m_{i_m} by $\frac{1}{|C_{i_m}| + |C_{j_m}|}(|C_{i_m}| m_{i_m} + |C_{j_m}| m_{j_m})$
5:     Assign points in C_{j_m} to cluster C_{i_m}
6:     Delete m_{j_m} (and remove C_{j_m})
7:     Update K
8: **end if**
9: Identify $|C_{k_i}| = \min_k |C_k|$ (index $k_i \in \{1, 2, \ldots, K\}$)
10: **if** $|C_{k_i}| < N_{\min}$ **then**
11:     Define all points in C_{k_i} as 'noise/outlier'
12:     Delete m_{k_i} (and remove C_{k_i})
13:     Update K
14: **end if**
15: **return** m_k and C_k, $k = 1, \ldots, K$.
***

One cluster may be added (one at a time) by splitting the cluster with maximum hypervolume $\mathcal{V}_k$ [7], where

$$\mathcal{V}_k = \left(\det \left(\frac{1}{|C_k|} \sum_{X_i \in C_k} (X_i - m_k)(X_i - m_k)^T \right) \right)^{1/2}. \tag{2}$$

However, our strategy is to allow the cluster with maximum volume to be split only if its volume is not smaller than a target value η_V. The value of this parameter is found to be problem dependent and is given by

$$\eta_V = \frac{1}{|C_k|} \left(\sum_{k=1}^{K} \mathcal{V}_k + \frac{a}{a-1} \sum_{k=1}^{K} Z_k \right) \text{ with } Z_k = \frac{1}{a} \sum_{j=1}^{a} \sigma_{k,j}^2 \qquad (3)$$

and the vector $\sigma_k \in \mathbb{R}^a$ contains the deviations of the vectors directed from m_k to every point $X_i \in C_k$. These deviations are computed componentwise as follows [15]:

$$\sigma_{k,j} = \frac{1}{|C_k|} \left(\sum_{X_i \in C_k} (X_{i,j} - m_{k,j})^2 \right)^{1/2} \qquad \text{for } j = 1, \dots, a. \qquad (4)$$

After the cluster to be split has been identified, e.g. the cluster C_{k_i}, center m_{k_i} is modified and a new center, m_{K+1}, is created out of m_{k_i}. Let σ_{k_i,j_M} be the largest component of the vector σ_{k_i} in (4). The only component modified in the center m_{k_i} is j_M; similarly, the component of the new center m_{K+1} that differs from m_{k_i} is m_{K+1,j_M}:

$$m_{k_i,j_M} = m_{k_i,j_M} + 1.5\sigma_{k_i,j_M} \text{ and } m_{K+1,j_M} = m_{k_i,j_M} - 1.5\sigma_{k_i,j_M}.$$

Algorithm 4 describes the main steps of the splitting process.

Algorithm 4. Splitting Algorithm

Require: K, m_k, C_k, for $k = 1, \dots, K$

1: **for** $k = 1$ to K **do**
2:     Compute $\mathcal{V}_k$ using (2)
3:     Compute the vector σ_k using (4)
4: **end for**
5: Compute η_V using (3)
6: Identify the cluster, C_{k_i}, with maximum volume $\mathcal{V}_{k_i}$, (index $k_i \in \{1, 2, \dots, K\}$)
7: **if** $\mathcal{V}_{k_i} \geq \eta_V$ **then**
8:     Modify center m_{k_i} and create the new center m_{K+1} as previously described
9:     Assign the points in cluster C_{k_i} to the new centers m_{k_i} and m_{K+1} using Algorithm 2
10:     Update K;
11: **end if**
12: **return** m_k and C_k, $k = 1, \dots, K$.

2.2   Fitness Probability Scores

In line 10 of Algorithm 1, improved cluster centers are obtained using an optimization method. Evolutionary algorithms and metaheuristics have been suggested for similar purposes. Unlike other proposals [7,13,16], among others, our algorithm does not optimize all the current cluster centers. Only a few are selected for optimization. This way a reduction in computational effort is notable.

To choose the centers to be optimized, a fitness probability score ('FPscore') of the center is used. This 'FPscore' is a measurement of the cluster vicinity and fitness relative to the data points that have been assigned to that cluster. Thus, clusters with lower 'FPscore' are considered to have least fitted centers and undergo an optimization process; whereas the clusters with higher 'FPscore' have fitter centers and need not to be optimized. The 'FPscore' are computed as follows. Based on the current K cluster centers $m_1, m_2, \ldots, m_K$, the *fitness function*

$$\mathcal{F}_k = \frac{1}{|C_k|} \sum_{X_i \in C_k} \|X_i - m_k\|_2 \quad \text{with} \quad S = \sum_{k=1}^{K} \mathcal{F}_k$$

is used to define the 'FPscore', as follows:

$$FPscore_k = \frac{1}{K-1} \frac{S - \mathcal{F}_k}{S}. \tag{5}$$

We note that

- the sum of the $FPscore$ of the cluster centers is equal to one;
- a cluster center with a lower fitness $\mathcal{F}_k$ value is awarded a higher $FPscore$; thus allocating to a fitter cluster a *higher probability of selection* to be maintained to the next iteration;
- a cluster center with a larger $\mathcal{F}_k$ value is awarded a lower $FPscore$; thus allocating to a least fitted cluster center a *smaller probability of selection* so that the center position (relative to the data points that have been assigned to it) should be improved during optimization.

The idea is to maintain for the next iteration cluster centers that have a $FPscore$ higher than p_{FP}, set as the average of the $FPscore$ of the current cluster centers, and optimize the remaining cluster centers using an optimization method, e.g., the differential evolution (DE) algorithm, using the objective function known as 'sum of within-cluster distances'

$$WCD = \sum_{i=1}^{n} d_{i,k_i} \tag{6}$$

where the index k_i represents the index of cluster center closest to data point X_i, as described in (1). This optimization process is described in Algorithm 5.

2.3   Problem Dependent Parameters

In this subsection, we summarize the paper contributions concerning with the definition of problem dependent parameters for the proposed clustering algorithm:

- number of centers for initialization, $K = \max\{2, \lceil 0.01n \rceil\}$;
- minimum number of points in a cluster, $N_{\min} = \max\{2, \lceil 0.05n \rceil\}$ (for Algorithm 3);

- a threshold value for the smallest distance between centers, η_D - minimum amplitude (relative to the attributes) divided by current number of clusters (for Algorithm 3);
- a target value for the cluster with maximum hypervolume, η_V, as defined in (3) (for Algorithm 4);
- p_{FP} - average value of the $FPscore$ of the current cluster centers - defined in (5) (for Algorithm 5).

Algorithm 5. Optimization Algorithm

Require: m_k, C_k for $k = 1, \ldots, K$;
1: Compute $\mathcal{F}_k$ and $FPscore_k$ for $k = 1, \ldots, K$ using (5)
2: Compute $p_{FP} = \frac{1}{K} \sum_{k=1}^{K} FPscore_k$
3: Select the fitter cluster centers by checking if $FPscore_k \geq p_{FP}$, $k = 1, \ldots, K$ and save the indices in $\mathcal{K}$
4: Compute new cluster centers m_k^*, $k = 1, \ldots, K$, $k \notin \mathcal{K}$, using the centers $m_k, k \in \mathcal{K}$ as constant values,

$$\min_{m_k, k=1,\ldots,K, \, k \notin \mathcal{K}} WCD$$

5: Set $m_k \leftarrow m_k^*$
6: **return** m_k, $k = 1, \ldots, K$.

---

3   Computational Results

In this preliminary study, the algorithms are coded in MATLAB®. Two sets of data points with two attributes (see Subsect. 3.1 below), one set with four attributes (known as 'Iris') and one set with thirteen attributes (known as 'Wine') are used to compute and visualize the partitioning clustering.

In line 10 of Algorithm 5, the DE algorithm is used. This algorithm is run for 5 iterations and the size of population is 20 (and 50 for 'Iris' and 'Wine' problems). The other DE parameters are $\beta_m = 0.2$, $\beta_M = 0.8$ (bounds of the scaling factor), $p_{CR} = 0.2$ (crossover probability).

Some comparisons are included to evaluate the goodness of our clustering. The DBSCAN clustering algorithm [2] as well as the K-means clustering are used. DBSCAN is a density-based spatial clustering algorithm and depends on two parameters: ϵ (a numeric scalar that defines a neighborhood search radius around each point) and $MinPts$ (a positive integer the gives the minimum number of neighbors required for a core point). The code[1] has been used in our comparisons [17]. Our experience solving a large variety of data sets seem to show that DBSCAN clustering is very sensitive to variations on the parameters, in particular ϵ. The code that implements the K-means clustering [18] is also used for comparative purposes, although with K-means the number of clusters

---

[1] https://www.mathworks.com/matlabcentral/fileexchange/52905-dbscan-clustering-algorithm.

K had to be specified in advance. The performances of the tested clustering algorithms are measured in terms of a cluster validity measure, the Davies-Bouldin (DB) index [19]. The DB index aims to evaluate intra-cluster similarity and inter-cluster differences by computing

$$DB = \frac{1}{K} \sum_{i=1}^{K} \max_{j=1,\ldots,K, j \neq i} \left\{ \frac{S_i + S_j}{d_{i,j}} \right\} \qquad (7)$$

where S_i (resp. S_j) represents the average of all the distances between the center m_i (resp. m_j) and the points in cluster C_i (resp. C_j) and $d_{i,j}$ is the distance between m_i and m_j. The smallest DB index indicates a valid optimal partition. We note that when the number of clusters is one, the DB index is 0.

3.1   Data Sets

The first two problems have data randomly generated from particular distributions, have two attributes and have been drawn from MATLAB online manual. The last two problems are well-known in the literature.

Problem 1. 600 data points with $a = 2$.

```
mu1 = [2 2]; sigma1 = [0.9 -0.0255; -0.0255 0.9]; mu2 = [5 5];
sigma2 = [0.5 0 ; 0 0.3]; mu3 = [-2, -2]; sigma3 = [1 0 ; 0 0.9];
X = [mvnrnd(mu1,sigma1,200); mvnrnd(mu2,sigma2,200);
mvnrnd(mu3,sigma3,200)];
```

Problem 2. 2000 data points with $a = 2$.

```
mu1 = [1 2]; Sigma1 = [2 0; 0 0.5]; mu2 = [-3 -5]; Sigma2 = [1 0; 0 1];
X = [mvnrnd(mu1,Sigma1,1000); mvnrnd(mu2,Sigma2,1000)];
```

Problem 3. 'Iris' with 150 data points. It contains three categories (types of iris plant) with 4 attributes (sepal length, sepal width, petal length and petal width) [20].

Problem 4. 'Wine' with 178 data points. It contains chemical analysis of 178 wines derived from 3 different regions, with 13 attributes [20].

3.2   Results

Plots to visualize the clustering are included in Figs. 1 and 2. The results for Problems 3 and 4 are shown in Tables 1 and 2.

We show in Fig. 1 six plots. The first 3 plots correspond to the clustering that is obtained with our algorithm. Case (a) shows the clustering obtained after the assign, delete, split and delete processes on the initial centers randomly generated. Case (b) shows the centers obtained by the first call to DE, where only the center of cluster 2 (green in the plot) has been optimized (thus, it is the least fitted cluster center among the three). From iteration 2 to iteration 3, only the cluster center of cluster 1 (red in the plot) is optimized - the other two are then considered as having a good fitter according to the corresponding clusters. Plots (d) and (e) display the clustering obtained by DBSCAN using $\epsilon = 0.5$ and $\epsilon = 0.75$ respectively. As it can be seen, DBSCAN with $\epsilon = 0.5$ considers a large number of points in the data set as 'noise'. Finally, plot (f) shows the clustering obtained with K-means when $K = 3$ is provided to the algorithm.

The six plots in Fig. 2 correspond to the clustering process applied to Problem 2. The visualized 3 centers in plot (a) have been randomly generated in the space of the points (during initialization) and were the only ones preserved after the assign, delete, split and delete processes. Comparing plots (a) and (b), it is possible to conclude that the 3 centers were selected to be optimized by the optimization algorithm. Based on their new positions, and the processes assign, delete, split and delete, one of the centers has been deleted. The iterative process ended at the 6th iteration with two cluster, and comparing with plot (b), the center of cluster 2 (the light blue one) has not been moved. For comparative purposes, we include plots (d) and (e) with the clustering obtained by DBSCAN, for $\epsilon = 0.5$ and $\epsilon = 1$ respectively. We note that clustering in (d) contains a large number of points coined as 'noise' which makes the DB index to be reduced. The plot (f) contains the result of K-means clustering when $K = 2$ is provided.

The results of our clustering algorithm, when solving Problems 3 and 4, are compared with those of [10] (that uses a particle swarm optimization (PSO) approach to the clustering) and [12] (an enhanced genetic algorithm (EGA)), see Table 1. To compare the performance, our algorithm was run 30 times for each data set. When solving the 'Iris' problem, our algorithm finds the 3 cluster in 100% of the runs (30 successful runs out of 30). When solving the problem 'Wine', 22 out of 30 runs identified 3 clusters. In the table, we show the optimal objective function value WCD (the best, the average (avg.) and the worst values over the successful runs). Although our values of WCD are slightly higher than those registered in [10] and [12], the WCD of the best runs are of the same order of magnitude than their competitors. We also note that the variation between the best, avg. and worst WCD values is larger than the variations reported in the papers in comparison. Since the basic DE algorithm is applied to optimize the cluster centers during the iterative automatic clustering, whereas the PSO and EGA algorithms (in [10] and [12]) have been specifically designed and modified to integrate the clustering process (with assign, remove and split processes) into the heuristic algorithm, explains the differences in objective function variations.

Unlike the PSO approach in [10], our clustering methodology does not seem to be affected by the dimension of the data set $\mathbf{X}$ as far as computational time is concerned (see 'time' - in seconds - in Table 1). Table 2 shows the cluster centers obtained in our best clustering.

From the reported experiments, we may conclude that the clustering strategy herein proposed presents satisfactory results, very similar to those in comparison, is effective and robust. In most of the tested runs, the number of expected/optimal clusters is found after a steady number of iterations and time.

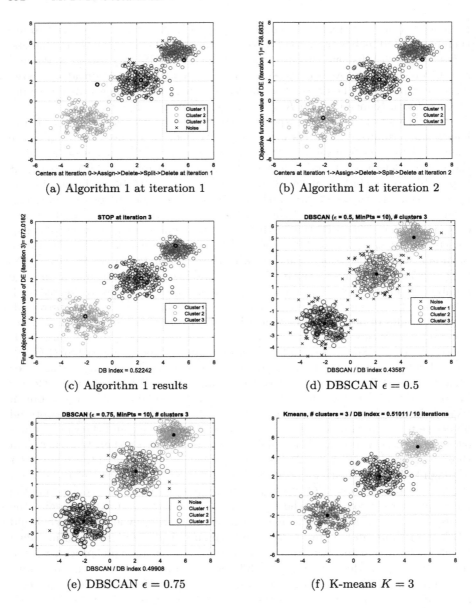

(a) Algorithm 1 at iteration 1   (b) Algorithm 1 at iteration 2

(c) Algorithm 1 results   (d) DBSCAN $\epsilon = 0.5$

(e) DBSCAN $\epsilon = 0.75$ (f) K-means $K = 3$

Fig. 1. Visualization of the results for Problem 1 (Color figure online)

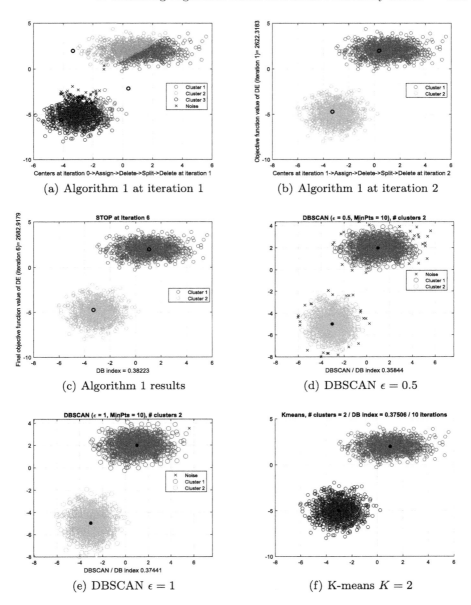

(a) Algorithm 1 at iteration 1

(b) Algorithm 1 at iteration 2

(c) Algorithm 1 results

(d) DBSCAN $\epsilon = 0.5$

(e) DBSCAN $\epsilon = 1$

(f) K-means $K = 2$

Fig. 2. Visualization of the results for Problem 2 (Color figure online)

Table 1. Clustering results for Problems 3 and 4

Problem		Algorithm 1				Results in [10]		Results in [12]
		WCD	It	Time	Suc.	WCD	Time	WCD
'Iris'	Best	97.4149	4	1.107	100%	97.22	0.343	97.1170
	Avg.	98.0501	4.2	1.252		97.22	0.359	97.0395
	Worst	99.3268	6	1.758		97.22	0.375	97.3259
'Wine'	Best	16540.69	5	1.063	73%	16530.54	2.922	16499.32
	Avg.	17013.92	8.0	1.941		16530.54	2.944	16527.50
	Worst	17998.60	10	2.752		16530.54	3.000	16555.68

Table 2. Centers of best clustering obtained by Algorithm 1, for Problems 3 and 4

'Iris'			'Wine'		
Center 1	Center 2	Center 3	Center 1	Center 2	Center 3
6.70740e+00	4.97307e+00	5.90988e+00	1.37146e+01	1.34037e+01	1.25181e+01
3.05717e+00	3.40055e+00	2.88684e+00	4.22842e+00	2.72431e+00	1.59380e+00
5.62126e+00	1.43060e+00	4.32993e+00	2.39641e+00	1.36000e+00	2.73048e+00
2.12030e+00	2.57315e−01	1.36495e+00	1.55840e+01	2.07645e+01	1.74152e+01
			7.97346e+01	1.07011e+02	1.08444e+02
			1.08178e+00	1.90686e+00	9.80000e−01
			2.55062e+00	2.27351e+00	2.64061e+00
			6.07698e−01	3.08006e−01	4.28489e−01
			8.66250e−01	2.13267e+00	8.28290e−01
			1.07218e+01	7.35849e+00	7.65873e+00
			1.46198e+00	1.28529e+00	9.60483e−01
			1.43378e+00	2.10639e+00	2.55457e+00
			4.54128e+02	6.85721e+02	1.14131e+03

4   Conclusions

The preliminary experiments, carried out with the proposed methodology to the clustering process of a set of given patterns, show that the clustering algorithm based on the fitness probability scores to select the cluster centers that should undergo an optimization process is effective and robust. The clustering methodology is an iterative process and relies on five sequentially applied main processes, namely: i) assign points of the data set to the current cluster centers; ii) delete a cluster center if the number of points of the correspondent cluster is very small and merge two clusters if their distance is below a threshold; iii) split the cluster with maximum hypervolume if its value exceeds a target; iv) delete a center and merge two clusters if it appropriate; and v) optimize a specifically selected set of the cluster centers using an optimization algorithm, e.g., the DE algorithm.

The tested problems have compact and well separated clusters, except two of the clusters in the 'Wine' problem, but in the future, patterns with non-convex clusters, clusters with different shapes and sizes will be addressed. Our proposal is to integrate a kernel function into our clustering approach.

We aim to further investigate the dependence of the parameter values of the algorithm on the number of attributes, in particular, when highly dimensional data sets should be partitioned. The set of tested problems will also be enlarged to include patterns with larger number of clusters than those in analysis, patterns with a large number of attributes, and patterns of different shapes and non-convex.

Acknowledgments. The authors wish to thank two anonymous referees for their comments and suggestions to improve the paper.

References

1. MacQueen, J.B.: Some methods for classification and analysis of multivariate observations. In: Le Cam, L.M., Neyman, J. (eds.) Proceedings of the fifth Berkeley Symposium on Mathematical Statistics and Probability, University of California Press, vol. 1, pp. 281–297 (1967)
2. Ester, M., Kriegel, H.-P., Sander, J., Xu, X.: A density-based algorithm for discovering clusters in large spatial databases with noise. In: KKD-1996 Proceedings, pp. 226–231. AAAI Press (1996)
3. Mohammed, J.Z., Meira, Jr., W.: Data Mining and Machine Learning: Fundamental Concepts and Algorithms, 2nd (edn.). Cambridge University Press, Cambridge (2020)
4. Mirkin, B.: Clustering For Data Mining: A Data Recovery Approach. Computer Science and Data Analysis Series. Chapman & Hall/CRC, Boca Raton (2005)
5. Higham, D.J., Kalna, G., Kibble, M.: Spectral clustering and its use in bioinformatics. J. Comput. Appl. Math. **204**, 25–37 (2007)
6. Haraty, R.A., Dimishkich, M., Masud, M.: An enhanced k-means clustering algorithm for pattern discovery in healthcare data. Int. J. Distrib. Sens. Netw. **2015**, Article ID 615740, p. 11 (2015)
7. Sarkar, M., Yegnanarayana, B., Khemani, D.: A clustering algorithm using evolutionary programming-based approach. Pattern Recogn. Lett. **18**, 975–986 (1997)
8. Das, S., Abraham, A., Konar, A.: Automatic clustering using an improved differential evaluation algorithm. IEEE Trans. Syst. Man Cyber. Syst. **38**, 218–237 (2008)
9. Kwedlo, W.: A clustering method combining differential evolution with K-means algorithm. Pattern Recogn. Lett. **32**, 1613–1621 (2011)
10. Cura, T.: A particle swarm optimization approach to clustering. Expert Syst. Appl. **39**, 1582–1588 (2012)
11. Patel, K.G.K., Dabhi, V.K., Prajapati, H.B.: Clustering using a combination of particle swarm optimization and K-means. J. Intell. Syst. **26**(3), 457–469 (2017)
12. El-Shorbagy, M.A., Ayoub, A.Y., Mousa, A.A., El-Desoky, I.M.: An enhanced genetic algorithm with new mutation for cluster analysis. Comput. Stat. **34**, 1355–1392 (2019)
13. Ezugwu, A.E.-S., Agbaje, M.B., Aljojo, N., Els, R., Chiroma, H., Elaziz, M.A.: A comparative performance of hybrid firefly algorithms for automatic data clustering. IEEE Access **8**, 121089–121118 (2020)

14. He, Z., Yu, C.: Clustering stability-based evolutionary K-means. Soft. Comput. **23**, 305–321 (2019)
15. Memarsadeghi, N., Mount, D.M., Netanyahu, N.S., Le Moigne, J.: A fast implementation of the ISODATA clustering algorithm. Int. J. Computat. Geom. Appl. **17**(1), 71–103 (2007)
16. Prabha, K.A., Visalakshi, N.K.: Improved particle swarm optimization based K-means clustering. In: International Conference on Intelligent Computing Applications, pp. 59–63. IEEE Publisher CPS (2014). https://doi.org/10.1109/ICICA.2014.21
17. Heris, M.K.: Evolutionary Data Clustering in MATLAB. https://yarpiz.com/64/ypml101-evolutionary-clustering Yarpiz (2015)
18. Asvadi, A.: K-means Clustering Code. Department of ECE, SPR Lab., Babol (Noshirvani) University of Technology (2013). http://www.a-asvadi.ir/
19. Davies, D.L., Bouldin, D.W.: A cluster separation measure. IEEE Trans. Pattern Anal. Mach. Intell. PAMI-1(2), 224–227 (1979)
20. Dua, D., Graff, C.: UCI machine learning repository http://archive.ics.uci.edu/ml. University of California, School of Information and Computer Science, Irvine (2019)

Solving a Logistics System for Vehicle Routing Problem Using an Open-Source Tool

Filipe Alves[1,2(✉)], Filipe Pacheco[2], Ana Maria A. C. Rocha[1], Ana I. Pereira[2], and Paulo Leitão[2]

[1] ALGORITMI Center, University of Minho, 4710-057 Braga, Portugal
arocha@dps.uminho.pt,a32657@alunos.ipb.pt
[2] Research Centre in Digitalization and Intelligent Robotics (CeDRI), Instituto Politécnico de Bragança, Campus de Santa Apolónia, 5300-253 Bragança, Portugal
{filipealves,apereira,pleitao}@ipb.pt

Abstract. The growing demand for logistics services for deliveries, collections, or home health services, have significantly increased. However, there is a need to have a technologically innovative information system for digitizing data in the operational logistics of these services, required for an increasingly better vehicle route planning. Unsurprisingly, for many years, there has been an increasing and steady growth in the interest and development of optimization tools to solve real-world problems, namely in the logistic domain. The evolution and support of computational power and the fact that advances in optimization solvers have allowed many of them to be developed as free or open-source software, to the detriment of some classic numerical calculation software. The main issue arises in the dynamic search for solutions obtained by open-source solvers and how they can be useful in solving complex combinatorial problems in real life, such as the optimal allocation of routes in logistics planning services. This work proposes an application that integrates the Google OR-Tools software and the Google Maps and Distance Matrix API. The approach developed in this work uses a VRP mathematical model to minimize the maximum route (considering as objective function the time or the distance) and provide a workload balancing, with the use of a cloud application to reduce costs and an online map service. Experimental results were obtained on simulated VRP instances in the district of Porto, where the quality of the computational solution is analyzed for training and easy usability in logistics problems.

Keywords: Logistics system · VRP · Open-source solver

This work has been supported by FCT – Fundação para a Ciência e a Tecnologia within the R&D Units Projects Scope: UIDB/00319/2020. Filipe Alves is supported by FCT Doctorate Grant Reference SFRH/BD/143745/2019.

1   Introduction

Nowadays, sharing and "on demand" economy, the number of available services and the demand for them have increased. New services, such as Uber have emerged. One of the benefits of such a system is the ability to develop optimization logic that increases profits for partners, and decreases the costs for customers [14]. It is no different in logistics, where solving routing problems makes delivery of goods more efficient by optimizing fleets of vehicles - allowing them to deliver more orders and helping each driver to complete more deliveries. Problems such as the Travelling Salesman Problem (TSP) or Vehicle Routing Problem (VRP) have always received a lot of attention in the literature. TSP was first explored by Flood [6] and VRP was introduced using the example of optimum routing of a fleet of gasoline delivery truck by Dantzig et al. [5]. Ever since, these two problems have been important in the field of operations research.

Any process that requires transportation and visit planning is among the most important tasks of operational and strategic management, whether in a product company or in home visits by informal caregivers. The complex problem of route planning consists of the proper and optimal rationalization of the process of allocation and distribution of resources offered by the network in question.

In operational research, the route planning is usually included in the class of VRP. The VRP is a problem of combinatorial optimization and integer programming, which normally tries to organize a set of routes to satisfy constraints and requirements, minimizing the cost of global transportation (monetary, distance or other context). VRP, nowadays, is already studied taking into account several factors that can affect it, such as vehicle capacity, number of depots, traffic conditions or time restrictions (time windows). These factors make route optimization and scheduling increasingly difficult in reasonable time. In fact, VRP is an NP-hard problem, which means that, in practice, it is not possible to build an expert algorithm that will always provide optimal solutions in an acceptable amount of time. However, recent advances on Information and Communications Technologies (ICT) - increasing use of GPS, traffic map, distributed systems - open up new possibilities to optimize the process of planning and scheduling routes in several domains. New technologies combined with optimization techniques allow the practical development and implementation of new solutions to support decision-making in the operational logistic. The increase in computing power and the development of new solvers using classical algorithms, have enabled the development of efficient tools capable of solving many routing issues, especially those that can be represented in the form of VRP.

This research work focuses on the development of a cloud application based on an open-source tool for solving VRP. The application integrates the Google OR-Tools for VRP optimization, the Google Maps and the Google Distance Matrix API as external services. The Google OR-Tools software is detailed, and has gained great popularity as an efficient optimization package for several combinatorial problems. Another contribution of this work is the experimental results of the application on simulated instances of VRP in the district of Porto.

The paper is divided as follows: Sect. 2 briefly introduces the related literature, while Sect. 3 shows the architecture of the system to be developed. Section 4 presents the mathematical formulation of the VRP. The open-source solver tool used to solve the VRP is described in Sect. 5. The computational experiments, data collection and strategies of VRP are presented and discussed in Sect. 6. Finally, Sect. 7 rounds up the main conclusions and future work.

2 Related Literature

The vehicle routing problem [3], a well-known combinatorial optimization [17] problem, is defined as a fleet of vehicles in a network seeking to serve a set of customers, starting from a single depot. The typical VRP objectives are to minimize the total distances travelled by all vehicles or to minimize the travel costs while serving every customer. The VRP has been studied in applied mathematics and computer science for decades. Dantzig et al. [5], have the first record in the VRP literature, where they studied a relatively large scale travelling salesman problem and proposed the mathematical programming formulation and algorithmic approach to solve the problem of delivering gasoline to service stations.

VRP is known to be a NP-hard problem for which many exact and heuristic algorithms have been proposed. However providing fast and reliable solutions is still a challenging task. Basically, a single or a fleet of vehicles are responsible for delivering items or perform something to multiple customer nodes, starting and returning at a given node, called the depot. The main objective is to optimize the set of routes in order to attain the maximum possible reward, optimizing the use of resources and try to obtain the best workload balance. The VRP problem is computationally difficult to solve to optimality, but throughout the time, there have been many proposed solutions, such as, exact methods. For example, one of the first exact method proposed was the branch-and-bound algorithm [2]. However, many of the literature in exact methods relate the work only for up to 360 crossing points, which may be insufficient in some cases [15]. For an overview of the VRP, see, for example, [8,11,12,19].

The evolution in the operational research was considering metaheuristics, in order to improve the sub-optimal solutions. Examples of efficient metaheuristics, include genetic algorithms [10], local search [13] or ant colony optimization [7].

In terms of software, there are some classic and commercial solutions, such as Gurobi [9], LocalSolver [20] and IBM CPLEX [4], which are used to solve VRP problems. However, they require high computational effort, are commercial licenses and generally used in an academic context. Currently, there are cloud optimization applications that solve VRP problems, such as OptimoRoute,[1] Badger Maps,[2] Route4Me,[3] Routific tools,[4] and many others. These software provide systems for optimizing routes, supported by API, but they are in a commercial scope, with closed source and subscription plan fees. In this sense, Google OR-Tools [16], an open source Google optimization tool for VRP issues with an active community and several libraries, has recently emerged. The tool is completely free, customizable and capable of commercial and academic applications.

---

[1] https://optimoroute.com/.
[2] https://www.badgermapping.com/.
[3] https://www.route4me.com/.
[4] https://routific.com/.

3   System Architecture

This project aims to develop a dynamic and innovative application based on a robust system for digitized data manipulation and integrated use of open-source tools as external services to use optimization algorithms and real maps. The architecture leverages back-end data models, with integration into a database, and integrates a well-structured tool, namely Google OR-Tools as external service, to contribute to the optimized route planning and simulation of logistical cases. The structure of the system has a cloud architecture to facilitate flexibility between the different modules and components. On the other hand, the creation of the application programming interface (API) allows routines and patterns of access to the system by the developed dashboard (front-end). In this way, the architecture provides a service capable of being used by different users, adapting the data according to the problems and monitoring/accessing the routing and scheduling solutions through an interface. The communication of the system to its different parts can be seen in the Fig. 1.

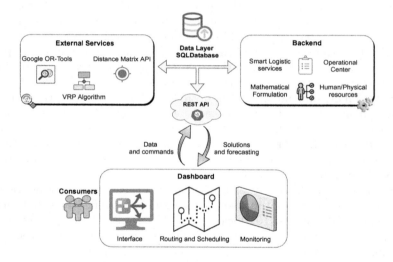

Fig. 1. System architecture approach.

The module integrated with external services, will have optimization skills to provide mechanisms for optimized solutions, using VRP algorithms implemented on the Google OR-Tools platform, with easily edited cognitive models and with different solution search strategies. On the other hand, the use of Google Distance Matrix service allows to compute the distance and duration of the trip between multiple origins and destinations for a given problem. In this sequence, the Google Maps API will offer customization and use of static and dynamic maps, where users will be able to obtain real-time data and advanced information from specific locations for a greater reality of the project. The mathematical formulation on the back-end will assist the VRP engine to search for the optimal solution taking into account the needs, distance or duration of the routes under study. The dashboard module provides a connection to the platforms using a user-friendly interface, which allows real-time monitoring of the solution state.

4   VRP Formulation

The main idea is to solve a logistics system for VRP using a well-known algorithm embedded in an open-source solver. The approach is to consider a scenario where a number of points (locations) are distributed over a certain area (Portugal), each of which demands some kind of services. The service provider has a fleet of vehicles, typically homogeneous and initially located at a single location, called the depot. Each of these vehicles can provide service trying to guarantee equity of services, that all vehicles have an assigned route and that it has a good workload-balancing. Keeping in mind the recent concern towards the environment and the fact that the service provider wishes to distribute work equally among all the vehicles, a mathematical model has been applied to minimize the total time and distance for the routes. The problem is to find a set of routes, one route for each of the vehicles such that the route distance or the route time are minimized.

The routes consist of a set of nodes which are arranged sequentially in that particular order in which they are visited. Each route starts and ends at the same depot, and each node is serviced by one vehicle. The classic VRP formulation was taken into account and adapted to guarantee the proper flow of vehicles [18]. The mathematical model to describe this approach is presented below:

- n: number of nodes to be serviced (locations),
- v: total number of vehicles used,
- d_{ij}: cost (distance) to go from i to j,
- t_{ij}: cost (time) to go from i to j.
- u_i^k: place in the sequence of visits of vehicle k for the customer i.

The binary variables take the form:

$$x_{ijk} = \begin{cases} 1, \text{ if the vehicle } k \text{ visits } j \text{ immediately after } i; \\ 0, \text{ otherwise.} \end{cases}$$

The objective function that could be minimized is

$$\min \quad D = \sum_{k=1}^{v}\sum_{i=0}^{n}\sum_{j=0}^{n} x_{ijk}d_{ij} \tag{1}$$

or based on the minimization of the maximum routing time

$$\min \quad T = \sum_{k=1}^{v}\sum_{i=0}^{n}\sum_{j=0}^{n} x_{ijk}t_{ij} \tag{2}$$

Some constraints are assumed as listed below:

$$\sum_{k=1}^{v}\sum_{j=0}^{n} x_{ijk} = 1, \quad \forall i \in N; \tag{3}$$

$$\sum_{j=0}^{n} x_{0jk} = 1, \quad \forall k \in K; \tag{4}$$

$$\sum_{i=0}^{n} x_{jik} - \sum_{j=0}^{n} x_{ijk} = 0, \forall i \in N; \forall k \in K; i \neq j \tag{5}$$

$$u_j^k \geq u_i^k - C(1 - x_{ij}^k) + 1, \quad \forall i,j \in N; \forall k \in K; i \neq j \tag{6}$$

$$x_{ijk} \in \{0,1\}, \quad \forall i,j \in N; \forall k \in K; \tag{7}$$

where N represents the index set of all locations $N = \{1, ..., n\}$ and K represents the index set associated to the vehicles $K = \{1, ..., v\}$.

The constraints in (3) state that each customer is visited exactly once, while constraints (4) and (5) ensure that each vehicle is used exactly once and that flow conservation is satisfied at each customer vertex. Finally, the sub-circuit elimination are expressed by constraints (6). Alternative formulations of VRP are already explored by Bektas [1]. Thus, taking into account this mathematical model, it will be able to optimize the use of vehicles and minimize the assigned routes, leveraging a better balancing workload and empowering the user to select the route based on their preferred objective function (time or distance).

5　Open Source Solver

There are many barriers and difficulties related to the development of algorithms to solve classic VRP problems, either due to the different characteristics, specific requirements, or even the closed source code of commercial software. These barriers also hamper the development of distributed and decentralized systems with little cooperation in supplier software. Nowadays, more open source tools and libraries are available to solve different types of VRP. One of the great examples of this, with recent activity and high trust from users and researchers, is Google OR-Tools. This suitable library to solve a particular and practical VRP, presents statistical data of reasonable speed, programming environment, flexibility, functionality and easy to use in different programming languages. Many of the criteria chosen for the use of this platform, are related to the access and applicability in many real-world scenarios, such as:

- Adjusted to handle the most difficult problems in vehicle routing, flows, integer and linear programming, and constraint programming.
- Flexibility in choosing and adding the modified algorithm itself (generating an initial solution) and repairing or evolving an algorithm (heuristic and/or metaheuristic strategies).

- Choice and definition the objective function by the user.
- Flexibility in defining soft or specific constraints, and execution speed (especially for large problem instances).
- Quality of produced solutions.
- Integration skills with external systems or online services (Google Maps API, and others) as well as visualization systems.
- Testing tools with abilities of use benchmark sets and different datasets in several formats (csv, xlsx, json, sql, and others).

By having a programming environment and integration of different external services, the tool provides customization and mechanisms for different test scenarios in dynamic environments. Thus, it is also interesting to understand the steps of the procedure for the proper functioning of the model and its algorithmic execution in the open-source solver (see the flowchart presented in Fig. 2).

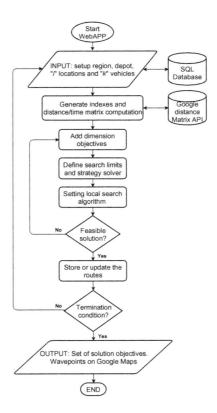

Fig. 2. Sequential procedure for executing the VRP adapted on the OR-Tools platform.

In general, OR-Tools is an open-source package from Google, fast and portable software suite for solving complex and simple combinatorial optimization problems, which allows the use for specific real-world problems [16]. It supports various several programming languages, including C++, C#, Java and Python. OR-Tools can solve many types of VRP, including problems with pickups and deliveries, heterogeneous fleets, multiple depots, time windows, different start and end locations, multiple capacity dimensions, initial loads, skills, scheduling problems, and so on. Obviously, there are some limitations on solving VRP as they are inherently intractable for larger instances. Therefore, OR-Tools sometimes returns solutions that are good, but are not optimal. Sometimes better solutions can be found by changing the search options for the solver. The first solution strategy is used to find an initial solution (one can also specify a set of already found initial routes).

The platform presents several first solution strategies. Some strategies let the solver detect the strategy to be used according to the model being solved, where other strategies iteratively build a solution by inserting the cheapest node at its cheapest position; the cost of insertion is based on the arc cost function. In the topic of decision strategies, the user is also given the possibility to incorporate local search options. This strategy considers six examples of search options, such as greedy descent, simulated annealing, and tabu search.

The documentation of OR-Tools is available with plenty of examples and API documentation. Google OR-Tools is very promising, recent, with an extensive and intensive network of development in operational research by one of the largest companies in the world, which makes available the software for solving various VRP problems.

6   Computational Experiments

This section describes the Google OR-Tools optimization tool applied to different designed and simulated cases of logistics VRP.

6.1   Data Collection

The dataset was prepared to allocate different locations in the district of Porto, as an example, where operational and logistics services in the delivery or collection of products and/or provision or follow-up of health care are increasingly urgent and necessary. However, the experiments can be easily replicated in other regions or countries. Even more with the pandemic situation of COVID 19, more and more people are requesting these logistics services, either from local units or from social solidarity institutions. The data allow replicating daily cases of operational visit planning and are inserted and saved according to the development of a database on the platform (SQLserver). The datasets can be chosen at random during the analysis.

Each dataset generated randomly comprises the locations and the depot and represents cases of a logistics system, being able to provide simulations of routing and task planning in operational services of the kind. The dataset was generated using the database and it was possible to generate a set of tests with different instances, which can be assigned to a single day or divided over several days.

To evaluate the robustness of the open-source tool (OR-Tools), multiple problem sizes with different number of vehicles were provided, making a total of 3 instances, where the dimension of each instance can be seen in Table 1.

Table 1. List of test instances.

Parameters		
Dataset	Locations (n)	Vehicles (v)
Case 1	10	2
Case 2	20	4
Case 3	30	6

It should be noted that the different locations are dynamically instantiated in a time/distance matrix between all start and end points.

In this sense, a sensitivity analysis will be conducted considering two optimization strategies. The first one involves heuristics and the other uses local search strategies based on metaheuristcs.

The tests are conducted on a Lenovo Yoga, with an Intel(R) Core(TM) M-5Y71 CPU 1.4GHz with 8.0 GB of RAM. The development of a user-friendly web application makes it possible to digitize the entire process of managing information and routes, enabling the system to dynamically insert data, vehicles, locations and other information. It should be noted that the calculations of distance and time, use the Google Maps cloud, which provides the facility to keep accurate locations and routes through comprehensive data and real-time traffic. In turn, the distance matrix provides travel times and distances to one or more locations, useful for the combinatorial calculation of the OR-Tools.

6.2   Strategies to Solve VRP

The method involves going through all the crossing points and health or technical professionals represented by each vehicle, along with the constraints to the Google Optimization Tools solver, choosing the main strategy and treating its output as the final solution. In the development platform, unit tests were structured for the entire application, both in data entry and in the output of solutions. The use of this approach allows, in general, different strategies to be tested using the OR-tools library. Thus, when invoking the Google Optimization Tools Routing library, different parameters were used, namely, the description of some options for the Routing Solver, in order to enhance the diversification of the solutions used.

In this sense, the first aspect to be taken into account is the search limits, which end when the solver reaches a specific limit, such as the maximum length

Table 2. Summary of search limits.

Parameter	Value	Description
Solution limit	∞	Limit to the number of solutions generated during the search
Time limit	5000	Limit in seconds of the time spent in the search
Lns time limit	100	Limit in seconds of the time spent on the completion search for each local search neighbor

of time, or number of solutions found. It is possible to set a search limit using the search parameters of the solver, as shown in Table 2.

In this context, after the search limits definition, it is important to address the first solutions strategies, that is, the methods that the solver uses to find an initial solution. Table 3, lists the six different types of options (out of a total of thirteen, some similar to each other), chosen for the problem under study.

Table 3. Summary of first solution strategies.

Strategy option	Description
Automatic	Lets the solver detect which strategy to use according to the model being solved
Path_Cheapest_Arc	Starting from a route "start" node, connect it to the node which produces the cheapest route segment, then extend the route by iterating on the last node added to the route
Savings	Savings algorithm (Clarke & Wright)
Christofides	Christofides algorithm (Nicos Christofides)
Best insertion	Iteratively build a solution by inserting the cheapest node at its cheapest position
Global cheapest arc	Iteratively connect two nodes which produce the cheapest route segment

The user can check the status returned by the method while the search unfolds, such as, "routing_not_solved", "routing_success - problem solved successfully", "routing_fail - no solution found for the problem", or for example, "routing_invalid".

In turn, the user also has local search options at his disposal. These options can change the search approach and provide better results, especially for more complex problems, than the first search options listed above. Table 4 presents the three local search strategies chosen as the object of study (out of a total of six), which can be used to set and cover a larger space for searching for solutions.

As a final parameter to end the call to Google Optimization Tool library, set the parameter that controls the propagation "Use Light Propagation" as true. This parameter describes the use of the constraints with light propagation in routing model. The "Extra propagation" control is only necessary when using depth-first search or for models which require strong propagation to finalize the

Table 4. Summary of local search strategies.

Local search	Description
Guided Local Search	Uses guided local search to escape local minima
Simulated annealing	Simulated annealing algorithm
Tabu search	Tabu search algorithm

value of secondary variables. Changing this setting to true will slow down the search in most cases and increase memory consumption in all cases.

The setting of the different parameters and options will generate different outputs and routes. In the same sequence, the performance will also be distinct, which will contribute to a sensitivity and metric analysis: runtime, maximum time/distance of the routes and the number of vehicles that are used. The main goal is to optimize the maximum time/distance, at a reduced runtime, without much impact on the workload balance between the vehicles.

6.3   Results

In this section, the solutions found using the open-source Google optimization tool (OR-Tools) are presented.

Thus, different first solution strategies, from Table 3, were applied to VRP instances. After the first layer of tests, the optimal routes were generated to minimize the length of the longest route among all vehicles. In the three instances of the tests, the results corresponding to the routing of operational logistics using the first solutions strategies based on heuristics are presented in Table 5.

Table 5. List of results for the first solution strategies based on Heuristics.

Heuristics	Case 1		Case 2		Case 3	
	Route time (min)	Runtime (ms)	Route time (min)	Runtime (ms)	Route time (min)	Runtime (ms)
Automatic	72	75	77	133	100	238
Best insertion	–	–	–	–	–	–
Christofides	82	13	77	100	78	375
Global cheapest arc	72	8	76	87	86	313
Path cheapest arc	72	12	77	67	100	186
Savings	72	16	100	54	86	325

Considering the objective function selected by the user $(\min T)$, a set of routes for the vehicles are generated with the total distances of the operational planning. It is possible to verify that the runtime increase as long as the complexity of the instances increase. In addition, there was a slight increase in terms of the time of the route and scheduling solution as long as the complexity and instances increase, mostly in Case 3.

When considering the local search strategies based on metaheuristics, the operational solutions obtained are shown in Table 6.

Table 6. List of results of the local search strategies based on metaheuristics.

Metaheuristics	Case 1		Case 2		Case 3	
	Route time (min)	Runtime (ms)	Route Time (min)	Runtime (ms)	Route Time (min)	Runtime (ms)
Guided Local Search	72	1001	74	5001	75	5001
Simulated annealing	72	1001	77	5001	75	5000
Tabu search	72	1002	77	5001	77	5005

The results are consistent when compared to the ones from Table 5, although were obtained better solutions for Case 2 and Case 3 in terms of route time. Note that, the OR-Tools allows to specify a runtime limit when using metaheuristcs, allowing to increase the chances of finding better solutions. Thus, different runtime values were selected. In general, the "Guided Local Search" metaheuristic strategy presents the best results in terms of routing time.

Figure 3 presents graphically the obtained results in Table 5. The graph shows on the x-axis the different strategies for first solutions (heuristics) with their respective color and grouped by the 3 cases under study. In turn, the y-axis presents the results of each of the strategies in the order of the route time (in minutes).

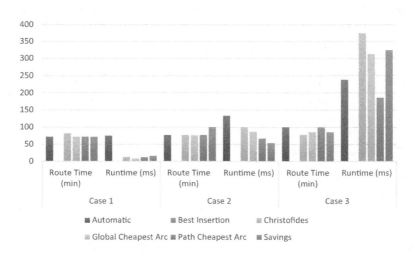

Fig. 3. Heuristics results for each case study.

The "Best Insertion" heuristic was not able to solve any case problem proposed. In a simplified way, it is possible to verify that the maximum route solutions obtained by the different strategies do not differ much from case to case. However, it is possible to verify that the runtime of Case 3, when compared to Cases 1 and 2, has undergone a noticeable increase, possibly due to the increased in dimension and complexity.

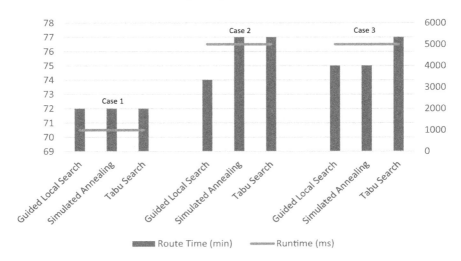

Fig. 4. Metaheuristics results for each case study.

The solutions obtained by the local search strategies (metaheuristics), in Table 6, will be represented for a better visualization of the optimization process, in Fig. 4. The values on the left vertical axis are related to the routing time, while the values on the right vertical axis refer to the runtime. Therefore, there is a slight increase in the maximum routes from Case 1 to the remaining cases.

Regarding the metaheuristic, it is possible to suggest the "Guided Local Search" as the best choice, due to its better performance (essentially in Case 2) relatively to the others. According to this suggestion, the scheduling and routing for Case 2 is presented in Table 7.

Table 7. Scheduling and routing using Guided Local Search for Case 2.

Guided Local Search		
Vehicles	Routes	Route time
Vehicle 0	0 ->17 ->16 ->11 ->2 ->3 ->0	72 min
Vehicle 1	0 ->15 ->12->13 ->4 ->7 ->10 ->0	72 min
Vehicle 2	0 ->8 ->1 ->18 ->19 ->0	74 min
Vehicle 3	0 ->5 ->9 ->6 ->14 ->0	73 min
Maximum route time: 74 min		
Runtime: 5001		

Location 0 represents the depot, where all vehicles start and end routes. As soon as the results are obtained, it is available for the user to view any of the VRP solutions and also has the availability to access any of the gantt graphics for recall via WiFi and inform each of the vehicles, of their respective route. It should be noted that all requests seek to establish an improved workload-balance between all the vehicles, to facilitate distribution and acceptance by logistics managers.

Since access via the app is facilitated with quick access to solutions, the user will be able to, after viewing the schedule, interact dynamically by sending the specific coordinates of the route of one of the vehicles to its user and customize the real-time information according to google maps and places to visit. Figure 5 illustrates the route and tracking of the locations to be visited by one of the vehicles for Case 2. The experience of using this app becomes real, with the possibility in obtaining updated reports, optimized directions and geolocation (using google maps API service included in the system).

Fig. 5. Route map wave-points.

The user will always be able to monitor any of the routes and interact with it, being able to return to the main interface, viewing the remaining solutions of the different strategies.

In turn, it is important to highlight the fact that the results presented above are according to the search and optimization of problems according to the objective of minimizing the time in routes. The user when defining the dimensions of the objectives, defining the solver strategies and respective algorithms will have the opportunity to decide whether to compute the matrix dimension between the localities, according to distance or time. The Google matrix service automatically generates the matrix according to the user's decision, being able to change the objectives of the problem whenever he/she wishes. In this case, minimizing the distance, and with the possibility of data input in real-time, the results would be different, but in any case, the whole process of calculations and combinations in obtaining solutions is the same. The idea is to enhance a system that provides the best solutions and in turn enables the user to support decision making in logistical VRP problems.

The proposed system architecture has significant potential to be used in real-world problems with further improvements, even in the application of the other VRP variants.

7 Conclusion

This research shows the extreme usefulness of a recent and popular open-source optimization tool for solving a logistics system for VRP in a specific region in Portugal, namely in the district of Porto. The developed system revealed some interesting properties of the considered optimization toolkit, as well as in the digitization of information in a user-friendly way.

The different case studies and instances revealed a very balanced solution behavior, with very good quality in the results and in the runtime, the latter often considered as the essential performance parameter for the choice and adoption of any optimization solver for real application. The system also presented different and valid configurations according to the optimization strategies of the initial solution, heuristics and metaheuristics, providing a weighted choice to the user.

The ease of integration in programming environments (in this case C#), plus the use of the Google Maps and Distance Matrix API service, integrated with the development of the database for the engine, retrieve and manage information, created a potential future prototype for more application cases. The application can be used to provide guidance on real VRP in the Porto district or replicated in other places. Embedding this system and optimization resources in the cloud, combined with artificial intelligence, namely multi-agent systems, may in the future, enable the distribution of dynamic and reactive VRP, thus managing emergencies and unexpected events in real-time.

References

1. Bektas, T.: The multiple traveling salesman problem: an overview of formulations and solution procedures. Omega **34**(3), 209–219 (2006)
2. Christofides, N., Eilon, S.: An algorithm for the vehicle-dispatching problem. J. Ope. Res. Soc. **20**(3), 309–318 (1969)
3. Clarke, G., Wright, J.W.: Scheduling of vehicles from a central depot to a number of delivery points. Oper. Res. **12**(4), 568–581 (1964)
4. Cplex, I.I.: V12.1: user's manual for CPLEX. Int. Bus. Mach. Corp. **46**(53), 157 (2009)
5. Dantzig, G.B., Ramser, J.H.: The truck dispatching problem. Manage. Sci. **6**(1), 80–91 (1959)
6. Flood, M.M.: The traveling-salesman problem. Oper. Res. **4**(1), 61–75 (1956)

7. Gambardella, L.M., Taillard, É., Agazzi, G.: MACS-VRPTW: a multiple colony system for vehicle routing problems with time windows. In: New Ideas in Optimization. Citeseer (1999)

8. Golden, B.L., Raghavan, S., Wasil, E.A.: The Vehicle Routing Problem: Latest Advances and New Challenges, vol. 43. Springer, Boston (2008). https://doi.org/10.1007/978-0-387-77778-8

9. Gurobi Optimization, L.: Gurobi optimizer reference manual (2021). http://www.gurobi.com

10. Karakatič, S., Podgorelec, V.: A survey of genetic algorithms for solving multi depot vehicle routing problem. Appl. Soft Comput. **27**, 519–532 (2015)

11. Laporte, G.: The vehicle routing problem: an overview of exact and approximate algorithms. Eur. J. Oper. Res. **59**(3), 345–358 (1992)

12. Laporte, G., Gendreau, M., Potvin, J.Y., Semet, F.: Classical and modern heuristics for the vehicle routing problem. Int. Trans. Oper. Res. **7**(4–5), 285–300 (2000)

13. Nagata, Y., Bräysy, O.: Efficient local search limitation strategies for vehicle routing problems. In: van Hemert, J., Cotta, C. (eds.) EvoCOP 2008. LNCS, vol. 4972, pp. 48–60. Springer, Heidelberg (2008). https://doi.org/10.1007/978-3-540-78604-7_5

14. Nguyen, H.N., Rintamäki, T., Saarijärvi, H.: Customer value in the sharing economy platform: the Airbnb case. In: Smedlund, A., Lindblom, A., Mitronen, L. (eds.) Collaborative Value Co-creation in the Platform Economy. TSS, vol. 11, pp. 225–246. Springer, Singapore (2018). https://doi.org/10.1007/978-981-10-8956-5_12

15. Pecin, D., Pessoa, A., Poggi, M., Uchoa, E.: Improved branch-cut-and-price for capacitated vehicle routing. Math. Programm. Comput. **9**(1), 61–100 (2016). https://doi.org/10.1007/s12532-016-0108-8

16. Perron, L., Furnon, V.: OR-Tools (2019). https://developers.google.com/optimization/

17. Sbihi, A., Eglese, R.W.: Combinatorial optimization and green logistics. 4OR **5**(2), 99–116 (2007). https://doi.org/10.1007/s10479-009-0651-z

18. Toth, P., Vigo, D.: An overview of vehicle routing problems. In: The Vehicle Routing Problem, pp. 1–26 (2002)

19. Toth, P., Vigo, D.: The Vehicle Routing Problem. SIAM (2002)

20. Zhang, Y., Qi, M., Miao, L., Wu, G.: A generalized multi-depot vehicle routing problem with replenishment based on LocalSolver. Int. J. Ind. Eng. Comput. **6**(1), 81–98 (2015)

Feature Selection Optimization of Risk Factors for Coronary Heart Disease

Ana Rita Antunes⬤, Lino A. Costa(✉)⬤, Ana Maria A. C. Rocha⬤,
and Ana Cristina Braga⬤

ALGORITMI Center, University of Minho, 4710-057 Braga, Portugal
id9069@alunos.uminho.pt,{lac,arocha,acb}@dps.uminho.pt

Abstract. Cardiovascular disease is a worldwide problem and is the main cause of mortality when coronary heart disease leads to a heart attack. Hence, it is important to evaluate how to prevent this disease considering the symptoms description and physical examinations.

This study points out the application and comparison of different performance measures for the classification of heart disease. Firstly, a feedforward neural network was applied to classify heart disease risk, using the well-known Framingham database. Feature selection optimization was performed to identify the most important variables to take into consideration, minimizing the Type II error and maximizing the accuracy. In addition, a multi-objective optimization algorithm was carried out to simultaneously optimize both performance measures. A set of non-dominated solutions representing the trade-offs between objectives were obtained, and gender, age, systolic blood pressure, and glucose level emerged as the principal factors to take into consideration to predict heart disease. The results obtained are promising and show the importance of considering more than one criterion to identify the most important variables.

Keywords: Feature selection · Optimization · Neural network · Heart disease

1 Introduction

Cardiovascular diseases are the main cause of mortality in the world and it is expected to be the most important cause of death by 2030 [28], despite recently the number of deaths caused by cardiovascular diseases has been decreasing over the decades [8]. Coronary heart disease (CHD) and coronary artery disease are cardiovascular diseases that involve heart and blood vessels, where CHD is a result of coronary artery disease [32]. CHD leads to a heart attack which occurs when the blood flow to the heart is cut off and there is a decrease in the supply of oxygen and nutrients [28].

This work has been supported by FCT – Fundação para a Ciência e Tecnologia within the R&D Units Project Scope: UIDB/00319/2020.

© Springer Nature Switzerland AG 2021
O. Gervasi et al. (Eds.): ICCSA 2021, LNCS 12953, pp. 413–428, 2021.
https://doi.org/10.1007/978-3-030-86976-2_28

In the European Union, Portugal has presented a low-risk of CHD for decades, but, in 2013, it was the second most common cause of death [25,30]. Therefore, it is essential to prevent heart attacks, taking into account raised blood pressure and glucose, physical inactivity, overweight, obesity, and tobacco use, since they are some risk factors [15,28].

Thus, to identify heart disease it is important to describe symptoms and make physical examinations [3]. In 2015, a study was carried out to identify which factors can be associated with the development of the disease, where high blood pressure, overweight, and hypercholesterolemia showed large increases in the incidence of heart disease [15]. Systolic, diastolic, and pulse pressure are risk factors that lead to heart failure, but systolic and pulse pressure have more impact [19].

Over the years, some authors have used the well-known Framingham database to study the factors that influence CHD. This database contains information about the residents of the city of Framingham, in Massachusetts, and comprises 15 variables on the demographic, behavioral, and medical history of more than 4000 patients. With this information, it is intended to verify whether the patient is at risk for future CHD [14]. According to Dawber and Kannel (1996), this was the first successfully detailed epidemiological study on heart disease and provided useful information [13]. However, a limitation of this study is that if other regions wish to classify the risk of CHD using Framingham data as a training dataset, they can not estimate the risk well, since the study uses only a restricted population, with daily habits that vary from region to region [11].

Since cardiovascular disease is a worldwide problem, it is important to understand what factors can be analyzed to prevent CHD. This work aims to identify which combinations of variables are capable of predicting whether the patient is at risk for future CHD, using the Framingham database. First, a feedforward neural network will be trained to learn with the available data. Then, a feature selection optimization will be carried out to identify the best subset of variables capable to predict the risk for future coronary heart disease. Finally, a multi-objective approach will be conducted to maximize accuracy and minimize Type II error, simultaneously. The computational environment MatLab® (version R2020b) will be used to obtain the results.

This paper is structured as follows. Section 2 presents a literature review, where some related works about cardiovascular diseases, feature selection, neural networks and performance measurement criteria are explained. Thereafter, the methods implemented and the parameters defined are in Sect. 3. The descriptive analysis and discussion of the results are presented in Sect. 4 and the main conclusions are reported in Sect. 5.

2   State of the Art

In this section, an analysis of some works related to cardiovascular diseases is presented to understand which methodologies were used and for what purpose.

Then, feature selection, neural networks, and performance measurement criteria are briefly described.

2.1   Cardiovascular Disease Studies

Cardiovascular diseases are the main cause of death worldwide and over the years this theme has been studied in several countries with different applications [28]. In most studies, the main purpose was to diagnose cardiovascular, heart, or artery diseases regarding the given datasets using different approaches. Some authors applied several machine learning techniques in order to evaluate the classification performance of different models taking into account performance measures such as accuracy, precision, recall, specificity, F-measure, and area under the ROC curve (AUC) [4,24,29]. In [5,6], a Genetic Algorithm (GA) was considered to optimize the weights of a Neural Network (NN) in order to improve performance. Feature selection using correlation matrix or Particle Swarm Optimization (PSO) was studied in [17,23]. Furthermore, cross-validation by splitting data into training, validation and test sets are also common in these works. The main goal of these models is learning from the available data.

A system that uses GA to optimize the NN weights to predict the risk of cardiovascular diseases is proposed in [6]. The dataset consists of heart disease information, the data was divided into training and test sets and the performance was measured in terms of accuracy. The accuracy reported for the test set was 94.17% [6].

A new hybrid model of NN and GA, using risk factors data of 50 patients, is used to diagnose heart diseases. The aim is to optimize the connection weights of the NN to improve performance. Data was divided into training, test, and validation and the accuracy obtained was 96.2%, 92%, and 89%, respectively [5].

PSO and NN feedforward backpropagation were used to rank factors of cardiovascular diseases. PSO was applied to minimize cost and maximize precision to select the most relevant features. The data is about Cleveland clinic and it was divided into training and test sets. Accuracy, recall, and precision were used to measure the performance of the model. The results achieved were an accuracy of 91.94%, a recall of 93% and a precision of 91.9% [17].

A system to predict the risk of cardiovascular disease, using data from 689 patients with cardiovascular disease symptoms, was developed in [29]. The data set was divided into training, validation and testing, and a logistic regression, Bayesian classification and quantum NN were applied to the Framingham dataset for validation purposes. In this work, the authors concluded that quantum NN obtained the best accuracy result (98.57%).

In [23], a NN was applied to predict CHD risk through feature selection, considering the correlation analysis. Korea's national health and nutrition examination survey was used to conduct the analysis and the performance was compared with the Framingham risk scores. Data were divided into training and validation sets, where the accuracy was 89% and 82.51%, respectively. Several methods (for example, Naive Bayes, Random Forest, NN) were studied to diagnose coronary artery disease, using three publicly available data, and different measures, like sensitivity, specificity, F-measure, AUC, and running time. It is shown that accuracy is not the unique important measure to use to determine the performance of a classifier [24].

To predict the CHD risk in the Korean population, a deep NN was used in [4]. Tenfold cross-validation was used to split data. The model was compared with different algorithms, such as Naive Bayes, K-Nearest Neighbor, Support Vector Machine, Decision Tree, and Random Forest. Moreover, different measures were used to assess the performance of the models (accuracy, precision, recall, specificity, F-measure, and AUC). The proposed deep NN achieved the best performance measure values, with the exception of specificity.

2.2   Feature Selection

Feature Selection is the process of selecting the best subsets of features to improve predictor performance. Nowadays, it is used in different research areas due to the exponential increase of data, where there are many variables to study. According to Iguyon and Elisseeff [18], feature selection can also help to understand the data to be analyzed. There are different methods capable of extracting variables, in which some include variable ranking and others the similarity between the variables. The most common methods for feature selection can be divided into filter, wrapper, or embedded [18,21,34].

In the filter method, the focus on the selection of features is based on a performance measure, where the first step is to find the best subset of features. Some well-known performance measures are correlation between variables, Chi-square and Fisher score [21]. In this method, the variables are ranked considering the measure chosen and the variables selected have useful information [12]. After the feature selection, the variables are used in the model. This method is also called the preprocessing step [18].

In the wrapper method, different combinations of features are used to find the model with the best performance, for example, with the highest accuracy [34]. This method uses the predicting performance to find the best subset of features [18]. In general, this method allows to obtain better results than the filter method since the subsets of features are evaluated using a modeling algorithm [21].

In the embedded method, the selection of features is made in the training process, without split data into training and testing, and aims to reduce the computation time [12]. The selection is made during the modeling algorithm's execution. Some methods consider objective functions to minimize fitting errors and a penalty is assigned to the features that do not contribute to the model [21]. Since the data is not split, a better use of the available data is observed and it is possible to obtain a faster solution when compared to the filter and wrapper methods [18].

2.3   Neural Networks

In order to make better decisions, many researchers investigate how to diagnose heart disease problems using intelligent systems such as Neural Networks [3]. NN is widely used in this area since it can extract more information about the system in the study due to the learning process [6].

In a NN, a neuron, also known as a unit or node, is the basic computational unit that can receive signals from other neurons and multiplies each signal by the corresponding weight (the connection strength). The weighted signals are then summed and passed through an activation function [27]. In Fig. 1 it is shown an individual neuron architecture.

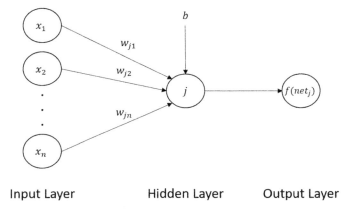

Fig. 1. Individual neuron architecture (based on [22]).

NN can have several different layers of neurons. In theoretical terms, the input layer is the first layer, the intermediate layer(s) is known as the hidden layer(s) and the last one is the output layer. Therefore, the output layer takes into account the number of values to be predicted. Thus, in Fig. 1 there is an input layer with n neurons, one hidden layer with one neuron, and one output layer. The input signal is denoted by a vector $\mathbf{x}$ (x_1, x_2, ..., x_n) and corresponds to the independent variables present in the data. Moreover, the weights of the neuron j are denoted by w_j (w_{j1}, w_{j2}, ..., w_{jn}) and f is the activation function. The *net* input to the neuron j is described in (1), where b is called bias [7,22].

$$net_j = \sum_n w_{jn} x_n + b \tag{1}$$

Most of the activation functions are nonlinear and the most widely used are hyperbolic tangent, sigmoidal and gaussian [7,22].

A multilayer NN has more than one hidden layer. In a feedforward NN the information propagates along the forward direction [7,22]. It is difficult to choose the appropriate network size, i.e., the number of layers in the NN and the number of neurons per layer. Hence, the quality of the solution found, using NN, depends on the network size that can affect the complexity, learning time, and the ability to produce accurate results [10].

A NN can be used for supervised and unsupervised learning. In supervised learning, for each input, the target output is known. The NN weights are adjusted to produce the smallest error possible, considering the actual output and the predicted output. Furthermore, the generalized delta rule is used to minimize the error. In contrast, in unsupervised learning the NN adjusts the weights without knowing the associated output and the NN learns how to classify input patterns [3,10]. Backpropagation learning is the most common type of supervised learning used to optimize the weights. According to Ding, Su, and Yu [16] this optimization process can be stuck in a local minimum. The combination of backpropagation with a GA is one solution to this problem, since GA is a global optimization method. GA is an optimization algorithm that considers the principles of natural genetics and can escape from local minimums. The combination of a GA with the learning NN can provide a better predictive accuracy [6].

2.4   Performance Measures

The performance of classifier models, for a given dataset, can be assessed by different evaluation measures to describe how well the classification is done and to compare different models [1].

Thereby, inferential statistics are used to detect the effects of the independent variables regarding the variability that is inherent in the variable being measured (the dependent variable). Thus, hypothesis tests are, in general, used in inferential statistics in order to extract more information about the data under study. Two types of errors can be committed in the decisions, known as Type I and Type II errors. Type I error is committed when the null hypothesis is rejected, when in fact it is true. In contrast, Type II error is deciding not to reject the null hypothesis when it is actually false [9]. These types of errors have to be minimized but it is not always easy to do it. Type I error is the level of significance and can be controlled since it is the amount of risk that the authors are willing to take. On the other hand, the Type II error is related to the sample size, since it is sensitive to the number of observations in the sample. Thus, if the number of observations increases, the Type II error decreases [31].

A confusion matrix is a well-known tool for evaluating the classifier and takes into account the number of positive and negative instances correctly classified, also known as True Positive (TP) and True Negative (TN), respectively [1,9,33]. Hence, the confusion matrix also considers the number of instances that are predicted to be negative, but are actually positive, known as False Negatives (FN), and the number of instances that are predicted to be positive when they are negative, known as False Positives (FP) [1,20]. Table 1 presents an example of a confusion matrix that considers the hypotheses in the study and the decision made.

Table 1. Example of a confusion matrix

	Hypothesis	
	H_0	H_1
Decision		
Retain H_0	TP	FN (Type II Error)
Reject H_0	FP (Type I Error)	TN

FP and FN are the Type I and Type II Errors, respectively [33]. Therefore, the ratio for each error can be express as (2) and (3).

$$\text{Type I Error } (\%) = \frac{FP}{FP + TN} \qquad (2)$$

$$\text{Type II Error } (\%) = \frac{FN}{TP + FN} \qquad (3)$$

Another measure to take into account is the accuracy [33], in (4), which considers the ratio of observations that the model correctly classifies.

$$\text{Accuracy } (\%) = \frac{TP + TN}{TP + FN + FP + TN} \qquad (4)$$

Accuracy does not consider instances that are misclassified. It can have serious implications, for example, in the health area. This can be an important limitation [20]. However, there are measures capable of filling this gap such as precision, recall rate, also known as sensitivity, specificity, F-Measure, and AUC. These measurements can be computed from a confusion matrix [20,33].

3   Methods

This section addresses the feature selection procedure, explaining the steps needed to achieve the main goals of the work. Besides that, the implementation details to identify the parameters considered are described.

3.1   Feature Selection Procedure

Feature selection optimization requires several steps in order to identify the subset of independent variables with better performance for classification. Figure 2 shows an overall summary of the different steps involved and what is defined in each step.

The first step refers to the definition of the independent and dependent variables. After that, the data is split into training (80%) and test (20%) sets, using the holdout method, in order to construct the feedforward NN and optimize the objective functions. This split intends to prevent overfitting to the Framingham dataset. Thereafter, the genetic algorithm is carried out to obtain the best subset of variables capable to predict the risk of CHD.

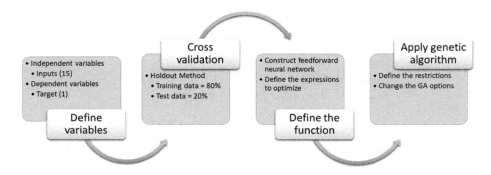

Fig. 2. Steps to build the solution for the feature selection optimization problem.

According to the literature review, accuracy is not the only measure to take into account to find the performance of a classifier [24]. Therefore, in this study, two criteria were selected to be optimized: maximization of accuracy and minimization of Type II error. Moreover, using the wrapper method it is expected to find the best subset of variables that can explain risk of CHD. The hypotheses defined were:

H_0: The patient does not have risk of CHD;
H_1: The patient has risk of CHD.

Thereby, Type II error is committed when the model predicted that the patient does not have risk of CHD, but he has. This type of situation should not happen and must be minimized. It provides incorrect information and it can be detrimental to patient health. Conversely, Type I error happens when the model predicts that the patient has risk of CHD, but he does not have. This situation is a false alert. These two situations can affect the patient's health, but also the time of doctors and the resources available. Considering these details, Type II error leads to a worse situation than Type I error. For this reason, Type II error and accuracy were the measures to take into account.

3.2   Implementation Details

In order to implement the proposed methodology, the software MatLab® [26] was used.

Firstly, a single-objective optimization was conducted, using the **ga** function from the Global Optimization Toolbox. In this approach, the objective functions were maximizing accuracy and minimizing type II error, separately. Three different feedforward NN were performed to predict the risk of CHD, using **feedforwardnet** function. The number of layers and the number of neurons per layer are the following: one hidden layer with eight neurons (NN_1), two hidden layers with eight and four neurons (NN_2), respectively, and three hidden layers with eight, four and two neurons (NN_3). With these three feedforward NN it is intended to evaluate which one has the best performance. Besides that, the number of epochs was set to 750 and the training ratio parameter was defined as 1 to consider the same training set along the optimization. As a consequence, the validation and test ratio were defined as 0. Relatively to the optimization parameters concerning the genetic algorithm, the default values were considered, except the population size option set to 100.

Thereafter, a multi-objective optimization was addressed to maximize accuracy and minimize Type II error, simultaneously. The multi-objective optimization was performed using the `gamultiobj` function, where the standard options were used, except the use of the adaptive feasible mutation and the population size set to 100.

4   Results

This section begins by making a descriptive analysis of the Framingham dataset to be used in this work. Thereafter, a feature selection optimization using the feedforward neural network was performed. The results for single and multi-objective optimization are presented and discussed.

4.1   Dataset Description

Framingham dataset [2] contains information about 4240 patients. There are cases where variables are missing, so these cases were not considered in this study. Thus, only information about 3658 patients was analyzed. Table 2 presents the description of Framingham variables, where the Risk of CHD is the dependent variable and all the others are independent variables. The independent variables contain different types of information, namely demographic, behavioral and medical information. A codification for each variable is given in Table 2 to facilitate the identification of the selected variables.

In this data, 55.63% are women and 15.23% of patients were diagnosed with the risk of future CHD. The youngest patient is thirty-two years old and the oldest is seventy years old. Figure 3 shows the risk of CHD by gender. It can be observed that more men were diagnosed with the risk of future CHD, approximately, 18.92%. In contrast, 12.29% of women were diagnosed with CHD. With this representation, there are, by far, more patients that were diagnosed with no risk of CHD.

Table 2. Description of Framingham variables.

Type of information	Variable	Codification
Demographic	Gender	G
	Age	A
	Education level	EL
Behavioral	Current Smoker (Yes or No)	CS
	Cigarettes per day	CPD
Medical	Blood pressure medication (Yes or No)	BPM
	Had a stroke (Yes or No)	HS
	Hypertensive (Yes or No)	HYP
	Diabetes (Yes or No)	DIAB
	Total cholesterol level	TCL
	Systolic blood pressure	SBP
	Diastolic blood pressure	DBP
	Body mass index	BMI
	Heart rate	HR
	Glucose level	GL
	Risk of CHD (Yes or No)	CHD_Risk

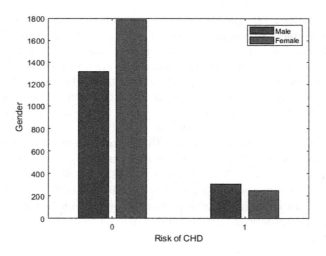

Fig. 3. Risk of CHD by gender.

4.2 Single-Objective Optimization

The different models constructed and the respective results for the single-objective optimization are presented in Table 3. First column reports the NN characterization showing the number of layers and the number of neuron per layer. The following columns present the variables retained and the percentage values for Type II error and accuracy.

Table 3. Type II error and accuracy results for NN_1, NN_2 and NN_3.

NN	Variables	Type II Error	Accuracy
8	G, A, HYP, DBP, GL	–	84.82%
	G, A, EL, CS, CPD, HYP, DIAB, TCL, SBP, DBP BMI, GL	80.73%	–
8,4	BPM, HS, HYP, DIAB	–	85.64%
	G, A, EL, HYP, DIAB, SBP, DBP, BMI, HR, GL	84.11%	–
8,4,2	BPM, HS, HYP, DIAB	–	85.64%
	G, A, EL, CS, CPD, HYP, DIAB, SBP, DBP, BMI, GL	78.90%	–

The lowest value for Type II error was obtained with NN_3 and the highest value for accuracy was achieved with NN_2 and NN_3. Thereby, when the NN size increases the accuracy value is established. However, for the variation of Type II error was different. The Type II error value in NN_2 was the worst and it improves with NN_3. The results showed that Type II error criterion requires more variables than the accuracy criterion to predict the risk of CHD.

If it is important to just maximize accuracy, BPM, HS, HYP, and DIAB are the subset of variables to be taken into account. These variables are all qualitative. When the answer for these variables is no, there are 2206 in 3658 patients that do not have the risk of CHD. On the other hand, when minimizing the Type II error, G, A, EL, CS, CPD, HYP, DIAB, SBP, DBP, BMI, and GL are the variables to be taken into consideration. These results are in accordance with the literature that refers to the association of high blood pressure, overweight, and high cholesterol with large increases in the incidence of heart disease [15,19]. Type II error considers blood pressure (SBP and DBP) and overweight (BMI) as the most important variables.

4.3   Multi-objective Optimization

In the multi-objective optimization, the NN_3 with the best performance for single-objective optimization (see Table 3) was considered.

The Pareto front, in Fig. 4, provides information about the seven different non-dominated solutions achieved. This curve allows to analyze the trade-offs between solutions. It can be seen that the solution corresponding to a Type II error of 70.64% and an accuracy of 85.50% is a good compromise between the two criteria.

Table 4 presents the variables retained, Type II error and accuracy values for each non-dominated solution.

According to the results, it can be concluded that when the Type II error increases, the accuracy value also increases. Thus, G, A, SBP, and GL variables are present in the seven solutions. While the variables CS, CPD, BPM, and BMI

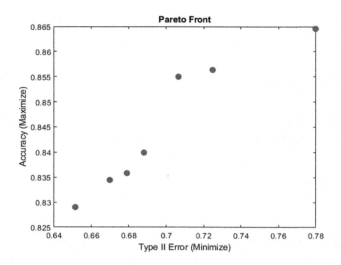

Fig. 4. Pareto front: Type II Error against Accuracy.

Table 4. Multi-objective optimization results.

Variables	Type II Error	Accuracy
G, A, EL, HS, HYP, DIAB, TCL, SBP, DBP, HR, GL	65.14%	82.90%
G, A, EL, SBP, DBP, HR, GL	66.97%	83.45%
G, A, EL, HS, SBP, DBP, HR, GL	67.89%	83.58%
G, A, EL, HS, HYP, DIAB, TCL, SBP, DBP, HR, GL	68.81%	83.99%
G, A, CPD, HYP, DIAB, SBP, DBP, HR, GL	70.64%	85.50%
G, A, CPD, HYP, SBP, DBP, GL	72.48%	85.64%
G, A, HS, TCL, SBP, HR, GL	77.98%	86.46%

do not enter into any model. Moreover, the variable TCL is only used in three solutions.

In addition, there are two solutions with the same variables, but the criteria values are different. The NN weights were optimized in each solution and this can be the reason for these results. The best values for Type II error and accuracy were 65.14% (accuracy is equal to 82.90%) and 86.46% (Type II error is equal to 77.98%), respectively. The "best" solution depends on whether the decision-maker gives more importance to Type II error or accuracy.

4.4   Discussion of Results

CHD leads to heart attacks, hence the importance of analyzing what factors can be measured to prevent this from happening. Over the years, different expensive applications have been developed to assist the decision-making.

Different machine learning techniques were carried out to assess which one presents the best results. Moreover, NN is commonly applied in the healthcare sector. Some researchers used optimization methods to optimize the NN weights and perform different feature selection methods. In this particular situation, it is more important to identify and understand the risk factors that lead to CHD. Kim and Kang identified that triglyceride and chronic renal failure were related to CHD [23]. In another study, sex, age, cholesterol, fasting blood sugar, resting electrocardiograph results, angina experience, ST depression, and slope of the peak exercise were the best subset of variables to predict heart disease [17]. Besides that, high blood pressure, overweight, hypercholesterolemia, SBP, DBP, and pulse rate were also identified as risk CHD factors [15,19].

This study combines a machine learning technique (NN) and feature selection optimization, whose objectives were to maximize accuracy and minimize Type II error. When a NN is performed in MatLab, the weights are optimized to minimize the mean square error. The wrapper method was performed to identify the best subset of variables capable to predict CHD.

In a first approach, a single-objective optimization was conducted and, an interesting remark is that Type II error requires more variables to predict the risk of CHD than the accuracy criterion. Moreover, the NN_3, with three layers, presented the best results in both cases (85.64% for accuracy and 78.90% for Type II error). Thereby, if it is intended to maximize accuracy, the variables to take into consideration are BPM, HS, HYP, and DIAB, whereas if only Type II error is taken into account, it considers G, A, EL, CS, CPD, HYP, DIAB, SBP, DBP, BMI and GL.

Furthermore, using multi-objective optimization, seven different solutions were obtained. In terms of risk CHD factors, G, A, SBP and GL variables are included in all of these solutions. This means these variables must be controlled to prevent CHD. Some other variables can be added to this list, but it depends on whether the Type II error is more important than accuracy or vice versa. The Type II error values are too high (65.14%–77.98%), which may be related to the sample size [31]. In Fig. 3 it is possible to see that there are more patients without risk of CHD, where only 15.23% of the patients were diagnosed at risk for CHD.

5 Conclusions

The main goal of this paper is to identify the best subset of risk factors that can be used to prevent CHD. In this study, the Framingham dataset was used for validation purposes. Firstly, a single-objective optimization was carried out in order to minimize the Type II error and maximize accuracy. Secondly, a multi-objective optimization was conducted to simultaneously optimize both objectives. Thereby, the wrapper method was used to obtain the more important risk factors.

Three NN characterizations were used in single-objective optimization, considering different numbers of layers and neurons per layer, in order to assess which one gets the best results. In this approach, one interesting remark is that Type II error considers more variables than accuracy. The lowest and highest value for Type II error and accuracy was 78.90% and 85.64%, respectively. Risk factors G, A, EL, CS, CPD, HYP, DIAB, SBP, DBP, BMI, and GL must be taken into account when the criterion is to minimize Type II error. On the other hand, the subset of the variables BPM, HS, HYP, and DIAB must be considered when the criterion is to maximize accuracy. All of these variables are qualitative.

In the multi-objective optimization, seven non-dominated solutions were obtained, where G, A, SBP and GL variables belong to all of them. Therefore, these variables can be considered the risk factors to pay more attention to prevent CHD.

As future work, the implementation of different machine learning techniques can be performed, like logistic regression, support vector machine, and random forest, to identify which method has better results. Moreover, a distinct feature selection method, such as the embedded method, and the selection of other performance measurement criteria can also be implemented.

References

1. Aggarwal, C.C.: Data Classification: Algorithms and Applications, 1st edn. Chapman and Hall/CRC, Boca Raton (2014)
2. Ajmera, A.: Framingham heart study dataset (2018). https://www.kaggle.com/amanajmera1/framingham-heart-study-dataset. Accessed 03 Dec 2020
3. Al-Milli, N.: Backpropogation neural network for prediction of heart disease. J. Theor. Appl. Inf. Technol. **56**(1), 131–135 (2013)
4. Amarbayasgalan, T., Van Huy, P., Ryu, K.H.: Comparison of the framingham risk score and deep neural network-based coronary heart disease risk prediction. In: Smart Innovation, Systems and Technologies (2020)
5. Amin, S.U., Agarwal, K., Beg, R.: Genetic neural network based data mining in prediction of heart disease using risk factors. In: 2013 IEEE Conference on Information and Communication Technologies, ICT 2013 (2013)
6. Amma, N.G.: Cardiovascular disease prediction system using genetic algorithm and neural network. In: 2012 International Conference on Computing, Communication and Applications, ICCCA 2012 (2012)
7. Annema, A.J.: Feed-Forward Neural Networks. Springer, Boston (1995). https://doi.org/10.1007/978-1-4615-2337-6
8. Araújo, F., Gouvinhas, C., Fontes, F., La Vecchia, C., Azevedo, A., Lunet, N.: Trends in cardiovascular diseases and cancer mortality in 45 countries from five continents (1980–2010). Eur. J. Prev. Cardiol. **21**(8), 1004–1017 (2014)
9. Bakeman, R., Robinson, B.F.: Understanding Statistics in the Behavioral Sciences. Psychology Press, Hove (2005)
10. Bebis, G., Georgiopoulos, M.: Feed-forward neural networks. IEEE Potentials **13**(4), 27–31 (2002)
11. Brindle, P., et al.: Predictive accuracy of the Framingham coronary risk score in British men: prospective cohort study. BMJ **327**(7426), 1267 (2003)
12. Chandrashekar, G., Sahin, F.: A survey on feature selection methods. Comput. Electr. Eng. **40**(1), 16–28 (2014)

13. Dawber, T.R., Kannel, W.B.: The Framingham study. An epidemiological approach to coronary heart disease. Circulation **34**(4), 553–555 (1966)
14. Dawber, T.R., Meadors, G.F., Moore, F.E.: Epidemiological approaches to heart disease: the Framingham Study. Am. J. Public Health **41**(3), 279–286 (1951)
15. Dawber, T.R., Moore, F.E., Mann, G.V.: II. Coronary heart disease in the Framingham study. Int. J. Epidemiol. **44**(6), 1767–1780 (2015)
16. Ding, S., Su, C., Yu, J.: An optimizing BP neural network algorithm based on genetic algorithm. Artif. Intell. Rev. **36**(2), 153–162 (2011)
17. Feshki, M.G., Shijani, O.S.: Improving the heart disease diagnosis by evolutionary algorithm of PSO and feed forward neural network. In: 2016 Artificial Intelligence and Robotics, IRANOPEN 2016 (2016)
18. Guyon, I., Elisseeff, A.: An introduction to variable and feature selection. J. Mach. Learn. Res. **3**, 1157–1182 (2003)
19. Haider, A.W., Larson, M.G., Franklin, S.S., Levy, D.: Systolic blood pressure, diastolic blood pressure, and pulse pressure as predictors of risk for congestive heart failure in the Framingham Heart Study. Ann. Intern. Med. **138**(1), 10–16 (2003)
20. Japkowicz, N., Shah, M.: Evaluating Learning Algorithms: A Classification Perspective. Cambridge University Press, Cambridge (2011)
21. Jović, A., Brkić, K., Bogunović, N.: A review of feature selection methods with applications. In: 2015 38th International Convention on Information and Communication Technology, Electronics and Microelectronics, MIPRO 2015 - Proceedings (2015)
22. Kamruzzaman, J., Begg, R., Sarker, R.: Overview of artificial neural networks and their applications in healthcare. In: Neural Networks in Healthcare: Potential and Challenges. Idea Group Publishing (2006)
23. Kim, J.K., Kang, S.: Neural network-based coronary heart disease risk prediction using feature correlation analysis. J. Healthcare Eng. (2017)
24. Kolukisa, B., et al.: Evaluation of classification algorithms, linear discriminant analysis and a new hybrid feature selection methodology for the diagnosis of coronary artery disease. In: Proceedings - 2018 IEEE International Conference on Big Data, Big Data 2018 (2019)
25. Levi, F., Lucchini, F., Negri, E., La Vecchia, C.: Trends in mortality from cardiovascular and cerebrovascular diseases in Europe and other areas of the world. Heart **88**(2), 119–124 (2002)
26. MATLAB: version 9.9.0.1495850 (R2020b). The MathWorks Inc., Natick, Massachusetts (2020)
27. McCulloch, W.S., Pitts, W.: A logical calculus of the ideas immanent in nervous activity. Bull. Math. Biophys. **5**(4), 115–133 (1943)
28. Mendis, S., Puska, P., Norrving, B.: Global atlas on cardiovascular disease prevention and control. World Health Organization (2011)
29. Narain, R., Saxena, S., Goyal, A.K.: Cardiovascular risk prediction: a comparative study of framingham and quantum neural network based approach. Patient Prefer. Adherence **10**, 1259 (2016)
30. Pereira, M., et al.: Explaining the decline in coronary heart disease mortality in Portugal between 1995 and 2008. Circ. Cardiovasc. Qual. Outcomes **6**(6), 634–642 (2013)
31. Salkind, N.J.: Statistics for People Who (Think They) Hate Statistics: Excel 2007 Edition. SAGE Publications, Inc., Thousand Oaks (2010)

32. Sanchis-Gomar, F., Perez-Quilis, C., Leischik, R., Lucia, A.: Epidemiology of coronary heart disease and acute coronary syndrome. Ann. Transl. Med. **4**(13), 256 (2016)
33. Sokolova, M., Lapalme, G.: A systematic analysis of performance measures for classification tasks. Inf. Process. Manag. **45**(4), 427–437 (2009)
34. Yu, L., Liu, H.: Efficient feature selection via analysis of relevance and redundancy. J. Mach. Learn. Res. **5**, 1205–1224 (2004)

Predicting the Need for Adaptive Radiotherapy in Head and Neck Patients from CT-Based Radiomics and Pre-treatment Data

Natália Alves[1](✉), Joana Dias[2,3], Tiago Ventura[4], Josefina Mateus[4], Miguel Capela[4], Leila Khouri[5], and Maria do Carmo Lopes[2,4]

[1] Faculty of Science and Technology, Physics Department, University of Coimbra, Coimbra, Portugal
[2] Institute of Computer and Systems Engineering, Coimbra, Portugal
[3] Faculty of Economics, University of Coimbra, Coimbra, Portugal
[4] Medical Physics Department, Instituto Português de Oncologia de Coimbra Francisco Gentil, EPE, Coimbra, Portugal
[5] EPE, Radiotherapy Department, Instituto Português de Oncologia de Coimbra Francisco Gentil, Coimbra, Portugal

Abstract. Although adaptive radiotherapy can reduce the negative dosimetric and clinical impacts of anatomical changes during head and neck treatments, evidence shows that it is not equally beneficial for all patients. This makes it important to electively schedule adaptation ahead of time to optimize clinical resources and patient benefit. The purpose of this study is to assess the feasibility of using both pre-treatment patient features and radiomic features extracted from a pre-treatment contrast enhanced computed tomography scan to predict the need for adaptive radiotherapy. Seventy-two patients were included in the analysis, of which 36 required adaptation. 36 pre-treatment semantic features as well as 351 radiomic features extracted from the gross target volume were considered. Three support vector machine models were developed: 1) considering only semantic features; 2) considering only radiomic features; 3) using a combination of features from 1 and 2. A robustness analysis of the selected radiomic features was also conducted. The best classification results were obtained considering 6 features (4 semantic and 2 radiomic) with median accuracy and area under the receiver operating characteristic curve of 0.821 and 0.843, respectively.

Keywords: Adaptive radiotherapy · Radiomics · Head and neck cancer

1 Introduction

Head and neck (H&N) cancer is one of the most common type of cancer worldwide, with approximately 1.5 million new cases and 0.9 million deaths in 2018 alone [1]. In current clinical practice, the vast majority of patients with locally advanced H&N cancer require radiotherapy (RT), with or without concurrent chemotherapy. Intensity modulated radiotherapy (IMRT) is the gold standard treatment technique [2]. The highly

© Springer Nature Switzerland AG 2021
O. Gervasi et al. (Eds.): ICCSA 2021, LNCS 12953, pp. 429–444, 2021.
https://doi.org/10.1007/978-3-030-86976-2_29

conformal dose distributions produced by IMRT lead to steep dose gradients in the borders of the target volumes, which are extremely sensitive to positional errors and anatomic changes, especially in H&N cases, since there are several critical structures very close to the tumor.

Several studies have shown that significant anatomical alterations in both the target volumes and the organs at risk (OAR) may occur during RT treatments, leading to deviations between the planned and the delivered doses [3–6]. These might cause underdose the target volume, with loss of tumor control, and/or overdose of the normal structures, originating unexpected side effects [6, 7].

In order to correct for day-to-day positioning errors relative to the planning CT (p-CT), most centers perform Image Guided Radiotherapy (IGRT). This consists of daily position verification through imaging, and the performance of couch shifts to correct for deviations between the daily image and the p-CT. However, one of the main limitations of IGRT is that internal changes in size, shape or relative position of the target volumes or OARs compared with the initial p-CT cannot be corrected by rigid translational and/or rotational couch shifts [8].

A possible solution is Adaptive Radiotherapy (ART), which aims to correct for the anatomical modifications by adapting the initial target volumes and planning to the current patient status [4–9]. This process requires repeated imaging with sufficient quality for treatment planning, re-contouring and re-planning, and can be done either offline, between treatment fractions, or online immediately prior to a fraction, while the patient is laying on the treatment couch [9, 10]. The most frequently implemented type of ART is offline ART since online ART requires advanced tools such as automatic segmentation and planning which are not yet commonly available in most centers. In this work, the term ART refers to offline ART.

Although several studies have successfully established both the clinical and dosimetric benefits of ART application [11–17], its implementation into the clinical practice is still a rather labor-intensive and time-consuming process, making it impossible for most clinics to implement it for every patient [9]. Furthermore, evidence shows that ART is not equally important for all patients, potentially being an unnecessary effort for some [18], with the percentage of patients that benefit from ART reported to range from 21% to 66% [19, 20]. This means that electively scheduling adaptive replanning when initiating treatment would be extremely important to optimize clinical resources and the benefit for the patient.

With this goal, many studies have investigated the statistical relationship between different pre-treatment factors and the need for ART [4], but to this date there is relatively few work on developing multi-variable models with the objective of predicting the need for ART [21–23]. The main issue with performing the selection of predictive factors based on correlation tests alone is that these only take into account the linear relationship between individual variables and the endpoint, not-considering multi-variable or non-linear interactions that could potentially improve prediction.

Radiomics is a field with rapidly increasing popularity in radiation oncology, consisting of the high-throughput extraction of quantitative biomarkers (features) from medical images, which can then be applied in mathematical models for several purposes, such as aid in diagnosis or prediction of outcome [24–29].

The purpose of this study is to assess the feasibility of using both pre-treatment patient features and radiomic features from a pre-treatment contrast enhanced CT scan to predict the need for ART in H&N patients. Three models were developed: 1) considering only pre-treatment clinical data from the patient; 2) considering only radiomic features extracted from the gross target volume (GTV); 3) using a combination of features from 1 and 2.

2   Materials and Methods

2.1   Sample Description

The study sample consisted of 72 (66 male and 6 female) H&N patients from the Portuguese Institute of Oncology Clinic Francisco Gentil in Coimbra, Portugal, which were treated with helical IMRT delivered by a Tomotherapy HD (Accuray) unit, with (58 patients) or without (14 patients) concomitant chemotherapy.

The vast majority (63 out of 72) of patients were prescribed 69.96 Gy to the tumor planning target volume (PTV-T), with 2 patients being prescribed 59.4 Gy. The prescription to the lymphatic nodes' PTVs (PTV-N) was either 50.4 Gy, 54 Gy or 59.4 Gy. Regarding the adenopathies, 48 patients were prescribed 69.96 Gy, 4 patients were prescribed 66 Gy, one patient was prescribed 50 Gy and one patient 59,4 Gy. The remaining patients did not present any adenopathies. There were 3 patients with a prescription of 50.4 Gy for both the PTV-T and the PTV-N, and 4 patients with dose prescribed to the PTV-T only (50 Gy for 3 patients and 70Gy for 1 patient). Depending on the prescription scheme the treatment was delivered in either 33 (65 patients), 28 (4 patients) or 20 (3 patients) fractions.

2.2   Patient Imaging

For diagnostic purposes, patients underwent a contrast enhanced CT (d-CT) prior to the first appointment with the radiation oncologist (at a median of 27 days before the planning CT). The d-CT scan is often acquired at different external centers, leading to varying acquisition parameters, namely slice thickness and reconstruction kernels. The d-CT was available for 67 patients.

All patients had a planning CT (p-CT) scan in treatment position acquired at a median of 14.5 days before the start of the treatment, on which the target volumes and OAR were delineated either manually (targets) or through an auto-segmentation software (OAR). This CT scan was acquired using the scanner Somatom Sensation Open from Siemens, with a 3 mm slice thickness.

2.3   Adaptive Radiotherapy Scheme

All patients underwent a daily Megavoltage CT (MV-CT) scan, before each treatment fraction, to assess for differences between the current position and the one in the p-CT. A rigid registration was then performed between the MV-CT and the p-CT, and a transformation vector calculated, which translated into rigid couch and roll angle shifts to correct for positional errors.

If significant discrepancies could be observed after the rigid transformation, the medical physicist was alerted, and a dose calculation was performed on the daily scan using the Planned Adaptive software module from Accuray. This dose distribution was then revised by the responsible radiation oncologist, which determined the need for a new treatment plan. If a replan was required, a second CT (re-CT) was acquired, and both the target volumes and OAR were propagated from the p-CT to the re-CT by rigid and deformable image registration. These volumes were then manually corrected by the radiation oncologist and a new plan was designed by the responsible medical physicist.

From the 72 patients included in the study, 36 had at least one replan during treatment (ART group), with 3 requiring 2 replans. The remaining 36 patients were used as the control group for comparison and model development.

2.4 Semantic Features

Thirty-six pre-treatment factors (features), which could potentially be predictive for the need of ART were acquired for each patient.

Initially, statistical tests were performed to determine whether there were significant differences between the replan and control groups for each factor. For continuous features (as initial weight, GTV volume/surface area, parotid glands volume/surface area, or prescription doses) first the normality and homogeneity of the variance were assessed using the Shapiro-Wilk normality test and Levene's test respectively, in order to determine whether parametric or non-parametric tests were suitable. Then, the t-test and Wilcoxon sign ranked test were used to assess statistical significance in the parametric and non-parametric continuous features, respectively.

For categorical features (as drinking habits, smoking habits, TNM staging, or chemotherapy) the chi-squared test was used. As a real clinical dataset was considered in this study, there was some missing data and not all parameters had the information for all patients.

2.5 Radiomics

The radiomic analysis was performed in MATLAB R2019b. The adopted workflow was based on the guidelines provided by the Image Biomarker Standardization Initiative (IBSI) [30], regarding both image pre-processing and feature extraction, as implemented by the Standardized Environment for Radiomics Analysis (SERA) [31]. SERA is a MATLAB-based framework developed at Johns Hopkins University in 2019, that can handle CT, PET, SPECT or MRI images, and extracts standardized radiomic features in compliance with the IBSI's guidelines. A simplified global representation of the adopted radiomics workflow can be seen in Fig. 1.

Image segmentation was done from the manual contour of the GTV by the radiation oncologist in the p-CTs. Rigid and deformable image registration of the GTV from the p-CT was performed using the Velocity AI v. 3.2. software from Varian to define the region of interest (ROI) in the d-CT.

To correct for differences in voxel spacing and slice thickness on the d-CTs, all images were interpolated to an isotropic voxel spacing of 1 mm x 1 mm x 1 mm, using

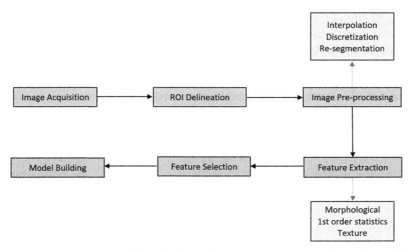

Fig. 1. General Radiomics workflow. The boxes in green represent steps where the actual images and/or ROI mask are considered. The orange boxes represent steps where vectors of the quantitative features extracted from the images are considered.

the tri-linear interpolation algorithm. Furthermore, the intensity range of the ROI was re-segmented to include only voxels between -150 and 180 Hounsfield units, eliminating all bone and air voxels [32], and voxels with outlier intensities (outside the range of $\pm$ 3 standard deviations) were removed. Lastly, intensities inside the ROI were discretized in a fixed bin number approach considering 32 bins.

Having completed these pre-processing steps, 351 radiomic features (as defined by the IBSI [30]) were extracted from each ROI, which are summarized in Table 1.

2.6   Feature Selection and Model Building

Feature selection was made by a greedy search algorithm, which at each iteration eliminates one feature based on the performance of the classification. This was done considering four different classifiers: support vector machines (SVM), naïve-Bayes, decision trees (DT) and multi adaptive regression splines (MARS). At each iteration, the impact of removing each available feature was tested using leave one out cross-validation (LOO) and assessing the accuracy, true positive rate (TPR) and true negative rate (TNR) of the classification. The feature set with better performance moves on to the next iteration of the algorithm and the whole process is repeated until there is only one feature left. Applying this method with different classifiers will produce possibly different feature selected sets, since the classification performance will be the best one obtained for the particular classifier used.

This process was done for the semantic features alone, for the radiomic features alone, and then for a combination of both, using the 20 last-standing features from each. For the semantic features, all the missing values were replaced by the mean value of the existing data for that factor.

Regarding the radiomic features, all features were normalized (z-normalization) after extraction and hierarchical clustering was performed to prevent redundancy. The clustering was based on the Spearman correlation coefficient, meaning that highly correlated features were assigned to the same cluster, and all feature clusters with intra-cluster correlation > 0.9 were replaced by a meta-feature which corresponded to the average of all features in the cluster. This reduced set of non-redundant features was finally fed to the feature selection algorithm previously described.

After determining a suitable set of variables, hyper-parameter optimization was conducted for the SVM using only the selected variables. The parameters considered for optimization were the box-constraints and the kernel scale, and a Bayesian optimization algorithm implemented in the built-in SVM function of MATLAB was used, considering a 5-fold cross-validation.

Table 1. Extracted radiomic features.

Feature family	Number
Morphological	29
Local Intensity	2
Intensity-based statistics	18
Intensity Histogram	23
Intensity-Volume Histogram	7
Gray Level Co-occurrence Matrix (GLCM) 2D/2.5D/3D	100
Gray Level Run Length Matrix (GLRLM) 2D/2.5D/3D	64
Gray Level Size Zone Matrix (GLSZM) 2D/3D	32
Gray Level Distance Zone Matrix (GLDZM) 2D/3D	32
Neighbourhood Grey Tone Difference Matrix (NGTDM) 2D/3D	10
Neighbouring Grey Level Dependence Matrix (NGLDM) 2D/3D	34
TOTAL	351

The classification was then performed with 30 repetitions of leave-one-out cross-validation. Mean accuracy, sensitivity, specificity, and area under the ROC curve were evaluated. The presented workflow is schematically represented in Fig. 2.

2.7 Robustness Analysis

Radiomic feature's robustness to variations in patient positioning, different degrees of noise in the image, and variation in the ROI delineation was assessed using the framework proposed by Zwanenburg, et al. [33]. Based on the results obtained by the authors for a H&N squamous cell carcinoma cohort, four types of image perturbations were selected: rotation, gaussian noise addition, volume adaption an contour randomization [33]. These perturbations were chained using varying degrees for the angle θ of rotation around the z-axis, namely θ ∈ [−10°, −6°, −2°, 2°, 6°, 10°], as well as varying fractions β for growth/shrinkage of the ROI mask in volume adaption, namely β ∈ [−0.2, −0.1, 0, 0.1, 0.2,]. The combination of these parameters resulted in 30 perturbed images per patient, on which features selected in the previous step were calculated. The intra-class correlation coefficient ICC(1,1) [34] was then computed to assess feature robustness.

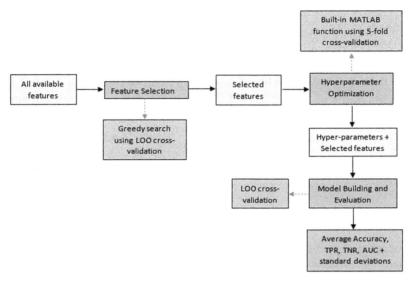

Fig. 2. Adopted workflow from feature selection to model building. The yellow boxes represent features and hyper-parameters, which are inputs/outputs of the different processes; the blue boxes represent the algorithmic processes, with a brief description in the grey box, and the orange box represents the final result. (Color figure online)

3   Results

3.1   Statistical Analysis

From all the analyzed variables the only ones that showed a statistically significant difference between the control and the ART groups were the planned minimum dose to the GTV (Dmin GTV) and both the volume and the surface area of the initial GTV. These results as well as some other pre-treatment features that were considered relevant are shown in Table 2.

Table 2. Statistical analysis for pre-treatment factors. The mean ± standard deviation for each group is shown for the continuous variables age, initial weight, Dmin GTV, prescribed dose to the adenopathies (Dpresc ADNs) and GTV volume (vol)/surface area (sa). The drinking habits correspond to 1- marked drinking habits, 2- moderate drinking habits, 3- no drinking habits and 4- ex-drinking habits.

Feature	Control	ART	p-value
Age	57.28 ± 8.77	61.19 ± 10.24	0.102
Gender (M/F)	34/2	32/4	0.157
T stage (1/2/3/4)	2/4/12/18	1/1/10/24	0.243
N stage (0/1/2/3/X)	4/5/25/1/1	4/1/26/5/0	0.242
Drinking Habits (1/2/3/4)	6/10/3/17	14/3/8/11	0.213
Initial Weight (Kg)	67.05 ± 14.14	62.39 ± 14.59	0.140
Dpresc ADNs (Gy)	52.14 ± 30,55	52.8 ± 29,50	0,889
Dmin GTV (Gy)	67.47 ± 4.44	64.78 ± 6.67	0.031*
GTV vol (cm3)	47.10 ± 46.02	85.56 ± 69.95	0.006*
GTV sa (mm2)	4284.08 ± 3157,49	6367.05 ± 3778.02	0.007*

3.2 Feature Selection and Model Building

For the semantic features, after performing several experiments using SVM, DT, MARS, and Bayes classification methods (referred in Sect. 2.6) the SVM presented the best results so it was the selected classifier.

The best balance between accuracy, TPR and TNR was found with six selected variables using the greedy search method with LOO cross-validation. These features were: age, initial weight, prescription dose to adenopathies (Dpresc ADNs), Dmin GTV, and the binary variables T stage = 1 and marked drinking habits.

After optimizing the box constraints and kernel scale parameters for the SVM classifier with the selected variables, the results achieved for 30 repetitions of LOO cross validation for the accuracy, TPR, TNR, and area under the receiver operating characteristic (ROC) curve (AUC) can be seen in Table 3.

Table 3. Results of the classification using 6 semantic features.

Accuracy			TPR		
Mean	Med	Std	Mean	Med	Std
0.799	0.806	0.014	0.778	0.778	0.023
TNR			**AUC**		
Mean	Med	Std	Mean	Med	Std
0.820	0.819	0.016	0.803	0.803	0.004

For the radiomic features, after the hierarchical clustering, the original set of 351 features extracted from the GTV delineated in the d-CT was reduced to a non-redundant initial set of 88 features. Several tests for feature selection were done with three different classifiers: DT, Bayes and SVM, with the best results arising for SVM, which was again the selected method.

The best balance between accuracy, TPR and TNR was found for six selected features (R1-R6 Table 4). From the six selected features, features R4, R5 and R6 corresponded to original extracted features and R1, R2 and R3 to clustered features. Feature R2 consists of a cluster containing eighteen highly correlated features Table 5 presents these results, as well as the ones obtained considering only 3 features.

Table 4. 6 selected features from the GTV in the dCT.

Feature(s)		Feature Family
R1	Grey level non uniformity normalised	GLSZM 2D GLDZM 2D
R2	Cluster with 18 features (described in the text)	GLRLM 2D/2.5D/3D (8 features) GLSZM 2D/3D (4 features) GLDZM 2D/3D (2 features) NGLDM 2D/3D (4 features)
R3	10th percentile Intensity at 90	Intensity-based statistics Intensity-volume histogram
R4	Centre of mass shift	Morphology
R5	Flatness	Morphology
R6	Small distance low grey level emphasis	GLDZM 3D

Figure 3 shows the ROC curves obtained for each set of variables considering LOO cross-validation from 3 to 6 features in total. The 3-feature model corresponds to.

features R1 to R3 from Table 4, the 4-feature model to features R1 to R4, and so on for the models with five and six features.

As for the combination of semantic and radiomic features, the best results for the feature selection were again achieved with six selected features, from which four were the semantic features: age, prescription dose to ADNs, Dmin to the GTV and marked drinking habits, and two were the radiomic features: a clustered feature comprising the zone-size non-uniformity normalized and the small-zone emphasis from the GLSZM 3D (feature R7), and feature R1 from Table 4. The results obtained for 30 repetitions LOO cross-validation for the models with 6 and 3 features are shown in Table 6. The last three features standing after the greedy search were the Dmin to the GTV, R1 and R7.

3.3 Robustness Analysis

Regarding the robustness analysis, the ICC (1,1) was above 0.77 for all radiomic features except R1, which presented an ICC (1,1) of 0.602 (95% CI of 0.523–0.690). Features R2 and R5 were the most reproducible across the different image perturbations with ICCs (1,1) of 0.985 (95% CI of 0.980–0.990]) and 0.954 (95% CI of 0.937–0.968) respectively. Features R7 and R4 also obtained good reproducibility with ICCs of 0.887 (95% CI of 0.850–0.920) and 0.858 (95% CI of 0.813–0.898) respectively. Finally, the ICC values for features R3 and R6 were 0.785 (95% CI of 0.725–0.842) and 0.775 (95% CI of 0.713–0.834).

Table 5. Results obtained for the 6-feature and 3-feature radiomic models

Accuracy				TPR		
	Mean	Med	Std	Med	Mean	Std
6 features	0.783	0.776	0.008	0.755	0.758	0.009
3 features	0.761	0.761	0.000	0.727	0.727	0.000
TNR				**AUC**		
	Mean	Med	Std	Mean	Med	Std
6 features	0.810	0.824	0.015	0.798	0.799	0.004
3 features	0.794	0.794	0.000	0.765	0.765	0.003

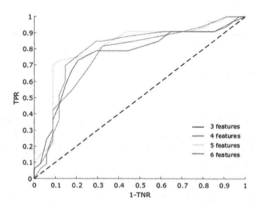

Fig. 3. ROC curves obtained for the models with 3 to 6 radiomic features using LOO cross-validation.

Table 6. Results obtained for the 6-feature and 3-feature mixed models

Accuracy				TPR		
	Mean	Med	Std	Mean	Med	Std
6 features	0.817	0.821	0.016	0.778	0.788	0.029
3 features	0.726	0.731	0.009	0.672	0.667	0.011
TNR				**AUC**		
	Mean	Med	Std	Mean	Med	Std
6 features	0.856	0.853	0.014	0.844	0.843	0.005
3 features	0.779	0.779	0.015	0.777	0.776	0.005

4   Discussion

In this study, three separate models based on SVM were built with the purpose of predicting the need for ART in H&N patients prior to the beginning of treatment: 1) considering only pre-treatment clinical data from the patient; 2) considering only radiomic features extracted from pre-treatment CT images; 3) using a combination of features from 1 and 2.

The idea of applying radiomics to predict the need for ART is very recent, with only two published papers on the topic so far [35, 36]. The first study to explore radiomics for ART patient eligibility was published by Ramella et al. [35] in 2018 and investigated the ability to predict tumor reduction during chemoradiotherapy for a cohort of 91 non-small cell lung cancer patients. The authors considered both radiomic and semantic features, and were able to obtain an AUC of 82% (95% CI of 73%-91%), an accuracy of 78% (95% CI of 69.5%-86.5%), a precision of 77.8% (95% CI 69.95%-86%), a sensitivity of 84% (95% CI of 75.7%-92.2%), and a PPV and NPV of 65.7% (95% CI of 60.7%-70.7%) and 86.9% (95% CI 83.4%-90.4%) respectively, considering 12 (5 semantic and 7 radiomic) features. It was also reported that the scores obtained using the semantic features alone were considerably lower than with the radiomic signature, showing a decrease of 4% in AUC and 6% in accuracy [35]. Another more recent study, by Yu et al. [36], was published in October 2019 and had the objective of predicting ART eligibility for advanced nasopharyngeal carcinoma patients (NPC), using radiomic features extracted from multi-parametric MR images. The study cohort included 70 NPC patients treated with radical radiotherapy, from which 13 had a replan sometime during treatment. Using Least Absolute Shrinkage and Selection Operator algorithm for both feature selection and for classification, the authors obtained an average AUC value in the testing sets of 93% (95%CI of 92.8%-93.3%) with 6 selected features. No semantic features were included in the predictive models for this study. These studies show that there is potential in exploring radiomic and semantic features to build models capable of predicting the need for ART.

As can be seen from the statistical analysis (Table 2), the planned minimum dose to the GTV is significantly lower in the ART group. However, when comparing the ratio between the Dmin to the GTV and the prescribed dose to the PTV-T no differences were found between the two groups, which indicates that the PTV-T underdosage is not significantly larger in the ART group than it is in the control group.

Furthermore, statistically significant differences were found for the initial GTV volume and surface area between the two groups, with the ART group presenting on average an 82% higher initial volume when compared to the control group. These results are in line with several published studies that identify higher initial volumes to be associated with greater anatomical changes in the course of treatment [4–7, 22, 23]. Nevertheless, the initial GTV volume was not identified as a predictive factor in any of the models, which suggests that it would not add additional predictive information to the interactions between the selected variables.

Regarding the first predictive model, the features selected by the greedy-search algorithm using only pre-treatment semantic features were age, initial patient weight, the prescribed dose to the ADNs, T stage, the planned minimum dose to the GTV and whether the patient had marked drinking habits or not. These features are clinically relevant and in conformance with previously published results. Different studies have shown patient age to be predictive of both tumor [22] and parotid [37] shrinkage, as well as reported tumor staging to be significantly correlated with anatomical/dosimetric changes [4, 23].

As is shown in Table 3, using the six selected variables in an SVM classifier and performing 30 repetitions of LOO cross-validation we were able to obtain a median accuracy of 80.6%, TPR of 77.8%, TNR of 81.9% and AUC of 80.3%. These results demonstrate that it is possible to obtain a reliable prediction for the need of ART using only pre-treatment semantic variables. LOO cross-validation was chosen since the study cohort is relatively small and it is important to use as much as possible the available samples for training. Furthermore, using, for instance, an 80/20 split could make the results too biased towards the training set. As the final goal is to classify new samples using the whole of the cohort for training, the LOO cross-validation results are a good representation of the classifier performance.

Moving to the radiomics model, the best predictive performance was obtained for six selected features from the GTV volume in the d-CT. As the selected radiomic variables are highly dependent on the imaging modality, the cancer site and classification endpoint, and this is the first study to assess CT radiomics for prediction of ART, more studies of this nature with different cohorts are needed to assess the consistency of the selected features.

The results obtained with LOO cross-validation for these six features presented a median accuracy of 77.6%, a median TPR of 75.8%, a median TNR of 82.4% and finally a median AUC of 79.9%, all with standard deviations ranging from 0.4% to 1.5%.

It is very interesting to note that only three radiomic features are needed, namely the three previously mentioned meta-features, to reach very similar results: a median accuracy of 76.1%, TPR of 72.7%, TNR of 79.4% and AUC of 76.5% with standard deviations lower than 0.3%. This observation is not valid considering semantic features, where it is clear that much more information is lost when the total number of features is reduced. It seems reasonable to conclude that the radiomic model could have a higher ability of generalization considering new data, since the use of fewer features decreases the possibility of overfitting. Nevertheless, the results obtained using just radiomics are in general weaker than the ones considering just the semantic features.

A mixed model was also built using the information obtained from the feature selection procedure based on both the semantic features and the radiomic features. The feature selection algorithm showed the best performance for a set of six features, including four semantic and two radiomic features. The selected semantic features were also selected for the first model, confirming their predictive power. As for the radiomic features, one of them was the meta-feature including the grey level non uniformity normalized obtained from both the 2D grey level size and distance zone matrixes, which had also been selected in the radiomic-only model and which was the last standing feature in the radiomic greedy search, indicating its high predictive capacity. The other selected radiomic feature was also a clustered feature comprising the zone-size non-uniformity normalized and the small-zone emphasis from the GLSZM 3D, which on the contrary was not selected for the radiomic-model alone. This mixed model presented the best results out of the three models, indicating that a mixture of both semantic and radiomic variables is the most likely to be able to predict whether a given patient will need ART during treatment. Nonetheless, the model built using only the three last standing variables, and the two radiomic features could not match the performance of the 3-feature model using only radiomic features.

One of the potential drawback of using a radiomics approach is that some features' values have shown to be affected by factors such as patient positioning, image acquisition parameters and segmentation [26, 38]. In this way, it could be difficult to achieve a set of reproducible features, which in turn are able to generate generalizable models, if a robustness analysis is not included in the radiomic studies.

In this study, a robustness analysis was performed by applying different image perturbations, namely noise addition, rotations, volume adaptations and contour randomizations, to mimic the effects of the above mentioned factors on the calculated features, as proposed by Zwanenburg et al. [33]. From the results of this analysis, 6 out of the 7 radiomic features included in the models presented an ICC higher than 0.75, indicating a good reproducibility across the perturbed images for each patient.

The main limitation of this study is the fact that the sample cohort has a small number of patients and they were all treated at the same health institution. It would be interesting to assess the predictive capability of these models on unseen patients coming from different clinics. Despite this fact, the number of selected variables was six, which is a relatively low number for the size of the dataset, respecting the rule of thumb of having 10–15 samples per feature [39]. Furthermore, because the diagnostic CTs were used, which are acquired at different centers with different equipment and, consequently, varying acquisition parameters, it is reasonable to infer that our models are likely not overfitting to a given set of imaging parameters, which is a major concern in radiomics studies as the extracted features have shown to be affected by these factors [40]. Additionally, by performing the robustness analysis it is also guaranteed that the selected radiomic features are not dependent on specific image orientations (rotation perturbation), contours of the region of interest (volume adaption/ contour randomization perturbation), or overfitting to noise in the images, since they show good robustness to varying degrees of added random gaussian noise.

To the best of our knowledge this is the first study to use radiomic features from CT images to build a model to predict the need for ART in H&N patients. Furthermore, we compared the radiomic model with both a non-radiomic model built only with semantic features and a mixed model using a combination of radiomic and non-radiomic features. This is a hypothesis-generating study as although several steps were taken to improve the generalizability of the developed models, these do not eliminate the need for external validation.

These results are very promising and in conformity with the ones reported by Ramella et al. [35] and Yu et al. [36], suggesting the ability of using radiomics and pre-treatment factors to predict the need for ART in a clinical H&N cancer dataset.

5   Conclusion

The presented study successfully demonstrated the ability to predict the need for ART in H&N patients from both pre-treatment semantic features and radiomic features extracted from the GTV of a contrast-enhanced CT scan acquired prior to the beginning of treatment. The best classification results were obtained considering 6 features, of which 4 were semantic and 2 radiomic features. A comparable result was achieved considering only 3 radiomic features. A robustness analysis showed that 6 out of the 7 radiomic features that were used in the models presented good robustness across perturbed images. These models could be valuable to optimize the ART workflow and the clinic's resources. Future work is needed to validate the proposed models using an independent patient cohort preferably from a different institution, in order to incorporate them into clinical practice.

References

1. Bray, F., Ferlay, J., Soerjomataram, I., Siegel, R., Torre, L., Jemal, A.: Global cancer statistics 2018: GLOBOCAN estimates of incidence and mortality worldwide for 36 cancers in 185 countries. CA: A Cancer J. Clini. **68**, 394–424 (2018)
2. Chin, D., Boyle, G., Porceddu, S., Theile, D., Parsons, P., Coman, W.: Head and neck cancer: past, present and future. Expert Rev. Anticancer Ther. **6**, 1111–1118 (2006)
3. Castadot, P., Lee, J., Geets, X., Grégoire, V.: Adaptive radiotherapy of head and neck cancer. Semin. Radiat. Oncol. **20**, 84–93 (2010)
4. Brouwer, C., Steenbakkers, R., Langendijk, J., Sijtsema, N.: Identifying patients who may benefit from adaptive radiotherapy: does the literature on anatomic and dosimetric changes in head and neck organs at risk during radiotherapy provide information to help? Radiother. Oncol. **115**, 285–294 (2015)
5. Mnejja, W., et al.: Dosimetric impact on changes in target volumes during intensity-modulated radiotherapy for nasopharyngeal carcinoma. Rep. Pract. Oncol. Radiother. **25**, 41–45 (2020)
6. Yousuf, A., Qureshi, B., Hussain, A., Qadir, A., Abbasi, N.: SU-E-J-81: Adaptive Radiotherapy for IMRT Head & Neck Patient in AKUH. Med. Phys. **42**, 3282 (2015)
7. Barker, J., et al.: Quantification of volumetric and geometric changes occurring during fractionated radiotherapy for head-and-neck cancer using an integrated CT/linear accelerator system. Int. J. Radiat. Oncol.* Biol.* Phys. **59**, 960–970 (2004)
8. Yan, D., et al.: Computed tomography guided management of interfractional patient variation. Semin. Radiat. Oncol. **15**, 168–179 (2005)
9. Böck, M.: On adaptation cost and tractability in robust adaptive radiation therapy optimization. Med. Phys. **47**, 2791–2804 (2020)

10. Green, O., Henke, L., Hugo, G.: Practical clinical workflows for online and offline adaptive radiation therapy. Semin. Radiat. Oncol. **29**, 219–227 (2019)
11. Schwartz, D., et al.: Adaptive radiotherapy for head and neck cancer—dosimetric results from a prospective clinical trial. Radiother. Oncol. **106**, 80–84 (2013)
12. Zhao, L., Wan, Q., Zhou, Y., Deng, X., Xie, C., Wu, S.: The role of replanning in fractionated intensity modulated radiotherapy for nasopharyngeal carcinoma. Radiother. Oncol. **98**, 23–27 (2011)
13. Zhang, P., et al.: Optimal adaptive IMRT strategy to spare the parotid glands in oropharyngeal cancer. Radiother. Oncol. **120**, 41–47 (2016)
14. Yang, H., Hu, W., Wang, W., Chen, P., Ding, W., Luo, W.: Replanning During Intensity Modulated Radiation Therapy Improved Quality of Life in Patients with Nasopharyngeal Carcinoma. Int. J. Radiat. Oncol. *Biol.*Phys. **85**, e47-e54 (2013)
15. Lindsay, P., et al.: SU-GG-T-50: dosimetric impact of anatomy variations and benefits of mid-course replanning for head and neck IMRT. Med. Phys. **35**, 2737 (2008)
16. Poon, E., Shenouda, G., Parker, W.: SU-E-J-209: dosimetric benefits of replanning for IMRT treatment of head and neck cancer. Med. Phys. **40**, 199 (2013)
17. Shang, Q., et al.: SU-E-J-74: Dosimetric advantages of adaptive radiotherapy for head and neck cancer are confirmed with weekly CBCT images. Med. Phys. **42**, 3281 (2015)
18. Capelle, L., Mackenzie, M., Field, C., Parliament, M., Ghosh, S., Scrimger, R.: Adaptive radiotherapy using helical tomotherapy for head and neck cancer in definitive and postoperative settings: initial results. Clin. Oncol. **24**, 208–215 (2012)
19. Ahn, P., et al.: Adaptive planning in intensity-modulated radiation therapy for head and neck cancers: single-institution experience and clinical implications. Int. J. Radiat. Oncol.*Biol.*Phys. **80**, 677–685 (2011)
20. Hansen, E., Bucci, M., Quivey, J., Weinberg, V., Xia, P.: Repeat CT imaging and replanning during the course of IMRT for head-and-neck cancer. Int. J. Radiat. Oncol.*Biol.*Phys. **64**, 355–362 (2006)
21. Brown, E., et al.: Predicting the need for adaptive radiotherapy in head and neck cancer. Radiother. Oncol. **116**, 57–63 (2015)
22. Surucu, M., et al.: Decision trees predicting tumor shrinkage for head and neck cancer. Technol. Cancer Res. Treat. **15**, 139–145 (2015)
23. Brouwer, C., et al.: Selection of head and neck cancer patients for adaptive radiotherapy to decrease xerostomia. Radiother. Oncol. **120**, 36–40 (2016)
24. Lambin, P., et al.: Radiomics: Extracting more information from medical images using advanced feature analysis. Eur. J. Cancer **48**, 441–446 (2012)
25. Gillies, R., Kinahan, P., Hricak, H.: Radiomics: images are more than pictures they are data. Radiology **278**, 563–577 (2016)
26. Kumar, V., et al.: Radiomics: the process and the challenges. Magn. Reson. Imaging **30**, 1234–1248 (2012)
27. Song, J., et al.: TU-AB-BRA-10: prognostic value of intra-radiation treatment FDG-PET and CT imaging features in locally advanced head and neck cancer. Med. Phys. **42**, 3588–3589 (2015)
28. Bagher-Ebadian, H., et al.: Application of radiomics for the prediction of HPV status for patients with head and neck cancers. Med. Phys. **47**, 563–575 (2020)
29. Oh, J., et al.: WE-E-17A-03: FDG-PET-based radiomics to predict local control and survival following radiotherapy. Med. Phys. **41**, 507–508 (2014)
30. Zwanenburg, A., et al.: The image biomarker standardization initiative: standardized quantitative radiomics for high-throughput image-based phenotyping. Radiology **295**, 328–338 (2020)
31. Ashrafinia, S.: Quantitative Nuclear Medicine Imaging using Advanced Image Reconstruction and Radiomics, Ph.D. Dissertation, Johns Hopkins University (2019)

32. Leger, S., et al.: CT imaging during treatment improves radiomic models for patients with locally advanced head and neck cancer. Radiother. Oncol. **130**, 10–17 (2019)

33. Zwanenburg, A., et al.: Assessing robustness of radiomic features by image perturbation. Sci. Rep. **9**(1) (2019)

34. Shrout, P.E., Fleiss, J.L.: Intraclass correlations: uses in assessing rater reliability. Psychol Bull. **86**(2), 420–428 (1979). https://doi.org/10.1037//0033-2909.86.2.420

35. Ramella, S., et al.: A radiomic approach for adaptive radiotherapy in non-small cell lung cancer patients. PLOS ONE **13**(11), p. e0207455 (2018)

36. Yu, T., et al.: Pretreatment prediction of adaptive radiation therapy eligibility using MRI-based radiomics for advanced nasopharyngeal carcinoma patients. Front. Oncol. **9** (2019)

37. Sanguineti, G., Ricchetti, F., Thomas, O., Wu, B., McNutt, T.: Pattern and predictors of volumetric change of parotid glands during intensity modulated radiotherapy. Br. J. Radiol. **86**(1031), 20130363 (2013)

38. Traverso, A., Wee, L., Dekker, A. and Gillies, R.: Repeatability and reproducibility of radiomic features: a systematic review. Int. J. Radiat. Oncol.*Biol.*Phys. **102**(4), 1143–1158 (2018)

39. Yip, S., Aerts, H.: Applications and limitations of radiomics. Phys. Med. Biol. **61**(13), R150–R166 (2016)

40. Rai, R., et al.: Multicenter evaluation of MRI-based radiomic features: a phantom study. Med. Phys. **47**(7), 3054–3063 (2020)

Measuring Plantar Temperature Changes in Thermal Images Using Basic Statistical Descriptors

Vítor Filipe[1,2(✉)] 📷, Pedro Teixeira[1] 📷, and Ana Teixeira[1,3] 📷

[1] University of Trás-os-Montes e Alto Douro, Quinta de Prados, 5001-801 Vila Real, Portugal
{vfilipe,ateixeir}@utad.pt
[2] INESC TEC - INESC Technology and Science, 4200-465 Porto, Portugal
[3] Mathematics Centre CMAT, Pole CMAT – UTAD, Vila Real, Portugal

Abstract. One of the principal complications of patients that suffer from Diabetes Mellitus (DM) and that can lead to ulceration is the Diabetic foot. As tissue inflammation causes temperature variation, several studies show that thermography can be used to detect complications in diabetic foot and help predicting the risk of ulceration. It is known that, although healthy individuals present characteristic plantar temperature variation patterns, the same does not happen with diabetic patients, for which a particular pattern can not be found; thus, making the measurement of the temperature variation more difficult. Given that, it is important to research in this field in order to obtain methods that can detect atypical variations of the temperature in the sole of the foot. With this in mind, the objective of this work is to present a methodology to analyze the distribution of temperature in thermograms of the foot's plant and classify it as belonging to a DM individual with risk of ulceration or a healthy individual. After foot partitioning with a clustering algorithm, basic statistical descriptors are computed for each cluster. A binary classifier to predict the risk of ulceration in the diabetic foot was evaluated with the different descriptors; both a quantitative temperature index and a classification threshold are calculated for each descriptor. To evaluate the performance of the classifier, experiments were conducted using a public dataset (containing 45 thermograms of healthy individuals and 122 images of DM ones); the following metrics were obtained: Accuracy = 78%, AUC = 86% and F-measure = 84%, with the best descriptor.

Keywords: K-means · Descriptors · Classification · Diabetic foot · Thermogram

1 Introduction

Diabetes Mellitus (DM) is a chronic disease that affects many people and causes many deaths. In 2017, approximately 3.2 to 5.0 million deaths were associated with this disease [1].

DM individuals frequently develop a pathology, named Diabetic foot (DF), that is characterized by a variety of foot injuries, like ulceration and/or destruction of deep

© Springer Nature Switzerland AG 2021
O. Gervasi et al. (Eds.): ICCSA 2021, LNCS 12953, pp. 445–455, 2021.
https://doi.org/10.1007/978-3-030-86976-2_30

tissues that can be related with neuropathy or vascular disease [2]. The development of ulcers can cause infections, that, when severe, may lead to limb amputation [3]. DF problems are directly linked to abnormal changes of the temperature in the plantar region; thus, justifying the temperature monitoring and the identification of characteristic patterns as well as the measurement of thermal changes. A specific spatial temperature pattern, called butterfly pattern, can be found in the feet of healthy individuals, while, in the groups of the diabetic patients an extensive diversity of spatial patterns can be detected [4–6].

Infrared thermography (IRT) is a non-contact, non-invasive and fast method that permits to observe the distribution of the temperature of the sole of the foot and to analyze the thermal alterations that take place [7].

The use of IRT to automatically identify a foot as belonging to a diabetic individual captured the attention of a number of researchers for some time now, for example [4–11]. As the foot does not have an uniform temperature, it is of significance to consider a partition of the foot in regions, in order to obtain more detailed information concerning temperature variation, in addition to the analysis of the temperature of the entire foot [12]. Some authors present a thermal analysis based on the observation of specific points, or specific regions. For example, in [13, 14], 33 regions were considered, considering the points of the foot that are most likely to ulcer. Another approach that has been quite used and discussed recently [4–6, 15, 16] splits the plant of the foot in four areas and it is based on the concept of angiosome (region of tissue which has blood supply through a single artery); its use is justified by the fact that the reduction in blood supply is one of the leading causes of DF ulceration.

Additionally, only a few studies on this topic propose quantitative information to estimate the plantar temperature variation; for example, in [15] the temperature difference of the matching regions of the right and left foot are considered, while in [4], an index involving both the temperature difference between the regions and the temperature interval of the control group (constituted of healthy individuals) is computed.

In [17] a quantitative index based on the average values of the temperature in clusters regions was presented. The present work is a sequel of the one in [17], where a clustering algorithm was used to split the foot in regions and the average temperature descriptor is used to predict diabetic foot.

In this work, a method that analyzes thermographic photos of the plant of the foot and gives a quantitative temperature index is proposed. To obtain the quantitative temperature index, each foot is divided into clusters and a statistical descriptor measure of the temperature of each cluster is considered. The index measures the temperature deviations in respect to the control group allowing to classify the foot in one of the categories *risk of ulceration* or *healthy*. The final stage of the method implements a binary classifier by thresholding the quantitative temperature index with the optimum threshold that separates the two classes.

A clustering method groups similar values of the temperature in a cluster; therefore, isolating the different areas (clusters) of the foot that present approximate temperature values [18], being the range of temperatures within each one of the clusters low; thus, it is expected to obtain an index capable of measuring thermal variations in respect to the control group. Notice that a lower value index is obtained when low variation of temperature values occur within the same region.

In this article, the k-means algorithm is used to obtain the clusters. Moreover, two new temperature descriptors are calculated in the regions found by the clustering algorithm. Using the new proposed descriptors, two new indexes, called minimum cluster temperature index and maximum cluster temperature index, are computed.

To measure the classifiers' performance, experiments using a public database [12] were performed, being the performance metrics Accuracy, Area Under the Curve, F-measure, Precision, Sensitivity and Specificity used to assess and validate the presented classification method. Furthermore, the average cluster temperature index, presented in [17], was compared with the two new indices implemented in this work; a generalized improvement in the evaluation metrics could be observed when the minimum cluster temperature index was used to classify the thermographic images of the used public dataset.

This paper is organized as follows. In Sect. 2 the proposed method is described. In Sect. 3 the used data set is introduced and the obtained results are presented and analyzed. In Sect. 4 the conclusions and the guidelines for future work are presented.

2 Methodology

The proposed method has three phases of processing: temperature clustering, index computation and classification. In the first phase, a clustering algorithm divides the foot into five regions (clusters), based on the temperature values. In the second phase, for each cluster, regional descriptors of temperature are calculated (namely, average, standard deviation, maximum and minimum values), as well as an index concerning the variation of the temperature in respect to a reference value. Finally, applying a thresholding procedure on the index, the subject is classified in one of the classes: healthy or risk of ulceration.

2.1 Clustering

Clustering is an important technique for data mining, with applications ranging from statistics, computer science, biology to social sciences [18, 19].This technique consists of grouping data samples in groups based on a certain similarity measure, being a lot of clustering algorithms cited in the literature [20, 21]. The dataset is divided into groups so that data points in the same group are similar while data points in different groups are dissimilar to each other.

The most popular clustering algorithms are the centroid based, including K-means [22]; that is the algorithm used in the first phase of the presented method.

K-means is one of the most used clustering algorithms, with a straightforward implementation and being computationally efficient, even when applied on large datasets. The algorithm splits the original data into k non overlapping groups, defined as clusters of data points exhibiting similar properties. The number of clusters (k parameter) is specified by the user depending on the problem to be solved. The K-means algorithm through an iterative process converges to a solution where subsets of data points are assigned into k clusters. The final cluster configuration is determined by the minimization of the sum of the distances of each data point to the cluster centroid, in all clusters.

The algorithm consists in two steps designated expectation-maximization. In the expectation step each observation is assigned to the nearest cluster centroid. In the next step, named as maximization, for each cluster the new centroid is determined by averaging the all data points belonging to the cluster. The algorithm proceeds as follows:

1. Specify the number of clusters, k, and randomly choose the initial centers (centroids).
2. **Repeat**
3. Each data point is assigned to the cluster with the closest centroid.
4. Compute the new centroid.
5. **Until** all the clusters centroid stop moving (k-means has converged).

One advantage of K-means is that it easily scales to large data set, as for example high resolution images. However, due to his non-deterministic characteristic, the algorithm can produce different cluster configurations from two separate runs even if the data points are the same. The final results strongly depend of the arbitrary selection of the initial centroid [22, 23]. Figure 1 shows the results of two runs of the K-means in the same dataset, which obtained different final configurations.

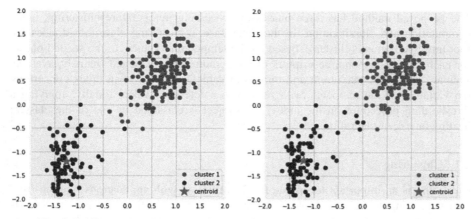

Fig. 1. Different cluster configurations in two runs of K-means in the same dataset.

2.2 Computation of Cluster Temperature Indexes

After the foot partition using K-means, each cluster can be described by a set of basic statistical descriptors, such as average, maximum, and minimum value of temperature. These descriptors extracted from each cluster can be used to estimate how much the foot temperature of an individual deviates from the reference temperature calculated in the control group, formed by healthy feet.

In this work we proposed new quantitative indexes to measure the foot temperature changes in respect to the control group. The statistical descriptors of each clusters are used to calculate three indexes named as Cluster Temperature Indexes (CTIs).

Each index is calculated as the average of the positive differences between the temperatures of an individual (IND) and the correspondent reference values ($\overline{CTR}$) obtained using the average of the data from the control group, as in (1), where $\overline{CTR}_i$ is the average value of the reference temperature descriptor for cluster i and IND_i is the value of the temperature descriptor of the individual (IND) in study for cluster i.

$$CTI = \frac{\sum_{i=1}^{5} \left| \overline{CTR}_i - IND_i \right|}{5} \tag{1}$$

When the average descriptor is used, the index in (1) will be called as Average CTI (ACTI); similarly, when the maximum and the minimum descriptors are considered the Maximum CTI (MCTI) or the minimum CTI (mCTI) are obtained from (1).

The value of each CTI index is an indicator of variations in the temperature pattern of a subject's foot in relation to the normal temperature pattern (butterfly pattern). It is expected that higher index values are related with greater values of temperature variation; therefore, flagging the subject as having higher risk of appearing of foot lesions. Thus, these indexes can be used to classify each foot as belonging to a healthy or a DM individual with risk of ulceration.

2.3 Classification

In the last stage of the method the thermograms are classified in one of the categories: *healthy* or *risk of ulceration*, based on the thresholding of the CTI values. The success of the classification depends on the selection of an optimum cluster threshold value (CTT - Cluster Temperature Threshold); for each descriptor a CTT is computed.

During the experiments several performance metrics were calculated: *Sensitivity* (Se), *Specificity* (Sp), *Precision, Accuracy, F-measure*, and *Area Under the Curve* (AUC), defined by (2) to (6), where TP, FP, TN and FN represent the number of cases of *True Positive, False Positive, True Negative* and *False Negative*, respectively:

$$Sensitivity = \frac{TP}{TP + FN} \tag{2}$$

$$Specificity = \frac{TN}{FP + TN} \tag{3}$$

$$Precision = \frac{TP}{TP + FP} \tag{4}$$

$$Accuracy = \frac{TP + FN}{TP + TN + FP + FN} \tag{5}$$

$$F_{measure} = \frac{2 * TP}{2 * TP + FP + FN} \tag{6}$$

The Receiver Operating Characteristic (ROC) curve is a way to show in a graphic the connection between the true positive rate (sensitivity) and the false positive rate (1-specificity) for different cut-off (threshold) of CTI.

As the method is used to detect the risk of lesion, *sensitivity* and *specificity* are the most relevant metrics to assess the performance [24]. The balance between these two-performance metrics can be achieved if a cut-point is determined as the threshold to classify the foot as *healthy* or in *risk of ulceration*. The value was chosen using an approach known as the point closest-to-(0,1) corner in the ROC plane, which defines the optimal cut-point as the point that minimizes the Euclidean distance between the ROC curve and the (0,1) point, denominated as ER criteria [25]. In this criteria, the "optimal" cut-point is obtained using (7).

$$ER = \sqrt{(1 - Se)^2 + (1 - Sp)^2} \tag{7}$$

To summarize the entire location of the ROC curve the AUC is used, as it is an effective and combined measure of sensitivity and specificity that describes the inherent validity of diagnostic tests, rather than depending on a specific operating point [26].

3   Experimental Results

To evaluate the classifier, a public database that contains 334 individual plantar thermographic photos, of 167 individuals (being 45 of healthy subjects and 122 of DM individuals with risk of ulceration) [12]. All the computational experiences were carried out using version R2020b of the software MATLAB.

In this section the results of the classification using the clustering algorithm described in Sect. 2 are presented. It is important to notice that, as reported in [17], several experiments were carried out to determine the number of clusters that should be used in order to obtain the best classification, starting with three clusters and increasing this number until six. From these experiments it was possible to observe that better metric results are obtained with four clusters than with three and even better ones were obtained with five clusters, but the same does not happen when six clusters are considered; thus, it has been concluded that the best results were obtained when considering foot division in five clusters.

The classification indexes (1), are based on reference temperature values. For each descriptor, the reference average values of the temperature per cluster ($\overline{CTR}$) and the correspondent standard deviation (Std. dev.), both measured in Celsius degrees (°C), as well as the reference CTI average values (ACTI, mCTI and MCTI) and correspondent standard deviation are presented in Table 1.

As the performance of the method depends on the threshold value used to determine whether the thermogram is from a healthy or a DM individual, various threshold values were tested, considering the reference CTI value obtained with each descriptor. In order to obtain a threshold that balances sensibility and sensitivity metrics, the ER measure approach was used. The value 1.9 was selected as the threshold to classify the thermogram as risk ulceration or healthy using the average descriptor, the value 1.84 was chosen when using the minimum and 2.22 was set for the maximum.

Table 1. Average and standard deviation of the temperature (°C) for the control group, per cluster, after the k-means clustering, with different descriptors.

Descriptor	Cluster	1	2	3	4	5	CTI
Average	$\overline{CTR}$	23,93	25,52	26,59	27,61	28,88	1,23
	Std. dev	1,75	1,60	1,56	1,50	1,44	0,91
Minimum	$\overline{CTR}$	21,38	24,72	26,06	27,11	28,25	1,31
	Std. dev	2,07	1,66	1,58	1,52	1,46	0,79
Maximum	$\overline{CTR}$	24,71	26,05	27,10	28,25	29,80	1,31
	Std. dev	1,66	1,58	1,52	1,46	1,57	0,79

Analyzing the results obtained with the different descriptors, presented in Table 2, it can be observed that both the average and the maximum present similar metric results, but the maximum descriptor presents a more unbalanced sensibility and sensitivity. Furthermore, it can be concluded that the minimum is the descriptor that presents the best results, obtaining in some metrics, like F-measure or Accuracy an increase of 4% when compared with the algorithm that presents the worst metric results. To compare the performance of the classifiers (represented by the AUC metrics), the ROC curves and the CTT obtained for the three descriptors, are illustrated in Fig. 2.

Table 2. Metrics scores using K-means, for the 3 descriptors.

Descriptor	CTT	Accuracy	Se	Sp	Precision	AUC	F-measure	ER
AVERAGE	1,9	74%	73%	78%	90%	84%	81%	0,350
MIN	1,84	78%	77%	81%	92%	86%	84%	0,297
MAX	2,22	72%	66%	88%	94%	83%	77%	0,361

Observing Fig. 2 it is perceptible that, although all the AUC results are higher than 83%, the best results in classification, with the highest AUC values and best balance between sensibility and sensibility are obtained with the minimum descriptor.

In order to better illustrate the comparison between the used descriptors, in Table 3, information concerning three feet thermograms is presented. The first case is a thermogram from the control group, where the butterfly pattern is easily detected (CG005 from [12]), the second example was chosen to exemplify a case when the butterfly pattern is not so well defined (DM051 from [12]), and, finally, in the third case a thermogram of a foot that can clearly be characterized as belonging to a DM individual was chosen (DM010 from [12]). Additionally, the columns of Table 3 contain information concerning: the subject's identification (Subject), the thermographic image (Thermal), the image obtained after k-means clustering (K-means), the index value for each descriptor (ACTI, mCTI and MCTI), as well as the measures identification (Measures) and the corresponding values for the entire foot (General).

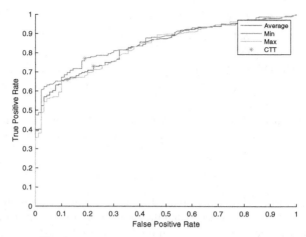

Fig. 2. ROC curves for all the three descriptors.

Table 3. CTI's and temperature measure values, per cluster, for some feet thermograms of the control and the DM groups in [12].

Subject	Thermal	K-means	ACTI	mCTI	MCTI	Measures	General
CG005			0,24	0,50	0,20	Min	22,94
						Max	29,90
						Average	26,75
						Std dev	1,64
DM051			1,62	2,15	1,34	Min	25,65
						Max	30,04
						Average	28,49
						Std dev	0,75
DM010			7,50	7,76	7,13	Min	30,26
						Max	35,58
						Average	34,31
						Std dev	0,61

The thermal analysis of the feet allowed to observed that, when the average temperature values of the clusters of a foot are close to the ones of the control reference (Table 1), low values of the CTI's are obtained and the foot distribution temperature approximates the butterfly pattern, typical of non-diabetic subjects, as can be observed in the thermogram of subject CG005 (Table 3). Generally, the method classifies accurately these type of feet for all the descriptors.

Thermal changes in the feet of the diabetic subjects can vary from marginally dissimilar from the butterfly pattern to a totally diverse pattern. This fact reflects in the CTI's value, being that, wide variations of the CTI indexes' values can be observed. As shown in Table 3, when minor temperature deviations occur, the CTI's values are closer to the reference CTI's values, as in DM051 (Table 3). In this case, it appears that when using the average and the maximum descriptors, the obtained CTI's shows more difficulty in classify the foot as belonging to a healthy or a diabetic individual. On the other hand, it seems that when using the minimum descriptor, the method is able to find the small thermal changes, showing a pattern marginally dissimilar from the butterfly pattern and that correspond to the transition between the two classes; thus, leading to a better performance of the classifier for these type of feet than the one obtained when using the other two descriptors.

As variations start to be more accentuated, the CTI's values increase, moving further away from the reference CTI's values. Additionally, it can also be observed that, when the hot spots evolve, they not only become wider, but also warmer; thus, higher CTI's values are achieved. The hot spots may even cover the entire plantar region, reaching very high temperature values and presenting very high CTI's values, as in DM010 (Table 3). In general, and similarly to what happens with the first group of feet, this method classifies accurately these type of feet for all the descriptors.

4   Conclusions

In this work, a method that uses thermographic photos of the sole of the foot to analyze the multiplicity of thermal changes in the plantar region, is presented. In this approach, the clustering concept is used to obtain different descriptors and, for each one, a quantitative temperature index and a classification temperature threshold are obtained. In the classification stage, for each descriptor the optimum threshold value was set finding a balance between the sensitivity and specificity metrics.

According to the presented results, the method proved to be effective in helping to measure temperature variations in the plant of the feet, and the obtained indexes can detect these changes, being that a higher value of the index corresponds to greater values of temperature variation. Additionally, the determined thresholds allow to classify an individual as having risk of ulceration or being healthy.

When comparing the different descriptors, it can be noticed that, in general, the presented method is able to correctly classify the feet, for all the descriptors, when the temperature distribution of the plant of the foot preserves the butterfly pattern, or when the hot spots are visible and may, even, cover the entire plantar area and reach high temperature values. On the other hand, using the minimum descriptor, the method is able to find small thermal changes, which are slightly different from the butterfly pattern and correspond to the transition between the two classes. Therefore, it can be concluded that the classifier's performance using the minimum descriptor surpasses the one obtained by the classifier when using the other two descriptors.

With this work, another step is taken in order to obtain an effective classification tool that can assist in medical diagnosis, thus, helping in the prevention of ulcerations and in the early detection of the risk of injuries.

As future work it is intended to balance the number of the photos of diabetic and healthy and DM subjects, by extending the dataset.

Acknowledgments. This work was supported by the project "WalkingPAD - Patient education on a quantified supervised home-based exercise therapy to improve walking ability in patients with peripheral arterial disease and intermittent claudication" (PTDC/MEC-VAS/31161/2017) funded by Fundação para a Ciência e a Tecnologia (FCT), Portugal.

References

1. Diabetes, (n.d.): https://www.who.int/en/news-room/fact-sheets/detail/diabetes. Accessed 4 Apr 2021
2. Leung, P.: Diabetic foot ulcers - a comprehensive review. Surgeon. (2007). https://doi.org/10.1016/S1479-666X(07)80007-2
3. Glaudemans, A.W.J.M., Uçkay, I., Lipsky, B.A.: Challenges in diagnosing infection in the diabetic foot. Diabet. Med. **32**, 748–759 (2015). https://doi.org/10.1111/dme.12750
4. Hernandez-Contreras, D., Peregrina-Barreto, H., Rangel-Magdaleno, J., Gonzalez-Bernal, J.A., Altamirano-Robles, L.: A quantitative index for classification of plantar thermal changes in the diabetic foot. Infrared Phys. Technol. **81**, 242–249 (2017). https://doi.org/10.1016/j.infrared.2017.01.010
5. Nagase, T., et al.: Variations of plantar thermographic patterns in normal controls and non-ulcer diabetic patients: Novel classification using angiosome concept. J. Plast. Reconstr. Aesthetic Surg. **64**, 860–866 (2011). https://doi.org/10.1016/j.bjps.2010.12.003
6. Mori, T., et al.: Morphological pattern classification system for plantar thermography of patients with diabetes. J. Diabetes Sci. Technol. **7**, 1102–1112 (2013). https://doi.org/10.1177/193229681300700502
7. Pereira, C.B., Yu, X., Dahlmanns, S., Blazek, V., Leonhardt, S., Teichmann, D.: Infrared thermography. In: Abreu de Souza, M., Remigio Gamba, H., Pedrini, H. (eds.) Multi-Modality Imaging, pp. 1–30. Springer, Cham (2018). https://doi.org/10.1007/978-3-319-98974-7_1
8. Frykberg, R.G., et al.: Diabetic foot disorders: a clinical practice guideline (2006 revision). J. Foot Ankle Surg. **45** (2006). https://doi.org/10.1016/S1067-2516(07)60001-5
9. Ring, F.: The Herschel heritage to medical thermography. J. Imaging. 2 (2016). https://doi.org/10.3390/jimaging2020013
10. Hernandez-Contreras, D., Peregrina-Barreto, H., Rangel-Magdaleno, J., Gonzalez-Bernal, J.: Narrative review: diabetic foot and infrared thermography. Infrared Phys. Technol. **78**, 105–117 (2016). https://doi.org/10.1016/j.infrared.2016.07.013
11. Adam, M., Ng, E.Y.K., Tan, J.H., Heng, M.L., Tong, J.W.K., Acharya, U.R.: Computer aided diagnosis of diabetic foot using infrared thermography: a review. Comput. Biol. Med. **91**, 326–336 (2017). https://doi.org/10.1016/j.compbiomed.2017.10.030
12. Hernandez-Contreras, D.A., Peregrina-Barreto, H., Rangel-Magdaleno, J.D.J., Renero-Carrillo, F.J.: Plantar thermogram database for the study of diabetic foot complications. IEEE Access. **7**, 161296–161307 (2019). https://doi.org/10.1109/ACCESS.2019.2951356
13. Macdonald, A., et al.: Thermal symmetry of healthy feet: a precursor to a thermal study of diabetic feet prior to skin breakdown. Physiol. Meas. **38**, 33–44 (2017). https://doi.org/10.1088/1361-6579/38/1/33

14. Macdonald, A., et al.: Between visit variability of thermal imaging of feet in people attending podiatric clinics with diabetic neuropathy at high risk of developing foot ulcers, Physiol. Meas. 40 (2019). https://doi.org/10.1088/1361-6579/ab36d7
15. Peregrina-Barreto, H., Morales-Hernandez, L.A., Rangel-Magdaleno, J.J., Avina-Cervantes, J.G., Ramirez-Cortes, J.M., Morales-Caporal, R.: Quantitative estimation of temperature variations in plantar angiosomes: a study case for diabetic foot. Comput. Math. Methods Med. 2014 (2014). https://doi.org/10.1155/2014/585306
16. Peregrina-Barreto, H., Morales-Hernandez, L.A., Rangel-Magdaleno, J.J., Vazquez-Rodriguez, P.D.: Thermal image processing for quantitative determination of temperature variations in plantar angiosomes. Conf. Rec. - IEEE Instrum. Meas. Technol. Conf. 816–820 (2013). https://doi.org/10.1109/I2MTC.2013.6555528
17. Filipe, V., Teixeira, P., Teixeira, A.: A clustering approach for prediction of diabetic foot using thermal images. In: Gervasi, O., et al. (eds.) ICCSA 2020. LNCS, vol. 12251, pp. 620–631. Springer, Cham (2020). https://doi.org/10.1007/978-3-030-58808-3_45
18. Omran, M.G.H., Engelbrecht, A.P., Salman, A.: An overview of clustering methods. Intell. Data Anal. 11, 583–605 (2007). https://doi.org/10.3233/ida-2007-11602
19. Ben Ayed, A., Ben Halima, M., Alimi, A.M.: Adaptive fuzzy exponent cluster ensemble system based feature selection and spectral clustering. IEEE Int. Conf. Fuzzy Syst. (2017). https://doi.org/10.1109/FUZZ-IEEE.2017.8015721.
20. (PDF) Survey on clustering methods : Towards fuzzy clustering for big data, (n.d.). https://www.researchgate.net/publication/280730634_Survey_on_clustering_methods_Towards_f uzzy_clustering_for_big_data. Accessed 24 Mar 2021
21. Berkhin, P.: A survey of clustering data mining techniques. In: Group. Multidimens. Data Recent Adv. Clust., pp. 25–71. Springer, Heidelberg (2006). https://doi.org/10.1007/3-540-28349-8_2
22. Dhanachandra, N., Manglem, K., Chanu, Y.J.: Image segmentation using k-means clustering algorithm and subtractive clustering algorithm. Procedia Comput. Sci. 54, 764–771 (2015). https://doi.org/10.1016/j.procs.2015.06.090
23. Tremblay, N., Loukas, A.: Approximating spectral clustering via sampling: a review. In: Ros, F., Guillaume, S. (eds.) Sampling Techniques for Supervised or Unsupervised Tasks. USL, pp. 129–183. Springer, Cham (2020). https://doi.org/10.1007/978-3-030-29349-9_5
24. Taha, A.A., Hanbury, A.: Metrics for evaluating 3D medical image segmentation: analysis, selection, and tool. BMC Med. Imaging. 15 (2015). https://doi.org/10.1186/s12880-015-0068-x
25. Unal, I.: Defining an optimal cut-point value in ROC analysis: an alternative approach. Comput. Math. Methods Med. 2017 (2017). https://doi.org/10.1155/2017/3762651
26. Hajian-Tilaki, K.: Receiver operating characteristic (ROC) curve analysis for medical diagnostic test evaluation. Casp. J. Intern. Med. 4, 627–635 (2013)

On Local Convergence of Stochastic Global Optimization Algorithms

Eligius M. T. Hendrix[1]([envelope])[iD] and Ana Maria A. C. Rocha[2][iD]

[1] Computer Architecture, Universidad de Málaga, 29080 Málaga, Spain
eligius@uma.es
[2] ALGORITMI Center, University of Minho, 4710-057 Braga, Portugal
arocha@dps.uminho.pt

Abstract. In engineering optimization with continuous variables, the use of Stochastic Global Optimization (SGO) algorithms is popular due to the easy availability of codes. All algorithms have a global and local search character, where the global behaviour tries to avoid getting trapped in local optima and the local behaviour intends to reach the lowest objective function values. As the algorithm parameter set includes a final convergence criterion, the algorithm might be running for a while around a reached minimum point. Our question deals with the local search behaviour after the algorithm reached the final stage. How fast do practical SGO algorithms actually converge to the minimum point? To investigate this question, we run implementations of well known SGO algorithms in a final local phase stage.

Keywords: Stochastic global optimization · Evolutionary algorithms · Convergence · Nonlinear optimization

1 Introduction

In many engineering applications [6], we consider a black-box global optimization problem

$$f^* = \min_{x \in X} f(x), \tag{1}$$

where $f(x)$ is a continuous function and $X \subset \mathbb{R}^n$ is a feasible region. The idea of the black-box optimization is that function evaluations imply running an external (black-box) routine that may take minutes or hours to provide the evaluated objective function value. In engineering applications, often the question is to obtain a good, but not necessarily optimal solution within a day, several days, or a week.

The choice of engineers for solution algorithms is often driven by ease of availability and the attractiveness of the intuitive behaviour. Therefore, Stochastic

This paper has been supported by The Spanish Ministry (RTI2018-095993-B-I00) in part financed by the European Regional Development Fund (ERDF) and by FCT – Fundação para a Ciência e Tecnologia within the Project Scope: UIDB/00319/2020.

O. Gervasi et al. (Eds.): ICCSA 2021, LNCS 12953, pp. 456–472, 2021.
https://doi.org/10.1007/978-3-030-86976-2_31

Global Optimization (SGO) algorithms based on evolutionary equivalences have been most popular over the last decades. According to the generic description of [13], a new iterate to be evaluated is generated according to:

$$x_{k+1} = \mathrm{Alg}(x_k, x_{k-1}, \ldots, x_0, \xi), \tag{2}$$

where ξ is a pseudo-random variable and index k is the iteration counter. Description (2) represents the idea that a next point x_{k+1} is generated based on the information in all former points $x_k, x_{k-1}, \ldots, x_0$ and a random effect ξ based on generated pseudo-random numbers.

If the algorithm behaves well, it might converge to a global optimum solution or even several of them. In our investigation, we focus on the situation where an algorithm converges to one of the global minimum points $x^* \in \mathrm{argmin}_{x \in X} f(x)$ which is interior with respect to the feasible region. In fact, it is better to switch to a nonlinear optimization algorithm from the iterate or one of the population points in that case. However, as the user is not always aware that the algorithms reached the final stage, it may continue for a while up to reaching a predefined stopping criterion.

In nonlinear optimization, the concept of convergence speed is well defined, see e.g., [3]. It deals with the convergence limit of the series x_k. Let $x_0, x_1, \ldots, x_k, \ldots$ converge to point x^*. The largest number α for which

$$\lim_{k \to \infty} \frac{\|x_{k+1} - x^*\|}{\|x_k - x^*\|^\alpha} = \beta < \infty \tag{3}$$

gives the order of convergence, whereas β is called the convergence factor. In this terminology, the special instances are

- linear convergence with $\alpha = 1$ and $\beta < 1$
- quadratic convergence with $\alpha = 2$ and $0 < \beta < 1$
- superlinear convergence: $1 < \alpha < 2$ and $\beta < 1$, i.e. $\beta = 0$ if $\alpha = 1$ in (3).

How is this limit behaviour for SGO algorithms? First of all, we are dealing with (pseudo-)random iterates that may or not behave in a Markovian way in the limit situation. Second, many SGO algorithms are population algorithms as sketched in the generic Algorithm 1. This means that stopping criteria in limit (when no maximum number of evaluations is set) may be based on the convergence of the distance in the population (swarm) $\max_{p,q \in \mathcal{P}} \|p - q\|$, or the function value $\max_{p,q \in \mathcal{P}} |f(p) - f(q)|$. The first criterion is not appropriate when

---

Algorithm 1. GPOP(X, f, N)

Generate set $\mathcal{P} = \{p_1, \ldots, p_N\}$ of N random points in X and evaluate
repeat
    Generate a set of trial points $\mathcal{X}$ based on $\mathcal{P}$ and evaluate
    Replace $\mathcal{P}$ by a selection of points from $\mathcal{P} \cup \mathcal{X}$
until (stopping criterion)

---

the population clusters around several minimum points. In [5], the convergence behaviour of Controlled Random Search (CRS) is studied also for the case where we have convergence to several minimum points.

In this study, we focus on the behaviour of six SGO algorithms for convergence to one minimum point of a smooth function. This facilitates considering the limit situation as the behaviour over a convex quadratic function

$$f(x) = f(x^*) + \frac{1}{2}x^T H(x^*)x, \tag{4}$$

where $H(x^*)$ is the Hessian in the minimum point x^*.

According to [5], the speed of convergence of a SGO algorithm is determined by the so-called success rate

$$S_k := P\left(f(x_{k+1}) < \max_{p \in \mathcal{P}} f(p)\right), \tag{5}$$

as the probability that the next generated iterate is better than the worst function value in the population. Our research question is how S_k is behaving when practically used population SGO algorithms solve problem (4). Specifically

1. Are the algorithms going to behave in a stationary way, i.e. is S_k converging?
2. How do the algorithms compare with respect to convergence speed on the same Hessian?
3. How do the algorithms behave for varying dimension and condition number of the Hessian $H(x^*)$ and are algorithms sensitive to rotation, i.e. does their behaviour depend on the eigenvectors?

The latter is related to the roundness of the ellipsoidal level sets of function (4).

To investigate these questions, in Sect. 2, we describe the experimental design of instances that vary in dimension and condition number of the Hessian. Section 3 provides pseudo-code for each investigated algorithm and presents its convergence behaviour. Section 4 summarizes our findings.

2   Experimental Setting

In order to measure the convergence, we focus on the worst function value in the population $\mathcal{P}_k$ at iteration k

$$\text{fworst}_k := \max_{p \in \mathcal{P}_k} f(p)$$

and measure the success rate as the number of points in the population, that are better than the worst value of the last population $\mathcal{P}_{k-1}$:

$$S_k := \frac{1}{N} \sum_{p \in \mathcal{P}_k} (f(p) < \text{fworst}_{k-1}), \tag{6}$$

where N is the population size. The starting population $\mathcal{P}_0$ consists of a uniform random sample over the level set defined by $\mathcal{P}_0 := \{x \in \mathbb{R}^n | x^T H x \leq 1\}$. The same starting population is used over different SGO algorithms. The population algorithms have different moments to update the population. CRS [11] updates the population after every iteration (function evaluation), i.e. $|\mathcal{X}| = 1$. It decides to replace the worst point in the population or not. In an algorithm based on swarms, the population is updated after all points in the population have been moved, i.e. $|\mathcal{X}| = N$. For the latter type of algorithms, we will update the measured success rate after replacement of the population.

The condition number and eigenvectors of the Hessian H allow us to vary the ellipsoidal shape of the initial population and the experimental setting. We are going to use 7 instances as depicted in Table 1, where the dimension n of the problem and the roundness of the level set are varied. The latter is related to the condition number of the Hessian which is the ratio of the largest and smallest eigenvalue in our context, [3].

For the two dimensional cases, we consider 3 instances of the Hessian; the identity matrix I_n, the Hessian of the Trid[1] quadratic function H_{Tn}, which is said to be difficult for population algorithms and a skewed matrix H_S in two dimensional space: $H_{T2} := \begin{pmatrix} 2 & -1 \\ -1 & 2 \end{pmatrix}$ and $H_S := \begin{pmatrix} 101 & -99 \\ -99 & 101 \end{pmatrix}$. Moreover, we also extend the identity matrix and Trid function to dimension $n = 2, 5, 10$. In general, we inspect the development of the indicators up to complete convergence, i.e. the final population is practically one point, or at most up to $1000 \times n$ function evaluations. We use the same seed for the generated pseudo-random numbers for all experiments with a long run instead of repeating the run several times. This implies that the starting population $\mathcal{P}_0$ is the same for each algorithm.

Table 1. Experimental setting varying the Hessian in the minimum point

Hessian	I_2	I_5	I_{10}	H_S	H_{T2}	H_{T5}	H_{T10}
n	2	5	10	2	2	5	10
cond nr	1	1	1	100	3	13.92	48.37

3 Evaluation of Algorithms

We investigate the behaviour of a total of six stochastic population algorithms. In the sequel, we leave out the iteration counter k from their pseudo-code description.

---

[1] https://www.sfu.ca/~ssurjano/trid.html.

3.1   Controlled Random Search

Price [11] introduced CRS in 1979. It has been widely used and also modified into many variants by himself and other researchers. Investigation of the algorithm shows mainly numerical results. Algorithm 2 describes the initial scheme. It generates points in a Nelder-Mead-way on randomly selected points from the current population.

Algorithm 2. CRS(f, X, N)

Generate and evaluate a set $\mathcal{P}$ of N random points uniformly on X

repeat

    Find the worst point q in the population $\mathcal{P}$, $q \leftarrow \mathrm{argmax}_{p \in \mathcal{P}} \, f(p)$

    fworst $\leftarrow f(q)$

    select at random a subset $\{y_0, \dots, y_n\}$ from $\mathcal{P}$

    $x \leftarrow \frac{2}{n} \sum_{i=1}^{n} y_i - y_0$ and evaluate $f(x)$

    if $(f(x) < \text{fworst})$

        Replace, in $\mathcal{P}$, point q by x

until (stopping criterion)

In later versions, the number of parents $n + 1$ is a parameter m of the algorithm. A so-called secondary trial point, which is a convex combination of the parent points is generated when the first type of points does not lead to sufficient improvement. In that version, a rule keeps track of the success rate.

Table 2. Order of magnitude reached function value for the worst point in the population fworst after $1000n$ evaluations and average success rate $\overline{S}$ for CRS

Hessian	I_2	I_5	I_{10}	H_S	H_{T2}	H_{T5}	H_{T10}
dim n	2	5	10	2	2	5	10
pop N	50	50	100	50	50	50	100
fworst	10^{-11}	10^{-10}	10^{-8}	10^{-9}	10^{-9}	10^{-10}	10^{-7}
$\overline{S}$	0.47	0.43	0.47	0.47	0.47	0.43	0.47

We run the algorithm over all test instances. The population size is $N = 50$ for $n \leq 5$ and $10n$ otherwise. Figure 1 gives insight in the course of the algorithm for the Trid function in dimension $n = 2$. In all dimensions the algorithm practically converges to the minimum point. In dimension $n = 2$ after 500 evaluations and in dimension $n = 10$ after 3000 iterations, the maximum value of the population reaches a value of about 0. The average success rate is $\overline{S} = 0.469$ for both cases H_{T10} and I_{10}, as illustrated in Fig. 2. This is no coincidence. The specific behaviour if CRS is that the generation mechanism with the same (pseudo) random numbers is the same if dimension and population size N is fixed *independent*

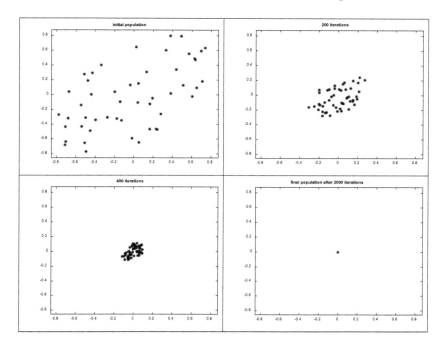

Fig. 1. Population development of CRS for the Trid Hessian H_{T2}, $N = 50$.

of the shape of the Hessian. This means, for $n = 2$, the same average success rate is reached for I_2, H_{T2} and H_S, i.e. $\overline{S} = 0.466$. In 5-dimensional space, for both H_{T5} and I_5, the reached value fworst after 5000 iterations is about fworst$\approx 10^{-10}$, but the average success rate is exactly the same, i.e. $\overline{S} = 0.430$.

What we learn from this experiment is that the local search behaviour of CRS is independent of the Hessian in the minimum point and that the average success rate, although varying, does not reveal a trend during the iterations. Moreover, it is quite independent of the dimension n and population size N. Of course the speed of convergence goes down with the population size N as analyzed in [5]. We expect this constant behaviour to be quite unique among the stochastic population algorithms.

3.2 Uniform Covering by Probabilistic Rejection

An alternative for CRS which focuses on only generating points around global minimum points to get a uniform cover of the lower level set is called Uniform Covering by Probabilistic Rejection (UCPR) introduced in 1994, [9]. The method has mainly been developed to be able to cover a level set $S(f^* + \delta)$ which represents a confidence region in nonlinear parameter estimation. The idea is to cover with a sample of points $\mathcal{P}$ as if they are from a uniform distribution or with a so-called Raspberry set $R := \{x \in X \mid \exists p \in \mathcal{P}, \|x - p\| \le c \times r\}$, where

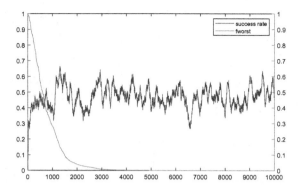

Fig. 2. Development of CRS for the Trid Hessian H_{T10}. In orange the reached function value of the worst point in the population and in blue the success rate.

r is a small radius following the idea of the average nearest neighbor distance for approximating the inverse of the average density of points over S and c a parameter, see Algorithm 3. We will use a value of $c = 1.3$ in the experiments as suggested in [4].

Algorithm 3. UCPR(f, X, N, c)

Generate and evaluate a set $\mathcal{P}$, of N random points uniformly on X
repeat
    Find the worst point q in the population $\mathcal{P}$, $q \leftarrow \text{argmax}_{p \in \mathcal{P}} f(p)$
    fworst$\leftarrow f(q)$
    determine the average inter-point distance r in $\mathcal{P}$
    Raspberry set $R := \{x \in X \mid \exists p \in P, \|x - p\| \le c \times r\}$
    Generate and evaluate x from a uniform distribution over R
    if $(f(x) <$fworst$)$
        Replace, in $\mathcal{P}$, point q by x
until (stopping criterion)

Like CRS, the UCPR algorithm has a theoretical fixed success rate with respect to spherical functions that does not depend on level fworst$= \max_{p \in P} f(p)$ that has been reached. The success rate goes down with increasing dimension, as the probability mass goes to the boundary of the level set if dimension n increases. Therefore, more of the Raspberry set sticks out. Moreover, it suffers more from highly skewed Hessians, i.e. the condition number differs from 1.

We are going to measure these effects running the algorithm for the 7 instances in Table 1 using the same population size as for CRS. First, the development of the population for the highest condition number case H_S is sketched in Fig. 3. One can observe a fast convergence and the aim to cover all the level set with the population.

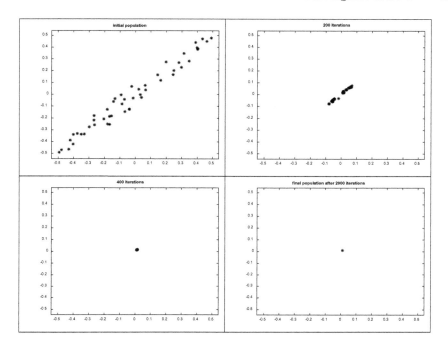

Fig. 3. Population development of UCPR on Hessian H_S.

The results for the 7 instances in Table 3 show us that UCPR has a strong local search behaviour, but in contrast to CRS, the success rate is going down with the dimension. Moreover, we can observe, that the behaviour is far more affected by the condition number. Actually, for the 2-dimensional cases, the algorithm converges too fast to a non-optimal point. For the largest cases, it seems not to have reached the optimum after 10,000 evaluations, due to a low success rate. Probably the algorithm requires a better tuning of the parameter c to the dimension n. In the presented theory, this should be correct automatically due to the nearest neighbour distance concept. Figure 4 depicts the relatively constant behaviour of the success rate for the Trid instance H_{T5}.

Table 3. Order of magnitude reached function value for the worst point in the population fworst after $1000n$ evaluations and average success rate $\overline{S}$ for UCPR

Hessian	I_2	I_5	I_{10}	H_S	H_{T2}	H_{T5}	H_{T10}
dim n	2	5	10	2	2	5	10
pop N	50	50	100	50	50	50	100
fworst	10^{-2}	10^{-8}	0.40	10^{-4}	0.01	10^{-8}	0.14
$\overline{S}$		0.94	0.41	0.05	0.92	0.93	0.40	0.09

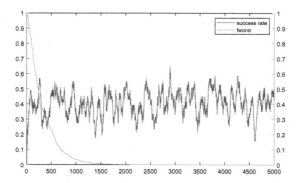

Fig. 4. Development of UCPR for the Trid Hessian H_{T5}. In orange the reached function value of the worst point in the population and in blue the success rate.

3.3   Genetic Algorithm

Although evolutionary algorithms existed before, Genetic Algorithms (GA) became known after the appearance of the book by Holland in 1975 [7] followed by many other works such as [2]. The generic population algorithm generates at each iteration a set of trial points based on a terminology from biology and nature: evolution, genotype, natural selection, reproduction, recombination, chromosomes etc. For instance, the average inter-point distance in a population is called diversity. The basic concepts as depicted in Algorithm 4 are the following

- the objective function is transformed into a fitness value,
- the points in the population are called individuals,
- points of the population are selected for making new trial points: parent selection for generating offspring,
- candidate points are generated by combining selected points: crossover,
- candidate points are varied randomly to become trial points: mutation,
- new population is composed from selecting from old and new points.

Algorithm 4. GA(f, X, N, M)

Generate and evaluate a set $\mathcal{P}$, of N random points uniformly on X
repeat
        Parent selection: select points used for generating candidates
        Crossover: create M candidates from selected points
        Mutation: vary candidates towards M trial points (offspring)
        Selection: create a new population out of $\mathcal{P}$ and the M trials
until (stopping criterion)

The fitness $F(x)$ of a point giving its objective function value $f(x)$ to be minimized can be taken via a linear transformation using extreme values $\max_{p \in \mathcal{P}} f(p)$ and $\min_{p \in \mathcal{P}} f(p)$. A higher fitness provides a higher probability to be selected as a parent. The probability for selecting point $p \in P$ is often taken as $\frac{F(p)}{\sum_{q \in \mathcal{P}} F(q)}$. Parameters of the algorithm deal with choices on: fitness transformation, the way of probabilistic selection, the number of parents, etc. We used the ga function from MATLAB2018b® implementation with the default values for the parameters to measure the convergence. Actually, we found that we have to include bounds to the search space in a box (bounds on the variables) around the initial population $\mathcal{P}_0$ in order to have convergence of the complete population. The observed convergence values can be found in Table 4.

In earlier experiments, we were surprised to observe that using smaller population size, it appeared possible that duplicates of the same points appeared in the population. Probably therefore, every now and then a refreshment of the population takes place, as can be observed very well for the higher dimensional cases in Fig. 5. It may be clear that the algorithm, in contrast to CRS and UCPR, also accepts points that are worse in the population. Basically, the behaviour means that up to a stopping criterion is reached, GA keeps on a global search behaviour, even when the population settled around the minimum point. This can be observed very well for the H_{T10} case in Fig. 5, where the population converged after evaluation 8000 and then diverged again towards the total search space. There is no notable distinction with respect to the condition number of the Hessian.

Table 4. Order of magnitude reached function value fworst for the worst point in the population after $1000n$ evaluations and average success rate $\overline{S}$ for GA

Hessian	I_2	I_5	I_{10}	H_S	H_{T2}	H_{T5}	H_{T10}
dim n	2	5	10	2	2	5	10
pop N	50	50	200	50	50	50	200
fworst	10^{-5}	10^{-5}	0.05	10^{-4}	10^{-6}	10^{-6}	11.04
$\overline{S}$	0.98	0.98	0.99	0.98	0.93	0.97	0.97

3.4   Particle Swarm Algorithm

Kennedy and Eberhart in 1995 [8], came up with an algorithm with a terminology of "swarm intelligence" and "cognitive consistency". In each iteration of the algorithm, each member (particle) of the population $\mathcal{P}$, called swarm, is modified and evaluated. The traditional nonlinear programming modification by direction and step size is termed "velocity". Instead of considering $\mathcal{P}$ as a set, one better thinks of a list of elements, $p_j, j = 1, \ldots, N$. So we will use the index j for the particle. Besides its position p_j, also the best point z_j found by p_j is stored.

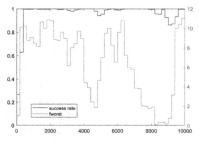 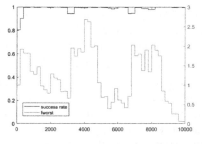

Hessian based on Trid, H_{T10} Identity matrix I_{10}

Fig. 5. Behaviour of GA for $n = 10$. In orange the reached function value fworst of the worst point in the population and in blue the success rate.

A matrix of modifications (velocities) $[v_1, \ldots, v_N]$ is updated at each iteration containing random effects. The velocity v_j is based on points p_j, z_j and the best point found so far $x_b = \operatorname{argmin}_j f(z_j)$ in the complete swarm. In the next iteration, simply $p_j \leftarrow p_j + v_j$ as sketched in Algorithm 5. We will use the notation $D(x)$ for a diagonal matrix with the elements of x on the diagonal.

Algorithm 5. PSO(f, X, N, ω)

Generate and evaluate a set $\mathcal{P}$, of N random points uniformly on X
$\mathcal{Z} \leftarrow \mathcal{P}$; $v_j \leftarrow 0$, $j = 1, \ldots, N$
repeat
    $x_b \leftarrow \operatorname{argmin}_{z \in \mathcal{Z}} f(z)$, $f_b \leftarrow f(x_b)$
    for $(j = 1$ to $N)$ **do**
        generate vectors r and u uniformly over $[0, 1]^n$
        $v_j \leftarrow \omega v_j + 2D(r)(z_j - p_j) + 2D(u)(x_b - p_j)$
        $p_j \leftarrow p_j + v_j$; evaluate $f(p_j)$
        if $(f(p_j) < f(z_j))$
            $z_j \leftarrow p_j$
until (stopping criterion)

To study its convergence behaviour, we used the `particleswarm` function from MATLAB2018b® with its default parameter values. Like for GA, we also put bounds on the search space around the initial population $\mathcal{P}_0$ to avoid the swarm to go far away from the initial population. We were surprised by a far stronger local search behaviour of the swarm towards the minimum point than the GA algorithm. Very small values were reached. This effect is not directly clear from the pseudo-code description in Algorithm 5. The question with respect to the condition number, is very relevant for the PSO algorithm, as we can observe in Fig. 6. The geometric mechanism of generating new points is not insensitive to scaling of the swarm. First of all, we were surprised by the strange acceptance of worse points for I_{10} after about 2400 iterations. This is not a random effect,

Table 5. Order of magnitude reached function value fworst of the worst point in the population after $1000n$ evaluations and average success rate $\overline{S}$ for PSO

Hessian	I_2	I_5	I_{10}	H_S	H_{T2}	H_{T5}	H_{T10}
dim n	2	5	10	2	2	5	10
pop N	20	50	100	20	20	50	100
fworst	10^{-20}	10^{-12}	10^{-6}	10^{-9}	10^{-24}	10^{-10}	3.25
$\overline{S}$	0.97	0.98	0.98	0.97	0.97	0.98	0.98

i.e. we repeated the same run with many random numbers and observed the same bubble in the graph, corresponding to a diversity action. More impressive is the behaviour with respect to instance H_{T10}. It seems the swarm keeps on expanding cyclically hindering a clear convergence like for instance I_{10}.

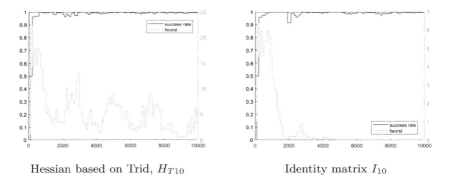

Hessian based on Trid, H_{T10} Identity matrix I_{10}

Fig. 6. Behaviour of PSO for dimension $n = 10$. In orange the reached function value of the worst point in the population and in blue the success rate.

3.5 Differential Evolution

The algorithm, published by Storn and Price in 1997 [12], has a big impact on application in engineering environments. Probably its schedule is very attractive due to its simplicity. For each point p in the population, a trial point is created based on three other points in the population using a so-called differential weight β, which we will draw uniformly from a box. Each component i is replaced with a certain so-called crossover probability γ. If the new trial point is better, then individual p is replaced by the trial point.

This means that like in CRS and UCPR, only better points are allowed in the new population. Like in these algorithms, when the population $\mathcal{P}$ is caught by a basin around a minimum, no global search in other regions is done. One can find an analysis of the non-convergence from some specific populations in [10]. This

---

Algorithm 6. DE$(f, X, N, \gamma, [\underline{B}, \overline{B}])$

Generate and evaluate a set $\mathcal{P}$, of N random points uniformly on X
repeat
    for $(p \in \mathcal{P})$ **do**
        draw three points (a, b, c) randomly from $\mathcal{P}$
        pick component j uniformly from $\{1, \ldots, n\}$
        generate β uniformly over $[\underline{B}, \overline{B}]^n$
        trial point $x \leftarrow p$ and set component $x_j \leftarrow a_j + \beta_j(b_j - c_j)$
        for the other components $(i \neq j)$ **do**
            with probability γ set component $x_i \leftarrow a_i + \beta_i(b_i - c_i)$
        if $(f(x) < f(p))$
            $p \leftarrow x$
until (stopping criterion)

---

is in contrast to the Genetic algorithm we have seen and the Particle Swarm algorithm. In a Markovian sense, the basin around the minimum works as an attraction state set. This means that we expect a strong local search behaviour of the algorithm.

Table 6. Order of magnitude reached function value fworst for the worst point in the population after $k = 1000n$ evaluations and average success rate $\overline{S}$ for DE

Hessian	I_2	I_5	I_{10}	H_S	H_{T2}	H_{T5}	H_{T10}
dim n	2	5	10	2	2	5	10
pop N	20	50	100	20	20	50	100
fworst	10^{-23}	10^{-9}	10^{-4}	10^{-5}	10^{-17}	0.04	0.61
$\overline{S}$	0.99	0.99	0.99	0.96	0.98	0.98	0.99

A description of the used experimental variant[2] is depicted in Algorithm 6. The population size was taken as $N = \min(10n, 100)$, the crossover probability was taken as $\gamma = 0.2$ and the differential weight is taken from the interval $[\underline{B}, \overline{B}] = [0.2, 0.8]$.

The strong local search behaviour after the population reaches a minimum point can be observed in Table 6. From the reproduction mechanism, it is more clear than for the PSO or GA algorithms that the process is thought of component-wise. This means that the population does not automatically adapt to the shape of the level set. We can observe this effect very well in Fig. 7. For the high condition number instance H_{T10}, the algorithm does not find improvements easily for the worst point in the population for a long time. For the instance I_{10} with spherical level sets, the probability of finding better points is relatively constant.

---

[2] Taken from https://yarpiz.com/231/ypea107-differential-evolution.

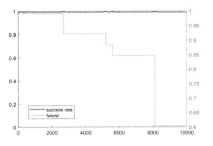 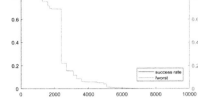

Hessian based on Trid, H_{T10} Identity matrix I_{10}

Fig. 7. Behaviour of DE for dimension $n = 10$. In orange the reached function value of the worst point in the population and in blue the success rate.

3.6 Firefly Algorithm

The Firefly algorithm (FA) was introduced by Yang in 2008 [14], as a variant of the PSO algorithm based on nature inspired mechanisms. Each point in the population is moved towards all better points having a so-called higher lightness in the population adding a random mutation. Then all individuals are evaluated again.

Algorithm 7. FA$(f, X, N, \alpha, \beta, \gamma)$

Generate a set $\mathcal{P}$ of N random points uniformly on X
repeat
    Evaluate and rank $f(p)$ for all $p \in \mathcal{P}$
    for all $(p \in \mathcal{P})$ **do**
        for all $(q \in \mathcal{P}$ with $f(q) \leq f(p))$ **do**
            generate a pseudo random number ε from the Normal distribution
            $p \leftarrow p + \beta e^{-\gamma \|p-q\|^2} + \alpha \varepsilon$
until (stopping criterion)

For the experiments, we used the MATLAB code that Yang published in [14] with parameter values $\alpha = 0.25$ (randomness), $\beta = 0.20$ (attraction parameter) and $\gamma = 1$ (absorption coefficient). These last two parameters are used in the exponential function for calculating the attractiveness between fireflies. The implementation requires bounds on the variables in order to use a good scaling. However, we found that for the instances we use this is not relevant due to the way the initial population is taken uniformly over the level set with a function value of 1. Actually, the algorithm can easily be extended to deal with constrained problems, [1].

In contrast to the particle swarm algorithm, no moves are based on the best point in the population. Basically, the population focuses towards the center of the population with only additional random effects. Therefore, we expect

Table 7. Order of magnitude reached function value fworst of the worst point in the population after $1000n$ evaluations and average success rate $\overline{S}$ for FA

Hessian	I_2	I_5	I_{10}	H_S	H_{T2}	H_{T5}	H_{T10}
dim n	2	5	10	2	2	5	10
pop N	20	50	100	20	20	50	100
fworst	10^{-7}	10^{-4}	0.20	10^{-6}	10^{-7}	10^{-4}	0.32
$\overline{S}$	0.98	0.99	0.99	0.97	0.98	0.98	0.99

the algorithm like UCPR to shape better along the level set of the function. This effect can be observed in Fig. 8, where the algorithm seems not affected by the condition number of the Hessian. We observe however, that for the high dimensional cases the population initially deviates from the initial level set. As depicted in Table 7, it has a strong convergence to the minimum point.

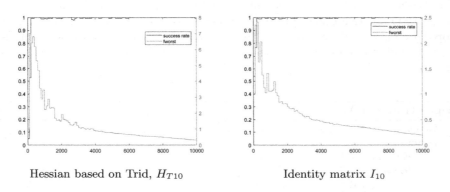

Hessian based on Trid, H_{T10} Identity matrix I_{10}

Fig. 8. Behaviour of FA for dimension $n = 10$. In orange the reached function value of the worst point in the population and in blue the success rate.

4 Conclusions

We investigated the convergence behavior towards a minimum point of 6 population metaheuristics when the initial population starts around the point. We varied the dimension and condition number of the Hessian in the minimum point. The algorithms CRS, UCPR and DE only accept better points within the new population, whereas GA, PSO and FA keep a global search behavior. For GA, this is due to periodic refreshment of the population. We found that GA and PSO require a bounding around the initial population in order not to diverge.

CRS appears completely insensitive to the shape of the Hessian and converges strongly to one point, whereas UCPR and DE are far more sensitive and for the highest condition number converge much slower. The FA algorithm converges slow for all cases, whereas the GA and PSO do not converge well when the level sets around the minimum are not round.

References

1. Costa, M.F.P., Francisco, R.B., Rocha, A.M.A.C., Fernandes, E.M.G.P.: Theoretical and practical convergence of a self-adaptive penalty algorithm for constrained global optimization. J. Optim. Theory Appl. **174**, 875–893 (2017)
2. Davis, L.: Handbook of Genetic Algorithms. Van Nostrand Reinhold, New York (1991)
3. Gill, P.E., Murray, W., Wright, M.H.: Practical Optimization. Academic Press, New York (1981)
4. Hendrix, E.M.T., Klepper, O.: On uniform covering, adaptive random search and raspberries. J. Glob. Optim. **18**, 143–163 (2000)
5. Hendrix, E.M.T., Ortigosa, P., Garcia, I.: On success rates for controlled random search. J. Glob. Optim. **21**, 239–263 (2001)
6. Hendrix, E.M.T., Tóth, B.G.: Introduction to Nonlinear and Global Optimization. Springer, New York (2010). https://doi.org/10.1007/978-0-387-88670-1
7. Holland, J.H.: Adaptation in Natural and Artificial Systems. University of Michigan Press, Ann Arbor (1975)
8. Kennedy, J., Eberhart, R.C.: Particle swarm optimization. In: Proceedings of IEEE International Conference on Neural Networks, pp. 1942–1948. Piscataway, NJ (1995)
9. Klepper, O., Hendrix, E.M.T.: A comparison of algorithms for global characterization of confidence regions for nonlinear models. Environ. Toxicol. Chem. **13**(12), 1887–1899 (1994)
10. Locatelli, M., Vasile, M.: (Non) convergence results for the differential evolution method. Optim. Lett. **9**(3), 413–425 (2014). https://doi.org/10.1007/s11590-014-0816-9
11. Price, W.: A controlled random search procedure for global optimization. Comput. J. **20**, 367–370 (1979)
12. Storn, R., Price, K.: Differential evolution - a simple and efficient heuristic for global optimization over continuous spaces. J. Glob. Optim. **11**(4), 341–359 (1997)
13. Törn, A., Žilinskas, A. (eds.): Global Optimization. LNCS, vol. 350. Springer, Heidelberg (1989). https://doi.org/10.1007/3-540-50871-6
14. Yang, X.S.: Nature-Inspired Metaheuristic Algorithms. Lunivers Press, Bristol (2008)

International Workshop on Cities, Technologies and Planning (CTP 2021)

MilanoAttraverso.
Telling the Story of Social Inclusion of Milan Through Digitised Archives Linked to Historical Cartography

Letizia Bollini[(⊠)] [iD]

Free University of Bozen-Bolzano, 39100 Bolzano, Italy
`letizia.bollini@unibz.it`

Abstract. In the last two decades, Milan has undergone profound transformations from both an urban and social perspective. The online project *MilanoAttraverso*, promoted by ASP Golgi Redaelli and by a network of local private and public archives and institutions, wants to give back to the community the history of Milan as the centre of a network of solidarity and social inclusion, from National Unity to today. The knowledgebase open to citizenship includes the digitised and curated primary archival and documentary sources displayed and presented according to three structural organisation criteria: the narrative paths and stories, the protagonists – people, institutions and communities, and the historical cartographies were documents – texts, images, multimedia, maps and objects – are geo-based and contextualised according to space and time criteria. The paper presents and critically discusses the case study and, in particular, the three modes of navigation/experience – logical, narrative and visual – offered as an access point to users.

Keywords: Geo-based narrative · Storytelling design in the field of Cultural Heritage · Digitized archives · User experience design

1 Introduction: *Milan l'è un gran Milan*

Milano is known for being the "European capital" of Italy: a dynamic, contemporary metropolis looked at like an attractive place for innovations, talents, rich of opportunities and leading in different sectors, among those, finance, design and fashion.

In the last two decades, many important areas have been progressively changing thanks to urban planning and economic dynamics [1]. Zona *Garibaldi-Isola*, with the new skyscrapers district, has become one of the most hipster and innovative places. The transformation of some dismissed industries has created new cultural poles, and university campuses – i.d. Politecnico-Bovisa, Pirelli-Bicocca [2] – the old Fiera (ex Expo area) is now *CityLife*, a rich and modern residential suburb, and Prada with the Fondazione is writing a new chapter in a peripheral railway transit and cargo hub [3]. Some other places are emerging, more spontaneously and according to a bottom-up process, as interesting nodes with their own personality: *Porta Venezia District*, the LGTB + friendly zone, Via Tortona and then Ventura-Lambrate "invaded" by the *FuoriSalone*, or *NoLo* (North of

© Springer Nature Switzerland AG 2021
O. Gervasi et al. (Eds.): ICCSA 2021, LNCS 12953, pp. 475–488, 2021.
https://doi.org/10.1007/978-3-030-86976-2_32

Loreto) with its ethnicity melting-pot, to mention few. As stated in a recent publication, these enclaves "quite apart from the rhetoric that would have the suburbs as the most degraded place or as the territory that has been reconciled and recomposed thanks to the action of its inhabitants, I think it is interesting to see in these places a potential expressed in terms of generating new citizenship and local welfare. [Neighbourhoods that also become] places for experimenting new practices of coexistence between different people, for example in intergenerational and intercultural terms." [4]. Besides, it is also famous for attractive events such as the *Milano Design Week (Salone Internazionale del Mobile)*, the Universal Expo held in 2015 – the place is now to become the new campus of Milan State University and a research center – and the Olympics Winter Games planned in 2026. all of them have deeply internationalised the city and transformed it into a plausible touristic destination.

On the one hand, the massive and progressive evolution has (had) a massive impact on the social structure. The urban transformation has pushed many citizens and small businesses away from their original locations due to renovations or the unaffordable increase in rental prices and property costs. Furthermore, as almost every place attractive for city-users and (mass)tourism, Milano is suffering from gentrification [5]. The phenomena according to the territories are shaped more by the needs of temporary visitors rather than by inhabitants themselves. On the other hand, the working and studying opportunities [6] offered continued to attract the population to the metropolis since the 1950s. Milano has welcomed immigrants from peripheral areas and the south of Italy.

In the last 30 years, the trend has concerned new European citizens, largely from Eastern Europe and the Balkan Peninsula since the 1990s, and migrants from outside the EU geographical boundaries, from developing countries or the so-called Third World. The successive waves of migration are a continuous process that fluctuates between the two extremes of the spectrum, which means marginalisation and integration. The city and the vast urban area (Città Metropolitana) has been an osmotic space in which the phenomenon of urbanisation and migration has given rise to divergent dynamics. Milan has demonstrated an excellent capacity for welcoming and offering better living conditions for many new inhabitants, but it has also meant exclusion, marginalisation and the formation of enclaves where the poor mixing of historical residents and newcomers, tradition and new cultures has created friction in social terms. A contradiction that has often found a deep mismatch between reality and its representation in political propaganda. Flattened by a debate that risks reducing it to a distorted image of contemporaneity that gives a partial view of the complexity and sedimentation that makes it, on the contrary, so articulated and different from other Italian cities crystallised in their historical and artistic past.

Nevertheless, the evolution of Milano is short and *long* at the same time. The metropolitan area – the original settlement was established around 600 BC and conquered by Romans in 222 BC, who named it *Mediolanum* – has been limited to the inner ring road, defined by the *Spanish Walls* (dating back 1550) for centuries [7]. It's only in 1873, with the inclusion of external areas, nearby villages, farms, and small municipalities – the *Annessione dei Corpi Santi,* i.e. peripheral spaces outside the walls were people, the *martyrs* in the early Christian era, where buries – that the city starts to expand outside the historical boundaries. The further transformation is fast and astonishing. Less than a century later, the city has reached the full expansion of the nowadays limits of the actual municipality (the metropolitan area includes other towns in a vast *continuum* of the conurbation and expands in many directions: see Fig. 1).

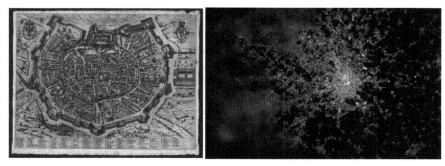

Fig. 1. Comparison between the map of Milano drawn by Mario Cartaro in 1581 (Source: Biblioteca Nacional de Portugal in Lisbon) and Milan by night photographed by astronaut Paolo Nespoli from the International Space Station (ISS) (Source: Flickr author profile). The original historical city-centre of the map on the left corresponds to the brightest centre of the image on the right.

At the same time, the presence of Italian internal migration phenomena [8] or the establishment of foreign communities is not as recent as believed by many. As reminded by Bigatti in the text *Milan and migrants from Unification to the present day*: "In the mid-19th century, Milan [...] was a city of about 150,000 inhabitants. Of these, almost 10% were the so-called floating population, 'poor, uncouth, importunate, uncivilised people'. People who had a seasonal relationship with the city, often living in its immediate suburbs, until 1873 a separate municipality, sleeping in makeshift lodgings or in simple barns. [...] In the decades following the Unification of Italy there were no significant changes in this respect. The town grew, changed, expanded and continued to attract people from outside. [...] Between 1881 and 1911, a period marked by significant growth in the industrial fabric, the number of residents rose from 321,839 to 599,200. After the Great War, the population continued to grow. In 1921 the number of inhabitants exceeded 700,000, rising to over a million ten years later, thanks in part to the aggregation of eleven small municipalities in the metropolitan belt." [9] This is the period in which Milan becomes the industrial city that will make the suburbs grow and which, together with other northern centres, especially Turin, will become a pole of attraction after the Second World War. At the beginning of the 1960s, it was these flows that radically changed the way people moved around, both in terms of the scale of the phenomenon and the problems of integration and integration that it caused for urban structures and the labour market.

Peasant Italy was transformed into an industrial country and Milan – as sung by Gaber and Jannacci – began the process of tertiarisation that was to turn it into the "Milano da bere" [*Milan to drink*] of the 1980s. It is from this period that the immigration process changes, and internal flows are joined by those from non-EU countries in successive waves that also characterise the contemporary city.

2 *MilanoAttraverso*: Telling the Story of Social and Urban Transformation

The project *MilanoAttraverso. People and places that transform the city* [10] established by the *Azienda di Servizi alla Persona "Golgi Redaelli"* under the direction of the dott. Bescapè, director of the *Servizio Archivio e Beni Culturali* [Archives and historical heritage service] and the supervision of dott.ssa Aiello, financially supported by Fondazione Cariplo and Fondazione AEM and shared by numerous Milanese institutions and cultural associations – here presented as a case study – intends to bring to the attention to a broad public the less known history of hospitality, inclusion and philanthropism of many individuals, public and private institutions thanks to documents and maps stored in different civic, private archives joining and sharing a partnership (https://www.mil anoattraverso.it/soggetti-della-rete/). The project, which is part of the broader context of urban narrative, aims to bring together the real city with its representation – toxic or triumphalist – in order to create awareness of the complexity and richness of the debate on its territory and its social vocation, not only in urban and economic terms. The project also indirectly addresses the issue of the gap between the real and the perceived, which in the period 2018–19 – the same period in which the portal was conceived, developed and published online – has been exploited in Italian politics to steer and manipulate public opinion [11]. *MilanoAttraverso*, by approaching the topic from a historical point of view and perspective, inserts that physiological temporal detachment that allows for a more objective and documented focus on the topic and, at the same time, uses social tools of participation to bring citizens closer to a different storytelling of the phenomena.

The project "wants to give back to the community the history of Milan as the centre of a network of solidarity and social inclusion, from national unity to the present day. Since the nineteenth century, Milan has been able to invent innovative structures and tools to welcome people in search of better living conditions and to meet the social needs of the 'new Milanese'. MilanoAttraverso makes today's citizens aware of the richness of the past experiences of Milanese solidarity, which can also be interpreted as a starting point to read the present differently. [Besides] the network, made up of organisations with strong territorial roots, aims to bring to light the patterns of assistance and social inclusion that run through the history and face of Milan. The project will emerge through stories of encounters, of gratitude, but also of transformations and transitions. [...] The project is guided by a dynamic and valuing research of sources and involves the public trying to activate processes of critical awareness. All the experiences are collected in the web platform, while the activation of dedicated social channels keeps the dialogue with the city open." [12].

The case study *MilanoAttraverso* has the peculiarity of narrating the contemporary and intercepting the possible future social and urban trends of the city of Milan through its history and its past topology. Based on a solid network of archives already operating on the territory, on the availability of widespread editorial group and on an archival heritage already partially digitised and curated, the project creates common ground through an interdisciplinary approach: historians – specialised on different topics e.d. photography – archivists, designers, developers, social media experts and people operating in the social and voluntary world with a strong connection with the territories have been involved in producing a shared vision collectively.

Besides, working with a network of public and private bodies has made it possible to exploit the potential offered by digital and hypertext notation [13]. In other words, the possibility of relocating and migrating chunks of information from their physical location, in this case, the document and archive, and clustering them according to "meaningful" criteria [14]. Moreover, the richness of the archives involved – containing not only textual documents such as correspondence, texts, but also paintings, photographs, historical cartographic images, relics, objects and multimedia content – offers a vast repertoire of narrative possibilities as proposed by Withelaw when mentioning the *generous* interfaces [15] approach to be applied in the field of digital heritage.

3   The Storytelling Matrix and the People Assessment

The initial research phase, aimed at delimiting the scope of research and mapping best practices in the field, outlined the state of the art and critically defined some significant patterns. In particular, the survey started by identifying and analysing a number of case studies in order to define, on the one hand, similar experiences and, on the other hand, possible suggestions and solutions [16].

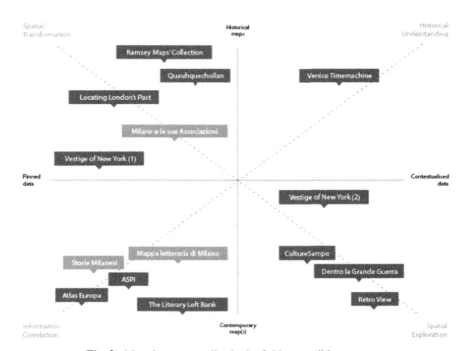

Fig. 2. Mapping case studies in the field: a possible taxonomy

The proposed taxonomy organises (see Fig. 2, above) the case studies along two axes which consider the two macro-criteria adopted in the project as differential. The first refers to the territory and the way of relating the data to their spatial location. On one extreme, the simple "pin" is understood as pure positioning; on the other, "contextualization", i.e. the ability to integrate the data – document, image, text, fragment – in relation to a conceptual, cultural and social location. The second axis, on the other hand, considers temporal aspects and their representation on contemporary cartographies (in fact Google Maps) or referred to the historical thresholds examined to which the information and documents refer. Crossing these two parameters along the diagonals outlines possible keys to interpretation which have been summarised in 4 key words/concepts under which some patterns identified from the research and case study analysis can be clustered. The latter outline possible applications and developments and as many interpretations of the evolution of urban and social transformation phenomena.

Furthermore, among the case studies taken into consideration, similar experiences already developed with reference to the Milan territory were investigated and, specifically, the *Literary Maps of Milan* (a), the *Milanese Stories* (b) and *Milan and its associations* (c).

The second phase research activities focused mainly on the information architecture [17] of the system that means "we arrange the parts of something to make it understandable" as stated by Abby Covert [18]. The aim was to make the contents accessible in both cultural and technical terms, as well from different perspectives to a wide public allowing people to find their personal paths to knowledge, addressing their needs, behaviors and motivations. The end result is a rich and articulated multi-path navigation allowing the contents to be approached from different sides.

In fact, hypertext structures are generally organised according to a hierarchical pattern that allows one to descend, from *global* to *local*, into the information until one reaches the last leave/node. The different levels use criteria – Location, Alphabet, Time, Category and Hierarchy – as described by Wurmann [19] to cluster homogeneous contents. The experience offered is *logic*: the structure progressively leads the user following a rational and vertical process that leads from an *overview* – Protagonists, i.e. i) People; ii) Institutions; iii) Communities – to *detail:* the card of every document listed in the knowledge-base, although stored elsewhere. Each *leaf* proposes and opens up new explorations thanks to an associative system – the contextual navigation – which supports learner orientation in the digital environment and nudge people to jump around [20]. In addition to this possibility, readers are introduced to the themes of *MilanoAttraverso* thanks to a series of thematic essays edited by historians who deal with evolution of the city in a *narrative* way. For instance, the path about *Migrants. Milan and migrants from the Unification to today* [9] brings the user into the stories of people and their experience in Milano: *The 'circulating libraries' for Italian emigrants, Residential course on emigration, Michele Fortunato's 'eagerness'* or *A house for the Trentino people* are just some of the narratives that translate the official history into individual stories, bringing out the social, human and emotional component (Fig. 3).

Finally, the system uses historical cartographies to show visually and diachronically co-presences, phenomena and transformations. The selected maps cover the time span from 1856 to the present day (Google Maps) in 8 historical thresholds (1856, 1884,

Fig. 3. Historical images illustrating the card *Milan and Caporetto*

1906, 1928, 1943, 1965, 2000 and 2021). Each map represents, among the possible and available ones, a significant transitional moment in the transformation of the city and its social corpus (see Fig. 4). The possibility of superimposing them and displaying them transparently, one on top of the other, makes the morphological changes in the urban fabric visible and comparable. Besides, the maps also become an opportunity to "interrogate" the knowledgebase by correlating documents and cards to the space in which they are historically constituted. The filters – categories of institutions, types of documents, tags referring to urban areas and clusters, and historical-cartographic thresholds – help users, including experts, to relate the contents to the space that temporally generated them [21].

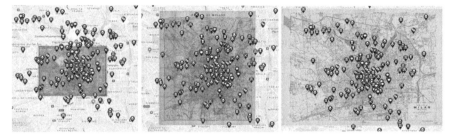

Fig. 4. Viewing maps from 1865 (a), 1906 (b) and 1928 (c) respectively, in which the rapid expansion of the city beyond the Spanish Walls is always very evident.

The three navigation systems identified, tested and implemented represent as many communication possibilities. The three approaches, *logical, narrative* and *visual* [22, 23], offer different types of users and users with different "needs" to access and interact with the stories and documents in specific ways, as well as the consultation strategies and experiences are modelled on different criteria: *association, exploration* and *filtering*, shaped by the different types of contents (Table 1).

Among the many aspects considered within the project, a few issues, in particular, emerged as priorities, both from a conceptual point of view as well as the users' experience.

The main topics addressed by the research have been:

Table 1. The Information Architecture/storytelling/experience matrix

Navigation	Content (typology)	Experience modalities
Logic	Protagonists: People, Institutions, Communities	Association
Narrative	Paths and Narratives	Exploration
Visual	Historical cartography and Google Maps	Filtering

- The active engagement on a cognitive as well on a more emotional level of a broader public to activate processes of critical awareness and participated citizenship
- Create a common platform for a distributed editorial staff to present, curate and connect the primary sources stored in the archives of the subjects joining the network
- Valorise and make documents open and accessible also to a public with no specific knowledge in the field
- Telling the history of the Milan territory, people and communities from the XIX century to the contemporaneity
- Connect documents with the historical cartography to better represent the urban evolution and transformation thanks to historical primary sources.

Therefore, the project is situated in terms of methodological approach in the area of practice-driven research in the field of design [24] and digital-humanities and approaches the experience from the point of view of human-centred design.

Among the possible methods [16], three different approaches in the field of qualitative/user research [25] were chosen, taking into account on the one hand the needs of the stakeholders and on the other hand those of the end users. This was done in a participatory manner [26]. A first exploratory phase involved domain experts - historians, archivists, editors, curators etc. – in an expert-walk through and evaluation of existing case studies identified among those analysed in the initial phase.

In the design phase, it was decided to co-design part of the solutions – especially the visualisation of documents on historical maps – together with the stakeholders, facilitating collaboration through paper prototyping [27], as presented in Fig. 5. A low-tech approach, where technology is often perceived as a barrier, brought out the implicit skills and knowledge of the experts – historians, curators and archivists, mainly – and transferred them into interactions and interfaces in a first prototype (see Fig. 6), which was then tested with users [28].

According to the Human-centered approach adopted in the project, after the co-design activities, a first working prototype was produced to be used both to validate the hypotheses made on the information architecture of the entire system, in its three navigation possibilities – logic, narrative, visual – and to verify the critical points and the overall experience with the stakeholder and end-users [29].

A sample of research participants has been selected to reflect the possible user-personas of the project: people age 18–54 among scholars, archivists, historians, fine art and art history students, architects and professionals in the field of the third sector, Ong, and social workers and volunteers. Internal stakeholders, such as the editors who are

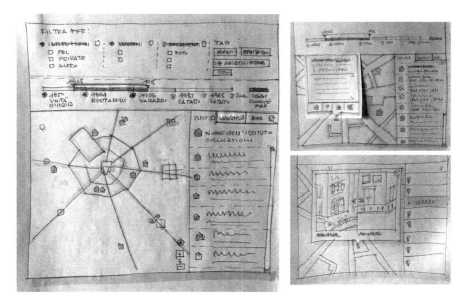

Fig. 5. Paper prototyping in co-design activities

part of the project consortium, as well as external people from heterogeneous audiences were involved in the evaluation sessions (for a discussion of this experimental phase and the results, see the article presented at EARTH 2018 [10]). The 24 participants were divided in two groups and asked to navigate the portal using two different approaches: a) the narrative/textual and the logic/hierarchical navigation and b) the visual one, namely the maps.

Four tasks have been proposed and verified: 1) access the historical evolution of an institution; 2) find the extended card about a person relating he/she to the institution; 3) contextualize and link both the information to time and space thanks to the historical cartography; 4) cluster group of institutions or document typologies according to common criteria in a specific time span to be compared with the current urban morphology.

The definition of "usability" established by the ISO 9241–11 (1998) has been adopted as evaluation criteria, to define, assess and qualify/quantify the overall experience. In particular, a) *efficiency* has been parameterised in terms of execution time, i.e. time taken to perform the given task; b) *efficacy* as the ability to complete a task and/or the number of errors made in doing so; c) *satisfaction*, investigated through a final narrative interview, as a qualitative feed-back on the overall experience. The results of the user tests were according to 3 further criteria: 1) the frequency with which certain problems or errors occurred in the performance of the tasks; 2) the types of problems and errors were then clustered according to Norman's interaction principles [30], i.e. a) visibility b) feedback c) constraints d) mapping e) consistency f) affordance; and finally 3) the type of intervention is prioritised in relation to the test results i.e. a) blocking, b) important, c) improvement.

As a spin-off of the verification and evaluation activity, a second iterative design cycle was conducted to develop the beta version of the system. In the second version, in particular, the filter system in the visual navigation mode was redefined both in terms of functionality and the terminology used to define concepts and categories (Figs. 7 and 8).

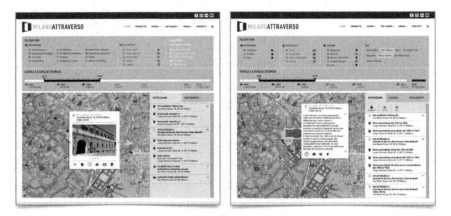

Fig. 6. First pilot version tested with users

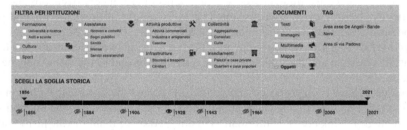

Fig. 7. Detail of the map filtering system: among possible criteria: Institutions, Type of historical-archival documents, Cartographic time thresholds and Tags

A final workshop was conducted together with all representatives of the archives that are part of the project network and consortium. In particular, the people who would later use the system to insert, integrate, edit and publish the contents – mainly document cards and cartographic location – on the website were involved. This last participatory activity, before the online publication and official launch of the project, served as a final check with the stakeholders and to align the members of the widespread editorial staff who, with their work and contribution, determine the real success of the project.

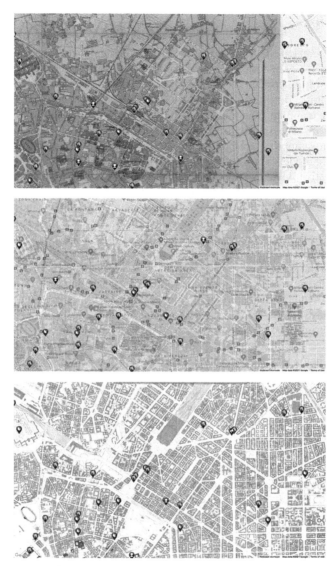

Fig. 8. The relocation of Milan's Central Station: Detail of overlapped maps thanks to the transparency effect. Top: the station built in 1864 in what is now Piazza della Repubblica shown on the 1906 map (the year of the International Expo of Sempione); In the middle: the current station (opened in 1931) on the 1928 Vallardi map, visible thanks to the transparency overlay effect aimed to compare maps; Bottom: the 2000 map.

4   Conclusions

The experience carried out on the case study *MilanoAttraverso*, follows a path undertaken to model the design of historical-archival-cultural heritage that introduces, in the process and as a driver of the project, the theme of storytelling [31] on the one hand and on the other the possibility to offer a rich and multimodal experience to users and it does it thanks to story-mapping. The metaphor of *generous* interfaces has been interpreted as the possibility of accessing data and the knowledge base from various touch points, choosing the most appropriate exploratory mode, both for the purpose and for the metal and experiential models of people. It has been further supported by the three-way access – logical, narrative, visual – offered to fulfil the user needs and expectations. Besides, the interdisciplinary combined approach of theory and practice-based research has been a way to frame the cultural and design hypothesis on the subject and then to assess them thank to the ideation, development, test and publication of the final version of the case study according to a modelling process that is both inductive and deductive and which, in tackling a real project, develops it concretely and formalises it, while making it replicable, at the same time.

Secondly, the network's potential to reconnect dispersed and dislocated fragments in a hypertextual manner was explored by creating a system of aggregation from entities, archives and institutions located throughout the Milan area. The approach has made it possible to bring together and connect heterogeneous and specific sources, giving a choral dimension to both the project and its contents: no longer vertical information on a single topic belonging to a specific collection or archive, but fragments in dialogue with others to recompose a complex, articulated and profound image of the city and its protagonists in space and time. In addition, the participatory experience of the editors and curators and their active involvement offered a common, fertile and inclusive ground for contaminating, integrating and *augmenting* the individual contributions in a choral and polyphonic narrative.

Thirdly, the decision to use not only geo-localisation but also historical cartography has made it possible to contextualise and narrate, also visually, the evolution of an area undergoing transformation, not only from an urban point of view but also, and above all, from a social one. The superimposition of the different historical thresholds, significant for the evolution of Milan, and the choice of corresponding and significant cartographies makes the of the transformation visible. The possibility of fading – the map's transparency/opacity effect – makes these visualisations easily comparable and highlights the changes in urban morphology.

Finally, among the possible developments of the project, a particularly promising one is the introduction of *user-generated contents* that will make the population of the city participate and be involved in a process of identity construction, not only from the historical perspective but also from bottom-up: a story not only written by the official protagonists, but also and above all, by the witnesses of the daily experience of transformation.

Acknowledgements. The activity presented in the paper is part of the research project promoted by the Azienda di Servizi alla Persona "Golgi Redaelli". Special thanks to Marco Bescapè and Lucia Aiello, leaders and coordinators of the project and the partner associations network. Thank you to Sara Radice, Fabio Sturaro and Michele Zonca with whom we designed and developed both the archive and the historical maps section; thanks to all the archivists and users who helped us to test, assess and improve the project: www.milanoattraverso.it.

References

1. Pasqui, G.: Politiche urbane, sviluppo locale e produzione di "immagini strategiche" del cambiamento territoriale, pp. 16–25. Franco Angeli, Milano (2000)
2. Bollini, L.: Territories of digital communities. Representing the social landscape of web relationships. In: Murgante, B., Gervasi, O., Iglesias, A., Taniar, D., Apduhan, B.O. (eds.) ICCSA 2011. LNCS, vol. 6782, pp. 501–511. Springer, Heidelberg (2011). https://doi.org/10.1007/978-3-642-21928-3_36
3. Fondazione Prada. https://www.fondazioneprada.org/mission. Accessed 10 Oct 2020
4. Cognetti, F., De Martiis, F., Gambino D., Lareno Faccini J.: Periferie del cambiamento. Traiettorie di rigenerazione tra marginalità e innovazione a Milano. Macerata Quodlibet (2020)
5. Carlucci, M., Chelli, F.M., Salvati, L.: Toward a new cycle: short-term population dynamics, gentrification, and re-urbanization of Milan. Sustainability **10**(9), 3014 (2018)
6. Viesti, G.: Nuove migrazioni. Il "trasferimento" di forza lavoro giovane e qualificata dal Sud al Nord, in il Mulino, Rivista bimestrale di cultura e di politica 4/2005, pp. 678–688
7. Della Peruta F.: (ed.) Storia illustrata di Milano, Elio Sellino Editore Verona (1993)
8. Panichella, N.: The Italian internal migration in the last century: old versus new migrations Stato e mercato. Rivista quadrimestrale **2**(2012), 255–282 (2012)
9. Bigatti, G.: Migrations. Milan and migrants from Unification to the present day. (2018). https://www.milanoattraverso.it/migrazione. Accessed 10 Oct 2020
10. Bollini, L.: Representing a space-based digital archive on historical maps: a user-centered design approach. In: Luigini, A. (ed.) EARTH 2018. AISC, vol. 919, pp. 599–607. Springer, Cham (2019). https://doi.org/10.1007/978-3-030-12240-9_62
11. Pelligra, V.: Migranti, il divario tra percezione e realtà. Il Sole 24Ore (2018). https://www.ils ole24ore.com/art/migranti-divario-percezione-e-realta-AEQa67IF. Accessed 10 Oct 2020
12. MilanoAttraverso. www.milanoattraverso.it. Accessed 10 Oct 2020
13. Bollini, L.: The digital space of knowledge: from archival forms to cultural knowledge-bases. Aggregations, narrations and migrations. In: Trocchianesi, R., Lupo, E.(eds.) Design & Cultural Heritage, vol. 3, pp. 53–66 (2013)
14. Ausubel, DP.: The psychology of meaningful verbal learning. (1963)
15. Whitelaw, M.: Towards generous interfaces for archival collections. In: Proceedings of International Council on Archives Congress (2012)
16. Hall, E.: Just Enough Research, 2nd edn. A Book Apart, San Francisco (2019)
17. Rosenfeld, L., Morville, P., Arango, J.: Information Architecture: For the Web and Beyond, 4th edn. O'Reilly Media, San Francisco (2015)
18. Covert, A.: How to Make Sense of Any Mess: Information Architecture for Everybody. CreateSpace Independent Publishing Platform (2014)
19. Wurman R. S.: Information Architects. Graphis Inc. (1997)
20. Bollini, L.: A Human-centered perspective on interactive data visualization. A digital flâneries into the documentation of Historical Italian Mind Science Archive. In: Ceccarelli, N., Jiménez-Martínez, C. (eds.) 2CO Communicating Complexity 2017, pp. 106–114. Santa Cruz de Tenerife: Universidad de La Laguna (2020)

21. Bollini, L., Begotti, D.: The time machine. cultural heritage and the geo-referenced storytelling of urban historical metamorphose. In: Gervasi, O., et al. (eds.) ICCSA 2017. LNCS, vol. 10406, pp. 239–251. Springer, Cham (2017). https://doi.org/10.1007/978-3-319-62398-6_17

22. Bollini, L., and Cerletti, V.: Knowledge sharing and management for local community: logical and visual georeferenced information access. In: International Conference on Enterprise Information Systems and Web Technologies (EISWT-09), pp. 92–99. ISRST (2009)

23. Bollini, L: The urban landscape and its social representation. A cognitive research approach to rethinking historical cultural identities. In: Amoruso, G. (ed.) Putting Tradition into Practice: Heritage, Place and Design, pp.834–842. INTBAU 2017. Lecture Notes in Civil Engineering, vol. 3. Springer, Cham (2018). https://doi.org/10.1007/978-3-319-57937-5_86

24. Eleven lessons. A study of the design process. Design Council. http://www.designcouncil.org.uk/sites/default/files/asset/document/ElevenLessons_Design_Council%20(2).pdf. Accessed 5 Oct 2020

25. Portigal, S.: Interviewing Users. How to Uncover Compelling Insights. Rosenfeld Media, New York (2013)

26. Rizzo, F.: Strategie di co-design. Teorie, metodi e strumenti per progettare con gli utenti. Franco Angeli, Milano (2009)

27. Todd Zaki Warfel: Prototyping. A Practitioner's Guide. Rosenfeld Media, New York (2009)

28. Tomer, S.: Validating Product Ideas. Through Lean User Research. Rosenfeld Media, New York (2016)

29. Krug, S.: Rocket Surgery Made Easy: The Do-It-Yourself Guide to Finding and Fixing Usability Problems. New Riders, San Francisco (2009)

30. Norman, D.: The Design of Everyday Things: Revised and, Expanded Basic Book, New York (2013)

31. Quesenbery, W.: Storytelling for User Experience. Crafting Stories for Better Design. Rosenfeld Media, New York (2010)

Space in Socio-technical Systems: Exploring the Agent-Space Relation

Maria Rosaria Stufano Melone[1]([⊠]), Stefano Borgo[2], and Domenico Camarda[1]

[1] Polytechnic University of Bari, Via Re David 200, 70125 Bari, Italy
{mariarosaria.stufanomelone,domenico.camarda}@poliba.it
[2] CNR-ISTC, Via alla Cascata 56/c, 38123 Trento, Italy
stefano.borgo@cnr.it

Abstract. Socio-technical systems (STS) described in literature today rely on multiple and different interaction patterns for their characterization. With the development of multi-agent systems (MAS) and formal interaction languages, the logical modeling of STS has improved. Yet these rich ongoing approaches require perspective changes and new features.

Developing within a research line on spatial urban studies, this paper takes physical space experience as a core perspective in the analysis of STS. Space experience is naturally central in human understanding and acting, and human spatial cognition provides therefore a powerful approach. This study explores the kind of knowledge that is centered on space in STS, and questions whether and how its variety can be managed and formalized.

In particular, the paper explored aspects of the configuration and relationships of the agentive and spatial components of urban environments, from an STS perspective, toward possible MAS-based prototypes of decision support architectures in urban contexts.

Keywords: Socio-technical systems · Ontological analysis · Spatial cognition · Multi-agent systems

1 Introduction

The characterization of socio-technical systems (STS) in the literature moves along these lines: "systems that involve a complex interaction between humans, machines and the environmental aspects of the work system" [7] and have five key characteristics [4, 7]: (i) have interdependent parts; (ii) adapt to and pursue goals in external environments; (iii) have an internal environment comprising separate but interdependent technical and social sub-systems; (iv) their goals can be achieved by more than one means; (v) their performance relies on the joint optimisation of the technical and social subsystems.

The first part of the STS description ("interaction between humans, machines and environmental aspects") is explicitly focusing on interactions and components, and the

---

The present study was carried out by the authors as a joint research work. Nonetheless, S.Borgo wrote §1, D.Camarda wrote §2 and §4, M.R.Stufano Melone wrote §3.

© Springer Nature Switzerland AG 2021
O. Gervasi et al. (Eds.): ICCSA 2021, LNCS 12953, pp. 489–502, 2021.
https://doi.org/10.1007/978-3-030-86976-2_33

view of STS as made of components is the center of the characterizations (i) and (iii). Points (ii) and (v) qualify the interactions as aiming to some goals (here understood as selected or desired states). Having multiple ways to achieve a goal, as stated in (iv), implies that different interaction patterns may achieve the sought state.

With the development of multi-agent systems and of formal languages for interaction [9], the logical modeling of socio-technical systems has improved. These rich approaches are still under development and require a change of perspective and thus the introduction of new features. Briefly, their potentialities today are only partially understood. To help in this endeavor, we investigate a fundamental issue that, unfortunately, has been largely disregarded in this literature: the notion of space. Of course, there is plenty of literature on space representation (geometrical and cognitive), space as environment (for navigation, perception and action), space as organization (spatial planning, decision science), and so on. Yet, socio-technical systems are complex entities with many facets, and any choice of a spatial approach from these viewpoints would look arbitrary. What we need is a holistic view of space in STS. (An analogous observation can be made about time.) Furthermore, the development of space in the listed communities presents a technical issue: these analyses developed specialized formalizations which we cannot assume are optimal, or even suitable, for a general theory of STS.

This paper falls within a research line on spatial urban studies. It takes physical space and its experience as a core perspective in the analysis of socio-technical systems. Physical space is naturally at the core of human understanding of reality and at the core of human acting in it. Moreover, the human cognitive module that deals with spatial structures is a powerful tool that humans exploit to model a variety of topics. Among the fundamental questions this research line aims to address is the kind of knowledge that is centered on space. Given the variety of roles that space takes in socio-technical systems, a further question is whether and how this variety can be integrated (managed and formalized). Of course, this also depends on the formalisms that have been explored so far and on the foreseeable developments. Finally, one wonders how one could test a general theory that tries to encompass all the space-related aspects of socio-technical system. We close this introduction noticing that the listed topics are nothing more than special cases of the following much broader research questions: I) How should we understand multi-faceted dimensions in socio-technical systems? II) How could we generate an integrated model for each dimension starting from existing formalisms? III) How could we test that the resulting theory is satisfactory and can be exploited alongside with theories for other dimensions?

The work explores particularly dimensions, instances and peculiarities of the relationships between the agentive/social element and the spatial/environmental element. These are elements that are individually endowed with intrinsic granularity, which allows them to be individually integral but also articulated, disaggregated - or possibly disaggregated.

In a socio-technical system, the possibility of maintaining a complex formalization of this organizational complexity guarantees a formidable support to aware decision-making, planning and management processes of the system itself. This is clearly a homothety (organizational complexity vs. representative complexity), desirable but also difficult to achieve operationally, based on an extended range of instances and attributes (typological, behavioral, attitudinal, dimensional, hierarchical data, etc.), even dynamically variable. However, research in the literature today increasingly reflects on the use of ontologies as a descriptor intrinsically consistent with the complexity of the sociotechnical system.

The present study is therefore placed in this ontological perspective, trying with a fine-grained approach to shed light on the relational aspects between agent and space, which seem fundamental in this perspective.

The aims of this paper within this domain is to discuss how space can and should be understood in cities here considered as a special class of socio-technical systems. The choice of cities as application case is driven by our previous analysis of these complex objects [10] and the need to make the resulting view accessible to urban planning study and modeling. The discussion remains mainly at the conceptual level with some observations into the processes of model development and formalization.

The paper is structured as follows. Section 2 deals with roles, configurations and interactions of the individual and social agents' level in spatial environments, with particular reference to decision-oriented tasks. Therefore, Sect. 3 discusses the representation of space at the knowledge level, first reasoning on a dynamic individual-collective dialectic toward space and then exploring approaches and methods toward space conceptualization. Brief remarks conclude the paper, envisioning the potentials of building formal models that seem not at our reach.

2   The Agentive/Social Level in Space

Social issues have been addressed within urban organizations and management from different points of view. Many perspectives are traditionally connected to sociological, anthropological and political aspects that have represented an indistinct magma often (mis-) interpretable only through political and sometimes even rhetorical filters [11]. Hence, for an analysis of the agentive level of space as an interactive place of connection and action, these perspectives seem logically not well objectifiable. In fact, they are vague or too aggregate to express clearly representable classes or agentive properties. Yet, especially since the middle of the last century, there is a growing interest in the field of decision theory in the individual behavioral dimension, as an essential element towards 'reasonable' rather than rational decisions in a collective arena of public interest [36]. In this context, there is an interesting articulation proposed by Forester (Fig. 1) [17] concerning the multiform limits that the relational organization between agents of a community can impose on the classic model of rational decision. This intriguing configuration, originated to operationally argue Simon's bounded rationality model, actually gives useful account of a complex system of agents, agencies and agent contexts - although mainly oriented towards an arena of institutional governance. In these arguments, space is present rather unusually as an actively determining element in accompanying, determining and sometimes participating in the relationships between the various agents that structure the decision-making dynamics. The relations between human agents and the space in this simplified world proposed by Forester are certainly of a mutually bidirectional type - whereas certain traditional domain models instead relegate space unfortunately to roles of inactive support for actions (and transformations) by agents that populate spaces. By closing doors and connecting environments, communication flows transfer information and determine relational ties between individuals, dynamically reprogramming decision-making contexts and, therefore, the activities of individuals themselves. A decision made in the solitude (or in the company) of an enclosed space is affected by knowledge limited to self-centered or self-connected relationships: only in this case (perhaps) does space take on typical features of an inactive static context. But it is a temporary and fleeting inactivity. The opening of passages immediately conveys new awareness, new arenas, new relationships and new levels of interaction. It determines new skills and new roles for the agents involved - not always and not necessarily emancipatory but also of decision-making risk and obstacle [17].

Type of Boundedness of Rationality	Conditions of Administrative/Planning Actions						
	Agent	Setting	Problem	Information	Time	Practical Strategy
Comprehensive (Unbouded)	Rational Actor	One Room (Closed System)	Well-defined Problem	Perfect Information	Infinite	Optimize/solve (algorithm, technique)
Simon: Cognitive Limits, e.g., (Bounded I)	Fallible Actor	Room Open to Environment	Ambiguous Scope, Basis of Evaluation	Imperfect	Limited	Satisfice/hedge, lower expectations
Socially Differentiated (Bounded II)	Several; Varying skills, insight; cooperative	Several rooms, phones, socially differentiated	Varying Interpretations	Varying Quality, Location, Accessibility	Varying with Actors	Network/search and satisfice
Pluralist (Lindblom) (Bounded III)	Actors in competing interest groups	Rooms in Organizations Variable access	Multiple Problem Definitions (Senses of Value, Right, Impacts)	Contested, Withheld, Manipulated	Time is Power	Bargain/ increment, acjust/check
Structurally Distorted/ Political-Economic (Habermas) (Bounded IV)	Actors in Political-Economic Structures of Inequality	Rooms in Relations of Power: Differential resources, skill, status	Ideological Problem definitions; Structurally Skewed	(Mis)information Ideological; contingent upon participation, "consciousness"	Time Favors "Haves"	Anticipate/ counteract, organize/ democratize

Fig. 1. Rationality and practice in administration and planning [17, p.27]

The evolution of these economic studies then goes on to point out the various collective decision contexts, increasingly specifying cognitive, relational and political-structural limits and the consequent final operational viability of a purely rational approach [2, 37]. In particular, through his well-known logical-mathematical theorem, Arrow shows the impossibility of a collective multi-agent decision based on the classic axioms of rationality, unless some of them is weakened or abandoned [1]. The typical formulation of this theorem starts from five axioms, namely: universal decidability of preferences, reachability of results, inadmissibility of choices imposed authoritatively, absolute transitivity of preferences, independence from irrelevant alternatives. Indeed, the mathematical development shows that the solution attempts depend either on a relativization of the transitivity of the preferences (the outcome depends on the different order in which the preferences are expressed, the so-called Condorcet paradox) [18] or on a final decision imposed by an agent who alone determines the result (the dictator of Arrow [1]). In fact, this circumstance implies that it is impossible to devise a system that fully conforms to the axiomatics of classical rationality, meaning that no strictly rational system is able to aggregate individual preferences into social choices, unless some of the conditions are loosened. The operating model emerging from this certified substantial unattainability of a pareto-optimal decision [41] takes on the less abstract, more 'reasonable' features of a behavioural approach, which is oriented towards decidability objectives that are not rationally optimal but satisfactory for the levels of effective operations required by the decision in a collective arena [37]. The research in literature subsequently focuses on attempts to overcome the limits to the rational approach, using qualitative political analysis models such as muddling-through or mixed-scanning approaches [14, 23]. However, the level of formalization introduced by Arrow remains quite useful in an ontological analysis perspective, such as that of the present work. This also in consideration of the growing interest in pure and applied mathematics research, which have produced further interesting reflections. A particularly innovative elaboration was built starting from the field of System Theory with the possibilistic function of Zadeh [46]. Following fuzzy logic, scholars have explored solutions to Arrow's theorem by proposing the aggregability of individual preferences according to different membership degrees, ordered within the typical fuzzy range [0; 1]. Interesting results have emerged from these attempts, which are still formally viable even if not yet fully shared and consolidated [16, 19, 26].

Even with a structurally oriented approach, the reflection on decision-making contexts presents an agentive dimension that connotes space beyond its prerogative of a simple background, towards a complex interactive and proactive essence. The urban space, the theme of this contribution, is a context of extremely varied agentive decisions that characterize a real 'system' of agents [6, 31]. In a sociospatial domain this shows up as an area of mutual multidimensional and multidirectional relationships between human agents, between human agents and non-human, biotic and abiotic, natural and artificial agents, etc. In addition to a multiplicity in terms of agent's type and nature, other elements can usefully be highlighted in the characterization of agents. According to consolidated literature, a multi-agent system (MAS) is a set of agents located in a certain environment and interacting with each other through a suitable organization [15, 42, 44]. In a MAS located in a socio-spatial environment that is defined in this way, some key characterizing problems can be highlighted, useful for representing the agentive/social level in urban space [15]:

1) The action-that is, the ways in which a set of agents acts simultaneously in a multi-characterized, fragmented space, and with which the space in turn interacts in response to the agents.
2) The cognitive model available to the agent - that is, the ways in which the cognitive structure of the agent relates to space.
3) The nature of interactions - intended as a source of both opportunities and constraints, in relation to the modalities (e.g. the language/s used) and the forms (e.g. collaboration, cooperation, altruism, selfishness) of relationship between agents.
4) Adaptation dynamics - both at an individual level (for example in terms of learning) and at a collective level (in terms of evolution-or involution).
5) The implementation processes - that is, the definition of formalization rules for spatial relationships and knowledge representation.
   Further questions can be added to these ones, concerning:
6) Multiple levels of operations - that is, different level activities that can be concentrated in a single agent, for example when circumstances cause specific agents to start high level functions in addition to routine activities.

7) Types of agents. According to Jacques Ferber, a classification of agents can be made through two criteria: a typological one (cognitive/reactive agents) or a behavioral one (teleonomic/reflex behavior). The typological distinction basically concerns the agent's representation of the world. A cognitive agent is able to draw reasoning from its symbolic representation of the world, while a reactive agent can only draw perceptions, that is, subsymbolic representations. The behavioral distinction, on the other hand, discriminates between the methods of action of the agents. A teleonomic behavior is connected to intentional actions towards explicit objectives, while a reflex behavior is connected to perceptual tendencies coming from the agents themselves or from the external environment [15].

8) The environmental agent. The space-environment can play different roles in a MAS model. Intended both as an artificial computer-based infrastructure and as a natural framework for the interaction between agents, the space-environment represents an essential part of the system. As mentioned above, it is often traditionally seen as a static field with zero or merely reactive attitudes towards external stimuli. However, even if only reactive attitudes are available, it can be categorized as a type of agent within a MAS model, with relations with external agents that explicitly require further investigation and formalization (Ferber and Muller, 1996). Moreover, in recent times the environment has also been interpreted as a proactive agent in some situations, with interesting attempts at modeling transactions interacting through theories and logical rules [22, 43]. In particular, in anthropic transformation processes with an impact on natural resources, environmental characteristics tend to be enhanced and can be elevated as proxies of environmental agents, for example in an environmental conservation perspective [30].

In this context, and in a perspective of analysis or possible construction of ontological models of urban space, a final digression may therefore be useful. It concerns the outcomes that the previous analytical-taxonomic premises have induced in the traditional field of development and deepening of the MAS. We are obviously referring to the domain of computer science and artificial intelligence, which in recent decades has produced complex and advanced MAS-based operating models and architectures. A multi-agent architecture in this context consists of agents characterized in particular by some peculiar connotations, including the following [5]:

1) Agents own decision systems. Decision theory, which we discussed earlier, is the main source for a study of this field. This also happens in particular in terms of relations with the context of space-environment, with the related cognitive problems embedded in navigation and exploration tasks [12, p.45].

2) Agents need a cognitive model. One of the models often used in this field is the classic BDI model (Beliefs-Desires-Intentions) [45, p.21].

3) Agents should have a communication system. Here the problem of languages matters, which can typically be common (e.g. oral, symbolic, gestural etc.) or specialized (e.g. Knowledge Query and Manipulation Language, KQML, or the FIPA-ACL standard, Agent Communication Language) [34].

Clearly, these are key characters that inevitably and reiteratively occur. By analyzing and observing the prerogatives of these system architectures, interesting suggestions can emerge. They are important for the definition, almost from a de/reconstructive perspective, of an interpretative process of the agentive/social level, useful in the ontological perspective of spatial analysis addressed in this work.

3   A System of Representation of the Spatial Knowledge Level

3.1   Toward a 'Diffuse Individuality' or the New Individual-Collective Sight in City

This writing aims to be a hinge between the conceptualization of the city as a physical artefact immersed in material reality and a more abstract conceptualization of the city as a set of different spaces. In the last decades, the study of cities has become more and more inclusive of the immaterial aspects that, with today new consciousness of the phenomena, are clearly relevant for the city. These aspects even though not material are defined and definable and not less real than the physical aspects of the city, these are for example the dynamics of living that insist on the city, that inhabit it, animate it and shape its specific identity. In turn, these dynamics involve (and are generated by) individuals and organizations. The tension inside certain activities take place around and thanks to the spaces/places of the city. The double term of 'space/place' we use is about the definition of spaces dense and rich in lived meaning, and that is plenty of sense beyond their physical matter. These spaces/places sometimes are shaped during durable times. They are inherited through the centuries or sometimes formed in a few decades.

The city is a modified topological and geographical space in the sense of being a specific place in a physical region with geographical characteristics and affordances, and this region has embedded the physical transformations due to the activities of the city-system itself [38]. Previously we have posed and carried out an ontology-driven analysis of cities distinguishing three layers in the city: the modified place layer, the agentive layer and the knowledge layer [10].

Our aim here is to offer a way to read and interpret how space enters the layers that "make" the city through the method of ontological analysis, the aim in this paper (and more generally in our research path) is to deepen our knowledge of the city. In fact, the general aim is to make it clearer, less ambiguous and more sharable among all the actors (human and non-human agents) involved in a planning process.

In any of these cases we have to consider all the external causalities that forge the development of cities: their histories, their shapes, maybe their intrinsic tendencies towards certain types of evolution (often luckily changeable).

Intrinsic limits for planning processes are due principally to: (i) the limited rationality of the planners (a single agent or as a team, a collective agent) that are involved; (ii) the long duration needed to produce an answer and to implement a responsive tool for the city (as for an example plan, as analysis, as strategies); (iii) the almost complete lack of ad hoc monitoring and the consequent inability of reacting to plan deviations, or to rethink solutions when a previously unknown factor bursts into the scene.

External limits and external causalities to the planning process take an important part in drawing heavy limits to the effectiveness of a plan or of a strategy or a proposal for the organization of the city. These external limits deal with how our social systems are stated: (i) the political and decisional power and volition, and (ii) the economic pressure profit-oriented.

As architects and planners, we are used to conceiving the space around us as something physical, material, and metrical, even though intangible; something to model, to organize, to design, to conquer, to inhabit: a kind of void to populate with objects useful (or at least necessaire) to afford human inhabiting needs. Anyway, we have to recognize the necessity to integrate the different layered meanings that exist in the city, i.e., the abstract urban object in its wholeness, a complex and dynamic abstractness and materiality that are coexistent.

At any rate, already the philosophical reflection about space deals with the matter of the relation among parties that are there and participate in the space in different states. As an example, the nature of the relation between abstract geometry and its practical expression has been considered [20]. Space can be thought of as composed of all (actual and possible) positions of objects; pure space is space with all solid bodies removed, and distance the primitive concept we use to discuss the separation between bodies [20, 24]. The space of the city has always coexisted with a socio-technical system. Technologies have evolved in time by becoming increasingly widespread and activating dematerialized connections. The city is an increasingly dense and stratified socio-technical system. As an analogy, roads have formed one of the first infrastructure of the territory and cities, they have become more complex, larger, specialized, reaching levels of ever greater sophistication. Over time, other socio-technical networks were imposed on the environment, the territory and the city. Here, we have in mind the long evolution and stratification of various networked technological systems, from aqueducts to railways, from electrical networks, to oil and gas pipelines, telegraphic and telephone lines, radio, television, satellite transmissions, the world wide web, and all subsequent technologies.

We live in a mixed space that is increasingly growing: the digital revolution interweaves our reality with a pervasive plot of circuits that produces a material/virtual universe, expanding our consciousness to a new sense of intangible proximity [29].

Social contexts–and especially urban systems–can be seen nowadays as socio-technical systems (STSs), constituted of technical artefacts, social artefacts, and living beings (humans and not humans). As the complexity of such systems increases, their governance must be proportionally addressed, especially to face unexpected critical situations and guarantee overall system resilience [21].

The city is a complex whole made of human and non-human beings, made of physical material objects and intangible objects, the city as a unicum made of dynamics, relations, actions. But to understand the city in general, and specifically a particular one, we have to warp the weft that makes it and look inside, trying to interpret with a different sight, the individual's sight about the city and inside the city, and the individual/collective habits in the city. It is a matter of perspective and granularity too.

It is necessary to conceive that the sense of the comprehension of space, and specifically of a city is in the sight (and in the mind) of the agent who sees it, get on it, gives it a sense. In the different repetition that takes place in the making of the city developing it across space and the time it is generated as a relation, we test a tension between the city's parts, the agents, the city's knowledge itself (for each of the individual subjective knowledge and as a sum of distinct individual knowledge).

About the sight from inside of the molecular elements that form the city itself, it is useful not to forget the relationship between voids and solids that compose the city network structure. This relationship can be represented by imaging the tense flowing among spaces connecting them: they are the vectors (line) and nodes of this structure/network in some way never firm, dynamic, if not mobile. With new technologies, we deal with new model of abstract connections model a new abstract space (in and out of the city) that in some sense overlays the physical space itself. Connections made possible by computers and sensors are windows across the physical space, this re-model the relations between the material points in a new virtual space.

There is another level of space to be considered, in some sense, this is more material, and is about a kind of micro granularity of the scenario: it corresponds to the repeated gestures (lives) of every single agent, for example going back home and going out to work, to shopping, to definite places (the square, the seaside, the belvedere). Those habits trace infinite personal, individual maps that do not fit with the geographical, topological maps we usually deal with.

3.2   Exploring Theoretical and Pragmatic Methods

Cities are stratifications in time that stand side by side and overlap (Rossi, 1966). Their analysis could be an opportunity to engage in a new way to map space. But does this give an interpretation of space analogous to the one the inhabitants of that city have? And what is to be an inhabitant? Is it just being constantly present at the site? Does it make sense to talk about aggregates in the form of cities? Or must we take into account the 'n' near-infinite units (for example modules - points - nodes - trajectories) more or less mobile (with degrees of variability) that coincide with a modus of conscious and active individual identity? Does this individual identity in turn reinterpret inhabitants and models?

With the awareness of the problems posit by these questions, we begin to re-identify the aggregate spatial, agentive, relational, cognitive form of the city and reconsider it in a co-individual form of a community that inhabits a city (space-place-place).

Maybe at this point it could be useful to study more in-depth the distinction between space and place, to better affirm our interest in considering the city composed by the layer of place, that participate of space, and to better analyze what is the concept of space in the three-layer we identified (elicited) in previous contributions [10, 39].

In literature, we can find references to the multidimensionality of place and discussions about its different aspects in geography [33]. One interpretation is about the subjective and objective interpretation of both space and place. The subjective dimension embraces individualistic meanings attached to place basically in the representational level whereas the objective denotes the 'naturalistic qualities of place' [33]. This reflection brought [13] to define the "betweenness of places", as a place where meanings and objective reality encounter [33]. Anyway, the reading of a space-place as proposed by Pasini [29] leads to the definition of a 'symbiotic field' that refers to space, *topos* and *chora* [25, p.99] or locus [32, p.103] and spatium [8, p.403], where anthropogenic and geogenic [3] systems intersect, producing the multilayered cognitive construct we are dealing with [29].

Cities have been and remain dynamic, polycentric systems [10, 27], new technologies populate the environment of nets, links, dynamics, that have knots in a physical place but at the same time can spread all around the world.

New technological infrastructures could implement the quality of the socio-technical system giving to decision-makers new opportunities, and giving people a chance to control the system they are in. What is needed is the ability to understand how their input relates to the relevant systemic components, which may concern structural, functional, normative, environmental, or strategic aspects, and navigate their mutual relationships [21]. Especially in a crisis, people's input may be related to a faulty component, a broken communication link, an absurd rule, an ineffective business strategy. A good model should be able to give them, at least in principle, the possibility to understand how their specific input relates to the whole system, and hopefully how they can contribute to the global resilience [21]. Here again, we can see how the ontological approach could be useful and how it is needed to develop an ontological theory of Socio-technical Systems aimed at describing the various aspects above and their complex relationships, by expanding and integrating existing foundational theories of technical, social and legal artefacts. This could integrate our 'knowledge system' about the city. To know a city, the starting point is delving into the neighborhood, the set of places around the agent begins to form a map, where interiors and exteriors flow ones into each other or stop in front of doors, private portals, walls without access to the inside.

Paradoxically, we have to consider that there will always be a more central center, although several 'centers' coexist, they could be indifferent to other centralities. Also, they could be interpreted as connected in a sort of network of centralities.

The concept of space often remains founded on its geometrical reading, which gives us back its Euclidean measurability, the rigorousness of the postulated V, which has been joined in the centuries by non-Euclidean geometries. These have revealed a new complexity of the spatial fact, albeit abstract where the parallels multiply, the 'saddles' deform the perspective. Perhaps this could be intended as a metaphor for real complexity of the urban spaces that overlapped, layered, erased in the time, which have preserved previous memories, intuitions of future space and have been structured beyond walls, squares and public halls, symbolic monuments, geographical and geological signs forfeited in functions and symbolic signs of the city, in the city. The city's space itself it is realized in a social collectivity, in collective knowledge, and expresses a knowledge extraneous to itself beyond the individuals and the single stone that articulates it.

There is a first attempt here to propose an interpretation for the reading of the shape of the city which, takes into account the fluid interaction between the inside and the outside which in their setting define the overall shape of the city in finer granularity.

Traditionally the study of the shape of the city is called morphology. Urban morphology has known an important 'scientific' development in the 1950s thanks to Saverio Muratori research and subsequently by the so-called 'Scuola Romana'. Anyway, the word morphology existed previously, in fact, it was first proposed by Johann Wolfgang Von Goethe (1749–1832). Goethe used the word morphology to designate the 'science that deals with the essence of forms' [28, p.2].

The natural context is the first condition for the establishment and organization of the different elements of urban form. The land relief, the quality and suitability of soil and subsoil, the climate, the solar and wind exposure, the type of natural landscape [28]. As an example, the Persian life, art, and architecture Tavassoli affirms to be shaped by mountainous and desert [40].

A renewed interpretation of the urban morphology comprises the study of urban forms, of agents and processes responsible for their transformation; the urban form refers to the main physical, geographical, topological elements that structure and shape the city and then by urban tissues, streets (and squares), urban plots, buildings, to name the most important [28]). Different granularities take part to the complex game of being of the city, the making of it and then transforming it.

An analysis of the city for effective support to the decision and interpretation for the city has to consider: a harmonious integration of mass and space; consideration to origin; environmental knowledge; aesthetic knowledge; aesthetic experience; development problems; principles of urban spatial organization. This is a proposal by Tavassoli derived from his attentive reading to the geographical and climate as the point of the origin of the city's shape and identity. He looks back to the origin of forms operating a confrontation between coeval cities in different geographical areas: European cities, Chinese cities, Persian cities [40]. It is interesting to point it out here the importance of 'where' the city is founded (or is born) to have an a-priori lens for the relations that shape it.

The awareness of the non-homogeneous nature of time, of how time flows with different rhythms for different individuals and social groups, for different activities and on different occasions and places has perhaps become the real problem of the twentieth-century city and its project adds new layers of analysis [35].

4   Final Remarks

This work is part of the studies for the creation of cognition-based models to support spatial decisions in urban planning and management contexts. In particular, the paper explored aspects of the configuration and relationships of the agentive and spatial components of the city, from an STS perspective.

The study analyzed the agentive dimension, aiming to capture and highlight the characters of relationship and spatial contextualization in decision-making actions. The analysis began by reflecting on the potential actions of agents in the multiformity of multi-agent decision-making contexts - of which STS are intrinsically characterized. Reflections developed in the economic and partly environmental literature were taken into consideration, proposing model layouts referable to MAS architectures with cognitive characterization. A particularly intriguing aspect of this characterization is the modeling of the 'environmental agent', whose intrinsic multidimensional complexity represents a specific topic for reflection in MAS approaches - although still debated.

The spatial dimension of the environment was therefore specifically investigated in the paper, as a complex stratification and representation of metric but also behavioral and emotional, agent-inspired features. The analysis induces to highlight aspects of the characterization of the space as aggregated entity and/or entities in the organization of the

STS. However, the analysis also emphasizes the relevance of aspects of disaggregation of the space into components and of mutual relationality between components, and between disaggregated elements towards aggregate entities. In particular, the second part of the analysis focuses on the identification of possible formal characterizations of the spatial components/elements in their aspects of individual granularity and scaling. As a result, the study seems to add a deeper and more articulated insight to these spatial entities, apparently and traditionally simple and instead of great intrinsic complexity. It seems to integrate the results of significant complexity already emerged within the previous agentive analysis, possibly exasperating the general complex layout.

However, the traditional synthetic and reductionist approach that exalts a standard stereotype of citizens and an urban environment as a passive theater of their actions is no longer suitable today. The city today appears to be more and more consciously complex and difficult to manage through aggregate and undifferentiated approaches. Today we deal with 'smart city' but the network approach included in this concept needs to embed the fine understanding of the parts, attributes, instances, nodes and relationships of the urban object, to which the network itself must adhere, in order to function and be effective. STS today can take advantage of smart supports and grid-oriented infrastructures, which allow systems to evolve towards functionalities more consistent with the organizational and relational contexts of current urban communities.

In this framework, the disaggregated analysis carried out here is able to prefigure the suitability of this approach in ontological terms, in order to investigate this complexity in an analytical and fine-tuned way. In fact, the ontological approach is also intended as a potential tool for formalizing features, instances and relationships, within this STS [21]. It is evident that these efforts are still prodromal to a real ontological modeling, oriented to investigate in advance the scope of work of an ontological analysis - which is large and articulated, and increasingly extends almost fractally after each new reflection.

However, it is an extremely useful and interesting perspective in reasoning on the smart city. In fact, in this framework the follow up of this study envisions the possibility of creating MAS-based prototypes of decision support architectures in urban contexts. Therefore, the development of this research will be oriented towards these objectives in the near future.

References

1. Arrow, K.J.: A difficulty in the concept of social welfare. J. Political Econ. **58**, 328–346 (1950)
2. Arrow, K.J.: Social Choice and Individual Values. Wiley, New York (1963)
3. Baccini, P., Brunner, P.H.: Metabolism of the Anthroposphere: Analysis, Evaluation Design. MIT Press, Cambridge (2012)
4. Badham, R., Clegg, C., Wall, T.: Socio-technical theory. In: Handbook of Ergonomics, John Wiley, New York (2000)
5. Balke, T., Gilbert, N.: How do agents make decisions? A survey. J. Artif. Soc. Soc. Simul. **17**, 13 (2014)
6. Batty, M.: Agents, cells, and cities: new representational models for simulating multiscale urban dynamics. Environ Plan A **37**, 1373–1394 (2005)
7. Baxter, G., Sommerville, I.: Socio-technical systems: from design methods to systems engineering. Interact. Comput. **23**, 4–17 (2011)

8. Böhme, G.: Atmosphere as the subject matter of architecture. In: Ursprung, P. (ed.) Natural Histories. Lars Müller, Zurich (2006)
9. Borgo, S.: An ontological view of components and interactions in behaviorally adaptive systems. J. Integr. Des. Process. Sci. **23**, 17–35 (2019)
10. Borgo, S., Borri, D., Camarda, D., Stufano Melone, M.R.: An ontological analysis of cities, smart cities and their components. In: Nagenborg, M., Stone, T., González Woge, M., Vermaas, P.E. (eds.) Technology and the City. PET, vol. 36, pp. 365–387. Springer, Cham (2021). https://doi.org/10.1007/978-3-030-52313-8_18
11. Davoudi, S.: Planning as practice of knowing. Plan. Theory **14**, 316–331 (2015)
12. Dennett, D.C.: The Intentional Stance. MIT Press, Cambridge (1989)
13. Entrikin, J.N.: The Betweenness of Place. Springer, London (1991). https://doi.org/10.1007/978-1-349-21086-2_2
14. Etzioni, A.: Mixed-scanning: a "third" approach to decision-making. Public Adm. Rev. **27**, 385–392 (1967)
15. Ferber, J.: Multi-Agent Systems: An Introduction to Distributed Artificial Intelligence. Addison-Wesley, London (1999)
16. Fono, L.A., Donfack-Kommogne, V., Gabriel Andjiga, N.: Fuzzy arrow-type results without the Pareto principle based on fuzzy pre-orders. Fuzzy Sets Syst. **160**, 2658–2672 (2009)
17. Forester, J.: Bounded rationality and the politics of muddling through. Public Adm. Rev. **44**, 23–31 (1984)
18. Gehrlein, W.V.: Condorcet's paradox. Theory Decis. **15**, 161–197 (1983)
19. Gibilisco, M.B., Gowen, A.M., Albert, K.E., Mordeson, J.N., Wierman, M.J., Clark, T.D.: Arrow and the aggregation of fuzzy preferences. In: Fuzzy Social Choice Theory. SFSC, vol. 315, pp. 53–87. Springer, Cham (2014). https://doi.org/10.1007/978-3-319-05176-5_4
20. Gray, J.: The epistemology of geometry. In: Zalta, E.N. (ed.) The Stanford Encyclopedia of Philosophy (2019). https://plato.stanford.edu/archives/fall2019/entries/epistemology-geometry//. Accessed 19 May 2021
21. Guarino, N., Bottazzi, E., Ferrario, R., Sartor, G.: Open ontology-driven sociotechnical systems: transparency as a key for business resiliency. In: De Marco, M., Te'eni, D., Albano, V., Za, S. (eds.) Information systems: crossroads for organization, management, accounting and engineering, pp. 535–542. Springer, Heidelberg (2012). https://doi.org/10.1007/978-3-7908-2789-7_58
22. Le Page, C., Becu, N., Bommel, P., Bousquet, F.: Participatory agent-based simulation for renewable resource management: the role of the Cormas simulation platform to nurture a community of practice. J. Artif. Soc. Soc. Simul. **15**, 10 (2012)
23. Lindblom, C.E.: The science of "muddling through." Public Adm. Rev. **19**, 79–88 (1959)
24. Locke, J.: An Essay Concerning Human Understanding. Penguin Books Limited, London (1997)
25. Montaner, J.M.: Espacio. In: de Solá-Morales, I. (ed.) Introducción a la arquitectura. Conceptos fundamentales. Universitat Politécnica de Catalunya, Barcelona (2000)
26. Mordeson, J.N., Clark, T.D.: Fuzzy Arrow's theorem. New Math. Nat. Comput. **05**, 371–383 (2009)
27. Okner, T., Preston, R.: Smart cities and the symbiotic relationship between smart governance and citizen engagement. smart cities: foundations, principles and applications, pp. 344–372 (2017)
28. Oliveira, V.: Urban Morphology: An Introduction to the Study of the Physical Form of Cities. Springer, Cham (2016). https://doi.org/10.1007/978-3-319-32083-0
29. Pasini, R.: Landscape Paradigms and Post-urban Spaces: A Journey Through the Regions of Landscape. Springer International Publishing, Cham (2018). https://doi.org/10.1007/978-3-319-77887-7

30. Phillips, R.A., Reichart, J.: The environment as a stakeholder? a fairness-based approach. J. Bus. Ethics **23**, 185–197 (2000)
31. Rabino, G.A.: Processi Decisionali e Territorio nella Simulazione Multi-Agente. Società Editrice Esculapio, Milano (2005)
32. Rossi, A.: The Architecture of the City. MIT Press, Cambridge (1984)
33. Saar, M., Palang, H.: The dimensions of place meanings. Living Rev. Landscape Res. **3**, 5–24 (2009)
34. Searle, J.R.: Social ontology: some basic principles. Anthropol. Theory. **6**, 12–29 (2006)
35. Secchi, B.: La città europea contemporanea e il suo progetto. Territorio. **20**, 78–92 (2002)
36. Simon, H.A.: Administrative Behavior: A Study of Decision-making Processes in Administrative Organization. Macmillan, London (1945)
37. Simon, H.A.: The Sciences of the Artificial. MIT Press, Cambridge (1969)
38. Stufano, R., Borri, D., Camarda, D., Borgo, S.: Knowledge of places: an ontological analysis of the social level in the city. In: Papa, R., Fistola, R., Gargiulo, C. (eds.) Smart Planning: Sustainability and Mobility in the Age of Change. GET, pp. 3–14. Springer, Cham (2018). https://doi.org/10.1007/978-3-319-77682-8_1
39. Stufano, R., Borri, D., Camarda, D., Borgo, S.: Knowledge of places: an ontological analysis of the social level in the city. In: Gervasi, O., et al. (eds.) Computational Science and Its Applications – ICCSA 2017. LNCS, vol. 10407, pp. 687–694. Springer, Cham (2017). https://doi.org/10.1007/978-3-319-62401-3_50
40. Tavassoli, M.: Form, Space and Design: From the Persian to the European Experience. Springer, Cham (2019). https://doi.org/10.1007/978-3-030-15831-6
41. Thompson, E.A.: A Pareto optimal group decision process. Pap. Non-Market Decis. Making. **1**, 133–140 (1966)
42. Weiss, G.: Multiagent Systems: A Modern Approach to Distributed Artificial Intelligence. The MIT Press, Cambridge (2000)
43. Weyns, D., Holvoet, T.: Synchronous versus asynchronous collaboration in situated multi-agent systems. In: Proceedings of the Second International Joint Conference on Autonomous Agents and Multiagent Systems (AAMAS 2003), Melbourne, Australia. ACM (2003)
44. Wooldridge, M.: An Introduction to Multi-Agent Systems. Wiley, London (2002)
45. Wooldridge, M.: Reasoning About Rational Agents. MIT Press, Cambridge (2003)
46. Zadeh, L.: Fuzzy sets. Inf. Control **8**, 338–353 (1965)

Project e-Space: Building a Digital Platform for Spatial and Urban Planning and Development in Serbia

Ljiljana Živković[(✉)]

Ministry of Construction, Transport and Infrastructure, Belgrade, Serbia

Abstract. Besides supporting the general idea and goals of sustainable development in every aspect of a modern life, there are many other reasons for accelerating digitalization efforts within the public sector in Europe. These efforts are also notable in the spatial and urban planning and development domain, where a majority of the European cities and countries following the common policies, strategies and accepted standards (like, INSPIRE, TA2030, Digital Europe, Urban agenda for the EU, ESPON, etc.) have already established or are in development of the different digital databases and platforms for the spatial and urban planning data management, as well as their usage for a various and improved internal and public services provision. The purpose of this article is to present a Project "Improving spatial planning and development in the Republic of Serbia by establishment of e-Space digital platform", i.e. the e-Space project, launched in March 2021 by the Serbian Ministry of Construction, Transport and Infrastructure, which aim is to establish the so-called e-Space digital platform that would support the spatial and urban planning and development process and related services provision in Serbia, both on national and local level. While increasing the efficiency and effectiveness of the public decision-making and territorial/land policy management, this platform should additionally improve, streamline and make more transparent the current spatial and urban planning and development practice in Serbia in general. Thus, starting from the identified problems and obstacles within the spatial and urban planning and development domain in Serbia today, as well as needs of the public sector, businesses and citizens to have easy access to the territorial/land development related information, as well as adequate tool for participation and efficient services provision, the general concept, objectives and main functionalities and components of the future e-Space digital platform have been described in this article. Besides number of the direct advantages that establishment of this digital platform would bring to the domain of sustainable territorial/land management and other domains in Serbia (gender equality, investment, taxation, etc.), it could be assumed that several obstacles still need to be resolved or managed during this project implementation in the coming years.

Keywords: Sustainable development · Public sector digitalization · Spatial and urban planning and development · e-Space project · Serbia

O. Gervasi et al. (Eds.): ICCSA 2021, LNCS 12953, pp. 503–518, 2021.
https://doi.org/10.1007/978-3-030-86976-2_34

1 Introduction

In order to support and manage a rapid urbanization and dynamic urban development process, the public administrations on all levels in the European countries are transforming their operating models, increasing at the same time a number and type of channels for public demands receiving as well as the capacities for understanding those various and changing citizens', businesses' and other end-users' needs [1, 2]. One of the dominant approaches to these challenges responding involves digital transformation of the public services and their provisions using the new technologies and their advantages [3, 4].

Relying on the commonly agreed policies, strategies and standards [5–8], a type of public services that is noticeably and increasingly transforming in the recent years in the European cities is that related to the spatial planning and construction domain [4, 34]. Similar to digitalization of the other public administration and service domains, digital transformation of this domain has brought the easier access, lower production costs, shorten times for providing services and overall improved quality of services, like issuance of construction permits, location information provision, etc. [4].

However, mainly due to the lack of funds and lack of staff with necessary skills, not all European cities have reached the same status of digital transition related to the digital solutions implementation for the spatial planning and development and construction [4, 9, 10]. Therefore, setting up of the digital plan registers -or databases- and digitalization of the spatial and urban planning process in some European countries have taken place -also or initially- on the national level [10]. In both local and national approaches to the digital transformation, digital plan databases and digital spatial and urban planning procedures and services are reflecting strongly the specifics of countries' planning practices, while creating capabilities for analyzing the quality of spatial and urban plans, and opening possibilities for understanding digital plan data and digital transformation influence on the spatial and urban development policy management in general [4, 9–12].

In order to reap advantages of the new technologies as well as to respond to growing demands for the transparent, streamlined and truly-participatory spatial and urban planning and development domain in Serbia [13], the Ministry for Construction, Transport and Infrastructure (MCTI) [14] has initiated and launched together with partners the Project "Improving spatial planning and development in the Republic of Serbia by establishment of e-Space digital platform", i.e. the e-Space project. The aim of this project is to digitally transform spatial and urban planning and development process in Serbia by building a centralized –national- digital plan database and digitizing planning procedures, which integrated within the e-Space digital platform with the other relevant databases would improve the efficiency and effectiveness of spatial and urban development decision-making and policy management, both on national and local level [15].

Since the initial project activities has just started in March 2021, namely preparation of the project idea document before a pilot launching, the purpose of this article is to present the general concept of e-Space digital platform and approach to its establishment, and to describe this project foreseen results and significance in light of the current spatial and urban planning digital transformation and related services digital transition in the other European countries.

Thus, the article starts with the overview of a current status related to the digitalization of spatial and urban planning domain in Europe. Afterwards, situation and challenges within the spatial and urban planning and development domain in Serbia today are presented, followed by the chapter introducing purpose, main aim and objectives of the e-Space project. Methods and materials used for the project concept determination are described in the Methodology chapter, after which the assumed project activities, outputs and outcomes are presented in the Expected project results chapter. Finally, the article ends with the Conclusions chapter.

2 Digitalization of Plans Data and Related Services in Europe

In order to grasp the proven advantages of new technologies and, thus, increase efficiency of the industries and production in general, the European Union (EU) has been stimulating implementation of the digital solutions and creation of the digitalization benefits for businesses and citizens in Europe by supporting development of the different e-initiatives (like, e-government, e-health, e-transport, etc.), as well as by providing the clear directions, frameworks, incentives and leadership within its strategic documents [3, 4]. As a result, digital interaction between the individuals and public authorities over the Internet via different digital public services, from searching for the right information to usage of the provided administrative procedures, has been increased significantly, particularly in Northern and some parts of Western Europe comparing to the Eastern and Southern parts of Europe. These discrepancies in the digital transition of public services between the European countries, regions and cities are due to the several common reasons or barriers, which are thus impeding the cohesive and sustainable urbanization and urban development in Europe (Fig. 1).

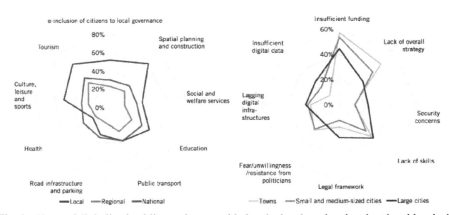

Fig. 1. Share of digitalized public services provided at the local, regional and national levels, by type (left); Factors constraining the digital transition of public services in Europe (right) [4]

Among those commonly provided digital public services by the authorities on different administration levels are those related to the spatial and urban planning and development domain. According to the ESPON survey about the digital transition of cities from

Table 1. Share of digitalized public services related to the spatial planning and construction at the level of towns (T), small and medium-sized cities (S) and large cities (L); at regional level (R) and national level (N) [4]

Spatial planning and construction services		Find information via website	Apply for planning and building permits	Explore land use plans and proposals via dedicated GIS services	Obtain land use and cadaster data online via land registry	Participate in online public consultations on plans
Northern Europe	T					
	S					
	L					
	R					
	N					
Eastern Europe	T					
	S					
	L					
	R					
	N					
Southern Europe	T					
	S					
	L					
	R					
	N					
Western Europe	T					
	S					
	L					
	R					
	N					

Share of service digitalization:

0-10%		50-60%	
10-20%		60-70%	
20-30%		70-80%	
30-40%		80-90%	
40-50%		90-100%	

2017 [4], mentioned digital services were provided mostly on the local levels, where the Northern Europe countries had a higher share of these services provided also on the national level, as observed in Table 1. Among the digital services for spatial and urban planning and development domain in Europe, services for the online application for construction permits, as well as GIS-based services for accessing the land use information and development proposals, had the high shares. Also, reflecting the existing spatial and urban planning and development practices in different countries, digital public services related to the online public consultations for proposed draft plans as well as public participation in the planning processes in general, have been more advanced in the Northern and Eastern parts of Europe.

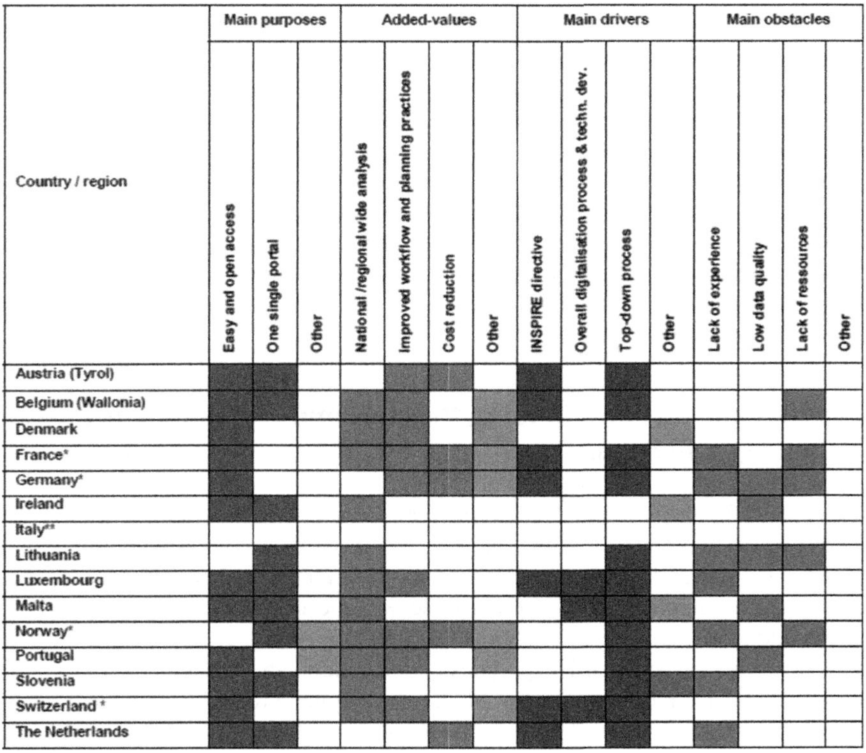

Country / region	Main purposes			Added-values				Main drivers				Main obstacles			
	Easy and open access	One single portal	Other	National /regional wide analysis	Improved workflow and planning practices	Cost reduction	Other	INSPIRE directive	Overall digitalisation process & techn. dev.	Top-down process	Other	Lack of experience	Low data quality	Lack of ressources	Other
Austria (Tyrol)															
Belgium (Wallonia)															
Denmark															
France*															
Germany*															
Ireland															
Italy**															
Lithuania															
Luxembourg															
Malta															
Norway*															
Portugal															
Slovenia															
Switzerland *															
The Netherlands															

Fig. 2. Overview of the digitalisation process of plan data in 15 cases across Europe [10]

In 2020, the ESPON DIGIPLAN project [10] revealed that digitalization efforts within the spatial and urban planning and development domain in Europe is continuing, while the barriers for digital transition of public services in this domain have still remain prevailingly the same, that is, lack of skills and lack of resources, besides some others, like a low quality of data (Fig. 2). However, despite the identified obstacles, qualitative research about the digitalization of plan data in Europe has stressed some key findings [10]:

– The eagerness of spatial planning actors to provide harmonised and standardised plan data on a digital and open platform from the 2010s onwards;

- An improved workflow and planning practices contributing to cost-reduction;
- Differences in the organisation and publication of digital plan data reflect differences in spatial planning traditions and competences;
- Digital plan data, that have been harmonised and standardised, allows for innovative practises; etc.

Also, in line with the findings related to the need of local level to cooperate and/or look for a support from the national level for digital transition and provision of spatial and urban planning and development services digitally, DIGIPLAN project's interim results emphasize also 1) the national level as one of the main drivers for digitalization of public services, and 2) the centralized -national- digital plan databases role for assessment and improvement of the existing spatial and urban planning practices and plans quality. Further, the interim DIGIPLAN project results confirmed also that the national digital plan databases could provide needed input for a better territorial/land development policy and other sectoral policies creation and management, besides being a valuable tool for spatial analysis performance. Therefore, besides the fact that majority of sustainable land planning and development-oriented activities and services are delivering on the local level, this project highlights the importance of building the national databases for spatial and urban planning and development practice improvement and national-wide sustainable development goals achievement [34].

3 Spatial and Urban Planning Practice and Development Domain Challenges in Serbia

Two decades after the political changes in 2000, and decision of Serbia to set on the path towards European integration, negative legacy of the socialist system within the spatial and urban planning and development domain has been abandoned, but further adaptations towards the contemporary, market-oriented, democratic and transparent spatial and urban planning and land management system need to be completed. These changes should be thus in line with the relevant EU policies and standards and, besides the other things, have to include also requirements for the more integrated urban development [13].

Further, COMPASS report for Serbia [10] stresses a lack of tools for the measurement of plans quality and how successful they are in the implementation, particularly on the local level, as one of issues within the current spatial and urban planning practice in Serbia. Also, the problems include a lack of comprehensive viability study before the plans preparation, as well as a situation when the plans are initiated by the individual investments and not by the strategic development plan for certain area, introducing so-called 'investor urbanism' phenomenon [16]. Other problems identified within the spatial and urban planning and development domain in Serbia include the frequent changes of legal framework and lack of trust in the system; long-lasting issues of informal development; as well as lack of meaningful public dialogue and development stakeholders participation in the early stage of plans preparation.

Regarding digitalization of the spatial and urban plans and planning domain in general, Serbia planning practice is experiencing the same obstacles like the other European countries towards the digital provision of an easy access to plans data and related public

Fig. 3. Access to the urban plans for the City of Belgrade territory is today divided between the two Web GIS platforms with different functions: URBEL for the plans data visualization (up) [19] and BEOLAND for the plans implementation monitoring and urban land development in general (down). [20] These two platforms and their functions would be replaced in future by the e-Space digital platform, as a main national platform for spatial and urban planning

services. Despite the plans are preparing in digital format using the GIS and CAD technologies, plans data generally have low quality, lack standardization and are not open nor easily accessible in vector or digital map formats (.pdf format prevails), both on national and local level (Fig. 3). Also, there is a general lack of staff with the appropriate digital skills and experience, particularly on local level, while the municipalities prevailingly poor still refuse to pool their resources and provide modernized public services in cooperation with the other neighboring cities and municipalities [17]. Finally, related to the need for digital transformation of the spatial and urban planning and development process in Serbia, it should be mentioned that today there are many, sometimes too long, costly and complicated administrative procedures within this domain, which are occasionally hardly applicable in practice and, generally, lack transparency and efficiency required for a timely and informed development decision-making and establishment of an inclusive and participatory planning model.

Therefore, taking into account proven advantages of the new technologies implementation within the other European countries' planning systems and practices [4, 9, 10, 18], planned digital transformation of the spatial and urban planning and development domain in Serbia could directly support changes within the identified 'fields of improvement' [13]:

- The need for stronger market orientation and improved collaboration between public and private sector, as well as protection of the public interest;
- The need for improvement of budget planning;
- The need for better integration of sustainability principles in the formal planning framework; and
- The need for transparent and wide inclusion of all relevant stakeholders in the planning process.

4   Project e-Space: Aim and Objectives

In order to respond to the identified spatial and urban planning and development challenges in Serbia by implementing the proven new technologies' advantages through a digital transformation of this domain, MCTI has launched the Project "Improving spatial planning and development in the Republic of Serbia by establishment of e-Space digital platform", so-called e-Space project [15].

The aim of this Project is to establish the digital platform –named e-Space- as a standardized, reliable and open G2G, G2C and G2B solution for the spatial and urban planning and development process management, based on the relevant international and national data management standards and sustainable development initiatives (like, NUA, Urban Agenda for EU, TA2030, INSPIRE, ESPON, etc.) [15]. In other words, the aim of this Project is a digital transformation of spatial and urban planning and development domain in Serbia, focused on the improvement of its efficiency and effectiveness related to the public decision-making and territorial/land development policy management, both on national and local level (Fig. 4).

Based on the e-Space project aim and scope, the next general objectives have been identified to be reached during the project implementation [15]:

- Development of a national spatial and urban planning data standard, and establishment of the centralized –national- digital plans database;
- Digitalization of the procedures for spatial and urban planning documents preparation/revision, adoption and implementation;
- Establishment of the e-Space digital platform that would include links to the other relevant national databases/registers, development of the advanced geovisualization capabilities and building to the needs adjusted communication tools/channels for the territorial/land development stakeholders;
- Training and building necessary capacities of the spatial and urban planning and development stakeholders; and
- Creating appropriate legal and institutional framework for the Project results sustainability.

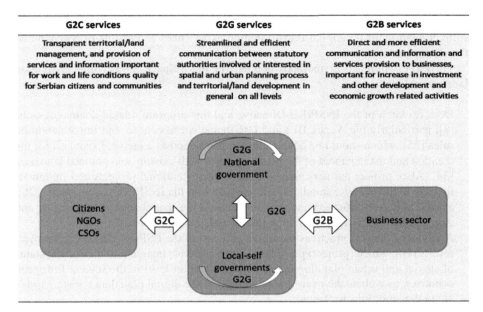

G2C services	G2G services	G2B services
Transparent territorial/land management, and provision of services and information important for work and life conditions quality for Serbian citizens and communities	Streamlined and efficient communication between statutory authorities involved or interested in spatial and urban planning process and territorial/land development in general on all levels	Direct and more efficient communication and information and services provision to businesses, important for increase in investment and other development and economic growth related activities

Fig. 4. Project e-Space: expected outcomes

The e-Space project duration is estimated to 3 years (2021–2023), at least for a pilot or initial solution establishment, where the main project partners include: MCTI [14], Republic Geodetic Authority (RGA) [21], National Alliance for Local Economic Development (NALED) [22], Office for information technologies and e-Government (ITE) [23] and, internationally, Lantmäteriet [31] and Swedish International Development Cooperation Agency (SIDA) [32].

5   Methodology

In order to identify a right approach to digital transformation of the spatial and urban planning and development domain in Serbia, and to achieve identified project aim and objectives, MCTI has started from the current challenges within this domain [13, 15, 17]. In parallel, towards creating the appropriate e-Space digital platform concept and solutions for the planned digital transformation, MCTI has analyzed the relevant EU documentation and other materials related to this domain practices and their level of digitalization in the other European countries, trying to identify the common points and best practices valuable for Serbia. This approach has been taken due to Serbia status of the EU candidate country and ongoing negotiation process, on one side, but also due to the confirmed similarity of the European spatial and urban planning systems, which is increasing even more with the digitalization [4, 18, 24].

Although materials related to the digitalization and digital transformation in the spatial and urban planning and development domain are rather scarce (at least in English language), MCTI has based the e-Space digital platform concept and expected project results on a comprehensive desk study of literature and documentations reading, as well as direct analysis of the digital transformation experiences and results of Sweden and other European countries.

Therefore, approach or methods applied for the e-Space project implementation planning included:

1. Desk research of the INSPIRE Directive and this program related documentations [8], particularly the Annex III Land Use theme specifications and implementation rules [25], which should be adapted and implemented as a national standard for the creation and management of the plan data layer with existing and planned land uses [34]. Also, project partners analyzed the previous national projects and initiatives focused to the land use standardization in line with the INSPIRE requirements [26], as well as current situation and specific needs of the spatial and urban planning and development practice and planning instruments in Serbia [13, 17];

2. Analysis of the best practices presented as a part of the ESPON DIGIPLAN project results [10], which (project) provides a comprehensive insight into the current status of spatial and urban planning practices digitalization level in the several European countries, as well as the overview of a usage of the digital plan data registers today along the ambitions for future;

3. Desk research targeted at collecting data through a direct experience with the already established or developing relevant digital platforms, databases/registers and other e-initiatives in the public sector internationally [10] and in Serbia, like e-Permit [27], e-Government [28], Central Register of Planning Documents (CRPD) [29], and particularly NSDI initiative and its geoportal GeoSerbia [30], and other related Web sites, geoportals and platforms; and

4. Finally, application of a thematic workshop method with Swedish partners [31, 32] for learning about the Swedish national digital platform for a territorial/land development (https://www.lantmateriet.se/en/webb/smartare-samhallsbyggnadsprocess/) and sharing of lessons learnt from this platform establishment.

Finally, since digital transformation includes the various changes and adaptations of an existing system to the selected new technologies solution, the e-Space project planning has assumed necessary socio-technical approach to the spatial and urban planning and development domain transformation in Serbia. This approach should secure optimal usage of the e-Space digital platform and its operating framework from the very beginning; it should provide necessary scalability of the solution needed for its national and local level setting up; and, finally, it should deliver project results that would ensure e-Space digital platform sustainability in the future.

6 Expected Project Results

Based on the project aim, objectives and applied methodology, validation criteria for the e-Space project results have been focused on 1) providing online accessibility and increased quality of the spatial and urban plans data, 2) more economical, participatory, transparent and inclusive spatial and urban planning and development process in Serbia, as well as 3) enabling sustainable growth and increasing economic activities, both on national and local level [36].

Therefore, the main output of this project, i.e. e-Space digital platform, must include in one place –centralized- all spatial and urban plans in Serbia, and be able to provide on-demand comprehensive information on the existing and planned territorial/land development proposals, potentials and/or limitations on any area or location, to all development stakeholders and interested parties. Also, this assumes that e-Space digital platform should incorporate the relevant digital processes which would support transparency, communication, participation and, particularly, online cooperation between the responsible statutory authorities and other development stakeholders, enforcing thus the national and local development rules and procedures faster, less costly and more accurate (like, issuing of construction permit).

In next three headlines, expected project results and their outcomes are generally presented.

6.1 Centralized Digital Plans Database

In order to overcome identified problems of the spatial and urban plans and planning process in general in Serbia, MCTI has defined the creation of centralized –national- database with the spatial and urban plans digital data as the first activity and result of the e-Space project. Creation of this national digital plans database, which would be a core element and starting point for the e-Space digital platform establishment, would require several outputs to be created:

- National land use dataset specification in accordance with the INSPIRE standards and specific needs of Serbia;
- Spatial and urban plans standardized data and metadata models for the national database creation;
- Off-line templates –i.e. distributed database- for spatial and urban plans data collection and conversion to a standardized data model; and
- Web-based application for spatial and urban plans digital data verification and uploading into the national database.

Results created in this first activity of the e-Space project would allow simple and efficient preparation/revision of the plans, by using the templates with already defined standard land uses and data for each type of the spatial and urban plans; after which the digital plans data quality would be easily verified before they are uploaded into the centralized database. This approach is important for overcoming the identified challenges related to the preparation and management of digital plans data in Serbia, especially the lack of skilled staff and financial resources on the local level.

Besides establishment of the e-Space digital platform, as the major future tool for territorial/land development domain in Serbia, this new national database for digital plans would be an initial element for establishment of both national and local ISs for spatial and urban planning and development (Fig. 5), as prescribed by the Law on Planning and Construction [33]. Compared to the e-Space digital platform that would be oriented towards communication, public services and information provision, the role of these ISs

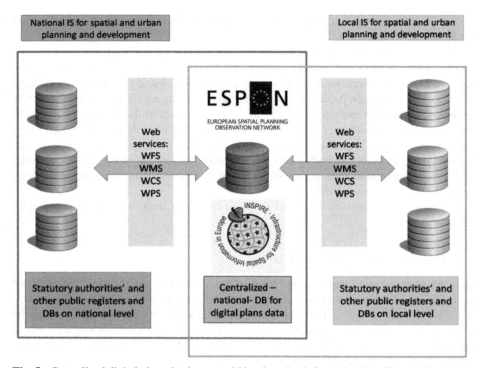

Fig. 5. Centralized digital plans database would be also a basis for national and local information systems (ISs) for spatial and urban planning and development establishment

would be focused on the strategic decision-making as well as planning methodology and plans quality improvement for a better integration of sustainability principles (through different spatial analysis, scenarios development and testing, etc.).

6.2   E-Space Digital Platform

After creating the centralized digital plans database, the next step towards establishment of the e-Space digital platform would include 1) linking this national database with the other relevant databases and registers within the NSDI initiative, and 2) development of a geovisualization application and its integration with the other digital procedures or functionalities that would support and improve the spatial and urban planning and development process and practice in Serbia. Expected functionalities of the e-Space digital platform would include the building of next outputs:

- Web-based module for collecting data and information on the development conditions from the relevant statutory authorities (national and local ones);
- Connection with the national distribution information system for NSDI – Geosrbija 2.0;
- Development of authentication and authorization module with the different user roles for each digital platform functionality;

- Web-based module for e-participation during the early public hearing and the public hearing of draft plans;
- Web-based user interface(s) for services provision and communication between those responsible for the spatial and urban planning and development and 1) relevant statutory authorities and administrations (G2G), 2) private sector or businesses (G2B), and 3) citizens and local communities (G2C) (Fig. 4); and
- Web-based application for the construction permit applications submission and procedure tracking (e-Permit).

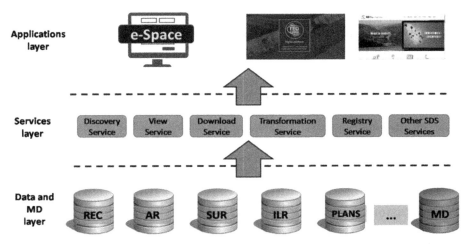

Fig. 6. E-Space digital platform as part of the Serbian NSDI initiative: national plans database would be linked to the other national databases and registers, like real estate cadastre (REC), address register (AR), spatial units register (SUR), investment location register (ILR), etc.

Planned to be developed as a part of the NSDI initiate in Serbia (Fig. 6), digital platform e-Space would rely on this initiative's evolving standards and resources (people, data, services, technologies, procedures, agreements, etc.), and use them for overcoming the previously already identified lack of skills and financial resources within the spatial and urban planning and development domain, particularly on the local level.

In other words, the centralized digital plans database (6.1) along the e-Space digital platform would help in overcoming the general digitalization gap or operations incompatibility between the national and local administrations (top-down), where situation in the other European countries is mainly characterized by building the national plans databases and portals using the bottom-up approach.

Also, comparing to the similar initiatives in Europe, the e-Space digital platform has also ambitious to provide functionalities that are usual for the spatial and urban planning digital portals (like communication, visualization, participation, public hearing, etc.), but also to provide the construction permit service point on one place, i.e. on e-Space digital platform.

6.3   Legal and Organizational Frameworks and Capacity Building for e-Space

Following the emphasized socio-technical approach to the digital transformation of spatial and urban planning and development domain in Serbia, three other project activities would be run in parallel to the previously described expected project results related to the technical solution development (6.1 and 6.2). These three activities would support the technical solution optimal functioning and project results sustainability in future, and they include:

– Legal framework – as part of this activity, the Law on Planning and Construction and its bylaws would be amended to reflect changes introduced by the centralized digital plans database and e-Space digital platform. Also, this new national database and e-Space digital platform solution would be implemented and managed by a separate bylaw that would be based on the knowledge created during the project implementation;
– Organizational framework – assumes establishment of the relevant legal entities structure with their roles, which would delegate clear responsibilities and ownership over data and procedures within the digitally transformed spatial and urban planning and development system in Serbia; and
– Capacity building – activity would include development of the various manuals and other technical documentations for the e-Space model and its components, as well as a number of promotional and capacity building events, directed to the knowledge and skills development of all planning and development stakeholders in Serbia.

7   Conclusions

The main aim of here presented the e-Space project is digital transformation of the spatial and urban planning and development domain in Serbia and establishment of the e-Space digital platform, directed at improvement of the efficiency and effectiveness of public decision-making and management of territorial/land development policy, both on national and local level. This digital transformation will include first standardization and digitalization of the urban and spatial plans and related planning procedures, and then establishment of the e-Space digital platform. The basic structural element of the e-Space digital platform will be thus a newly built national digital plans database, which linked with the other digital databases/registers and supported by the digital procedures and services within the NSDI as well as e-Government and other initiatives in Serbia, would ensure on-line communication and exchange of data and information between statutory authorities, business sector and citizens via e-Space digital platform. Besides these direct results, it is expected that this recently launched 3-year Project will enhance also the quality of planning practice and planning documents in general, creating conditions for overcoming the existing inefficiencies and non-transparency of existing planning process and provision of services for the sustainable territorial/land development and management in Serbia. Additionally, the Project will reduce the number of days and costs for obtaining location requirements and construction permits, which will lead to a better position of the Republic of Serbia on the Doing Business list of the World Bank as well [35].

References

1. New Urban Agenda. http://habitat3.org/wp-content/uploads/NUA-English.pdf
2. Urban Agenda for the EU. https://ec.europa.eu/futurium/en/urban-agenda
3. Digital Europe Programme. https://digital-strategy.ec.europa.eu/en/activities/digital-pro gramme
4. ESPON Territorial and urban dimensions of digital transition in Europe, Luxembourg: ESPON EGTC (2018). ISBN 978-99959-55-14-4. https://www.espon.eu/sites/default/files/attachments/ESPON%20Policy%20Brief%20on%20Digital%20Transition.pdf
5. Cohesion Policy 2021–2027. https://ec.europa.eu/regional_policy/en/2021_2027/
6. Territorial Agenda of the European Union 2030. https://www.territorialagenda.eu/files/age nda_theme/agenda_data/Territorial%20Agenda%20documents/TerritorialAgenda2030_201 201.pdf
7. EC Digital Agenda Investing in the future digital transformation 2021–2027 - Why is this a priority? (2021). https://euagenda.eu/upload/publications/untitled-199893-ea.pdf
8. INSPIRE Infrastructure for spatial information in Europe. http://inspire.ec.europa.eu/
9. ESPON COMPASS – Comparative Analysis of Territorial Governance and Spatial Planning Systems in Europe (2018). https://www.espon.eu/planning-systems
10. ESPON DIGIPLAN-Evaluating Spatial Planning Practices with Digital Plan Data (2020). https://www.espon.eu/sites/default/files/attachments/ESPON%20DIGIPLAN%20I nterim%20report.pdf
11. Fertner, C., Aagaard Christensen, A., Andersen, P.S., et al.: Emerging digital plan data–new research perspectives on planning practice and evaluation. Geografisk Tidsskrift-Danish J. Geogr. **119**(1), 6–16 (2019). https://doi.org/10.1080/00167223.2018.1528555
12. Larsen, H.: Nye plandata–nye muligheder. Geoforum Danmark (2018). https://geoforum.dk/nye-plandata-nye-muligheder/
13. ESPON COMPASS – Comparative Analysis of Territorial Governance and Spatial Planning Systems in Europe, Final Report - Additional vol. 5-Additional Countries Feasibility Report (2018). https://www.espon.eu/sites/default/files/attachments/6.%20Volume_5_Addi tional_countries.pdf
14. Ministry of construction, transport and infrastructure (MCTI). http://mgsi.gov.rs/
15. MCTI/RGA e-Space: Spatial and Urban Planning Information System–An e-Planning Platform for e-Government, internal document (project concept draft) (2020)
16. Živković, L.: Monitoring urban development: national register of investment locations as a tool for sustainable urban land use management in Serbia. In: Gervasi, O., et al. (eds.) Computational Science and Its Applications – ICCSA 2020. LNCS, vol. 12251, pp. 820–835. Springer, Cham (2020). https://doi.org/10.1007/978-3-030-58808-3_59
17. Krunić, N.: Analiza postojećih geografskih informacionih sistema (GIS) u gradovima i opštinama i kapaciteta lokalnih uprava za upravljanje geoprostornim podacima sa predlozima za unapređenje, Stalna konferencija gradova i opština (SKGO). Republika Srbija, Savez gradova i opština (2020)
18. Soria-Lara, J.A., Zúñiga-Antón, M., Pérez-Campaña, R.: European spatial planning observatories and maps: merely spatial databases or also effective tools for planning?, Environ. Plann. B Plann. Des. **42**(5), 904–929 (2015). http://journals.sagepub.com/doi/abs/10.1068/b130200p
19. URBEL Web GIS application. https://qgiscloud.com/urbel/GranicePlanova_2/
20. BEOLAND Web GIS application. https://gis.beoland.com/smartPortal/gisBeoland
21. Republic geodetic authority (RGA). http://en.rgz.gov.rs/
22. National Alliance for Local Economic Development (NALED). https://naled.rs/
23. Office for information technologies and e-Government (ITE). https://www.ite.gov.rs/

24. Živković, L.: A proposal for the spatial planning monitoring system in Serbia. In: Gervasi, O., et al. (eds.) Computational Science and Its Applications – ICCSA 2017. LNCS, vol. 10407, pp. 555–570. Springer, Cham (2017). https://doi.org/10.1007/978-3-319-62401-3_40
25. INSPIRE LU. https://inspire.ec.europa.eu/theme/lu
26. Živković, L., Đorđević, A.: Building a GIS platform for sustainable land management: a case study of the city of Čačak. Serbia J. Urban Technol. (2016). https://doi.org/10.1080/10630732.2015.1102420
27. e-Dozvola. http://gradjevinskedozvole.rs/
28. Portal eUprave Republike Srbije. https://euprava.gov.rs/
29. Central Registry of Planning Documents (CRPD) http://www.crpd.gov.rs/RegistarPlanskihDokumenata/Default.aspx
30. NSDI geoportal Geosrbija. https://geosrbija.rs/en/
31. Lantmäteriet. https://www.lantmateriet.se/sv/
32. Swedish International Development Cooperation Agency (SIDA). https://www.sida.se/
33. Law on Construction and Planning, Official Gazette of the Republic of Serbia 9-2020. https://mgsi.gov.rs/cir/dokumenti/zakon-o-planiranju-i-izgradnji
34. Hersperger, A.M., Fertner, C.: Digital plans and plan data in planning support science–article commentary. Environ. Plann. B Urban Analytics City Sci. **48**(2), 212–215 (2021). https://doi.org/10.1177/2399808320983002
35. Program za unapređenje pozicije Republike Srbije na rang listi Svetske banke o uslovima poslovanja-Doing Business za period 2020–2023. godine sa Akcionim planom za njegovo sprovođenje. https://www.pravno-informacioni-sistem.rs/SlGlasnikPortal/eli/rep/sgrs/vlada/drugiakt/2020/89/1/reg
36. Sustainable urban development strategy of the Republic of Serbia 2030. https://www.mgsi.gov.rs/cir/dokumenti/urbani-razvoj/

Strategic Planning and Web-Based Community Engagement in Small Inner Towns: Case Study Municipality of Nemea – Greece

Maria Panagiotopoulou$^{(\boxtimes)}$ and Anastasia Stratigea 🆔

Department of Geography and Regional Planning, School of Rural and Surveying Engineering,
National Technical University of Athens, Athens, Greece
stratige@central.ntua.gr

Abstract. The present paper aims at supporting small settlements, located in the countryside, towards paving long-term sustainable development pathways. To this end, a methodological framework is developed and implemented in a specific case study area, the lagging-behind region of Nemea. The ultimate goal is the mobilization of local assets in order for the place's attractiveness to be enhanced and ambitious trajectories of economic growth, but also social and territorial cohesion, to be accomplished. The proposed framework is grounded in the concept of place-based approach and strategic planning; and integrates various planning processes, techniques and tools such as spatial data management, scenario planning, as well as F2F and ICT-enabled community engagement. The empirical results unveil the small settlements and rural communities' deficit in online interaction, governance schemes and community engagement practices, a gap that needs to be bridged so as attractiveness and future sustainable development objectives, in a European territory of equal opportunities, to be attained.

Keywords: Small inner towns · Place-based approach · Strategic planning · Scenario planning · Citizens' engagement · Territorial cohesion

1 Introduction

The concept of *participation* appeared in the urban and regional planning theory during the sixties. However, its role and contribution have been greatly acknowledged in recent few decades, since it has vigorously permeated the planning and policy-making realm [23, 24, 30, 34, 42, 44, 45]. Current recognition of its value goes hand in hand with the gradually evolving *planning paradigm* and the transition from a top-down to a bottom-up approach [5, 22, 35, 44, 45]. This implies a shift from an obsolete, regulatory, command and control-driven governmental scheme to a more democratic and inclusive governance model [30], giving prominence to cooperative efforts at the urban and regional context. Furthermore, *participation* lies at the heart of the presently prevalent *smart city paradigm* and the consequent rapid proliferation of technological applications that stem from its adoption; while community empowerment and more substantial engagement are also promoted. In such scenery, the scope and value added to

© Springer Nature Switzerland AG 2021
O. Gervasi et al. (Eds.): ICCSA 2021, LNCS 12953, pp. 519–534, 2021.
https://doi.org/10.1007/978-3-030-86976-2_35

the democratization of planning and decision-making practices through the deployment of participation is remarkably broadened. Moreover, mature and user-friendly *digital mediation tools*, capable of bridging decision-making processes and communities, are brought to the forefront [34, 42] in order to craft more sustainable, well-defined, widely acceptable and bottom-up urban and regional strategies.

The above transitions – smart governance, bottom-up decision-making models and community engagement – have been mainly advocated by key *sustainability concerns* at a glocal (global/local) scale; and have streamlined planning approaches during the last two decades [42]. Such approaches emanate from the realization that *sustainability* and *participation* seem to be two tightly interwoven concepts, with the latter being perceived as an enabler of the former. Indeed, as Dalal-Clayton and Bass [13] claim, pursuing sustainability objectives is a rather complex and challenging endeavor, cross-cutting spatial scales; and demands multi- and inter-disciplinary cooperation as well as cross-fertilization of knowledge that emerges from the interaction of various actors, who are associated with a given local ecosystem. It also calls for the cultivation of culture in interaction among all actors and stakeholders involved in each single step of decision-making procedures. The establishment of a new participatory philosophy targets at setting the ground for negotiation and consensus-building in the spatial planning process with regard to a commonly agreed future vision and the pathways for reaching it. This, in turn, strengthens dedication to more aware and responsible patterns of community behavior, as a result of trust and commitment to both the planning process and related outcomes [21, 24, 30, 42, 44. 45].

While the aforementioned noticeable transitions seem to be at the epicentre of discussions on the *ICT-enabled* and *innovation-driven* urban context, a certain *gap* is detected when downscaling to small and medium-sized towns (SMSTs – population between 5.000–50.000 inhabitants) [40]. The gap is further widened when it comes to *very small towns* (VSTs – population < 5.000 inhabitants), thereby realizing that in a high-tech era where competitiveness, embeddedness, social innovation, unimpeded accessibility, networking and interaction are almost exclusively enabled by ICTs and their applications, these types of regions remain – to an extended degree – *neglected, overlooked* or *under-addressed* and largely *'invisible'* to the European policy-making and academic smart research agenda [29, 40]. This inconsistency, as highlighted by numerous researchers, is a critical one, taking into consideration the polycentric structure of the European settlement network and its high dependence on small-scale urban constellations [20, 46]. Furthermore, Naldi et al. [32] point out that although *smart, sustainable* and *inclusive growth* (i.e., ambitious policy-oriented targets) have laid the foundations of the European Union's (EU) strategy, as reflected in the ten-year vision 'Europe 2020', the way this could fit a diverse set of SMSTs remains rather obscure. Pursuant to a substantial share of the research community, in order to fulfil these targets, one should abandon the 'one size fits all' and adopt a more *place-based* approach [19, 20]. However, apart from the distinct categories of urban contexts, a place-oriented rationale brings also to the surface the different types of SMSTs that greatly diversify from one another with respect to their proximity to larger urban centers, access to resources and markets, socio-economic conditions and structure, physical attributes and spatial identity, etc. Moreover, it illuminates the peripheral, isolated and disadvantageous position of SMSTs in terms of riding the *technological 'wave'* of recent decade as a prerequisite for paving smart, sustainable and inclusive future pathways [43], lacking thus potential for endogenous development [4]. Additionally, smart growth policies are void of specific focus on the peculiar attributes of these regions, especially the rural ones; and therefore, applications tailored to their contexts and/or needs are nonexistent.

Nonetheless, grasping the role and significance of SMSTs, as parts of the urban mosaic and the unique structure of the European settlement network [10], but also the functions offered by them, leads to the conclusion that the 'invisibility' imposed on smaller urban constellations – perceived as falling short in terms of developmental potential, glory etc. and being, in most cases, severely neglected in favor of larger cities – has to be remedied. This way, aspects of socio-economic and territorial cohesion that are in alignment with *smart, sustainable, resilient* and *inclusive growth* objectives, are optimally served. This necessity is further justified by *facts*. More particularly, SMSTs provide essential services in their surrounding rural areas. Actually, as *core centers* of functional regions [20] in the countryside, they possess a much more important role than their size might suggest, while they also impede depopulation of rural areas [10]. Moreover, peripheral and isolated SMSTs constitute vital elements of the European history [40]; while VSTs are deemed to be integral and essential parts of Europe as a predominantly rural region, according to the work of Dijkstra and Poelman [16] on the structural typology of NUTS 3 regions. The share of dwellers living in these types of regions is of equal significance, since they accommodate almost half of the European population. Pursuant to the study of Servillo et al. [38], about 27% of Europeans resides in SMSTs (approximately 8.350 towns with a population density ranging from 300 to 1.500 inhabitants/km^2); while another 19% lives in VSTs.

In harmony with the above discussion, the focus of the present paper is placed on SMSTs located in the countryside that are characterized by morphological, administrative and functional attributes [15, 39, 41]. In this respect, an attempt to explore a series of issues, via empirical results obtained from a Greek small inner town case study, is undertaken, namely:

- How mature and user-friendly ICT applications can underpin *governance* and *cooperation/interaction* of decision-making bodies with community actors in such an urban context?
- How can these applications broaden *community engagement* towards more informed decision-making regarding the future development paths that sustainably exploit these regions' territorial capital and support their functional role in rural territories?
- How transformational potential of *participatory planning* can build consensus on promising future developmental perspectives that ensure: territorial, social and economic cohesion of these lagging behind areas; new chances for gaining attractiveness; extroversion and competitive advantage by means of their territorial capital and historical trajectory?

Bearing the above questions in mind, this work proceeds with the establishment of a strategic planning framework for featuring future development pathways of a SMST. The paper is structured as follows: Sect. 2 elaborates on key methodological concerns of current territorial cohesion policy, i.e., a place-based approach; Sect. 3 delineates the framework's discrete steps, that are developed and applied on the specific case study of this work, namely the municipality of Nemea which includes the town of Nemea (a Greek SMST); Sect. 4 concisely presents the empirical results that emerge from the implementation of the proposed framework; while finally, Sect. 5 provides some key concluding remarks.

2 'Territory Matters' – The Place-Based Approach as a Frame of Territorial EU Policy

Inequalities and polarized development, observed in the EU, constitute critical obstacles to the realization of the shared aspiration of a united Europe [19]. Despite the ample EU regional development policies implemented so far, polarization still persists, taking the form of constantly escalating economic and social disparities between places and between people, along with environmental pressures and threats [19]. According to Görmar et al. [26], polarized development is roughly appearing as: an increasing *population concentration* in and around large cities, coupled with trends of population decline that occurs in other regions; *accumulation* of investments and economic resources in a few capital and metropolitan areas, leaving behind the rest of cities and regions in the EU; a spatially and socially *uneven distribution of wealth*, which leads to a trust deficit in the European construction, overall frustration of population and a sense of detachment from an inclusive European future vision.

In the age of information society and the surge of the *smart city paradigm*, these inequalities and polarized development are considerably broadened, giving prominence mostly to large urban environments (global cities, mega cities, metropolises, etc.). Conversely, *SMSTs seem to drop behind*, despite the fact that their critical functional and socioeconomic role in the European urban-rural system in general, and the rural development in particular is greatly recognized [11, 17, 29, 48].

This category of *less-favored urban constellations* has recently gained high attention at the policy level, by being incorporated in the EU Cohesion and Territorial Development policy agenda in 2015, during the Latvian Presidency [40]. Nowadays, policy directions regarding such regions are grounded in their valuable *local assets* and *spatial qualities* that are deemed as core factors for appealing to economic agents and guiding local development strategies [37].

In this respect, the issue of small and medium-sized cities' *attractiveness* as a policy concept [25, 36], based on the variety of their assets and territorial capital, is immensely emphasized in the post-2000 period and has enriched the discussion for both EU's territorial cohesion as well as the new strategy and vision for rural Europe towards 2040. What actually seems to be sought is the mobilization of territorial assets and the boosting of attractiveness in order to strengthen competitiveness and attenuate local disparities.

Coping with imbalances and regional backwardness brings to the fore the concept of *place-based approach* as a form of public policy [3, 19, 20] and a *new paradigm* [2] for achieving long-term sustainability objectives, founded on the endogenous development of territorial assets [19, 20, 36]. Such an approach seeks a wiser utilization or motivation of local assets, so that economic efficiency but also social inclusion or equity objectives to be attained. It also sheds light on the tight relationship between every single spatial context (region) on the one hand; and the nature of efficiency and equity problems that need to be dealt with, as well as the necessity to propose tailor-made interventions on the other hand. Stated differently, as Barca [2:9] suggests, a place-based approach refers to *"...a policy strategy aimed at promoting development from outside (the place) by means of interventions tailored to contexts"*, implying thus the need for a *spatially-aware developmental policy.* Beer et al. [3:5] provide a broader definition of the term by claiming that it *"... embodies an ethos about, and an approach to, the developments of economy and society that acknowledge that the context of each and every city, region and rural district offers opportunities for enhancing well-being. It advocates for a development approach tailored to the needs of each"*. They also state that no settlement can be grasped as too small or too remote for planning its own progress; while they enrich the term 'place' by attributing to it the human dimension, meanings and emotions [3], vital aspects that are critically linked to motivation of community groups and institutional settings. Servillo et al. [39] describe place-based approach as a genuine perspective for putting small towns in their local and regional context, combined with an effort to establish relationships and interaction of these towns with other spatial scales (national and international).

In the post-2000 period, the significance of the place-based approach towards addressing socio-economic and territorial cohesion objectives is remarkably acknowledged; while it is mentioned in numerous strategic documents, thereby forming a *mainstream* in dealing with territorial policies in the EU [12, 18, 19, 36]. This approach can be applied to a variety of territorial typologies including urban contexts, small and medium-sized towns, rural constellations, insular regions, peripheral and sparsely-populated areas. Its key constituents are the use of social capital and territorial assets, coupled with the building of innovation and smart specialisation strategies. The ultimate goal of the place-based or territorial approach is to abrogate inefficiency of resource utilization and social exclusion in terms of income and other well-being features [2].

All the above have provided precious food for thought on the development of the appropriate methodological approach, followed in the specific case study – Nemea locality –, which is marked by: an explicit focus on 'locale' – *place-based approach* – [19, 20], taking into consideration all local assets and the value attached to them by the local community, as well as the full set of opportunities that stem from the broader decision environment; an *integrated approach* [19, 20], attempting to identify and strengthen sectoral interaction and creation of value chains; a *participatory view* – both face-to-face (F2F) and ICT-enabled –, inherent in the place-based approach [12, 19, 20], so that distributed knowledge to be embedded in the planning endeavour and the widest possible consensus, as to the potential future development pathways, to be ensured; a *strategic view* (i.e., a results-oriented, long-term planning approach), targeting future, desirable, identity-based and locally-driven pathways that can offer short but mostly robust medium and longer term inclusive growth. The steps of the proposed framework are described in the following section.

3   Steps of the Methodological Framework

Adopting a place-based approach, the methodological framework for policy analysis of Nemea case study attempts to get a deep insight into the economic, social and spatial peculiarities of the local context – *the internal environment*. It also delves into the area's broader context – *the external environment* – by exploring potential relationships and interactions with different spatial scales (national and international), as well as challenges and opportunities that emanate from this context. Key drivers for discovering potential future developmental pathways are: quantitative and qualitative spatial data management regarding distinctive *territorial assets* for informing long-term perspectives of sustainable development strategies; a *scenario planning* process, which builds upon a specific combination of territorial assets, integrates distinct community interests and demonstrates spatial choices of scenarios that are transparent, verifiable, forward-looking and can be subjected to citizens' scrutiny; and F2F as well as ICT-enabled *community engagement* for assessing both the current state of the study region and the preferences, with regard to the proposed future pathways, which are expressed during the application of the scenario planning exercise. The steps of the methodological framework are illustrated in Fig. 1.

More specifically, *Stage 1* focuses on a preliminary identification of *problems* and *critical issues* in seeking a sustainable and resilient future of the locality, but also on their relative *prioritization*. To this end, successive interaction processes between the research team and the local community are carried out. Engagement, at this stage, involves specific target groups such as: the mayor and the members of the municipality's council, key municipal employees (directors of municipality's departments) and local community groups.

Stage 2 refers to the shaping of the local *vision* for the future development of Nemea. This task is, initially, accomplished by the research team, by taking into consideration the pieces of information that are collected at Stage 1, the elaboration on the elements of the internal environment, as well as the challenges and opportunities that emanate from the external environment; while it is further detailed at Stage 6, where this vision and a proposed strategic plan for its implementation are scrutinized.

Stage 3 attempts to illuminate the *peculiar attributes* of the study area. Natural and cultural resources, local economic structure, employment pattern, social environment, infrastructures, etc. are explored in this respect. Mapping of pertinent resources and key infrastructures is also carried out as a complementary task for both the planning exercise and the effective communication/interaction with the local community. The insight gained reveals the comparative advantages, but also the weaknesses of the region. This, combined with knowledge gathered at Stage 4 – the external environment – provides valuable input to Stage 2, thereby sharpening the vision by throwing light on constraints, opportunities and risks of the external environment.

Stage 4 regards the deciphering of the key drivers of the *external environment*, elucidating thus the decision context in which the region's strategic objectives will be pursued. Developments of these key drivers may induce either positive or negative effects on the study area. Strategic planning should take advantage of the positive influences and efficaciously handle the negative ones at the same time, in order to secure a sustainable and resilient future. The study of the external environment is based on the *PESTLE analysis* (Political – Economic – Social – Technological – Legal – Environmental) [1, 6]; and elaborates on issues such as climate change, technological developments, economic recession, to name but a few. Furthermore, *developmental* and *strategic spatial choices*

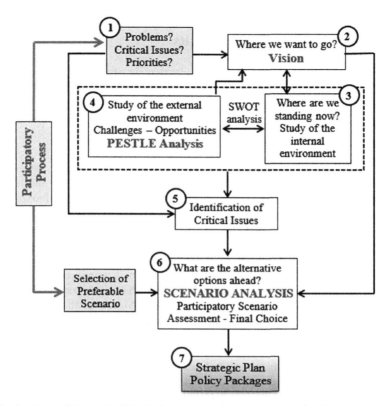

Fig. 1. Steps of the methodological approach of Nemea's strategic planning exercise

that emerge from hierarchically higher policy making levels are taken into account, e.g., the national or regional level.

Stage 5 identifies the *critical issues* that are expected to arise during the study area's 'journey' towards the desirable end state. This is accomplished through the qualitative assessment of information gathered at all the previous stages; whereas the issues illuminated at this step give input into the stage of scenario building.

Stage 6 elaborates on *future alternative scenarios*, capable of attaining a visionary end state, as this is articulated at Stage 2. In the context of the particular spatial planning endeavour, the scenario building process follows the *two uncertainty axes* rationale [14, 47, 49].

Finally, *Stage 7* comprises the policy paths that can bring the selected scenario to life.

4 Featuring Future Development Perspectives of Nemea Municipality – Case Study Results

The particular section presents indicative results that are obtained from the implementation of the previously analyzed framework, while a succinct description of Nemea's municipality profile is also provided.

4.1 The Study Region – The Internal Environment

The study area, i.e., municipality of Nemea (Region of Peloponnese, Greece) has a population of 10.954 inhabitants, according to the 2011 Greek census; and falls under the category of *inner regions*, as these are defined by Servillo et al. [40]. Pursuant to this view, inner regions are mountainous or rural places, at a distance from large urban centers or capitals, that include functionally autonomous small towns. They usually exhibit low or negative job creation rates in all sectors and low level of services, as well as deficient educational/recreation amenities and poor quality of life. Therefore, they are perceived as *marginal territories* in terms of territorial dynamics but also socio-economic frontiers.

Municipality of Nemea is situated in a relatively plain territory surrounded by mountains, hence its characterization as mountainous region. Moreover, the soil composition, the geology, the altitude and the sub-arid and sub-humid climate of the area are conducive to the development of viticulture. Indeed, Nemea possesses the largest vineyard zone met in the Balkans and constitutes the greatest red wine producer and exporter in Greece. It is also endowed with a remarkably wealthy cultural capital, composed of significant archaeological sites, monuments of various historical periods, modern art, local habits and customs as well as well-established cultural events (e.g., Nemean Games) and pertinent infrastructures.

The local economy is strongly contingent on the primary sector with 48,77% of the workforce being engaged in it, whereas 11,32% is involved in the secondary and 39,91% in the tertiary sector. As far as the basic demographical and social characteristics are concerned, the following can be mentioned: Nemea exhibits considerable tendencies of population decline; a substantial share of its citizens (13%) has not completed primary education; unemployment rates remain low compared to the national average; the labor force is considered well-educated; the area is equipped with all the necessary social infrastructures. Additionally, its accessibility is rather problematic due to the inefficiencies and the bad quality of the road network; while a great degree of dependence between Nemea and the nearby urban centers is pretty obvious, a fact that seriously obstructs its developmental perspective and dynamics.

4.2 The Context of Community Engagement

In the context of Nemea's spatial planning exercise, community engagement takes place in two distinct stages of the methodological framework, namely (Fig. 2):

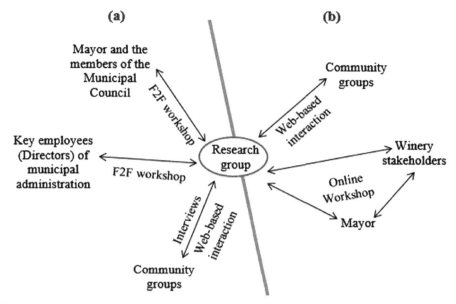

Fig. 2. Target groups and means of interaction between the research group and the community of Nemea at: (a) Stage 1 and (b) Stage 6

- Stage 1 (Fig. 1), where the focus is placed on the identification of *problems, critical issues* and *priorities*, as these are grasped by various local actors and community groups;
- Stage 6 (Fig. 1), where *scenario preferences* of the local community are explored.

More specifically, at *Stage 1*, the participatory approach is implemented through successive interaction procedures that intend to get insight into diversifying views on the *problems, critical issues* and their *prioritization*. This whole process involves the following target groups and means of interaction:

- A F2F workshop of the research group with the *mayor* and the *members of the municipal council*, i.e., those in charge of setting up local policies.
- A F2F workshop with *key municipal employees*, who represent the heads of various departments and handle locality's everyday issues and inefficiencies.
- Interaction with local community groups, conducted through a limited number of interviews with Nemea's residents and entrepreneurs (10 persons).

Based on the responses and views that emerge from the traditional interaction (previously described F2F workshops and interviews with community groups), a *Web questionnaire* is structured as a means for extending the participatory process to the local community; and engaging lay people and local entrepreneurs, in order to enrich and therefore improve the planning process and outcome. The *online interaction* is hosted by the municipality's website, where the Web questionnaires are uploaded and responses, as to the problems, critical issues and priorities, are collected in a time span of one month (from the beginning of August to the beginning of September 2020).

Additionally, at *Stage 6*, the constructed scenarios are communicated by the research team to:

- the *local community* through a Web-based exercise that takes place in September 2020. In this respect, textual description of each scenario narrative and their respective visualization (maps) are embedded in a Google form and uploaded to the municipal website. Afterwards, community groups are asked to express their views as to which one better meets their preferences.
- *influential stakeholders* of the wine sector through an online workshop (October 2020) in order for their preferences, concerning the proposed scenarios, to be explored. The workshop is attended by five of the most important and powerful local winery owners and the mayor of Nemea.

4.3   Building Attractive Future Development Pathways for Nemea Region

"Increasingly, competitiveness and prosperity depend on the capacity of the people and businesses located there to make the best use of all of territorial assets."

Green Paper on Territorial Cohesion, 2008:3

Following the above statement, an endeavor to mobilize the study area's territorial assets towards *sustainable future images*, which are capable of opening up new opportunities for social, economic and territorial cohesion for local people and businesses, but also for external investments and visitors, is undertaken and is briefly delineated in this section. Development of these future images or scenarios is greatly dependent on the *critical issues* identified in previous stages of the methodological framework (Stage 5), and they principally refer to the: protection of the highly productive agricultural land and the multifunctional exploitation of the wine sector (wine tourism and gastronomy, educational node in wine cultivation and production, wine production clusters, innovation and entrepreneurship); brand creation/place marketing, founded on wine and alternative cultural tourism; development, digitization and promotion of cultural routes – virtual wineries' route, virtual cultural route that links the local archaeological sites, revival of famous myths (land of Hercules); empowerment of local community and ICT skills acquisition; governance – active engagement of local community in decision-making processes; extraversion by means of complementarity and synergies' creation with adjacent cultural tourism destinations.

The above-mentioned critical issues provide substantial food for thought and decisively contribute to the structuring of the study region's future development scenarios. From the set of available methodologies, the *two uncertainty axes* scenario building approach, whose rationale is illustrated in Fig. 3, is applied. Such an approach is based on two uncertainty axes, which reflect two particular objectives of the study region that exhibit the highest degree of uncertainty. More specifically, the *two key uncertainties* used for constructing Nemea's future development scenarios, mostly perceived as the main vehicles for its future perspective, relate to the role of the:

- traditional and well-rooted wine production of the region that ranges from a medium rate of exploitation (current state) to a fully dynamic and innovative sector, a vital component of a strong place branding;
- sustainable exploitation of territorial capital – natural and cultural – that ranges from a mild capitalization of cultural heritage to a more dynamic entry in niche tourist markets, by providing alternative, authentic, multi-thematic and experience-based tourism products.

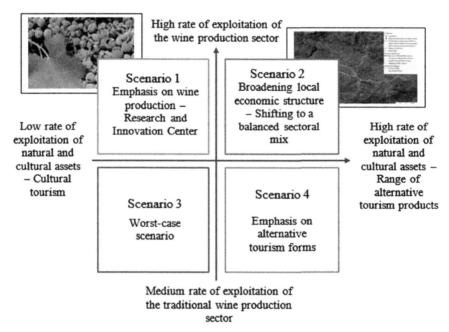

Fig. 3. The 'two uncertainty axes' scenario building approach

Qualitative evaluation of the four scenarios leads to the exclusion of scenarios 3 and 4. In fact, Scenario 3 is perceived as the worst-case scenario and 4 as a scenario that defies the region's long wine tradition and dynamism. The prevailing scenarios 1 and 2 reflect two qualitative, normative and well-differentiated future images. *Scenario 1* – Nemea as a Research and Innovation Center of wine production – aims at triggering innovation, extraversion and productivity of the wine sector (agricultural and winery community), being conceived thus as the cornerstone of the local economic scheme and a 'vehicle' for future growth. *Scenario 2* – Nemea as a multidimensional alternative tourism destination - development and establishment of various of cultural routes – represents a sectoral-balanced, socially-equitable and spatially-deconcentrated future development pattern, totally harmonised with the prominent wine sector. The scenario attempts to combine the long wine tradition with a range of alternative tourism pathways that are built upon the remarkable local natural and cultural assets and comparative advantages.

4.4 Key Results of Nemea's Spatial Planning Exercise

The particular section shortly presents the results that emerge from the community engagement processes of Stage 1 and Stage 6.

Regarding the online questionnaires of the first stage, only 61 of them were submitted. Although the sample can by no means be considered as representative, the obtained results are finally used. This is mainly justified by the research teams' opinion that the degree of online engagement is relatively satisfactory, given the lack of participatory and technological culture of the local people, the significant time constrains (time span and date of conduction) and new priorities' setting due to the outburst of COVID-19. The key findings that stem from the elaboration of the collected questionnaires mainly refer to the: poor quality of life, community's ignorance of projects under progress thereby revealing their 'distance' from local decision-making processes, insufficient and -in many cases- superficial participation in local affairs, extremely limited deployment of municipal e-services and indifferent, low-skilled and rude municipal employees.

Concerning the citizens and stakeholders' viewpoint on the most suitable scenario (Stage 6), 81 responses are gathered. As regards the first scenario (Nemea as a Research and Innovation Center of wine production), 89% of participants fully agree or agree with its fundamentals, whereas 11% disagree, fully disagree or have no opinion on the matter. The second scenario (Nemea as a multidimensional alternative tourism destination – creation of cultural routes) manages to provoke even more positive reactions, since 91% of the participators fully agree or agree with its principal idea, while only 9% holds indifferent or negative opinion. It should be stressed that extensive workshop discussion with the influential stakeholders of the wine sector uncovers a certain preference towards the second scenario, because it is deemed to be the one that better utilizes Nemea's extraordinary cultural resources and optimally fits local competencies, while at the same time it offers new chances for enlarging their marketing footprint. Interesting suggestions on efficient ways of integrating well-established and extroverting viticulture with cultural tourism and local gastronomy, strengthening thus local value chains' creation, are also provided by them.

5   Conclusions

In the era of perpetual and unexpected changes, intense and multifaceted pressures of all kinds, imperative demands and constantly growing needs, every region is called to build and implement a flexible, consistent and integrated developmental strategic plan that seeks to form and maintain a *sustainable, resilient and inclusive* future. In this respect, various planning approaches that incorporate all the above alterations occurring in society, economy, environment, institutions, technology, etc., can be followed for crafting these plans. *Strategic planning*, as such an approach, systematically endeavors to: (a) gain a more detailed insight into a place by demarcating its advantages, disadvantages, strengths and weaknesses (internal environment); (b) identify the opportunities and risks that stem from the broader -external- environment; and (c) promote participation by embedding civic engagement into every stage of the planning process. Additionally, strategic planning is mainly oriented towards action undertaking, effective implementation/monitoring of results and alignment with the desirable outcomes; and thus, it constitutes an essential tool for shaping a *locale's future state* over a long-term horizon, managing at the same time severe complexity and uncertainty and contributing to the realization of enticing future developments.

The process of creating Nemea's strategic plan reveals a series of crucial issues that may raise interesting questions or instigate vivid discussions; and therefore, they should be taken into serious consideration. To begin with, Nemea is immensely lagging behind in terms of *governance maturity*, *online participation culture* as well as *penetration and assimilation of technology* in general, compared to larger Greek cities. This is a dominant trend at national, but also at European and international level, since small and medium-sized urban environments tend -inter alia- to exhibit poor technological performance. The main reason behind this remark lies at the root of the prevalent contemporary neoliberal notion that perceives large cities as dynamic marketplaces, which can efficaciously serve the interests of particular companies (mostly technological) and states [28]. For over a decade, colossal industries have been monopolizing the diffusion of technology and the development of 'smart' urban environments. Attention is paid almost exclusively to large cities and metropolises because these have the capacity to develop economies of scale and constitute much more attractive investement environments, compared to smaller cities and the limited economic benefits these entail [31]. As a consequence, the critical issue of *digital divide* and the predicament of those who have limited to no access to ICT infrastructures, or are void of the necessary skills [7, 43] is emerging; and is gradually gaining importance among planners and decision makers, as it leads to a certain kind of social inequality and social exclusion [9], thereby nurturing discussions on *technological* [33] and *spatial justice* [27]. Sudden adverse circumstances, such as the COVID-19 pandemic outbreak, may severely exacerbate the problem, since access to technology, especially during such turbulent, uncertain and restrictive periods, constitutes the *only window to the outer world*.

It should also be mentioned that in recent years, rural policy, in its effort to effectively address and support the specific needs and aspirations of rural places and their citizens, has decisively moved towards a more integrated, society empowering, multi-sectoral and *place-based approach*. This actually reflects the constantly increasing significance of ensuring the: participation of local stakeholders in the decision-making process; detection and assessment of local assets and their sustainable exploitation in favor of rural development; shift from a subsidy- to an investment-oriented approach; and the shift from policy interventions that redistribute local income to the identification of new economic opportunities as well as an *inclusive* and *just* transition towards the smart era [8], based on the available but untapped local capital [43].

References

1. Achinas, S., Horjus, J., Achinas, V., Jan Willem Euverink, G.: A PESTLE analysis of biofuels energy industry in Europe. Sustainability **11**, 5981 (2019). https://doi.org/10.3390/su1121 5981
2. Barca, F.: An agenda for a reformed cohesion policy. A Place-Based Approach to Meeting European Union Challenges and Expectations. European Commission, Brussels (2009)
3. Beer, A., Mckenzie, F., Blazek, J., Sotarauta, M., Ayres, S.: Every place matters: towards effective place-based policy. Regional Studies Policy Impact Books, Regional Science Association (2020). ISBN: 978-0-367-62649-5 (print)

4. Bilbao-Osorio, B., Rodríguez-Pose, A.: From R&D to innovation and economic growth in the EU. Growth Change **35**(4), 434–455 (2004)
5. Bishop, J.: Collaboration and consensus. Town Country Plann. **67**(3), 111–114 (1998)
6. Boyce, P.: PESTLE analysis - definition and template (2020). https://boycewire.com/pestle-analysis-definition-and-template/. Accessed 5 June 2020
7. Brabham, C.D.: Crowdsourcing the public participation process for planning projects. Plan. Theory **8**(3), 242–262 (2009)
8. Burch, S.: Accelerating a just transition to smart, sustainable cities. Center for International Governance Innovation, Policy Brief No. 164 - February, pp. 1–8 (2021)
9. Carver, S., Evans, A., Kingston, R., Turton, I.: Public participation, GIS, and cyber-democracy: evaluating on-line spatial decision support systems. Environ. Plann. B. Plann. Des. **28**(6), 907–921 (2001)
10. COM(2008)616: Green Paper on Territorial Cohesion - Turning Territorial Diversity into Strength. Communication from the Commission to the Council, the European Parliament, the Committee of the Regions and the European Economic and Social Committee, Brussels, 6 October (2008)
11. Courtney, P., Moseley, M.: Determinants of local economic performance: experience from rural England. Local Econ. **23**, 305–318 (2008)
12. CSIL Centre for Industrial Studies: Territorial Agenda 2020 put in practice - enhancing the efficiency and effectiveness of cohesion policy by a place-based approach. Synthesis Report, vol. I. European Commission (2015)
13. Dalal-Clayton, B., Bass, S. (eds.): Sustainable Development Strategies: A Resource Book. Earthscan Publications Ltd., London (2002)
14. Dawson, M., et al.: Strategic thinking – scenario planning for an uncertain future. In: OzWater Conference, Brisbane, 8–10 May. Australian Water Association, Swinburne Research Bank (2018)
15. De Noronha, T., Vaz, E.: Theoretical foundations in support of small and medium towns. Sustainability **12**, 5312 (2020). https://doi.org/10.3390/su12135312
16. Dijkstra, L., Poelman, H.: Remote rural regions: how proximity to a city influences the performance of rural regions. Regional Focus, 01/2008. European Commission, Brussels (2008)
17. Elisei, P. (ed.): Strategic Territorial Agenda for Small and Middle-sized Towns and Urban Systems. Urban Planning Institute of the Republic of Slovenia (UIRS), Ljubljana (2014)
18. European Commission (EC): Territorial agenda of the European Union 2020 - towards an inclusive, smart and sustainable Europe of diverse regions (2011)
19. European Commission (EC): Territorial Agenda 2030 - #TerritorialAgenda a future for all places. In: Informal Meeting of Ministers Responsible for Spatial Planning and Territorial Development and/or Territorial Cohesion, Germany, 1 December (2020)
20. European Commission (EC): The New Leipzig Charter – The Transformative Power of Cities for the Common Good. In: Adopted at the Informal Ministerial Meeting on Urban Matters on 30 November (2020)
21. Evans-Cowley, J., Hollander, J.: The new generation of public participation: internet-based participation tools. Plan. Pract. Res. **25**(3), 397–408 (2010)
22. Fishkin, S.J.: The Voice of the People, Public Opinion and Democracy. Yale University Press, New Heaven (1995)
23. Friedmann, J.: Planning in the Public Domain: From Knowledge to Action. Princeton University Press, Princeton (1987). https://doi.org/10.1515/9780691214009
24. Garau, C.: Citizen participation in public planning: a literature review. Int. J. Sci. **1**, 21–44 (2012)

25. Garau, C., Desogus, G., Stratigea, A.: Territorial cohesion in insular contexts: assessing exter-
    nal attractiveness and internal strength of major Mediterranean islands. Eur. Plan. Stud. **28**(12),
    1–21 (2020). https://doi.org/10.1080/09654313.2020.1840524
26. Görmar, F., Lang, T., Nagy, E., Raagmaa, G.: Re-thinking regional and local policies in
    times of polarisation: an introduction. In: Lang, T., Görmar, F. (eds.) Regional and Local
    Development in Times of Polarisation. NGE, pp. 1–25. Springer, Singapore (2019). https://
    doi.org/10.1007/978-981-13-1190-1_1
27. Jones, R., Moisio, S.M., Weckroth, M.T.K., Luukkonen, J.M., Mayer, F., Miggelbrink, J.: Re-
    conceptualising territorial cohesion through the prism of spatial justice: critical perspectives
    on academic and policy discourses. In: Lang, T., Görmar, F. (eds.) Regional and Local Devel-
    opment in Times of Polarisation: Re-thinking Spatial Policies in Europe, pp. 1–24. Palgrave
    Macmillan, Singapore (2019)
28. Kitchin, R.: Decentering the smart city. In: Flynn, S. (Ed.) Equality in the City: Imaginaries
    of the Smart Future. Intellect, Bristol (2021). https://progcity.maynoothuniversity.ie/wp-con
    tent/uploads/2021/01/PC-45-Decentring-the-smart-city.pdf. Accessed 22 Mar 2021
29. Malý, J.: Small towns in the context of "borrowed size" and "agglomeration shadow" debates:
    the case of the South Moravian region (Czech Republic). Eur. Countryside **4**, 333–350 (2016).
    https://doi.org/10.1515/euco-2016-0024
30. Marava, N., Alexopoulos, A., Stratigea, A.: Barriers to empowering and engaging youth in
    sustainable urban development endeavours – experience gained from Korydallos municipality
    – Greece. Geogr. Res. Forum **40**(1), 89–107 (2020). In: Ronen, O., Purian, R. (Eds.) Smart,
    Sustainable and Fair Cities, Special Issue
31. Muro, M., Whiton, J.: Big cities, small cities - and the gaps, October 2017. https://www.
    brookings.edu/blog/the-avenue/2017/10/17/big-cities-small-cities-and-the-gaps/. Accessed 4
    Feb 2019
32. Naldi, L., Nilsson, P., Westlund, H., Wixe, S.: What is smart rural development? J. Rural.
    Stud. **40**, 90–101 (2015)
33. Ortega, A., Pérez, F.A., Turianskyi, Y.: Technological justice: a G20 agenda. Economics
    Discussion Papers, No. 2018-58, Kiel Institute for the World Economy (IfW), Kiel (2018)
34. Przeybilovicz, E., et al.: Citizen participation in the smart city: findings from an international
    comparative study. Local Gov. Stud. 1–26 (2020). https://doi.org/10.1080/03003930.2020.
    1851204
35. Rhodes, R.A.W.: Understanding Governance - Policy Networks, Governance, Reflexivity and
    Accountability. Open University Press, Philadelphia (1997). ISBN: 0-335-19727-2
36. Russo, A., Smith, I., Atkinson, R., Servillo, L., Madsen, B., Van der Borg, J.: ATTREG -
    the attractiveness of European regions and cities for residents and visitors. Applied Research
    2013/1/7, Scientific Report. ISBN: 978-2-919777-26-6, ESPON 2013 Programme (2012)
37. Servillo, L., Atkinson, R., Russo, A.P.: Territorial attractiveness in EU urban and spatial
    policy: a critical review and future research agenda. Eur. Urban Reg. Stud. **19**(4), 349–365
    (2012). https://doi.org/10.1177/0969776411430289
38. Servillo, L., Atkinson, R., Smith, I., Russo, A.P., Sykora, L., Demaziere, C.: Small and medium
    sized towns in Europe. Interim Report. ESPON, Luxemburg (2013)
39. Servillo, L., et al.: TOWN - Small and Medium Sized Towns in their Functional Territorial
    Context. Applied Research 2013/1/23, Final Report, Version 6, November 2014
40. Servillo, L., Russo, A.P., Barbera, F., Carrosio, G.: Inner peripheries: towards an EU place-
    based agenda on territorial peripherality. Ital. J. Plann. Pract. **VI**(1), 42–75 (2016)
41. Servillo, L., Atkinson, R., Hamdouch, A.: Small and medium-sized towns in Europe: concep-
    tual, methodological and policy issues. Tijdschr. Econ. Soc. Geogr. **108**(4), 365–379 (2017).
    https://doi.org/10.1111/tesg.12252
42. Somarakis, G., Stratigea, A.: Guiding informed choices on participation tools in spatial
    planning: an e-decision support system. Int. J. E-Plann. Res. **8**(3), 38–61 (2019)

43. Stratigea, A.: ICTs for rural development: potential applications and barriers involved. NETCOM **25**(3–4), 179–204 (2011)
44. Stratigea, A.: Theory and Methods of Participatory Planning. Greek Academic Electronic Books, Athens (2015). ISBN: 978-960-603-241-7 (in Greek)
45. Stratigea, A., Somarakis, G., Panagiotopoulou, M.: Smartening-up communities in less-privileged urban areas – the 'DemoCU' participatory cultural planning experience in Korydallos – Greece Municipality. In: Stratigea, A., Kyriakides, E., Nicolaides, Ch. (Eds.) Smart Cities in the Mediterranean - Coping with Sustainability Objectives in Small and Medium-Sized Cities and Island Communities, pp. 85–111. Springer, Switzerland. ISBN 987-3-319-54557-8 (2017). https://doi.org/10.1007/978-3-319-54558-5
46. Stratigea, A., Leka, A., Nicolaides, C.: Small and medium-sized cities and insular communities in the Mediterranean: coping with sustainability challenges in the smart city context. In: Stratigea, A., Kyriakides, E., Nicolaides, C. (eds.) Smart Cities in the Mediterranean. PI, pp. 3–29. Springer, Cham (2017). https://doi.org/10.1007/978-3-319-54558-5_1
47. Van der Heijden, K.: Scenarios – The Art of Strategic Conversation, 2nd edn. Wiley, Chichester (2005)
48. Van Leeuwen, E.: Urban-rural Interactions: Towns as Focus Points in Rural Development. Springer, Heidelberg (2010). ISBN 978-3-7908-2407-0. https://doi.org/10.1007/978-3-7908-2407-0
49. Van't Klooster, S.A., Van Asselt, M.B.A.: Practising the scenario-axes technique. Futures **38**(1), 15–30 (2006)

15-Minute City in Urban Regeneration Perspective: Two Methodological Approaches Compared to Support Decisions

Ginevra Balletto[1]([⊠]) [iD], Michèle Pezzagno[2] [iD], and Anna Richiedei[2] [iD]

[1] DICAAR – Department of Civil and Environmental Engineering and Architecture, University of Cagliari, Via Marengo, 2, Cagliari, Italy
`balletto@unica.it`

[2] DICATAM – Department of Civil, Environmental, Architectural Engineering and Mathematics, University of Brescia, via Branze, 43, Brescia, Italy
`{michele.pezzagno,anna.richiedei}@unibs.it`

Abstract. Among the interesting topics concerning urban regeneration, there are reconversion of disused public buildings and widespread neighbourhood facilities maintenance. The proposal of effective solutions about these topics is also a common subject for the construction of the 15-Minute City. Starting from a 15-Minute city review, a lack in the organic vision on the theme in the literature emerges, together with numerous interesting field studies, applications and experimentations in practice still to be deepened. The paper presents a comparison between different methodological approaches for the analysis of the accessibility of open spaces in order to support practitioners and policy-makers to improve walkability. The comparison between the two Italian case studies (Cagliari and Brescia) identifies the values of the systematic methodological approach based on description of context, design data collection, data analysis, indexing, to be used for co-construction of knowledge to support contemporary 15-Minute city (The paper is part of the activities of the Interdepartmental Center "Cagliari Accessibility Lab" of the University of Cagliari.).

Keywords: Urban walkability · 15-Minute city · Decision-makers support

1 Introduction

1.1 Motivations

The construction of the 15-Minute city is a subject of topicality and renewed interest for public administrations, also but not only due to the Covid-15 pandemic, as it plans to transform or live the open spaces differently. The experiences of medium and large cities that experiment plans based on the 15-Minute city principles are many, while the scientific literature, in the face of a past season of in-depth study on walkability,

---

The original version of this chapter was revised: the names of the authors are written bibliographically correct. The correction to this chapter is available at
https://doi.org/10.1007/978-3-030-86976-2_50

O. Gervasi et al. (Eds.): ICCSA 2021, LNCS 12953, pp. 535–548, 2021.
https://doi.org/10.1007/978-3-030-86976-2_36

pedestrianism and proximity, does not yet seem to systematically address the theme (see Literature review). Among the emerging themes in urban regeneration [1–3], understood as the transformation of building fabrics, services, open spaces, but also of social relations, in contexts that tend to contain land consumption, can certainly be included:

- The recovery of large abandoned buildings;
- The maintenance of small residential fabrics (also to be redeveloped) and the network of services connected to them.

The redevelopment of public real estate assets has long been at the center of research attention, both for historical-architectural stylistic aspects and for spatial-urban ones: services - cultural, health, ecosystem services, [4, 5] - and mobility - walkability, cycling, e-mobility [6]. However, this is a difficult task, also due to the economic crisis, which together with the health crisis do not facilitate, on the one hand, the federalism of this asset [7], and on the other its related requalification, although considered fundamental for improving urban, social and environmental quality [8, 9].

In this synthetic framework, the planning of proximity services, which is inspired by small municipalities, is capable of determining high levels of livability that guarantee a balanced relationship between services and communities, greater sustainability of mobility and generate-consolidate a network of community relations [10]. The transposition of the proximity services of the small town in the medium-large city can be represented through the 15-Minute city [11]. However, in the medium-large sized cities the proximity services are often "hosted" by obsolete buildings and infrastructures that need to be renovated or regenerated according to energy, safety and environmental aspects.

Furthermore, the lack of a structured 15-Minute vision on the city in the academic field, or updated to the modern context, as shown by the literature analysis, and the themes of interest for urban regeneration have led to propose in the present paper a comparison between methodological approaches for the analysis of the accessibility/walkability of open spaces to support decision-makers to identify the most effective and significant characteristics that could become the strengths for design the 15-Minute city. Two case studies were then selected to compare the methods used in the field of disused public building (in Cagliari) and residential urban fabrics and related services (in Brescia). The two identified themes are intentionally different from each other, in order to highlight more considerations. We characterize these works along a continuum ranging from communicative planning to planning technologist" [12] his paper proposes two techniques GIS-based to visualize and locate problems supporting the decisions of policy-makers [13, 14]. GIS is also used as Geospatial/Geovisual Decision Support Systems [12].

Aim of this paper is addressing the issue related to the 15-Minute city, analysing it from the literature review point of view, and also proposing two different methods of analysis, applied to two different cities in Italy (Brescia and Cagliari). In particular, the idea was that of selecting some particular neighbourhood in the two areas, observing the availability - or lack - of services according to two different approaches: Space Syntax in the case of Brescia, and the development of suited-for-purpose basic indices of porosity (PI), crossing (CI) and attractiveness (AI), and combined index Walkability through Big Building (WBBI) of urban 'enclave' in the case of Cagliari. In the present case, the two areas were analysed following two different approaches, while the idea developed throughout the realization of the present research, for future activities, will be that of combining the two methods applying them all to different case studies.

The rest of the paper is organized as follows. A literature review is carried on in Sect. 1.2. Section 2 addresses a comparison of methodological approaches. It contains a description of the different methods adopted and the two study areas, together with a discussion and comparison of the areas, methods and results obtained. Section 3 on final considerations concludes the paper.

1.2 Literature Review

Cities are complex organisms that live thanks to substructures that are not always in an organic relationship with each other. The evidence is often that of apparently uncontrolled growth and conditioned by the income from infrastructural investments, rather than by the quality of life. On more than one occasion, the positivity of urban schemes that are based on accessibility to services or stops of Local Public Transport has been recognized. As a matter of example, the case of Stockholm, which won the EU green capital award for this reason: still, the case of Freiburg which based integrated urban planning and transport on these principles. In small urban areas, access to essential services should take place within a period suitable for non-motorized travel (hence the idea of "15-Minute cities"), while in larger urban areas that should be the maximum time for access to a transport system that connects the city.

In the face of the wide and consolidated academic and technical literature relating to Transit-Oriented Development (TOD), even if limited to urban studies (e.g. [15–28]), the well-known importance of a strong public transport system is for structuring more sustainable cities from the point of view of mobility [29–35]. We want to investigate the system of services and relationships between the different urban functions that revolve around the concept of proximity. Some pushes on this approach starting from the TOD are present in Chatman, Ratner & Goetz, Boarnet & Compin and Freilich [36–39] and the so-called "15-Minute City". The scientific literature that clearly deals with 15-Minute City using this term properly is practically nil (Web of Science, Scopus, Franco Angeli, etc.). On the other hand, there are many references of an experimental nature and best practices applied at the planning level which are included in reports evaluating the performance of the cities [40]: for example, Edinburgh, Utrecht and Ottawa; Melbourne had an urban plan called "twenty-minutes neighbourhood", while in Copenhagen the new zero-emission district of Nordhavnen is nicknamed "five minutes to everything" and Paris started the Plan "Ville du quart d'heure". The studies that analyse the area that can be reached in 15 min on foot can represent an indirect reference to the concept, but they are mainly specialized, not generalist and systematic studies. The case studies that analyze a specific phenomenon aim to find technical solutions for accessibility and its development opportunities [6, 41–43]. It can be deduced that the topic is of interest to society and little dealt with systematically from the academic perspectives, so the topic is original.

Furthermore, to frame the topic in general terms, it is appropriate to consider some references that, by extension, concern the same approach with different taxonomy, such as the concept of "proximity" in the city or "soft city". The literature in this sense is very rich [28, 44–58], but less known by practitioners and little applied at an operational level in the last century.

2 Comparison of Methodological Approaches to Walkability

2.1 Analysis and Comparison

In this paragraph, the selected case studies are compared. The two case studies are different and complementary in the typical Italian cities. So a case study (in the city of Cagliari) deals with the issue of largely dismissed buildings, while the second case (in the city of Brescia) concerns the relation between (vulnerable) city-users and services in a residential context.

The elements compared in the analysis are: topic (problem to solve), subject (area investigated in the case study), preliminary information/knowledge (planning tool or data at the base of the case study), methodological approach (the method used in the study). The comparison after the analysis allows to identify the strengths and weaknesses of both approaches and it will allow clarifying which methodological aspects can be more significant for the 15-Minute city and urban redevelopment in general terms.

2.2 Methodology of the Case Study of Cagliari

The Cagliari case study (558,684 inhabitants in 2019, in the case of the Metropolitan City, Region of Sardinia) refers to the historic center of the main municipality divided into four districts, within which there are urban enclaves resulting from the abandonment of big buildings.

The proposed method, extrapolated from a previous research always tested on the city of Cagliari [6] is based on the elaboration of a series of indices, considered useful and interesting to evaluate the capacity of disused public buildings to act as potential public spaces. This constitutes one of the main challenges for the city of Cagliari and for contemporary cities in general. Therefore, indicators have been developed to support walkability in contexts characterized by urban enclaves.

In particular, with three basic main indices of porosity (PI), crossing (CI) and attractiveness (AI), and the combined index of Walkability through Big Building (WBBI), they are functional to the reduction of the above-said urban enclave effect. In particular, Porosity Index (PI) is the weighted coverage ratio, between the building area and the pertinent free land area; Crossing index (CI) represents the level of crossability that characterizes each public property and that allows people to reach different parts of the city. This index, in fact, depends on the architectural morphology of the building, in particular on the number of crossings and paths that connect the various entrances to the property; The attractiveness index (AI) refers to both the number and variety of central locations located in the area that can be walked in 15 min from the enclave.

Therefore, for the calculation of this index, the Simpson diversity index was taken as a reference, which allows us to give weight to the diversity of urban boundary functions. The Simpson index is applied to represent ecological diversity, but is also applied by analogy in the urban context [6, 59], that is to describe the diversity of urban services. The proposed methodology is applied in the focus of disused public buildings of the Strategic Plan of the metropolitan city of Cagliari (2020).

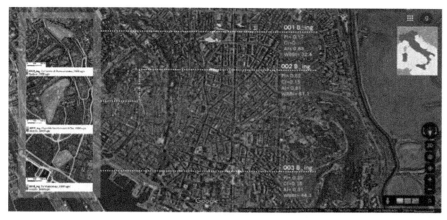

Fig. 1. City of Cagliari, - Sardinia - main enclaves deriving from disused public buildings (001, 002, 003 B_ing).

The method required:

1. the assessment of the strategies the urban plan of the historic center;
2. the assessment of the urban context, urban morphology and the community for the definition of service groups (movement, welfare and trade);
3. use of the OSMR1 algorithms referring to Google maps for the determination of the isochrones.

After evaluating the strategies of the urban plan of the historic center, public works plan of the Municipality of Cagliari and carrying out a number of inspections both in the abandoned buildings and in the immediate context, the quantitative evaluation of the services was carried out.

The first analyzes concerned the equipment and pedestrian accessibility of the proximity services of the selected enclaves (001, 002, 003 B ing) through a qualitative assessment of the walkability deriving from digital traces, (strava.com) and the quantity of services divided by categories (google maps).

Once the data was collected and georeferenced, it was possible to evaluate the indices: porosity (PI), crossing (CI) and attractiveness (AI) and Walkability Big Building (WBBI) of each disused public building area (Fig. 1). Though these indicators were contextualized by specific context weights, it is intended to measure the intrinsic and extrinsic characteristics of disused public building areas, in particular of large dimensions and extensions. The proposed approach allows us to represent the quality of the public space and therefore its potential in the city of 15 min. In particular, these indexes make it possible to relate intrinsic elements (PI and CI) with extrinsic elements (AI) of a given decommissioned real estate asset with big-sized dimensional characteristics. This is in order to act in the redevelopment of abandoned assets to obtain maximum walkability, knowing that the ideal reference benchmark is given by squares and urban parks. In fact, PI, CI = 1 and AI = 1 (WBBI = 100) occur in an open space, which can be crossed in several directions and with a relative diversified attractiveness. In doing so, WBBI can support decisions in order to evaluate the intervention priorities aimed at making urban contexts, today characterized as enclaves from abandoned public buildings. In particular, we have intended to evaluate the possibilities of making the "central places" of the past, such as ancient factories, hospitals etc., accessible in pedestrian terms in a logical and flexible network, where the "walkability" can renew the quality of life.

2.3   Methodology of the Case Study of Brescia

The case study of Brescia (196,134 inhabitants in 2019, Lombardy Region) concerns a specific district of the city: an economic-popular housing neighborhood with clearly identifiable and rather homogeneous typological characteristics, attributable to the experience of Father Marcolini, called "Villaggio Prealpino" (4,417 inhabitants). It is located in the North of the capital city on the territory of two municipalities (Brescia and Bovezzo) and built by the Cooperative "La Famiglia" between 1958 and 1972.

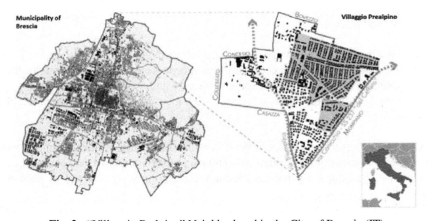

Fig. 2. "Villaggio Prelpino" Neighborhood in the City of Brescia (IT)

The methodology proposed in this case study carried out in 2019 is strongly civitas-oriented (focus on the civitas, the "city of people" and the city of the urban life, not on the urbs, the "city of stone", the built one [60, 61]): it places people and his relationships at the centre [62]. The analysis uses GIS software (QGIS). The alphanumeric data at the beginning processing phase needed to be georeferenced and therefore become usable for subsequent processing with QGIS. The method required the following steps:

- Analysis of demographic factors and urban load georeferentiation;
- Organization of existing services into categories and georeferentiation;
- Cartographic definition of the pedestrian mobility network;
- Proximity analysis through the GIS Space syntax plugin;
- Identification of the imbalance in the supply-demand ratio by type of service in the study area.

The analysis of demographic factors focused on the resident population by sex and age group and in particular on the elderly population (over 65 years old). Once the data had been collected and geo-referenced, it was possible to create the board in Fig. 3 which shows the urban load for each building and to evaluate the presence of buildings with an elderly population only.

The analysis of public services present in the Villaggio Prealpino was developed based on the Municipal urban plan which reports, in the Service Plan ("Piano dei Servizi"), the provision of existing public services. This information was implemented by additional open-source data (Google Maps, White Pages website, specific websites for commercial activities) and by site inspections. In the analysis, health and social assistance services were privileged (clinics, clinics also in the third sector), parks and gardens, religious and cultural services (including the library), childcare services and schools and a selection of administrative services to identify the spaces and services essential for the daily life (and health) of the elderly. Besides, small neighborhood shops were included in the analysis, considered essential to encourage pedestrian mobility. Information was collected on nearly 50 services. An example regarding the collection and mapping of the green area is shown in Fig. 3.

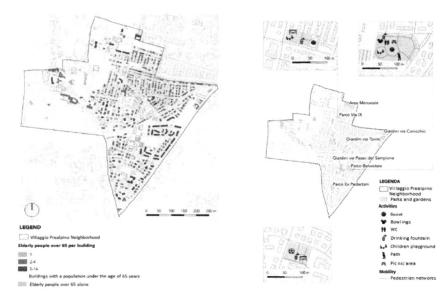

Fig. 3. Urban load per building with a particular focus on the elderly, on the left, and a sample of services analysis about green areas, on the right.

Once the places of the departure and potential arrival of the population were defined, we proceeded with the design of the pedestrian network to know the potential flows. The *Space Syntax*[1] tool was used to carry out this analysis. It is based on a set of techniques for analysing spaces (be they buildings or urban areas) and the human activity that takes place in them. The theories holding this methodology were put forward around the Seventies by Hillier and Hanson [63], and then it was implemented until the creation of software, usable in QGIS (see also [64]). At the basis of this system is the awareness of the close link between society and the environment in which it operates and lives. Space is an intrinsic sign of human activity itself, and what happens in a limited area can be strictly influenced by the relationship between that single space and the network of spaces with which it is connected.

Space Syntax enables you to analyse the relationship between spatial elements (points, segments, areas, etc.) starting from their configuration, in various ways. The result is a spatial model from which it is possible to carry considerations regarding urban mobility (but also other phenomena) through a process that starts from the analysis and, in some cases, also permits us to forecast future dynamics and behaviours[2], albeit with limits [65].

The plugin made it possible to view the range of influence of some services based on the present paths (consisting of the pedestrian mobility network), overcoming the concept of approximate "radius" traditionally represented by a circle. In fact, the "Catchment analyser" function of Space Syntax allows calculating the distance travelled on the pedestrian network (Network layer) starting from the chosen service (Origin layer). The first step to perform this operation is the validation of the Network layer: all errors (indicated in a specific window) must be corrected. The operation can be quite laborious and require the partial or total re-tracing of the network through specific criteria. After validation, in the "Catchment Analyzer" window it is possible to specify the chosen shapefiles and the desired distances for a chromatic representation scale (in this case 0, 150, 300, 400 and 500 m). The starting layers and the result of the processing were then loaded into a special folder using the *QPackage plugin* and imported into the general project file (within QGIS 3.4.6)[3]. The outcome of the processing for example for medical clinics is shown in Fig. 4.

---

[1] The plugin is called Space Syntax Toolkit. It is available at: https://spacesyntax.net/software/.

[2] Space Syntax website https://www.spacesyntax.org/.

[3] Space Syntax Toolkit is not compatible with the latest versions of QGIS, therefore all processing related to spatial analysis was performed in the version 2.18.17.

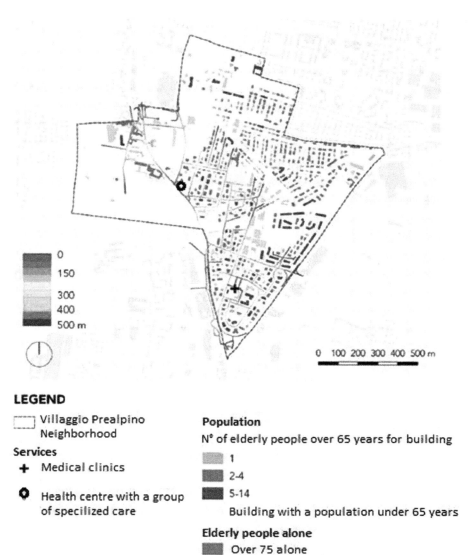

LEGEND

[____] Villaggio Prealpino
       Neighborhood

Services

\+ Medical clinics

⚫ Health centre with a group
    of specilized care

Population
N° of elderly people over 65 years for building

▨ 1

▨ 2-4

▨ 5-14

   Building with a population under 65 years

Elderly people alone

▨ Over 75 alone

▨ Over 65 alone

Fig. 4. Mapping via *space syntax tool* of the distance of services from users

2.4 Highlights from the Two Methodological Approaches

The comparison between the two methods has the purpose of highlighting any point of contact and/or elements that could allow an improvement for both, also through the identification of the relative strengths and weaknesses.

The explanatory table of the comparison between the two case studies for the elements identified in Sect. 2.1 is shown below.

	Cagliari	Brescia
Topic	Accessibility potential of large abandoned public spaces	Accessibility to existing services by residents (vulnerable users - the elderly)
Subject	Abandoned public space with a relative area of relevance ("service area")	Neighbourhood (Marcolini village)
Preliminary information/knowledge	Metropolitan Strategic Plan, Urban plan of the historic center; Cagliari public works plan	Service Plan and its update (offer of service)
Methodological approach	1. Service area identification for each site 2. Analysis and organization in categories of existing services 3. Analysis of the basic data for the construction of the indices and assignment of the weights 4. Calculation of indices (Porosity, Crossing i, Attractivity) 5. Calculation of the composite index (Walkable Big Building Index) 6. Comparison between sites 7. Ranking and identification of weaknesses of each site	1. Analysis of demographic factors and georeferencing of the urban load 2. Organization in categories of existing services and georeferencing 3. Cartographic definition of the pedestrian mobility network 4. Proximity analysis - Space syntax 5. Identification of the imbalance in the supply-demand ratio by type of service in the neighbourhood

2.4.1 Strengths and Weaknesses

Among the strengths of the method proposed in the Brescia case study is the immediate understanding of the outcome of the analysis. The chromed scale that highlights accessibility to the service is simple and easy to read. The size of the influence range can be easily changed to produce different scenarios. The weaknesses of the method concern the difficulties of acquiring the initial data, data processing requires specific software and specialized knowledge. A public administration does not always have the availability of these resources and therefore such decision support can only be provided by an external body.

On the other side, the strengths of the method proposed in the Cagliari case study is the immediate understanding of the results of the evaluations, simple and easy to read. The proposed indices allow to represent the context and support decisions. The weak points of the method concern the difficulties of geo-spatial representation of context data, which require a thorough knowledge of Geographic Information System and Google Maps, Google earth, Google Earth studio applications.

3 Final Consideration

These methods are useful for viewing problems and proposing scenarios, but the use of the methodology is only one of the steps in a decision process that must involve citizens. After carrying out the analysis (from a theoretical point of view), a confrontation is required both with the decision-makers and with the population living in the neighbourhood. Effective design, even for the 15-Minute city, must necessarily be set on a community-based approach (Community-Based Research e.g. [66]).

The walkability of a place becomes an indicator of the social and economic status of its community [67, 68], playing a role in: accessibility to services and inclusiveness and social equity. Furthermore, in the 15-Minute city, the interactions-relationships that can be generated by pedestrian movements in strengthening the sense of community consolidate the 'common goods' of public space and health and well-being.

In fact, the methods used, although different from each other, also to better adapt to the context, are based on these principles, obtaining as out-put maps for the case of Brescia and indices for the case of Cagliari. In this sense, the next step will be to combine the two methods in both cases to evaluate how their combined action is.

Author Contributions. G.B., A.R., M.P Sects. 1.1, 2.1, 2.4, 2.4.1, 3; G.B. Sect. 2.2; A.R., M.P Sect. 2.3; A.R. Sect. 1.2.

References

1. Colantonio, A., Dixon, T.: Measuring socially sustainable urban regeneration in Europe. Oxford Institute for Sustainable Development (OISD), School of the Built Environment, Oxford Brookes University (2009)
2. Lehmann, S.: The ten strategies for an urban regeneration. In: Urban Regeneration, pp. 133–156. Springer, Cham (2019). https://doi.org/10.1007/978-3-030-04711-5_5
3. Natividade-Jesus, E., Almeida, A., Sousa, N., Coutinho-Rodrigues, J.: A case study driven integrated methodology to support sustainable urban regeneration planning and management. Sustainability **11**, 4129 (2019)
4. Balletto, G., Milesi, A., Fenu, N., Borruso, G., Mundula, L.: Military training areas as semicommons: the territorial valorization of Quirra (Sardinia) from easements to ecosystem services. Sustainability **12**, 622 (2020)
5. Ladu, M., Balletto, G., Milesi, A., Mundula, L., Borruso, G.: Public real estate assets and the metropolitan strategic plan in Italy. In: Gervasi, O., et al. (eds.) The Two Cases of Milan and Cagliari. International Conference on Computational Science and Its Applications, ICCSA 2020. LNCS, vol. 12255, pp. 472–486. Springer Cham (2020) https://doi.org/10.1007/978-3-030-58820-5_35
6. Balletto, G., Ladu, M., Milesi, A., Borruso, G.: A methodological approach on disused public properties in the 15-minute city perspective. Sustainability **13**, 593 (2021)
7. Bruno, S.A., Petraroia, P.: Capitale culturale, resilienza territoriale e pandemia: un approccio sussidiario alla gestione delle sfide/Cultural capital, territorial resilience and the pandemic: a subsidiary approach to manage challenges. IL CAPITALE CULTURALE. Stud. Value Cult. Herit. **11**, 425–446 (2020)

8. Opoku, A., Akotia, J.: Uban regeneration for sustainable development. Constr. Econ. Build. **20** (2020)
9. Liu, J.Y., Deng, X.Z., Liu, M.L., Zhang, S.W.: Atudy on the spatial patterns of land-use change and analyses of driving forces in northeastern china during 1990–2000. Chin. Geogra. Sci. **12**, 299–308 (2002)
10. Pezzagno, M., Richiedei, A.: La riqualificazione dei tessuti consolidati: una proposta per i villaggi Marcolini a riconferma del loro ruolo identitario nella città. Planum. J. Urban. **27** (2013)
11. Aree interne e covid. Lettera Ventidue, Siracusa (2020)
12. Bailey, K., Grossardt, T.: Toward structured public involvement: justice, geography and collaborative geospatial/geovisual decision support systems. Ann. Assoc. Am. Geogr. **100**(57–86), 68 (2010)
13. Befani, B.: Choosing Appropriate Evaluation Methods: A Tool for Assessment and Selection (version 2) (2020)
14. Creswell, J.W.: Research Design: Qualitative, Quantitative, and Mixed Methods Approaches. Sage publications, London (2013)
15. Menotti, V.J.: The new transit town: best practices in transit-oriented development. J. Am. Plan. Assoc. **71**, 111 (2005)
16. Lund, H., Willson, R.W., Cervero, R.: A re-evaluation of travel behavior in California TODs. J. Architect. Plan. Res. **23**, 247–263 (2006)
17. Cervero, R.: Transit-oriented development in the US: Contemporary practices, impacts and policy directions. Incentives, Regulations and Plans: the Role of States and Nation-States in Smart Growth Planning, pp. 149–167 (2007)
18. Searle, G., Darchen, S., Huston, S.: Positive and negative factors for transit oriented development: case studies from Brisbane, Melbourne and Sydney. Urban Policy Res. **32**, 437–457 (2014)
19. Qvistrom, M., Bengtsson, J.: What kind of transit-oriented development? Using planning history to differentiate a model for sustainable development. Eur. Plan. Stud. **23**, 2516–2534 (2015)
20. Wey, W.M., Zhang, H., Chang, Y.J.: Alternative transit-oriented development evaluation in sustainable built environment planning. Habitat Int. **55**, 109–123 (2016)
21. Yang, K., Pojani, D.: A decade of transit oriented development policies in Brisbane, Australia: development and land-use impacts. Urban Policy Res. **35**, 347–362 (2017)
22. Thomas, R., Pojani, D., Lenferink, S., Bertolini, L., Stead, D., van der Krabben, E.: Is transit-oriented development (TOD) an internationally transferable policy concept? Reg. Stud. **52**, 1201–1213 (2018)
23. Dirgahayani, P., Choerunnisa, D.N.: IOP: development of methodology to evaluate TOD feasibility in built-up environment (Case Study: Jakarta and Bandung, Indonesia). In: 1st ITB Centennial and 4th PlanoCosmo International Conference. Iop Publishing Ltd., Bristol (Year)
24. Jamme, H.T., Rodriguez, J., Bahl, D., Banerjee, T.: A twenty-five-year biography of the TOD concept: from design to policy, planning, and implementation. J. Plan. Educ. Res. **39**, 409–428 (2019)
25. Carlton, I.: Transit planners' transit-oriented development-related practices and theories. J. Plan. Educ. Res. **39**, 508–519 (2019)
26. Scherrer, F.P.: Assessing transit-oriented development implementation in Canadian cities: an urban project approach. J. Plan. Educ. Res. **39**, 469–481 (2019)
27. Quintero-Gonzalez, J.R.: Sustainable transit-oriented development (STOD) a prospective for Colombia. Bitacora Urbano Territor. **29**, 59–68 (2019)
28. Stojanovski, T.: Urban design and public transportation - public spaces, visual proximity and Transit-Oriented Development (TOD). J. Urban Des. **25**, 134–154 (2020)

29. Liu, K., Qiu, P.Y., Gao, S., Lu, F., Jiang, J.C., Yin, L.: Investigating urban metro stations as cognitive places in cities using points of interest. Cities **97**, 13 (2020)
30. Paulsson, A.: The city that the metro system built: urban transformations and modalities of integrated planning in Stockholm. Urban Stud. **57**, 2936–2955 (2020)
31. Campos-Sanchez, F.S., Abarca-Alvarez, F.J., Serra-Coch, G., Chastel, C.: Comparative evaluation of the level of Transport-Oriented Development (DOT) around transport hubs of large cities: complementary methods of decision support. Eure-Revista Latinoamericana De Estudios Urbano Regionales **45**, 5–29 (2019)
32. Pal, S.: Measuring transit oriented development of existing urban areas around metro stations in Faridabad City. Int. J. Built Environ. Sustain. **5**, 115–126 (2018)
33. Loo, B.P.Y., du Verle, F.: Transit-oriented development in future cities: towards a two-level sustainable mobility strategy. Int. J. Urban Sci. **21**, 54–67 (2017)
34. Hasibuan, H.S., Soemardi, T.P., Koestoer, R., Moersidik, S.: The role of transit oriented development in constructing urban environment sustainability, the case of Jabodetabek, Indonesia. In: Utama, N.A., et al. (eds.) 4th International Conference on Sustainable Future for Human Security Sustain 2013, vol. 20, pp. 622–631. Elsevier Science Bv, Amsterdam (2014)
35. Borg, M., Orsini, R.: Transit oriented development - integrating land-use and transport in small island states. Urban Transport Xiv: Urban Transport and the Environment in the 21st Century, vol. 101, pp. 457–466 (2008)
36. Chatman, D.G.: Does TOD need the T?: on the importance of factors other than rail access. J. Am. Plan. Assoc. **79**, 17–31 (2013)
37. Ratner, K.A., Goetz, A.R.: The reshaping of land use and urban form in Denver through transit-oriented development. Cities **30**, 31–46 (2013)
38. Boarnet, M.G., Compin, N.S.: Transit-oriented development in San Diego County - the incremental implementation of a planning idea. J. Am. Plan. Assoc. **65**, 80–95 (1999)
39. Freilich, R.H.: The land-use implications of transit-oriented development: controlling the demand side of transportation congestion and urban sprawl. Urban Lawyer **30**, 547–572 (1998)
40. Laurenti, M., Bono, L.: Ecosistema urbano. Rapporto sulle performance ambientali delle città 2020. Legambiente (2020)
41. Ma, F.: Spatial equity analysis of urban green space based on spatial design network analysis (sDNA): a case study of central Jinan, China. Sustain. Cities Soc. **60**, 102256 (2020)
42. Abd El Karim, A., Awawdeh, M.M.: Integrating GIS accessibility and location-allocation models with multicriteria decision analysis for evaluating quality of life in Buraidah City, KSA. Sustainability **12**, 1412 (2020)
43. Pezzagno, M., Richiedei, A., Tira, M.: Fast analysis methods to evaluate urban requalification and regeneration opportunities in widespread area/Applicazione di metodi di analisi speditiva per valutare le opportunità di rigenerazione urbana nei territori diffusi delle risorse tra progetti di forestazione urbana]. Valori e Valutazioni **27**, 9 (2021)
44. Perry, C.A.: The neighborhood unit, a scheme of arrangement for the family-life community. Neighborhood and Community Planning, Regional Plan of New York and Its Environs. Committee on Regional Plan of New York and Its Environs, New York (1929)
45. Bleiker, A.H.: Proximity model and urban social relations. Urban Anthropol. **1**, 151–175 (1972)
46. Columbo, V.: La ricerca urbanistica. Organica urbanistica. Giuffrè, Milano (1983)
47. Lynch, K.: Good City Form. The MIT Press, Cambridge (1994)
48. Krizek, K.J., Johnson, P.J.: Proximity to trails and retail: Effects on urban cycling and walking. J. Am. Plan. Assoc. **72**, 33–42 (2006)
49. Jones, P., Evans, J.: Urban regeneration, governance and the state: exploring notions of distance and proximity. Urban Stud. **43**, 1491–1509 (2006)

50. Roda, M.: Icona urbana e spazio pubblico. Territorio **45**, 69–80 (2008)
51. Andreotti, A., Le Gales, P., Fuentes, F.J.M.: Controlling the Urban Fabric: the complex game of distance and proximity in European upper-middle-class residential strategies. Int. J. Urban Reg. Res. **37**, 576–597 (2013)
52. Basso, S.: In comune : percorsi di ricerca per un nuovo progetto di prossimità nella città pubblica. Territorio **72**, 18–20 (2015)
53. Basso, S.: Ripensare la prossimità nella città pubblica : strumenti per la ricomposizione degli spazi, oltre l'alloggio. Territorio **72**, 75–82 (2015)
54. Di Campli, A.: Comfort urbano : tre direzioni di ricerca attorno ad un nuovo progetto di prossimità. Territorio **72**, 51–58 (2015)
55. Pellegrini, M.: Un percorso tra quartieri pubblici e campagne urbane: relazioni di prossimità nelle frange periurbane di Trieste sud-est. Territorio **79**, 70–73 (2016)
56. Ardeshiri, A., Willis, K., Ardeshiri, M.: Exploring preference homogeneity and heterogeneity for proximity to urban public services. Cities **81**, 190–202 (2018)
57. Sim, D.: Soft City: Building Density for Everyday Life. Island Press, Washington, DC (2019)
58. Coppetti, B.: Architettura e paesaggio tra prossimità e distanza. Territorio **63**, 91–98 (2020)
59. Borruso, G., Porceddu, A.: A tale of two cities: density analysis of cbd on two midsize urban areas in Northeastern Italy. In: Murgante, B., Borruso, G., Lapucci, A. (eds.) Geocomputation and Urban Planning, pp. 37–56. Springer, Berlin Heidelberg, Berlin, Heidelberg (2009)
60. Sennett, R.: The Conscience of the Eye, the Design and Social Life of Cities. Norton & Company, London (1990)
61. Romano, M.: Ascesa e declino delle città europee. Raffaello Cortina Editore, Milano (2010)
62. Kindon, S., Pain, R., Kesby, M.: Participatory Action Research Approaches and Methods: Connecting People, Participation and Place. Routledge, London (2007)
63. Hillier, B., Hanson, J.: The Social Logic of Space. Cambridge University Press, Cambridge (1984)
64. Scorza, F., Fortunato, G., Carbone, R., Murgante, B., Pontrandolfi, P.: Increasing urban walkability through citizens'partecipation process. Sustainability **13**(11), 1–29 (2021)
65. Ratti, C.: Space Syntax: Some Inconsistencies. Environ. Plan. B Plan. Des. **31**, 487–499 (2004)
66. Macaulay, A., Jagosh, J., Pluye, P., Bush, P., Salsberg, J.: Quantitative methods in participatory research: being sensitive to issues of scientific validity, community safety, and the academic-community relationship. Nouvelles pratiques sociales **25**, 159–172 (2013)
67. Gullón, P., Bilal, U., Cebrecos, A., Badland, H.M., Galán, I., Franco, M.: Intersection of neighborhood dynamics and socioeconomic status in small-area walkability: the Heart Healthy Hoods project. Int. J. Health Geogr. **16**(1), 1–9 (2017). https://doi.org/10.1186/s12942-017-0095-7
68. Zeynep, T.: Walking beyond the socioeconomic status in an objectively and perceptually walkable pedestrian environment. Urban Stud. Res. 1–15 (2015). https://doi.org/10.1155/2015/919874

Interactive Maps of Chorems Explaining Urban Contexts to Align Smart Community's Actors

Pietro Battistoni📧, Michele Grimaldi📧, Marco Romano(✉)📧,
Monica Sebillo📧, and Giuliana Vitiello📧

University of Salerno, 84084 Fisciano, SA, Italy
{pbattistoni,migrimaldi,marromano,msebillo,gvitiello}@unisa.it

Abstract. The actualization of the three pillars of the Open Government paradigm, namely transparency, participation and collaboration, motivates the importance for a smart city administration to share decisions with citizens to receive real support and legitimize the decisions made. A way to engage citizens is to make available government data as open. This allows achieving a higher transparency in decision-making that also fosters citizens to support the strategic objectives of the city and improve the individual and collective quality of life. The goal of this paper is to show the effectiveness of chorems as a communication and support tool for understanding the dynamic realities of a territory. When used to visually synthesize urban contexts, maps of chorems can produce a territorial schematic representation, which eliminates details not useful to the map comprehension, and emphasizes relevant information to enable decision makers, experts and ordinary citizens to share knowledge about complex phenomena occurring in urban areas. A use case is built, which describes how the urban heat island phenomenon and the factors involved in its development are analyzed through a set of chorems and operators. This phenomenon is invisible but typically present in most of the modern cities. It is composed of different urban elements present on the urban territory and its understanding implies technical and scientific knowledge not common among citizens and administrators. By visually interacting with chorems, it is possible support data manipulation by expert users, and data interpretation by citizens, thus aligning the different actors of a smart community towards a shared sustainability goal.

Keywords: GeoVisualization · Smart communities · Urban heat islands · Chorems

1 Introduction

Nowadays, the topic of the smart cities is increasingly central in the dynamics of management, transformation and redesign of modern cities, and is strongly

Partially supported by MIUR PRIN 2017 grant number 2017JMHK4F_004, and MIUR 2019 grant number AIM1872991-2.

O. Gervasi et al. (Eds.): ICCSA 2021, LNCS 12953, pp. 549–564, 2021.
https://doi.org/10.1007/978-3-030-86976-2_37

related to the concept of smart communities. In [14] the authors synthetize a smart city as *"a city exploiting IT services to connect people to each other, to city services, infrastructures and organizations with the goal to create a common conscience or knowledge that can improve the community life of the same city"*. Speaking of smart community, instead, it is defined as a *"community in which government, business, and residents understand the potential of information technology, and make a conscious decision to use that technology to transform life and work in their region in significant and positive ways"* [18]. Although in both those contexts, technology is imagined as the main objective [17], many researchers and local administrators prefer to put the citizen at the center, and consider technology a mere support for the community to share common visions and reach common goals. Such an approach is in line with the actualization of the three pillars of the Open Government (OG) paradigm, namely transparency, participation and collaboration [11], which motivate the importance for a smart city administration to share decisions with citizens to receive real support and legitimize the decisions made.

As explained in [10,17] a way to engage citizens is to make available government data as open. Open data allows the administration to achieve a higher transparency in decision-making and foster citizens to support the strategic objectives of the city by building a network for improving the individual and collective quality of life. However, data and information used to make administrative decisions and involve citizens can sometimes represent complex territorial phenomena and processes, which therefore require specific knowledge to be interpreted. Problems may arise, in particular, when data and information are related to phenomena that are implicitly complex by nature. This is the case of phenomena in which several and different by nature parameters concur, which can also have a different weight depending on the scale with which they are evaluated.

Failing this sharing goal means to generate a misalignment of purposes among the different community's actors, which represents a typical problem of any public or private goal-oriented organization. To deal with it, organizations generally use the so-called alignment diagrams [8]. These are visual artifacts designed to help organizations align their internal people towards shared goals with the aim to generate a unique value. However, such diagrams are not adequate when dealing with huge amounts of data underlying complex spatio-temporal phenomena, even if some of their principles could be taken into account to design a more suitable artifact, such as the ability to represent both an overview of a scenario that is self-explanatory, and multiple dimensions for a multilevel analysis.

The goal of this paper is to show the effectiveness of chorems as a communication and support tool for understanding the dynamic realities of a territory. When used to visually synthesize urban contexts, maps of chorems can produce a territorial schematic representation, which eliminates details not useful to the map comprehension, and emphasizes relevant information to enable decision makers, experts and ordinary citizens to share knowledge about complex phenomena occurring in urban areas. In particular, to show the efficacy of chorems, in this paper they are adopted to represent the complex phenomenon of urban heat island (UHI).

The phenomenon of urban heat islands is invisible but typically present in most of the modern cities. It is composed of different elements present on the urban territory and its understanding implies technical and scientific knowledge not common among citizens and administrators, although it is a phenomenon affecting all of us daily. Then, in order to explain how factors involved in the occurrence of the phenomenon can be managed to reduce its impact, it is necessary to identify a visual paradigm that can be easily understood and used both by decision-makers, who have to interface with technical staff, and by citizens, who have to understand the reasons for the actions taken by the administration to mitigate the phenomenon.

Maps of chorems can represent a solution. They offer a synthetic global view that is suitable to guarantee such requirements.

The paper is organized as follows. Section 2 recalls the definition of *chorem* and briefly describes the set of operators defined to manage and analyze maps of chorems. In Sect. 3, the UHI phenomenon is described along with factors involved in its development. A model to determine criticality maps is recalled, which is used as a possible source for UHI chorems. Section 4 is addressed to show how chorems can be used to visually synthesize a urban context and some relevant phenomena and elements related to it. In particular, it depicts how the urban heat islands phenomenon can be investigated by manipulating a map of chorems. Two scenarios are depicted in Sect. 5 whose goal is to show how decision-makers and citizens can take advantages of maps of chorems in investigating urban contexts and understanding environmental phenomena affecting them. Concluding remarks and Future work are drawn in Sect. 6.

2   Chorems as Visual Synthesis of Spatio-Temporal Phenomena

The concept of *chorem* was first introduced in 1986 by the French geographer Brunet as a schematic territory representation, which eliminates details not useful to the map comprehension [3]. Since then, the concept has evolved over the years, although the proliferation of *ad hoc* solutions, due to the lack of a rigorous approach for chorem creation and composition, caused failing in conveying the information they were meant to [1,2,12].

Figure 1 shows a set of chorems, including industrial zones and big poles, which make up a thematic map referring to Spain. A definition and classification of chorems as visual syntheses of geographic database contents was first provided in [6], to homogenize chorem construction and usage and to provide a usable framework for computer systems. According to it, chorems can be grouped into three main categories, namely:

– Geographic chorems,
– Phenomenal chorems and
– Annotation chorems.

Geographic chorems represent geographic data with associated simple geometries, such as points, lines, polygons, and objects made up of their combinations, such as networks. Phenomenal chorems describe spatio-temporal phenomena involving one or more geographic chorems, and, when useful, they can be further classified in Flow, Tropism, and Spatial Diffusion. A Flow chorem represents objects movement between geographic chorems. A Tropism chorem represents an homogeneous attractive or repulsive space, around a geographic chorem. A Spatial Diffusion chorem represents a spatial progression or regression, from a geographic chorem along a given direction. Finally, an Annotation chorem represents map labels or remarks, useful to provide users with additional information about the map.

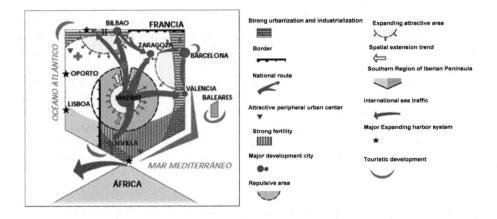

Fig. 1. A Map containing chorems about Spain (a) and its legend (b) [6]

Figure 2 depicts the underlying structure of a chorem, which was first described in [6]. It takes into account the complex nature of geographic data and phenomena by visually integrating the iconic and the property components. As for the former, the iconic representation assemblies a graphical component, corresponding to the visual representation, and a meaning, referring to the semantic component. In such a way, users can quickly perceive the meaning associated with data and use it properly. As for the property component of a chorem, it is divided into two parts, a type attribute specifying the category the chorem belongs to, namely geographic, phenomenal or annotation, and a source indicating where data could be retrieved (such as a table or a view name, a SQL query or a function). It is worth to notice that, in case of a phenomenal chorem, the type attribute also contains information about the geographic chorems which it is related to.

Based on this structure, a different classification can be provided that inherits the structural organization, typical of the well-established model used in GIS for managing spatial data, namely feature layer, layer and map.

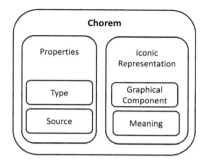

Fig. 2. The structure of chorems [6]

In particular, the concept of Chorem element, Chorem and Chorematic Map were introduced as follows:

- a Chorem element is a basic element representing either a single geographic object, such as a city and a road, or a single phenomenon, such as people migration and car mobility;
- a Chorem is a set of homogeneous chorem elements. For instance, the set of the most important Italian cities, or the set of the main flows between such cities.
- a Chorematic Map is a set of chorems, which schematize data of interest related to a specific place or region. A legend can be associated with a chorematic map, which explains the meaning of each chorem.

This classification emphasizes the relationships existing among a single instance of a chorem, the group to which it belongs, and the whole scenario where different chorems can be spatially arranged.

The potentiality of chorems was discussed by Laurini et al. in [5], where a list of the different roles that chorems may play is given. The authors state that chorems can be used to represent geographic knowledge, to visually summarize database contents and finally to underlie the creation of a novel entry system for geographic databases.

Following this line, in [4,6], the authors demonstrated how chorems can represent the starting point for further processing tasks aimed to derive spatial analysis data, and to support expert users in decision making. In particular, they introduced a set of operators, both geographic and semantic, to derive spatial knowledge, useful to help domain experts face and get rapid and exhaustive responses in critical situations.

Based on the Ben Shneiderman's mantra and on Keim's adaptation to the Visual Analytics domain [9,16], applying these operators allows users to navigate a chorematic map from an initial overview to a detail, as follows.

Geographic Zoom
This operation corresponds to the traditional map zooming (in/out) operator. When applied to a chorematic map, it acts exclusively on the visual aspect of the chorem, by changing the size of the visible details of the involved chorem elements, leaving them unchanged, also in terms of structure.

Semantic Zoom
Generally speaking, a semantic zoom (in/out) changes the type and meaning of information associated with chorems. When applied, it allows accessing to a different level of information, that is, it analyzes the chorem and its elements by (dis)aggregating and visualizing them in detail. In particular, when the operation is applied to geographical chorems, they are simply split up (resp., aggregated), by showing a new level of geographic data abstraction. The chorem structure is modified accordingly, by properly substituting the corresponding iconic representation component, both in terms of graphical component and meaning. When a semantic zoom is applied to a Phenomenal chorem, it is decomposed (resp., aggregated) along with the Geographic Chorems related to it. In this case, the chorem structure is differently modified. In fact, even if the output chorem still corresponds to the initial phenomenal chorem, its meaning changes, being referred to a different abstraction of the territory.

Geographic Filter
This operation allows the user to select Phenomenal Chorems elements by using the graphical component of one or more Geographic Chorems elements as spatial filter. In this case, the condition corresponds to the territory of interest where phenomenal chorems elements have to be analyzed. The output of the operation consists of one or more phenomenal chorems that satisfy the condition. The resulting chorems structure does not change in terms of properties and iconic representation, whereas the number of phenomenal chorem elements may vary in order to satisfy the condition.

Semantic Filter
This operation allows users to filter chorem elements that satisfy a particular condition, by directly operating on the semantics associated to them.

In order to show how the visual representation based on chorems can be useful to handle the information associated to the UHIs, the following Section briefly describes this environmental phenomenon and presents a model to process a set of parameters associated with it.

3   The Urban Heat Islands Phenomenon

The increase in temperature occurring in public urban areas with respect to surrounding outlying and rural areas determines a thermal anomaly known as Urban

Heat Island. This phenomenon can have significant differences between cities with a comparable population, and varies considerably according to weather conditions, season and time of day: it turns out to be a more significant phenomenon at night and in summer. Its most relevant effects are:

- an increase in energy consumption,
- high emissions of pollutants and so-called greenhouse gases,
- a worsening of the life and thermal comfort of the population, and
- an increase in storm phenomena in the urban area.

Together, these effects have a significant impact on the outdoor air quality, making UHI an important phenomenon to consider to improve urban life quality.

To reach this goal, it is necessary to take into account that urban areas are known to be richer in energy than rural areas, and this imbalance is even more fragile due to additional heat sources. The factors that influence a UHI are divided into three groups:

- factors related to the environmental context;
- factors related to the human component;
- factors related to the urban structure.

The first two components are defined in [13] as uncontrollable, while the causes linked to the anthropic modification of the territory, defined as controllable variables, are urban geometry, properties of urban materials and urban green.

The urban geometry contributes to the UHI phenomenon through the so-called urban canyons, consisting of the high building walls that face each other along the streets. Here, the solar radiation is reflected several times from the road surface and the walls of the buildings, remaining trapped inside the canyon and causing a rise in temperatures. The materials used in urban areas modify the energy balance mainly through the albedo, which indicates the fraction of incident radiation that is reflected off a surface and varies considerably in relation to the color and type of surface. The materials present in the city are characterized by a much lower albedo than in the countryside. The presence of green areas, on the other hand, offers a mitigating contribution to the phenomenon. The crowns of the trees are able to shield the solar radiation and use a part of this for photosynthesis.

Based on the analysis of these factors, it is possible to identify specific mitigation actions, i.e. interventions that should:

- modify the morphology and adopt materials with lower thermal admittance, thus reducing the flow of heat stored in the urban structure;
- increase the albedo of the surfaces and modify the geometry of the buildings, thus reducing the net radiation;
- increase the permeability of surfaces and the presence of vegetation;
- reduce the vehicular traffic and improve energy efficiency, thus reducing the flow of anthropogenic heat.

As for the visual representation of the UHI phenomenon, its inner complexity implies that components to be visually analyzed must be selected depending on the scale by which the phenomenon is investigated. In [7] the authors studied more than 250 scientific articles on urban heat mapping indicators, and mapping techniques. They found that one hundred thirty-three articles did use a cartographic map to indicate UHIs. However, although it is popular to visually analyze the UHI phenomenon with mapping, it is still challenging to represent a single complex indicator derived by multi-variate data. In reason of this complexity, the chorem paradigm, with its geographic and sematic operators, appears to be a valuable mechanism for a more immediate understanding of the causes of the phenomenon at any scale.

In the following Section, the controllable variables are modelled in terms of chorems and are used to visually express the basic features of the critical zones identified by a model underlying the structure of the UHI chorem.

4   Chorematic Maps to Visually Synthesize and Analyze Urban Contexts

Starting from the basic elements previously mentioned, and representing them through proper chorems, it is possible to design and build chorematic maps to support decision makers in their monitoring activities conceived to improve citizens' life.

The goal of this Section is twofold. First, it is addressed to describe a set of chorems specifically conceived to visually synthesize a urban context and some relevant phenomena and elements related to it. Then, it is shown how geographic and semantic operators can be applied to the built chorematic maps in order to investigate the UHI phenomenon.

4.1   Chorems for the Urban Context

Figure 3 shows the list of chorems associated with the UHI phenomenon and each factor contributing to its development, namely Urban Area, Urban Greenery, Urban Geometry and Albedo. They are structured as described in Fig. 2 and, when applicable, a classification of their possible values is given in terms of ranges. The Urban Area geographic chorem represents the visual synthesis of a urbanized area to which several phenomena can be associated. As an example of instances, districts and quarters can be considered.

The Urban Greenery geographic chorem represents the visual synthesis of public landscaping and urban forestry created to let citizens benefit from environmental green spaces. Arboretum, parks and urban vegetable gardens are instances of Urban Greenery.

Associated with the Urban Area chorem, Urban Geometry and Albedo are Spatial Diffusion chorems. The Urban Geometry source is calculated as the average urban complexity, which takes into account some spatial indices, such as size,

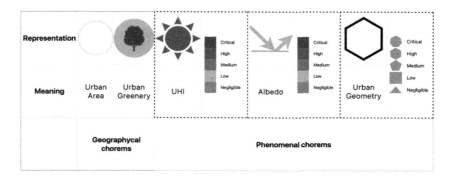

Fig. 3. Chorems for the UHI phenomenon (Source: Authors' elaboration)

shape, skyline and openess of the area of interest. It is represented by a polygon whose number of sides ranges from 3 (negligible geometry) to 7 (critical urban geometry), thus increasing with the criticality performed.

As for the Albedo chorem, its iconic representation is similar to a *tick* made up of two arrows, whose colour shows the capability of the associated area to absorb/reflect the solar light.

Finally, UHI is a Spatial Diffusion chorem associated with the Urban Area chorem. The UHI source corresponds to the calculation performed on the factors as defined in Sect. 3. Its iconic representation is a *sun* whose colour intensity indicates the level of criticality.

In addition to the above chorems, the urban context is also characterized by a set of phenomena whose presence and intensity can affect one or more factors underlying the UHI phenomenon, such as the average temperature of the area, pollution, wind, traffic and the quality of the urban greenery. Then, to derive a complete scenario of the urban context, it is necessary to associate a chorem representation with each of them. This approach allows decision makers both to obtain a global overview of an area of interest, and analyse every single object and phenomenon featuring it.

Figure 4 collects chorems modelled to this aim, namely Pollution, Winds, Traffic, Temperature and Urban Greenery Quality. They are Spatial Diffusion chorems associated with the Urban Area chorem. In particular, Pollution, Winds and Traffic represent elements that can affect the temperature, and their sources are the sensors located in the area of interest, along with sensors for temperature. The iconic representation of Temperature is given also by a numeric annotation, showing that the arrow moves in clockwise (resp., counterclockwise) when the average temperature measured in the area is higher (resp., lower) than the city average temperature.

Finally, the Urban Greenery Quality indicates the quality of the vegetation in the depicted area, which can depend on the seasons and the care of the plants. The high quality of the urban greenery alleviates the impact of the heat island. Its source is a database frequently updated with a quality index ranging from 1 to 10 and estimated with data from satellite images or field inspections. Its iconic representation is made up by two concentric circles containing a tree. The outer circle represents the extension of the green, the inner one the quality, whose size is directly proportional to the quality index.

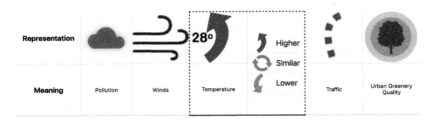

Fig. 4. Chorems affecting the UHI phenomenon (Source: Authors' elaboration)

4.2   Analysing the UHI Phenomenon

A chorematic map is able to emphasize important aspects of a territory, which are useful for a better comprehension of the visualized phenomena. It offers a synthetic global overview that can be further investigated to analyze specific spatio-temporal information built upon large sets of source data, otherwise difficult to manage. In particular, by zooming and filtering tasks in terms of geographic and semantic operators, users may gradually reduce the search space and select a subset of data in agreement with the visual information-seeking paradigm based on the Shneiderman's mantra and Keim's interpretations. Then, users can select and query a chorem element in order to obtain descriptive information related to it.

As the map scale (ranging from 2 km to 500 m), the north indicator, and the map source (Google 2021) are not meaningful to the current purpose, in the following, all figures have been clipped from the map viewer to obtain a better visualization for readers.

Figure 5 (on the left) shows a chorematic map containing seven UHI chorems, different for intensity.

A geographic zoom-in derives the scenario depicted on the right. By applying a semantic zoom-in to the red UHI chorem, it is disaggregated according to the parameters described in Sect. 3, while the given scale still holds, as shown in Fig. 6. In particular, it shows the involved chorems, namely Urban Area, Albedo, Urban Geometry and Urban Greenery, where the area represents the extension of the UHI phenomenon, the color of the Albedo chorem indicates the medium level of the albedo in that area, the level of average urban geometry is high, being represented by an hexagon, and the presence of urban greenery is indicated by two chorems, differently sized to represent their different impact on the heat island. Finally, the average temperature of the area is reported and the red arrow indicates the increment of the temperature with respect to the average temperature of the city.

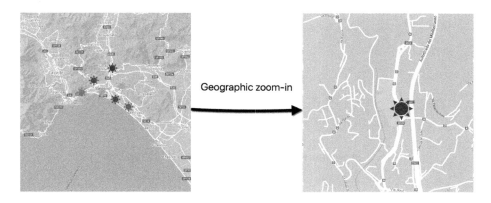

Fig. 5. A geographic zoom-in (Source: Authors' elaboration)

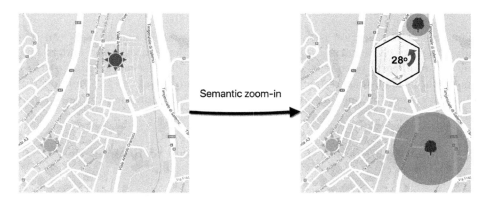

Fig. 6. A semantic zoom-in (Source: Authors' elaboration)

Figure 7 shows a semantic filter applied to derive UHIs whose criticality is higher than "Low".

Figure 8 displays a chorematic map where instances of each type of chorems previously introduced occur for the UHI chorem under investigation. Here, data about lines of traffic, air pollution, temperature, the presence of winds, and the quality of the urban greenery is acquired through the proper sensors distributed on the territory.

Finally, Fig. 9 shows a chorematic map resulting from a semantic zoom-in applied to two UHIs. This map allows users to investigate the phenomenon

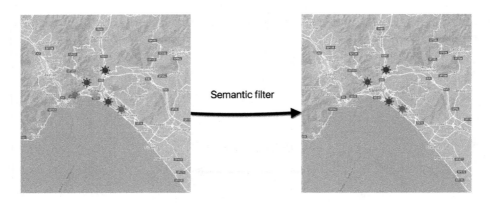

Fig. 7. A semantic filter (Source: Authors' elaboration)

occurring in two different areas by comparing the corresponding factors in the form of chorems.

5   A Chorem-Based Approach to Get Citizens Involved in Decision Making

The goal of this Section is to show how decision-makers and citizens can take advantages of chorematic maps in investigating urban contexts and understanding environmental phenomena impacting on them. Two scenarios are described in which decision-makers are supported in designing plans and communicating them to citizens through a simple visual language based on the expressive power of chorems.

5.1   Identify a Portion of Territory on Which to Rethink the Urban Greenery

Today, political decision-makers design and plan installation and renovation of urban green parks and tree-lined avenues often considering them as street furniture or leisure areas instead of strategic urban elements. Various criteria come into play in these design activities, such as the cost of work, the possible complications for mobility and the possibility of recovering degraded spaces, while others, equally relevant for their impact, are not sufficiently considered, such as the urban heat islands. This discrepancy is mainly due to the reduced availability of simple methods and tools that can be used to study complex phenomena, as well as the lack of knowledge to understand factors influencing them.

A chorem-based approach can represent a solution to bridge te gap. Decision-makers, who aim to explore city areas, can adopt chorematic maps and analyze specific contexts to identify complex phenomena, such as UHIs in the urban area, without any effort. In fact, the criticism of each UHI is represented by its own color and decision-makers can apply a semantic filter to identify those areas whose criticality overcomes a given threshold. Then, the areas affected by these UHIs can be taken into main consideration with respect to the others for the reorganization of the urban greenery. Moreover, a semantic zoom-in on a selected UHI, allows decision-makers to know the extension of the critical area and the presence of the greenery nearby, whose level of quality can be observed, in turn. Hence, the adopted chorematic map simplifies and highlights the comprehension of the UHI phenomenon and facilitates its use as an additional criterion to identify the portion of territory where intervening.

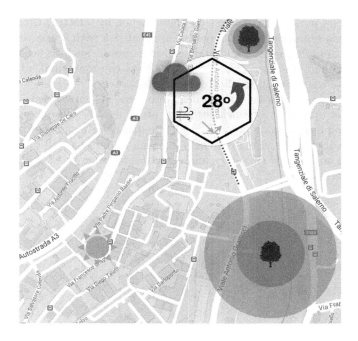

Fig. 8. Chorems in a urban context (Source: Authors' elaboration)

Finally, the adoption of chorematic maps as communication tool can be useful for sharing the planned urban works, and in particular the urban green redesign plans, with citizens. A map, in fact, can support citizens' understanding of the project by showing them how the proposed interventions are useful for addressing the UHI phenomenon that occur in urban areas, thus improving the well-being of the entire community and avoiding the general regret due to the lack of understanding of the reasons why the planned interventions involve one area of the city rather than another.

5.2   Designing Targeted Interventions for the Prevention of Heatwaves to Protect the Health of the Elderly and Children

During the summer, the elderly and children can be severely prone to heat waves, which can cause serious health risks. The municipal administration arranges for the deployment of ambulances and mobile medical points in various areas to quickly bring help. They can also set up points for the administration of water bottles and arrange sun covers in the avenues. Finally, they may want to communicate to the population to stay at home and avoid some particularly affected areas. Making such a plan involves a great waste of time and resources.

Based on chorematic maps, the city administration can easily identify the areas of the city most prone to the UHI phenomenon by selecting the most serious ones through a semantic filter. Moreover, areas at risk with sensitive sites can be detected by applying geographic and semantic zooms, such as schools, nursing homes, parks and squares. This approach allows the municipal administration to allocate its resources in the best way.

As for citizens, in order to let them know the resources distribution, it is possible to set up public totems in strategic areas, such as bus and subway stops, where running a chorematic map showing the main UHIs and the corresponding temperature increment. This can help citizens understand the gravity of the phenomenon and plan their routes and activities for the rest of the day avoiding the riskiest areas.

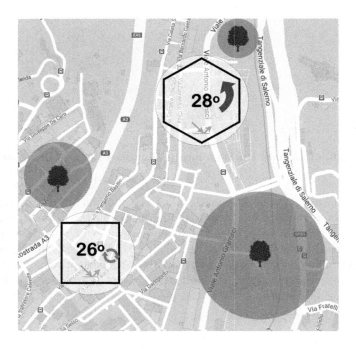

Fig. 9. Comparing UHIs (Source: Authors' elaboration)

6   Conclusions and Future Work

Generally speaking, by performing map overview and querying tasks, it is possible to obtain a global view of a scenario featuring a domain of interest. However, visual and interactive methods may be not adequate when dealing with large amounts of data because of the high risk of getting lost inside the original data collection. In this case, it is reasonable to apply first some analysis computations and then provide an overview of the resulting relevant contents and details on demand.

Chorematic maps for urban contexts follow this paradigm. Namely, they visually summarize relevant objects and phenomena of an area of interest and, when manipulated by geographic and semantic operators, they provide users with information useful to better understand what characterizes a scenario.

In this paper, the focus is on the UHI phenomenon and chorems have been adopted to represent both it and factors determining it. The model used to process those factors and calculate the extension of the critical zone is a "work in progress" from a physics point of view. Nevertheless, every its possible improvement can be revisited in terms of chorems thanks to the level of abstraction of their structure, which expresses each component in a way abstract enough to be independent of specific implementations. This feature also paves the way for the use of chorems to build "what if?" scenarios where the interaction is addressed to simulate the presence/absence of phenomena and the modification of parameters to evaluate possible outcomes.

As for a prototype specifically conceived to manage chorems and chorematic maps, the SAFE (SAfety for Families in Emergency) system described in [15] is under revision to embed a section where different typologies of users can interact, apply operators and pose queries on chorems and chorematic maps. SAFE is a spatial decision support system, developed to provide users with data (the user as a consumer) and acquire information from them (the user as a producer), thus increasing knowledge about a territory. Besides monitoring activities, SAFE was designed to improve certified procedures. Then, it is especially suitable to handle emergency procedures, both planned and extraordinary, and involve citizens in the identification of risks on a territory and in the planning of needs.

References

1. Arreghini, L.: La modélisation graphique dans la réalisation des atlas pour le développement. Les atlas pour le développement en coopération, pp. 1–10 (1995)
2. Batardy, C.: Le berry antique-de la carte au modèle-chorème. Revue archéologique du Centre de la France **43**, 253–258 (2005)
3. Brunet, R.: La carte-modèle et les chorèmes. Mappemonde (1986)
4. De Chiara, D., Del Fatto, V., Laurini, R., Sebillo, M., Vitiello, G.: A chorem-based approach for visually analyzing spatial data. J. Vis. Lang. Comput. **22**(3), 173–193 (2011)

5. Del Fatto, V., et al.: Potentialities of chorems as visual summaries of geographic databases contents. In: Qiu, G., Leung, C., Xue, X., Laurini, R. (eds.) VISUAL 2007. LNCS, vol. 4781, pp. 537–548. Springer, Heidelberg (2007). https://doi.org/10.1007/978-3-540-76414-4_52

6. Del Fatto, V., Laurini, R., Lopez, K., Sebillo, M., Vitiello, G.: A chorem-based approach for visually synthesizing complex phenomena. Inf. Vis. **7**(3–4), 253–264 (2008)

7. de Groot-Reichwein, M.A.M., van Lammeren, R.J.A., Goosen, H., Koekoek, A., Bregt, A.K., Vellinga, P.: Urban heat indicator map for climate adaptation planning. Mitig. Adapt. Strat. Glob. Change **23**(2), 169–185 (2015). https://doi.org/10.1007/s11027-015-9669-5

8. Kalbach, J.: Mapping Experiences. O'Reilly Media, Sebastopol (2020)

9. Keim, D.A., Mansmann, F., Schneidewind, J., Ziegler, H.: Challenges in visual data analysis. In: Tenth International Conference on Information Visualisation (IV 2006), pp. 9–16. IEEE (2006)

10. Morozov, E., Bria, F.: Rethinking the Smart City. Democratizing Urban Technology. Rosa Luxemburg Stiftung. City Series, no. 5 (2018)

11. Obama, B.: Transparency and open government: memorandum for the heads of executive departments and agencies (2009). Accessed 6 Sept 2016

12. Patrick, C.: Modélisation graphique et chorèmes: la gestion des parcours collectifs à massaroca (brésil du nordeste). Mappemonde **62** (2001)

13. Rizwan, A.M., Dennis, L.Y., Liu, C.: A review on the generation, determination and mitigation of urban heat island. J. Environ. Sci. **20**(1), 120–128 (2008)

14. Romano, M., Díaz, P., Aedo, I.: Emergency management and smart cities: civic engagement through gamification. In: Díaz, P., Bellamine Ben Saoud, N., Dugdale, J., Hanachi, C. (eds.) ISCRAM-med 2016. LNBIP, vol. 265, pp. 3–14. Springer, Cham (2016). https://doi.org/10.1007/978-3-319-47093-1_1

15. Sebillo, M., Vitiello, G., Grimaldi, M., De Piano, A.: A citizen-centric approach for the improvement of territorial services management. ISPRS Int. J. Geo-Inf. **9**(4) (2020)

16. Shneiderman, B.: The eyes have it: a task by data type taxonomy for information visualizations. In: Proceedings 1996 IEEE Symposium on Visual Languages, pp. 336–343 (1996). https://doi.org/10.1109/VL.1996.545307

17. Vives, A.: Smart City Barcelona: the Catalan quest to improve future urban living. Int. J. Iberian Stud. **33**(1), 103–104 (2018)

18. Wilson, P.: Smart communities guidebook. Governor of California, CA, USA (1997)

Public Participation with Fuzzy Cognitive Maps to Assess Safety Perception in Urban Regeneration

Dario Esposito[✉] and Maria Giovanna Ciaccia

Polytechnic University of Bari, 70125 Bari, Italy
dario.esposito@poliba.it, mariagiovannaciaccia@gmail.it

Abstract. In urban regeneration it is essential to promote civic engagement through public participatory processes because stakeholder involvement ensures democracy, legitimacy and effectiveness of decisions. Nevertheless, this entails dealing with a mass of fragmented qualitative information which, in the case of the public's perception of safety, is intangible, uncertain and ambiguous. Experts need supportive methods to process this in order to make it more understandable and manageable. This paper discusses the work conducted in a case study of urban regeneration of a degraded, historical central square in the city of Bari (Italy). It presents a process designed with Scenario Workshop consultations and conducted by leveraging the Fuzzy Cognitive Map approach to model shared knowledge. This aimed to achieve a collaborative problem-solving decision-making environment to address differing intentions in situations where means and ends are confused. The development of what-if intervention scenarios enabled the evaluation of counter-intuitive cause-effect links, the recognition of critical causal loops and unintended consequences and the identification of feasible choices. The results demonstrate the suitability of the proposed process as a decision support system in the field of urban policy making to facilitate learning and negotiation, allowing for innovative solutions to emerge and for the empowerment of local communities.

Keywords: Fuzzy Cognitive Maps · Participatory process · Urban regeneration · Decision support system · Public policy making · Urban safety perception

1 Introduction

Safety and its perception from the point of view of citizens is a key theme in assessing the liveability of cities and is an increasingly significant factor in urban planning choices. The interaction between a social system and that of a city's spatial urban-architecture influences, by fostering or hindering, the perception of threats and consequently the need for greater safety. In order to obtain effective urban regeneration, analytical methods must be applied which are able to take into account the complexity of intangible elements such as those that are psycho-social or cognitive and related to the shared perception of danger. These approaches reveal how these elements can be assessed and integrated

© Springer Nature Switzerland AG 2021
O. Gervasi et al. (Eds.): ICCSA 2021, LNCS 12953, pp. 565–577, 2021.
https://doi.org/10.1007/978-3-030-86976-2_38

with the technical analysis of physical features to provide effective support in operation and management decisions.

Given this background, this study investigates the perception of safety in public areas, considering the combined effect of both social aspects and the built environment, for the case study of the historic Piazza Umberto square in Bari (Italy). It was developed through the public participatory process headed by researchers from the Polytechnic University of Bari in 2019. This procedure involved focus groups on thematic issues aimed towards blending knowledge from the local community, institutions and experts. The choice of this case study was based on the opportunity to regenerate the area of the square and restore its public use. Indeed, despite its central location and its historical value, the area had become notorious as an unsafe place to avoid, given its degraded state. The purpose of this paper is to present the proposed participatory process, along with the methodology to structure shared knowledge and also to evaluate to what extent this was able to make the perception of safety, an intangible aspect, more definite. The method used to formalize collected opinions is described; these were modelled with a process based on fuzzy logic, i.e. Fuzzy Cognitive Maps (FCM), with Mental Modeler (MM) software [1]. Subsequently, hypothesized intervention choices were simulated within what-if scenarios to support decision management for urban planning and to verify that their effects met people's requests [2].

Although limited by a tight schedule, the results obtained were of great interest. The FCMs were able to visually represent people's thoughts and it was possible to express the ambiguity and uncertainty inherent in multi-agent spatial systems [3]. The developed approach proved to be suitable as a method for problem structuring and formalization, since it generates useful knowledge to support public decision-making. The creation of what-if intervention scenarios gave us the opportunity to visualize the cascade impacts of decisions aimed toward increasing the perceived safety of users and, at the same time, allowed us to verify the effectiveness of the FCM approach. Indeed, the dynamic elaboration of FCMs was useful in identifying possible unintended consequences of choices to plan mitigation strategies in advance.

The paper is structured as follows: following the introduction, a background section links the study to the participatory process practices and explains the FCM approach within the framework of problem-structuring methods. The following section presents the case study. Subsequently, the methodology for data acquisition and analysis in the context of the participatory workshop is described. This is followed by an analysis of the thematic map representing the what-if scenario of safety and a discussion on findings. A concluding paragraph reports limitations and recommendations with considerations on the potential of the proposed approach and future developments of the work.

2   Background

In land use planning, problems are ambiguous and must be understood from fragmented information about situations in which the means and ends are confusing and contradictory [4]. Thanks to public consultation, critical issues are identified through interaction between different stakeholders and no longer by examining solely urban and regulatory aspects. Participatory processes are a way of informing, listening, assessing and making decisions which allow the knowledge process to be extended to non-rational components [5]. The choice of how to structure these and the methods for formalizing information and results is a consequence of the evaluation of elements such as the territorial scale, the purpose of the process, the number of participants and the resources available. In this work, a Scenario Workshop (SW) approach integrated with information structuring and analysis using Fuzzy Cognitive Maps (FCM) is adopted. The SW was applied as a public consultative method, implemented in the presence of a limited number of problem-aware/participants, on a specific issue with a strong local impact and for the prior assessment of the consequences of choices. This served to examine and contextualize the problem, hypothesize related issues and identify combined patterns of solutions through concrete actions applicable at topical moments of change [6]. A technique for formalizing information was essential to facilitate communication and consensus among stakeholders and to inform later public debate. Problem-structuring methods map the nature of the situation to be changed by modelling the knowledge of stakeholders to create a formal, shared representation of reality and develop new understanding. In this field, FCMs are a parameterized form of concept mapping in which it is possible to transform qualitative static models, for example, environmental, social or ecological concepts, into dynamic and semi-quantitative ones. These can be visualized in the form of a matrix or graph [7]. In this case, the FCM analysis method was developed to describe the problem, the solutions based on the proposed actions and their mutual impacts. A cognitive map (CM) (also called mental map) is an adaptable graphical representation of perception on a particular topic [8]. Graphically, it is a network of nodes connected with arrows, where the direction of the arrow implies the assigned causality. It can be used to encode, store, acquire, transmit and decode information about a phenomenon, as well as a specific and spatially defined environmental problem. However, the CM, while able to represent the mutual influences between the elements of a system, is not able to express the ambiguity of causal relationships typical of complex social systems. Therefore, its integration with the theory of fuzzy logic is designed to overcome this limit. Kosko introduces FCMs to make CMs more flexible and appropriate for the more vague knowledge systems and uncertain reasoning that reflect real-world case studies [9]. Indeed, fuzzy logic was developed as an extension of dual logic to deal with real-world problems in which the absence of defined classification criteria is a source of uncertainty [10]. This is a multi-valued logic, since the true and false values of bivalent logic become the extremes of a continuous domain. With this principle, it is possible to analyse an uncertain (fuzzy) set and estimate partial membership of elements in that set. Thus, while in traditional logic the degree to which an element belongs to a set is expressed in binary terms (i.e. an element belongs to it or not), with fuzzy logic the degree of belonging is within an interval ranging from 0 to 1. FCM consists of nodes and arcs where the nodes represent concepts and the arcs represent the causal influences between them. The centrality value of each node reflects the role of the concept itself in the network. The relationships between concepts are expressed by positive or negative signs and with a weight for the influence value expressed with fuzzy values between -1 and 1 [11].

FCMs are widely used to support group decision-making processes where it is necessary to consider and integrate the knowledge of experienced and non-experienced actors. In the field of urban planning, FCMs are considered suitable tools to graphically represent stakeholder concepts such as issues, policies, priority events and core values. An FCM dynamic analysis leads to insights about the system in question, particularly predictions about future states that are not possible with statistical methodologies [12]. Specifically, FCMs help predict the evolution of the system to which they are applied by simulating its behaviour with a causal progression that answers what-if questions. In practice, once an FCM of a certain problem domain has been realized, the answer of the system to set up conditions can be simulated in order to test the evolution of impacts and support public debate and decision-making. In the present study, the FCMs were modelled using Mental Modeler software, which made it possible to parameterize the relationships between the components and develop and analyse thematic what-if scenarios created on identified criticalities and needs.

3   Case Study

The city of Bari is located in the south of Italy and covers about 116 km^2. The original nucleus of the city is today's old town. 1813 saw expansion outside the defensive walls that encircled it and in 1816 Joachim Murat issued a decree to construct the "new town", now the Murattiano district, with an orthogonal grid. Here, numerous buildings are protected, given their historical and architectural value. The present study refers to the redevelopment of the historical Piazza Umberto I and of the Goccia del Latte building located inside it (see Fig. 1). Piazza Umberto I is located in the heart of the Murat district, in a strategic position between the pole of the railway station (1865) and the main axis of Via Sparano. This is a non-fenced square with a public garden resulting from the merging of two previous gardens. The older of these was designed in 1866 by the Neapolitan architect Giovanni Castelli, together with the university building Palazzo dell'Ateneo and as part of its property. The second took shape in a later period as a scenic setting for the equestrian statue of Umberto I, a tribute to the assassinated Italian king, which was inaugurated in 1905. The garden still retains its original architectural setting, with pedestrian paths that wind through flower beds bordered by low brick fences, where the paths define a more or less regular grid, typical of Italian architecture. Upon completion of the construction of the Apulian Aqueduct, a large fountain with an oval basin was installed at the axis of the main University entrance. Inside the garden there is a small pavilion in Art Nouveau style. This building originally housed Caffè Umberto and in 1921 became the headquarters of the association Goccia di Latte and Maternal Assistance until the 1970s. This carried out charity work in favour of disadvantaged children. Currently, the building is a municipal property. After a long period of abandonment followed by recent renovation, it was entrusted to the FIDAS blood donation association.

Fig. 1. Area under study: Piazza Umberto square - red, train station - yellow, university - blue, Via Sparano - pink and on the right the Goccia del Latte building. (Color figure online)

4 Methodology

To provide an analysis of safety perception, an integrated path was designed and proposed. This was based on the active involvement of stakeholders to identify socio-economic and organizational measures, as well as any interventions on the built physical, functional and managerial environment. The methodology to formalize collective knowledge supported the participatory process through the development of what-if scenarios. This allowed us to analyse the demand for safety according to a process whereby the participatory identification of the nodal criteria of the problem leads to a definition of a decision support framework. This was carried out through an evaluation of the effects of actions which aimed to improve the liveability of the square and acted at the same time on the perception of risk, the sense of belonging and the role of informal citizen control. The developed approach allowed for the combined analysis of the configuration and usability of public space, with the aim of introducing elements of detailed knowledge into tools for administrative management to support the adaptation of places over time to satisfactory levels of safety, mitigating factors of danger. The design process consisted of five phases. The present paper refers to the first three of these which have already been carried out and are presented here for the case study. These phases were implemented with the support of the FCM method to structure problems and with a

Table 1. Design process for information collection, elaboration and analysis

Objectives of the process phase	Operational phases
Shared problem formulation	Knowledge Structuring with FCM
Generation of alternative redevelopment visions	Thematic map definition and elaboration
Actionable solution identification	What-if scenario analysis to identify priorities
Resulting choice-set collective validation and assessment	Shared problem formulation and building criteria to assess fulfilment of objectives
Decision support	Recommendation, formalization and integration with technical analysis

variable involvement of domain experts. Table 1 relates objectives identified within the participatory decision-making process to the operational phases of the project.

4.1 Knowledge Structuring with FCM

Stakeholder involvement was conducted during two meetings attended by several associations, public administrators and citizens interested in the redevelopment of the square, the building and the surrounding area; they were asked to share their knowledge and their views and ideas. Clearly the limited number of/participants was not enough to represent a large, democratic consultation. Indeed, the aim of the process was more aimed towards the creation of a collaborative environment where a wide variety of selected stakeholder types could share/well informed knowledge which could be elaborated publicly. Interesting physical and social issues emerged from the discussion, as well as numerous factors that influenced them. It was unanimously recognized that the square was an unsafe place due to the presence of criminal activities, such as drug dealing, fights and vandalism and the widespread state of physical neglect (see Fig. 2). In addition, the importance of intervention for regeneration as part of a broader and coherent district redevelopment was stressed. Nevertheless, despite substantial agreement on the most pressing problems, disagreements on and opposition to suggested solutions followed. This common situation reveals brainstorming deficiency as an effective method for generating alternative solutions, so confirming the need for a formalized expert-driven process for the comparison of choices and the identification of satisfactory and shared solutions.

Fig. 2. Scenario workshop with citizens and evidence of Piazza Umberto I degradation.

For this phase of the participation process an innovative methodology was triggered, with the aim of organizing, processing and visualizing contributions collected during the workshops. The construction of FCMs was based on elicited knowledge with the aim of obtaining a structured and tractable picture of the reality shared by stakeholders, experts and non-experts, through which more clearly salient features of the system and nodal problems could be identified and possible alternative scenarios compared [13]. Hence, Mental Modeler software was used to create the map of concepts brought up by stakeholders during the debate. These were later grouped for reasons of clarity into three distinct classes of components: reference principles for redevelopment, critical elements that emerged from the analysis of the current situation and proposed possible solutions and their mutual impacts (see Fig. 3). Influences are depicted with links between components and quantified with fuzzy values, varying in a continuum between − 1 and 1, depending on whether the influence is negative or positive.

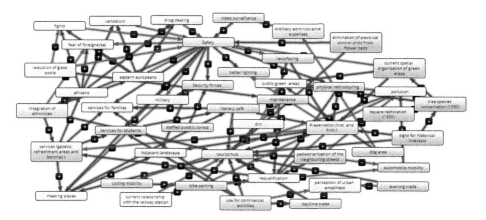

Fig. 3. Fuzzy Cognitive Map drawn up during the workshop.

In the accurate representation of knowledge that emerged from focus groups, the critical issues identified act as inputs to the system. Through the suggested actions these influence the guiding principles for the redevelopment of the area, which in turn play the role of outputs, i.e. effects derived from a certain combination of actions. In the map it is possible to follow the path of impact of each action on the principles to which it is connected. Moreover, those that influence several principles at the same time are crucial in the analysis and are called transitional, since they correlate different visions of redevelopment [14]. Nevertheless, the accurate representation made with the main map of the state of knowledge on the context and its problems is not particularly useful since it does not allow for the addition of new knowledge; consequently, thematic maps were created.

4.2 Thematic Map Elaboration

In the main map, it is not easy to speculate on exemplary future scenarios that enhance one vision of interest over the others and consequently this does not allow us to derive priorities for actions to be implemented. Thematic maps, centred on detailed scenarios of interest, were extracted from the main map with the objective of identifying the set of actions needed to achieve a single guiding principle. These new maps have a leading vision for redevelopment as a starting node that serves as a system input and nodes and links to related actions and criticalities are also contemplated. Thus, because of the implemented reversal of the causal link, actions in the thematic maps become the effects of the scenario. In addition to the proposed solutions, isolated concepts and above all transition elements were identified in the map. In the present study the map developed to simulate the scenario on the theme of safety is shown. This is intended as the perception of being able to enjoy a functional area freely and peacefully, without risk or fear of feeling in danger of violence or crime (see Fig. 4).

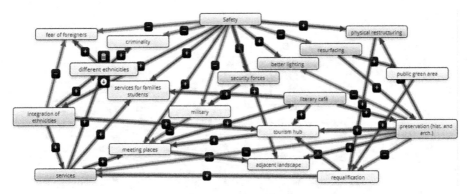

Fig. 4. FCM of safety perception scenario: principles - orange, criticalities - green and actions - blue. (Color figure online)

4.3   What-If Scenario Analysis

Once the thematic map was created, the scenario analysis was conducted according to hypothetical what-if configurations, each consisting of specific starting combination values of system factors. Subsequent inferences were automatically generated by software. This simulated the reaction of the system to various possible imposed conditions. Thanks to this kind of modelling, the real situation develops according to different paths. Indeed, the analysis does not examine a single image of the future but is expressed in different future outcomes. The most interesting aspect is to try to validate (or refute) the starting hypotheses and support (or reject) the resulting decisions. In fact, for each configuration an attempt is made to suppose the range of upcoming results and forecast an understanding of what these mean. Subsequently, to test the hypotheses in the scenario interface, the scenario is activated simulating the effects that derived from decisions. The impact on the system is visualized with a histogram that indicates how components react. Specifically, it presents the variation of each component depending on the value imposed on others and according to the causal relationships defined in the mapping interface.

For the case under investigation, operating on the key theme of the map, i.e. safety, enables us to appreciate how the scenario dynamically reshapes, visualizing the impact that the driving element had on the transition actions and how these in turn act on other principles. This process allows us to detect emerging and counterintuitive effects and it is possible to understand the impacts associated with possible changes and those responding to the greater number of needs that minimize undesired effects. Thus, it is easier to identify any side effects due to the impacts that a certain choice causes on other elements of the system and strategies can be developed to mitigate the negative effects so that more resilient choices can be implemented. Furthermore, this elaboration process trains experts to conceptualize the types of situations that arise from the choices made, which will need to be managed in the future and for which they will need to plan ahead. Below a case is reported in which the weight assigned to the safety component (a value of each element of the map which transforms it from qualitative to quantitative) was increased to its maximum. This is to simulate combined impacts of this what-if configuration, as well as all the side effects on the system as a result of policies aimed at maximizing safety. Figure 5 shows the histogram produced by the software in the scenario interface. The graph represents how the components react to the assumption. Principles and actions are on the x axis, while on the y axis the returned variations are shown.

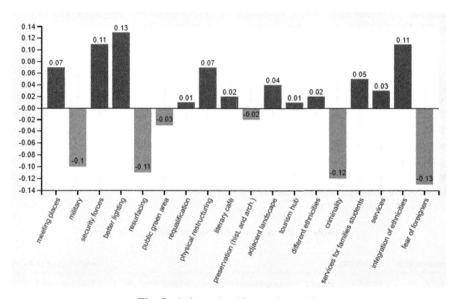

Fig. 5. Safety what-if scenario graph.

5   Results

An analysis of the histogram of safety scenario enables us to draw up a number of interesting evaluations. Indeed, in the plot of the scenario configuration in which the safety element is the main driver, elements aimed at restoring urban decorum have increased values. These aspects are related to the physical renovation of the square, better lighting and the resurfacing of paving and borders of flowerbeds, whereas the effect of the choice to transform the Goccia Di Latte building into a literary café shows a minimal positive impact. The condition of decreasing public green areas is an unexpected collateral phenomenon because of its relative implicit reduction in the importance of the preservation of the historical and architectural heritage of the square. In addition, the scenario displays a growth in the social cohesion level due to the reduction of the perception of danger and also the increased possibility of using the square as a meeting place for students and families, while only a minimal positive secondary effect impact is evident on the cultural integration of different ethnic groups. Finally, the assumption that the prevention of crime (in particular predatory crime) can be achieved by reinforcing police control would imply more than simply increasing their presence, but a better distribution throughout the area with a view to reducing military presence. These minor variations demonstrate the reliability of the model in representing the complexity of the real system, in which the components, although connected through secondary effects, impact only slightly on each other because of the non-linearity of the interactions. The dynamic problem analysis assists in the development of decisions and measures for problem solving correlated with urban regeneration. In fact, in the later stages of the process, based on the outlined scenarios, an action guide in the form of a list of priorities and urgent measures will be compiled to develop management and intervention strategies.

6 Discussion

The collaborative decision-making process was designed since collaboratively dealing with divergent intentions and conflictual objectives is essential to facilitate negotiation in complex social environments. Moreover, this allows for innovative solutions to emerge [15]. Therefore, with the help of the FCM methodology from a stakeholders' engagement, an attempt was made to reach empowerment as much as possible. This was achieved by moving from a phase of information sharing and adding to this to reach active collaboration, following the layout in Table 2.

Table 2. Phases for participatory involvement.

Phase action	Description	Involvement Level
Inform	Inspiring, informing and supporting a learning process among stakeholders	Engagement
Consult	Actively listening to views, concerns and insights of others	↓
Collaborate	Working together to solve problems, drawing on expertise and knowledge of others	Empowerment

Although part of a highly specific environmental and urban context, characterized by non-polarized preferences and from a short-term project perspective, the results obtained are more structured and qualitatively better than the reports produced in traditional participatory workshops, or compared with those obtained from observations collected through public consultation activities. The proposed approach has proved satisfactory in formalizing the problem, overcoming a linear cause-effect logic and managing the multiplicity of variables of interest at stake. In detail, the use of FCM to model and process the fragmented qualitative knowledge collected and the simulation of scenarios supported the process of reasoning and learning about causal loops and unintended consequences of choices.

From a methodological perspective, it is necessary to consider that in the modern practice of urban planning, the analytical phase of stakeholders' knowledge plays a central role. This is the result of the activities of collection and elaboration of information distributed among local actors. As a matter of fact, a meaningful description of an urban system requires the processing of a mass of data that a single individual can barely manage and understand. An expert can attempt to understand the relationships between two single factors in a complex system, or investigate how a certain factor affects others, but cannot understand the dynamic interaction of numerous elements all at once. Thus, structuring information with FCM was essential to make available data more manageable and to identify critical issues and feasible solutions. Nevertheless, due to the countless physical and socio-economic variables that come into play in urban situations, exact predictions are impossible. The scenario analysis applied is consistent with the need to obtain plausible projections to guide decision makers in defined context characterized by ambiguity, uncertainty and conflict. Indeed, the proposed approach addresses these complexities by incorporating multiple possibilities into the set of scenarios themselves. These will be used in forthcoming public debates to understand more clearly the complexity of the interdependence between possibilities, above all cases in which these alternatives are found to be incompatible. Thanks to this formalization, a more general shared reflection on the impossibility of reaching a single, unique and optimal solution can be developed. Conversely, a definition of a satisfactory trade-off between the multiple needs and priorities of stakeholders can arise.

7 Conclusion

In this paper the methodology designed to support the public participatory process developed for an urban regeneration programme is described. This was aimed at semi-quantitatively structuring the qualitative knowledge collected in meetings with stakeholders about perceived safety in the case of a defined, distinctive, but degraded public space in the heart of the city of Bari (Italy). It is shown how a traditional scenario workshop approach can be integrated by more innovative information processing with FCM formalized with MM software to elaborate collected data. This has the aim of addressing critical issues in terms of actual and perceived safety, encouraging the collective re-appropriation of places and promoting changes.

Every public policy is a strategic decision that aims to achieve defined goals in a certain time frame and this involves a set of linked elementary measures designed to address problems of a public nature. Stakeholder engagements on the decision-making process are necessary to avoid later conflicts, protests and resistance. Indeed, if involved, the decision phase can become much longer and non-linear, but it is a process that greatly facilitates subsequent implementation phases. As FCM uses a neutral approach, it can easily adapt to the context, mirroring this accurately. At the same time, it is useful to focus attention on central and critical issues, as well as on pivotal solutions for transition. Moreover, as it fosters the creation of temporary and mixed groups, it helps to empower participants and build trust in the participatory process itself. Finally, the FCM approach ensures that both the participatory and decision-making processes at least partially overlap (where one usually precedes or follows the other). This is because the process involves discussion, choice and (after scenario development led by an expert) an analysis phase that endorses or refutes and modifies the outputs, with the aim of providing results that are immediately available for decision support.

Although the proposed process alone cannot fulfil the need for a large-scale, democratic public consultation, e.g. due to the limits of the sample size which can be managed due to the workshop nature of the meetings, it may represent an informed preliminary step. Indeed, in the near future, thematic scenario elaborations will guide a public debate with citizens to facilitate the understanding of causal links and the effects of desirable and undesirable choices, and thus to imagine more clearly the outcomes of the redevelopment of places. This will be used to define strategies and actions to make decisions more concrete, thus likely avoiding the risks of unintended consequences or implementing appropriate additions for their mitigation. However, prior to the goal of arriving at final shared decisions, public reprocessing of the results of the analysis is essential to build the process of collective learning, which in turn provides a larger number of stakeholders with access to more knowledge and so enables their empowerment.

The application of this approach for data analysis in the field of spatial planning offers promising opportunities for the study of complex environmental and territorial systems. It seems appropriate for building scenarios suitable for dealing with the kind of intuitive, nuanced knowledge that seeks to understand uncertainty rather than ignore it; this is an indispensable aspect of formulating effective strategies in today's multicultural and multifaceted cities and thus for public administration support. A limitation found in the approach is the inability to contemplate unknown future variables and thus the unexpected impacts of additional factors that may occur in the long term. For this reason, the FCM approach can be seen as a problem-oriented phase to evaluate possible solutions in contingent situations as part of a larger pathway aimed at building future development strategies. However, it is useful in narrowing the gap between research and practice and can make the added value produced by public participation quantifiable. The findings are extremely interesting, with significant potential in the field of urban governance to open new perspectives of applied research to support decision-making problems and urban public policy design.

Author Contributions. Conceptualization, methodology, formalization, writing, review and editing D.E.; case study investigation and visualization D.E. and M.G. All authors have read and agreed to the published version of the manuscript.

References

1. Gray, S.A., Gray, S., Cox, L.J., Henly-Shepard, S.: Mental modeler: a fuzzy-logic cognitive mapping modeling tool for adaptive environmental management. In: Proceedings of the Annual Hawaii International Conference on System Sciences, pp. 965–973 (2013). https://doi.org/10.1109/HICSS.2013.399

2. Borri, D., Camarda, D., Pluchinotta, I., Esposito, D.: Supporting environmental planning: knowledge management through fuzzy cognitive mapping. In: Luo, Y. (ed.) CDVE 2015. LNCS, vol. 9320, pp. 228–235. Springer, Cham (2015). https://doi.org/10.1007/978-3-319-24132-6_29
3. Pluchinotta, I., Esposito, D., Camarda, D.: Fuzzy cognitive mapping to support multi-agent decisions in development of urban policymaking. Sustain. Cities Soc. **46**, 101402 (2019). https://doi.org/10.1016/j.scs.2018.12.030
4. Schön, D.: The Reflective Practitioner: How Professionals Think in Action (1993)
5. Nanz, P., Fritsche, M.: La partecipazione dei cittadini: un manuale. Metodi partecipativi: protagonisti, opportunita' e limiti, https://www.researchgate.net/publication/272418040_La_partecipazione_dei_cittadini_un_manuale_Metodi_partecipativi_protagonisti_opport unita%27_e_limiti. Accessed 07 Feb 2021
6. Barbanente, A., Khakee, A., Puglisi, M.: Scenario building for metropolitan Tunis. Futures **34**, 583–596 (2002). https://doi.org/10.1016/S0016-3287(02)00002-2
7. Eden, C.: Analyzing cognitive maps to help structure issues or problems. Eur. J. Oper. Res. **159**, 673–686 (2004). https://doi.org/10.1016/S0377-2217(03)00431-4
8. Tolman, E.C.: Cognitive maps in rats and men. Psychol. Rev. **55**, 189–208 (1948). https://doi.org/10.1037/h0061626
9. Kosko, B.: Fuzzy cognitive maps. Int. J. Man Mach. Stud. **24**, 65–75 (1986). https://doi.org/10.1016/S0020-7373(86)80040-2
10. Zimmermann, H.-J.: Fuzzy set theory. Wiley Interdiscip. Rev. Comput. Stat. **2**, 317–332 (2010). https://doi.org/10.1002/wics.82
11. Aguilar, J.: A survey about fuzzy cognitive maps papers (invited paper). Int. J. Comput. Cogn. **3**, 27–33 (2005)
12. Stach, W., Kurgan, L., Pedrycz, W.: Expert-based and computational methods for developing Fuzzy Cognitive maps. In: Studies in Fuzziness and Soft Computing, pp. 23–41. Springer, Heidelberg (2010). https://doi.org/10.1007/978-3-642-03220-2_2
13. Groumpos, P.P.: Fuzzy cognitive maps: basic theories and their application to complex systems. In: Studies in Fuzziness and Soft Computing, pp. 1–22. Springer, Heidelberg (2010). https://doi.org/10.1007/978-3-642-03220-2_1
14. Santoro, S., Esposito, D., Camarda, D., Borri, D.: A hybrid approach for the acquisition and analysis of distributed knowledge on spatial planning: the case study of the master plan for Brindisi (Italy). In: La Rosa, D., Privitera, R. (eds.) INPUT 2021. LNCE, vol. 146, pp. 195–204. Springer, Cham (2021). https://doi.org/10.1007/978-3-030-68824-0_21
15. Giordano, R., Vurro, M.: Fuzzy cognitive map to support conflict analysis in drought management. In: Studies in Fuzziness and Soft Computing, pp. 403–425. Springer, Heidelberg (2010). https://doi.org/10.1007/978-3-642-03220-2_17

International Workshop
on Computational Astrochemistry
(CompAs-tro 2021)

The CH_2CH_2 + OH Gas Phase Reaction: Formaldehyde and Acetaldehyde Formation Routes

Andrea Lombardi[1,2($\boxtimes$)] (iD), Luca Mancini[1,2] (iD),
Emília Valença Ferreira de Aragão[1,2] (iD), and Lisa Giani[1]

[1] Dipartimento di Chimica, Biologia e Biotecnologie, Università degli Studi di Perugia, Via Elce di Sotto 8, 06123 Perugia, Italy
andrea.lombardi@unipg.it
[2] Master-Tec srl, Via Sicilia 41, 06128 Perugia, Italy

Abstract. In this work we assess the viability of the CH_2CH_2+OH gas phase exothermic route as a mechanism for the formation of formaldehyde and acetaldehyde in the Interstellar Medium. The relevant features of the potential energy surface of the system have been characterized by accurate quantum chemical calculations, identifying the available pathways as a sequence of minimum and transition state structures, with no entry barriers. Preliminary theoretical kinetics calculations have been performed at the low temperature range characteristic of the spatial environments where such neutral-neutral reactions could be of interest.

Keywords: Astrochemistry · Rate constant · Transition state

1 Introduction

Complex Organic Molecules (COMs), defined as organic species made up by more than a few atoms, are routinely detected in the Interstellar Medium (ISM) [1]. The investigation of their reaction mechanisms is a major task of astrochemistry, functional to the explanation of the abundances of the observed molecules and to the identifications of the processes that mostly contribute to their formation. COMs have been discovered under a variable range of extreme conditions typical of different spatial environments, such as cold clouds [2], protostellar envelopes [3] or protoplanetary disks [4], to mention some of them.

The two main types of phenomena allowing for molecules to be generated are (i) grain chemistry, where the surface of dust grains interacts with molecules promoting product formation and (ii) gas-phase reactions upon collisions.

The ISM is characterized by very low temperatures and densities, which essentially reduce the viable gas phase processes to exothermic reactions and to pathways with not too high energy barriers. Even so, there are many fundamental aspects of gas-phase processes that have to be known in detail, among them, the reactive rate coefficients have to be quantified as accurately as possible, for the

O. Gervasi et al. (Eds.): ICCSA 2021, LNCS 12953, pp. 581–593, 2021.
https://doi.org/10.1007/978-3-030-86976-2_39

many possible reactive channels. Moreover, since reactive dynamics and kinetics of the molecular systems are a manifestation of the underlying potential energy surface, an accurate characterization of the electronic states at relevant geometries and energy profiles of the most relevant pathways is a prerequisite to obtain reliable theoretical results. Typical approaches for gas phase reactivity therefore integrate accurate quantum chemical calculations, dynamics simulations and kinetic modelling.

Two important molecules in the ISM, formaldehyde (HCOH) and acetaldehyde (CH_3COH), are the object of this work. Formaldehyde has been detected for the first time in 1969 trough the analysis of ground state rotational transitions against numerous galactic center and extragalactic radio sources, including, as an example, SgrA and SgrB2 [5]. Since that moment the molecule has been detected in a variety of environments, including cold and warm regions. Fomaldehyde, and its deuterated analogue HDCO, has been detected in 1995 toward the Orion Molecular Cloud (OMC-1)[6], while later in the 2000s different regions have been analyzed, including solar-type protostars [7]; Class 0 protostars [8]; cold, dense pre-protostellar cores [9], young stellar objects [10] and Photodissociation regions [11,12]. Most of the models built in order to constrain the abundances of the aforementioned molecule include the formation of formaldehyde through subsequent processes in the surface of the grains, followed by the injection in the gas phase as a consequence of the evaporation of the grain mantles when the temperature reaches 100K. The other target molecule in this work, acetaldehyde is considered as an important precursor for the synthesis of prebiotic species such as carbohydrates and amino acids [13,14]. The first detection of the molecule has been reported in 1973 [15] and later confirmed in 1974 trough the observation of the 211–212 transition in the SgrB2 region [16]. Since that moment, several works revealed the presence of acetaldehyde in different regions including the Orion Molecular Cloud (OMC-1) [17] but also low mass protostars [18,19], cold prestellar cores [20,21] (where the temperature can reach values near 10K) and in the L1157-B1 shock region [22], also related to high-mass protostars [23]. In the last years, the analysis of some data coming from the ALMA telescope allowed the identification of acetaldehyde in Dark clouds [24]. In 2019 new observations have been performed through the vertically resolved disk around a protostar [25], while last year a survey analysis of 31 starless and prestellar cores in the Taurus Molecular Cloud [26] has been reported, together with the detection of acetaldehyde in the shocked material associated with low-mass protostellar outflows [27].

Considering the huge variety of environments in which the CH_3COH molecule has been detected, together with the strong prebiotic potential showed, several formation mechanisms have been proposed in order to understand the possible origin of this species. In particular different gas phase neutral-neutral and ion-neutral reactions have been proposed in the past years starting from dimethyl ether [28], ethyl radical [29] and methanol [30]. A work from Skouteris et al. in 2018 shows the possible formation route of CH_3COH starting from the chemical activation of the ethanol molecule [31], followed by the reaction with atomic oxygen, while a recent analysis performed by Vazart et al. [32] revised the possible C$_2$H$_5$+O(^{3}P) and CH$_3$OH+CH reactions in order to provide the values of the rate constant in the 7–300 K range of temperature. Other processes can be invoked as possible formation mechanisms of HCOH and CH$_3$OH in the gas-phase, including the OH+C$_2$H$_4$ reaction.

A theoretical analysis of the aforementioned process has been performed by S.J. Klippenstein and collaborators [33] through ab-initio calculations for portions of the PES, together with a kinetic analysis using the two-transition state model, in order to reproduce the experimental data. The calculations showed two possible reaction pathways: (i) the formation of a van der Waals adduct coming from the association of the two species and (ii) an hydrogen abstraction process, leading to the formation of a water molecule. The possible competition between the formation of acetaldehyde and its isomer, vinyl alcohol, is also examined. Similar results have been obtained by R.S. Zhu and coworkers at the PMP2/aug-cc-pVQZ//MP2/cc-pVTZ level of theory coupled with RRKM calculations [34]. A different analysis has been performed by Z.F. Xu et al. and B.J. Ratliff et al. starting from the CH$_3$CHOH and CH$_2$CH$_2$OH radicals respectively [35,36], leading to the formation of C$_2$H$_4$ + OH, together with other possible combinations of products, including acetaldehyde and formaldehyde.

In the present work the attention has been focused on the first possible pathway, namely the interaction of the two reactants followed by the formation and evolution of a vdW adduct.

The paper is organized as follows. In Sect. 2 the theoretical and computational methods used for the characterization of the potential energy surface and its relevant stationary points are described. The potential adopted to model the intermolecular interactions characterizing the vdW adduct formation is detailed and a brief description of the kinetic theory is given.

2 Methodology

Here we describe the theoretical approach to the calculation of the stationary points in the reactive pathways of the OH + C$_2$H$_4$ system and the rate coefficients for the various elementary steps leading to formaldehyde and acetaldehyde formation. The initial step at the beginning of the two reactive pathways is mediated by the formation of a van der Waals adduct between ethene and the hydroxyl radical, which can subsequently evolve to the hydroxyethyl radical (HER). The adduct formation, a barrierless process, has been modelled by capture theory.

2.1 Electronic Structure Calculations

The OH + C$_2$H$_4$ reaction has been analyzed adopting a computational strategy already used in the past for several systems [37–43]. In particular the doublet potential energy surface has been investigated through optimization of the most stable stationary points at the DFT level of theory using the B3LYP functional

[44, 45] in conjunction with the correlation consistent valence polarized set aug-cc-pVTZ [46]. The same level of theory has been used to perform harmonic vibrational frequency calculations, in order to determine the nature of each stationary point, classified as minimum if all the frequencies were real and as a first order saddle point (representative of a transition state) if there was a single imaginary frequency. The identified saddle point structures have been assigned using Intrinsic Reaction Coordinate calculations (IRC) [47, 48]. Finally refined energy values for each identified stationary point have been obtained using coupled cluster theory, including single and double excitations as well as a perturbative estimate of connected triples CCSD(T) with the same aug-cc-pVTZ basis set [49–51]. All the energies have been corrected by adding the zero point energy, computed using the scaled harmonic vibrational frequencies as obtained at the B3LYP/aug-cc-pVTZ level of theory. All the calculations have been performed using GAUSSIAN09 [52], while the analysis of the vibrational frequencies have been carried out using Avogadro[53].

2.2   Van der Waals Interaction Potential

The initial bimolecular association process is the vdw dimer formation driven by intermolecular forces. A semi-empirical potential function has been adopted to model these interactions and to evaluate the C_6 coefficient used for the kinetic calculations. In details, the overall potential V_{tot} is assumed to be a combination of two terms, as follows:

$$V_{tot} = V_{ILJ} + V_{elect} \tag{1}$$

where V_{elect} is the electrostatic interaction contribution and V_{ILJ} (see next for the subscript acronym) is the contribution due to size repulsion and dispersion attraction, usually named as the vdW term. The electrostatic contribution has been evaluated considering the Coulombic interactions between pairs of charges (see Table 1) obtained from the CCSD(T)/aug-cc-pVTZ calculations for each atom of the two interacting fragments:

$$V_{elect}(r) = \frac{1}{4\pi\varepsilon_0} \sum_{i=1}^{6} \sum_{j=1}^{2} \frac{q_i q_j}{r_{ij}} \tag{2}$$

The non-electrostatic term V_{ILJ} has been evaluated using the so called Improved Lennard-Jones (ILJ) potential function, which provides a better reproduction with respect to the classical Lennard-Jones model over both short- and long-range distances [54]. The ILJ potential, for a pair of interacting centers at a distance r, can be expressed as:

$$V_{ILJ}(r) = \varepsilon \left[\frac{m}{n(r) - m} \left(\frac{r_m}{r} \right)^{n(r)} - \frac{n(r)}{n(r) - m} \left(\frac{r_m}{r} \right)^{m} \right] \tag{3}$$

where ε and r_m are the well depth and position of the potential, respectively, m=6 for neutral-neutral systems and $n(r)$ can be expressed as follows:

Table 1. Mulliken partial charges obtained from the CCSD(T)/aug-cc-pVTZ calculations.

Atom	Mulliken partial charges (CCSD(T))
C	−0.899
H	0.449
O$_{rad}$	−0.275
H$_{rad}$	0.275

Table 2. ε and r$_m$ parameters used to obtain the non-electrostatic potential.

Interacting pair	r$_m$ (Å)	ε (meV)
C-O$_{rad}$	3.62	5.21
H-O$_{rad}$	3.31	2.61
C-H$_{rad}$	3.47	2.05
H-H$_{rad}$	3.07	1.26

$$n(r) = \beta + 4.0 \left(\frac{r}{r_m} \right)^2 \tag{4}$$

The β parameter is set equal to 8 in our case. The r_m and ε parameters can be obtained considering the polarizability of the two interacting partners [55]. Their values for this system are listed on Table 2.

2.3 Kinetic Calculations

Kinetic calculations have been performed to derive the rate coefficients for the formation of the two identified products, using a code developed for this purpose in our group. In order to get a rate coefficient for the first step leading to the van der Waals adduct formation, capture theory has been used assuming the following expression for the entrance attractive potential $V(R)$:

$$V(r) = -\frac{C_n}{r^n} \tag{5}$$

where n is equal to 6 in the case of neutral-neutral systems ($n = 4$ for ion-neutral processes), R is the distance between the two particles and C_n is the interaction coefficient between the two species. Subsequently, RRKM theory has been used in order to evaluate all the unimolecular processes, the rate coefficient at a specific energy, $K(E)$, being obtained as follows:

$$K(E) = \frac{N(E)}{h\rho(E)} \tag{6}$$

where $N(E)$ is the sum of states at an energy E, $\rho(E)$ is the density of states, and h is the Planck's constant. A master equation has been solved including all the unimolecular rate coefficients in order to obtain the branching ratios for the formation of the two products.

3   Results

3.1   Electronic Structure Calculations

A schematic version of the Potential Energy Surface (PES) obtained for the OH + C_2H_4 reaction is reported in Fig. 1. For simplicity, only the CCSD(T) energies corrected with the zero-point energy have been reported in the figure. The first step of the reaction appears to be the interaction of the OH radical with the ethylene molecule, leading to the formation of a van der Waals adduct, named INT1, located 7.9 kJ mol^{-1} below the reactant energy asymptote, where the distance between the two interacting fragments is around 2.5 Å. A small barrier of 0.4 kJ mol^{-1} must be overcome in order to form the INT2 intermediate (hydroxyethyl radical), in which is possible to notice the formation of a new C-O chemical bond, with a relative energy of -109.2 kJ mol^{-1}. The related transition state, TS1, clearly shows the rotation of the OH radical and the interaction of the O atom with one of the two carbon atoms of the ethylene molecule. Once INT2 is formed, it can isomerize to INT3 by transferring an hydrogen atom from the oxygen to the carbon. The new intermediate is located 100 kJ mol^{-1} below the reactant energy asymptote, nevertheless a barrier of 131.8 kJ mol^{-1} must be overcome. As a consequence the above mentioned process appears to be endothermic. Tunneling effects can be invoked in order to explain the crossing of the barrier at low temperature conditions when the crossing is classically forbidden. Once INT3 is formed, it can easily undergo dissociation in order to produce the formaldehyde molecule, together with the CH_3 radical. The transition state TS3, which clearly shows the breaking of the C-C bond, is located 25.5 kJ mol^{-1} below the reactant energy asymptote, while the HCOH + CH_3 products show an exothermicity of -53.1 kJ mol^{-1} with respect to the reactants. A different fate can affect INT3: a hydrogen elimination process leading to the formation of acetaldehyde, located 34.3 kJ mol^{-1} below the reactant energy asymptote. The analysis of the vibrational frequencies calculated for the related transition state TS4, which shows a relative energy of -7.5 kJ mol^{-1}, clearly shows the breaking of a C-H bond. In Figs. 2, 3, 4 are reported the geometries of all the stationary points identified along the potential energy surface, together with the reactants and the possible products, obtained at the B3LYP/aug-cc-pVTZ level of theory, while in Table 3 are reported the enthalpy changes and the barrier heights for each step, computed at the CCSD(T)/aug-cc-pVTZ level.

3.2   Van der Waals Interaction Potential

The overall interaction potential $V(r)$, in kJ mol^{-1}, as a function of the distance between the two reactants is reported in Fig. 5. The plot clearly shows a minimum in the potential at a distance between the H atom of the OH radical and the center of mass of the ethylene molecule of 2.6 Å, which appears to be in agreement with the data coming from electronic structure calculations, where the distance between the two interacting atoms of the fragments is $d_{C-H} = 2.517$ Å, while the energy coming from the semi-empirical potential appears to be 6.95 kJ mol^{-1} lower than the

Table 3. Enthalpy changes and barrier heights (kJ mol^{-1}, 0 K) computed at the CCSD(T)/aug-cc-pVTZ level of theory for the system OH + C$_2$H$_4$.

Reaction path	ΔH_0^0 kJ mol^{-1}	Barrier Heights kJ mol^{-1}
OH + C$_2$H$_4$ → INT1	−7.9	
INT1 → INT2	−101.3	0.4
INT2 → INT3	9.2	131.8
INT3 → CH$_3$ + HCOH	46.9	74.5
INT3 → H + HCOCH$_3$	65.7	92.6

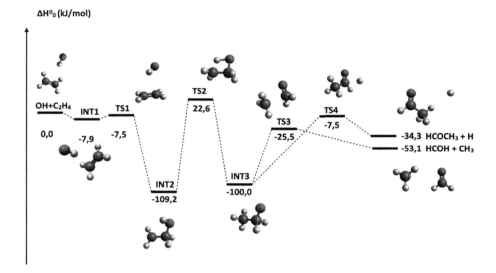

Fig. 1. Schematic version of the Potential Energy Surface including the energies obtained at the CCSD(T)/aug-cc-pVTZ level of theory.

CCSD(T)/aug-cc-pVTZ energy. The data related to the long-range interaction, particularly the range of distances from 2 Å to 5 Å, have been used in a fitting procedure in order to obtain the value of the C$_6$ coefficient, to be included in the kinetics calculations for the estimation of the branching ratios.

3.3 Kinetic Calculations

According to our analysis, the first step of the reaction is the interaction of the two reactants and the barrierless formation of a van der Waals adduct. A small barrier leads to the formation of an intermediate with a new C-O bond. Alternatively the adduct has the option of undergoing back dissociation to the reactants. The RRKM analysis has been carried out on the PES described in the previous sections. In the case of back dissociation, the rate is proportional

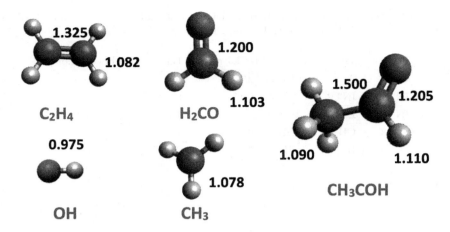

Fig. 2. Main distances (in Å) of the reactants and products for the OH+C$_2$H$_4$ reaction obtained at the B3LYP/aug-cc-pVTZ level of theory.

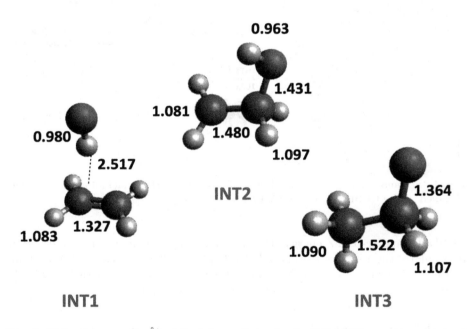

Fig. 3. Main distances (in Å) of the intermediates for the OH+C$_2$H$_4$ reaction obtained at the B3LYP/aug-cc-pVTZ level of theory.

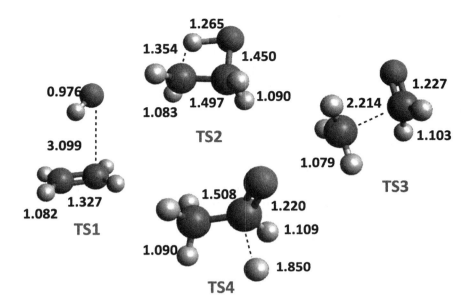

Fig. 4. Main distances (in Å) of the saddle points for the OH+C$_2$H$_4$ reaction obtained at the B3LYP/aug-cc-pVTZ level of theory.

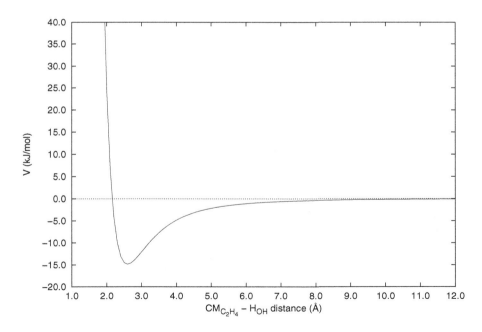

Fig. 5. Interaction potential [kJ mol^{-1}] as a function of the distance between the two reactants [Å].

to the density of states of the reactants. The obtained branching ratios for the formation of the two products are reported in Table 4. As it can be noticed, in the range of temperatures between 1 and 300 K the % of formation of the two products is almost negligible, while the only possible process appears to be the back dissociation. This is due to the presence of TS2, located 22.6 kJ mol^{-1} above the energy of the reactants, which makes the reaction inefficient under the conditions of the Interstellar Medium. Only a small fraction of the reactive flux can lead to the formation of formaldehyde at 10K. This process can be explained considering the possibility of tunneling at low temperatures, allowing the system to reach the configuration of INT3. Once INT3 is formed, it can dissociate to form both acetaldehyde and formaldehyde. The breaking of the C-C bond appears to be favourable, due to the lower barrier heights. As a consequence the formation of formaldehyde is preferred with respect to acetaldehyde.

Table 4. Branching ratios (%) obtained for the formation of the two products identified in the PES

Temperature (K)	HCOH + CH$_3$ (%)	CH$_3$CHO + H (%)
10	3.255	0.0196
50	0.0377	0.0002
100	0.0056	0.00004
200	0.0012	0.00001
300	0.0008	0.00001

4   Conclusions and Future Works

In the present work we analyzed the reaction between the OH radical and the ethylene molecule. Theoretical quantum chemical calculations allowed us to describe the formation of two different products: formaldehyde and acetaldehyde. An initial barrierless association process has been identified, nevertheless an endothermic transition state has been found to be related to a rearrangement process, fundamental for the formation of the title products. As a consequence the investigated reaction pathways can not be considered the main formation mechanisms of the two aforementioned species under the harsh conditions of the Interstellar Medium, given the inefficiency of the processes. A more detailed analysis will be performed in the future in order to identify other possible reaction pathways, including the H-abstraction channel.

Acknowledgments. The work presented in this paper has received funding from the European Union's Horizon 2020 research and innovation programme under the Marie Skłodowska-Curie grant agreement No 811312 for the project "Astro-Chemical Origins" (ACO). EVFA thanks the DICA (Dipartimento di eccellenza) of University of Perugia for allocated computing time. AL and NFL thank the Dipartimento di Chimica, Biologia e Biotecnologie dell'Università di Perugia (FRB, Fondo per la Ricerca di Base

2019 and 2020) and the Italian MIUR and the University of Perugia for the financial support of the AMIS project through the program "Dipartimenti di Eccellenza". AL acknowledges the Italian Space Agency (ASI) Life in Space project (ASI N. 2019-3-U.0). AL and NFL thank the OU Supercomputing Center for Education & Research (OSCER) at the University of Oklahoma, for allocated computing time.

References

1. Caselli, P., Ceccarelli, C.: Our astrochemical heritage. Astron. Astrophys. Rev. **20**, 56 (2012)
2. Aikawa, Y., et al.: AKARI observations of ice absorption bands towards edge-on young stellar objects. A&A **538**, A57 (2012)
3. Aikawa, Y., Nomura, H.: Physical and chemical structure of protoplanetary disks with grain growth. Astrophys. J. **642**(2), 1152–1162 (2006)
4. Aikawa, Y., Umebayashi, T., Nakano, T., Miyama, S.M.: Evolution of molecular abundances in protoplanetary disks with accretion flow. Astrophys. J. **519**(2), 705–725 (1999)
5. Snyder, L.E., Buhl, D., Zuckerman, B., Palmer, P.: Microwave detection of interstellar formaldehyde. Phys. Rev. Lett. **22**, 679 (1969)
6. Sutton, E., Peng, R., Danchi, W., Jaminet, P., Sandell, G., Russell, A.: The distribution of molecules in the core of OMC-1. Astrophys. J. Suppl. Ser. **97**, 455–496 (1995)
7. Ceccarelli, C., Loinard, L., Castets, A., Tielens, A., Caux, E.: The hot core of the solar-type protostar IRAS 16293-2422: H$_2$CO emission. Astron. Astrophys. **357**, L9–L12 (2000)
8. Maret, S., et al.: The H2CO abundance in the inner warm regions of low mass protostellar envelopes. Astron. Astrophys. **416**, 577–594 (2004)
9. Young, K.E., Lee, J.E., Evans, N.J., II., Goldsmith, P.F., Doty, S.D.: Probing pre-protostellar cores with formaldehyde. Astrophys. J. **614**, 252 (2004)
10. Araya, E., Hofner, P., Goss, W., Linz, H., Kurtz, S., Olmi, L.: A search for formaldehyde 6 cm emission toward young stellar objects. II. H2CO and H110α observations. Astrophys. J. Suppl. Ser. **170**, 152 (2007)
11. Guzmán, V., et al.: The IRAM-30 m line survey of the horsehead PDR-IV. comparative chemistry of H2CO and CH3OH. Astron. Astrophys. **560**, A73 (2013)
12. Guzmán, V., Pety, J., Goicoechea, J., Gerin, M., Roueff, E.: H2CO in the horsehead PDR: photo-desorption of dust grain ice mantles. Astron. Astrophys. **534**, A49 (2011)
13. Pizzarello, S., Weber, A.L.: Prebiotic amino acids as asymmetric catalysts. Science **303**, 1151 (2004)
14. Córdova, A., Ibrahem, I., Casas, J., Sundén, H., Engqvist, M., Reyes, E.: Amino acid catalyzed neogenesis of carbohydrates: a plausible ancient transformation. Chem.-A Eur. J. **11**, 4772–4784 (2005)
15. Gordon, M., Snyder, L., Chaisson, E.J.: Molecules in the galactic environment. Phys. Today **28**, 74 (1975)
16. Fourikis, N., Sinclair, M., Robinson, B., Godfrey, P., Brown, R.: Microwave emission of the 211–212 rotational transition in interstellar acetaldehyde. Aust. J. Phys. **27**, 425–430 (1974)
17. Blake, G.A., Sutton, E., Masson, C., Phillips, T.: Molecular abundances in OMC-1: the chemical composition of interstellar molecular clouds and the influence of massive star formation. Astrophys. J. **315**, 621–645 (1987)

18. Cazaux, S., et al.: The hot core around the low-mass protostar IRAS 16293–2422: scoundrels rule! Astrophys. J. Lett. **593**, L51 (2003)
19. Bianchi, E., et al.: The census of interstellar complex organic molecules in the class i hot corino of SVS13-a. Mon. Not. R. Astron. Soc. **483**, 1850–1861 (2019)
20. Bacmann, A., Taquet, V., Faure, A., Kahane, C., Ceccarelli, C.: Detection of complex organic molecules in a prestellar core: a new challenge for astrochemical models. Astron. Astrophys. **541**, L12 (2012)
21. Vastel, C., Ceccarelli, C., Lefloch, B., Bachiller, R.: The origin of complex organic molecules in prestellar cores. Astrophys. J. Lett. **795**, L2 (2014)
22. Lefloch, B., et al.: L1157-B1, a factory of complex organic molecules in a solar-type star-forming region. Mon. Notices Royal Astron. Soc.: Lett. **469**, L73–L77 (2017)
23. Csengeri, T., Belloche, A., Bontemps, S., Wyrowski, F., Menten, K., Bouscasse, L.: Search for high-mass protostars with alma revealed up to kilo-parsec scales (sparks)-II. Complex organic molecules and heavy water in shocks around a young high-mass protostar. Astron. Astrophys. **632**, A57 (2019)
24. Sakai, T., et al.: *Alma* observations of the IRDC clump G34.43+00.24 MM3: complex organic and deuterated molecules. Astrophys. J. **857**, 35 (2018)
25. Lee, C.F., Codella, C., Li, Z.Y., Liu, S.Y.: First abundance measurement of organic molecules in the atmosphere of HH 212 protostellar disk. Astrophys. J. **867**, 63 (2019)
26. Scibelli, S., Shirley, Y.: Prevalence of complex organic molecules in starless and prestellar cores within the taurus molecular cloud. Astrophys. J. **891**, 73 (2020)
27. De Simone, M., et al.: Seeds of life in space (SOLIS)-X. interstellar complex organic molecules in the NGC 1333 IRAS 4A outflows. Astron. Astrophysi. **640**, A75 (2020)
28. Wakelam, V., et al.: A kinetic database for astrochemistry (KIDA). Astrophys. J. Suppl. Ser. **199**, 21 (2012)
29. McElroy, D., Walsh, C., Markwick, A., Cordiner, M., Smith, K., Millar, T.: The UMIST database for astrochemistry 2012. Astron. Astrophys. **550**, A36 (2013)
30. Vasyunin, A.I., Caselli, P., Dulieu, F., Jiménez-Serra, I.: Formation of complex molecules in prestellar cores: a multilayer approach. Astrophys. J. **842**, 33 (2017)
31. Skouteris, D., et al.: The genealogical tree of ethanol: gas-phase formation of glycolaldehyde, acetic acid, and formic acid. Astrophys. J. **854**, 135 (2018)
32. Vazart, F., Ceccarelli, C., Balucani, N., Bianchi, E., Skouteris, D.: Gas-phase formation of acetaldehyde: review and new theoretical computations. Mon. Not. R. Astron. Soc. **499**, 5547–5561 (2020)
33. Senosiain, J.P., Klippenstein, S.J., Miller, J.A.: Reaction of ethylene with hydroxyl radicals: a theoretical study. J. Phys. Chem. A **110**, 6960–6970 (2006)
34. Zhu, R., Park, J., Lin, M.C.: Ab initio kinetic study on the low-energy paths of the HO+C2H4 reaction. Chem. Phys. Lett. **408**, 25–30 (2005)
35. Xu, Z.F., Xu, K., Lin, M.C.: Ab initio kinetics for decomposition/isomerization reactions of C2H5O radicals. ChemPhysChem **10**, 972–982 (2009)
36. Ratliff, B.J., Alligood, B.W., Butler, L.J., Lee, S.H., Lin, J.J.M.: Product branching from the CH2CH2OH radical intermediate of the OH+ ethene reaction. J. Phys. Chem. A **115**, 9097–9110 (2011)
37. de Petris, G., Cartoni, A., Rosi, M., Barone, V., Puzzarini, C., Troiani, A.: The proton affinity and gas-phase basicity of sulfur dioxide. ChemPhysChem **12**(1), 112–115 (2011)
38. Leonori, F., et al.: Observation of organosulfur products (thiovinoxy, thioketene and thioformyl) in crossed-beam experiments and low temperature rate coefficients for the reaction S (1 D)+ C 2 H 4. Phys. Chem. Chem. Phys. **11**(23), 4701–4706 (2009)

39. de Petris, G., Rosi, M., Troiani, A.: SSOH and HSSO radicals: an experimental and theoretical study of [s2oh] 0/+/-species. J. Phys. Chem. A **111**(28), 6526–6533 (2007)

40. Rosi, M., Falcinelli, S., Balucani, N., Casavecchia, P., Skouteris, D.: A theoretical study of formation routes and dimerization of methanimine and implications for the aerosols formation in the upper atmosphere of titan. In: Murgante, B., et al. (eds.) ICCSA 2013. LNCS, vol. 7971, pp. 47–56. Springer, Heidelberg (2013). https://doi.org/10.1007/978-3-642-39637-3_4

41. Skouteris, D., et al.: Interstellar dimethyl ether gas-phase formation: a quantum chemistry and kinetics study. Mon. Not. R. Astron. Soc. **482**(3), 3567–3575 (2019)

42. Sleiman, C., El Dib, G., Rosi, M., Skouteris, D., Balucani, N., Canosa, A.: Low temperature kinetics and theoretical studies of the reaction CN+ CH 3 NH 2: a potential source of cyanamide and methyl cyanamide in the interstellar medium. Phys. Chem. Chem. Phys. **20**(8), 5478–5489 (2018)

43. Berteloite, C., et al.: Low temperature kinetics, crossed beam dynamics and theoretical studies of the reaction s (1 D)+ CH 4 and low temperature kinetics of S (1 D)+ C 2 H 2. Phys. Chem. Chem. Phys. **13**(18), 8485–8501 (2011)

44. Becke, A.D.: Density functional thermochemistry. III. The role of exact exchange. J. Chem. Phys. **98**(7), 5648–5652 (1993)

45. Stephens, P.J., Devlin, F.J., Chabalowski, C.F., Frisch, M.J.: *Ab Initio* calculation of vibrational absorption and circular dichroism spectra using density functional force fields. J. Phys. Chem. **98**(45), 11623–11627 (1994)

46. Dunning Jr, T.H.: Gaussian basis sets for use in correlated molecular calculations. I. the atoms boron through neon and hydrogen. J. Chem. Phys. **90**(2), 1007–1023 (1989)

47. Gonzalez, C., Schlegel, H.B.: An improved algorithm for reaction path following. J. Chem. Phys. **90**(4), 2154–2161 (1989)

48. Gonzalez, C., Schlegel, H.B.: Reaction path following in mass-weighted internal coordinates. J. Phys. Chem. **94**(14), 5523–5527 (1990)

49. Bartlett, R.J.: Many-body perturbation theory and coupled cluster theory for electron correlation in molecules. Annu. Rev. Phys. Chem. **32**(1), 359–401 (1981)

50. Raghavachari, K., Trucks, G.W., Pople, J.A., Head-Gordon, M.: A fifth-order perturbation comparison of electron correlation theories. Chem. Phys. Lett. **157**(6), 479–483 (1989)

51. Olsen, J., Jørgensen, P., Koch, H., Balkova, A., Bartlett, R.J.: Full configuration-interaction and state of the art correlation calculations on water in a valence double-zeta basis with polarization functions. J. Chem. Phys. **104**(20), 8007–8015 (1996)

52. Frisch, M., et al.: Gaussian 09, Revision A. 02, 2009, Gaussian. Inc., Wallingford CT (2009)

53. Hanwell, M.D., Curtis, D.E., Lonie, D.C., Vandermeersch, T., Zurek, E., Hutchison, G.R.: Avogadro: an advanced semantic chemical editor, visualization, and analysis platform. J. Cheminform. **4**(1), 1–17 (2012)

54. Pirani, F., Brizi, S., Roncaratti, L.F., Casavecchia, P., Cappelletti, D., Vecchiocattivi, F.: Beyond the lennard-jones model: a simple and accurate potential function probed by high resolution scattering data useful for molecular dynamics simulations. Phys. Chem. Chem. Phys. **10**(36), 5489–5503 (2008)

55. Cambi, R., Cappelletti, D., Liuti, G., Pirani, F.: Generalized correlations in terms of polarizability for van der Waals interaction potential parameter calculations. J. Chem. Phys. **95**(3), 1852–1861 (1991)

Free-Methane - from the Ionosphere of Mars Towards a Prototype Methanation Reactor: A Project Producing Fuels via Plasma Assisted Carbon Dioxide Hydrogenation

Stefano Falcinelli[1]($\boxtimes$) (iD), Marzio Rosi[1,2], Marco Parriani[1], and Antonio Laganà[2,3]

[1] Department of Civil and Environmental Engineering, University of Perugia,
Via G. Duranti 93, 06125 Perugia, Italy
{stefano.falcinelli,marzio.rosi}@unipg.it
[2] SCITEC, CNR,
Via Elce di Sotto 8, 06123 Perugia, Italy
[3] Department of Chemistry, Biology and Biotechnologies, University of Perugia,
Via Elce di Sotto 8, 06100 Perugia, Italy

Abstract. A major challenge in the scientific research for strategies that use low-cost renewable energy is to design and develop heterogeneous /homogeneous catalysis processes that use waste CO_2 to produce fuels in a circular economy regime. In this paper a theoretical and experimental study aiming at reusing CO_2 and implementing a validated laboratory technology based on a prototype methanation reactor producing carbon neutral methane through the chemical conversion of CO_2 waste flue gases using renewable energies, is presented. The first operational line of the work is the theoretical, computational and experimental treatment of elementary reactive and non-reactive molecular processes occurring inside the reactor in order to optimize its operating conditions and to identify possible technological improvements that are more compatible with the environment. Experimental determinations of methane yield by the reactor have been carried out using CO_2 either taken from commercial bottles or produced from fermentation of wine and vegetable exhausted materials. To this end we have also undertaken a computational and experimental investigation of a new methanation pathway aimed at avoiding the use of the solid catalyst, by exploring mechanisms involving a plasma generation by electrical discharges or by vacuum ultraviolet (VUV) photons on $CO_2 + H_2$ gas mixtures. The measurements performed using a microwave discharge beam source developed in our laboratory gave useful indications on how to proceed to develop alternative solutions to the present Ni catalysed apparatus by resorting to a gas-phase-only process for the reduction of CO_2 to CH_4. These results demonstrate that the chemical reactivity of plasmas containing CO_2 should be strongly increased thanks to the presence of CO^+ and O^+ ions having a very high kinetic energy. These ionic species are produced via Coulomb explosion of CO_2^{2+} molecular dications by the same process responsible for the erosion of the atmosphere of Mars.

© Springer Nature Switzerland AG 2021
O. Gervasi et al. (Eds.): ICCSA 2021, LNCS 12953, pp. 594–607, 2021.
https://doi.org/10.1007/978-3-030-86976-2_40

Keywords: Carbon dioxide · Fuels · Methanation · Renewable energy · Circular economy · Molecular dications · Coulomb explosion · Planetary ionospheres · Ion escape · Atmospheric erosion

1 Introduction

The global warming environmental problem is mainly due to strategy globally used in the production of energy employing fossil fuels [1, 2] with the subsequent emission in atmosphere of carbon dioxide which is the greenhouse gas responsible for the estimated increase in the average temperature of the Earth of about 1 °C. Because of this we brought together a team of scientists and technologists having the expertise necessary to design and build an apparatus converting waste carbon dioxide into (re-usable) methane. This effort gathered around the research laboratories of the University of Perugia - Italy (UPG), some Spanish scientists from the University of the Basque Country in Vitoria (EHU), the University of Barcelona (UB), the University of Toulouse – France (UT) as well as some technologists from Italian research institutions and companies: ENEA, EOS Energetics s.r.l.s. - Roma (EOSE), Master-up s.r.l. - Perugia (MUP), PLC System s.r.l. – Acerra (PLCS), FASAR Elettronica s.r.l. - Senigallia (FE) and RDPower s.r.l. - Terni (RDP). The collaboration between these partners provides both the skills on the theoretical-computational treatment of elementary molecular processes [3–5] and the measuring of molecule-(atom)molecule and light-(atom)molecule collision cross section and rate coefficient [6–8] and the capacity of designing and assembling computer controlled apparatuses. As a result, the project "Free-methane (Fuel from Renewable Energies – methane) was worked put and submitted to the Horizon 2020 Call H2020-LCE-2016-2017 (COMPETITIVE LOW-CARBON ENERGY) as a Research and Innovation Action (Proposal number: 763936-1). The project, aimed at building a solid background for the assembling of a novel apparatus using renewable energies to produce carbon neutral fuels through a chemical catalytic conversion of carbon dioxide waste flue gases was levering:

1) a first operational line based on the design of the molecular processes involved in the various stages of the apparatus: (A) the electrolytic production of H_2, (B) the Paul-Sabatier (PS) catalytic reduction of CO_2 to CH_4, (C) the formation of CH_4 clathrate hydrates from a water solution supported by the relevant theoretical, computational and experimental treatment of elementary reactive and non-reactive molecular processes (see the sketch of Fig. 1);
2) a second operational line on the design and implementation of the technological components of the low-cost hydrogen generation (Department of Enterprise Engineering - University of Rome "Tor Vergata", EOSE) and methane production steps (with the related automation and numerical control (FE)). Despite the failure of the proposal, we built the prototype apparatus PROGEO (thanks to the additional financial and technical support of the company PLCS).

2 The PROGEO Prototype Reactor

The PROGEO apparatus built at the PLCS site is a 30 kW (scalable to 1 MW) innovative prototype reactor [3, 9]. It is based on a validated laboratory technology for the production of carbon neutral methane using electricity from the public net and hydrogen generated by a commercial electrolyser (optimized to maximize the H_2 production rather than its purity) to feed the catalytic conversion of a CO_2 flux originating from any kind of sources (including off-line filled bottles). As already mentioned, such indirect use of H_2 as an energy vector (the direct and systematic use of H_2 is more difficult because of its low viscosity and high diffusivity) reduces the carbon dioxide on a Nickel based commercial catalyser levering so far the scientific and technological skills of the consortium members. In particular, the hinge of the scientific components of the project were the know-how of ENEA, EOSE and UPG (Dipartimento di Ingegneria Civile ed Ambientale (DICA) and Dipartimento di Chimica, Biologia e Biotecnologie (DCBB)) on the theoretical-computational treatment of elementary molecular processes and the expertise on molecule-(atom)molecule and light-(atom)molecule collision cross section and rate coefficient measurements [4–8]. In addition, the project levered also the electronic structure calculation competences of LCPQ [10], the fitting and modelling of potential energy surfaces together with their use for dynamical calculations by EHU [11] and the integration of coupled kinetic equations related to the mechanism of catalysed reactions of UB [12]. Technological competences of ENEA, EOSE, FE, MUP, RDP and PLCS [13, 14] were also extensively exploited.

More in detail the component "Theoretical and computational investigations of the molecular processes" has consisted in: a) high level accurate and approximate ab initio and model calculations of the electronic structure of the involved molecular systems; b) fitting ab initio values to a suitable functional form or, for heavier or more complex systems, formulate the interaction in terms of force fields; c) performing accurate quantum, quantum-classical, quasi-classical dynamical calculations of the detailed dynamical properties of the system on the assembled potential energy surface; d) statistically averaging the detailed outcomes of dynamical calculations over the unobserved parameters (e.g. thermal distributions over initial internal energy) in order to provide realistic estimates of physical observables; e) modelling the temperature dependence of thermal rate coefficients for their composition in complex kinetic schemes; f) compare the outcomes of the simulation with measurements of the apparatus yields to validate the model; g) learn from the analysis of the results of the calculations on the rate determining steps of the simulation for possible improvements of the process.

At the same time, the component "Designing and assembling the laboratory apparatuses" has consisted in: a) designing the composition of the different hardware components of the overall PROGEO apparatus; b) selecting and integrating the commercial electrolyser for the production of H_2; c) setting the characteristics of the Paul Sabatier reactor so as to maximize the recovery of the heat produced by the process (the process is exoergic with $\Delta G_{298K} = -130.8$ kJ/mol and this makes the reaction self-sustainable with no need of external energy supply other than the activation one at the beginning of the reaction process); d) adopting the solid state catalyser (KATALCOJM 11-4MR, a Ni based metal alloy commercialized by Johnson Matthey [15]); e) measuring typical yields of the PROGEO apparatus.

The measured yields of PROGEO are given in a previous publication [3] for different values of the CO_2/H_2 ratios and were recorded at the operating conditions of 2 bar and 300 °C. Optimizations can be obtained by: a) introducing automated control procedures for temperature by pre-warming the reactants reusing the heat released by the process and b) regulating the hydrogen/carbon dioxide molar ratio in excess to the stoichiometric one.

3   Computational Results

The first important goal of the PROGEO project was to compare accurate theoretical simulations to the experimental outcomes of a low-level agile demonstrator of the technology and provide a flexible test bed for enabling both a scale up and an improvement of the process. To this end the Kinetic Monte Carlo Method (KMC) [16] was used to simulate the kinetics of the (surface) catalyzed process by solving the set of differential equations arising from the proposed mechanism. In the KMC approach the catalyst is represented as a symbolic grid of sites on which the different elementary processes happen at a rate in general proportional (through a rate coefficient) to the concentration of the intervening species powered to the reaction partial order and consequently forming and

Step	E_a forward (kJ/mol)	E_a reverse (kJ/mol)
$CO_2 + * \leftrightarrow CO_2^*$	0.0	8.3
$H_2 + 2* \leftrightarrow 2H^*$	4.0	77.1
$CO + * \leftrightarrow CO^*$	0.0	127.7
$H_2O + * \leftrightarrow H_2O^*$	0.0	49.0
$CO_2^* + H^* \leftrightarrow COOH^* + *$	113.1	155.6
$CO_2^* + 2H^* \leftrightarrow C(OH)_2^* + 2*$	292.3	217.8
$CO_2^* + * \leftrightarrow CO^* + O^*$	93.7	169.3
$COOH^* + * \leftrightarrow CO^* + OH^*$	306.8	308.7
$C(OH)_2^* + H^* \leftrightarrow CH_2O^* + OH^*$	98.7	125.7
$CH_2O^* + H^* \leftrightarrow CH_2^* + OH^*$	163.7	154.1
$CO^* + * \leftrightarrow C^* + O^*$	237.4	111.8
$CO^* + 2H^* \leftrightarrow CH^* + OH^* + *$	221.4	146.1
$2CO^* \leftrightarrow CO_2^* + C^*$	339.6	109.0
$C^* + H^* \leftrightarrow CH^* + *$	69.2	154.1
$CH^* + H^* \leftrightarrow CH_2^* + *$	68.2	61.9
$CH_2^* + H^* \leftrightarrow CH_3^* + *$	71.4	105.6
$CH_3^* + H^* \rightarrow CH_4 + 2*$	137.4	178.7
$O^* + H^* \leftrightarrow OH^* + *$	137.9	116.0
$OH^* + H^* \leftrightarrow H_2O^* + *$	137.9	99.9
$H^* + * \leftrightarrow * + H^*$	13.0	13.0
$CO^* + * \leftrightarrow * + CO^*$	10.0	10.0
$O^* + * \leftrightarrow * + O^*$	48.0	48.0
$OH^* + * \leftrightarrow * + OH^*$	21.0	21.0

Fig. 1. Elementary processes intervening in the $H_2 + CO_2$ and related activation energies (with the source reference in the rhs) for the forward and reverse process. Species with an asterisk (*) aside refer to adsorbed ones, meanwhile asterisk by their own refer to free adsorption sites.

consuming the involved species weighted by the adsorbed fraction. The Fig. 1 shows the considered elementary processes with related forward and backward activation energy.

Despite the complexity of the system of elementary processes involved in the PS reaction, a very important contribution of our computational investigations to the rationalization of its mechanism, was the singling out that the rate-determining step is the intermediate adsorption of CO on the surface of the catalyser which accounts for the almost totality of the produced methane.

Further investigations will be carried out to understand whether the adsorbed CO goes through a dissociation into C and O first before adding H_2 to form CH_4 or the adsorbed CO undergoes a disproportion or gets hydrogenated directly. After all such result indicates that the stretching of the CO bond is a preliminary condition for the production of CH_4 and is a clear indication that any research effort spent in enhancing processes weakening the CO bond directly in the gas phase (as we have already anticipated in Ref. [3]) shall provide valid alternatives to the heterogenous catalysis.

4   The Plasma Assisted Catalysis

In this section very recent progress made in the DICA laboratory on the generation and characterization of different microwave discharge plasmas containing CO_2/H_2 mixtures are discussed. By such an experimental strategy we have been able to convert carbon dioxide into various hydrocarbons such as: methane, formic acid and/or dimethyl ether as well as small amounts of HCO^+, H_2CO^+, H_3CO^+, HCO_2^+ ions. In addition, CO^+ and O^+ ions, are also generated in the plasmas with a high content of translational energy ranging between 2 and 6 eV. These ionic species are the fragmentation products of the Coulomb explosion of CO_2^{2+} molecular dications: i.e. the same process responsible for the erosion of the atmosphere of Mars as demonstrated by our research group in a recent study (see for instance Ref. [3] and references therein). The high kinetic energy of the CO^+ and O^+ ions formed increases the chemical reactivity of the generated microwave discharge plasmas using gaseous CO_2/H_2 mixtures and allows us to consider the plasma-assisted technique as a pivotal strategy for the CO_2 conversion into CH_4 fuel in the field of chemical engineering master plans for new emerging catalysts development.

The relevant experimental investigation is based on two main steps: i) an experimental characterization of the main operative working conditions of the prototype methanation reactor PROGEO (see Fig. 2); ii) the production and relative chemical characterization of generated microwave plasmas containing CO_2/H_2 mixtures having different chemical compositions (1:3 and 1:5, respectively).

As mentioned above, for the generation of CO_2/H_2 containing plasmas a microwave discharge beam source specially built in our laboratory and jointly working with a molecular beam apparatus operating at high vacuum conditions ($\sim 10^{-7}$–10^{-8} mbar) has been employed. Such an experimental apparatus, able to perform chemical characterization of generated plasmas by mass spectrometry [17, 18] and fully described elsewhere [19–21], is showed in the upper (a) panel of Fig. 3, while in the lower panel (b) of the same Figure a scheme of the microwave discharge can be seen. The latter is essentially made by a cylindrical quartz pipe (5 cm in length and 2 cm of diameter) inside a brass and water-cooled resonant cavity (2450 MHz and 70–200 kW typical operating power range) by a klystron and a devoted electronic control unit specially developed by FE.

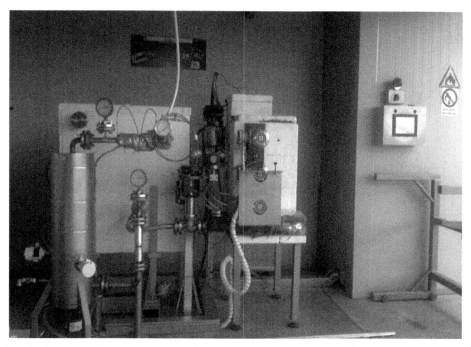

Fig. 2. The PROGEO apparatus: a methanation prototype reactor working in the Laboratory of Chemical Technologies of the DICA – University of Perugia (Italy).

The analysis of the best working conditions for the PROGEO reactor, allowed us to record the yields of carbon dioxide methanation when using a Ni-based solid catalyst as a function of the CO_2/H_2 molar ratio [3].

To verify the possibility that the methanation reaction can take place via a plasma catalytic conversion by a plasma assisted version of the PROGEO apparatus, we explored the generation of various CO_2/H_2 plasma mixtures using our microwave discharge device shown in Fig. 3. With a 1:1, 1:3, and 1:5 CO_2:H_2 composition, we determined the percentage of CO_2 dissociation according to the following reactions:

$$CO_2 + e^- \rightarrow CO + O + e^- \tag{1}$$

$$O + O \rightarrow O_2 \tag{2}$$

Figure 4a reports such data (see the upper panel) as a function of the applied power to the microwave discharge.

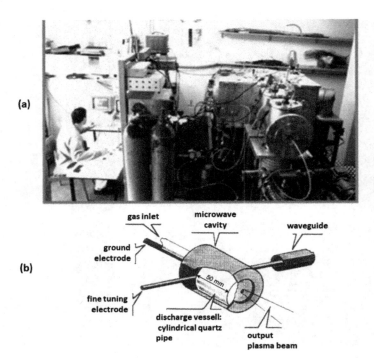

Fig. 3. (a) The molecular beam apparatus used for CO_2/H_2 plasmas generation; (b) A scheme of the microwave discharge plasma source designed and built in the Laboratory of the University of Perugia (see text).

The data shown in Fig. 4 were obtained by determining the CO_2 dissociation percentage (%CO_2diss) from the recording the CO_2^+ ion intensity in the two experimental conditions of microwave discharge off (I_{off}) and on (I_{on}) via the following relation:

$$\%CO_2\text{diss} = 100(I_{off} - I_{on})/I_{off} \tag{3}$$

The obtained data of Fig. 4a are in very good agreement with previous measurements performed in our and other laboratories [22, 23]. They clearly point out that the dissociation of CO_2 is growing when the concentration of H_2 increases: it is of about 50% higher in the case of the CO_2:H_2 1:5 mixture than the 1:1 one, reaching its maximum value of about 62% for a 200 W applied power. Such data agree with previous determinations by de la Fuente *et al.* [24]. Indeed, these authors found higher CO_2 decomposition values when the CO_2:H_2 concentration ratio decrease and reaches up to about 80% for a CO_2:H_2 ratio of 1:3, since H_2 is able to act as a "catalyst" for such a process.

Using the crossed beam apparatus showed in Fig. 4 and the procedure described above, we were able to analyze and characterize from a chemical point of view our generated plasmas [25]. In Fig. 4b (see the lower panel) is showed the recorded mass spectrum of the plasma having a 1:5 CO_2:H_2 composition. Such a spectrum clearly reveals the generation of: i) various hydrocarbons: methane, formic acid and/or dimethyl ether; ii) small amounts of HCO^+, H_2CO^+, H_3CO^+, HCO_2^+ ions; iii) considerable amounts of

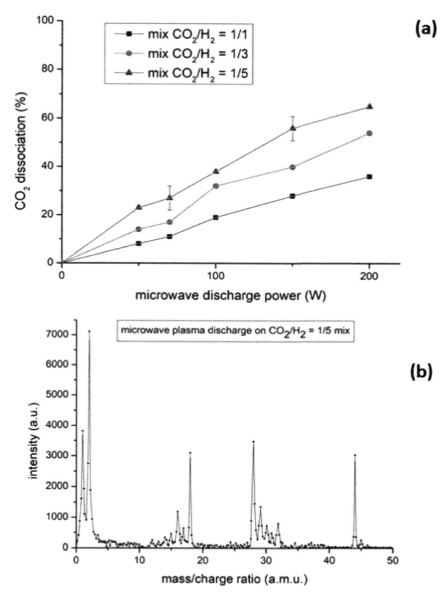

Fig. 4. (a) The CO_2 dissociation experimentally determined at different values of the applied microwave discharge power. The inlet gas pressure is kept at a constant value of ~1800 Pa and for three different plasmas using 1:1, 1:3 and 1:5 CO_2:H_2 gas mixtures (see text). (b) The mass spectrum collected by the microwave discharge plasma with a 1:5 CO_2:H_2 gas mixture composition (applied microwave discharge power ~180 W; inlet gas pressure ~1800 Pa).

the following ionic species: H^+, H_2^+, H_2O^+, CO^+ and CO_2^+. Our results are in fairly good agreement with previous data from Hayashi *et al.* [26] who were able to produce methane, dimethyl ether and formic acid as well as several intermediate species as O, OH, and CO in their surface discharge experiments. Furthermore, our data confirm also the observations by de la Fuente *et al.* [24] who detected H^+, H_2^+, H_2O^+, CO^+ and CO_2^+ ions and small amounts of methanol and ethylene in their microwave plasma reactor.

5 From Distributed to Cloud Computing Activities

The above reported evolution of our theoretical, computational and experimental research on chemical reactions and its applications has since the beginning levered the advantages of distributed and collaborative computing. For this purpose, we have implemented in the past the Simulator of Molecular Beam Experiments (SIMBEX) [27] and Grid Empowered Molecular Simulator (GEMS) [28] assembled out of computer programs distributed over the Grid aimed at modelling the efficiency of chemical processes under the different conditions of accuracy sensitive applications (e.g. astro-chemistry, combustion, environment, etc.). To this end we levered in the past the work carried out using infrastructures and services established by the members of the Molecular Science (MS) community within the COMPCHEM VO [29], CMMST VRC [30], D23 [31] and D37 [32] COST Actions, ECTN [33], EGEE III [34] and EGI Inspire [35] initiatives. More recently these activities have evolved into the Open Molecular Science Cloud (OMSC) ones [36] as part of the European Open Science Cloud (EOSC) initiative [37] and its application oriented EOSC-Pillar [38] infrastructural activities whose operational schema is given in Fig. 5.

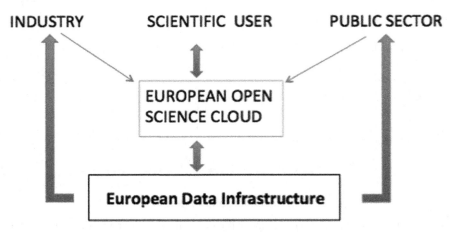

Fig. 5. The basic scheme of EOSC.

As shown in Fig. 5, EOSC provides the support of the European governments' network infrastructure to the private companies, public sector and scientific community the support necessary to share on the cloud the scientific knowledge made available by the members. In particular, within EOSC-Pillar, we have made available to the OMSC community the cloud services of the MOSEX (Molecular Open Science Enabled Cloud

Services) project [39, 40] related to the efficiency of elementary gas phase processes. Related blocks of the MOSEX operational diagram inspired to the GEMS simulator are:

i)   the construction of the potential energy surface governing the process out of the implemented electronic structure calculations,
ii) the evaluation of the rate coefficient of the reactive process out of the cloud implemented integration of the dynamical equations of the involved atomic nuclei,
iii) the Data Handling cloud services for making available to the users the validated efficiency parameters.

In particular MOSEX is meant to provide the cloud support [41] for:

a) producing/discovering and downloading data for the open collaborative and fully re-usable databases and repositories (like those of the already implemented EChemTest® service of the European Chemistry Thematic Network (ECTN) for assessing chemical competences at school, University and Life-Long-Learning levels [42]);
b) running/checking/correcting (where possible) or discarding and validating data through iterative cycles collaboratively undertaken by the members of the community (like the Learning Objects of ECTN);
c) annotating/curating/preserving data of service for a more efficient re-use (see e.g. [43–49]);
d) evaluating the quality of services provided by the members of the MS community;
e) offsetting debits with credits of the adopted Prosumer (Producer + Consumer) model (at present experimented only for the electronic assessment EChemtest® product) in which the community members are at the same time users (making debits for used services) and producers (gaining credits against produced services) [42].

6   The Prosumer Model and Circular Economy

The MOSEX theoretical, computational and experimental activities for the post PRO-GEO development of renewable energies storage pursues not only the research illustrated in Sect. 4 but also the implementation of its circular economy and Prosumer articulation. An illustration of the circularity plan discussed with some colleagues of the Agricultural Faculty [50] and Technological Park [51], is given in Fig. 6.

In Fig. 6 the scheme of an experimental plant agreed among the partners for enriching biogas produced by agricultural feedstock by converting the fraction (about 50%) of the biogas generated by fermentation. To this end the previous composition of the informal consortium has been reformulated for establishing, under the coordination of DICA, a formal consortium with DCBB and some companies. It will operate within the MOSEX project in particular for implementing on the cloud circular economy initiatives based on the Prosumer model levering on Green Chemistry. As already mentioned in item (e) of the MOSEX mission illustrated above, the Master-UP member of the PROGEO consortium has already adopted the Prosumer scheme for implementing the cloud service of EChemTest® running the Self Evaluation Sessions for the assessment of Chemistry

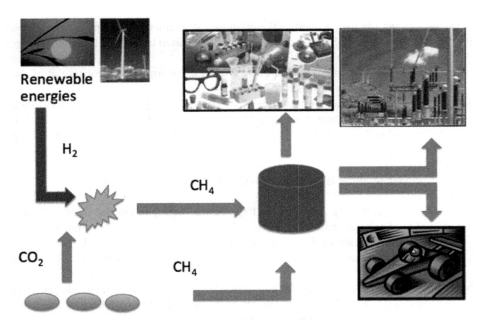

Fig. 6. The scheme of the circular economy Prosumer for PROGEO. In the lower-left corner of the figure the production of biogas is schematized: CO_2 and CH_4 main components, after a proper purification by specific membrane filtration technologies, are sent to the methanation reactor (vertical arrow), and to the gaseous fuel storage tank (horizontal arrow), respectively.

competences using the ECTN libraries of Questions and Answers and for acting as an ECTN Agency [48].

The implementation of a green chemistry circular economy initiative for PROGEO-like activities has been already proposed in Ref. [43] for the simpler case of a large winery wishing to convert to methane the carbon dioxide accumulated from the fermentation of wines during the related season (the higher simplicity of the considered case lies in the fact that the accumulated CO_2 is virtually pure and does not require costly filtering technologies. In that case it was found that the company gets positive returns out of the innovation and will be also encouraged to increase the quantity of CO_2 to convert because this increases the production efficiency. The process will continue, in fact, to produce at standard methods (still satisfying the market demand) while investing at the same time on R&D to increase the productivity of the production factors and shift the isoquant to higher efficiency when moving to next steps (the Research and development variable cost can be kept unaltered thanks to its positive effect on a perspective of profit increase even further in subsequent steps. This means that the circular economy reuse of energy guarantees, through the registering of patents and the consequent temporary monopolistic situations, the fulfilment of the conditions of Positive Ecological Externality for the involved societies and clusters of companies.

7 Conclusions

A prototype reactor (PROGEO) devoted to carbon dioxide methanation was developed to produce carbon neutral methane via chemical conversion of CO_2 waste flue gases using renewable energy, in a circular economy strategy. It was characterized in its best operative conditions determining yields of methanation by the Sabatier reaction of about 84%, where a Ni-based solid catalyst has been employed.

Furthermore, an experimental effort aimed to investigate a new reaction pathway without the use of the solid catalyst, has been undertaken. Interesting and promising data collected exploring mechanisms via plasma generation using microwave discharges over $CO_2 + H_2$ gas mixtures are presented and discussed. They demonstrate the generation in the exploited plasmas of simple hydrocarbons as methane, formic acid and/or dimethyl ether, small amount of HCO^+, H_2CO^+, H_3CO^+, HCO_2^+ ions, and considerable quantities of CO^+ and O^+ ions, with high kinetic energy content, ranging between 2 and 6 eV. These ionic species are produced via Coulomb explosion of CO_2^{2+} molecular dications by the same process responsible for the erosion of the atmosphere of Mars as demonstrated by our previous investigations [52–54]. Indeed, CO^+ and O^+ ions formed by Coulomb explosion of CO_2^{2+} molecular dications, could be the responsible of the enhanced chemical reactivity of the generated plasmas. Further theoretical and experimental efforts will be done by our group in two directions: i) to make the use of the PROGEO prototype suitable to be employed in the industrial chain in order to treat waste gases and convert them into valuable fuels in a circular economy logic: to do this it will be necessary to develop a new type of low-cost hydrogen gas generator through a project that EO is working on; ii) to develop a hybrid plasma-catalytic solid system or a homogeneous gas-phase reaction where CO_2/H_2 reagent mixtures activated by a plasma generation could realize the methanation reaction by new microscopic mechanisms more favorable from both a kinetic and energetic point of view.

In conclusion, we expect that new theoretical method able to fully describe state-to state prototype oxidation processes [55, 56], as well as experimental efforts on the characterization of microscopic dynamics of elementary reactions [57–60], will provide reliable data useful for a better understanding and perspectives for innovative carbon neutral technologies as reported in various interesting papers [61–63]. Industry and regional authorities could include them into future energy strategy and systems for innovation and environmental-sustainable development, as well as for new catalysts able to maximize the products yield in plasma assisted reactions.

Acknowledgments. This work was supported and financed with the "Fondo Ricerca di Base, 2018, dell'Università degli Studi di Perugia" (Project Titled: Indagini teoriche e sperimentali sulla reattività di sistemi di interesse astrochimico). Support from Italian MIUR and University of Perugia (Italy) is acknowledged within the program "Dipartimenti di Eccellenza 2018-2022".

References

1. Cook, J., et al.: Environ. Res. Lett. **8**, 2 (2013)
2. Oreskes, N.: Science **306**(5702), 1686 (2004)

3. Falcinelli, S., et al.: Fuel **209**, 802–811 (2017)
4. Laganà, A., Riganelli, A.: Reaction and Molecular Dynamics. Springer, Heidelberg (1999). https://doi.org/10.1007/978-3-642-57051-3. ISBN: 3-540-41202-6
5. Laganà, A., Parker, G. A.: Chemical Reactions Basic Theory and Computing. Springer, New York (2018). https://doi.org/10.1007/978-3-319-62356-6. ISBN: 978-3-319-62355-9
6. Falcinelli, S., Pirani, F., Vecchiocattivi, F.: Atmosphere **6**(3), 299–317 (2015)
7. Falcinelli, S., Bartocci, A., Cavalli, S., Pirani, F., Vecchiocattivi, F.: Chem. Eur. J. **22**(2), 764–771 (2016)
8. Falcinelli, S., Rosi, M., Cavalli, S., Pirani, F., Vecchiocattivi, F.: Chem. Eur. J. **22**(35), 12518–12526 (2016).
9. PROGEO by PLC System. https://www.plc-spa.com/en/plc-system-progeo.php. Accessed 11 Mar 2021
10. Laboratoire de Chimie et Physique Quantiques - UMR5626. http://www.lcpq.ups-tlse.fr/?lang=fr. Accessed 11 Mar 2021
11. Rampino, S., Skouteris, D., Laganà, A., Garcia, E., Saracibar, A.: Phys. Chem. Chem. Phys. **11**, 1752–1757 (2009)
12. Prats, H., Gamallo, P., Illas, F., Sayós, R.: J. Catal. **342**, 75–83 (2016)
13. L'Energia che crea il tuo futuro by PLC System. https://www.plc-spa.com/it/index.php. Accessed 11 Mar 2021
14. RadioAstroLab. https://www.radioastrolab.it/. Accessed 11 Mar 2021
15. Chemical Processes by Johnson Matthey. http://www.jmprotech.com/methanation-catalysts-for-hydrogen-production-katalco. Accessed 16 Mar 2021
16. Martì Aliod, C.: Networked computing for ab initio modelling the chemical storage of alternative energy, ITN-EJD-TCCM Ph.D. thesis. Università degli Studi di Perugia (Italy) and Universitè P. Sabatier de Toulouse (France), 14 December 2018
17. Pei, L., Carrascosa, E., Yang, N., Falcinelli, S., Farrar, J. M.: J. Phys. Chem. Lett. **6**(9), 16841689 (2015)
18. Brunetti, B., et al.: Chem. Phys. Lett. **539–540**, 19–23 (2012)
19. Falcinelli, S., Vecchiocattivi, F., Pirani, F.: Phys. Rev. Lett. **121**, 163403 (2018)
20. Balucani, N., et al.: Chem. Phys. Lett. **546**, 34–39 (2012)
21. Leonori, F., et al.: Phys. Chem. Chem. Phys. **11**(23), 4701–4706 (2009)
22. Dobrea, S., Mihaila, I., Popa, G.: Carbon dioxide dissociation in a 2.45 GHz microwave discharge. In: Proceedings of 1st ICPIG, Granada, Spain, vol. 14 (2013)
23. Dobrea, S., Mihaila, I., Tiron, V., Popa, G.: Roman Rep. Phys. **66**, 1147–1154 (2014)
24. de la Fuente, J.F., Moreno, S.H., Stankiewicz, A.I., Stefanidis, G. D.: Int. J. Hydrogen Energy **41**, 21067–21077 (2016)
25. Falcinelli, S.: Catal. Today **348**, 95–101 (2020)
26. Hayashi, N., Yamakawa, T., Baba, S.: Vacuum **80**, 1299–1304 (2006)
27. Gervasi, O., Laganà, A.: SIMBEX: a portal for the a priori simulation of crossed beam experiments. Futur. Gener. Comput. Syst. **20**(5), 703–716 (2004)
28. Laganà, A., et al.: Virt&l-Comm.10.2016.6. http://services.chm.unipg.it/ojs/index.php/virtlcomm/article/view/151. Accessed 16 Mar 2021
29. Laganà A., Riganelli A., Gervasi O. (2006) On the Structuring of the computational chemistry virtual organization COMPCHEM. In: Gavrilova, M., et al. (eds.) Computational Science and Its Applications - ICCSA 2006. ICCSA 2006. Lecture Notes in Computer Science, vol. 3980. Springer, Heidelberg. https://doi.org/10.1007/11751540_70
30. Towards a CMMST VRC team project report. https://wiki.egi.eu/wiki/Towards_a_CMMST_VRC. Accessed 16 Mar 2021
31. European Cost Action D23: Metalaboratories For Complex Computational Applications in Chemistry. https://www.cost.eu/actions/D23/#tabslName:overview/. Accessed 16 Mar 2021

32. European Cost Action D37: Grid Computing in Chemistry. https://www.cost.eu/actions/D37/#tabs|Name:overview/. Accessed 16 Mar 2021
33. European Chemistry Thematic network. http://ectn.eu/. Accessed 16 Mar 2021
34. Enabling Grids for E-sciencE III (EGEE III). https://cordis.europa.eu/project/rcn/87264/factsheet/en. Accessed 16 Mar 2021
35. EGI-Inspire. https://wiki.egi.eu/wiki/EGI-InSPIRE:Main_Page. Accessed 16 Mar 2021
36. Laganà, A.: Virt&l-Comm.16.2019.5. http://services.chm.unipg.it/ojs/index.php/virtlcomm/article/view/210. Accessed 16 Mar 2021
37. European Open Science Cloud. https://ec.europa.eu/research/openscience/index.cfm?pg=open-science-cloud. Accessed 16 Mar 2021
38. EOSCpilot. https://eoscpilot.eu/. Accessed 16 Mar 2021
39. Vitillaro, G., Laganà, A.: Virt&l-Comm.20.2020.7. http://services.chm.unipg.it/ojs/index.php/virtlcomm/article/view/248. Accessed 2 Apr 2021
40. Laganà, A., Garcia, E.: Virt&l-Comm.18.2019.3. http://services.chm.unipg.it/ojs/index.php/virtlcomm/article/view/219. Accessed 16 Mar 2021
41. Skouteris, D., Balucani, N., Faginas-Lago, N., Falcinelli, S., Rosi, M.: A&A **584**, A76 (2015)
42. EChemTest by ECTN. http://ectn.eu/committees/virtual-education-community/echemtest/. Accessed 16 Mar 2021
43. Laganà, A., di Giorgio, L.: Lecture Notes in Computer Science, vol. 10962, pp. 549–562 (2018)
44. QCArchive. https://qcarchive.molssi.org/. Accessed 16 Mar 2021
45. NIST Chemical Kinetics Database. http://kinetics.nist.gov. Accessed 16 Mar 2021
46. Wakelam, V., et al.: AstroPhys. J. Suppl. Ser. **199**, 21 (2012)
47. McElroy, D., Walsh, C., Markwick, A.J., Cordiner, M.A., Smith, K., Millar, T.J.: A&A **550**, A36 (2013)
48. Laganà, A., Gervasi, O., Tasso, S., Perri, D., Franciosa, F.: The ECTN virtual education community prosumer model for promoting and assessing chemical knowledge. In: Gervasi, O., Murgante, B., Misra, S., Stankova, E., Torre, C.M., Rocha, A.M.A.C., Taniar, D., Apduhan, B.O., Tarantino, E., Ryu, Y. (eds.) ICCSA 2018. LNCS, vol. 10964, pp. 533–548. Springer, Cham (2018). https://doi.org/10.1007/978-3-319-95174-4_42
49. Álvarez-Moreno, M., de Graaf, C., López, N., Maseras, F., Poblet, J.M., Bo, C.: J. Chem. Inf. Model. **55**(1), 95–103 (2015)
50. I.S.A.FO.M. by CNR, Perugia. http://www.iro.pg.cnr.it/. Accessed 16 Mar 2021
51. 3A Parco Tecnologico Agroalimentare Dell'Umbria, Pantalla Todi (Italy). http://www.parco3a.org. Accessed 16 Mar 2021
52. Alagia, M., et al.: Phys. Chem. Chem. Phys. **12**, 5389–5395 (2010)
53. Falcinelli, S., Pirani, F., Alagia, M., Schio, L., Richter, R., et al.: Chem. Phys. Lett. **666**, 1–6 (2016)
54. Falcinelli, S., Rosi, M., Candori, P., Farrar, J.M., Vecchiocattivi, F., et al.: Planet. Space Sci. **99**, 149–157 (2014)
55. Falcinelli, S., Vecchiocattivi, F., Pirani, F.: Commun. Chem. **3**(1), 64 (2020)
56. Falcinelli, S., Farrar, J. M., Vecchiocattivi, F., Pirani, F.: Acc. Chem. Res. **53**, 2248–2260 (2020)
57. Leonori, F., et al.: Chem. A **113**(16), 4330–4339 (2009)
58. De Petris, G., Cartoni, A., Rosi, M., Barone, V., Puzzarini, C., Troiani, A.: ChemPhysChem **12**(1), 112–115 (2011)
59. Alagia, M., et al.: Lincei Sci. Fis. Nat. **24**(1), 53–65 (2013)
60. Podio, L., et al.: MNRAS **470**(1), L16–L20 (2017)
61. Thema, M., Bauer, F., Sterner, M.: Power-to-Gas: Renewable & Sustainable Energy Reviews **112**, 775–787 (2019)
62. Vogt, C., Monai, M., Kramer, G.J., Weckhuysen, B.M.: Nat. Catal. **2**(3), 188–197 (2019)
63. George, A., et al.: Renew. Sustain. Energy Rev. **135**, 109702 (2021)

Ab initio Calculation of Binding Energies of Interstellar Sulphur-Containing Species on Crystalline Water Ice Models

Jessica Perrero[1](✉)(iD), Albert Rimola[1](iD), Marta Corno[2](iD), and Piero Ugliengo[2](iD)

[1] Departament de Química, Universitat Autònoma de Barcelona, 08193 Bellaterra, Catalonia, Spain
{jessica.perrero,albert.rimola}@uab.cat
[2] Dipartimento di Chimica, Università degli Studi di Torino, via P. Giuria 7, 10125 Torino, Italy
{marta.corno,piero.ugliengo}@unito.it

Abstract. There are different environments in the interstellar medium (ISM), depending on the density, temperature and chemical composition. Among them, molecular clouds, often referred to as the cradle of stars, are paradigmatic environments relative to the chemical diversity and complexity in space. Indeed, there, radio to far-infrared observations revealed the presence of several molecules in the gas phase, while near-infrared spectroscopy detected the existence of submicron sized dust grains covered by H_2O-dominated ice mantles. The interaction between gas-phase species and the surfaces of water ices is measured by the binding energy (BE), a crucial parameter in astrochemical modelling. In this work, the BEs of a set of sulphur-containing species on water ice mantles have been computed by adopting a periodic *ab initio* approach using a crystalline surface model. The Density Functional Theory (DFT)-based B3LYP-D3(BJ) functional was used for the prediction of the structures and energetics. DFT BEs were refined by adopting an ONIOM-like procedure to estimate them at CCSD(T) level toward complete basis set extrapolation, in which a very good correlation between values has been found. Moreover, we show that geometry optimization with the computationally cheaper HF-3c method followed by single point energy calculations at DFT to compute the BEs is a suitable cost-effective recipe to arrive at BE values of the same quality as those computed at full DFT level. Finally, computed data were compared with the available literature data.

Keywords: ISM · Sulphur · Binding energy

1 Introduction

The interstellar medium (ISM) is the region between stars constituted by matter and radiation. The interstellar matter consists of either gaseous (atoms and

© Springer Nature Switzerland AG 2021
O. Gervasi et al. (Eds.): ICCSA 2021, LNCS 12953, pp. 608–619, 2021.
https://doi.org/10.1007/978-3-030-86976-2_41

molecules) or solid (dust grains of silicate or carbonaceous material) components. Several environments can be defined in the ISM according to their physical conditions, amongst them the dense molecular clouds, cold (10 K) and rarefied ($10^3 cm^{-3}$–$10^7 cm^{-3}$) regions in which stars form. Because of the very low temperature, species heavier than He disappear from the gas phase due to freeze-out (adsorption) on dust grain surfaces, forming a thick layer of ices. The ice composition is dominated by H_2O ice, but also by small molecules like CO, CO_2, CH_3OH, CH_4 and NH_3 [4]. The significant presence of hydrogenated species on the ice mantles is due to the hydrogenation reactions taking place on the ice surfaces and involve atoms and small molecules that are adsorbed on grains [6].

Dust grains play a fundamental role in the chemistry of the ISM. Beyond their physical properties, like UV absorption and radio emission, they can help the occurrence of chemical reactions in three ways: i) they can concentrate chemical species on the surfaces, facilitating the encountering of the reactive species; ii) they can act as chemical catalysts, decreasing the activation energy of chemical reactions; and iii) they can be a third body, allowing the dissipation of the energy released by exothermic reactions without undermining the stability of the products.

Molecules on the grain surfaces require some energy to desorb. This energy can be thermal, chemical or radiative, but it has to exceed the interaction energy between the molecule and the surface since the evaporation rate is proportional to $exp[-E_B/(k\,T_{dust})]$, where $T_{dust} < 10$ K and the binding energies are typically $E_B > 1000$ K. If the amount of energy is a fraction of the binding energy, species can diffuse on the surfaces, which is one of the prerequisite for their subsequent reactivity [9]. Accordingly, one of the most important parameters in the description of the ISM are the binding energies (BEs), i.e., the interaction energy of chemical species on dust grains. Molecules adsorbed on grains can interact with them in two main ways: through rupture/formation of chemical bonds, so-called chemisorption, or through weak interactions, resulting in physisorption. This latter mechanism is the focus of this work and what our BEs are referred to. BE governs whether molecules remain stick on the grain surfaces as well as whether they diffuse and, therefore, react with other species. Thus, BEs hugely affect the gas and ices composition. Moreover, they are essential parameters to run astrochemical models at large aimed to understand the chemical composition of the ISM.

The importance of a careful estimation of BEs is thus evident. However, they have usually been estimated simply as a sum of the BEs of the single atoms or functional groups forming the molecule (in turn estimated from their polarizability when interacting with bare grain surfaces). In addition, the experimental procedure to collect BEs is not completely trustworthy, considering the impossibility to reproduce properly the ISM conditions in a laboratory chamber [9,18]. Ferrero et al. (2020) [11], have used quantum chemical computations as an alternative way to obtain accurate BE values for a set molecular species on water ices. The aim of this work is to enlarge the network of BEs, focusing on eight sulphur-containing molecules that play a major role in the dense clouds.

2   Methods

We adopted a periodic approach to model the adsorption of the sulphur-containing molecules (all of them being closed-shell species) on the ice surface. The hybrid B3LYP DFT functional [2,3,16], with the addition of Grimme's D3 empirical correction with Becke-Johnson (BJ) damping scheme to account for the dispersion interactions [13,14,19], in combination with the Ahlrichs triple zeta quality VTZ basis set, supplemented with a double set of polarization functions (Ahlrichs-VTZ*), was used for geometry optimizations and *BE* calculations (hereafter referred to as full B3LYP-D3(BJ) theory level).

Because of the high computational cost of DFT calculations, we also adopted the computationally cheaper semi-empirical HF-3c method in two ways [19]. This method is based on the Hartree-Fock (HF) energy computed with a minimal basis set, to which three empirical corrections (3c) are added. In the first case, HF-3c was used both in the optimization and the *BE* calculation (HF-3c//HF-3c theory level). In the second one, DFT single point energy calculations on the HF-3c optimized geometries were performed to compute *BEs* (B3LYP-D3(BJ)//HF-3c theory level). The latter approach was used to validate its performance in prevision of applying the same approach in amorphous ice models, which are prohibitively too expensive to be simulated at full DFT level.

Finally, to prove that DFT *BEs* are accurate enough, the single- and double-electronic excitation coupled-cluster method with an added perturbative description of triple excitations (CCSD(T)), in combination with a correlation consistent basis set extrapolated to complete basis set (CBS) limit, was used by applying a local correction at this level adopting an ONIOM2-correction approach [8], in which a small part of the system (i.e., the adsorbed molecule plus a few interacting water molecules) was treated at CCSD(T), while the rest at B3LYP-D3(BJ).

The *BE* is defined as the opposite of the interaction energy ΔE, which were corrected for the basis set superposition error (BSSE), due to using a finite basis set of localized gaussian functions.

$$BE = -\Delta E^{CP} \tag{1}$$

$$\Delta E^{CP} = \Delta E - BSSE \tag{2}$$

All periodic calculations were performed with the CRYSTAL17 code [10], while CCSD(T) calculations were performed with the GAUSSIAN16 code [12].

3   Results

Interstellar ices are thought to be mostly formed by amorphous solid water [4]. We, however, have chosen a crystalline model for two main reasons: (i) crystalline structure are well defined due to symmetry constraints and computationally cheap, and (ii) no definite structure of an amorphous ice model is available. Nevertheless, regions rich in crystalline ices have been observed in protoplanetary disks and stellar outflows [17,20]. Our ice surface model derives from the bulk of the proton-ordered P-ice, which was cut along the (010) surface defining a 2D periodic slab model [5,22]. The thickness of the ice (10.9 Å) was chosen to converge its surface energy. The (010) P-ice supercell slab model consists of twelve atomic layers (24 water molecules) and its cell parameters are $|a| = 8.980$ Å and $|b| = 7.081$ Å. The structure of the ice is such as to ensure a null electric dipole along the non-periodic z-axis. This is a direct consequence of the symmetry of the system, which shows two identical faces both at the top and at the bottom of the model. Therefore, the adsorption was modeled only onto one face of the system.

3.1   BEs of the S-Containing Species

Here the *BEs* of 8 sulphur-containing species, i.e., H_2S, CH_3SH, H_2S_2, H_2CS, C_3S, SO_2, CS and OCS, on the crystalline (010) water ice surface model were computed. Figures 1a and 1b show the optimized geometries of the computed complexes at full B3LYP-D3(BJ) level, while Table 1 reports the computed *BE* for these species.

According to the adsorption geometries, these species can be divided in two groups: i) molecules that can act as both hydrogen bond (H-bond) acceptors and donors, given the presence of an electronegative sulphur atom and one or more hydrogen atoms (H_2S, CH_3SH, H_2S_2 and H_2CS); and ii) molecules that can only act as H-bond acceptors, through an electronegative atom which is never the sulphur one (C_3S, SO_2, CS and OCS). We would like to highlight that this classification does not always correspond with the electrostatic (non dispersive) contribution to the *BEs*. Indeed, not only H-bond contributes to the definition of the electrostatic energy, but also the interaction between permanent dipoles and higher order multipoles. Additionally, dispersive forces are stronger as the volume of the molecule and the interaction surface with the ice increase, resulting in the articulated panorama appearing in Table 1. While the molecules both accepting and donating an H-bond show a *BE* spanning the limited range between 40 and 52 kJ mol^{-1}, the other group presents more variability. In fact, not only these molecules show very different dipoles, but they also differentiate in their mass and shape, giving rise to a dispersive force that can account for between 50% and 100% of the *BE*. The case of OCS is of particular interest because, by having the smallest dipole moment in the set of molecules, it is the less bound species to the ice. Not only it has the smallest binding energy, but also its interaction with the ice is almost completely (>90%) due to the dispersive forces.

3.2   HF-3c Method

As mentioned above, interstellar ice grains are mostly considered as amorphous solid water (ASW) systems. Unfortunately, ASW can only be simulated by requesting unit cells large enough to provide sufficient structural variability to mimic the amorphous nature. This increases the request of computer resources, making DFT methods almost impractical. Therefore, here we check our DFT

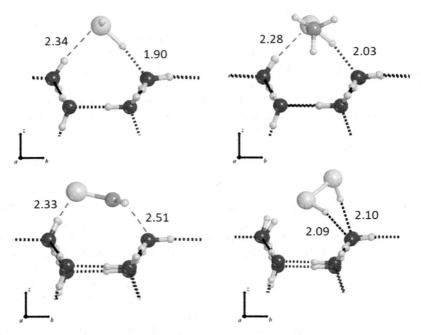

(a) Side view of B3LYP-D3(BJ)/Ahlrichs-VTZ* optimized geometries of H₂S, CH₃SH, H₂CS and H₂S₂.

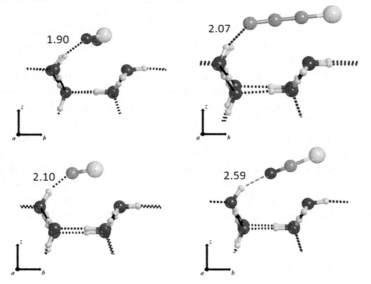

(b) Side view of B3LYP-D3(BJ)/Ahlrichs-VTZ* optimized geometries of SO₂, C₃S, CS and OCS.

Fig. 1. Optimized geometries of the 8 S-bearing species adsorbed on the ice crystalline slab (010). Hydrogen bond distances are given in Angstrom. Color legend: red, O; yellow, S; white, H; brown, C. (Color figure online)

Table 1. B3LYP-D3(BJ)/Ahlrichs-VTZ* computed BEs (in kJ mol^{-1}) of the sulphur-containing species on the P-ice (010) (2×1) super cell model. The dispersive and non-dispersive contribution to the BE are also listed. Whenever more than one adsorption geometry was found, all BEs are listed and separated by a slash.

Molecule	Total BE	No dispersion	Only dispersion (%)
H_2S	43.8	27.7	16.1 (37%)
CH_3SH	51.4	24.6	26.8 (52%)
H_2CS	40.3/51.9	18.5/23.7	21.8 (54%)/28.2 (54%)
H_2S_2	45.2/51.2	13.5/16.1	31.7 (70%)/35.1 (69%)
SO_2	57.2	30.0	27.2 (48%)
CS	38.1	13.3	24.8 (65%)
C_3S	50.2/55.9	13.0/17.7	37.2 (74%)/38.2 (68%)
OCS	25.0/28.6	−1.8/2.8	26.8 (107%)/25.8 (90%)

results against those obtained with HF-3c, a much cheaper methodology to potentially be used when dealing with amorphous systems.

From the optimized DFT structures, we proceeded through the two HF-3c ways explained in the Methods section, i.e., at HF-3c//HF-3c and at B3LYP-D3(BJ)//HF-3c theory levels. The obtained results are summarized in Table 2. Figure 2a (left panel) shows the comparison between the BE computed at full B3LYP-D3(BJ) with the results computed at HF-3c//HF-3c. The correlation is only coarse, as it would be expected from the various approximations included in the HF-3c definition. In contrast, the performance of the B3LYP-D3(BJ)//HF-3c method is very good (see Fig. 2a, right panel), showing its applicability to compute BEs on amorphous surface models in terms of computational cost and quality of the results, allowing moreover a wide exploration of different binding sites in an affordable way.

Table 2. Summary of the computed BEs (in kJ mol^{-1}) of the set of chosen species using the P-ice (010) (2×1) supercell.

Molecule	DFT//DFT	HF-3c//HF-3c	DFT//HF-3c
H_2S	43.8	31.0	38.9
CH_3SH	51.4	34.0	44.4
H_2CS	40.3/51.9	25.1/37.2	35.4/46.9
H_2S_2	45.2/51.2	40.8	41.8
SO_2	57.2	71.6	49.3
CS	38.1	23.6	32.1
C_3S	50.2/55.9	36.9/35.6	47.1/51.1
OCS	25.0/28.6	22.9	23.2

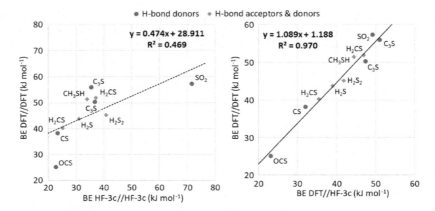

(a) Left panel: correlation between *BEs* computed at HF-3c//HF-3c level versus B3LYP-D3(BJ)//B3LYP-D3(BJ). Right panel: correlation between *BEs* computed at B3LYP-D3(BJ)//HF-3c level versus B3LYP-D3(BJ)//B3LYP-D3(BJ). *BEs* are in kJ mol^{-1}.

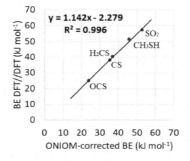

(b) Correlation between ONIOM-corrected *BEs* versus B3LYP-D3(BJ)//B3LYP-D3(BJ) computed energies. *BEs* are in kJ mol^{-1}. The four species were chosen in order to span the entire range of *BEs* computed in this work and in order to select two species form each group.

Fig. 2. Correlation of DFT//DFT *BEs* versus two approaches involving HF-3c (panel a) and versus ONIOM-corrected *BEs* (panel b).

3.3   CCSD(T) Correction

We finally performed some calculations at CCSD(T)/CBS (ONIOM2-correction, see Sect. 2) to check the accuracy of the B3LYP-D3(BJ) functional in describing the local interactions between the species and the ice and, at the same time, to refine the computed *BEs*. We chose to compute the correction only for some species, with the aim to span as much as possible the range of *BEs* and to sample geometries due to different contributions of dispersion forces. We are aware of the fact that five points are few for a meaningful statistics. However, when plotting the ONIOM2-corrected CCSD(T)/CBS *BEs* against those computed at the full B3LYP-D3(BJ) level, one can see an almost perfect correlation between the values, regardless of the nature of their interaction (see Fig. 2b). Therefore, our results evidence the accuracy and reliability of the full B3LYP-D3(BJ) procedure adopted and, by extension, of the B3LYP-D3(BJ)//HF-3c scheme.

4   Discussion

Our computed *BEs* have been compared with the available literature data in Fig. 3. In 2017, Penteado et al. [18] presented a list of recommended *BEs*, collecting data from previous works and adding an uncertainty range to each value. For H_2S, OCS and SO_2, the *BEs* were estimated from the experimental work of Collings et al. (2004) [7], while for all other species, data were based on the work of Hasegawa and Herbst (1993) [15], which collected *BEs* from previous works, including Allen & Robinson 1977 [1]. The uncertainty range for these values was set to half the *BE* value for species whose *BE* is less than 1000K and to 500K for all other cases. Comparison between these *BE* estimates with our computed *BEs* shows discrepancies, our values being systematically larger. This inconsistency should be taken with care, given the origin of the data published by Penteado et al. (2017). The cases of H_2S, OCS and SO_2, the ones extrapolated from thermal desorption process (TPD) experiments by Collings et al. (2004), are of interest. In the experiments, the species were deposited onto a pre-existing film of H_2O at 8–10 K with an exposure that ensured a multilayer growth of each species. This is at variance with our assumption of a submonolayer adsorption. Therefore, while for OCS the difference amounts to about 30%, for H_2S and SO_2 this percentage goes up to almost 60%. An additional reason explaining these large differences

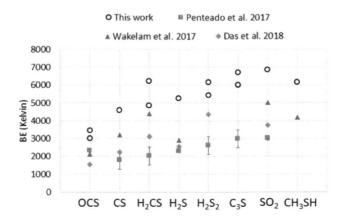

Fig. 3. *BEs* of the 8 S-bearing species (in Kelvin) at B3LYP-D3(BJ)//B3LYP-D3(BJ) level compared with those published by Wakelam et al. (2017) (red triangles), Das et al. (2018) (blue rhombus) and Penteado et al. (2017) (green squares, with error bars). [9,18,21] (Color figure online)

can be tracked down to the crystalline nature of our computer model compared to experimental data measured for AWS ice. The paucity of different adsorption sites at the crystal ice and the enhanced hydrogen bond cooperativity compared with amorphous ices give *BEs* values higher than any experimental estimate. Additionally, the fact that our *BE* values do not account for zero-point energy (ZPE) corrections contributes to enlarge the discrepancies. The comparison with values based on the additive principle by Allen and Robinson in 1997 [1] present an average difference of 50%. Given the huge difference in the theoretical background standing behind these values, it is not straightforward explaining the differences. However, we can advance that the additive principle employed by Allen and Robinson [1] to estimate the *BEs*, although being a reasonable approach in 1977, it is currently not suitable to obtain *BEs* since the interaction of a molecule with a surface cannot be described as the sum of the interactions of the single atoms constituting the molecule.

In 2017, Wakelam et al. proposed a new chemical model to compute the binding energies [21]. Given the difficulty to reproduce a reliable structure of an amorphous ice, it was assumed that *BEs* on ASW are proportional to the interaction energy with one single water molecule, without ZPE nor BSSE correction. The approximate nature of this model was recovered by correcting the computed *BEs* through a scaling factor from the best fit with selected experimental *BE* values. The general trend by comparing our computed *BE* values with those of Wakelam et al. (2017) is a percentage difference of about 30%, the our values being larger. Although being corrected, it seems clear that using one water molecule to model an entire water ice surface is not a suitable choice since different important aspects such as H-bond cooperativity and surface long-range effect are neglected.

In 2018, Das et al. [9] simulated the water surface using four, and in some cases, six water molecules. For S-bearing species, only H_2O and OCS were considered at MP2/aug-cc-pVDZ level on the water tetramer. Comparison of these values with our results with shows large differences. Reasons are twofold: i) the P-ice (010) surface exploits full hydrogen bond cooperativity, largely missing in the water tetramer; and ii) the adopted quantum mechanical methods are significantly different. Moreover *BEs* by Das et al. (2018) were not corrected for BSSE, which sure contribute to these discrepancies, nor for the ZPE [9].

The work of Ferrero et al. (2020) [11], presented for a set of chemical species a *BE* distribution by modeling their adsorption on both a crystalline and an amorphous surface ice models. Results showed that those on the crystalline ice were usually in the upper region of the range. Thus, we expect a similar behaviour for the adsorption of S-bearing species. Therefore, literature values should then be included in the range spanned by the distributions. With that being said, it is clear that the computation of *BEs* on an amorphous water ice model is necessary and already scheduled for the future, especially because these values have a pivotal role in the accuracy of the predictions provided by astrochemical models that deal with the chemical evolution in the ISM.

5 Conclusions

In this work we computed the *BEs* of 8 astrochemically-relevant S-containing species (i.e., H_2S, CH_3SH, H_2S_2, H_2CS, C_3S, SO_2, CS and OCS) on water ice surfaces by means of quantum chemical calculations. We followed the same approach proposed by Ferrero et al. (2020) [11], in which the interstellar water ice was simulated through the (010) surface of the crystalline P-ice [5] as first step to subsequent studies in which amorphous ice systems will be employed. It is found that the S-containing species can be categorized in two groups: those acting as both H-bond acceptors and donors (H_2S, CH_3SH, H_2S_2, H_2CS), and those acting only as H-bond acceptors (C_3S, SO_2, CS and OCS), in which the S atoms dos not participate in the interaction. Although *a priori* one could think that the former group would present larger *BEs* than the later ones, B3LYP-D3(BJ) results indicate that this is not the case since dispersive interactions are actually important, specially in the second group. CCSD(T) refinements on the *BE* values adopting an ONIOM2-correction approach indicate that those obtained at full B3LYP-D3(BJ) level are accurate enough. Similarly, comparison between B3LYP-D3(BJ)//HF-3c and full B3LYP-D3(BJ) *BE* values indicate that the former method is an optimum cost-effective method to compute *BEs*, in that case to be applicable in larger systems like the amorphous ones.

When comparing the computed *BEs* with experimental and other theoretical values from the literature we found major discrepancies. They arise from: i) the adoption of a crystalline ice model, which emphasizes the H-bond cooperativity compared with the amorphous ones, and ii) the different accounting for of long range order effects, highly present in crystalline systems while lost in the random network of the amorphous ice. Furthermore, the paucity of adsorption sites due to symmetry constraints as provided by the crystalline systems gives *BE* values that are at the upper extreme of the ranges compared with the larger surface morphological variability present in the amorphous ices. Such a constraint does not allow us to establish a statistical distribution of the *BEs* values, which is compulsory if a fair comparison with the experimental TPD data is foreseen. It is clear that the uncertainties on these values require more studies on the subject, especially because the binding energies have a pivotal role in the description of the chemistry occurring in the ISM.

Acknowledgment. This project has received funding from the European Research Council (ERC) under the European Union's Horizon 2020 research and innovation programme (grant agreement No. 865657) for the project "Quantum Chemistry on Interstellar Grains" (QUANTUMGRAIN). MINECO (project CTQ2017-89132-P) DIUE (project 2017SGR1323) are acknowledged for financial support. This work is related to the project "Astro-Chemical Origins" (ACO) associated with the European Union's Horizon 2020 research and innovation programme under the Marie Sklodowska-Curie grant agreement No. 811312. A. R. is indebted to the "Ramón y Cajal" program. The authors wish to thank the anonymous reviewers for their valuable suggestions.

References

1. Allen, M., Robinson, G.W.: The molecular composition of dense interstellar clouds. Astrophys. J. **212**, 396–415 (1977)
2. Becke, A.D.: Density-functional exchange-energy approximation with correct asymptotic behavior. Phys. Rev. A **38**, 3098–3100 (1988)
3. Becke, A.D.: Density-functional thermochemistry. iii. The role of exact exchange. J. Chem. Phys. **98**(7), 5648–5652 (1993)
4. Boogert, A.A., Gerakines, P.A., Whittet, D.C.: Observations of the icy universe. Ann. Rev. Astron. Astrophys. **53**(1), 541–581 (2015)
5. Casassa, S., Ugliengo, P., Pisani, C.: Proton-ordered models of ordinary ice for quantum-mechanical studies. J. Chem. Phys. **106**, 8030–8040 (1997)
6. Caselli, P., Ceccarelli, C.: Our astrochemical heritage. Astron. Astrophys. Rev. **20**(1), 56 (2012)
7. Collings, M.P., et al.: A laboratory survey of the thermal desorption of astrophysically relevant molecules. Mon. Not. R. Astron. Soc. **354**(4), 1133–1140 (2004)
8. Dapprich, S., Komáromi, I., Byun, K., Morokuma, K., Frisch, M.: A new ONIOM implementation in gaussian98. Part I. The calculation of energies, gradients, vibrational frequencies and electric field derivatives. Comput. Theor. Chem. **461–462**, 1–21 (1999). DOI: https://doi.org/10.1016/S0166-1280(98)00475-8
9. Das, A., Sil, M., Gorai, P., Chakrabarti, S.K., Loison, J.C.: An approach to estimate the binding energy of interstellar species. Astrophys. J. Suppl. Ser. **237**(1), 9 (2018)
10. Dovesi, R., et al.: Quantum-mechanical condensed matter simulations with crystal. WIREs Comput. Mol. Sci. **8**(4), e1360 (2018)
11. Ferrero, S., Zamirri, L., Ceccarelli, C., Witzel, A., Rimola, A., Ugliengo, P.: Binding energies of interstellar molecules on crystalline and amorphous models of water ice by ab initio calculations. Astrophys. J. **904**(1), 11 (2020)
12. Frisch, M.J., et al.: Gaussian16 Revision C.01. Gaussian Inc., Wallingford CT (2016)
13. Grimme, S., Antony, J., Ehrlich, S., Krieg, H.: A consistent and accurate ab initio parametrization of density functional dispersion correction (DFT-D) for the 94 elements H-Pu. J. Chem. Phys. **132**(15), 154104 (2010)
14. Grimme, S., Ehrlich, S., Goerigk, L.: Effect of the damping function in dispersion corrected density functional theory. J. Comput. Chem. **32**(7), 1456–1465 (2011)
15. Hasegawa, T.I., Herbst, E.: New gas-grain chemical models of quiscent dense interstellar clouds?: the effects of H2 tunnelling reactions and cosmic ray induced desorption. Montly Not. Roy. Astron. Soc. **261**, 83–102 (1993)
16. Lee, C., Yang, W., Parr, R.G.: Development of the Colle-Salvetti correlation-energy formula into a functional of the electron density. Phys. Rev. B **37**, 785–789 (1988)
17. Molinari, S., Ceccarelli, C., White, G.J., Saraceno, P., Nisini, B., Giannini, T., Caux, E.: Detection of the 62 micron crystalline H_2O ice feature in emission toward HH 7 with the infrared space observatory long-wavelength spectrometer. Astrophys. J. **521**(1), L71–L74 (1999)
18. Penteado, E.M., Walsh, C., Cuppen, H.M.: Sensitivity analysis of grain surface chemistry to binding energies of ice species. Astrophys. J. **844**(1), 71 (2017)
19. Sure, R., Grimme, S.: Corrected small basis set Hartree-Fock method for large systems. J. Comput. Chem. **34**(19), 1672–1685 (2013)
20. Terada, H., Tokunaga, A.T.: Discovery of crystallized water ice in a silhouette disk in the M43 region. Astrophys. J. **753**(1), 19 (2012)

21. Wakelam, V., Loison, J.C., Mereau, R., Ruaud, M.: Binding energies: new values and impact on the efficiency of chemical desorption. Mol. Astrophys. **6**, 22–35 (2017)
22. Zamirri, L., Casassa, S., Rimola, A., Segado-Centellas, M., Ceccarelli, C., Ugliengo, P.: IR spectral fingerprint of carbon monoxide in interstellar water-ice models. Mon. Not. R. Astron. Soc. **480**(2), 1427–1444 (2018)

A Computational Study on the Attack of Nitrogen and Oxygen Atoms to Toluene

Marzio Rosi[1]([✉]), Stefano Falcinelli[1], Piergiorgio Casavecchia[2], Nadia Balucani[2], Pedro Recio[2], Adriana Caracciolo[2], Gianmarco Vanuzzo[2], Dimitrios Skouteris[3], and Carlo Cavallotti[4]

[1] Department of Civil and Environmental Engineering, University of Perugia, 06125 Perugia, Italy
{marzio.rosi,stefano.falcinelli}@unipg.it
[2] Department of Chemistry, Biology and Biotechnologies, University of di Perugia, 06123 Perugia, Italy
{piergiorgio.casavecchia,nadia.balucani, gianmarco.vanuzzo}@unipg.it
[3] Master-Tec, 06128 Perugia, Italy
[4] Department of Chemistry, Materials and Chemical Engineering, Politecnico di Milano, 20131 Milano, Italy
carlo.cavallotti@polimi.it

Abstract. The interaction between nitrogen atoms in their first electronically excited state ^2D and oxygen atoms in their ground state ^3P or in the first electronically excited state ^1D with toluene has been characterized by electronic structure calculations. We focused our attention, in particular, on the different sites of attack of nitrogen or oxygen to toluene using different methods. Our results suggest that, while for geometry optimizations DFT methods are adequate and different DFT methods provide comparable results, in order to compute accurate energies higher level of calculations, as CCSD(T), are necessary, in particular when strong correlation effects are present.

Keywords: Computational chemistry · Ab initio calculations · DFT methods · Combustion · Fuels · Chemistry of planetary atmospheres · Computational astrochemistry · Astrobiology

1 Introduction

Toluene represents the major aromatic found in gasoline. Development of detailed chemical kinetic models of toluene oxidation requires knowledge of the primary products and branching fractions (BFs) for the bimolecular reaction $O(^3P)+C_6H_5CH_3$ as a function of temperature (T) and pressure (p). Despite extensive kinetic studies [1–4], little is known about the mechanism and BFs for this reaction. We have therefore undertaken a synergistic experimental/theoretical investigation of $O(^3P)$+toluene by exploiting the same approach recently successfully used to identify all primary products and determine the

© Springer Nature Switzerland AG 2021
O. Gervasi et al. (Eds.): ICCSA 2021, LNCS 12953, pp. 620–631, 2021.
https://doi.org/10.1007/978-3-030-86976-2_42

BFs for the multichannel $O(^3P)$ reactions with a variety of unsaturated aliphatic hydrocarbons [5–8], namely the crossed molecular beam (CMB) technique with soft electron ionization mass spectrometric detection and time-of-flight analysis. These experimental results are combined to high-level electronic structure calculations of the underlying triplet and singlet potential energy surfaces (PESs) and statistical RRKM/Master Equation computation of product distribution as a function of collision energy, E_c, as well as T and p, with intersystem crossing (ISC) taken into account, in order to get important information for improved kinetic modeling of toluene combustion.

Toluene is important also in other contexts, in particular in astrochemical contexts, as in the atmosphere of Titan which, being composed mainly by dinitrogen and simple hydrocarbons [9, 10], is somewhat reminiscent of the primordial atmosphere of Earth [11, 12]. Among the species identified by Cassini Ion Neutral Spectrometer (INMS) [13] in Titan atmosphere, benzene shows a relatively important mole fraction, being 1.3×10^{-6} at 950 km [14]. Toluene is efficiently produced in Titan's atmosphere since C_6H_5, the main product of the photodissociation of benzene, reacts with the radicals most abundant in Titan's atmosphere, which are H and CH_3 [15]. Molecular dinitrogen, in its closed shell electronic configuration, cannot react with hydrocarbons in the atmosphere of Titan because of the presence of relatively high activation energy barriers, but atomic nitrogen in its first electronically excited ^2D state can be produced [16] and it shows a significant reactivity with several molecules identified in the atmosphere of Titan. We have already investigated the reactions of $N(^2D)$ with aliphatic hydrocarbons, like CH_4, C_2H_2, C_2H_4, C_2H_6 [17–22]. More recently, we started the investigation of the reaction between $N(^2D)$ and aromatic hydrocarbons like benzene [23–25]. In this study we will report preliminary calculations on the interaction of $N(^2D)$ with toluene comparing the attack of $N(^2D)$ with that of $O(^3P)$ or $O(^1D)$ to toluene, paying attention to the computational requirements. Indeed, the ab initio study of these systems is computationally very challenging and a compromise between chemical accuracy and computational resources is necessary.

2 Computational Details

The stationary points, both minima and transition states, were localized on the Potential Energy Surface (PES) performing Density Functional Theory (DFT) calculations using the ωB97X-D [26, 27] or the B3LYP [28, 29] functional, in conjunction with the 6-311+G(d,p) basis set [30, 31]. The Basis Set Superposition Error (BSSE) has been previously estimated and computed to be 1.1 kcal/mol [24]. At the same level of theory we have computed the harmonic vibrational frequencies. The assignment of the saddle points was performed using intrinsic reaction coordinate (IRC) calculations [32, 33]. The geometry of all the species was optimized without any symmetry constraints. For all the stationary points, the energy was computed also at the higher level of calculation CCSD(T) [34–36] using the correlation consistent aug-cc-pVTZ basis set [37] and the DFT optimized geometries, following a previously applied computational scheme [38–49]. Both the DFT and the CCSD(T) energies were corrected to 0 K by adding the zero point energy correction computed using the scaled harmonic vibrational frequencies evaluated at DFT level. The energy of $N(^2D)$ was estimated by adding the experimental [50] separation $N(^4S) - N(^2D)$ of 55 kcal mol^{-1} to the energy of $N(^4S)$ at all levels of calculation. All calculations were done using Gaussian 09 [51] while the analysis of the vibrational frequencies was performed using Molekel [52, 53].

3   Results and Discussion

3.1   N(^{2}D) + Toluene

Figure 1 reports the optimized geometries of the isomers deriving from the interaction of N(^{2}D) with toluene. We have three different isomers depending on the carbon atoms interacting with nitrogen. Nitrogen forms two σ bonds with two adjacent carbon atoms, as expected because nitrogen has two electrons with opposite spin in different p orbitals which can interact with the two electrons with opposite spin involved in the π bond of the two carbon atoms. The energy required for breaking the π bond is more than compensated by the energy associated to the formation of the two σ bonds between nitrogen and carbon. The breaking of the π bond is shown by the C—C bond distance reported in Fig. 1 which corresponds to that of a single bond for the carbon atoms interacting with nitrogen. In Fig. 1 we have reported both the optimized geometry at B3LYP/6-311+G(d,p) and at ωB97XD/6-311+G(d,p) level in order to compare the two functionals. From Fig. 1 we can notice that the optimized geometries obtained with the two functionals are very similar, the difference in bond distances being within 0.01 Å and that in bond angles within 1°. In Table 1 we have reported the relative energies of these species with respect to N(^{2}D) + toluene computed both at DFT level and at the more accurate CCSD(T) level. From Table 1 we can notice that the three isomers are almost degenerate, with a slight preference for 2NMIN1. We can also notice that the binding energy of N(^{2}D) to toluene at DFT level is slightly higher at ωB97XD/6-311+G(d,p) level with respect to the B3LYP/6-311+G(d,p) level, the difference being however less than 2 kcal/mol. At the more accurate CCSD(T) level the binding energies computed using the two different optimized geometries are almost the same, the difference being less than 0.5 kcal/mol. At the B3LYP/6-311+G(d,p) level when N(^{2}D) interacts with toluene there is the formation of an initial van der Waals adduct, whose geometry is shown in Fig. 2. We can notice that the distance between the nitrogen and the closest carbon is 3.03 Å, while the binding energy is computed to be 30.2 kcal/mol at the B3LYP/6-311+G(d,p) level, as reported in Table 1. This value is very high for a van der Waals interaction, confirming that the B3LYP functional tends to overestimate the long range interactions. This adduct (2NMIN0) isomerizes to 2NMIN1 through the saddle point whose geometry is reported in Fig. 2; the barrier height for this isomerization is 2.6 kcal/mol, as reported in Table 1. It was not possible to localize on the PES this adduct at ωB97XD/6-311+G(d,p) level. This is similar to what recently found by Chin et al. for N(^{2}D) + benzene [54]: they were not able to find any initial adduct at ωB97XD/6-311+G(d,p) level, while our group could localize this adduct at B3LYP/6-311+G(d,p) level [24]. It is well known that B3LYP cannot describe very accurately dispersion forces and it is possible that it somewhat overestimates weak interactions.

Starting from 2NMIN1 we can consider the H loss and CH$_3$ loss channels; in Fig. 3 we have reported the optimized geometries for the transition states and the products, computed both at ωB97XD/6-311+G(d,p) and at B3LYP/6-311+G(d,p) levels, while in Table 1 we have reported the enthalpy changes and barrier heights for these reactions.

From Fig. 3 we can notice that the optimized geometries obtained with the two methods are comparable, the only significant difference being in the breaking bond. Since this bond (C—C in the CH_3 loss and C—H in the H loss) is almost broken the dependence of the energy from the distance is very small and the localization of the minimum is more difficult. From Table 1 we can notice that the DFT methods tends to overestimate the binding energies with respect to the values computed at CCSD(T) level, with the B3LYP results in slight better agreement with the more accurate CCSD(T) results.

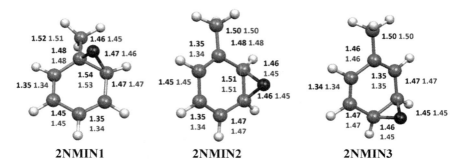

Fig. 1. Optimized geometries at B3LYP/6-311+G(d,p) (in black) and ωB97XD/6-311+G(d,p) (in red) level of the minima for the attack of $N(^2D)$ to toluene. Bond lengths in Å. Carbon in green, nitrogen in blue, hydrogen in white. (Color figure online)

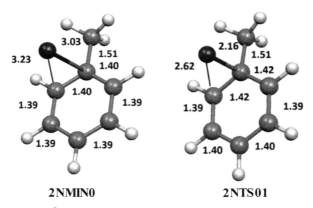

Fig. 2. Initial attack of $N(^2D)$ to toluene in *ipso*. Optimized geometries at B3LYP/6-311+G(d,p). Bond lengths in Å. Carbon in green, nitrogen in blue, hydrogen in white. (Color figure online)

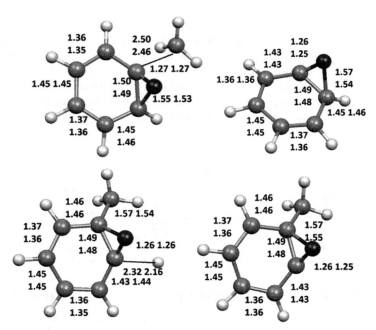

Fig. 3. Optimized geometries at B3LYP/6-311+G(d,p) (in black) and ωB97XD/6-311+G(d,p) (in red) level of the stationary points for the exit channels leading to CH₃ or H from 2NMIN1. Bond lengths in Å. Carbon in green, nitrogen in blue, hydrogen in white. (Color figure online)

3.2 O(^{3}P) + Toluene

In Fig. 4 we have reported the optimized geometries of the isomers obtained from the interaction of O(^{3}P) and toluene. The O(^{3}P) interacts only with one carbon atom, since it has the two electrons in singly occupied p orbitals with parallel spin; these electrons cannot break a π bond and form two σ bonds with two adjacent carbon atoms, like N(^{2}D). There are therefore four possible isomers, depending on the site of attack of the oxygen: *ipso*, *ortho*, *meta* and *para* with respect to the carbon center bonded to CH₃. For all isomers, there is first the formation of a van der Waals adduct which isomerizes, through a transition state, to the stable minimum. Figure 4 shows the optimized geometries computed at ωB97XD/6-311+G(d,p) level for all these species; for the *ipso* isomer we have optimized the geometries also at B3LYP/6-311+G(d,p) level, for comparison. In Table 2 we have reported the enthalpy changes and barrier heights for these reactions. From Fig. 4 considering the *ipso* isomer, we can notice that the optimized geometries at ωB97XD/6-311+G(d,p) level and at B3LYP/6-311+G(d,p) level compare very well, the only significant difference being in the distance between oxygen and carbon in the van der Waals adduct. From Table 2 we can notice that the binding energies of the four isomers are very similar, although the *ipso* isomer is slightly more stable than the others. It is also interesting to notice that the formation of all four isomers shows at CCSD(T) level an energy barrier above the reactants. From Table 2 we can notice also that the *ipso* isomer can loose a methyl radical in an exothermic reaction, while the loss

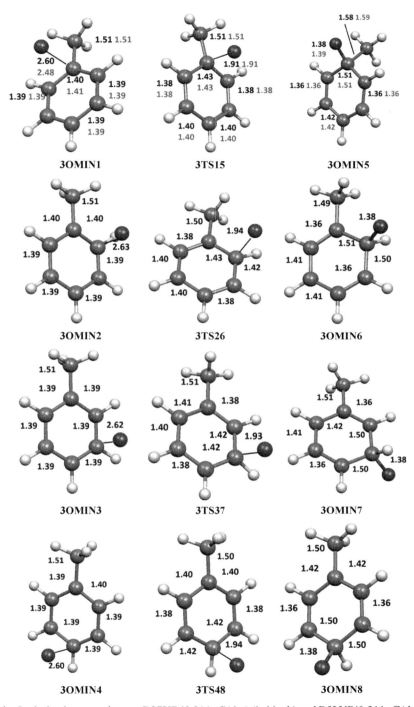

Fig. 4. Optimized geometries at ωB97XD/6-311+G(d,p) (in black) and B3LYP/6-311+G(d,p) (in red) level of the initial van der Waals adducts, the saddle points and the minima for the attack of $O(^3P)$ to toluene. Bond lengths in Å. Carbon in green, oxygen in red, hydrogen in white. (Color figure online)

of an hydrogen atom from the *ortho*, *meta* or *para* isomers is an almost thermoneutral process, but with an energy barrier higher than 10 kcal/mol. In Fig. 5 we have reported the optimized geometries of the saddle points for the loss of CH_3 from the *ipso* isomer and for the loss of H from the *ortho* isomer. In both cases CH_3 or H leave the system in a direction almost perpendicular with respect to the plane of the molecule.

3.3 $O(^1D)$ + Toluene

Figure 6 reports the optimized geometries of the isomers deriving from the interaction of $O(^1D)$ with toluene. We have three different isomers depending on the carbon atoms interacting with oxygen. $O(^1D)$ forms two σ bonds with two adjacent carbon atoms, as expected because it has two electrons with opposite spin in different p orbitals which can interact with the two electrons with opposite spin involved in the π bond of the two carbon atoms. The energy required for breaking the π bond is more than compensated by the energy associated to the formation of the two σ bonds between oxygen and carbon. The breaking of the π bond is shown by the C—C bond distance reported in Fig. 6 which corresponds to that of a single bond for the carbon atoms interacting with oxygen. In Table 2 we have reported the relative energies of these isomers with respect to oxygen in its ground state and toluene; this is a spin forbidden reaction which has been reported only to compare the energy of the singlet isomers with that of the triplet ones. We can notice that the three isomers are almost degenerate with a slight preference for the first isomer. It is worth noting also that the DFT and CCSD(T) energies are in very good agreement suggesting that for the study of larger systems it could be possible to use DFT calculations. The loss of CH_3 or H from the very stable minimum 1OMIN1 are endothermic processes, as expected, as we can see from the values reported in Table 2.

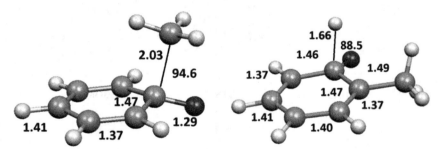

Fig. 5. Optimized geometries at ωB97XD/6-311+G(d,p) level of the saddle points for the loss of CH_3 from the ipso isomer (3OMIN5) and H from the *ortho* isomer (3OMIN6) in the $O(^3P)$+toluene PES. Bond lengths in Å, angles in degrees. Carbon in green, oxygen in red, hydrogen in white. (Color figure online)

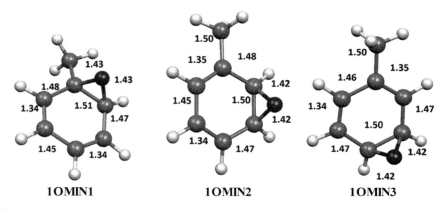

1OMIN1   **1OMIN2**   **1OMIN3**

Fig. 6. Optimized geometries at ωB97XD/6-311+G(d,p) level of the minima for the attack of O(^{1}D) to toluene. Bond lengths in Å. Carbon in green, oxygen in red, hydrogen in white. (Color figure online)

Table 1. Enthalpy changes and barrier heights (kcal/mol, 0 K) computed at the ωB97X-D/6-311+G(d,p), B3LYP/6-311+G(d,p), CCSD(T)/aug-cc-pVTZ//ωB97X-D/6-311+G(d,p) and CCSD(T)/aug-cc-pVTZ//B3LYP/6-311+G(d,p) levels of theory for selected reactions of N(^{2}D) + toluene system.

	ΔH^0_0	
	ωB97X-D (CCSD(T))	B3LYP (CCSD(T))
N(^{2}D)+C$_6$H$_5$CH$_3$ → 2NMIN1	−80.5 (−75.6)	−78.8 (−75.9)
N(^{2}D)+C$_6$H$_5$CH$_3$ → 2NMIN2	−80.1 (−74.9)	−78.6 (−75.2)
N(^{2}D)+C$_6$H$_5$CH$_3$ → 2NMIN3	−79.6 (−74.9)	−78.6 (−75.2)
	ΔH^0_0	Barrier height
B3LYP		
N(^{2}D)+C$_6$H$_5$CH$_3$ → 2NMIN0	−30.2	
2NMIN0 → 2NMIN1	−48.6	2.6
ωB97X-D (CCSD(T))		
2NMIN1 – CH$_3$ → products	47.4 (43.4)	47.9 (45.3)
2NMIN1 – H → products	55.1 (51.8)	58.0 (53.3)
B3LYP		
2NMIN1 – CH$_3$ → products	40.4	43.6
2NMIN1 – H → products	53.7	54.6

Table 2. Enthalpy changes and barrier heights (kcal/mol, 0 K) computed at the ωB97X-D/6-311+G(d,p) and CCSD(T)/aug-cc-pVTZ//ωB97X-D/6-311+G(d,p) levels of theory for selected reactions of $O(^3P, {}^1D)$ + toluene system. In parentheses CCSD(T) results.

	ΔH^0_0	Barrier height
$O(^3P)+C_6H_5CH_3 \rightarrow 3OMIN1$	−2.7 (−1.6)	
$O(^3P)+C_6H_5CH_3 \rightarrow 3OMIN2$	−2.5 (−1.4)	
$O(^3P)+C_6H_5CH_3 \rightarrow 3OMIN3$	−2.3 (−1.2)	
$O(^3P)+C_6H_5CH_3 \rightarrow 3OMIN4$	−2.3 (−1.2)	
$3OMIN1 \rightarrow 3OMIN5$	−14.5 (−11.2)	2.7 (6.8)
$3OMIN2 \rightarrow 3OMIN6$	−15.7 (−11.5)	2.7 (6.1)
$3OMIN3 \rightarrow 3OMIN7$	−14.5 (−10.4)	3.6 (7.0)
$3OMIN4 \rightarrow 3OMIN8$	−14.8 (−10.3)	6.7 (9.9)
$3OMIN5 - CH_3 \rightarrow$ products	−7.2 (−7.0)	7.7 (8.1)
$3OMIN6 - H \rightarrow$ products	0.5 (0.5)	13.2 (11.5)
$3OMIN7 - H \rightarrow$ products	0.1 (0.1)	13.5 (11.8)
$3OMIN8 - H \rightarrow$ products	0.6 (0.7)	13.7 (12.1)
$O(^3P)+C_6H_5CH_3 \rightarrow 1OMIN1$	−55.1 (−55.4)	
$O(^3P)+C_6H_5CH_3 \rightarrow 1OMIN2$	−53.7 (−53.6)	
$O(^3P)+C_6H_5CH_3 \rightarrow 1OMIN3$	−53.3 (−53.5)	
$1OMIN1 - CH_3 \rightarrow$ products	94.7 (95.1)	
$1OMIN1 - H \rightarrow$ products	100.6 (99.8)	

4 Conclusions

The study at *ab initio* level of the interaction of $N(^2D)$, $O(^3P)$ and $O(^1D)$ with toluene, performed using different methods in order to find a reasonable compromise between chemical accuracy and computational costs suggests that, while for geometry optimizations DFT methods are adequate, for energies, calculations of higher level are necessary in order to obtain accurate quantitative results, although even DFT methods can provide reasonable semi-quantitative results.

Acknowledgments. We acknowledge the MUR (Ministero dell'Università e della Ricerca) for "PRIN 2017" funds, project "Modeling and Analysis of carbon nanoparticles for innovative applications Generated dIrectly and Collected DUring combuSTion (MAGIC DUST)", Grant Number 2017PJ5XXX. SF and MR acknowledge the project "Indagini teoriche e sperimentali sulla reattività di sistemi di interesse astrochimico" funded with Fondo Ricerca di Base of the University of Perugia. MR thanks the Department of Civil and Environmental Engineering of the University of Perugia for allocated computing time within the project "Dipartimenti di Eccellenza 2018–2022".

References

1. Brezinsky, K.: The high-temperature oxidation of aromatic hydrocarbons. Prog. Energy Combust. **12**, 1–24 (1986)
2. Atkinson, R., Pitts, J.N.: Rate constants for the reaction of $O(^3P)$ atoms with benzene and toluene over the temperature range 299–440 K. Chem. Phys. Lett. **63**, 485–489 (1979)
3. Nicovich, J.M., Gump, C.A., Ravishankara, A.R.: Rates of reactions of $O(^3P)$ with benzene and toluene. J. Phys. Chem. **86**, 1684–1690 (1982)
4. Tappe, M., Schliephake, V., Wagner, H.G.: Reactions of benzene, toluene and ethylbenzene with atomic oxygen $O(^3P)$ in the gas phase. Z. Phys. Chem. **162**, 129–145 (1989)
5. Cavallotti, C., et al.: Relevance of the channel leading to formaldehyde + triplet ethylidene in the $O(^3P)$+propene reaction under combustion conditions. J. Phys. Chem. Lett. **5**, 4213–4218 (2014)
6. Leonori, F., et al.: Experimental and theoretical studies on the dynamics of the $O(^3P)$+propene reaction: primary products, branching ratios, and role of intersystem crossing. J. Phys. Chem. C **119**, 14632–14652 (2015)
7. Gimondi, I., Cavallotti, C., Vanuzzo, G., Balucani, N., Casavecchia, P.: Reaction dynamics of $O(^3P)$+propyne: II. Primary products, branching ratios, and role of intersystem crossing from ab initio coupled triplet/singlet potential energy surfaces and statistical calculations. J. Phys. Chem. A **120**, 4619–4633 (2016)
8. Caracciolo, A., et al.: Combined experimental and theoretical studies of the $O(^3P)$+1-butene reaction dynamics: primary products, branching ratios and role of intersystem crossing. J. Phys. Chem. A **123**, 9934–9956 (2019)
9. Hörst, S. M.: Titan's atmosphere and climate. J. Geophys. Res. Planets **122**, 432–482 (2017)
10. Vuitton, V., Yelle, R.V., Anicich, V.G.: The nitrogen chemistry of Titan's upper atmosphere revealed. Astrophys. J. **647**, L175–L178 (2006)
11. Vuitton, V., Dutuit, O., Smith, M.A., Balucani, N.: Chemistry of Titan's atmosphere. In: Mueller-Wodarg, I., Griffith, C., Lellouch, E., Cravens, T. (eds.) Titan: Surface, Atmosphere and Magnetosphere, Cambridge University Press (2013)
12. Balucani, N.: Elementary reactions of N atoms with hydrocarbons: first steps towards the formation of prebiotic N-containing molecules in planetary atmospheres. Chem. Soc. Rev. **41**, 5473–5483 (2012)
13. Brown, R., Lebreton, J.P., Waite, J. (eds.): Titan from Cassini-Huygens. Springer, Nethelands (2010). https://doi.org/10.1007/978-1-4020-9215-2
14. Vuitton, V., Yelle, R.V., Cui, J.: Formation and distribution of benzene on Titan. J. Geophys. Res. **113**, E05007 (2008)
15. Loison, J.C., Dobrijevic, M., Hickson, K.M.: The photochemical production of aromatics in the atmosphere of Titan. Icarus **329**, 55–71 (2019)
16. Lavvas, P., et al.: Energy deposition and primary chemical products in Titan's upper atmosphere. Icarus **213**, 233–251 (2011)
17. Balucani, N., et al.: Combined crossed molecular beam and theoretical studies of the $N(^2D)$ + CH_4 reaction and implications for atmospheric models of Titan. J. Phys. Chem. A **113**, 11138–11152 (2009)
18. Balucani, N., et al.: Cyanomethylene formation from the reaction of excited nitrogen atoms with acetylene: a crossed beam and ab initio study. J. Am. Chem. Soc. **122**, 4443–4450 (2000)
19. Balucani, N., Cartechini, L., Alagia, M., Casavecchia, P., Volpi, G.G.: Observation of nitrogen-bearing organic molecules from reactions of nitrogen atoms with hydrocarbons: a crossed beam study of $N(^2D)$ + ethylene. J. Phys. Chem. A **104**, 5655–5659 (2000)
20. Balucani, N., et al.: Formation of nitriles and imines in the atmosphere of Titan: combined crossed-beam and theoretical studies on the reaction dynamics of excited nitrogen atoms $N(^2D)$ with ethane. Faraday Discuss. **147**, 189–216 (2010)

21. Balucani, N., et al.: Combined crossed beam and theoretical studies of the $N(^2D) + C_2H_4$ reaction and implications for atmospheric models of Titan. J. Phys. Chem. A **116**, 10467–10479 (2012)

22. Rosi, M., Falcinelli, S., Balucani, N., Casavecchia, P., Skouteris, D.: A theoretical study of formation routes and dimerization of methanimine and implications for the aerosols formation in the upper atmosphere of Titan. Lect. Notes Comp. Sci. **7971**, 47–56 (2013)

23. Balucani, N., Pacifici, L., Skouteris, D., Caracciolo, A., Casavecchia, P., Rosi, M.: A theoretical investigation of the reaction $N(^2D) + C_6H_6$ and implications for the upper atmosphere of Titan. Lect. Notes Comp. Sci. **10961**, 763–772 (2018)

24. Rosi, M., et al.: A computational study on the insertion of $N(^2D)$ into a C—H or C—C bond: the reactions of $N(^2D)$ with benzene and toluene and their implications on the chemistry of Titan. Lect. Notes Comp. Sci. **12251**, 744–755 (2020)

25. Balucani, N., et al.: A computational study of the reaction $N(^2D) + C_6H_6$ leading to pyridine and phenylnitrene. LNCS **11621**, 316–324 (2019)

26. Chai, J.-D., Head-Gordon, M.: Long-range corrected hybrid density functionals with damped atom-atom dispersion corrections. Phys. Chem. Chem. Phys. **10**, 6615–6620 (2008)

27. Chai, J.-D., Head-Gordon, M.: Systematic optimization of long-range corrected hybrid density functionals. J. Chem. Phys. **128**, 084106 (2008)

28. Becke, A.D.: Density functional thermochemistry. III. The role of exact exchange. J. Chem. Phys. **98**, 5648–5652 (1993)

29. Stephens, P.J., Devlin, F.J., Chablowski, C.F., Frisch, M.J.: Ab initio calculation of vibrational absorption and circular dichroism spectra using density functional force fields. J. Phys. Chem. **98**, 11623–11627 (1994)

30. Krishnan, R., Binkley, J.S., Seeger, R., Pople, J.A.: Self-consistent molecular orbital methods. XX. A basis set for correlated wave functions. J. Chem. Phys. **72**, 650–654 (1980)

31. Frisch, M.J., Pople, J.A., Binkley, J.S.: Self-consistent molecular orbital methods 28. Supplementary functions for Gaussian basis sets. J. Chem. Phys. **80**, 3265–3269 (1984)

32. Gonzalez, C., Schlegel, H.B.: An improved algorithm for reaction path following. J. Chem. Phys. **90**, 2154–2161 (1989)

33. Gonzalez, C., Schlegel, H.B.: Reaction path following in mass-weighted internal coordinates. J. Phys. Chem. **94**, 5523–5527 (1990)

34. Bartlett, R.J.: Many-body perturbation theory and coupled cluster theory for electron correlation in molecules. Ann. Rev. Phys. Chem. **32**, 359–401 (1981)

35. Raghavachari, K., Trucks, G.W., Pople, J.A., Head-Gordon, M.: Quadratic configuration interaction. A general technique for determining electron correlation energies. Chem. Phys. Lett. **157**, 479–483 (1989)

36. Olsen, J., Jorgensen, P., Koch, H., Balkova, A., Bartlett, R.J.: Full configuration–interaction and state of the art correlation calculations on water in a valence double-zeta basis with polarization functions. J. Chem. Phys. **104**, 8007–8015 (1996)

37. Dunning, T.H., Jr.: Gaussian basis sets for use in correlated molecular calculations. I. The atoms boron through neon and hydrogen. J. Chem. Phys. **90**, 1007–1023 (1989)

38. de Petris, G., Cacace, F., Cipollini, R., Cartoni, A., Rosi, M., Troiani, A.: Experimental detection of theoretically predicted N_2CO. Angew. Chem. **117**, 466–469 (2005)

39. De Petris, G., Rosi, M., Troiani, A.: SSOH and HSSO radicals: an experimental and theoretical study of $[S_2OH]^{0/+/-}$ species. J. Phys. Chem. A **111**, 6526–6533 (2007)

40. Bartolomei, M., et al.: The intermolecular potential in NO–N_2 and (NO–$N_2)^+$ systems: implications for the neutralization of ionic molecular aggregates. PCCP **10**, 5993–6001 (2008)

41. Leonori, F., et al.: Observation of organosulfur products (thiovinoxy, thioketene and thioformyl) in crossed-beam experiments and low temperature rate coefficients for the reaction $S(^1D) + C_2H_4$. PCCP **11**, 4701–4706 (2009)

42. Leonori, F., et al.: Crossed-beam and theoretical studies of the $S(^1D) + C_2H_2$ reaction. J. Phys. Chem. A **113**, 4330–4339 (2009)
43. De Petris, G., Cartoni, A., Rosi, M., Barone, V., Puzzarini, C., Troiani, A.: The proton affinity and gas-phase basicity of sulfur dioxide. ChemPhysChem **12**, 112–115 (2011)
44. Berteloite, C., et al.: Low temperature kinetics, crossed beam dynamics and theoretical studies of the reaction $S(^1D) + CH_4$ and low temperature kinetics of $S(^1D) + C_2H_2$. Phys. Chem. Chem. Phys. **13**, 8485–8501 (2011)
45. Rosi, M., Falcinelli, S., Balucani, N., Casavecchia, P., Leonori, F., Skouteris, D.: Theoretical study of reactions relevant for atmospheric models of Titan: interaction of excited nitrogen atoms with small hydrocarbons. LNCS **7333**, 331–344 (2012)
46. Skouteris, D., Balucani, N., Faginas-Lago, N., Falcinelli, S., Rosi, M.: Dimerization of methanimine and its charged species in the atmosphere of Titan and interstellar/cometary ice analogs. Astron. Astrophys. **584**, A76 (2015)
47. Falcinelli, S., Rosi, M., Cavalli, S., Pirani, F., Vecchiocattivi, F.: Stereoselectivity in autoionization reactions of hydrogenated molecules by metastable gas atoms: the role of electronic couplings. Chem. Eur. J. **22**, 12518–12526 (2016)
48. Troiani, A., Rosi, M., Garzoli, S., Salvitti, C., de Petris, G.: Vanadium hydroxide cluster ions in the gas phase: bond-forming reactions of doubly-charged negative ions by SO_2-promoted V-O activation. Chem. Eur. J. **23**, 11752–11756 (2017)
49. Rosi, M., et al.: An experimental and theoretical investigation of 1-butanol pyrolysis. Front. Chem. **7**, 326 (2019). https://doi.org/10.3389/fchem.2019.00326
50. Moore, C. E.: Atomic Energy Levels, Natl. Bur. Stand. (U.S.) Circ. N. 467. U.S., GPO, Washington (1949)
51. Frisch, M. J., et al.: Gaussian 09, Revision A.02, Gaussian, Inc., Wallingford (2009)
52. Flükiger, P., Lüthi, H. P., Portmann, S., Weber, J., MOLEKEL 4.3, Swiss Center for Scientific Computing, Manno (Switzerland), 2000–2002
53. Portmann, S., Lüthi, H.P.: MOLEKEL: an interactive molecular graphics tool. Chimia **54**, 766–769 (2000)
54. Chin, C.-H., Zhu, T., Zhang, J.Z.H.: Cyclopentadienyl radical formation from the reaction of excited nitrogen atoms with benzene: a theoretical study. PCCP (2021), online version. https://doi.org/10.1039/d1cp00133g

Computing Binding Energies of Interstellar Molecules by Semiempirical Quantum Methods: Comparison Between DFT and GFN2 on Crystalline Ice

Aurèle Germain[1]([✉]) [iD], Marta Corno[1,2] [iD], and Piero Ugliengo[1,2] [iD]

[1] Dipartimento di Chimica, Università degli Studi di Torino,
via P. Giuria 7, 10125 Torino, Italy
aureleroger.germain@unito.it
[2] Nanostructured Interfaces and Surfaces (NIS) Centre, Università degli Studi di
Torino, via P. Giuria 7, 10125 Torino, Italy

Abstract. Interstellar Grains (IGs) spread in the Interstellar Medium (ISM) host a multitude of chemical reactions that could lead to the production of interstellar Complex Organic Molecules (iCOMs), relevant in the context of prebiotic chemistry. These IGs are composed of a silicate-based core covered by several layers of amorphous water ice, known as a grain mantle. Molecules from the ISM gas-phase can be adsorbed at the grain surfaces, diffuse and react to give iCOMs and ultimately desorbed back to the gas phase. Thus, the study of the Binding Energy (BE) of these molecules at the water ice grain surface is important to understand the molecular composition of the ISM and its evolution in time. In this paper, we propose to use a recently developed semiempirical quantum approach, named GFN-xTB, and more precisely the GFN2 method, to compute the BE of several molecular species at the crystalline water ice slab model. This method is very cheap in term of computing power and time and was already showed in a previous work to be very accurate with small water clusters. To support our proposition, we decided to use, as a benchmark, the recent work published by some of us in which a crystalline model of proton-ordered water ice (P-ice) was adopted to predict the BEs of 21 molecules relevant in the ISM. The relatively good results obtained confirm GFN2 as the method of choice to model adsorption processes occurring at the icy grains in the ISM. The only notable exception was for the CO molecule, in which both structure and BE are badly predicted by GFN2, a real pity due to the relevance of CO in astrochemistry.

Keywords: Interstellar medium · Interstellar icy grains · Complexes organic molecules · Semiempirical quantum methods · GFN2

1 Introduction

Astronomical observations tell us that the Interstellar Medium (ISM) is rich in molecules that may become relevant in the prebiotic context.

© The Author(s) 2021
O. Gervasi et al. (Eds.): ICCSA 2021, LNCS 12953, pp. 632–645, 2021.
https://doi.org/10.1007/978-3-030-86976-2_43

These molecules can be produced by diverse chemical processes inside the gas phase of the ISM, but some molecules like H_2 (the most abundant molecule in the ISM [15,17]) cannot be formed by simple gas-phase process [15,17]. However, the presence inside the ISM of micron-sized particles called Interstellar Grains (IGs), made of a silicate core covered by several layers of amorphous ice mantles [3,12,18], are the place where H atoms get adsorbed and the excess energy dispersed into the grain when H_2 is finally formed. Indeed, these IGs host chemical reactions producing interstellar Organic Molecules (iCOMs) by absorbing the excess of energy due to the bond formation of the iCOMs [13], while also acting, in specific cases, as a catalyst by reducing the activation energy [7,14]. Thus, chemical reactions at the surfaces of IGs could explain the presence in the ISM of molecules not feasible through gas phase processes.

The information about binding energies (BEs) of interstellar molecules on the grain is, therefore, essential for understanding the adsorption, movement, and desorption of iCOMs. All this is essential in order to understand the amount and distribution of iCOM in the gas-phase, as the BE controls both the diffusivity and the velocity of desorption from the grain towards the gas-phase where further processing of the iCOM will occur. Numerical models are, indeed, based on these data to provide the chemical composition of the ISM.

The BEs can be worked out in terrestrial laboratory by temperature programmed desorption (TPD), but the extreme conditions of the ISM (low temperature, low pressure, and very long time scale) hinders the real possibility to mimic the actual interstellar conditions. Quantum computation can be adopted as a useful complementary tool to the experimental data, provided that proper comparison between TPD extracted BE and those computed by quantum mechanical methods are properly made [8].

2   Methodology

2.1   Computational Method

In this work we aim at benchmarking a recently developed semiempirical quantum mechanical method (SQM) called GFN-xTB and more precisely the GFN2 method [1,2]. This method is being developed by the Grimme's group at the Bonn University and can be almost three orders of magnitude faster than conventional DFT methods; it can be used efficiently on simple desk computers and, indeed, every result showed in this paper was computed using a laptop computer equipped with an Intel i5 CPU and 8 GB of RAM.

We chose to use GFN-xTB not only because it is inexpensive in time and computational power, but also because it is particularly well suited for the system we want to study (IG made mostly of water ice), owning to its excellent performance in treating systems dominated by non-covalent interactions (H-bonds included), as it is the case of iCOMs adsorbed on water ice.

In a previous work [10], we showed that the method was accurate to deal with small water clusters for both energy and structures; here, we extended the applicability of the GFN2 method to model the interaction between a large number of relevant iCOMs adsorbed on a crystalline model of water ice. Our target is to establish whether GFN2 can compete with more robust and accurate DFT methods, as recently adopted by some of us [8], to model realistic and amorphous water clusters close to the real grains compared to the crystalline ice adopted here.

2.2   Computational Dataset

The set of data used to benchmark the GFN2 method for the computation of BEs was taken from Ferrero et al. 2020 work [8].

In that work Ferrero et al. [8] computed the BEs of 21 interstellar molecules, four of which were radicals. The BEs were computed using DFT/A-VTZ* method (M06-2X for radicals and B3LYP-D3 for closed shell ones).

In contrast to other computational chemistry work on BEs which use grain models composed of a few water molecules [6,16], Ferrero et al. [8] used a crystalline (010) slab model of proton-ordered ice (P-ice) [4] to simulate the grain structure, within the paradigm of the periodic boundary conditions. This crystalline model does not properly represent IGs, known to be amorphous. Nonetheless, the periodic boundaries used in the work by Ferrero et al. [8] indicated that the hydrogen bond cooperativity, too often underestimated in small water clusters mimicking the icy grains, is accurately represented.

Ferrero et al. [8] also adopted an amorphous periodic water model to study the BEs. This amorphous water slab is closer to the expected structure of IGs compared to a crystalline structure, but is not taken into account here as it is too difficult to simulate by a finite cluster (*vide infra*) as we did for the crystalline ice model.

2.3   Crystalline Slab Model

We cannot perform a one by one comparison with the Ferrero et al. [8] results as the periodic boundary condition (PBC) implementation in GFN-xTB does not include the GFN2 hamiltonian. Furthermore, the PBC coding in the xTB program is still under development. Therefore, we prefer to use a large molecular cube envisaging 84 water molecules (see Fig. 1) cut out from the periodic crystalline slab by Ferrero et al. [8].

This slab ensures that the dangling hydrogen (dH) and oxygen (dO) shown in Fig. 1, and acting as a binding sites, are properly embedded within surrounding layers of water molecules.

To simulate geometric constraints due to the long-range effects of the periodic boundaries applied to the a and b axis, we fixed the H atoms of the water molecules at the border of the cluster to the periodic conditions, while leaving free to move the H atoms within the core of the cluster. This ensures that the dangling hydrogen dH, used in partnership with the dangling oxygen dO as a binding site for the different chemical species, is unconstrained and free to move.

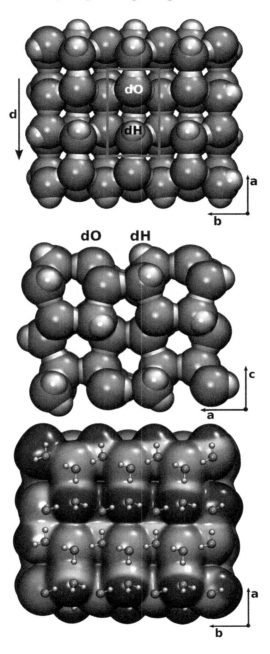

Fig. 1. Slab cut from the proton-ordered P-ice crystal used by Ferrero et al. 2020 [8]. Top: Slab seen from the ab plane with the dO and dH binding sites indicated inside the blue rectangle. The net dipole moment is indicated by a black arrow. Center: Slab seen from the ac plane. Bottom: Electrostatic potential mapped on the electron density of the slab. Negative regions are in red and positive regions are in blue. (Color figure online)

These constrains will also avoid the collapse of the structure during geometry optimisation due to the missing water molecules at the frontiers of the cluster.

2.4   Binding Energies and Role of the ZPE Correction

For each chemical species to be studied we performed a GFN2 optimisation using the "extreme" level of optimisation of GFN-xTB. For each molecule, three optimisations were performed, one for the molecule alone, one for the slab alone, and one for both the slab and the molecule in interaction. The starting positions of the molecules above the binding site were as similar as possible to that adopted by Ferrero et al. 2020 [8] and optimised using GFN2 to check if the GFN-xTB positions after optimisation matched that of the DFT/A-VTZ* calculations. If the final position were significantly different, the starting position of the molecule was changed by trying to reproduce the final position of Ferrero et al. [8] instead of the initial one. The computation was then restarted (in the remainder of this article results for which the final position has been used will be followed by the suffix "-end". For example N_2 indicates results using the starting position and N_2-end indicates results using the final position). This way, we were able to check if the method could maintain this position as a stable one.

The BEs of these chemical species were computed as follow:

$$BE = E_{mol} + E_{slab} - E_{mol+slab} \tag{1}$$

Where E_{mol}, E_{slab}, and $E_{slab+mol}$ are the GFN2 energies after optimisation of the molecule, the 84 water molecules slab with the constrains applied, and the molecule interacting with the slab, respectively.

To confirm that the optimised geometries are minima on the potential energy surface we computed the harmonic vibrational frequencies and checked that all frequencies were real. In case of imaginary frequencies, xTB provides a perturbed geometry which, after optimisation and further vibrational frequency calculation, may end up in a minimum.

From the set of frequencies, also the zero point energy (ZPE) is provided for each component of the BE as:

$$\Delta ZPE = ZPE_{slab+mol} - ZPE_{mol} - ZPE_{slab} \tag{2}$$

We can then obtain the zero point energy corrected binding energies BE(0) by subtracting ΔZPE to the original BE:

$$BE\,(0) = BE - \Delta ZPE \tag{3}$$

In general, the ΔZPE is a positive quantity, therefore the $BE\,(0)$ is always smaller than the uncorrected one.

3   Results and Discussion

The adoption of a finite water cluster to mimic the PBC is not drawback-free. The first one, is the presence of a dipole moment of 14.4 Debye in the a-b plane of the slab and directed along the a cell axis (see Fig. 1). This dipole moment is exactly cancelled out when rigorous PBC are adopted, as in the work by Ferrero et al. [8]. In our case it could alter the behaviour of the most dipolar molecules of the set. The second one, is the fact that even if we try to mimic the long range effects imposed by the periodic boundaries conditions by applying constrains on the slab, this does not include the infinite hydrogen bond cooperativity of the real crystalline material. As a result, the final positions of these molecules could also be impacted.

Table 1. GFN2 BE, zero point energy corrected BE(0) and ΔZPE values (in kJ/mol) for all considered species. For H_2CO and $HCONH_2$ "SC1" and "SC2" refer to different initial positions used for the molecules on the binding sites by Ferrero et al. 2020 [8].

Species	BE		BE(0)		ΔZPE	
	GFN2	DFT	GFN2	DFT	GFN2	DFT
H_2	8.47	9.90	3.48	2.40	5.0	7.5
O_2	40.6	8.50	47.8	6.80	−7.1	1.7
N_2	16.8	13.0	12.6	10.4	4.2	2.6
N_2-end	15.6	13.0	13.1	10.4	2.5	2.6
CH_4	21.9	14.0	16.2	11.2	5.8	2.8
CO	39.6	19.6	35.5	15.7	4.1	3.9
CO_2	32.7	28.6	29.4	25.6	3.3	3.0
OCS	27.8	28.9	25.4	26.5	2.4	2.4
HCl	66.4	54.1	58.2	47.4	8.2	6.7
HCN	35.5	42.6	31.2	41.6	4.2	1.0
H_2O	70.0	70.1	58.1	56.3	11.9	13.8
H_2S	44.2	47.2	35.0	38.2	9.2	9.0
NH_3	59.6	61.3	50.0	50.1	9.6	11.2
CH_3CN	52.9	62.8	47.0	56.6	6.0	6.2
CH_3OH	70.7	72.2	62.7	62.6	8.0	9.6
H_2CO-SC1	53.0	48.8	42.5	39.6	10.5	9.2
H_2CO-SC2	43.8	53.0	36.0	43.9	7.8	9.1
$HCONH_2$-SC1	84.0	79.9	75.1	69.5	8.9	10.4
$HCONH_2$-SC2	80.8	83.8	71.2	71.3	9.6	12.5
HCOOH	86.4	78.5	81.5	71.7	4.9	6.8
OH	115	54.4	127	43.3	−11.8	11.1
HCO	38.5	28.9	31.4	20.2	7.1	8.7
CH_3	35.8	21.3	29.8	14.3	6.0	7.0
CH_3-end	23.8	21.3	17.4	14.3	6.4	7.0

The binding energy values are given in Table 1.

GFN2 results are in good agreement with the DFT ones except for some unusual cases, mainly: CH_3, CO, HCO, OH, and O_2. All of them, except CO, are radicals (the ground state of O_2 is a triplet) making them highly reactive. Thus, they demand a level of theory that GFN2 cannot provide.

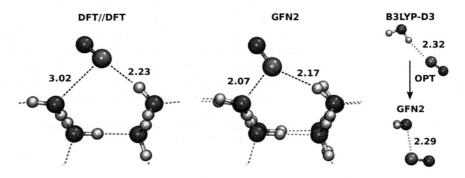

Fig. 2. Left: DFT//DFT results for CO. From Ferrero et al. 2020 [8]. Centre: GFN2 results for CO. Right: $H_2O - CO$ dimer with the starting geometry from B3LYP-D3/aug-cc-pVTZ on top and the GFN2 optimised geometry at the bottom. Dotted lines were added to emphasise the H--C and C--O interactions.

The particularly intriguing electron configuration of CO gives to the molecule a very weak dipole moment (with the negative pole located at the C atom) and a large quadrupole. The experimental dipole moment is 0.11 D [11], with carbon atom carrying the negative end despite being less electronegative than oxygen (see Ref. [9]). GFN2 overestimates the dipole moment (0.615 D) and swaps the charges (+0.0049 e on carbon) with respect to accurate calculations. This affect the results as, usually, CO interacts preferentially from the C-end when involved in H-bond interactions (see Fig. 2 Left) or with net charges like Na^+. Unfortunately, GFN2 is unable to treat such a delicate bonding situation for CO interacting with the grain (see Fig. 2 Centre). Even when CO is put in interaction with a single water molecule, the optimised structure differs dramatically from the optimum B3LYP-D3/aug-cc-pvTZ one taken as internal reference, due to the bad description of the electronic structure of CO (see Fig. 2 Right). This is very unfortunate, owning to the general good performance of GFN2, and due to the extreme relevance of CO in the astrochemical context (the second most abundant gas-phase molecule in the ISM).

Figure 3 shows the comparison between the structures of a subset of the considered molecules computed at GFN2 with that resulting by the DFT optimization by Ferrero et al. The agreement is, in general, very good considering the speedup due to GFN2. Also, the critical case of the methyl radical is well reproduced.

Figure 4 compares the GFN2 BEs against the DFT ones. We exclude from the correlation these unusual cases: O_2, CO, OH, CH_3, simply showing the more common molecules of the set. For both the BE and BE(0) the linear correlation is close to the "ideal line", i.e. the trend line we would have obtained if the GFN2

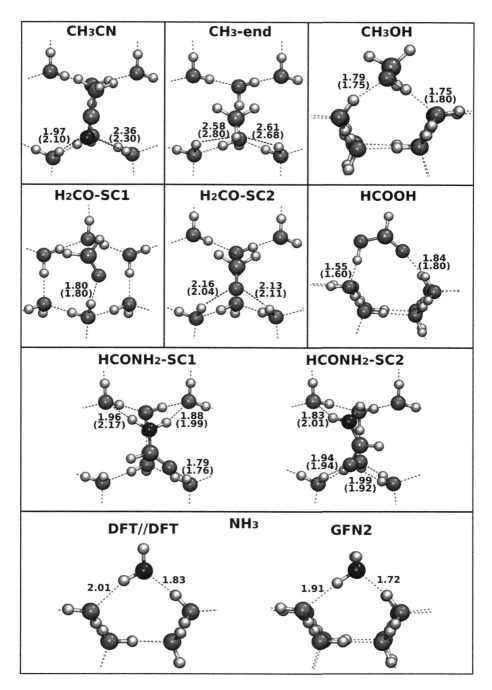

Fig. 3. Comparison between DFT structures (in parenthesis) from Ferrero et al. 2020 [8] and GFN2 results for selected molecules. Distances in unit of Å.

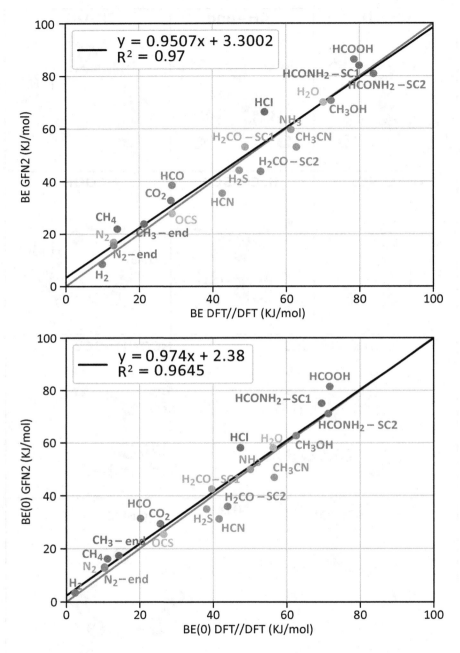

Fig. 4. Up: Linear fit (black line) between BEs using DFT//DFT results available in Ferrero et al. 2020 [8] and BEs using GFN2. The grey line represents the "ideal line". Down: Same as up except the BEs are ZPE corrected in both cases.

results were exactly equal to the DFT ones computed by Ferrero et al. [8]. The good agreement is also evidence that the relative high dipole moment in the crystalline ice plane does not affect the GFN2 BE to a significative extent.

Fine analysis of data in Fig. 4 allows to detect specific cases with larger deviations, namely:

- HCl: +12.2 kJ/mol (22.6%) for the BE (when compared to DFT//DFT results) and +10.8 kJ/mol (22.7%) for the ZPE corrected BE(0) (when compared to ZPE corrected DFT//DFT results)
- HCN: −7.14 (16.8%) for the BE and −10.4 (24.9%) for the BE(0)
- CH$_3$CN: −9.85 (15.7%) for the BE and −9.64 (17.0%) for the BE(0)
- H$_2$CO-SC2: −9.22 (17.4%) for the BE and −7.95 (18.1%) for the BE(0)
- HCOOH: +7.86 (10.0%) for the BE and +9.76 (13.6%) for the BE(0)

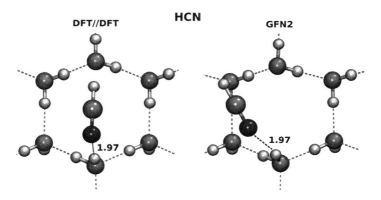

Fig. 5. Left: DFT//DFT results for HCN. From Ferrero et al. 2020 [8]. Right: GFN2 results for HCN.

In this list, only HCN shows a significant difference in the final molecule position compared to Ferrero et al. 2020 [8] (as can be seen on Fig. 5). The nitrogen is still accepting the hydrogen bond from the dH, but the HCN hydrogen does not make a H-bond with the dO going toward an adjacent dangling oxygen. This is due to the delicate balance between the H-bond donor/acceptor geometrical features which is handled differently by GFN2 compared to DFT. Therefore, HCN is probably a critical molecule for GFN2 for the same reasons explained for the CO case, as the triple bond electronic features are difficult to describe.

Correcting the BE for ZPE is important in the astrochemical context of the cold (10K) molecular clouds. Unfortunately, the frequency calculations can be quite demanding, due to the calculation of the expensive Hessian matrix. Therefore, it is important to establish how much the BE are affected by the ZPE correction. Figure 6 shows, indeed, that a very robust linear correlation exists between the two set of BE and BE(0) values. This implies that BE(0) values can be arrived at without actually computing the vibrational frequencies,

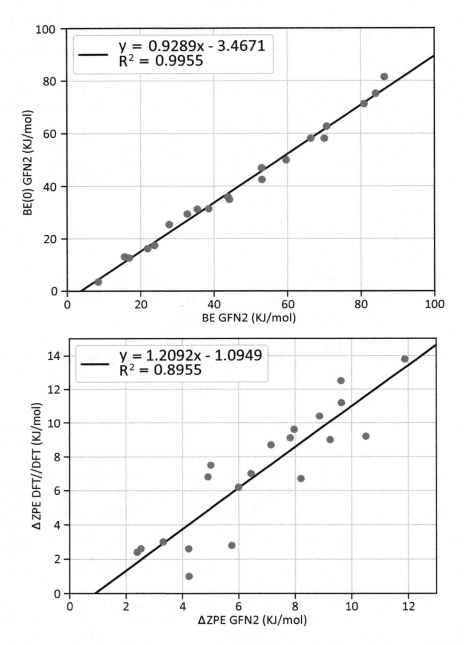

Fig. 6. Top: Linear fit between GFN2 BE and BE(0). Bottom: Linear fit between GFN2 ΔZPE and DFT//DFT ΔZPE.

by a simple re-scaling of the BE values. This has important consequences for the future calculations in which the BE of iCOMs will be computed with respect to large amorphous icy grains than the present crystalline model. Even more important is to establish whether the ΔZPE computed by GFN2 (very cheap) correlates with the corresponding DFT ones reported by Ferrero et al. [8] (very expensive). The graph in the bottom part of Fig. 6 reveals that the correlation is only coarse: unfortunately, one cannot adopt the GFN2 ΔZPE to correct the DFT BE.

4 Conclusion

In this work we benchmarked the GFN2 method provided by the GFN-xTB program developed by the Grimme's group at the Bohn university, against DFT results from the work by Ferrero et al. 2020 [8]. The benchmark consisted in comparing structures and binding energies (BE) of a large set of interstellar molecules adsorbed at the surface of a crystalline, proton ordered ice cluster grain model. This cluster was cut out from the periodic P-ice adopted by Ferrero et al. [8] as a crystalline model for the interstellar ice. We also extended the comparison to study the role of zero point energy correction to the electronic BEs. The comparison is biased by the adoption of a molecular cluster of 84 water molecules to represent an otherwise periodic crystalline model as reported by Ferrero et al. 2020 [8]. Nevertheless, the results showed excellent performance of the GFN2 for both structures and BE, with some important exceptions, namely radical species and the CO molecule. As many radical species are also challenging for DFT functionals, we did not expect good GFN2 performance. The bad behaviour for CO is, instead, much more serious, due to the relevance of this molecule in the ISM. Unfortunately, GFN2 badly fails in predicting even the corrected structure, in which CO is H-bonded through its carbon end with the dH of the ice surface.

We also showed that the zero point energy corrected BE(0) nicely correlates with the uncorrected BE ones, allowing to skip the very expensive calculation of the Hessian matrix in future applications of GFN2 for the larger icy grain models.

In conclusion, we are optimistic about the application of the GFN2 method to model large icy grain models closer in size to the real grain than what has been simulated up to now. The excellent performance for structures and BE also allows to use GFN2 as a promising low model method in a refined ONIOM approach [5], in which high DFT/MP2/CCSD(T) level of theory for a limited portion of the icy grain where the adsorption takes place are adopted to compute very accurate BE values. This is the subject of future work by our group.

Acknowledgements. This project has received funding from the European Union's Horizon 2020 research and innovation programme under the Marie Skłodowska-Curie grant agreement No 811312 for the project "Astro-Chemical Origins" (ACO).

Images of 3D molecule rendering were made with VMD. VMD is developed with NIH support by the Theoretical and Computational Biophysics group at the Beckman Institute, University of Illinois at Urbana- Champaign.

References

1. Bannwarth, C., et al.: Extended tight-binding quantum chemistry methods. WIREs Comput. Mol. Sci. **11**(2), 1–49 (2021). https://doi.org/10.1002/wcms.1493
2. Bannwarth, C., Ehlert, S., Grimme, S.: GFN2-xTB - An accurate and broadly parametrized self-consistent tight-binding quantum chemical method with multipole electrostatics and density-dependent dispersion contributions. J. Chem. Theory Comput. **15**(3), 1652–1671 (2019). https://doi.org/10.1021/acs.jctc.8b01176
3. Boogert, A.C., Gerakines, P.A., Whittet, D.C.: Observations of the icy universe. Ann. Rev. Astron. Astrophys. **53**(1), 541–581 (2015). https://doi.org/10.1146/annurev-astro-082214-122348
4. Casassa, S., Ugliengo, P., Pisani, C.: Proton-ordered models of ordinary ice for quantum-mechanical studies. J. Chem. Phys. **106**(19), 8030–8040 (1997). https://doi.org/10.1063/1.473813
5. Chung, L.W., et al.: The oniom method and its applications. Chem. Rev. **115**(12), 5678–5796 (2015). https://doi.org/10.1021/cr5004419
6. Das, A., Sil, M., Gorai, P., Chakrabarti, S.K., Loison, J.C.: An approach to estimate the binding energy of interstellar species. arXiv **237**(1), 9 (2018). https://doi.org/10.3847/1538-4365/aac886
7. Enrique-Romero, J., Rimola, A., Ceccarelli, C., Ugliengo, P., Balucani, N., Skouteris, D.: Reactivity of HCO with CH$_3$ and NH$_2$ on water ice surfaces. A comprehensive accurate quantum chemistry study. ACS Earth Space Chem. **3**(10), 2158–2170 (2019). https://doi.org/10.1021/acsearthspacechem.9b00156
8. Ferrero, S., Zamirri, L., Ceccarelli, C., Witzel, A., Rimola, A., Ugliengo, P.: Binding energies of interstellar molecules on crystalline and amorphous models of water ice by ab-initio calculations. Astrophys. J. **904**(1), 11 (2020). https://doi.org/10.3847/1538-4357/abb953
9. Frenking, G., Loschen, C., Krapp, A., Fau, S., Strauss, S.H.: Electronic structure of CO-an exercise in modern chemical bonding theory. J. Comput. Chem. **28**(1), 117–126 (2007). https://doi.org/10.1002/jcc.20477
10. Germain, A., Ugliengo, P.: Modeling interstellar amorphous solid water grains by tight-binding based methods: comparison between GFN-XTB and CCSD(T) results for water clusters. In: Gervasi, O., et al. (eds.) ICCSA 2020. LNCS, vol. 12253, pp. 745–753. Springer, Cham (2020). https://doi.org/10.1007/978-3-030-58814-4_62
11. Muenter, J.: Electric dipole moment of carbon monoxide. J. Mol. Spectrosc. **55**(1–3), 490–491 (1975). https://doi.org/10.1016/0022-2852(75)90287-8
12. Oba, Y., Miyauchi, N., Hidaka, H., Chigai, T., Watanabe, N., Kouchi, A.: Formation of compact amorphous H$_2$O ice by codeposition of hydrogen atoms with oxygen molecules on grain surfaces. Astrophys. J. **701**(1), 464–470 (2009). https://doi.org/10.1088/0004-637X/701/1/464
13. Pantaleone, S., Enrique-Romero, J., Ceccarelli, C., Ugliengo, P., Balucani, N., Rimola, A.: Chemical desorption versus energy dissipation: insights from ab-initio molecular dynamics of HCO formation. arXiv **897**(1), 56 (2020). https://doi.org/10.3847/1538-4357/ab8a4b
14. Rimola, A., et al.: Can formamide be formed on interstellar ice? An atomistic perspective. ACS Earth Space Chem. **2**(7), 720–734 (2018). https://doi.org/10.1021/acsearthspacechem.7b00156
15. Vidali, G.: H$_2$ formation on interstellar grains. Chem. Rev. **113**(12), 8762–8782 (2013). https://doi.org/10.1021/cr400156b

16. Wakelam, V., Loison, J.C., Mereau, R., Ruaud, M.: Binding energies: new values and impact on the efficiency of chemical desorption. Mol. Astrophys. **6**, 22–35 (2017). https://doi.org/10.1016/j.molap.2017.01.002
17. Wakelam, V., et al.: H_2 formation on interstellar dust grains: the viewpoints of theory, experiments, models and observations. Mol. Astrophys. **9**, 1–36 (2017). https://doi.org/10.1016/j.molap.2017.11.001
18. Watanabe, N., Kouchi, A.: Ice surface reactions: a key to chemical evolution in space. Prog. Surf. Sci. **83**(10–12), 439–489 (2008). https://doi.org/10.1016/j.progsurf.2008.10.001

Autoionization Processes Involving Molecules of Atmospheric Interest: A Computational Test for Ne*-N2 System

Stefano Falcinelli[1]([⊠]) [iD], Franco Vecchiocattivi[1], and Fernando Pirani[2,3]

[1] Department of Civil and Environmental Engineering, University of Perugia,
Via G. Duranti 93, 06125 Perugia, Italy
stefano.falcinelli@unipg.it, franco@vecchio.it
[2] Department of Chemistry, Biology and Biotechnologies, University of Perugia,
Via Elce di Sotto 8, 06100 Perugia, Italy
fernando.pirani@unipg.it
[3] ISTM-CNR, 06123 Perugia, Italy

Abstract. This paper provides basic aspects of the stereodynamics of autoionization reactions, triggered by collisions of N_2 molecules with metastable neon atoms, $Ne^*(^3P_{2,0})$, that are of great relevance for the balance of phenomena occurring in atmospheric environments under various conditions. A computational analysis based on the long-range intermolecular forces involved, some of chemical and other of physical origin, allows a first attempt in order to reproduce experimental data from our and other laboratories. This is a good test of the reliability of our recently proposed semiclassical model for atom-atom self-ionization processes and here extended to a simple atom-molecule system.

Keywords: Autoionization · Stereo-dynamics · State to state · Charge transfer · Transition state · Electron spectroscopy · Astrochemistry

1 Introduction

It is well known that the stable-closed shell nature of noble gas atoms Ng (Ng = He, Ne, Ar, Kr and Xe) explains their chemical inertness [1]. On the other hand, when Ng is excited in electronic metastable states (producing Ng^* atom) it assumes an open shell structure and because of its high energy content becomes extremely reactive. In general, Ng^* atoms live for a time sufficient long to give several collisions with other partners even under gaseous rarefied conditions of pressure [2–6]. Ng^* can be formed by collisions of Ng atoms with cosmic rays and/or energetic electrons and their two body collisions with neutral atomic/molecular M partners can promote autoionization reactions, from sub-thermal (cold chemistry) [7], of relevance in astrochemistry [8, 9], up to hyper-thermal (hot chemistry) conditions, of importance in combustion and flames [10, 11], with the formation of NgM^+ (associate ion) and/or $Ng + M^+$(Penning ion) + electrons as products. Highest energetic He^* and Ne^* atoms trigger autoionization with

© Springer Nature Switzerland AG 2021
O. Gervasi et al. (Eds.): ICCSA 2021, LNCS 12953, pp. 646–657, 2021.
https://doi.org/10.1007/978-3-030-86976-2_44

most part of neutral species and in the case of molecular partners also ions coming from the fragmentation of parent M^+ can be formed [2–4].

Because of their relevance in the balance of microscopic processes occurring in plasmas, electric discharges and laser systems, autoionization reactions have been investigated in bulk, and under single collision conditions with the molecular beam technique [2–6]. Important experimental findings have been provided by measuring the collision energy dependence of total and partial (i.e., referred to specific reaction channels) ionization cross sections and of Penning ionization electron spectra (PIES). All these findings depend on different features of the optical potential, formerly introduced for the description of nuclear reactive collisions [12], whose real part drives the collision dynamics while its imaginary part, triggering the passage from neutral reagents to ionic products, accounts for the "opacity" of the system [3, 4]. However, up to day information on important details of the intermolecular forces controlling the optical potential, as their nature and their dependence on the relative orientation of involved partners, and consequently on their effect on the reaction stereo-dynamics, is rather limited.

Recently, we have proposed an applied a new/original method for the detailed representation of autoionization processes promoted by collisions of $Ne^*(^3P_{2,0})$ with Ar, Kr and Xe and such study provided an internal consistent rationalization of available experimental findings [13–15]. In particular, the proper characterization of the intermolecular forces that drive the atom-atom reaction dynamics casted light on basic/innovative aspects concerning rearrangement and angular momentum coupling of valence electron. Obtained results must be considered of general interest for the control of many other elementary chemical reactions. In particular, the application of our method suggests that autoionization can occur through the competition of two alternative (*direct/indirect*) reaction mechanisms driven by the selectivity of intermolecular forces of different nature [14, 15]. The *direct mechanism*, dominant at short separation distances of reagents, is basically controlled by chemical forces due to charge (electron) transfer (CT) effects. The *indirect mechanism*, prevalent at large separation distances, originates from weaker forces of more physical origin, as those due to dispersion, induction-polarization contributions and those promoting spin-orbit and centrifugal-Coriolis effects. Moreover, while the *direct mechanism* controls the evolution of prototype elementary *oxidation reactions* [14, 15], the *indirect mechanism* triggers typical *radiative (photo)-ionization processes* [16, 17].

The present target is to extend this method to study autoionization reactions of molecules and a preliminary objective to be achieved is the correct identification of nature and strength of intermolecular forces controlling structure and stability of the reaction transition state (TS). It is of relevance to note that intermolecular forces involved in autoionization reactions involving molecules are usually stronger, more anisotropic and including additional components respected to the atom-atom case [13, 14].

2 Modelling the Internuclear Interaction

The computational model used to describe both atom-atom and atom-molecules autoionization reactions is based on the Optical Potential Model (OPM) proposed by Hans Bethe in 1940 [12], where a complex potential W is used to describe the microscopic autoionization dynamics according to the following equation:

$$W = V - \frac{i}{2}\Gamma \tag{1}$$

V is the real part describing the $Ng^* + M$ interaction in the incoming collision (where M can be an atomic or molecular target) and Γ is the imaginary part that takes into account the probability of the autoionization of the intermediate collisional complex $[Ng\text{---}M]^*$, which is the transition state (TS) of the reaction [16, 18, 19].

The novelty of our semiclassical treatment, already proposed and successfully applied to simple atom-atom autoionization processes [13–15, 20, 21] consider the two V and Γ components as interdependent [6, 14, 15]. The general treatment can be found in details in refs. [14, 22] pointing out the differences with previous adopted models for autoionization processes [23, 24]. Its application and obtained results in the description of state-to-state $Ne^*(^3P_{2,0})$-Ar, Kr and Xe atom-atom autoionizing systems are reported in refs. [13–15]. The selectivity of the electronic rearrangements triggering the two microscopic mechanisms operative in such atom-atom auotionization reactions (see the *direct* and *indirect mechanisms* mentioned above) has been related to the angular momentum couplings by Hund's cases and is fully described in ref. [23]. Here, in the following subsection, a first computational attempt to extend our treatment to the atom-molecule case is done, considering the simple Ne^*-N_2 system which is relevant for an atmospheric point of view. Further details concerning the computational procedure and the modelling of the intermolecular potential are given in refs. [25, 26].

2.1 Extension to Autoionization Reactions Involving Molecules

Preliminary, it is convenient to consider N_2 and N_2^+ as isotropic partners. According to the general features discussed in details in refs. [14, 22], also for atom-molecule autoionizing systems is important to evaluate only C_x (C_x and C_y are the radial dependence of the Σ character coefficients in entrance, $[Ng\text{---}M]^*$, and in exit, $[Ng\text{---}M]^+$, channels, respectively [14]): $C_y = 1$ is assumed to hold at all internuclear distances, R, as suggested by the electronic structure of the N_2^+ product, extending the previous relations obtained in the case of atom-atom autoionization:

$$V_{|2,0>}, V_{|2,1>} = cos^2\alpha V_\Sigma + sin^2\alpha V_\Pi \tag{2}$$

$$V_{|0,0>} = sin^2\alpha V_\Sigma + cos^2\alpha V_\Pi \tag{3}$$

$$V_{|2,2>} = V_\Pi \tag{4}$$

$$cos^2\alpha = \frac{1}{2} + \frac{\left(1 - \frac{9V_2}{5\Delta}\right)}{4\sqrt{2}\sqrt{1 + \left[\left(\frac{1-\frac{9V_2}{5\Delta}}{2\sqrt{2}}\right)\right]^2}} \tag{5}$$

Where, for all channels: the effective adiabatic potential energy curves are expressed as $V_{|J;\Omega>}$ (J is the total electronic angular momentum quantum number, defining also the spin orbit level, while Ω quantizes the absolute projection of the $\mathbf{J}$ along R); the coupling terms $A_{\Lambda-\Lambda'}$ between entrance and exit channels (i.e. $A_{\Sigma-\Sigma}, A_{\Pi-\Pi}, A_{\Sigma-\Pi}$ and $A_{\Pi-\Sigma}$), on the basis of Σ and Π molecular character of initial and final states of the system involved in the electron exchange have been adopted (Σ ($\Lambda = 0$) and Π ($\Lambda = 1$) are the molecular states of different symmetry and accessible to the colliding system – see ref. [14] for more details); for both entrance and exit channels, V_2, that we have identified with the anisotropic configuration interaction between entrance and exit channels (see refs. [14, 15]), has been represented by an exponential decreasing function, defined by a pre-exponential factor A and an exponent α which is given by Eq. (5); Δ is the energy splitting SO between fine atomic sublevels, identified by the quantum number J.

For such reactions it can be assumed that only $A_{\Sigma-\Sigma}$ and $A_{\Pi-\Sigma}$ couplings are effective for the electron rearrangements, since they are also the most important couplings in atom-molecule processes of present interest. Here, it is convenient to identify $A_{\Sigma-\Sigma}$ and $A_{\Pi-\Sigma}$ with A_{DM} and A_{IM}. They represent, respectively, the coupling that promotes the *direct mechanism* (*DM*), through the control the chemical reactivity, and the *indirect mechanism* (*IM*) to which important contributions come from polarization, that stimulates photo-ionization, spin-orbit and Coriolis couplings *effects*.

Accordingly, the following relations are obtained for state-to-state Γ components:

$$\Gamma_{|0,0\rightarrow ions>} = A_{DM}\, C_x + +A_{IM}\,(1 - C_x) \tag{6}$$

$$\Gamma_{|2,0\rightarrow ions>} = A_{DM}\,(1 - C_x) + A_{IM}\, C_x \tag{7}$$

$$\Gamma_{|2,1\rightarrow ions>} = A_{DM}\,\frac{3}{4}(1 - C_x) + A_{IM}\left(\frac{3}{4}C_x + \frac{1}{4}\right) \tag{8}$$

$$\Gamma_{|2,2\rightarrow ions>} = A_{IM} \tag{9}$$

On this ground, it is possible to obtain the Γ dependence only on $\mathbf{J}$ of the entrance channels and averaged on Ω:

$$\Gamma_{|0\rightarrow ions>} = A_{DM}\, C_x + +A_{IM}\,(1 - C_x) \tag{10}$$

$$\Gamma_{|2\rightarrow ions>} = \frac{1}{2}[A_{DM}\,(1 - C_x) + A_{IM}\,(1 + C_x)] \tag{11}$$

The Γ averaged on the spin orbit states of reagents is given by:

$$\Gamma_{|ions>} = w_0[A_{DM}\, C_x + A_{IM}\,(1 - C_x)] + \frac{w_2}{2}[A_{DM}\,(1 - C_x) + A_{IM}\,(1 + C_x)] \tag{12}$$

If it is assumed that $\frac{w_0}{w_2} = \frac{1}{3}$ (the statistical weight ratio in the case of ^3P_J open shell atomic species like $Ne^*(^3P_{2,0})$, see ref. [14]), the final relation is obtained

$$\Gamma_{|ions>} = \frac{1}{8}[A_{DM}\,(3 - C_x) + A_{IM}\,(5 + C_x)] \tag{13}$$

Now, if we can assume that only $A_{\Pi-\Pi}$ and $A_{\Sigma-\Pi}$ are effective for the reaction we obtain the same equation with inverted coefficients is otained. Specifically:

$$\Gamma_{|0,0\rightarrow ions>} = A_{IM} C_x + +A_{DM} (1 - C_x) \tag{14}$$

$$\Gamma_{|2,0\rightarrow ions>} = A_{IM} (1 - C_x) + A_{DM} C_x \tag{15}$$

$$\Gamma_{|2,1\rightarrow ions>} = A_{IM} \frac{3}{4}(1 - C_x) + A_{DM} \left(\frac{3}{4}C_x + \frac{1}{4}\right) \tag{16}$$

$$\Gamma_{|2,2\rightarrow ions>} = A_{DM} \tag{17}$$

Accordingly, also previous equations modify consistently. For instance:

$$\Gamma_{|ions>} = w_0[A_{DM} (1 - C_x) + A_{IM} C_x] + \frac{w_2}{2}[A_{DM} (1 + C_x) + A_{IM} (1 - C_x)] \tag{18}$$

2.2   Modelling the Intermolecular Interaction on Ne*-N$_2$ Autoionizing System

A proper study of autoionization processes involving molecules must include also the dependence on the molecular orientation. For all the components of the interaction (see the real part V of the OPM of Eq. (1)) an expansion in Legendre polynomials is adopted, where $P_0 = 1$ and θ defines the orientation of the molecules respect the Ne* atom ($\theta = 0$ indicates a collinear approach):

$$P_2(\cos \theta) = \frac{3\cos^2(\theta) - 1}{2} \tag{19}$$

This procedure concerns both the real and the imaginary part of the optical potential.

2.2.1   The [Ne---N$_2$]* Entrance Channel

For atom-atom systems a manifold of potential energy curves, properly coupled and depending on R, describes the dynamical evolution of the processes. For atom-molecule systems the dynamics is controlled by a manifold of potential energy surfaces, whose main features are here obtained extending the atom-atom treatment.

In the formulas of the intermolecular potentials $V_{|J,\Omega>}$ introduced for atom-atom systems [14], the term $V_0(R)$ ($V_0 = \frac{1}{3}(V_\Sigma + 2V_\Pi)$), describing the spherical average interaction component, is now replaced by:

$$V_0(R, \theta) = V_{nel}^{i-n}(R, \theta) + V_{elect}(R, \theta) \quad \text{when } R < R_0 \tag{20}$$

$$V_0(R, \theta) = V_{nel}^{n-n}(R, \theta) \quad \text{when } R > R_0 \tag{21}$$

where $V_{nel}^{i-n}(R, \theta)$ and $V_{nel}^{n-n}(R, \theta)$ are the components of the potential representing for ion-neutral and neutral-neutral interactions, respectively. For them it is used an

Improved Lennard Jones (ILJ) [25–28] function having the $\varepsilon(meV)$ and $R_m(\text{Å})$ parameters defined as it follows in terms of the polarizability of the neutral and ionic species involved:

$$-n - n \text{ case } R_m(\theta) = 5.70 + 0.00 \, P_2(\cos\theta); \, \varepsilon(\theta) = 3.15 + 0.00 \, P_2(\cos\theta) \quad (22)$$

$$-i - n \text{ case } R_m(\theta) = 2.96 + 0.35 \, P_2(\cos\theta); \, \varepsilon(\theta) = 114.0 + 16.0 \, P_2(\cos\theta) \quad (23)$$

The further contribution $V_{elect}(R, \theta)$ here added describes the electrostatic interaction between the ion Ne^+, nascent as a consequence of the $3s$ electron polarization of Ne^* in the collision complex, and the electric permanent quadrupole of N_2. For the term $V_{elect}(R, \theta)$, given in meV, the formulation adopted in the case of the Ar^+-N_2 interaction [29] has properly extended, leading to:

$$V_{elect}(R, \theta) = -\frac{3996}{R^3} P_2(\cos\theta) \quad (24)$$

As previously done for the atom-atom case [14], the two types of interactions must be combined with a Fermi function dependent on R_0 and d. Also here, $R_0 = 3.72$ Å is the distance where the two combined limiting potential forms have the same weight, while $d = 0.5$ Å describes how fast the transition occurs.

In the adiabatic formulation of $V_{|J,\Omega>}$ appears also the V_2 term, $V_2 = \frac{5}{3}(V_\Sigma - V_\Pi)$, due to the electronic anisotropy of the P atom and related to the charge transfer (CT) term [14]. In the atom-atom case has been used a simple $V_2(R)$, while now for the atom-molecule systems a function $V_2(R, \theta)$ must be adopted. For the Ne^*-N_2 system with the formation of the N_2^+ ion in its ground electronic state ($^2\Sigma$) the following parameterization, estimated on the basis of the noble gas systems already investigated and the couplings identified for the prototype $(Ar-N_2)^+$ system [29], can be used:

$$V_2(R, \theta) = (1.4 \cdot 10^7 + 4.0 \cdot 10^6 \cdot P_2(\cos\theta)) \cdot e^{-4.32 \cdot R} \quad (25)$$

2.2.2 The [Ne—N₂]⁺ Exit Channel

In this case, the representation of the real part V of the OPM (see Eq. (1)) is easier than before being facilitated by the fact that there is no spin-orbit coupling that mixes the states with different electronic symmetry. Therefore, in the case of N_2^+ formation in its ground electronic state $^2\Sigma$, we can use directly the following expression:

$$V_t(R, \theta) = V_{nel}^{i-n}(R, \theta) + V_{CT}(R, \theta) \quad (26)$$

Note that the Eq. (26) also includes the coupling for CT with the excited electronic state $^2\Pi$ of N_2^+ which, even if it cannot be formed by autoionization since Ne^* does not have enough energy, is part of the configuration interaction [14, 15].

For the $V_{nel}^{i-n}(R, \theta)$ term the following parameters can be used:

$$R_m(\theta) = 3.30 + 0.35 \, P_2(\cos\theta); \, \varepsilon(\theta) = 30.0 - 13.2 \, P_2(\cos\theta) \quad (27)$$

While the $V_{CT}(R, \theta)$ term becomes equal to $\simeq -\frac{2}{5} V_2(R, \theta)$.

In the case of the formation of N_2^+ in the $^2\Pi$ excited electronic state, the formulation of $V_{nel}^{i-n}(R, \theta)$ term remains the same than before, while the $V_{CT}(R, \theta)$ term becomes equal to $\simeq -\frac{3}{5} V_2(R, \theta)$, as suggested by the greater overlap and greater proximity between the entrance and exit ionic state, as demonstrated previously for the prototype system $(Ar-N_2)^+$ [29].

2.2.3 Definition of $\Gamma(R,\theta)$ and Autoionization Probability

The $V_2(R, \theta)$ term, defined in Eq. (25), it is also used to calculate the coefficient C_x which appears in the weight of the *direct* and *indirect* mechanisms, i.e. in the weight with which to combine the A_{DM} e A_{IM} couplings terms necessary to determine the imaginary part Γ of the OPM in its various components according to Eqs. (6)–(18). The definition of the couplings terms can be done as it follows:

$$A_{DM}(meV) = (5.0 \cdot 10^6 + 5.0 \cdot 10^5 \cdot P_2(\cos\theta)) \cdot e^{-4.32 \cdot R} \tag{28}$$

$$A_{IM}(meV) = (1.9 \cdot 10^3 + 3.8 \cdot 10^2 \cdot P_2(\cos\theta)) \cdot e^{-2.20 \cdot R} \tag{29}$$

The full representation of Γ allows for the evaluation of the probability of self-ionization for the system under consideration based on the general treatment extensively described elsewhere [24, 26]. Indeed, along the element dR, at the distance R, during a collision with asymptotic speed g and a collision energy E, with impact parameter b, the probability that the system ionizes is given by Eq. (30) below

$$P(R)dR = \frac{\Gamma(R)}{\hbar g \left[1 - \frac{V(R)}{E} - \frac{b^2}{R^2} \right]^{\frac{1}{2}}} dR. \tag{30}$$

3 Experimental Determination of the Cross Sections

In our laboratory we are able to measure either total and partial ionization cross sections discriminating all the possible product ions by mass spectrometry in a crossed beam apparatus, which has been presented in detail in previous papers [30–33]. Shortly, such apparatus consists of two beams, one of metastable rare gas atoms, generated by electron bombardment (two possible effusive and supersonic beam sources are available with the possibility to change the nozzle temperature and to use the seeded beams technique as described in refs. [34–36]), and the other one of the target molecules in the ground state, that cross at 90°. The product ions are extracted from the scattering volume by an electric field (usually $\approx$150 V/cm).

For the total ion intensity measurement, the ions are directly detected by a channel electron multiplier. For the mass analysis the product ions are focused, mass analyzed by a quadrupole filter, and detected by another channel electron multiplier.

A time-of-flight device was used to obtain the velocity (or collision energy) dependence of cross sections, including those of interest for the present study. A scheme of our crossed molecular beam device is reported in Fig. 1.

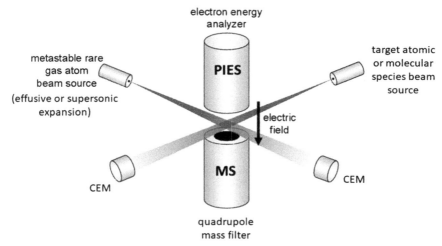

Fig. 1. The crossed molecular beam apparatus working in the Perugia laboratory coupled with mass spectrometry (MS) and Penning ionization electron spectroscopy (PIES). To monitor the metastable rare gas atom beam and the target atomic or molecular species beam, two channel electron multipliers (CEM) are used.

4 Computational Results and Comparison with Experimental Cross Sections

A first attempt has been done in the calculation of the manifold of potential energy surfaces for the $Ne^*(^3P_{2,0})$-N_2 used as a test system applying the computational procedure described in Sect. 2. Involved interaction potentials have been used to calculate the cross sections for the two open channels in the experimentally investigated collision energy range (30–120 meV in our laboratory [37] and 8–60 meV by the Osterwalder group [38]) that are reported below:

$$Ne^*\left(^3P_{2,0}\right) + N_2 \rightarrow Ne + N_2^+ + e^- \text{ (Penning ionization)} \tag{31}$$

$$\rightarrow NeN_2^+ + e^- \text{ (associative ionization)} \tag{32}$$

The results obtained are shown in Fig. 2 where a direct comparison between experimental and computational data can be done.

From Fig. 2 is evident that the experimental data obtained in the Perugia laboratory [37] indicate that in our case the production of the associative ionization (see Eq. (32)) is very low. This is a clear indication that in our experiment performed at thermal collision energy (30–120 meV) there is a prevalent dissociation of the NeN_2^+ ion produced by the autoionization reaction between Ne^* and N_2. On the other hand, the data from the Losanna laboratory obtained in the sub-thermal regime of the collision energy (8–60 meV) [38] are much higher than both our previous experimental determinations and the computational calculations performed according to the procedure illustrated in Sect. 2. This could be an evidence that for this system a clear orientational effect emerges

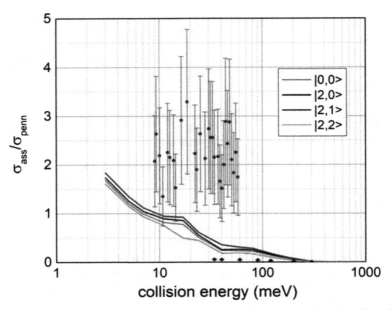

Fig. 2. The ratio between associative and Penning ionization cross sections (see Eqs. (31) and (32)) as a function of the collision energy for the $Ne^*(^3P_{2,0})$-N_2. The curves are the result of the computational calculation based on our model at a state-to-state level for the various $|J,\Omega\rangle$ states (see text). The points are the experimental data obtained in the Losanna laboratory (blue color) [38] and in the Perugia laboratory (black color) [37]. (Color figure online)

when low collision energies are probed. To clarify these effects, further investigations will have to be made, extending this first test on the Ne^*-N_2 system by investigating different angles of approach between the reagents. To this end, further studies are in progress in our laboratory.

5 Conclusions

The present paper extends a new semiclassical method recently proposed by our research group and succesfully applied to autoionization reactions involving Ne^* metastable atoms and simple atomic targets as Ar, Kr and Xe [14, 15] to the stereodynamical study of autoionization reactions of molecules in a quantum state-to-state condition. As a preliminary test has been investigated the $Ne^*(^3P_{2,0})$-N_2 system and useful comparison between experimental data and computational calculations of the Penning and associative ionization is reported showing that a clear orientational effect emerges when low collision energies are probed in the sub-thermal regime. Obtained results are encouraging and open the possibility to apply the proposed computational methodology to the autoionization reactions involving more complex molecules which are of great interest in several fields, including the balance of phenomena occurring in interstellar environments [39–41] and planetary atmospheres [42–44].

Acknowledgments. This work was supported and financed with the "Fondo Ricerca di Base, 2018, dell'Università degli Studi di Perugia" (Project Titled: Indagini teoriche e sperimentali sulla reattività di sistemi di interesse astrochimico). Support from Italian MIUR and University of Perugia (Italy) is acknowledged within the program "Dipartimenti di Eccellenza 2018–2022".

References

1. Nunzi, F., Pannacci, G., Tarantelli, F., Belpassi, L., et al.: Leading interaction components in the structure and reactivity of noble gases compounds. Molecules **25**(10), 2367 (2020)
2. Hotop, H., Illenberger, E., Morgner, H., Niehaus, A.: Penning electron spectra from ionization of hydrogen atoms by He(21S) and He(23S) metastables. Chem. Phys. Lett. **10**(5), 493–497 (1971)
3. Haberland, H., Lee, Y.T., Siska, P.E.: Scattering of noble-gas metastable atoms in molecular beams. Adv. Chem. Phys. **45**(2), 487–585 (1981)
4. Siska, P.E.: Molecular-beam studies of penning ionization. Rev. Mod. Phys. **65**, 337 (1993)
5. Brunetti, B., Vecchiocattivi, F.: Autoionization dynamics of collisional complexes. In: Ng, C.Y., Baer, T., Powis, I. (eds.) Current Topic on Ion Chemistry and Physics, pp. 359–445. Wiley, New York (1993)
6. Falcinelli, S., Pirani, F., Candori, P., Brunetti, B.G., Farrar, J.M., Vecchiocattivi, F.: A new insight on stereo-dynamics of penning ionization reactions. Front. Chem. **7**, 445 (2019). https://doi.org/10.3389/fchem.2019.00445
7. Dulieu, O., Osterwalder, A.: Cold Chemistry. Molecular Scattering and Reactivity Near Absolute Zero, pp. 1–670. Royal Society of Chemistry, Cambridge (2018)
8. Alagia, M., Balucani, N., Candori, P., Falcinelli, S., Pirani, F., Richter, R., et al.: Production of ions at high energy and its role in extraterrestrial environments. Rendiconti Lincei Scienze Fisiche e Naturali **24**(1), 53–65 (2013)
9. Falcinelli, S., Pirani, F., Vecchiocattivi, F.: The possible role of penning ionization processes in planetary atmospheres. Atmosphere **6**(3), 299–317 (2015)
10. Calcote, H.F.: Electrical properties of flames. Symp. Combust. Flame Explosion Phenom. **3**(1), 245–253 (1948)
11. Sugden, T.M.: Excited species in flames. Annu. Rev. Phys. Chem. **13**(1), 369–390 (1962)
12. Bethe, H.A.: A continuum theory of the compound nucleus. Phys. Rev. **57**(12), 1125–1144 (1940)
13. Falcinelli, S., Vecchiocattivi, F., Pirani, F.: Adiabatic and nonadiabatic effects in the transition states of state to state autoionization processes. Phys. Rev. Lett. **121**, 163403 (2018)
14. Falcinelli, S., Vecchiocattivi, F., Pirani, F.: General treatment for stereo-dynamics of state-to-state chemi-ionization reactions. Commun. Chem. **3**, 64 (2020)
15. Falcinelli, S., Farrar, J.M., Vecchiocattivi, F., Pirani, F.: Quantum-state controlled reaction channels in chemi-ionization processes: radiative (optical–physical) and exchange (oxidative–chemical) mechanisms. Acc. Chem. Res. **53**(10), 2248–2260 (2020)
16. Miller, W.H., Morgner, H.: A unified treatment of Penning ionization and excitation transfer. J. Chem. Phys. **67**(11), 4923–4930 (1977)
17. Gregor, R.W., Siska, P.E.: Differential elastic scattering of Ne*(3s 3P2,0) by Ar, Kr, and Xe: optical potentials and their orbital interpretation. J. Chem. Phys. **74**(2), 1078–1092 (1981)
18. Brunetti, B., Candori, P., Falcinelli, S., Pirani, F., Vecchiocattivi, F.: The stereodynamics of the Penning ionization of water by metastable neon atoms. J. Chem. Phys. **139**(16), 164305 (2013)
19. Falcinelli, S., Candori, P., Pirani, F., Vecchiocattivi, F.: The role of charge transfer in the stability and reactivity of chemical systems from experimental findings. Phys. Chem. Chem. Phys. **19**(10), 6933–6944 (2017)

20. Falcinelli, S., Vecchiocattivi, F., Pirani, F.: Electronic rearrangements and angular momentum couplings in quantum state-to-state channels of prototype oxidation processes. J. Phys. Chem. A **125**(7), 1461–1467 (2021)

21. Falcinelli, S., Vecchiocattivi, F., Farrar, J.M., Pirani, F.: Chemi-ionization reactions and basic stereodynamical effects in collisions of atom-molecule reagents. J. Phys. Chem. A **125**(16), 3307–3315 (2021)

22. Falcinelli, S., Vecchiocattivi, F., Pirani, F.: The electron couplings in the transition states: the stereodynamics of state to state autoionization processes. J. Chem. Phys. **150**(4), 044305 (2019)

23. Nakamura, H.: Theoretical considerations on penning ionization processes. J. Phys. Soc. Jpn. **26**(6), 1473–1479 (1969)

24. Miller, W.H.: Theory of penning ionization. I. Atoms. J. Chem. Phys. **52**(7), 3563 (1970)

25. Falcinelli, S., Rosi, M., Candori, P., Vecchiocattivi, et al.: ICCSA 2013, Part I, Lecture Notes in Computer Science LNCS 7971, pp. 69–83. Springer, Cham (2013) https://doi.org/10.1007/978-3-642-39637-3_6

26. Falcinelli, S., Pirani, F., Rosi, M., Vecchiocattivi, F.: Theoretical and computational analysis at a quantum state level of autoionization processes in astrochemistry. In: Gervasi, O., et al. (eds.) ICCSA 2020. LNCS, vol. 12251, pp. 693–706. Springer, Cham (2020). https://doi.org/10.1007/978-3-030-58808-3_50

27. Candori, P., Falcinelli, S., Pirani, F., Tarantelli, F., Vecchiocattivi, F.: Interaction components in the hydrogen halide dications. Chem. Phys. Let. **436**(4–6), 322–326 (2007)

28. Lombardi, A., Lago, N.F., Laganà, A., Pirani, F., Falcinelli, S.: A bond-bond portable approach to intermolecular interactions: simulations for N-methylacetamide and carbon dioxide dimers. In: Murgante, B., et al. (eds.) ICCSA 2012. LNCS, vol. 7333, pp. 387–400. Springer, Heidelberg (2012). https://doi.org/10.1007/978-3-642-31125-3_30

29. Candori, R., et al.: Structure and charge transfer dynamics of the (Ar–N2)+ molecular cluster. J. Chem. Phys. **115**(19), 8888–8898 (2001)

30. Brunetti, B., Candori, P., De Andres, J., Pirani, F., Rosi, M., et al.: Dissociative ionization of methyl chloride and methyl bromide by collision with metastable neon atoms. J. Phys. Chem. A **101**(41), 7505–7512 (1997)

31. Biondini, F., Brunetti, B.G., Candori, P., De Angelis, F., et al.: Penning ionization of N2O molecules by He*(2(3,1)S) and Ne*(3P2,0) metastable atoms: theoretical considerations about the intermolecular interactions. J. Chem. Phys. **122**(16), 164308 (2005)

32. Brunetti, B., et al.: Energy dependence of the Penning ionization electron spectrum of Ne* (3P2,0)+Kr. Eur. Phys. J. D **38**(1), 21–27 (2006)

33. Falcinelli, S., Bartocci, A., Cavalli, S., Pirani, F., Vecchiocattivi, F.: Stereodynamics in the collisional autoionization of water, ammonia, and hydrogen sulfide with metastable rare gas atoms: competition between intermolecular halogen and hydrogen bonds. Chem. A Eur. J. **22**(2), 764–771 (2016)

34. Brunetti, B.G., Candori, P., Cappelletti, D., Falcinelli, S., et al.: Penning ionization electron spectroscopy of water molecules by metastable neon atoms. Chem. Phys. Lett. **539–540**, 19–23 (2012)

35. Balucani, N., Bartocci, A., Brunetti, B., Candori, P., et al.: Collisional autoionization dynamics of Ne∗(3P2,0)–H2O. Chem. Phys. Lett. **546**, 34–39 (2012)

36. Alagia, M., Biondini, F., Brunetti, B.G., Candori, P., et al.: The double photoionization of HCl: An ion–electron coincidence study. J. Chem. Phys. **121**(21), 10508–10512 (2004)

37. Aguilar, A., Brunetti, B., González, M., Vecchiocattivi, F.: A crossed beam study of the ionization of molecules by metastable neon atoms. Chem. Phys. **145**(2), 211–218 (1990)

38. Zou, J., Gordon, S.D.S., Osterwalder, A.: Sub-Kelvin stereodynamics of the Ne(3P2)+N2 reaction. Phys. Rev. Lett. **123**, 133401 (2019)

39. Skouteris, D., Balucani, N., Faginas-Lago, N., et al.: Dimerization of methanimine and its charged species in the atmosphere of Titan and interstellar/cometary ice analogs. Astron. Astrophys. **584**, A76 (2015)
40. Skouteris, D., Balucani, N., Ceccarelli, C., Faginas Lago, N., et al.: Interstellar dimethyl ether gas-phase formation: a quantum chemistry and kinetics study. MNRAS **482**, 3567–3575 (2019)
41. Pei, L., Carrascosa, E., Yang, N., Falcinelli, S., Farrar, J.M.: Velocity map imaging study of charge-transfer and proton-transfer reactions of CH3 Radicals with H3+. J. Phys. Chem. Lett. **6**(9), 1684–1689 (2015)
42. Alagia, M., Candori, P., Falcinelli, S., Pirani, F., et al.: Dissociative double photoionization of benzene molecules in the 26–33 eV energy range. Phys. Chem. Chem. Phys. **13**(18), 8245 (2011). https://doi.org/10.1039/c0cp02678f
43. Falcinelli, S., Pirani, F., Alagia, M., Schio, L., Richter, R., et al.: The escape of O+ ions from the atmosphere: an explanation of the observed ion density profiles on Mars. Chem. Phys. Lett. **666**, 1–6 (2016)
44. Falcinelli, S., Rosi, M., Candori, P., Farrar, J.M., Vecchiocattivi, F., et al.: Kinetic Energy Release in molecular dications fragmentation after VUV and EUV ionization and escape from planetary atmospheres. Planet. Space Sci. **99**, 149–157 (2014)

Computational Investigation on the Thermodynamics of $H_2CO + NH_2 \rightarrow NH_2CHO + H$ on Interstellar Water Ice Surfaces

Berta Martínez-Bachs[✉] and Albert Rimola

Departament de Química, Universitat Autònoma de Barcelona,
08193 Bellaterra, Catalonia, Spain
berta.martinez@uab.cat

Abstract. Formamide has a key role in prebiotic chemistry as it is the simplest molecule containing the four most important atoms from a biological point of view: hydrogen, carbon, nitrogen and oxygen. Due to its importance, the formation of this molecule has been studied and different pathways have been considered both in gas-phase and on ices of dust grains since it was first detected. In the present work, the thermodynamics of the formation route of formamide starting from NH_2 and H_2CO, a reaction channel proposed to occur in the gas phase, has been theoretically investigated in the scenario taking place on icy dust grains modelled by both a cluster and a periodic approach. Different DFT functionals have been employed to obtain accurate energy values for the mechanistic steps involved in the reaction.

1 Introduction

Interstellar complex organic molecules (iCOMs) are carbon-bearing molecules containing at least six atoms that have been detected in the interstellar medium (ISM). iCOMs are a turn out in chemical complexity and diversity, being the next group of chemical compounds after the simplest inorganic species detected [1, 2].

Formamide (NH_2CHO) was first detected in 1971 in the ISM [3]. It is not only interesting due to its iCOM nature but also because it is the simplest molecule that contains the four most important elements from a biological point of view, hydrogen, carbon, nitrogen and oxygen, and the simplest molecule containing the amide bond O-C-NH, the group that join amino acids forming peptides. This turn out in chemical complexity increases its interest from the standpoint of prebiotic chemistry [4, 5].

Different pathways for the formation of formamide have been discussed in the recent years, including routes in the gas phase and on the surfaces of icy dust grains, which have conducted a vivid debate. The formation of formamide on ice mantles has been studied by reaction of the radical CN with H_2O molecules of the ice itself [4]. Other on-grain routes postulate the radical-radical coupling between NH_2 and HCO [6] adopting the general scheme for iCOM formation recurrently used in gas-grain astrochemical modelling [7].

© Springer Nature Switzerland AG 2021
O. Gervasi et al. (Eds.): ICCSA 2021, LNCS 12953, pp. 658–666, 2021.
https://doi.org/10.1007/978-3-030-86976-2_45

The formation of formamide has also been analysed from gas-phase scenarios, considering its formation by reaction between NH_2 and H_2CO [5]. In this route, the pathway goes through the formation of a radical intermediate NH_2CH_2O which dissociates to give formamide and hydrogen, i.e.,:

$$NH_2 + CH_2O \rightarrow NH_2CH_2O \rightarrow NH_2CHO + H.$$

In this mechanism, the intermediate was found to be the most stable species, i.e., the energetics of the overall reaction are disfavoured because the products are more unstable than the intermediate. However, since the reaction is associated with the release of a H atom, kinetic calculations based on the RRKM approach indicated a relatively fast overall reaction highlighting its feasibility in the ISM. This formation route, however, has not been considered on the ice mantles. Interestingly, the interaction of the reactive species with the surfaces can modify the energetic features of the reactions, by increasing/decreasing the energy barriers and favouring/disfavouring their thermodynamics.

In this work, we address this formamide formation route occurring on interstellar water ice mantles considering only its thermodynamics, that is, accounting for the relative energies of the different minima stationary points (i.e., the reactants, the intermediate and the products). This has been studied by means of quantum chemical calculations according to different situations: in the absence of water ice and in their presence in order to determine whether water ice infers any influence on the energetics of the reaction. Water ice surfaces have been modelled using two different approaches: a cluster consisting of three water molecules, and a periodic water ice surface of a crystalline system. For all the cases, different DFT methods have been employed to check their accuracy with the goal to identify the most accurate one (with respect to CCSD(T) results), which will be used in future studies including the kinetics aspects.

2 Methods

Molecular calculations have been performed with the Gaussian16 software package, while periodic simulations with the CRYSTAL17 program. Both codes use gaussian functions centred to the atoms as basis set, in this way ensuring a reasonable comparison of the results.

For both molecular and periodic calculations, the formation of formamide has been analysed by optimising the structures of the reactants, intermediate and products. The following DFT functionals have been used in these geometry optimisations: the pure gradient generalized approximations (GGA) PBE, the non-local B3LYP hybrid functional that includes a 20% of exact exchange in its definition, and the meta-hybrid M06-2X functional, which incorporate a 45% of exact exchange. To take into account dispersive forces, for all the DFT functionals, the D3-based Grimme's correction term was added: for B3LYP and PBE the D3 Becke-Johnson (D3(BJ)) correction, while for M06-2X the zero-damping (D3), since the BJ parameters are not computed for this functional [8–13]. The basis sets used among these DFT calculations were: 6-311 + G(d, p) for molecular systems, and 6-311G* for periodic systems.

Coupled Cluster (CC) is a family of the most accurate methods in quantum chemistry, but due to their extremely cost they can only be applied to small systems [14]. In this study, the CCSD(T) method, a truncated CC with first and second excitations and the third ones added perturbatively, has been used to compute single point energy calculations on the DFT optimized geometries for the systems in the absence of water ice and in the presence of the 3-water cluster model. For these calculations the Dunning aug-cc-pVTZ basis set has been used.

Truncated Coupled Cluster methods are the most accurate methods in quantum chemistry but due to its expensive cost they can only be applied to small systems. In this study CCSD(T) a truncated CC with first and second excitations and the third ones added perturbatively have been used to compute single point energy calculations of the optimized geometries with DFT functionals for the gas-phase scenario optimizations and the cluster model optimization [14].

For the periodic calculations, additionally, the semi-empirical HF-3c method [15], which is based on the original HF combined with a MINIX basis set that include three corrections to alleviate the deficits caused by the approximations employed, was used to optimize the geometries. Subsequently, single point energy calculations on the HF-3c optimized geometries at the different DFT theory levels were carried out, the results of which were compared with those obtained at the full DFT level.

Interstellar water ice surfaces were modelled by adopting two different approaches: i) a cluster model made up by three water molecules, and ii) a crystalline periodic slab model. For this later case, the model is based on the crystalline P-ice structure. It has been generated by cutting out the P-ice 3D periodic bulk structure perpendicular to the [010] direction, resulting with the (010) slab surface model, which consists of twelve atomic layers (a thickness of 10.784 Å) [16, 17]. Additionally, different unit cells were considered aiming to study the effect of the lateral interactions between species belonging to adjacent cells: a 1×1 cell, consisting of 24 water molecules (72 atoms), and a 2×2 cell, consisting of 96 water molecules (288 atoms).

3   Results

As mentioned above, the reactants, intermediate and products geometries have been optimized on the absence and in the presence of water ice.

In the absence of ice models (namely, a gas-phase reaction), the reactants, the intermediate and the products were optimized using the three different DFT functionals mentioned above: B3LYP-D3(BJ), PBE-D3(BJ) and M06-2X-D3. Additionally, CCSD(T) single point energy calculations on all the DFT optimized geometries were performed to check the accuracy of the DFT methods.

Figure 1 shows the optimized stationary points at these DFT methods. Table 1 reports their relative energies with respect to the reactants, including the single point CCSD(T) values. Significant differences can be observed in the relative energies between the three DFT functionals, although changes in geometries are almost insignificant, less than 0.1 Å. Indeed, all DFT results indicate the intermediate as the most stable species along the path with some significant differences between DFT energy values specially with PBE-D3(BJ) results. In contrast, CCSD(T) energy values are almost in perfect

Reactants   Intermediate   Products

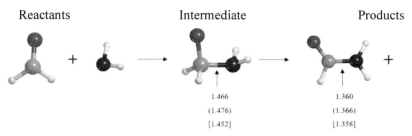

	1.466		1.360
	(1.476)		(1.366)
	[1.452]		[1.358]

Fig. 1. Optimized structures of the reactants, intermediate and products of the studied reaction. Distances are in Å. Bare values correspond to those at B3LYP-D3(BJ), in brackets to those at PBE-D3(BJ) and in square brackets to those at M06-2X-D3. Atom color legend: red, O; blue, N; green, C white, H. (Color figure online)

Table 1. Relative energies (in kJ/mol) of the stationary points with respect to the reactants for the reaction in absence of water ice computed at the different DFT functionals used for geometry optimizations and considering the single point energy calculation at CCSD(T).

Geometry optimization functional	B3LYP-D3(BJ)		PBE-D3(BJ)		M06-2X-D3	
Single point calculation	B3LYP-D3(BJ)	CCSD(T)	PBE-D3(BJ)	CCSD(T)	M06-2X-D3	CCSD(T)
Reactants	0.0	0.0	0.0	0.0	0.0	0.0
Intermediate	−80.7	−63.2	−105.9	−62.6	−83.0	−63.8
Products	−43.4	−37.2	−77.4	−37.1	−59.0	−37.3

agreement irrespective of the optimized geometry level and underline a general trend: the intermediate species is more stable than the products, in line with published works [5].

Aiming to characterize this formation route on water ice mantles, as a first step, geometry optimizations of the stationary points on a water trimer have been performed adopting the three DFT methods, which were subsequently computed at CCSD(T). Results are shown in Fig. 2 and Table 2.

In this scenario, regarding the geometry optimizations, significant differences are found between optimizations at B3LYP-D3(BJ) and M06-2X-D3 compared with those at PBE-D3(BJ). Indeed, in this later case H-bond interactions connecting the NH_2CH_2O species with the cluster are significantly shorter (by 0.2 Å) than those computed at the other levels (see Fig. 2). Despite these geometry differences, relative energies indicate now that the intermediate and the products present a more similar stability than in the gas-phase scenario, the former species being somewhat more stable. However, single point CCSD(T) results do not follow the general trend observed in the absence of water ice, in which the intermediate was the most stable species of the route. In PBE-D3(BJ)

Reactants	Intermediate	Products

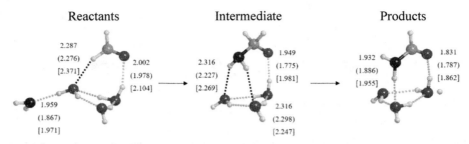

Fig. 2. Optimized structures of the reactants, intermediate and products of the studied reaction in the presence of a 3-H$_2$O cluster. Distances are in Å. Bare values correspond to those at B3LYP-D3(BJ), in parenthesis to those at PBE-D3(BJ), and in brackets to those at M06-2X-D3.

Table 2. Relative energies (in kJ/mol) of the stationary points with respect to the reactants for the reaction under study in the presence of a 3-H$_2$O cluster computed at the different DFT functionals and at CCSD(T) single point energy calculation on the DFT optimized geometries.

Geometry optimization functional	B3LYP-D3(BJ)		PBE-D3(BJ)		M06-2X-D3	
Single point calculation	B3LYP-D3(BJ)	CCSD (T)	PBE-D3(BJ)	CCSD (T)	M06-2X-D3	CCSD (T)
Reactants	0.0	0.0	0.0	0.0	0.0	0.0
Intermediate	−64.1	−53.5	−92.6	−32.8	−74.4	-55.0
Products	−39.8	−37.0	−72.9	−37.3	−51.3	-35.6

optimized geometries case, the situation is reversed, giving the products more stable than the intermediate (see Table 2).

Characterization of the energetic features of this mechanistic path has also been performed on a more realistic ice surface by adopting a periodic approach. In this case, the geometry optimizations have been performed on the crystalline (010) slab surface model of P-ice using the three different DFT functionals and the cost-effective HF-3c method.

Optimized geometries of the stationary points on the 1x1 crystalline slab model are shown in Fig. 3 and the computed energetics are reported in Table 3. Considering the energy values obtained with the three DFT functionals, it can be underlined that the B3LYP-D3(BJ) and the M06-2X-D3 functionals present the products as the most stable structures (see Table 3), predicting accordingly the reactions as exoergic processes. In contrast, this is not observed for the PBE-D3(BJ) functional, which is attributed to an overstabilization of the spin delocalization in the intermediate structures (usually in GGA functionals), as the spin density on the O atom of NH$_2$CH$_2$O is 0.35 while for the other two functionals almost all the spin density is on the O atom.

Although HF-3c optimized geometries are in good agreement with DFT functionals, energy values are dramatically different, providing reaction energies largely endoergic.

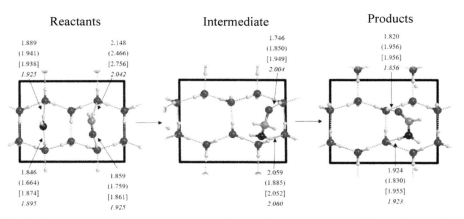

Fig. 3. Optimized structures of the reactants, intermediate and products of the studied reaction on the 1x1 crystalline water slab model. Distances are in Å. Bare values correspond to those at B3LYP-D3(BJ), in parenthesis to those at PBE-D3(BJ), in brackets to those at M06-2X-D3 and in italics to those at HF-3c.

Table 3. Relative energies (in kJ/mol) of the stationary points with respect to the reactants for the reaction under study on the 1 × 1 crystalline slab model computed at the different DFT functionals and at the HF-3c level and considering the single point energy calculation at the different DFT functionals on the optimized HF-3c geometries.

Geometry optimization functional	B3LYP-D3(BJ)	PBE-D3(BJ)	M06-2X-D3	HF-3c			
Single point calculation	B3LYP-D3(BJ)	PBE-D3(BJ)	M06-2X-D3	HF-3c	B3LYP-D3(BJ)	PBE-D3(BJ)	M06-2X-D3
Reactants	0.0	0.0	0.0	0.0	0.0	0.0	0.0
Intermediate	−19.1	−42.4	−26.1	−113.6	−15.7	−34.6	−31.8
Products	−24.9	−22.2	−45.9	86.0	−18.4	−59.8	−38.3

This behaviour could be due to the bad description of HF-3c in computing the binding energies of the involved species. That is, for H2CO, NH2CHO, the error in the BE computed at HF-3c//HF-3c compared to those at DFT//DFT is 20%, 38% and 35%, clearly pointing out the accuracy limitations of HF-3c in relation to the energetics. Presents results shown in Table 3 indicate that HF-3c is a very good cost/effective method for geometry optimizations but not for computing energetics. For this reason, single point energy calculations with the three DFT functionals have been carried out on the optimized HF-3c geometries. Obtained results clearly indicate that the reaction is exoergic, in which products is the most stable species, with no exception. Thus, these results indicate that the presence of water ice surfaces reverts the thermodynamics compared with the gas phase situation. This is probably due to the fact that the products (NH_2CHO + H) are stabilised by favourable interactions with the surface (namely, H-bonds and dispersion), which are absent under strict gas-phase conditions. However, it is worth mentioning that the computed energetic values are significantly dependent on the functional method, in which the stability of the intermediate as well as the exoergicity of the processes follows the trend of (from more to less) PBE-D3(BJ) > M06-2X-D3 > B3LYP-D3(BJ). The significant stabilization of the intermediates and products exhibited by the PBE-D3(BJ) functional is probably due to its propensity to stabilize electron delocalized situations, as mentioned above. These results, additionally, indicate that, although energy values of HF-3c method are actually unreliable, performing DFT single point energy calculations on the HF-3c optimized geometries is a robust approach to obtain accurate results.

Finally, to assess possible lateral interaction effects between species belonging to adjacent cells (caused by the small unit cell size of the slab model), calculations on a slab model with a 2×2 unit cell (obtained by increasing by a factor 2 the a and b cell parameters) have been performed. In this case, to speed up the calculations, we optimized the systems at HF-3c followed by DFT single point calculations on them. Optimized geometries of the stationary points are shown in Fig. 4 and the energetic values in Table 4.

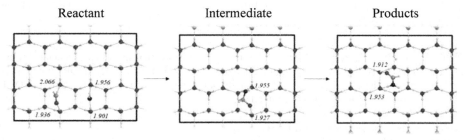

Fig. 4. HF-3c optimized structures of the reactants, intermediate and products of the studied reaction in on the 2×2 crystalline water slab model. Distances are in Å.

Table 4. Relative energies (in kJ/mol) of the stationary points with respect to the reactants for the studied reaction on the 2×2 crystalline slab model computed by considering single point energy calculations with the HF-3c method for geometry optimizations and considering DFT single point energy calculations on the HF-3c optimized geometries. Energetics calculated at HF-3c are also shown.

Single point calculation	HF-3c	B3LYP-D3(BJ)	PBE-D3(BJ)	M06-2X-D3
Reactants	0.0	0.0	0.0	0.0
Intermediate	−115.6	−15.5	−35.0	−26.8
Products	85.4	−19.0	−50.1	−36.3

As far as the geometries is concerned, no significant changes have been observed when they are compared (at HF-3c only) with those on the 1×1 crystalline slab model, variations being less than 0.1 Å. In the same way, computed energetics are also in line with those computed by adopting the 1x1 unit cell, all the cases indicating the products as the most stable species. Additionally, the trend of exoergicity of the reaction as a function of the DFT methods is kept. Accordingly, we can conclude that there are no lateral interaction effects and thus the 1×1 crystalline slab model is large enough to study the thermodynamics of this reaction by employing a periodic approach.

4   Conclusions

In this contribution, theoretical results relative to the formation of formamide by adopting the reaction of $NH_2 + H_2CO \rightarrow NH_2CHO + H$, which has been proposed to be a main synthetic route in the gas-phase, has been computed considering that it occurs on interstellar water ice surfaces. Water ice surfaces have been represented by modelled by adopting two different approaches: a water cluster consisting of three water molecules and a periodic surface of a crystalline water slab in which both 1×1 and 2×2 unit cell sizes have been used.

Simulations in absence of water ice and in the presence of the 3-H_2O cluster model, have been performed using three different DFT functionals (B3LYP-D3(BJ), PBE-D3(BJ) and M06-2X-D3), in which, to check their accuracy, CCSD(T) single point energy calculations have been performed on the DFT optimized geometries. Simulations on the periodic 1x1 crystalline surface model, the same DFT methods have been performed, in which the semi-empirical HF-3c method has also been used to optimize the geometries followed by DFT single point calculations. On the periodic 2×2 crystalline model, this later methodology was only used to speed up the calculations.

In absence of water ice and in the presence of the 3-H_2O cluster model the overall reaction is predicted to be endoergic, as the NH_2CH_2O intermediate is more stable than the $NH_2CHO + H$ products. In contrast, on both the 1×1 and 2×2 periodic surfaces, for B3LYP-D3(BJ) and M06-2X-D3 results show that the final products are more stable than the intermediate species, indicating that the presence of the water surfaces revert the energetic trends observed in the gas phase and in the presence of the 3-H_2O cluster.

This is because the extended surfaces provide an extra-stability to the products due to the intermolecular forces (i.e., H-bond and dispersion) established with the "NH_2CH_2O + H" species. Interestingly, this is not observed in PBE-D3(BJ) results because the functional, due to its definition as GGA functional, over stabilizes the intermediate species due to its propensity to favour electron delocalized situations.

Finally, the energetics provided by the HF-3c method are dramatically inaccurate. However, optimized geometries are similar to those at the DFT level and accordingly results from DFT single point energy calculations are very similar to those at full DFT level. Moreover, the unit cell size does not affect the results (i.e., those for the 1×1 and 2×2 unit cells are similar) and accordingly lateral interactions (if present) are not significant in the 1×1 unit cell, both surface models providing accurate thermodynamics for formamide formation on interstellar water icy grains.

Acknowledgments. This project has received funding from the European Research Council (ERC) under the European Union's Horizon 2020 research and innovation programme (grant agreement No. 865657) for the project "Quantum Chemistry on Interstellar Grains" (QUANTUMGRAIN). MINECO (project CTQ2017-89132-P) DIUE (project 2017SGR1323) are acknowledged for financial support. A.R. is indebted to the "Ramón y Cajal" program.

References

1. Ceccarelli, C., et al.: Seeds of life in space (SOLIS): the organic composition diversity at 300–1000 au scale in solar-type star-forming regions*. Astrophys. J. **850**, 176 (2017). https://doi.org/10.3847/1538-4357/aa961d

2. Herbst, E., van Dishoeck, E.F.: Complex organic interstellar molecules. Annu. Rev. Astron. Astrophys. **47**(1), 427–480 (2009). https://doi.org/10.1146/annurev-astro-082708-101654

3. Rubin, R.H., Swenson, G.W.J., Benson, R.C., Tigelaar, H.L., Flygare, W.H.: Microwave detection of interstellar formamide. Astrophys. J. **169**, L39 (1971). https://doi.org/10.1086/180810

4. Rimola, A., et al.: Can formamide be formed on interstellar ice? An atomistic perspective. ACS Earth Sp. Chem. **2**(7), 720–734 (2018). https://doi.org/10.1021/acsearthspacechem.7b00156

5. Barone, V., et al.: Gas-phase formation of the prebiotic molecule formamide: insights from new quantum computations. Mon. Not. R. Astron. Soc. Lett. **453**(1), L31–L35 (2015). https://doi.org/10.1093/mnrasl/slv094

6. Enrique-Romero, J., Rimola, A., Ceccarelli, C., Ugliengo, P., Balucani, N., Skouteris, D.: Reactivity of HCO with CH3 and NH2 on water ice surfaces. a comprehensive accurate quantum chemistry study. ACS Earth Sp. Chem. **3**(10), 2158–2170 (2019). https://doi.org/10.1021/acsearthspacechem.9b00156

7. Garrod, R.T., Herbst, E.: Formation of methyl formate and other organic species in the warm-up phase of hot molecular cores. Astron. Astrophys. **457**(3), 927–936 (2006). https://doi.org/10.1051/0004-6361:20065560

8. Becke, A.D.: A new mixing of Hartree-Fock and local density-functional theories. J. Chem. Phys. **98**(2), 1372–1377 (1993). https://doi.org/10.1063/1.464304

9. Becke, A.D.: Density-functional exchange-energy approximation with correct asymptotic behavior. Phys. Rev. A **38**(6), 3098–3100 (1988). https://doi.org/10.1103/PhysRevA.38.3098

10. Zhao, Y., Truhlar, D.G.: A new local density functional for main-group thermochemistry, transition metal bonding, thermochemical kinetics, and noncovalent interactions. J. Chem. Phys. **125**(19), 194101 (2006). https://doi.org/10.1063/1.2370993

11. Perdew, J.P., Burke, K., Ernzerhof, M.: Generalized Gradient Approximation Made Simple (1996). Accessed: 09 Jun 2019. https://doi.org/10.1103/PhysRevLett.77.3865. https://journals-aps-org.are.uab.cat/prl/pdf/

12. Grimme, S.: Accurate description of van der Waals complexes by density functional theory including empirical corrections. J. Comput. Chem. **25**(12), 1463–1473 (2004). https://doi.org/10.1002/jcc.20078

13. Grimme, S., Ehrlich, S., Goerigk, L.: Effect of the damping function in dispersion corrected density functional theory. J. Comput. Chem. **32**(7), 1456–1465 (2011). https://doi.org/10.1002/jcc.21759

14. Tsuneda, T.: Density functional theory in quantum chemistry, vol. 9784431548256. Springer Japan (2013)

15. Sure, R., Grimme, S.: Corrected small basis set Hartree-Fock method for large systems. J. Comput. Chem. **34**(19), 1672–1685 (2013). https://doi.org/10.1002/jcc.23317

16. Zamirri, L., Casassa, S., Rimola, A., Segado-Centellas, M., Ceccarelli, C., Ugliengo, P.: IR spectral fingerprint of carbon monoxide in interstellar water-ice models. MNRAS **480**, 1427–1444 (2018). https://doi.org/10.1093/mnras/sty1927

17. Pisani, C., Casassa, S., Ugliengo, P.: Proton-ordered ice structures at zero pressure. A quantum-mechanical investigation. Chem. Phys. Lett. **253**(3–4), 201–208 (1996). https://doi.org/10.1016/0009-2614(96)00228-X

International Workshop on Advanced Modeling E-Mobility in Urban Spaces (DEMOS 2021)

Uptake of e-Scooters in Palermo, Italy: Do the Road Users Tend to Rent, Buy or Share?

Tiziana Campisi[1]($\boxtimes$) (iD), Nurten Akgün-Tanbay[2]($\boxtimes$) (iD), Kh. Md Nahiduzzaman[3] (iD), and Dilum Dissanayake[4] (iD)

[1] University of Enna Kore, Cittadella Universitaria, 94100 Enna, Italy
`tiziana.campisi@unikore.it`
[2] Faculty of Engineering and Natural Sciences, Bursa Technical University, 16330 Bursa, Turkey
`nurten.akgun@btu.edu.tr`
[3] Faculty of Applied Science, School of Engineering, The University of British Columbia, Okanagan, BC V1V 1V7, Canada
[4] School of Engineering, Newcastle University, Room 2.19, Cassie Building, Newcastle upon Tyne N1 7RU, UK

Abstract. The uptake of micro-mobility, particularly the use of e-scooters has exponentially grown in Europe. The EU strategies have led to promote the decisions of purchasing, renting and/or sharing e-scooters by making some vital changes to the infrastructure. Several companies have made it possible to rent or share vehicles, while many manufacturers have marketed different models. During the COVID-19 pandemic, e-scooters have become widely popular for short distance travel in Italy as they allow the potential to maintain a social distancing. This paper aims to explore the uptake of e-scooters with an attention to propensity to buy, rent or share those sustainable urban mobility alternatives as well as user perceptions and frequency of use by comparing the periods before and during the third phase of the pandemic. Two sets of surveys were carried out with 200 participants who habitually use e-scooters in Palermo, Italy. 77.5% of the participants had to commute to work during the third phase of the pandemic. Majority of the participants preferred e-scooters as they were economic and environmentally friendly. Road users tended to buy or rent e-scooters during the third phase of the pandemic but they hesitated to share. The results of this study will enhance our understanding of the demand for micro-mobility in the context of interest and will allow for a better planning in consideration to the available options to purchase, share and rent.

Keywords: E-scooters · Renting · Shared mobility · COVID-19 · Sustainable transport

1 Introduction

The COVID-19 pandemic has affected the whole world in many aspects, particularly transport activities. The pandemic has dramatically altered our daily life, including the ways of getting around within a city [1]. A series of measures, such as restricting the

© Springer Nature Switzerland AG 2021
O. Gervasi et al. (Eds.): ICCSA 2021, LNCS 12953, pp. 669–682, 2021.
https://doi.org/10.1007/978-3-030-86976-2_46

movement of people and the suspension of economic activities were defined as non-essential, were adopted by the national governments [2]. Several recommendations have been made by the governments and public transport companies. They include fundamental aspects such as keeping social distance in public vehicles, continuous sanitation of vehicles and waiting areas, using sustainable travel modes, particularly walking, cycling and micro-mobility [3, 4]. A survey [5] was carried out in Italy and the results showed that more than 50% of road users do not feel comfortable while travelling by public transport such as metro and bus due to the personal health concerns during the pandemic. As a consequence, public transport has also been severely restricted across Europe [6]. Complying with the social distancing rules issued by governments has reduced the transport capacity by 15% to 35%. This reduction did not cause any major disruption during the lockdown periods, but now with industries reopening, people are looking for fast, safe and efficient alternatives. Therefore, alternative travel modes, especially micro-mobility, started to be preferred by road users.

The term micro-mobility refers to small, lightweight vehicles that people can drive themselves, including electric bicycles and scooters. These are more convenient and environmentally friendly alternatives compared to traditional means of transport, and help to reduce the level of traffic congestion [7]. E-scooters are considered to be at low risk of spreading the virus, as there are fewer places where people put their hands, compared to public transits e.g., buses, trains and trams. In addition, e-scooters can only be used by one person at a time and the rider is in total control of his/her position on the road, which means that it is easier to comply with the social distancing rules [8]. E-scooters are also easy to use for both work and leisure travels [9]. Moreover, they contribute to the EU's zero climate impact strategy for 2050 [10].

Governments and local authorities need to employ strategies for improving infrastructure in order to encourage the trend to prefer e-scooters for short trips. Former studies [11, 12] showed that Brussels established specific zones where the traffic was limited to 20 km/h and the vulnerable road users can travel safely. Creating limited traffic zones should allow a reduction in the use of private vehicles by encouraging sustainable modes of transport. Preventive studies in micro-simulation can help assess the level of service and choose between the best design alternatives for this infrastructural improvement [13, 14]. In addition, the design of shared-use infrastructures should focus on appropriate measures to minimise points of interaction and especially points of conflict between pedestrians and cyclists and also micro-mobility users [15, 16]. However, the infrastructural improvements need a proper urban planning attention and financial resources. Therefore, it is necessary to gain a deeper understanding of the trend of using e-scooters in urban areas. Does the increase of using e-scooters occur due to the first shock of the pandemic conditions, or is it a permanent change of our mobility choices? This study aimed to answer these questions and focus on a statistical evaluation obtained through the administration of an online survey to a sample of e-scooter users in the city of Palermo. This city has been the subject of studies in the last few years regarding both the propensity of people to rent scooters [17] and the importance of the democratic participation of people in the planning of urban interventions for the improvement of the e-scooter service [18].

2 Use of E-Scooters in Palermo, Italy

The new rules for e-scooters were first implemented in 2019 in Italy. It was the year in which the Italian Parliament spent much effort to regularise the use of e-scooters on public road. Following this, the new Italian regulation on the use of e-scooters came into force. From the end of July 2020, the Italian municipalities had largely put these regulations into practice. These actions helped local authorities and road users choose e-scooters as a daily travel mode in urban cities during the COVID-19 pandemic. The severe pandemic condition affected the use of public transport; this means that alternative means of transport capable of guaranteeing greater safety were beginning to be more popular in 2020. Since the lockdown from 9th March 2020 and the partial reopening from 4th May 2020, the use of e-scooters has gained significant importance and become a strategic mean of travel in the city of Palermo. The measure and recommendations, which were promoted by the Ministry of the Environment in agreement with the Ministry of Infrastructure and Transport, aimed to encourage sustainable modes of transport that guaranteed people's right to have mobility in urban areas during this period of COVID-19 emergency. Shared e-scooters started to be used commonly in the urban areas of Palermo, particularly the historic centre since March 2020. A large part of the city falls within the restricted traffic zone, which is referred as ZTL in Italy, and is characterised by a low gradient.

It is planned that, shared e-scooter service will be improved by introducing new regulations and safe and improved infrastructures in Palermo. It is aimed to increase the number of shared e-scooters with more than 1,600 new vehicles, and users will be able to rent via a smartphone app and/or integrated platforms. Rental will be banned for children under the age of 14; therefore, the shared e-scooter is planned to be an adult mobility mode. In order to encourage citizens to use e-scooters, some companies will provide a promotional rate consisting of 0.50 cents and 100 min of free travel by entering a promotional code.

Encouraging the use of e-scooters in urban areas is an important target for local authorities and transport planners. However, it is also a complicated situation. Road users showed a great favour for choosing micro-mobility vehicles, particularly e-scooters, as a daily travel mode during the COVID-19 pandemic. Nevertheless, it is uncertain that increase of using e-scooters might be a temporary behaviour for a period of time. It should be noted that improving infrastructures needs high amount of budget and time. Therefore, critically evaluation of the interest on using e-scooter is essential for decision makers as this links to reform the urban transport beyond the pandemic.

Former studies [3, 19–22] investigated the change of travel behaviour during the COVID-19 pandemic. They have concluded that there has been an increase of using e-scooters in urban city due to the health concerns. However, there has been no study to date focusing on investigating the resistance of this change on road users' preferences. Therefore, the study in this paper investigates the aspects related to the use of private and/or rented or shared scooters in order to explore and investigate how to optimise the services and related infrastructures. In the city of Palermo, it is possible to rent e-scooters from several private shops for a period of time, while the companies that provide the e-scooter sharing service are Helbiz and Lime. Thus, both renting and sharing options are available in the city of Palermo. These concepts are further scrutinized in the analysis section.

3 Methodology

The aim of this research is to analyse the trend in the use of e-scooters in the city of Palermo. A questionnaire was carried out through the Google survey platform. This methodology eliminates the need for paper and allows for greater response and enhances accuracy [23]. In addition, during the pandemic period, it was not possible to conduct face-to-face surveys with respondents. It is easy to implement and the greatest benefit is obtained from online data collection by increasing productivity and saving time. The data is instantly available and can easily be transferred into specific statistical software or spread sheets if more detailed analysis is required. Furthermore, it is essential that the online survey is responsive for mobile devices to be perfectly visible and usable on any platform. According to market research experts, majority of the users prefer responding to online surveys to written questionnaires or telephone interviews [24]. Therefore, the creation and dissemination of online surveys can be complementary to traditional survey methods via telephone interviews and face-to-face surveys. Finally, the structure of an online questionnaire makes it easy to change the order of questions, or by introducing skip logic based on their answers to the previous questions. In this way, the survey and response path can be tailored to each user. Specifically, the sample was randomly selected from regular micro-mobility users belonging to sector associations in the city of Palermo.

3.1 Study Area

The context related to Italian mobility in 2020 highlights on the one hand a decrease of long-distance trips and on the other hand an increase of short-distance trips especially for leisure. Alongside the increase in car use, there is also an increase in soft mobility, especially in exchange mode: it is increasingly common, for example, to arrive by car at a car park and from there use a bicycle or scooter, even in sharing mode, to cover the last part of the journey. In general, 2 out of 3 Italians rate the spread of scooters for short journeys in the city positively.

The area investigated in this study is the metropolis of Palermo (Sicily) in southern Italy. According to the statistical data recorded for this city, a number of residents as of 2019 of 647,422, of which 23,904 are foreigners. According to the Municipality of Palermo, the connection areas between Favorita, Mondello and Zisa (usually consider like the main tourist attraction areas of Palermo) had a limited parking areas while the pedestrian areas have been characterised by a limited speed, remotely managed (which cannot exceed 25 kms per h) like described in Fig. 1.

Approximately 15.3% of the citizens have a higher educational qualification. Considering the job position, the number of employed men are 115,438 while 74,507 are women. From the point of view of transport dynamics, the city of Palermo is characterised by an intense vehicular traffic along the main roads that circumscribe the limited traffic area of the historic centre. On average, the inhabitants of the city of Palermo walk

Fig. 1. The case study area: Palermo (Source: OpenStreetMap)

0.68 km considering that the average distance that people in Palermo walk every day in one direction, for example going back home or to work, is 3 km [17].

The percentage of people in Palermo who walk more than 1 km every day to reach a specific destination, for example to or from work, is 17%. In the last two years, through the adaptation of the urban sustainable mobility plan, the local authorities have authorised the use of private, rented and shared micro-mobility in some areas of the city, both central and peripheral. These vehicles can only circulate in urban areas and must comply with the speed limits of local and national legislation. Furthermore, it has been established that the devices authorised for experimental circulation can be parked in the areas and parking spaces designated for bicycles and motorbikes, and in any case in places where there is no interference with pedestrians and other vehicles, and in other parking areas that the Administration is identifying with special ordinances. The drivers of the devices must comply with these regulations regarding the parking of vehicles. All services are used in more or less the same way. To rent a scooter, you need to download the app and register for the service. Within the app there is a map showing where the scooters are located and ready to rent.

The vehicles have a QR code which is unlocked with the app and allows you to use the vehicle immediately. The payment of the corresponding tariff is also made via the app. Figure 2 shows some of the points where it is possible to find and share electric scooters in Palermo.

The data recorded by the Moovit digital platform [25] on micromobility in 2019 and 2020 in the city of Palermo show a slight increase in the propensity to use scooters and the like, as described in Fig. 3, where the frequency of use is shown.

Other data provided by the above mentioned platform show that the main motivation for moving in 2020 in micro-mobility was related to the eco-friendly vision of these means of transport, while in the previous year the majority of the interviewed users preferred electric scooters because they are faster than walking. The main reasons for non-use in 2019 and 2020 are related to the absence of bicycle lanes and poor road maintenance.

The purchase of scooters by private individuals has risen sharply since December 2019 due to governmental incentives. In Italy, more than 600,000 purchases of bicycles and scooters have been registered (614,000 to be precise) due to a specific bonus. The rental of electric scooters in Palermo started in 2020 through some shops or specialised

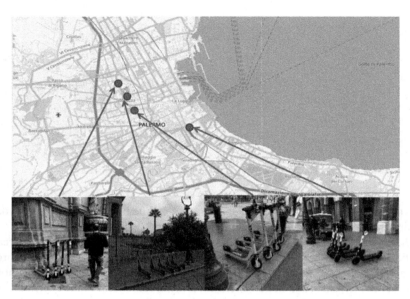

Fig. 2. Dockless e-scooters and the areas where they are predominantly located (Source: OpenStreetMap)

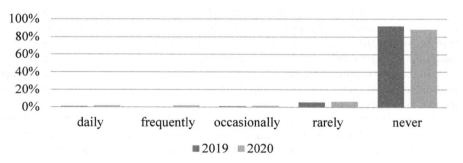

Fig. 3. Comparing the frequencies of using e-scooters between years 2019 and 2020

centres, but also some hotels or B&Bs have made available some electric modes to cover short distances. The service of sharing electric scooters in Palermo is to be paid for by credit card or cash at authorised points of sale, is totally sustainable and constitutes an alternative for private travel in the city in accordance with European measures that will make an important contribution to the ecological and sustainable mobility of the city of Palermo. The sharing service has started with four different operators that could potentially become nine.

3.2 Data Collection

The sample has been characterised by 200 users as better described below instead the survey has foreseen the creation of 3 sections:

1. Socio-demographic data (6 questions).
2. The judgment on the use of e-scooter (8 questions of Likert Scale 1 to 5)
3. The movement habits before and after the COVID-19 with the e-scooter with a judgement on a Likert scale for 7 different questions.

The survey was planned to collect data during the period January-March 2021, close to the discovery of the COVID vaccinations. Table 1 shows the variables investigated and the possible responses.

Table 1. Survey and relative sections

Section 1 - Sociodemographic variables

Gender	Age groups	Ownership (yes-no)	Employment
Male	18–24	Car	Worker
Female	25–39	Bike	Student
	40–54	e-scooter	Other
	55–65		
	≥65		

Section 2 – e-scooter using habits

How economically advantageous do you think is moving with e-scooter?	Using a Likert scale from 1 to 5 where: 1 = completely disagree
How eco-friendly do you consider moving with e-scooter?	2 = disagree 3 = neutral
How inclined are you to rent an e-scooter?	4 = agree 5 = completely agree
How inclined are you to buy an e-scooter?	
How inclined are you to share an e-scooter?	
How useful do you think GPS is when using e-scooter?	
How useful do you think a platform/social community or where is possible to add experiences with e-scooter?	
Do you think your propensity to use e-scooter has increased post-COVID?	
How economically advantageous do you find moving with e-scooter?	

Section 3 - Travel frequency before and after COVID-19

How often did you use your e-scooter?		Likert frequency scale from 1 to 5 1 = I tried it once,
before COVID-19 H-W	after COVID-19 H-W	2 = Less than once a month; 3 = Several times per month;
before COVID-19 H-L	after COVID-19 H-L	4 = Several times per week; 5 = Daily
before COVID-19 H-BN	after COVID-19 H-BN	
Did you use teleworking after COVID?		1 = yes 2 = no 3 = partially

4   Results

The results obtained from the first section showed that the sample was well balanced in terms of the gender of the users with 47% female and 53% male. The age-related distributions showed a higher percentage of users aged between 40–54 years and about 72% of the sample was characterised by working professionals (users) as shown in Fig. 4.

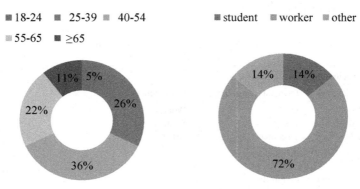

Fig. 4. Demographic distribution by age and status

The first section also investigated car ownership (left), which characterised the largest proportion of the sample, bicycle ownership (centre) and micro-mobility (right), obtaining the following distributions respectively defined by Fig. 5.

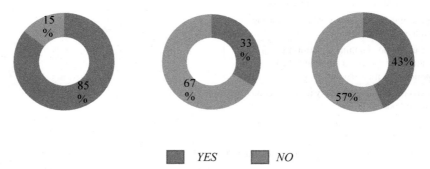

Fig. 5. Ownerships of car, bicycle and micro-mobility

Section 2 investigated through a judgment expressed on a Likert scale from 1 (completely disagree) to 5 (completely agree) with the vision of e-scooters as economically advantageous and eco-friendly means, obtaining the comparative distribution of Fig. 6, which shows a positive response on a scale value of 4 for both variables, with a slightly higher value for the economic aspect compared to the environmental one.

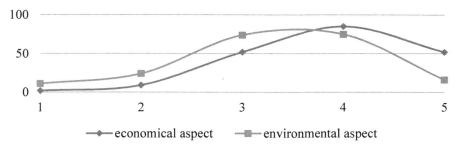

Fig. 6. The values associated with economic and environmental aspects

Using the same rating scale, the usefulness of the use of GPS systems for vehicle geolocation and the use of digital platforms for booking or release was investigated considering the concept of Mobility as a Service - Maas. The data showed the trends shown in Fig. 7.

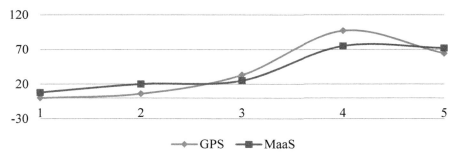

Fig. 7. Usefulness of GPS systems for vehicle geolocation and digital platforms for booking or release

The distribution of the propensity to buy, rent and share electric scooters on a Likert scale from 1 (strongly disagree) to 5 (strongly agree) correlates with the trend in Fig. 8. There is a preponderance of neutral or positive responses with a greater trend towards rating 3 for sharing and rating 4 and 5 for renting. Probably part of the results is due to the testing of the shared service from March 2021.

The third section investigated the frequency of use of the electric scooter before (before March 2020) and after the pandemic (after March 2020 until today) obtaining the following distributions for various reasons of travel and with reference to.

– Home-work trip (H-W)
– Home-work displacement (H-L)
– Home shopping (H-BN)

Fig. 8. Propensity distribution to buy, rent and share electric scooters

Specifically, with regard to home-work travel (H-W), the trend shown in Fig. 9 was obtained, where more than 100 users had a favourable opinion of the electric scooter before COVID, but this value fell during COVID, with a neutral opinion. This is closely linked on the one hand to the closure of certain work activities and on the other hand to the introduction of teleworking.

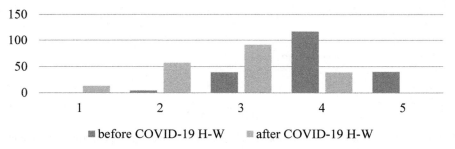

Fig. 9. Home-Work travel (H-W) scenarios before and after COVID-19

These data reflect the general trend of the city of Palermo recorded in March 2021 compared to March 2020 in the pre-pandemic phase with a value of −24% of trips for work [26]. These trends also reflect the regional trend that refers on average to the 9 capital cities. With regard to travel for home-work reasons, Fig. 10 shows that the neutral response prevails both before and after COVID: this is due to the fact that the scooter is useful for short journeys and that there are no recharging stations in the city to power it. In addition, during the pandemic period, the restrictions and recommendations provided by the government have reduced travel in general.

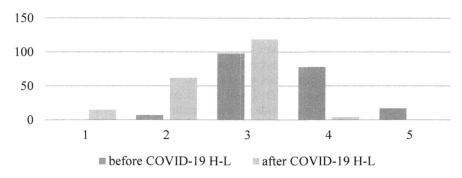

Fig. 10. H-L scenarios before and after COVID-19

With regard to travel for the purchase of basic necessities such as medicines or food, the results obtained are described in Fig. 11, which shows a largely neutral response for the pre-COVID period and a favourable response (4) in the post-pandemic phase. This trend is due to the fact that the purchase of basic necessities in the pre-pandemic phase took place mainly over long distances because of the positioning of the large food distribution chains, whereas in the pandemic phase people preferred to buy goods close to home or via e-commerce. The biggest purchases in the pandemic phase were medicines, sanitation products and masks.

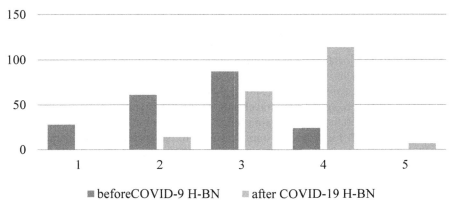

Fig. 11. H-BN scenarios before and after COVID-19

Finally, the respondents were asked to express whether their work activities are proceeding by teleworking, with the result that about 63% carry out their activities partially from home and about 22% completely from home. A small percentage of them (15%) continue to go to work. This answer also partly justifies the trends in Fig. 9. The trends shown in the previous figures also reflect the general travel trends in the city recorded in March 2021 [27] with 28% of trips for retail and leisure and +5% for trips for purchasing essential goods (groceries and pharmacies).

5   Discussion and Conclusions

Scooter sharing has been getting more attention from transport users in Palermo since March 2020. A few days after the service was activated, many people have tested the service offered by various companies in compliance with the measures on distancing and crowding of areas to reduce COVID-19 infections. In the meantime, another 800 e-scooters will be on their way, with the authorisation of two new companies. The local administration's urban mobility planning and design activities fit in well with the expansion of the city's network of cycle paths and the creation of new parking areas for mobility, taking into account the favourable climatic conditions that the city enjoys several months a year.

Strategies are aiming at the expansion of pedestrian areas, traffic zones and cycle paths to improve citizens' living conditions and policies on sustainability and decarbonisation. The present work shows a first step of investigation on the propensity to use e-scooters, considering purchase, rental and sharing. The results suggested a positive notion for renting, which is higher than for sharing. They can be justified by the fact that rental companies provide more scooters than shared scooter companies and are able to maintain them more easily.

Furthermore, the data refer to the first months in which the sharing services were activated, there is a phase of first approach by Palermo inhabitants to sharing e- scooters. The results also show that the use of the scooter was more successful for home-work transfers, especially during the pandemic period in the case of short distances (less than 2 km). Moreover, a positive trend was also observed to use e-scooters for trips associated with basic necessities. Therefore, an increasing tendency emerges to use these means during the post-pandemic period as well that respects social distancing as well as establishes its perception/branding as eco-friendly which is faster than walking. The use of technology, geo-localisation and digital platforms for booking vehicles was found to be strongly correlated with the use of these modes of transport. Although the research focused on a small sample size, it shows that despite COVID-19 has reduced travel volume, users are changing their travel habits with a preference for short (distances) trips using slow mobility and micro-mobility, thus limiting the use of private vehicles. Future research will focus on the statistical-descriptive evaluation of a larger sample as well as investigating the users' propensity to use the services provided by different sharing companies operating in the city of Palermo.

Acknowledgments. The authors acknowledge the financial support from the MIUR (Ministry of Education, Universities and Research [Italy]) through a project entitled WEAKI TRANSIT: WEAK-demand areas Innovative TRANsport Shared services for Italian Towns (Project code: 20174ARRHT/CUP Code: J74I19000320008), financed with the PRIN 2017 (Research Projects of National Relevance) program. We authorize the MIUR to reproduce and distribute reprints for Governmental purposes, not-withstanding any copyright notations thereon. Any opinions, findings, and conclusions or recommendations expressed in this material are those of the authors and do not necessarily reflect the views of the MIUR.

This paper is the result of the joint work of the authors. 'Abstract' 'Introduction' 'Methodology' and 'Results' were written jointly by the authors. TC and KMN discussed on the state of the art. NAT and TC designed the methodological approach and discussion. Supervision and research funding DD, and TC.

Funding. This research work was partially funded by the MIUR (Ministry of Edu-cation, Universities and Research [Italy]) through a project entitled WEAKI TRANSIT.This research work was partially funded by the MIUR (Ministry of Edu-cation, Universities and Research [Italy]) through a project entitled WEAKI TRANSIT.

Conflicts of Interest. The authors declare no conflict of interest.

References

1. Shrestha, N., et al.: The impact of COVID-19 on globalization. One Health **11**, 100180 (2020)
2. Vaughan, A.: Italy in lockdown. New Sci. **245**(3273), 7 (2020)
3. Campisi, T., Basbas, S., Skoufas, A., Akgün, N., Ticali, D., Tesoriere, G.: The impact of COVID-19 pandemic on the resilience of sustainable mobility in sicily. Sustainability **12**(21), 8829 (2020)
4. Nahiduzzaman, K., Lai, S.-K.: What does the global pandemic COVID-19 teach us? Some reflections. J. Urban Manage. **9**(3), 261 (2020)
5. STATISTA (2020). https://www.statista.com/statistics/1123287/post-covid-intercity-public-transport-use-frequency-intentions-in-italy/
6. Newman, A.O.: COVID, cities and climate: historical precedents and potential transitions for the new economy. Urban Sci. **4**(3), 32 (2020)
7. Campisi, T., Nahiduzzaman, K.M., Ticali, D., Tesoriere, G.: Bivariate analysis of the influencing factors of the upcoming personal mobility vehicles (PMVs) in palermo. In: Gervasi, O., et al. (eds.) ICCSA 2020. LNCS, vol. 12250, pp. 868–881. Springer, Cham (2020). https://doi.org/10.1007/978-3-030-58802-1_62
8. Dickson, I.: Social distancing: a COVID conundrum for commuters or a dawning for e-scooters? (2020). https://360.here.com/covid-19-electric-scooters
9. Gössling, S.: Integrating e-scooters in urban transportation: problems, policies, and the prospect of system change. Transp. Res. Part D Transp. Environ. **79**, 102230 (2020)
10. Møller, T.H., Simlett, J.: Micromobility: moving cities into a sustainable future. EYGM Limited (2020). https://assets.ey.com/content/dam/ey-sites/ey-com/en_gl/topics/automotive-and-transportation/automotive-transportation-pdfs/ey-micromobility-moving-cities-into-a-sustainable-future.pdf
11. Hubert, M., Corijn, E., Neuwels, J., Hardy, M., Vermeulen, S., Vaesen, J.: From pedestrian area to urban project: assets and challenges for the centre of Brussels. BSI synopsis. In: Brussels Studies. La revue scientifique électronique pour les recherches sur Bruxelles/Het elektronisch wetenschappelijk tijdschrift voor onderzoek over Brussel/The e-journal for academic research on Brussels (2017)
12. Raptopoulou, A., Basbas, S., Stamatiadis, N., Nikiforiadis, A.: A first look at e-scooter users. In: Nathanail, E.G., Adamos, G., Karakikes, I. (eds.) Advances in Mobility-as-a-Service Systems: Proceedings of 5th Conference on Sustainable Urban Mobility, Virtual CSUM2020, June 17-19, 2020, Greece, pp. 882–891. Springer International Publishing, Cham (2021). https://doi.org/10.1007/978-3-030-61075-3_85
13. Campisi, T., Canale, A., Tesoriere, G., Lovric, I., Čutura, B.: The importance of assessing the level of service in confined infrastructures: some considerations of the old ottoman pedestrian bridge of mostar. Appl. Sci. **9**(8), 1630 (2019)
14. Basbas, S., Campisi, T., Canale, A., Nikiforiadis, A., Gruden, C.: Pedestrian level of service assessment in an area close to an under-construction metro line in Thessaloniki, Greece. Transp. Res. Procedia **45**, 95–102 (2020)

15. Nikiforiadis, A., et al.: Quantifying the negative impact of interactions between users of pedestrians-cyclists shared use space. In: Gervasi, O., et al. (eds.) ICCSA 2020. LNCS, vol. 12250, pp. 809–818. Springer, Cham (2020). https://doi.org/10.1007/978-3-030-58802-1_58

16. Nikiforiadis, A., Basbas, S., Garyfalou, M.I.: A methodology for the assessment of pedestrians-cyclists shared space level of service. J. Cleaner Prod. **254**, 120172 (2020)

17. Campisi, T., Akgün, N., Tesoriere, G.: An ordered logit model for predicting the willingness of renting micro mobility in urban shared streets: a case study in Palermo, Italy. In: Gervasi, O., et al. (eds.) ICCSA 2020. LNCS, vol. 12250, pp. 796–808. Springer, Cham (2020). https://doi.org/10.1007/978-3-030-58802-1_57

18. Campisi, T., Akgün, N., Ticali, D., Tesoriere, G.: Exploring public opinion on personal mobility vehicle use: a case study in Palermo, Italy. Sustainability **12**(13), 5460 (2020)

19. Tarasi, D., Daras, T., Tournaki, S., Tsoutsos, T.: Transportation in the Mediterranean during the COVID-19 pandemic era. Global Transit. **3**, 55–71 (2021). https://doi.org/10.1016/j.glt.2020.12.003. ISSN 2589-7918

20. Bereitschaft, B., Scheller, D.: How might the COVID-19 pandemic affect 21st century urban design, planning, and development? Urban Sci. **4**, 56 (2020). https://doi.org/10.3390/urbansci4040056

21. Almannaa, M.H., Alsahhaf, F.A., Ashqar, H.I., Elhenawy, M., Masoud, M., Rakotonirainy, A.: Perception analysis of e-scooter riders and non-riders in Riyadh, Saudi Arabia: survey outputs. Sustainability **13**, 863 (2021). https://doi.org/10.3390/su13020863

22. Li, A., Zhao, P., He, H., Axhausen, K.W.: Understanding the variations of micro-mobility behavior before and during COVID-19 pandemic period. Arb. Verk. Raumplan. **2020**, 1547 (2020)

23. Richardson, A.J., Ampt, E.S., Meyburg, A.H.: Survey Methods for Transport Planning, pp. 75–145. Eucalyptus Press, Melbourne (1995)

24. Wright, K.B.: Researching Internet-based populations: advantages and disadvantages of online survey research, online questionnaire authoring software packages, and web survey services. J. Comput.-Mediat. Commun. **10**(3), JCMC1034 (2005)

25. Moovit (2020). www.moovitapp.com

26. Moslem, S., Campisi, T., Szmelter-Jarosz, A., Duleba, S., Nahiduzzaman, K.M., Tesoriere, G.: Best–worst method for modelling mobility choice after COVID-19: evidence from Italy. Sustainability **12**(17), 6824 (2020)

27. Google. Google mobility reports, Italy (2020). https://www.google.com/covid19/mobility/index.html?hl=it

An Estimation of Emission Patterns from Vehicle Traffic Highlighting Decarbonisation Effects from Increased e-fleet in Areas Surrounding the City of Rzeszow (Poland)

Tiziana Campisi[1]($\boxtimes$) , Maksymilian Mądziel[2] , Andreas Nikiforiadis[3] ,
Socrates Basbas[3] , and Giovanni Tesoriere[1]

[1] Faculty of Engineering and Architecture, University of Enna Kore, Cittadella Universitaria,
94100 Enna, Italy
tiziana.campisi@unikore.it
[2] Faculty of Mechanical Engineering and Aeronautics, Rzeszow University of Technology,
35-959 Rzeszow, Poland
[3] Department of Transportation and Hydraulic Engineering, School of Rural and Surveying
Engineering, Faculty of Engineering, Aristotle University of Thessaloniki,
54124 Thessaloniki, Greece

Abstract. After several months of lockdown and the freezing of many human activities, Europe has entered phase III of the management of the COVID19 emergency. The pandemic made necessary to give great attention in the economic recession and also to give emphasis on the decarbonisation of our economy. While the European Commission reaffirms its determination to move forward with the European Green Deal and announces a green recovery plan, many governments are rapidly putting in place public stimulus programmes to boost the economy and restore jobs. After years of rising CO_2 emissions from road transport and the lack of investment in clean technologies, in the early 2020s an unprecedented growth in sales of zero and low emission cars was observed in the EU. The three main pillars for the success of e-mobility are the spread of electric vehicles, the carbon-neutral production processes and the use of energy from renewable sources. The present work shows the usefulness of traffic simulation tools for the comparison of existing and future scenarios, paying particular attention to the variation of the percentage of electric vehicles in the fleet. More specifically, a specific emission model is being used in the case of a roundabout in the city of Rzeszow, Poland and the results underline the importance of preventive analysis for the implementation of optimal transport decarbonisation strategies, as well as they lay the groundwork for future research steps.

Keywords: Electric vehicles · Decarbonisation strategies · Emission models · Traffic simulation · Roundabout

© Springer Nature Switzerland AG 2021
O. Gervasi et al. (Eds.): ICCSA 2021, LNCS 12953, pp. 683–698, 2021.
https://doi.org/10.1007/978-3-030-86976-2_47

1   Introduction

The European Union is implementing a series of strategies to achieve a reduction in pollutant emissions from vehicle traffic by 2030 and 2050. The fact that the European Union highly prioritizes the significant reduction of CO_2 emissions is being already understood with the 2011 White Paper on Transport [1] and it became even clearer with the recent European Green Deal [2]. In the epicentre of the activities for achieving this important objective is the promotion of electromobility. However, the effective reduction of emissions requires the utilization of renewable energy sources for vehicles' charging [3].

The compatibility of electric vehicles with renewable energy sources has motivated many businesses, governments and non-governmental organisations to introduce electric vehicles in their fleets to drastically reduce oil consumption, reduce carbon pollution, eliminate local air pollution and stimulate economic development. Long-term planning scenarios indicate that the global vehicle fleet needs to be almost entirely made up of electric vehicles, powered mostly by renewable sources, for avoiding the worst-case scenarios of the global climate change in 2050.

The present paper aims to quantify the benefits of introducing electric vehicles, by applying simulation tools and emission models. Through this quantification, it is sought to understand the potential of electromobility for contributing in the environmental sustainability of the road transport sector.

The case study examined in this paper refers to a roundabout which is a very effective traffic management "tool" used worldwide to achieve a satisfactory level of service for motorized traffic and to secure a high level of road safety for vulnerable road users [4–6]. In addition, roundabouts have a significant effect in the environmental conditions since they are expected to reduce air pollutants like CO_2 and noise emissions [7, 8].

Another important aspect is the forthcoming introduction of autonomous and connected vehicles in the daily operation of roundabouts where the use of algorithms and simulation techniques is essential to assess the impact of the new technologies [9, 10]. For all the above-mentioned reasons, it is considered very interesting to test the simulation scenarios concerning the e-fleet in a roundabout which is a crucial element of the road network and will continue to be in the future.

2   The Spread of e-mobility in Europe

In recent decades, various regulations have been implemented for setting restrictions regarding the use of high-polluting vehicles. The regulations concern both technological and taxation aspects.

The efforts for limiting the use of high-polluting vehicles also include the introduction of electric vehicles, which do not directly emit air pollutants or CO_2. As of 2010 a number of actions have been implemented to improve the environmental performance of vehicle fleets and it is anticipated that the electric vehicles market will rise due to European CO_2 targets. These targets have motivated the formation of national plans that ban the sale of new cars with internal combustion engines, for example in Norway, the Netherlands, Ireland, Slovenia, France and the UK [11–13]. The increase of new zero-emission vehicles on the market will also lead to a greater availability of these vehicles to second-hand vehicle buyers.

Despite the goals that European Union has set for the reduction of emissions coming from the transport sector, it has been observed that significant differences exist between the European regions. More specifically, Northern, Central and Western European countries have the most environmentally friendly vehicle fleets, with less CO_2 emissions on average. On the other hand, the vehicles in the South-Eastern, Central-Eastern and Southern European countries emit greater CO_2 volumes on average.

Vehicle trade flows also follow different patterns among the different European regions. For instance, the Northern and Central European countries export far more used vehicles than they import; since the total number of vehicles is not being shrinked, it becomes clear that the difference is being covered by new vehicles. On the contrary, the South-East and the Central-East countries are the main importers and, in many cases, they import vehicles with relatively high air pollutants and CO_2 emissions.

One of the most influential factors for these differences between the European regions is the household income, which differs significantly and determines to a large extent the penetration rate of electric vehicles [14].

Except for the income, national regulations and taxation systems have a significant role to play in the motivation of users for purchasing a low-emission vehicle or even an electric. However, in countries such as Serbia, Bosnia-Herzegovina and Hungary, bans on the import of old vehicles or on vehicles with low European emission standards, did not led to the import of higher-value vehicles. These countries in particular import vehicles that have a low price and also average emissions (e.g. due to high mileage travelled or technological inefficiencies). However, further research is needed to better understand the impact of various import bans on the vehicle fleet and its environmental-friendliness.

The penetration of electric vehicles in the European market is well defined by Fig. 1. It can be clearly seen that Norway and Northern European countries in general have the highest rates (15–25% or even more), while very low penetration rates of around 1–3% are observed in countries such as Poland.

The diffusion of shared mobility with electric vehicles is accompanied by various campaigns that raise awareness [15] and by strategies that encourage the use of electric vehicles for both taxis [16, 17] and DRT [18–20].

2.1 The development of electric mobility in Poland.

Poland is one of the countries with the highest levels of pollution from road traffic [21, 22]. It is currently characterized by a national traffic composition defined on Table 1 considering different fuelling types per vehicle category in Poland in 2019–2020.

The Polish Ministry of Energy proposed in its electromobility development plan, which was adopted in September 2016, an ambitious target to see 1 million electric vehicles on Polish roads by the end of 2025. This programme is divided into two independent components: one aiming at the development and production of electric buses and one that focuses on the design and production of a Polish electric car. Moreover, the Polish Ministry plans to create a system of incentives in order to promote electric vehicles at this level.

In 2018, laws were adopted in favour of electromobility and alternative fuels. A number of actions were implemented regarding the facilitation of electric mobility, including the formation of a framework for basic infrastructure for alternative fuels (electricity,

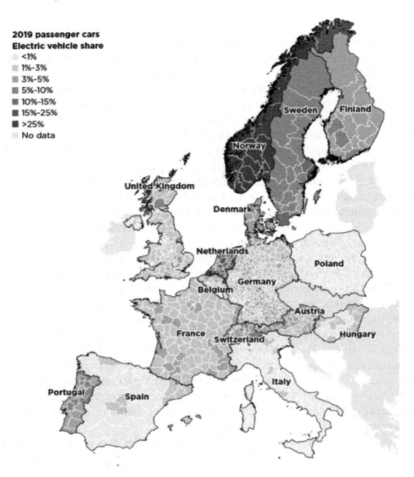

Fig. 1. Electric share of 2019 new passenger car registration in 16 European countries (source: https://theicct.org/publications/european-electric-vehicle-factbook-20192020).

Table 1. Distribution of different fueling vehicle type in Poland.

Vehicle category	Diesel	petrol (including bi-fuel)
Passenger cars	60,5%	39,5%
Commercial vehicles	86,0%	14,0%
Trucks	99,7%	0,2%
Coaches	99,4%	0,6%
Public transport	100,0%	0,0%
Buses (Light commercial vehicles)	100,0%	0,0%

LNG, CNG and hydrogen). Additional measures that have been implemented to promote electric vehicles in Poland are the allowance of installing charging stations without building permits and the establishment of a law that exempts suppliers from the obligation to obtain a licence for electricity trading in the case of charging services. Also, fiscal benefits are in place with exemption from excise duty for electric and hydrogen vehicles.

From an infrastructural point of view, parking spaces dedicated to electric vehicles during charging have been designed and implemented in paid parking zones. Polish legislation also indicates a minimum number of charging points to be installed per municipality. In addition, electric vehicles will be allowed in bus lanes until 1 January 2026. A main challenge is also the installation of public charging stations along TEN-T roads.

Recent surveys show that between 28% and 45% of citizens and businesses in Poland would consider buying an electric car and consumers have a generally positive opinion of electric vehicles, but they expect that the purchase of electric vehicles should be supported. [23, 24]. At the same time, registrations of new electric cars in Poland have shown a positive trend. In 2019, a total of about 2,600 new electric cars were registered in Poland, a share of 0.5%. In July 2020, the number of electric passenger cars in Poland amounted to over 13 thousand, an increase of 12% since May 2020. The battery electric vehicles (BEV) accounted for 35–38% of the electric cars market as of July 2020 [22, 25] as it is presented in Fig. 2.

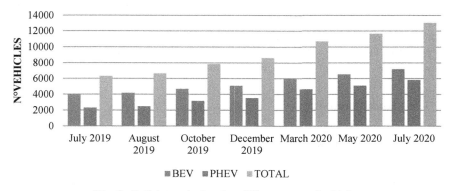

Fig. 2. Polish trend related to different type of vehicle.

Poland has the largest concentration of battery production plants for electric vehicles in Europe. Several strategies are available in the literature to study the demand and supply of transport with particular reference to electric mobility. In order to understand which strategies can be put in place to improve electric mobility, several investigative steps are necessary: on the one hand, the distribution of surveys to the population could highlight some criticalities related to the use of electric vehicles and difficulties in travel habits; on the other hand, an evaluation with simulation software could highlight some criticalities related to the types of infrastructure currently present in the area.

After a brief analysis of the literature and of the trends in electric mobility in Poland, this manuscript focused on the analysis of a roundabout intersection with an average high traffic flow due to the presence of numerous commercial and other activities and on the possibility of comparing traffic scenarios with constant increases in electric vehicles through the use of traffic microsimulation as a preventive evaluation and possible mitigation tool of environmental impacts. Several traffic scenarios were compared and the results yielded useful conclusions for the implementation of decarbonisation policies in the area examined.

3   Methodology

3.1   Microsimulation Approach

The comparison of multiple hypothetical scenarios was possible through a microsimulation evaluation. Microsimulation tools allow the assessment of traffic scenarios, which include fluctuations of the vehicle's composition, and changes in geometric and functional characteristics of the infrastructure [26]. There are numerous tools that allow the surrogate evaluation of safety parameters [27], but also the level of service assessment for vehicular flows or even pedestrian flows [28, 29]. Moreover, they can provide an estimation regarding the produced emissions [30, 31]. The study was carried out using the VISSIM software and the RoundaboutEM emission model [32, 33], comparing different layouts with the same intersection geometry but with different percentages of electric vehicles in the fleet, and estimating the CO_2 concentrations that are being produced. The selected area is located in the northern part of the city of Rzeszow, which is in the south-eastern part of Poland. In particular, a two-lane roundabout intersection on the ring road was identified, characterised by medium-intense traffic linked to the various activities in the vicinity of the investigated area.

3.2   Case Study Analysis

Congestion phenomena that are being caused by vehicle traffic have started playing a significant role in the area connected to the city of Rzeszow. One of the main reasons for the increase in traffic congestion in Rzeszow is the fast growth of the city area (since 2006, the city has expanded its administrative boundaries six times) and the relocation of inhabitants from the city centre to the suburbs.

As a result, the increasing number of people working in Rzeszow are forced to commute every day, which results in increased traffic and leads to traffic congestion [32]. Moreover, there are no ring roads (north-south) and motorways (north-south) and comparing with other cities in Poland, Rzeszow has a very low share of bicycles.

Thus, further decisive action is needed from the municipal authorities to promote cycling. The investments in bicycle lanes [33, 34], that were implemented in recent years, were not supplemented by appropriate actions to change mobility habits. On the public transport side, the increase in the number of passengers has been greater than the growth of the city's population in recent years. This was achieved largely due to measures taken by the city's authorities to reduce public transport journey times and make traffic flow smoother in congested areas.

Improving the energy efficiency of public transport, the negative effects on the environment can be reduced, especially with regard to the emission of greenhouse gases and other toxic substances. The introduction of electric buses on these routes would lead to a decrease in fuel consumption and it would limit the emission of harmful substances into the atmosphere.

The present study shows a comparison of scenarios (actual and theoretical) in one of the roundabouts located in the city of Rzeszow, in the East part of city like, as it shown in Fig. 3.

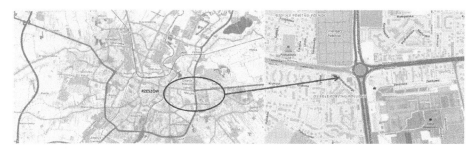

Fig. 3. Location of the examined roundabout (source: https://www.openstreetmap.org/#map=15/50.0360/22.0211&layers=T).

This area was selected because it is characterised by a high level of vehicle traffic and the presence of various commercial and other activities in the proximity. An assessment of the emissions generated by an increasing percentage of light vehicles, starting from the composition of the local fleet, has allowed us to understand the benefits of the spread of electric mobility in terms of the concentration of pollutants. The roundabout intersection was initially analysed in terms of functional geometry and was reproduced by defining arcs using VISSIM software. The city of Rzeszow bears witnesses to practically all unfavourable effects of urban development related to the functioning of transport. The increase in the number of vehicles and traffic intensity contributes to road congestion and higher journey times [26]. In particular a functioning roundabout with four arms and double lanes was selected like described on Fig. 4. The daily traffic is about 1000 veh/h during the peak hour 08:00–09:00 in the morning of weekdays. The roundabout is named Rond Pobitno and it connects an urban with a national road. The intersection is characterized by the presence on both directions of cycle paths. The secondary direction is defined by ul. Lwowska (East to West and vice versa), while the main direction is defined in the south part by al. Armii Krajowej and in the northern part by al. Żółnierzy i Armii Wojska Polskiego (North to South and vice versa) (see Fig. 4).

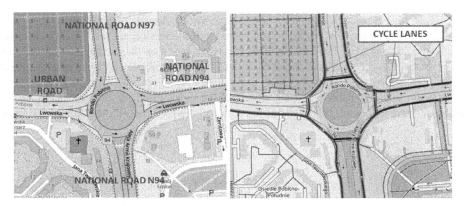

Fig. 4. Roads classification and bike lane (on blue) location. (Color figure online)

The outer diameter of the roundabout is 84 m. The road width in inlets and outlets is 4.15 m and, in the roundabout, it is 4.28 m. The roundabout is located next to supermarkets, a hospital and actually enables to enter the city from suburban areas, while it is also a crossing node of national roads. Due to its importance, the specific roundabout was chosen for the research. Figure 5 presents the real and the simulated roundabout.

Fig. 5. The real and the simulated geometrical scheme of the analyzed roundabout.

Five scenarios have been selected, one of which is the current scenario and the others assume an increase of 5–10–15 and 30% in the share of electric vehicles. These scenarios do not envisage 100% of electric vehicles on the road, as reaching this figure is a long way off. However, the scenarios are quite consistent with European strategies, with an action horizon of the next few decades. In particular these scenarios were selected after considering the European strategies described in Table 2.

Table 2. Target for inclusion of electric vehicles in European strategies

	A	B	C	D	E	F	G	H
2025	50%	15%	20%	50%	10%	10%	5%	70%
2030	100%	40%	50%	100%	25%	30%	30%	80%
2035		100%			50%	80%	80%	90%
2050		100%						

A = motorcycles and mopeds B = passenger cars C = vans D = urban buses
E = coaches F = HGVs < 16t G = HGVs < 16t H = rail

4   Results

The Vissim software enables vehicle movement simulation based on a discrete time step and a stochastic microscopic model, which includes Wiedemann car following psycho-physical driver behavior. In this way, it was possible to create a CO_2 concentration map for the studied area in VERSIT+ calculation model. The roundabout scheme, which is analysed, is characterised by a main direction of vehicular flow (North-South) and secondary direction (East-West), as it can be seen in Fig. 6.

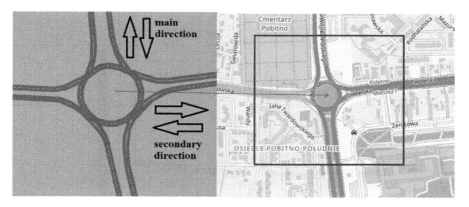

Fig. 6. Definition of the case study area and relative traffic directions.

The first analysed scenario expresses the existing situation, in which there are no electric vehicles. Figure 7 shows the distribution of CO_2 emissions, where the darker colour corresponds to a higher emission.

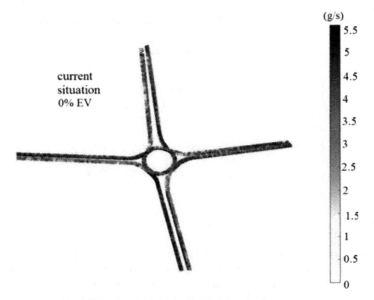

Fig. 7. Current scenario without e-fleet.

For the second scenario, the electric fleet was increased by 5%, by replacing a proportion of the combustion-powered light vehicles. The results are shown in Fig. 8.

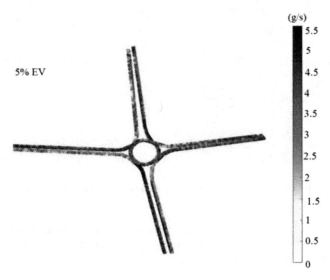

Fig. 8. Increase of 5% of EV on current vehicle fleet.

Then, a 10% increase (comparing with the existing situation), of electric vehicles was assumed. The results are presented in Fig. 9.

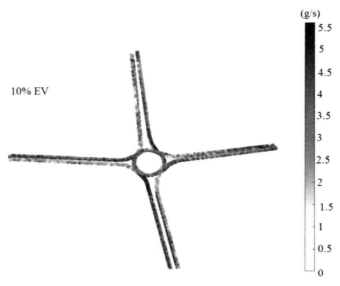

Fig. 9. Increase of 10% of EV on current vehicle fleet.

Figure 10 presents the results for the fourth scenario, with a 15% of the electric fleet.

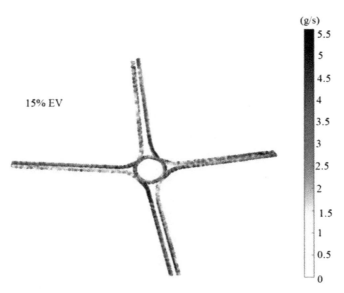

Fig. 10. Increase of 15% of EV on current vehicle fleet.

Finally, an insertion of 30% in accordance with European strategies was considered and the layout that is presented in Fig. 11 shows a substantial reduction in emissions.

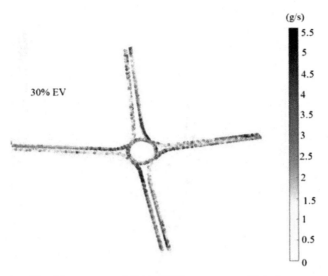

Fig. 11. Increase of 30% of EV on current vehicle fleet.

To summarize the results, Fig. 12 compares the CO_2 concentrations in the five scenarios. It shows that a 30% share of electric vehicles in the fleet could reduce CO_2 emissions from about 340 to about 220 (g/km).

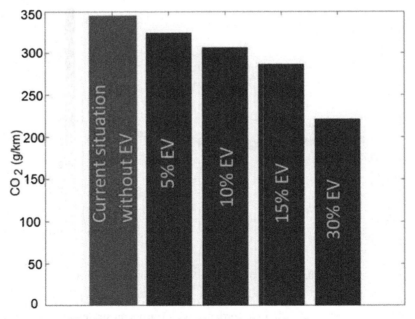

Fig. 12. Comparion of results in relation with e-fleet rate.

5   Conclusion and Discussion

Air pollution that is produced by the road transport sector, is one of the greatest threats for the environment. This is due to the predominance of road transport modes over other modes of transport, but also due to the fact that the emission of pollutants is being concentrated mainly on dense urban areas. This is also an outcome of the increased mobility of people and goods in modern societies.

Several strategies have been implemented worldwide to discourage the use of internal combustion engine vehicles and to encourage the use of greener means of transport, such as walking or cycling. Also, a great effort is being made to replace high-emission vehicles with low-emission ones and especially with electric vehicles, either private or public.

However, the increased mobility needs are directly linked with an increased negative impact on the environment. The demographic development, the expansion of urban agglomerations and the centralisation of services and activities in urban centres have led to extremely increased traffic volumes. In turn, this has led to frequent phenomena of congestion and therefore to a deterioration of the air quality. The monitoring of air pollution makes possible to obtain very precise information on the pollutants' concentrations and to make valuable comparisons.

However, this approach is generally applied for the detection of a limited number of pollutants (e.g. COx and NOx) comparing with the number of different pollutants that are being released into the atmosphere (e.g. aromatic compounds, heavy metals, etc.). Furthermore, this approach is not able to provide information for all areas, due to an unavailability of sensors, as well as for future scenarios. For a more holistic approach regarding the identification of the environmental conditions and degradation, it is particularly useful to combine the abovementioned sensors with simulation tools (models). Therefore, in the context of these general considerations, the present paper investigates the improvement of the air quality due to the introduction of electric vehicles and quantifies the CO_2 savings, using a specific micro-simulation software.

The simulation results prove that the introduction of electric vehicles in the fleets reduce significantly the CO_2 emissions. Even a 10% of electric vehicles in the total fleet can provide a substantial reduction of emissions, while a 30% penetration of electric vehicles can have an extremely positive impact. The specific conclusion shows that the efforts for the promotion of electromobility need to be enhanced, by providing adequate subsidies to the users. The purchasing cost of electric vehicles remain the greatest obstacles in adopting electromobility, but it is anticipated that this obstacle can be overcome with the subsidies' aid. Additionally, the implementation of complete charging networks is considered as a prerequisite for increasing electric vehicles' penetration. However, countries such as Norway, Sweden and the Netherlands have already showed the path, proving that the right measures can have a positive impact.

This research lays the foundations for future investigation considering not only light but also heavy electric vehicles for showing in a preventive way the benefits related to the reduction of internal combustion engine vehicles.

Acknowledgments. The authors acknowledge financial support from the MIUR (Ministry of Education, Universities and Research [Italy]) through a project entitled WEAKI TRANSIT: WEAK-demand areas Innovative TRANsport Shared services for Italian Towns (Project code:

20174ARRHT/CUP Code: J74I19000320008), financed with the PRIN 2017 (Research Projects of National Relevance) program. We authorize the MIUR to reproduce and distribute reprints for Governmental purposes, notwithstanding any copyright notations thereon. Any opinions, findings, and conclusions or recommendations expressed in this material are those of the authors and do not necessarily reflect the views of the MIUR.

Funding. This research work was partially funded by the MIUR (Ministry of Education, Universities and Research [Italy]) through a project entitled WEAKI TRANSIT.

Author Contributions. Conceptualization, T.C., S.B. and M.M.; methodology M.M and T.C.; software, M.M.; validation, T.C and M.M.; formal analysis, A.N.; resources M.M.; data curation, T.C.; writing—original draft preparation, T.C., S.B. and A.N.; writing—review and editing, S.B. and A.N.; visualization, T.C.; supervision, G.T.; project administration, T.C. All authors have read and agreed to the published version of the manuscript.

Conflicts of Interest. The authors declare no conflict of interest.

References

1. European Commission: White Paper: Roadmap to a Single European Transport Area – Towards a competitive and resource efficient transport system, Brussels (2011)
2. European Commission: The European Green Deal, Brussels (2019)
3. Pietrzak, K., Pietrzak, O.: Environmental effects of electromobility in a sustainable urban public transport. Sustainability **12**, 1052 (2020)
4. Campisi, T., Deluka-Tibljaš, A., Tesoriere, G., Canale, A., Rencelj, M., Šurdonja, S.: Cycling traffic at turbo roundabouts: some considerations related to cyclist mobility and safety. Transp. Res. Procedia **45**, 627–634 (2020)
5. Hydén, C., Várhelyi, A.: The effects on safety, time consumption and environment of large scale use of roundabouts in an urban area: a case study. Accid. Anal. Prev. **32**(1), 11–23 (2000)
6. Gavanas, N., Pitsiava-Latinopoulou, M., Basbas, S.: Pedestrian safety requirements at urban roundabouts: a case study in three roundabouts in Greece. ICASTOR J. Eng. **3**(3), 223–238 2010 (2010)
7. Lakouari, N., Oubram, O., Bassam, A., Pomares Hernandez, S.E.R., Ez-Zahraouy, M.H.: Modeling and simulation of CO2 emissions in roundabout intersection. J. Comput. Sci. **40**, 101072 (2020). https://doi.org/10.1016/j.jocs.2019.101072
8. Fernandes, P., et al.: Impacts of roundabouts in suburban areas on congestion-specific vehicle speed profiles, pollutant and noise emissions: an empirical analysis. Sustain. Cities Soc. **62**, 102386 (2020)
9. Martin-Gasulla, M., Elefteriadou, L.: Traffic management with autonomous and connected vehicles at single-lane roundabouts. Transp. Res. Part C Emerg. Technol. **125**, 102964 (2021)
10. Gonzalez, D., Pérez, J., Milanés, V.: Parametric-based path generation for automated vehicles at roundabouts. Expert Syst. Appl. **71**, 332–341 (2017)
11. Velten, E.K., Brauer, C., Thie, J.E.: Used vehicle trade and fleet composition in Europe (2019)
12. Wawer, M., et al.: Traffic-related pollutants in roadside soils of different countries in Europe and Asia. Water Air Soil Pollut. **226**(7), 1–14 (2015)
13. Łowicki, D.: Landscape pattern as an indicator of urban air pollution of particulate matter in Poland. Ecol. Ind. **97**, 17–24 (2019)

14. Chen, T.D., Wang, Y., Kockelman, K.M.: Where are the electric vehicles? a spatial model for vehicle-choice count data. J. Transp. Geogr. **43**, 181–188 (2015)
15. Tesoriere, G., Campisi, T.: The benefit of engage the "crowd" encouraging a bottom-up approach for shared mobility rating. In: Gervasi, O. et al. (eds) Computational Science and Its Applications – ICCSA 2020. ICCSA 2020. Lecture Notes in Computer Science, vol 12250. Springer, Cham (2020). https://doi.org/10.1007/978-3-030-58802-1_60
16. Kaya, Ö., Alemdar, K.D., Çodur, M.Y.: A novel two stage approach for electric taxis charging station site selection. Sustain. Cities Soc. **62**, 102396 (2020)
17. Askari, S., Peiravian, F., Tilahun, N., Yousefi Baseri, M.: Determinants of users' perceived taxi service quality in the context of a developing country. Transp. Lett. **13**(2), 125–137 (2021)
18. Papanikolaou, A., Basbas, S.: Analytical models for comparing demand responsive transport with bus services in low demand interurban areas. Transp. Lett. **13**, 1–8 (2020)
19. Abdullah, M., Ali, N., Shah, S.A.H., Javid, M.A., Campisi, T.: Service quality assessment of app-based demand-responsive public transit services in Lahore Pakistan. Appl. Sci. **11**(4), 1911 (2021)
20. Campisi, T., Canale, A.,Ticali, D., Tesoriere, G.: Innovative solutions for sustainable mobility in areas of weak demand. Some factors influencing the implementation of the DRT system in Enna (Italy). In AIP Conference Proceedings, vol. 2343, pp. 090005. AIP Publishing LLC March 2021. https://doi.org/10.1063/5.0047765
21. Bienias, K., Kowalska-Pyzalska, A., Ramsey, D.: What do people think about electric vehicles? an initial study of the opinions of car purchasers in Poland. Energy Rep. **6**, 267–273 (2020)
22. https://www.statista.com/statistics/1081299/poland-number-of-electric-passenger-vehicles/. Accessed 1 Dec 2020
23. Campisi, T., Tesoriere, G., Sanfilippo, L., Brignone, A., Canale, A.: Exploring the TTMS's impact to the accessibility of a long distance stretch using micro-simulation approach. In: Gervasi O. et al. (eds) Computational Science and Its Applications – ICCSA 2020. ICCSA 2020. Lecture Notes in Computer Science, vol. 12250. Springer, Cham July 2020. https://doi.org/10.1007/978-3-030-58802-1_55
24. Tesoriere, G., Campisi, T., Canale, A., Zgrablić, T.: The surrogate safety appraisal of the unconventional elliptical and turbo roundabouts. J. Adv. Transp. (2018)
25. Rotaris, L., Giansoldati, M., Scorrano, M.: The slow uptake of electric cars in Italy and Slovenia. Evidence from a stated-preference survey and the role of knowledge and environmental awareness. Transp. Res. Part A Policy Pract. **144**, 1–18 (2021)
26. Campisi, T., Mrak, I., Canale, A., Tesoriere, G.: The surrogate safety measures evaluation of a staggered crossing on the delta area of Rijeka. In: AIP Conference Proceedings, vol. 2186, no. 1, p. 160006. AIP Publishing LLC, December 2019
27. Basbas, S., Campisi, T., Canale, A., Nikiforiadis, A., Gruden, C.: Pedestrian level of service assessment in an area close to an under-construction metro line in Thessaloniki, Greece. Transp. Res. Procedia **45**, 95–102 (2020)
28. Tollazzi, T., Tesoriere, G., Guerrieri, M., Campisi, T.: Environmental, functional and economic criteria for comparing "target roundabouts" with one-or two-level roundabout intersections. Transp. Res. Part D Transp. Environ. **34**, 330–344 (2015)
29. Mądziel, M., Campisi, T., Jaworski, A., Tesoriere, G.: The development of strategies to reduce exhaust emissions from passenger cars in Rzeszow city—Poland a preliminary assessment of the results produced by the increase of e-fleet. Energies **14**(4), 1046 (2021)
30. Jaworski, A., Mądziel, M., Lejda, K.: Creating an emission model based on portable emission measurement system for the purpose of a roundabout. Environ. Sci. Pollut. Res. **26**(21), 21641–21654 (2019). https://doi.org/10.1007/s11356-019-05264-1

31. Madziel, M., Jaworski, A., Savostin-Kosiak, D., Lejda, K.: The impact of exhaust emission from combustion engines on the environment: modelling of vehicle movement at roundabouts. Int. J. Automot. Mech. Eng. **17**(4), 8360 (2020). https://doi.org/10.15282/ijame.17.4.2020.12.0632
32. Gębarowski, M., Wiażewicz, J.: Transport Congestion (in Polish Cities)–Rzeszow in Comparison to the Biggest Cities in Poland
33. Smieszek, M., Dobrzanska, M., Dobrzanski, P.: Rzeszow as a city taking steps towards developing sustainable public transport. Sustainability **11**(2), 402 (2019)
34. Dobrzański, P.D., Smieszek, M.S., Dobrzańska, M.D.: Rzeszow as a City Taking Steps towards Developing Sustainable Public Transport (2019)

Exploring the Factors that Encourage the Spread of EV-DRT into the Sustainable Urban Mobility Plans

Tiziana Campisi[1] , Elena Cocuzza[2] , Matteo Ignaccolo[2] , Giuseppe Inturri[3] ,
and Vincenza Torrisi[2(✉)]

[1] Faculty of Engineering and Architecture, University of Enna Kore, Cittadella Universitaria,
94100 Enna, Italy
`tiziana.campisi@unikore.it`
[2] Department of Civil Engineering and Architecture, University of Catania,
Cittadella Universitaria, 95125 Catania, Italy
`{ecocuzza,vtorrisi}@dica.unict.it`
[3] Department of Electric Electronic and Computer Engineering, University of Catania,
Cittadella Universitaria, 95125 Catania, Italy

Abstract. The development of sustainable mobility is linked to technological developments and different forms of vehicle power supply. Despite all the difficulties brought by the COVID-19 pandemic, therefore, it is necessary to provide road users with an adequate network of public recharging infrastructures and to facilitate the setting-up of private recharging stations through shared and participatory development plans between the stakeholders and all the institutions involved. The present work introduces an analysis of some of the European Sustainable Urban Mobility Plans (SUMPs) and the transport supply connected to several cities. After an evaluation of the macro areas of intervention, factors and criteria for the deployment of the electric vehicle linked to the demand responsive transport choice (EV-DRTs) have been defined in terms of user classification and environmental factors, but also considering the services and infrastructures for electric charging. The identification of these factors and criteria allows an exemplification in the development and adaptation of the planning and design concept.

Keywords: Electric vehicle · SUMPs · Demand Responsive Transport (DRT) · Shared mobility

---

This paper is the result of the joint work of the authors. 'Abstract' and 'Conclusion' were written jointly by all authors. Vincenza Torrisi wrote "Introduction" and "Background". Tiziana Campisi wrote "Methodology". Tiziana Campisi and Elena Cocuzza wrote the paragraph title "SUMPs analysis ". Matteo Ignaccolo and Giuseppe Inturri supervised and founded the work.

O. Gervasi et al. (Eds.): ICCSA 2021, LNCS 12953, pp. 699–714, 2021.
https://doi.org/10.1007/978-3-030-86976-2_48

1 Introduction

One of the main objectives of the European Union is to achieve climate neutrality by 2050. One of the main sources of emissions and greenhouse gases (GHG) is transport. By 2030, it is expected that there will be about 10% less travel by private car. In addition, the rise of the sharing economy, multi-modality and autonomous vehicles, as well as the global ageing of the population, will drastically reduce the need to own a car. This decrease will be offset by compensated by a progressive increase in the use of public transport [1], bicycles and walking [2–4], as well as by a transition to more sustainable and ecological transport systems [5]. New mobility habits related to increased cycling and walking for short distances (<2 km) and the use of public or shared mobility for medium and long distances (>2 km) are supported by many projects such as the extension of cycle paths, the implementation of sharing systems, pedestrianization projects and the improvement of public transport [6, 7].

Investing in the use of technologies for urban mobility will be decisive in facilitating the transition towards more agile and sustainable solutions in the next 10 years [8, 9].About 40% of people globally are inclined to the idea of using more innovative transport solutions. But not all cities are prepared for a radical transformation of mobility [8, 9]. Among the technologies and mobility solutions with the greatest potential to meet the needs of tomorrow's commuters there are:

- Mobility as a Service (MaaS) This model integrates different transport modes, including buses, trams, bicycles and car sharing, and combines them in a single ticket or in a single app. In this way, the multimodal travel experience can be optimized into a unique user experience that has the same convenience as a trip in your own car [10];
- Mobility hubs: located in the peripheral areas of cities, these stations allow commuters to switch from their polluting cars to vehicles with zero emissions, such as electric buses, e-bikes and scooters, so as to contribute to the reduction of pollution and decongestion urban area [12];
- Autonomous parcel delivery vehicles: vehicles with automatic parcel delivery such as mobile stations, where the customer can activate the delivery via an app, in order to direct the vehicle to a predetermined place and autonomously retrieve the package from it. This system helps to limit trips with unsuccessful delivery, significantly reducing traffic and ensuring greater effectiveness [13].

Within this framework, the main aim of this paper is to define factors and criteria for the deployment of EV-DRTs, in terms of user classification and environmental factors, but also considering the services and infrastructures for electric charging. The determination of these factors and criteria allows an exemplification in the development and adaptation of the planning and design concept. The work focused on the research steps defined by Figure 1:

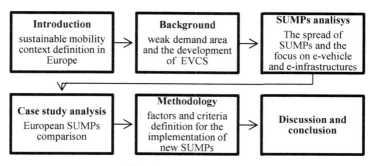

Fig. 1. Steps of research

2 Background

Low demand areas are located in urban or interurban contexts and are generally characterised by low or medium-low transport demand. These areas are notable for their spatial and temporal dispersion.

The "weak demand" attribute is directly related to the number of travels but can also refer to the degree of fragmentation of the demand for which small groups of users generate low levels of demand for mobility. The identification of these areas must be carried out considering the presence within the municipal area of a large number of villages or scattered houses that require to be connected to the main urban center of the Municipality (where, e.g. commercial businesses, offices, transport hubs are located). These types of settlements should not be served by conventional public transport systems, which would be expensive and inefficient for the level of mobility of the area. Indeed, it may be necessary to combine different routes with many stops, long distances to be covered with low load factors, reinforcing the need to adopt more flexible forms of local public transport [14, 15].

In this context, the Demand Responsive Transport (DRT) represents an innovative solving solution. It consists in using a fleet of small-sized public transport (e.g. minivans) capable of making personalized trips based on user requests (with origin and destination chosen each time), bringing a certain number of users and managing the concatenation of paths with a good level of flexibility to satisfy all requests [16, 17].

The DRT must be able to plan the route of each vehicle used based on the requests received. The models used to manage these systems are also adaptable to the transport of goods, albeit with a slightly higher level of rigidity [18]. In general, the implementation of DRT tries to satisfy two opposing needs:

- Minimization of operating costs (which can increase in the case of maximum flexibility);
- Maximization of the level of service offered to the user (which decreases if waiting or travel times become longer).

Therefore, in the absence of a local public transport service, the innovations brought about by both new technologies and the new shared mobility paradigm can help to bridge the gap by redefining the concept of public transport.

The new mobility paradigm provides for an on-demand transport service, which allows users distributed in an area to book and make a trip and allows to transport operators to perform the service reducing the waiting time for users, the number of vehicles and the travelled kilometres, thanks to the sharing of the ride with the same vehicle among multiple users. However, to the concept of weak demand areas, which have low demand for mobility only at certain hours of the day or periods of the year, is evolving in the light of the pandemic caused by COVID-19, which has made it essential to strengthen the service in lines with higher demand.

Thus, it is possible to consider a different perspective regarding the temporal dimension. This means that a DRT system can also be useful in cities with a high demand for transport, also characterized by possible daily peaks. In this case, the DRT can act as an integration to public transport, in order to increase the capacity of the service, maintaining lower seat-load factor and answering to the requests for social distancing [19, 20].

The significant increase in electric vehicles in Europe should be related to the charging infrastructure which should adapt to these innovative forms of mobility. The evolution of these services and the increasing demand for their use must be the subject of planning tools for optimizing the benefits for the user and the surrounding environment. Therefore, European planning instruments at local, regional and national scales must consider these developments.

3 SUMPs Analysis

In Europe, two main planning tools have been defined to develop local strategies integrating electric mobility, namely Sustainable Energy Action Plans (SEAPs) and Sustainable Urban Mobility Plans (SUMPs).

A SEAP is a document related to cooperation between cities (called Pact of Mayors) in which activities and measures are defined to reduce CO_2 emissions by 2020 according to certain targets. Since 2005, EU projects have considered SUMPs and they are now an essential part of European policy [21, 22]. Unfortunately, the deployment of electric vehicles in Europe has so far a minimal impact on the strategic objectives of a SUMP. This is related to the duration of the SUMP (5–10 years) and thus the time correlation with a full adoption of e-mobility. In addition, some of the operational e-mobility objectives, such as capacity and local network use, are still difficult to link to SUMP objectives. Nevertheless, a state-of-the-art SUMP that, together with other measures, considers the introduction of e-mobility as an objective to achieve improved air quality, energy efficiency and reduced greenhouse gas emissions.

Several research studies deal with the topic of e-mobility and emissions by comparing scenarios and mitigating possible effects [23] and by analysing citizens' opinions on private use [24] or renting or sharing [25]. Therefore, this section analyses and compares on the one hand the diffusion of SUMP urban mobility plans and forms of electric mobility in some European contexts with reference to shared mobility [26] and DRT [17, 27, 28]. Secondly, it defines the factors and evaluation criteria that can be used to draw up a SUMP with a future and increasing focus on electric mobility.

3.1 Evolving Urban and Electric Mobility Planning Tools in Europe

Urban mobility planning is complex and focuses on new concepts that not only cover transport, but also integrate many related areas (land use, environment, economic development, social policy, health, safety, energy, etc.).

A sustainable urban mobility plan is a strategic plan designed to meet the mobility needs of people and businesses in and around cities for a better quality of life. It builds on existing planning and considers integration, participation and evaluation principles. The objectives focus on both traffic congestion and space consumption but also address safety, dependence on certain resources and local and global emissions. Promoting a sustainable [29], resilient [30] and smart city [31].The evolution of the latter is closely related to the diffusion of alternative mobility and in shared and on-demand mobility with electric or hybrid type engines [32]. Unfortunately, the EU does not have an overall strategic road map for e-mobility, the availability of publicly accessible charging stations varies considerably from country to country, payment systems are not harmonised, and no information is available.

Rechargeable electric and hybrid vehicles are growing but charging networks are not developing at the same pace Indeed they can act as first and last mile solutions for passengers and freight, especially when combined with electric infrastructure, as electric vehicles are suitable for short distances (see also use cases of transport networks for electric vehicles and electric charging infrastructure).

Furthermore, the charging time depends mainly on the type of vehicle battery and the capacity of the charging point, also on the battery capacity and other variables described in Table 1.

Table 1. Different charging stations details (Source: [33])

Charger speed and type	Power rating	Approximate time to charge
Slow (single-phase AC)	3–7 kW	7–16 h
Normal (three-phase AC)	11–22 kW	2–4 h
Fast (DC)	50–100 kW	30–40 min
Ultra-fast (DC)	> 100 kW	< 20 min

The definition of the SUMP [34] must therefore consider the development of the Mobility on Demand (MoD) [35] for combustion and electric fuels and the MaaS digital platforms [36], underlining the benefits and weaknesses according to the infrastructure (charging stations and parking areas) and the type of vehicle:

- Private (car, bike, micro-mobility)
- Public (bus)
- Shared mobility (car, bike, micro-mobility)
- DRT

DRT can replace low-frequency and low-frequency services, shuttling users between them and the wider public transport network.

To better plan both the infrastructure of charging stations and the inclusion of shared electric mobility (in relation to other forms of alternative electric mobility) in the SUMP, this work has defined a preliminary comparison between urban mobility planning tools and the presence of electric mobility, considering the definition showed in Table 2.

Table 2. Distribution of SUMPs in different European cities (Our elaboration. Data source from [37, 38])

City	Country	SUMP period	Local rules	EVCS (2020)	ECS	EBS	DRT
Athens	GR	n.d	SUMP	5	yes	yes	no
Barcelona	ES	2013–2018	PMUS	45 (fast)	yes	yes	partial
Berlin	DE	2025	UTDP	728	yes	yes	yes
			STEP				
Bremen	DE	2025	VEP	> 100	yes	yes	yes
Budapest	HU	2014–2030	BMT	262	yes	yes	no
Copenaghen	DK	2016–2020	SUMP	600	yes	yes	no
:eneva	SW	n.d	SUMP	57	yes	yes	no
Hamburg	DE	2013–2015	VEP	600	yes	yes	yes
			SMP 2.0				
Helsinki	FI	2015	HLJ	110	yes	yes	yes
Ljubljana	SL	2015	SUMP	80	yes	yes	no
Madrid	ES	2014	PMUS	148	yes	yes	yes
		2025	PEMSCAM				
Malmö	SE	2001–2032	SUMP	150	yes	yes	no
			TRAST				
			TROMP				
Milan	IT	2013–2018	PUMS	156	yes	yes	yes
			PUT				
Oslo	NO	2020	SUMP	400	yes	yes	yes
			SUT				

Furthermore, in the digital age, there are numerous ways to improve the efficiency of DRT systems through software and hardware solutions such as intelligent sensors, big-data or artificial intelligence. Indeed, using easy-to-use apps and their mutual connectivity with superior platforms of transport providers, the customer experience can be enhanced while maintaining or increasing the efficiency of DRT systems at the same time. An important aspect to watch out for is the introduction and use of autonomous vehicles. This technology has the potential to change the public transport landscape, especially in rural areas [39].

Therefore, the following are some European case studies defining good practices related to e-mobility deployment and sustainability and urban resilience strategies.

3.2 The Evolution of European Best Practices on e-Mobility

In the last years, European countries encourage electric mobility. However, there are not a single approach and the same policies adopted and different measures were implemented by different cities to achieve the objectives of the related SUMP. Germany has significantly implemented the number of public charging points for electric vehicles in recent years and Munich is the German city with the largest number, equal to 1,185. It has set itself the goal of optimally coordinating services such as public transport and car sharing and connecting them to an efficient electricity network. Already in 2018, to better integrate the new Domagkpark district, mainly residential and suburban, with the center, to discourage the use of private vehicles, flexible and sustainable alternative mobility[1] have been tested, such as car sharing, electric scooters and electric bicycle rental. At the same time, a charging infrastructure was implemented to support electro-mobility (Fig. 2). In particular it is consisting of charging points and mobility stations (in which different charging points for bicycles, electric scooters and cars are located) that combine and provide integrated services shared mobility with access to public transport services, such as trams and buses. The innovative concept introduced in Munich is the design of mobility stations as an integral part of traffic planning and urban mobility. Another objective pursued in Munich is the optimal coordination of services such as public transport and with new shared mobility services different forms of shared mobility and the respective connection to an intelligent electricity network. In this context, a best practice is the Mobility Station Freiheit Munchen[2], that integrates public transport (subway, bus, tram,) with taxi services, car sharing e bicycle rental. Also in this case, the electric charging infrastructure was planned as an integral part to support the services offered. In fact, there are both electric charging areas and parking spaces dedicated to vehicles of e-car sharing and bicycle parking facilities.

In 2019, Oslo was the first Green Capital of Europe and was among the first cities in Europe to promote electric mobility, having set itself the goal of drastically reducing carbon gas emissions by 95% by 2030 (compared to 1990). Therefore, it has combined several local and national measures. According to Norway's goal of eliminating sales of petrol or diesel-powered vehicles by 2025, the City has launched a program of electrification of road mobility, including buses and taxi. Locally it has banned the traffic of cars powered by fossil fuels in the central areas. Free parking areas have been created that offer the possibility of connecting vehicles to the electricity grid and recharging the

---

[1] They are implemented as part of the project ECCENTRIC by CIVITAS, also financed from the European Union's Horizon 2020 research and innovation programme, tried new sustainable mobility solutions.

[2] The result of a joint project of the City of Munich in collaboration with Münchner Verkehrsge-sellschaft (MVG), a municipally owned company responsible for operating public transport in Munich, which operates buses, the tramway and the U-Bahn, and Stadtwerke München GmbH (SWM), a company owned by the city of Munich which offers public services for the city and the region of Munich.

Fig. 2. Domagkpark charging point (Source: [40])

batteries for free. An innovative element is the creation in the parking areas reserved for taxis of a recharging network using induction plates. Furthermore, to reduce urban traffic congestion, electric car sharing services have been implemented and have been created the "Green Mobility Houses", areas that offer e-car sharing services, charging points, bicycle parking, e-scooters. A common action undertaken is the installation of charging infrastructures in public areas that exploit clean energy by renewable energy source (Fig. 3).

Fig. 3. Oslo charge & drive stations (Source: [41])

Barcelona in recent years has been promoting the use of cleaner, cheaper and more sustainable modes of transport and alternative energies, improving public transport systems and encouraging electric mobility and the mobility sharing services to improve environmental quality. According to the Strategy for electric mobility, the Catalan city aims to have 80% of the municipal fleet, buses and taxis, electric by 2024. The municipality has an efficient bike sharing service. As part of the Green Charge[3] project, actions have been implemented that aim to encourage intermodality and easily accessible forms

---

[3] The project Green Charge by CIVITAS (https://www.greencharge2020.eu/), also financed from the European Union's Horizon 2020 research and innovation programme, aims to create an electricity-based transport system and has started pilot projects in Oslo, Barcelona and Bremen.

of individual mobility and reduce externalities such as the use of public space by private vehicles. One goal pursued is the replacement of fossil fuel-powered scooters with light electric vehicles (LEVs), such as e-bike and e-scooters.

Therefore, they were installed charging location in office and public areas: over 500 charging points distributed in numerous stations and car parks in all districts, currently (February 2021) there are 555 electric charging points located in the city, 25 of which are fast charging points.

4   Methodology

This paragraph focuses on the definition of macro-areas of action. By identifying the factors and criteria, this paragraph allows the assessment of the evolution of electric infrastructures and EV-DRT in order to foster greater sustainability in transport planning and promote decarbonisation strategies.

4.1   Setting Criteria for Planning and Designing Electric Mobility

The European Commission has adopted a wide-ranging strategy which, in its rich artic-ulation of actions, pursues the objective of reducing Europe's dependence on oil imports and reducing carbon dioxide emissions in transport by 60% by 2050. To achieve this result, a makeover of the current European transport system will be necessary. To allow adequate development of electric mobility, consistent with the objectives set by the European Union for 2030, planning tools with a 2030 time-horizon will have to define possible scenarios defining private vehicle fleets, public fleets, company fleets and shar-ing services, respectively. In general, electric mobility brings energy, environmental and economic advantages, which are summarised in Table 3.

Table 3. Macro-areas definition and relative benefits (Our elaboration)

Energy	Environmental	Economy
Greater efficiency compared to a vehicle with a combustion engine	Decreasing environmental emissions or particulate matter (PM10, NOx, CO, CO2)	Increasing the development of smart energy networks
Reduced dependence on oil-based energy		Promotion of an innovative industrial sector
Integration of renewable energies in mobility	Decreasing acoustic emissions	Territorial rebalancing
Increased distributed generation and self-sufficiency		Promotion of connectivity and interaction with ICTs

About the DRT, it is observed that it can:

• Replace low-frequency routes with a dynamic service that responds to demand, which can reduce the overall costs of providing the service;

- Reduce road deterioration and maintenance costs by increasing the number of economic vehicles on the road instead of heavier, low-frequency vehicles;
- Reduce the need for additional capital investment as the use of existing road infrastructure can be optimised;
- Increase economic, social and environmental values;
- Reduce emissions by replacing inefficient fixed services with flexible and adaptable services that optimise service use;
- Encourage modal shift from private car use with convenient shared mobility options that are tailored to the specific needs of the user.

The implementation of electric mobility with DRT is closely linked to the planning of charging areas. In general, DRT operations based on electric vehicles present a more complex environment in terms of mathematical modelling and decision analysis, because battery autonomy and charging constraints need to be addressed.

It is possible to define some criteria related to both service and infrastructure to identify which criteria need to be analysed to easily plan and implement an EV-DRT service. According to [42], four aspects are necessary for the implementation of a Demand Responsive Transport system, namely the definition of the area and the potential demand preferably between 3000 and 5000 users [43], the users (e.g. elderly, young people, families and their children, etc.) and the reason for the trip, that would determinethe type of vehicle to bechosen. Furthermore, for the optimisation of an electric service, it is necessary to consider the driving style, the environmental and morphological characteristics of the area (such as slopes), the urban evolution and activities and the location of the charging stations [44] In order to implement an EV-DRT service.

The main critical issues to be analysed are related to:

- How to efficiently design and manage the integrated EV-DRT system, aiming at energy efficiency and considering the challenges of stochastic demand and charging operations;
- How DRT can best augment/replace mass transport by improving adaptation to spatial and temporal variations in demand, ensuring high quality of service and limiting operational costs;
- Define the expected benefits of an integrated EV-DRT system in terms of ridership, reduced emissions and operational costs.

Strategic planning must therefore be undertaken to decide on the provision of projects that address infrastructure gaps and future development needs (changing the use of parking, stops, stations, network; monetising the use of public infrastructure for private providers). Results-based regulation of DRT provision must also be implemented to serve the policy of integration and development/optimisation of mass transport infrastructure.

Governments need strategic network planning, commercial and project management capabilities to understand and address infrastructure gaps (physical, electrical and digital) to integrate such solutions with existing transport and energy service provision and develop the commercial framework to support the transition to results-based provision [45]. Therefore, to proceed to the infrastructure phase, it is essential to first carry out analyses at a territorial level, to identify potential users, define usage scenarios and the corresponding recharging requirements. In this case, a New York architecture firm carried out important research on its territory, where it analysed the correlation between infrastructure locations, geographical and demographic data, and current policies to highlight the main trends in location, define recommendations for maximising the use of facilities and indicate further areas for study [46].

4.2 Development of Aspects and Criteria for Planning and Designing Electric Mobility

The analysis of mobility demand and supply (infrastructures) is constantly being developed [47] and requires the identification of actions to be implemented in the short, medium and long term. This makes it possible to make the sector's regulatory process effective, to identify what actions need to be taken to improve and disseminate technical data, and finally to implement a series of actions and incentives to raise awareness among the population of the use of electric mobility. Table 4 below highlights the main action points for improving infrastructure and increasing the propensity to use electric mobility.

Table 4. Definition of actions for the improvement of SUMP in regulatory, technical and socio-cultural terms (Our elaboration)

Area	Definition	
Legal Aspects	SUMP update	Greater uniformity between European regulations on charging infrastructure
	Increasing car sharing with electric vehicles and reducing pollutant emissions and congestion	
Technical Aspects	Site selection	Public land use permits
	Connection to the electricity grid	Capacity of connection to the local network
	Type of charging station	Spatial configuration of car parks
	Parking regulations and signage	Urban design
	Type configurations for different areas	Accelerating the development of a publicly accessible charging network
	Expanding charging possibilities in residential and business premises	
Socio-cultural Aspects	Incentives to use shared or dial-a-ride mobility	Awareness campaigns
	Participatory planning	Stimulate the introduction of electric vehicles in the most effective and practicable mobility segments

The actions also make it possible to define criteria for describing electric vehicle DRT (EV_DRT) mobility. Therefore, a series of criteria have been identified in Table 5 to be used to characterise and thus improve the connection between the infrastructures and services relating to the supply of electric demand-responsive transport, as well as the environment and the users that make up demand.

Table 5. Criteria for the definition of the electric DRT service (Our elaboration)

Criteria	Definition	
Infrastructure	Infrastructure quality index	Number of recharging stations at local and regional level
	Type of charging station	Presence of maps and geo-localization tools
	Presence of parking spaces reserved for electric mobility	Presence and implementation of green mobility development plans
	Presence and implementation of maintenance plans for electrical infrastructure	
Service	Incentives for customers to Use electric mobility	Availability of electric vehicles (n. of e-vehicle/fleet)
	Multimodality	Presence of digital MaaS platforms
	Partnerships with other companies	Monitoring through survey campaigns
	Definition of performance and service quality indicators	Possible integration with PT
	Sustainable pricing	
User	Estimation of resident and commuter population	Socio-demographic characterization
	Income	Driving license possession
	Car/van ownership	Bicycle/micromobility ownership
	Democratic participation in planning	Presence of psycho-social barriers limiting the use of e-mobility (handicap, religion…)
	Educational and awareness campaigns	
Environment	Monitoring of acoustic and environmental parameters (pollutants)	Presence of green energy sources
	Presence of aquifers or lakes	Presence of green areas
	Presence of steep areas (slope)	

5   Conclusions

Sustainable mobility planning strategies are generally linked to a set of planning and design tools that dictate their characteristics, critical aspects or encourage their use. SUMPs include among their objectives the progressive replacement of the public transport fleet with electrically powered vehicles, the dissemination of incentive measures for private transport and the dissemination of measures in support of shared and on-demand mobility with a time horizon of 2030 and/or 2050. The diffusion of DRT makes it possible to address several critical issues that have recently been affecting public transport. The implementation of electric DRT services makes it possible to reach areas of weak demand and to discourage the use of private vehicles.. The evolution of these vehicles and thus the possibility of disseminating EV-DRT services depends not only on the present infrastructure (charging stations) but also on the propensity of users to use electric mobility.

This research work aims to introduce an exploratory and comparative survey on the evolution of SUMP in different European cities and the correlation of the evolution of planning tools with the diffusion of charging infrastructure and the spread of shared transport services (bike and car) and DRT.

After an introduction on the current development of the electric car market in Europe, the analysis of the transport offer was examined considering the spread of electric charging stations and the spread of alternative forms of mobility. The comparison of several case studies and the relative facts made it possible to outline the macro areas of investigation to be taken into consideration when discussing the variables that determine the benefits and criticalities of the spread of electric mobility and in particular of EV-DRTs. It emerges that it is necessary to entrust the managers of collective and shared transport services and the managers of recharging services with the task of progressively and constantly investigating the process of planning and monitoring electric mobility, with the aim of guaranteeing the capillarity of electric columns in the city context, as well as ensuring the adaptation to evolutionary standards in terms of sockets and installed power.

To encourage the above-mentioned spread of the infrastructure, a series of national and other measures and strategies will have to be disseminated to obtain the national and European funds necessary to improve the quality and quantity of the recharging systems present in the territory. The dissemination of service conferences for the extension of the infrastructure of charging points should be promoted by participatory planning and by mapping them. This is aimed at making the infrastructural progress public to citizens and operators, in line with the objectives of the Urban Plan for Sustainable Mobility (PUMS) and the Guidelines for the location of infrastructures for the recharging of electrically powered vehicles on public land for public use and subsequent amendments/integrations. In the final part the criteria linked respectively the infrastructure, the transport service, the user and the context have been defined in order to be able to analyse in the next research steps the weights to be attributed to each factor and therefore to be able to study through a multi-criteria analysis the diffusion of EV-DRTs.

Acknowledgement. This study was supported by the MIUR (Ministry of Education, Universities and Research [Italy]) through a project entitled WEAKI TRANSIT: WEAK-demand areas Innovative TRANsport Shared services for Italian Towns (Project code: 20174ARRHT /CUP Code: E44I17000050001), financed with the PRIN 2017 (Research Projects of National Relevance) programme. We authorize the MIUR to reproduce and distribute reprints for Governmental purposes, notwithstanding any copy-right notations thereon. Any opinions, findings and conclusions or recommendations expressed in this material are those of the authors, and do not necessarily reflect the views of the MIUR.

References

1. Awad-Núñez, S., Julio, R., Gomez, J., Moya-Gómez, B., González, J.S.: Post-COVID-19 travel behaviour patterns: impact on the willingness to pay of users of public transport and shared mobility services in Spain. Eur. Transp. Res. Rev. **13**(1), 1–18 (2021). https://doi.org/10.1186/s12544-021-00476-4
2. Bergantino, A.S., Intini, M., Tangari, L.: Influencing factors for potential bike-sharing users: an empirical analysis during the COVID-19 pandemic. Res. Transp. Econ. **86**, 101028 (2021)
3. Torrisi, V., Ignaccolo, M., Inturri, G., Tesoriere, G., Campisi, T.: Exploring the factors affecting bike-sharing demand: evidence from student perceptions, usage patterns and adoption barriers. Transp. Res. Procedia **52**, 573–580 (2021). https://doi.org/10.1016/j.trpro.2021.01.068
4. Garau, C., Annunziata, A., Yamu, C. A walkability assessment tool coupling multi-criteria analysis and space syntax: the case study of Iglesias, Italy. Eur. Plan. Stud. 1–23 (2020)
5. Campisi, T., Ignaccolo, M., Inturri, G., Tesoriere, G., Torrisi, V.: The growing urban accessibility: a model to measure the car sharing effectiveness based on parking distances. In: Gervasi, O., et al. (eds.) ICCSA 2020. LNCS, vol. 12255, pp. 629–644. Springer, Cham (2020). https://doi.org/10.1007/978-3-030-58820-5_46
6. Rossetti, S., Tiboni, M.: In field assessment of safety, security, comfort and accessibility of bus stops: a planning perspective. Eur. Transp. **8**(80) (2020). https://doi.org/10.48295/ET.2020.80.8. ISSN 1825-3997
7. Tiboni, M., Rossetti, S., Vetturi, D., Torrisi, V., Botticini, F., Schaefer, M.D.: Urban policies and planning approaches for a safer and climate friendlier mobility in cities: strategies. Initiatives Some Anal. Sustain. **13**(4), 1778 (2021). https://doi.org/10.3390/su13041778
8. Torrisi, V., Ignaccolo, M., Inturri, G.: Innovative transport systems to promote sustainable mobility: developing the model architecture of a traffic control and supervisor system. In: Gervasi, O., et al. (eds.) ICCSA 2018. LNCS, vol. 10962, pp. 622–638. Springer, Cham (2018). https://doi.org/10.1007/978-3-319-95168-3_42
9. Torrisi, V., Ignaccolo, M., Inturri, G.: Analysis of road urban transport network capacity through a dynamic assignment model: validation of different measurement methods. Transp. Res. Procedia **27**, 1026–1033 (2017). https://doi.org/10.1016/j.trpro.2017.12.135
10. Canale, A., Tesoriere, G., Campisi, T.: The MAAS development as a mobility solution based on the individual needs of transport users. In: AIP conference proceedings, vol. 2186, no. 1, p. 160005. AIP Publishing LLC, December 2019
11. Wong, Y.Z., Hensher, D.A., Mulley, C.: Mobility as a service (MaaS): charting a future context. Transp. Res. Part A Policy Pract. **131**, 5–19 (2020)
12. Bell, D.: Intermodal mobility hubs and user needs. Soc. Sci. **8**(2), 65 (2019)
13. Schlenther, T., Martins-Turner, K., Bischoff, J.F., Nagel, K.: Potential of private autonomous vehicles for parcel delivery. Transp. Res. Rec. **2674**(11), 520–531 (2020)
14. Quadrifoglio, L., Dessouky, M.M., Ordóñez, F.: A simulation study of demand responsive transit system design. Transp. Res. Part A Policy Pract. **42**(4), 718–737 (2008)
15. Calabrò, G., Inturri, G., Le Pira, M., Pluchino, A., Ignaccolo, M.: Bridging the gap between weak-demand areas and public transport using an ant-colony simulation-based optimization. Transp. Res. Procedia **45**, 234–241 (2020)
16. Campisi, T., Canale, A., Ticali, D., Tesoriere, G.: Innovative solutions for sustainable mobility in areas of weak demand. Some factors influencing the implementation of the DRT system in Enna (Italy). In AIP Conference Proceedings, vol. 2343, no. 1, p. 090005. AIP Publishing LLC, March 2021
17. Abdullah, M., Ali, N., Shah, S.A.H., Javid, M.A., Campisi, T.: Service quality assessment of app-based demand-responsive public transit services in Lahore Pakistan. Appl. Sci. **11**(4), 1911 (2021)

18. Calabrò, G., Torrisi, V., Inturri, G., Ignaccolo, M.: Improving inbound logistic planning for large-scale real-world routing problems: a novel ant-colony simulation-based optimization. Eur. Transp. Res. Rev. **12**(1), 1–11 (2020). https://doi.org/10.1186/s12544-020-00409-7

19. Ahangari, S., Chavis, C., Jeihani, M.: Public transit ridership analysis during the COVID-19 pandemic. medRxiv (2020)

20. Torrisi, V., Inturri, G., Ignaccolo, M.: Introducing a mobility on demand system beyond COVID-19: Evidences from users' perspective. In: International Conference of Computational Methods in Sciences and Engineering ICCMSE 2020 (2021). https://doi.org/10.1063/5.0047889

21. Torrisi, V., Ignaccolo, M., Inturri, G.: Toward a sustainable mobility through a dynamic real-time traffic monitoring, estimation and forecasting system: the RE.S.E.T. project. Town and Infrastructure Planning for Safety and Urban Quality - Proceedings of the 23rd International Conference on Living and Walking in Cities, LWC 2017, pp. 241–247 (2018).https://doi.org/10.1201/9781351173360-32

22. Torrisi, V., Garau, C., Ignaccolo, M., Inturri, G.: Sustainable urban mobility plans: key concepts and a critical revision on SUMPs guidelines. In: Gervasi, O., et al. (eds.) ICCSA 2020. LNCS, vol. 12255, pp. 613–628. Springer, Cham (2020). https://doi.org/10.1007/978-3-030-58820-5_45

23. Mądziel, M., Campisi, T., Jaworski, A., Tesoriere, G.: The development of strategies to reduce exhaust emissions from passenger cars in Rzeszow city—Poland a preliminary assessment of the results produced by the increase of e-fleet. Energies **14**(4), 1046 (2021)

24. Campisi, T., Nahiduzzaman, K.M., Ticali, D., Tesoriere, G.: Bivariate analysis of the influencing factors of the upcoming personal mobility vehicles (PMVs) in Palermo. In: Gervasi, O., et al. (eds.) ICCSA 2020. LNCS, vol. 12250, pp. 868–881. Springer, Cham (2020). https://doi.org/10.1007/978-3-030-58802-1_62

25. Campisi, T., Ignaccolo, M., Tesoriere, G., Inturri, G., Torrisi, V.: The Evaluation of Car-Sharing to Raise Acceptance of Electric Vehicles: Evidences from an Italian Survey among University Students, no. 2020–24–0021. SAE Technical Paper (2020)

26. Torrisi, V., Campisi, T., Inturri, G., Ignaccolo, M., Tesoriere, G.: Continue to share? an overview on italian travel behavior before and after the COVID-19 lockdown. In AIP Conference Proceedings, vol. 2343, no. 1, p. 090010. AIP Publishing LLC, March 2021

27. Campisi, T., Canale, A., Ticali, D., Tesoriere, G.: Innovative solutions for sustainable mobility in areas of weak demand. Some factors influencing the implementation of the DRT system in Enna (Italy). In: AIP Conference Proceedings, vol. 2343, no. 1, p. 090005. AIP Publishing LLC, March 2021

28. Dlugosch, O., Brandt, T., Neumann, D.: Combining analytics and simulation methods to assess the impact of shared, autonomous electric vehicles on sustainable urban mobility. Inf. Manage. 103285 (2020)

29. Bibri, S.E., Krogstie, J.: Smart sustainable cities of the future: an extensive interdisciplinary literature review. Sustain. Urban Areas **31**, 183–212 (2017)

30. Campisi, T., Basbas, S., Skoufas, A., Akgün, N., Ticali, D., Tesoriere, G.: The impact of COVID-19 pandemic on the resilience of sustainable mobility in sicily. Sustainability **12**(21), 8829 (2020)

31. Azzari, M., Garau, C., Nesi, P., Paolucci, M., Zamperlin, P.: Smart city governance strategies to better move towards a smart urbanism. In: Gervasi, O., et al. (eds.) Computational Science and Its Applications – ICCSA 2018, pp. 639–653. Springer International Publishing, Cham (2018). https://doi.org/10.1007/978-3-319-95168-3_43

32. Hu, T.Y., Zheng, G.C., Liao, T.Y.: Smart mobility: evaluation of demand-responsive transit systems in chiayi city. In: 2017 International Smart Cities Conference (ISC2), pp. 1–6. IEEE, September 2017

33. Transport and environment (2020): Recharge EU: how many charge points will Europe and its member states need in the 2020s. T&E, January 2020
34. Torrisi, V., Garau, C., Inturri, G., Ignaccolo, M.: Strategies and actions towards sustainability: encouraging good ITS practices in the SUMP vision. In: International Conference of Computational Methods in Sciences and Engineering ICCMSE 2020 (2021). https://doi.org/10.1063/5.0047897
35. Shaheen, S., Cohen, A.: Mobility on demand (MOD) and mobility as a service (MaaS): early understanding of shared mobility impacts and public transit partnerships. In Demand for Emerging Transportation Systems, pp. 37–59. Elsevier (2020)
36. Canale, A., Tesoriere, G., Campisi, T.: The MAAS development as a mobility solution based on the individual needs of transport users. In AIP Conference Proceedings, vol. 2186, no. 1, p. 160005. AIP Publishing LLC, December 2019
37. https://www.eltis.org/mobility-plans/sumpconcept
38. https://lukasfoljanty.medium.com/mapping-the-global-on-demand-ridepooling-market-f8318de1c030
39. Friedrich, M., Hartl, M.: MEGAFON—Modellergebnisse Geteilter Autonomer Fahrzeugflotten des Oeffentlichen Nahverkehrs. In: Verband Deutscher Verkehrsunternehmen e.V., Stuttgarter Straßenbahnen A.G., Verkehrs- und Tarifverbund Stuttgart GmbH, Stuttgart, Germany (2016)
40. https://civitas.eu/measure/e-mobility-stations-domagkpark-district-and-centre-periphery-integration
41. https://www.sustaineurope.com/oslo-european-green-capital-2019-20191023.html
42. Brost, M., et al.: Development, implementation (pilot) and evaluation of a demand-responsive transport system. World Electr. Veh. J. 9(1), 4 (2018)
43. Klima, U.: Energie GmbH Handbuch zur Planung flexibler Bedienungsformen im ÖPNV: Ein Beitrag zur Sicherung der Dasseinsvorsorge in Nachfrageschwachen Räumen; Bundesministerium für Verkehr, Bau und Stadtentwicklung (BMVBS), Berlin (2009)
44. Camacho, D., et al.: Electric vehicles in rural demand-responsive systems: findings of two demand responsive transport projects for the improvement of service provision. World Electr. Veh. J. 9(2), 32 (2018)
45. https://www.gihub.org/resources/showcase-projects/demand-responsive-transport/
46. WXY Architecture + Urban design: Assessment of current EVSE and EV de-ployment. Electric vehicle supply equipment support study. New York State Energy Research, Development Authority, Trasportation and Climate Initiative (2012)
47. Wirges, J.: Planning the Charging Infrastructure for Electric Vehicles in Cities and Regions. KIT Scientific Publishing, Karlsruhe (2016)
48. EC: New guidelines for sustainable urban mobility planning (2019). https://ec.europa.eu/transport/themes/urban/news/2019-10-02-new-guidelines-sump_en

Exploring European Strategies for the Optimization of the Benefits and Cost-Effectiveness of Private Electric Mobility

Giovanna Acampa[1]($\boxtimes$) (iD), Tiziana Campisi[1]($\boxtimes$) (iD), Mariolina Grasso[1] (iD), Giorgia Marino[1] (iD), and Vincenza Torrisi[2]($\boxtimes$) (iD)

[1] Faculty of Engineering and Architecture, University of Enna Kore, Cittadella Universitaria, 94100 Enna, Italy
{giovanna.acampa,tiziana.campisi}@unikore.it
[2] Department of Civil Engineering and Architecture, University of Catania, 95125 Catania, Cittadella, Italy
vtorrisi@dica.unict.it

Abstract. All over the world the e-mobility phenomenon is expanding, both on the supply and demand side. Leading global car manufacturers have introduced electric models at increasingly competitive prices and many people are interested in benefits and cost-effectiveness that the new technology could bring them. Even if from March to June 2020, due to the COVID-19 mobility restrictions, sales of electric cars have fallen below 2019's levels, in the last few months the rate of sales recovered strongly. Governments of various countries, in compliance with EU directives, have introduced strict rules to reduce CO2 emission. For the same purpose, to increase the demand for private electric vehicles they are providing incentives and subsidies to encourage EV sales. The paper focuses on private electric vehicles total costs and investigates the European and United Kingdom tax benefits and purchase incentives. The aim is to understand how the demand growth is related with the policies of the European countries by analyzing existing data referred to all EU member states. Whether subsidies policies prove insufficient to achieve the set objectives, it will be appropriate to plan educational strategies to promote environmentally sustainable habits for citizens.

Keywords: Electric vehicles benefits · Cost-effectiveness · European incentives

This paper is the result of the joint work of the authors. 'Abstract' and 'Results' were written jointly by all authors. Tiziana Campisi and Giorgia Marino wrote 'Introduction'; Giovanna Acampa and Vincenza Torrisi wrote 'Materials and Methods' and Giovanna Acampa and Mariolina Grasso wrote 'Results and discussion'; Tiziana Campisi and Vincenza Torrisi wrote "Conclusions". Tiziana Campisi supervised the manuscript and funded.

1   Introduction

Climate change is a central focus of the Intergovernmental Panel's special report [1], which highlights the 1.5 °C increase in global warming as one of the critical environmental issues. Compared to the levels monitored in 2015, this report suggests that CO2 emissions from transport must be reduced by at least 70% to 80% to meet the targets set in the Paris Agreement.

The climate change is one of the most important environmental issues and transport contributes about one quarter of the EU's total greenhouse gas emissions. Reducing the environmental impact of transport can be addressed by reducing the demand for travel, presenting cleaner technologies and shifting towards less ecologically damaging transport modes [2]. Therefore, it is central to track this sector in detail and project changes in GHG emissions based on the reductions possible with policy measures that have already been adopted or are planned in the EU member States.

Figure 1 shows the evolution of EU greenhouse gas emissions from transport the 1990–2020 period as reported by member states:

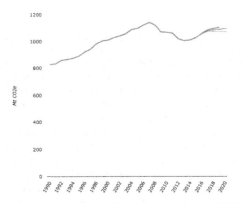

Fig. 1. Greenhouse gas emissions from transport in the EU (Source: [3])

According to preliminary estimates, the EU's transport emissions increased in 2020 by 0.8%. This follows a 0.9% increase in 2018. These rates of increase are the slowest since 2014. Figure 2a shows how road transport account for 72% of total greenhouse gas emissions of the sector. Railway emissions establish only a small portion of overall transport emissions (below 1%) such as domestic navigation emissions which constitute under 2% of overall transport emissions. If only the part relating to road transport is analysed, the percentages are divided as follows (Fig. 2b): motorcycles (0.9%), heavy duty trucks and buses (19.2%), light duty trucks (8.7%) and cars (44.3%).

In this context, a sustainable trail for the transport sector is possible using a mix of policy actions to reduce the need for transport trips, encouraging changes toward more efficient transport modes, and improve vehicle efficiency through low-carbon technologies [4, 5].

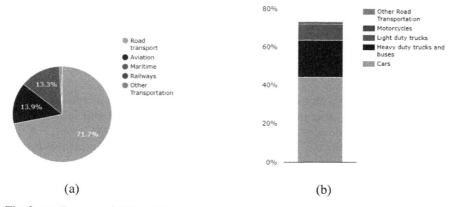

(a)   (b)

Fig. 2. (a) Transport GHG and (b) Road Transport GHG emission EU27 + UK (Source: [3])

An integrated way to plan the mobility system serving people in cities is through sustainable mobility planning [6, 7]. The SUMP not only focus on a coordinated transport system but also how the system impacts its users [8–11].

The European Green Deal published by the European Commission in December 2019, states that by 2025, will reinforce the CO2 targets for passenger cars and light-commercial vehicles to bring them in line with the EU's ambition to cut greenhouse gas emissions by at least 55% by 2030. Table 1 shows an overview of EV policies in EU 2018/2019.

Table 1. Overview of EV policies in the European Union (Source: Elaboration from [12])

Country	Policy type	Description
European Union	**Regulations** (Vehicles)	Tightened CO2 emissions standards for LDVs in 2025 and 2030 with credits for EV sales, following the 95 g Co2/km requirement for 2021; C02 emissions standards for trucks in 2025 and 2030; Clean vehicle Directive mandates public procurement for clean LDVs and HDVs; Increasing number of number states announcing ICE and diesel bans
	Incentive (Vehicles)	Incentives schemes for zero and low emission PDLVs in 33 European countries
	Industrial policy	European Battery Alliance to promote the development of a battery industry in Europe
	Regulation (Chargers)	Energy Performance of Buildings Directive approved in the EU mandates EV charges for new and renovated buildings
	Targets (Chargers)	Through the AFI Directive, EU member states have set EVSE deployment targets for 2020, 2025 and 2030

1.1   European Strategies for Sustainable Mobility in the Post-pandemic Phase

European decarbonisation policies have promoted several interventions in infrastructure and mobility services. Unfortunately, the transport sector has come to a standstill due to the recent pandemic and has faced new challenges in ensuring essential services and safe travel.

Since March 2020 with the advent of the pandemic in Europe and the first case in Italy, several mobility strategies have been put in place, trying to build sustainable and innovative models while promoting actions for resilient mobility [13].

On-board restrictions and the respect of social distancing have had a disruptive impact on people's travel habits with a particular effect on the public transport sector. In the short to medium term public transport has not been the primary choice of many citizens. This had repercussions on urban traffic in large cities, which was already at the limit of sustainability before the emergency [14–16].

In the coming years, the spread of digital platforms and MaaS (Mobility as a Service) will facilitate people's travel choices [17] and there will be an increasing use of electric vehicles as forms of private and shared mobility.

Several studies in Europe show that the private car has historically been the default mode of transport in many areas, affecting road capacity in a negative way [18, 19]. This has influenced the design of infrastructure and the surrounding working environment over the years [20, 21].

Reducing car traffic is indispensable to rapidly reduce pollution. Several European cities have invested in infrastructure measures such as new bicycle lanes and the creation of 30 zones. The European Commission has promoted the growth of shared mobility with the aim of reaching about 80% of the service with electric vehicles by 2040. In this sense, several European governments are incentivising electric mobility, through tax deductions, bureaucratic advantages or benefits related to traffic restrictions. However, while direct incentives create immediate benefits, tax credits are beneficial in the medium term, after three to four years on average.

In the literature, several studies focus on evaluating the benefits of a higher percentage of electric vehicles in the fleet and present the results obtained by comparing scenarios using traffic micro-simulation tools [22] or multicriteria analysis [23] or by administering questionnaires and interviews to gain information on the travel habits of different types of users [24, 25]. These studies show a lower CO_2 emission into the environment including the e-in the daily vehicle fleet and a greater tendency among young people to rent or use shared mobility services including electric vehicles such as scooters or vehicles.

To improve infrastructures and the location of recharging areas, it is necessary also to spread the digital representation of physical and functional characteristics through I-BIM (infrastructures Building information modelling) in order to be able to evaluate in an integrated way the different steps of construction and maintenance of infrastructures, also considering the aspects of safety and service level [26, 27].

The present work, following an accurate examination of the correlation between transport demand and the growth of the offer of electric mobility services, focuses on the statistical evaluation of the benefits produced by the diffusion of electric mobility in the different European countries and in the UK, focusing on policies and strategies for the promotion of sustainable mobility.

2   Materials and Methods

2.1   Correlation Analysis for Electric Vehicles Demand Growth

On a global scale, there are some good practices adopted by various countries to encourage the purchase or use of EVs. China is the largest market in the world for the sale of electric cars thanks to low-cost supply and a wider choice, as well as a strong incentive policy. Moreover, electric vehicles are not subject to registration restrictions (although the number of new license plates in China is limited) or driving bans on certain days. Purchase incentives vary according to battery capacity and lasted until 2020. The US encourages the purchase of electric cars by cancelling federal taxes that depend on fuel consumption. In Europe, in particular Norway represents a forerunner in the introduction of e-mobility and it is currently a leader in the production of renewable energy that powers its energy grid. Electric cars are not subject to the 25 percent VAT on motor vehicles, and other benefits include limited use of bus lanes in select areas and savings on ferry crossings, tolls and parking. In the Netherlands, there are no registration taxes for pure electric cars, which are based on the CO_2 emissions of a vehicle. As in Germany, there are tax benefits for company car drivers who also privately use the vehicles. Plug-in vehicle grants of up to £ 3,500 are available to all consumers purchasing a pure electric vehicle in the UK. Surprisingly, Romania is one of the countries offering the most significant government subsidies for electric cars and is currently the strongest incentive policy in the whole of the EU (Fig. 3).

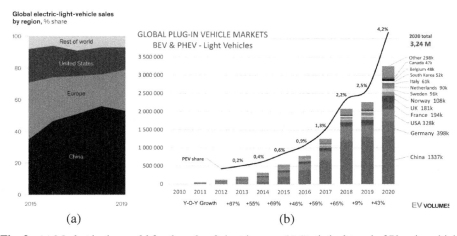

(a)   (b)

Fig. 3. (a) Market in the world for the sale of electric cars; (b) Statistical trend of Plug-in vehicle sales in the world. (Source: [28])

Based on this short premise, the paper will focus on private electric vehicles total costs and investigates the European and United Kingdom tax benefits and purchase incentives in order to understand how the demand growth is related with the policies of the European countries (see Fig. 4).

Fig. 4. Methodological framework (source: Authors elaboration)

2.2   BEVs Purchase, Management and Maintenance Costs Analysis

To investigate about the purchase, management and maintenance cost of Battery Electric Vehicle (BEV) among Europe and UK a research has been carried out on the 10 best sellers BEV. The ranking in Fig. 5 shows the top 10 best sellers BEV in EU countries and UK.

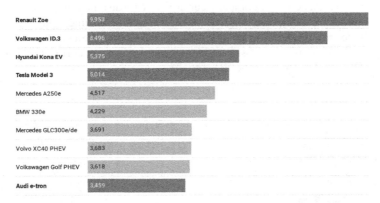

Fig. 5. Top 10 best sellers BEV in EU and UK (November 2020). (Source: [29])

In the electric car ranking, Renault Zoe holds on to its top spot. In November 2020, the main market was Germany (4,287 units), followed by France (2,944), with Italy (555 units) and the UK (450 units) also helping along [28].

Considering the first BEV in ranking (Renault Zoe) it has been carried out an investigation about the price list among the main EU countries and UK, the purchase cost after deducting e-mobility subsidies (if provided), the management cost with particular reference to battery charge cost (both with public and private charge stations), the maintenance cost (during 6 years) and last but not least the cost for battery replacement (necessary after 8 years or 160.000/200.000 km) (Table 2).

First, what immediately show up is the battery replacement cost which is equal to approximately 90% of the total cost of the vehicle (necessary after only 8 years).

Also, another interesting data concerns the battery charge cost. As regard charging with public energy, the cost differs from one country to another (min value 0,21 €/kWh

Table 2. Investigation about BEV (Renault Zoe) purchase, management and maintenance cost. (Sources: [30]).

			Renault Zoe			
Countries	Price list	Purchase cost (after deductig all e-mobility subsidies)	Management cost (battery charge 41kWh - Autonomy 300 KM) - Public charge	Management cost (battery charge 41kWh - Autonomy 300 KM) - Private charge	Mantainance cost (total for 6 years)	Battery replacement (after 8 years or 160.000/200.0
Austria	30.590 €	25.190 €	0,21 €/kWh	0,15 €/kWh	700 €	
Belgium	28.990 €	-	0,35 €/kWh	0,20 €/kWh	-	
Denmark	30.800 €	-	0,50 €/kWh	0,30 €/kWh	-	
Estonia	33.000 €	28.000 €	0,21 €/kWh	-	-	
Finland	33.500 €	31.500 €	0,28 €/kWh	0,09 €/kWh	-	
France	28.000 €	23.000 €	0,30 €/kWh	0,18 €/kWh	580 €	
Germany	32.550 €	25.300 €	0,53 €/kWh	0,27 €/kWh	680 €	
Grecee	34.000 €	-	0,42 €/kWh	-	-	
Hungary	33.500 €	29.075 €	0,37 €/kWh	-	-	
Ireland	32.200 €	27.200 €	0,39 €/kWh	-	-	
Italy	33.880 €	27.380 €	0,45€/KWh	0,23€/kWh or (0,07€/kWh with solar power system)	675 €	20.000/22.000 €
Netherlands	29000 €	-	0,30 €/kWh	0,14 €/kWh	-	
Norway	33.000 €	-	0,21 €/kWh	0,10 €/kWh	750 €	
Poland	33.800 €	25.300 €	0,29 €/kWh	-	-	
Portugal	31.800 €	28.800 €	0,46 €/kWh	-	-	
Romania	32.200 €	22.200 €	0,24 €/kWh	-	-	
Slovakia	28.800 €	20.800 €	0,33 €/kWh	-	-	
Slovenia	30.000 €	22.500 €	0,55 €/kWh	-	-	
Spain	33.880 €	29.380 €	0,54 €/kWh	0,35 €/kWh	700 €	
Sweden	32.200 €	26.300 €	0,22 €/kWh	-	-	
UK	28.670£ (33.280€)	25.670£ (29.798€)	0,20£/KWh (0,23€/kWh)	0,09 €/kWh	750£ (870€)	

in Austria, Estonia and Norway – max value 0,55 €/kWh in Slovenia). In each country charging the car battery with private charge energy is much cheaper than the public ones. The difference can be up to 50% if the private plant is solar powered (photovoltaic plant). Finally, maintenance costs (for those countries where data are available) are homogeneous and not particularly expensive.

2.3 The Spread of Electric Vehicles in Europe and UK: Statistical Data

The spread of BEV in Europe is increasing, in line with the EU objectives of emissions reduction derived by transport sector. Figure 6 shows the electric cars registered in the EU-27 and UK from 2010 to 2019. An increase in the number of electric vehicles is evident. However, the market penetration ok BEV remains relatively low. In 2019, it is possible to observe that the electric vehicle registrations have been close to 550.000 cars (i.e. 3.5% of the total), compared to 300.000 in 2018 (i.e. 2% of the total). Moreover, comparing the plug-in hybrid vehicles (PHEVs) and BEV, the latter represent the majority in terms of registrations in 2019.

The notable increase in BEV new registrations between 2018 and 2019 can be associated with the high increase of electric vehicles recorded in Norway, where around 60.000 BEVs have been registered. Considering the various countries of Europe, the

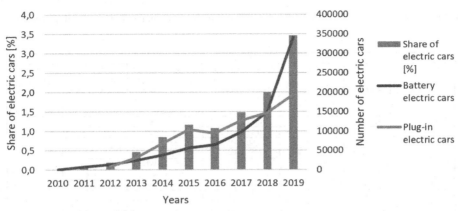

Fig. 6. Electric cars registered in the EU-27 and UK from 2010 to 2019. (Authors elaboration, Data Source: [31])

highest shares of BEVs have been found after Norway (i.e. 56%), in Netherlands (i.e. 16%) followed by Sweden (i.e. 12%), while in Italy and Spain the percentage of BEVs remained less than 1% of the total fleet.

According to the report "Making the Transition to Zero-Emission Mobility", sales of electric-charging cars in the EU have benne increased by 110% over the past three years. However, during the same period, the number of charging points only grew by 58%, demonstrating that investments in infrastructure are not at the same level with the increase in sales of electric vehicles.

Despite the pandemic's effect on the economy and restrictions on people's travel habits, global adoption of electric vehicles increased in 2020. According to data from EV Volumes, global sales of electric vehicles have been increased, marking a + 43% for a total of 3.24 million vehicles placed on the market.

But the real evidence of the year 2020 is that Europe has overtaken China as the engine of electric vehicle growth, with Norway's record. Europe is ahead in terms of the share of electric vehicles: BEV and PHEVs increased from 3.5% in 2019 to 10.2% of the fleet in 2020, counting the EU countries including the United Kingdom. The share in China increased from 5.1% to 5.5% during the same period (see Fig. 7).

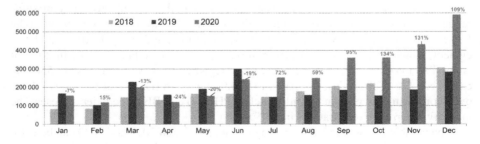

Fig. 7. Monthly Plug-in vehicle sales in the world. (Source: [28])

3   Results and Discussions

3.1   Comparison Among EU and UK Policies and BEVs Spread

Electric cars — battery electric vehicles (BEVs) are gradually penetrating the EU market. However, despite a steady increase in the number of new electric car registrations annually, from 700 units in 2010 to about 550 000 units in 2020, they still account for a market share of only 3.5% of newly registered passenger vehicles [33]. According to Schmidt Automotive Research it will accelerate again in 2025 to a market share of 13%. The analysis carried out in paragraph 2.1 showed that the higher purchase costs for electric vehicles compared to combustion-powered vehicles remain a barrier. Therefore, the policies adopted by the different countries should be crucial to encourage BEV purchase uptakes [33]. In Figs. 8 are shown the purchase incentive for BEV among the main EU countries and UK.

Fig. 8. Purchase incentive for BEV among EU countries and UK. (Authors elaboration, Data Source [34])

Comparing Figs. 8 and 9 it is interesting to note that the ratio between GDP and purchase incentives for BEV is quite proportional except in Italy and Germany (low GDP – high incentives).

In Table 3 is shown a comparison between policies (focusing on restrictions and tax exemptions) and the percentage of BEVs registration on the total automotive registration among main EU countries and UK.

Purchase incentive and annual national tax breaks on vehicle registration and operation are common where electric shares are high—for example in Austria, Finland, France, Germany, Ireland, Portugal, Sweden and UK.

Fig. 9. GDP (2019) among EU Countries and UK. (Authors elaboration, Data Source [35])

Yet, even though many countries like Italy, Spain, Greece, Hungary, Poland, Romania, Slovakia and Slovenia provides both purchase and tax incentives, the registration percentage is still set on low levels. (Fig. 8).

Analyzing Fig. 8 it shows up that Norway, Netherlands, Denmark do not provide any incentive or scrapping bonus, yet the percentage of BEV registrations reached the highest level (Table 3). This is probably due to the general attention of the population towards environmental sustainability issues. Regardless of the number of incentives available, the purchase of an electric vehicle contributes to environmental respect.

3.2 Policies and Educational Strategies to Promote Sustainability

From the analysis of the data obtained in Sect. 3.1, by comparing Figs. 8 and 9 and Table 3, the following remarks can be made:

- In most Eastern European Countries (Romania, Slovakia, Poland, Slovenia), although both GDP and incentives for purchasing electric vehicles are set on high levels, the registration rate of BEV is among the lowest percentage in Europe.
- In Italy, where GDP in 2019 has been among the lowest levels within European Union and incentives for the purchase of electric vehicles are high, still the registration rate for BEV is set on low percentage.

Table 3. Comparison between policies and uptake of private electric vehicles among main EU countries and UK. (Source [36]).

Country	Restrictions	Exemption ownership tax	Exemption registration tax	% of BEV registrations on the total automotive registrations in each country 2019
Austria	Gross list price of ≤ €60.000	Yes		3,3
Belgium		Flanders: Yes Brussels and Wallonia: minimum rate (€76.32 + 10% municipal tax).		2,8
Denmark	-	Yes	Reductions of 40.000 DDK and payment in instalments	3,6
Estonia	Gross list price of ≤ €50.000	-	-	0,3
Finland	Gross list price of ≤ €50.000	Minimum rate	Minimum rate	5,6
France	-	-	Yes	2,5
Germany	-	Temporary VAT reduction 16% to 19%	10 years	2,6
Grecee	-	Yes	Yes	0,3
Hungary	Gross list price of ≤ €44.000	Yes	Yes	1,7
Ireland	-	Reduction up to 5.500€	Minimum rate	3,5
Italy	Gross list price of ≤ €50.000	for 5 years then 75% reduction	-	0,7
Netherlands	-	Yes	Yes	10,1
Norway	-	Yes	Yes	56,2
Poland	Gross list price of ≤ 150.000PLN (32.000€)	Yes	-	0,5
Portugal	-	VAT deduction	Yes	4,7
Romania	-	Yes	-	0,6
Slovakia	-	Yes	-	0,4
Slovenia	-	-	Minimum rate (0,5%)	0,8
Spain	Gross list price of ≤ €35.000	Reduction of 75% in the main cities (eg. Madrid, Barcelona, Zaragoza, Valencia)	Yes	1,3
Sweden	-	Reduction on annual road tax (360 SEK - 35€)	-	11,3
UK	Gross list price of ≤ £50.000 (58.000€)	Yes	Yes	2,1

– In northern European countries such as the Netherlands, Norway and Sweden, whose GDP is set on average level and the BEV's purchase incentives are low or non-existent the registration rate for electric vehicles is among the highest percentage in Europe (Norway 56.2%, Sweden 11.3%, Netherlands 10.1%). As mentioned above, this trend is probably due to the culture of these populations perceiving environmental sustainability aspects as paramount.

Whether subsidies policies prove insufficient to achieve the set objectives, it will be appropriate to plan educational strategies to promote environmentally sustainable habits for citizens. To tackle the crisis, a structural approach is needed: it is a multi-year incentive plan, with a much longer horizon than the current one, which must be characterized by favoring low-impact cars, to lead towards the reduction of emissions.

Structural policies in this direction would also contribute to modernizing the vehicle fleet which has a strong negative impact not only on the environment but also on traffic safety, as shown by the death rates due to road accidents:

– Incentives for the purchase of new zero-emission cars;
– Scrapping of old vehicles and dealer bonus;
– Incentives for sharing and rental services;
– Integration of charging infrastructures.

With reference to these last two points, even in a highly critical economic phase, the rental confirms the innovative charge and the role of driving force for the diffusion of electrified cars in our countries. The electric turnaround can only pass from a wider spread of "pay-per-use" mobility. Indeed, rental is a strategic element of the circular economy, thanks to a fleet of latest generation cars and the ability to put on the second-hand market every year safe and low-emission vehicles (at the end of the rental more polluting. Furthermore, the role of charging infrastructures is an essential factor for the transition towards zero-emission mobility. Equally fundamental is the capillarity of the territorial distribution of infrastructures, both in terms of accessibility (public / private) and in terms of number of charging stations. This technological adaptation is necessary to keep up with the growth in the diffusion of the electric car. But that's still not enough: the user must be able to quickly and easily identify the location of the infrastructures in order to make the most of them. Integration is the key word: research and use of public charging stations through a few apps able to offer standardized services ranging from booking to unblocking the charging up to payment (often online), interfacing with charging networks spread globally.

Finally, to be able to raise awareness with a bottom-up approach, the issue of sustainability must be strengthened through constant training activities, correct dissemination information, communication campaigns, sharing and promotion of good practices in the area, in addition to university and scientific research that allow the development of new knowledge and technologies and the identification of intelligent and more efficient mobility systems.

4   Conclusions

In the coming years, mobility will be one of the biggest environmental challenges, especially in terms of emissions. It is hoped that increasingly sustainable solutions and new technologies can be proposed and promoted by investing in electric mobility.

The current European e-mobility market has connected to the Green Economy in all European countries. Several strategies will have to be implemented by the automotive industry to reduce high production costs, low range and non-zero environmental impacts from vehicle production, circulation and recycling. However, "local emissions" are zero, making this technology useful for urban mobility, where there is often a high population density. Furthermore, e-mobility is useful within the new forms of mobility stimulated by the deployment of MaaS, which could emphasize the strengths of e-mobility and reduce its weaknesses.

The shift towards more sustainable transport modes will also be encouraged through incentives and reward mechanisms (i.e. incentives for the purchase of low-impact vehicles or for the installation of devices capable of reducing pollutant emissions; incentives for public transport passes; provision of minimum requirements and reward criteria referring to sustainable mobility). In addition, several actions may be adopted to encourage users to use e-mobility. Considering a short-medium time horizon, the awareness-raising campaigns addressed to different age population groups, focused on the theme of sustainability and green mobility, can encourage the propensity of transport demand to use electric vehicles.

However, in the medium-long term,, the implementation of an improved recharging infrastructure and the exemplification of the procedures (i.e. waiting times and types of charging stations) can be a strategy to support the spread of e-mobility.

There is certainly still a long way to go. But the year 2021 can truly be the "driving force" to ensure that the trends recorded for electric vehicles in 2020 become structural. In this direction, this study lays the foundations for in-depth research aimed at analyzing the measures put in place for 2021 by the State and Regions to encourage the use of e-mobility. The comparison between the spread of shared and private e-mobility will highlight the critical points in both mobility sectors. At the same time, a more in-depth analysis of recharging infrastructures will increase the study of the electric mobility sector in terms of both transport demand and supply, promoting new strategies for the spread of sustainable mobility in different time horizons.

Acknowledgments. This study was also supported by the MIUR (Ministry of Education, Universities and Research [Italy]) through a project entitled WEAKI TRANSIT: WEAK-demand areas Innovative TRANsport Shared services for Italian Towns (Project code: 20174ARRHT; CUP Code: J74I19000320008) financed with the PRIN 2017 (Research Projects of National Relevance) programme. We authorize the MIUR to reproduce and distribute reprints for Governmental purposes, notwithstanding any copyright notations thereon. Any opinions, findings and conclusions or recommendations expressed in this material are those of the authors, and do not necessarily reflect the views of the MIUR.

References

1. Intergovernmental Panel on Climate Change - IPCC (2021). https://www.ipcc.ch/
2. European Commission: A European Strategy for low-emission mobility (2021). https://ec.europa.eu/clima/policies/transport_en
3. European Environment Agency (2021). https://www.eea.europa.eu/
4. Acampa, G., Grasso, M., Ticali, D.: MCDA to evaluate alternative paths for urban electric micromobility. In: International Conference of Computational Methods in Sciences and Engineering ICCMSE 2020, Crete, Greece (2021)
5. Torrisi, V., Inturri, G., Ignaccolo, M.: Introducing a mobility on demand system beyond COVID-19: evidences from users' perspective. In: International Conference of Computational Methods in Sciences and Engineering ICCMSE 2020 (2021). https://doi.org/10.1063/5.0047889
6. Tiboni, M., Rossetti, S., Vetturi, D., Torrisi, V., Botticini, F., Schaefer, M.D.: Urban policies and planning approaches for a safer and climate friendlier mobility in cities: strategies. Initiatives Some Anal. Sustain. **13**(4), 1778 (2021). https://doi.org/10.3390/su13041778
7. Tira, M., Tiboni, M., Rossetti, S., De Robertis, M.: Smart planning to enhance nonmotorised and safe mobility in today's cities. In: Papa, R., Fistola, R., Gargiulo, C. (eds.) Smart Planning: Sustainability and Mobility in the Age of Change. GET, pp. 201–213. Springer, Cham (2018). https://doi.org/10.1007/978-3-319-77682-8_12
8. Acampa G., Marino G., Parisi C.M.: Social network as tool for the evaluation of sustainable urban mobility in Catania (Italy). In: Bevilacqua C., Calabrò F., Della Spina L. (eds.) New Metropolitan Perspectives. NMP 2020. Smart Innovation, Systems and Technologies, vol 178. Springer, Cham (2021). https://doi.org/10.1007/978-3-030-48279-4_23
9. Torrisi, V., Garau, C., Inturri, G., Ignaccolo, M.: Strategies and actions towards sustainability: Encouraging good ITS practices in the SUMP vision. In: International Conference of Computational Methods in Sciences and Engineering ICCMSE 2020 (2021). https://doi.org/10.1063/5.0047897
10. Torrisi, V., Garau, C., Ignaccolo, M., Inturri, G.: "Sustainable urban mobility plans": key concepts and a critical revision on SUMPs guidelines. In: Gervasi, O., et al. (eds.) ICCSA 2020. LNCS, vol. 12255, pp. 613–628. Springer, Cham (2020). https://doi.org/10.1007/978-3-030-58820-5_45
11. Acampa, G., Contino, F., Grasso, M., Ticali, D.: Evaluation of infrastructure: application of TOD to Catania underground metro station. In: AIP conference proceedings, vol. 2186, no. 1, p. 160010. AIP Publishing LLC, December 2019
12. Global EV Outlook: Scaling up the transition to electric mobility. Technology Report, May 2019
13. Campisi, T., Basbas, S., Skoufas, A.C., Akgün, N., Ticali, D., Tesoriere, G.: The impact of COVID-19 pandemic on the resilience of sustainable mobility in sicily. Sustainability **12**(21), 8829 (2020)
14. Bonaccorsi, G., et al.: Economic and social consequences of human mobility restrictions under COVID-19. Proc. Natl. Acad. Sci. **117**(27), 15530–15535 (2020)
15. Moslem, S., Campisi, T., Szmelter-Jarosz, A., Duleba, S., Nahiduzzaman, K.M., Tesoriere, G.: Best–worst method for modelling mobility choice after COVID-19: evidence from Italy. Sustainability **12**(17), 6824 (2020)
16. Torrisi, V., Campisi, T., Inturri, G., Ignaccolo, M., Tesoriere, G.: Continue to share? An overview on italian travel behavior before and after the COVID-19 lockdown. In: International Conference of Computational Methods in Sciences and Engineering ICCMSE 2020 (2021). https://doi.org/10.1063/5.0048512

17. Canale, A., Tesoriere, G., Campisi, T.: The MAAS development as a mobility solution based on the individual needs of transport users. In: AIP conference proceedings, vol. 2186, no. 1, p. 160005. AIP Publishing LLC, December 2019
18. Noussan, M., Hafner, M., Tagliapietra, S.: The evolution of transport across world regions. In: The Future of Transport Between Digitalization and Decarbonization. SE, pp. 1–28. Springer, Cham (2020). https://doi.org/10.1007/978-3-030-37966-7_1
19. Torrisi, V., Ignaccolo, M., Inturri, G.: Analysis of road urban transport network capacity through a dynamic assignment model: validation of different measurement methods. Transp Research Procedia **27**, 1026–1033 (2017). https://doi.org/10.1016/j.trpro.2017.12.135
20. Shiftan, Y., Kaplan, S., Hakkert, S.: Scenario building as a tool for planning a sustainable transportation system. Transp. Res. Part D: Transp. Environ. **8**(5), 323–342 (2003)
21. Kaya, Ö., Alemdar, K.D., Campisi, T., Tortum, A., Çodur, M.K.: The development of decarbonisation strategies: a three-step methodology for the suitable analysis of current EVCS locations applied to Istanbul, Turkey. Energies **14**(10), 2756 (2021). https://doi.org/10.3390/en14102756
22. Mądziel, M., Campisi, T., Jaworski, A., Tesoriere, G.: The development of strategies to reduce exhaust emissions from passenger cars in Rzeszow city—Poland a preliminary assessment of the results produced by the increase of e-fleet. Energies **14**(4), 1046 (2021)
23. Wątróbski, J., Małecki, K., Kijewska, K., Iwan, S., Karczmarczyk, A., Thompson, R.G.: Multi-criteria analysis of electric vans for city logistics. Sustainability **9**(8), 1453 (2017)
24. Campisi, T., Ignaccolo, M., Tesoriere, G., Inturri, G., Torrisi, V.: The Evaluation of Car-Sharing to Raise Acceptance of Electric Vehicles: Evidences from an Italian Survey among University Students no. 2020-24-0021. SAE Technical Paper (2020)
25. Campisi, T., Akgün, N., Ticali, D., Tesoriere, G.: Exploring public opinion on personal mobility vehicle use: a case study in Palermo. Italy Sustain. **12**(13), 5460 (2020)
26. Acampa, G., Bona, N., Grasso, M., Ticali, D.: BIM: building information modeling for infrastructures. In: AIP Conference Proceedings, vol. 2040, no. 1, p. 140008. AIP Publishing LLC, November 2018
27. Campisi, T., Acampa, G., Marino, G., Tesoriere, G.: Cycling master plans in Italy: the I-BIM feasibility tool for cost and safety assessments. Sustainability **12**(11), 4723 (2020)
28. Electric Vehicle World Sales Database (2020). https://www.ev-volumes.com/
29. Europe Plug-In Vehicle Sales. (2020). https://cleantechnica.com/2020/12/29/record-electric-vehicle-sales-in-europe/
30. https://www.sicurauto.it/news/auto-elettriche-ibride/
31. European Environmental Agency: New registrations of electric vehicles in Europe (2020). https://www.eea.europa.eu/data-and-maps/indicators/proportion-of-vehicle-fleet-meeting-5/assessment
32. Focus UE/EFTA mercato autovetture ad alimentazione alternativa (2019). 1569419668494_A.pdf, https://www.ansa.it/documents/1569419668494_A.pdf
33. Wappelhorst, S., Hall, D., Nicholas, M., Lutsey, N.: Analyzing policies to grow the electric vehicle market in European cities (2020)
34. European Automobile Manufacturers Association: Electric vehicle purchase incentives per country in Europe (2019). https://www.acea.be/statistics/article/interactive-map-electric-vehicle-incentives-per-country-in-europe-2018
35. https://www.corriere.it/economia/finanza/19_luglio_10/pil-2019
36. Transport and Environment. Recharge EU. How many charge point will Europe and its Member States need in the 2020s (2020). https://www.transportenvironment.org/sites/te/files/publications/01%202020%20Draft%20TE%20Infrastructure%20Report%20Final.pdf

Correction to: 15-Minute City in Urban Regeneration Perspective: Two Methodological Approaches Compared to Support Decisions

Ginevra Balletto⊙, Michèle Pezzagno⊙, and Anna Richiedei⊙

Correction to:
Chapter "15-Minute City in Urban Regeneration Perspective: Two Methodological Approaches Compared to Support Decisions" in: O. Gervasi et al. (Eds.): *Computational Science and Its Applications – ICCSA 2021*, **LNCS 12953, https://doi.org/10.1007/978-3-030-86976-2_36**

In the originally published version, the authors of the paper "15-Minute City in Urban Regeneration Perspective: Two Methodological Approaches Compared to Support Decisions" had their first and last names inverted. The correctly written names are "Balletto, Ginevra", "Pezzagno, Michéle", and "Richiedei, Anna". Author names has been updated in chapter.

The updated version of this chapter can be found at
https://doi.org/10.1007/978-3-030-86976-2_36

© Springer Nature Switzerland AG 2021
O. Gervasi et al. (Eds.): ICCSA 2021, LNCS 12953, p. C1, 2021.
https://doi.org/10.1007/978-3-030-86976-2_50

Author Index

Printed in the United States
by Baker & Taylor Publisher Services